Clinical Neurology of Aging

CLINICAL NEUROLOGY OF AGING

Edited by
MARTIN L. ALBERT, M.D.
Boston University School of Medicine
and
Boston Veterans Administration Medical Center

New York   Oxford
OXFORD UNIVERSITY PRESS
1984

Library of Congress Cataloging in Publication Data
Main entry under title:
Clinical neurology of aging.
Includes bibliographies and index.
1. Geriatric neurology. I. Albert, Martin L.
[DNLM: 1. Nervous system—Physiology. 2. Aging.
3. Nervous system diseases—In old age. WL 102 C639]
RC346.C54   1984   618.97'68   82-18815
ISBN 0-19-503287-X

Printing (last digit): 9 8 7 6 5 4 3 2 1
Printed in the United States of America

Foreword

"Do not cast me off in the time of old age; forsake me not when my strength is spent." This poignant plea was raised centuries ago in the Seventy-first Psalm. Unfortunately, the response has improved only slightly. The government has been remiss in providing financial support, municipalities continue to segregate the elderly against all professional advice, and the medical profession in general has neglected this group.

This book will go a long way toward rectifying the problem among physicians who care for elderly people with nervous system dysfunction. By taking fundamental research data from up-to-date studies on the neurobiology of aging and by translating these data into practical diagnostic and therapeutic terms of benefit to the clinician, this book successfully serves a dual purpose. First, it provides the scientific and clinical foundations necessary for the management of elderly patients with neurologic disorders. Second, it explicitly recognizes the emerging field of geriatric neurology, a new field consisting of an identifiable body of knowledge and skills. The book systematically, comprehensively, and clearly presents this body of knowledge. Pediatricians exerting their territorial imperative often stated children are not just little adults. To some extent, physicians have now learned that old people are not just shrinking adults.

The editor of this volume, Dr. Martin Albert, has considerable experience with description and quantification of disorders of the nervous system, especially in elderly populations. This was not gained by isolation in a research laboratory, but by active engagement with patients. The selection of contributors reflects his own training and efforts—they are skilled clinicians, careful observers, and concerned people.

ROBERT J. JOYNT, M.D., Ph.D.

Professor and Chairman
Department of Neurology
Rykenboer Professor of Neurophysiology
University of Rochester

Preface

"Let us recognize ourselves in this old man or in that old woman. It must be done if we are to take upon ourselves the entirety of our own humanity."

SIMONE DE BEAUVOIR

Is growing old worth the effort? Are elderly people doomed to relentless deterioration and consequent suffering? Or is there something that concerned clinicians can offer the older patient that will assist in the maintenance of physical and psychological well-being and the ability to participate comfortably in life's activities. By providing the scientific foundations necessary for diagnosis and treatment of nervous system dysfunction in aging patients, this book is designed to help clinicians help the elderly. Although many books on the neurobiology of aging have been published during the past decade, few have been directed toward the clinician. One major goal of this book is to share with practicing clinicians the experience and knowledge of clinician-scientists who have unusually high levels of expertise in fundamentals of the neurobiology of aging and in the application of these fundamentals to everyday problems of elderly people with neurologic disorders.

In 1970 about 11% of the population of the United States was over age 65. By the year 2030 this percentage is expected to increase to 20%, or about 50 million elderly people in this country alone. Since more than half of the medical incapacitation of people over age 65 is accounted for by neurologic diseases, there is a rapidly increasing need for clinicians to develop a special awareness of the neurology of old age.

The clinical neurology of aging is more than just the practice of general adult neurology within the expanding elderly population. Geriatric neurology, like pediatric neurology before it, is emerging as a distinctive discipline with distinctive clinical and neuroscientific features. Charcot demonstrated in 1867 that the same disease of the nervous system may affect an older patient quite differently from a young adult, and, moreover, that older people are subject to certain neurologic diseases not usually found in younger populations. This book attempts to document the specificity of geriatric neurology by providing a systematic, up-to-date review of the neurobiology of aging as applied to the clinical practice of neurology in the elderly.

No published work of this magnitude could be produced without the practical and moral support of many friends and colleagues. I thank once again the contributors of each chapter for the considerable effort they put into this work. I am also grateful to the two major institutions that supported me while this project was taking shape—Boston University Medical School and the Veterans Administration. At Boston University, Robert Feldman, Chairman of the Department of Neurology, has continually supported and encouraged me; and Dean John Sandson has demonstrated unusual sensitivity and goodwill in his support. Thanks are also due to my associates and colleagues at the Boston VA Medical Center for their encouragement during this project. The Veterans Administration granted me a six-month extended educational leave during which much of the final editorial work on this book was carried out.

Special thanks should be given to Janice Knoefel, geriatric neurologist, and Martha Windrem, philosopher of science and neurolinguist, for their excellent and much appreciated editorial assistance. I am grateful to Jennifer Sandson and Jane Litter for their review of the proofs and to Suzanne Ruscitti, my secretary, for her valuable and reliable assistance.

Much of the editorial work on this book was carried out in Paris while I was visiting the I.N.S.E.R.M. Research Laboratory for Neuropsychological Studies. I thank Pierre Rondot, Director of the Laboratory, for his friendly welcome. Members of the I.N.S.E.R.M. Laboratory for Gerontologic Studies, in particular its former Director, F. Bourlière, and current Director, Y. Courtois, were particularly helpful to me, and I am most appreciative. Our friends Jean and Jan Haegel provided consistent moral and material support which greatly facilitated my task and for which I am grateful.

Thanks are also due to Jeffrey House, editor for medical and scientific publications at Oxford University Press, whose calm and thoughtful advice was always available. I wish especially to thank Phyllis, David, Michael, and Rachel Albert for all their goodwill.

Boston   M.L.A.
October 1, 1983

Contents

III   MENTAL STATUS

IV   SPECIAL SENSES

V   MOTOR SYSTEM AND SENSATION

VI   COMMON NEUROLOGICAL DISORDERS

List of Contributors

Raymond D. Adams, Professor of Neuropathology (Emeritus), and Senior Neurologist and Chief of Neurology (Emeritus), Massachusetts General Hospital, Boston, Massachusetts.

Martin L. Albert, Professor of Neurology and Director, Behavioral Neurosciences and Geriatric Neurology, Boston University School of Medicine and Boston Veterans Administration Medical Center, Boston, Massachusetts.

Phyllis C. Albert, Associate Professor of Socio-Medical Sciences (History), Boston University School of Medicine, Boston, Massachusetts, and Research Associate, Center for European Studies, Harvard University, Cambridge, Massachusetts.

Michael P. Alexander, Associate Professor of Neurology, Boston University School of Medicine, and Chief, Aphasia/Behavioral Unit, Boston Veterans Administration Medical Center, Boston, Massachusetts.

Jack Antel, Associate Professor of Neurology, Department of Neurology, University of Chicago Division of Biological Sciences, Pritzker School of Medicine, and Bernard Mitchell Hospital of the University of Chicago, Chicago, Illinois.

Barry G.W. Arnason, Professor and Chairman, Department of Neurology, University of Chicago Division of Biological Sciences, Pritzker School of Medicine, and Bernard Mitchell Hospital of the University of Chicago, Chicago, Illinois.

Sanford H. Auerbach, Assistant Professor of Neurology, Boston University School of Medicine, and Director, Behavioral Neurology, University Hospital, Boston, Massachusetts.

Robert W. Baloh, Professor of Neurology and Surgery (Head and Neck), University of California at Los Angeles Medical School, and Director, Neurotology Laboratory, University of California at Los Angeles Medical Center, Los Angeles, California.

J. Gregory Cairncross, Assistant Professor, Departments of Clinical Neurological Sciences and Radiation Oncology, Ontario Cancer Treatment and Research Foundation, and University of Western Ontario, Toronto, Ontario.

Donna Cohen, Associate Professor, Department of Psychiatry, Head, United Division of Aging and Geriatric Psychiatry, Albert Einstein College of Medicine and Montefiore Medical Center, New York, New York.

Michael M. Cohen, Assistant Professor of Neurology (Neuropathology), Medical College of Pennsylvania (Philadelphia), Associate Attending Neuro-ophthalmologist, and Chief, Neurology Service, Veterans Administration Medical Center, Philadelphia, Pennsylvania.

William C. Dement, Professor of Psychiatry and Behavioral Sciences, and Director, Sleep Disorders Center, Stanford University School of Medicine, Stanford, California.

David A. Drachman, Professor and Chairman of Neurology, University of Massachusetts Medical School, and Chief of Neurology, University of Massachusetts Medical Center, Worcester, Massachusetts.

Carl Eisdorfer, Professor, Departments of Psychiatry and Neuroscience, Albert Einstein College of Medicine, and President, Montefiore Medical Center, New York, New York.

Morris Freedman, Lecturer, Faculty of Medicine, University of Toronto, and Neurologist, Mount Sinai Hospital and Baycrest Centre for Geriatric Care, Toronto, Ontario.

Norman Geschwind, James Jackson Putnam Professor of Neurology, Harvard Medical School, and Neurologist-in-Chief, Beth Israel Hospital, Boston, Massachusetts.

Bennet S. Gurian, Associate Professor of Psychiatry, Harvard Medical School, and Director of Geriatrics, Massachusetts Mental Health Center, Boston, Massachusetts.

Richard N. Harner, Associate Professor of Neurology, University of Pennsylvania Medical School, and Director, Department of Electroencephalography and Neurophysiology, The Graduate Hospital, Philadelphia, Pennsylvania.

Deborah Hayes, Assistant Professor of Audiology, Baylor College of Medicine, Houston, Texas.

Gail Hochanadel, Research Fellow, Department of Psychology, Clark University, and Clinical Neuropsychology Consultant, Department of Neurology, Lahey Clinic Medical Center, Burlington, Massachusetts.

C. Louise Holm, University of Washington School of Medicine, Seattle, Washington.

James Jerger, Professor of Audiology, Baylor College of Medicine, and Director, Audiology and Speech Pathology Service, The Neurosensory Center of the Methodist Hospital of Houston, Houston, Texas.

William B. Kannel, Professor of Medicine, Chief, Section of Preventive Medicine and Epidemiology, and Adjunct Professor of Public Health, Boston University School of Medicine, Attending Physician, University Hospital, Boston, Massachusetts.

Edith Kaplan, Associate Professor of Neurology (Neuropsychology), Boston University School of Medicine, and Neuropsychologist, Boston Veterans Administration Medical Center, Boston, Massachusetts.

Carlos S. Kase, Associate Professor of Neurology, University of South Alabama College of Medicine and University of South Alabama Medical Center, Mobile, Alabama.

Richard I. Katz, Clinical Associate Professor of Neurology, Temple University Medical School, and Director of Laboratory of Electroencephalography, Albert Einstein Medical Center, Philadelphia, Pennsylvania.

Thomas L. Kemper, Professor of Neurology and Anatomy, Boston University School of Medicine, and Director of Neuropathology Laboratory, Boston City Hospital, Boston, Massachusetts.

Harold L. Klawans, Jr., Professor of Neurology and Pharmacology, Rush Medical College, and Associate Chairman, Department of Neurological Sciences, Rush-Presbyterian, St. Luke's Medical Center, Chicago, Illinois.

Janice E. Knoefel, Instructor in Neurology, Boston University School of Medicine and Director, Geriatric Assessment Unit, Boston Veterans Administration Medical Center, Boston, Massachusetts.

Kenneth S. Kosik, Instructor in Neurology, Harvard Medical School, and Assistant Neuropathologist, McLean Hospital, Belmont, Massachusetts.

Simmons Lessell, Professor of Ophthalmology, Neurology and Anatomy, Boston University School of Medicine, and Director, Ophthalmology Service, Boston City Hospital, Boston, Massachusetts.

Harvey L. Levine, Associate Professor of Radiology, Tufts University School of Medicine, and Chief, Section of Neuroradiology, Boston Veterans Administration Medical Center, Boston, Massachusetts.

Zibigniew J. Lipowski, Professor of Psychiatry, University of Toronto, and Psychiatrist-in-Chief, Psychosomatic Medicine Unit, Clarke Institute of Psychiatry, Toronto, Ontario.

Randall R. Long, Savannah Neurological Associates, Savannah Neurodiagnostic Laboratory, Savannah, Georgia.

John Stirling Meyer, Professor of Neurology, Baylor College of Medicine, and Director, Cerebrovascular Research Center, Veterans Administration Medical Center, Houston, Texas.

Laughton E. Miles, Clinical Assistant Professor of Medicine, Stanford University Medical Center, and Director, Vitalog Monitoring Center, Palo Alto, California.

J.P. Mohr, Sciarra Professor of Clinical Neurology, College of Physicians and Surgeons, Columbia University, New York Neurological Institute, and The Presbyterian Hospital, New York, New York.

Theodore L. Munsat, Professor of Neurology, Tufts University School of Medicine, and Director, Neuromuscular Research Unit, New England Medical Center, Boston, Massachusetts.

Margaret A. Naeser, Assistant Research Professor of Neurology, Boston University School of Medicine, and Research Neurolinguist, Aphasia Research Center, Boston Veterans Administration Medical Center, Boston, Massachusetts.

Loraine K. Obler, Associate Research Professor of Neurology, Boston University School of Medicine, and Research Associate in Neurolinguistics, Boston Veterans Administration Medical Center, Boston, Massachusetts.

John Polich, Research Psychologist, Division of Neurology, Scripps Clinic and Research Foundation, La Jolla, California.

Jerome B. Posner, Vice-Chairman, Department of Neurology, Cornell University Medical College, and Chairman, Department of Neurology, Memorial Sloan-Kettering Cancer Center, New York, New York.

Thomas D. Sabin, Professor of Neurology and Psychiatry, Boston University School of Medicine, and Director, Neurological Unit, Boston City Hospital, Boston, Massachusetts.

John E. Sarno, Professor, Clinical Rehabilitation Medicine, New York University School of Medicine, Institute of Rehabilitation Medicine, and New York University Medical Center, New York, New York.

Dennis J. Selkoe, Associate Professor of Neurology, Harvard Medical School, Associate Neuropathologist, McLean Hospital, and Associate Neurologist, Brigham and Women's Hospital, Boston, Massachusetts.

Terry G. Shaw, Assistant Director, rCBF Laboratory, Department of Neurology, Baylor College of Medicine, and Assistant Chief, Cerebrovascular Research Center, Veterans Administration Medical Center, Houston, Texas.

Arnold Starr, Professor, Departments of Neurology and Psychobiology, University of California at Irvine School of Medicine, Irvine, California.

Kari Stefansson, Assistant Professor of Neurology, Department of Neurology, University of Chicago Division of Biological Sciences, Pritzker School of Medicine, and Bernard Mitchell Hospital of the University of Chicago, Illinois.

Caroline M. Tanner, Assistant Professor of Neurology, Rush Medical College and Rush-Presbyterian, St. Luke's Medical Center, Chicago, Illinois.

Nagagopal Venna, Assistant Professor of Neurology, Boston University School of Medicine, and Associate Director, Neurological Unit, Boston City Hospital, Boston, Massachusetts.

Joel Verter, Biostatistician, National Heart, Lung, and Blood Institute, Mathematical and Applied Statistics Branch, Division of Heart and Vascular Disease, Bethesda, Maryland.

Philip A. Wolf, Professor of Neurology, Research Professor of Medicine, Boston University School of Medicine, and Visiting Physician in Neurology, Boston University Medical Center, Boston, Massachusetts.

I
Clinical Neurosciences

1. History and Scope of Geriatric Neurology

PHYLLIS C. ALBERT

MARTIN L. ALBERT

Geriatric Neurology embraces all intersecting points between the disciplines of geriatrics and neurology. Its clinical dimensions include the diagnosis and treatment of neurological conditions specifically associated with old age and the processes of aging. From its basic science perspective, the field is concerned with the neurobiology of aging. Just as pediatric neurology can be distinguished from adult neurology by its specific neurobiological and clinical characteristics, so geriatric neurology is emerging as a distinctive discipline because its range of clinical and neuroscientific features are sufficiently different from those of general adult neurology to warrant special study. The modern field of geriatric neurology could be said to have originated in the middle of the nineteenth century when Charcot, France's first professor of neurology, declared in his lectures on diseases of old age and chronic sickness, "The importance of a special study of diseases of old age would not be contested at the present day" (Charcot, 1867). The current volume is designed to provide further evidence in support of this claim.

The Aging Population

Although today it is banal to talk about the rapid increase of the elderly population, this phenomenon is relatively new and tends to be limited in geographic scope to the modern industrial societies. The dramatic increase of the aging population can be seen, for example, in France or in the United States, but not in Brazil or in India. In France, estimates of the population over age 60 are 6 to 7% for the 1600s and 18% for the 1980s (Coulbert, 1982; Bourlière, in press). In the United States, it has been estimated that in 1870 approximately 2% of the population was over age 65, in 1910 approximately 4%, and in 1970 approximately 11%; this percentage is expected to increase to 20% by the year 2030, when there will be 50 million Americans over the age of 65 (Besdine, 1980). Caird and his colleagues estimate that neurological diseases account for about 50% of the incapacitation seen over age 65 (Akhtar et al., 1973).

The geographic differences in this phenomenon are amply demonstrated by a comparison of percentages of the population 60 years of age and older in various countries in 1980: Sweden, 22.2%; England, 19.7%; United States, 15.7%; Egypt, 5.7%; Brazil, 5.3%; and India, 5.3% (Bourlière, in press). We emphasize this point, to which we shall return, to forewarn both the clinician and the basic scientist that factors of human ecology, such as climate, nutrition, pollutants, physical exercise, and psychosocial stress must not be ignored in the search for the specific chemical molecules that may contribute to pathological changes in the aging nervous system.

In terms of human suffering—for the patient, the family, and society at large—the cost of neurological disease in elderly people is clear, well known, and tragic. The financial cost is also great. Consider, for example, the financial costs of only one of the neurological diseases found in old people, senile dementia of the Alzheimer type. The Epidemiology, Demography, and Biometry Program personnel of the National Institute of Aging estimated expenditures in the United States for senile dementia of the Alzheimer type. Admittedly using an incomplete data base, they determined that direct costs, in nursing homes alone, for senile dementia of all types (of which senile dementia of the Alzheimer type represents about one-half) was $5.1 billion. To this must be added other direct costs for acute hospitalization, indirect costs of care provided in homes by family, friends, nurses, etc., or indirect costs reflecting loss of earning power (Cowell, 1983).

Neuroepidemiology of Aging

Disorders of nervous system function are among the commonest causes of disability in old age. Certain neurological diseases or certain sets of neurological signs and symptoms, for example, dizziness, falls, gait disorders, mental deterioration, and strokes, become more frequent, more obvious, or more severe with aging. These problems are discussed in detail in this book. As examples, two such problems, dementias and falls, are considered briefly here.

The diagnosis of dementia is a behavioral diagnosis at present. Thus, confusing and occasionally contradictory data relating to the frequency of this disease appear in the literature. Estimates of the percentage of the elderly population that has a mild dementia range from 2.6 to 15%. Severe dementia is estimated variously between 1.0 and 7.2%. The total frequency of dementia of all forms is con-

sidered to be within the range of 10 to 18% (Kay, 1977). All specialists in the field agree that dementia occurs with greatest frequency in the oldest age groups (Bergmann, 1975; Gruenberg, 1978) and that the incidence of dementia increases with increasing age (several chapters in Katzman et al., 1978). Over the age of 80, the risk of moderate or severe dementia is 15 to 20% (Jarvik, 1980; Campbell et al., 1983).

Disorders of balance and stability, leading to falls, are among the common complaints of the elderly. It is estimated that about 35% of people over the age of 65 experience one or more falls in a year (Gryfe et al., 1977; Campbell et al., 1981). The clinical approach required for evaluating the problem of falling in elderly populations can serve as an example of the distinctive clinical requirements of geriatric neurology. Many of these elderly people are referred to a neurologist for evaluation. The neurologist who examines these patients by looking only at the nervous system (neurological examination, computerized tomography, positron emission tomography, nuclear magnetic resonance studies of the brain, etc.) will be ignoring one of the essential basic principles of geriatric neurology. The causes of neurological signs and symptoms in the elderly are usually multiple, and usually involve minor or major dysfunction of several systems at the same time. Thus, for example, most falls in the elderly result from a combination of factors, including postural hypotension, seizures, anemia, transient vertebrobasilar insufficiency, visual impairment, dysfunction of the vestibular system, arthritic disorders of the hips and back, reaction to medication, and poor judgment. The specialist in geriatric neurology must have expertise in more than just diseases of the nervous system.

Historical Background

New disciplines in the clinical and basic sciences emerge in response to increasing knowledge, technological advances, and the needs of society. To write a thorough history of the emerging discipline of geriatric neurology would be a formidable undertaking. One would first have to study the history of gerontology (the study of aging) and geriatrics (the clinical branch of medicine concerned with the diagnosis and treatment of diseases of old age), then of neuroscience, and neurology, and finally interweave these various stories at appropriate junctures. For this book we wish only to point out some of the main lines leading to the current status of the field.

We can consider the development of both geriatrics and neurology within three major historical periods: ancient (the period when the art of medicine predominated over the science), modern (the anatomoclinical period, when the art and the science of medicine confronted each other openly), and contemporary (the technological period, when the art of medicine is subordinated to the science).

Since the earliest periods of history, fear of senescence, and in particular fear of neurological deterioration in old age, has been common. We even have ancient clinical descriptions of neurological disability in the elderly. For example, *The Teachings of Ptahhotep,* written in about 2600 B.C. by the 110-year-old Chief Judge and Vizir to King Izezi in the Fifth Dynasty of the Old Egyptian Empire, contain the following: "When old age descends upon you, slowness of movement appears; . . . the eyes become dim; the ears hard of hearing; . . . muscles become weak, every movement is difficult; . . . and the spirit is forgetful and cannot even remember yesterday. . . ." (free translation of the French translation by François Daumas in Bourlière, 1979).

In ancient times, and even current times in some cultures, philosophical and religious conceptions in medicine predominated over scientific conceptions based on observation and experience, and recourse to magic and sorcery was standard medical practice. In such societies, attempts to prevent or cure the neurological deterioration of old age took the form of medico-religious or medico-philosophical approaches. Thus, for example, we have the story of King David in biblical days trying to restore his physical strength and "vital heat" in his old age by a combination of prayers and the breathing in of the breath

of young girls (Grmek, 1958). In ancient India, gold salts taken as part of a religious ritual were thought to restore strength and memory (Grmek, 1958). To preserve the intellect, in China in the first century, powders of gold, sulfur, jade, mercury, and lead, accompanied by religious incantations, were recommended (Huard and Wong, 1959). Even the intellectual revolution during the Renaissance failed to influence the general approaches to the prevention or cure of disease. Especially influential throughout many centuries were the teachings of Hippocrates ("moderation in all things") and Galen ("maintain physical activity into old age; take warm baths and massages regularly; and eat wisely, especially fish, wine, figs, prunes, and honey") (Grmek, 1958).

The early modern period saw the beginnings of scientific medicine. As early as the first decades of the sixteenth century, attempts were made to relate certain neurological signs and symptoms of old age to specific anatomical changes. Leonardo da Vinci (1452–1519) carried out a postmortem examination of an aged man who died peacefully and without obvious cause at the Santa Maria Nuova Hospital in Florence. Da Vinci was struck by the senile changes in the old man's arteries, when compared to the arteries of a young man, and he provided a detailed and didactic description of the differences in his *Dell'anatomia* (Bourlière, 1979).

Through the seventeenth and eighteenth centuries, increasingly frequent attempts were made to provide systematic analyses of clinical signs of neurological dysfunction in the elderly and to relate them systematically to anatomopathological observations. There were many painstakingly detailed descriptions of anatomoclinical correlations. Thus, for example, in the eighteenth century, Giovanni Batista Morgagni described cerebral atherosclerosis in old age. He also confirmed that cerebral hemorrhage was the cause of "apoplexy" in the elderly. Also in the eighteenth century, Gerhard van Swieten described the progressive hardening and flattening of the intervertebral discs with age (Grmek, 1958).

The histories of neurology and geriatrics

were never more intimately linked than in the middle of the nineteenth century, when Charcot, possibly Europe's most famous neurologist, produced his *Lessons on Diseases of Old Age and on Chronic Diseases* (1867). Highly successful, they were translated into English in 1881. Charcot distinguished three categories of medical problems in the elderly. The first, which he called involutional diseases, included cerebral atrophy and cerebral arteriosclerosis. Charcot emphasized that, with increasing age, the line between normal age-related changes and abnormal disease-related changes becomes more difficult to discern. Charcot's second category included illnesses that may occur at any age but that have a different evolution and prognosis in the elderly. He cited pneumonia as an example. His third category consisted of the illnesses older people tolerate better than younger people. Charcot put tuberculosis here.

During the last quarter of the nineteenth century and the first quarter of the twentieth century, many scientists believed that senescence resulted from the involution or failure of a neural or neuroendocrinological control mechanism (e.g., Hodge, 1894; Lorand, 1904; Gley, 1922). Notable among the experiments carried out at this time were those done on himself by the famous neurologist Brown-Sequard. In 1889, believing that the reduction of male sex hormones was at the basis of senile dementia, he tried to achieve rejuvenation by injecting himself subcutaneously with a liquid extract of ground testicles from dogs and guinea pigs. There is no clear evidence that his experiments were successful.

Despite the influence of Charcot on the early history of geriatric neurology, the historical development of the independent fields of neurology and geriatrics diverged after his work. From the end of the nineteenth century to the present, they were distinctly separate fields, and only now have they begun to converge again. The history of neurology is particularly well told in the books by Young, 1970; Clarke and O'Malley, 1968; Clarke and Dewhurst, 1972; Hécaen and Lanteri-Laura, 1977; and Spillane, 1981. For American neurology, the reader is referred to the splendid recent

book by De Jong (1982). In the field of neurology there were steady advances both in knowledge and in interest into the contemporary period, when subspecialization and technological breakthroughs have progressed rapidly.

The same cannot be said for geriatrics. In the twentieth century, geriatrics has developed by fits and starts, with brief bursts of enthusiasm interspersed with long periods of disinterest (Robbins et al., 1982). In 1914, Nascher, who introduced the term "geriatrics," published the first American textbook of geriatric medicine. Between the two world wars there was relatively little interest in the field, perhaps because physicians could not earn enough practicing geriatrics (Robbins et al., 1982), perhaps because of the disdain of scientists confronted with an abundance of pseudoscientific research on rejuvenation (Bourlière, 1979), perhaps because the elderly were not yet a sufficiently large, vocal, and politically and economically important group within society.

Following World War II, the efforts of a handful of individuals, such as Cowdry (1888–1975) in the United States, Korenchevsky (1880–1959) in England, Binet (1891–1971) in France, and Bürger (1885–1966) in Germany, provided the impetus for a limited new growth of the field. It was not until the 1960s, however, that the field of geriatrics entered its major period of growth.

In the contemporary period, three major forces have combined not only to spur the development of the individual disciplines of neurology and geriatrics, but also to encourage their merger into the new field of neurogeriatrics. One of these forces is our increasing knowledge. The current volume is evidence of the wealth of new knowledge in this area obtained within the past decade. The second force is technological advances. New techniques in the study of the nervous system have opened the way to important new depths of understanding of pathophysiological mechanisms of neural function. The third force is the changing needs of society. A growing aged population, accompanied by an increase in manifestations of neurological disease, has forced the scientific and political communities to seek concrete solutions to the problems these demographic and epidemiological changes are introducing.

The Scope of Geriatric Neurology

Geriatric neurology is an identifiable body of knowledge and skills. Without pretending to provide a definitive definition of the field or its limits, we shall try to indicate the specificity of the discipline. A few examples may illustrate some of the distinctive aspects of the field.

If we consider human cerebral anatomy, for example, we see that, with normal aging, a series of specific changes occurs in the brain; these include reduction of brain weight, loss of neurons, deposition of amyloid, appearance of senile plaques and neurofibrillary tangles, occurrence of granulovacuolar degeneration, and a linear increase in lipofucsin accumulation. Certain parts of the neuron may be especially sensitive to aging, for example, dendritic spines in the hippocampal regions. These anatomical changes are linked to the specific motoric and other behavioral signs associated with normal aging.

One question that may be asked is how the normal neuroanatomical changes of aging are related to disturbed function in the elderly. Studies of neurochemistry and neuroimmunology in the elderly may help provide some links between anatomy and physiology. Complex neurochemical and neuroimmunological changes specific to aging have been described, but whether a causal relationship exists between these basic neuroscientific changes and neurological diseases in the elderly is a pressing question in geriatric neurology.

If we turn to clinical examples, we find problems that were perhaps unexpected. As Charcot demonstrated in 1867, the same (or apparently similar) disease of the nervous system may affect a young adult quite differently from an older patient. In patients with aphasia-producing strokes, for example, the older the patient, the greater the likelihood of a Wernicke-type aphasia, compared with a Broca-type aphasia. In the area of sleep–wake cycles, sleep patterns are different in elderly people. In psychiatry, manifestations of depression are often quite different in elderly people; depressive psuedodementia, for example, is more common in older than in younger subjects. The list of distinctive clinical differences could be extended throughout all subsystems of the nervous system.

Even the approach to neurological evaluation must be different for the older patient. In the aged individual, the significance of clinical findings may be difficult to determine. Once it has been determined that a sign or symptom is clinically significant, the causes must be sought differently, since individual signs and symptoms in the elderly often have multiple causes. To an even greater extent than in other age groups, the evaluation of environmental influences on older people is especially important. This includes recent loss of a loved one, life-long environmental or psychosocial stress, and the effects of therapy for non-neurological diseases. As this book documents repeatedly, for each nervous system function, there is a set of problems specific to the elderly population.

Whether or not the fields of geriatrics and neurology continue to grow together sufficiently to provide an independent and officially recognized subspecialty, the cross-disciplinary clinical and research field of geriatric neurology already exists, and its existence holds the promise of important new discoveries to benefit the aging population. Among the major benefits resulting from the development of the specialty of pediatric neurology were enhancement of the field of clinical neurochemistry and development of the field of neurogenetics. Among the benefits already arising from the recent interest in the clinical neurology of aging include intensified activity in the study of neurotransmitters, burgeoning research on neuropeptides, and studies of the links between neural control mechanisms and behavior. Probably research on neural plasticity will be stimulated, and questions of neural regeneration reopened. Additionally, as noted, one of the major areas for research will be the question of individual differences in aging (Bourlière, 1983). Much of this book, and indeed much of the work to date on aging, is concerned with group similarities. Studies of individual differences, however, have already begun in gerontology and should be one of the key areas of research in geriatric neurology in the next decade.

References

Akhtar, A.J., Broe, G.A., Crombie, A., McLean, W.M.R., Andrews, G.R., and Caird, F.I. (1973). Disability and dependence in the elderly at home. Age and Ageing 2, 102–110.

Bergman, K. (1975). The epidemiology of senile dementia. Br. J. Psychiatr. 9, 100–109.

Besdine, R. (1980). Geriatric Medicine: An Overview. In Annual Review of Gerontology and Geriatrics, C. Eisdorfer, Ed. Vol. 1, Springer, New York.

Bourlière, F. (1979). Histoire de la Gérontologie. In Histoire de la Médecine, J. Poulet, J-C. Sournia, and M. Martiny, Eds. Vol. VI. Soc. Française d'éditions professionnelles, médicales, et scientifiques, Paris.

Bourlière, F. and Vallery-Masson, J. (1983). Epidemiology and ecology of aging. In Textbook of Geriatric Medicine and Gerontology, 3rd Ed. J.C. Brocklehurst, Ed. Churchill-Livingstone, London.

Brown-Sequard, C. (1889). Des effets produits chez l'homme par des injections sous-cutanées d'un liquide retiré des testicules frais de cobayes et de chiens. C.R. Soc. Biol. Paris 41, 415–422.

Campbell, A., Reinken, A.B. and Martinez, G. (1981). Falls in old age: A study of frequency and related clinical factors. Age and Ageing 10, 264–270.

Campbell, A., McCosh, L., Reinken, J., and Allen, B. (1983). Dementia in old age and the need for services. Age and Ageing 12, 11–16.

Charcot, J-M. (1867). Leçons sur les Maladies des Viellards et les Maladies Chroniques., Paris.

Clarke, E. and O'Malley, C. (1968). The Human Brain and Spinal Cord. A Historical Study. University of California Press, Los Angeles.

Clarke E. and Dewhurst, K. (1972). An Illustrated History of Brain Function. Sandford Publications, Oxford.

Coulbert, P. (1982). La Vie Quotidienne des Paysans Français au XVIIIᵉ Siecle. Hachette, Paris.

Cowell, D. (1983). Senile dementia of the Alzheimer type: A costly problem. J. Amer. Geriatr. Soc. 31, 61.

De Jong, R. (1982). A History of American Neurology. Plenum Press, New York.

Gley, E. (1922). Sénescence et endocrinologie. Bull. Acad. Méd. Paris 87, 285–291.

Grmek, M. (1958). On Ageing and Old Age. Monograph in series Monographiae Biologicae, F.S. Bodenheimer and W.W. Weisbach, Eds. Vol V No. (2). Uitgeverij Dr. W. Junk, Den Haag.

Gruenberg, E.M. (1978). Epidemiology of senile dementia. In Advances in Neurology, B.S. Schoenberg, Ed. Raven Press, New York.

Gryfe, C.I., Ames, A., and Ashley, M.J. (1977). A longitudinal study of falls in an elderly population: I. Incidence and morbidity. Age and Ageing 6, 201–210.

Hécaen, H. and Lanteri-Laura, G. (1977). Evolution des Connaissances et des Doctrines sur les Localisations Cérébrales, Desclée de Brouwer, Paris.

Hodge, C.F. (1894). Changes in human ganglion cells from birth to senile death. Observations on man and honey-bee. J. Physiol. 17, 129–134.

Huard, P. and Wong, M. (1959). La Médecine Chinoise au Cours des Siécles, Flammarion, Paris.

Jarvik, L. (1980). Diagnosis of dementia in the elderly: A 1980 perspective. In Annual Review of Gerontology and Geriatrics, Vol. 1, C. Eisdorfer, Ed. Springer, New York.

Katzman, R., Terry, R.D., and Bick, K. (Eds.) (1978). Alzheimer's Disease: Senile Dementia and Related Disorders. Raven Press, New York.

Kay, D.W.K. (1977). The epidemiology of brain deficit in the aged. In The Cognitively and Emotionally Impaired Elderly. C. Eisdorfer and R.O. Friedel, Eds. Yearbook Medical Publisher, Chicago.

Lorand, A. (1904). Quelques considérations sur les causes de la sénilité, C.R. Soc. Biol. Paris 57, 500–502.

Nascher, I.L. (1914). Geriatrics: The Diseases of Old Age and Their Treatment, P. Blakiston's Son and Co., Philadelphia.

Robbins, A., Mather, J., and Beck, J. (1982). Status of geriatric medicine in the United States. J. Amer. Geriatr. Soc. 30, 211–218.

Spillane, J.D. (1981). The Doctrine of the Nerves. Oxford University Press, New York.

Young, R. (1970). Mind, Brain, and Adaptation in the Nineteenth Century. Clarendon Press, Oxford.

2. Neuroanatomical and Neuropathological Changes in Normal Aging and in Dementia

THOMAS KEMPER

In this chapter, many different changes found in the brain with age and with senile and Alzheimer's presenile dementia are described. Emphasis is placed on their distribution and possible interrelationships. In some of the reports reviewed in this chapter, the data were expressed according to cytoarchitectonic areas. In order to visualize these areas readily, we have made dot saturation templates in which the density of the dots indicates the relative density of the change in different areas. Because of the uncertainty surrounding the cytoarchitectonic criteria used in some of these studies, the extent of the areas had to be approximated. In the concluding section of the chapter, the data are summarized and the relationship of many of the changes to the connectivity of the brain is explored. For the latter, data from primate experiments are used whenever possible.

Brain Weight, Gyral Atrophy, and Ventricular Dilation

Age-related decreases in adult brain weight have been well documented. In the older literature, brain weight was generally stated to peak in the third decade (see von Braunmühl, 1957, for a review), whereas in the recent study of Dekaban and Sadowsky (1978), an earlier peak weight was

noted, occurring in the male between 19 and 21, and in the female between 16 and 18. This latter finding is consistent with the observation of Kretchmann et al. (1979) that the rate of brain growth in their series collected between 1966 and 1976 was more rapid than in a comparable series from the turn of the century. Brain weight then decreases, with the timing of this decrease varying from series to series. Bischoff (1880) and Marchand (1902) noted little change in brain weight until the sixth and seventh decade, Chernyshev (1911) reported a gradual decline until age 55 and then a more rapid decline, and Pearl (1905) and Peress et al. (1973) described a steady decline into old age. The Peress et al. (1973) study is a large series (7579 autopsies), including many cerebra from the 10th decade. From a statistical analysis, they concluded that both the supratentorial and the infratentorial brain weight for both sexes showed a steady decline from the third to the tenth decade "without alteration in the linear pattern." Dekaban and Sadowsky (1978) summarized their own series and six other large series of brain weights, comparing brain weight in the third and the eighth decade. The average decline in male brain weight during this time was 92 grams (range 51–131 grams) and in female brain weight 94 grams (range 69–144 grams). The variation in rate of decline and timing of the decline in brain weight may be due to the fact that each of these series was collected over a relatively short period of time from individuals with a wide range of birth dates. Miller and Corsellis (1977) reported increases in adult brain weight and body length of both males and females in the 80-year period between 1860 and 1940. The increases in brain weight during this time were 52 grams for the male and 23 grams for the female. Miller et al. (1980) took these factors into account and measured the volume of the cerebral hemispheres in 47 male and 44 female brains from ages 20 to 98 years and found no change until age 50, and then a 2% decrease per decade for both sexes. This was accompanied by an increasing ratio between the gray and white matter, suggesting that the predominant loss was from white matter.

Measurements of brain volume and cranial capacity in the same individual further confirm the presence of an atrophic process occurring in the brain with increasing age. A disparity between cranial capacity and brain volume was noted by Rudolph (1914), in a small series, and more recently by Davis and Wright (1977), in a larger series of 87 autopsies of carefully selected mentally normal individuals ranging in age from 22 to 94 years. In this series, there was no significant decrease in cranial capacity with age. Disparity between this measurement and brain volume then increased after age 55, and became striking after age 60.

Gross morphological correlates of this atrophic process are gyral atrophy and ventricular dilation. The term gyral atrophy is preferred to cortical atrophy, since it is not clear whether the cortex, the underlying white matter, or both are responsible for the change. At autopsy, gyral atrophy, when present, is generally described as involving the convexities of the frontal lobes, parasagittal region, and temporal and parietal lobes (von Braunmühl, 1957; Hooper and Vogel, 1976; Tomlinson et al., 1968). von Braunmühl (1957) noted that temporal lobe involvement is more likely to be on the left, particularly the polar region. The base of the brain and the

occipital pole are generally spared. Although von Braunmühl (1957) recognized generalized gyral atrophy as a separate pattern, it is apparently uncommon; Tomlinson et al. (1968) failed to note this finding in any of their carefully studied brains of 28 non-demented elderly individuals. In contrast, Yakovlev (1962) noted in whole brain serial sections that the median and paramedian limbic regions bear the brunt of this process. This observation agrees with that of McMenemey (1958), who emphasized a predilection for the insula.

Age-related gyral atrophy in CT scans begins at about age 40 (LeMay, 1980; Carlen et al., 1981) and shows significant correlation with increasing age (Earnest et al., 1979; Gyldensted, 1977). There is, however, marked individual variation noted both at autopsy (Tomlinson et al., 1968) and with the CT scan (Huckman et al., 1975). According to Tomlinson et al. (1968), atrophy begins in the parasagittal region where, as Gyldensted (1977) states, it shows a strong statistical correlation with aging.

The other grossly evident, age-related atrophic change, ventricular dilation, may be a process independent of gyral atrophy (Gyldensted, 1977). Estimation of ventricular size in autopsy material is potentially less accurate than CT scan determination. Artifacts that must be taken into account include agonal states, brain swelling before death, and swelling of the brain during formalin fixation (Last and Tompsett, 1953; Blinkov and Glezer, 1968; Messert et al., 1972). Last and Tompsett (1953) noted no age-related increase in volume in a small series of carefully prepared ventricular casts in 24 brains from individuals aged 29 to 73 years. This series, however, contained only three individuals over 65 years of age and the range of variation was marked (7.4 to 56.6 cubic centimeters). In a much larger series of 423 brains of patients with "physiological" aging, Morel and Wildi (1952) measured the volume of the lateral ventricles of the formalin-fixed brain of individuals aged 55 to 99. They noted a progressively increasing capacity in the male until about age 80, in the female about age 85, and then a decrease. Knudsen (1958) measured the volume of the lateral ventricles of 85 male and 98 female brains aged 20 to 90 years and found a similar increase up to the seventh decade, followed by a marked increase, with the female brain then showing a less striking further increase than the male brain. In agreement with Last and Tompsett (1953), ventricular size did not correlate with brain weight.

The observation of Morel and Wildi (1952) and Knudsen (1958) of age-related increases in ventricular size is confirmed by CT scan, but the decrease in ventricular size noted in extreme old age by Morel and Wildi (1952) is not confirmed. These CT studies are done by either making linear measurements at selected levels or planimetric measurement of ventricular size, generally at the maximum ventricular extent shown on the scan. Barron et al. (1979) planimetrically measured the lateral ventricle and the inner table of the skull in seven females and eight males per decade and found a gradual increase in the ratio of ventricular to skull volume between the third and seventh decade, followed by a marked increase in the eighth and ninth decade. In this latter group, there was marked individual variation, a finding in agreement with both Huckman et al. (1975) and Tomlinson et al. (1968). Earnest et al. (1979) also found a statistically significant increase in size of the lateral ventricles in 80- to 99-year-olds, as compared to 60- to 75-year-olds, and Gyldensted (1977) showed the same relationship when 41- to 86-year-old patients were compared to those 17 to 40 years of age. In

this latter study, the width of the third ventricle was also found to be significantly increased in 41- to 86-year-old individuals.

Gyral atrophy, loss in brain weight, and ventricular enlargement are all accentuated in patients with senile dementia of the Alzheimer type (SDAT), with a wide range of individual variation and frequent overlap with age-matched controls. In a relatively small series of brains of carefully studied patients with SDAT, brain weight has been reported as both nonsignificantly different from controls (Tomlinson et al., 1970) and significantly different from controls (Terry et al., 1981). In larger series in which the neurofibrillary tangle has been used as a diagnostic criteria for SDAT, there appears to be a clearer relationship between brain weight and the dementing process. Morel and Wildi (1952) compared the hemispheric weight of 79 cerebra with both neurofibrillary tangles and senile plaques with 187 cerebra with only senile plaques. Their results are replotted, from their Tables 2 and 3, in Figure 2-1. In all but the tenth decade, the hemispheric weights were less in the brains with both changes. A study of Constantinidis (1978) provides further support for a correlation between the neurofibrillary tangle and decreased brain weight in SDAT. In this study, 648 cerebra were classified into seven groups, each of which had at least 58 cerebra. His group VII showed neither senile plaques nor neurofibrillary tangles, group VI senile plaques only, and group V to I increasing extension of the neurofibrillary tangles from the allocortex to the neocortex. These groups showed a steady decrease in brain weight from group VII to

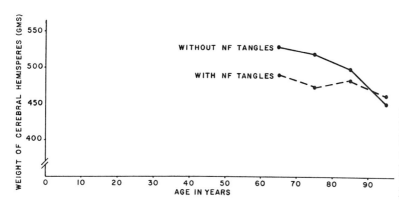

Figure 2-1. Graph of cerebral hemisphere weight of brains with and without neurofibrillary tangles. Replotted from Morel and Wildi (1952, Tables 2 and 3).

I, with a 146-gram difference between the extremes. It thus appears that, morphologically, SDAT is associated with a loss of brain weight and that the neurofibrillary tangle may play a key role.

In the careful autopsy study of Tomlinson et al. (1970), gyral atrophy was more prominent in SDAT than in controls, and moderate to severe degrees were seen only in their demented patients. In this study and in the CT study of Huckman et al. (1975), however, many dements failed to show recognizable gyral atrophy. In Huckman et al. (1975), the percentage of such patients was 25% and in Tomlinson et al. (1970), 40%. Gyral atrophy, when present, was most prominent in the parasagittal area in the demented patients. This is the same region most affected by normal aging (Tomlinson et al. (1970). Atrophy of the temporal lobes, which occurred in 14 of their 50 demented patients, was not seen in their controls. von Braunmühl (1957) indicates that, unlike Pick's disease, the entire extent of the superior temporal gyrus is involved in SDAT. Goodman (1953) noted a predilection in Alzheimer's disease for the frontal lobes, followed by the temporal lobe, with 13% of 23 cases showing a reversal of this pattern. According to Poppe and Tennsted (1969), the rank order of predilection of gyral atrophy in Alzheimer's disease is frontal>parietal>temporal>occipital lobe.

Ventricular enlargement is also more prominent in SDAT than in age-matched controls (Tomlinson et al., 1970; Huckman et al., 1975; Fox et al., 1975). Patients with SDAT showing normal ventricular size were found in only 6% of the autopsy series of Tomlinson et al. (1970) and in 6% of the CT series of Huckman et al. (1975). Many, however, showed slight degrees of enlargement (respectively, 24% and 37% in these two series). According to the CT study of Roberts and Caird (1976), the size of the lateral ventricle shows only a "broad relationship" to measured intellectual impairment and no clear relationship to gyral atrophy. This latter point was also noted by Tomlinson et al. (1970). Enlarged lateral ventricles, like brain weight, also appear to be correlated with the neurofibrillary tangle. Morel and Wildi (1952) have shown that brains with senile plaques and neurofibrillary tangles have larger ventricles than those with only senile plaques (Figure 2-2).

In summary, an atrophic process occurs in the brain with increasing age—the pace, initially, is gradual and then accelerates during the sixth or seventh decade. It has, as its grossly evident correlates, decreased brain weight, gyral atrophy, and ventricular enlargement. The latter two are poorly correlated with each other and may be independent processes. In SDAT, these features are accentuated, with a wide range of individual variation and often broad overlap with controls. The available evidence points to a major role for the neurofibrillary tangle in the pathogenesis of these atrophic processes.

Cortical Thickness

The width of the neocortex appears to be little affected by either aging or SDAT. von Ecomono and Koskinas (1925) sum-

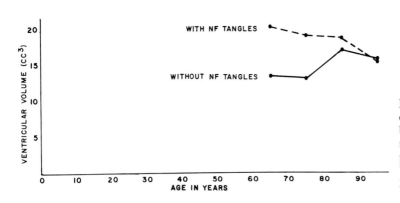

Figure 2-2. Graph of lateral ventricular volume of brains with and without neurofibrillary tangles. Replotted from Morel and Wildi (1952, Tables 2 and 3).

marized the data from Kaes (1907) on cortical thickness in 12 different cortical areas from the third postnatal month to ninety-seven years. There was a period of growth in width in the fourth and fifth decade, a decrease in the sixth decade, and then essentially no change thereafter. Brody's (1955) data on the effect of age on the thickness of five different cortical areas again shows no decrease in cortical thickness in his 95-year-old individual as compared to younger individuals. These observations were confirmed by Colon (1972), in a small series of brains, and by Henderson et al. (1980), in an extensive study of five different gyral locations in 66 brains from individuals aged 16 to 95. Both studies found no evidence of age-related decrease in cortical width. Shefer (1972) and Terry et al. (1981) also failed to show a decrease in width of the neocortex in patients with SDAT when compared to controls. In contrast, in the allocortex Shefer (1976) noted a 28% decrease in width of the subiculum with "old age" that was further accentuated in SDAT.

Neuronal Cell Loss

Neuronal cell loss in the human neocortex with increasing age has been well documented and noted in all areas studied. These studies can be divided into two categories, those that report their data according to gyral location and those that use cytoarchitectonic areas. In the former category is the classic study of Brody (1955), in which manual cell counts were made throughout the thickness of the cerebral cortex from birth to 95 years of age, with the most extensive data for the precentral and postcentral gyrus, superior temporal gyrus, and visual cortex. In these four areas, all but the postcentral gyrus showed significant progressive age-related cell loss. (See Hanley, 1974 for statistical calculations.) When the data for the 16- to 21-year-olds were compared to that for the 70- to 95-year-olds, the losses for the three areas showing significant cell loss were 32%, 49%, and 34%. In a later, comparable study of the frontal pole of the superior frontal gyrus, Brody (1970) noted a 48% neuronal cell loss from the fifth to the ninth decade. Henderson et al. (1980) repeated these studies for the precentral and postcentral gyrus and superior temporal gyrus together with the inferior temporal gyrus and gyrus rectus, using a larger sample and a computerized imaging system. Over the age range studied (16 to 95 years), all areas showed significant progressive loss of nerve cells greater than 19 micra in diameter within the narrow range of 44 to 53%. Smaller cells (12–19 micra in diameter) showed significant loss only in the precentral and postcentral gyrus and the superior temporal gyrus, ranging from 34 to 41%. An apparent exception is the study of Cragg (1975), in which he failed to show significant age-related cell loss in the frontal and temporal cortex. In this study, however, comparable areas may not have been used and the material was technically not comparable, since the younger specimens were all surgical biopsies and the older ones, autopsies.

A problem with using gyral topography as the only criterion is the uncertainty that the investigator is always dealing with the same architectonic area in each sample. It has recently been shown that there is a marked individual variation in the extent of some of these areas within the gyri, as well as right–left differences (Galaburda and Sanides, 1980). The use of cytoarchitectonic areas as a reference point obviates these problems. Colon (1972) noted an overall loss of 44% of neurons in areas 4, 10, 17, and 24 by the eighth decade, as compared to cerebra from the 18 to 39 age group. Shefer (1972), in a much larger series, studied the "absolute amount [of neurons] in the thickness of the cortex" according to cytoarchitectonic area and compared five 19- to 28-year-olds with a non-demented older age group (10 cerebra) with a mean age of 77 years. In the latter age group, the most marked cell losses occurred in area 10, a frontal polar cortex (28%); area 6, a premotor cortex (22%); and area 21, an association cortex in the temporal lobe (23%). The other three areas studied showed losses of 12 to 15%. These included area 40, a somesthetic association area; area 18, a primary visual association cortex; and area 21/38, temporal limbic area (Figure 2-3).

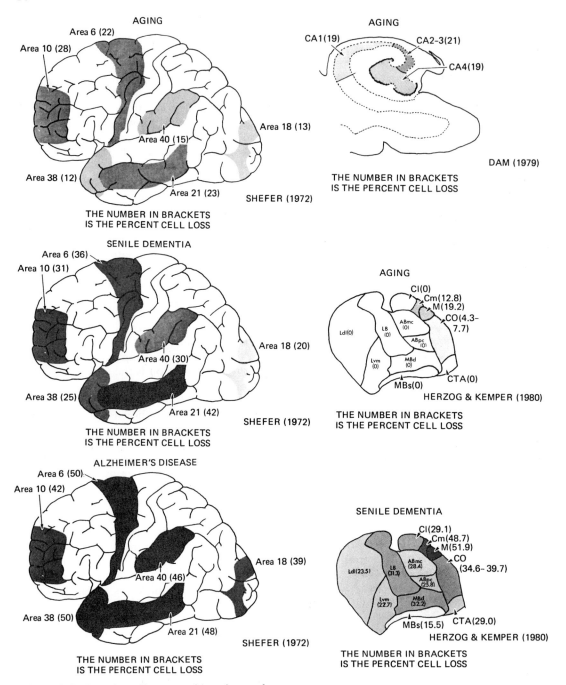

Figure 2-3. Template diagrams of location and extent of neuronal cell loss.

Although consistency in the extent of cell loss in comparable areas in the various studies is lacking, presumably reflecting the many technical problems inherent in such studies, there are certain consisten-

cies within the data of the individual studies. Brody (1955, 1970) and Shefer (1972) studied all four lobes of the brain; in these studies, the most severe cell loss was noted in the frontal and temporal lobes. These three studies also provide data for primary cortices and their respective association cortices. In Brody's studies, neuronal cell loss was greater in the frontal pole than in the primary motor cortex. In Shefer's study, neuronal cell loss was greater in the frontal polar cortex (area 10) than in the premotor cortex (area 6), and greater in the high-order visual association cortex in the temporal lobe (area 21) than in the primary visual association cortex (area 18). These data suggest a trend, with increasing neuronal cell loss from primary cortices to higher-order association cortices.

All areas of the hippocampal formation also show age-related neuronal cell loss. In a serial section study using nucleolar cell counts of all fields of the hippocampus and subiculum, Ball (1977) found a 27% loss of cells from the fifth to the ninth decade. In the subiculum, Shefer (1972, 1976) noted a 29% neuronal loss when 19- to 28-year-olds were compared to older individuals (mean age 77 years). Dam (1979), in a series of 30 brains from the third to the eleventh decade, using nuclear counts, noted, in the seventh to tenth decade, significant neuronal cell loss in all hippocampal fields within the narrow range of 19 to 25% (Figure 2-3). He noted a lesser, nonsignificant loss in the granule cells of the fascia dentate. Thus, within the hippocampal formation, neuronal cell loss is widespread without striking predilection for any of its subdivisions.

In contrast to these neo- and allocortical areas, subcortical forebrain, brain stem, and cerebellar formations show highly selective neuronal loss. In the putamen, Bugiani et al. (1978) compared 16- to 49-year-old individuals with individuals 55 to 65 years of age, using cell counts without correction for cell size, and found a 30% loss of small cells and a 27% loss for large cells. In the amygdala, Herzog and Kemper (1980), using series sections and nucleolar counts, found a 4.3 to 19.2% neuronal loss confined to the medial central, medial, and cortical nucleus (Figure 2-3). In the hypothalamus, von Buttlar-Brentano (1954) noted no cell loss in the supraoptic and paraventricular nuclei on visual inspection; Wilkinson and Davies (1978) found no significant neuronal loss in the medial mammillary nucleus (mammillary body) in a serial section study. The majority of brain stem studies used nucleolar counts and serial sectioning. This technique has shown no age-related cell loss in trochlear nerve nucleus (Vijayashankar and Brody, 1973), ventral cochlear nucleus (Konigsmark and Murphy, 1970), or the inferior olive (Monagle and Brody, 1974). In contrast, Maleci (1934) found a 15% decrease in neurons in the facial nerve nucleus from the third to the ninth decade, which, according to Hanley's (1974) recalculation of the data, is highly significant. Age-related neuronal loss in the locus coeruleus has been documented in three studies (Vijayashankar and Brody, 1973; Tomonago, 1979; Tomlinson et al., 1981), with close agreement as to percentage loss by the eight and ninth decade of 30 to 40%. McGeer et al. (1977), in a serial section study of the substantia nigra, noted an approximate 50% cell loss by the ninth and tenth decade (estimated from their graph). In the cerebellum, both Ellis (1920, 1921) and Hall et al. (1975) have reported age-related loss of Purkinje cells, which, according to the careful study of Hall et al. (1975), occurs at the rate of 2.5% per decade. The dentate and other roof nuclei have shown no evidence of age-related neuronal loss (Hopker, 1951; Heidary and Tomasch, 1969).

Thus, cell loss with increasing age appears to be widespread in cortical and hippocampal areas, whereas in other areas of the brain it is selective, affecting the striatum, the phylogenetically older regions of the amygdala, the facial nerve nucleus, the monoaminergic nuclei in the brain stem, and the Purkinje cells of the cerebellum.

In patients with senile dementia, and particularly in patients with presenile Alzheimer's disease, this cell loss is accentuated. Shefer (1972) found the average percent neuronal loss for the six neocortical areas studied in the aged brain, SDAT, and Alzheimer's disease to be, respectively, 19%, 31%, and 46% (Figure 2-3). For the subiculum (Shefer, 1972, 1976), the comparable cell losses were 29%, 48%, and 53%. Colon (1973), in a study of three patients with Alzheimer's presenile dementia, noted an overall 60% cell loss in areas 4, 10, 17, and 24 that was most marked in the deeper cortical layers. The four controls for this study were 18 to 39 years of age. Terry et al. (1981) compared 18 patients with SDAT (aged 70–89 years) to 12 age-matched controls, and noted, in the frontal and temporal cortex, a respective loss of 26% and 22% for all neuronal cell sizes and a 40% and 46% loss of large cells, indicating a more marked loss of large than small neurons. In SDAT, Ball (1977) noted a 47% decrease in neurons in all fields of the hippocampus and subiculum combined, a finding in close agreement with Shefer's (1972, 1976) data on the subiculum. In the amygdala in SDAT (Herzog and Kemper, 1980), all subdivisions showed a 23% to 52% decrease in cell packing density, with the most marked deficit in those nuclei showing age-related cell loss, the medial, medial central, and cortical nucleus (Figure 2-3). In the thalamus, on visual inspection, Simma (1951) noted no evidence of cell loss in SDAT, whereas there was cell loss in Alzheimer's disease in specific cortical projection nuclei. Very little information is available for subcortical structures. Wilkinson and Davies (1978) found no cell loss in the mammillary nucleus in senile dementia. Tomonaga (1979), Mann et al. (1980), and Tomlinson et al. (1981) found evidence of greater cell loss in the locus coeruleus in patients with SDAT than in controls. In a single case of Alzheimer's disease, Whitehouse et al. (1981) noted marked cell loss in the nucleus basalis of Meynert.

Thus, in SDAT and Alzheimer's presenile dementia, further cell loss occurs in areas showing age-related cell loss and, in the case of the amygdala, in areas that failed to show age-related cell loss.

Glia

With increasing age, glial cells also decrease in number, but not to the extent shown by neurons. Shefer (1976) noted a 20 to 50% decrease in the subiculum in old and demented individuals, and Henderson et al. (1980), in a variety of cortical areas, a 14% decrease from age 20 to age 90. Terry et al. (1981) used a computer-imaging system to compare SDAT with age-matched controls and found no significant increase in glial cells in SDAT. In this study, cells less than 40 square microns in surface area were assumed to be glial cells.

Cellular, Nuclear, and Nucleolar Size

A decrease in size of the neuronal perikaryon, nuclei, and nucleoli with increasing age has been shown in several studies. A decrease in neuronal cell size has been reported in the subiculum beginning in the sixth decade (Uemura and Hartmann, 1979), in layer III pyramidal neurons in the frontal cortical area 9 in the mid-seventh decade (Uemura and Hartmann, 1978a), and in the hypoglossal nucleus (Uemura and Hartmann, 1978b) and the dentate nucleus (Treft, 1974) in the ninth decade. The only data on neuronal nuclear size is that of Mann et al. (1981a), who noted that it was decreased in temporal lobe pyramidal cells of patients 78 to 85 years old, as compared to those in their fifth to seventh decade. An age-related decrease in nucleolar size has been noted for hippocampal pyramidal cells, Purkinje cells, and neurons in the dentate nucleus and inferior olive by Mann et al. (1978). In a series of three patients, Uemura and Hartmann (1978a) noted no effect of SDAT on the size of cortical pyramidal cells. In the Mann et al. study (1981a), a reduction in nuclear size was noted in both SDAT and Alzheimer's disease, with the decrease in any one cell proportionate to their estimate of the amount of atrophy of the cell. Mann et al. (1981a) also noted a decrease in nucleolar size in SDAT. Mann et al. (1980) noted a similar, but less marked decrease in nucleolar volume of the locus coeruleus neurons, but no significant change in the substantia nigra in SDAT. In autopsy studies, both Dyan and Ball (1973) and Mann et al. (1981b) noted that the reduction in nucleolar size was greater in cells with neurofibrillary tangles than in those without this change, whereas in biopsies of Alzheimer's disease patients, Mann et al. (1981b) failed to find this difference. This observation presumably is due to an earlier stage of the disease in the patient biopsied.

Neuronal Processes

A closer view of age-related changes in individual neurons is provided by the Golgi method. The most complete staining of the neuronal processes is found in material fixed by vascular perfusion and stained with the rapid Golgi method, a procedure obviously limited to animal studies. Human studies, therefore, must be interpreted with caution, and allowance made for artifacts due to agonal states, delays in fixation (Williams et al., 1978), effects of minor trauma to unfixed tissue (Cammermeyer, 1960), and probably the Golgi staining technique used. Scheibel et al. (1975, 1976, 1977) and Scheibel (1979) made qualitative studies of the temporal and middle frontal gyrus, motor cortex, and hippocampus and adjacent cortex in aged and demented individuals. They described a characteristic sequence of changes. The initial stage was an irregular swelling and "lumpiness" of the cell body and proximal apical shaft, followed by spine loss. The horizontal dendritic processes then disappeared, with "amputation" of basal branches and loss of apical dendritic branches. In the end stage, fragmentation and disappearance of the apical shaft occurred. In these studies, the Betz cells of the motor cortex showed the most striking vulnerability, followed by the hippocampal and neocortical pyramidal cells. The granule cells of the fascia dentata were least effected. Certain regional peculiarities were noted, such as a "wind-swept" appearance of hippocampal pyramids and a spindle-shaped enlargement of the apical dendrites in the adjacent subiculum and entorhinal area. This latter observation, presumably representing focal accumulation of lipofuscin in subicular pyramidal cells, was reported by Braak (1972). In contrast to these regressive changes, Buell and Coleman (1979), in a quantitative study of parahippocampal pyramidal cells with the Cox–Golgi stain, noted an increase in the extent of apical and basal dendrites when 44- to 55-year-olds were compared to 68- to 92-year-olds. They failed to note this late life dendritic growth in SDAT, which suggested either a failure of growth or a regressive change. Mehra-ein et al. (1975), in a quantitative study, compared pyramidal cells in the cingulate cortex and the hippocampal and Purkinje cells in the cerebellum in patients with SDAT with non-demented controls. In SDAT, they noted a significant loss of dendritic spines and a decreased number and extent of Purkinje cell dendrites. In presenile Alzheimer's disease, these changes were more marked than in senile dementia. Further, Scheibel and Tomiyasu (1978) noted in two cases of familial Alzheimer's disease, "lawless" spine-covered clusters of new dendritic growth on Betz cells.

Support for many of these observations on the cerebral cortex can be found in animal models of aging in which perfusion fixation is used. Age-related decreases in dendritic synaptic spines, in dendritic length and width, as well as the loss of entire dendrites ("debranching"), have been noted in the monkey (Culp and Uemura, 1980; Uemura, 1980), dog (Mervis, 1978), and rat (Feldman and Dowd, 1975; Feldman, 1976, 1977; Vaughan, 1977). Cupp and Uemura (1980) noted, in layer III and layer V pyramidal neurons from the superior temporal gyrus in the monkey, dendritic growth in the 18- to 20-year-olds compared to the 7- to 12-year-olds, followed by a decrease in dendritic extent at 27 to 28 years of age. In the apical dendrite, this dendritic growth involved both increases in the number of dendrites as well as in the branch length; in the basal dendrite, only length was increased, and that primarily in the distal segments. In the oldest monkeys, both number and segment length decreased, particularly in the distal branches. In contrast, in the rat, there is a progressive age-related decrease in dendritic length (Feldman, 1977), which suggests a species-specific difference. A striking observation in the dog (Mervis, 1978) and rat (Feldman and Dowd, 1975; Feldman, 1976) is the presence of cells showing advanced age-related change next to unchanged cells. Abnormal dendritic growths also have been noted in aged dogs (Lafora, 1914; Mervis, 1978). Varicose-like swellings of dendrites and distortions of cell body shape are absent from the animals in these studies, with the exception of the Mervis (1978) study, which suggests that these abnormalities may be artifacts in the human material.

Myelin

Several lines of evidence indicate that significant changes occur in white matter with both aging and SDAT. Miller et al. (1980), in a serial section study of the cerebral hemispheres of normal individuals aged 20 to 98 years, noted after age 50 a decline in the volume of the hemisphere that was associated with an increased gray matter to white matter ratio, indicating a loss of myelin. In SDAT, they noted a further decline in hemispheric volume without any change in the gray matter to white matter ratio, which suggests a further decrease in both. Tomlinson et al. (1970) found a reduction of myelin in the cores of gyri in SDAT, and the electron microscopic studies of Terry et al. (1964) and Terry and Wisniewski (1972) have shown evidence of Wallerian degeneration and primary demyelination in Alzheimer's disease.

In the whole brain serial sections in the Yakovlev Collection (now at the Armed Forces Institute of Pathology), (Figure 2-4) the older normative brains show a pallor of myelin staining in the forebrain that appears to be confined to the corona radiata and stratum sagittale interna (personal observation), subcortical fiber systems with long postnatal cycles of myelination (Yakovlev and Lecours, 1967). In

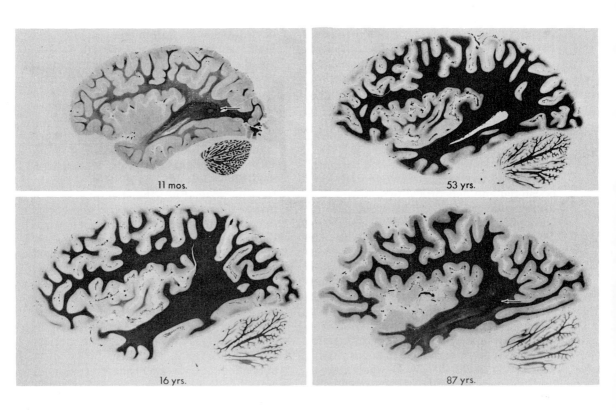

Figure 2-4. Macrophotograph of age-related pallor of myelin staining. Note the similarity of the myelination of the 11-month-old infant and the 87-year-old non-demented individual. Arrow indicates early myelinating visual radiations. The later myelinating stratum sagittale interna within the visual radiations and the corona radiata outside of them have longer cycles of myelination and show age-related pallor.

contrast, myelinated fiber systems with shorter postnatal cycles of myelination, such as the visual radiations and the internal capsular fibers, show no evidence of age-related pallor. In this same material, Yakovlev (1962) made similar observations in the brain stem, noting that the reticular formation, which has the longest cycle of myelination in this location (Yakovlev and Lecours, 1967), also showed age-related pallor of myelin staining. The same phenomenon can be seen in the plates of the atlas of Kaes (1907), which illustrates intracortical myelination for 12 different areas according to age. The primary cortices (motor, somesthetic, visual, and auditory), in which myelination is completed earlier than in the association and limbic cortices, show few age-related changes. In contrast, both the association and limbic cortices show age-related loss of myelin (Figure 2-5). Thus, age-related loss of myelin appears to be directly related to the length of the cycle of myelination, and

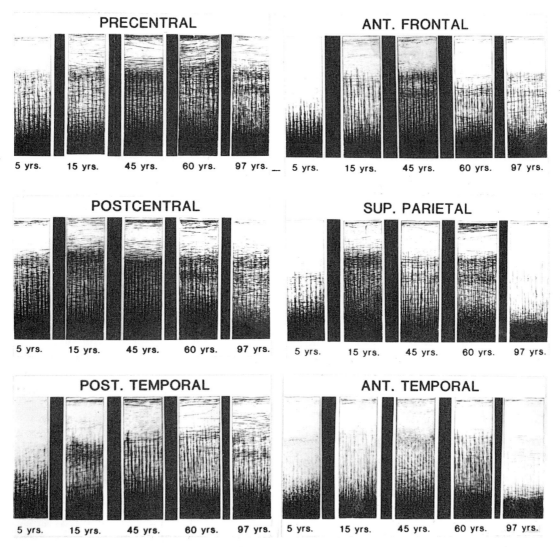

Figure 2-5. Composite illustration from Kaes (1907) of intracortical myelination. The primary cortices (left) show little age-related loss of myelin; the association cortices (right) show marked age-related loss of myelin.

in the forebrain, it occurs primarily in the association and limbic cortices and the cortico-cortical fiber systems of the corona radiata.

Amyloid

Amyloid infiltrates are frequently observed in brains of normal elderly individuals. These infiltrates occur in pial and penetrating blood vessels; in senile plaques, as subependymal and subpial deposits; and in the choroid plexus. Vascular amyloid was first described in detail by Scholz (1938), and his observations have been confirmed in many subsequent studies. In leptomeningeal blood vessels, amyloid primarily affects arteries 21 to 100 microns in diameter, with some arteries up to 1000 microns also affected (Morimatsu et al., 1975). Veins are rarely affected, and then usually only small veins in cases with extensive cerebrovascular amyloidosis (Morimatsu et al., 1975; Mandybur, 1975). The infiltrate is generally segmental (Wright et al., 1969; van Bogaert, 1970; Mandybur, 1975; Kurucz et al., 1981a) and may be associated with a local swelling (van Bogaert, 1970; Mandybur, 1975). Deposition of amyloid begins in the media of the arterial wall just beneath the adventitia; it then extends throughout the media and into the adventita (Scholz, 1938; Wright et al., 1969; Morimatsu et al., 1975; Tomonaga, 1981a) and is associated with regressive changes in the cellular elements and loss of collagen (Scholz, 1938). The intima is unaffected. The elastica initially becomes stretched, thin, and reduplicated and later fragments and may disappear (Scholz, 1938; Mandybur, 1975). When penetrating vessels are affected, they are generally less than 50 microns in diameter (Morimatsu et al., 1975). In these vessels, the entire wall may show loss of cellular structure, with extension of the amyloid into brain tissue (Scholz, 1938; Pantelakis, 1954; Wright et al., 1969; Mandybur, 1975). Capillaries are usually spared, according to Mandybur (1975). When capillaries are involved, they show amorphous globular masses, semilu-

nar nodules, and circumferential deposits with ill-defined borders (Figure 2-6). From these capillaries and from penetrating small arteries, amyloid may extend into the brain tissue where it is often associated with "free" deposits (Scholz, 1938; Pantelakis, 1954; Margolis and Pickett, 1959; Mandybur, 1975; Morimatsu et al., 1975). This latter phenomenon was called *drusige Entarturg* by Scholz (1938) and dyshoric angiopathy by Morel and Wildi (1952). Pantelakis (1954) proposed the term congophilic angiopathy for blood vessels in which the amyloid is confined to the vessel wall with the glial limiting membrane preserved.

Vascular amyloid within the cerebral cortex is most abundant in the occipital and temporal lobes (Mandybur, 1975; Tomonaga, 1981), with the most striking involvement of the dyshoric angiopathy in layer IVc of the visual cortex (Scholz, 1938; Pantelakis, 1954; Surbek, 1961; Mandybur, 1975), where, according to Surbek (1961), it occurs without evidence of a cellular reaction. According to Pantelakis (1954), the congophilic angiopathy shows less striking predilection for this area and may occur in areas 18 and 19 to the exclusion of area 17. It has also been noted in the gray matter of the cerebellum, basal ganglia, diencephalon, brain stem and spinal cord, and, rarely, in the white matter (Scholz, 1938; Pantelakis, 1954; Mandybur, 1975; Tomonaga, 1981). According to Scholz (1938), vascular amyloid is relatively frequent in cerebellum, with only the molecular layer remaining unaffected (Pantelakis, 1954).

The age of onset of vascular amyloid is generally reported as the seventh decade (Scholz, 1938; Surbek, 1961; Wright et al., 1969; Morimatsu et al., 1975). However, Morel and Wildi (1952) first noted it at age 58 and Pantelakis (1954) at age 71. The incidence subsequently increases with age (Pantelakis, 1954; Surbek, 1961; Wright et al., 1969; Morimatsu et al., 1975; Tomonaga, 1981; Kurucz, 1981). Tomonaga (1981), in a series of 128 brains from a geriatric hospital, found an incidence of 8% in the seventh decade, 23% in the eighth decade, 37% in the ninth

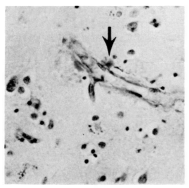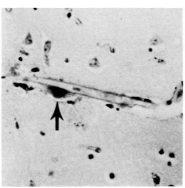

Figure 2-6. Small deposits of amyloid in close relationship to small blood vessels (arrows). PAS stain. 250X.

decade, and 58% after the ninth decade. In the older brains, it appears to be etiologically related to softening and hemorrhage.

The incidence of amyloid change with regard to sex is not clear. Surbek (1961) found it slightly more prevalent in males, but Morimatsu et al. (1975) noted a female preponderance. Surbek (1961) suggested a hereditary factor, since he had observed it in all six brains from two different families.

Brain amyloid appears to correlate with age-related amyloid deposits in the heart, aorta, and pancreas (Wright et al., 1969; Schwartz, 1970; Shirahama et al., 1982), rather than generalized systemic amyloidosis. Mathews (1954) found only two of ninety-eight cases of systemic amyloidosis with cerebral vascular amyloidosis and only five with choroid plexus amyloidosis. In contrast, Wright et al. (1969), in a systematic study of autopsies from the fourth to the tenth decade, noted age-related amyloid in cerebral blood vessels and senile plaques in 50% of all cerebra over 60 years of age, 63% over age 70 and 85% over age 80. In this study, the brain was the most frequently involved organ. This relationship is further supported by the recent observation that cerebral vascular and senile plaque amyloid show some of the same immunocytochemical properties as senile amyloid (Shirahama et al., 1982). No relation to atherosclerosis (Scholz, 1938; Morel and Wildi, 1952; Pantelakis, 1954; Surbek, 1961; Mandy-

bur, 1975) or to hypertension (Morel and Wildi, 1952) has been found. However an association with hyalinosis has been noted by Surbek (1961) and Tomonaga (1981), and with angionecrosis by Tomonaga (1981). According to Kurucz et al. (1981), vascular amyloid is more frequent in areas of vascular softening.

The incidence of vascular amyloid in most studies is more frequent in senile dementia and Alzheimer's disease as compared to controls. Pantelakis (1954) emphasized its relationship to dementia, observing it in three out of four cases of Alzheimer's disease and in 48% of his twenty-five cases of senile dementia. It was present in all 12 cases of Alzheimer's disease studied by von Braunmühl (1957), and in Surbek's series (1961), all patients with this change were demented. Mandybur (1975) noted it in 13 out of 15 cases of SDAT. Thus, as emphasized by Mandybur (1975), it is a common, but not consistent finding in SDAT. Further, although of greater severity in severely demented individuals, vascular amyloid is less strikingly correlated with dementia than the neurofibrillary tangle (Morimatsu et al., 1975).

A close relationship of amyloid deposition to the senile plaque has been postulated since 1909, when Oppenheim found a similar, metachromatically staining, glassy hyaline material in both brain capillaries and senile plaques. The early history of thinking about this relation has been reviewed by Margolis and Pickett (1959),

Surbek (1961), Schwartz et al. (1964), Wright et al. (1969), and Schwartz (1970). Recent studies, however, indicate no obligate relationship. Mandybur (1975) found no evidence of amyloid angiopathy in two of fifteen cases of SDAT with marked senile plaque formation. Morimatsu et al. (1975) found a lower incidence of amyloid angiopathy than of senile plaques in their study of 146 autopsies, and Kurucz et al. (1981) found no evidence of amyloid angiopathy in 30 of 96 brains with senile plaques. Further, Tomonaga (1981) noted in 8.7% of brains with amyloid angiopathy that there was no evidence of senile plaques, and both Surbek (1961) and Kurucz et al. (1981) found no topographic relationship between the angiopathy and the senile plaque.

In 1954, Corsellis and Brierley called attention to an atypical form of Alzheimer's disease in which marked amyloid vascular deposits and unusually prominent senile plaques occurred. The report included two new cases and reviewed four similar ones published earlier. The clinical picture was of a progressive presenile dementia with spastic paraparesis, often with cerebellar signs. All but one case had a family history of a similar condition. At autopsy, the brain showed slight or absent gyral atrophy, marked amyloid deposits in pial and penetrating blood vessels, abundant senile plaques, neurofibrillary tangles in the neocortex and hippocampus, and a marked loss of central myelin in the cerebral hemispheres. In a clinical report of 10 patients, over three generations, Worster-Drought et al. (1940) noted an age of onset of 44 to 48 years, with one case at 57 years, and a marked preponderance in females. In 1970, Hollander and Strich reported six cases with neuropathological changes similar to those reported by Corsellis and Brierley (1954), with, however, an apparent acute onset following an "intracranial catastrophe."

Senile (Neuritic) Plaque

Senile (neuritic) plaques are discrete structures in the neuropil, with an average diameter of 70 microns (Wisniewski and Terry, 1973), that occur in largest numbers in the neocortex and amygdala. They were first described by Blocq and Marinesco (1892) as sclerotic plaques of microglia and later by Redlich (1898) as miliary sclerosis. Following the early detailed description by Fischer (1907), who used the Bielschowsky stain for axis cylinders, they were then frequently referred to as the military plaques of Fischer. The term senile plaques was coined by Simchowicz (1911). In order to emphasize degenerating small axons and dendrites noted in electron microscope studies, Wisniewski et al. (1973) have proposed the name neuritic plaque.

Light and electron microscope appearances allow classification into three types (Fischer, 1907; van der Horst et al., 1960; Wisniewski and Terry, 1973; Shefer, 1977). The smallest type consists of a sharply circumscribed granular deposit of amyloid (Figure 2-7A), with an average diameter of 8.9 millimeters (Shefer, 1977). The axons and myelinated fibers in the surrounding tissue are displaced, but show little or no other evidence of abnormality. Reactive cells are either absent or infrequent. The other two types of plaques are larger and are usually referred to as typical (or classical) plaques (Figure 2-7B, C) and primitive plaques (Figure 2-7D). The typical plaque consists of a central core of amyloid surrounded by a corona of reactive astroglial cells, microglia, macrophages, degenerating axons, and occasional dendrites (Figure 2-7B,C). The primitive plaque lacks the central core of amyloid. It consists of a spherical mass of intermixed degenerating neuronal processes, amyloid, and reactive cells. Early workers had suggested a close relationship to blood vessels (Fischer, 1907; Oppenheim, 1909), but this was not substantiated by later studies (Fuller, 1911; Margolis and Pickett, 1959; Kidd, 1964; Wisniewski and Terry, 1973). The presence of various forms of plaques suggests that the forms represent different stages in evolution. Based on light microscopic studies, most authors, following Fischer (1907), considered the small focal accumulation of

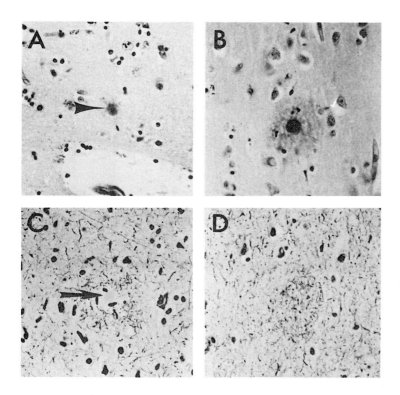

Figure 2-7. Senile plaques. At A, a "burned-out" plaque represented by a small focal deposit of amyloid (arrowhead). B, a classical plaque with reactive cells surrounding the amyloid deposit. C, a classical plaque with degenerating axons surrounding focal deposit of amyloid (arrow). D, a primitive plaque with degenerating axons throughout the plaque. A and B, H & E stain; C and D, Bodian stain. 250X.

amyloid to be the initial stage (Scholz, 1938; van der Horst et al., 1960; Shefer, 1977), but the electron microscopic studies of Wisniewski and Terry (1973) indicate that this is an end stage, a "burned-out plaque." The amyloid nature of this deposit has been shown with the light microscope using congo red and thioflavin staining (Divry, 1927, 1952; Schwartz, 1970) and with the electron microscope (Kidd, 1964; Terry et al., 1964; Wisniewski and Terry, 1973). Many details of the axonal pathology were elucidated in silver-stained preparations by early workers (Fischer, 1907; Bouman, 1934; Cajal, 1968), particularly Fischer (1907). In small plaques, axons appear to be displaced by the amyloid deposit, whereas in larger plaques, there are a variety of reactive and degenerative changes. The most frequently described change in these studies are single or multiple club-like swellings, at times with thread-like endings. Axons that approach the central amyloid core turn abruptly

away from it, with their swellings directed toward the periphery of the plaque. Axons that tangentially traverse the edge of the plaque often have offshoots of similar swellings directed toward the center of the plaque. Cajal (1968) and Bouman (1934) both felt that these swellings represented abortive attempts at regeneration. According to Fischer (1907), Bouman (1934), and Tomlinson et al. (1970), similar swellings of axons are present in the neuropil in areas where plaques are not present. Under the electron microscope (Kidd, 1964; Terry et al., 1964; Suzuki and Terry, 1967; Wisniewski and Terry, 1973), abnormalities in both dendrites and axons, collectively referred to as neurites, can be seen. These neurites have laminated dense bodies, dense bodies, paired helical filaments, and, occasionally, bundles of neurofilaments. In the primative plaques, these abnormal neurites and reactive cells are intermixed with wisps of amyloid; in the classical plaques, they surround a central core of amyloid (Wisniewski and Terry, 1973).

Early thinking on the etiology of the senile plaque has been summarized by Fuller (1911), Uyematsu (1923), Ferraro (1931), and McMenemey (1958). Early workers, following the original studies of Blocq and Marinesco (1892), thought that these plaques arose from degenerating glial reticulum. Fischer (1907) and Fuller (1911), however, suggested that they arose from degenerating nerve fibers; Herxheimer and Gierlich (1907) and Bonfiglio (1908), from degenerating nerve cells; von Braunmühl (1932) and Marinesco (1911), from the intracellular ground substance; and Urechina and Elekes (1925) and Ferraro (1931), from degenerating oligodendroglial and microglial cells. In 1927, Divry identified amyloid in senile plaques and implicated it in their pathogenesis, a view shared by Bouman (1934) and van der Horst et al. (1960) and recently championed by Schwartz (1970). Many modern workers have suggested that the initial insult is to the neuronal perikaryon, with resultant abnormal neurites and secondary amyloid deposits (Suzuki and Terry, 1967; Wisniewski and Terry, 1973). A possible role for the monoaminergic system in their pathogenesis is suggested by the study of Tomlinson et al. (1981), in which they found that cell loss in the nonadrenergic locus coeruleus in SDAT significantly correlated with the number of senile plaques in the neocortex, but not with the neurofibrillary tangle or the degree of dementia.

The senile plaque is found in many human diseases and in aged animals. In man, it occurs in Pick's disease (Wisniewski and Terry, 1973), Guam ALS–Parkinson–dementia complex (Hirano et al., 1966), Creutzfeldt–Jakob disease (Traub et al., 1977), and kuru (Klatzo et al., 1959; Field et al., 1969). Its occurrence in the latter two diseases, together with the finding of typical plaques in scrapie-infected mice (Fraser and Bruce, 1973; Wisniewski et al., 1975), suggest a viral etiology.

In animals, the plaques differ from those found in man only the absence of the paired helical filaments (Terry et al., 1972). Plaques have been noted in monkeys 16 to 23 years of age (Wisniewski et al., 1973), in dogs from 12 years of age (Schwartz, 1970; Wisniewski et al., 1970), and in rats 28 to 30 months of age (Vaughan and Peters, 1981). In rats, they occurred in association with a spongiform encephalopathy, which also suggests a viral etiology.

Density of senile plaques is not correlated with neuronal cell loss in the neocortex (Henderson et al., 1980; Terry et al., 1981), cortical thickness, or brain weight (Terry et al., 1981). Most authors have noted a predilection for superficial cortical layers (Redlich, 1898; Fischer, 1907; Fuller, 1911), particularly in the banks (Fuller, 1911) and depths of sulci (Tomlinson et al., 1968, 1970). However, Tomlinson et al. (1968, 1970) have indicated that there is a preference for layers III and V, and Mandybur (1975) has shown regional differences in the laminar distribution of senile plaques. These plaques also occur in small numbers in subcortical white matter (Fuller, 1911).

The plaques show no right–left differences (Jamada and Mehraein, 1968) and no male–female differences (Matsuyama and Nakamura, 1978). Jordan (1971) found an increased incidence in cancer patients, whereas Matsuyama and Nakamura (1978) found no clear relation between occurrence of plaques and the presence of malignancy.

As an age-related change, the senile plaque was first noted as an occurrance of old age by early workers (Simchowicz, 1911). However, in more recent studies, it was first noted in the fifth decade (Jordan, 1971), with an increasing incidence with increasing age (Dayan, 1970a; Jordan, 1971; Morimatsu et al., 1975). According to Jordan (1971), two-thirds of all cerebra show senile plaques by the ninth decade. As an age-related change, plaques occur in small numbers, with an apparent predilection for the neocortex, but the extent of their subcortical distribution is unknown. Matsuyama and Nakamura (1978) noted, in a study of the hippocampus and all four lobes of brains, a predilection for the parahippocampal and occipitotemporal (fusiform) gyrus, with less frequent involvement of the frontal and insular cortex. Tomlinson et al. (1968), who also studied all four lobes of the brain, noted their first appearance in the occipital lobe and observed that when more than two senile plaques per high power field were present in this location, all four lobes of the brain would be involved.

In demented individuals, the full extent of the distribution of the senile plaque is seen, with patients with Alzheimer's disease showing a higher density of plaques in any one area as well as a more extensive distribution throughout the areas of predilection (Mutrux, 1947; Jamada and Mahraein, 1968) (Figure 2-8). The relationship of the senile plaque to senile dementia is, however, not as clear as for the neurofibrillary tangle. Dayan (1970b), in a quantitative study of the hippocampus and frontal lobe, noted no significant difference in the density of plaque in SDAT as compared to controls. Similarly, Tomlinson et al. (1970), in a study of all four lobes of brains, noted no significant difference in the number of cases with senile plaques as compared to controls. In nine of their twenty-five demented patients, plaque counts were within or just above the control range. In contrast, Roth et al. (1966), in a study of all four lobes of brain, and Morimatsu et al. (1975), in a study of the hippocampus, found a significant increase in senile plaques in SDAT. Further, Morimatsu et al. (1975) found no significant difference in plaque counts between less and more severely demented individuals. Of the various clinical features of SDAT, Morimatsu et al. (1975) found a correlation with emotional incontinence and Kurucz et al. (1981) found a correlation with disorientation and age of the patient.

Within the neocortex in senile dementia and in Alzheimer's disease, the senile plaque is most frequent in the temporal lobe (Goodman, 1953; Hooper and Vogel, 1976; Matsuyama and Nakamura, 1978), with the highest concentrations in the association cortices of the middle and inferior temporal gyri (Mutrux, 1947; Goodman, 1953) (Figure 2-9). Mutrux (1947) noted a gradient of increasing density of plaques from the primary auditory cortex (area TC) to its immediate association cortex (area TB), with a still greater concentration in the higher-order association cortical area TA. Senile plaque density in area TE in the middle and inferior temporal gyri, in turn, exceeds that of area TA. According to Goodman (1953), area TA has a higher concentration of plaques than has area 38, a transitional limbic cortex in the temporal pole. Thus, within the temporal lobe, there is a gradient of increasing plaque density from the primary auditory cortex to higher-order association cortices.

Although studied in less detail, a similar gradient appears to be present in the other three lobes of the brain. Goodman (1953) studied nine neocortical areas in Alzheimer's disease and found the three lowest plaque counts in the primary motor (area 4), primary sensory (areas 3, 1, 2), and primary visual (area 17) cortex. In the frontal lobe in this study, area 10 (frontal pole) and area 44 (Broca's area) showed higher plaque counts than area 4, with Broca's areas showing the highest average plaque count, approximately three and one-half times higher than the motor cortex. In the study of Jamada and Mehraein (1968), area 9 (a prefrontal cortex) showed a higher plaque count than area 4. In the parietal lobe, Goodman (1953) found the plaque count in the angular gyrus (area 39) to be almost twice the average density of that found in areas 3, 1, and 2. Although comparable data are not available for the occipital lobe, Jamada and Mehraein (1968) have indicated that the average plaque count in the visual association area, area 19, is comparable to that found in frontal and temporal association areas. The density of senile plaques in the limbic cortices relative to other neocortical areas is not as clear. According to Jamada and Mehraein (1968), senile plaque density is comparable to the density in cortical association areas in the frontal, temporal, and occipital lobes, although Hooper and Vogel (1976), found it to be

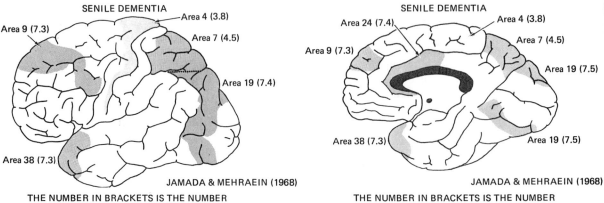

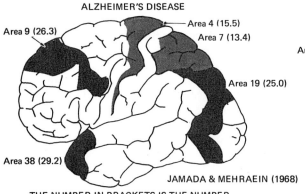

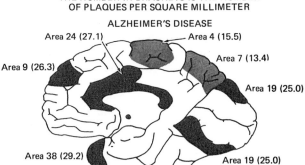

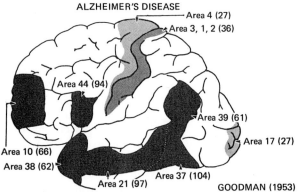

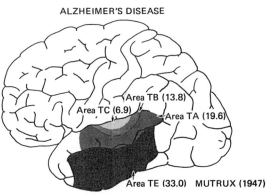

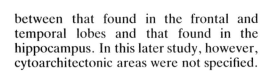

Figure 2-8. Template diagrams of location and density of senile plaques in the neocortex in SDAT and Alzheimer's disease.

between that found in the frontal and temporal lobes and that found in the hippocampus. In this later study, however, cytoarchitectonic areas were not specified.

These neocortical areas have a higher concentration of plaques than areas in the hippocampal complex (Goodman, 1953; Jamada and Mehraein, 1968; Hooper and

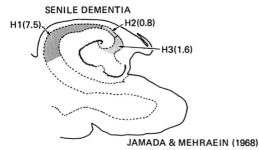

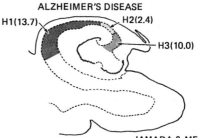

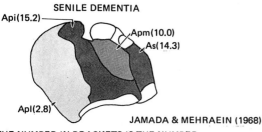

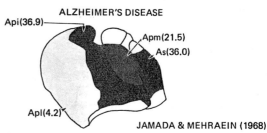

Figure 2-9. Template diagrams of location and density of senile plaques in the hippocampus and amygdala in SDAT and Alzheimer's disease.

Vogel, 1976). Within the latter, they are more frequent in H1 (Sommer's sector), subiculum, and presubiculum than in fields H2 and H3 (Jamada and Mehraein, 1968) (Figure 2-9).

The amygdala shows the highest plaque counts documented for any region of the brain in SDAT (Jamada and Mehraein, 1968) (Figure 2-9). There is a striking predilection for the cortical and small-celled part of the basal nucleus, particularly the medial basal and lateral basal nucleus (Brockhaus, 1938; Jamada and Mehraein, 1968; Hooper and Vogel, 1976), and according to Brockhaus (1938), the central nucleus also. The lateral nucleus shows a much lower plaque count with a density comparable to that found in Sommer's sector of the hippocampus (Jamada and Mahraein, 1968).

In the thalamus, according to Simma (1951), senile plaques can be seen in Alzheimer's disease, but not in senile dementia. In the basal forebrain and brain stem they are infrequent, but are occasionally noted in the nucleus basalis, nucleus raphe dorsalis, and mammillary body (Jamada and Mehraein, 1977). They are rare in the cerebellum, where they occur mainly in cases of familial Alzheimer's disease; there they resemble the plaques seen in kuru and Creutzfeld–Jakob disease (Pro et al., 1980).

Although the senile plaque and the neurofibrillary tangle commonly occur together, they are apparently not closely related to each other. Matsuyama and Nakamura (1978), in a study of 617 brains without evidence of "psychosis," noted that there was a wider distribution of plaque than of tangle and that the severity of these changes appeared to be unrelated. Goodman (1953) also noted this disparity in Alzheimer's disease. Further, he noted the relative rarity of the senile plaque in Sommer's sector and in Arnold's glomeruli of the entorhinal cortex, areas of marked predilection for the neurofibrillary tangle. Jamada and Mahraein (1968) made the same observations with regard to Sommer's sector. In addition, Goodman (1953) cites a case of Alzheimer's disease with a large number of neurofibrillary tangles without a single senile plaque and another with a large number of senile plaques and only a single neurofibrillary tangle. Also in the Guam ALS–Parkinsonism–dementia complex, typical neurofibrillary tangles are abundant and senile plaques rare and limited to elderly individuals (Hirano et al., 1966).

Neurofibrillary Tangle

The neurofibrillary tangle (NFT) is an intraneuronal fibrillary structure best seen with silver stains (Figure 2-10). The earliest form of this abnormality is identified as a darkly stained thick band, often irregularly traversing the cytoplasm from the apical end to a basal dendrite (Figure 2-10A). At later stages, the numbers of bands increase and, becoming twisted and whorled, often displace the nucleus and distort the cell body. At late stages, the NFT appears even more extensive and is less argentophilic; the cell membrane and nucleus fail to stain, giving the NFT an appearance that persists after cell death (Figure 2-10C). In pyramidal cells, they are triangular or flame shaped (Figure 2-10A, B, C); in subcortical formations, they usually resemble a coarse ball of string (Figure 2-10D). With Nissl stain, the NFT appears as an unstained negative image and is often associated with a loss of Nissl granules (Spielmeyer, 1922; von Braunmühl, 1957; McMenemey, 1958). Under the electron microscope, the NFT is composed of paired helical filaments (PHF) of "infinite" length and approximately 10 nanometers in diameter, with a periodic twist every 80 nanometers, and occasionally intermixed with normal-appearing filaments and tubules (Kidd, 1963, 1964; Wisniewski et al., 1970; Terry and Wisniewski, 1972; Wisniewski and Soiser, 1979; Terry and Davis, 1980). In these studies, the cytoplasm of the cell appears to be otherwise little affected, except for displacement by the PHF and an apparent loss of mitochochondria and ribosomes (Kidd, 1963, 1964; Terry and Wisniewski, 1972; Wisniewski and Soiser, 1979, Terry and Davis, 1980).

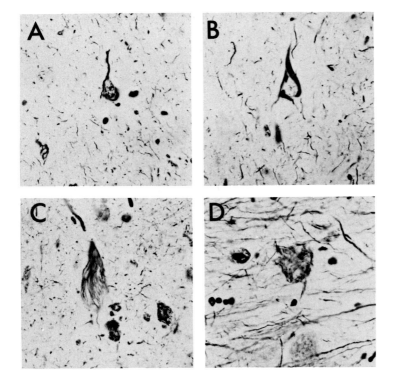

Figure 2-10. Neurofibrillary tangles. A, a small pyramidal cell with early neurofibrillary degeneration. B, a later stage. C, a neurofibrillary tangle with no recognizable cell membrane or nucleus. Note the flame shape of the neurofibrillary tangle in these three pyramidal cells. D, the ball-like appearance of the neurofibrillary tangle in a subcortical neuron. Bodian stain. 250X.

The etiology of the NFT is unsettled. Alzheimer (1907), who originally described the change in a 51-year-old woman with a disease later called Alzheimer's disease by Kraepelin, suggested that the NFT was due to disease-transformed neurofilaments, with deposition of a morbid product of neuronal metabolism. This view was shared by Spielmeyer (1922) and von Braunmühl (1932), the former adding that he felt it might also involve the deposition of a substance foreign to the cell and the latter that it was due to aging changes in colloid. Bielschowsky (1912, 1932), who noted that the NFT appeared to develop independent of the neurofibrillary network of the cell, thought it was due to deposition of a foreign substance. Divry (1934) and Schwartz et al. (1964) noted that the NFT had the same staining and birefringent qualities as amyloid and suggested that it might be due to deposition of this substance within the cell. This view was recently supported by Glenner (1979) and Shirahama et al. (1982). In this regard, it is of interest to note that King (1942), Margolis and Pickett (1959), and Schwartz et al. (1964) have reported a halo staining for amyloid around NFT-containing neurons. Electron microscopic studies, however, fail to support an amyloid etiology for this change (Kidd, 1963, 1964; Krigman et al., 1965; Schlote, 1968; Wisniewski and Terry, 1973). Wisniewski and Soiser (1979) reviewed the available neurochemical studies and suggested four possible etiologies for the NFT: (1) They may form from tubulin, a protein that accounts for 10% of brain protein and 75 to 90% of the microtubule; (2) they arise from pre-existing neurofilaments; (3) they are an altered form of tubulin or neurofilament; and (4) a new protein is produced. Dahl et al. (1982), in a report of their own studies and those of others, have provided evidence for a cross-reactivity of the NFT with neurofilament protein(s). A possible infectious cause has been suggested by the transmission of a viral-like agent from two cases of familial Alzheimer's disease to primates. These primates, however, develop spongiform changes rather than the histological features of Alzheimer's disease (Traub et al., 1977). The observation of Crapper et al. (1976) of increased aluminum in the brain of patients with senile and presenile dementia suggested a possible role for it in the pathogenesis of the NFT. However their original observations have not been confirmed (Wisniewski and Soiser, 1979; McDermott et al., 1979; Traub et al., 1981), and, further, although aluminum in experimental animals does produce the NFT, they fail to show the PHF with the electron microscope (Crapper et al., 1976).

The neurofibrillary tangle with the PHF, although unique to man, is not specific for either aging or SDAT. It has been reported in the Guam Parkinsonism–dementia complex, dementia pugilistica, Down's syndrome, postencephalitic Parkinsonism, subacute sclerosing panencephalitis, tuberous sclerosis, Hallervorden–Spatz disease, and pigment variant lipofuscinosis (Iqbal et al., 1977).

A striking feature of the NFT in aging and dementia is its predilection for certain cell groups and its rarity or absence in others. The lesion is rare in the Betz cells of the motor cortex; putamen; caudate; globus pallidus; specific cortical projection nuclei of the thalamus; subthalamic nucleus; entire cerebellar circuits, including the red nucleus; third nerve nucleus; dorsal cochlear nucleus; and spinal cord (Simchowicz, 1911; Hirano and Zimmerman, 1962; Jellinger, 1971; Jamada and Mehraein, 1977). In cortical formations, nearly all authors emphasize involvement of the hippocampus and the adjacent entorhinal cortex (Simchowicz, 1911; Spielmeyer, 1922; von Braunmühl, 1957; Hirano and Zimmerman, 1962; Jamada and Mehraein, 1968; Tomlinson et al., 1970; Hirano, 1973; Hooper and Vogel, 1976; Matsuyama and Nakamura, 1978; Kemper, 1978; Ball, 1978). In this region, its areas of predilection are CA1 (Sommer's sector), the subiculum, and the entorhinal cortex (Jamada and Mahraein, 1968; Ball, 1978; Kemper, 1978), particularly the lateral entorhinal area (McLardy, 1970; Kemper, 1978). In this area, the NFT occur predominantly in superficial clumps of large neurons, often referred to as Arnold's glomeruli. These glomeruli, according to Goodman (1953), show the

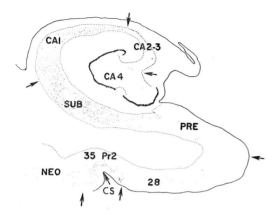

Figure 2-11. Camera lucida drawing of the distribution of neurofibrillary tangles according to cytoarchitecture in SDAT. Each dot represents a single tangle. CS, collateral sulcus.

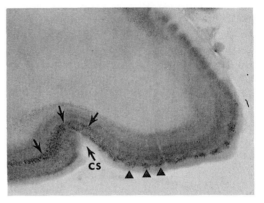

Figure 2-12. Lipofuscin-stained, 900-micron-thick section of the parahippocampal gyrus of the transentorhinal cortex. Note the clumped lipofuscin-filled cells in the lateral entorhinal cortex (arrowheads) and the transition of these cells into layer IIIC pyramids (arrows) in the depth of the collateral sulcus (CS). Compare the position of these cells to those containing neurofibrillary tangles in Figure 2-11.

highest density of NFT's in the cortex in Alzheimer's disease. It can be seen in Figure 2-11 that, at progressive depths in the collateral sulcus, the NFT-containing neurons occur at progressively deeper cortical layers, eventually aligning with layer IIIc pyramidal cells in the adjacent area 35 (of Brodmann). In the human brain stained for lipofuscin, the position of the NFT-containing neurons corresponds to a band of heavily pigmented neurons that traverse these two areas (Figure 2-12), regions collectively referred to as the transentorhinal cortex by Braak (1980). According to Braak, with the Golgi stain, these heavily pigmented neurons are basically the same cell type with a progressively elaborated apical dendrite, suggesting that the NFT may have a high degree of specificity for a particular cell type.

The NFT shows no male–female or right–left predilection (Ball, 1976; Matsuyama and Nakamura, 1978) and appears to be little affected by systemic illness (Matsuyama and Nakamura, 1978).

As an age-related change, the NFT appears in increasing numbers with increasing age, with the greatest density in CA1 (Sommer's sector), the subiculum, and the entorhinal cortex; its highest density and earliest appearance are in the lateral entorhinal cortex (Figure 2-9) (Hirano and Zimmerman, 1962; Tomlinson et

al., 1968; Ball, 1978; Kemper, 1978; Matsuyama and Nakamura, 1978). In these locations, it is more common in anterior than posterior levels (Ball, 1976; Matsuyama and Nakamura, 1978). It is first found here in the fourth decade (Matsuyama and Nakamura, 1978). If only the presence or absence of the NFT is noted, there is then a steady increase in the percent of brains showing this change until the ninth decade when all (Matsuyama et al., 1966) or almost all brains (Jordan, 1971; Matsuyama and Nakamura, 1978) show the NFT. If, however, the data are expressed as the percent of brains with over 10 NFT (Peress et al., 1973) or 50 NFT (Matsuyama et al., 1966, Jordan, 1971; Matsuyama and Nakamura, 1978) in the histological section, then the rate of increase in percent of affected brains is less, with those surviving to the tenth decade and beyond showing a smaller percent of affected brains than found in the ninth decade.

As an age-related change, the NFT is either rare or absent in the neocortex (Tomlinson et al., 1968; Kemper, 1978; Matsuyama and Nakamura, 1978). In a series of 617 control brains, Matsuyama and Nakamura (1978) found only five brains with the NFT in this location.

In the brain stem, the NFT is often reported as absent or rare as an age-related change (Gellerstedt, 1933; Hirano and Zimmerman, 1962; Ishii, 1966; Ishino and Otsuki, 1975). Forno and Alvord (1971), however, observed it in the locus coeruleus beginning in the fourth decade and in the substantia nigra in the sixth decade. In patients 60 years of age and older, the percentage of brains with this change in these locations, respectively, is 44% and 9%. At over 90 years of age, almost all patients in this study had NFT's in the locus coeruleus. Similarly, Tomonago (1979) found the NFT in the locus coeruleus in 10 to 20% of patients aged 60 to 90 years and in all patients over 100 years. According to Ishii (1966) and Ishino and Otsuki (1975), the NFT is rare as an age-related change in the basal forebrain.

In SDAT, the entire extent of the distribution pattern of the NFT is seen with a greater concentration in presenile Alzheimer's disease than in senile dementia, in both cortical (Goodman, 1953; Mutrux, 1947; Jamada and Mehraein, 1968, 1977) and subcortical areas (Ishino and Otsuki, 1975; Jamada and Mehraein, 1968, 1977). These differences, based on the data from Jamada and Mehraein (1968, 1977), are most marked in the neocortex where, in the six areas studied, the presenile Alzheimer patients showed a 5- to 6-time greater density for NFT than the senile dementia patients. Comparative calculations for the amygdala and brain stem are three to four times and for the hippocampal formation one to two times greater density in Alzheimer's disease.

Numerous studies have shown that the density of the NFT in the neocortex and hippocampus in SDAT is significantly greater than in controls (Tomlinson et al., 1970; Dayan, 1970b; Morimatsu et al., 1975; Ball, 1976). Dayan (1970b) differentiated cases of SDAT from non-demented controls by the concentration of the NFT in the hippocampus. Ball (1978) showed 20.6, 40.7, and 29.3 times increases in NFT in his hippocampal fields H1 and H2 and in

the subiculum, respectively, in patients with SDAT as compared to age-matched controls. The comparative figures from Kemper (1978) for CA1 (H1) and the subiculum were 27.4 and 9.8 times (Figure 2-13).

Quantitative and semiquantitative data for the distribution of the NFT in the neocortex come from Morel (1944), Mutrux (1947), Goodman (1953), Jamada and Mehraein (1968), Hooper and Vogel (1976), and Kemper (1978) (Figure 2-14). In the studies of Jamada and Mehraein (1968), Hooper and Vogel (1976), and Kemper (1978), the density of the NFT in the neocortex in SDAT was less than that of the hippocampus. However, Goodman (1953) found areas 37 and 39 of Brodmann, areas not investigated in the other studies, to have a greater density than that in the hippocampus. The lowest densities noted in these studies were in the primary sensory and motor cortices. Morel (1944), studying a single case of Alzheimer's disease, noted that the primary visual area, area OC, and the adjacent area OB showed a lower density of the NFT than the higher-order association area, area OA. Mutrux (1947) noted a similar gradient from the primary auditory cortex (area TC) to its association areas (TB and TA) in five cases each of senile dementia and Alzheimer's disease (Figure 2-14). In this study, area TE, a visual association cortex, showed the highest average density. In an extensive study of nine neocortical areas in Alzheimer's disease, Goodman (1953) noted lower densities of the NFT in the motor (area 4), primary somesthetic (areas 3, 1, 2) and visual (area 17) cortices, with the lowest density in the motor cortex. In this study, the highest density was in area 39 (the angular gyrus) followed by the temporal lobe association areas, areas 37 and 21. Intermediate between these extremes was the frontal polar cortex (area 10), Broca's area (area 44), the temporal polar cortex (area 38), and the insula (area not given) (Figure 2-14). Jamada and Mahraein (1968) similarly found the lowest density of the NFT in both Alzheimer's disease and senile dementia in the motor cortex, the only primary cortex included in their six areas (Figure 2-14). These studies

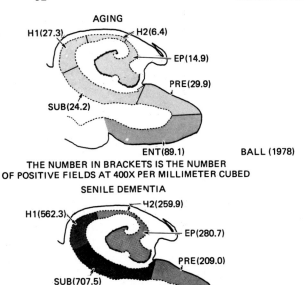

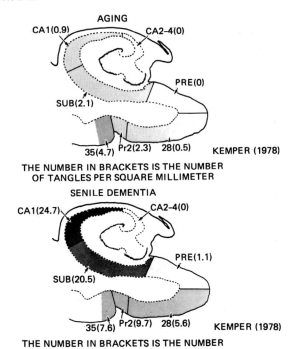

Figure 2-13. Template diagrams of location and density of neurofibrillary tangles in the hippocampus and parahippocampal gyrus in aging and in SDAT.

showed marked individual variation, and many of these differences were not statistically significant (Jamada and Mehraein, 1968). The common finding in all of them, however, that the lowest density of the NFT occurred in the primary cortices, suggests that these areas are relatively resistant to this change. The limbic cortex also appears to be an area of vulnerability. Hooper and Vogel (1976) noted a higher density of the NFT here than in the cortex of the frontal and temporal lobes, and Jamada and Mehraein, in their 22 cases of Alzheimer's disease, found a density as high as any association area. In senile dementia, the density was intermediate between areas 9 and 38 and areas 4, 17, and 19 (Figure 2-14).

There is also a marked predilection of the cortical and small-celled part of the basal nucleus of the amygdala for the NFT (Brockhaus, 1938; Jamada and Mehraein, 1968; Corsellis, 1970). In the quantitative study of Jamada and Mehraein, the highest

density of NFT was in the cortical nucleus (area As) and area Api (corresponding to the medial and lateral basal nuclei), in Alzheimer's disease, and in these two areas, plus the accessory basal nucleus (area Apm), in SDAT (Figure 2-15). These densities were not significantly different in this study from those in field H1 (Sommer's sector) of the hippocampus (Figure 2-15). In this study, the lateral nucleus (area Apl) showed a decidedly lower density of the NFT.

In the basal forebrain, diencephalon, and brain stem, the NFT shows a predilection for specific nuclei with a density considerably less than in the cerebral cortex, hippocampal formations, and amygdala (Jamada and Mehraein, 1977). Here their density in SDAT did not overlap with the control densities (Ishii, 1966; Ishino and Otsuki, 1975). In these locations, the major site of predilection is the serotoninergic nuclei in the brain stem, the nuclei raphe dorsalis and centralis

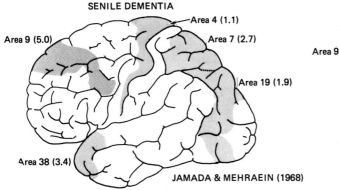

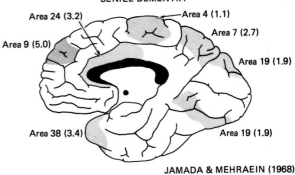

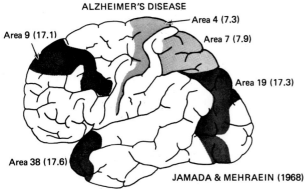

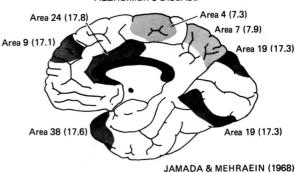

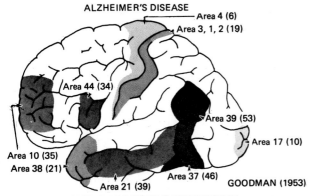

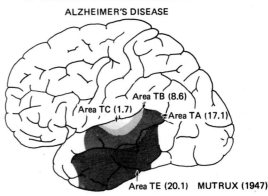

Figure 2-14. Template diagrams of location and density of neurofibrillary tangles in the neocortex in SDAT and Alzheimer's disease.

superior (Ishii, 1966; Jellinger, 1971; Ishino and Otsuki, 1975; Jamada and Mehraein, 1977). The other monoaminergic nuclei at brain-stem level show a less marked involvement, with the noradrener-

gic locus coeruleus being more involved than the dopaminergic substantia nigra (Ishii, 1966; Jellinger, 1971; Jamada and Mehraein, 1977). The other brain stem area of predilection is the reticular forma-

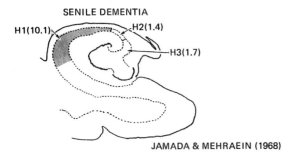

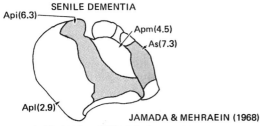

Figure 2-15. Template diagrams of the location and density of neurofibrillary tangles in the hippocampus and amygdala in SDAT and Alzheimer's disease.

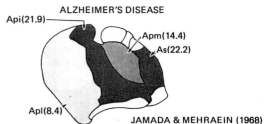

tion, particularly the nucleus magnocellularis (Jellinger, 1971; Jamada and Mehraein, 1977). In the basal forebrain and diencephalon, the areas of predilection are the mammilloinfundibular nucleus (Ishii, 1966; Ishino and Otsuki, 1975) and the nucleus basalis of Meynert (Ishii, 1966; Jellinger, 1971; Ishino and Otsuki, 1975; Jamada and Mehraein, 1977), with the degree of involvement of the acetylcholinergic nucleus basalis of Meynert (substantia innominata) less than that of the serotoninergic nuclei raphe dorsalis and centralis superior (Jellinger, 1971; Ishii, 1966; Jamada and Mehraein, 1977).

In summary, the available data indicate that, as an age-related change, the NFT occurs primarily in the lateral entorhinal area, the CA1 of the hippocampus, the subiculum, and the monoaminergic nuclei of the brain stem. In these areas, it is first found in the fourth decade, with virtually every brain involved by the tenth decade. However, when the percent of brains with moderate numbers of NFT are plotted against age, this progressive increase is reversed in the tenth decade and beyond. In SDAT, there is a marked increase in density of the NFT in these areas, and it is found throughout the neocortex, amygdala, basal forebrain, and brain stem, with greater concentrations in the presenile age group than in the senile group. In the neocortex, the areas of predilection are the association and limbic cortices, with relative sparing of the primary motor and sensory cortices; in the amygdala, the cortical and small-celled part of the basal complex; in the basal forebrain, the mammilloinfundibular nucleus and cholinergic nucleus basalis of Meynert; and in the brain stem, the monaminergic nuclei and reticular formation.

Granulovacuolar Degeneration

Granulovacuolar degeneration (GVD) is apparently unique to man. It is a neuronal intracytoplasmic vesicle measuring 1 to 5 microns in diameter, with a central dark granule measuring 0.5 to 1.5 microns in diameter (Hirano et al., 1961; Woodard,

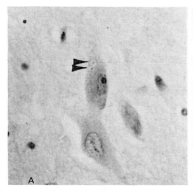
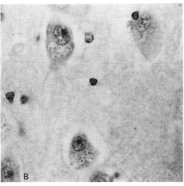

Figure 2-16. Granulova-cuolar degeneration in hippocampal pyramidal cells. A, two granules are indicated by arrowheads; B, three neurons with multiple granules. H & E stain. 250X.

1962; Tomlinson and Kitchener, 1972; Wisniewski and Terry, 1973) (Figure 2-16). Under the electron microscope, it has a similar appearance, with a membrane-bound vesicle and electron-dense center (Hirano et al., 1968; Terry and Wisniewski, 1972; Wisniewski and Terry, 1973). Its resemblance to an autophagic vacuole has been noted by Terry and Wisniewski (1972) and Wisniewski and Terry (1973), and the similarity of its central electron-dense core to lipofuscin has been commented upon by Wisniewski and Terry (1973). Simchowicz (1911) first described GVD in hippocampal pyramidal cells in senile dementia. In this location, individual neurons may show multiple GVD, with some neurons containing up to 12 to 20 vesicles in a 5-micron thick paraffin section; the shape of the neuronal cell body is often distorted. An accompanying reduction in the amount of Nissl substance in the adjacent perikaryon has been noted by Tomlinson and Kitchener (1972) and Ball and Lo (1977), and a reduction in the amount of lipofuscin by Margolis and Pickett (1959).

Granulovacuolar degeneration is not unique to aging or SDAT. It has been reported as a frequent finding in it's areas of predilection in the Guam ALS–Parkinsonism–dementia complex (Hirano et al., 1961) and Down's syndrome (Ellis et al., 1974). In progressive supranuclear palsy, GVD has been noted in the brain stem and cerebellum (Steele et al., 1964). Hirano et al. (1968) observed it in a parietal tumor in a girl with tuberous scleroses, where it

occurred in association with the NFT and the Pick body.

The site of predilection for GVD is Sommer's sector of the hippocampus (Morel and Wildi, 1952; Woodard, 1962, 1966; Tomlinson et al., 1968, 1970; Tomlinson and Kitchener, 1972; Hooper and Vogel, 1976; Ball and Lo, 1977) (Figure 2-17), with a greater concentration in the posterior than in the anterior hippocampus (Tomlinson and Kitchener, 1972; Ball and Lo, 1977). According to Tomlinson and Kitchener (1972), when few areas are involved, GVD is essentially confined to fields H1 and H2, occurring only occasionally in the subiculum and prosubiculum. When approximately 10% of the neurons in H1 and H2 are involved, it can then be found in all hippocampal fields, with the end plate (H4 and H5) more involved than H3. In brains with heavy involvement of the subiculum and prosubiculum, there may be a rare vesicle in the neocortex, amygdala, hypothalamus, and paramedian nuclei of the midbrain. Right–left and male–female differences have not been found (Woodard, 1966; Tomlinson and Kitchener, 1972; Ball and Lo, 1977).

As an age-related change, GVD has been first noted in the third decade, but it is uncommon before age 60 (Tomlinson and Kitchener, 1972). According to Dayan (1970a), after age 60, approximately 20% of brains show GVD, and according to Tomlinson and Kitchener (1972), there is a 75% incidence after age 80. However, when the data are expressed as the percent of cells with this change or as their number per cubic millimeter, there is little increase

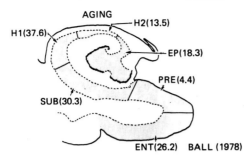

AGING

H1(37.6)

H2(13.5)

EP(18.3)

PRE(4.4)

SUB(30.3)

ENT(26.2)   BALL (1978)

THE NUMBER IN BRACKETS IS THE NUMBER
OF POSITIVE FIELDS AT 400X PER MILLIMETER CUBED

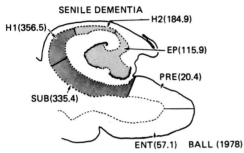

SENILE DEMENTIA

H1(356.5)

H2(184.9)

EP(115.9)

PRE(20.4)

SUB(335.4)

ENT(57.1)   BALL (1978)

THE NUMBER IN BRACKETS IS THE NUMBER
OF POSITIVE FIELDS AT 400X PER MILLIMETER CUBED

Figure 2-17. Template diagrams of location and density of granulovacuolar degeneration in the hippocampus and parahippocampal gyrus in aging and SDAT.

in density with increasing age (Woodard, 1962; Tomlinson et al., 1968; Ball and Lo, 1977). Peress et al. (1973) has reported a decreased incidence in the tenth decade. The percent of affected cells reported in the hippocampal formation in elderly individuals depends on the area sampled. Tomlinson et al. (1968) and Tomlinson and Kitchener (1972), who studied fields H1 and H2, areas of marked predilection, noted, respectively, none with greater than 7 or 9% of the cells with GVD. Woodard (1962, 1966), studying an area corresponding to part of CA1(H1) and the subiculum (his ventrolateral region), noted that less than 9% of the cells were affected. Ball and Lo (1977), who studied all hippocampal fields and the subiculum, found no brains with over 1% of the cells involved with GVD.

In SDAT, the percentage of cells with this change is markedly increased. Woodard (1962), in 200 consecutive autopsies from a mental institution, found 62 brains with an incidence of 9 to 60% of cells with

GVD in his "ventrolateral' region of the hippocampal formation. All but two cases were considered to be SDAT. The two exceptions were cases of Pick's disease. In a later, larger follow-up study, Woodard (1966) made similar observations. Blessed et al. (1970) also stressed that in SDAT the incidence of GVD was greater than in any of their controls. Further, Tomlinson and Kitchener (1972) noted in 25 documented cases of SDAT that 22 cases showed a greater than 9% involvement of cells in fields H1 and H2 of the hippocampus and subiculum as compared to age-matched controls.

The relationship of GVD to the senile plaque, the neurofibrillary tangle, and neuronal cell loss is not clear. At the level of individual neurons, Woodard (1962) noted that although GVD and the NFT may occur in the same cell, this is not the rule. Both Tomlinson et al. (1968) and Dayan (1970a) noted, in quantitative studies, the lack of a clear relationship between the density of GVD and that of the NFT and senile plaques. Further, Tomlinson and Kitchener (1972) noted that GVD may occur in high concentrations without either the NFT or senile plaques, and found this combination in six out of thirty-nine brains from individuals over 70 years of age. In a series of 219 routine autopsies of individuals aged 14 to 98 years, they noted thirty-five brains with the NFT, but not GVD, in the hippocampus, and seven brains with GVD without the NFT. In contrast, Ball and Lo (1977) and Ball (1977), in a study of the entire hippocampal complex, noted, in age-matched groups of brains with and without SDAT, a strong correlation between the concentration of GVD and both the NFT and neuronal cell loss.

Thus, GVD is not specific for either aging or SDAT. With increasing age, it occurs at a steadily increasing frequency and a slowly increasing concentration. It shows a predilection for Sommer's sector of the hippocampus, particularly the posterior part. In this location, in the vast majority of aged brains, it occurs in less than 9% of the cells. In contrast, in SDAT, there is a marked increase in the concentration of GVD in this location, with a spread to other fields of the hippocampus, particularly the subiculum, with a rare GVD in other areas of the brain. Although usually associated with NFT and senile plaques, the available evidence suggest that GVD may be independent of them.

Hirano Body

The Hirano body is a highly refractile, eosinophilic, spindle-shaped, fusiform, or spheroidal intracytoplasmic inclusion (Figure 2-18). It was first described by Hirano (1965) in Sommer's sector of the hippocampus in the Guam ALS–Parkinsonism–dementia complex and later called the Hirano body by Schochet et al. (1969). In cross section, these bodies measure up to 15 microns in diameter, and in longitudinal section, up to 30 microns in length. Although generally homogeneous, they may show striations (Hirano et al., 1966; Ogata et al., 1972; Schochet and McCormick, 1972; Gibson and Tomlinson, 1977) (Figure 2-18D). Under the electron microscope, they appear crystalline or paracrys-

talline, with two dominent patterns. In one pattern, densely arranged parallel smooth filaments, measuring approximately 100 Angstroms in diameter, are separated by intervals of approximately 120 Angstroms, in a circular, interlacing, or herring-bone-like pattern. In the other pattern, the filaments are replaced by electron-dense particles of similar diameter (Hirano, 1965; Hirano et al., 1968; Wisniewski et al., 1970; Ogata et al., 1972; Schochet and McCormick, 1972; Terry and Wisniewski, 1972; Wisniewski and Terry, 1973; Tomonaga, 1974). According to Schochet and McCormick (1972) and Tomonaga (1974), these two forms are the same basic structure, differing only in plane of section. Schochet and McCormick (1972) state that the appearance of these filaments under the electron microscope is different than that of the PHF, amyloid, and the normal neurotubule or neurofilament. Under the electron microscope, they are intraneuronal in either the perikaryon or more often in its processes (Schochet and McCormick, 1972; Ogata et al., 1972). This latter

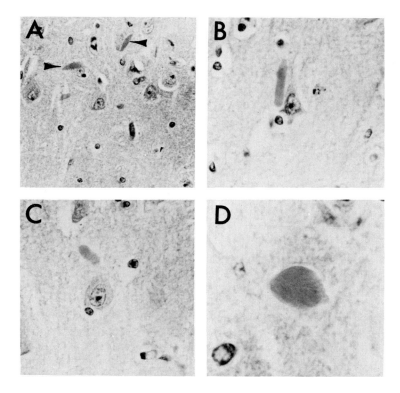

Figure 2-18. Hirano bodies in Sommer's sector of the hippocampus. A, location indicated by arrowheads. B and C, higher magnification. D, an Hirano body at a still higher magnification to show striations. H & E stain. A, 100X; B and C, 250X; D, 400X.

observation would be in keeping with their frequent occurrence in the stratum lacunosum in Sommer's sector (Gibson and Tomlinson, 1977; Ogata et al., 1972), a zone containing relatively few neuronal cell bodies. Many authors have confirmed their predilection for Sommer's sector of the hippocampus (Hirano et al., 1966; Schochet and McCormick, 1972; Ogata et al., 1972; Hirano, 1973; Gibson and Tomlinson, 1977; Ball, 1978) (Figure 2-19). According to Schochet and McCormick (1972) and Ball (1978), Hirano bodies are also found in the adjacent subiculum.

The presence of Hirano bodies is not unique to either aging or SDAT. They have also been described in the hippocampal formation in Pick's disease (Rewcastle and Ball, 1968; Schochet et al., 1968; Schochet and McCormick, 1972) and the Guam ALS–Parkinsonism–dementia complex (Hirano, 1965, 1973; Hirano et al., 1966, 1968). In ALS, they have been seen in the proximal axons of motor neurons (Chou et al., 1969), in anterior horn cells (Schochet et al., 1969), and adjacent to a cerebral tumor (Ramsey, 1967). A possible viral etiology is supported by its presence in kuru-infected humans and chimpanzees (Field et al., 1969) and in the cerebral cortex of scrapie-infected mice (David-Ferriera et al., 1968).

As an age-related change, these bodies begin to appear in the second decade, occur in small numbers up to the sixth decade, and then markedly increase (Ogata et al., 1972; Gibson and Tomlinson, 1977). In a series of "aged brains" from a geriatric hospital, Tomonaga (1974) noted their occurrence in 50% of the brains, and according to Ogata et al. (1972), they occur in all brains of individuals over 80 years of age. As an age-related change, these bodies first appear in the pyramidal cell layer and later in the stratum lacunosum. In the latter they show a maximum incidence in the fourth to sixth decade, and then a decline at older ages. This decline may be related to the association of degeneration of neuronal processes with this change, as noted by Schochet and McCormick (1972). According to Gibson and Tomlinson (1977), there are no right–left differences. When compared to age-

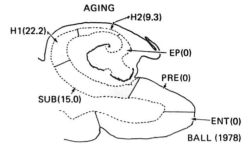

THE NUMBER IN BRACKETS IS THE NUMBER OF POSITIVE FIELDS AT 400X PER MILLIMETER CUBED

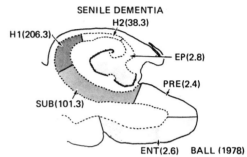

THE NUMBER IN BRACKETS IS THE NUMBER OF POSITIVE FIELDS AT 400X PER MILLIMETER CUBED

Figure 2-19. Template diagrams of the distribution and density of Hirano bodies in the hippocampus and parahippocampal gyrus in aging and SDAT.

matched controls, SDAT brains show a higher concentration of Hirano bodies, with a broad overlap between SDAT patients and controls (Gibson and Tomlinson, 1977; Ball, 1978).

Thus the Hirano body in man occurs as an age-related change and as an expression of several dementing illnesses, including SDAT. Although its relationship to GVD is unknown, it shares with the latter its striking predilection for Sommer's sector of the hippocampus. It apparently has no obligate relationship to the senile plaque, since the latter is rare in the Guam ALS–Parkinson–dementia complex, in which the Hirano body is frequently seen.

The Lewy Body

The Lewy body, a neuronal intracytoplasmic eosinophilic inclusion body in the central nervous system, is most frequently seen as a spheroid with a dense central core and a less dense surround (Figure

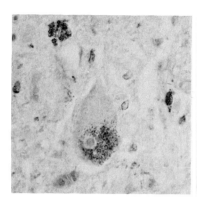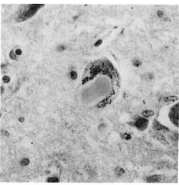

Figure 2-20. Lewy bodies in the locus coeruleus. H & E stain. 250X.

2-20). Some bodies appear uniformly dense throughout, whereas others appear as multiple concentric rings. In the autonomic ganglia, where they occur in nerve cell processes, they are most frequently elongated. Under the electron microscope, they show no limiting membrane and are seen as a variable mixture of fibrillary and granular material, with shifts in density corresponding to those noted under the light microscope (Duffy and Tennyson, 1965; Roy and Wolman, 1969; Forno and Norville, 1976). This change was first noted in idiopathic Parkinsonism by Lewy (1912) in the substantia innominata and the dorsal motor nucleus of the vagus, and later in this same disease by Tretiakoff (1919) in the substantia nigra. Although subsequent studies have emphasized its close relationship with this disease (Beheim-Schwartzbach, 1952; Greenfield and Bosanquet, 1953; Lipkin, 1959; den Hartog Jager and Bethlem, 1960; Earle, 1968; Forno and Alvord, 1971), the Lewy body is specific for it. It has been described in decidedly less frequency in postencephalitic Parkinsonism, Guam Parkinson–dementia complex, Hallervorden–Spatz disease, striato-nigral degeneration, progressive supranuclear palsy, and in aging and senile dementia (see Ohama and Ikuta, 1976, for a review). Although more frequently noted and most throughly studied in the pigmented nuclei of the brain stem, it has a wide distribution within the nervous system (den Hartog Jager and Bethlem, 1960; Ohama and Ikuta, 1976). Ohama and Ikuta (1976), in a detailed study of three cases of idiopathic

Parkinsonism, noted twenty different nuclei that were consistently involved, with seven others involved in individual cases. Of these 20 nuclei, only 12 were pigmented, indicating a lack of obligate relationship to melanin. In contrast, 19 of these 20 nuclei contained monoaminergic cell bodies. The single exception was the intermediolateral column, the source of sympathetic outflow from the spinal cord. In close agreement to their predilection for monoaminergic neurons within the central nervous system, Lewy bodies also occur in peripheral autonomic ganglia (Wohlwill, 1925; Herzog, 1926; Hechst and Nussbaum, 1931; Forno and Norville, 1976). In autonomic ganglia, they are most frequently encountered in idiopathic Parkinsonism (Hechst and Nussbaum, 1931; Forno and Norville, 1976). This close relationship is illustrated by the study of Forno and Norville (1976) of the stellate ganglion. They observed them in all nine patients with idiopathic Parkinsonism, but failed to find these bodies in nine Parkinsonians without central nervous system Lewy bodies and in seventeen controls aged 36 to 102 years. Their relationship to aging and dementia in this location is unknown.

In the central nervous system, the Lewy body is occasionally noted in aged individuals without clinical evidence of idiopathic Parkinsonism; in these cases it first appears in the sixth (Beheim-Schwarzbach, 1952; Forno and Alvord, 1971) or the seventh decade (Woodard, 1962; Forno, 1969). In small series, it is generally not noted (Bethlem and den Hartog Jager, 1960—20 patients; Greenfield and Bosanquet, 1953—19 patients), whereas in larger series they are. Lipkin (1959) found an incidence of 4.6% in 206 patients, 159 of whom were 62 years of age or older. Woodard (1962) found an incidence of 6.7% in 400 consecutive patients autopsied in a mental hospital, 26% of whom had Parkinson's disease, yielding an incidence of 4.5% in non-Parkinsonian brains. Forno (1969), in an unselected series of 1090 autopsies from a VA hospital, noted Lewy bodies as an incidental finding in 4.6% of the brains. Forno and Alvord (1971), in a series of 330 brains from aged individuals without Parkinsonism, noted an 11% incidence, and Tomonaga (1979) a 12.2% incidence in aged brains, with 33% of patients over age 90 years showing this change.

The distribution of the Lewy body in the aged brain closely parallels its distribution in idiopathic Parkinsonism (Forno, 1969). The area of greatest predilection is the locus coeruleus (Lipkin, 1959; Forno, 1969; Forno and Alvord, 1971). In this location, Tomonaga (1981b), in a serial section study of a 96-year-old patient, noted that 0.07% of the cells were affected. Next in frequency is the substantia nigra and the dorsal motor nucleus of the vagus, which in brains with Lewy bodies elsewhere, are involved in two-thirds to three-fourths of the cases (Forno, 1969; Forno and Alvord, 1971). In approximately one-fourth of these brains, the tegmentum of the pons and mesencephalon, the hypothalamus, and the nucleus basalis of Meynert are also involved (Forno, 1969). Less frequently involved are the cerebral cortex, thalamus, subthalamus, septum and caudate nucleus, nucleus of Roller, Edinger-Westphal nucleus, and inferior olive (Lipkin, 1959; Woodard, 1962; Forno, 1969). As was noted above in regard to idiopathic Parkinsonism, this change in the aged brain does not show an obligate relationship to pigmented neurons (Forno, 1969).

Although the distribution pattern of the Lewy body in the subcortex and brain stem closely parallel that of the NFT (Hirano, 1973), the relationship of the Lewy body to dementia is not clear. In Forno's 1969 study of fifty patients with Lewy bodies as an incidental finding, four were diagnosed clinically as senile dementia and two-thirds showed evidence of mental deterioration. Woodard (1962) also found a disproportionately increased incidence of Lewy bodies in patients with the onset of "mental symptoms" after age 50 and in cases of Alzheimer's disease, particularly those with paranoid and affective symptoms. In a series of 100 cases of SDAT, Woodard (1966) found 14% with Lewy bodies.

Thus, the Lewy body shows a predilection for subcortical formations containing monoaminergic neurons. It is considered to be diagnostic of idiopathic Parkinsonism when present in large numbers. In patients without clinical evidence of idiopathic Parkinsonism, it occurs in small numbers as an apparent age-related change, with a similar distribution pattern. It is not known whether these represent subclinical cases of Parkinsonism. The relationship of the Lewy body to SDAT is also unknown, but the available evidence suggests an increased number in this condition.

Lipofuscin/Melanin

Lipofuscin accumulates with age in most nerve cells in the human brain, with each cell type showing a characteristic amount at any one age, location within the cell body, time of onset, and rate of progression (Braak, 1978). This consistency is sufficient to permit reliable parcellation of the human cerebral cortex (Braak, 1980). Quantitative studies on its rate of accumulation in hippocampal pyramidal cells, lateral geniculate body, Purkinje cells, dentate nucleus, and anterior horn cells of the spinal cord have shown that the increase in lipofuscin is linear with increasing age (Mann and Yates, 1974a; Mann et al., 1978; West, 1979). In these studies, there was no sex difference in its rate of accumulation (Mann et al., 1978; Mann and Sinclair, 1978). A somewhat different pattern has been noted by Braak (1979) in layer IIIab pyramidal cells in the neocortex. Here spindle-shaped, lipofuscin-filled appendages in the region of the axon hillock appear in small numbers in the third to the sixth decade and then dramatically increase in number. In quantitative studies, both Jamamda and Mehraein (1968) and Mann and Sinclair (1978) found no increase in lipofuscin in SDAT as compared to controls. The rate of accumulation is also unaffected by Down's syndrome, phenylketonuria, progeria, and transneuronal atrophy (West, 1979), further suggesting that lipofuscin accumulation is primarily a time marker.

Melanin pigment in the locus coeruleus and substantia nigra also shows a linear increase with increasing age until about age 60, and then a decrease. This decrease has been attributed to the loss of heavily pigmented cells (Mann and Yates, 1974b). The melanin content of these neurons, according to Mann et al. (1980), is unaffected by Alzheimer's disease or senile dementia.

Summary

A wide variety of changes have been described in aging, senile dementia of the Alzheimer type, and Alzheimer's disease. All are of uncertain relationship to one another. Cortical thickness is unchanged by either aging or the dementias. Lipofuscin accumulation appears to be linear with increasing age and is unaffected by the dementias. Of the remaining changes, the most extensive data are available for decreased brain weight, gyral atrophy, ventricular dilation, loss of neurons, amyloid deposits, senile plaques, neurofibrillary tangles, granulovacular degeneration and Hirano bodies. Based on the extent of the change and its distribution in aging and in the dementias, these can be divided into three groups. In the first group are decreased brain weight, loss of neurons (and probably myelin), gyral atrophy, ventricular dilation, and amyloid accumulation. These prominent age-related changes show a further increase in the dementias, with, however, a broad overlap with controls. In the second group are granulovacuolar degeneration and the neurofibrillary tangle. These occur only in small numbers and in relatively restricted locations as age-related changes and show striking increase in density and extent of distribution in the dementias. These two changes provide the clearest morphological separation of the dementias from normative aging. Intermediate between these two groups is the senile plaque and the Hirano body.

In senile dementia and Alzheimer's disease, no new change appears. The morphological expression of these dementias is an increase in density and extent of distribution of age-related changes, with, as noted above, the most marked increase occurring in changes that are relatively inconspicuous in the aged brain. Thus, it can be argued that these dementias are not simply an accentuation of aging, but rather reflect a specific disease process, a process that is more marked in Alzheimer's disease than in senile dementia. Further support for this can be seen in the data for the neurofibrillary tangle and granulovacuolar degeneration, both of which show marked increases in the dementias compared to controls. As age-related changes, these two steadily increase until the ninth decade and then, rather than increasing further, decrease.

Analysis of the distribution pattern of the change that shows the most marked increase in these dementias, the neurofibrillary tangle, shows that it is not randomly distributed. Instead, when viewed in terms of connectivity of the brain, it is strategically placed in a closely interconnected system. This is shown schematically in Figure 2-21, with the details of connectivity of the hippocampal complex shown in Figure 2-22. In Figure 2-21, the density is graded on a scale from zero (none or rare) neurofibrillary tangles to four plus (maximum density). In the cerebral cortex, there is a progressive increase in density from the primary cortices (motor, sensory, visual, and auditory) to their respective primary and secondary association cortices, with the highest density in the multimodal association area, the angular gyrus (area 39). The secondary association cortices and the multimodal association areas are reciprocally related to the heavily involved limbic neocortex. The limbic and association cortices are, in turn, reciprocally related to the hippocampal complex and amygdala, all of which are also areas of predilection for the neurofibrillary tangle. Figure 2-7 shows that the density of

ALZHEIMER'S DISEASE

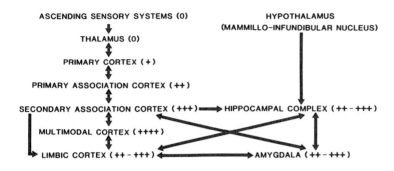

Figure 2-21. Diagram to show the relationship of cortical connectivity to the density of distribution of the neurofibrillary tangles. "O," rare or absent neurofibrillary tangles; ++++, maximum density of tangles. Cortical circuit diagram adapted from Pandya and Seltzer (1982).

the neurofibrillary tangle within the hippocampus is greatest in two zones. One surrounds the collateral sulcus and comprises Brodmann's area 35 and the adjacent lateral entorhinal area, area Pr 2. This is a major site of afferent projections from the limbic and secondary association cortices (Figure 2-22). The other zone, which is more heavily involved in the dementias, is the subiculum and CA1 (Sommer's sector or H1), the former with a heavy projection from the latter. The subiculum, which also receives projections from the limbic and association cortices, is, in turn,

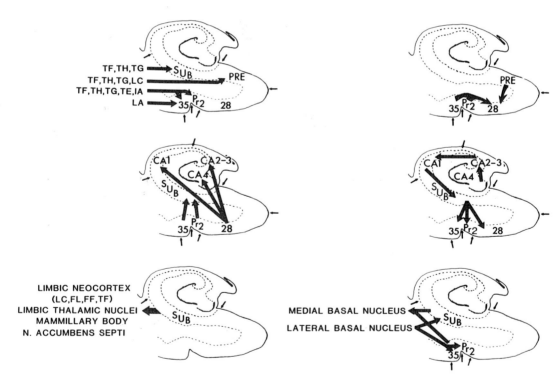

Figure 2-22. Diagram of afferent and efferent projection and local circuits within the hippocampus and parahippocampal gyrus. (From Herzog and van Hoesen, 1976; Krettek and Price, 1978; Pandya et al., 1973; Pandya et al., 1981; Rosene and van Hoesen, 1977; Turner et al., 1978; van Hoesen and Pandya, 1975; and van Hoesen et al., 1972.)

the origin of projections back to the limbic neocortex, as well as subcortical limbic formations, including the amygdala. Between these two zones is a complex series of intermediary circuits with decidedly less densely distributed neurofibrillary tangles. The highest concentrations of the neurofibrillary tangles in the basolateral complex of the amygdala occur in a region corresponding to the lateral basal and medial basal nuclei (area Api), with relative sparing of the accessory basal nucleus. All three of these nuclei show widespread interconnections with the limbic and association cortices (Nauta, 1961; Pandya et al., 1973; Herzog and van Hoesen, 1976; Rosene and van Hoesen, 1977; Krettek and Price, 1978; Aggleton et al., 1980; Turner et al., 1978; Mufson et al., 1981; Pandya et al., 1981; Porrino et al., 1981). Only the heavily involved lateral basal and medial basal nucleus connect to the hippocampus (Herzog and van Hoesen, 1976; Rosene and van Hoesen, 1977; Aggleton et al., 1980). A similar relationship to the hippocampus exists for the heavily involved cortical nucleus of the amygdala. Its major source of afferents are from the olfactory bulb (Turner et al., 1978), and it, in turn, projects to the hippocampal complex (Krettek and Price, 1978). The same pattern can be discerned in the hypothalamus. The neurofibrillary tangles are most abundant in the mammillo-infundibular nucleus, which is the cellular origin of the hypothalamic projection to the hippocampus (Pasquier and Reinoso-Swarez, 1976). In the basal forebrain and brain stem, the areas of predilection are the cholinergic and monoaminergic nuclei, nuclei that diffusely project to all these areas. Neurofibrillary tangles are absent or rare in the spinal cord, the ascending subcortical sensory systems, the basal ganglia, and the entire cerebellar circuitry.

Many of the other changes also show predilection for the same regions of the brain shown by the neurofibrillary tangle. Granulovacuolar degeneration and the Hirano body are almost totally confined to the subiculum and area CA1 of the hippocampus. The senile plaque shows a similar, but not identical distribution pattern to the neurofibrillary tangle. Neuronal cell loss and loss of myelin within the neocortex is more marked in the association and limbic cortices than in the primary cortices. Loss of subcortical myelin is most conspicuous in the long cortico-cortical association fibers of the corona radiata. In the basal forebrain and brain stem, neuronal cell loss, neurofibrillary tangles, and the Lewy body all share a predilection for the cholinergic and monoaminergic nuclei. Gyral atrophy, ventricular dilation, and amyloid angiopathy bear an uncertain relationship to this overall scheme. An apparent exception is loss of Purkinje cells, a widespread process in aged animals (Dayan, 1971).

References

Aggleton, J.P., Burton, M.J., and Passingham, R.E. (1980). Cortical and subcortical afferents to the amygdala of the rhesus monkey (*Macaca mulatta*). Br. Res. 190, 347–368.

Alzheimer, A. (1907). Über eine eigenartige Erkrankung der Hirnrinde. Allg. Ztschr. Psychiat. 64, 146–148.

Ansari, K.A. and Loch, J. (1975). Decrease myelin basic protein content of the aged human brain. Neurology 25, 1045–1050.

Ball, M.J. (1976). Neurofibrillary tangles and the pathogenesis of dementia: A quantitative study. Neuropath. Appl. Neurobiol. 2, 395–410.

Ball, M.J. (1977). Neuronal loss, neurofibrillary tangles and granulovacuolar degeneration in the hippocampus with ageing and dementia. Acta Neuropath. 37, 111–118.

Ball, M.J. and Lo, R. (1977). Granulovacuolar degeneration in the ageing brain and in senile dementia. J. Neuropath. Exp. Neurol. 36, 474–487.

Ball, M.J. (1978). Histopathology of cellular changes in Alzheimer's disease. In Senile Dementia: A Biomedical Approach. K. Nandy, Ed., Elsevier, New York.

Barron, S.A., Jacobs, L., and Kinkel, W.R. (1979). Changes in size of normal lateral ventricles during aging determined by computerized tomography. Neurology 28, 1011–1013.

Beheim-Schwarzbach, P. (1952). Über Zelleibveränderungen im Nucleus coeruleus bei Parkinson-Symptomen. J. Nerv. Ment. Dis. 116, 619–632.

Berlet, H.H. and Volk, B. (1980). Studies of

human myelin proteins during old age. Mech. Ageing Dev. 14, 211–222.

Bethlem, J. and den Hartog Jager, W.A. (1960). The incidence and characteristics of Lewy bodies in idiopathic paralysis agitans (Parkinson's disease). J. Neurol. Neurosurg. Psychiat. 23, 74–80.

Bielschowsky, M. (1912). Zur Kenntnis der Alzheimerschen Krankheit (präsenile Demenz mit Herdsymptomen). J. Psychol. Neurol. 18, 273–292.

Bielschowsky, M. (1932). Histopathology of nerve cells. In Cytology and Cellular Pathology of the Nervous System. W. Penfield, Ed. Hoeber, New York.

Bischoff, T. (1880). Hirngewicht des Menschen, anatomische, physiologische and physikalische Tabellen. Bonn.

Blinkov, S.M. and Glezer, I.I. (1968). The Human Brain in Figures and Tables. Basic Books, New York.

Blocq, P. and Marinesco, G. (1892). Sur les lésions et la pathogénie de l'epilepsie dite essentielle. Semaine Med. 12, 445–446.

van Bogaert, L. (1970). Cerebral amyloid angiopathy and Alzheimer's disease. In Alzheimer's Disease and Related Conditions. A Ciba Foundation Symposium. G.E.W. Wolstenholme, and M. O'Connor, Eds. J. and A. Churchill, London.

van Bogaert, L., Maere, M., and de Smedt, E. (1940). Sur les formes familiales précoces de la maladie d'Alzheimer. Mschr. Psychiat. Neurol. 102, 249–301.

Bonfiglio, F. (1908). Di speciali reperti in un caso di probabile sifilide cerebrale. Riv. Sper di Freniatria 34, 1–3.

Bouman, L. (1934). Senile plaques. Brain 57, 128–142.

Braak, H. (1972). Zur Pigmentarchitektonik der Grosshirnrinde des Menschen. II. Subiculum. Z. Zellforsch. 131, 235–254.

Braak, H. (1978). On the pigmentarchitectonics of the human telencephalic cortex. In Architectonics of the Cerebral Cortex. M.A.B. Brazier and H. Petsche, Eds. Raven Press, New York.

Braak, H. (1979). Spindle-shaped appendages of IIIab-pyramids filled with lipofuscin: A striking pathological change of the senescent human isocortex. Acta Neuropath. 46, 197–202.

Braak, H. (1980). Studies of Brain Function, Vol 4. Architectonics of the Human Telencephalic Cortex. Springer-Verlag. Berlin, Heidelberg, New York.

von Braunmühl, A. (1932). Kolloidchemische Betrachtungs weise seniler and präseniler Gewebseränderung. Das Hysteretische Syndrom als Cerebral Reaktionsform. Ztschr. ges. Neurol. Psychiat. 142:1.

von Braunmühl, A. (1957). Alterserkrankungen des Zentralnervensystems. In Handbuch der Speziellen Pathologischen Anatomie and Histologie, Vol. 13. H. Lubarsch, F. Henke, and R. Rossle, Eds. Springer-Verlag, Berlin, pp. 337–539.

Brockhaus, H. (1938). Zur Anatomie des Mendelkerngebietes. J. Psychol. Neurol. 49, 1–136.

Brody, H. (1955). Organization of the cerebral cortex III. A study of aging in the human cerebral cortex. J. Comp. Neurol. 102, 511–556.

Brody, H. (1970). Structural changes in the aging nervous system. In Interdisciplinary Topics in Gerontology, Vol. 7. S. Karger, Basal.

Buell, S.J. and Coleman, P.D. (1979). Dendritic growth in the aged human brain and failure of growth in senile dementia. Science 206, 854–856.

Bugiani, O., Salvarani, F., Perdelli, G.L., Mancardi, G.L., and Leonardi, A. (1978). Nerve cell loss with aging in the putamen. Eur. Neurobiol. 17, 286–291.

Buttlar-Brentano, K. von (1954). Zur Lebensgeschichte des Nucleus basalis, tuberomammillaris, supraopticus und paraventricularis unter normalen und pathogenen Bedingungen. J. Hirnforsch. 1, 337–419.

Cajal, S. Ramon Y. (1968). Degeneration and Regeneration of the Nervous System. Hafner, London, New York.

Cammermeyer, J. (1960). The post-mortem origin and mechanism of neuronal hyperchromatosis and nuclear pyknosis. Exp. Neurol. 2, 379–405.

Carlen, P., Wilkinson, D.A., Wortzman, G., Holgate, R., Cordingley, J., Lee, M.A., Huszar, L., Moddel, G., Singh, R., Kiraly, L., and Rankin, J.G. (1981). Cerebral atrophy and functional deficits in alcoholics without clinically apparent liver disease. Neurology 31, 377–385.

Chernyshev, S.P. (1911). The Weight of the Human Brain. (Cited by Blinkov and Glezer, 1968).

Chou, S.M., Martin, J.D., Gutrecht, J.A., and Thompson, H.G. (1969). Axonal balloons in subacute motor neuron disease. Neuropathol. Exp. Neurol. 29, 141–142.

Colon, E.J. (1972). The elderly brain—a quantitative analysis in the cerebral cortex of two cases. Psychiat. Neurol. Neurochir. 75, 261–270.

Colon, E.J. (1973). The cerebral cortex in

presenile dementia—a quantitative analysis. Acta Neuropath. 23, 281–290.

Constantinidis, J. (1978). Is Alzheimer's disease a major form of senile dementia? Clinical, anatomical, and genetic data. In Alzheimer's Disease: Senile Dementia and Related Disorders. Vol. 7. Aging. R. Katzman, R.D. Terry, and K.L. Bick, Eds. Raven Press, New York, pp. 15–25.

Corsellis, J.A.N. and Brierley, J.B. (1954). An unusual type of pre-senile dementia (atypical Alzheimer's disease with amyloid vascular change). Brain 77, 571–587.

Corsellis, J.A.N. (1970). The limbic areas in Alzheimer's disease and in other conditions associated with dementia. In Alzheimer's Disease and Related Conditions. G.E.W. Wolstenhome and M. O'Connor, Eds. J. A. Churchill, London, pp. 37–45.

Cragg, B.G. (1975). The density of synapses and neurons in normal, mentally defective and ageing human brains. Brain 98, 81–90.

Crapper, D.R., Krishman, S.S., and Quittkat, S. (1976). Aluminum neurofibrillary degeneration and Alzheimer's disease. Brain 99, 67–80.

Cupp, C.J. and Uemura, E. (1980). Age-related changes in prefrontal cortex of *Macaca mulatta:* Quantitative analysis of dendritic branching patterns. Exp. Neurol. 69, 143–163.

Dahl, D., Selkue, D.J., Poro, R.T., and Bignami, A. (1982). Immunostaining of neurofibrillary tangles in Alzheimer's senile dementia with neurofilament antisera. J. Neurosci. 2, 113–119.

Dam, A.M. (1979). The density of neurons in the human hippocampus. Neuropath. Appl. Neurobiol. 5, 249–264.

David-Ferreira, J.F., David-Ferreira, K.L., Gibbs, C.J., and Morris, J.A. (1968). Scrapie in mice: Ultrastructural observations in the cerebral cortex. Proc. Soc. Exp. Biol. 127, 313–320.

Davis, P.J.M. and Wright, E.A. (1977). A new method for measuring cranial cavity volume and its application to the assessment of cerebral atrophy at autopsy. Neuropath. Appl. Neurobiol. 3, 341–358.

Dayan, A.D. (1970a). Quantitative histological studies on the aged human brain I. Senile plaques and neurofibrillary tangles in "normal" patients. Acta Neuropath. 16, 85–94.

Dayan, A.D. (1970b). Quantitative histological studies on the aged human brain II. Senile plaques and neurofibrillary tangles in senile dementia. Acta Neuropath. 16, 95–102.

Dayan, A.D. (1971). Comparative neuropathology of ageing. Studies on the brains of 47 species of vertebrates. Brain 94, 31–42.

Dayan, A.D. and Ball, M.J. (1973). Histometric observations on the metabolism of tangle-bearing neurons. J. Neurol. Sci. 19, 433–436.

Dekaban, A.S. and Sadowsky, B.S. (1978). Changes in brain weights during the span of human life: Relation of brain weights to body heights and body weights. Ann. Neurol. 4, 345–356.

Divry, P. (1927). Etude histochemique des plaques séniles. J. Neurol. Psychiat. 27, 643–657.

Divry, P. (1934). De la nature de l'altération fibrillaire d'Alzheimer. J. Belge Neurol. Psychiat. 34, 197–201.

Divry, P. (1952). La Pathochimie Générale et Cellulaire des Processus Séniles et Préséniles. Proc. 1st Internat. Congr. Neuropath. (Rome) Vol. 2. Turin, Rosenberg and Sellier, pp. 313–345.

Duffy, P.E. and Tennyson, V.M. (1965). Phase and electron microscopic observations of Lewy bodies and melanin granules in the substantia nigra and locus coerulus in Parkinson's disease. J. Neuropath. Exp. Neurol. 24, 398–414.

Earle, K.M. (1968). Studies on Parkinson's disease including X-ray fluorescent spectroscopy of formalin fixed brain tissue. J. Neuropath. Exp. Neurol. 27, 1–14.

Earnest, M.P., Heaton, R.K., Wilkinson, W.E., and Manke, W.F. (1979). Cortical atrophy, ventricular enlargement and intellectual impairment in the aged. Neurology 29, 1138–1143.

Economo, C. vm. and Koskinas, G.N. (1925). Die Cytoarchitektonik der Hirnrinde des Erwachsenen Menschen. Springer, Wien, Berlin.

Ellis, R.S. (1920, 1921). Norms for some structural changes in the human cerebellum from birth to old age. J. Comp. Neurol. 32, 1–33.

Ellis, W.G., McCulloch, J.R., and Corley, C.L. (1974). Presenile dementia in Down's syndrome. Ultrastructural identity with Alzheimer's disease. Neurology 24, 101–106.

Feldman, M.L. and Dowd, C. (1975). Loss of dendritic spines in aging cerebral cortex. Anat. Embryol. 148, 297–301.

Feldman, M.L. (1976). Aging changes in the morphology of cortical dendrites. In Neurobiology of Aging. R.D. Terry and S. Gershon, Eds. Raven Press, New York.

Feldman, M.L. (1977). Dendritic changes in aging rat brain: Pyramidal cell dendrite length and ultrastructure. In The Aging Brain and Senile Dementia. K. Nandy and I. Sherwin, Eds. Plenum Press, New York.

Ferraro, A. (1931). The origin and formation of senile plaques. Arch. Neurol. Psychiat. 25, 1042–1060.

Field, E.J., Mathews, J.D., and Raine, C.S. (1969). Electron microscopic observations on the cerebellar cortex in Kuru. J. Neurol. Sci. 8, 209–224.

Fischer, O. (1907). Miliare Nekrosen mit Drusigen Wucherungen der Neurofibrillen, eine regelmässige Veränderung der Hirnrinde bei seniler Demenz. Monatschr. Psychiat. Neurol. 22, 361–372.

Forno, L.S. (1969). Concentric hyalin intraneuronal inclusions of Lewy type in the brains of elderly persons (50 incidental cases): Relationship to Parkinsonism. J. Amer. Geriatr. Soc. 17, 557–575.

Forno, L.S. and Alvord, E.C., Jr. (1971). In Recent Advances in Parkinson's Disease. Contemporary Neurology Series, No. 8. Part I. Some New Observations and Correlations. F.H. McDowell and Ch. H. Markham, Eds. F.A. Davis Co., Philadelphia Pa., pp. 120–130.

Forno, L.S. and Norville, R.L. (1976). Ultrastructure of Lewy bodies in the stellate ganglion. Acta Neuropath. 34, 183–197.

Fox, J.H., Topel, J.L., and Huckman, M.S. (1975). The use of computerized tomography in the diagnosis of senile dementia. J. Neurol. Neurosurg. Psychiat. 38, 948–953.

Fraser, H. and Bruce, M.E. (1973). Argyrophilic plaques in mice inoculated with scrapie from particular sources. Lancet i, 617–618.

Fuller, S.C. (1911). A Study of the miliary plaques found in brains of the aged. Amer. J. Insanity 68, 147–219.

Galaburda, A. and Sanides, F. (1980). Cytoarchitectonic organization of the human auditory cortex. J. Comp. Neurol. 190, 597–610.

Gellerstedt, N. (1933). Zur Kenntnis der Hirnveränderungen bei der Normalen Alterinvolution. Upsula Läkareforen. Förhandl. 38, 194–408.

Gibson, P.H. and Tomlinson, B.E. (1977). Numbers of Hirano bodies in the hippocampus of normal and demented people with Alzheimer's disease. J. Neurol. Sci. 33, 199–206.

Glenner, G.G. (1979). Congophilic microangiopathy in the pathogenesis of Alzheimer's syndrome (presenile dementia). Med. Hypotheses 5, 1231–1236.

Goodman, L. (1953). Alzheimer's disease: A clinicopathologic analysis of 23 cases with a theory on pathogenesis. J. Nerv. Ment. Dis. 118, 97–130.

Greenfield, J.G. and Bosanquet, F.D. (1953). The brain-stem lesions in Parkinsonism. J. Neurol. Neurosurg. Psychiat. 16, 213–226.

Gyldensted, C. (1977). Measurement of the normal ventricular system and hemispheric sulci of 100 adults with computed tomographs. Neuroradiology 14, 183–192.

Hall, T.C., Miller, A.K.H., and Corsellis, J.A.N. (1975). Variation in human Purkinje cell population according to age and sex. Neuropath. Appl. Neurobiol. 1, 267–292.

Hanley, T.C. (1974). Neuronal fall-out in the ageing brain: A critical review of the quantitative data. Age and Ageing 3, 133–151.

den Hartog Jager, W.A., and Bethlem, J. (1960). The distribution of Lewy bodies in the central and autonomic nervous system in idiopathic paralysis agitans. J. Neurol. Neurosurg. Psychiat. 23, 282–290.

Hechst, B. and Nussbaum, I. (1931). Beiträge zur Histopathologie der sympathischen Ganglien. Archiv. Psychiat. Nervenkr. 95, 556–583.

Heidary, H. and Tomasch, J. (1969). Neuron numbers and perikaryon areas in the human cerebellar nuclei. Acta Anat. 74, 290–296.

Henderson, G., Tomlinson, B.E., and Gibson, P.H. (1980). Cell counts in human cerebral cortex in normal adults throughout life using an image analysing computer. J. Neurol. Sci. 46, 113–136.

Herxheimer, G. and Gierlich N. (1907). Studien über die Neurofibrillen im Centralnervensystem. Wiesbaden. (Cited by Fuller, 1911.)

Herzog, E. (1926). Beitrag zur normalen uncl pathologischen Histologie des Sympathicus. Z. Neurol. 103, 75.

Herzog, A.G. and Van Hoesen, G.W. (1976). Temporal neocortical afferent connections to the amygdala in the rhesus monkey. Br. Res. 115, 57–69.

Herzog, A.G. and Kemper, T.L. (1980). Amygdaloid changes in aging and dementia. Arch. Neurol. 37, 625–629.

Hirano, A. (1965). Pathology of amyotrophic lateral sclerosis. In Slow, Latent and Temperate Virus Infection. D.C. Gajdusek, C.J. Gibbs, and M. Alpers, Eds. NINDB Monograph 2. Washington, National Institute of Health, pp. 23–37.

Hirano, A. (1973). Progress in the pathology of motor neuron disease. In Progress in Neuropathology Vol. II. H.M. Zimmerman, Ed. Grune & Stratton, New York and London.

Hirano, A., Dembitzer, H.M., Kurland, L.T., and Zimmerman, H.M. (1968). The fine structure of some intraganglionic alterations. Neurofibrillary tangles, granulovacuolar bodies and "rod-like" structures as seen in Guam amyotrophic lateral sclerosis and Parkinson-dementia complex. J. Neuropath. Exp. Neurol. 27, 167–182.

Hirano, A., Malamud, N., Elizan, T.S., and Kurland, L.T., (1966). Amyotrophic lateral sclerosis and Parkinsonism-dementia complex on Guam. Arch. Neurol. 15, 35–51.

Hirano, A., Malamud, N., and Kurland, L.T. (1961). Parkinson-dementia complex, an endemic disease on the Island of Guam. II—Pathological features. Brain 84, 662–679.

Hirano, A., Tuazon, R., and Zimmerman, H.M. (1968). Neurofibrillary changes, granulovacuolar bodies and argentophilic globules observed in tuberous sclerosis. Acta Neuropath. 11, 257–261.

Hirano, A. and Zimmerman, H.M. (1962). Alzheimer's neurofibrillary changes. Arch. Neurol. 7, 227–242.

Hollander, D. and Strich, S.J. (1970). Atypical Alzheimer's disease with congophilic angiopathy presenting with dementia of acute onset. In Alzheimer's Disease and Related Conditions. A Ciba Foundation Symposium. G.E.W. Wolstenholme and M. O'Connor, Eds. J. and A. Churchill, London.

Hooper, M.W. and Vogel, F.S. (1976). The limbic system in Alzheimer's disease. Amer. J. Path. 85, 1–13.

Hopker, W. (1951). Das Altern des Nucleus dentatus. Z. Altersforsch. 5, 258–277.

van der Horst, L., Stam, F.C., and Wigboldus, J.M. (1960). Amyloidosis in senile and presenile involutional processes of the central nervous system. J. Nerv. Ment. Dis. 130, 578–587.

Huckman, M.S., Fux, J., and Topel, J. (1975). The validity of criteria for the evaluation of cerebral atrophy by computed tomography. Radiology 116, 85–92.

Hunziker, O. Abdel'Al, S., Frey, H., Veteau, M.J. and Meier-Ruge, W. (1978). Quantitative studies in the cerebral cortex of aging humans. Gerontol. 24, 27–31.

Iqbal, K., Wisniewski, H.M., Grundke-Iqbal, I., and Terry, R.D. (1977). Neurofibrillary pathology; an update. In The Aging Brain and Senile Dementia, K. Nandy and I. Sherwin, Eds. Plenum Press, New York.

Ishii, T. (1966). Distribution of Alzheimer's neurofibrillary changes in the brain stem and hypothalamus of senile dementia. Acta Neuropath. 6, 181–187.

Ishino, H. and Otsuki, S. (1975). Frequency of Alzheimer's neurofibrillary tangles in the basal ganglia and brain-stem in Alzheimer's disease, senile dementia and the aged. Folia Psychiat. Neurol. Jap. 29, 279–287.

Jamada, M. and Mehraein, P. (1968). Verteilungsmuster der senilen Veränderungen im Gehern. Die Beteiligung des limbischen Systems bei hirnatrophischen Prozessen des Senium und bei Morbus Alzheimer. Arch. Psychiat. Neurol. 211, 308–324.

Jamada, M. and Mehraein, P. (1977). Verteilungsmuster der senilen Veränderungen in den Hirnstammkernen. Folia Psychiat. Neurol. Jap. 31, 219–224.

Jellinger, K. (1971). Progressive supranuclear palsy (subcortical argyrophilic dystrophy). Acta Neuropath. 19, 347–352.

Jordan, S.W. (1971). Central nervous system. Human Pathol. 2, 561.

Kaes, T. (1907). Die Grosshirnrinde des Menschen in ihren Massen und in ihrem Fasergehalt. Gustav Fischer, Jena.

Kemper, T. (1978). Senile dementia: A focal disease in the temporal lobe. In Senile Dementia: A Biomedical Approach. K. Nandy, Ed. Elsevier, New York, pp. 105–113.

Kidd, M. (1963). Paired helical filaments in electron microscopy of Alzheimer's disease. Nature 197, 192–192.

Kidd, M. (1964). Alzheimer's disease—an electron microscopical study. Brain 87, 307–320.

King, L.S. (1942). Pathology of senile brains 1. Silver-reducing structures in the hippocampus. Arch. Neurol. Psychiat. 48, 241–256.

Klatzo, I., Gajdusek, D.E., and Zigas, V. (1959). Pathology of kuru. Lab. Invest. 8, 799–847.

Knudsen, P.A. (1958). Ventrikeles atorrelsesforhold: anatomisk normale hjerner fru voksne mennsker. (Cited by Blinkov and Glezer, 1968.)

Konigsmark, B. and Murphy, E. (1970). Neuronal populations in the human brain. Nature 228, 1335–1336.

Kretschmann, H.J., Schleicher, A., Wingert, F., Zilles, K., and Löblich, H.J. (1979). Human brain growth in the 19th and 20th century. J. Neurol. Sci. 40, 169–188.

Krettek, J.E. and Price, J.L. (1978). A description of the amygdaloid complex in the rat and cat with observations on the intraamygdaloid axonal connections. J. Comp. Neurol. 178, 255–280.

Krigman, M.R., Feldman, R. G., and Bensch, K. (1965). Alzheimer's presenile dementia: A histochemical and electron microscopic study. Lab. Invest. 14, 381–396.

Kurucz, J., Charbonneau, R., Kurucz, A., and Ramsey, P. (1981a). Quantitative clinicopathological study of cerebral amyloid angiopathy. J. Amer. Geriatr. Soc. 29, 61–69.

Kurucz, J., Charbonneau, R., Kurucz, A., and Ramsey, P. (1981b). Quantitative clinicopathological study of senile dementia. J. Amer. Geriatr. Soc. 29, 158–163.

Lafora, G.A. (1914). Neuronal dentritic neoformations and neurological alterations in the senile dog. Trabajos del Laboratorio de Investigaciones Biologica de la Universidad de Madrid 12, 39–53.

Last, R.J. and Tompsett, D.H. (1953). Casts of the cerebral ventricles. Br. J. Surg. 40, 525.

LeMay, M. (1980). Neurological aspects of language disorders in the elderly: An anatomical overview. In Language and Communication in the Elderly. L.K. Obler and M. Albert, Eds. Lexington Books, Heath. Lexington, Mass., Toronto.

Lewy, F.H. (1912). Paralysis Agitans. I. Pathologische Anatomie. In Handbuch der Neurologic, M. Lewanclowsky, Ed. Springer, Berlin.

Lipkin, L. (1959). Cytoplasmic inclusions in ganglion cells associated with Parkinsonian states. A neurocellular change study in 35 cases and 206 controls. Amer. J. Path. 35, 1117–1133.

McDermott, J.R., Smith, I., Igbal, K., and Wisniewski, H.M. (1979). Brain aluminum in aging and Alzheimer disease. Neurology 29, 809–814.

McGeer, P.L., McGeer, E.G., and Suzuki, P.S. (1977). Aging and extrapyramidal function. Arch. Neurol. 34, 33–35.

McLardy, T. (1970). Memory function in hippocampal gyri but not in hippocampi. Intern. J. Neurosci. 1, 113–118.

McMenemey, W.H. (1958). The Dementias and Progressive Diseases of the Basal Ganglia. In Neuropathology. J.G. Greenfield et al., Eds. Edward Arnold, London.

Maleci, O. (1934). Contributo all conoscenza della variazioni quantitative delle cellule nervose nelle senescenza. Arch. Ital. Anat. 33, 883.

Mandybur, T. (1975). The incidence of cerebral amyloid angiopathy in Alzheimer's disease. Neurology 25, 120–126.

Mann, D.M.A., Lincoln, J., Yates, P.O., Stamp, J.E., and Toper, S. (1980). Changes in the monamine containing neurons of the human CNS in senile dementia. Br. J. Psychiat. 136, 533–541.

Mann, D.M.A., Neary, D., Yates, P.O., Lincoln, J., Snowden, J.S., and Stanworth, P. (1981a). Alterations in protein synthetic capability of nerve cells in Alzheimer's disease. J. Neurol. Neurosurg. Psychiat. 44, 97–102.

Mann, D.M.A., Neary, D., Yates, P.O., Lincoln, J., Snowden, J.S., and Stanworth, P. (1981b). Neurofibrillary pathology and protein synthetic capability in nerve cells in Alzheimer's disease. Neuropath. Appl. Neurobiol. 7, 37–47.

Mann, D.M.A. and Sinclair, K.G.A. (1978). The quantitative assessment of lipofuscin pigment, cytoplasmic RNA and nucleolar volume in senile dementia. Neuropath. Appl. Neurobiol. 4, 129–135.

Mann, D.M.A. and Yates, P.O. (1974a). Lipoprotein pigments—their relationship to ageing in the human nervous system I. The lipofuscin content of nerve cells. Brain 97, 481–488.

Mann, D.M.A. and Yates, P.O. (1974b). Lipoprotein pigments—their relationship to ageing in the human nervous system II. The melanin content of pigmented nerve cells. Brain 97, 489–498.

Mann, D.M.A., Yates, P.O., and Stamp, J.E. (1978). Relationship between lipofuscin pigment and ageing in the human nervous system. J. Neurol. Sci. 37, 83–93.

Marchand, F. (1902). Über das Hirngewicht des Menschen. (Cited in Blinkov and Glezer, 1968.)

Margolis, G. and Pickett, J.P. (1959). Senile cerebral disease. A critical survey of traditional concepts based upon observations with new techniques. Lab. Invest. 8, 335–370.

Marinesco, G. (1911). Sur la structure des plaques dites séniles dans l'ecorce cérébrale des sujets atteints d'affection mentales. Compt. rend. Soc. Biol. 70, 609.

Mathews, W.H. (1954). Primary systemic amyloidosis. Amer. J. Med. Sci. 228, 317–333.

Matsuyama, H. and Nakamura, S. (1978). Senile changes in the brain in the Japanese: Incidence of Alzheimer's neurofibrillary change and senile plaque. In Alzheimer's Disease: Senile Dementia and Related Disorders. Vol. 7. Aging. R. Katzman, R.D. Terry, and K.L. Blick, Eds. Raven Press, New York, pp. 287–297.

Matsuyama, H., Namiki, H., and Watanabe, I.

(1966). Senile changes in the brain in the Japanese. Incident of Alzheimer's Neurofibrillary Change and Senile Plaques. In Proceedings of the 5th International Congress of Neuropathology. F. Luthy and A. Bischoff, Eds. Excepta Medico Series No. 100, Zurich.

Mehraein, P., Yamada, M., and Tarnowska-Dziduszko, E. (1975). Quantitative study on dendrites and dentritic spines in Alzheimer's disease and senile dementia. In Advances in Neurobiology, Vol 12. G.W. Kreutzberg, Ed. Raven Press, New York, pp. 453–458.

Mervis, R. (1978). Structural alterations in neurons of aged canine neocortex: A Golgi study. Exp. Neurol. 62, 417–432.

Messert, B., Wannamaker, B.B., and Dudley, A.W. (1972). Reevaluation of the size of lateral ventricle of the brain. Neurology 22, 941–951.

Miller, A.K.H., Alston, R.L., and Corsellis, J.A.N. (1980). Variations with age in the volumes of grey and white matter in the cerebral hemispheres of man: Measurements with an image analyser. Neuropathol. Appl. Neurobiol. 6, 119–132.

Miller, A.K.H. and Corsellis, J.A.N. (1977). Evidence for a secular increase in human brain weight during the past century. Ann. Human Biol. 4, 253–257.

Monagle, R.D. and Brody, H. (1974). The effects of age upon the main nucleus of the inferior olive in human. J. Comp. Neurol. 155, 61–66.

Morel, F. (1944). (Cited by Mutrux, S., 1947.)

Morel, F. and Wildi, E. (1952). General and cellular pathochemistry of senile and presenile alterations of the brain. Proc. 1st Intl. Congr. Neuropath. Rome, pp. 347–374.

Morimatsu, M., Hirai, S., Muramatsu, A., and Yoshikawa, M. (1975). Senile degenerative brain lesions and dementia. J. Amer. Geriatr. Soc. 23, 390–406.

Mufson, E.J., Mesulam, M-M., and Pandya, D.N. (1981). Insular interconnections with the amygdala in the rhesus monkey. Neuroscience 6, 1231–1248.

Mutrux, S. (1947). Diagnostic differentiel histologique de la maladie d'Alzheimer et de la démence sénile: Pathophobie de la zone de projection corticale. Mschf. Psychiat. Neurol. 113, 100–107.

Nauta, W.J.H. (1961). Fibre degeneration following lesions of the amygdaloid complex in the monkey. J. Anat. 95, 515–531.

Ogata, J., Budzilovich, G.N., and Cravioto, H. (1972). A study of rod-like structures (Hirano bodies) in 240 normal and pathological brains. Acta Neuropath. 21, 61–67.

Ohama, E. and Ikuta, F. (1976). Parkinson's disease: Distribution of Lewy bodies and monamine nervous system. Acta Neuropath. 34, 311–319.

Oppenheim, G. (1909). Über "drusige Nekrosen" in der Grosshirnrinde. Neurol. Zbl. 28, 410–413.

Pandya, D.N. and Seltzer, B. (1982). Association areas of the cerebral cortex, Trends in Neurosci. 5, 386–390.

Pandya, D.N., Van Hoesen, G.W., and Domesick, V.B. (1973). A cingulo-amygdaloid projection in the rhesus monkey. Br. Res. 61, 369–373.

Pandya, D.N., Van Hoesen, G.W., and Mesulam, M-M. (1981). Efferent connections of the cingulate gyrus in the rhesus monkey. Exp. Brain Res. 42, 319–330.

Pantelakis, S. (1954). Un type Particulier d'angiopathie sénile du système Nerveux Central: l'Angiopathie congophile. Topographie et fréquence. Mschr. Psychiat. Neurol. 128, 219–256.

Pasquier, D.A. and Reinoso-Suarez, F. (1976). Direct projections from hypothalamus to hippocampus in the rat demonstrated by retrograde transport of horseradish peroxidase. Br. Res. 108, 165–169.

Pearl, T. (1905). Biometrical studies on man. Variations and correlations in brain weight. Biometrika 4, 13–104.

Peress, N.S., Kane, W.C., and Aronson, S.M. (1973). Central nervous system findings in a tenth decade autopsy population. Prog. Br. Res. 40, 473–483.

Poppe, W. and Tennstedt, A. (1969). Studie über hirnatrophische Prozesse unter besonderer Berücksichtigung des Morbus Pick und des Morbus Alzheimer. Fischer, Jena.

Porrino, L.J., Crane, A.M., and Goldman-Rakic, P.S. (1981). Direct and indirect pathways from the amygdala to the frontal lobe in rhesus monkeys. J. Comp. Neurol. 198, 121–136.

Pro, J.D., Smith, C.H., and Sumi, S.M. (1980). Presenile Alzheimer disease: Amyloid plaques in the cerebellum. Neurology 30, 820–825.

Ramsey, M.J. (1967). Altered synaptic terminals in cortex near tumor. Amer. J. Path. 51, 1093–1109.

Redlich, E. (1898). Ueber Miliare Sklerose der Hirnrinde bei seniler Atrophie. Jahrbucher Psychiat. Neurol. 17, 208–216.

Rewcastle, N.B. and Ball, M.J. (1968). Electron microscopic structure of the "inclusion bodies" in Pick's disease. Neurology 18, 1205–1213.

Roberts, M.A. and Caird, F.I. (1976). Computerized tomography and intellectual impairment in the elderly. J. Neurol. Neurosurg. Psychiat. 39, 986–989.

Rosene, D.L. and van Hoesen, G.W. (1977). Hippocampal efferents reach widespread areas of cerebral cortex and amygdala in the rhesus monkey. Science 198, 315–317.

Roth, M., Tomlinson, B.E., and Blessed, G. (1966). Correlation between scores for dementia and counts of "senile plaques" in cerebral grey matter of elderly subjects. Nature 209, 109–110.

Roy, S. and Wolman, L. (1969). Ultrastructural observations in Parkinsonism. J. Path. 99, 39–44.

Rudolph, O. (1914). Untersuchungen über Hirngewicht, Hirnvolumen, Schädelkapazität. Beitr. Path. Anat. 58, 48–87.

Scheibel, A.B. (1979). The hippocampus: Organizational patterns in health and senescence. Mech. Ageing Dev. 9, 89–102.

Scheibel, A.B. and Tomiyasu, U. (1978). Dendritic sprouting in Alzheimer's presenile dementia. Exp. Neurol. 60, 1–8.

Scheibel, M.E., Lindsay, R.D., Tomiyasu, U., and Scheibel, A.B. (1975). Progressive dendritic changes in aging human cortex. Exp. Neurol. 47, 392–403.

Scheibel, M.E., Lindsay, R.D., Tomiyasu, U., and Scheibel, A.B. (1976). Progressive dendritic changes in the aging human limbic system. Exp. Neurol. 53, 420–430.

Scheibel, M.E., Tomiyasu, U., and Scheibel, A.B. (1977). The aging human Betz cell. Exp. Neurol. 56: 598–609.

Schlote, W. (1968). Polarisationsoptisch differenzierbare Stadien der intraneuronalen "Amyloid" Bildung bei Morbus Alzheimer. Verh. Deutsch. Ges. Path. 52, 204–209.

Schochet, S.S. and McCormick, W.F. (1972). Ultrastructure of Hirano bodies. Acta Neuropath. 21, 50–60.

Schochet, S.S., Lampert, P.W., and Lindenberg, R. (1968). Fine structure of the Pick and Hirano bodies in a case of Pick's disease. Acta Neuropath. 11, 330–337.

Schochet, S.S., Hardman, J.M., Ladewig, P.P., and Earl, K.M. (1969). Intraneuronal conglomerates in sporadic motor neuron disease. Arch. Neurol. 20, 548–553.

Scholz, W. (1938). Studien zur Pathologie der Hirngefässe II. Die drusige Entartung der Hirnarterien und -capillaren. (Ein form seniler Gafässerkrankung.) Z. ges. Neurol. Psychiat. 162, 694–715.

Schwartz, P. (1970). Amyloidosis. Causes and Manifestation of Senile Deterioration. Charles C. Thomas, Springfield, Ill.

Schwartz, P., Kurucz, J., and Kurucz, A. (1964). Recent observations on senile cerebral changes and their pathogenesis. J. Amer. Geriatr. Soc. 12, 908–922.

Shefer, V.F. (1972). Absolute number of neurons and thickness of the cerebral cortex during aging, senile and vascular dementia and Pick's and Alzheimier's disease. Zh. Nevropat. Psikhiatr. Korsakov. 72, 1024–1029.

Shefer, V.F. (1976). Hippocampal pathology as one of the possible factors in the pathogenesis of several dementias of old age. Zh. Nevropat. Psikhiatr. 76, 1032–1036.

Shefer, V.F. (1977). Development of senile plaques in the human brain. Arkh. Anat. Gistol. Embriol. 73:97–103.

Shirahama, T., Skinner, M., Westermark, P., Rubinow, A., Cohen, A., Brun, A., and Kemper, T.L. (1982). Senile cerebral amyloid: Prealbumin as a common constituent in the neuritic plaque, in the neurofibrillary tangle and in the microangiopathic lesion. Amer. J. Pathol. 107, 41–50.

Simchowicz, T. (1911). Histologische Studien über die senile Demenz. In Histologische und histopatholische Arbeiten über die Grosshirnrinde mit besonderer Berücksichtigun der pathologischen Anatomie der Geisteskrankheiten. F. Nissle and A. Alzheimer, Eds. Gustav Fischer Verlag, Jena.

Simma, K. (1951). Über Thalamusveränderungen bei seniler Demenz und bei der Alzheimierschen Krankheit. Monatschr. Psychiat. Neurol. 122, 156–178.

Spielmeyer, W. (1922). Histopathologie des Nervensystems. Julius Springer, Berlin.

Steele, J.C., Richardson, J.C., and Olszewski, J. (1964). Progressive supranuclear palsy. Arch. Neurol. 10, 333–359.

Surbek, B. (1961). L'angiopathie dyshorique (Morel) de l'ecore cérébrale. Etude anatomo-clinique et statistique, aspect génétique. Acta Neuropath. 1:168–197.

Suzuki, K. and Terry, R.D. (1967). Fine structural localization of acid phosphatase in senile plaques in Alzheimer's presenile dementia. Acta Neuropath. 8, 276–284.

Terry, R.D. and Davis, P. (1980). Dementia of the Alzheimer type. Ann. Rev. Neurosci. 3, 77–95.

Terry, R.D. and Wisniewski, H.M. (1972). Ultrastructure of senile dementia and of experimental analogs. In Advance in Behavior Biology, Vol. 3 Aging and the

Brain. C.M. Gaitz, Ed. Plenum Press, New York.

Terry, R.D., Gonatas, N.K., and Weiss, M. (1964). Ultrastructural studies in Alzheimer's presenile dementia. Amer. J. Path. 44, 269–281.

Terry, R.D., Peck, A., DeTeresa, R., Schechter, R., and Horoupian, D.S. (1981). Some morphometric aspects of the brain in senile dementia of the Alzheimer type. Ann. Neurol. 10, 184–192.

Tomlinson, B.E. and Kitchener, D. (1972). Granulovacuolar degeneration of hippocampal pyramidal cells. J. Path. 106, 165–185.

Tomlinson, B.E., Blessed, G., and Roth, M. (1968). Observations on the brains of non-demented old people. J. Neurol. Sci. 7, 331–356.

Tomlinson, B.E., Blessed, G., and Roth, M. (1970). Observations and the brains of demented old people. J. Neurol. Sci. 11, 205–242.

Tomlinson, B.E., Irving, D., and Blessed, G. (1981). Cell loss in the locus coeruleus in senile dementia of Alzheimer's type. J. Neurol. Sci. 49, 419–428.

Tomonago, M. (1974). Ultrastructure of Hirano bodies. Acta Neuropath. 28, 365–366.

Tomonago, M. (1979). On the morphological changes in locus coeruleus in the senile human brain. Jap. J. Geriatr. 16, 545–550.

Tomonago, M. (1981a). Cerebral amyloid angiopathy in the elderly. J. Amer. Geriatr. Soc. 29, 151–157.

Tomonago, M. (1981b). Neurofibrillary tangles and Lewy bodies in the locus ceruleus neurons of the aged brain. Acta Neuropath. 53, 165–168.

Traub, R.D., Gajkusek, D.C., and Gibbs, C.J. (1977). Transmissible virus dementia: The relation of transmissible spongiform encephalopathy to Creutzfeldt-Jakob disease. In Aging and Dementia. M. Kinsbourne and L. Smith, Eds. Spectrum, Flushing, N.Y., pp. 91–146.

Traub, R.D., Rains, T.C., Garruto, R.M., Gajdusek, D.C., and Gibbs, C.J. (1981). Brain destruction alone does not elevate brain aluminum. Neurology 31, 986–990.

Treft, W. (1974). Das Involutionsmuster des Nucleus dentatus cerebelli. Eine morphometrische Analysis. In Platt Altern. (Cited by Hunziker et al., 1978.)

Tretiakof, C. (1919). J. Pathol. 99, 39–44. (Cited by Roy and Woman, 1969.)

Turner, B.H., Gupta, K.C., and Mishkin, M. (1978). The locus and cytoarchitecture of the projection areas of the olfactory bulb in *Macaca mulatta*. J. Comp. Neurol. 177, 381–396.

Uemura, E. (1980). Age-related changes in prefrontal cortex of *Macaca mulatta:* Synaptic density. Exp. Neurol. 69, 164–172.

Uemura, E. and Hartmann, H.A. (1978a). RNA content and volume of nerve cell bodies in human brain I. Prefrontal cortex in aging normal and demented patients. J. Neuropath. Exp. Neurol. 37, 487–496.

Uemura, E. and Hartmann, H.A. (1978b). Age-related changes in RNA content and volume of the human hypoglossal neuron. Br. Res. Bull. 3, 207–211.

Uemura, E. and Hartmann, H.A. (1979). RNA content and volume of nerve cell bodies in human brain II. Subiculum in aging normal patients. Exp. Neurol. 65, 107–117.

Urechina, G.I. and Elekes, N. (1925). Contribution a l'etude des plaques seniles. Role de la Microglie. Bull. Acad. Med. Paris 3; 94, 795–803.

Uyematsu, S. (1923). On the pathology of senile psychosis. The differential diagnostic significance of Redlich-Fischer's military plaques. J. Nerv. Ment. Dis. 57, 1–25, 131–156, 237–260.

van Hoesen, G.W. and Pandya, D.N. (1975). Some connections of the entorhinal (area 28) and perirhinal (area 35) cortices of the rhesus monkey I. Temporal lobe afferents. Br. Res. 95, 1–24.

van Hoesen, G.W., Pandya, D.N., and Butters, N. (1972). Cortical afferents to the entorhinal cortex of the rhesus monkey. Science 175, 1471–1473.

van Hoesen, G.W., Rosene, D.L., and Mesulam, M.-M. (1979). Subicular input from temporal cortex in rhesus monkey. Science 205, 608–610.

Vaughan, D.W. (1977). Age-related deterioration of pyramidal cell basal dendrites in rat auditory cortex. J. Comp. Neurol. 171, 501–516.

Vaughan, D.W. and Peters, A. (1981). The structure of neuritic plaques in the cerebral cortex of aged rats. J. Neuropath. Exp. Neurol. 40, 472–487.

Vijayashankar, N. and Brody, H. (1973). The neuronal population of the nuclei of the trochlear nerve and the locus coeruleus in the human. Anat. Rec. 172, 421–472.

Vijayashankar, N. and Brody, H. (1977). A study of aging in the human abducens nucleus. J. Comp. Neurol. 173, 433–438.

West, C.D. (1979). A quantitative study of lipofuscin accumulation with age in normals and individuals with Down's syndrome, phenylketonuria, progeria and transneuronal atrophy. J. Comp. Neurol. 186, 109–116.

Whitehouse, P.J., Price, D.L., Clark, A.W., Coyle, J.T., and DeLong, M.R. (1981). Alzheimer disease: Evidence for selective loss of cholinergic neurons in the nucleus basalis. Ann. Neurol. 10, 122–126.

Wilkinson, A. and Davies, I. (1978). The influence of age and dementia on the neuron population of the mamillary bodies. Age and Aging 7, 151–160.

Williams, R.S., Ferrante, R.J., and Caviness, V.S. (1978). The rapid Golgi method in clinical neuropathology: The morphological consequences of suboptimal fixation. J. Neuropathol. Exp. Neurol. 37, 13–33.

Wisniewski, H.M. and Soiser, D. (1979). Neurofibrillary pathology: Current status and research perspectives. Mech. Ageing Dev. 9, 119–142.

Wisniewski, H.M. and Terry, R.D. (1973). Morphology of the aging brain, human and animal. In Progress in Brain Research, Vol. 40, Neurobiological Aspects of Maturation and Aging. D.H. Ford, Ed. Amsterdam, Elsevier, pp. 167–186.

Wisniewski, H.M., Bruce, M.E., and Fraser, H. (1975). Infectious etiology of neuritic (senile) plaques in mice. Science 190, 1108–1109.

Wisniewski, H.M., Ghetti, B., and Terry, R.D. (1973). Neuritic (senile) plaques and filamentous changes in aged rhesus monkeys. J. Neuropath. Exp. Neurol. 32, 566–584.

Wisniewski, H.M., Johnson, A.B., Raine, C.S., Kay, W.J., and Terry, R.D. (1970). Senile plaques and cerebral amyloidosis in aged dogs. A histochemical and ultrastructural study. Lab. Invest. 23, 287–296.

Wohlwill, F. (1925). Pathologisch-anatomische Befunde an excidierten sympathischen Malsganglien bei Asthma bronchiale. Klin. Wschr. 4, 107.

Woodard, J.S. (1962). Clinicopathologic significance of granulovacuolar degeneration in Alzheimer's disease. J. Neuropath. Exp. Neurol. 21, 85–91.

Woodard, J.S. (1966). Alzheimer's disease in late adult life. Amer. J. Pathol. 49, 1157–1169.

Worster-Drought, C., Greenfield, J.G., and McMenemey, W.H. (1940). A form of familial presenile dementia with spastic paralysis. Brain 63, 237–254.

Wright, J.R., Calkins, E., Breen, W.J., Stolte, G., and Schultz, R.T. (1969). Relationship of amyloid to aging. Review of literature and systematic study of 83 patients from a general hospital population. Medicine 48, 30–60.

Yakovlev, P.I. (1962). Morphological criteria of growth and maturation of the nervous system in man. Res. Pub. ARMND 39, 3–46.

Yakovlev, P.I. and Lecours, A.R. (1967). The myelogentic cycles of regional maturation of the brain. In Regional Development of the Brain in Early Life. A. Minkowski, Ed. Blackwell Scientific Publications, Oxford.

3. Neurochemical Changes with Aging

DENNIS SELKOE

KENNETH KOSIK

It has been estimated that humans lose 100,000 neurons each day. The significance of this continuous attrition in a population of more than 20 billion neurons in the human brain is not yet clear. The loss of neurons is not topographically random; the hippocampus, temporal lobes, and frontal poles (Critchley, 1931; Brody, 1955) are considerably more vulnerable than many brainstem structures. Cell loss is not confined to cortical structures; cell loss as a function of age has been well documented in the locus coeruleus and the intermediolateral column of the spinal cord. Certain parts of the neuron may be especially vulnerable to the effects of age, for example, the dendritic domains of hippocampal neurons (Scheibel and Scheibel, 1975). These age-associated morphological alterations provide points of reference for the biochemist interested in molecular changes during normal and pathological aging.

The data on neurochemical changes linked to the aging process consist of a body of diverse observations and do not relate easily to any of the major theories concerning the nature of cellular aging. These theories include (1) encoding of aging in DNA; (2) progressive breakdown in accuracy of protein synthesis; (3) cross-linkage of macromolecules; (4) "attack" of the immune system (in higher organisms) on self-antigens; (5) damage by free radi-

cal reactions to macromolecules. The enormity of the literature about age-related brain phenomena precludes consideration of the subject in its entirety; we shall therefore limit our treatment to human findings, referring to animal and cell culture data only when such data are relevant.

Difficulties Inherent in Neurochemical Studies of Human Brain Aging

Measurements and interpretation of biochemical alterations that occur as a function of age are subject to many problems. Special difficulties complicate human studies, so that multivariate analysis with several control populations is often required. We will now review some of the factors that must be considered in assessing biochemical studies of human brain aging.

THE POSTMORTEM INTERVAL

The time between death and the freezing of tissue is a critical parameter. To complicate further the effects of this parameter, the degradation kinetics of various brain substrates is neither uniform nor constant. For example, the rate at which a particular substrate is degraded postmortem is determined by its subcellular localization. If an enzyme or a structural protein is located in the cytosol (soluble, nonparticulate) fraction of cytoplasm, it is more apt to be degraded by proteolytic enzymes than if it is protected in the hydrophobic environment of a membranous organelle. Dopamine-stimulated adenylate cyclase activity has been shown to decrease markedly during the first 5 hours, postmortem, but, if one measures activity in a washed membrane preparation, it changes very little over a 10-hour period (Nicol et al., 1981). A similar observation has been reported with the brain structural protein tubulin (Carlin et al., 1982; Kosik et al., 1982), the subunit of microtubules. An occasional problem in studies of tissue from aged individuals is the difficulty in ascertaining the exact time of death.

THE PREMORTEM AGONAL PERIOD

The healthy patient who dies suddenly must be considered quite apart from the patient who suffers a prolonged agonal period. The importance of this consideration is most clearly seen in the patient whose cardiovascular system is supported by a respirator, but who has brain death. In such patients, tissue degradation is grossly apparent. However, tissue degradation almost certainly begins while the outward signs of life persist in the hypoxic patient with pneumonia or in the poorly perfused patient with severe cardiac failure. The quantitation of these factors is difficult. At present, one of the best indicators of the length of the agonal period appears to be the levels of glutamic acid dehydrogenase in brain (Bird and Iversen, 1974; Bowen et al., 1977). Creatine kinase, an enzyme of intermediary metabolism and therefore less likely to be affected by a patterned neuronal degeneration, also appears to indicate the duration and severity of the preterminal illness (Maker et al., 1981).

THE UNDERLYING DISEASE STATE

It has been amply demonstrated that certain neurological illnesses change specific proteins and neurotransmitters. These changes often parallel age-related changes qualitatively, but are greater in magnitude. Losses of neurotransmitters and their synthetic enzymes in the dopaminergic system in Parkinson's disease and in the cholinergic system in Alzheimer's disease are examples. An underlying systemic disease also affects certain biochemical parameters. For example, hypothyroidism, uremia, diabetes, and hepatic insufficiency can affect brain function and therefore must be considered in the interpretation of data.

DRUG HISTORY

The patient's exposure to drugs has important implications for studies of neurotransmitter functions. Many drugs commonly used in the elderly population, such as psychotropic agents and the antihypertensives, are known to affect one or more of the classical neurotransmitter systems. The action of such drugs, however, may extend beyond their effects on synaptic biochemistry. For example, the phenothiazines have been shown to interact with brain-specific structural proteins (Marshak et al., 1981).

GENETIC VARIABILITY

Subtle differences of human brain proteins occur from individual to individual. Polymorphisms or degree of heterozygosity per genetic locus for the human population have been estimated to average 6.7% (Harris and Hopkins, 1972). For human fibroblasts, in which a considerably smaller percentage of the genome is expressed, such polymorphisms average 1.2% (Walton et al., 1979). Genetic variation in neurotransmitter function has also been documented in animal studies (Fink and Reis, 1981). The forty-fold range of maximum life-span among mammalian species suggests major genetic determinants of age-related biochemical and functional changes. Thus, extension of animal data to humans becomes problematic unless a correction for the total life span of the population being studied is included. Genetically based heterogeneity of life span among human populations is likely to exist. In fact, it is well known that chronological age does not accurately reflect physiological age, so "age-matched controls" may not always represent ideal controls.

HANDLING OF POSTMORTEM TISSUE

There is great variation in the way human brain postmortem tissue is processed, but the establishment of regional brain banks may bring some uniformity to postmortem tissue handling. The freezing process itself is one variable. McGeer and McGeer found that freezing and thawing interfered with the assay of glutamic acid decarboxylase, tyrosine hydroxylase, and DOPA decarboxylase (McGeer, 1978). The authors have recently shown that the use of frozen brain tissue as opposed to fresh postmortem tissue can introduce selective, freezing-related artifactual changes in protein migration on gel electrophoresis (Kosik et al., 1982). The rate at which tissue is frozen introduces yet another variable (Hardy, 1983). The temperature at which tissue is stored, which may range from 0° C to −182°C (the temperature of liquid nitrogen), is also a variable.

REGIONAL VARIABILITY OF BRAIN CONSTITUENTS

Biochemical studies have begun to reveal systems of brain organization that do not always parallel the boundaries of tracts and nuclei of classical neuroanatomy. Although the microtopography of neurotransmitters has revealed increasingly fine levels of organization (Pope et al., 1964; Graybiel and Ragsdale, 1978), regional variability of brain constituents even within the limits of classical neuroanatomy is often problematic. Thus, the nucleus basalis, with its many cortical cholinergic efferents, was found to be severely depleted of neurons in a case of Alzheimer's disease (Whitehouse et al., 1981). To a lesser degree, the cell population of this nucleus is affected by normal aging (Hassler, 1965). The actual boundaries of this nucleus however remain ill defined, and variation in its neuronal population among normal subjects has not been determined. A more clearly age-related cell loss occurs in the intermediolateral column of the spinal cord and may be responsible for

idiopathic orthostatic hypotension in the elderly (Low et al., 1978).

When a particular brain area is considered to be selectively vulnerable to the aging process or to a degenerative disease, a number of correlative studies must be performed to document this consideration. These include (1) immunohistochemical localization of particular functional classes of neurons; (2) quantitative determinations of neurotransmitters and their respective enzyme activities, using a small sample technique over a defined anatomical area; and (3) cell counts of the area in question. When an anatomically well-defined area loses cells, associated biochemical losses are not surprising. Hence, loss of dopamine from the substantia nigra in Parkinson's disease and cholecystokinin (CCK) loss from the caudate in Huntington's disease (Emson et al., 1980) are not unexpected.

CELL-TYPE SPECIFICITY OF AGE-RELATED CHANGES

Brain cells often vary greatly in their susceptibility to age-related changes. For example, neurofibrillary tangles occur selectively within the hippocampus, affecting CA1 and subiculum most prominently, while usually sparing the dentate and CA3 and CA4 (Kemper, 1978). Corpora amylacea accumulate around the ventricles and near the subarachnoid space. The greater cell loss among neurons compared to glia reflects, biochemically, as a relative enhancement of glial-specific constituents. The glial fibrillary acidic protein is enhanced in the caudate in Huntington's disease and, very likely, the cerebellum in Joseph's disease, as a consequence of the marked gliosis and the increased density of filament bundles within the glia in these diseases (Rosenberg et al., 1981; Selkoe et al., 1982).

VARIATION IN ASSAY TECHNIQUE OF BRAIN CONSTITUENTS

Methodologies for determining many of the most important constituents that might reflect neuronal aging are still being debated and revised. Some recent innovations (Langlais et al., 1980) have improved the accuracy of the liquid chromatographic measurement of 3-methoxyphenylglycol, the major metabolite of norepinephrine. Aquilonius and Eckernäs (1976) found that the choline acetyltransferase activity in cerebrospinal fluid (CSF) must be considered falsely high because in earlier methodologies, nonenzymatically catalyzed formation of acetylcholine, which affects such activity substantially, was not considered. Furthermore, the critical evaluation of such data requires attention to how calculations are made; for example, whether values are expressed per milligram wet weight of tissue or per milligram of protein.

THE AGING CURVE

When a brain substance is shown to decline with age, it can be graphed over time. The choice of time points will be critical in determining the shape of the curve. Many brain substances have a curvilinear function with age, which means that they decline most during childhood and adolescence, and thereafter there is little or no change. Hence, although there are age-related alterations, they are often not associated with the senescent end of the aging curve. In other words, aging is a process that should be considered as spanning development and adulthood in addition to senescence.

Molecular Genetic Aspects of Aging

It is generally agreed that postmitotic cells, e.g., the neuron and the muscle cell, may play a special role in the aging process. However, because *in vitro* systems to study these cells are limited, there is a paucity of cell and molecular biological data regarding the changes such cells undergo over the life-span of the organism. A large body of data does exist on untransformed mitotic cells in culture, and it has been utilized as a model of *in vitro* aging (Hayflick, 1977). Such cells (usually fibroblasts) have a predictable number of cell doublings until, ultimately, cell division ceases in the senescent cell; and the number of population doublings the cells undergo correlates inversely with the age of the donor

(Schneider and Mitsui, 1976; Hayflick, 1977). The location of this biological "clock," thought to reside in the cell nucleus, was deduced from experiments in which *in vitro* aged nuclei were reinserted into low passage-number cytoplasts, and vice versa. In such experiments, the age of the nucleus determined the number of population doublings remaining (Wright and Hayflick, 1975). Loss of replicative capacity, however, is not thought to be a primary mechanism of aging in humans, although many of the changes that such cells undergo before cell division ceases mimic changes seen in less rapidly dividing cells. Loss of replicative capacity may be important in such age-related changes as reduction in immune responsiveness.

The changes in nucleic acids in the aging brain have recently been reviewed by von Hahn (1981). Studies in this area generally fall into two categories: (1) quantitative DNA and RNA changes and (2) structural and functional nucleic acid changes.

For the quantitative studies, there is general agreement that once maturity is reached there is no significant quantitative change in the DNA content of the brain (von Hahn, 1981). This appears to be the case for all species and brain regions studied to date. As with DNA, whole RNA from various brain regions does not appear to change in either man or experimental animal once maturity is reached (von Hahn, 1981). However, measurement of brain RNA content is more problematic, since, unlike DNA content, cellular RNA content does not remain constant over the life-span of the organism. Measurements have been obtained, in part, by the ultramicroanalytic techniques of Hydén (1960). For example, the RNA content of motor neurons from the ventro-lateral nucleus of human spinal cord at C_5 increases until the fifth decade and then steadily declines from the seventh to tenth decade (Hydén, 1970). A similar trend was reported by Uemura and Hartmann (1978), who, in single human hypoglossal neurons, found an increasing RNA content until age 10, a plateau until age 50, and a steady decline thereafter. An analogous pattern has been described in rat studies, in which Ringborg (1966) found a decrease in the RNA content of single hippocampal pyramidal cells after maturity. In certain age-associated diseases, a loss of both cytoplasmic RNA and nucleolar volume in specific brain regions also occurs. This is seen in the locus coerulus of patients dying with Alzheimer's disease (Mann et al., 1980) and in the anterior horn cells in patients with amyotrophic lateral sclerosis (Davidson and Hartmann, 1981).

When one moves from quantitative studies to the investigation of structural and functional nucleic acid changes, experimental conditions severely limit studies in humans. Age-related changes in DNA polymerases, enzymes that synthesize DNA, have been detected in human *in vitro* systems (Petes et al., 1974). These enzymes synthesize DNA during the S phase of the cell cycle, as well as during continuous DNA repair processes, and this may complicate interpretation of data. What may be more relevant to the aging process is the fidelity of the DNA polymerase. Errors in the genetic code may be introduced even in postmitotic cells during DNA repair processes. Evidence in favor of the existence of this process, which indirectly supports the well-known "error-catastrophe" theory of Orgel (1973), comes from late-passage human lung fibroblast DNA polymerase. Using various synthetic templates, Linn et al. (1976) found that DNA polymerase from late-passage cells was more error-prone than that of early-passage cells.

Animal studies suggest that with aging there may be a change and/or a reduction in the genes being transcribed and translated. Such data are obtained by determining both the age-related shifts in nucleic acid base ratios and the DNA/RNA hybridization levels. The results indicate that a decrease in template activity of brain chromatin occurs with advancing age. Support for this concept derives in large measure from the growing body of research on DNA damage and rates of DNA repair associated with aging, a subject recently reviewed by Williams and Dearfield (1981).

Structural damage to the DNA double helix may be responsible for its decreased biological activity with age. For instance, single-strand breaks, which are physical discontinuities in the linear DNA single strands of the double helix, appear to accumulate (Price et al., 1971; Chetsanga et al., 1977). Other modifications that can impair the function of DNA are interstrand cross-links and cross-links between DNA and cellular proteins. The few brain studies in which these phenomena have been observed can be summarized as follows: Autopsied human brain from senescent individuals (age 78–85) showed an age-associated increase in nucleosomal repeat length of base-pairs and a decrease in the amount of DNA digested by micrococcal nuclease (Ermini et al., 1978). Increasing nuclease S_1 sensitivity, which indicates single-strand breaks, has been detected in mice after 20 months of age (Chetsanga et al., 1977). This finding has been extended with the immunofluorescent detection of an age-associated increase in single-stranded regions in mouse brain DNA, using anticytidine antibody (Nakanishi et al., 1979). There are a number of known mechanisms of DNA repair, and Robbins has proposed that some neuronal degenerations may result from defective DNA repair mechanisms (Robbins, 1978; Andrews et al., 1978), which cause a gradual increase in the number of transcription errors.

Certain inherited diseases have a demonstrated or hypothesized defect in DNA repair mechanisms, and if an impairment of DNA repair is related to aging, then accelerated aging may be seen in these disease states. Diseases for which there is good current evidence for a repair deficiency include xeroderma pigmentosum, ataxia telangiectasia, and Fanconi's anemia. Martin (1978) has studied a number of indices of aging in patients with these disorders, and although such patients are susceptible to the neoplasms characteristic of aging populations, an overall pattern of accelerated aging does not emerge.

Sequential activation and repression of genes has been proposed by Kanungo and Thakur (1977) as a general mechanism controlling growth, differentiation, and aging. That is, damage to genetic information itself is not so much responsible as are failures of the regulatory mechanisms that control the genes. For example, alterations in the regulation of transcription may occur secondary to modification in histone and nonhistone nucleoproteins, and age-related decrements in histone phosphorylation and acetylation have also been reported (Thakur et al., 1965; Kanungo and Thakur, 1977).

Proteins

Because the neuron is a postmitotic cell, the process of neuronal aging has somewhat different implications than has aging in the many other cells that retain their ability to divide. By-products of the neuron's synthetic machinery as well as proteins that may contain errors in their amino acid sequences may accumulate in the neuron during the life of the individual. Dilution of the products of cellular aging among the offspring as seen in dividing cells would not be expected to occur in the postmitotic neuron. On the one hand, the neuron incurs cumulative insults over its entire life-span, but, on the other hand, it is spared the molecular burden of maintaining a proliferative cell cycle.

The effects of senescence on translation have been studied using cell-free protein synthesis. This system translates at only 1% of the *in vivo* rate (Henshaw et al., 1971; Waterlow, 1975), so one must be cautious drawing conclusions about protein synthesis rates from such studies. Ekstrom et al. (1980) found that there was a 56% decrease in cell-free protein synthesis in brain from rats 6 to 32 months of age; however, only 15% of this decrease occurred after 14 months. Dwyer and Wasterlain (1978) found a significant decrease in the incorporation of radioactive lysine in brain from rats up to 23 months old. The decline in rat brain protein synthesis continues during post-developmental aging (Dwyer et al., 1980). Thus, protein synthesis decreases significantly during brain maturation, following which protein synthesis continues to decline, but at a considerably slower rate. Investigating possible mechanisms of this decline, Frazer and Yang (1972), Mariotti and Ruscitto (1977),

Mays et al. (1979), and Wust and Rosen (1972) have reported on age-related decline in the aminoacylation of transfer RNA (*t*RNA) due to a decrease in the ability of *t*RNA to accept amino acids. Protein synthesis from skeletal muscle in old animals decreases 60% in mice 18 to 29 months old (Britton and Sherman, 1975). An interesting study (Chatterjee et al., 1981) that bears repeating in brain is the identification of senescence marker proteins from *in vitro* translation products of rat liver. An age-dependent regulation of messenger RNA (*m*RNA) was postulated because, among other changes, a 26,000 molecular weight protein appeared in senescence.

In a series of studies, Gershon et al. (1979) documented a decrease in brain enzyme activity with age. They determined the catalytic activity per unit of enzyme antigen in rodents of various ages and demonstrated declines that ranged from 30 to 70%. Declines in enzymatic activity have been described for some enzymes of intermediary metabolism, such as aldolase A and B, catalase, tyrosine aminotransferase, and lactic dehydrogenase, as well as for some neurotransmitter synthetic and degradative enzymes. The enzyme superoxide dismutase, which protects the cell from the effects of the free radical superoxide, undergoes a similar decline. Although the specific activity of this enzyme is unchanged per milligram of protein of aged rat and mouse brain, its catalytic activity per antigenic unit of enzyme does decrease (Reiss and Gershon, 1976). The authors postulated a compensatory mechanism during brain aging in which the cells in old animals synthesize more enzyme molecules to compensate for the partial loss of activity per molecule. Age-related changes in enzymatic activities vary considerably among species; there is, as well, topographic variability within species. Nor is this decline in activity universally true for all enzymes. Adenyl cyclase activity and phosphodiesterase activity are unchanged in aged rat cortex.

Enzymes that do decline in activity often do so only in certain parameters, particularly as regards their specific catalytic activity and heat stability. Most enzymes do not change with age in their affinity for substrate (K_m), affinity for specific inhibitors (K_i), electrophoretic mobility, molecular weight, and antigenic identity (Rothstein, 1977; Gershon, 1979). The kinds of molecular alterations that could cause a specific decline in enzyme activity are not yet understood. For example, an amino acid substitution might induce a charge shift in the enzyme, which should be detectable by isoelectric focusing; however, no such shifts have been described. Using lens protein as a model, Truscott and Augusteyn (1977) have suggested how enzyme activity could change without a charge shift. For example, formation of the senile cataract could involve oxidation of methionine to methionine sulfoxide, which would not involve a charge shift.

Chainy and Kanungo (1978) have suggested that it is not so much the enzyme molecule that changes with age, but rather the ability to induce the enzyme. For example, androgenic and estrogenic stimulation have differential effects on pyruvate kinase in the cerebral hemispheres relative to the age of the animal. Static measurements as a function of age for many brain and CSF enzymes have recently been tabulated (Wilson, 1981).

The mechanisms by which the neuronal cell body maintains its axon are under intense investigation. Whether transport of materials down the axons changes in aging has been the subject of several studies. The protein constituents involved in axonal transport have been classified as slow and fast, based on their rates of transport. Most age-associated changes in transport so far described indicate a further slowing of the slow component (Droz and LeBlond, 1963; Lasek, 1970; Jablecki and Brimijoin, 1975); this slow component is made up of many of the cytoskeletal proteins, such as actin, tubulin, and the neurofilament polypeptides. Geinisman et al. (1977) have presented data that suggest that an age-related reduction in the amount and/or rate of axonal transport of glycoproteins occurs in the septohippocampal pathway.

A major, age-related brain protein alteration is the formation of the neurofibrillary tangle (NFT). This lesion is found in normal aged individuals as well as in patients with Alzheimer's disease. The NFT seen in Alzheimer's disease are indistinguishable from those in the brains of normal individuals; the difference is a quantitative one. The Alzheimer brain shows a greater density and wider distribution of these lesions (see Chapter 2). The NFT is a mass of abnormal fibrils occupying much of the neuronal cytoplasm, particularly within the perikaryon and in the axon terminal found in the rim of the senile plaque. Electron microscopically, the abnormal fibers consist of pairs of helically wound 10-nanometer filaments. They therefore bear some resemblance to normal 10-nanometer neurofilaments, which are, however, unpaired and straight.

The protein composition of the NFT and its paired helical filaments are under investigation. Identification by immunocytochemistry has been problematic, since there is conflicting data on whether antibodies to neurofilaments stain the NFT. One major problem is that immunological cross reactivity of proteins is based on shared antigenic determinants that may constitute only a small part of the proteins.

In our laboratory, we have recently utilized the techniques of analytical protein chemistry to characterize further the molecular nature of the paired helical filaments (Selkoe et al., 1982). We have subjected highly enriched preparations of paired helical filaments to such harsh protein denaturants as sodium dodecyl sulfate, urea, and guanidine hydrochloride. The results obtained imply that the paired helical filaments are highly insoluble, rigid protein polymers apparently held together by strong noncovalent and perhaps covalent bonds. Strong bonds similar to those within paired helical filaments occur in other proteins as a function of increasing age. Such bonds or protein cross-links have been described in collagen, in lens protein during senile cataract formation, and in the red blood cell membrane as the red cell approaches the end of its life-span.

Another protein that accumulates in brain during aging is amyloid, a protein found in many parts of the body under many different conditions. It occurs as a

twisted β-pleated sheet, which, under po-
larized light after Congo red staining,
shows a green birefringence. In brain,
amyloid forms the core of the senile plaque
and is sometimes seen in the walls of small
intracortical blood vessels in congophilic
angiopathy. Although it is known that the
amyloid fibrils in primary systemic amyloidosis are composed of immunoglobulin
light chain fragments, the composition of
brain amyloid is still unknown.

Neurotransmitter Metabolism

The parameters that make the study of aged
human brain tissue difficult (see the section
on difficulties inherent in neurochemical
studies) are especially important in analyses of neurotransmitter function. In contrast to such structural proteins, as neurofilaments, which are relatively stable, the
enzymatic proteins regulating synaptic
transmission, and transmitter molecules,
may be altered by pharmacological agents
administered before death and by agonal
and postmortem processes. In studying the
classical neurotransmitters, most investigators have assessed the activities of synthetic
and degradative enzymes, rather than the
amines themselves, which are less reliably
measured in small postmortem tissue
samples. All investigators observed that enzyme levels vary more in human than in
animal tissue. Nevertheless, several workers have reported little significant effect of a
postmortem interval of several hours on
assays of most of the classical transmitter
enzymes (McGeer and McGeer, 1976a;
McGeer, 1978). The premortem state of
the patient, particularly if the patient is hypoxic or comatose, appears to be a more
important variable. Even with reproducible
data, however, interpretation of changes in
specific transmitter systems during aging
and in dementia has become increasingly
complex. Many new putative neurotransmitters, including certain neuropeptides
and amino acids, have been discovered.
The fact that a particular neuron may store
and release more than one type of molecule
further complicates the analyses.

During aging in apparently normal individuals, sizable declines in the activities of

catecholamine synthetic enzymes, particularly tyrosine hydroxylase and DOPA decarboxylase, have been reported in some
brain regions (Cote and Kremzner, 1974;
McGeer and McGeer, 1976b; McGeer,
1978). However, most of the decline occurs between 5 and 30 years (Figure 3-1).
After age 60, which is our interest here,
there is only a modest decline of these two
enzymes, with some elderly subjects showing no significant loss compared to individuals in late middle age. As would be
expected, the areas in which the major loss
of tyrosine hydroxylase (the rate-limiting
step in catecholamine synthesis) and
DOPA decarboxylase occurs have high
densities of dopaminergic nerve endings or
axons (e.g., the caudate and putamen)
(McGeer, 1978). The cell bodies of many
of these dopaminergic terminals are in the
substantia nigra, and this region shows a
decrease in dopaminergic neurons from
approximately 400,000 per nigra at birth to
250,000 by age 60 (McGeer et al., 1977).
In Parkinson's disease, the latter figure
decreases to around 60,000 to 120,000
cells. A similar age-related decline in the
number of noradrenergic neurons in human locus coeruleus has also been reported (Brody, 1976; Vijayashanker and
Brody, 1979). Other brain-stem nuclei
show little or no apparent perikaryal loss
with age (Brody, 1976), which suggests
that catecholaminergic cells may be particularly vulnerable to the effects of aging.
It is of interest that in aged rats there is no
significant loss of locus coeruleus neurons
(Goldman and Coleman, 1980). An age-
related decline in the intensity of norepinephrine fluorescence of these neurons has
been observed in 3- versus 20-month-old
rats; however, a further decline in senescence, that is, between 20 and 30 months
of age, was not consistently observed
(Sladek and Blanchard, 1981).

The enzyme that converts dopamine to
norepinephrine, dopamine-β-hydroxylase,
has been little studied in human brain,
with one group reporting no significant
age-related change (Grote et al., 1974).
On the other hand, there have been
several reports of an increase with age in
the activity of the catecholamine degrada-

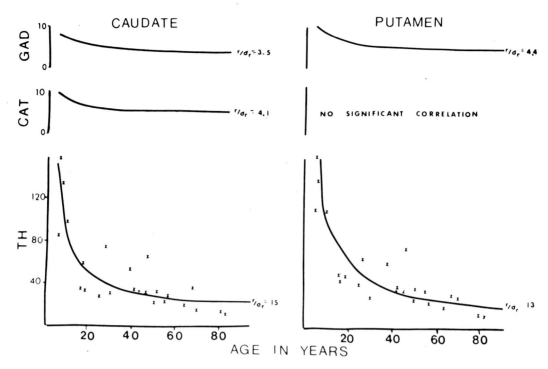

Figure 3-1. Calculated curves for glutamate decarboxylase (GAD), choline acetyltransferase (CAT) and TH activities as a function of age in caudate and putamen from humans dying without neurological illness. Individual values are also shown for TH. TH: nanomoles/hour/100 mg protein. GAD and CAT: micromoles/hour/100 mg protein. The TH in nucleus accumbens showed a similar curve (TH = 22.5 + 455/age;r/$^\delta$r = 14). [From McGeer, E.G. (1978). Aging and neurotransmitter metabolism in human brain. In Alzheimer's Disease: Senile Dementia and Related Disorders. R. Katzman, R.D. Terry, and K.L. Bick, Eds. Raven Press, New York, pp. 427–440.]

tive enzyme monoamine oxidase (MAO) (Robinson et al., 1972; Samorajski and Rolsen, 1973; Crote and Kremzner, 1974; Grote et al., 1974; Gottfries et al., 1975). The best correlations between age and increased MAO activity appear to occur in the globus pallidus, the hippocampus, the substantia nigra, and certain neocortical areas (Grottfries et al., 1975; Robinson et al., 1977). As in the case of the decline of tyrosine hydroxylase activity, it must be emphasized that most of the increase in MAO activity in human brain occurs prior to late middle age, with the rate of increase dropping off in the senium (Samorajski and Rolsten, 1973). The gradual loss of

synthetic capacity, and the corresponding increase in catabolic activity, for the catecholamines would be expected to lead to a progressive deficiency, which could contribute to certain motoric and intellectual manifestations of normal aging (Barbeau, 1973).

The synthetic enzyme for serotonin, tryptophan hydroxylase, is less active and less stable than tyrosine hydroxylase and has not yet been well studied in humans (McGeer, 1978). Results from studies of the levels of serotonin itself, and its metabolite, 5-hydroxyindoleacetic acid, in aged human and rodent brain, have been contradictory. Glutamic acid decarboxylase, the enzyme that synthesizes γ-aminobutyric acid (GABA), has been found to decline with age in numerous human brain regions, particularly the thalamus, but the loss is again more rapid in younger age groups (McGeer, 1978).

Among the classical neurotransmitters, acetylcholine has received the most attention because of the finding by three independent groups in 1976 of a marked and apparently selective loss of choline acetyltransferase (ChAT) in the brains of presenile and senile Alzheimer patients (Table 3-1) (Davies and Maloney, 1976; Perry et al., 1977; Spillane et al., 1977). Figure 3-1 depicts ChAT activity during normal aging in human striatum; no significant change is observed in late life. However, in other brain regions, particularly the cerebral cortex, there is a moderate decline of ChAT in nondemented aged patients (McGeer, 1978). The loss is far greater in Alzheimer's disease, however, with decreases of up to 60 to 90% of the cortical ChAT activity reported in the cerebral cortex of age-matched, normal subjects (Davies and Maloney, 1976; Perry et al., 1977; Spillane et al., 1977; Terry and Davies, 1980). The decline in cortical ChAT levels has been quantitatively corre-lated with both the degree of intellectual impairment and the density of cortical neuritic plaques. However, decreased ChAT activity has also been found in the striatum in Alzheimer's disease, an area containing few neuritic plaques or NFT's.

The cell bodies of the cholinergic terminals that innervate the cerebral cortex of mammals are in the nucleus basalis of Meynert (Divac, 1975; Mesulam, 1976), a small subcortical gray area lying ventromedial to the globus pallidus and anterior commissure. Whitehouse et al. (1982) demonstrated a marked (>75%) loss of neurons in this nucleus in Alzheimer's disease, thus providing an explanation for the decrease in presynaptic cholinergic markers in the neocortex. A similar loss of cholinergic cell bodies has been reported in the medial septal nucleus (Nakano and Hirano, 1982), a major source of cholinergic projections to the hippocampus. Some of the remaining neurons in these deep cholinergic nuclei contain NFT's (Nakano and Hirano, 1982; Whitehouse et al., 1982b). It has been hypothesized that the altered axonal endings found in cortical neuritic plaques in Alzheimer's disease may represent the cholinergic terminals of nucleus basalis neurons (Struble et al.,

Table 3-1. Neurotransmitter-related enzymes in Alzheimer's disease brain.

Enzyme	Brain region	Percentage of activity in age-matched normals
Choline acetyltransferase	Frontal cortex	10–30
	Hippocampus	10–30
	Caudate	40–80
Acetylycholinesterase	Frontal cortex	10–50
	Hippocampus	10–50
	Caudate	30–60
Pseudocholinesterase	Frontal cortex	130–180
Glutamic acid decarboxylase	Frontal cortex	60–130
	Hippocampus	60–120
	Caudate	60–110
Tyrosine hydroxylase	Frontal cortex	80–100
	Hippocampus	80–100
Aromatic amino acid decarboxylase	Frontal cortex	100 ± 20
	Whole temporal lobe	100 ± 20
Dopamine-β-hydroxylase	Frontal cortex	90–130
Monoamine oxidase	Frontal cortex	80–150

Adapted from Terry, R.D. and Davies, P. (1980) Ann. Rev. Neurosci. 3, 77–95.

1982). Loss of neuronal perikarya in the nucleus basalis is not restricted to Alzheimer's disease, but has also been reported in Pick's disease (Hilt et al., 1982) and in Parkinsonism with dementia (Whitehouse et al., 1982a).

No significant loss of muscarinic acetylcholine receptors in Alzheimer cortex has yet been documented on the other side of the cholinergic synapse (Davies and Verth, 1977; Perry et al., 1977; Spillane et al., 1977). This finding has led to therapeutic trials of dietary choline precursors, particularly lecithin, and other cholinergic agents in Alzheimer patients, thus far without notable benefit to memory and other intellectual functions. The profound loss of cholinergic perikarya recently observed in Alzheimer brains may indicate that too great a loss of cholinergic synthetic capacity has occurred in many Alzheimer patients to make augmentation of precursor useful. Other complex neuropharmacological alterations in Alzheimer neurons, for example, in choline uptake, may render this therapy ineffective. The loss of ChAT activity in Alzheimer cortex has also been putatively linked to decreases in the activity of the pyruvate dehydrogenase complex (Sorbi et al., 1982), which is the major source of the acetyl-CoA needed for acetylcholine synthesis.

Most investigators agree that there is no compelling evidence for a significant disease-related deficiency in the synthesis of dopamine, serotonin, or GABA in Alzheimer's disease (Terry and Davies, 1980), although some loss of receptors for these compounds has been reported (Reisene et al., 1978; Bowen et al., 1979). A selective decrease of neurons in the locus coeruleus, the principal source of noradrenergic projections to the cerebral cortex, has been observed in some Alzheimer patients (Mann et al., 1980; Bondareff et al., 1981). This alteration may be associated with more severe dementia and earlier death in these patients than in patients without significant locus coeruleus cell loss. An associated decrease in norepinephrine in several brain regions, notably the hypothalamus, was found in Alzheimer patients displaying attrition in the locus coeruleus (Mann et al., 1980).

Neuropeptides

Knowledge about the biochemistry and putative transmitter functions of the small peptide molecules found within neurons has rapidly expanded in the past few years (Hökfelt et al., 1980). However, evidence for specific changes in neuropeptide metabolism during aging and age-related diseases in human brain has not yet accumulated sufficiently to draw definitive conclusions. This is now an important area of investigation for those interested in the neurobiology of senescence. Recently, Davies et al. (1980) reported a roughly 70% decrease in somatostatin-like immunoreactivity (using a radioimmunoassay for synthetic somatostatin) in severely affected Alzheimer neocortex and hippocampus. The decline was quantitatively similar to the loss of ChAT activity in the same brain regions. These investigators and others (Buck et al., 1981) did not observe an alteration of somatostatin-like immunoreactivity with age in normal human brain. Perry et al. (1981) found a decline of somatostatin and cholecystokinin immunoreactivities, and an increase in substance P reactivity in Alzheimer cortex, but felt these changes occurred at later stages of the disease process. Perry and coworkers also noted an increase in vasoactive intestinal peptide immunoreactivity between ages 60 and 90 years in non-demented subjects. Buck et al. (1981) studied the levels of substance P and neurotensin as a function of age in normal human brain and observed a selective decrease in substance P in the putamen, but not in several other brain regions, including the frontal cortex. Neurotensin levels were found to decline with age only in the substantia nigra (Buck et al., 1981). The significance of these early findings of peptidergic neuronal abnormalities and their relationship to the loss of cholinergic neurons and their terminals in Alzheimer's disease remain to be determined.

Cerebral Metabolism

It is generally believed that total cerebral blood flow (CBF) and cerebral metabolic rate (i.e., total cerebral oxygen consumption) show little or no significant decline into the eighth decade of life if subjects are carefully selected to be free of vascular or neurological disease (Sokoloff, 1966). In senile dementia, however, reductions in both cerebral oxygen consumption and total CBF have been well documented (Lassen et al., 1960; Sokoloff, 1966; Hachinski et al., 1975; Blass, 1980). Interpretations of this decline vary, but the consensus seems to be that the changes are secondary: neuronal degeneration leads to a decrease in total neuronal metabolism and a secondary fall in oxygen utilization.

More recent studies using regional CBF techniques have demonstrated that there is a decrease in the volume of brain tissue having "fast flow" (an approximation of fast-clearing tissue, primarily gray matter) in patients with primary degenerative dementia (presumably Alzheimer's disease) or with multi-infarct dementia (Hachinski et al., 1975). This decrease in gray matter volume correlates with the pathologically documented loss of cerebral gray matter in both degenerative and vascular dementias. However, only the patients with multi-infarct dementia have significant decreases in actual total hemispheral flow, initial flow, and fast flow (Hachinski et al., 1975). These parameters did not change in patients with degenerative dementia. Among multi-infarct dementia patients, mean fast flow and cognitive test scores were inversely correlated whereas no such relationship was evident in the degenerative group. It can be concluded that the degree of dementia is related to the decrease in gray matter blood flow when cerebrovascular disease rather than neuronal degeneration is the apparent cause of the dementia. Since CBF is measured per 100 grams of brain tissue, a loss of cortical neurons in Alzheimer's disease would not of itself decrease flow as long as the metabolic demands of the remaining neurons were near normal.

In addition to total oxygen consumption, several other global measures of cerebral metabolism have been determined in freshly biopsied cortex of Alzheimer patients and have largely been found not to be altered. Cerebral rates of glycolysis, lactate production, acetate incorporation into lipids, and total amino acid incorporation into proteins do not appear to be significantly decreased in patients with Alzheimer's disease (Terry and Davies, 1980). However, these *in vitro* data are from older studies in which there were numerous methodological pitfalls. The advent of positron emission tomography has very recently allowed study of the regional cerebral metabolism of specific compounds during physiological aging and in degenerative diseases in living human subjects. This powerful new methodology, the early results of which are being reported at the time of this writing (for example, Foster et al., 1982), will no doubt provide major new insights into the metabolic events accompanying brain aging.

The activity of numerous enzymes of intermediary metabolism has been determined in autopsied cerebral cortex of Alzheimer patients and compared to normal aged tissue. Terry and Davies (1980) have recently summarized the results of such investigations (Table 3-2), many of which were conducted by Bowen et al. (1973, 1974, 1976a,b) and by Pope and Embree (1976). Interpretation of quantitative changes in these enzymatic activities and in various other structural and metabolic components of human brain tissue (e.g., total protein, cerebroside, ganglioside, acid phosphatase) is complex. Many of the changes appear to be secondary to loss of neurons. However, the enzymes and structural components assayed are not restricted to one cell type. Lack of precise knowledge of their relative distribution among various cells (glia, neurons, vascular cells) in an organ as heterogeneous as human brain appears to preclude specific conclusions regarding the mechanisms of brain aging based on quantitative compositional analyses.

Lipids

It is generally accepted that brain lipid content and metabolism decline with aging. The lipid constituents and the topography of this loss have not been fully elucidated. There is great variability in lipid composition and age-related changes in lipids; therefore, animal studies have limited ap-

Table 3-2. Enzymes related to energy metabolism in Alzheimer's disease brain.

Parameter in whole temporal lobe	Percentage of activity in age-matched normals
Hexokinase	"May be altered"
Phosphohexose isomerase	55–56
Phosphofructokinase	"May be altered"
Aldolase	55–56
Phosphotriose isomerase	73–74
Glyceraldehyde-3-phosphate dehydrogenase	77–81
Phosphoglycerokinase	100 ± 20
Phosphoglyceromutase	60–70
Enolase	100 ± 20
Pyruvate kinase	77–81
Lactate dehydrogenase	77–81
Alcohol dehydrogenase	73–74
Succinate dehydrogenase	60–80
6-Phosphogluconate dehydrogenase	100 ± 20
Total ATPase	77–81
Mg^{2+}-ATPase	73–74
Na^+, K^+-ATPase	100 ± 20
Total protein kinase	100 ± 20
cAMP-independent protein kinase	"May be altered"

Adapted from Terry, R.D. and Davies, P. (1980) Ann. Rev. Neurosci. 3, 77–95.

plicability even among closely related species. Myelin loss occurs with advanced age, and hence those lipids that are relatively concentrated in myelin contribute in greater proportion to the overall loss of lipid constituents with aging. Furthermore, since total brain weight progressively decreases, myelin is lost relatively faster than total brain mass during aging. Lipids with high concentrations in myelin, such as the sphingoglycolipids, galactocerebrosides, and sulfatides, have the highest rates of loss. Although the saturated fatty acids of most of the myelin fractions decrease slightly with age, the monoenoic acids remain constant or increase slightly (Svennerholm, 1978). This increase is most notable among the ethanolamine glycerophospholipids. Thus, the proportion of monoenoic acids increases into senescence and indicates continued metabolic activity of these lipid pools throughout life. Although lipid loss is not confined to myelin

constituents, most lipids found in gray matter, such as phosphatidyl ethanolamines and choline glycerophospholipids, show only small decreases in senescence. A small decrease with age in polyunsaturated acyl groups has been noted by Bowen et al. (1973) in human frontal gray matter. Mansson et al. (1978) report that fatty acid composition of gangliosides may also have an age-specific pattern similar to that noted in myelin. Berlet and Volk (1980) have substantiated a continued loss of myelin into senescence in frontal cortical white matter and corpus callosum. An age-related loss in 2', -3'-cyclic nucleotide 3'-phosphodiesterase activity, considered a marker of myelination, correlates with the loss of myelin. Furthermore, Wisniewski and Terry (1973) have observed a loss of myelin with sparing of axons in aged individuals. Peripheral myelin is also lost with age (Spritz et al., 1973); this is reflected in a slowing of nerve conduction velocities in both motor and sensory nerves (Dorfman and Bosley, 1979) of elderly subjects.

Studies that are more difficult, but that provide more dynamic information than the above compositional studies are those that are designed to measure age-related alterations in lipid synthesis and turnover. The nature of such studies precludes their being performed in humans. It is known that brain lacks an enzyme for the degradation of cholesterol, an important membrane constituent. Cholesterol is actively taken up by the brain during myelination and, unlike other organs in which turnover of cholesterol is continuous, the brain retains the cholesterol for life. This has been most clearly demonstrated in newly hatched chicks injected with radioactive cholesterol. The activity remains in brain cholesterol indefinitely, whereas in liver and plasma it disappears in three to eight weeks (Lehninger, 1982). These authors propose that a static pool of brain membrane cholesterol may be more susceptible to free radical reactions, which may secondarily interfere with membrane fluidity. In contrast to cholesterol, other brain lipids are metabolized at widely varying rates. For example, galactocerebrosides, have a very slow turnover once myelination is complete, whereas phosphoinositides turn over rapidly.

A finding that has intrigued investigators for almost 100 years is the age-related accumulation of an intraneuronal pigmented material called lipofuscin. The association of lipofuscin with aging was first suggested by Koneff in 1886. Histochemically, lipofuscin can be shown to contain an acidic lipid moiety, ethylenic groups, and 1,2-glycols (Glees and Hasan, 1976). A good recent review of the biochemistry of lipofuscin is that of Horrocks et al. (1981).

Lipofuscin is believed to derive either from lysosomes or mitochondria or both. Electron microscopists have noted transitional forms between normal mitochondria and lipofuscin in which fragments of mitochondrial cristae have been found. Some lipofuscin granules have been seen to be delimited by a double membrane. Although such mitochondrial enzymes as cytochrome oxidase, succinate dehydrogenase, and glucose-6-phosphate dehydrogenase have been detected in lipofuscin, the lipid composition of the two organelles differs. Lysosomal enzymes, including acid phosphatase, cathepsin B, β-galactosidase, β-hexosaminidase, and AMP-hydrolase, have also been found in lipofuscin. Other studies have focused on the postmitotic state of the neuron to explain the derivation of lipofuscin. This hypothesis suggests that autophagic vacuoles become lipofuscin in the nondividing neuron because the cell is incapable of exocytosis. Using both glial and neuroblastoma cell cultures, several investigators have concluded that the accumulation of lipofuscin is inversely related to the rate of cell division; the latter process lowers the cellular concentration of lipofuscin (Brunk et al., 1973; Nandy and Schneider, 1978; Collins and Brunk, 1978).

Chemically, lipofuscin consists of 50% lipid and 30% protein; however, the composition of the remaining 20% has not been completely characterized. The component lipids are cholesterol esters, triglycerides, cholesterol, cephalins, lecithins, and sphingomyelins. After acid hydrolysis, the remaining fraction is an insoluble resinous material. Siakotos and Armstrong (1975) and Siakotos et al. (1976) further characterized lipofuscin by isolating large quantities of the material. Using two-dimensional thin-layer chromatography, they found that lipofuscin contained a large amount of a non-polar lipid polymer. This polymer, which fluoresced under ultraviolet light, was a heterogeneous substance containing phospholipids and amino acids; no galactolipids could be detected (Taubold et al., 1975). Its unsaturated fatty acid moieties had presumably undergone oxidation, perhaps by free radical reaction and subsequent polymerization. This process can damage lipid membranes as well as inactivate proteins and nucleic acids.

More recently, certain long chain carbon compounds known as dolichols have received increasing interest from researchers concerned with brain aging. These compounds are part of a family of isoprenoid lipids that occur widely in living organisms and participate as carriers of oligosaccharides in biosynthetic processes involving cell membranes. On the basis of nuclear magnetic resonance spectra of lipofuscin, Goebel et al. (1979) postulated that this pigment contained dolichol complexes. Although dolichols are found in endoplasmic reticulum membrane, they are not found in mitochondrial or plasma membranes. Dolichols have been studied in human aging and disease because they are excreted in the urine and thus readily measurable. Recently, Pullarkat and Reha (1982) and Wolfe and Ng Ying Kin (1982) have shown that urinary dolichol excretion is linearly related to chronological age in both humans and rats. Dolichol excretion can also be used clinically, according to Wolfe and Ng Ying Kin, to diagnose neuronal ceroid lipofuscinosis. Studies to determine dolichol values in Alzheimer disease patients are ongoing.

Several lines of evidence indirectly support the notion that cells with the highest metabolic activities accumulate the most lipofuscin. Friede (1962) found that those human brain nuclei with the most lipofuscin also reacted most strongly for oxidative enzyme activity. Furthermore, in rodents, enucleation of one eye results in less oxidative enzyme activity and less lipofusin in the layers of lateral geniculate projecting from that eye (Friede, 1962). The functional consequences of the lipofuscin accumulation remain unknown. There does not appear to be a compromise in energy metabolism in regions with such accumulations (Ferrendelli et al., 1971), nor were improvements in learning found in rats with diminished brain lipofuscin following vitamin E treatments (Freud, 1979). However, treatment with centrophenoxine, another lipofuscinolytic agent, was associated with improved T-maze learning in 1-year-old mice (Nandy, 1978).

Metallic Ions

Interest in the role of metallic ion toxicity in age-related human brain degeneration has been sparked in large part by reports of a possible relationship between intraneuronal aluminum deposition and NFT formation in Alzheimer's disease. This observation arose from experimental studies of aluminum-induced encephalomyelopathy in rabbits and cats, which, although far from ideal, is perhaps the best available pathological and behavioral model of neurofibrillary degeneration. It has been known for several decades that aluminum paste can be injected intracortically to produce experimental epileptogenic foci. In 1965, Klatzo et al. serendipitously discovered that such lesions contained argyrophilic intraneuronal filamentous bundles that bore a striking light-microscopic resemblance to human NFT. A major ultrastructural difference was the fact that the aluminum-induced filaments were similar to normal straight neurofilaments and were not helically wound as are the Alzheimer paired helical filaments (Terry and Pena, 1965).

When aluminum salts are injected into the brain or subarachnoid space of rabbits, the animals are asymptomatic for 10 to 15 days and then develop a rapidly progressive encephalomyelopathy, marked by seizures and quadriparesis, leading to death from status epilepticus or inanition, in a few days. Crapper et al. (1973) studied the early course of the intoxication, when the animals were asymptomatic, and found that their performance on a task requiring retention of new information (an analogue of short-term memory) progressively declined and that the level of performance correlated inversely with cortical aluminum levels. Rabbit neurons undergoing such neurofibrillary degeneration induced by aluminum have recently been isolated and their filaments have been shown by biochemical and immunocytochemical techniques to be highly similar if not identical to normally occurring neurofilaments (Selkoe et al., 1979).

Moving from experimental to human pathology, Crapper and coworkers (1973) assayed aluminum in biopsied and autopsied cortex of four patients with verified Alzheimer's disease and found levels three to four times that of control cortex in some areas. The highest levels were noted in the mesial frontal and temporal cortex. A later study by the same Canadian group (Crapper et al., 1976) extended these observations to 12 demented patients, including two with Down's syndrome with neurofibrillary degeneration; again they found significantly elevated aluminum levels in an average of 28% of the cortical samples from each of the 12 brains. The distribution of cortical aluminum levels closely matched the topographic distribution of the NFT, although it did not seem to correlate with the presence of senile plaques.

A similar study conducted in Great Britain failed to show any difference in cortical aluminum levels between patients with senile dementia and age-matched controls (McDermott et al., 1977). However, the latter study did document an age-related elevation of brain aluminum in both demented and normal persons over 75 years old. Furthermore, areas particularly susceptible to neurofibrillary degeneration (frontal and temporal cortex and hippocampus) showed significantly higher aluminum content than did other cortical areas in these elderly subjects. Other studies in the United States (Markesberry et al., 1981) have also not duplicated the findings of selectively increased aluminum levels in Alzheimer cortex made by Crapper and coworkers in Canadian patients. The discrepancies between such studies raise the question of differences in environmental exposure to aluminum among Alzheimer patients residing in various geographical loci and also suggest the possibility that aluminum deposition, when it occurs, could be a secondary event following neuronal injury and tangle formation. An alternative explanation is that significant differences in the methods of assaying aluminum in postmortem brain samples, which is not a technically simple process, led to the variable results reported to date.

The putative association between aluminum and human neurofibrillary degeneration has been significantly strengthened by the recent experiments of Perl and Brody (1980), using an elegant combination of scanning electron microscopy and X-ray spectrometry. They determined the presence of intraneuronal aluminum in both tangle-bearing and non-tangle-bearing neurons in Alzheimer hippocampal sections and found that a very high percent (91%) of the former cells contained peaks for aluminum, compared to only 4% of the latter. Moreover, they observed that 89% of the occasional tangle-bearing hippocampal neurons of nondemented, age-matched subjects also contained foci of aluminum, compared to 6% of adjacent normal neurons (Perl and Brody, 1980). The aluminum was localized in focal deposits within the nuclei of the neurons rather than in the cytoplasmic tangles themselves. This nuclear localization, is in agreement with subcellular fractionation studies by Crapper et al. (1980), which showed that aluminum content per gram of DNA was significantly increased in nuclear and heterochromatin fractions in presenile Alzheimer's disease compared to age-matched controls. In the report by Perl and Brody (1980), tangle-bearing neurons were also more likely to display significant peaks for magnesium and silicon than were morphologically normal perikarya, but the differences for these elements were much less impressive than those for aluminum. In view of these intriguing findings, studies are under way to assess the extent of intraneuronal aluminum accumulation in patients residing in geographical loci with remarkably high prevalences of neurofibrillary degeneration and to determine whether the cation level of the environment could affect patterns of trace metal deposition in brain.

Recently, we have reported (Kosik et al., 1983) a further analogy between aluminum-induced lesions and Alzheimer's disease. Axons projecting from cell bodies containing numerous neurofibrillary tangles show a marked reduction in ChAT activity over the entire length of the axon. This biochemical deficit occurs in spite of the fact that the axon maintains its morphological integrity.

It is important to emphasize that an association between aluminum or other metals and age-related NFT formation, even if definitively documented, may well not be etiological. Indeed, the pathological significance of aluminum accumulation in neurons that may already be lesioned is not known. In demented patients with dialysis encephalopathy, many of whom have cortical aluminum levels as high as or higher than those measured in Alzheimer brains, no neurofibrillary pathology is observed. An abnormally high incidence of dementia or other neurological disorders has not been observed in aluminum workers. Aluminum is ubiquitous in the earth's crust and many natural foods contain this element, so that an unusually high exposure to this element in aged subjects or sporadic Alzheimer patients need not be hypothesized at present.

Several other metallic ions have been associated with the pathology of Alzheimer's disease. Even before the current interest in aluminum, Nikaido, Austin, and colleagues reported high levels of silicon in the rims and cores of senile plaques, although not in other organs or body fluids of Alzheimer patients (Nikaido et al., 1971; Austin et al., 1973). Elevated manganese levels in serum and brain were found in a demented patient whose cortical biopsy tissue contained numerous plaques and tangles (Banta and Markesbery, 1977). This element has also been associated with the occurrence of a Parkinsonian syndrome in manganese miners in South America (Mena et al., 1976). There has been a report of parenterally administered lead salts leading to a neurofibrillary degeneration in rats (Niklowitz, 1975), although the ultrastructural verification of these lesions as filamentous has not been firmly established. Careful epidemiological studies relating chronic metallic ion exposure to the development of sporadic dementing illness have yet to be done.

Conclusion

A review of the diverse and fragmentary data presently available about the biochemistry of normal human brain tissue during physiological aging provides no clear picture of the mechanisms or even the results of normal, age-related neuronal attrition and thus does not permit the formulation of unifying hypotheses about brain aging at the cellular and molecular level. Perhaps the simplest message derived from published studies is that, in the absence of a specific pathological condition, human brain aging proceeds with little or no significant disruption in a number of biochemical systems as we presently assay them. In contrast, completed and ongoing

neurochemical studies in senile dementia of the Alzheimer type indicate an accelerated, topographically selective loss of certain functional classes of neurons, with the death of cholinergic neurons and their terminals representing the most dramatic such change noted to date. Further research may well demonstrate that our current ideas about the pathogenesis and degree of selectivity of the neurotransmitter changes documented to date are naively simple. The precise molecular nature of the striking morphological changes that accompany normal and pathological brain aging, including paired helical filament formation, amyloid deposition, and lipofuscin accumulation, remain to be determined. In this regard, emerging information suggests a hypothesis of progressive and irreversible accumulation of rigid insoluble polymers during aging of human brain cells. Since the pathological distinction between normal aged brain tissue and Alzheimer tissue is quantitative rather than qualitative, knowledge about the molecular changes preceding death of neurons in Alzheimer's disease may ultimately shed light on the mechanisms of neuronal aging in general.

References

Andrews, A.D., Barrett, S.F., and Robbins, J.H. (1978). Xeroderma pigmentosum neurological abnormalities correlate with colony-forming ability after ultraviolet radiation. Proc. Natl. Acad. Sci. USA 75, 1984–1985.

Aquilonius, S.- M. and Eckernäs, S.Å. (1976). Choline acetyltransferase in human cerebrospinal fluid: Non-enzymatically and enzymatically catalysed acetylcholine synthesis. J. Neurochem. 27, 317–318.

Austin, J.H., Rinehard, R., Williamson, T., Burcar, P., Russ, K., Nikaido, T., and Lafrance, M. (1973). Studies in aging of the brain. III. Silicon levels in postmortem tissues and body fluids. Progr. Brain Res. 40, 485–495.

Banta, R.G. and Markesbery, W.R. (1977). Elevated manganese levels, associated with dementia and extrapyramidal signs. Neurology 27, 213–216.

Barbeau, A. (1973). Aging and the extrapyramidal system. J. Amer. Geriatr. Soc. 21, 145–149.

Berlet, H.H. and Volk, B. (1980). Age-related microheterogeneity of myelin basic protein isolated from human brain. In Aging of the Brain and Dementia, L. Amaducci, A.N. Davison, and P. Antuono, Eds. Raven Press, New York, pp. 81–90.

Bird, E.D. and Iversen, L.L. (1974). Huntington's chorea: Postmortem measurement of glutamic acid decarboxylase, choline acetyltransferase and dopamine in basal ganglia. Brain 94, 457–472.

Blass, J.P. (1980). Metabolic dementias. In Aging of the Brain and Dementia, L. Amaducci, A.N. Davison, and P. Antuono, Eds. Raven Press, New York, pp. 261–270.

Bondareff, W., Mountjoy, C.Q., and Roth, M. (1981). Selective loss of neurones of origin of adrenergic projection to cerebral cortex (nucleus locus coeruleus) in senile dementia. Lancet i, 783–784.

Bowen, D.M., Smith, C.B., and Davison, A.N. (1973). Molecular changes in senile dementia. Brain 96, 849–856.

Bowen, D.M., Flack, R.H.A., White, P., Smith, C.B., and Davison, A.N. (1974). Brain-decarboxylase activities as indices of pathological change in senile dementia. Lancet i, 1247–1248.

Bowen, D.M., Smith, C.B., White, P., and Davison, A.N. (1976a). Neurotransmitter-related enzymes and indices of hypoxia in senile dementia and other abiotrophies. Brain 99, 459–495.

Bowen, D.M., Smith, C.B., White, P., and Davison, A.N. (1976b). Senile dementia and related abiotrophies: Biochemical studies on histologically evaluated human postmortem specimens. In Neurobiology of Aging, Vol. 3. Aging. R.D. Terry and S. Gershon, Eds. Raven Press, New York, pp. 361–378.

Bowen, D.M., Smith, C.B., White, P., Goodhardt, M.J., Spillane, J.A., Flack, R.H.A., Davison, A.N. (1977). Chemical pathology of organic dementias. I. Validity of biochemical measurements on human postmortem brain specimens. Brain 100, 397–426.

Bowen, D.M., Spillane, J.A., Curzon, G., Meier-Ruge, W., White, P., Goodhardt, M.J., Iwangoff, P., and Davison, A.N. (1979). Accelerated ageing or selective neuronal loss as an important cause of dementia? Lancet i, 11–14.

Britton, G.W. and Sherman, F.G. (1975). Altered regulation of protein synthesis during aging is determined by *in vitro* ribosomal assays. Exp. Gerontol. 10, 67.

Brody, H. (1955). Organization of the cerebral cortex. III. A study of aging in cerebral cortex. J. Comp. Neurol. 102, 511–556.

Brody, H. (1976). An examination of cerebral cortex and brainstem aging in Neurobiology of Aging Vol. 3, Aging, R.D. Terry and S. Gershon, Eds. Raven Press, New York, pp. 177–181.

Brunk, U., Ericsson, J.L.E., Ponten, J., and Westermark, B. (1973). Residual bodies and "aging" in cultured human glial cells. Effects of entrance into phase III and prolonged periods of confluence. Exp. Cell Res. 79, 1–14.

Buck, S.H., Deshmukh, P.P., Burks, T.F., and Yamamura, H.I. (1981). A survey of substance P, somatostatin and neurotensin levels in aging in the rat and human central nervous system. Neurobiol. Aging 2, 257–264.

Carlin, R.K., Grab, D.J., and Siekevitz, P. (1982). Postmortem accumulation of tubulin in postsynaptic density preparations. J. Neurochem. 38, 94–100.

Chainy, G.B. and Kanungo, M.S. (1978). Induction and properties of pyruvate kinase of the cerebral hemisphere of rats of various ages. J. Neurochem. 30, 419–247.

Chatterjee, B., Surend Nath, T., and Roy, A.K. (1981). Differential regulation of the messenger RNA for three major senescence marker proteins in male rat liver. J. Biol. Chem. 256, 5939–5941.

Chetsanga, C., Tuttle, M., Jacoboni, A., and Johnson, C. (1977). Age-associated structural alterations in senescent mouse brain DNA. Biochim. Biophys. Acta 474, 180–187.

Collins, V.P. and Brunk, U. (1978). Quantitation of residual bodies in cultured human glial cells during stationary and logarithmic growth phases. Mech. Ageing Develop. 8, 139–152.

Cote, L.J. and Kremzner, L.T. (1974). Changes in neurotransmitter systems with increasing age in human brain. Trans. Am. Soc. Neurochem. 5, 83.

Crapper, D.R., Krishnan, S.S., and Dalton, A.J. (1973). Brain aluminum distribution in Alzheimer's disease and experimental neurofibrillary degeneration. Science 180, 511–513.

Crapper, D.R., Krishnan, S.S., and Quittkat, S. (1976). Aluminum, neurofibrillary degeneration and Alzheimer's disease. Brain 99, 67–80.

Crapper, D.R., et al. (1980). Intranuclear aluminum content in Alzheimer's disease, dialysis encephalopathy and experimental aluminum encephalopathy. Acta Neuropathol. (Berl.) 50, 19–24.

Critchley, M. (1931). The neurology of old age. Lancet i, 1119.

Davidson, T.J. and Hartmann, H.A. (1981). RNA content and volume of motor neurons in amyotrophic lateral sclerosis. II. The lumbar intumescence and nucleus dorsalis. J. Neuropathol. Exp. Neurol. 40, 187–192.

Davies, P., Katzman, R., and Terry, R.D. (1980). Reduced somatostatin-like immunoreactivity in cerebral cortex from cases of Alzheimer disease and Alzheimer senile dementia. Nature 288, 279–280.

Davies, P. and Maloney, A.J.F. (1976). Selective loss of central cholinergic neurons in Alzheimer's disease. Lancet ii, 1403.

Davies, P. and Verth, A.H. (1977). Regional distribution of muscarinic acetylcholine receptor in normal and Alzheimer's type dementia brains. Brain Res. 138, 385–392.

Divac, I. (1975). Magnocellular nuclei of the basal forebrain project to neocortex, brainstem and olfactory bulb. Review of some functional correlates. Brain Res. 93, 385–398.

Dorfman, L.J. and Bosley, T.M. (1979). Age-related changes in peripheral and central nerve conduction in man. Neurology 29, 38–44.

Droz, B. and Leblond, C.P. (1963). Axonal migration of proteins in the central nervous system and peripheral nerves as shown by radioautography. J. Comp. Neurol. 121, 325–337.

Dwyer, B.E., Fardo, J.L., and Wasterlain, C.G. (1980). Rat brain protein synthesis declines during postdevelopmental aging. J. Neurochem. 35, 746–749.

Dwyer, B.E. and Wasterlain, C.G. (1978). Brain protein synthesis declines with age. Age 1, 163 (Abstr.).

Ekstrom, R., Liu, D.S.H., and Richardson, A. (1980). Changes in brain protein synthesis during the life span of male Fischer rats. Gerontology 26, 121.

Emson, P.C., Rehfeld, J.F., Langevin, H., and Rossor, M. (1980). Reduction in cholecystokinin-like immunoreactivity in the basal ganglia in Huntington's disease. Brain Res. 198, 497–500.

Ermini, M., Moret, M., Reichmeier, K., and Dunne, T. (1978). Age-dependent structural changes in human neuronal chromatin. Aktuel Gerontol. 8, 675–

Ferrendelli, J.A., Sedgwick, W.G., and Suntzeff, V. (1971). Regional energy metabolism and lipofuscin accumulation in mouse brain during ageing. J. Neuropathol. Exp. Neurol. 30, 638–649.

Fink, S.J. and Reis, D.J. (1981). Genetic variations in midbrain dopamine cell number: Parallel with differences in response to dopaminergic agonists and in naturalistic behaviors mediated by central dopaminergic systems. Brain Res. 222, 335–349.

Foster, N.L., Patrones, N.J., De La Paz, R., Di Chiro, G., Brooks, R., Chase, T.N., Fedio, P., Denaro, A., and Durso, R. (1982). PET studies of Alzheimer disease. Neurology 32, A167 (Abstr.).

Frazer, J.M. and Yang, W.K. (1972). Isoaccepting transfer ribonucleic acids in liver and brain of young and old BC3F$_1$ mice. Arch. Biochem. Biophys. 153, 610.

Freud, G. (1979). The effect of chronic alcohol and vitamin E consumption on aging pigments and learning performance in mice. Life Sciences 24, 145–152.

Friede, R.L. (1962). The relation of the formation of lipofuscin to the distribution of oxidative enzymes in the human brain. Acta Neuropathol. 2, 113–125.

Geinisman, Y., Bondareff, W., and Telser, A. (1977). Diminished axonal transport of glycoproteins in the senescent rat brain. Mech. Age Dev. 6, 363–378.

Gershon, D. (1979). Current status of age-altered enzymes: Alternative mechanisms. Mech. Age Dev. 9, 189–196.

Gershon, D., Reznick, D., and Reiss, V. (1979). Characterization and possible effects of age-associated alterations in enzymes and proteins. In Physiology and Cell Biology of Aging, A. Cherkin, C.E. Finch, N. Karasch, T. Makinodon, F.L. Scott, and B.S. Strehler, Eds. Raven Press, New York, pp. 21–26.

Glees, P. and Hasan, M. (1976). Lipofuscin in neuronal aging and diseases. Normale Path. Anat. 32, 1–68.

Goebel, H.H., Zeman, W., Patel, V.K., Pullarkat, R.K., and Leonard, H.G. (1979). On the ultrastructural diversity and essence of residual bodies in neuronal ceroid-lipofuscinosis. Mech. Ageing Dev. 10, 53–70.

Goldman, G. and Coleman, P.D. (1980). The Fischer 344 rat as a model of aging human brain: Neuron counts in locus coeruleus. Neurobiol. Aging 2, 33–36.

Gottfries, C.G., Orland, L., Wiberg, A., and Winblad, B. (1975). Lowered monoamine oxidase activity in brains from alcoholic suicides. J. Neurochem. 25, 667–673.

Graybiel, A.M. and Ragsdale, C.W. (1978). Histochemically distinct compartments in the striatum of human, monkey and cat demonstrated by acetylcholinesterase staining. Proc. Natl. Acad. Sci. USA 75, 5723–5726.

Grote, S.S., Moses, S.G., Robins, E., Hudgens, R.W., and Croninger, A.B. (1974). A study of selected catecholamine metabolizing enzymes: A comparison of depressive suicides and alcoholic suicides with controls. J. Neurochem. 25, 667–673.

Hachinski, V.C., Iliff, L.D., Zilhka, E., et al. (1975). Cerebral blood flow in dementia. Arch. Neurol. 32, 632–637.

Hardy, J.A., Dodd, P.R., Oakley, A.E., Perry, R.H., Edwardson, J.A., and Kidd, A.M. (1983). Metabolically active symptosomes can be prepared from fragmented human brain. J. Neurochem. 40, 608–614.

Harris, H. and Hopkins, D.A. (1972). Average heterozygosity per locus in man: an estimate based on the incidence of enzyme polymorphism. Ann. Hum. Genet. 36: 9–20.

Hassler, R. (1965). Extrapyramidal control of the speed of behavior and its change by primary age processes. In Behavior, Aging and the Nervous System, A.T. Welford and J.T. Birrin, Eds. Charles C. Thomas, Springfield, Ill. pp. 284–306.

Hayflick, L. (1977). The cellular basis for biological aging. In Handbook of the Biology of Aging, C.E. Finch and L. Hayflick, Eds. Van Nostrand Reinhold, San Francisco, pp. 159–186.

Henshaw, E.C., Hirsch, C.A., Morton, B.E., and Hiatt, H.H. (1971). Control of protein synthesis in mammalian tissues through changes in ribosome activity. J. Biol. Chem. 246, 436.

Hilt, D.C., Uhl, G.R., Hedreen, J.C., Whitehouse, P.J., and Price, D.L. (1982). Pick disease: Loss of neurons in the nucleus basalis. Neurology 32, A229 (Abstr.).

Hökfelt, T., Johansson, O., Ljungdahl, A., Lundberg, J.M., and Schultzberg, M. (1980). Peptidergic neurones. Nature 284, 515–521.

Horrocks, M., Van Rollins, M., and Yates, A.J. (1981). Lipid changes in the aging brain. In The Molecular Basis of Neuropathology, A.N. Davison and R.H.S. Thompson, Eds. Edward Arnold Ltd., London, pp. 601–630.

Hydén, H. (1960). The neuron. In The Cell, Vol. 1. J. Brachet and A.E. Mirsky, Eds. Academic Press, New York, pp. 215–324.

Hydén, H. (1970). Biochemical and molecular aspects of learning and memory. In Biological and Clinical Aspects of the Central Nervous System. Sandoz Symposium, Basel, pp. 17–58.

Jablecki, C. and Brimijoin, S. (1975). Axoplasmic transport of choline acetyltransferase activity in mice: Effect of age and neurotomy. J. Neurochem. 25, 583–593.

Kanungo, M.S. and Thakur, M.K. (1977). Phosphorylation of chromosomal proteins as a function of age and its modulation by calcium. Biochem. Biophys. Res. Comm. 79, 1031–1036.

Kemper, T.L. (1978). Senile dementia: A focal disease in the temporal lobe. In Senile Dementia: A Biochemical Approach, K. Nandy, Ed. Elsevier North Holland Biomedical Press, New York.

Klatzo, I., Wisniewski, H., and Streicher, E. (1965). Experimental production of neurofibrillary degeneration. I. Light microscopic observations. J. Neuropath. Exp. Neurol. 24, 187–199.

Kosik, K.S., Bradley, W.G., Good, P.F., Rasool, C.G., Selkoe, D.J. (1983). Cholinergic function in lumbar aluminum myelopathy. J. Neuropath. Exp. Neurol. 42, 365–375.

Kosik, K.S., Gilbert, J.M., Selkoe, D.J., and Strocchi, P. (1982). Characterization of postmortem human brain proteins by two-dimensional gel electrophoresis. J. Neurochem. 39, 1529–1538.

Langlais, P.J., McEntee, W.J., and Bird, E.D. (1980). A rapid, liquid chromatographic measurement of 3-methoxy phenylglycol and other monoamine metabolites in human cerebrospinal fluid. Clin. Chem. 26, 786–788.

Lasek, R.J. (1970). Axonal transport of proteins in dorsal root ganglion cells of growing cat: A comparison of growing and mature neurons. Brain Res. 20, 121–126.

Lassen, N.A., Feinberg, I., and Lane, M.H. (1960). Bilateral studies of cerebral oxygen uptake in young and aged normal subjects and in patients with organic dementia. J. Clin. Invest. 39, 491–500.

Lehninger, A.L. (Ed.) (1975). *Biochemistry, Molecular Bases of All Structures and Functions*, 2nd ed., Worth, New York.

Linn, S., Karis, M., and Holliday, R. (1976). Decreased fidelity of DNA polymerase activity isolated from aging human fibroblasts. Proc. Natl. Acad. Sci. USA 73, 2818–2822.

Low, P.A., Thomas, J.E., and Dyck, P.J. (1978). The splanchnic autonomic outflow in Shy-Drager and idiopathic orthostatic hypotension. Ann. Neurol. 4, 511–514.

Maker, H.S., Weiss, C., Weissbarth, S., and

Silides, D.J. (1981). The perimortem variation of glutamate decarboxylase and creatine kinase in human brain. (Abstr.) 8th Meeting International Society for Neurochemistry, Nottingham, U.K., p. 340.

Mann, D.M.A., Lincoln, J., Yates, P.O., Stamp, J.E., and Toper, S. (1980). Changes in the monoamine containing neurons of the human CNS in senile dementia. Br. J. Psych. 136, 533–541.

Mansson, J.E., Vanier, M.T., and Svennerholm, L. (1978). Changes in the fatty acid and sphingosine composition of the major gangliosides of the human brain with age. J. Neurochem. 30, 273–275.

Mariotti, D. and Ruscitto, R. (1977). Age-related changes of accuracy and efficiency of protein synthesis machinery in rat. Biochim. Biophys. Acta 475, 96–102.

Markesbery, W.R., Ehmann, W.D., Hossain, T.I.M., Alauddin, M., and Goodin, M.S. (1981). Instrumental neutron activation analysis of brain aluminum in Alzheimer disease and aging. Ann. Neurol. 10, 511–516.

Martin, G. (1978). Genetic syndromes in man with potential relevance to the pathobiology of aging. In Genetic Effects on Aging, D. Bergsma and D. Harrison, Eds. Alan R. Liss, Inc., New York, pp. 5–39.

Marshak, D.R., Watterson, D.M., and Van Eldik, L.J. (1981). Calcium-dependent interaction of S100b, troponin C, and calmodulin with immobilized phenothiazine. Proc. Natl. Acad. Sci. USA 78, 6793–6797.

Mays, L.L., Lawrence, A.E., Ho, R.W., and Ackley, S. (1979). Age-related changes in function of transfer ribonucleic acid in rat livers. Fed. Proc. 38, 1984.

McDermott, J.R., Smith, A.I., Iqbal, K., et al. (1977). Aluminum and Alzheimer's disease. Lancet ii, 710.

McGeer, E.G. (1978). Aging and neurotransmitter metabolism in human brain. In Alzheimer's Disease: Senile Dementia and Related Disorders, R. Katzman, R.D. Terry, and K.L. Bick, Eds. Raven Press, New York, pp. 427–440.

McGeer, P.L. and McGeer, E.G. (1976a). Enzymes associated with the metabolism of catecholamines, acetylcholine and GABA in human controls and patients with Parkinson's disease and Huntington's chorea. J. Neurochem. 26, 65–70.

McGeer, E.G. and McGeer, P.L. (1976b). Neurotransmitter metabolism in the aging brain. In Aging, Vol. 3, R.D. Terry and S. Gershon, Eds., Raven Press, New York, pp. 389–403.

McGeer, P.L., McGeer, E.G., and Suzuki, J.S. (1977). Aging and extrapyramidal function. Arch. Neurol. 34, 33–35.

Mena, I., Marin, O., Fuenzalida, S., and Cotzins, G.C. (1967). Chronic manganese poisoning: Clinical picture and manganese turnover. Neurology 17, 128–136.

Mesulam, M.M. and Van Hoesen, G.W. (1976). Acetylcholinesterase-rich projections from the basal forebrain of the rhesus monkey to neocortex. Brain Res. 109, 152–157.

Nakanishi, K., Shima, A., Fukada, M., and Fujita, S. (1979). Age-associated increase of single-stranded regions in the DNA of mouse brain and liver cells. Mech. Ageing Dev. 10, 273–281.

Nakano, I. and Hirano, A. (1982). Loss of large neurons of the medial septal nucleus in an autopsy case of Alzheimer's disease. J. Neuropath. Exp. Neurol. 41, 341 (Abstr.).

Nandy, K. (1978). Centrophenoxine: Effects on ageing mammalian brain. J. Amer. Ger. Soc. 16, 74–81.

Nandy, K. and Schneider, H. (1976). Lipofuscin pigment formation in neuroblastoma cells in culture. In Neurobiology of Aging, R.D. Terry and G. Gershon, Eds. Raven Press, New York, pp. 245–264.

Nicol, S.E., Senogles, S.E., Caruso, T.P., Hudziak, J.J., McSwigan, J.D., and Frey, W.H. (1981). Postmortem stability of dopamine-sensitive adenylate cyclase, guanylate cyclase, ATPase and GTPase in rat striatum. J. Neurochem. 37, 1535–1539.

Nikaido, T., Austin, J., Rinehart, R., et al. (1971). Studies in aging of the brain. I. Isolation and preliminary characterization of Alzheimer's plaques and cores. Arch. Neurol. 25, 198–211.

Niklowitz, W.J. (1975). Neurofibrillary changes after acute experimental lead poisoning. Neurology 25, 927–934.

Orgel, L.E. (1973). Aging clones of mammalian cells. Nature 243, 441–445.

Perl, D.P. and Brody, A.R. (1980). Alzheimer's disease: X-ray spectrometric evidence of aluminum accumulation in neurofibrillary tangle-bearing neurons. Science 208, 297–301.

Perry, E.K., Blessed, G., Tomlinson, B.E., Perry, R.H., Crow, T.J., Cross, A.M., Dockney, G.J., Dimaline, R., and Arregui, A. (1981). Neurochemical activities in human temporal lobe related to aging and Alzheimer-type changes. Neurobiol. Aging 2, 251–256.

Perry, E.K., Perry, R.H., Blessed, G., et al. (1977). Necropsy evidence of central nervous system cholinergic deficits in senile dementia. Lancet i, 189–190.

Petes, T.D., Farber, R.A., Tarrant, G.M., and Holliday, R. (1974). Altered rate of DNA replication in aging human fibroblast cultures. Nature 251, 434–436.

Pope, A. and Embree, L.J. (1976). Neurochemistry of dementia. In Handbook of Clinical Neurology, P.J. Vinken and G.W. Bruyn, eds. Vol. 27, Metabolic and Deficiency Diseases of the Nervous System, Pt. I. Harold L. Klawans, Ed. North Holland, Amsterdam. Chap. 21, pp. 477–501.

Pope, A., Hess, H.H., and Lewin, E. (1964). Studies on the microchemical pathology of human cerebral cortex. In Morphological and Biological Correlates of Neural Activity, M.M. Cohen and R.S. Snider, Eds. Harper/Hoeber, New York, pp. 98–111.

Price, G.B., Modak, S.P., and Makinodan, T. (1971). Age-associated changes in the DNA of mouse tissues. Science 171, 917–920.

Pullarkat, R.K. and Reha, H. (1982). Accumulation of dolichol in brains of elderly. 13th Annual Meeting, American Society of Neurochemistry, p. 165.

Reisine, T.D., Yamamura, H.I., Bird, E.D., Spokes, E., and Enna, S.J. (1978). Pre- and postsynaptic neurochemical alterations in Alzheimer's disease. Brain Res. 159, 477–481.

Reiss, U. and Gershon, D. (1976). Comparison of cytoplasmic superoxide dismutase in liver, heart and brain of aging rats and mice. Biochem. Biophys. Res. Comm. 73, 255–262.

Ringborg, U. (1966). Composition and content of RNA in neurons of rat hippocampus at different ages. Brain Res. 2, 296–298.

Robbins, J.H. (1978). ICN-UCLA Symposia on Molecular and Cellular Biology, Vol. IX, DNA Repair Mechanisms, P.C. Hanawalt, E.C. Friedberg, and C.F. Fox, Eds. Academic Press, New York.

Robinson, D.S., Nies, A., Davies, H.N., Bunney, W.E., Davis, J.M., Colburn, R.W., Bourne, H.R., Shaw, D.M., and Coppen, A.J. (1972). Aging, monoamines and monoamine oxidase levels. Lancet i, 290–291.

Robinson, D.S., Sourkes, T.L., Nies, A., Harris, L.S., Spector, S., Bartlett, D.L., and Kaye, I.S. (1977). Monoamine metabolism in human brain. Arch. Gen. Psychiat. 34, 89–92.

Rosenberg, R.N., Ivy, N., Kirkpatrick, J., Bay, C., Nyhan, W., and Baskin, F. (1981). Joseph disease and Huntington disease: Protein patterns in fibroblasts and brain. Neurology (N.Y.) 31, 1003–1014.

Rothstein, M. (1977). Recent developments in the age-related alteration of enzymes: A review. Mech. Aging Dev. 6, 241–257.

Samorajski, T. and Rolsten, C. (1973). Age and regional differences in the chemical composition of brains of mice, monkeys and humans. Progr. Brain Res. 3, 253–265.

Scheibel, M.E. and Scheibel, A.B. (1975). Structural changes in aging brain. In Clinical, Morphologic and Neurochemical Aspects in the Aging Central Nervous System, H. Brody, D. Harman, and J.M. Ordy, Eds. Raven Press, New York.

Schneider, E.L. and Mitsui, Y. (1976). The relationship between *in vitro* cellular aging and *in vivo* human age. Proc. Natl. Acad. Sci. USA 73, 3584–3588.

Selkoe, D.J., Ihara, Y., and Salazar, F.J. (1982). Alzheimer's disease: Insolubility of partially purified paired helical filaments in sodium dodecyl sulfate and urea. Science 215, 1243–1245.

Selkoe, D.J., Liem, R.K.L., Yen, S.H., and Shelanski, M.L. (1979). Biochemical and immunological studies of neurofilaments in aluminum-induced neurofibrillary proliferation. Brain Res. 163, 235–252.

Selkoe, D.J., Salazar, F.J., Abraham, C., and Kosik, K.S. (1982). Huntington's disease: Changes in striatal proteins reflect astrocytic gliosis. Brain Res. 245, 117–125.

Siakotos, A.N. and Armstrong, O. (1975). Age pigment, a biochemical indicator of intracellular ageing. In Neurobiology of Aging, J.M. Ordy and K.R. Brizzee, Eds. Plenum Press, New York, pp. 369–399.

Siakotos, A.N., Armstrong, D., Koppang, N., and Muller, J. (1976). Biochemical significance of age pigment in neurones. In The Ageing Brain and Senile Dementia, K. Nandy and I. Sherwin, Eds. Plenum Press, New York, pp. 99–118.

Sladek, Jr., J.R. and Blanchard, B.C. (1981). Age-related declines in perikaryal monoamine histofluorescence in the Fischer 344 rat. In Brain Neurotransmitters and Receptors in Aging and Age-Related Disorders, S.J. Enna, T. Samorajski, and B. Beer, Eds. Raven Press, New York, pp. 13–21.

Sokoloff, L. (1966). Cerebral circulatory and metabolic changes associated with aging. Res. Publ. Assoc. Res. Nerv. Ment. Dis. 41, 237–253.

Sorbi, S., Amaducci, L., Blass, J.P., and Bird, E.D. (1982). Pyruvate dehydrogenase complex and choline acetyltransferase in aging and dementia. In The Aging Brain, Giacobini et al., Eds. Raven Press, New York, pp. 223–229.

Spillane, J.A., White, P., Goodhardt, M.J., Flack, R.H.A., Bowen, D.M., and Davison, A.N. (1977). Selective vulnerability of neurones in organic dementia. Nature (Lond.) 266, 558–559.

Spritz, N., Singh, H., and Geyer, B. (1973). Myelin from human peripheral nerves: Quantitative and qualitative studies in two age groups. J. Clin. Invest. 52, 520–523.

Struble, R.G., Cork, L.G., Whitehouse, P.J., and Price, D.L. (1982). Cholinergic innervation in neuritic plaques. Science 216, 413–415.

Svennerholm, L., Jungbjer, B., and Vanier, M.T. (1978). Changes in fatty acid composition of human brain myelin lipids during maturation. J. Neurochem. 30, 1383–1390.

Taubold, R.D., Siakotos, A.N., and Perkins, E.G. (1975). Studies on chemical nature of lipofuscin (age pigment) isolated from normal human brain. Lipids 19, 383–390.

Terry, R.D. and Davies, P. (1980). Dementia of the Alzheimer type. Ann. Rev. Neurosci. 3, 77–95.

Terry, R.D. and Pena, C. (1965). Experimental production of neurofibrillary degeneration. II. Electron microscopy, phosphate histochemistry and electron probe analysis. J. Neuropath. Exp. Neurol. 24, 200–210.

Thakur, M.K., Das, R., and Kanungo, M.S. (1978). Modulation of acetylation of chromosomal proteins of the brains of rats of various ages by epinephrine and estradiol. Biochem. Biophys. Res. Comm. 81, 828–831.

Truscott, R.J.W. and Augusteyn, R.C. (1977). Oxidative changes in human lens protein during senile nuclear cataract formation. Biochim. Biophys. Acta 492, 43–53.

Uemura, F. and Hartmann, H.A. (1978). Age-related changes in RNA content and volume of the human hypoglossal neuron. Brain Res. Bull. 3, 207–211.

Vijayashankar, N. and Brody, H. (1979). A quantitative study of the pigmented neurons in the nuclei locus coeruleus and subcoeruleus in man as related to aging. J. Comp. Neurol. 38, 490–497.

von Hahn, H.P. (1981). Nucleic acids in the ageing brain and the concept of ageing. In The Molecular Basis of Neuropathology, A.N. Davison and R.H.S. Thompson, Eds. Edward Arnold Ltd., London, pp. 579–590.

Walton, K.E., Styer, D., and Gruenstein, E.I. (1979). Genetic polymorphism in normal human fibroblasts as analyzed by two-dimensional polyacrylamide gel electrophoresis. J. Biol. Chem. 254, 7951–7960.

Waterlow, J.C. (1975). Protein turnover in the whole body. Nature (Lond.) 253, 157.

Whitehouse, P.J., Hedreen, J.C., White, C., DeLong, M., and Price, D.L. (1982a). Loss of neurons in nucleus basalis in the dementia of Parkinson disease. Neurology 32, A228 (Abstr.).

Whitehouse, P.J., Price, D.L., Clark, A.W., Coyle, J.T., and De Long, M.R. (1981). Alzheimer disease: Evidence for selective loss of cholinergic neurons in the nucleus basalis. Ann. Neurol. 10, 122–126.

Whitehouse, P.J., Price, D.L., Struble, R.G., Clark, A.W., Coyle, J.T., and De Long, M.R. (1982b). Alzheimer's disease and senile dementia: Loss of neurons in the basal forebrain. Science 215, 1237–1239.

Williams, J.R. and Dearfield, K.L. (1981). DNA damage and repair in aging mammals. In Handbook of Biochemistry in Aging, J.R. Florini, Ed. CRC Press, Inc., Boca Raton, Fla., pp. 25–48.

Wilson, P.D. (1981). Enzyme levels in animals of various ages. In Handbook of Biochemistry and Aging, J.R. Florinic, Ed. CRC Press, Inc., Boca Raton, Fla., pp. 163–194.

Wisniewski, H.M. and Terry, R.D. (1973). Morphology of the aging brain, human and animal. Progr. Brain Res. 40, 167–186.

Wolfe, L.S. and Ng Ying Kin, M.K. (1982). Dolichols in neuronal ceroid lipofuscinosis and in aging brain (Abstr.). 13th Annual Meeting, American Society of Neurochemistry.

Wright, W.E. and Hayflick, L. (1975). Nuclear control of cellular aging demonstrated by hybridization of anucleate and whole cultured normal human fibroblasts. Exp. Cell Res. 96, 113–121, 1975.

Wust, C.J. and Rosen, L. (1972). Aminoacylation and methylation of *t*RNA as a function of age in the rat. Exp. Gerontol. 7, 331–343.

4. Neuroimmunology of Aging

KARI STEFANSSON   JACK ANTEL
BARRY G. W. ARNASON

The nervous system and the immune system interact with each other in many ways, any of which may be affected by the aging process. In this survey, the following selected aspects of these interactions are emphasized:

1. Antigens shared by nervous and lymphoid tissue may permit both to become targets of a single autoimmune attack, particularly as immune surveillance decreases with age
2. Age-related changes in immune function may lead to the synthesis of abnormal immune products that contribute to neurological disease or may increase susceptibility to infection
3. A possible relationship between age-dependent changes in the nervous system and the alterations in immune regulation that accompany aging may implicate a role of the nervous system in immune regulation

Antigens Shared between Brain and Lymphoid Cells

Evidence for the existence of antigens shared by human brain and lymphoid cells has come from such studies as those of Brouet and Toben (1976), who demon-

strated that one could, by immunizing animals with human brain homogenates, raise polyclonal antisera that reacted with brain and lymphoid elements, but with no other tissues. Absorption with brain removed both brain and lymphocyte reactive antibodies, as did absorption with lymphocytes. Polyclonal antisera usually contain antibodies against many antigenic determinants. For this reason, it is possible to argue that even though antigenic determinants in brain and on lymphocytes are detected, the antigenic determinants need not be identical in both tissues, particularly since absorption experiments pose technical problems. Recently, the existence of a surprisingly large number of antigens common to brain and lymphoid cells has been proven unequivocally by the use of monoclonal antibodies, a finding, in our view, of considerable importance. Monoclonal antibodies are obtained by fusing splenic lymphocytes from immunized animals with mouse myeloma cells to form hybrids. The hybridoma technique permits one to isolate a single cell that produces antibody reactive with a single antigenic determinant; to grow this cell and its progeny (a clone), and, in this way, to obtain a virtually unlimited supply of antibody possessing a unique specificity.

Perhaps the most thoroughly characterized antigen shared by brain and lymphoid

Supported by U.S. Public Health Service Grant #AGO 1798 from the National Institute of Health.

cells is the Thy-1 antigen, first described in the mouse by Reif and Allen (1964). This antigen has now been studied immunohistochemically with both polyclonal and monoclonal antibodies. Thy-1 homologues have been found in several species, including man, dog, and rat. Striking species differences in the distribution of this antigen exist (Acton et al., 1974; Dalchau and Fabre, 1979; McKenzie and Fabre, 1981). An outline of Thy-1 distribution is given in Table 4-1. In lymphoid tissue Thy-1 is abundant at birth; in brain it is low at birth and increases as the central nervous system matures. Certain determinants on Thy-1 have been highly conserved during evolution, permitting cross-species identification of the antigen. Other determinants are species-restricted. The density of Thy-1 antigen on mouse lymphocytes decreases with age (Brennan and Jaroslow, 1975), but it is not known whether this occurs in man.

Recently, Kennet and Gilbert (1979) demonstrated that the monoclonal antibodies raised by them against neuroblastoma cells react with B lymphocytes. Kernshead et al. (1981) showed that the monoclonal antibodies M1/N1 raised against human neuroblastoma also react with human neurons and with mature myeloid cells (polymorphonuclear leukocytes). Hogg et al. (1981) found that their monoclonal antibodies to human acute monoblastic leukemia cells react not only with human monocytes *in situ* (and in culture), but also with neurons in rat cerebellar cultures. Oger et al. (1982) have shown that the monoclonal antibody known as OKT8 (Orthoclone, Inc.), which is routinely used to identify T suppressor lymphocytes (T_S) in man, recognizes determinants on ovine oligodendrocytes. These results suggest that T_S cells and oligodendrocytes share an antigen that may make them both vulnerable to the same autoimmune attack, thus offering an attractive explanation for the loss of oligodendrocytes within multiple sclerosis (MS) plaques over the course of the disease and the loss of T_S cells from the blood during exacerbations of MS (Antel et al., 1979).

Further evidence for shared antigens between neural and lymphoid tissues has come from studies of human diseases in which antibodies that recognize lymphoid cells and nervous system elements can be demonstrated. Patients with systemic lupus erythematosus (SLE) have been shown to have serum antibodies that react with brain and with lymphoid structures. Anti-brain antibodies in serum from SLE patients can be absorbed out with lymphocytes, at least in large part. Anti-brain antibodies are found most frequently in sera from SLE patients with central nervous system (CNS) manifestations of the disease. Anti-brain antibodies demonstrated in spinal fluid during attacks of CNS–SLE can also be absorbed out with lymphocytes (Bluestein et al., 1981). Antilymphocyte antibodies are usually detected by their capacity to lyse lymphocytes at room temperature in the presence

Table 4-1. Tissue distribution of Thy-l in mouse, rat, dog, and man.

Organ	Species			
	Mouse	Rat	Dog	Man
Brain*	+ + + +	+ + + +	+ + + +	+ + + +
Thymus	+ + + +	+ + + +	+ + +	+ (peripheral lobule)
Spleen	+ + +	+ +	+ +	+ (marginal zone)
Lymph node	+ + +	−	+ +	+ (post-capillary venule)
Bone marrow	−	−	+ +	+ +
Kidney	−	−	+ +	+ +
PBL-T cells	+ + + +	−	+ + +	−
Liver, heart	−	−	−	−

*On neurons and fibrous astrocytes, but not on oligodendrocytes.

of complement. If the same cytotoxicity assay is performed at body temperature (37 °C), very little lysis of cells ensues; presumably a metabolically active cell can defend itself from an attack by activated complement components. For this reason, it is not possible to state what pathogenic significance such antilymphocyte antibodies may have *in situ*. It should also be noted, however, that some investigators have been unable to find an association between anti-brain or anti-lymphocyte antibodies and CNS involvement in SLE (Huntley et al., 1977).

Paraneoplastic syndromes affecting the nervous system comprise another group of disorders in which antigens shared by neural and non-neural tissues may play a major role in pathogenesis of disease. One may postulate that if either humoral or cell-mediated immune responses are generated against a neoplasm, these responses may cross-react with those neural elements that share antigens with the neoplasm. The existence of antigens shared by neural tissues and non-neural, non-lymphoid malignancies has been demonstrated. Oat cell carcinoma (OCC) of the lung is the neoplasm most commonly encountered in paraneoplastic syndromes of the nervous system. It is of interest that OCC derives from the Kulschitsky cell, which is held to be of neural crest origin and which migrates into the lungs during fetal life. Bell and Seetharam (1977) immunized rabbits with plasma membrane isolated from OCC. The rabbit serum, after extensive absorption, reacted with OCC and Schwann cells only. No reactivity against normal lung or other tissues was detected.

The S-100 protein is specific to neural tissue and chondrocytes (Stefansson et al., 1982a,b). In the CNS, it has been found in astrocytes, oligodendrocytes, and, possibly, neurons. In the peripheral nervous system, it is only detectable in Schwann cells and satellite cells of the sensory and autonomic ganglia. Using immunohistochemical methods, we looked for S-100 protein in an insulinoma from a patient who had both an insulinoma and a neuropathy, a rare, but well-described syndrome (Stefansson et al., 1981a). We also looked for S-100 in several normal pan-

creas and five other insulinomas not accompanied by neuropathy; S-100 was not detected in the islets nor in the exocrine portion of normal pancreas, and the only islet cell tumor containing S-100 was the insulinoma from the patient with the neuropathy.

Several groups have reported the presence of circulating anti-neural antibodies in patients with paraneoplastic syndromes of the nervous system. Wilkinson (1964) and Wilkinson and Zeromski (1965) demonstrated anti-neural antibodies in sera of several patients with OCC and subacute sensory neuropathy by means of a complement fixation assay. In subacute sensory neuropathy, dorsal root ganglion neurons die. Wilkinson and Zeromski (1965), and subsequently Zeromski (1970), showed, by immunohistochemistry, that these antibodies were directed against cytoplasm of neurons in dorsal root ganglion, but that reactivity was not confined to dorsal root ganglion neurons, since it was also seen in the neurons of spinal cord and brain. As a general rule, antibodies to surface components are more likely to kill or damage cells than are antibodies to intracellular structures. For this reason, the true meaning of intracellular binding of antibodies from sera of patients with sensory neuropathy is unclear at this time, and the relative nonspecificity of the antibody reactivity detected is disturbing. In myasthenia gravis, intracellular anti-muscle antibodies were known to be present many years before the pathogenetically significant immune response directed against the acetylcholine receptor on the muscle surface at the myoneural junction was discovered. In retrospect, the intracellular antibody in myasthenia can be looked upon as the forerunner of the clinically relevant antibody. The same may be true in subacute sensory neuropathy.

Trotter et al. (1976) demonstrated antibodies against Purkinje cells in serum from a patient with subacute cerebellar degeneration on a background of Hodgkin's disease. In this condition, Purkinje cells die; in some instances, the loss of nerve cells may be more extensive, with the brain stem and cortical neurons also affected. We have shown (again by indirect immunofluorescence studies) antibodies against cerebral and cerebellar neurites in serum from another patient with subacute cerebellar degeneration and Hodgkin's disease (Stefansson et al., 1981b). We have also studied five cases of subacute cerebellar degeneration occurring with neoplasm using immunoblotting (Latov et al., 1981b). This technique permits solubilizing of cell membrane components and allows for the determination of the molecular weight of the antigens against which the autoantibodies are directed. All five of our patients had antibodies against the same neural antigen; the molecular weight was 75,000 daltons. The antigen is found in the gray matter of the human CNS.

The Lambert–Eaton syndrome occurs most commonly as a complication of OCC, although in 30% of the cases there is no underlying tumor. The condition is characterized by weakness and by failure of release of acetylcholine from the terminal motor axon. Recently, there have been reports (Newsom-Davis et al., 1982) of successful response to plasmapheresis in the Lambert–Eaton syndrome. Plasmapheresis removes circulating antibody, and the finding therefore provides indirect evidence that the Lambert–Eaton syndrome is likely to have an immunological basis presumably because antibody binding to the terminal axon blocks acetylcholine release.

In general, the paraneoplastic syndromes affecting the nervous system have been associated either with tumors of probable neuroectodermal origin or with lymphoid tumors (Arnason, 1979). With neuroectodermal tumors, the basis for antigens shared with neural elements is not too difficult to discern; for lymphoid tumors, the basis is likely to be antigens shared by lymphoid and neural elements as discussed above. Rare cases of paraneoplastic syndromes associated with breast and other types of tumors may also be tied to shared antigens, but there is no evidence at present to support this.

An immunological basis for paraneoplastic syndromes is, in our opinion, of great interest despite the rarity of these conditions. In the paraneoplastic syndromes, as we have stressed, nerve cells die. In aging man, nerve cells die, and selective neuronal cell death characterizes most so-called degenerative diseases. The finding points up a need for a careful immunological investigation of senile dementia of the Alzheimer's type (SDAT), amyotrophic lateral sclerosis, and other sporadically occurring degenerative disorders. The finding of anti-brain antibodies in SLE is also of interest. Cerebral lupus is variable in its presentation, with acute psychoses predominating. Cerebral lupus is reversible, which argues, perhaps, that anti-brain antibodies may sometimes affect function without causing cell death, and without obvious morphological lesions.

Age-Related Changes in Immune Function

For purposes of this discussion, the immune system can be considered as functionally distinct subsets of cells that interact with each other. In simple terms, the immune system consists of B lymphocytes, which produce antibodies and mediate humoral immunity, and T lymphocytes, which can be subdivided into T effector lymphocytes and T regulator lymphocytes. T effector lymphocytes mediate cellular immunity; T regulator lymphocytes can either amplify (T helper) or suppress (T suppressor) both cellular and humoral immune responses. A third cell type, the macrophage, presents antigens to lymphoid cells and also contributes to the regulation of responses by lymphocytes. Most of what we know about the immune system has come from studies of lymphocytes and macrophages that have been isolated and kept in culture. Study of cells in a controlled environment has obvious advantages, even though certain artifacts may be present.

It has been recognized from the time of Hippocrates that old people are more prone than young ones to develop diseases that, in more recent times, have been found to be infectious. Since the immune system provides the principal defense against infections, age-related deterioration of the immune system is likely to be one of the reasons for the increased susceptibility of the elderly to infectious agents. The incidence of neoplasia is also greater in the old than the young, and there is an inverse relationship between immune activity and the tendency to develop neoplasia. Certain inflammatory diseases that can affect the nervous system and that are widely considered to be autoimmune in nature occur with increased frequency in the elderly. These include polyarteritis nodosa and temporal arteritis.

Cell-Mediated Immunity

This form of immunity has long been held to be particularly affected by the aging process. Skin test responses to a variety of antigens are reduced in the elderly, even though the number of circulating T lymphocytes is only modestly reduced, when elderly individuals are compared with young adults. The response of T lymphocytes from elderly individuals to substances that increase DNA synthesis and, ultimately, the rate of cell division (mitogens) has been found to be reduced compared to the response of T lymphocytes from young adults (Antel et al., 1980). Our studies of mitogen-stimulated T lymphocytes using flow cytometry, a technique in which individual cells can be analyzed, indicate that fewer lymphocytes from elderly donors enter the cell cycle and that those that do pass through the cell cycle more slowly than do cells from younger donors.

There are reasons to believe that there are two discrete mechanisms involved in the response of T lymphocytes to mitogens, particularly concanavalin A (Con A) (Dropcho et al., 1982; Lohrmann et al., 1974). One system responds to low concentrations of Con A, but requires the presence of accessory cells (e.g., macrophages). The other system is independent of accessory cells, but requires high concentration of Con A. The two systems may involve different Con A receptors, one of low affinity, the other of high affinity. The presence on human lymphocytes of multiple Con A receptors with various affinities has been shown by binding assays (Krug et al., 1973). Whether the receptors involved in the two systems reside on different T lymphocyte subpopulations or

on a single cell type has not been determined. In any case, both mechanisms of T lymphocyte activation by mitogens are impaired in the aged (Antel et al., 1980). This finding may be contrasted with our experiences in MS, in which the response requiring accessory cells seems to be preferentially impaired, and in myasthenia gravis, in which only the direct T lymphocyte activation response is defective (Dropcho et al., 1982). The age-related impairment in the accessory cell requiring activation system can be ascribed to a defect in the T lymphocytes themselves, since accessory cells from old donors will support a normal mitogenic response by T lymphocytes from young individuals, whereas accessory cells from young donors cannot restore the T lymphocyte responses of the elderly.

A number of age-related changes in cell membrane properties or in intracellular functions can be implicated in the changes in T lymphocyte activity just described. The density of mitogen receptors on lymphocytes, particularly for phytohemagglutinin, probably increases with age (Hung et al., 1975), making it unlikely that the reduced response of lymphocytes from the elderly to mitogens can be explained by a reduced interaction of mitogens and receptors. The same may not apply to other types of receptors on lymphocytes (see discussion below). The viscosity of the plasma membrane does increase with age; increased viscosity, likely reflecting changes in the cholesterol to phospholipid ratio, correlates directly with reduced mitogen-induced cell activation (Rinvay et al., 1980). The increased viscosity likely accounts for the age-related reduction in the process of lymphocyte "capping" (Noronha et al., 1980; Gilman et al., 1981; Naeim and Walford, 1980), which involves interaction of a ligand such as Con A with a surface receptor and redistribution of the entire complex to one pole of the cell, the complex then being either internalized or shed.

Intracellular changes both in quiescent and in mitogen-stimulated T lymphocytes are found with aging. Tam and Wolford (1980) reported a significant decrease in cyclic AMP and an increase in cyclic GMP in T lymphocytes from the elderly; an altered ratio of these cyclic nucleotides is known to influence cell activation. Other cell activation processes, particularly those that depend on calcium, are affected during aging (Kennes et al., 1981). These changes in lymphocyte properties appear to far outweigh the modest shifts in lymphocyte subset numbers seen with aging and are likely to account for the better part of the alterations in T lymphocyte activation that accompany aging.

IMMUNE REGULATION OF T LYMPHOCYTE RESPONSES

Age-related changes in T suppressor and T helper lymphocytes can be appreciated both by enumerating each of the T lymphocyte subsets and by *in vitro* assays of regulator lymphocyte activity. The number of Tγ lymphocytes, a lymphocyte subset that contains T suppressor lymphocytes, is increased with age (Gupta and Good, 1979). In our experience, no major shift in T suppressor or T helper lymphocytes as defined by monoclonal antibodies that recognize each of these subsets (OKT8 and OKT4, Orthoclone, Inc.) is found with age. *In vitro* assays comparing activity of T suppressor lymphocytes from young and old individuals have given results that at first sight may appear to be somewhat contradictory. It is possible to activate T suppressor lymphocytes by exposing them in culture to the mitogen Con A. The suppressive activity of lymphocytes so activated can then be determined by adding freshly obtained lymphocytes and measuring the extent to which response of the fresh lymphocytes to a mitogenic lectin is blunted by the presence of the activated T suppressor lymphocytes. We have found that T suppressor lymphocyte activity induced by a 96-hour incubation with Con A and directed toward responder lymphocytes from the same individual (autologous responder cells) is increased in the elderly (Antel et al., 1978a), a finding recently confirmed by Miller et al. (1981). Miller and coworkers also demonstrated that this increase was even greater in elderly individuals with senile dementia of the Alzheimer type (SDAT).

In our experience, elderly MS patients show greater autologous suppressor activity than young MS patients (Antel et al., 1978b). Young patients with MS are most often subject to attacks separated by quiescent periods, but as they grow older, the disease tends to become slowly, but more inexorably progressive; this is also seen in patients with middle life onset of the disease. It is distinctly possible that changes in the function of regulator lymphocytes may be involved in the altered clinical course of MS that accompanies aging.

In seeming contrast to our results, Hallgren and Yunis (1977) found that Con A-induced suppressor activity was reduced in the elderly. These workers used a heterologous lymphocyte (lymphocytes from unrelated donors) system, that is, they tested suppressor function of the elderly on responder lymphocytes from another donor, usually young. The apparent conflict with our results may be explained, at least in part, by the fact that effector lymphocytes from the elderly are extremely sensitive to suppressor influences (Antel and Arnason, 1979); thus, culture supernatants of Con A-activated lymphocytes from the elderly that actively suppressed their own responder lymphocytes suppressed DNA synthesis by cell lines less well than supernatants of lymphocytes from young donors. The data suggest that, although the amount of suppressor factor released by T suppressor lymphocytes from elderly donors is less than that released by cells from young donors, it is more than counter balanced by an augmented sensitivity of effector lymphocytes from the elderly to suppressor signals, with the net result, in an autologous (self–self) system, being an increased suppressor effect. The net result of *in vitro* assays for suppressor function depends on both the production of suppressor factors and the sensitivity of the responder cells to such factors.

T regulator influences on B cell responses may be mediated by cell subsets other than those that affect T effector cells. In this regard, Burns et al. (1981) demonstrated that, in certain cases of suppressor cell leukemia, the suppressor influence is marked on T cell responses, but not on B lymphocyte responses.

Humoral-Mediated Immunity

The number of circulating B lymphocytes (Becker et al., 1979) is relatively unaffected by aging, but serum concentrations of IgG and IgA tend to increase with age; the concentration of IgM remains constant or decreases slightly (Radl et al., 1975; Buckley et al., 1974). *In vitro* assays of B lymphocyte activity utilize two major categories of lymphocyte activators, namely thymus independent (TI) activators, which stimulate B lymphocytes directly, and thymus dependent (TD) activators, which require not only B lymphocytes for the response, but also T regulator lymphocytes. In our hands (Wrabetz et al., 1982), B lymphocytes from the elderly respond to TI activators by synthesizing comparable amounts of IgA, lesser amounts of IgG, and much lesser amounts of IgM than do lymphocytes from the young under identical conditions. This reduction in TI-induced IgG and IgM synthesis by B lymphocytes from the elderly suggests that the intrinsic capabilities of the B lymphocytes have themselves changed.

REGULATION OF HUMORAL IMMUNE RESPONSES

Prior studies of Con A-activated T suppressor lymphocytes on responses of heterologous B lymphocytes (usually from young donors) have indicated that suppressor influences on B lymphocytes are reduced in the elderly. In a follow-up to these studies, we have compared responses of elderly donors to TD activators with their responses to TI activators (Wrabetz et al., 1982). We have found that lymphocytes from the elderly respond to TD activators by generating the same amount of IgA and IgG as do lymphocytes from the young, although somewhat less IgM is generated. The preservation of the TD–IgG response, taken together with the previously mentioned reduced TI–IgG response, suggests that a decline in T suppressor influences over B lymphocytes in the elderly, even in the face of reduced B

lymphocyte synthesizing capacity, can preserve or even augment net immunoglobulin production.

Our studies comparing Ig secretion in TD-stimulated crossover cultures between B and T lymphocytes of elderly and young donors with Ig secretion by autologous T–B cultures further indicated the complex nature of the interplay of a number of factors that determine overall immune reactivity. Both in the young and the old age groups, a proportion of individuals respond poorly to TD activators. In young donors, this "non-response" reflects strong T suppressor influences. Our finding that T lymphocytes from elderly "non-responders" support high levels of Ig secretion by heterologous B lymphocytes taken from young donors indicates that non-response is not attributable in this elderly group to the same mechanism as it is in the young group, and likely reflects B lymphocyte properties. Such properties could include a heightened sensitivity of the old donors' B lymphocytes to suppressor influences that overrides a decrease in synthesis of suppressor factors, intrinsic changes in the B lymphocytes, or both. Thus, the wide range of *in vitro* immune responses characteristic of the elderly are not unexpected. Lymphocytes from some of the old people we studied did not respond to TI activators, but did respond to TD activators; none of the old people responding to TI activators did not respond to TD activators. In contrast, lymphocytes from some young individuals responded to TI, but not to TD activators. This suggests that the lack of response to TD activators by lymphocytes from young donors may relate to an override of functionally intact B lymphocytes by T regulator lymphocytes. Other data suggest that, in some old donors, T helper cell function is defective. These studies indicate that results that appear to be a simple increase or decrease in immunoglobulin synthesis really reflect complex changes in the immunological network. (See Table 4-2).

Down's Syndrome

This syndrome, associated with an increased incidence of SDAT, has been

Table 4-2. Summary of how some of the parameters of the immune system in the old compare to the young.

Number of T lymphocytes →

Response of T lymphocytes to mitogens ↓

Influence of T suppressor lymphocytes on autologous T effector lymphocytes ↑

Influence of T suppressor lymphocytes on heterologous T effector lymphocytes ↓

Sensitivity of T effector lymphocytes to suppression ↑

Number of B lymphocytes →

Serum IgG and IgA →

Serum IgM ↓

Response of B lymphocytes to TI activators ↓

Response of B lymphocytes to TD activators →

Influence of T suppressor lymphocytes on B lymphocytes ↓

Key: → unchanged, ↑ increased, ↓ decreased.

considered to reflect a state of accelerated aging (Naeim and Walford, 1980; Tavolato and Argentiero, 1979). In this regard, many of the changes in immune function described as being characteristic of the chronologically aged have been found in Down's syndrome patients. Such patients show reduced numbers of total T lymphocytes, T lymphocyte hyporeactivity to mitogens, an increased incidence of autoantibodies, and an inferred deficiency of T suppressor lymphocyte function. In addition, lymphocyte capping is reduced. These findings further emphasize the need to correlate changes in the brain with changes in the immune system, as well as the need to determine whether cause–effect relationships between the two systems exist.

Aberrant B Lymphocyte Products in the Elderly

One result of altered humoral immune function in the elderly is the production of abnormal immune products that may induce disease of the nervous system. Autoantibodies are more frequently found in the sera of the elderly than of young adults. Among such autoantibodies are those directed against DNA, nuclear proteins, thyroglobulin, and immunoglobulins (Shu et al., 1975; Diaz-Jouanen et al., 1975; Roberts-Thomson et al., 1974). We have looked for antibodies against neural tissue in sera from old and young people,

using immunohistochemical techniques, and find them more often in the old (Table 4-3). Within the aged population, there is a marked heterogeneity with regard to the antigens recognized by the antibodies. There are elderly subjects whose sera recognize mainly neuronal elements (soma, axons), or astrocytes, or both. Whether these autoantibodies play a role in the genesis of diseases of the elderly or in the aging process itself has yet to be determined.

The prevalence of "benign" monoclonal gammopathy increases with age (Waldenström, 1973; Radl and Hollander, 1974; Radl et al., 1975). Benign monoclonal gammopathy is rarely found in people through the fourth decade, whereas 19% of people in the tenth decade of life have monoclonal gammopathy without an underlying B lymphocyte malignancy (Axelsson et al., 1966). The B lymphocyte malignancies that give rise to monoclonal gammopathies (multiple myeloma, Waldenstrom's macroglobulinemia) are also diseases of the elderly (Mackenzie and Fudenberg, 1972; Alexanian et al., 1980). The significance of monoclonal gammopathies to neurological disease has become increasingly apparent with the demonstration of the association between these conditions and peripheral neuropathies (Victor et al., 1958; Swash et al., 1979; Latov et al., 1981a,b; Besinger et al., 1981). Even though peripheral neuropathy is not the commonest complication of

Table 4-3. Distribution of serum antibody binding in patients with detectable anti-neural antibodies.

| Age | Peripheral nerve | Neuron | | Brain Astrocytes | Axons | Liver | Kidney |
		Cytoplasm	Nuclei				
71	+	+		+			+
74	+						
60	+						
85		+					
80	+	+			+		
94	+						
25			+				

Using indirect immunofluorescence we looked for anti-neural antibodies in sera from two groups of asymptomatic individuals; one with 20 persons over 59 years of age, the other with 16 persons less than 40 years of age. Six old patients and the one young patient had detectable anti-neural antibodies.

monoclonal gammopathies, up to 10% of chronic peripheral neuropathies of unknown etiology are said to be associated with monoclonal gammopathies. The neuropathies of monoclonal gammopathies can be divided into two major groups on the basis of histological alterations in the affected nerves.

SEGMENTAL DEMYELINATION

In this form of neuropathy, the pathology is segmental demyelination, accompanied by varying degrees of axonal degeneration, sometimes with infiltrates of mononuclear cells, but without significant amyloid deposits (Kelly et al., 1981). Immunoglobulins with the same heavy and light chain types as the circulating monoclonal immunoglobulins can be found in the diseased nerves (Propp et al., 1975; Julien, et al., 1978; Dalakas and Engel, 1981). Latov et al. (1980, 1981a) have reported that the monoclonal immunoglobulins circulating in four of the twenty patients with neuropathy and monoclonal gammopathy they studied bind specifically to peripheral nerve. More recently, they have demonstrated that the monoclonal immunoglobulins from these four patients recognize a myelin protein (MW ~ 100,000 daltons) that is found both in the peripheral and the central nervous system (Latov et al., 1981b). Dellagi et al. (1979) had reported earlier that the circulating monoclonal immunoglobulins in five

of their sixteen patients with Waldenstron's macroglobulinemia and neuropathy were probably directed against the same antigenic determinant.

The mere presence of monoclonal antibodies against the same myelin protein in sera from several patients with monoclonal gammopathy and peripheral neuropathy does not prove that the monoclonal antibodies are responsible for the neuropathy. Besinger et al. (1981), however, demonstrated that repeated injections of monoclonal immunoglobulins from patients with monoclonal gammopathy and neuropathy intraperitoneally into rats caused segmental demyelination of peripheral nerves, whereas injection of monoclonal immunoglobulins from patients with monoclonal gammopathy unaccompanied by polyneuropathy did not. This work leads us to conclude that the monoclonal immunoglobulins in sera from a significant proportion of patients with monoclonal gammopathy and peripheral neuropathy may be involved in the genesis of the neuropathy. Given this formulation, two questions can be posed. Why do autonomous but benign B lymphocyte clones and malignant B lymphocyte clones so often secrete antibodies against the same myelin protein? and which is primary, the autoimmune process or the monoclonal gammopathy? It is conceivable that these monoclonal gammopathies begin as a polyclonal autoimmune attack during the course of which a clone of B lymphocytes becomes autonomous or malignant. Transformation to autonomy or malignancy may be favored by the failure of immune regulation that accompanies aging. The hypothesis that these monoclonal gammopathies originate as autoimmune processes is perhaps strengthened by the fact that many of the myelomas accompanied by neuropathies present with neuropathy as the sole clinical manifestation some considerable time before the "classical" signs of myeloma appear (Kelly et al., 1981). The hypothesis also receives some support from the work of Latov et al. (1981b), who showed that one of their patients with circulating monoclonal IgM and peripheral neuropathy had not only monoclonal IgM directed against the myelin protein, but also IgG. This IgG could be a remnant of the "original polyclonal humoral immune response" against the myelin protein.

Why are myelin proteins such a common target of autoimmune attack in the elderly? Do autoimmune responses against these particular proteins for some reason favor transformation of B lymphocytes to an autonomous or a malignant state? The spectrum of these neuropathies associated with gammopathies is still incompletely defined. We have, for example, encountered a patient with monoclonal gammopathy and neuropathy whose monoclonal immunoglobulins were directed against axons of peripheral nerves, but not myelin, and Dellagi et al. (1982), have reported on two patients with monoclonal gammopathy and neuropathy who had their monoclonal immunoglobulins directed against intermediate filaments in astrocytes, Schwann cells, kidney, muscle, and liver, but not axons. We (Sweet et al., 1982) have also recently seen two patients with a syndrome of monoclonal gammopathy, peripheral neuropathy, and pseudotumor cerebri.

AMYLOID DEPOSITS

The pathology of an additional form of neuropathy of the elderly that accompanies monoclonal gammopathies is characterized by amyloid deposits in affected nerves. The amyloid can be in epineurium, in endoneurium, and in vessel walls (Cohen and Benson, 1975). Axonal degeneration is marked, segmental demyelination less prominent (Kelly et al., 1979). This form of neuropathy is said to be uncommon in patients with B cell malignancies (Davies-Jones and Esiri, 1971, Trotter et al., 1977) and is most often encountered in patients with what used to be called "primary amyloidosis" (Cohen, 1967), but is now termed monoclonal protein (MP) amyloidosis and is classified conjointly with the amyloidosis of multiple myeloma as amyloidosis of immunocyte dyscrasias (Glenner, 1980). The distinction between multiple myeloma accompanied by amyloidosis and the immunocyte dyscrasia of MP amyloidosis is somewhat arbitrary and often only quantitative* (Alexanian et al., 1980), as, for that matter, is the distinction between multiple myeloma and benign monoclonal gammopathy. Amyloid deposits in the amyloidosis of immunocyte dyscrasias are composed of the variable regions of monoclonal light chains of immunoglobulins (Glenner et al., 1971a), which are in each case identical to the variable region of circulating monoclonal light chains (Terry et al., 1973). Monoclonal light chains therefore appear to be circulating precursors of the amyloid deposits. Approximately 50% of patients with peripheral neuropathy of MP amyloidosis did not suffer from involvement of other organs by amyloid at the time of diagnosis (Kelly et al., 1979). This tendency of the light chains to form amyloid selectively in peripheral nerves is unexplained; it could be governed by a particular affinity these light chains may have for nerves. Affinity of monoclonal light chains for peripheral nerves would be most easily explained if the antigen-binding sites of the light chains recognized some determinant in the nerves. Despite a lack of supporting evidence, it is tempting to postulate that the

*The diagnosis of multiple myeloma is favored by lytic lesions on X-rays, plasma cells > 15% of cells in bone marrow, monoclonal B cell product in serum > 3G/dl or monoclonal B cell product excreted in urine > 3G/24h, reduced serum levels of polyclonal immunoglobulins, and anemia.

amyloid neuropathy that accompanies monoclonal gammopathies is, like its non-amyloid counterpart, caused by a monoclonal humoral *immune* response against the nerves themselves. It would not be difficult to explain why these responses sometimes give rise to amyloid deposits and sometimes not. The amyloid of immunocyte dyscrasias is formed from circulating free light chains (Glenner et al., 1973), and it is likely that only some patients with monoclonal gammopathy and neuropathy will generate significant amounts of free light chains (Paladini et al., 1980). It is also known both from clinical data (Stone and Frenkel, 1975) and from *in vitro* experiments (Glenner et al., 1971b) that only some monoclonal free light chains have a tendency to form amyloid.

CEREBRAL AMYLOID

Not only is peripheral nerve amyloid of immunocyte discrasias more commonly encountered in the elderly, but the incidence of brain-limited amyloid also increases with age (Wright et al., 1969). Amyloid deposits in brain are found most often in senile plaques and in the walls of blood vessels (Glenner, 1980). Both of these lesions are found in "normal" old people, but are more prevalent in patients with SDAT (Wright et al., 1969). It is important to recall that patients with Down's syndrome are affected at a very early age with a dementia that is characterized by CNS histopathology almost identical to that found in patients with SDAT, including amyloid deposits (Wolstenholme and O'Connor, 1970; Malamud, 1972). It is also of relevance that cerebrovascular amyloidosis has recently been recognized as one of the conditions that predispose to cerebral hemorrhage (Gudmundsson et al., 1972; Jellinger, 1977).

Amyloid consists of proteins with the twisted β-pleated sheet fibril conformation. A considerable number of proteins can adopt this conformation and therefore may serve as amyloid precursors. The two most prominent precursors of amyloid in man are (1) light chains of immunoglobulins that form what is now called AL amyloid and is found in amyloidosis of immunocyte dyscrasias and (2) AA protein (the antigenically related serum protein is called SAA) that forms the so-called AA amyloid and is found in systemic reactive amyloidosis (secondary amyloidosis). Other possible amyloid precursors include prealbumin and precalcitonin.

The nature of the precursor(s) of the amyloid found in senile plaques and cerebral blood vessels is disputed (Probst et al., 1980; Powers et al., 1981; Torack and Lynch, 1981; Ishii and Haga, 1975, 1976; Vuia, 1978), as is the nature of the proteins that form amyloid in senile plaques and in congophilic cerebral blood vessels. Recent histochemical studies indicate that the precursors of the amyloid found in these two locations may be the same (Probst et al., 1980). Ishii and Haga (1976) and Ishii et al. (1975), using immunohistochemical techniques, detected IgG in senile plaques and argued for the AL nature of the amyloid found there. Other investigators have reported both direct and indirect evidence for the presence of immunoglobulins in senile plaques (Torack and Lynch, 1981; Probst et al., 1980; Vuia, 1978; Powers et al., 1981). Both kappa and lambda light chains are found in the same plaques, according to Powers et al. (1981), yet AL amyloid is formed from monoclonal light chains. The study of Powers et al. (1981) suggests that the mere presence of IgG in senile plaques can no longer be taken as evidence favoring an AL origin of the amyloid (Glenner, 1980). The AA protein does not appear to be a significant component of amyloid in the aged brain (Probst et al., 1980), and several investigators have postulated that the amyloid in senile plaques may be formed from locally produced proteins rather than from circulating precursors (Miyakawa et al., 1974; Terry et al., 1964; Powers and Spicer, 1977). Mice infected with scapie develop amyloid plaques in their brains that appear to be identical to senile plaques in humans (Fraser and Bruce, 1973; Wisniewski et al., 1975). How the infectious agent induces amyloid formation and from which precursor protein the amyloid is formed is unknown.

We have studied some properties of peripheral blood lymphocytes (PBL's) from patients of an Icelandic kindred in which cerebrovascular amyloidosis is inherited as an autosomal dominant disease. The patients suffer intracerebral hemorrhage, sometimes at an early age, and at autopsy, amyloid is found in the walls of the cerebral blood vessels. There is no amyloid outside the CNS and there are no senile plaques in the brain (Gudmundsson et al., 1972). In these patients, a significantly greater proportion of PBLs carry surface membrane immunoglobulins (SmIg+PBLs) capping of PBLs with Con A is significantly lower, and the PBLs mitogenic response to Con A is suggestively reduced (Stefansson et al., 1980). We are not in a position to claim that these changes in the PBLs prove that the cerebrovascular amyloid is AL amyloid or that there is some causal relationship between the brain disease and the changes in the PBLs. It is nevertheless tempting to postulate such a relationship, since the patients have increased numbers of SmIg+PBLs and the precursor proteins of AL amyloid are produced by SmIg+ cells (B lymphocytes, plasma cells).

From what has been stated above, it is obvious that the chemical nature of cerebral amyloid has yet to be determined, but it is of interest that SDAT, Down's syndrome, and autosomal dominant cerebrovascular amyloidosis are marked by accumulation of cerebral amyloid and by alterations in function of peripheral blood lymphocytes.

The Role of the Nervous System in Immune Regulation

The role of the CNS in immune regulation has been studied by lesioning brain nuclei. Lesions in the hypothalamus and reticular formation of rats are followed by considerable changes in immune function (Szentivanyi and Filipp, 1958; Polyak et al., 1969), including reduction in humoral immunity as measured by Arthus reactivity and reduced formation of antibodies to bovine serum albumin (Jankovic and Isakovic, 1973). More recently, it has been demonstrated that lesions in the anterior hypothalamus prevent anaphylaxis (Stein et al., 1980). Changes in the architecture

of the lymphoid organs accompany these lesions. The thymus gland is depleted of lymphocytes, with thinning of the cortex and indistinct corticomedullary junctions. The spleen and the lymph nodes contain fewer lymphocytes, fewer plasma cells, and no germinal centers.

Evidence for reciprocal communication between the immune system and hypothalamic nuclei has also been reported. Immunized rats have an increased neuronal firing rate in ventromedial, but not anterior hypothalamic nuclei during the peak of the immune response (Besedovsky et al., 1977, 1979). How hypothalamic lesions might influence the immune response is unclear; hormonal and neuroendocrine mechanisms have been proposed, but the hypothalamic effect could also be mediated through the peripheral sympathetic and parasympathetic nervous systems. In patients with SDAT, there are changes in the brain regions involved with control of the autonomic nervous system and changes in immune function. Might the two be linked?

The concentration of noradrenaline and the specific activity of choline acetyltransferase have been reported to decrease in the hypothalamus of patients with SDAT (Yates et al., 1981; Mann et al., 1980). In SDAT, there is a loss of neurons from the locus coeruleus (Mann et al., 1980; Bondareff et al., 1981), which, along with other mesencephalic nuclei, contain perikarya of noradrenergic neurons that project to the hypothalamus (Lindvall and Bjorklund, 1978). Of interest is the fact that the profound loss of neurons from the locus coeruleus in patients with SDAT appears to be associated with particularly severe dementia and early death (Bondareff et al., 1981). Recently Whitehouse et al. (1982) reported on the loss of neurons from the nucleus basalis of Meynert in patients with SDAT. The nucleus basalis contains perikarya of cholinergic neurons that project primarily to the cortex, but also to the hypothalamus. Loss of neurons from the nucleus basalis may account for the reduction in the specific activity of choline acetyltransferase in the hypothalamus of SDAT patients.

The peripheral sympathetic nervous system (SNS) also appears to play a role in immune regulation. Selective destruction of the peripheral SNS in mice with 60H dopamine causes definite changes in immune function, but reports in the literature are somewhat contradictory as to what the changes are (Kasahare et al., 1977; Besedovsky et al., 1979; Miles et al., 1981). Miles et al. (1981) found that ablation of the peripheral SNS augmented the response of lymphocytes to Con A, a T lymphocyte mitogen that also activates suppressor lymphocytes. The augmented response to Con A observed in mice could reflect either loss of suppressor lymphocyte function or increased responsiveness of T helper lymphocytes. Response of B lymphocytes to antigens that do not require T helper lymphocytes, but that are influenced by T suppressor lymphocytes (Baker, 1975), is increased three- to fivefold by SNS axotomy. This increase in response could depend on an increase in responsiveness of B lymphocytes or a loss of T suppressor lymphocyte activity. Both the change in the response to Con A and to antigens would be explained, if T suppressor function were selectively compromised by SNS ablation.

Most studies examining the role of the SNS in immune regulation have been short-term ones. It is possible that long-term experiments would give different results. Monjan and Collector (1976) have emphasized that short-term "stress" blunts immune response, but that long-term stress augments it. The obvious analogy to denervation sensitivity springs to mind. Were this to be the case, the increased T suppressor function found in SDAT might be logically explained.

One mechanism by which the peripheral SNS could influence immune responses is through release of neurotransmitters. Functional receptors for neurotransmitters are present on lymphocytes. Lymphocytes have β-adrenergic receptors (Williams et al., 1976), and the inhibitory effects of catecholamines on cytotoxic activity of T lymphocytes *in vitro* can be suppressed by β-, but not by α-adrenergic agonists (Melmon et al., 1974). Inflammatory responses (Bourne et al., 1974) and lysosomal enzyme release from neutrophils (Ignarro and George, 1974) are also inhibited by catecholamines. The β-adrenergic receptors are reported to decrease in density with age, not only in brain (Weiss et al., 1979), but also on lymphocytes (Schocken and Roth, 1977). Failure in receipt of "messages" from the peripheral SNS to lymphocytes caused by a reduction in the density of β-adrenergic receptors may be one of the reasons why alterations in immune regulation accompany aging.

Lymphocytes have both H_1 and H_2 histamine receptors, which mediate the complex and somewhat counteractive influences of histamine on lymphocytes (Ogden and Hill, 1980). It is not known whether the histamine receptors on lymphocytes change with age. Lymphocytes have also been shown to possess both nicotinic and muscarinic acetylcholine receptors (Richman and Arnason, 1979; Strom et al., 1973). Nicotinic agonists appear to inhibit lymphocyte activation (Richman and Arnason, 1979); muscarinic agonists facilitate the response (Macmanus et al., 1975). Richman et al. (1982) have demonstrated that carbamyl choline in concentrations similar to those that inhibit lymphocyte activation, induces T suppressor cell activity. The density of muscarinic acetylcholine receptors decreases with age both in cerebral and cerebellar cortices (James and Kanungo, 1976), but whether the muscarinic receptors on lymphocytes are influenced by aging remains to be shown. There are now numerous examples of how the ailing nervous system can be helped through manipulation of neurotransmitters (Peters and Levin, 1979; Muramoto et al., 1979). Since some functions of lymphocytes can be influenced by the same transmitters, it may be feasible to attempt to rejuvenate the aging immune system through similar manipulations.

Conclusion

The human aging process is accompanied by a complex series of changes in immune function and by a number of both well-defined and not-yet-defined disorders of the nervous system. Whether an interrelation exists between derangements of immune function and nervous system disease is a central issue in defining the neuroimmunology of aging. The increasingly well-delineated syndromes of immune-mediated neuropathies illustrate that deranged immune function can selectively affect the nervous system. The demonstration that presumably primary disorders of the nervous system, particularly senile dementia of the Alzheimer type, are associated with the more marked changes in immune function found in the aged population at large emphasizes that the nervous system can influence the immune system. In addition, the presence of shared antigens or receptors for the same transmitter substances may result in the nervous system and immune system being susceptible to common disease processes. As one defines the contribution of each of the above-mentioned mechanisms to the development of neurological or immunological disorders of aging, attention can then be focused on the development of pharmacological therapies to restore normal function.

References

Acton, R.T., Morris, R.J., and Williams, A.F. (1974). Estimation of the amount and tissue distribution of rat Thy-1. Eur. J. Immunol. 4, 598.

Alexanian, R., et al. (1980). Multiple myeloma. In Harrison's Principles of Internal Medicine. K.J. Isselbacher, R.D. Adams, E. Braunwald, R.G. Petersdorf, and J.D. Wilson, Eds. New York, McGraw-Hill, pp. 333–338.

Antel, J.P. and Arnason, B.G.W. (1979). Circulating suppressor cells in man: Evidence for altered sensitivity of responder cells with age. Clin. Immunol. Immunopath. 13, 119–124.

Antel, J.P., Arnason, B.G.W., and Medof, M.E. (1979). Suppressor cell function in multiple sclerosis: Correlation with clinical disease activity. Ann. Neurol. 5, 338–342.

Antel, J.P., Oger, J.J-F., Dropcho, E., Richman, D.P., Kuo, H.H., and Arnason, B.G.W. (1980). Reduced T-lymphocyte cell reactivity as a function of human aging. Cell. Immuno. 54, 184–192.

Antel, J.P., Weinrich, M., and Arnason, B.G.W. (1978a). Circulating suppressor cell activity in man as a function of age. Clin. Immun. Immunopath. 9, 134–141.

Antel, J.P., Weinrich, M., and Arnason, B.G.W. (1978b). Mitogen responsive and suppressor cell function in multiple sclerosis: Influence of age and disease activity. Neurology 28, 999–1003.

Arnason, B.G.W. (1979). Paraneoplastic syndromes of muscle, nerve and brain. In Clinical Neuroimmunology F. Clifford Rose, ed., Oxford: Blackwell Scientific Publications, pp. 421–443.

Axelsson, U., Bachman, R., and Hellen, J. (1966). Frequency of pathological proteins (M components) in 6995 sera from an adult population. Acta Med. Scand. 179, 235–247.

Baker, P.M. (1975). Lymphocyte subpopulations in thymus. Transplant Rev. 26, 3–20.

Becker, M.J., Farakas, R., Schneider, M., Drucker, I., and Klajman, A. (1979). Cell-mediated cytotoxicity in humans: Age-related decline as measured by a xenogeneic assay. Clin. Immunol. Immunopath. 14, 204.

Bell, C.E. and Seetharam, S. (1977). Identification of the Schwann cell as peripheral nervous system cell possessing a differentiation antigen expressed by human lung tumor. J. Immunol. 118(3), 826–831.

Besedovsky, H.O., del Rey, A., Sorkin, E., DaPrada, M., and Keller, H.H. (1979). Immunoregulation by the sympathetic nervous system. Cell Immunol. 48, 346–355.

Besedovsky, H.O., Sorkin, E., Felix, D., et al. (1977). Hypothalamic changes during the immune response. Eur. J. Immunol. 7, 323–325.

Besinger, U.A., Toyka, K.V., Antzil, A.P., Fateh-Moghadam, A., Rauscher, R., and Heininger, K. (1981). Myeloma neuropathy: Passive transfer from man to mouse. Science 213, 1027–1030.

Bluestein, H.G., Williams, G.W., and Steinberg, A.D. (1981). Cerebrospinal fluid antibodies to neuronal cells: Association with neuropsychiatric manifestations of systemic lupus erythematosus. Amer. J. Med. 70, 240–245.

Bondareff, W., Mountjoy, C.Q., and Roth, M. (1981). Selective loss of neurons of origin of adrenergic projection to cerebral cortex (nucleus locus coeruleus) in senile dementia. Lancet i, 783–784.

Bourne, H.R., Lichtenstein, L.M., Melman, K.L., Henny, C.S., Weinstein, Y., and Shearer, G.M. (1974). Modulation of inflammation and immunity by cAMP. Science 184, 19–28.

Brennan, P.C. and Jaroslow, B.N. (1975). Age-associated decline in theta antigen on spleen thymus-derived lymphocytes of B6 CFl mice. Cell Immunol. 15, 51–56.

Brouet, J.C. and Toben, H. (1976). Characterization of a subpopulation of human T lymphocytes reactive with heteroantiserum to human brain. J. Immunol. 116, 1041.

Buckley, C.G., Buckley, E.G., and Dorsey, F.C. (1974). Longitudinal changes in serum immunoglobulin levels in older humans. Fed. Proc. Fed. Am. Soc. Exp. Biol. 33, 2036.

Burns, J.B., Antel, J.P., Haren, J.M., and Hopper, J.E. (1981) Human T-cell lymphoma with suppressor effects of the mixed lymphocyte reaction (MLR). II. Functional *in vitro* lymphocyte analysis. Blood 57, 642–648.

Cohen, A.S. (1967) Amyloidosis. N. Engl. J. Med. 277, 522–530, 574–583, 628–638.

Cohen, A.S. and Benson, M.D. (1975). Amyloid neuropathy. In: Peripheral Neuropathy, P.J. Dyck, P.K. Thomas, and E.H. Lambert, Eds. Philadelphia, Saunders, pp. 1067–1091.

Dalakas, M.C. and Engel, W.K. (1981). Polyneuropathy with monoclonal gammopathy: Studies of 11 patients. Ann. Neurol. 10, 45–52.

Dalchau, R. and Fabre, J.W. (1979). Identification and unusual tissue distribution of the canine human and homologues of Thy-l. J. Exp. Med. 49, 576–591.

Davies-Jones, G.A.B. and Esiri, M.M. (1971). Neuropathy due to amyloid in myelomatosis. Brit. Med. J. 2, 244.

Dellagi, K., Brouet, J.C., Danan, F. (1979). Cross-idiotypic antigens among monoclonal immunoglobulin M from patients with Waldenstrom's macroglobulinemia and polyneuropathy. J. Clin. Invest. 64, 1530–1534.

Dellagi, K., Brouet, J.C., Perreau, J., and Paulin, D. (1982). Human monoclonal IgM with autoantibody activity against intermediate filaments. Proc. Natl. Acad. Sci. USA 79, 446–450.

Diaz-Jouanen, E., Williams, R.C., Jr., and Strickland, R.G. (1975). Age related changes in T and B cells. Lancet i, 688–689.

Dropcho, E.J., Richman, D.P., Antel, J.P., and Arnason, B.G.W. (1982). Defective mitogenic responses in myasthenia gravis and multiple sclerosis. Ann. Neurol. 11, 456–462.

Fraser, H. and Bruce, M.E. (1973). Argyrophilic plaques in mice inoculated with scrapie from particular sources. Lancet i, 617.

Gilman, S.C., Woda, B.A., and Feldman, J.D. (1981). T. lymphocytes of young and aged rats. I. Distribution identity and capping of T antigens. J. Immunol. 127, 149–153.

Glenner, G.G. (1980). Amyloid deposits and amyloidosis. New Engl. J. Med. 302(23), 1283–1292; 302(24), 1333–1343.

Glenner, G.G., Terry, W., Haroda, M., Isersky, C., and Page, D. (1971a). Amyloid fibril proteins: Proof of homology with immunoglobulin light chains by sequence analyses. Science 172, 1150–1151.

Glenner, G.G., Ein, D., Eanes, E.D., Bladen, H.A., Terry, W., and Page, D.L. (1971b). Creation of "amyloid" fibrils from Bence Jones proteins *in vitro*. Science 174, 712–714.

Glenner, G.G., Terry, W.D., and Isersky, C. (1973). Amyloidosis: Its nature and pathogenesis. Semin. Hematol. 10, 65–86.

Gudmundsson, G., Hallgrimsson, J., Jonasson, T.A., and Bjarnason, O. (1972). Hereditary cerebral hemorrhage with amyloidosis. Brain 95, 387–404.

Gupta, S. and Good, R.A. (1979). Subpopulations of human T lymphocytes. X. Alterations in T, B, third population cells and T cells with receptors for immunoglobulin M(Tμ) or G(Tγ) in aging humans. J. Immunol. 122, 1214–1219.

Hallgren, H.M. and Yunis, E.J. (1977). Suppressor lymphocytes in young and aged humans. J. Immunol. 118, 2004–2008.

Hogg, N., Slusarenko, M., Cohen, J., and Reiser, J. (1981). Monoclonal antibody with specificity for monocytes and neurons. Cell. 24, 875–885.

Hung, C.Y., Perkins, E.H., and Yang, W.K. (1975). Age-related refractoriness of PHA-induced lymphocyte transformation. II. [125]I PHA binding to spleen cells from young and old mice. Mech. Ageing Dev. 4, 103.

Huntley, A.C., Fletcher, M.P., Ikeda, R.M., and Gershwin, M.E. (1977). Shared antigenic determinants between rabbit antihuman brain and rabbit antihuman thymocyte sera: Relationship to the lymphocytotoxic antibodies of systemic lupus erythematosus. Clinical Immunol. Immunopath. 7, 269–280.

Ignarro, L.J. and George, W.J. (1974). Hormonal control of lysosomal enzyme release from human neutrophils; elevation of cyclic nucleotide levels by autonomic neurohormones. Proc. Nat. Acad. Sci. 71, 2027–2031.

Ishii, T. and Haga, S. (1976). Identification of components of immunoglobulins in senile plaques by means of fluorescent antibody technique. Acta Neuropath. 36, 243–249.

Ishii, T., Haga, S., and Shimizu, F. (1975). Immuno-electron microscopic localization of immunoglobulins in amyloid fibrils of senile plaques. Acta Neuropath. 32, 157–162.

James T.C. and Kanungo, M.S. (1976). Alterations in atropine sites of the brain of rats as a function of age. Biochem. Biophys. Res. Commun. 72, 170–175.

Jankovic, B.D. and Isakovic, K. (1973). Neuroendocrine correlates of immune response. I. Effects of brain lesions on antibody production, Arthus reactivity and delayed sensitivity in the rat. Int. Arch. Allergy 45, 360–372.

Jellinger, K. (1977). Cerebrovascular amyloidosis with cerebral hemorrhage. J. Neurol. 214, 195–206.

Julien, J., Vital, C., Vallat, J.M., et al. (1978). Polyneuropathy in Waldenstrom's macroglobulinemia: Deposition of M component on myelin sheaths. Arch. Neurol. 35, 423–425.

Kasahare, K., et al., (1977). Suppression of the primary immune response by chemical sympathectomy. Res. Comm. Chem. Pathol. Pharmacol. 16, 687–697.

Kelly, J.J., Kyle, R.A., O'Brien, P.C., and Dyck, P.J. (1979). The natural history of peripheral neuropathy in primary systemic amyloidosis. Ann. Neurol. 6, 1–7.

Kelly, J.J., Kyle, R.A., Miles, J.M., O'Brien, P.C., and Dyck, P.J. (1981). The spectrum of peripheral neuropathy in myeloma. Neurology (Minneap.) 31, 24–31.

Kennes, B., Huber, C., Brohee, D., and Neve, P. (1981). Early biochemical events associated with lymphocyte activation in aging. I. Evidence that Ca^{2+} dependent processes induced by PHA are impaired. Immunology 42, 119–126.

Kennet, R.H. and Gilbert, F. (1979). Hybrid myeloma producing antibodies against a human neuroblastoma antigen present on fetal brain. Science 201, 1120–1121.

Kernshead, J.T., Bicknell, D., and Greaves, M.T. (1981). A monoclonal antibody detecting an antigen shared by neural and granulocytic cells. Ped. Res. 15, 1282, 1286.

Krug, R., Hollenberg, M.D., and Cuatrecasas, P. (1973). Changes in the binding of concanavalin A and wheat germ agglutinin to human lymphocytes during *in vitro* transformation. Biochem. Biophys. Res. Commun. 52, 305–312.

Latov, N., Braun, P.E., Gross, R.B., Sherman, W.H., Penn, A.S., and Chess, L.

(1981b). Plasma cell dyscrasia and peripheral neuropathy: Identification of the myelin antigens that react with human paraproteins. Proc. Nat. Acad. Sci. 78 (11), 7139–7142.

Latov, N., Gross, R.B., Kastelman, J., Flanagan, T., Lamme, S., Alkaitis, D.A., Olarte, M.R., Sherman, W.H., Chess, L., and Penn, A.S. (1981a). Complement-fixing anti-peripheral nerve myelin antibodies in patients with inflammatory polyneuritis and with polyneuropathy and paraproteinemia. Neurology 31, 1530–1534.

Latov, N., Sherman, W.H., Nemni, R., Galassi, G., Shuong, J.S., Penn, A.S., Chess, L., Olarte, M., Rowland, L.P., and Osserman, E.F. (1980). Plasma-cell dyscrasia and peripheral neuropathy with monoclonal antibody to peripheral nerve myelin. N. Engl. J. Med. 303, 618–621.

Lindvall, Q. and Bjorklund, A. (1978). Organization of catecholamine neurons in the rat central nervous system. In Handbook of Psychopharmacology, Vol. IX, L.L. Iversen, S.D. Iversen, and S.H. Snyder, Eds. New York, Plenum, pp. 139–231.

Lohrmann, H.P., Novikivs, L., and Graw, R.G. (1974). Cellular interactions in the proliferative response of human T and B lymphocytes to phytomitogens and allogenic lymphocytes. J. Exp. Med. 139, 1553–1567.

McKenzie, J.L. and Fabre, J.W. (1981). Human Thy-l unusual localization and possible functional significance in lymphoid tissues. J. Immunol. 126, 843–850.

Mackenzie, M.R. and Fudenberg, H.H. (1972). Macroglobulinemia: An analysis of forty patients. Blood 39, 874–889.

Macmanus, J.P., Bounton, A.L., Whittfield, J.F., Gillian, D.J., and Isaacs, R.J. (1975). Acetylcholine-induced initiation of thymic lymphoblast DNA synthesis and proliferation. J. Cell Physiol. 85, 321–330.

Malamud, N. (1972). Neuropathology of organic brain syndromes associated with aging. In Advances in Behavioral Biology, Vol. III. C.M. Gaitz, Ed. New York, Plenum Press.

Mann, D.M.A., Lincoln, J., Yates, P.O., Stamp, J.E., and Toper, S. (1980). Changes in the monoamine containing neurons of the human CNS in senile dementia. Br. J. Psychiat. 136, 533–541.

Melmon, K.L., Bourne, H.R., Weinstein, Y., Shearer, G.M., Kram, J., and Bauminger, S. (1974). Hemolytic plaque formation by leukocytes *in vitro*. J. Clin. Invest. 53, 13–21.

Miles, K., Quintans, J., Chelmicka-Schorr, E., and Arnason, B.G.W. (1981). The sympathetic nervous system modulates antibody response to thymus-independent antigens. J. Neuroimmunol. 1, 101–105.

Miller, A.E., Neighbour, A., Katzman, R., Aronson, M., and Lipkowitz, R. (1981). Immunological studies in senile dementia of the Alzheimer type: Evidence for enhanced suppressor cell activity. Ann. Neurol. 10, 506–510.

Miyakawa, T., Sumiyoshi, S., Murayama, E., and Deshimaru, M. (1974). Ultrastructure of capillary plaque-like degeneration in senile dementia: Mechanism of amyloid production. Acta Neuropath. (Berl.) 29, 229–236.

Monjan, A.A. and Collector, M.I. (1976). Stress-induced modulation of the immune response. Science 196, 307–308.

Muramoto, O., Sugishita, M., Sugita, H., and Toyokura, Y. (1979). Effect of physostigmine on constructional and memory tasks in Alzheimer's disease. Arch. Neurol. 36, 501–503.

Naeim, F. and Walford, R.L. (1980). Disturbance of redistribution of surface membrane receptors on peripheral mononuclear cells of patients with Down's syndrome and of aged individuals. J. Gerontol. 35:650–655.

Newsom-Davis, J., Lang, B., Wray, D., Murray, N., Vincent, A., and Gwilt, M. (1982). Clinical and experimental evidence for a humoral factor in the myasthenic (Eaton-Lambert) syndrome. Neurology 32(2), A 221–222.

Noronha, A.B.C., Antel, J.P., Roos, R.P., and Arnason, B.G.W. (1980). Changes in concanavalin A capping of human lymphocytes with age. Mech. Ageing Dev. 12, 331–337.

Ogden, B.E. and Hill, H.R. (1980). Histamine regulates lymphocyte mitogenic responses through activation of specific H_1 and H_2 histamine receptors. Immunology 41, 107–114.

Oger, J., Szuchet, S., Antel, J.P., and Arnason, B.G.W. (1982). A monoclonal antibody against human T suppressor lymphocytes bind specifically to the surface of cultured oligodendrocytes. Nature 295, 66–68.

Paladini, G., Sala, P.G., and Santini, P.A. (1980). Benign Bence Jones gammopathy. Acta Haemat. 63, 241–246.

Peters, B.H. and Levin, H. (1979). Effects of physostigmine and lecithin on memory in Alzheimer disease. Ann. Neurol. 6, 219–221.

Polyak, A.I., Rumbesht, L.M., and Sinichkin, A.A. (1969). Antibody synthesis following electrocoagulation of the posterior hypothalamic nucleus. Zh. Microbiol. Epidemiol. Immunobiol. 46(3), 52–56.

Powers, J.M. and Spicer, S.S. (1977). Histochemical similarity of senile plaque amyloid to Apudamyloid. Virch. Arch. (Path. Anat.) 376, 107–115.

Powers, J.M., Schlaepfer, W.W., Willingham, M.C., and Hall, B.J. (1981). An immunoperoxidase study of senile cerebral amyloidosis with pathogenetic considerations. J. Neuropathol. Exp. Neurol. 40, 592–612.

Probst, A., Heitz, U., and Ulrich, J. (1980). Histochemical analysis of senile plaque amyloid and amyloid angiopathy. Virch. Arch. (Path. Anat.) Histol. 388, 327–334.

Propp, R.P., Means, E., Deibel, R., et al. (1975). Waldenstrom's macroglobulinemia and neuropathy: Deposition of M-component on myelin sheath. Neurology (Minneap.) 25, 980–988.

Radl, J. and Hollander, C.F. (1974). Homogeneous immunoglobulins in sera of mice during aging. J. Immunol. 112, 2271–2272.

Radl, J., Sepers, J.M., Skvaril, F., Morell, A., and Hymans, W. (1975). Immunoglobulin patterns in humans over 95 years of age. Clin. Exp. Immunol. 22, 84–90.

Reif, A.E. and Allen, J.M.V. (1964). The AKR thymic antigen and its distribution in leukemias and nervous tissue. J. Exp. Med. 120, 413.

Richman, D.P. and Arnason, B.G.W. (1979). Nicotinic acetylcholine receptors: Evidence for a functionally distinct receptor on human lymphocytes. Proc. Natl. Acad. Sci. USA 76, 4632–4635.

Richman, D.P., Antel, J.P., Burns, J.B., and Arnason, B.G.W. (1982). Nicotinic acetylcholine receptor on human lymphocytes. Ann. N.Y. Acad. Sci. 377, 427–435.

Rinvay, B., Bergman, S., Shinitzky, M., and Globerson, A. (1980). Correlation between membrane viscosity, serum cholesterol, lymphocyte activation and aging in man. Mechan. of Aging Develop. 12, 119–126.

Roberts-Thomson, F., Whittingham, S., Youngchaiyud, U., and Mackay, I.R. (1974). Aging, immune response and mortality. Lancet ii, 368–370.

Schocken, D.D. and Roth, G.W. (1977). Reduced B-adrenergic receptor concentrations in aging man. Nature (Lond.) 267, 856–858.

Shu, S., Nisengard, R.J., Hale, W.L., and Beutner, E.H. (1975). Incidence and titers of antinuclear, antismooth muscle and other autoantibodies in blood donors. J. Lab. Clin. Med. 86, 259–265.

Stefansson, K., Antel, J.P., Oger, J., Burns, J., Noronha, A.B.C., Roos, R.P., Arnason, B.G.W., and Gudmundsson, G. (1980). Autosomal dominant cerebrovascular amyloidosis: Properties of peripheral blood lymphocytes. Ann. Neurol. 7, 436–440.

Stefansson, K., Antel, J.P., Wollmann, R.L., Levin, K.H., Larson, R., and Arnason, B.G.W. (1981b). Anti-neural antibodies in serum of a patient with Hodgkin's disease and cerebellar ataxia. Neurology 31, 163.

Stefansson, K., Wollmann, R.L., and Arnason, B.G.W. (1981a). S-100 protein in an insulinoma accompanied by peripheral neuropathy. J. Neuropath. Exp. Neurol. 40, 320.

Stefansson, K., Wollmann, R.L., and Moore, B.W. (1982a). Distribution of the S-100 protein outside the central nervous system in humans and rats. Brain Res. 234, 309–317.

Stefansson, K., Wollmann, R.L., Moore, B.W., and Arnason, B.G.W. (1982b). S-100 protein in human chondrocytes. Nature 295, 63–64.

Stein, M., Schiavi, R.C., and Camerino, M. (1976). Influence of brain and behavior on the immune system. Science 191, 435–440.

Stone, M.J. and Frenkel, E.P. (1975). The clinical spectrum of light chain myeloma: A study of 35 patients with special reference to the occurrence of amyloidosis. Am. J. Med. 58, 601–619.

Strom, T.B., Carpenter, C.B., Garavoy, M.R., Austen, K.F., Merill, J.P., and Kaliner, M. (1973). The modulating influence of cyclic nucleotides upon lymphocyte-mediated cytotoxicity. J. Exp. Med. 138, 381–395.

Swash, M., Perrin, J., and Schwartz, M.S. (1979). Significance of immunoglobulin deposition in peripheral nerve in neuropathies associated with paraproteinemia. J. Neurol., Neurosurg., Psychiat. 42, 179–183.

Sweet, D.L., Variakojis, D., Antel, J., and Kluskens, L. (in press). Multicentric giant lymph node hyperplasia, pseudotumor cerebri, neuropathy and dysproteinemia: A new clinicopathologic entity. Blood

Szentivanyi, A. and Filipp, G. (1958). Anaphylaxis and the nervous system. Parts II and IV. Ann. Allergy 16, 143–151, 389–392.

Tam, C.F. and Walford, R.L. (1980). Alterations in cyclic nucleotides and cyclase-specific activities in T lymphocytes of aging normal humans and patients with Down's syndrome. J. Immunol. 125, 1665–1670.

Tavolato, B. and Argentiero, V. (1979). Immunological deficiency in the Down's syndrome: Importance of the age factors. In Humoral Immunity in Neurological Diseases. D. Karcher, A. Lowenthal, and A.D. Strosberg, Eds. Plenum Press, New York, pp. 645–652.

Terry, R.D., Gonatas, N.K., and Weiss, M. (1964). Ultrastructural studies in Alzheimer's presenile dementia. Amer. J. Path. 44, 269–297.

Terry, W.D., Page, D.L., Kimura, S., Isobe, T., Osserman, E.F., and Glenner, G.G. (1973). Structural identity of Bence Jones and amyloid fibril proteins in a patient with plasma cell dyscrasia and amyloidosis. J. Clin. Invest. 52, 1276–1281.

Torack, R.M. and Lynch, R.G. (1981). Cytochemistry of brain amyloid in adult dementia. Acta. Neuropath. 53, 189–196.

Trotter, J.L., Engel, W.K., and Ignaczak, T.F. (1977). Amyloidosis with plasma cell dyscrasia: An overlooked cause of adult onset sensorimotor neuropathy. Arch. Neurol. 34, 209–214.

Trotter, J.L., Hendin, B.A., and Osterland, C.K. (1976). Cerebellar degeneration with Hodgkin's disease: An immunological study. Arch. Neurol. 33, 660–661.

Victor, M., Banker, B.Q., and Adams, R.D. (1958). The neuropathy of multiple myeloma. J. Neurol. Neurosurg. Psychiat. 21, 73–88.

Vuia, O. (1978). Paraproteinosis and amyloidosis of the cerebral vessels and senile plaques. J. Neurol. Sci. 39, 37–46.

Waldenström, J.G. (1973). Benign monoclonal gammapathies. In Multiple Myeloma and Related Disorders, Vol. 1. A. Azar and M. Potter, Eds. Hagerstown, Md., Harper & Row, p. 247.

Weiss, B., Greenberg, L., and Cantor, E. (1979). Age-related alterations in the development of adrenergic denervation supersensitivity. Fed. Proc. 38, 1915–1921.

Whitehouse, P.J., Price, D.L., Struble, R.G., Clark, A.W., Coyle, J.T., and Delong, M.R. (1982). Alzheimer's disease and senile dementia: Loss of neurons in the basal forebrain. Science 215, 1237–1239.

Wilkinson, P.C. (1964). Serological findings in carcinomatous neuropathy. Lancet i, 1301–1303.

Wilkinson, P.C. and Zeromski, J. (1965). Immunofluorescent detection of antibodies against neurons in sensory carcinomatous neuropathy. Brain 88, 529–538.

Williams, L.T., Snyderman, R., and Lefkow-
  itz, R.J. (1976). Identification of B-adrenergic receptors in human lymphocytes by
  (-)^{3}H alprenolol binding. J. Clin. Invest.
  57, 149–155.
Wisniewski, H.M., Bruce, M.E., and Fraser,
  H. (1975). Infectious etiology of neuritis
  (senile) plaques in mice. Science 190,
  1108–1110.
Wolstenholme, G.E.W. and O'Connor, M.
  (1970). Alzheimer's Disease and Related
  Conditions. London, Churchill.
Wrabetz, L.G., Antel, J.P., Oger, J., Arnason,
  B.G.W., Goust, J-M., and Hopper, J.E.
  (in press). Age-related changes in *in vitro*
  immunoglobulin secretion: Comparison of
  response to T-dependent and T-indepen-
dent polyclonal activators. Cellular Immunology.
Wright, J.R., Calkins, E., Breen, W.J., Stolte,
  G., and Schulte, R.T. (1969). Relationship
  of amyloid to aging. Review of the literature and systematic study of 83 patients
  derived from a general hospital population. Medicine 48(1), 39–60.
Yates, C.M., Ritchie, J.M., Simpson, J., Maloney, A.F.J., and Gordon, A. (1981). Noradrenaline in Alzheimer-type dementia and
  Down's syndrome. Lancet, 39–40.
Zeromski, J. (1970). Immunological findings of
  sensory carcinomatous neuropathy: Application of peroxidase labeled antibody.
  Clin. Exp. Immunol. 6, 633–637.

II
Clinical Examination
and Diagnostic Studies

5. Neurological Evaluation of the Elderly Patient

DAVID A. DRACHMAN

RANDALL R. LONG

Among the elderly, symptoms and signs of neurological dysfunction are commonplace. Impairment of memory, intellect, strength, sensation, balance, and coordination are well known. Caird (1966) and others (Akhtar et al., 1973; Broe et al., 1976) have shown that neurological disorders are the most common causes of disability in the elderly, accounting for almost 50% of the incapacitation beyond the age of 65 and over 90% of serious dependency. (In addition to the references cited later in the chapter, see Brewis et al., 1966; Gilbert and Levee, 1971; Jerome, 1959; Kinsbourne, 1977.)

Why should the nervous system, more than any other system, be susceptible to debilitating deterioration with age? In large part, this is because the nervous system consists of exclusively postmitotic neuronal elements; every neuron present in the octogenarian was present at the time of birth (Strehler, 1976). We know less about the persistence of neural connections and their replaceability during life, although axons and dendrites are likely to be relatively permanent components of the nervous system (Raisman, 1978). Strehler (1976) has pointed out the teleological advantage of this arrangement: it permits an individual to retain information that has been acquired. If neural elements were constantly replaced, accumulation of memories would be markedly diminished.

One of the consequences of this arrangement is the inevitable deterioration of the system over time. Elements that wear out cannot be replaced, nor can those that are damaged. Even in a system with a large "safety factor," or excess of neural elements, the ability to compensate for losses—either present or past—declines as its reserve diminishes (Laurence and Stein, 1978; Stein and Firl, 1976).

For these reasons, neurological deterioration in the elderly should be viewed as the cumulative summation of four factors:

1. "Normal" neuronal attrition (involution over time)
2. Previous neural damage
3. Decline in neural reserve, or "plasticity"
4. Specific disease(s) of the nervous system present at the time of evaluation

Among individuals, the rate of involutional change, the burden of previous damage, the amount of neural reserve, and the presence and extent of nervous system disease may vary considerably. Clinical neurological disorders become evident when any or all of these factors reach the threshold of clinical deficit. In practice, this threshold may depend not only upon the initial endowment of the individual and the summation of his neural losses, but also upon the demands of the particular situation in which a deficit becomes apparent. Thus, a clinically apparent deficit may be the result of rapidly advancing involution alone; specific disease alone (e.g., a major stroke); previous traumatic injury combined with "normal" involution; or a mild new disease process (e.g., a vascular lacune) combined with other factors; etc.

Some of the difficulties in assessing the neurological status of the elderly are due to the simultaneous operation of multiple, sometimes unknown, factors in producing clinical deterioration. These include variability in the rate of involution among different individuals; injuries to the nervous system that were unnoticed or forgotten; and the differing physical and mental challenges to aged individuals.

In approaching the neurological problems of the elderly, physicians must adopt diagnostic strategies appropriate to both the variations in individual performance and the multiple factors contributing to deficits. First, they must be able to distinguish between *normal* and *abnormal* neurological function commensurate with the individual's age. Second, they must determine whether the neurological impairment is the result of a *specific disease state, neural attrition, previous damage,* or *loss of neural reserve*. Finally, they must attempt to identify those features of the patient's condition that contribute to his or her disability in an effort to modify as many of the problems that limit function as possible.

Normal and Abnormal Functions: Health and Disease

"Normal" function, most simply, is regarded as the mean performance on a given test, ±2 standard deviations, for an individual of a given age. As reasonable as this concept of *normal*—that is, equivalent to average—may seem, it presents many problems (Andres, 1967). First, there is much scatter of function in the aged compared with young adults, leading to a less homogeneous pattern of performance. Certain findings commonly seen in the aged (e.g., decreased glucose tolerance; diminished ankle jerk reflexes) are considered to be abnormalities or even diseases in the young. Indeed, the fact that 75% of individuals over the age of 65 have at least one serious chronic illness (Confrey and Goldstein, 1960) makes it impossible to equate normal (average) function in the elderly with a state of health or the absence of disease.

The difficulties arising from this concept of normality have led to two other definitions of normal function. The first of these restricts the definition of *normal* to the average performance of *healthy* aged individuals; that is, those functioning independently, who are free of known disease. Although a useful compromise, the difficulty of defining a healthy person and the circular, self-fulfilling nature of the definition give it limited value. The second defines *normal* function in the elderly as equivalent to *ideal* function for all healthy adults. Viewed in this way, findings that occur even quite frequently in an aged population may be considered *abnormal* if they fail to meet some definable minimum standard.

All three concepts of normality must be considered in order to evaluate the neurological status of aged individuals and to attempt to distinguish neurological *disease* from *non-disease*. The physician must recognize that in some aged patients normal involution masquerades as a disease state; in others, actual disease is concealed in the guise of the normal aging process. Since specific diseases are often treatable, whereas involution usually is not, this distinction is of central importance in the neurological assessment.

The Neurological Evaluation

The neurological evaluation of any adult, young or old, includes a history, the neurological examination, and a series of laboratory tests. These are well described elsewhere and will not be given in detail here (Adams and Victor, 1981; De Jong, 1969; Mayo Clinic and Mayo Foundation, 1976). However, in the elderly, a different range of problems is likely to be encountered, and the question of the clinical significance of neurological symptoms or findings becomes more difficult to resolve. The implications of a numb hand or of Babinski signs are therefore quite different in the 75-year-old than in the 25-year-old.

Neurological History

In addition to recording each neurological complaint and obtaining the standard historical information related to the present illness, it is important to document carefully the rate of decline of function, to assess *the pace of involutional processes,* or to diagnose a new neurological disease. A past history of neurological injury (e.g., head trauma, stroke, encephalitis) establishes the extent of *previous neural losses.* Finally, a review of the neurological system should be carried out; it should cover the use of alcohol or other drugs, episodes of loss of consciousness, and specific inquiries into cranial nerve, motor, and sensory functions (Table 5-1).

In obtaining the neurological history of an aged patient, the physician must be prepared to deal with a number of special pitfalls. Largely, these derive from the plethora of neurological symptoms "normally" seen in the elderly, making it

Table 5-1. Review of the neurological system.

Head and Mental Function
    Headaches
    Dizziness
    Mental or memory change
    Cerebrovascular accidents
    Head trauma
    Seizures
    Loss of consciousness
    Alcoholism

Cranial Nerves
    Loss of smell
    Blurring or loss of vision
    Diplopia
    Numbness or weakness of the face
    Hearing loss, tinnitus
    Difficulty in swallowing or speaking

Motor and Coordination
    Difficulty in walking
    Clumsiness
    Weakness of an arm or a leg

Reflexes
    Involuntary spasms of legs

Sensation
    Numbness of or abnormal sensation in limbs

difficult for both the physician and the patient to distinguish between involutional inevitabilities and real disease. Some of the problems in making this distinction are listed in Table 5-2.

1. *Paucity of accurate history due to memory loss.* Particularly in the dementing disorders, but also in "benign senescent forgetfulness," the patient himself may be either unaware of his intellectual deficits or may deny them, and the history is then obtainable only from the patient's family (Paulson, 1977). Of course, other aspects of the neurological history also become unreliable, and the physician cannot depend on reported drug usage or the absence of headache, gait disturbance, etc. Paradoxically, those patients who do complain of memory loss or of intellectual impairment are less likely to be significantly demented; more often they are in a depressive state.

2. *Varying expectations for the aged.* Because families' expectations of elderly patients' performance may vary widely, their judgment regarding intactness or degree of impairment may be misleading. The patient who is "very sharp" may be considered so because he remembers his grandchildren's names, whereas the aged person with a "poor memory" may no longer be able to make as astute business decisions as he once did, though otherwise he is functioning at a high level. For this reason, it is especially important to ask questions ranging from the ability of the patient to care for his personal needs to his competence in playing bridge or discussing world events. *Impairment of memory* is most frequently recognized by both patients and their families as the initial deficit

Table 5-2. Pitfalls in the neurological history of the aged.

1. Paucity of accurate history due to memory loss
2. Varying expectations for the aged
3. Sudden change versus revealing events
4. Denial; excessive somatic concern
5. Impact of environmental changes
6. Activity decline versus depression
7. Sensory deprivation

in most forms of dementia. If it is determined that a degree of dementia exists, additional questions must be asked to help clarify the nature of the underlying disorder.

3. *Sudden change versus "revealing events."* Ordinarily, a sudden change in neurological function is an appropriate cause for concern and medical investigation. In the elderly, however, gradual changes may be suddenly brought to the patient's or family's attention when the circumstances change. A slowly dementing patient may abruptly become totally disoriented on vacation in an unfamiliar place; one whose balance has gradually declined may begin to fall when he must walk to the store, following the death of his wife, to shop. Close inquiry is needed to determine the true rate of onset of such events.

4. *Excessive somatic concerns versus denial of illness.* These polar approaches become more confusing as disability and disease increase with age. Perfectionists report every decline as a probable disease requiring medical investigation; however, those who are too prepared for deterioration fail to regard even serious and debilitating disease as worthy of mention.

5. *Impact of environmental changes.* The resources of the elderly—personal, professional, social, and financial—modify the perception and effect of normal aging and disease. The octogenarian who moves to the Sunbelt may suddenly lose all his sources of support and knowledge of his environment acquired over a lifetime. Deprived of friends, family, and transportation, and with a diminished capacity to adapt readily, his minor disabilities become major obstacles to coping with his environment.

6. *Diminished activity versus depression.* Ordinarily decreased energy, interests, and activities; disordered sleep, bowel, and sexual function; and feelings of helplessness are regarded as evidence of depression. These complaints may be physiological in some elderly individuals. The line between appropriately decreased activity and psychopathological withdrawal is a fine one, and the distinc-

tion requires the physician's careful judgment.

7. *Sensory deprivation.* Loss of hearing, vision, and other senses are discussed below. The cumulative impact of *multisensory* isolation may have a global effect on the patient's capacity to absorb new information, in addition to the expected impairment of primary sensations. Frequently, the deaf may be regarded as demented, and those with visual impairments as having balance disorders.

Neurological Examination

In the neurological examination of the elderly patient, the physician assesses the integrity of the central and peripheral nervous system by the use of a standard series of maneuvers, described elsewhere (Adams and Victor, 1981; R. DeJong, 1969; Mayo Clinic and Mayo Foundation, 1976) (Table 5-3).

Assessment of the elderly patient requires that standards of performance be adjusted in accordance with the patient's age and that particular attention be given to certain areas. Areas of special interest are memory function; vision and hearing; gait; frontal release signs; axial and limb tone; diminution of ankle jerks and distal vibratory sensation; and presence of cervical or cranial arterial bruits. The significance of these findings is discussed below, and elsewhere in this volume.

Laboratory Studies

Table 5-4 lists a number of laboratory studies that are useful in the evaluation of aged patients with a variety of complaints. It is by no means complete, yet, even a superficial discussion of the techniques and interpretations is beyond the scope of this chapter. The tests listed provide the means of evaluating the anatomical integrity of the aged patient's nervous system, intellectual performance, hearing, visual acuity, cerebral blood flow, etc. Numerous other studies are often needed to evaluate the effects of the cardiac, renal, respiratory, and other systems on neurological functions.

Table 5-3. Examination of the nervous system.

Mental Status
State of consciousness
Orientation
Information
Memory
Calculation
Language function
Special testing for aphasia, apraxia, or agnosia

Cranial Nerves
Sense of smell
Visual acuity, visual fields, optic fundi, ocular motility, pupillary response
Facial sensation, corneal reflexes, jaw movement, jaw jerk
Facial movement and symmetry, taste
Hearing (air, bone conduction), gag reflex, swallowing, phonation
Sternocleidomastoid and trapezius movement
Tongue motion

Motor and Coordination
Gait, station, walking on heels and toes, tandem gait
Direct testing of strength, tone, and coordination in extremities

Reflexes
Deep tendon reflexes, plantar reflexes, abdominal reflexes

Sensation
Primary (touch, pinprick, vibration, and position sense)
Cortical (face-hand, double simultaneous stimulation, etc.)

Vascular
Carotid palpation, auscultation for bruits

Neurobiological Changes with Age

Clinically significant neurological changes occurring with age in an undiseased population can be attributed to neurobiological deterioration. Anatomical, biochemical, physiological, pharmacological, and support-system changes appear to underlie the progressive involution of the nervous system with age. Of all the changes, the anatomical have been most extensively studied and are best understood (Brody, 1975, 1976; Corsellis 1976; Terry and Wiesniewski, 1975, 1977; Tomlinson, 1977, 1980; Tomlinson and Henderson, 1976). Grossly, the weight of the brain declines with age, normally decreasing by about 10% from its maximum weight in early adult life to the ninth decade (Corsellis, 1976). There is enlargement of the ventricles and sulci, while both gray and white matter appear to decrease in volume. Neurons are said to be lost at the rate of approximately 50,000 per day. By the ninth decade, 30 to 50% of cortical neurons are lost in certain areas (Brody, 1955, 1975); brainstem neurons (with some ex-

ceptions) remain intact. It is not clear whether the dendritic branches of cortical neurons change significantly in normal aging. Scheibel et al. (Scheibel and Scheibel, 1975; Scheibel et al., 1975) have claimed that dendritic branches decrease both in number and extent, particularly the horizontal dendrites of the cortical pathways. Coleman, however, has shown that the dendritic arborizations of cortical neurons actually *increase* in normal old age (although declining in dementia) (Buell and Coleman, 1980). This issue and its implications for dysfunction of the aging brain remain to be resolved. Synaptic connections between neurons also decline in number, as demonstrated by the loss of both dendritic spines (Feldman, 1976) and synapses (Bondareff and Geinisman, 1976, Cragg, 1975). Senile plaques representing degraded dendrites and axons begin to appear with increasing frequency and in increasing numbers with advancing age, as do neurofibrillary tangles (Tomlinson, 1977; Tomlinson and Henderson, 1976). Selkoe et al. (1982) have recently shown that neurofibrillary tangles represent po-

Table 5-4. Neurological laboratory tests useful in the aged.

Neuroradiological Procedures
Non-invasive
CT scan
Radioisotope scan; isotope cisternography
Skull X-rays
Spine X-rays
Invasive
Angiogram
Myelogram

Electrophysiological Tests
Electroencephalogram
Electromyography; nerve conduction velocities
Audiometry
Electronystagmography

Psychometric Tests
WAIS
WMQ
MMPI
Rorschach
Reitan battery, etc.

Vascular Tests
Oculoplethysmography (OPG)
Phonoangiography
Ultrasound imaging

Neuro-Ophthalmological Tests
Visual acuity
Visual fields
Slit lamp

Lumbar Puncture

lymerized neurofilaments, comparable in some ways to the polymerization of protein that develops with advancing age in the eye (causing cataracts), in the skin and in red blood cells. It is by no means certain that loss of *cortical* neurons or their connections is directly responsible for decline in cognitive function, and there is some evidence that loss of neurons in the thalamus (Drachman et al., 1982), nucleus basalis (Whitehouse et al., 1982), locus ceruleus (Bondareff et al., 1982), and other subcortical locations (Albert, 1978) may account for some or much of the cognitive decline. The total number of motor units (anterior horn cells of the spinal cord and their related muscle fibers) decreases, and the number of muscle fibers declines as well. It is of interest that peripheral nerve fibers remain essentially unchanged with advancing age (Gutmann and Hanzlikova, 1972).

The biochemical basis for neurological deterioration is less well understood (see Bowen, et al., 1977a,b; Iqbal et al., 1976; McNamara and Appel, 1977; Meier-Ruge et al., 1975; Orgel, 1963; Selkoe et al., 1982; Shelanski, 1976). It has been hypothesized that neuronal proteins are inaccurately synthesized due to "transcription failure"; i.e., errors in copying from DNA to ribosomal RNA (Orgel, 1963). When important structural protein "building blocks" are inaccurately produced, the structure of the nerve cells becomes degraded (Meier-Ruge et al., 1976). Other biochemical mechanisms deteriorate as well; these include diminution of energy metabolism and the accumulation of lipofuscin. Physiologically, there is evidence that axoplasmic flow decreases with age (Geinisman, et al., 1977). Cerebral blood flow and cerebral metabolic rate of oxygen diminish, although not remarkably (Thompson, 1976). Central synaptic delays in reflex arcs are increased in the elderly (Botwinick, 1975), and evoked potential responses have prolonged latencies (Celesia and Daly, 1977). In aged subjects, the overall amount of spontaneous physical activity is reduced, a clinical observation that has been reproduced by determining "activity levels" in aged versus young rats (Gutmann and Hanzlikova, 1972). Pharmacological changes occur with aging, but in many cases only indirect measures of neurotransmitter function have been carried out in detail. It is known that cortical cholinergic receptors decrease with age (White et al., 1977), and choline acetyltransferase (ChAT) decreases in the very aged and in Alzheimer's dementia (Carlsson, 1981; Russor et al., 1981). The decline in cholinergic neural function has been shown to be closely related to impairment of cognitive function (Drachman, 1978; Drachman and Glosser, 1981). Enzymes involved in catecholamine and GABA synthesis diminish with age (McGeer and McGeer, 1976), whereas monoamine oxidase, which is concerned with catecholamine degradation, increases (Nies et al., 1973); it is not surprising that catecholamine levels decrease in the basal ganglia. Since the nervous system depends upon other organs for life support, it is important to note that there is also diminution of a wide variety of other functions, from cardiac output to basal metabolic rate.

Neurology of the "Normal" Aged in the Absence of Disease

As a result of these involutional processes, a variety of neurological changes occur in the absence of disease. Some are clinically evident to the patient; others may be detected only by the examining neurologist. Not only is the midpoint of the normal distribution curve shifted in the elderly, but the variance seems to increase considerably (Miles, 1931). As a result, the separation between the low end of normal function and a disease-induced abnormality becomes indistinct. The neurologist must often decide whether his findings represent a disease or simple involution, based on the context in which the signs appear. Thus, Babinski signs may be seen in the absence of disease in the elderly, but if they occur asymmetrically, and in the presence of weakness, they are most likely part of a disease process rather than

merely involution. It is in this light that neurological changes in the elderly should be interpreted.

Clinical Changes

MENTAL STATUS

Many elderly individuals complain of impairment of memory (Kahn et al., 1975). This complaint may actually include other disorders of cognitive function (Horn, 1975), but it is difficult for most patients to frame complaints about such aspects of mental performance as problem-solving. Immediate memory tends to be spared in the aged, as is retrieval by category; however, the ability to store new information (acquisition) clearly proceeds at a slower pace in the elderly (Caird, 1966; Drachman and Leavitt, 1972; Gilbert, 1941, 1973; Kral, 1966; Schneider et al., 1975). There is still some controversy as to whether the difficulty lies in retrieval of newly learned information (Laurence, 1967; Schonfield, 1967) or in its storage. The latter seems more likely (Drachman and Leavitt, 1972). The solving of complex novel problems (Schaie and Gribbin, 1975) and rapid responses under time constraints (Botwinick, 1975; Jones, 1959; Welford, 1959) are also impaired in the normal aged. *Fluid intelligence*—the type required for solving novel problems—is more often impaired than *crystallized intelligence*—the manipulation of previously learned information (Horn, 1975). Many standard tests have been used to measure intellectual function in both aged and young adults; the more "difficult" ones (Reitan, 1967) tend to show the greatest differences. In the Wechsler adult intelligence scale, which has been perhaps most widely used, the subtests of the Performance scale are notably impaired, whereas those of the Verbal scale remain largely intact. Nonetheless, the extent to which the "cerebral horsepower" of the aged is diminished overall is illustrated by the fact that, at age 75, one need obtain only about one-half as many correct answers on the age-corrected scale to achieve an IQ of 100, as at age 21! (Wechsler, 1955). Other observations indicate that the aged have diminished energy, tend to be cautious, and show decreased initiative (Botwinick, 1975).

It is often valuable, in assessing the aged patient's mental function, to observe both his performance in direct tests of mental status and his ability to function operationally within his own setting. Thus, the patient should be able to manage his personal, family, and financial affairs; to maintain knowledge of world events; and to keep up appropriately with his contemporaries in conversation, card games, etc. Any significant change in interactions with close family members is also noteworthy; the previously dominant husband who now turns to his wife for answers to questions, no longer trusting his memory or judgment, exemplifies this change. Finally, it is important to recognize that *depression,* common in the elderly, may often present as a cognitive disorder (pseudodementia). A high index of suspicion should be maintained for this functional disorder (Kiloh, 1961).

In many instances when the extent of mental deterioration, or its absence, requires documentation, it is useful to obtain a battery of psychometric tests as objective measures. In addition to the WAIS, the Wechsler Memory Quotient, Bender-Gestalt, Raven's Matrices, Trailmaking tests, Halstead-Wepman and Benton Visual Retention tests may be of value in assessing cognitive capacity and performance; the MMPI, Beck Depression Scale, and Rorschach and others are of value in diagnosing affective disorders (Wells and Buchanan, 1977). Reitan (1967) has developed a standard battery of tests that have proven of value in assessing cognitive functions. Compared with these tests, the clinical impression of the skilled physician may be, paradoxically, both cruder and more subtle. A skillful interview and mental status examination may detect minor disorders that affect objective tests minimally, if at all; yet it may miss surprisingly gross deficits of isolated cognitive functions in patients whose alertness and energy is retained.

SLEEP PATTERNS

The elderly frequently complain of insomnia or disrupted sleep and often do experience a change in sleep patterns. Typically the total sleep time per night does not change but aged individuals spend more time awake in bed than do young adults, and they awaken more frequently (Feinberg, 1976). The percent time spent in various EEG-determined sleep stages shifts with age, delta-wave deep sleep (stage 4) decreasing and stage 3 increasing. There is probably no significant change in the number or duration of REM cycles (Williams et al., 1974), although some studies have suggested a decrease in REM sleep.

CRANIAL NERVES

Significant alterations are seen in cranial sensory functions in the elderly. With age, impairment of visual accommodation for near objects is nearly universal; distant vision also requires corrective lenses by age 70 in most individuals (Botwinick, 1975). Dark adaptation diminishes with age (Weiss, 1959), and greater illumination is needed for accurate vision (Weale, 1965). Yellowing of the lens impairs color vision for the blue end of the spectrum (Gilbert, 1957). Centrally, visual evoked responses are delayed, suggesting slowing in the central visual pathways (Celesia and Daly, 1977). Pupillary responses are diminished or even absent in the elderly, and pupil size decreases, on the average (Howell, 1949; Weiss, 1959). Ocular motility tends to be slowed, and upward gaze is often limited. *Perception* of visual stimuli also diminishes in the elderly: critical flicker fusion frequency declines with age (Weiss, 1959), and embedded figures are less easily extracted from confusing pictures (Basowitz and Korchin, 1957). Hearing is similarly diminished in the aged, beginning about age 50 (Weiss, 1959). High frequencies are chiefly affected, and the suggestion has been advanced that this may be due to acoustic trauma suffered over a lifetime (Rosen et al., 1964). Dichotic auditory stimuli are less often correctly identified simultaneously (Drachman, 1977; Drachman et al., 1980); this observation suggests that central processing of auditory information becomes limited with advancing age. Diminution of the senses of taste and smell has been noted, but is less well documented (Botwinick, 1975; Weiss, 1959). Impairment of other cranial nerve functions may be seen with specific disease entitics, but is not common in the normal aging process. Occasionally, it may be difficult to distinguish between neurogenic dysarthria and that due to oral pathology (ill-fitting dentures, for example).

MOTOR SYSTEM

Second to impairment of mental function, deterioration of gait and motility are the most frequent neurological concomitants of the aging process (Hobson and Pemberton, 1955). The confident stride of youth changes to a hesitant, broad-based, small-stepped gait that has many of the characteristics of incipient Parkinsonism: stooped posture, diminished armswing, "en bloc" turns (Barbeau, 1973; Critchley, 1956). The demarcation between this gait change and various clinical disorders described below may be slight, although from a pragmatic viewpoint, it is the ability to walk without serious limitations or falling that distinguishes dysfunction from a normal aged gait. This change is believed to be due to central, probably extrapyramidal, deterioration (Barbeau, 1973), since the peripheral changes seen in normal aging—a minor decrease in nerve conduction velocity, no change in anterior horn cells, decrease in muscle mass (Gutmann and Hanzlikova, 1972)—are not sufficient to account for the disability. Tremor, although often regarded as a normal concomitant of the aging process, will be discussed later; its infrequency—less than 2% of the elderly (Hobson and Pemberton, 1955)—suggests that it should be regarded as neurological dysfunction. Increased muscle tone is often seen (Critchley, 1956); this may be in the form of mild axial rigidity, slight limb rigidity (resistance to passive stretch), or mild paratonic rigidity, usually in association with other evidence of frontal lobe signs. The role of mechanical changes involving arthritic joints, inelastic tendons or ligaments and other musculoskeletal restraints is difficult to assess; undoubtedly they contribute in a significant way to the restricted motility of the elderly (Critchley, 1956; Hobson and Pemberton, 1955).

REFLEXES

The reflex change most commonly noted in the aged is diminution or absence of the ankle jerks, which may occur in 10% of patients (Hobson and Pemberton, 1955). Whether this reflects a simple degenerative change or any of a variety of neuropathies (e.g., diabetic) is uncertain. However, the finding may occur in the absence of a typical peripheral neuropathy. Plantar reflexes may be neutral or extensor in about 5% of the aged (Hobson and Pemberton, 1955), and superficial abdominal reflexes are often absent. This latter finding is often attributed to obesity, abdominal surgery, or multiparity (Critchley, 1956). Suck and grasp reflexes, often regarded as signs of general cerebral or frontal lobe damage, occur in many elderly patients; and the snout reflex, a "corticobulbar" sign, is also frequently present (Paulson, 1977).

SENSATION

Vibratory sensation is regularly diminished or lost in the lower extremities, increasing from about a tenth of individuals at age 60 to a third to a half beyond age 75 (Hobson and Pemberton, 1955). An increase in the thresholds for touch and pinprick may be found, but this is not ordinarily present at the level of clinical testing. This dimunition may be due to changes in skin and connective tissue (Weiss, 1959). The face–hand test, a measure of cortical perceptual ability, may show extinction of the hand stimulus in the elderly (Bender et al., 1951). Other measures of cortical perception (stereognosis, graphesthesia, double simultaneous stimulation, etc.) ordinarily remain intact.

Laboratory Changes

ELECTROENCEPHALOGRAPHIC CHANGES

During normal aging, slowing of the background rhythm in the EEG characteristically occurs with a shift of the mean alpha frequency from 11 to 12 Hz to 7 to 8 Hz

(Wilson et al., 1977). In addition, temporal theta activity increases, particularly on the left side, and sharp waves may be seen in the same regions. By the age of 65, these findings are present in more than 50% of otherwise normal subjects. Drachman and Hughes (1971) have found that in normal "healthy" aged volunteer subjects, temporal sharp and slow activity correlates significantly with the psychological evidence of cognitive deterioration, while not reflecting specific disorders of the underlying hippocampal complexes.

COMPUTERIZED AXIAL TOMOGRAPHY

The CT scan shows mild enlargement of the ventricular system and widening of the sulci with advancing age (Pear, 1977; Lowry et al., 1977). The CT scan is useful in determining whether the degree of atrophy is excessive and likely to be related to dementia, although there is considerable overlap in the CT findings between normal and demented patients. In one study, for example, 60% of demented patients showed atrophy, whereas 15% of normal aged patients showed the same degree of change on the CT scan (Huckman et al., 1975). See Freedman et al., Chapter 7 for a detailed discussion. The CT scan remains of great value in the detection of destructive or space-occupying lesions in the aged patient.

Neurological Dysfunction due to Involution: Disability without Disease

Even in the absence of specific disease states, normal attrition of neural function may lead to a significant degree of disability in some individuals. This is the no-man's land in the neurology of aging: a statistical inevitability situated between normal involution and specific disease. Several conditions are worth noting because of their frequency of occurrence in a non-diseased population; these include normal dementia, dizziness, gait disorders, and cervical spondylosis.

NORMAL DEMENTIA

Much has already been said about the cognitive changes occurring with normal aging. Here, it should be stressed that the condition is not always benign (Kral, 1962), even when it occurs in the absence of disease. In fact, the very question of where normal neuronal attrition ends and Alzheimer's disease begins, is exceedingly difficult—perhaps it is more a philosophical than a medical problem (Drachman, 1982a). Tomlinson and his colleagues have shown that the relationship between senile plaques and normal or impaired mental functions in the elderly is a quantitative one and that senile plaques and neurofibrillary tangles accumulate in increasing numbers with advancing age in a non-diseased population (Tomlinson, 1976; Tomlinson and Henderson, 1976). It is clear that some individuals at 65 are no longer able to compete intellectually with their younger colleagues; past 75, only the exceptional individual is still able to perform at an intellectual level that permits him to remain employed. Although not a specific disease state, the cognitive impairment may prove disabling in the context of the patient's usual social or occupational requirements; it may then be termed "normal dementia of aging."

DIZZINESS

Dizziness, an exceedingly frequent complaint in the elderly, is commonly the result of involutional changes involving multiple sensory modalities (Drachman and Hart, 1973). We have indicated elsewhere that normal spatial orientation requires accurate visual, vestibular, proprioceptive, tactile, and auditory perception (Drachman, 1982b). Impairment of several of these orienting functions is perceived by patients as "dizziness," an elusive complaint that results from the patient's uncertainty of his position or motion in space. The elderly individual complaining of dizziness typically walks with a broad-based unsteady gait, with particular difficulty in turning and in walking on uneven ground. Carrying a cane or holding someone's arm improves balance somewhat. This multi-sensory dizziness appears to result from a combination of diminished sensation in several spheres: visual, vestibular, cervical proprioceptive, and peripheral nerve modalities. Deficits may be the result of involutional changes occurring with age; it is only when several occur simultaneously that the patient complains of dizziness, rather than a primary sensory problem.

There are, of course, many other causes of dizziness in the aged. Visual distortion produced by supplementary lenses after cataract extraction produces spatial disorientation and dizziness in the aged. A mild degree of positional vertigo also occurs with increased frequency in the elderly. And, since postural blood pressure adjustments occur more slowly in the aged, transient orthostatic hypotension on rapidly arising is common. Finally, pathological causes of dizziness due to specific disease states are also frequent, ranging from Ménière's disorder to brain-stem cerebrovascular accidents.

DISORDERS OF GAIT

When disorders of gait interfere with the elderly patient's independence, the distinction between an involutional process and a specific disease state must be carefully considered. In the absence of specific disease, gait disturbances produce disability in 13% of an aged population (Akhtar et al., 1973). The combination of an extrapyramidal syndrome, Bruns' frontal lobe gait apraxia, multisensory dizziness, and mechanical impairment due to joint degeneration often leads to significant disability. The gait may have characteristics of each of the components: small steps, stooped posture, a broad base, loss of balance on turning, retropulsion, and an entalgic component. Added to this composite picture is the patient's acquired cautiousness, often developed as a result of frequent falls. Neurological examination may reveal increased axial and limb tone, grasp and suck reflexes, and Myerson's glabellar sign, as well as the features of multisensory dizziness described above.

Diagnostically, it is important to determine whether any aspect of this combination of conditions is due to a specific disease state. In particular, diseases of the frontal lobes (brain tumor, subdural hematoma), normal pressure hydrocephalus,

drug intoxication, and cerebellar disorders should be ruled out with appropriate studies. The course of the gait disturbance should be followed long enough to confirm that no additional disease process is evolving.

CERVICAL SPONDYLOSIS

Degenerative changes of the cervical spine and the resulting symptoms occur so commonly that they deserve mention in the neurological assessment of the aged. Radiologically, more than 80% of individuals over the age of 55 show evidence of cervical disc degeneration, and by age 75 the finding is virtually universal (Brain and Wilkinson, 1967). Osteoarthritic changes of the zygapophyseal joints are almost as common as disc disease. Roughly 50% of patients with evidence of cervical spondylosis may experience symptoms of local cervical pain, nerve root or spinal cord compression. In all, signs of cervical spinal cord compression are uncommon; but some degree of bony degeneration of the cervical spine and accompanying pain can be expected as a frequent consequence of aging.

Exaggerated Vulnerability

DRUG SENSITIVITY

Although toxic effects of drugs are recognized in all age groups, the elderly are especially susceptible to these side effects (Hollister, 1981).

Two major mechanisms account for this vulnerability:

1. Altered pharmacokinetics, with delayed drug metabolism or excretion
2. Enhanced response to effects of certain drugs due to involutional losses of particular neuronal elements

As an example of the first mechanism, the half-life of diazepam is normally 48 hours, but may extend to twice this in elderly individuals. Since drugs continue to accumulate for approximately four half-lives, the steady-state blood level in elderly patients may be much higher than in younger individuals, even when they are given the same dose, repeated at the same intervals. With diazepam, the maximum plasma level of drug may not be achieved until one to two weeks after treatment is begun, and seemingly innocuous individual doses may eventually produce dangerous sedation.

The second mechanism is reflected in the confusion and hallucinations sometimes produced in elderly patients by even small doses of anticholinergic medications. Involutional and other losses of cholinergic neurons make the remaining cholinergic elements more susceptible to the effects of any centrally active anticholinergic medications. Small doses of tricyclic antidepressants, antihistamines, and scopolamine produce confusional states in the aged by this mechanism.

HEAD TRAUMA

Head injuries of moderate or severe degree are much more likely to result in lasting and severe neurological impairment and cognitive deficits in the aged than in young adults (Overgaard et al., 1973; Jennett and Teasdale, 1981). Whereas loss of consciousness without focal neurological deficit is usually benign in young adults, it is likely to result in permanent cognitive impairment in those over 60. The increased susceptibility to permanent injury after head trauma reflects both a diminished "neural reserve" in the elderly and a decrease in "plasticity," the ability to recover function following a deficit (Laurence and Stein, 1978; Stein and Firl, 1976).

CONFUSIONAL STATES

Metabolic alterations of many sorts may impair memory and cognitive function in the elderly. Hyponatremia, uremia, and hepatic encephalopathy are well-known systemic disorders that may produce confusional states. Aged patients may become disoriented and confused, particularly at night ("sun-downing"), or following surgery, during febrile episodes, or with myocardial infarctions, for reasons that are not entirely clear. The relationship of the alteration of mental status to the underlying metabolic derangement should be kept in mind; when the underlying condition resolves, the patient's mental status should return to normal, or another cause must be sought.

Recognition of Neurological Disease in the Aged

Most often the recognition of real neurological disease in the aged presents little difficulty: paralysis of the limbs, loss of speech, or onset of severe tremor and rigidity are easily recognized by both patient and physician. Yet, with other less obvious complaints, the determination of significant neurological disease becomes far more difficult. Diseases affecting the elderly are discussed in detail elsewhere in this volume; this section points out certain complaints and findings that should be recognized as especially likely to be related to significant neurological disease (Table 5-5).

HEADACHES

New headaches occurring in aged patients should always be regarded seriously. Although lifelong muscle-contraction headaches often persist through old age, neither these headaches nor migraine headaches are likely to appear *de novo* past age 50. The physician must always be alert for intracranial space-occupying lesions, cranial arteritis, and cranial neuralgias. A full scale evaluation is necessary whenever an elderly individual first develops new headache.

"BLACKOUTS"

Episodes of loss or alteration of consciousness in the aged require careful evaluation.

Table 5-5. Significant neurological symptoms in the aged.

1. Headache
2. "Blackout" spells
3. Transient neurological event
4. Uncorrectible visual impairment
5. Numb hand/weak hand
6. Lethargy
7. Acute mental change
8. Focal neurological deficits

Even in those patients who "fainted in church as children," loss of consciousness may indicate cardiac arrhythmias, seizures, orthostatic hypotension, or posterior circulation ischemia.

TRANSIENT NEUROLOGICAL EVENTS

Brief episodes of visual loss, difficulty finding words, weakness of an arm or a leg, and other neurological symptoms clearly require an evaluation for transient ischemic events and focal seizure disorders.

IMPAIRED VISION

Whenever loss in visual acuity is not easily restored by a refractive correction or diagnosable through the ophthalmoscope, a disorder of the visual and occasionally oculomotor pathways should be considered.

NUMB HAND OR WEAK HAND

Numbness or weakness of a hand may occur transiently in normal people, particularly after sleeping in an unusual position. In the absence of a precipitating cause, if the duration exceeds an hour or is progressive, neurological disease, from cortex to peripheral nerves, must be considered. Brain tumors, strokes, cervical spondylosis, thoracic outlet syndromes, amyotrophic lateral sclerosis, and peripheral neuropathies may present this way.

LETHARGY

Although the elderly can be expected to nap more frequently than young adults, lethargy—particularly increasing drowsiness or falling asleep at inappropriate times—requires evaluation. Possibilities range from brain tumors or subdural hematomas to sleep apnea and drug toxicity.

ACUTE MENTAL CHANGE

Although mild and gradual decline of memory and cognitive function may be "normal," to some extent, the sudden decline of intellectual function requires thorough evaluation. Poorly localized strokes, meningitis, subdural hematomas, and drug intoxication may all present in this manner.

FOCAL NEUROLOGICAL DEFICITS

Focal, localized or lateralized neurological deficits are always of significance at any age. With or without a history of neurological disease, the finding of a mild hemiparesis with motor, reflex, and sensory changes demands investigation. The allowances made for neurological changes with aging, described above, never imply that the physician should accept focal neurological signs as a consequence of the normal aging process.

Assessment and Management of Neurological Disorders of the Aged

Unlike the situation in the healthy young adult, in whom neurological symptoms and signs generally indicate significant disease, special care and judgment are required for the assessment and management of neurological complaints and findings in the elderly. As already indicated, the neurological status of the aged patient reflects the summation of multiple processes: some due to specific disease, some the result of involutional changes; some that are curable or treatable, some that are not; some that can be named, some that are nameless. How should the physician respond to a confusing array of complaints and signs when the specific combination of findings is often unique to the individual's genetic background and life history, as well as his present disease state?

The purpose of the neurological assessment must be sharply focused: *First,* the identification of specific disease processes, particularly those that are treatable or curable; *second,* the explanation of abnormal neurological symptoms or signs; *third,* relief or reduction of disability, whatever the cause. A final goal is the careful observation of presently untreatable conditions to derive insights, where possible, into the mechanism of the disorder, for the development of future rational treatment.

A few examples may serve to illustrate these points: In the dementing disorders, the majority of disabled patients have a diagnosis of Alzheimer's disease and a second large group have arteriopathic (multi-infarct) dementia. Fewer than 25% of dementing disorders are due to treatable disease, and in some populations, fewer than 10%. How far should an investigation be carried out, when the probability of identifying a treatable disease, such as a subdural hematoma, normal pressure hydrocephalus, extrapyramidal dementia, or depression, is relatively small? Aside from the humanitarian considerations, the cost of caring for a single patient in a nursing home environment for several years far exceeds that of many well-planned clinical evaluations. The overall benefits of reasonable investigations of dementia are therefore substantial, even when many patients are found to have disappointingly untreatable conditions. It is likely that the chance of a successful outcome exceeds that of the patient who is comatose following cardiac resuscitation, again at a fraction of the cost.

Explanation of the cause of symptoms or signs is often of great value as well. For example, the concerned professional who is disabled by fears that his memory is declining at 60, may be restored to normal function by assurance (based on an adequate evaluation) that his mental function is still superior compared with his coevals and that he does not have a brain tumor or a dementing process.

The reduction of disability due to noncurable disease, involution, or both, is also important. In multisensory dizziness, for example, where the underlying neuropathy, cervical spondylosis, and vestibular impairments cannot be cured, patients may often be restored to independent function by attention to details: the use of a cervical collar to eliminate excessive mobility and false proprioceptive inputs; training in cane-trailing to substitute hand sensation for impaired lower extremity sensation; the use of contact lenses in patients who have undergone cataract extractions, etc.

The ultimate goal of this neurological approach is not an attempt to eliminate the inevitable deterioration that must occur with aging. Rather, it is to maintain sufficient neural integrity in aging individuals so that they may function with acceptable independence and satisfaction, until the entire human machine wears down—a human counterpart of the Holmesian "wonderful one horse shay."

References

Adams, R.D. and Victor, M. (1981). Principles of Neurology. McGraw-Hill, New York.

Akhtar, A.J., Broe, D.A., Crombie, A., McLean, W.M.R., Andrews, G.R., and Caird, F.I. (1973). Disability and dependence in the elderly at home. Age and Aging 2, 102–110.

Albert, M. (1978). In Aging, Vol. 7, R. Katzman, R.D. Terry, and K.L. Bick Eds. Raven Press, New York, pp. 173–180.

Andres, R. (1967). Relation of physiologic changes in aging to medical changes of disease in the aged. Mayo Clin. Proc. 42, 674–684.

Barbeau, A. (1973). Aging and the extrapyramidal system. J. Amer. Geriatr. Soc. 21, 145–149.

Basowitz, H. and Korchin S.J. (1957). Age differences in the perception of closure. J. Abnorm. Soc. Psychol. 54, 93–97.

Bender, M.B., Fink, M., and Green, M. (1951). Patterns of perception on sumultaneous tests of face and hand. Arch. Neurol. Psychiat. 66, 355–362.

Bondareff, W. and Geinisman, Y. (1976). Loss of synapses in the dentate gyrus of the senescent rat. Amer. J. Anat. 145, 129–136.

Bondareff, W., Mountjoy, C.Q., and Roth, M. (1982). Loss of neurons of origin of the andrenergic projection to cerebral cortex in senile dementia. Neurology 32, 164–168.

Botwinick, J. (1975). Behavioral processes. In Aging, Vol. 2, S. Gershon and A. Raskin, Eds. Raven Press, New York, pp. 1–18.

Bowen, D.M., Smith, C.B., White, P., Goodhardt, M.J., Spillane, J.A., Flack, R.H.A., and Davison, A.N. (1977a). Chemical pathology of the organic dementias. I. Brain 100, 397–426.

Bowen, D.M., Smith, C.B., White, P., Flack, R.H.A., Carrasco, L.H., Gedye, J.L., and Davison, A.N. (1977b). Chemical pathology of the organic dementias. II. Brain 100, 427–453.

Brain, R. and Wilkinson, M. (1967). Cervical Spondylosis. Saunders, Philadelphia.

Brewis, M., Poskanzer, D.C., Rolland, C., and

Miller, H. (1966). Neurological disease in an English city. Acta Neurol. Scand. (Suppl. 24) 42, 1–89.

Brody, H. (1955). Organization of the cerebral cortex. III. A study of aging in the human cerebral cortex. J. Comp. Neurol. 102, 511–556.

Brody, H. (1975). The effects of age upon the main nucleus of inferior olive in the human. J. Comp. Neurol. 155(1), 61–66.

Brody, H. (1976). An examination of cerebral cortex and brainstem aging. In Aging, Vol. 3, R.D. Terry and S. Gershon, Eds. Raven Press, New York, pp. 177–181.

Broe, G.A., Akhtar, A.J., Andrews, G.R., Caird, F.I., Gilmore, A.J.J., and McLennan, W.J. (1976). Neurological disorders in the elderly at home. J. Neurol., Neurosurg., Psychiat. 39, 362–366.

Buell, S.J. and Coleman, P.D. (1980). Individual differences in dendritic growth in human aging and senile dementia. In The Psychobiology of Aging: Problems and Perspectives, D. Stein, Ed. Elsevier/North-Holland, New York.

Caird, W.K. (1966). Aging and short-term memory. J. Gerontol. 21, 295–299.

Carlsson, A. (1981). Aging and brain neurotransmitters. In Strategies for the Development of an Effective Treatment for Senile Dementia, T. Crook and S. Gershon, Eds. Mark Powley Associates, Inc., New Canaan, Conn.

Celesia, G.G. and Daly, R.F. (1977). Effects of aging on visual evoked responses. Arch. Neurol. 34, 403–407.

Confrey, E.A. and Goldstein, M.S. (1960). The health status of aging people. In Handbook of Social Gerontology, C. Tibbitts, Ed. University of Chicago Press, Chicago, pp. 165–207.

Corsellis, J.A.N. (1976). Aging and the dementias. In Greenfield's Neuropathology, 3rd ed., W. Blackwood and J.A.N. Corsellis, Eds. Year Book Medical Publishers, Chicago, pp. 1–42.

Cragg, B.G. (1975). The density of synapses and neurons in normal, mentally defective and aging human brains. Brain 98, 81–90.

Critchley, M. (1956). Neurologic changes in the aged. J. Chronic Dis. 3, 459–477.

DeJong, R.N. (1969). *The Neurologic Examination,* 3rd ed. Paul B. Hoeber, Inc., New York.

Drachman, D.A. (1977). Memory and the cholinergic system. In Neurotransmitter Function, Basic and Clinical Aspects, W.S. Fields, Ed. Symposia Specialists, Miami, pp. 353–372.

Drachman, D.A. (1978). Central cholinergic system and memory. In Psychopharmacology: A Generation of Progress, M.A. Lipton, A. Dimascio, and K.F. Killam, Eds. Raven Press, New York, pp. 651–662.

Drachman, D.A. (1982a). How normal aging relates to dementia: A critique and classification. In The Aging of the Brain, G. Toffano and D. Samuel, Eds. Raven Press, New York.

Drachman, D.A. (1982b). Dizziness and vertigo. In Cecil's Textbook of Medicine, 16th Ed. J.B. Wyngaarden and L.H. Smith, Eds. Saunders, Philadelphia, pp. 1961–1966.

Drachman, D.A., DeGirolami, U., and Ellis, J.M. (1982). Familial thalamic dementia and amyotrophy (FTDA). Neurology 32 (2), 168.

Drachman, D.A. and Hart, C.W. (1973). Multisensory dizziness. Neurology 23, 434.

Drachman, D.A. and Glosser, G. (1981). Pharmacologic strategies in aging and dementia: The cholinergic hypothesis. In Strategies for the Development of an Effective Treatment for Senile Dementia, T. Crook and S. Gershon, Eds. Mark Powley Associates, Inc., New Canaan, Conn., pp. 35–52.

Drachman, D.A., and Hughes, J.R. (1971). Memory and the hippocampal complexes. III. Aging and temporal EEG abnormalities. Neurology 21, 1–14.

Drachman, D.A. and Leavitt, J. (1972). Memory impairment in the aged: Storage versus retrieval deficit. J. Exp. Psychol. 93, 302–308.

Drachman, D.A., Noffsinger, D., Sahakian, B.J., Kurdziel, S., and Fleming, P. (1980). Aging, memory, and the cholinergic system: A study of dichotic listening. Neurobiol. Aging 1, 39–43.

Feinberg, I. (1976). Functional implications of changes in sleep physiology with age. In Aging, Vol. 3 R.D. Terry and S. Gershon, Eds. Raven Press, New York, pp. 23–41.

Feldman, M.L. (1976). Aging changes in the morphology of cortical dendrites. In Aging, Vol. 3, R.D. Terry and S. Gershon, Eds. Raven Press, New York, pp. 211–227.

Geinisman, Y., Bondareff, W., and Telser, A. (1977). Transport of (^{3}H) fucose labeled glycoproteins in the septo-hippocampal pathway of young adult and senescent rats. Brain Res. 125, 182–186.

Gilbert, J.C. (1941). Memory loss in senescence. J. Abnorm. Soc. Psychol. 36, 73–86.

Gilbert, J.G. (1957). Age changes in color matching. J. Gerontol. 12, 210–215.

Gilbert, J.G. (1973). Thirty-five year follow-up study of intellectual functioning. J. Gerontol. 28, 68–72.

Gilbert, J.G. and Levee, R.F. (1971). Patterns of declining memory. J. Gerontol. 26, 70–75.

Gutmann, E. and Hanzlikova, V. (1972). Age changes in the neuromuscular system. Scientechnica, Bristol.

Hobson, W. and Pemberton, J. (1955). The Health of the Elderly at Home. Butterworth, London, pp. 68–80.

Hollister, L. (1981). General principles of psychotherapeutic drug use in the aged. In Physicians' Handbook on Psychotherapeutic Drug Use in the Aged, T. Crook and G. Cohen, Eds. Mark Powley, Associates, New Canaan, Conn.

Horn, J.L. (1975). Psychometric studies of aging and intelligence. In Aging, Vol. 2, S. Gershon and A. Raskin, Eds. Raven Press, New York, pp. 19–43.

Howell, T.H. (1949). Senile deterioration of the central nervous system. Br. Med. J. 1, 56–58.

Huckman, M.S., Fox, J., and Topel, J. (1975). The validity of criteria for the evaluation of cerebral atrophy of computed tomography. Radiology 116, 85–92.

Iqbal, K., Grundke-Iqbal, I., Wisniewski, H., Korthals, J., and Terry, R. 1976. Chemistry of neurofibrous proteins in aging. In Aging, Vol. 3, R.D. Terry and S. Gershon, Eds. Raven Press, New York, pp. 23–41.

Jennett, B. and Teasdale, G. (1981). Management of Head Injuries. F.A. Davis, Philadelphia.

Jerome, E.A. (1959). Age and learning—experimental studies. In Handbook of Aging and the Individual, J.E. Birren, Ed. University of Chicago Press, Chicago, pp. 655–699.

Jones, H.E. (1959). Intelligence and problemsolving. In Handbook of Aging and the Individual, J.E. Birren, Ed. University of Chicago Press, Chicago, pp. 700–738.

Kahn, R.L., Zarit, S.H., Hilbert, N.M., and Niederehe, G. (1975). Memory complaint and impairment in the aged. Arch. Gen. Psychiat. 32, 1569–1573.

Kiloh, L.G. (1961). Pseudo-dementia. Acta Psychiat. Scand. 37, 336–351.

Kinsbourne, M. (1977). Cognitive decline with advancing age: An interpretation. In, W.L. Smith and M. Kinsbourne, Eds., Aging and Dementia, pp. 217–235. Spectrum Publishers, New York.

Kral, V.A. (1962). Senescent forgetfulness: Benign and malignant. Can. Med. Assoc. J. 86, 257–260.

Kral, V.A. (1966). Memory loss in the aged. Dis. Nerv. Sys. 27(7), 51–54.

Laurence M.W. (1967). Memory loss with age: A test of two strategies for its retardation. Psychonom. Sci. 9, 209–210.

Laurence S., and Stein, D.G. (1978). Recovery after brain damage and the concept of localization of function. In, S. Finger, Ed., Recovery from Brain Damage: Research and Theory, pp. 369–407. Plenum, New York.

Mayo Clinic and Mayo Foundation (1976). Clinical Examinations in Neurology, 4th Ed. W.B. Saunders, Philadelphia.

McGeer, E. and McGeer, P.L. (1975). Neurotransmitter metabolism in the aging brain. In, R.D. Terry and S. Gershon, Eds., Aging, Vol. 3, pp. 389–403. Raven Press, New York.

McNamara, J.O. and Appel, S.H. (1977). Biochemical approaches to dementia. In, C.E. Wells, Ed., Dementia, 2nd ed., pp. 155–168. F.A. Davis, Philadelphia.

Meier-Ruge, W., Reichlmeier, K., and Iwangoff, P. (1975). Enzymatic and enzyme histochemical changes of the aging animal brain and consequences for experimental pharmacology on aging. In, R.D. Terry and S. Gershon, Eds., Aging, Vol. 3, pp. 379–387. Raven Press, New York.

Miles, W.R. (1931). Measures of certain human abilities throughout the life span. Proc. Natl. Acad. Sci. 17, 627–633.

Nies, A., Robinson, D., Davis, J., and Ravaris, C.L. (1973). Changes in monoamine oxidase with aging. In, C. Eisdorfer and W.E. Fann, Eds., Psychopharmacology and Aging, pp. 41–54. Plenum, New York.

Orgel, L.E. (1963). The maintenance and the accuracy of protein synthesis and its relevance to aging. Proc. Natl. Acad. Sci. 49, 517–521.

Overgaard, J., Hvid-Hansen, O., Land, A.M., Pedersen, K., Christensen, S., Haase, J., Hein, O., and Tweed, W. (1973). Prognosis after head injury based on early clinical examination. Lancet, ii, 631–635.

Paulson, G.W. (1977). The neurological examination in dementia. In, C.E. Wells, Ed., Dementia, 2nd ed., pp. 169–188. F.A. Davis, Philadelphia.

Pear, B.L. (1977). The radiographic morphology of cerebral atrophy. In, W.L. Smith and M. Kinsbourne, Eds., Aging and Dementia, pp. 57–76. Spectrum Publishers, New York.

Raisman, G. (1978). What hope for repair of the brain? Ann. Neurol. 3, 101–106.

Reitan, R.M. (1967). Changes with aging and cerebral damage. Mayo Clin. Proc. 42, 653–673.

Rosen, S., Plester, D., El-Mofty, A., and Rosen, H.V. (1964). High frequency audiometry in presbycusis; A comparative study of the Mabaan tribe in the Sudan with urban populations. Arch. Otolaryngol. 79, 18–32.

Rossor, M.N., Iversen, L.L., Johnson, A.J., Mountjoy, C.Q., and Roth, M. (1981). Cholinergic deficit in frontal cerebral cortex in Alzheimer's disease in age dependent. Lancet, ii, 1422.

Schaie, K.W. and Gribbin, K. (1975). Adult development and aging. Ann. Rev. Psychol. 26, 65–96.

Scheibel, M.E., Lindsay, R.D., Tomiyasu, U., and Scheibel, A.B. (1975). Progressive dendritic changes in aging human cortex. Exp. Neurol. 47, 392–403.

Scheibel, M.E. and Scheibel, A.B. (1975). Structural changes in the aging brain. In Aging, Vol. 1, H. Brody, D. Harman, and J.M. Ordy, Eds. Raven Press, New York, pp. 11–37.

Schneider, N.G., Gritz, E.R., and Jarvik, M.E. (1975). Age difference in learning, immediate, and one week delayed recall. Gerontologia 21, 10–20.

Schonfield, D. (1967). Memory loss with age: Acquisition and retrieval. Psychol. Rts. 20, 223–226.

Selkoe, D.J., Ihara, Y., and Salazar, F.J. (1982). Alzheimer's disease: Insolubility of partially purified paired helical filaments in sodium dodecyl sulfate and urea. Science 215, 1243–1245.

Shelanski, M. (1976). Neurochemistry of aging: Review and prospectus. In Aging, Vol. 3, R.D. Terry and S. Gershon, Eds. Raven Press, New York, pp. 339–350.

Stein, D.G., and Firl, A.C. (1976). Brain damage and reorganization of function in old age. Exp. Neurol. 52, 157–167.

Strehler, B.L. (1976). Introduction: Aging and the human brain. In Aging, Vol. 3, R.D. Terry and S. Gershon, Eds. Raven Press, New York, pp. 1–22.

Terry, R.D. and Wiesniewski, H.M. (1975). Structural and chemical changes of the aged human brain. In Aging, Vol. 2, S. Gershon and A. Raskin, Eds. Raven Press.

Terry, R.D., and Wiesniewski, H.M. (1977). Structural aspects of aging of the brain. In Cognitive and Emotional Disturbances in the Elderly, C. Eisdorfer and R.O. Friedel, Eds. Year Book Medical Publishers, Chicago, pp. 1–9.

Thompson, L.W. (1976). Cerebral blood flow, EEG, and behavior in aging. In Aging, Vol. 3, R.D. Terry and S. Gershon, Eds. Raven Press, New York, pp. 103–120.

Tomlinson, B.E. (1977). Morphological changes and dementia in old age. In Aging and Dementia, W.L. Smith and M. Kinsbourne, Eds. Spectrum Publishers, New York, pp. 25–56.

Tomlinson, B.E. (1980). The structural and quantitative aspects of the dementias. In Biochemistry of Dementia, P.J. Roberts, Ed. Wiley, New York.

Tomlinson, B.E. and Henderson, G. (1976). Some quantitative cerebral findings in normal and demented old people. In Aging, Vol. 3, S. Gerson and R.D. Terry, Eds. Raven Press, New York, pp. 183–204.

Weale, R.A. (1965). On the eye. In Behavior, Aging, and the Nervous System, A.T. Welford and J.E. Birren, Eds. Charles C. Thomas, Springfield, Ill., pp. 307–325.

Wechsler, D. (1955). Manual for Wechsler Adult Intelligence Scale. The Psychological Corp., New York.

Weiss, A.D. (1959). Sensory functions. In Handbook of Aging and the Individual, J.E. Birren, Ed. University of Chicago Press, Chicago, pp. 503–542.

Welford, A.T. (1959). Psychomotor performance. In Handbook of Aging and the Individual, J.E. Birren, Ed. University of Chicago Press, Chicago, pp. 655–699.

Wells, C.E. and Buchanan, D.C. (1977). The clinical use of psychological testing in evaluation of dementia. In Dementia, 2nd Ed., C.E. Wells, Ed. F.A. Davis, Philadelphia, pp. 189–204.

White, P., Hiley, C., Goodhardt, M., Carasco, L.H., Keet, J.P., Williams, I.E.I., and Bowen, D.M. (1977). Neocortical cholinergic neurons in elderly people. Lancet i, 668–670.

Whitehouse, P.J., Price, D.L., Struble, R.G., Clark, A.W., Coyle, J.T., and DeLong, M.R. (1982). Alzheimer's disease and senile dementia: Loss of neurons in the basal forebrain. Science 215, 1237–1239.

Williams, R.L., Karacan, I., and Hursch, C.J. (1974). EEG of Human Sleep. Wiley, New York.

Wilson, W.P., Musella, L., and Short, M.J. (1977). The electroencephalogram in dementia. In Dementia, 2nd Ed., C.E. Wells, Ed. F.A. Davis, Philadelphia, pp. 205–222.

6. Electroencephalography in Aging

RICHARD I. KATZ

RICHARD N. HARNER

The clinical application of electroencephalography to disorders of the nervous system is never easy. This chapter will provide an appreciation of the variations in the normal EEG at mid-life and beyond as well as a set of principles upon which clinical EEG interpretation in the aging can be based. Since most EEGs are requested by nonspecialists to screen for the presence of neurological disease, it is not surprising that two-thirds of the EEGs interpreted in a general hospital setting turn out to be normal. This has been kept in mind in the subsequent discussions of normal variations, signs of disease, and the application of EEG to specific disorders. Those abnormalities that are particularly useful in the evaluation of patients will be emphasized.

A comprehensive review of EEG findings in specific disease states has not been included here, but rather may be found in the book by Kiloh et al. (1980), a useful reference. But, since patients present with symptom complexes, it is these symptoms with which the clinical electroencephalographer must deal and around which this chapter is organized.

Normal Variations in Mid-Life

The nomenclature of aging is neither uniform nor pleasing. We think that it is useful to speak in terms of decades, and, by mid-life, we mean the fifth decade. By this time, all trace of the developmental variability that characterizes the EEG of the first through the third decade is gone. And, the effects of senescence have not yet become apparent. Hence, variability in the EEG reaches a nadir at mid-life. Sometimes this can allow interpretation of a subtle EEG abnormality that would not be significant if encountered in a patient 30 years younger or older.

Alpha Rhythm

The alpha rhythm appears as rhythmic spindles of 9 to 11/second (sec) activity ranging from 20 to 100 microvolts (μV) in amplitude and distributed mainly in the occipital and parietal regions. In some individuals, alpha rhythm is restricted to the occipital region; in others, alpha extends well into the central areas. When alpha activity is extensive in posterior leads, recording to a relatively inactive reference, such as the mandible or the chin, will often demonstrate "frontal alpha activity" that merely reflects posterior activity. This is similar to the effect in electrocardiography of recording the QRS vector from the right and left precordium and noting inversion of the recorded event.

activity (PDA), is often quite low in amplitude and irregular in contour. Rhythmic delta activity is often 100 μV or more in amplitude and has a sinusoidal character. Although delta activity is characteristic of deep sleep and occurs in early life as a developmental feature, it is not normal in the waking adult, except for the occasional production of bilateral slow activity by hyperventilation.

Paroxysmal Activity

Paroxysmal activity is defined as those events that rise suddenly out of the background activity and that have amplitudes at least twice that of background waves of similar duration. Spikes have a duration of 30 to 80 msec, sharp waves a duration of 80 to 400 msec, spike-wave activity consists of linked spike–slow wave complexes that occur in isolation or recur at rates of from 1 to 6/sec. These events are included in discussion of normal rhythms, since they are not to be taken as absolute hallmarks of disease, however useful they may be in evaluation of patients with epilepsy.

Most difficult of all are sharp waves. A record may have a "sharp appearance" if the amplification is increased, if fast activity is excessive, or if superimposed muscle artifact is present. This occurs because the eye is attracted to high amplitudes and because mixing of fast and slow components can frequently result in a sharply contoured wave. In order for sharp waves to be significant, they must have a consistent contour, be distinct from the rhythmic sequence of background activity, and be consistently localizable to a group of electrodes in one or more brain regions. And, since almost every EEG contains some sharp activity, sharp activity must account for at least 5% of the record (that is, one sharp wave every 20 seconds or so) when no other abnormalities are present.

Even spikes can be difficult, since we now know that spikes may be distinct from background activity and yet be regarded as normal phenomena. Occurring in light sleep in children and young adults, 14 and 6/sec positive spikes are best recorded with long distance derivations and may appear in temporal regions in isolation. Even

worse are "small sharp spikes," which can reach amplitudes of 50 μV or more in temporal regions and may be extremely difficult to distinguish from spikes occurring in temporal lobe epilepsy (White et al., 1977). For the present, it is safe to term normal those spikes in the temporal region that occur only during the light phases of sleep, that are unassociated with local slow activity or background depression, and that tend to be broadly or even bilaterally distributed.

Spike-wave activity is not strictly normal, but can occur in individuals without neurological symptoms and may serve to distinguish them from others referred for EEG examination, particularly when the frequency of spike-wave activity is in the range of 5 to 6/sec. The 3/sec spike-wave complex, which may be seen in asymptomatic young adult relatives of patients with primary generalized (petit mal) seizures, is rare in mid-life.

Effects of Aging

The effects of aging on the electroencephalogram have been reviewed (Otomo and Tsubak, 1966; Harner, 1975; Obrist, 1976), as have the effects on normal sleep (Kales et al., 1967; Williams et al., 1974). These effects will be considered under four headings: slowing of alpha frequency, temporal slow wave activity, alteration of sleep onset, and altered distribution of sleep stages.

Alpha Frequency

It has been known for more than four decades that alpha frequency slows with advancing age. However, there has been a tendency by clinical electroencephalographers to overemphasize this "normal slowing" and thus to disregard the significance of alpha slowing outside the normal range.

Alpha frequency has been investigated in a clinical setting by comparing alpha frequencies in patients with minimal symptoms, with episodic vertigo, with transient neurological deficits, and with chronic intellectual impairment in the seventh, eighth, and ninth decades. Figure 6-1 compares the distribution of alpha fre-

Since alpha activity is often higher in amplitude over the right hemisphere, at least a 50% reduction over the left hemisphere is required before an asymmetry is considered to be abnormal. Over the right hemisphere, a smaller reduction of amplitude of alpha activity may be abnormal. Although alpha asymmetry can be a very important sign of disease, it is quite dependent upon (1) montage, (2) accurate placement of electrodes, (3) symmetrical positioning of the head, and (4) transmission characteristics of the dura, skull, and scalp. Thus, the interpreter should be cautious about reporting asymmetries as abnormal without checking these points and without observing confirming abnormalities of another type, however slight.

Alpha frequency may occasionally reach 12 to 13/sec without any known significance; however, alpha frequency as slow as 8/sec is extremely unusual in asymptomatic, fully alert adults. Persistent mean alpha frequency at 8/sec or below at this age usually represents an abnormality (see section on dementia syndromes).

In most adults, the alpha rhythm is very sensitive to eye-opening. It blocks within a few hundred milliseconds (msec) and returns quickly when the eyes are closed, often with a temporary increase in frequency and amplitude before returning to the base line. The unilateral impairment of alpha blocking can be a reliable sign of focal disease and has been called Bancaud's phenomena (Bancaud et al., 1953).

Mu Rhythm

The mu or wicket rhythm or *rythme en arceau* is an alpha frequency rhythm that occurs in the central region, sometimes with sharp components. This pattern has been related to an admixture of alpha and beta frequency activities (Gastaut et al., 1952; Cobb, 1963; Mundy-Castle, 1951). The mu rhythm appears mainly in central regions; it is not blocked by eye-opening, but it is blocked bilaterally with fist clenching, more so on the contralateral side. Sometimes the mu rhythm is quite asymmetrical, which has led some authors to suggest a relationship to head trauma or cerebrovascular disease. However, if the

asymmetry is recognized by the technician and blocked with a contralateral hand movement, the physiological nature of the finding can be confirmed.

Beta Activity

Beta activity ranges from 15 to 30/sec in frequency, 10 to 20 μV in amplitude, and is usually seen best in the frontal, central, and temporal scalp regions. It is most easily recorded from closely spaced electrode pairs, since the broad field of higher-amplitude alpha activity is reduced by such means. Beta activity represents the background activity of the frontocentral region, and persistent asymmetries are reliable indicators of disease. Again, careful attention to electrode placement, head position, and scalp transmission are essential. In the presence of phenobarbital, diazepam, or some other minor tranquilizer–hypnotic agent, beta activity may be doubled in amplitude and the mean frequency reduced from the usual 20 to 30/sec to 15 to 20/sec. This drug-induced beta activity, commonly seen in individuals without neurological disease, is also very symmetrical and can be used to evaluate the status of background rhythms in the frontal and central areas.

Theta Activity

Activity in the range of 4 to 7/sec in frequency and 20 to 40 μV in amplitude can be observed intermittently in all electroencephalograms, particularly in temporal and central areas. Theta activity shifts from side to side, is often rhythmic in nature, and is enhanced by drowsiness or hyperventilation. Although it is not a reliable indicator of disease at any age, theta activity found at mid-life, in the absence of drowsiness, and accounting for more than 30% of the EEG activity in one or more brain areas is not normal, particularly when accompanied by other abnormalities.

Delta Activity

The term delta activity applies to waves ranging in frequency from 0.5 to 3.5/sec. There are two types. Polymorphic delta

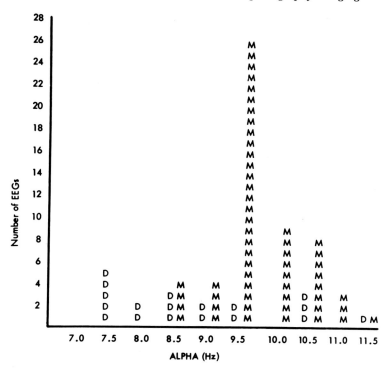

Figure 6-1. Mean alpha frequency in EEG's from dementia (D) patients and patients with minimal symptoms (M), age 60 to 79 years. (Reprinted from Psychiatric Aspects of Neurologic Disease, D. Frank Benson and Dietrich Blumer, Eds. 1975; with permission by Grune & Stratton, Inc.)

quencies for a group of patients in the seventh and eighth decades with minimal symptoms (M) and a group with symptoms of dementia (D). It is seen that the modal alpha frequency at this age is 9.5/sec and that no patient with minimal symptoms had an alpha frequency lower than 8.5/sec.

A prospective study of alpha frequency has been performed by Katz and Horowitz in 52 subjects carefully screened for absence of neurological or psychological impairment (Katz and Horowitz, 1981). Mean alpha frequency for such subjects in the eighth decade was 9.8/sec, even higher than that observed in the less rigorously controlled patients of the same age just described. Similar results were shown in the studies of Van Huffelen et al. (1980). Finally, anecdotal experience demonstrates the persistence of 10/sec alpha rhythm in ambulatory subjects well into the 90's (Figure 6-2) and even after 100 years of age (Hubbard et al., 1976).

Based on these studies, we can conclude that an alpha rhythm with a frequency less than 8/sec is not normal in the alert adult, with eyes closed, at any age, and the obligatory slowing of alpha as a function of age is not great.

Intermittent Temporal Slow Activity

Although initial important studies of EEG in aging by Obrist (1976) indicated that intermittent temporal delta activity could occur in the absence of symptoms, other studies (Harner, 1975) suggested a twofold incidence of 40 to 80 μV delta activity occurring for 20 to 40% of the record in patients with transient ischemic attacks compared to those with minor symptoms. The study of Katz and Horowitz (1981) is instructive in this regard. In 52 normal septuagenarians, these authors found only nine patients who had intermittent temporal slow activity but in no patient was such activity present for more than 1% of the time. Although more studies are required, it appears that delta activity of moderate amplitude is not normal when occurring for more than a minor portion of the record. We have arbitrarily chosen 5% as a threshold for abnormality for working purposes. Remember that this represents 1

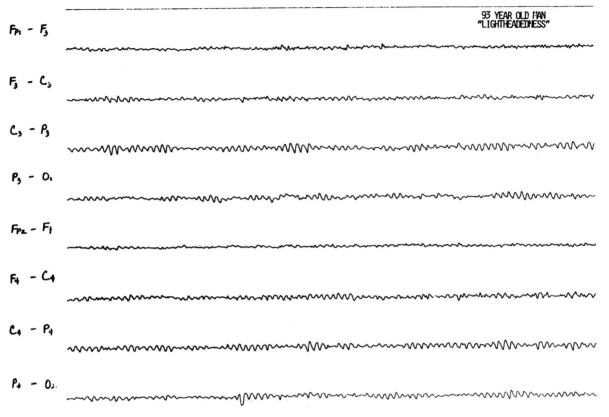

Figure 6-2. Alpha frequency of 10.5 Hz in 93-year-old man with nonspecific lightheadedness.

sec of delta activity every 20 sec, and a finding of this incidence could in no way be described as rare. Remember also, that low-amplitude irregular, as well as rhythmic theta activity may occur in temporal regions without significance, more often in the left hemisphere (Hughes and Coyaffa, 1977).

Sleep Onset

The onset of drowsiness in early childhood is often marked by dramatic, high-amplitude theta activity. With maturation to adulthood, drowsiness is characterized by alpha diminution, and the appearance of low-amplitude theta activity. This pattern persists through mid-life until, in the later decades, we begin to see a sleep onset that is again characterized by high-amplitude rhythmic activity, this time in the delta range. Sleep onset in the elderly can occur

very quickly without much change in background activity until, suddenly, 2 to 3/sec frontal intermittent delta activity occurs. Figure 6-3 shows an example of this sudden transition; Figure 6-4 shows a slower transition in the same individual that clarifies the relation of this delta activity to sleep onset. For this reason alone, it is important to be cautious in interpreting intermittent bilateral rhythmic delta activity in late life, particularly when the state of consciousness is not clearly defined.

Sleep Stages

The effects of advancing age on the development of sleep stages has been reviewed by Williams et al. (1974) and by Kales et al. (1967), who noted a general shortening of the total sleep time. Striking diminution of stage IV sleep occurs by the fourth

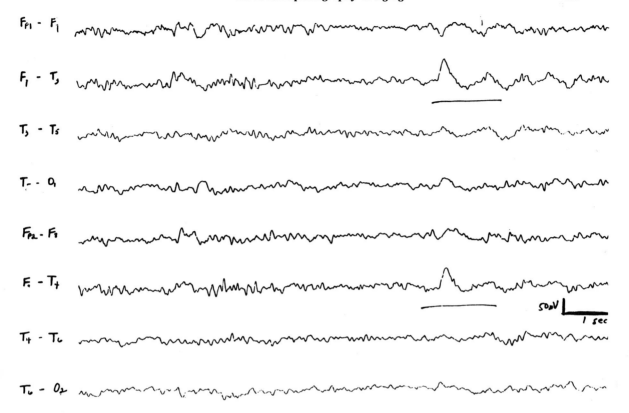

Figure 6-3. A normal 80-year-old subject with sudden sleep transition with frontal delta activity at onset.

decade, and by the fifth decade and beyond, stage IV sleep accounts for less than 5% of the total sleep time. The slight shortening of total rapid eye movement sleep from about 25 to 20% of the total sleep time evolves over the course of three decades beginning at age 50. For the clinical electroencephalographer, this means that sleep recordings in the elderly will consist mainly of brief periods of drowsiness and light sleep and that prolonged deep sleep with predominant delta activity is unusual as a normal finding.

Signs of Disease

In spite of the statistical complexity of the EEG signal and in part because of this complexity, the number of reliable signs of disease in EEG is small. Thus, it is sufficient to distinguish (1) alteration of intrinsic rhythms, (2) polymorphic delta and rhythmic slow activity, and (3) paroxysmal activity. It is the task of the clinical electroencephalographer to detect these signs according to consistently applied criteria, to determine their topographic distribution, and then to summarize the significance of EEG findings in relation to clinical symptoms for which the patient was referred.

Alteration of Intrinsic Rhythms

Three pathological alterations of background rhythms are recognized: slowing, accentuation, and depression.

SLOWING OF INTRINSIC ACTIVITY

This most often takes the form of an alpha rhythm that is slower than 8/sec. Although the concept of "slow alpha"—really in the theta frequency range—has been chal-

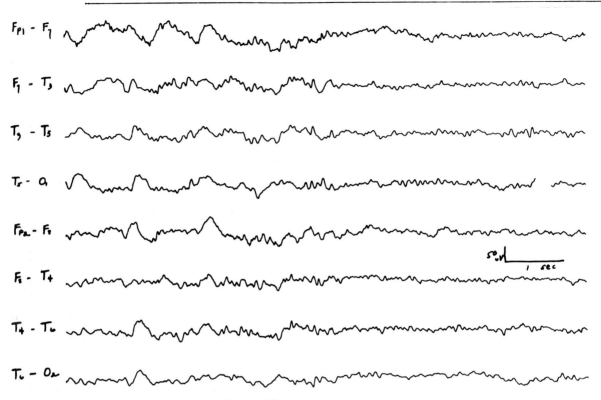

Figure 6-4. The same subject as in Figure 6-3 with a more gradual sleep transition with frontal delta activity at onset.

lenged in the past, the pragmatic value of this concept has been established. Slow alpha activity appears at a frequency of less than 8/sec, maintains the spindle-like characteristics of the alpha rhythm, is located in the posterior head regions, and usually blocks with eye-opening. When present bilaterally, alpha slowing is a reliable indicator of brain involvement that is usually diffuse and longstanding, and may be due to a variety of causes such as Alzheimer's disease, chronic barbiturate intoxication, hypothyroidism, and vitamin B_{12} deficiency. Localized slowing of alpha activity in one hemisphere may also occur, often as a result of lesions that are usually subcortical. Such alpha activity may be 1 to 2/sec slower than the opposite hemisphere and may be higher in amplitude, and unresponsive to eye-opening (Kiloh,

1980). Slowing of beta activity to less than 20/sec may also occur, usually as a bilateral finding, in response to sedation or minor tranquilizer medication.

ACCENTUATION OF INTRINSIC ACTIVITY

Although not a frequent occurrence, it can occur adjacent to focal brain lesions. Nonparoxysmal accentuation of beta activity occurs most often as a sign of focal brain involvement in patients with epilepsy. Although such accentuation of beta activity may be the most prominent sign of a lesion (Figure 6-5), it rarely stands as the sole abnormality (Harner, 1971; Jaffe and Jacobs, 1972). This single fact is useful in preventing overinterpretation of asymmetries that may arise as a result of normal variation or technical problems. The pre-

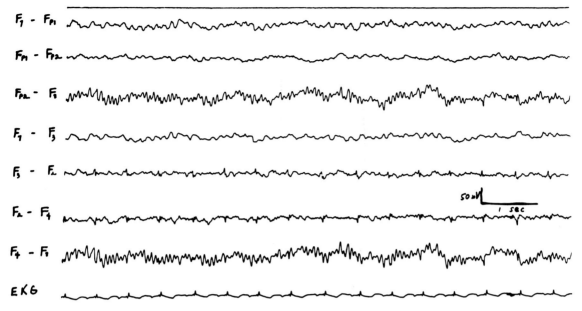

Figure 6-5. Prominent intermittent runs of rhythmic beta activity (18 Hz) over the right anterior temporal region in a 72-year-old man with recent onset of left-sided focal motor seizures. The CT brain scan and bilateral cerebral arteriography were normal.

sence of a skull defect can also produce striking accentuation of beta activity, which should not be interpreted as an abnormality unless slow waves or spikes are also present.

DEPRESSION OF INTRINSIC ACTIVITY

This is one of the most reliable signs of focal brain pathology. Background activity is taken to mean the most widespread normal activity present at any given time. This includes alpha and beta activity in the waking state, sleep spindles and vertex waves while the patient is asleep, and even diffuse rhythmic slow activity in a patient with a generalized metabolic disturbance. Since temporary asymmetries of all these features may occur during normal brain function, the interpreter must be sure that focal depression is a persistent finding.

Depression of rhythmic activity also occurs as the first and most striking response to cessation of cerebral blood flow or severe hypoxia. Sometimes it is difficult to distinguish depression of rhythmic activ-ity from the low voltage pattern that may occasionally be seen in normal EEG's. In this regard, it is helpful to increase amplification of the EEG signal and to examine fast activity that will always be present in normal records and absent in abnormal. Although depression of background activity may result from a variety of factors, including local accumulation of subdural or extracranial fluid, severe persistent loss of background activity due to an intracranial lesion indicates the loss of cortical function to that area, whatever the cause.

Slow Activity

Slow abnormalities in the EEG may be either rhythmic or irregular. Irregular slow activity is usually in the frequency range of 0.5 to 3.5/sec and is very unpredictable in contour from one wave to the next. The useful term polymorphic delta activity (PDA) has been applied (van der Drift and Magnus, 1961); PDA arises in cortex adjacent to local lesions or occurs as a widespread finding in relation to severe metabolic disturbance. Characteristically, PDA is associated with loss of intrinsic rhythms and may itself be quite low in amplitude. Some experience is required to recognize low-amplitude PDA as an important sign of local disease, particularly when higher-amplitude slow rhythms are present elsewhere in the brain.

Rhythmic slow activity usually ranges from 2 to 6/sec in frequency and is characterized by waves of similar contour occurring in groups of three or more. Rhythmic delta activity tends to be distributed near the frontal and temporal poles in adults, whereas rhythmic theta activity appears most often in the central and parietal areas. Although the exact significance of rhythmic slow activity is uncertain, it can be produced by lesions in the thalamus (Cobb and Gassel, 1961); in the cerebral hemispheres, and most often with subcortical lesions (Figure 6-6). Rhythmic slow activity is not a good sign of local brain involvement, since it often appears at a distance from a well-localized lesion. In addition, rhythmic slow activity occurs in such a wide variety of disturbances (including minor head trauma, metabolic encephalopathy, postictal state or drowsiness in the elderly) that it must be interpreted with great caution. Perhaps the best approach is to think of rhythmic slow activity as a flag indicating the need to search further for a possible cause of disturbed brain function.

Paroxysmal Activity

By paroxysmal activity we mean those sudden changes in amplitude or frequency

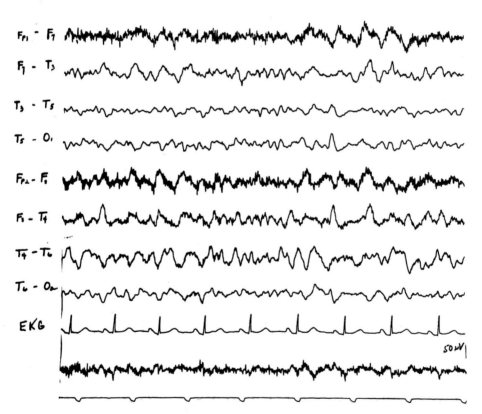

Figure 6-6. Runs of rhythmic slowing maximal over the right frontotemporal region, with occasional projection to the left frontal region, in a 72-year-old man with right thalamic hemorrhage.

of EEG activity, either focal or diffuse, that are visually and statistically distinct from the preceding background rhythm. Some truly paroxysmal activity is normal, such as lambdoidal waves in the occipital region, vertex waves in the central areas, "small sharp spikes" in the temporal regions, sleep spindles, and 14 and 6/sec positive spikes. However, by common usage, we have come to define paroxysmal activities as those unexpected EEG events that are associated with disease. We distinguish sharp waves, spikes, rhythmic ictal activity, spike-wave activity, and triphasic waves.

Only about two-thirds of EEGs with spikes and sharp waves are from patients with a history of epilepsy (Harner, 1971). For this reason, we believe that such events are better interpreted as "irritative features" than "epileptogenic" potentials. In the older age groups, spikes occur most frequently in relation to acute or recurrent cerebrovascular disease, but they are also seen as a sign of focal brain involvement in patients with cryptogenic seizures due to diverse cause. Widespread irritative features may occur in diffuse encephalopathies; periodic spikes occur in anoxic encephalopathy, Jakob–Creutzfeld disease, and endstage encephalopathy from a variety of etiologies (Kuriowa and Celesia, 1980).

Rhythmic ictal activity most often begins as low-amplitude beta or alpha activity and is associated with the onset of seizures, the majority of which are clinically evident on careful inquiry. However, the recurrent sequence of rhythmic ictal activity followed by bilateral spikes, periodic spike activity, and depression of background rhythms, particularly with a focal origin, constitutes sufficient evidence to describe a subclinical seizure, even in the absence of obvious clinical signs (Geiger and Harner, 1978).

Spike-wave activity in the older age group can occur rarely as an unexpected residua of genetically determined primary generalized epilepsy, usually expressed in the first through the third decade. In addition, it may be seen as a generalized disturbance in patients with severe encephalopathy, particularly that related to chronic dialysis, more specifically, dialysis dementia (Hughes and Schreeder, 1980).

Triphasic waves or repetitive sharp complexes appear bilaterally, but more in anterior regions in patients with metabolic encephalopathy (Figure 6-7). When blunt in contour, triphasic waves may resemble frontal intermittent delta activity, and when the contours are very sharp, the pattern resembles periodic spike activity. The main value of this abnormality is its recognition, in typical form, in a patient with unsuspected hepatic encephalopathy.

Technical Considerations

Certain technical considerations should be mentioned in light of the foregoing discussion. Since localized depression of intrinsic rhythm is such an important sign of focal brain disease, every effort should be made to detect it when the EEG is being performed. Two things are required. First, symmetry of electrode application and of inter-electrode distance is essential. Otherwise, so many asymmetries will develop because of asymmetrical placement that it will be impossible to detect reliable asymmetries of cerebral origin. Second, closely spaced anterior–posterior sequential bipolar montages show asymmetries to best advantage (Harner, 1974). Longer inter-electrode distances "erase" focal depression, since the difference between a depressed area and an active area recorded from widely separated electrodes in one hemisphere may actually be greater than the difference between two active areas in the opposite hemisphere. Similarly, transverse montages utilizing the vertex electrode or long-distance recording between homologous parasagittal areas reduces the number of electrode pairs that are likely to show the difference in background activity. From the interpreter's standpoint, asymmetries can best be appreciated when there is full data about head position and scalp consistency and when the suspected depression involves three or more electrodes.

A second area of technical concern is the proper recording of very low-amplitude, slow delta activity (less than 1/sec). The visualization of such activity, so important for the localization of focal brain lesions, depends upon amplification, band-pass filtering of the EEG in the low frequency

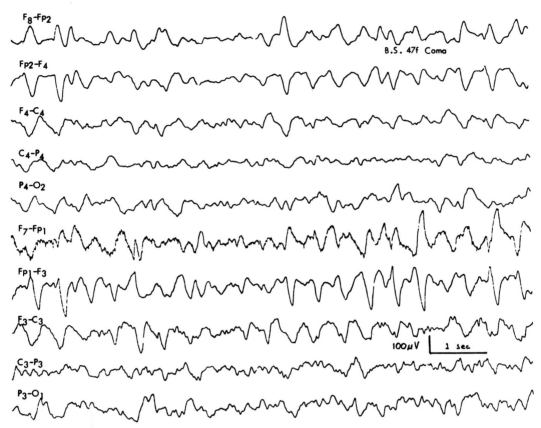

Figure 6-7. Prominent bifrontal triphasic waves, more on the left, in a 47-year-old patient with known hepatic failure who became comatose. Reduction of fast activity over the entire right hemisphere (upper five channels) led to the evacuation of a large, coexistent subdural hematoma. (Reprinted from Psychiatric Aspects of Neurologic Disease, D. Frank Benson and Dietrich Blumer, Eds. 1975; with permission by Grune & Stratton, Inc.)

range, and paper speed. Sometimes it is enough simply to increase the amplification. Additional gain can be obtained for low frequency activity by increasing the time constant (often termed the low frequency filter), so as to allow the passage of very slow activity below 1 Hz. Finally, the visualization of very long, low-amplitude waves is significantly improved by reducing the paper speed by one-half so that the height-to-width ratio is more acceptable to the eye. These techniques are essential when the EEG is used to screen for metastatic involvement in the absence of computed tomography (CT) or when suspected lesions are small or isodense on CT.

A third factor relates to the willingness to search for epileptogenic mechanisms of neurological symptoms. If the electroencephalograph is portable or otherwise accessible such that EEGs of critically ill patients can be recorded, a significant number of patients with "strokes" will turn out to have an epileptogenic mechanism. The ability to detect such treatable processes depends upon the availability of EEGs on a timely basis in the acute care area.

Finally, in the evaluation of intermittent disturbances of function, such as excessive daytime sleepiness, syncope, or seizure disorders, the technician in the laboratory must be prepared to monitor brain activity along with such other vital functions as heart rate, respiration, and body movement. Sometimes, this means special electrodes, video monitoring equipment, and the like. More often, the required commitment is that of time to wait for an event to occur; thoughtfulness to monitor EKG routinely, and other functions as needed; and a high level of interest on the part of the electroencephalographer and the clinical staff.

Clinical Application

The following sections will deal with the six major complaints for which patients in the older age group are referred for electroencephalography. Since EEG findings, clinical signs, specific symptoms or diseases are rarely directly correlated, some planning is required in order to obtain the maximum amount of information from an EEG investigation.

EEG interpretation should be viewed as a data-gathering process and one that should be performed initially without knowledge of more than the patient's age and state of consciousness. Thus, the alpha activity, beta activity, slowing, or paroxysmal events should all be described in terms that are as quantitative as possible before clinical correlation is attempted. The second step in interpretation is a statement of the degree of abnormality, its nature and location, e.g., "moderate left temporal slow abnormality." If a finding is considered questionable by the interpreter, it should probably be called normal. Experience shows that the risk of missing an important treatable lesion that could not be diagnosed by other means is less than the risk of overtreatment and overinvestigation of patients whose "brain waves were abnormal." This is particularly true in the older age group in whom adverse responses to diagnostic tests and even hospitalization are substantial.

The third step in the interpretive process is the correlation with clinical data. Sometimes the knowledge of the clinical history will occasion a review of the EEG findings to be certain that a minor feature was not overlooked. In making the clinical correlation, electroencephalographers will rarely have enough clinical data. Therefore, the best approach is to base the clinical correlation on the essential clinical feature or sometimes upon the question being asked by the clinician. For example, in a 50-year-old with a progressive headache for four weeks, the above "left temporal slow abnormality" should indicate the high likelihood of a mass in the left hemisphere. On the other hand, in a 70-year-old who had an episode of hemiparesis lasting 24 hours, two days before the EEG, a left temporal slow abnormality should be taken as evidence of residual effects of ischemia. Thus, EEG findings in the proper context provide the information sought by the clinician.

Dementia Syndromes

By dementia we mean the development of impaired intellect, particularly memory loss, that occurs in the adult and is progressive over a course of weeks to months. It is this rapid progression and occurrence at an unexpectedly early age that distinguishes dementia from the normal loss of computing power that occurs in us all. Dementia is not aphasia and the first use of the EEG is to screen for focal lesions that produce "confusion" that might be misinterpreted as more global intellectual impairment.

The second application of the EEG in dementia is in screening patients with dementia from treatable lesions. The great majority of such lesions produce significant EEG abnormalities by the time they are severe enough to cause intellectual impairment. This includes large meningiomas, subdural hematoma, and metabolic disorders such as hypothyroidism. Figure 6-1 shows that the major finding in dementia, alpha slowing, was not present in one-half of the patients with dementia. Thus, an early EEG has a better than even chance of being either normal or showing only mild alpha slowing. If mild alpha slowing is present, then the likelihood of a chronic diffuse encephalopathy is good. Some clinical evaluation and a few tests are required to be certain that hypothyroidism or vitamin B_{12} deficiency are not present. Several treatable abnormalities not screened by the EEG include lues, chronic meningitis, normal pressure hydrocephalus, and thiamine deficiency. Figure 6-8 shows progressive dementia over a six-month period, with associated progressive slowing of alpha activity; Figure 6-9 shows alpha slowing that responded to thyroid hormone therapy over a two-week period.

Sometimes the EEG may be a clue to the cause of dementia for which no treatment is presently available. Huntington's chorea characteristically shows low amplitude fast activity (Scott et al., 1972),

sometimes with superimposed movements that appear as artifact (Figure 6-10). The EEG in Creutzfeld–Jakob disease has recently been reviewed (Burger et al., 1972; Traub and Pedley, 1981). Figure 6-11 shows a case that was rapidly progressive over a one-month period in a 65-year-old man. The EEG shows typical periodic spike activity over the left hemisphere, but less activity on the right. Such asymmetries may occur at different stages of the disease. (This case may have been related to associated obstruction of the sagittal sinus, demonstrated by cerebral venography.) The EEG in well-developed Alzheimer's disease is severely slowed, with total loss of alpha activity and irregular delta activity in all areas. In the late

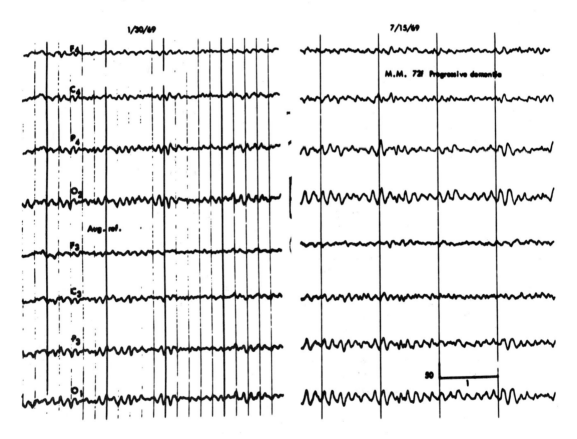

Figure 6-8. Reduction in occipital alpha frequencies from 9 to 7 Hz after six months of progressive dementia in a 72-year-old woman. (Reprinted from Psychiatric Aspects of Neurologic Disease, D. Frank Benson and Dietrich Blumer, Eds. 1975; with permission by Grune & Stratton, Inc.)

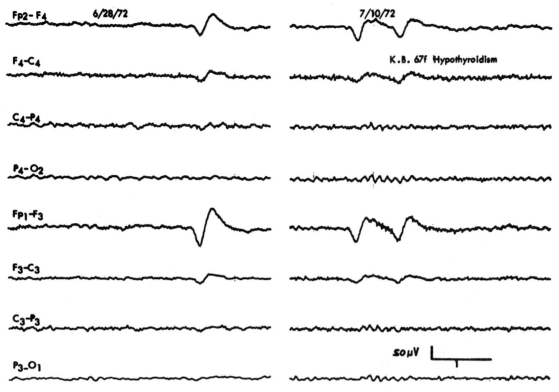

Figure 6-9. Hypothyroidism, before and after treatment. Low voltage rhythmic 4 to 6 Hz activity was associated with wakefulness on 6/28/72 (note eye blink artifact in channels one and five); 12 days later, after treatment, there was striking improvement, but alpha frequency was still only 7.5 Hz. (Reprinted from Psychiatric Aspects of Neurologic Disease, D. Frank Benson and Dietrich Blumer, Eds. 1975; with permission by Grune & Stratton, Inc.)

stages, triphasic waves may even develop (Muller and Kral, 1967).

Finally, a persistently normal EEG in the face of severe progressive functional impairment, lack of neurological signs, and normal CT, brain scan, and cerebrospinal fluid, would raise the possibility of a severe depression with pseudodementia that may respond dramatically to appropriate treatment.

Acute Delirium

The abrupt onset of confusion, disorientation, and varying degrees of agitation at mid-life or after can be a trying clinical problem for the physician. A wide variety of focal and diffuse encephalopathies may produce this clinical picture and some of them require immediate treatment. In this clinical setting, the EEG is rarely normal and may aid in the decision-making process if obtained in the first few hours after onset.

The most important use of EEG is the distinction between focal and nonfocal causes of delirium. The presence of a frontal slow wave focus or depression of rhythmic activity over one hemisphere immediately sets in motion the necessary

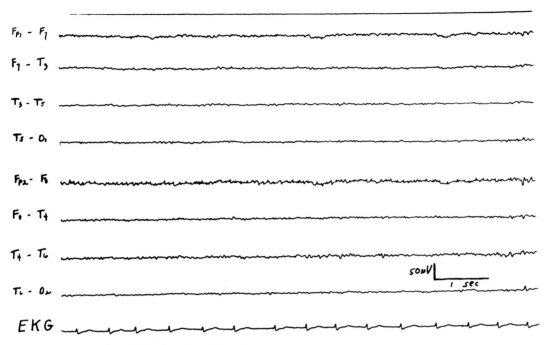

Figure 6-10. Waking EEG, showing diffuse low voltage fast activity of a 67-year-old woman with Huntington's chorea and dementia.

steps to define and treat *focal lesions*. In the older age group, cerebritis, subdural hematoma, left hemisphere infarction, or hemorrhage are examples of lesions that can present as "confusion."

The presence of excess beta activity leads directly to the possibility of sedative or minor tranquilizer intoxication. More difficult to detect are the effects of neuroleptic drugs, which may produce diffuse slowing, but may also produce paroxysmal wave forms and very low-amplitude fast activity without a significant change in the alpha rhythm. Perhaps the most common cause of this low-amplitude fast pattern of delirium is that of the alcohol withdrawal state.

Finally, about once a year, in our experience, a patient presents with acute confusion as a result of continuous spike-wave activity, the so-called spike-wave stupor or "petit mal status." Often there is a history of childhood seizures, but no recent convulsive activity or attention to anticonvulsant medication. The incidence of spike-

wave stupor is bimodal, occurring in the first two decades and again in later life (See review by Andermann and Robb, 1972).

Impaired Consciousness

The value of the EEG in the investigation of coma is twofold: to aid in the early differential diagnosis of coma and to provide prognostic information in the case of coma that is unresponsive to therapy.

Aid in the Differential Diagnosis of Coma

Differential diagnosis of the unresponsive state is a broad subject and has been reviewed elsewhere, particularly in the most recent edition of *Stupor and Coma* (Plum and Posner, 1980). The EEG provides useful information concerning the mechanism of unresponsiveness and the localization of disturbed brain function. There are three mechanisms of coma to which the EEG addresses itself. The first is

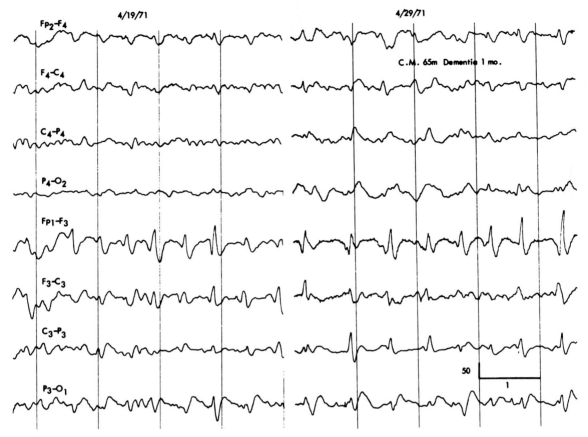

Figure 6-11. There is more periodic spike activity over the right hemisphere than the left in this 65-year-old man with Creutzfeld-Jacob disease. (Reprinted from Psychiatric Aspects of Neurologic Disease, D. Frank Benson and Dietrich Blumer, Eds. 1975; with permission by Grune & Stratton, Inc.)

diffuse encephalopathy with a widespread disturbance of cortical function. The second is a disturbance of upper brain-stem projections to the cerebral hemispheres. The third is a disturbance of the normal input and output to and from the brain.

The most common mechanism for disturbed consciousness is a diffuse encephalopathy that may be related to metabolic disturbances, hypoxia, drug intoxication, seizures or the postictal state, and infection. If the EEG shows diffuse symmetrical slow activity, this mechanism can be strongly suspected, but not necessarily to the exclusion of other mechanisms. Figure 6-12 shows an EEG from a poorly responsive patient with tuberculous meningitis,

which responded dramatically to therapy (Harner, 1975). If triphasic waves are present (Figure 6-7), the possibility of hepatic encephalopathy should be raised and, in our experience, will be found in about 50% of cases (Simsarian and Harner, 1972). Excess fast activity suggests the possibility of drug intoxication, whereas large amounts of paroxysmal activity raises the possibility of a seizure mechanism or of a disorder of metabolism that results in increased paroxysmal activity, such as renal failure. The EEG in metabolic coma has been reviewed in detail (Harner and Katz, 1975).

It has been known since the last century that the smallest lesions responsible for

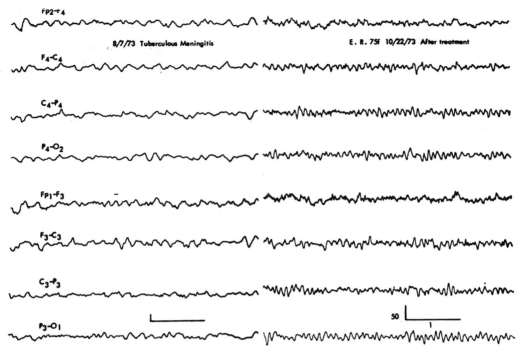

Figure 6-12. Tuberculous meningitis before and after treatment in a 75-year-old woman. Amplification on 8/7/73 was reduced by one-half. (Reprinted from Psychiatric Aspects of Neurologic disease, D. Frank Benson and Dietrich Blumer, Eds. 1975; with permission by Grune & Stratton, Inc.)

coma were in and around the midbrain (Carpenter, 1853). Lesions within or external compression of the neuraxis may lead to severe unresponsiveness. The presence of rhythmic slow EEG activity, often appearing in bursts, should raise this possibility. In addition, sleep spindles and other sleep transients that would be normal except for lack of response to stimulation may be seen in certain comatose states. For example, in the presence of head injury with impaired consciousness and without focal neurological involvement, slow wave sleep may appear (Chatrian, 1975). The asymmetric appearance of rhythmic delta activity has also been related to midbrain compression in patients with hemispheric lesions (Gloor et al., 1977).

Interest in the problem of disturbed input–output relations in coma can be dramatized by a normal or nearly normal appearing EEG in an apparently unrespon-

sive patient. The ability to detect nonconcordance between brain function and external responsiveness is one of the most important functions of the EEG. It should be remembered that clinical unresponsiveness may be due to a variety of extracerebral factors yielding a normal EEG in the face of "coma" e.g., prolonged recovery from anesthesia due to a pseudocholinesterase deficiency or a psychogenic coma in acute dissociative reactions.

A distinctive EEG pattern of "alpha coma" has been described in patients with lesions involving the brain stem at or below the pontomesencephalic junction; alpha activity as the principal EEG component of post-hypoxic–hypoxemic coma has been reported much less frequently. Typically, alpha activity is abundant and diffusely distributed with either central parietal or more anterior accentuation. To the extent that the two forms of alpha pattern coma can be distinguished, alpha reactivity, stimulus-evoked response, and at least partial preservation of variations with sleep make the diagnosis of pontomesencephalic infarction more likely (Westmoreland et al., 1975). The mechanism of generation of such rhythmic activity in patients with severe encephalopathy remains unknown, and although there are exceptions, prognosis is generally poor in both settings.

Cerebral Localization and Coma

One of the most useful dichotomies in the diagnostic evaluation of coma is the distinction between focal causes and diffuse causes. The EEG can provide useful information by suggesting the possibility of a focal brain lesion when indeed no focal signs are present on neurological evaluation. A brainstem lesion can be suggested, as noted above. More importantly, the presence of focal polymorphic delta activity or of unilateral suppression of intrinsic rhythms can suggest a treatable focal cause for coma. Figure 6-7 shows a patient with hepatic encephalopathy whose rhythmic activity including that related to the hepatic disease was depressed over the entire right hemisphere. This led to the diagnosis and subsequent removal of an associated subdural hematoma. The presence of focal paroxysmal activity, particularly if periodic spikes are observed, may lead to the consideration of ictal stupor or non-ketotic hyperglycemic coma or to the possibility of viral infection of the nervous system, if appropriate clinical signs are also present (Venna and Sabin, 1981).

With advances in techniques for neurological diagnosis, the EEG is probably not the first test to be used, but when the cause of coma remains unknown after the first hour of evaluation, EEG information can be extremely useful to the clinician, pointing the way for further investigation or treatment.

Prognosis and Coma

Prognosis in the comatose patient is related to a variety of factors, the most important of which are cause, severity, and duration. No EEG is required to determine that a patient with massive intracerebral hemorrhage who has been totally inactive and unresponsive for two days is unlikely to live out the week. However, the EEG may provide useful information in the evaluation of clinically unresponsive coma. The ability to sustain cardiovascular and pulmonary function for long periods in the absence of detectable brain function had led to an emergence of interest in the concept of cerebral death, and the prognosis for "cerebral life" (Silverman et al., 1969; Saunders, 1975; Bennett et al., 1976). First considered by Bichat (cited in Saunders, 1975) in the last century, the concept of cerebral death has attracted public and legal interest to the point where statutory cerebral death has been adopted, initially by Kansas and subsequently by an increasing number of other states (Saunders, 1975). There is now the possibility for adoption of a Uniform Death Act that embodies the principles of cerebral death. Central to the evaluation of cerebral death are the technical aspects of EEG recording, which have been reviewed by Silverman et al. (1969). The recent cooperative study by the National Institutes of Health (Bennett et al., 1976) indicate the value and reliability of a properly performed and interpreted EEG in determining the absence of cerebral function and the prognosis for subsequent recovery. [Information concerning the technical requirements for EEG recording in cerebral death have been widely circulated (Silverman, 1975; Harner, 1980).]

Headache

In the middle and later years of life, common causes of headache revolve around intracranial structures. The development of cervical arthritis, Paget's disease of bone, intraocular hypertension, nasal sinus obstruction, and temporal arteritis are but a few. Thus, the main role for the EEG is in screening for intracranial lesions, the great majority of which are focal. The patient who presents for EEG examination with the complaint of recent onset of headache should be evaluated

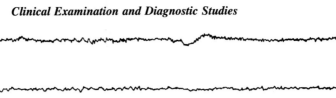

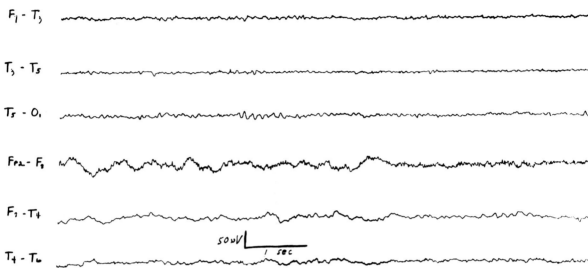

Figure 6-13. Severe right frontotemporal slowing, with associated hemispheric rhythm depression, in a patient with malignant glioma.

carefully; evidence of polymorphic delta activity, which may suggest an intra-axial lesion, or depression of rhythmic activity, with or without associated slowing that may belie the presence of subdural fluid collection, should be looked for. Figure 6-13 shows a severe slow abnormality in a patient with malignant glioma; Figure 6-14 shows a minor asymmetry in fast activity that can occur in association with subdural hematoma.

Headache related to increased intracranial pressure shows very few EEG findings if the responsible lesion is not in the cerebral hemisphere. However, bursts of rhythmic delta activity (FIRDA) appearing in the frontal regions of a patient with headache should raise the possibility of increased intracranial pressure, midbrain compression, or both.

Focal Neurological Deficit

The medical history and the clinical neurological examination together often provide accurate information about focal involvement of the nervous system. However, the clinical examination may not detect focal involvement of the frontal or temporal lobes; and even localization to the primary sensory and motor areas of the brain may be difficult, if there is partial involvement of a single system, for example, the clumsy hand syndrome (Fisher, 1967). In addition, it may be difficult to determine the mechanism of the symptom production by clinical examination of a patient who is aphasic or hemiparetic. The usefulness of the EEG is in the extension of the clinical examination to include areas of the brain that are "relatively silent," as far as the neurological examination is concerned, and to provide information about the mechanism of functional disturbance.

Stroke Syndrome

Figure 6-15 shows the EEG from a patient presenting with acute right hemiplegia

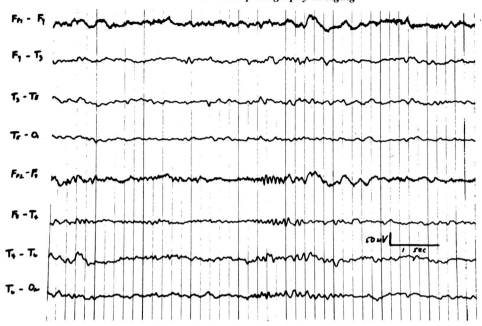

Figure 6-14. A relatively mild, fast activity asymmetry in an 80-year-old patient with left-sided subdural hematoma.

from a large hemispheric infarction: slow activity is often concentrated in the corresponding temporal region, with widespread depression of beta and alpha activity. Sometimes slow activity is present in the contralateral hemisphere, but whether this is related to an acute inter-hemispheric disconnection directly caused by the lesion or whether it is related to multifocal disease is unknown. Usually, this activity is maximum in the contralateral temporal region. If rhythmic delta activity appears bifrontally, the possibility of hemispheric swelling should be considered. The presence of this finding after more than 48 hours indicates severe infarction and a poorer prognosis for recovery of function.

The pattern of major intracerebral hemorrhage, may be similar but more marked in all respects. Characteristically, however, there is more rhythmic bifrontal slow activity and more disturbance of consciousness in the latter. Brain tumor may look similar, but may be more suspect if slowing and depression does not involve the entire hemi-

sphere. Subdural hematoma can also produce a hemispheric disturbance; however, the depression of background activity is ordinarily more striking and there is less polymorphic delta activity than in an acute infarction.

How then does one use the information obtained from the EEG? One approach is to correlate the severity of the clinical symptoms with the severity of the EEG abnormality. An acute hemiplegia and a severe contralateral hemispheric EEG disturbance suggest a hemispheric stroke, but if the hemiplegia is severe and the EEG is normal, or nearly so, then the lesion must be suspected as being deep in the corresponding internal capsule or perhaps even in the brain stem. On the other hand, if a hemispheric EEG disturbance is present, with no focal or only minor contralateral symptoms, an extra-axial lesion should be suspected. A lesion that involves frontal or temporal lobe may be inaccessible to the clinical examiner. In any case, the likelihood of a nonvascular lesion is greatly increased when EEG findings are dispro-

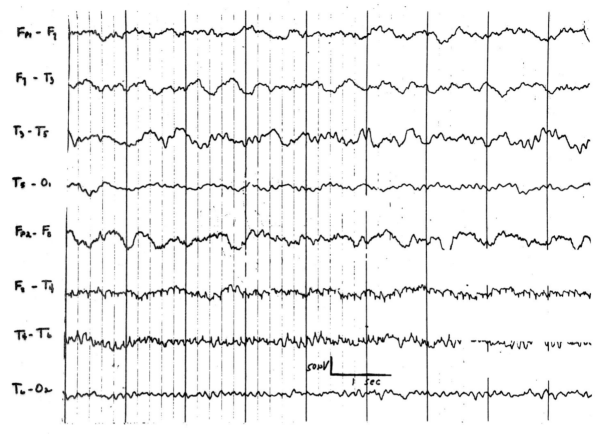

Figure 6-15. Marked, predominantly left frontotemporal slowing with associated widespread depression of beta and alpha activity in a patient presenting with acute right hemiplegia with hemispheric infarction.

portionately great in comparison to clinical findings.

Sometimes, the mere presence of an EEG abnormality is sufficient to aid the clinician. A contralateral delta focus will help the clinician decide that a "clumsy hand" is due to a cerebral and not a pontine lesion. The presence of focal delta activity following a "transient" ischemic attack will indicate the likelihood of residual infarction.

From the standpoint of immediate therapy, one important use of the electroencephalogram is to detect seizure states that are presenting as acute vascular disorders. In retrospect, after continuous paroxysmal activity on the EEG has indicated the likelihood of a seizure state, many patients are found to have intermittent, infrequent, clonic activity of the contralateral extremity (Figure 6-16).

Epilepsy

In the latter half of life, the onset of clinical seizures is clinically significant. Late recurrence of primary generalized epilepsy has been discussed above. More common than these are those seizures that recur in the ambulatory patient and those that occur in patients hospitalized for active medical or neurological disease.

First Seizure in the Ambulatory Patient

There are relatively few causes of seizures in this group of patients after the age of 40;

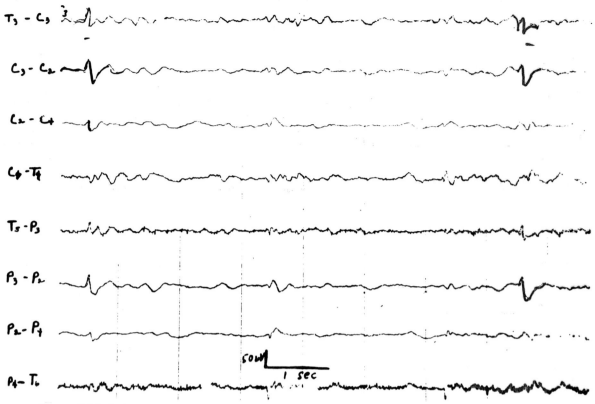

Figure 6-16. Left temporo-parietal spikes with associated global rhythm depression in a 71-year-old man, who presented with coma of "uncertain cause," rare right focal seizures with subsequent diagnosis of acute left middle cerebral artery territory infarction was made.

these include cerebrovascular or neurodegenerative disease, tumor, intoxication-withdrawal states, infection, and cardiac disease. Clinical seizures may herald the onset of cerebral infarction or cerebral hemorrhage and persistent electrographic seizure activity in the form of periodic lateralized epileptiform discharges (PLEDS) (Chatrian et al., 1964; Dauben and Adams, 1977) may contribute to the subsequent clinical neurological deficit. Epileptogenic foci may develop in the cerebral watershed regions around an area of ischemia; Naquet has described both paroxysmal EEG abnormalities as well as seizures that may occur weeks or months after a vascular insult (Naquet et al., 1961). Figure 6-17 shows PLEDS in a patient who presented with aphasia and

whose recovery was coincident with subsidence of the paroxysmal discharge upon treatment with Dilantin (Racy et al., 1980).

In the absence of a history of stroke and neurological deficit, the EEG can provide useful information. In a patient with a first seizure due to brain tumor or to localized brain infection, the EEG is almost always abnormal. Although spikes or periodic spikes may be present, it is the presence of polymorphic delta activity and the *absence* of paroxysmal activity that is the most ominous sign for an underlying structural lesion in this group.

On the other hand, in patients with seizures due to drug intoxication or alcohol withdrawal, EEG abnormalities of any type are rare and focal abnormalities are

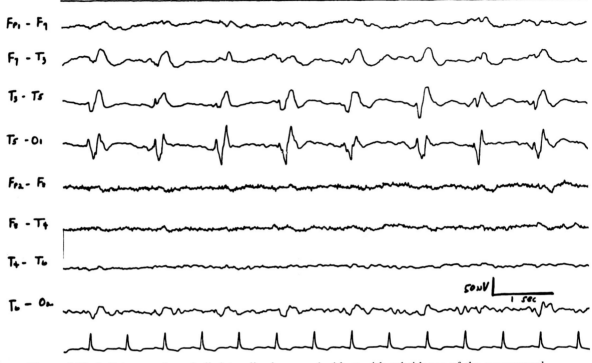

Figure 6-17. Left temporal, periodic lateralized epileptiform discharge in a patient who presented with aphasia and whose recovery was coincident with subsidence of the paroxysmal discharge under treatment with Dilantin.

extremely infrequent. In our experience, the finding of an abnormal EEG, particularly a focal EEG abnormality, in a patient with "withdrawal seizures" is reason to look for an underlying lesion, be it pre-existing head trauma or the development of a new and potentially treatable disorder.

The increased role of cardiac monitoring has led to the recognition that seizures in the older age group may be related to diminished cardiac output. However, seizure activity in the adult can also lead to cardiac arrest (Katz et al., in press). Prolonged asystole may evoke hypoxic seizures, and any transient drop in cardiac output and/or cerebral perfusion may trigger an ischemic seizure in a watershed area. It has become increasingly evident that cerebral and cardiac monitoring should be done in tandem.

Summary

The application of clinical electroencephalography to neurological diagnosis in mid- and late-life has been reviewed. We have learned that the effects of aging on the electroencephalogram occur within definite limits and that EEG findings in the elderly can be useful in the diagnosis and treatment of neurological disorders. The EEG extends the neurological examination to those regions not readily tested with traditional clinical methods and may provide information on disturbance of brain function that cannot be revealed by present radiological techniques. Information obtained by the electroencephalographic examination is best viewed in relation to the central clinical problem. Noncorrespondence between clinical findings and the expected EEG result may give additional clues to neurological localization, indicate a new mechanism of symptom production, and sometimes suggest a line of thought and investigation that may lead to the recognition of an unsuspected and potentially treatable disorder.

References

Andermann, F. and Robb, J.P. (1972). Absence status. A re-appraisal following review of 38 patients. Epilepsia 13, 177–187.

Bancaud, J., Block, V., and Paillard, J. (1953). Contribution EEG à l'étude des potentiels évoqués chez l'homme au niveau du vertex. Rev. Neurol. 89, 399–418.

Bennett, D.R., Hughes, J.R., Korein, J., Merlis, J.K., and Suter, C. (1976). Atlas of Electroencephalography in Coma and Cerebral Death. Raven Press, New York.

Burger, L.J., Rowen, J., and Goldensohn, E.S. (1972). Creutzfeld-Jakob Disease: An electroencephalographic study. Arch. Neurol. 26, 428–433.

Carpenter, W.B. (1853). Principles of Human Physiology. Blanchard and Lee, Philadelphia.

Chatrian, G.E. (1975). Electrographic and behavioral signs of sleep in comatose states. In Handbook of Electroenccphalography and Clinical Neurophysiology, Vol. 12, A. Remond, Ed. Elsevier, Amsterdam. pp. 63–77.

Chatrian, G.E., Shaw, C.M., and Leffman, H. (1964). The significance of periodic lateralized epileptiform discharges in EEG. An electrographic, clinical and pathologic study. Electroenceph. Clin. Neurophysiol. 17, 177–193.

Cobb, W. (1963). The normal adult EEG. In Electroencephalography, D. Hill and G. Parr, Eds. Macdonald, London, pp. 232–249.

Cobb, W.A. and Gassel, M.M. (1961). The EEG with lateral ventricle meningiomas. Electroencephal. Clin. Neurophysiol. (Suppl.) 19, 111–124.

Dauben, R.D. and Adams, A.H. (1977). Periodic lateralized epileptiform discharge in EEG: A review with special attention to etiology and recurrence. Clin. EEG (Electroenceph.) 8, 116–124.

Drift, J.H.A. Van der, and Magnus, O. (1961). The value of the EEG in the differential diagnosis of cases with cerebral lesions. Electroencephal. Clin. Neurophysiol. (Suppl.) 19, 183–196.

Fisher, C.M. (1967). A lacunar stroke. The dysarthria—clumsy hand syndrome. Neurology 17, 614–617.

Gastaut, H., Terzian, H., and Gastaut, Y. (1952). Etude d'une activité électroencephalographique meconnue: "le rythme rolandique en arceau." Marseille-med. 89, 296–310.

Geiger, L.R. and Harner, R.N. (1978). EEG patterns at the time of focal seizure onset. Arch. Neurol. 35, 276–286.

Gloor, P., Ball, G., and Schaul, N. (1977). Brain lesions that produce delta waves in the EEG. Neurology 27, 326–333.

Harner, R.N. (1971). The significance of focal hypersynchrony in clinical EEG. Electroenceph. Clin. Neurophysiol. 31, 293.

Harner, R.N. (1974). Interpretation of electroencephalograms. Amer. J. EEG Technol. 14, 211–217.

Harner, R.N. (1975). EEG evaluation of the patient with dementia. In Psychiatric Aspects of Neurologic Disease, Chap. 4, D.R. Benson, and D. Blumer, Eds. Grunne & Stratton, New York, p. 69.

Harner, R.N. (Ed.) (1980). Guidelines in EEG, American EEG Society, Atlanta, pp. 19–24.

Harner, R.N. and Katz, R.I. (1975). Electroencephalography in Metabolic Coma. In Handbook of Electroencephalography and Clinical Neurophysiology, Vol. 12, A. Remond, Ed. Elsevier, Amsterdam, pp. 47–62.

Hubbard, O., Sunde, D., and Goldensohn, E.J. (1976). The EEG in centenarians. EEG Clin. Neurophysiol. 40, 404–417.

Hughes, J.R. and Cayaffa, F.J. (1977). The EEG in patients at different ages without organic cerebral disease. Electroencephal. Clin. Neurophysiol. 42, 776–784.

Hughes, J.R. and Schreeder, M.T. (1980). EEG in dialysis encephalopathy. Neurology 30, 1148–1152.

Jaffe, R. and Jacobs (1972). The beta focus, its nature and significance. Acta. Neurol. Scand. 48, 191–203.

Kales, A., Wilson, T., et al. (1967). Measurements of all night sleep in normal elderly persons: Effects of aging. J. Amer. Geriatr. Soc. 15, 405–414.

Katz, R.I. and Horowitz, G.R. (1981). The septuagenarian EEG: Normative studies in a selected normal geriatric population. Electroenceph. Clin. Neurophysiol. 51, 55.

Katz, R.I., Tiger, M., and Harner, R.N. (in press). Epileptic cardiac arrhythnas: Sinoatrial arrest in two patients. A potential cause of sudden death in epilepsy? Electroenceph. Clin. Neurophysiol. (Abstr.).

Kiloh, L.G., McComas, A.J., and Ossleton, J.W. (1980). Clinical Electroencephalography, 3rd Ed. Butterworths, London.

Kuriowa, Y. and Celesia, G.G. (1980). Clinical significance of periodic EEG patterns. Arch. Neurol. 37, 15–20.

Muller, H.F. and Kral, V.A. (1967). The electroencephalogram in advanced senile dementia. J. Amer. Geriatr. Soc. 15, 415–426.

Mundy-Castle, A.C. (1951). Theta and beta rhythm in the electroencephalograms of normal adults. Electroenceph. Clin. Neurophysiol. 3, 477–486.

Naquet, R., Louvar, C., Rhodes, J., and Vigouroux, M. (1961). A propos de certaines décharges paroxystiques du carrefour parieto-temporo-occipital. Leur activation par L'hypoxie. Rev. Neurol. 105, 203–207.

Obrist, W.D. (1976). Problems of aging. In Handbook of EEG and Clinical Neurophysiology, Vol. 6, Pt. A, Sec. V, G.E. Chatrian and G.C. Lairy, Eds. Elsevier Scientific Amsterdam, The Netherlands, pp. 275–292.

Otomo, E. and Tsubak, T. (1966). Electroencephalography in subjects 60 years and older. Electroenceph. Clin. Neurophysiol. 20, 77–82.

Plum, F. and Posner, J.F. (1980). The Diagnosis of Stupor and Coma, 3rd Ed. F.A. Davis, Philadelphia.

Racy, A., Osborn, M.A., Vern, B.A., and Molinari, G.F. (1980). Epileptic Aphasia. Arch. Neurol. 37, 419–422.

Saunders, M.G. (1975). Medical-legal aspects of brain death. In Handbook of Clinical Electroencephalography and Clinical Neurophysiology, Vol. 12, Sec. XIV, A. Remond, Ed. Elsevier, Amsterdam.

Scott, D.F., Heathfield, K.W.G., Toone, B., and Margerison, J.H. (1972). The EEG in Huntington's chorea. A clinical and neuropathological study. J. Neurol. Neurosurg. & Psychiat. 36, 61–67.

Silverman, D. (1975). Electroencephalographic recording technique for suspected cerebral death. In Handbook of Electroencephalography and Clinical Neurophysiology. Vol. 12, Ch. 13, A. Ramond, Ed. Elsevier, Amsterdam, pp. 122–128.

Silverman, D., et al. (1969). Minimal electroencephalographic recording techniques in suspected cerebral death. Electroencephal. Clin. Neurophysiol. 27, 731.

Simsarian, J.P. and Harner, R.N. (1972). Diagnosis of metabolic encephalopathy: Significance of triphasic waves in the electroencephalogram. Neurology 22, 456.

Traub, R.D. and Pedley, T.A. (1981). Virus-induced electronic coupling: Hypothesis on the mechanism of periodic EEG Discharges on Creutzfeld-Jakob disease. Ann. Neurol. 10, 405–410.

VanHuffelen, A.C., Poortvliet, D.C.J., and Van der Wulp, C.J.M. (1980). Quantitative Electroencephalography in Cerebral Ischemia. TND Research Unit for Clinical Neurophysiology, The Hague.

Venna, N. and Sabin, T.D. (1981). Tonic focal seizures in nonketotic hyperglycemia of diabetes mellitus. Arch. Neurol. 38, 512–514.

Westmoreland, B., Klass, D.W., Sharbrough, F.W., and Reagan, T.J. (1975). "Alpha Coma": EEG. Clinical, pathologic and etiologic correlations. Arch. Neurol. 32, 713–718.

White, J.C., Langston, J.R., and Pedley, T. (1977). Benign epileptiform transients of sleep: Clarification of the small sharp spike controversy. Neurology 27, 1061–1068.

Williams, R.L., Karacan, I., and Hursch, C.J. (1974). Electroencephalography (EEG) of human sleep: Clinical applications. Wiley, New York.

7. Computerized Axial Tomography in Aging

MORRIS FREEDMAN   JANICE KNOEFEL
MARGARET NAESER   HARVEY LEVINE

By providing a non-invasive, readily accessible, safe means of viewing cerebral anatomy *in vivo,* computerized tomography (CT) has revolutionized the potential for studying the brain in its normal and diseased state. Before the introduction of CT scanning, information about cerebral structure in relation to aging and dementia came largely from autopsies and pneumoencephalograms. Computerized tomographic (CT) scanning is not only more readily available and easier to perform than these procedures, but it may also provide a more accurate representation of brain anatomy. Ventricular size, for example, may be smaller at autopsy as compared to the normal living state because of terminal agonal effects (Messert et al., 1972) and fixation artifacts (Blinkov and Glezer, 1968). Pneumoencephalography, however, may increase ventricular size (Le May, 1967). Thus, CT scanning has the advantage of providing an image of the brain in the living state without the introduction of exogenous materials (if done without contrast) that may distort tissue structure.

But CT scanning is not free of artifacts. An example is the apical artifact (Di Chiro et al., 1978), which produces falsely elevated CT density numbers on the higher CT slices. Another source of error is due to partial volume averaging (Wolpert, 1977), which can lead to over- or underestimates of ventricular size. The computer software is continuously being improved to try to minimize these inherent artifacts.

Several CT scan parameters have been evaluated in normal aging and dementia. These include prominence of cortical sulci and cerebral fissures, ventricular size, and CT density numbers. They will be discussed separately. The purely descriptive term prominent sulci and fissures will be used throughout this chapter instead of the more commonly used term "cortical atrophy." The relationship between the anatomical changes indicative of atrophy and the CT scan appearance of prominent sulci and fissures has not been sufficiently well defined to justify equating these entities at the present time. It should, however, be stressed that prominent cortical sulci do not necessarily represent irreversible changes in brain structure. A decrease in the prominence of cortical sulci has been documented in abstinent alcoholics (Carlen et al., 1978) and in patients during steroid withdrawal (Bentson et al., 1978). The actual measurements of the CT scan parameters will vary depending upon the type and generation CT scanner used. These measurements will therefore not be

Dr. Freedman was supported by a grant from the Ministry of Health of Ontario, Canada.

reported for each study cited, but can be found in the original articles.

With respect to dementia, the focus will be confined primarily to dementia of the Alzheimer type. Dementia secondary to other neurological disorders (e.g., hydrocephalus, Huntington's disease, Parkinson's disease) or secondary to structural lesions (e.g., infarction, tumor) will not be discussed.

Normal Aging

Prominent Sulci and Fissures

The most commonly reported quantitative indices of prominent cortical sulci in normal aging are measures of sulcal width. Other estimates of sulcal or fissure prominence or both include subjective impressions based upon clinical experience (Jacoby et al., 1980; Cala et al., 1981), peripheral fluid volume (Zatz et al., 1982a), and Sylvian fissure width (Soininen et al., 1982) (Table 7-1).

Cala et al. (1981) documented enlargement of the interhemispheric fissure in the frontal region by age 40 in nearly all of 115 normal volunteers. Sulci, however, were not prominent until after age 40. Gyldensted (1977) compared sulcal prominence in normal subjects over 40 with subjects below this age and found significantly more prominence in the older group. His sample consisted of 100 adults ranging in age from 17 to 86 years. Evidence for a gradient of increasing

prominent sulci with age beyond the fifth decade comes from Earnest et al. (1979), who evaluated normal subjects 60 to 99 years of age. Jacoby et al. (1980) showed similar findings in normal subjects aged 62 to 88 years.

Earnest et al. (1979), in addition to studying the relationship between prominent sulci and age in normal subjects, evaluated the relationships between neuropsychological test performance and age. These tests consisted of the Digit Symbol and Block Design subtests of the Wechsler Adult Intelligence Scale (WAIS), the Trail Making Test, and the Visual Reproduction subtest of the Wechsler Memory Scale. There was no relationship between prominent sulci and test performance. Cognitive function was studied in normal elderly (mean age 75 ± 7 years) by Soininen et al. (1982). The psychological examination involved tests of personal facts and current knowledge, orientation, praxis, expressive and receptive speech, memory, and general reasoning. Enlargement of the left Sylvian fissure (Figure 7-1), but not the right, was significantly correlated with a decline in intellectual function. There was no relationship between prominent sulci and psychological test performance.

In addition to objective linear measurements and subjective determinations of prominent sulci and fissures, semiautomated computer analyses have also been employed. Zatz et al. (1982a) used a semiautomated computer program to estimate fluid volume in the cortical sulci and

Table 7-1. Measurement parameters of prominent sulci and fissures in normal aging.

Parameters	References
Linear Measurements	
Maximum width of hemispheric sulci	Gyldensted (1977)
Sum of widths of four largest cortical sulci	Earnest et al. (1979)
Sum of widths of four largest cortical sulci on three highest cuts	Huckman et al. (1975); Gonzalez et al. (1978); Kaszniak et al. (1979)
Mean width of four largest sulci on highest cut	Soininen et al. (1982)
Maximum width of Sylvian fissure at insula on both sides	Soininen et al. (1982)
Subjective Rating	
Sum of four-point scale ratings at five cortical regions	Jacoby et al. (1980)
Four-point scale based on prominence of cortical sulci and interhemispheric fissure	Cala et al. (1981)
Semiautomated Computer Programs	
Peripheral fluid volume	Zatz et al. (1982a)

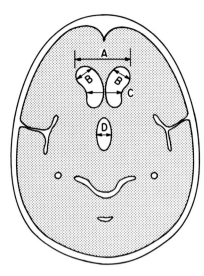

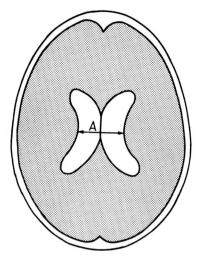

Figure 7-1. Schematic drawing of CT scan slice at level of third ventricle showing where linear measurements have been taken. (A) Bifrontal span; (B) anterior horn width; (C) bicaudate distance; (D) third ventricular distance.

Figure 7-2. Schematic drawing of a CT scan slice at the level of bodies of lateral ventricles showing where the width of the cella media (narrowest mid-portion of bodies of the third ventricles) was measured (A).

cerebral ventricles in normal subjects, age 23 to 88 years. An increase in sulcal volume was found only after age 60. According to the authors, their technique may have slightly underestimated the increase in fluid volume with increasing age, but they state that the error would not likely be of sufficient magnitude to alter their results. However, the possibility that minor increases in sulcal volume prior to age 60 may not have been noted cannot be excluded.

In summary, there is good evidence that prominent sulci and cerebral fissures on CT scans increase with advancing age. The age of onset of this change has not yet been firmly established and the significance of prominent sulci and cerebral fissures is not known. Sulcal prominence does not appear to be a useful predictor of cognitive function in normal subjects. Some data, however, suggest that enlargement of the left Sylvian fissure may correlate with decreased intellectual performance. Additional studies using well-designed neuropsychological protocols will be required to define further the relationship between mental status changes and CT scan findings of prominent sulci and fissures in normal elderly.

Ventricular Size

A variety of CT scan indices involving parameters of width, area, and volume have been used to estimate ventricular size (Table 7-2). Examples of common linear measurements include the widths of the frontal horns, third ventricle and cella media (midportion of the bodies of the lateral ventricles), the bifrontal span, the distance between the caudate nuclei (bicaudate distance), and Evans ratio (Figures 7-1 and 7-2). Evans ratio, originally defined on encephalograms, is the ratio of the transverse diameter of the frontal horns to the greatest internal transverse diameter of the skull (Evans, 1942). The linear measurements are often reported as a ratio of ventricular width to width of the brain or cranial cavity at the corresponding level. Wolpert (1977) has shown that the internal skull diameter on CT scan becomes larger with increasing window width. Caution should, therefore, be exercised in comparing measurements based upon the internal skull diameter without first taking into account the window setting. Ventricular area is measured by planimetry or semiautomated computer programs. Ventricular volume is determined using semiautomated computer programs.

Table 7-2. Measurement parameters of ventricular size in normal aging.

Parameters	References
Linear Measurements	
Lateral ventricles	Huckman et al. (1975); Gyldensted (1977); Hahn et al. (1977); Haug (1977); Gonzalez et al. (1978); Earnest et al. (1979); Kaszniak et al. (1979); Jacoby et al. (1980); Cala et al. (1981); Soininen et al. (1982)
Third ventricle	Gyldensted (1977); Haug (1977); Soininen et al. (1982)
Ventricular Area	
Lateral ventricles	Barron et al. (1976); Earnest et al. (1979); Jacoby and Levy (1980)
Semiautomated Computer Programs	
Ventricular volume	Zatz et al. (1982a)

Evidence that the ventricles increase in size with advancing age comes from several sources. Barron et al. (1976) found that the area of the lateral ventricles gradually increases over the first seven decades and then increases dramatically up to the ninth decade. During the second to third decade and the fourth to fifth decade, however, ventricle size remained stable. The data are based upon 135 normal volunteers from 9 months to 90 years of age. Earnest et al. (1979), studying normal subjects aged 62 to 88 years, and Soininen et al. (1982), studying normal subjects with a mean age of 75 ± 7, also showed that the lateral ventricles increased in size with age. Gyldensted (1977) found that the size of the third ventricle, as well as the lateral ventricle, increases with age. He studied subjects from the second to the ninth decade.

Zatz et al. (1982a), using a semiautomated computerized program to evaluate ventricular volume, found an increase in ventricular size only over the age of 60. However, their technique may have slightly underestimated the increase in fluid volume with increasing age. The authors state that the error would not likely be of sufficient magnitude to alter their results, but the possibility that minor increases in ventricular volume prior to age 60 may not have been noted cannot be excluded.

Others have failed to demonstrate that the ventricles become larger in normal aging. Cala et al. (1981) found no increase in ventricular size over the range of 15 to 44 years. However, their sample was limited to ages that overlapped considerably with the periods during which Barron et al. (1976) found no change in ventricular size. This may account for their negative findings. Hahn et al. (1977) and Jacoby et al. (1980) also found no relationship between age and ventricular size in patients aged 9 to 78 years and 62 to 88 years, respectively. The latter group did find nonsignificant trends toward a positive relationship between age and ventricular size.

Intellectual function has been correlated with ventricular size in normal elderly. Earnest et al. (1979) found that the Digit Symbol subtest of the WAIS was significantly related to lateral ventricular size independent of age. This test is multifactorial (Lezak, 1976) and is therefore sensitive to many deficits, including such noncognitive ones as motor slowing. Soininen et al. (1982) found that enlargement of the temporal horns of the lateral ventricle and the third ventricle correlated, independently of age, with decreasing cognitive performance (the psychological tests used in that study are described earlier in this chapter).

In summary, there are conflicting data about the relationship between ventricular size and normal aging. The evidence to date tends to favor the suggestion that the ventricular system does become larger as people get older, especially after the age of 60. However, the issue is by no means resolved. The data suggesting that increasing ventricular size may be a predictor of intellectual function must be interpreted very cautiously at this time.

Other Measurements

Additional parameters that have been evaluated in normal aging include (1) CT density numbers for brain tissue and (2) brain volume.

The CT density numbers are integral numbers that are directly proportional to the linear attenuation coefficients of X-rays in brain tissue (Peterson and Kieffer, 1976). Zatz et al. (1982b) examined the CT density numbers of white matter in the centrum semiovale in normal subjects aged 23 to 88 years. They reported a significant decrease with advancing age. The authors suggest that this may reflect either a primary change in the white matter or secondary axonal and glial changes following neural loss in the cortex.

Brain volume in normal subjects was estimated by Yamaura et al. (1980) using computerized analysis. They found a significant reduction in brain size after age 50. In a subsequent study by the same group, Ito et al. (1981) improved upon their own technique and were able to demonstrate a decrease in brain volume as early as 40 years of age. Ito and coworkers also evaluated intellectual function in their subjects, all of whom were normal and ranging in age from the third to the eighth decade. They used Hasegawa's dementia rating scale, which is a brief, eleven-item test that examines orientation, memory, general knowledge, and arithmetic. A significant correlation between a decrease in brain volume and impairment on this dementia scale was observed. This finding was age independent.

Computerized programs for analysis of CT data will likely play an increasingly important role in the study of age-related changes in the brain as technology continues to improve. Development in this direction is particularly appropriate, since quantitative and qualitative CT data are available in digital form for computerized analysis.

Prominent Cerebellar Sulci and Cisterns

The CT scan visualization of sulci in the cerebellar hemispheres does not correlate with age. Similarly, there is no relationship between enlargement of the superior cerebellar, cerebellopontine angle, quadrigeminal or lateral cisterns, the cisterna magna, or the fourth ventricle with age (Allen et al., 1979).

Sulci in the cerebellar vermis may appear on CT scans of healthy elderly individuals in the absence of prominent sulci in the cerebellar hemispheres or cerebral cortex (Koller et al., 1981). The same group found no association between the gait changes of aging and the visualization of sulci in the cerebellar vermis on CT scan.

Dementia

The age and diagnostic profiles of the dementia patients discussed below are given in Table 7-3.

Prominent Sulci and Fissures

Prominent sulci and fissures on CT scan in dementia have been studied with essentially the same quantitative techniques used in normal aging (Table 7-4). There is conflicting data correlating the size of the cerebral sulci and fissures with dementia.

De Leon et al. (1980) found a significant relationship between subjective measures of prominent sulci and cognitive function independent of age in patients with senile dementia of the Alzheimer type (SDAT). Cognitive function was assessed using tests of memory, perceptual-motor skills, and global measures. The global measures were the Guild Memory test, the vocabulary subtest of the WAIS, and a clinical interview by a psychiatrist. The percentages of cognitive measures that correlated with a subjective impression of prominent sulci were 25, 14, and 100 for the memory, perceptual-motor, and global tests, respectively. Prominent sulci, therefore, seemed to be a good predictor of performance on the global tests. Objective linear measurements of sulcal width and Sylvian fissure size did not correlate with cognitive function.

Jacoby and Levy (1980) used subjective measures in CT scans of patients with senile dementia to obtain a global rating of prominent sulci and fissures involving five

Table 7-3. Dementia groups studied.

Diagnostic Label	Age (Years) Range	Mean	References
No label*	62–90	—	Roberts and Caird (1976)
SDAT[1]	60–84	70.0±6.0	De Leon et al. (1980)
SD[2]	7th–9th decade	78.63±6.58	Jacoby and Levy (1980)
PD[3]	55–64	59.6±3.7	Naeser et al. (1980)
SDAT	68–84	77.6±5.9	Naeser et al. (1980)
PD	53–64	58.7±3.3	Albert et al. (1981)
SDAT	65–76	69.3±4.4	Albert et al. (1981)
AD[4]	—	60.4±9.4	Brinkman et al. (1981)
No label**	55–87	—	Ford and Winter (1981)
No label***	65+	75.4 ± 6.9	Hughes and Gado (1981)
SD	–	77.8±4.95	Bondareff et al. (1981)
SDAT	–	77 ± 6[†]	Soininen et al. (1982)
SDAT	65–76	69.3 ± 4.8	Naeser et al. (1982)

1. SDAT, senile dementia of the Alzheimer type
2. SD, senile dementia.
3. PD, presenile dementia (Alzheimer type)
4. AD, Alzheimer's disease.

*Dementia with no focal lesion.
**Dementia with no evidence of focal CT and neurological findings, stroke, or normal pressure hydrocephalus.
***Dementia with no evidence of cerebrovascular disease, head trauma, alcoholism, or previous intracranial surgery.
† Mean of patients with SDAT and multi-infarct dementia combined.

Table 7-4. Measurement parameters of prominent sulci and fissures in dementia.

Parameters	References
Linear Measurements	
Width of widest hemispheric sulcus (high cut)	Roberts and Caird (1976)
Mean width of four largest sulci on highest cut	Soininen et al. (1982)
Sum of widths of four largest sulci on upper three cuts	Fox et al. (1975); Huckman et al. (1975); Kaszniak et al. (1979); Hughes and Gado (1981)
Sum of widths of three most prominent cortical sulci	De Leon et al. (1980)
Sum of width of four largest sulci	Brinkman et al. (1981)
Width of largest sulcus plus maximum diameter of interhemispheric fissure	Ford and Winter (1981)
Maximum width of Sylvian fissure at insula on both sides	Soininen et al. (1982)
Width of Sylvian fissure on both sides	De Leon et al. (1980)
Subjective Rating	
Sum of four-point scale ratings at five cortical regions	Jacoby and Levy (1980)
Four-point rating scale	De Leon et al. (1980)
Subjective ranking	De Leon et al. (1980)
Semiautomated Computer Programs	
Fluid area	Naeser et al. (1980)
Fluid area and volume	Naeser et al. (1982)

regions: frontal, parietal, temporal, insula, and occipital. No relationship between the CT scan measures and degree of cognitive deficit was found. Intellectual function was assessed by a memory and orientation test, the Digit Copying Test, and the Digit Symbol subtest of the WAIS.

Findings similar to those of Jacoby and Levy were obtained by others using quantitative measures of prominent sulci (Roberts and Caird, 1976; Hughes and Gado, 1981; Soininen et al., 1982) and measures of prominent sulci combined with interhemispheric fissure size (Ford and Winter, 1981). Roberts and Caird studied patients with dementia who had no evidence of focal cerebral disease (age 62 to 90 years). They used the Crichton Geriatric Behavior Rating Scale and a test of memory and information to assess intellectual function. Hughes and Gado evaluated a group of demented patients who had no evidence of cerebrovascular disease, head trauma, alcoholism, or previous intracranial surgery (age range, 65+; mean age, 75.4 ± 6.9). They used a Clinical Dementia Rating score consisting of measures of memory, orientation, judgment and problem-solving, home life and hobbies, involvement in community affairs, and personal care to assess cognitive function. Soininen and coworkers studied patients with SDAT, using a battery of the psychological tests outlined earlier. Ford and Winter evaluated a population with dementia who had no evidence of focal CT scan findings, focal neurological findings, stroke, or normal pressure hydrocephalus (age range 53 to 87). Their cognitive assessment was based upon clinical parameters of orientation, language, praxis, and IQ.

Soininen et al. (1982), found that although prominent sulci did not correlate with degree of dementia in SDAT, the demented patients had significantly more sulcal prominence, as well as enlargement of the Sylvian fissure, than had controls. Similarly, Jacoby and Levy (1980) found that their measure of prominent sulci and fissure was significantly greater in demented patients compared to controls. However, there was considerable overlap between the groups. Brinkman et al. (1981), on the other hand, found no

relationship between prominent sulci and the presence of Alzheimer's disease (mean age, 60.4 ± 9.4 years).

In summary, there is conflicting data about the significance of prominent sulci and fissures on CT scan. These parameters cannot now be considered of value in predicting severity of dementia or in distinguishing between demented patients and normal subjects.

Ventricular Size

In contrast to the situation for prominent sulci and fissures, there is good agreement that ventricular size is increased in dementia (Roberts and Caird, 1976; Albert et al., 1981; De Leon et al., 1980; Soininen et al., 1982; Damasio et al., in press). The methods used to estimate ventricular size in dementia are the same as those used for normal aging (Table 7-5).

Soininen et al. (1982) and De Leon et al. (1980) found that the lateral and third ventricles become significantly larger as the severity of cognitive deficit increases in SDAT. De Leon and coworkers observed that the best correlation was with the size of the third ventricle. Roberts and Caird (1976) found a significant relationship between ventricular area and degree of cognitive impairment in their demented patients (62 to 90 years).

In addition to correlating with severity of dementia, ventricular size has also been found to distinguish between normal subjects and patients with dementia (Jacoby and Levy, 1980; Brinkman et al., 1981). Jacoby and Levy noted a great overlap in ventricular size between their patients with senile dementia and the controls. It is of interest that ventricular size did not correlate with degree of prominent sulci and fissures in the dementia group, but did in the control group. The authors raised the question as to whether this is consistent with the notion that the atrophy seen in dementia represents a different process than the changes seen in normal aging. Brinkman and coworkers measured ventricular size in Alzheimer's disease by a ventricle–brain ratio (VBR), defined as the area of the lateral ventricle taken at the largest representation above the caudate

Table 7-5. Measurement parameters of ventricular size in dementia.

Parameters	References
Linear Measurements	
Lateral ventricles	Fox et al. (1975); Huckman et al. (1975); Roberts and Caird (1976); Kaszniak et al. (1979); De Leon et al. (1980); Jacoby and Levy (1980); Brinkman et al. (1981); Soininen et al. (1982)
Third ventricle	Roberts and Caird (1976); De Leon et al. (1980); Brinkman et al. (1981); Soininen et al. (1982)
Ventricular Area	
Lateral ventricles	Jacoby and Levy (1980); Brinkman et al. (1981)
Slice showing largest area of ventricle	Roberts and Caird (1976)
Subjective Rating	De Leon et al. (1980); Brinkman et al. (1981)
Semiautomated Computer Programs	
Fluid area and volume	Albert et al. (1981); Naeser et al. (1982)

nuclei divided by the corresponding intracranial area, and also by the distance between the lateral wall of the third ventricle and the Sylvian fissure.

Albert et al. (1981) compared ventricular size in presenile and senile dementia with age-matched controls. They found that there was a significant increase in ventricular size in the presenile dementia patients (under age 65), but not in the senile dementia group (over age 65). The controls were primarily male, whereas the dementia patients were primarily female. The relationship between sex differences and ventricular size has not been well defined. Using semiautomated computer programs, Zatz et al. (1982a) found no difference in ventricular size between normal male and female subjects over an age range of 23 to 88 years. On the other hand, Gyldensted (1977), using linear measurements, found that the lateral ventricles were significantly larger in normal males in a sample ranging from 17 to 86 years. The findings of Albert et al. (1981) stress the importance of examining the relationships between CT scanning and dementia in various separate age groups. Whether their observations are due to (1) differences in disease processes between presenile and senile dementia, (2) an interaction between the effects of aging and dementia, (3) sex differences, or (4) other factors must await further study. These important questions need to be addressed. If the findings of Albert and coworkers are confirmed, they may prove useful diagnostically.

In summary, ventricular size does appear to correlate well with the presence of dementia and the degree of cognitive impairment in dementia. There is some question as to whether this is true at all ages.

Computerized Tomographic Density Numbers

The CT density numbers of cerebral grey and white matter have been evaluated in dementia (Naeser et al., 1980; Bondareff et al., 1981; Naeser et al., 1982).

Naeser et al. (1980) studied patients with presenile and senile dementia of the Alzheimer type. A significant decrease in CT density numbers, independent of age, was found in the white matter of the centrum semiovale. There was no overlap between the demented patients and the non-demented controls. It is of interest that age-related changes in the white matter in the dementia cases were not found (i.e., both the presenile and the senile group had low mean CT density numbers in the centrum semiovale). Zatz et al. (1982a) did find increasingly lower mean CT density numbers in the centrum semiovale in normal cases with advancing age.

In senile dementia, Bondareff et al. (1981) found a significant decrease in mean CT density numbers in several regions compared to normal subjects. The affected areas were the medial temporal lobes bilaterally, the anterior frontal lobe, and the head of the caudate.

Naeser et al. (1982), using a semiautomated computer program, found a decrease in CT density numbers in several brain regions in patients with SDAT as compared to age-matched controls. The parietal and frontal areas showed a significant decrease in CT density, bilaterally. This was most marked in the parietal area. There was also a significant decrease in CT density in the centrum semiovale and the mid-line thalamic nuclei.

In summary, CT density measurements in dementia appear to hold great promise for further advancements in our understanding of this condition. More research needs to be done before any statements can be made regarding the relationship of CT density to cognitive impairment.

Conclusion

Computerized tomography scanning has opened up a new dimension for the study of brain–behavior relationships. In normal aging, there appears to be a well-established relationship between prominent sulci and advancing age. The relationship between ventricular size and aging is still uncertain. Ventricle size may increase after age 60. The predictive value of CT scan findings with respect to cognitive function in normal elderly is not yet defined.

In dementia, there is a consensus that ventricular size increases. The significance of prominent sulci and fissures, on the other hand, is still unresolved. The mean CT density numbers in some brain regions appear to decrease in dementia.

Despite these CT profiles, there is considerable overlap between the findings in aging and dementia. Therefore, in the individual case, the CT scan findings cannot be used to determine whether dementia is present or not (Wells and Duncan, 1977). Dementia is a clinical diagnosis that, at this time, can be made only on the basis of a thorough evaluation and never on the basis of CT scan findings alone. This situation may change as CT scan technology improves.

References

Albert, M.S., Naeser, M.A., Kleefield, J., and Garvey, A.J. (1981). CT scan evaluation of patients with Alzheimer's disease. Paper read before the Gerontological Society Meeting, Toronto, Canada, November 8–12.

Allen, J.H., Marlin, J.T., and McLain, L.W. (1979). Computed tomography in cerebellar atrophic processes. Radiology 130, 379–382.

Barron, S.A., Jacobs, L., and Kinkel, W.R. (1976). Changes in size of normal lateral ventricles during aging determined by computerized tomography. Neurology (Minneapolis) 26, 1011–1013.

Bentson, J., Reza, M., Winter, J., and Wilson, G. (1978). Steroids and apparent cerebral atrophy on computed tomography scans. J. Computer Assisted Tomogr. 2, 16–23.

Bondareff, W., Baldy, R., and Levy, R. (1981). Quantitative computed tomography in senile dementia. Arch. Gen. Psychiat. 38, 1365–1368.

Blinkov, S.M. and Glezer, I.I. (1968). The Human Brain in Figures and Tables. Plenum Press, New York.

Brinkman, S.D., Sarwar, M., Levin, H.S., and Morris, H.H. (1981). Quantitative indexes of computer tomography in dementia and normal aging. Neuroradiology 138, 89–92.

Cala, L.A., Thickbroom, G.W., Black, J.L., Collins, D.W.K., and Mastaglia, F.L. (1981). Brain density and cerebrospinal fluid space size: CT of normal volunteers. Amer. J. Neuroradiol. 2, 41–47.

Carlen, P.L., Wortzman, G., Holgate, R.C., Wilkinson, D.A., and Rankin, J.G. (1978). Reversible cerebral atrophy in recently abstinent chronic alcoholics measured by computed tomography scans. Science, 200, 1076–1078.

Damasio, H., Eslinger, P.J., Damasio, A.R., Rizzo, M., Huang, H., and Demeter, S. (in press). Computed tomography in the diagnosis of dementia. Arch. Neurol.

De Leon, M.J., Ferris, S.H., George, A.E., Reisberg, B., Kricheff, I.I., and Gershon, S. (1980). Computed tomography evaluations of brain-behavior relationships in senile dementia of the Alzheimer's type. Neurobiol. Aging 1, 69–79.

Di Chiro, G., Brooks, R.A., Dubal, L., and Chew, E. (1978). The apical artifact: Elevated attenuation values toward the apex of the skull. J. Computer Assisted Tomogr. 2, 65–69.

Earnest, M.P., Heaton, R.K., Welkinson, W.E., and Manke, W.F. (1979). Cortical atrophy, ventricular enlargement and intellectual impairment in the aged. Neurology 29, 1138–1143.

Evans, W.A. (1942). An encephalographic ratio for estimating ventricular enlargement and cerebral atrophy. Arch. Neurol. Psychiat. 47, 931–937.

Ford, C.V. and Winter, J. (1981). Computerized axial tomograms and dementia in elderly patients. J. Gerontol. 36, 164–169.

Fox, J.H., Topel, J.L., and Huckman, M.S. (1975). Use of computerized tomography in senile dementia. J. Neurol., Neurosurg., Psychiat. 38, 948–953.

Gonzalez, C.F., Lantieri, R.L., and Nathan, R.J. (1978). The CT scan appearance of the brain in the normal elderly population: A correlative study. Neuroradiology 16, 120–122.

Gyldensted, C. (1977). Measurements of the normal ventricular system and hemispheric sulci of 100 adults with computed tomography. Neuroradiology 14, 183–192.

Hahn, F.J.Y., Rim, K., and Schapiro, R.L. (1977). A quantitative analysis of ventricular size on computed tomographic scans. J. Computer Assisted Tomogr. 1, 121–124.

Haug, G. (1977). Age and sex dependence on the size of normal ventricles on computed tomography. Neuroradiology 14, 201–204.

Huckman, M.S., Fox, J., and Topel, J. (1975). The validity of criteria for the evaluation of cerebral atrophy by computed tomography. Radiology 116, 85–92.

Hughes, C.P. and Gado, M. (1981). Computed tomography and aging of the brain. Radiology 139, 391–396.

Ito, M., Hatazawa, J., Yamaura, H., and Matsuzawa, T. (1981). Age-related brain atrophy and mental deterioration—a study with computed tomography. Br. J. Radiol. 54, 384–390.

Jacoby, R.J. and Levy, R. (1980). Computed tomography in the elderly 2. Senile dementia: Diagnosis and functional impairment. Br. J. Psychiat. 135, 256–269.

Jacoby, R.J., Levy, R., and Dawson, J.M. (1980). Computed tomography in the elderly 1. The normal population. Br. J. Psychiat. 136, 249–255.

Kaszniak, A.W., Garron, D.C., Fox, J.H., Bergen, D., and Huckman, M. (1979). Cerebral Atrophy, EEG slowing, age, education and cognitive functioning in suspected dementia. Neurology 29, 1273–1279.

Koller, W.C., Glatt, S.L., Fox, J.H., Kaszniak, A.W., Wilson, R.S., and Huckman, M.S. (1981). Cerebellar atrophy: Relationship to aging and cerebral atrophy. Neurology 31, 1486–1488.

Le May, M. (1967). Changes in ventricular size during and after pneumoencephalography. Radiology 88, 57–63.

Lezak, M.D. (1976). Neuropsychological Assessment. Oxford University Press, New York.

Messert, B., Wannamaker, B.B., and Dudley, A.W. (1972). Reevaluation of the size of the lateral ventricles of the brain. Neurology (Minneap.) 22, 941–951.

Naeser, M.A., Gebhardt, C., and Levine, H.L. (1980). Decreased computerized tomography numbers in patients with presenile dementia. Arch. Neurol. 37, 401–409.

Naeser, M.A., Albert, M.S., and Kleefield, J. (1982). New methods of CT scan diagnosis of Alzheimer's disease: Examination of white and gray matter mean CT density numbers. In "Alzheimer's Disease: A Report of Progress", Aging, Vol. 19. S. Corkin, K.L. Davis, J.H. Growden, E. Usden, and R.J. Wurtman, Eds. Raven Press, New York, pp. 63–78.

Peterson, H.O. and Kieffer, S.A. (1976). Neuroradiology (Addendum). In Clinical Neurology, A.B. Baker and L.H. Baker, Eds. Harper & Row, Philadelphia.

Roberts, M.A. and Caird, F.I. (1976). Computerized tomography and intellectual impairment in the elderly. J. Neurol., Neurosurg., Psychiat. 39, 986–989.

Soininen, H., Puranen, M., and Riekkinen, P.J. (1982). Computed tomography findings in senile dementia and normal aging. J. Neurol., Neurosurg., Psychiat., 45, 50–54.

Wells, C.E. and Duncan, G.W. (1977). Danger of overreliance on computerized cranial tomography. Amer. J. Psychiat. 134, 811–813.

Wolpert, S.M. (1977). The ventricular size on computed tomography. J. Computer Assisted Tomogr. 1, 222–226.

Yamaura, H., Ito, M., Kubota, K., and Matsuzawa, T. (1980). Brain atrophy during aging: A quantitative study with computed tomography. J. Gerontol. 35, 492–498.

Zatz, L.M., Jernigan, T.L., and Ahumada, A.J. (1982a). Changes on computed cranial tomography with aging: Intracranial fluid volume. Amer. J. Neuroradiol. 3, 1–11.

Zatz, L.M., Jernigan, T.L., and Ahumada, A.J. (1982b). White matter changes in cerebral computed tomography related to aging. J. Computer Assisted Tomogr. 6, 19–23.

8. Evoked Potentials in Aging

JOHN POLICH

ARNOLD STARR

With increased age, there is a concomitant change in the speed with which the nervous system responds to external stimuli. In general, there is a relatively rapid increase in neural transmission time as the human neonate matures into childhood and puberty, followed by a slowing as the adult human ages. These phenomena are well documented in the behavioral literature (e.g., Botwinick, 1977; Birren et al., 1979). During the last decade, however, electrophysiological measures have also been applied extensively to the analysis of aging effects. This approach has concentrated on the measurement of changes in the latency and amplitude of the primary sensory evoked potentials (e.g. Starr et al., 1978) and, more recently, on the measurement of cognitive changes as reflected by event-related brain potentials (e.g., Donchin et al., 1978). Because these measures reflect changes in neuroelectric activity, they are beginning to provide an accurate and informative index of how development and aging affect the transmission of sensory input and cognition.

This chapter surveys the data that have been obtained from evoked potential measures of aging. The general format consists of a description of evoked potentials to various sensory signals, including a discussion of the neural structures involved in the generation of the potentials. The effects of aging on the specific potential components will then be reviewed, with the focus on neonatal maturation and advanced age. The auditory, visual, and somatosensory modalities will be followed by an examination of the effects of aging on cognitive potentials. Table 8-1 portrays the primary components of interest for each sensory modality within their typical latency range. The longer-latency, event-related potentials generally can be obtained with all three sensory inputs and are listed according to their approximate peak latency. The effects of age on these measures will be discussed by comparing various age groupings across the primary evoked potential components.

Auditory Evoked Potentials

Presentation of an auditory stimulus at various rates and intensities elicits a series of auditory evoked potentials (AEPs), which can reflect changes in stimulus parameters as well as subject states (Picton et al., 1974). These potentials are typically classified by latency, as the top row of Table 8-1 illustrates. From 0 to 10 milliseconds, the auditory brainstem response

The writing of this chapter was supported by NIH Grant NS 11876-07 to the second author. Thanks to Patricia Merjanian and Carl Rosenberg for their helpful comments.

Table 8-1. Main components of sensory and cognitive potentials.

Modality	Sensory Potentials			Cognitive Potentials
	0–10 msec	10–80 msec	80 msec	~ 100–1000 msec
AUDITORY	ABR's Waves I–VII	Middle Latency Na, Pa, Nb, Pb, Nc	Long Latency N1, P2, N2	N100 (Attention) P200 (Early processing) N200 (Detection)
VISUAL	—	—	P100	P300 (Surprise, decision)
SOMATOSENSORY	N7 N10 P11 N13	N18 P30 P20 N40 N20/N22 N50 P60	—	CNV (Preparation)

(ABR) is observed with a highly consistent pattern of peaks typically labeled Waves I through VII (see Figure 8-1). The middle latency components are comprised of a series of peaks found within 10 to 80 milliseconds. The main potentials of interest in this range are most often labeled Na, Pa, and Nb, although later components (Nb, Nc) are also sometimes identified (see Figure 8-5a). The relatively long-latency components of the AEP are the N1, P2, and N2. These potentials are sensitive to changes in stimulus parameters and, additionally, reflect changes in the subject's states of consciousness (e.g., drowsiness increases the amplitude of the N2, as in Figure 8-6). When the long-latency potentials are elicited in psychologically relevant contexts, they can index changes in attention, decision-making, and other cognitive processes. Hence, they are listed in both the sensory and cognitive potential columns of Table 8-1. Each of these major categories of AEPs will be reviewed with respect to the effects of maturation and age.

Auditory Brainstem Response

The ABR reflects maturational changes in brainstem development. Differences in peak development, amplitude, and latency are readily apparent as the human neonate matures; they are illustrated in Figure 8-1. A series of studies (Salamy and McKean, 1976; Salamy et al., 1979; Salamy et al.,

1975; Salamy et al., 1978) has systematically examined changes in the ABR as a function of maturation. Based on the

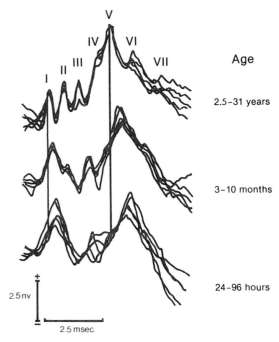

Figure 8-1. Maturational changes in the latency and waveform of the auditory brainstem response (ABR) from birth to adulthood. The vertical lines through Waves I and V emphasize the age-related shifts in latency. The superimposed tracings emphasize the consistent changes in the ABR waveform that take place as a function of age (after Salamy et al., 1975).

(a)

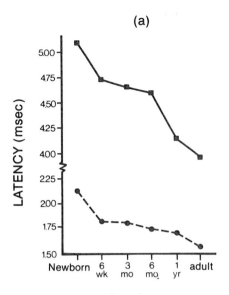

(b)

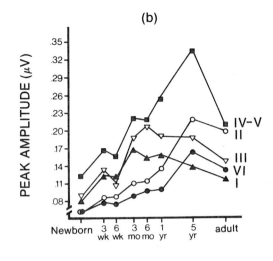

Figure 8-2. (a) Maturational trends for peripheral (Wave I latency, ●) and central (Wave V–I difference, ■) transmission time as a function of age. Each point represents the mean latency for each age group (after Salamy and McKean, 1976). (b) Mean amplitude of primary ABR components as a function of subject age group (after Salamy et al., 1979).

findings obtained from animal models (e.g., Achor and Starr, 1980; Buchwald and Huang, 1975; Jewett and Romano, 1972) and studies of brainstem neuropathology (e.g., Starr and Achor, 1975; Stockard and Rossiter, 1977), the latency of Wave I (reflecting activity of the eighth cranial nerve) from stimulus onset can be taken as a measure of peripheral transmission time, whereas the difference between Wave V (reflecting activity of midbrain auditory structures) and Wave I can be taken as a measure of central transmission time. As Figure 8-2a illustrates, these two measures of brainstem maturation change differentially with increased age up to about one year (Starr et al., 1977). Age effects are also reflected in changes in peak amplitudes for the major components of the ABR and are portrayed in Figure 8-2b.

As individuals continue to mature through middle age and into the later years, this pattern can reverse such that an increase in latency for both peripheral and central transmission times is observed (Patterson et al., 1981). Peak latencies for

the major ABR components across these older age groups are presented in Figure 8-3 and reflect differences in transmission time between the younger and older adults across the spectrum of ABR peaks. However, the nature of this latency increase appears to be quite variable, since several studies have reported only weak effects or no effect on peak latency with increased age (Jerger and Hall, 1980; Rosenhamer et al., 1980; Rowe, 1978; Stockard et al., 1978). Advanced age has been found to produce some shifts in amplitude, which are illustrated in Figure 8-4 (Harkins and Lenhardt, 1980). Both the latency and amplitude changes suggest a disorder in brainstem auditory conduction capability that may accompany the aging process.

Middle Latency Components

In contrast to aging studies of the ABR, the middle latency potentials have not been extensively investigated across the adult life-span (Polich and Starr, 1982), although some versions have shown prom-

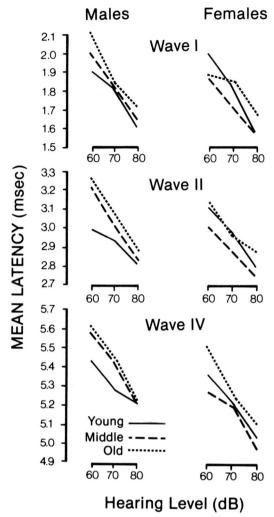

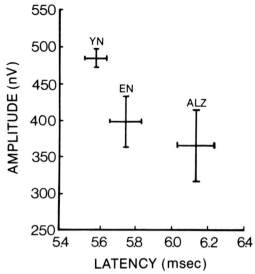

Figure 8-4. Effect of age and dementia on amplitude and latency of Wave V of the ABR. Since the groups (YN, young normal, 25 years; EN, elderly normal, 67 years; ALZ, Alzheimer's patients, 58 years) did not differ in latency of Wave I, the Wave V latency can be considered to reflect group differences in central transmission time. Bars represent one standard error (after Harkins and Lenhardt, 1980).

Figure 8-3. Effects of age and sex on latencies of ABR components obtained from 20 subjects in each group (young, 20–29; middle, 40–59; old, 60–79 years) (after Patterson et al., 1981).

ise for hearing evaluation (Galambos et al., 1981). An example of a normal adult middle latency AEP is presented in Figure 8-5a. As this figure indicates, these components are relatively sensitive to changes in stimulus intensity, in addition to other stimulus variables such as duration and presentation interval (Thornton et al., 1977; Mendel et al., 1975). The effects of early development are illustrated in Figure 8-5b and demonstrate a steady growth in amplitude and component definition dur-

ing the first few months of life. Although there has been difficulty in obtaining good middle component morphology in neonates (Davis et al., 1974; Skinner and Glattke, 1977), little difference between adult and infant waveforms, due to changes in intensity or rate of stimulus presentation, has been found (Goldstein and McRandle, 1976; Mendel et al., 1977).

Some slight but consistent differences between neonates and adults have been observed for the middle latency range. The primary difference is again slightly shorter latencies and smaller amplitudes for the neonates relative to adults. The Pa component appears to increase in amplitude with an increase in neonatal age from one to eight months with generally little significant activity observed beyond 50 milliseconds (Pb, Nc, Pc) for very young subjects, although the later components are often observed in adult subjects (Mendel, 1977; Wolf and Goldstein, 1978). Ipsilateral

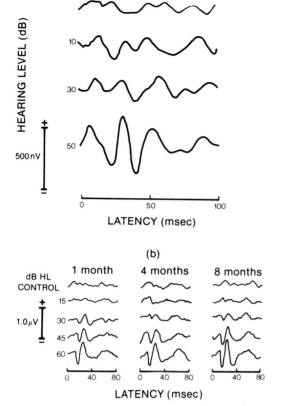

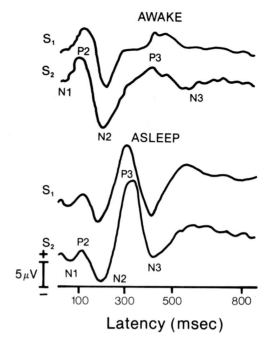

Figure 8-6. Comparison of long-latency auditory evoked potentials for two adult subjects between awake and asleep states (after Skinner and Antinoro, 1969).

Figure 8-5. (a) Effects of stimulus intensity on middle latency components of the auditory evoked potential compared to control for normal adult subject (after Wolf and Goldstein, 1978). (b) Middle-latency components for infants of various age groupings ($n = 6$) for different stimulus intensities (after Mendel et al., 1977).

stimulation produces larger amplitude components in the neonate than does contralateral stimulation. With adulthood, these amplitude differences become symmetrical (Wolf and Goldstein, 1980). Thus, the middle latency components appear to show relatively little change with early maturational development. How they may change with advanced age is not known.

Long-Latency Components

The long-latency AEPs depend both on the attributes of the signal and the sub-

ject's psychological processes (Picton et al., 1974; Picton and Hillyard, 1974). The latter attribute is illustrated in Figure 8-6, where the major components of the long-latency AEPs are plotted for two adult subjects in an awake and an asleep state. Stimulus variables such as intensity will increase both amplitude and latency of the N1-P2-N2 waveform (e.g., Picton et al., 1977; Davis, 1976), whereas greater amplitude P2-N2 components are observed for deeper sleep stages (Ornitz et al., 1974).

These considerations have led a number of investigators to employ the long-latency AEP as a measure of maturation and aging for both sensory and perceptual processes (e.g., Hillyard et al., 1978; Ford and Pfefferbaum, 1980). For infants, the effects of maturation on the long-latency AEPs produces systematic decreases in latency and increases in amplitude (Barnet et al., 1975; Ellingson et al., 1974). These effects are summarized in Figure 8-7 and suggest that the largest effect of early

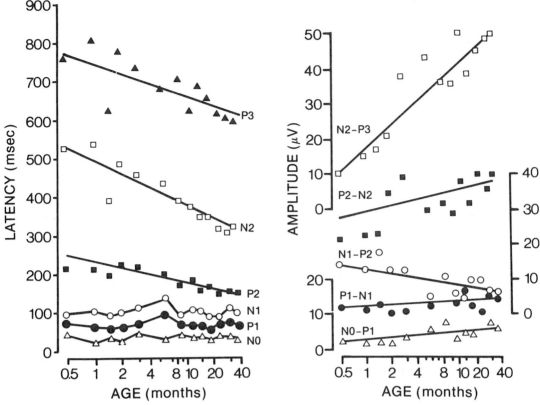

Figure 8-7. (a) Mean latencies of long latency auditory evoked potential components as a function of each age group ($n = 10$). Regression lines are drawn for those components that varied significantly with age. (b) Mean peak-to-peak amplitudes for the various components with respect to age. Regression lines are shown for each component. Left ordinates are for NO-P1 and N2-P3; the right ordinate is for P1-N1, N1-P2, and P2-N2 component amplitudes (after Barnet et al., 1975).

growth occurs within several months after birth. Such amplitude changes, however, have been associated with increased periods of "quiet" sleep as the newborn advances in age (Rapin and Graziani, 1967; Davis and Onishi, 1969). Maturational effects on the long-latency AEP appear more directly related to estimated postconceptual age rather than postnatal age (Graziani et al., 1974; Weitzman and Graziani, 1968). In addition, three-month-old female infants demonstrate higher-amplitude, left hemisphere long-latency components than male infants, suggesting the possibility of differential hemispheric development (Shucard et al., 1981).

As depicted in Figure 8-6, a similar variability in waveform morphology, amplitude, and latency is observed in sleep stages for adults (Weitzman et al., 1965; Taguchi et al., 1969). The effects of stimulus intensity on amplitude and latency for these components also change with age and are illustrated in Figure 8-8 for a group of young (20- to 30-year-old) and extraordinarily healthy, aged (70- to 80-year-old) subjects (Pfefferbaum et al., 1979). Although the stimulus intensities were adjusted systematically to sensation level threshold in this study, dramatic

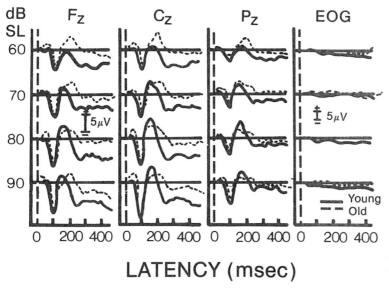

Figure 8-8. Average long-latency auditory evoked potentials for older (70–80 years) and younger (20–30 years) subjects ($n = 9$ each group) to stimuli of 60, 70, 80, and 90 dB SL recorded from Fz, Cz, and Pz electrode sites with associated EOG (after Pfefferbaum et al., 1979).

differences between the two age groups were observed. These differences, characterized in Figure 8-9, are most pronounced over the frontal electrode sites for the later P2 component. The differential effect of age on the various potentials and their scalp distributions suggests that aging does not reflect a general degradation of physiological processes. Unfortunately, because the neural generators for these components are largely unknown (cf. Knight et al., 1980; Vaughan and Ritter, 1970), strong inferences about the specific causes for these age effects are not possible. These components, however, do appear to provide a measure for assessing age-related neurophysiological changes for both sensory and perceptual processes before the manifestation of clinically relevant pathology.

Auditory Evoked Potentials and Aging

The effects of maturation and aging are well defined by the slowing of electrophysiological responsivity in the auditory system. Maturation into childhood stabilizes both amplitude and latency of the primary ABR components. Subsequently, throughout adult life, there is a slowing of these initial responses to auditory stimuli. Maturational changes are also reflected in

the middle- and long-latency AEPs, with advanced age evidenced by substantial slowing and a general decrease in component amplitude, at least for the long-latency AEPs. While the precise mechanisms for these changes are not yet well understood, both peripheral and central transmission rates of auditory stimuli are affected by age. The gross changes observed in the long-latency AEPs with advanced age suggest that the capacity of the cortical auditory processing centers to respond to auditory stimuli decreases, along with changes in receptor sites. Although the effects of aging on the various parameters of the AEP are still largely descriptive, their utility as a diagnostic tool is promising because of their precision and the comparative ease with which they can be acquired in clinical populations.

Visual Evoked Response

Presentation of a reversing checkerboard pattern to the human eye will reliably evoke consistent electrocortical activity. When averaged over as few as 25 to 50 such presentations, the visual evoked response (VER) recorded between the occipital and frontal sites is obtained with its characteristic negative-positive-negative deflection pattern. Examples of adult

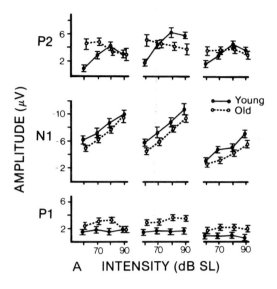

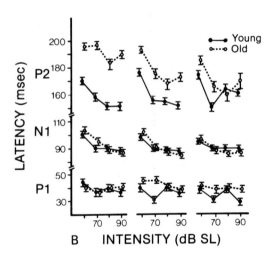

Figure 8-9. (A) Means and standard errors for amplitude of P1, N1, and P2 components of long-latency auditory evoked potentials for old and young subjects as in Figure 8-8. (B) Means and standard errors for latency of same components (after Pfefferbaum et al., 1979).

waveforms for several ages are presented in Figure 8-10. The prominent, positive-going peak occurring about 100 milliseconds after stimulus presentation is usually termed the P100 or P1 as indicated in the middle row of Table 8-1. This VER com-

ponent has proven valuable in the investigation of visual system pathology (Desmedt, 1977), particularly in the detection of asymptomatic optic neuritis in patients with multiple sclerosis (Halliday, 1978). Although some studies have employed a light flash stimulus to elicit a visual evoked potential for various age groups (e.g., Dustman and Beck, 1969; Ellingson et al., 1973; Callaway and Halliday, 1973; Blom et al., 1980), the waveforms obtained from this procedure are more complex and variable than those illustrated in Figure 8-10. Because pattern-shift stimulation is thought to activate the mammalian visual cortical processes responsive to contour and also yields similar evoked potential forms across the population, the checkerboard pattern is the preferred clinical test stimulus.

P100 Aging Effects

The major developmental application of VERs has been in the study of the early maturation for the visual system (infancy to young childhood to advanced age). The VER has been used to measure change in visual acuity in the maturing infant (e.g., Harter et al., 1977; Marg et al., 1976). The amplitude of P100 increases as the infant matures and also changes systematically as a function of check size which reflects the maturation of visual acuity. These effects, illustrated in Figure 8-11, show that detectable amplitudes are first observed for two-month-old infants with relatively large pattern sizes. The amplitudes of the P100 component increase with age and can be obtained for quite small check sizes at six months. These effects have been related to behavioral measures of acuity and have been successfully employed in clinical settings (Sokol, 1980). The amplitude of the P100 decreases significantly in size from early childhood until adolescence, when further decreases are minimal. Females during this age period show larger amplitudes than males, but sex differences are less apparent after 20 years of age (Snyder et al., 1981).

The latency of the P100 component also changes with maturation and stimu-

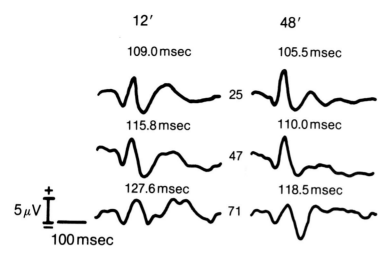

Figure 8-10. Visual evoked potentials for different-sized check patterns from three subjects of different ages (years). The P100 latency is given for each waveform (after Sokol et al., 1981).

lus (Sokol and Jones, 1979). As illustrated in Figure 8-12, there is a rapid decrease in P100 latency during the first three months as visual acuity develops, with relatively little change through childhood (Fenwick et al., 1981). Stimulus factors such as luminance level and check size also appear to affect increases in latency due to advanced age (Shaw and Cant, 1980; Celesia and Daly, 1977; Sokol et al., 1981). The importance of stimulus size on the P100 latency is illustrated in Figure 8-13 and may account for the different conclusions from various studies of P100 latency and aging effects (cf. Asselman et al., 1975; Hennerici et al., 1977; Shearer and Dustman, 1980; Stockard et al., 1979). Thus, just as overall acuity develops with maturation in the newborn and interacts with the latency of the P100 component of the VER, so too does advanced age affect the ability to resolve finer spatial frequencies.

Visual Evoked Responses and Aging

A number of optical, neural, and biochemical factors have been proposed to account for the changes observed in VER amplitude and latency that occur with maturation and aging (e.g., Harter et al., 1977; Ordy and Brizzee, 1979; Sokol and Jones, 1979). As the newborn infant matures, the retina becomes more sensitive to stimulation and myelination of the optic nerve increases. These changes have been associated with the increased amplitude and decreased latency for the P100 component of the VER during the first year of life. When taken together with the increase in spatial frequency resolution that also occurs with age (Figure 8-12), these findings suggest that development of the higher cortical centers is primarily responsible for the VER changes with maturation.

Optical considerations, such as retinal degeneration or decreases in pupil size that accompany age, do not appear to contribute to the significant changes in the VER with advanced age. Rather, the general slowing observed in the P100 for high spatial frequency stimuli suggests that there is a decrease in the number of axons in the optic nerve and that there may be biochemical changes in the lateral geniculate and occipital cortex. Although psychophysical studies of visual system aging support this suggestion, no direct connection between changes in the VER and the ability to resolve spatial frequency information has been determined. Despite the paucity of specific neurophysiological data, however, visual evoked potentials have provided a relatively precise means for assessing the effects of age on a primary human sensory and information processing system.

Somatosensory Evoked Potentials

Median nerve stimulation produces a variety of potentials that can be recorded from

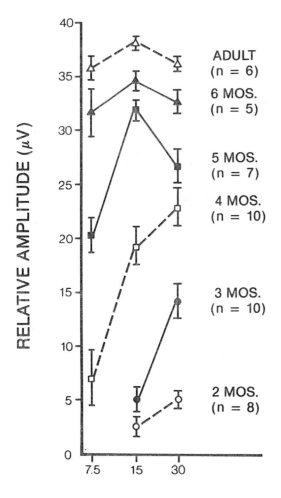

Figure 8-11. Relative amplitude of the visual evoked potential as a function of check size for infants of different ages and adult subjects. Data points represent the mean value of normalized amplitudes and one standard error (after Sokol and Dobson, 1976).

the scalp. These somatosensory evoked potentials (SEPs) were the first to be recorded with signal averaging techniques and have been extensively investigated (Cracco and Cracco, 1976; Desmedt and Brunko, 1980; Kritchevsky and Wiederholt, 1978). Some SEP components (N20, N40) are focally restricted to the somatosensory area contralateral to the stimulated side, whereas both the shorter (N10, N13) and the longer latency potentials

(N50, P60) have diffuse bilateral distribution (Goff et al., 1962; Desmedt, 1971; Desmedt and Brunko, 1980). These components are listed in the bottom row of Table 8-1 (see Figures 8-14 and 8-15) and are thought to reflect activity in the thalomocortical connections or the primary somatosensory cortex. The short-latency components in somatosensory stimulation can also be recorded over the peripheral nerve (Erb's point) and the cervical spine, which suggests that they are generated at these sites (Cracco, 1973; Mathews et al., 1974). Both the scalp and spinal recording sites produce SEPs that change with maturation and age, although the cortical locations have received the most attention (e.g., Noel and Desmedt, 1980; Desmedt et al., 1973). Although electrical stimulation is most often used to elicit SEPs, mechanically evoked somatosensory potentials can also be recorded and demonstrate similar, albeit attenuated waveform morphology (e.g., Pratt et al., 1979).

Cortical Somatosensory Evoked Potentials

Although normative data for SEPs is still being acquired, the components recorded over the postcentral gyrus have been found to change with maturation and age. Examples obtained from newborn infants are illustrated in Figure 8-14 and index the electrophysiological differences associated with stages of infant sleep. Of particular clinical interest, however, is the early negative component, or N1 potential (often labeled N20 when obtained from median nerve stimulation or N22 with digital stimulation in adults), which rapidly decreases in latency with maturation in infants and slowly increases in latency with advanced age. Representative recordings of these responses are presented in Figure 8-15 for infant, child, and adult waveforms, with similar recordings obtained from an elderly subject presented in Figure 8-16. As is apparent from these tracings, the general morphology and latency characteristics of the cortical SEPs demonstrates remarkable consistency across age after the first year of life (Desmedt and Cheron, 1980a; Desmedt et al., 1976).

Despite these overall similarities, how-

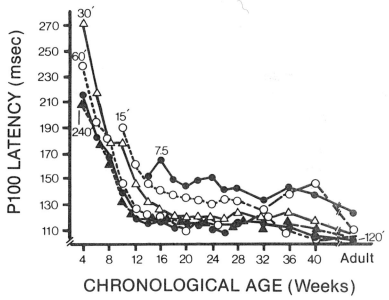

Figure 8-12. Mean latency for the P100 component of the visual evoked potential as a function of various age groups for different check sizes (after Sokol and Jones, 1979).

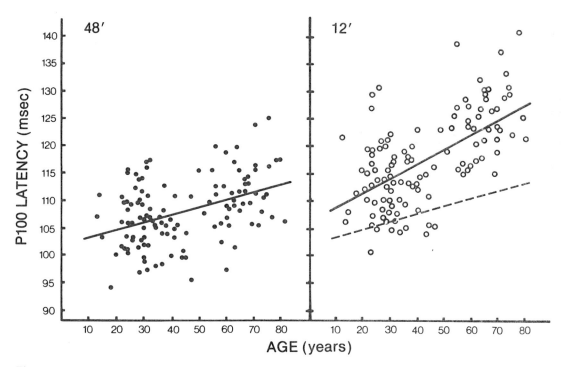

Figure 8-13. P100 latency for different check sizes as a function of age. Each data point is the mean latency of the right and left eye for each subject. For ease of comparison, the regression line for the 49-minute checks has also been plotted as a dashed line on the 12-minute graph (after Soko et al., 1981).

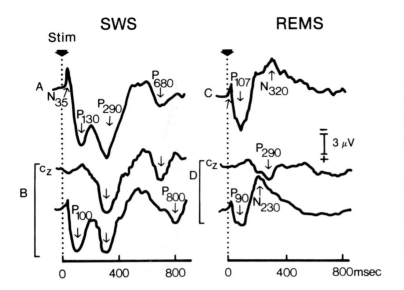

Figure 8-14. Comparison of somatosensory evoked potentials in two normal female newborns during slow wave sleep and rapid eye movement sleep. Waveforms A and C were recorded from the contralateral scalp parietal focus, whereas waveforms B and D were recorded from the vertex with both referenced to a midfrontal electrode (after Desmedt and Debecker, 1972).

ever, when concomitant factors associated with body growth are taken into account, distinct effects of maturation and aging emerge. The N1 component begins to decrease in amplitude and latency, while the following positive component increases in size. Although increased age does not shift the absolute latency of the N1 greatly, if the distance between the scalp recording site and the source of peripheral stimulation (fingers of the contralateral hand) is also considered, the resultant computation of neural conduction velocity demonstrates a considerable overall decrease. These effects, illustrated in Figure 8-17, indicate that adult conduction speeds are not obtained until eight years of age. Hence, the N1 onset latency clearly demarcates the relatively slow maturation of somatosensory afferent conduction compared to the auditory and visual sensory systems.

Detailed comparison of conduction velocities along the somatosensory pathway as a function of age suggests that changes in the central somatosensory axons are the major factor for changes in the onset of the SEP (Desmedt, 1971; Desmedt and Cheron, 1981; Desmedt et al., 1973). These effects are illustrated in Figure 8-18. The increase in latency for the N1 component of the cortical SEP can be attributed to slowing of afferent conduction with advanced age. However, in addition to a latency shift occurring in the elderly, this component also increases in amplitude, which suggests that the underlying mechanisms of these aging effects may be a reversal of the processes that contribute to maturation. If this suggestion is true, the apical synaptic connectivities in the neocortical pyramidal neurons, presumably reflected in the cortical SEP, may be critically related to the changes brought on by age (Desmedt and Cheron, 1980b,c; Hume and Cant, 1978).

Spinal Somatosensory Evoked Potentials

Evoked potentials to peroneal nerve stimulation recorded from surface electrodes placed over the spine progressively increase in latency from the lumbar to the cervical region. These potentials most likely arise in the dorsal roots of the cauda equina and spinal cord afferent pathways (Cracco et al., 1980). With maturation, there are marked changes in the spinal SEP in that the overall amplitude decreases as the infant matures without any major morphological changes. Examples of typical waveforms are presented in Figure 8-19 for a one-year-old and an adult. The larger diphasic amplitude observed for infants may reflect the shorter distance between the spinal cord and the recording electrode. The greater synchronization of the peroneal

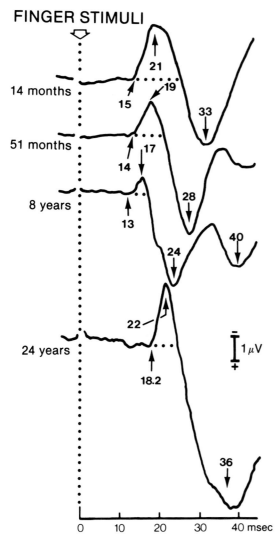

FINGER STIMULI

14 months

51 months

8 years

24 years

21
19
15
33
17
14
13
28
24
40
22
18.2
36

$1\,\mu V$

0   10   20   30   40 msec

Figure 8-15. Comparison of somatosensory evoked potentials for subjects of different ages. Active electrode was contralateral to the stimulated hand with a parietal focus and forehead reference while the subjects were awake with eyes open (after Desmedt et al., 1976).

newborns, 25 meters/second is the mean value; the adult value of about 65 meters/second is seen after four years of age. Figure 8-20 illustrates this trend. The increase in conduction velocity with age could reflect the increasing fiber diameter in peroneal nerve, dorsal root, and spinal afferent pathways associated with myelinization of peripheral nerve and spinal cord fibers (Cracco et al., 1975). However, conduction velocities over peripheral nerves and the cauda equina attain adult values at an earlier age than velocities over the spinal cord, suggesting that maturation of the spinal afferent pathway occurs at a slower rate than maturation of peripheral sensory fibers (Cracco et al., 1979).

Somatosensory Evoked Potentials and Aging

In contrast to AEPs and VERs, the neurophysiological locus of maturation and age effects for SEPs is somewhat better understood. Extensive analysis of conduction velocities for this sensory modality, based on comparatively precise neuroanatomical mechanisms, is beginning to provide insight into how age changes somatosensory functioning. Although the previously observed pattern of decreases in latency with maturation followed by latency increases with age is also observed for SEPs, understanding of this general trend is enhanced by our knowledge of the more easily traced anatomical pathways that somatosensory stimulation follows (e.g., Desmedt and Cheron, 1980a). Continued investigations of the somatosensory system employing these methodologies will doubtless provide an even more comprehensive assessment of aging effects for what Aristotle termed the "first" sense.

Cognitive Potentials

Cognitive potentials are obtained while the subject is engaged in the performance of a stimulus processing task. Although the types of tasks employed can be quite simple (e.g., counting a sequence of tones or pressing a button in response to a target stimulus), waveform variations are directly

nerve dorsal root impulses in infants also appears to be a factor in these morphology changes, since there is an increasing temporal dispersion of impulses in the maturing and, therefore, lengthening peripheral nerve fibers.

Conduction velocity measurements from the midlumbar to lower cervical recording sites also reflect the effects of aging. For

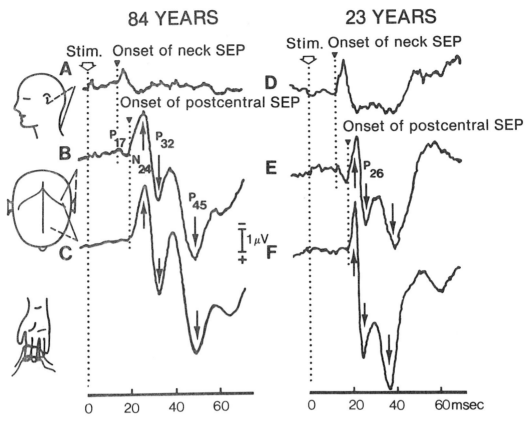

Figure 8-16. Comparison of somatosensory evoked potentials for a young and an old subject from electrode positions illustrated. The vertical dotted line indicates the onset of the cortical negative N24 component (after Desmedt and Cheron, 1980a).

related to the context in which they are elicited. Thus, these event-related potentials (ERPs) derive considerable investigative power because the tasks used in their generation often tap fundamental information-processing systems. When viewed in conjunction with behavioral responses, ERPs provide an additional metric in the analysis of normative and pathological mental processes (e.g., Callaway et al., 1978; Begleiter, 1979; Thatcher and John, 1977).

The primary components of the ERP are listed in the last column of Table 8-1, along with their associated psychological processes. Since these components primarily reflect cognitive or endogenous effects rather than sensory or exogenous effects, they generally can be obtained in each sensory modality. The number in the component label reflects the general latency of a specific component, although this value varies with the task situation, as does the amplitude magnitude for the positive or negative peaks. Cognitive ERPs are observed over all portions of the scalp, but their midline distribution of maximum amplitude differs from component to component and sometimes depends upon the modality of stimulus presentation (Picton et al., 1974; Simson et al., 1976, 1977). The N100, P200, N200, and P300 are often obtained in paradigms that require the subject to discriminate between different stimulus events, whereas the contingent negative variation (CNV) is generally obtained with the presentation of an initial warning

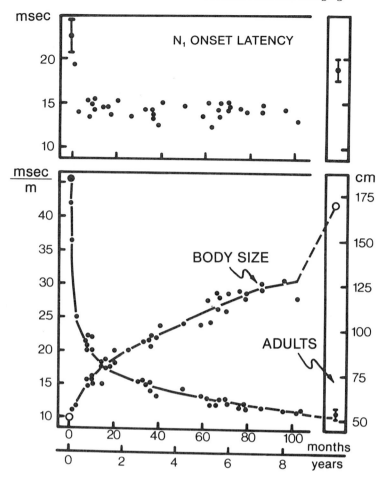

Figure 8-17. Changes in onset latency of the early cortical negative component of the somatosensory evoked potential with age. Upper graph, the onset latency with only the mean and one standard deviation indicated for newborns and adults; lower graph, the body size for the same subjects on the right side and the onset latency of the potential divided by body size on the left side (after Desmedt et al., 1976).

stimulus followed by the task stimulus. However, these components have been observed in a wide variety of processing tasks (Donchin, 1979, 1981; Donchin et al., 1978; Hillyard and Woods, 1979; Picton and Stuss, 1980; Pritchard, 1981; Tecce, 1972). Application of these potentials to the study of aging has centered on the P300 and associated cognitive potentials as well as CNV paradigms.

P300 Aging Effects

The P300 component (also referred to as the P3 or late positive complex) of the ERP is often obtained with an "oddball" stimulus discrimination paradigm. The subject is presented with a series of stimulus items and required to attend to and

discriminate one type of stimulus from the others. The less often the target stimulus occurs, the greater the amplitude of the P300. Thus, the "surprise" value as determined by the objective probability of the rarely presented or odd stimulus determines the magnitude of the P300 (e.g., Duncan-Johnson and Donchin, 1977), whereas its peak latency appears to vary with relative task difficulty and subject strategies (e.g., Squires et al., 1977; Kutas et al., 1977; McCarthy and Donchin, 1981). These effects have been obtained with the oddball paradigm for auditory, visual, and somatosensory stimuli (Desmedt et al., 1977; Donchin, 1981; Snyder et al., 1980).

Examples of ERP components illustrating the effects of maturation on overall

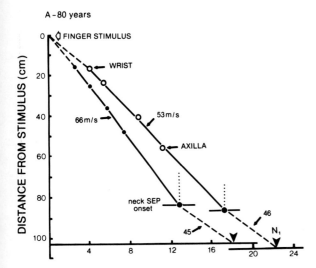

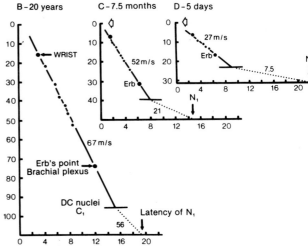

Figure 8-18. Peripheral and central afferent conduction of a sensory volley in subjects of different ages (A–D). The latency of the earliest component recorded at the peripheral nerve potential of cortical somatosensory potentials is plotted as a function of the distance traveled by the afferent volley from the finger stimulated. The peripheral afferent conduction velocity is extrapolated to the level of dorsal column nuclei; the dotted line corresponds to conduction for the dorsal column nuclei to the postcentral cortex (after Desmedt and Cheron, 1980c; Desmedt et al., 1973).

waveform morphology are presented in Figure 8-21. Similar data demonstrating the effects of aging on the P300 are given in Figure 8-22. As the young child matures, overall amplitude decreases along with latency, until the modal latency of 300 milliseconds is obtained in young adulthood. However, although the amplitude of the P300 is generally variable across the age span (Pfefferbaum et al., 1979), peak P300 latency appears to increase substantially for both the auditory (Goodin et al., 1978b; Ford et al., 1979) and visual (Beck et al., 1980) modalities. While the strongest effects for age are found in the P300, the earlier P200 and N200 ERP components also increase somewhat in latency; the N100 latency does not appear to change with age (Smith et al., 1980; Squires et al., 1979a). These effects are summarized in Figure 8-23; data are from an auditory oddball task.

Differences in overall ERP morphology associated with maturation in the young child have been attributed to changes in cognition accompanying development (Courchesne, 1981; Friedman et al., 1981). Moreover, because the various component amplitudes appear to change differentially with age, the negative and positive components corresponding to the typical adult morphology (i.e., N200, P300) are thought to specify the child's developing perceptual and decision-making capabilities, even though the exact correspondence between specific component development and aspects of cognitive growth is not known (e.g., Courchesne, 1977, 1978, 1979; Courchesnese et al., 1981). Clinically, these maturational ERP changes have been studied in conjunction with language development (e.g., Neville, 1977; Shelburne, 1973) and various forms of psychopathology (i.e., Friedman et al., 1979; Squires et al., 1979b).

The effects of advanced age on the

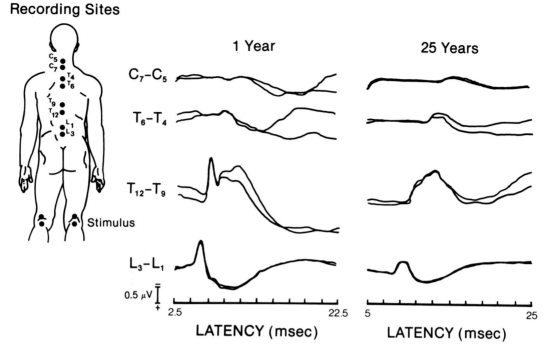

Figure 8-19. Comparison of somatosensory evoked potentials for an infant and adult subject obtained from peroneal nerve stimulation and recorded over the spinal cord (after Cracco et al., 1978).

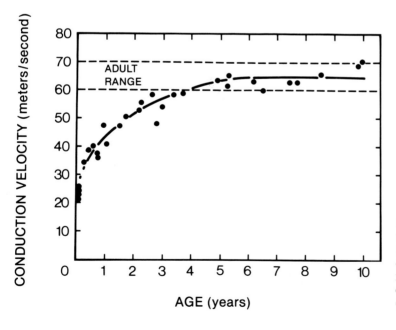

Figure 8-20. Conduction velocity as a function of age for the somatosensory evoked potential recorded from midlumbar to lower cervical recording sites (after Cracco et al., 1975).

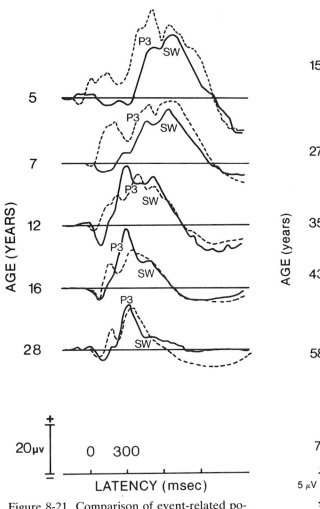

Figure 8-21. Comparison of event-related potentials recorded at Pz for younger and adult subjects obtained from a simple counting paradigm for auditory (——) and visual (----) stimuli. Note that the P3 or P300 and slow wave components change both in amplitude and latency as the age of the subject increases (after Courchesne, 1981).

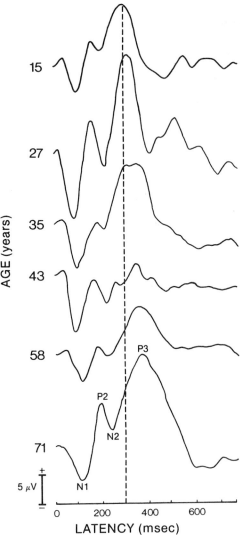

Figure 8-22. Comparison of event related potentials recorded at Cz for young and elderly subjects obtained from a simple counting paradigm with auditory stimuli. Although adult amplitudes vary considerably, latency appears to increase systematically with age (after Squires et al., 1979a).

components of the ERP produce a general slowing and shift toward more frontal activity (Pfefferbaum et al., 1980). These effects, illustrated in Figures 8-24 and 8-25, indicate that the latency and amplitude changes associated with age are particularly evident for the longer-latency components of the ERP (e.g., P300). When more complex stimulus processing tasks and single-trial analysis techniques are employed, it appears that elderly subjects are just as capable of attending to stimulus sequences as younger subjects, but exhibit differences in memory functioning and apply more conservative task performance strategies

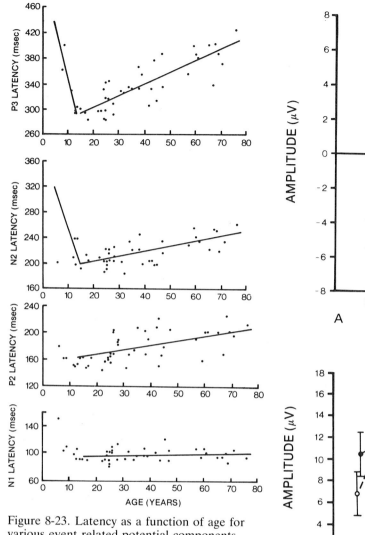

Figure 8-23. Latency as a function of age for various event related potential components obtained for a simple counting paradigm with auditory stimuli (after Goodin et al., 1978).

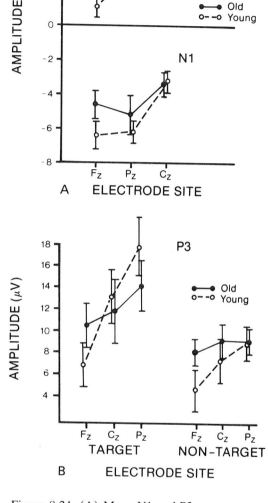

(Ford et al., 1982; Ford et al., 1979; Pfefferbaum et al., 1980).

Because the P300 is thought to reflect the cognitive events associated with changes in the stimulus sequences that are used to elicit this component (e.g., Squires et al., 1977; Squires et al., 1976), it is finding application in the study of disorders in which there is a cognitive decline, such as dementia and neurological trauma (Goodin et al., 1978a; Squires et al., 1980). Examples of these effects on P300 latency obtained from an oddball paradigm are presented in Figure 8-26. Al-

Figure 8-24. (A) Mean N1 and P2 component amplitudes for young (20–30 years) and elderly (70–80 years) subjects obtained from an auditory paradigm requiring a manual response to the target tones. (B) Mean P3 amplitudes for same subjects (after Pfefferbaum et al., 1980).

though the subject's task was simply to count silently the relatively rare (20%) occurrences of a high tone randomly pre-

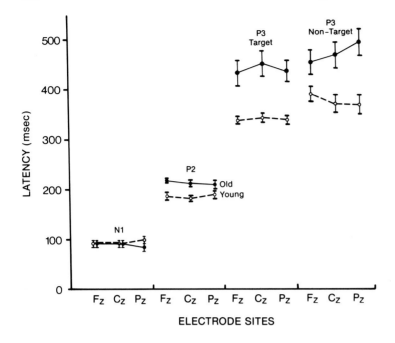

Figure 8-25. Mean component latencies for young and elderly subjects as in Figure 8-24 (after Pfefferbaum et al., 1980).

sented in a series of frequently presented low tones (80%), dramatic latency increases were observed for demented patients compared to normal subjects and nondemented patients, even though the behavioral counting performance was comparable for the various subject groups. An additional comparison of P300 latency to a mental status evaluation (Folstein et al., 1975) demonstrated a concomitant decrease in latency toward normal values and increased cognitive capability with therapy (Squires et al., 1980). These effects were attributed to fundamental changes in cognitive processing for this group of patients and demonstrate the clinical utility of ERPs in a neurological setting for a variety of age populations.

Contingent Negative Variation Aging Effects

In the usual form of a CNV paradigm, some type of warning signal is presented before a second stimulus to which the subject is required to respond. The interval between the two stimuli is constant over trials (typically 2 to 4 seconds) and a slow negative shift, or CNV, arises between the two signals. Although one of the earliest ERPs to be reported (Walter et

al., 1964), the exact nature of the CNV is still unclear. It is thought to reflect cognitive preparation in the form of attentional changes or arousal (Tecce, 1972; Tecce and Cole, 1976). Because of this possibility, CNV paradigms have been periodically employed as a measure of the ability of elderly subjects to maintain their cognitive readiness (Loveless and Sanford, 1974; Marsh and Thompson, 1973).

Waveforms obtained from a typical CNV task are presented in Figure 8-27. In this study, an interpolated memory task was presented under conditions that require the subject to recall the memory item some time after the occurrence of the second stimulus. The elderly subjects, while producing waveforms similar to the younger subjects, obtained lower-amplitude CNV waveforms across conditions. This decrease in amplitude was especially evident over the frontal electrode site, suggesting a selective dysfunction of the frontal lobes (Michalewski et al., 1980) in the aged. Similar effects have also been reported for other CNV tasks involving a memory factor for aged subjects (Tecce et al., 1980a). However, application of this approach to elderly patients with senile dementia suggested that such differences may be related to task performance strate-

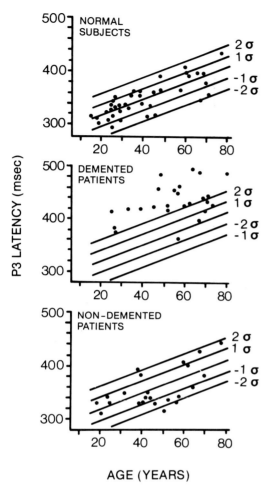

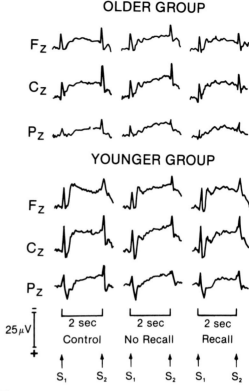

Figure 8-27. Overall contingent negative variation averages from older (60–70 years) and younger (20–30 years) subject groups for several task conditions (after Michalewski et al., 1980).

Figure 8-26. Latency of the P300 component at Cz obtained from a simple counting paradigm with auditory stimuli as a function of age for normal subjects and demented and non-demented patient populations (after Goodin et al., 1978).

gies for individual subjects (O'Conner, 1980a,b; Tecce et al., 1980b). Although these findings seem to imply differential effects of aging on cortical activity, they are not conclusive, since other reports have not obtained strong CNV differences between young and elderly subjects (e.g., Nakamura et al., 1979; Thompson and Nowlin, 1973).

Application of CNV paradigms to children is difficult because of the sustained attentional requirements between the initial stimulus and the task stimulus (Klorman et al., 1978). The few studies that have been performed (Cohen, 1973; Klorman, 1975) indicate that the waveform morphology of children is similar to that of adults and that adult amplitudes are reached by age 15. Additional work with children who show attentional or developmental deficits indicates decreased CNV activity, although the effects are not striking (Grunewald-Zuberbier et al., 1978; Cohen, 1976). However, as with CNV studies of elderly subjects, developmental differences for this ERP are not consistently found and are difficult to obtain in very young children in whom such differences may be more readily observed.

Event-Related Potentials and Aging

Maturation and aging produce clear differences of latency and amplitude in some of the components of ERPs. The effects associated with age appear to emerge for components of long latency, thereby reflecting endogenous factors of cognition and stimulus processing with strong influences from memory. The use of paradigms that yield the P300 component demonstrates the consistency of cognitive changes with age over a wide range of ages and task situations. Although the CNV also shows some effects in association with advanced age, they are not as clear cut, especially for developmental studies. However, the application of ERP methodologies to various populations is still relatively new, and the techniques show promise in their ability to differentiate the influences of the aging process with respect to different cognitive abilities.

Two major problems with the use of ERPs to study aging deserve comment. First, and perhaps foremost, is that the neuroanatomical origins of these cognitive potentials are largely unknown. Recent investigations employing depth electrodes in humans suggest that the locus of the P300 complex resides deep within the brain and is perhaps initiated by hippocampal processes (Halgren et al., 1980; Goff et al., 1980). The origins and functional significance of the CNV are also debated (Gaillard and Perdok, 1980). Hence, although variations in scalp topography for the various components of the ERP appear to change between task conditions and populations, a direct correspondence between sites of maximum scalp amplitude and differences for various age groups can only suggest the presumed cortical sites of generation. Second, because ERPs are obtained during a task performance situation, the variations in subject approaches to the task may be an important determinant of how the various components reflect age differences. While such differences between age groups are of interest, the fact that overall processing capability rather than a specific neurophysiological deficit may be producing the ERP difference further complicates the interpretation that these effects are due simply to physical age. More sophisticated psychological paradigms that manipulate cognitive and strategic differences across subject age

may be one means of resolving these ambiguities.

Summary

As this review indicates, maturation and aging are associated with profound changes in sensory evoked and event-related potentials. Their utility as tools for the study of the aging process is without parallel because they provide a relatively easy, noninvasive means for assessing sensory and psychological changes associated with aging. The consistency of the effects obtained for virtually all the measures across the life-span marks these electrophysiological indices as important to our understanding of how the sensory and cognitive systems develop, grow, and decline. Future applications of these techniques, based on the currently available data, should make possible even more insight into how the nervous system changes as it ages, especially as the anatomical sources for the various components become better known. Integration with findings from biochemical and animal research will advance this goal and the clinical utility of these measures. The diagnostic value of evoked and event-related potentials is already clear and will most likely evolve into a powerful tool for the assessment of aging effects and their associated pathologies.

References

Achor, L. and Starr, A. (1980). Auditory brain stem responses in the cat. II. Effects of lesions. Electroencephalogr. Clin. Neurophysiol. 48, 174–190.

Asselman, P., Chadwick, D., and Marsden, C. (1975). Visual evoked responses in the diagnosis and management of patients suspected of multiple sclerosis. Brain 98, 261–282.

Barnet, A., Ohlrich, E., Weiss, I., and Shanks, B. (1975). Auditory evoked potentials during sleep in normal children from ten days to three years of age. Electroencephalogr. Clin. Neurophysiol. 39, 29–41.

Beck, E., Swanson, C., and Dustman, R. (1980). Long latency components of the visually evoked potential in man: Effects of aging. Exp. Aging Res. 6, 523–545.

Begleiter, H. (Ed.) (1979). Evoked Brain

Potentials and Behavior. Plenum Press, New York.

Birren, J., Woods, A., and Williams, M. (1979). Speed of behavior as an indicator of age changes and the integrity of the nervous system. In F. Hoffmeister and C. Muller (Eds.), Brain Function and Old Age. Springer-Verlag, New York.

Blom, J. and Barth, P., and Visser, S. (1980). The visual evoked potential in the first six years of life. Electroencephalogr. Clin. Neurophysiol. 48, 395–405.

Botwinick, J. (1977). Intellectual abilities. In Handbook of the Psychology of Aging, J. Birren and K. Schaie, Eds. Van Nostrand Reinhold, New York.

Buchwald, J. and Huang, C.-M. (1975). Far-field acoustic responses: Origins in the cat. Science 189, 382–384.

Callaway, E. and Halliday, R. (1973). Evoked potential variability: Effects of age, amplitude and methods of measurement. Electroencephalog. Clin. Neurophysiol. 34, 125–133.

Callaway, E., Tueting, P., and Koslow, S. (Eds.) (1978). Event-related Brain Potentials in Man. Academic Press, New York.

Cohen, J. (1973). The CNV in children with special reference to learning disabilities. Electroencephalog. Clin. Neurophysiol. (Suppl.) 33, 151–154.

Cohen, J. Learning disabilities and conditional brain activity. In Developmental Psychophysiology of Mental Retardation, R. Karrer, Ed. C.C. Thomas, Springfield, Ill.

Celesia, G. and Daly, R. (1977). Effects of aging on visual evoked responses. Arch. Neurol. 34, 403–407.

Courchesne, E. (1977). Event-related brain potentials: A comparison between children and adults. Science 197, 589–592.

Courchesne, E. (1978). Neurophysiological correlates of cognitive development: Changes in long-latency event-related potentials from childhood to adulthood. Electroencephalog. Clin. Neurophysiol. 45, 468–482.

Courchesne, E. (1979). From infancy to adulthood: The neurophysiological correlates of cognition. In Progress in Clinical Neurophysiology: Cognitive Components in Event-Related Cerebral Potentials, Vol. 6, J.E. Desmedt, Ed. Karger Publishing, Basel.

Courchesne, E. (1983). The maturation of cognitive components of the event-related brain potential. In Tutorials in ERP Research: Endogenous Components, A.W.K.

Ritter, Ed. North-Holland Publishing, Amsterdam.

Courchesne, E., Ganz, L., and Norcia, A. (1981). Event-related brain potentials to human faces in infants. Child Develop. 52, 804–811.

Cracco, J., Cracco, R., and Graziani, L. (1975). The spinal evoked response in infants and children. Neurology, 25, 31–36.

Cracco, J., Cracco, R., and Stolove, R. (1979). Spinal evoked potential in man: A maturational study. Electroencephalogr. Clin. Neurophysiol. 46, 58–64.

Cracco, R. (1973). Spinal evoked response: Peripheral nerve stimulation in man. Electroencephalogr. Clin. Neurophysiol. 35, 379–386.

Cracco, R. and Cracco, J. (1976). Subcortical evoked potentials to median nerve stimulation recorded from the human scalp. Electroencephalogr. Clin. Neurophysiol. 40, 335.

Cracco, R., Cracco, J., Sarnowski, R., and Vogel, H. (1980). Spinal evoked potentials. In Progress in Clinical Neurophysiology: Clinical Uses of Cerebral, Brainstem and Spinal Somatosensory Evoked Potentials, Vol. 7, J.E. Desmedt, Ed. Karger Publishing, Basel.

Davis, H. (1976). Principles of electric response audiometry. Ann. Otol., Rhinol., Laryng. 85 (Suppl. 28), 1–96.

Davis, H., Hirsh, S., Shelnutt, J. and Dinges, D.A. (1974). Validation of clinical ERA at the Central Institute for the Deaf. Rev. Laryngol., Otol. Rhinol. 95, 475–480.

Davis, H. and Onishi, S. (1969). Maturation of auditory evoked potentials. Interntl. Audiol. 8, 24–33.

Desmedt, J. (1971). Somatosensory cerebral evoked potentials in man. Handbook of EEG and Clinical Neurophysiology, Vol. 9, A. Remond, Ed. Elsevier, Amsterdam.

Desmedt, J.E. (Ed.). (1977). Visual Evoked Potentials in Man: New Developments. Clarendon Press, Oxford.

Desmedt, J.E. and Brunko, E. (1980). Functional organization of far-field and cortical components of somatosensory evoked potentials in normal adults. In Progress in Clinical Neurophysiology: Clinical Uses of Cerebral, Brainstem and Spinal Somatosensory Evoked Potentials, Vol. 7, J.E. Desmedt, Ed. Karger Publishing, Basel.

Desmedt, J.E., Brunko, E., and Debecker, J. (1976). Maturation of the somatosensory evoked potentials in normal infants and children, with special reference to the early

N1 component. Electroencephalogr. Clin. Neurophysiol. 40, 43–58.

Desmedt, J.E., Brunko, E., and Debecker, J. (1980). Maturation and sleep correlates of the somatosensory evoked potential. In J.E. Desmedt (Ed.), Progress in Clinical Neurophysiology: Clinical Uses of Cerebral, Brainstem, and Spinal Somatosensory Evoked Potentials, Vol. 7. Basel, Karger Publishing.

Desmedt, J.E. and Cheron, G. (1980a). Somatosensory pathway and evoked potential in normal human aging. In Progress in Clinical Neurophysiology: Clinical Uses of Cerebral, Brainstem, and Spinal Somatosensory Evoked Potentials, Vol. 7, J.E. Desmedt, Ed. Karger Publishing, Basel.

Desmedt, J.E. and Cheron, G. (1980b). Central somatosensory conduction in man: Neural generators and interpeak latencies of the far-field components recorded from neck and right or left scalp and earlobes. Electroencephalogr. Clin. Neurophysiol. 50, 382–403.

Desmedt, J.E. and Cheron, G. (1980c). Somatosensory evoked potentials to finger stimulation in healthy octogenarians and in young adults: Wave forms, scalp topography and transit times of parietal and frontal components. Electroencephalogr. Clin. Neurophysiol. 50, 404–425.

Desmedt, J.E. and Cheron, G. (1981). The peripheral and central somatosensory pathway in healthy octogenerations. Neurology (Minne.).

Desmedt, J.E. and Debecker, J. (1972). The somatosensory cerebral evoked potentials of the sleeping newborn. In Sleep and the Maturing Nervous System, C.D. Clemente, D.P. Purpura, and F.E. Mayer Eds. Academic Press. New York.

Desmedt, J.E., Noel, P., Debecker, J., and Nameche, J. (1973). Maturation of afferent conduction velocity as studied by sensory nerve potentials and by cerebral evoked potentials. In New Developments in Electromyography and Clinical Neurophysiology, Vol. 2, J.E. Desmedt, Ed. Karger Publishing, Basel.

Desmedt, J.E., Robertson, D., Brunko, E., and Debecker, J. (1977). Somatosensory decision tasks in man: Early and late components of the cerebral potentials evoked by stimulation of different fingers in random sequences. Electroencephalogr. Clin. Neurophysiol. 43, 404–415.

Donchin, E. (1979). Event-related brain potentials: A tool in the study of human information processing. In Evoked Brain Poten-tials and Behavior, H. Begleiter, Ed. Plenum Press, New York.

Donchin, E. (1981). Surprise! . . . Surprise? Psychophysiology 18, 493–513.

Donchin, E., Ritter, W., and McCallum, C. (1978). Cognitive psychophysiology: The endogenous components of the ERP. In Brain Event-Related Potentials in Man, E. Callaway, P. Tueting, and S. Koslow, Eds. Academic Press, New York.

Duncan-Johnson, C.C., and Donchin, E. (1977). On quantifying surprise: The variation of event-related potentials with subjective probability. Psychophysiology 14, 456–467.

Dustman, R., & Beck, E. (1969). The effects of maturation and aging on the wave forms of visually evoked potentials. Electroencephalogr. Clin. Neurophysiol. 26, 2–11.

Ellingson, R., Danahy, T., Nelson, B., and Lathrop, G. (1974). Variability of auditory evoked potentials in human newborns. Electroencephalog. Clin. Neurophysiol. 36, 155–162.

Ellingson, R., Lathrop, G., Danahy, T., and Nelson, B. (1973). Variability of visual evoked potentials in human infants and adults. Electroencephalog. Clin. Neurophysiol. 34, 113–124.

Fenwick, P., Brown, D., and Hennesey, J. (1981). The visual evoked response to pattern reversal in 'normal' 6–11 year old children. Electroencephalogr. Clin. Neurophysiol. 51, 49–62.

Folstein, M., Folstein, S., and McHugh, P. (1975). "Mini-Mental State": A practical method of grading the cognitive state of patients for the clinician. J. Psychiat. Res. 12, 189–198.

Ford, J., Duncan-Johnson, C., Pfefferbaum, A., and Kopell, B. (1982). Expectancy for events in old age: Stimulus sequence effects on P300 and reaction time. J. Gerontol. 37, 696–704.

Ford, J., Hink, R., Hopkins, W., Roth, W., Pfefferbaum, A., and Kopell, B. (1979). Age effects on event-related potentials in a selective attention task. J. Gerontol. 34, 388–395.

Ford, J. and Pfefferbaum, A. (1980). The utility of brain potentials in determining age-related changes in central nervous system and cognitive functioning. In Aging in the 1980s: Psychological Issues, L. Poon, Ed. American Psychological Association, Washington, D.C.

Ford, J., Roth, W., Mohs, R., Hopkins, W., and Kopell, B. Event-related potentials recorded from young and old adults during a memory retrieval task. Electroencephalogr. Clin. Neurophysiol. 47, 450–459.

Friedman, D., Brown, C., Cornblatt, B., Vaughan, H., and Erlenmeyer-Kimling, L. (1981). Changes in the task-related brain potentials during adolescence. Ann. N.Y. Acad. of Sci.

Friedman, D., Vaughn, H., and Erlenmeyer-Kimling, L. (1979). Event-related potential investigations in children at high risk for schizophrenia. In Human Evoked Potentials: Applications and Problems. D. Lehmann and E. Callaway, Eds. Plenum Press, New York.

Gaillard, A. and Perdok, J. (1980). Slow brain potentials in the CNV paradigm. Acta Psychol. 44, 147–163.

Galambos, R., Makeig, S., and Talmachoff, P. (1981). A 40-Hz auditory potential recorded from the human scalp. Proc. Natl. Acad. Sci. 78, 2643–2647.

Goff, W., Rosner, B., and Allison, T. (1962) Distribution of somatosensory evoked responses in normal man. Electroencephalogr. Clin. Neurophysiol. 14, 697–713.

Goff, W., Williamson, P., Van-Gilder, J., Allison, T., and Fisher, T. (1980). Neural origins of long latency evoked potentials recorded from the depth and from the cortical surface of the brain in man. In Progress in Clinical Neurophysiology: Clinical Uses of Cerebral, Brainstem, and Spinal Somatosensory Evoked Potentials, J.E. Desmedt, Ed. Karger Publishing, Basel.

Goldstein, R. and McRandle, C. (1976). Middle components of the averaged electroencephalic response to clicks in neonates. In Hearing and Davis: Essays Honoring Hallowell Davis, S. Hirsh, D. Eldredge, I. Hirsh, and S. Silverman, Eds. Washington University Press, St. Louis.

Goodin, D., Squires, K., and Starr, A. (1978a). Long-latency event-related components of the auditory evoked potential in dementia. Brain 101, 635–648.

Goodin, D., Squires, K., Henderson, B., and Starr, A. (1978b). Age-related variations in evoked potentials to auditory stimuli in normal human subjects. Electroencephalogr. Clin. Neurophysiol. 44, 447–458.

Graziani, L., Katz, L., Cracco, R., Cracco, J., and Weitzman, E. (1974). The maturation and interrelationship of EEG patterns and auditory evoked responses in premature infants. Electroencephalogr. Clin. Neurophysiol. 36, 367–375.

Grunewald-Zuberbier, E., Grunewald, G., Rasche, A., and Netz, J. (1978). Contingent negative variation and alpha attenuation responses in children with different abilities to concentrate. Electroencephalogr. Clin. Neurophysiol. 44, 37–47.

Halgren, E., Squires, N., Wilson, C., Rohrbaugh, J., Babb, T., & Crandall, P. (1980). Endogenous potentials generated in the human hippocampal formation and amygdala by infrequent events. Science 210, 803–805.

Halliday, A.M. (1978). Clinical applications of evoked potentials. In Recent Advances in Clinical Neurology, Vol. 2, W. Matthews and G. Glaser, Eds. Churchill-Livingstone, Edinburgh.

Harkins, S., and Lenhardt, M. (1980). Brainstem auditory evoked potentials in the elderly. In Aging in the 1980s: Psychological Issues, L. Poon, Ed. American Psychological Association, Washington, D.C.

Harter, M.R., Deaton, F., and Odom, J.V. (1977). Maturation of evoked potentials and visual preference in 6–45 day old infants: Effects of check size, visual acuity, and refractive error. Electroencephalogr. Clin. Neurophysiol. 42, 595–607.

Hennerici, M., Wenzel, D., and Freund, H-J. (1977). The comparison of small-size rectangle and checkerboard stimulation for the evaluation of delayed visual evoked responses in patients suspected of multiple sclerosis. Brain 100, 119–136.

Hillyard, S., Picton, T., and Regan, D. (1978). Sensation, perception, and attention: Analysis using ERPs. In Event-Related Brain Potentials in Man, E. Callaway, P., Tueting, and S. Koslow, Eds. Academic Press, New York.

Hillyard, S. and Woods, D. (1979). Electrophysiological analysis of human brain function. In Handbook of Behavioral Neurobiology, Vol. 2, M. Gazzaniga, Ed. Plenum Press, New York.

Hume, A. and Cant, B. (1978). Conduction time in central somatosensory pathways in man. Electroencephalogr. Clin. Neurophysiol. 45, 361–375.

Jerger, J. and Hall, J. (1980). Effects of age and sex on auditory brainstem responses. Arch. Otolaryngol. 106, 384–391.

Jewett, D.L. and Romano, M.N. (1972). Neonatal development of auditory system potentials averaged from the scalp of the rat and cat. Brain Res. 36, 101–115.

Klorman, R. (1975). Contingent negative variations and cardiac deceleration in a long preparatory interval: A developmental study. Psychophysiology 12, 609–617.

Klorman, R., Thompson, L., and Ellingson, R.

(1978). Event related brain potentials across the life span. In Event-Related Brain Potentials in Man, E. Callaway, P. Tueting, and S. Koslow, Eds. Plenum Press, New York.

Knight, R., Hillyard, S., Woods, D., and Neville, H. The effects of frontal and temporal-parietal lesions in the auditory evoked potential in man. Electroencephalogr. Clin. Neurophysiol. 50, 112–124.

Kritchevsky, M. and Wiederholt, W. (1978). Short latency somatosensory evoked potentials in man. Arch. Neurol. (Chicago) 35, 706–711.

Kutas, M., McCarthy, G., and Donchin, E. (1977). Augmenting mental chronometry. Science 197, 792–795.

Loveless, N. and Sanford, A. (1974). Effects of age on the contingent negative variation and preparatory set in a reaction-time task. J. Gerontol. 29, 52–63.

Marg, E., Freeman, D., Pletzman, P., and Goldstein, P. (1976). Visual acuity development in human infants: Evoked potential measurements. Invest. Opthalmol. 15, 150–153.

Marsh, G., and Thompson, L. (1973). Effects of age on the contingent negative variation in a pitch discrimination task. J. Geront. 28, 56–62.

Mathews, W., Beauchamp, M., and Small, D. (1974). Cervical somato-sensory evoked responses in man. Nature 252, 230–232.

McCarthy, G. and Donchin, E. (1981). A metric for thought: A comparison of P300 latency and reaction time. Science 211, 77–80.

Mendel, M.I. (1977). Electroencephalic tests of hearing. In Audiometry in Infancy, S. Gerber Ed. Grune & Stratton, New York.

Mendel, M.I., Adkinson, C., and Harker, L. (1977). Middle components of the auditory evoked potentials in infants. Ann. Otolaryngol. Rhinol. Laryngol. 86, 293–299.

Mendel, M.I., Hosick, E., Windman, T., Davis, S., Hirsh, S., and Dinges, D. (1975). Audiometric comparison of the middle and late components of the adult auditory evoked potentials awake and asleep. Electroencephalogr. Clin. Neurophysiol. 38, 27–33.

Michalewski, H., Thompson, L., Smith, D., Patterson, J., Bowman, T., Litzelman, D., and Brent, G. (1980). Age differences in the contingent negative variation (CNV): Reduced frontal activity in the elderly. J. Geront. 35, 542–549.

Nakamura, M., Fukui, Y., Kadobayashi, I., and Katoh, N. (1979). A comparison of

CNV in young and old subjects: Its relation to memory and personality. Electroencephalogr. Clin. Neurophysiol. 46, 337–344.

Neville, H. (1977). Electroencephalographic testing of cerebral specialization in normal and congenitally deaf children: A preliminary report. In Language Development and Neurological Theory, S.J. Segalowitz and F. Gruber, Eds. Academic Press, New York.

Noel, P. and Desmedt, J.E. (1980). Cerebral and far-field somatosensory evoked potentials in neurological disorders involving the cervical spinal cord, brainstem, thalamus and cortex. In Progress in Clinical Neurophysiology: Clinical Uses of Cerebral, Brainstem and Spinal Somatosensory Evoked Potentials, Vol. 7, J.E. Desmedt, Ed. Karger Publishing, Basel.

O'Conner, K.P. (1980a). Slow potential correlates of attention dysfunction in senile dementia: I. Biol. Psychol. 11, 193–202.

O'Conner, K.P. (1980b). Slow potential correlates of attention dysfunction in senile dementia: II. Biol. Psychol. 11, 203–216.

Ordy, J.M., and Brizzee, K. (1979). Functional and structural age differences in the visual system of man and nonhuman primate models. In Sensory systems and communication in the elderly and aged, Vol. 10, J.M. Ordy and K. Brizzee, Eds. Raven Press, New York.

Ornitz, E., Tanguay, P., Forsythe, A., de la Pena, A., and Ghahremani, J. (1974). The recovery cycle of the averaged auditory evoked response during sleep in normal children. Electroencephalogr. Clin. Neurophysiol. 37, 113–122.

Patterson, J.V., Michalewski, H.J., Thompson, L.W., and Bowman, T.E. (1981). Age differences in brainstem auditory evoked response amplitudes and latencies. J. Gerontol. 36, 455–462.

Pfefferbaum, A., Ford, J., Roth, W., and Kopell, B. Age-related changes in auditory event-related potentials. Electroencephalogr. Clin. Neurophysiol. 49, 266–276.

Pfefferbaum, A., Ford, J., Roth, W., Hopkins, W., and Kopell, B. (1979). Event related potential changes in healthy aged females. Electroencephalog. Clin. Neurophysiol. 46, 81–86.

Picton, T., and Hillyard, S. (1974). Human auditory evoked potentials. II: Effects of attention. Electroencephal. Clin. Neurophysiol. 36, 191–199.

Picton, T., Hillyard, S., Krausz, H., and Galambos, R. (1974). Human auditory evoked potentials. I: Evaluation of components. Electroencephalogr. Clin. Neurophysiol. 36, 179–190.

Picton, T.W. and Stuss, D.T. (1980). The component structure of human event-related potentials. In Progress in Brain Research: Motivation, Motor and Sensory Processes of the Brain: Electrical Potentials, Behavior, and Clinical Use, Vol. 54, H.H. Kornhuber and L. Deecke, Eds. Elsevier, Amsterdam.

Picton, T., Woods, D., Baribeau-Braun, J., and Helay, T. (1977). Evoked potential audiometry. J. Otolaryngol. 6, 90–119.

Polich, J.M. and Starr, A. (1983). Middle, late and long latency auditory evoked potentials. In Bases of Auditory Brain Stem Evoked Responses, E.J. Moore, Ed. Grune & Stratton, New York.

Pratt, H., Starr, A., Amlie, R.N., and Politoske, D. (1979). Mechanically and electrically evoked somatosensory potentials in normal humans. Neurology 29, 1236–1244.

Pritchard, W. (1981). The psychophysiology of P300. Psychol. Bull. 89, 506–540.

Rapin, I. and Graziani, L. (1967). Auditory-evoked responses in normal, brain damaged, and deaf infants. Neurology 17, 888–894.

Rosenhamer, H., Lindstron, B., and Lundborg, T. (1980). On the use of click-evoked electric brainstem responses in audiological diagnosis. Scand. Audiol. 9, 93–100.

Rowe, J.R. (1978). Normal variability of the brain-stem auditory evoked response in young and old adult subjects. Electroencephalogr. Clin. Neurophysiol. 44, 459–470.

Salamy, A., Fenn, C., and Bronshvag, M. (1979). Ontogenesis of human brainstem evoked potential amplitude. Develop. Psychobiol. 12, 519–526.

Salamy, A. and McKean, C. (1976). Postnatal development of human brainstem potentials during the first year of life. Electroencephalog. Clin. Neurophysiol. 40, 418–426.

Salamy, A., McKean, C., and Buda, F. (1975). Maturational changes in auditory transmission as reflected in human brain stem potentials. Brain Res. 96, 361–366.

Salamy, A., McKean, C., Pettet, C., and Mendelson, T. (1978). Auditory brainstem recovery processes from birth to adulthood. Psychophysiology 15, 214–220.

Shaw, N. and Cant, B. (1980). Age-dependent changes in the latency of the pattern visual evoked potential. Electroencephalogr. Clin. Neurophysiol. 48, 237–241.

Shearer, D. and Dustman, R. (1980). The pattern reversal evoked potential: The need for laboratory norms. Amer. J. EEG Technol. 20, 185–200.

Shelbourne, A. (1973). Visual evoked responses to language stimuli in normal children. Electroencephalogr. Clin. Neurophysiol. 34, 135–143.

Shucard, J., Shucard, D., and Cummins, K. (1981). Auditory evoked potentials and sex-related differences in brain development. Brain Lang. 13, 91–102.

Simson, R., Vaughan, H., and Ritter, W. (1976). The scalp topography of potentials associated with missing visual or auditory stimuli. Electroencephalogr. Clin. Neurophysiol. 40, 33–42.

Simson, R., Vaughan, H., and Ritter, W. (1977). The scalp topography of potentials in auditory and visual go/no-go tasks. Electroencephalogr. Clin. Neurophysiol. 43, 864–875.

Skinner, P. and Antinoro, F. (1969). Auditory evoked responses in normal hearing adults and children before and during sedation. J. Speech Hear. Res. 12, 394–401.

Skinner, P. and Glattke, T. (1977). Electrophysiological response audiometry: State of the art. J. Speech Hear. Res. 42, 179–198.

Smith, D., Michalewski, H., Brent, G., and Thompson, L. (1980). Biol. Psychol. 11, 135–151.

Snyder, E., Dustman, R., and Shearer, D. (1981). Pattern reversal evoked potential amplitudes: Life-span changes. Electroencephalogr. Clin. Neurophysiol. 52, 429–434.

Snyder, E., Hillyard, S., and Galambos, R. (1980). Similarities and differences among the P3 waves to detected signals in three modalities. Psychophysiology 17, 112–122.

Sokol, S. (1980). Pattern visual evoked potentials: Their use in pediatric ophthalmology. Intl. Ophthal. Clinics 20, 251–268.

Sokol, S. and Dobson, V. (1976). Pattern reversal visually evoked potentials in infants. Invest. Ophthalmol. 15, 58.

Sokol, S. and Jones, K. (1979). Implicit time of pattern evoked potentials in infants: An index of maturation of spatial vision. Vision Res. 19, 747–755.

Sokol, S., Moskowitz, A., and Towle, V.L. (1981). Age-related changes in the latency of the visual evoked potential: Influence of check size. Electroencephalogr. Clin. Neurophysiol. 51, 559–562.

Squires, K., Chippendale, T., Wrege, K., Goodin, D., and Starr, A. (1980). Electrophysiological assessment of mental function in aging and dementia. Aging in the 1980s: Psychological Issues, L. Poon, Ed. American Psychological Association, Washington, D.C.

Squires, K., Goodin, D., and Starr, A. (1979a). Event related potentials in development, aging, and dementia. In Human Evoked Potentials: Applications and Problems, D. Lehman and E. Callaway, Eds. Plenum Press, New York.

Squires, K., Petuchowski, S., Wickens, E., and Donchin, E. (1977). The effects of stimulus sequence on event related potentials: A comparison of visual and auditory sequences. Percept. Psychophys. 22, 31–40.

Squires, K., Wickens, C., Squires, N., and Donchin, E. (1976). The effect of stimulus sequence on the waveform of the cortical event-related potential. Science 193, 1142–1146.

Squires, N., Donchin, E., Squires, K., and Grossberg, S. (1977). Bisensory stimulation: Inferring decision-related processes from the P300 component. J. Exp. Psychol.: Human Percep. Perform. 3, 299–315.

Squires, N., Galbraith, G., and Aine, C. (1979b). Event-related potential assessment of sensory and cognitive deficits in the mentally retarded. In Human Evoked Potentials: Applications and Problems, D. Lehmann and E. Callaway (Eds.). New York, Plenum Press.

Starr, A. (1978). Sensory evoked potentials in clinical disorders of the nervous system. Ann. Rev. Neurosci. 1, 103–127.

Starr, A. and Achor, L.J. (1975). Auditory brain stem responses in neurological disease. Arch. Neurol. 32, 761–768.

Starr, A., Amlie, R., Martin, W., and Sanders, S. (1977). Development of auditory function in newborn infants revealed by auditory brainstem potentials. Pediatrics 60, 831–839.

Starr, A., Sohmer, H., and Celesia, G. (1978). Some applications of evoked potentials to patients with neurological and sensory impairment. In Event-Related Brain Potentials in Man, E. Callaway, P. Tueting, and S. Doslow, Eds. Academic Press, New York.

Stockard, J., Hughes, J., and Sharbrough, F. (1979). Visually evoked potentials to electronic pattern reversal: Latency variations with gender, age, and technical factors. Amer. J. EEG Technol. 19, 171–204.

Stockard, J. and Rossiter, V. (1977). Clinical and pathological correlates of brain stem auditory response abnormalities. Neurology 27, 316–325.

Stockard, J., Stockard, J., and Sharbrough, F. (1978). Nonpathologic factors influencing brainstem auditory evoked potentials. Amer. J. EEG Technol. 18, 177–209.

Taguchi, K., Picton, T., Orpin, J., and Goodman, B. (1969). Evoked response audiometry in newborn infants. Acta Oto-Laryngol. Suppl. 252, 5–17.

Tecce, J.J. (1972). Contingent negative variation (CNV) and psychological processes in man. Psychol. Bull. 77, 73–108.

Tecce, J.J. and Cole, J. (1976). The distraction-arousal hypothesis, CNV, and schizophrenia. In Behavior Control and Modification of Physiological Activity, D.I. Mostofsky, Ed. Prentice-Hall, Englewood Cliffs, N.J.

Tecce, J.J., Yrchik, D., Meinbresse, D., Dessonville, C., and Cole, J. (1980a). CNV rebound and aging. I. Attention functions. In Progress in Brain Research: Motivation Motor and Sensory Processes of the Brain: Electrical Potentials, Behavior and Clinical Use, Vol. 54, H.H. Kornhuber and L. Deecke, Eds. Elsevier, Amsterdam.

Tecce, J.J., Yrchik, D.A., Meinbresse, D., Dessonville, C.L., Clifford, T.S., and Cole, J.O. (1980b). CNV Rebound and Aging. II. Type A and B CNV Shapes. In Progress in Brain Research: Motivation, Motor and Sensory Processes of the Brain: Electrical Potentials, Behavior and Clinical Use, Vol. 54, H.H. Kronhuber and L. Deecke, Eds. Elsevier, Amsterdam.

Thatcher, R. and John, E.R. (1977). Functional Neuroscience, Vol. 1, Foundations of Cognitive Processes. Erlbaum Publishers, Hillsdale, N.J.

Thompson, L. and Nowlin, J. (1973). Relation of increased attention to central autonomic nervous system states. In Intellectual Functioning in Adults, L.F. Jarvik, C. Eisdorder, and J.E. Blum, Eds. Springer, New York.

Thornton, A., Mendel, M.I., and Anderson, C. (1977). Effects of stimulus frequency and intensity on the middle components of the averaged auditory electroencephalic response. J. Speech Hear. Res. 20, 81–94.

Vaughan, H. and Ritter, W. (1970). The sounds of auditory evoked response recorded from the human scalp. Electroencephalography Clin. Neurophysiol. 28, 360–367.

Walter, W.G., Cooper, R., Aldridge, R., McCallum, W., and Winter, A. (1964). Contingent negative variation: An electric sign of sensorimotor association and expectancy in the human brain. Nature, 203, 380–384.

Weitzman, E., Fishbein, W., and Graziani, L. (1965). Auditory evoked responses obtained from the scalp electroencephalograms of full-term human neonate during sleep. Pediatrics 35, 458–462.

Weitzman, E. and Graziani, L. (1968). Maturation and topography of the auditory evoked response of the prematurely born infant. Develop. Psychobiol. 1, 79–80.

Wolf, K.E., & Goldstein, R. (1978) Middle component averaged electroencephalic response to tonal stimuli from normal neonates. Arch. Otolaryngol. 104, 508–513.

Wolf, K.E. and Goldstein, R. (1980). Middle component auditory evoked responses from neonates to low-level tonal stimulation. J. Speech Hear. Res. 23, 185–201.

9. Cerebral Blood Flow in Aging

JOHN STIRLING MEYER

TERRY G. SHAW

Physicians have long, and for the most part incorrectly, suspected that poor cerebral perfusion is the primary mediator of brain aging. This suspicion is based on the erroneous idea that cerebral atherosclerosis is a natural consequence of the aging process. Although cerebral atherosclerotic lesions are commonly found at necropsy among the elderly, atherosclerosis is not an invariable accompaniment of aging. Some elderly individuals have been reported to be virtually free of cerebral atherosclerotic change at autopsy, whereas severe involvement has frequently been observed in much younger individuals. Thus, cerebrovascular disease should not be considered synonomous with advancing age, but rather a disease that, like many others, occurs with increasing frequency among the aged.

The notion that aging itself is a cause of disease is now unanimously rejected by gerontologists and geriatricians (Reiff, 1980; Portnoi, 1980). In practice, however, it is often quite difficult to separate the effects of normal aging from disease. As the expected life-span in the United States steadily increases, and the elderly population begins to burgeon, a clear understanding of the difference between normal health and disease-related events becomes essential to an understanding of neurological complaints common among the elderly.

Early Studies of Cerebral Blood Flow and Aging

Examination of the relationship between aging and cerebral blood flow (CBF) was made possible almost 40 years ago when the nitrous oxide technique was developed by Kety and Schmidt (1948). This technique yielded an average value for blood flow and metabolic rate per unit of brain weight, and, for the first time, made possible the investigation of hemodynamic properties of the conscious human brain.

Early applications of this technique (Freyhan et al., 1951; Shenkin et al., 1953; Kennedy et al., 1954; Schieve and Wilson, 1953; Fazekas et al., 1952) were aimed at examining the influence of a variety of situational, disease-related, and therapeutic variables on CBF, including a somewhat cursory treatment of age-related variables. In 1956, Kety reviewed the existing literature, compiled data from 16 previous studies, and published the first definitive assessment of effects of advancing age on cerebral circulation. A combined analysis of these study groups indicated a rapid fall in cerebral circulation and metabolism in early adolescence, followed by gradual, but

This work was supported by USPHS Stroke Center Grant NS 09287 and the Veteran's Administration.

progressive declines from the third decade through senescence. Similar, but reciprocal relationships were found with cerebrovascular resistance. Care was taken to exclude subjects with gross vascular and/or neurological disorders from analysis; however, the older age groups were composed of hospitalized patients suffering or recovering from a variety of diseases that might influence or be related to cerebral circulatory and metabolic functions. Whether or not elderly individuals with asymptomatic or minimal vascular disease may have been included in these study groups was never clarified. Since between 70 to 85% of the elderly population have at least one or more chronic conditions, many of which increase the likelihood of cerebrovascular disease (e.g., hypertension, heart disease, diabetes mellitus, hyperlipidemia), the probability that Kety's data (1956) did not include data from subjects with atherosclerotic disease seems remote, and thus his data only approximate the normal aging process. By contrast, other investigators were unable to document an age difference in CBF measured in healthy individuals (Shenkin et al., 1953; Olesen, 1974) unless it was accompanied by such conditions as hypertension, atherosclerosis, and mental deterioration.

The unsettled question of the influence of age on CBF has many theoretical implications for understanding normal brain function. Given that reductions in CBF occur among the elderly, does this constitute a primary change due to cerebrovascular disease or changes secondary to normal alterations in the structural integrity of the brain? Specifically, does progressive reduction in CBF due to age-related atherosclerosis lead to cerebral hypoxia, tissue damage, and reduced cerebral metabolic rate, or does a normal, parenchymatous atrophy of the brain give rise to a reduced cerebral metabolic demand followed by a secondary readjustment of the circulation to the reduced demand of neuronal tissues? Although a variety of age-related changes in the cytoarchitecture of cerebral tissue populations have been documented (see later sections), these studies are similarly limited in their ability to differentiate accurately normal age changes in tissue from disease-related events.

In an effort to resolve this question, the National Institute of Mental Health, in the fifties, sponsored a large, multidisciplinary group of investigators from the behavioral, medical, and biological sciences for the express purpose of conducting a collaborative study on the effects of normal human aging (Birren et al., 1963). The study was specifically designed to eliminate and/or control for the effects of sickness, institutionalization, social adversity, and, in particular, vascular disease and to assess the effect of aging per se across a variety of functions. Following an extensive screening process, a final group of male candidates were dichotomized into young versus old, and, based on their documented degree of cerebrovascular involvement, they were ordinally graded into groups representative of normal, risk-factored, asymptomatic, and symptomatic populations. Since the normal elderly group did not significantly differ from their younger counterparts as far as CBF and cerebral oxygen metabolism ($CMRO_2$) were concerned (Table 9-1), the results of this study (Dastur et al., 1963) lend strong support to the notion that declines in CBF and oxygen consumption are not inevitable consequences of simple aging. When a decline occurs, it appears to be the result of vascular disease, however minimal it may be.

The contrast between the asymptomatic group with atherosclerosis and the symptomatic group with chronic brain syndrome is of particular interest. As shown in Table 9-1, reduced CBF in the asymptomatic group with atherosclerosis is accompanied by a normal $CMRO_2$. Although the demented group with "organic brain syndrome" had comparable blood flow values, they showed a reduced $CMRO_2$. Based upon the contrast between these two progressive dimensions of cerebrovascular disease, atherosclerotic-induced decreases in CBF appear to precede decrements in $CMRO_2$, and, according to Sokoloff (1966, 1979), such a sequence of change is consistent with the notion that poor cerebral circulation is probably the primary cause of brain degradation and

Table 9-1. Cerebral circulation and metabolism in normal subjects and asymptomatic patients with atherosclerosis and patients with "chronic brain syndrome" or dementia.

Group	Sample Size	Mean Age	Average CBF (ml/100 g/min)	Average CMRO$_2$ (ml/100 g/min)
Young normals	15	20.8	62	3.5
Elderly normals	26	71.0	58	3.3
Risk-factored elderly normals	5	71.2	55	3.6
Elderly patients with asymptomatic atherosclerosis	10	73.2	48**	3.2
Patients with chronic brain syndrome (dementia)	10	71.8	48**	2.7**

Adapted from Sokoloff, 1966.
**Statistically significantly different from normal young subjects (p <0.05); statistically significantly different from normal elderly men (p <0.05).

cell loss. On the other hand, in "organic brain syndromes" (presumably dementias of the parenchymatous degenerative type of Alzheimer), decreased CMRO$_2$ accompanies the reduced CBF and may be its cause.

Measurement of Cerebral Blood Flow

Intermediate Technological Advances

Over the past 30 years, a number of different technologies have evolved for measuring CBF. Following Kety and Schmidt's pioneering work with the nitrous oxide method, the techniques of intracarotid injection of radioactive krypton (^{85}Kr) (Lassen and Munck, 1955; Lassen, 1963) and intracarotid injection of radioactive xenon (^{133}Xe) (Glass and Harper, 1963; Harper et al., 1964; Ingvar et al., 1964) made it possible to simultaneously study CBF in multiple regions of the same hemisphere. Additional techniques that were subsequently developed include the hydrogen bolus method (Gotoh et al., 1966; Meyer and Welch, 1972), and the intravenous ^{133}Xe injection techniques (Agnoli et al., 1969; Austin et al., 1975).

The earlier techniques had their various advantages and disadvantages. The nitrous oxide technique, which was used to establish the early data base regarding the influence of aging on CBF, is inherently problematic. First, it should be pointed out that this method only estimates the average CBF and the cerebral metabolism, based on representative portions of the brain taken as a whole. It does not really provide information concerning the mean function of the total brain. Second, it does not take into consideration the changes in brain weight that usually occur with aging. Third, reproducibility error is large, being in the order of ±10%. And fourth, regional, age-related changes in brain function may not be seen with this technique. Despite the fact that the normal elderly group in the NIMH study displayed CBF and CMRO$_2$ values similar to those obtained in the young healthy group, differences in EEG frequency and cognitive/perceptual functions were evident (Birren et al., 1963), so that at least minor decreases in regional cortical or gray matter flow might be expected.

It should also be borne in mind that most of these earlier technologies were invasive. Almost all required carotid and/or jugular puncture, a procedure mainly limited to hospitalized patients undergoing angiographic examination. For ethical reasons, these techniques were not used in the majority of healthy volunteers whose larger numbers might have made minor differences more visible and possibly significant.

Regional CBF as measured by the noninvasive ^{133}Xe inhalation method was first introduced by Mallet and Veall in 1963 (Mallet and Veall, 1963, 1965), with subsequent modifications for abbreviated recording time and improved clinical application (Obrist et al., 1981; Risberg et al., 1975, 1977; Meyer et al., 1978).

As illustrated schematically in Figure 9-1, the inhalation method used in this laboratory is based on the Fick principle, whereby ^{133}Xe gas is inhaled as the inert, radioactive indicator for determining regional blood flow to the brain. Xenon-133 gas is inhaled as a mixture of 5 to 7 mCi/liter in air for 1 minute. After inhalation, the gas passes from the lungs via the pulmonary circulation to the heart and from the heart to the brain, where it diffuses rapidly to reach equilibrium. After

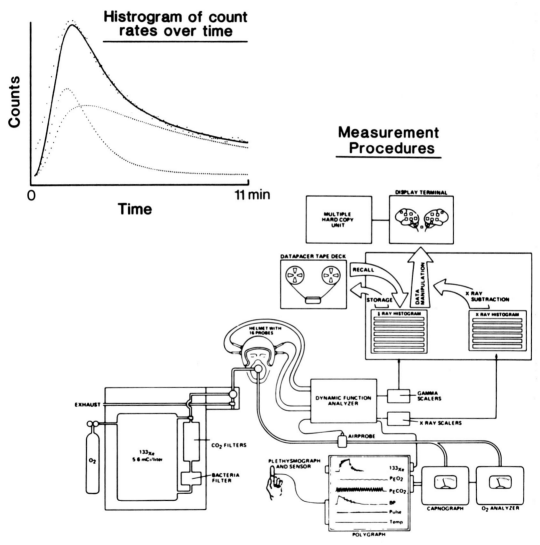

Figure 9-1. Xenon-133 inhalation method for measuring regional cerebral blood flow. Following inhalation of ^{133}Xe gas (5–7 mCi/liter) for 1-min, the collimated sodium iodide crystals held over the scalp monitor the clearance of the tracer from 16 different brain regions. Count rate histograms of washout are subjected to bi- compartmental analysis using standard computer algorithms for estimating faster-clearing gray matter and slower-clearing white matter compartments. Concurrent measures include EEG, EKG, end-tidal oxygen, carbon dioxide and xenon, respiration rate, blood pressure, pulse rate, and body temperature.

one minute, inhalation of ^{133}Xe is discontinued, and the brain tissues are allowed to desaturate while regional clearance curves are monitored by 16 collimated NaI crystal detectors mounted perpendicular to the scalp on a helmet. Desaturation curves are recorded for 10 minutes and recirculation from the arterial blood is corrected for by deconvoluting the head curves with the end-tidal ^{133}Xe curve, which may be assumed to be in equilibrium with arterial values.

Regional flow values are calculated using standard computer algorithms programmed according to a two-compartmental model (Obrist et al., 1975, 1981). The flow values are expressed as the fast component or gray matter flow (f_1) and the slow component or white matter flow (F_2), their respective weights (W_1 and W_2), and the mean 10-minute flow extrapolated to infinity (CBF_∞).

Some of the problems previously encountered with the earlier techniques, such as tissue overlap (i.e., spatial resolution), Compton scatter, slippage, temporal resolution, uncoupling of CBF and $CMRO_2$, and exposure to radiation are inherent in the non-invasive ^{133}Xe method using external probes. Additional problems peculiar to the ^{133}Xe inhalation technique have been identified and have either negligible effects or can be corrected/controlled. These include air sinus contamination (Obrist et al., 1975; Meyer, 1978), dissociation between arterial and end-tidal concentrations of the radioisotope, especially in chronic obstructive pulmonary disease, scalp contamination (Deshmukh and Meyer, 1978; Meyer et al., 1977), changes in tissue blood partition coefficients or solubility (λ), and detector artifacts (Baron et al., 1979). Furthermore, this technique does not measure the metabolic rate.

Nevertheless, the ^{133}Xe inhalation technique has distinct advantages. The most obvious advantage, from an ethical point of view, is that the procedure is atraumatic and can be repeated serially, if indicated, on subjects of any age and physical status safely and reliably. Additionally, this method yields suitable test-retest reliability coefficients (Sakai et al., 1979; Blauenstein et al., 1975) and is in good agreement with the data obtained by the ^{133}Xe intracarotid injection method. Finally, it provides for simultaneous recording of multiple, regional cerebral blood flow (rCBF) values for both the cerebral hemispheres and the brainstem–cerebellar region.

Contemporary Studies

With the improved technology for measuring CBF and the recognized need to eliminate or control for the effects of cerebrovascular disease in any analysis of age trends, many recent investigators have been able to demonstrate age-related reductions in CBF for normal healthy volunteers, consistent with Kety's original formulation (Davis et al., 1981; Naritomi et al., 1979, 1981; Shaw et al., 1981a,b; Shaw and Meyer, 1981; Yamamoto et al., 1980; Yamaguichi et al., 1980). A detailed analysis of the findings from each study would be beyond the scope of this review, and since the findings have been consistent among investigators, we have chosen to review this section using recent data obtained from our own laboratory. Detailed aspects of some of these data with reviews of the literature have been published elsewhere (see above); furthermore, the majority of data to be summarized here is new. To date, cross-sectional analysis of age-related changes in CBF has been completed among a group of 340 neurologically normal volunteers, with and without risk factors for atherosclerosis, representing the age groups between 30 and 98 years of age.

As shown in Figure 9-2, there is a progressive decline, when compared by cross-sectional analysis, of gray matter blood flow of both hemispheres, among healthy, right-handed males and females between the third to the eighth decade. Women have a significantly higher gray matter flow than men between the third to the fifth decade. This is partly attributed to an anti-aldosterone effect of the increased progesterone levels known to be present in the female, together with blood loss associated with the menstrual cycle. Both these

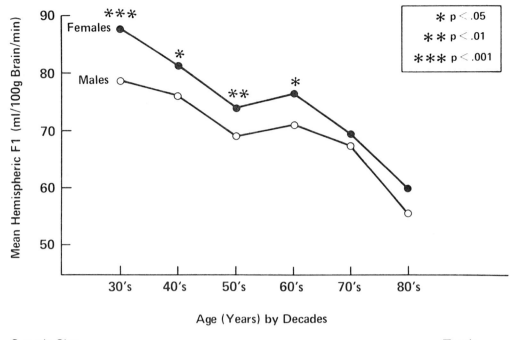

Sample Size

							Totals
Males:	23	7	25	13	7	2	77
Females:	20	16	49	17	22	8	132

Figure 9-2. Cross-sectional analysis of age-related trends showing progressive decrease in F_1 values for healthy women versus healthy men. Women have significantly higher CBF values through the menarche and up to age 60; thereafter, F_1 values for women decrease more rapidly and approach that of men.

factors have been shown to lower the hematocrit and decrease blood viscosity (Vellar, 1974; Thomas, 1977). The annual decline in gray matter flow for normal healthy subjects is in the order of 0.5 milliliter/100 grams of brain a minute and occurs in the absence of any clinically identifiable risk factors for cerebrovascular disease or abnormal cerebrovascular signs (bruit, transient ischemic attack, etc).

On a regional basis, it was apparent from Figure 9-3 that declines in hemispheric gray matter flow were not homogeneous throughout the brain. Although the left hemisphere in general had higher flows, they declined more rapidly than the right among these right-handed volunteers. Both prefrontal regions decline more rapidly with advancing age and to a greater extent than other regions (e.g., probes 1 and 9). On the other hand, the left precentral region (probe 2) and Sylvian region (probe 4) among these right-handers showed less decline with advancing age, suggesting that the speech and motor-hand areas for their dominant hemispheres change less with advancing age. This may be related to the relatively high functional activity of these cortical regions.

The only region of the right hemisphere that did not show a greater decline than homologous regions of the left hemisphere was the right parietal region. Such a finding was of special interest, since this region is commonly considered to be the dominant area for visuo-spatial function in right-handed individuals, and it may also be a region of relatively high functional

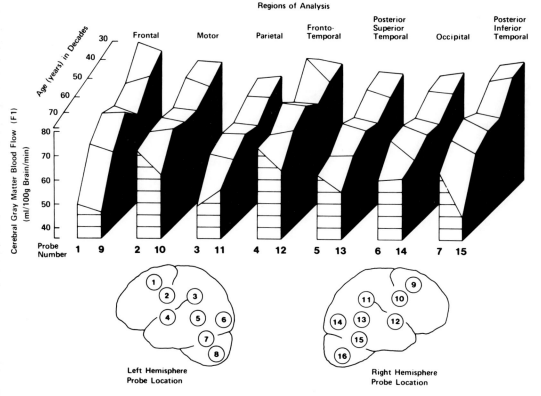

Figure 9-3. Cross-sectional analysis of regional reductions of F_1 values versus age in right-handed, healthy subjects. Prefrontal areas (1 and 9) and fronto-temporal speech areas (4 and 12), particularly for the left hemisphere, are relatively well preserved.

activity. These observations may be taken to support the hypothesis that sustained functional activity of the brain in the aged protects against structural decline. Conversely, inactivity associated with social withdrawal, depression, or premature retirement may hasten cerebral deterioration in the aged, and this has long been suspected, based on clinical observation.

As shown in Figure 9-4, it is also apparent that risk factors for cerebrovascular disease (hypertension, heart disease, diabetes mellitus, and hyperlipidemia), in otherwise normal volunteers, significantly enhance the rate and level of decline in gray matter flow, presumably by increasing the rate of cerebral atherogenesis.

The more recent findings of measurable reductions of CBF in healthy individuals without identifiable disease support the view that declines in cerebral circulation are a natural consequence of the aging process and are probably due to decreased cerebral metabolic demand. Although the above statement is in agreement with Kety's conclusions, it is not entirely consonant with the original position of the NIMH group (Birren et al., 1963; Dastur et al., 1963; Sokoloff, 1966). Both studies, however, agree that cerebrovascular disease accelerates the aging process of the brain. The reduced rCBF values observed in healthy elderly individuals could, in actuality, be due to subclinical cerebral artherosclerosis or to normal parenchymatous changes in the brain or a combination of both. Previous publications have cited evidence that both factors play a part

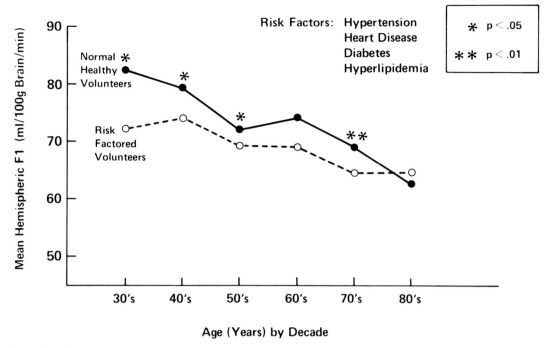

Figure 9-4. Cross-sectional analysis of the decrease in F_1 values with advancing age in normals with risk factors for atherothrombotic stroke compared to normal healthy volunteers without risk factors. The progressive reduction in CBF is significantly enhanced for risk-factored population.

(Myer et al., 1978; Naritomi et al., 1979; Nakajima et al., 1981a,b; Shaw et al., 1979, 1981a,b; Shaw and Meyer, 1981; Yamamoto et al., 1980, 1981; Yamaguchi et al., 1979, 1980; Sokoloff et al., 1977; Alavi et al., 1981), but in any case, the experimental designs employed in these studies have methodological shortcomings that should be overcome before this issue can be definitively resolved.

Design Considerations

Generally speaking, the purpose of aging research is to describe and explain how a complex living organism moves forward through time (Birren, 1959). Given that individuals age at variable rates, the pre-ferred method for the study of aging is a longitudinal design, whereby the same individuals are followed and observed over a given period of time. Since longitudinal studies have many practical difficulties in achievement* (Jones, 1958), investigators often rely on cross-sectional studies (different individuals of different ages are compared) or the "extreme groups" permutation of the cross-sectional design (individuals from opposite ends of the aging spectrum are compared). These options

---

*Longitudinal prospective studies require that the same individual return for repeated observation at intervals for several years. This results in loss by attrition due to illness, death, moving, lack of motivation, etc., and requires a stable and dedicated laboratory and staff.

are scientifically acceptable as long as the investigator is aware of and can tolerate the increased error: namely, cohort effects, selection bias, survivor effects, and, in general, the confusion between age change versus age differences (Schaie, 1968).

At present, most of our knowledge concerning age-related trends in CBF and $CMRO_2$ comes from cross-sectional or extreme group analyses. Kety's data (1956) and the more recent findings are exemplary of the cross-sectional approach, the NIMH study (Dastur et al., 1963) of the extreme groups design. Given their inability to differentiate between age change versus age difference, the possibility exists that neither analysis may depict the normal aging process accurately.

In order for conclusions drawn from data from such cross-sectional methods of assessment to be of clinical relevance, the data must be cross-validated by longitudinal studies. In this laboratory, most of the initial findings from cross-sectional analysis of resting CBF patterns have now been confirmed by longitudinal analysis of serial CBF measurements, carried out on many of the same subjects. Age-matched groups of healthy normal subjects ($N=44$), risk-factored normal subjects ($N=54$) and patients with a history of transient ischemic attacks (TIAs) ($N=34$), stroke ($N=9$), and multi-infarct dementia (MID) ($N=8$) have been examined at yearly intervals up to 42 months (Figure 9-5). Stepwise reductions in resting CBF were apparent between the groups listed above, with normal healthy subjects at one end of the spectrum of cerebrovascular health status and patients with MID at the other end.

All groups showed significant CBF reductions over the course of the 42-month interval. Although the normal healthy volunteers displayed the highest F_1 values across time, the rate of decline in CBF was essentially the same as that measured in the risk-factored, but otherwise normal subjects. The group with TIAs plus risk factors showed a similar, but more precipitous decline with advancing age. The most severe and rapid deterioration of gray matter flow with the passage of time was seen in subjects with completed stroke and/or MID (Figure 9-6).

The progressive reduction of F_1, apparent in the group of healthy normal subjects, should not be construed as a sign of pathology or compromised cerebral circulation. Instead, it should be viewed as a consequence of a normal age-related reduction in metabolic demand, separable from any effects attributable to cerebrovascular disease. The functional significance of this normal, age-related decline in F_1 is more realistictly viewed as a narrowing of the distance between resting CBF levels and the ischemic threshold (Shaw and Meyer, 1981). The presence and severity of cerebrovascular disease merely aggravates this relationship and increases the likelihood of ischemic changes in brain tissue.

Cerebral Vasomotor Responsiveness

Techniques developed for measuring CBF also provide a means of investigating changes in vasomotor capacitance in health and disease. The ability of cerebral vessels to constrict and/or dilate in response to induced changes in arterial concentrations of carbon dioxide and oxygen is an important indicator of cerebrovascular reserve and has received considerable attention (Kety and Schmidt, 1948; Novack et al., 1953; Schieve and Wilson, 1953; Lassen et al., 1957; Fazekas et al., 1953; Wolff and Lennox, 1930; Hayman et al., 1953; Nakajima et al., 1981).

Carbon dioxide is a potent cerebral vasodilator and plays a significant role in the normal physiological control of CBF, whereby an increased regional activity and metabolic demand results in regionally increased carbon dioxide production. In the presence of a healthy cerebrovascular substrate, this regional increase in carbon dioxide is met by regional increases in blood flow (Meyer and Welch, 1972). Since carbon dioxide responsiveness (hypercapnia) appears to be diminished in the presence of cerebrovascular disease (Meyer and Welch, 1972; Yamamoto et al., 1980; Yamaguchi et al., 1980; Novack et al., 1953; Schieve and Wilson, 1953),

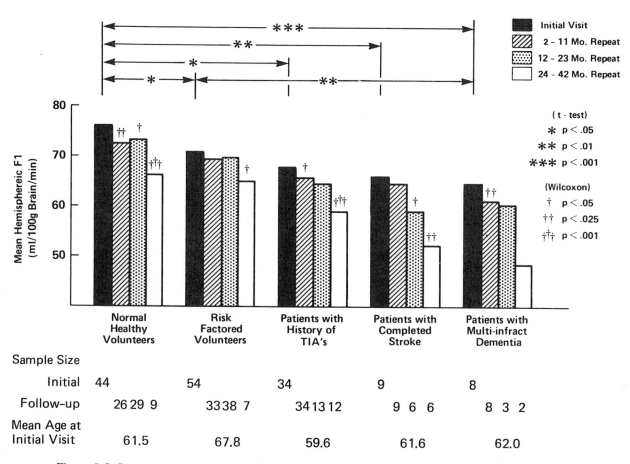

Figure 9-5. Intra-group comparisons of age-matched subjects demonstrate a significant decline in F_1 values measured prospectively across standard intervals of time in normal subjects with and without risk factors and patients with TIAs and with neurological deficits arising from stroke.

many investigators have proposed using hypercapnic responsiveness as a means of identifying patients with cerebrovascular disease and quantifying the degree of involvement. However, other investigators have found normal hypercapnic responses, as measured by cerebral arteriovenous differences, in patients with vascular dementia (Lassen et al., 1957).

The response to hypercapnia has also been reported to be reduced during normal aging. In early studies with the nitrous oxide technique the carbon dioxide responses were reduced in elderly patients

(Novack et al., 1953; Schieve and Wilson, 1953; Fazekas et al., 1953); however, the effects of normal aging versus symptomatic cerebral atherosclerosis were not clearly separated. Acknowledging the need to carefully screen individuals for the presence of cerebrovascular disease, investigators have more recently demonstrated a normal, age-related reduction in carbon dioxide responsiveness (Figure 9-7) in healthy volunteers (Yamamoto et al., 1980; Yamaguchi et al., 1980; Shaw and Meyer, 1981). The progressive loss of vasomotor capacitance to hypercapnia was

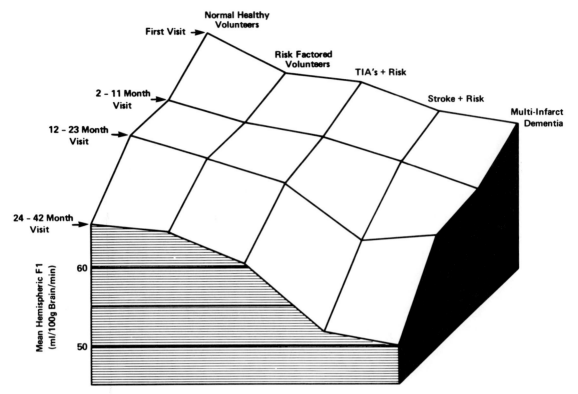

Figure 9-6. A contour map showing the interaction between advancing age and the degree of cerebrovascular disease on longitudinal measurements of F_1 values for normal healthy volunteers compared to (1) risk-factored volunteers; (2) patients with TIAs plus risk factors; (3) patients with stroke and (4) patients with MID. The decline in CBF becomes progressively exaggerated, as the degree of risk and/or severity of the neurological deficits arising from stroke become apparent.

further diminished in elderly individuals at risk for atherothrombotic stroke and was essentially lost in affected regions when cerebrovascular symptoms were present or when cerebral infarction had occurred.

It has also been known for over 50 years that increased arterial partial pressures of oxygen, induced by inhalation of 100% oxygen, constricts cerebral blood vessels (Wolff and Lennox, 1930) and reduces CBF (Kety and Schmidt, 1948; Hayman et al., 1953). In the absence of identifiable cerebrovascular disease, vasoconstrictor responses to hyperoxia also appear to be age dependent (Figure 9-8). Vasoconstriction is proportionately reduced in volunteers with

risk factors for atherothrombotic stroke, cerebral ischemia, and infarction; paradoxical vasodilation occurs in zones of maximal ischemia and in patients with long-standing cerebrovascular disease and/ or recent infarction (Nakajima et al., 1981a, b).

Collectively, these results indicate that, during normal aging, in healthy individuals without risk factors or identifiable disease, there is a reduction in resting CBF as well as a decrease in vasomotor capacitance during induced hypercapnia and hyperoxia. These graded, age-dependent changes are primarily attributed to normal neuronal loss with consequent decreases in cerebral metabo-

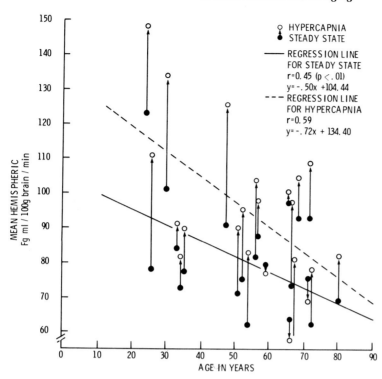

Figure 9-7. The cerebral vasodilator responsiveness during inhalation of 5% CO_2 becomes progressively reduced in healthy normal subjects without risk factors. Mean hemispheric flow gram values in the steady state (●) and during 5% CO_2 inhalation (○) are plotted against age.

lism as well as loss of elasticity of cerebral vessels. The presence and severity of cerebrovascular disease appears to accelerate these changes.

Applications in Dementia

A recurring issue in the study of human cerebral aging and CBF has been the relationship of dementia to normal senescence. Although dementia and normal aging are both occasioned by a variety of histopathological changes, including cerebral atrophy, neuritic plaque formation, accumulation of lipofuscin, and neurofibrillary degeneration, these changes are more extensive and widespread in dementia. Thus, aging and dementia are qualitatively similar, but quantitatively different. The quantitative differences are also reflected in measurements of CBF (Freyhan et al., 1951; Lassen et al., 1957; Ingvar and Gustafson, 1970; Simard et al., 1971; O'Brien and Mallet, 1970; Hachinski et al., 1975; Obrist et al., 1975). It is now generally accepted that CBF is signifi-

cantly reduced in patients with organic dementia. Furthermore, the degree of reduction in CBF appears to be related to the level of mental deterioration (Lassen et al., 1957; Obrist et al., 1975; Baer et al., 1976; Hagberg and Ingvar, 1976; Yamaguchi et al., 1980).

Quantitative neuropathological studies (Tomlinson et al., 1970; Tomlinson and Henderson, 1976), have revealed evidence of two distinct etiologies underlying the more frequent types of dementia in old age: a vascular or multi-infarct dementia, characterized by multiple cerebral infarcts, and the more common form known as Alzheimer's disease (AD) characterized by numerous senile plaques and neurofibrillary tangles. Alzheimer's disease is more than twice as prevalent than MID. Together the two forms account for 70 to 85% of all demented patients, and frequently AD and MID co-exist.

Differential diagnosis between MID and AD is not easily accomplished by neurological and psychological examination alone, although some degree of differentia-

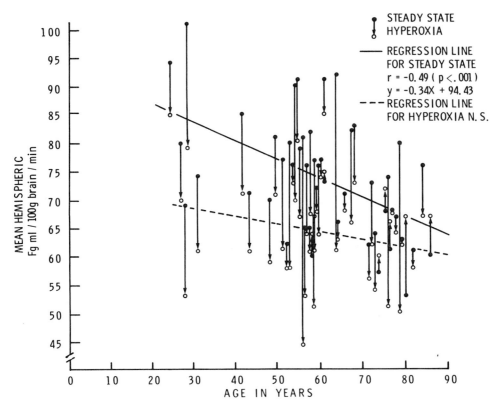

Figure 9-8. A decline in cerebral vasoconstrictor responsiveness during 100% oxygen inhalation occurs with normal healthy aging. Gray matter flow values during steady state (●) and during 100% oxygen inhalation (○) are plotted against age.

tion may be afforded by these evaluations combined with careful documentation of clinical history and course (Hachinski et al., 1974). O'Brien and Mallet (1970) were the first to suggest that measurements of CBF might provide an objective means of distinguishing between the two major types of dementia. Although some investigators have reported significantly lower overall CBF values in MID compared to AD (O'Brien and Mallet, 1970; Hachinski et al., 1975), others have found CBF to be equally reduced in both (Obrist et al., 1975; Ingvar and Gustafson, 1970). Failure to control for duration, severity, and possible combinations of the underlying pathologies in the various samples, no doubt contributed to such contradictions.

Although symmetrical frontal and temporal patterns of CBF reduction have been identified in AD (Yamaguchi et al., 1980; Obrist et al., 1975; Ingvar and Gustafson, 1970; Simard et al., 1971), and patchy reductions occur in MID, an innate and often large variability in blood flow values among demented populations of different types and severity make it highly unlikely that a particular resting CBF flow pattern or sets of values will be specific for each dementia type, particularly since, as noted, the two disorders often co-exist (Yamaguchi et al., 1980; Nakajima et al., 1981b; Simard et al., 1971).

Based on preliminary findings, Schieve and Wilson (1953) suggested that vasomotor responsiveness to carbon dioxide might differentiate MID from AD. Although early studies have met with mixed results (Lassen et al., 1957; Simard et al., 1971; Geraud et al., 1969; Dekoninch et al., 1975), small, but nonsignificant trends were apparent with hyperventilation-induced hypocapnia (Hachinski et al., 1975). More recently, clear-cut differences have been reported in hypercapnia (Yamaguchi et al., 1980) and hyperoxia (Nakajima et al., 1981b). Vasomotor responsiveness in MID appears to be patchily reduced during hypercapnia and paradoxically reversed during hyperoxia. By contrast, vasodilatory responses in patients with AD has been shown to be normal or excessive during hypercapnia, whereas vasoconstrictor responses to hyperoxia were diffusely diminished, but in the same direction as the normal response. If it is assumed that the latter findings are further confirmed, tests of vasomotor responsiveness appear to be a safe and reliable means of differentiating MID from AD as well as quantifying the severity of the process.

New Technological Frontiers

Although there are a number of advantages to the non-invasive ^{133}Xe inhalation methods for measuring CBF, there remain several shortcomings. Two of the more significant are (1) poor spatial resolution resulting from superimposition of signals from deep and superficial cerebral tissues and (2) possible uncoupling of oxygen delivery (CBF) and oxygen metabolism ($CMRO_2$) in pathological states. New technologies that circumvent these problems have recently been developed and are being applied to the study of brain function in aging.

Active brain cells are energy dependent on glucose oxidation, but will also accept labeled 2-deoxyglucose. However, once inside the cell, the tracer cannot be fully metabolized and is trapped. By introducing an intravenous bolus of radiolabeled carbon (^{14}C) deoxyglucose and exposing subsequent brain slices for autoradiographic determination of ^{14}C concentrations, Sokoloff et al. (1977) developed a quantitative method for measuring glucose utilization in all parts of the brain. As shown in Table 9-2, early results derived from this technique demonstrate an age-related reduction in cerebral glucose utilization in rats (Sokoloff, 1979). The unexpected observation that the elderly rats have higher values than their middle-aged counterparts is perplexing, but may well be due to the methodological inadequacies of cross-sectional designs (i.e., an inability to account for survivor/cohort effects). Nevertheless, the observed reductions were particularly evident in cortical regions corresponding to primary sensory systems and were most pronounced in cortical layer IV. This last observation correlates well with the neuropathological findings that neuronal drop-out is especially evident in layers II and IV of the cortex (Scheibel and

Table 9-2. Effects of aging on local cerebral glucose utilization in normal Sprague-Dawley rats determined by autoradiographic ^{14}C-labeled deoxyglucose method.

	Local cerebral glucose utilization (μmol/100 g/min)		
	Young (5–6 mos)	Middle-Aged ($\simeq$ 12 mos)	Aged ($\geq$ 2 yrs)
Cortical gray matter Average from nine regions	121.6	97.0	107.8
Subcortical gray matter Average from 21 regions	93.43	79.67	83.52
White matter Average from three regions	36.3	25.0	30.0

Modified from C. Smith, W.R. Fredricks, S.F., Rapoport, and L. Sokoloff and adapted from Sokoloff (1979).

Scheibel, 1975). Developmentally, these layers are the last to appear and, by virtue of their order of appearance, may be more susceptible to the aging process (Brody, 1978).

Although the autoradiographic ^{14}C-labeled deoxyglucose technique is limited to acute preparations of laboratory animals, a positron-emitting analogue has been developed and successfully applied to studies in man (Reivich et al., 1977). With the increasing availability of cyclotrons and linear accelerators to medical science, short-lived, positron-emitting radionuclides, such as $^{15}O_2$, ^{13}N, ^{11}C, ^{18}F, and $^{15}O_2$-labeled carbon dioxide have been utilized themselves or incorporated into metabolic compounds. By combining these substances with the imaging properties of positron emission tomography, scientists are now able to investigate brain metabolic activity in the conscious human noninvasively.

Using ^{18}F-labeled fluorodeoxyglucose as a positron-emitting analogue, several investigators have observed significant, age-related reductions in cerebral metabolic rates for glucose in normal elderly individuals (Alavi et al., 1981; Benson et al., 1981). The early data regarding dementia populations has not been supported by later data. Using the $^{15}O_2$-labeled carbon dioxide, other investigators have also reported age-related reductions in human CBF and oxygen consumption in a group of volunteers carefully screened to exclude significant medical antecedents (Lenzi et al., 1981).

Although analogues of the deoxyglucose technique will, in future, provide greater insight into the study of brain function and aging, the availability and cost of a cyclotron or linear accelerator is seen as a major limiting factor. For this reason, a number of investigators (Meyer et al., 1980, 1981a, b; Drayer et al., 1979, 1980; Kelcz et al., 1978) have attempted to develop methods that take advantage of the excellent resolving power of conventional X-ray transmission CT scanners by combining it with the contrast properties of stable, non-radioactive xenon gas to yield measures of local CBF and tissue solubility (i.e., blood/brain partition coefficients or Lλ). From early

results with this technique, it appears that the decrease of cortical and basal ganglia blood flow with advancing age in normal volunteers is further decreased by risk factors, TIA's, stroke, and dementia. Additionally, local Lλ values are reduced in zones of infarction or ischemia. In MID, zones of zero flow with reduced Lλ are evident. In AD, gray matter flow is diffusely reduced in excess of that of age-matched normals and appears to correlate linearly with the severity of the neurological deficits.

In AD, there also appears to be a loss of gray–white matter discriminability by plain CT scanning, as well as atrophy of the cortex and ventricular enlargement (George et al., 1981). This appears to be due to the reduction of local CBF in the cortex and the basal ganglia (since erythrocytes, which are numerous in gray matter, have higher CT attenuation than white matter), rather than to changes in composition of white matter, since the Lλ values remain normal (Meyer et al., 1981a).

Data from research using these newer technologies support the conclusions drawn from ^{133}Xe gas inhalation data and appear to be consistent with Kety's original formulation (1956), but longitudinal studies will still be necessary. Nevertheless, there is at least one consistent finding. Atherosclerosis is not the sole cause, nor is it necessarily the main cause, of the progressive atrophy of the brain. The brain can be expected to age and atrophy regardless of the state of the cerebral vasculature, but the appearance of concomitant cerebrovascular disease enhances, accelerates, and compounds its aging process.

References

Agnoli, A., Precipe, M., Priori, A.M. et al. (1969). Measurements of rCBF by intravenous injection of ^{133}Xe. A comparative study with the intra-arterial injection method. In Cerebral Blood Flow: Clinical and Experimental Results, M. Brock, C. Fieschi, D.H. Ingvar, N.A. Lassen, and K. Schurmann, Eds., Springer-Verlag, New York, pp. 31–34.

Alavi, A., Ferris, S., Wolf, A., Christman, D., Fowler, J., MacGregor, R., Farkas, T., Greenberg, J., Dann, R., and Reivich, M.

(1981). Determination of regional cerebral metabolism in dementia using F-18 Deoxyglucose and positron emission tomograph. Cerebral Vascular Disease 3,10th Salzburg Conference, International Congress Series 532, Excerpta Medica, pp. 109–112.

Austin, G., Laffin, D., and Hayward, W. (1975). Evaluation of fast component (gray matter) by 12 minute IV method using analog computer analysis. In Blood Flow and Metabolism in the Brain, A.M. Harper, W.B. Jennett, I.D. Miller, and J.O. Rowan, Eds. Churchill-Livingstone, Edinburgh, London, New York.

Baer, P.E., Faibish, G.M., Meyer, J.S., Mathew, N.T., and Rivera, V.M. (1976). Neuropsychological correlates of hemispheric and regional cerebral blood flow in dementia. In Cerebral Vascular Disease: 7th International Conference Salzburg, J.S. Meyer, H. Lechner, and M. Reivich, Eds. Thieme, Stuttgart, pp. 100–106.

Baron, J.C., Ackerman, R., Correia, J.A., Nelson, C.N., and Taveras, J. (1979). Artifactual curves with ^{133}Xe inhalation rCBF measurement. In Proceedings of the 9th International Symposium on cerebral blood flow and metabolism, Tokyo, Japan, F. Gotoh, H. Nagai, and Y. Tazaki, Eds. Acta Neurol. Scand. (Suppl. 72) 60, 238–239.

Benson, D., Kuhl, D., Phelps, M., Cummings, J., and Tsai, S. (1981). Positron emission computed tomography in the diagnosis of dementia. Ann. Neurol. 10, 76.

Birren, J.E. (1959). Principles of research on aging. In Handbook of Aging and the Individual. J.E. Birren, Ed. University of Chicago Press, Chicago, Ill.

Birren, J.E., Butler, R.N., Greenhouse, S.W., Sokoloff, L., and Yarrow, M.R. (Eds.) (1963). Human Aging: A Biological and Behavioral Study. U.S. Government Printing Office, Washington, D.C.

Blauenstein, U.W., Halsey, H.J., Wilson, E.M. et al. (1975). The ^{133}Xenon inhalation method. Analysis of reproducibility. In Blood flow and metabolism in the brain, M. Harper, B. Jennett, D. Miller et al., Eds. Churchill-Livingstone, Edinburgh, pp. 8.19–8.22.

Brody, H. (1978). Cell counts in cerebral cortex and brainstem. In Alzheimer's Disease: Senile Dementia and Related Disorders Aging, Vol. 7, R. Katzman, R.D. Terry, and K.L. Bick, Eds. Raven Press, New York.

Dastur, D.K., Lane, M.H., Hansen, D.B. et al. (1963). Effects of aging on cerebral circulation and metabolism in man. In Human Aging: A Biological and Biochemical Study, J.E. Birren, R.N. Butler, S.W. Greenhouse et al., Eds. USPHS Publication No. 986 Washington, D.C. U.S. Government Printing Office, pp. 59–76.

Davis, S.M., Ackerman, R.H., Correia, J.A., Alpert, N.M., Terrono, J., Buonanno, F., Chang, J.Y., Rosner, B., and Taveras, J.M. (1981). Cerebral blood flow and reactivity in stroke-age normal controls. J. Cerebral Blood Flow and Metabolism. (Suppl. 1), S547–548.

Dekoninch, W.J., Collard, M., and Jacquy, J. (1975). Comparative study of cerebral vasoactivity in vascular sclerosis of the brain in elder men. Stroke 6, 673–677.

Deshmukh, V.D. and Meyer, J.S. (1978). Noninvasive measurement of regional cerebral blood flow in man. Spectrum Publications, New York.

Drayer, B., Gur, D., Wolfson, S., and Dujovny, M. (1979). Regional blood flow in the posterior fossa. Xenon enhanced CT scanning. Acta Neurol. Scand. (Suppl. 2) 60, 218–219.

Drayer, B.P., Gur, D., Yonas, H., Wolfson, S.K., and Cook, E.D. (1980). Abnormality of the xenon brain: Blood partition coefficient and blood flow in cerebral infarction. An *in vivo* assessment using transmission computed tomography. Radiology 135, 349–354.

Fazekas, J.F., Alman, R.W., and Bessman, A.N. (1952). Cerebral physiology of the aged. Amer. J. Med. Soc. 223–245.

Fazekas, J.F., Bessman, A.N., Cotsonas, N.J. et al. (1953). Cerebral hemodynamics in cerebral arteriosclerosis. J. Gerontol. 8, 137–145.

Freyhan, F.A., Woodford, R.B., and Kety, S.S. (1951). Cerebral blood flow and metabolism in psychoses of senility. J. Nerv. Ment. Dis. 113, 449.

George, A.J., deLeon, M.J., Ferris, S.H., and Kricheff, I.I. (1981). Parenchymal CT correlates of senile dementia (Alzheimer's disease): Loss of gray-white matter discriminability. AJNR 2, 205–213.

Geraud, J., Bes, A., Delpla, M., and Marc-Vergnes, J.P. (1969). Cerebral arteriovenous oxygen differences: Reappraisal of their significance for evaluation of brain function. In Research on the Cerebral Circulation, J.S. Meyer, H. Lechner, and O. Eichhorn, Eds. C.C. Thomas, Springfield, Ill., pp. 209–222.

Glass, H.I. and Harper, A.M. (1963). Measurement of regional blood flow in cerebral cortex of man through intact skull. Br. Med. J. 1, 593.

Gotoh, F., Meyer, J.S., and Tomita, M. (1966). Hydrogen method for determining cerebral blood flow in man. Arch. Neurol. 15, 549–559.

Hachinski, V.C., Lassen, N.A., and Marshall, J. (1974). Multi-infarct dementia: A cause of mental deterioration in the elderly. Lancet ii, 207–210.

Hachinski, V.C., Iliff, L.D., Zilhka, E., Du-Boulay, G.H., McAllister, V.L., Marshall, J., Russell, R.W.R., and Symon, L. (1975). Cerebral blood flow in dementia. Arch. Neurol. 32, 632–637.

Hagberg, B., and Ingvar, D.H. (1976). Cognitive reduction in presenile dementia related to regional abnormalities of the cerebral blood flow. Br. J. Psychiatr. 128, 209–222.

Harper, A.M., Glass, H.I., Steven, J.L. et al. (1964). The measurement of local blood flow in the cerebral cortex from the clearance of xenon[133]. J. Neurol. Neurosurg. Psychiat. 27, 255–258.

Hayman, A., Patterson, Jr., J.L., Duke, T.W. et al. (1953). The cerebral circulation and metabolism in arteriosclerotic and hypertensive cerebrovascular disease. With observations on the effects of inhalation of different concentrations of oxygen. New Eng. J. Med. 249, 223–229.

Ingvar, D.H. and Gustafson, L. (1970). Regional cerebral blood flow in organic dementia with early onset. Acta Neurol. Scand. 43, 42–73.

Ingvar, D.H., Crouquist, R., Ekberg, K. et al. (1965). Normal values or regional cerebral blood flow in man during flow and weight estimates of gray and white matter. Acta Neurol. Scand. (Suppl. 14) 72–78.

Jones, H.E. (1958). Problems of method in longitudinal research. Vita Human 1, 93–99.

Kelcz, F., Hilal, S.K., Hartwell, P., and Joseph, P.M. (1978). Computed tomographic measurement of the xenon brain-blood partition coefficient and implication for regional cerebral blood flow: A preliminary report. Radiology 127, 385–392.

Kennedy, C., Sokoloff, L., and Anderson, W. (1954). Cerebral blood flow and metabolism in normal children. Am. J. Dis. Children 88, 813.

Kety, S.S. (1956). Human cerebral blood flow and oxygen consumption as related to aging. J. Chronic. Dis. 3, 478–486.

Kety, S.S. and Schmidt, C.F. (1948a). Nitrous oxide method for the quantitative determination of cerebral blood flow in man: Theory, procedure and normal values. J. Clin. Invest. 27, 476.

Kety, S.S. and Schmidt, C.F. (1948b). The effects of altered arterial tensions of carbon dioxide and oxygen on cerebral blood flow and cerebral oxygen consumption of normal young men. J. Clin. Invest. 27, 484–492.

Lassen, N.A., Hoedt-Rasmussen, K., Sorensen, K., et al. (1963). Regional cerebral blood flow in man determined by krypton[85]. Neurology 13, 719–727.

Lassen, N.A. and Munck, O. (1955). The cerebral blood flow in man determined by the use of radioactive krypton[85]. Acta Physiol. Scand. 33, 30–49.

Lassen, N.A., Munck, O., and Tottey, E.R. (1957). Mental function and cerebral oxygen consumption in organic dementia. Arch. Neurol. Psychiatr. 77, 126–133.

Lenzi, G., Jones, T., Frackowiak, R., Heather, J., and Rhodes, C. (1981). The quantification of regional cerebral blood flow and oxygen utilization in man with oxygen-15 and positron emission tomography. Cerebrovas. Dis. 3, 113–115.

Mallet, B.L. and Veall, N. (1963). Investigation of cerebral blood flow in hypertension using [133]xenon inhalation and extracranial recording. Lancet i, 1081–1082.

Mallet, B.L. and Veall, N. (1965). Measurement of regional cerebral clearance rates in man using [133]xenon inhalation and extracranial recording. Clin. Sci. 29, 179–191.

Meyer, J.S. (1978). Recent validation of ^{133}Xe inhalation. Stroke 9, 272.

Meyer, J.S., Deshmukh, V.D., Ishihara, N., Naratomi, H., Hsu, M., and Pollack, P. (1979). Noninvasive measurement of rCBF in man: Effects of x-ray correction, age and hemispheric differences. Stroke 8, 139.

Meyer, J.S., Hayman, L.A., Sakai, F., Yamamoto, M., Nakajima, S., and Armstrong, D. (1980). High resolution three dimensional measurement of localized cerebral blood flow by CT scanning and stable xenon clearance: Effect of cerebral infarction and ischemia. Trans. Amer. Neurol. Assoc. 104, 85–89.

Meyer, J.S., Hayman, L.A., Amano, T., Nakajima, S., Shaw, T., Lauzon, P., Derman, S., Karacan, I., and Harati, Y. (1981a). Mapping local blood flow of human brain by CT scanning during stable xenon inhalation. Stroke 12, 426–436.

Meyer, J.S., Hayman, L.A., Nakajima, S., Amano, T., Lauzon, P., Derman, S.,

Karacan, I., and Harati, Y. (1981b). Localized human cerebral blood flow in 3D in normals, brain tumor, stroke, epilepsy, sleep and activation by CT scanning and stable Xe inhalation. In Cerebral Vascular Diseases 3: Proceedings of the 10th International Salzburg Conference, International Conference Series No 532, September 24–27, 1980. Excerpta Medica pp. 130–135.

Meyer, J.S., Ishihara, N., and Deshmukh, V.D. (1978). An improved method for noninvasive measurement of regional cerebral blood flow by ^{133}Xe inhalation. Stroke 9, 195–210.

Meyer, J.S. and Welch, K.M.A. (1972). Relationship of cerebral blood flow and metabolism in neurological symptoms. In Progress in Brain Research, Vol. 35, J.S. Meyer and J.P. Schadé, Eds. Elsevier Publishing, New York, pp. 285–347.

Nakajima, S., Meyer, J.S., Amano, T., and Shaw, T. (1981b). Testing cerebral vasomotor responsiveness during oxygen inhalation in aging and cerebral ischemia. Arch. Neurol.

Nakajima, S., Meyer, J.S., Yamamoto, M., Amano, T., Trompler, A., Mortel, K., Shaw, T., and Cutaia, M. (1981a). Effects of normal aging and cerebral infarction on cerebral vasoconstrictor responsiveness to 100% oxygen inhalation. In Cerebral Vascular Disease 3. 10th Salzburg Conference Series No. 532, Excerpta Medical International Congress pp. 532, 166–177.

Naritomi, H., Meyer, J.S., Sakai, F., Yamaguchi, F., and Shaw, T. (1979). Effects of advancing age on regional cerebral blood flow: Studies in normal subjects and subjects with risk factors for atherothrombotic stroke. Arch. Neurol. 36, 410–416.

Novack, P., Shenkin, H.A., Bortin, L., Goluboff, B., and Soffe, A.M. (1953). The effects of carbon dioxide inhalation upon the cerebral blood flow and cerebral oxygen consumption in vascular disease. J. Clin. Invest. 32, 696–702.

O'Brien, M.D. and Mallet, B.L. (1970). Cerebral cortex perfusion rates in dementia. J. Neurol. Neurosurg. Psychiatr. 33, 497–500.

Obrist, W.D., Thompson, H.K. Jr., Wang, H.S. et al. (1975). Regional cerebral blood flow estimated by ^{133}xenon inhalation. Stroke 6, 245–256.

Obrist, W.D., Thompson, H.K. Jr., Wang, H.S. et al. (1981). A simplified procedure for determining fast compartment rCBF by ^{133}xenon inhalation. In Brain and Blood Flow, R.W. Russell, Ed. Proc. Fourth Intr. Symp. Pitman Medical and Scientific Publishing Co. Ltd., London, pp. 11–15.

Olesen, J. (1974). Cerebral blood flow. Methods for measurement regulation effects of drugs and changes in disease. Acta Neurol. Scand. 50 (Suppl. 57), 1–134.

Portnoi, V. (1980). Letter to the Editor (Aging, Natural Death, and the Compression of Morbidity). New Eng. J. Med. 303 (23), 1369.

Reiff, T.R. (1980). Biomedical aspects of aging and their relation to geriatric care. In Health Care of the Elderly: Strategies for Prevention and Intervention, G. Lesnoff-Caravaglia, Ed. Human Sciences Press, New York, pp. 19–46.

Reivich, M., Kuhl, D., Wolf, A., Greenberg, J., Phelps, M., Ido, T., Casell, V., Fowler, J., Gallagher, B., Hoffman, E., Alavi, A., and Sokoloff, L. (1977). Measurement of local glucose metabolism in man with ^{18}F-2-fluoro-2-deoxy-D-glucose. In Cerebral Function, Metabolism, and Circulation, D. Ingvar Lassen Eds. Munksgaard, Copenhagen, pp.190–191.

Risberg, J., Ali, Z.A., Wilson, E.M. et al. (1975). Regional cerebral blood flow by ^{133}Xe inhalation. Stroke 6, 142–148.

Risberg, J., Uzzell, B.P., and Obrist, W.D. (1977). Spectrum subtraction technique for minimizing extracranial influence on cerebral blood flow measurements by ^{133}xenon inhalation. Stroke 8, 380–382.

Sakai, F., Meyer, J.S., Karacan, I. et al. (1979). Narcolepsy: Regional cerebral blood flow during sleep and wakefulness. Neurology 29, 61–67.

Schaie, K.W. (1968). Age changes and age differences. In Middle Age and Aging. B.L. Neugarten, Ed. University of Chicago Press, Chicago, Ill., pp. 558–562.

Scheibel, M.D. and Scheibel, A.B. (1975). Structural changes in the aging brain. In Clinical Morphological and Neurochemical Aspects of the Aging Nervous System, H. Brody, D. Harmann, and J.M. Ordy, Eds. Raven Press, New York.

Schieve, J.F. and Wilson, W.P. (1953). The influence of age, anesthesia and cerebral arteriosclerosis on cerebral vascular activity to carbon dioxide. Amer. J. Med. 13, 171.

Shaw, T.G., Cutaia, M.M., Meyer, J.S., Mortel, K.F., Yamamoto, M., Nakajima, S., Karacan, I., and Derman, S. (1981b). Age related changes in regional cerebral blood flow during sleep in normals, sleep apneics and narcoleptics. In Cerebral Vascular

Disease 3. Proceedings of the international Salzburg Conference, Series No. 352, pp. 130–135.

Shaw, T.G., Cutaia, M.M., Mortel, K.F., Meyer, J.S., Nakajima, S., and Amano, T. (1981a). Prospective measurements of cerebral blood flow in normal and abnormal aging. Neurol. 31, (Suppl.) 102.

Shaw, T. and Meyer, J.S. (1981). Aging and cerebrovascular disease. In Diagnosis and Management of stroke and TIAs. J.S. Meyer and T. Shaw Eds. Addison-Wesley Publishers, Menlo Park, Calif., 318.

Shaw, T.G., Meyer, J.S., Sakai, F., Yamaguchi, F., Yamamoto, M., and Mortel, K. (1979). Effects of normal aging versus risk factors for stroke on regional cerebral blood flow (rCBF). Acta Neurol. Scand. (Suppl. 72) 60, 462–463.

Shenkin, H.A., Novak, P., Goluboff, B., Soffe, A.M., and Brotin, L. (1953). The effects of aging. Arteriosclerosis, and hypertension upon the cerebral circulation. J. Clin. Invest. 32, 459.

Simard, D., Olesen, J., Paulson, O.B., Lassen, N.A., and Skinjoh, E. (1971). Regional cerebral blood flow and its regulation in dementia. Brain 94, 273–288.

Sokoloff, L. (1966). Cerebral circulatory and metabolic changes associated with aging. Res. Publ. Assoc. Res. Nerv. Ment. Dis. 41, 237–254.

Sokoloff, L. (1979). Effects of normal aging on cerebral circulation and energy metabolism. In Brain Function in Old Age: Evaluation of Changes and Disorders, F. Hoffmeister and C. Muller, Eds.

Sokoloff, L., Reivich, M., Kennedy, C. et al. (1977). The {^{14}C} deoxyglucose method for the measurement of local cerebral glucose utilization: Theory, procedure, and normal values in the conscious and anesthetized albino rat. J. Neurochem. 28, 897–916.

Thomas, D.J., Marshall, J., Ross Russell, R.W., Weatherly, M.G., DuBoulay, G.H., Pearson, T.C., Symon, L., and Zylkha, E. (1977). Effect of hematocrit on cerebral blood flow in man. Lancet ii, 941.

Tomlinson, B.E., Blessed, G., and Roth, M. (1970). Observations on the brains of demented old people. J. Neurol. Sci. 11, 205–242.

Tomlinson, B.E. and Henderson, G. (1976). Some quantitative cerebral findings in normal and demented old people. In Neurobiology of Aging. R.D. Terry and S. Gershon, Eds. Raven Press, New York, pp. 183–204.

Vellar, O.D. (1974). Changes in hemoglobin concentration and hematocrit during the menstrual cycle. Acta Obst. Gynec. Scand. 53, 243–246.

Wolff, H.G. and Lennox, W.G. (1930). Cerebral circulation. XII. The effect on pial vessels of variations in the oxygen and carbon dioxide content of the blood. Arch. Neurol. Psychol. 23, 1097–1120.

Yamaguchi, F., Meyer, J.S., Sakai, F., and Yamamoto, M. (1979). Normal human aging and cerebral vasoconstrictive responses to hypocapnia. J. Neurol. Sci. 44, 87–94.

Yamaguchi, F., Meyer, J.S., Sakai, F., Yamamoto, M., Sakai, F., and Shaw, T. (1980). Noninvasive regional cerebral blood flow measurements in dementia. Arch. Neurol. 37, 410–418.

Yamamoto, M., Meyer, J.S., Sakai, F., and Yamguchi, F. (1980). Aging and cerebral vasomotor responses to hypercarbia. Responses in normal aging and in persons with risk factors for stroke. Arch. Neurol. 37, 489–496.

Yamamoto, M., Meyer, J.S., Sakai, F., Yamaguchi, F., Jacoby, R., and Shaw, T. (1981). Mechanisms of cerebral vasomotor responsiveness to carbon dioxide in health and disease. In Cerebrovascular Disease, Vol. 2. Excerpta Medica, Amsterdam, pp. 280–286.

10. Aspects of Sleep in Aging

WILLIAM DEMENT

LAUGHTON MILES

All human activities take place against the background of a fluctuating predisposition to sleep with a maximum and a minimum tendency occurring once every 24 hours. A comprehensive description of this compelling and pervasive rhythm, its components, and its determinants is still being developed, particularly in terms of changes over the life cycle. Nonetheless, a great deal of clinically useful information has been accumulated from investigations of sleep in elderly individuals.

It is well known that there are two entirely different kinds of sleep, REM (dreaming or rapid-eye-movement sleep) and NREM (non-REM sleep), the latter being subdivided into Stage 1, Stage 2, Stage 3, and Stage 4. The usual way of defining states and stages during sleep (Rechtschaffen and Kales, 1968) utilizes three measurements: brain-wave patterns or electroencephalogram (EEG), eye movement activity or electro-oculogram (EOG), and muscle activity or electromyogram (EMG). In NREM sleep, the brain is relatively inactive and the EEG is dominated by high-amplitude slow waves and/or "sleep spindles." Although bodily movements cease, the muscles continue to show electrical activity and reflex excitability is well maintained. In REM sleep, the brain is very active (by some measures, more active than in wakefulness) and the

EEG patterns are similar to those in the waking state. Although active eye movements occur, there is no EMG activity, and spinal reflexes can no longer be elicited. When normal human adults fall asleep, they invariably pass into NREM sleep. There is then a regular 90- to 100-minute alternation between NREM sleep and REM sleep, known as the basic sleep cycle.

Among the earliest publications describing the states and stages of sleep in elderly subjects were those by Kales et al. (1966) and Feinberg et al. (1967). In 1970, Williams et al. described sleep patterns across the entire human life-span. These investigators found that the elderly had greatly diminished NREM Stages 3 and 4 (slow-wave sleep, SWS) and increased nocturnal wakefulness. Their findings have been confirmed by many other workers.

More recently, several new trends in somnology have appeared. One is the extension of the routine, all-night polygraphic investigation to other physiological systems, notably cardiopulmonary and motor. A second trend is to study the entire 24 hours instead of just the nocturnal sleep period, in particular, by evaluating daytime sleepiness and performance. A third trend has been to study the powerful and fundamental circadian rhythm of sleep and wakefulness. Finally, interest in sleep pathology has increased, and a logical approach to the diagnosis and treatment of clinical sleep disorders has been developed. Sleep disorder centers have been established throughout the United States, and in 1976 The Association of Sleep Disorders Centers (ASDC) was founded. This organization has formulated standards for accrediting specialized clinical facilities for the diagnosis and treatment of patients with sleep/wake disorders, and has set up standards for nomenclature, diagnosis, and clinical testing (ASDC, 1978). In addition, the Association published the first standard nosology of sleep disorders, in which more than 100 specific diagnostic entities are defined and classified (ASDC, 1979). All these trends have been pursued in studying the sleep/wake function of elderly people.

All-Night Sleep Patterns in the Elderly

Introduction

By following the instructions in the Rechtschaffen and Kales manual (1968), each 30 seconds of the polysomnographic recording is scored as Stage 1, 2, 3, or 4, Stage REM, or Stage–wake. Unfortunately, the definitions of the various stages of polygraphic sleep rely upon age-dependent parameters, yet the coding system is not age adjusted. Figure 10-1, taken from Miles and Dement (1980), shows a schematic representation of the change in objective sleep parameters with age. This figure summarizes the results of studies that utilized relatively small samples. Even in the comprehensive atlas of Williams et al. (1970), each age group was represented

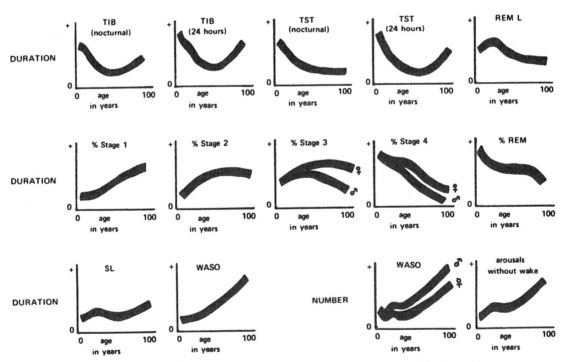

Figure 10-1. Representation of the trends of objectively recorded sleep parameters, all ages. In many situations, the data were conflicting or virtually non-existent, so that the patterns are speculative. TIB, time in bed; TST, total sleep time; SL, sleep latency; WASO, wake after sleep onset; REM L, REM latency. (Reprinted from Miles and Dement, 1980.)

by only 10 individuals. In addition, there was great individual variability in the results of most investigations, so statistically significant trends have rarely been demonstrated. The following discussion will emphasize those parameters that show a substantial change with aging. A more complete review may be found in the monograph of Miles and Dement (1980).

Time In Bed

Unless time in bed (TIB) is self-selected (ad-lib), the meaning of this parameter is uncertain. Nevertheless, elderly people do seem to spend more time (1) lying in bed at night without attempting to sleep, (2) in bed at night unsuccessfully trying to sleep, and (3) in bed resting or napping during the day. In one polygraphic study of sleep, performed in the homes of 12 healthy subjects aged 75 to 90 years, Prinz et al. (1975) found an average nocturnal TIB of 475.6 minutes.

Total Sleep Time

Since the elderly do tend to have increased nocturnal wakefulness (wake after sleep onset, WASO; see below), their total sleeping time (TST = TNREM + TREM) is especially vulnerable to imposed TIB, and polygraphic studies of their TST have yielded inconsistent data. Although usual WASO is excluded from TST, brief (for example, 2- to 15-second) arousals are not. The Williams et al. (1970) data show a slight, but nonsignificant reduction of TST in the elderly subjects; however, the variability of sleep time in middle-aged and elderly subjects increases significantly over that of younger subjects. This finding was particularly evident in male subjects. Feinberg et al. (1967) reported an average TST of 384.4 minutes in their normal aged subjects, a value not significantly different from that of younger people. The observational study of Webb and Swinburne (1971), on the other hand, reported much longer average nightly sleep times of 510 minutes in men and 438 minutes in women. Campbell and Webb (1980) investigated the length of the major sleep period by allowing 50- to 60-year-olds to

sleep as long as they could. Sleep termination in the morning was allowed following an awakening of more than 10 minutes. The mean sleep length was shorter and less variable than for younger adults (467 minutes versus 589 minutes). In general, it seems likely that TST per major sleep period is reduced, whereas the TST per 24 hours ultimately tends to increase.

Wake after Sleep Onset

Wake after sleep onset refers to the time spent awake from sleep onset until the final awakening. Many studies have found that the aged have increased amounts of WASO, and that the number of WASO is considerably higher for men than for women. The actual number of arousals may be even greater than usually reported, since it is possible for a wake episode as long as 28 seconds (spanning two standard scoring epochs) to be *not* scored as Stage-wake.

Such brief arousals may well be quite significant. Preliminary evidence suggests that the number of brief (2- to 15-second) wakes may more closely parallel changes in daytime function (Carskadon et al., 1982); and sleep disturbance reflected in nocturnal arousals without complete awakening has therefore been assessed by noting the frequency of shifts into Stage 1 sleep or the total number of changes from any sleep stage to any other.

Most authors consider this apparent change in the efficiency of sleep to be a change in the basic sleep process. However, in recent years, it has become apparent that many overt or occult sleep disorders share the dual distinction of being (1) more common in the elderly and (2) a cause of repeated arousal from sleep. The prevalence of these disorders in elderly volunteers is so astonishingly high that nearly every elderly person will show increased interruption of sleep even if the sleep process per se does not deteriorate.

States and Stages

NREM STAGE 1 SLEEP

An excessive total duration of Stage 1 sleep and an increase in the number of shifts into

Stage 1 sleep are both considered to be indications of sleep disturbance. The amount of TST spent in Stage 1 sleep appears to increase steadily throughout life. Men have a higher percentage of Stage 1 than women from puberty onward. Kales et al. (1967) found a fairly high percentage of TST spent in Stage 1 sleep in their elderly subjects on the first laboratory night (11.7%), with a substantial decine by night four (6.5%). Agnew et al. (1967) reported that late middle aged men spent an average of 10.91% of TST in Stage 1.

NREM STAGE 2 SLEEP

The mean percent of TST or sleep period time (SPT) spent in Stage 2 sleep approximates an inverted U-curve throughout life. The levels in old age are similar to those seen in early adult life and there is little sex difference. In the elderly, Stage 2 is less easy to score or interpret, since sleep spindles tend to be poorly formed and may appear less often. Sleep spindles or true episodes of Stage 2 tend to interrupt and fragment REM sleep.

RAPID-EYE-MOVEMENT SLEEP STATE

In general, absolute amounts of REM fall slightly, paralleling the change in nocturnal TST, but relative amounts of REM are well maintained until extreme old age, when they do decline somewhat. This reduction in the percentage of REM sleep may be due to the fact that the elderly tend to be awake in the latter part of the night when REM is usually most prevalent. However, this decline also appears to follow the trend of reduced intellectual function and relates to the presence of organic brain syndrome, changes in cerebral blood flow, and alpha frequency decline. When there is a decline in the amount of REM, there is also a decrease in the physiological changes associated with REM (muscular twitches, penile tumescence, rapid irregular respiration and heart rate, and increased cerebral blood flow).

SLOW WAVE SLEEP, NON-RAPID-EYE-MOVEMENT SLEEP STAGES 3 AND 4

Slow wave sleep (SWS) is defined by high-amplitude, delta wave EEG activity of 0.5 to 2 Hz. It is this EEG activity that defines sleep Stages 3 and 4. In the aged, there is an absolute and relative reduction in the time spent in Stage 4 sleep. Stage 3 sleep tends to be normal or even elevated in elderly females, and normal or reduced in elderly males. Sophisticated computer analyses indicate that these changes are mainly due to the fact that the amplitude of the delta waves is reduced from that in the young adult (Smith et al., 1977; Feinberg et al., 1978, 1980).

Sex Differences in All-Night Polygraphic Sleep Parameters

In general, elderly men appear to have more "abnormal" objective sleep parameters than elderly women, but these changes appears to be part of an increasing trend of sex differences already apparent in young adults. The most obvious differences are in SWS and WASO. A small, but significant number of elderly females continue to display sustained periods of Stage 4 sleep (Spiegel, 1981).

Daytime Sleepiness/Alertness and Related Functions in the Elderly

Introduction

It is not always clear what daytime symptoms besides sleepiness/alertness might specifically reflect the quality of sleep at night. Daytime symptoms and signs that have been ascribed to the aging processes and that might be a response to disturbed sleep include the loss of ability to perform highly skilled tasks in a rapid fashion, to resist fatigue, to maintain physical stamina, to unlearn or discard old techniques and habits, and to judge changing or emergency situations rapidly (Pfeiffer and Davis, 1971). The tendency for restricted activity, relative boredom, and dependence upon others probably favors giving in to daytime sleepiness.

Daytime Sleepiness/Alertness

Because healthy, noncomplaining elderly volunteers awaken frequently throughout the night, their total sleep time (per major sleep period) is reduced, and it is reasonable to expect that this sleep deprivation or fragmentation would cause increased drowsiness during the day. On the other hand, if the sleep changes occur because the elderly have less "need" for sleep, there would be no reason to propose a direct effect on daytime functioning. Resolution of this important question has been hampered by the fact that previous studies of nocturnal sleep in the elderly have not included concurrent measurements of daytime function, and no study of acute, total sleep deprivation has ever been carried out on elderly subjects.

Because the exact time of transition from wakefulness to sleep is relatively easy to specify in polygraphic recordings, it has been possible to design a standard test in which the momentary sleep tendency of an individual can be measured as the speed of falling asleep. The test has become known as the Multiple Sleep Latency Test (MSLT) (Carskadon and Dement, 1979; Richardson et al., 1978). The Stanford Sleep Research Center has begun to apply this approach to the study of daytime sleepiness in the elderly. A group of healthy elderly subjects have been recorded around-the-clock for two consecutive days (Carskadon et al., 1981). Nocturnal polysomnography was carried out before daytime testing, and MSLTs were administered at two-hour intervals from 0930 through 1930 (six tests daily). Of special interest was the fact that all subjects were in bed from 2200 to 0800 on both nights (10 hours per night). Thus, sleep was largely ad-lib, and a fairly wide range of nocturnal sleep times was seen.

As expected, nocturnal sleep tended to be seriously fragmented and interrupted. In many cases, this appeared to be due to either sleep apnea or nocturnal myoclonus (see section on sleep disorders in the elderly). About 60% of the subjects had more than 100 brief or prolonged arousals during a night's sleep.

Overall, these older subjects were more sleepy in the daytime than groups of younger subjects evaluated under identical circumstances, but there was a very wide range of individual scores. Several subjects showed daily average sleep latencies of 5 minutes or less on the MSLT. Such low sleep latencies are usually considered to be within the pathological range (Dement et al., 1978) and are invariably associated with impaired daytime performance. These sleepy subjects also had the most severe nocturnal respiratory disturbances. Overall, the number of brief arousals per hour of nocturnal sleep was the best predictor of the degree of daytime sleepiness. From these results it seemed that a substantial number of elderly presons must be extremely or pathologically sleepy in the daytime, even though they have no overt symptoms; they suggest that this sleepiness may usually be due to an occult sleep disorder.

Although it is not yet known whether elderly people can change their daytime alertness by increasing their nocturnal sleep time, the data obtained so far do not support the proposition that the fragmented sleep is due to decreased sleep "need."

Indirect Factors Influencing the Sleep/Wake Function of the Aged

Factors influencing the sleep/wake function of elderly people include excessive bed rest, suboptimal sleep environment, boredom, change in physical activity, physical and mental illness, feelings of rejection and uselessness, loss of loved ones, lack of family and friends, loneliness and social isolation, use of hypnotics and other CNS-active medication, use of other medication, socioeconomic changes, retirement, and the complex effects of menopause and sexuality.

Institutional care, such as in old-age or "rest" homes, has been an increasingly common way of caring for the non-self–sufficient aged. In order to function, these homes are often forced to establish quite rigid living regimens, which, in turn, lead to inappropriate and excessive use of sedative drugs, physical restraint, and confinement. Patients in these institutions are probably more liable to suffer depression, circadian rhythm abnormalities, and hypnotic-dependent insomnia, with a consequent further deterioration in sleep/wake function.

Biological Rhythms and Sleep/Wake Function in the Aged

The regular alternation of sleep and wakefulness is a fundamental endogenous biological rhythm that, in normal circumstances, is able to entrain other circadian rhythms. In addition, components of the sleep/wake cycle (such as the tendency for SWS and REM sleep, subjective sleepiness, and sleep latency) also vary with circadian periodicities (Mills and Hume, 1977; Webb, 1969; Webb and Agnew, 1971; Weitzman et al., 1970). Abnormalities of the sleep/wake cycle and changes in its relationship to other rhythms may well be responsible for many of the difficulties of old age.

Age-Related Changes in the Human Sleep/Wake Cycle

Circadian rhythm abnormalities in humans are very likely to present clinically as sleep/wake disorders (see ASDC, 1979). These conditions include acute and chronic shift work dyssomnia (Conroy et al., 1970; Halberg and Nelson, 1976; Walsh et al., 1978) and jet lag (McFarland, 1975), delayed sleep phase (Czeisler et al., 1981; Weitzman et al., 1981), advanced sleep phase (Kamei et al., 1979), non-24-hour circadian rhythms (Miles et al., 1977), reversed sleep/wake phase (Weitzman et al., 1970), and generally disorganized circadian rhythms.

With aging, there appears to be a breakdown of the biphasic pattern of sleep and wakefulness and a return to the polyphasic alternation of sleep and wakefulness encountered in an infant. The phase of the sleep/wake cycle may also change. Tune's study of 509 subjects of different ages showed that increasing age was associated with earlier times of falling asleep and awakening (Tune, 1968, 1969a,b).

There is some indication that elderly people may be less tolerant to phase-shifts of the sleep/wake cycle (Solberger, 1965). Preston (1973) reported sleep deficits in airline pilots operating on transmeridian routes, and found that the older the pilot, the greater the cumulative sleep loss. Winget et al. (1972) found that normal

(non-elderly) volunteers subjected to 56 days of absolute bed rest showed evidence of desynchronosis and free-running circadian rhythms of heart rate and body temperature. These abnormalities did not seem to be due to physical confinement or lack of exercise, but rather to be related to postural change. These findings on the effect of bed rest could have profound implication for sleep/wake function in the elderly and particularly for those confined in nursing homes.

Neuroendocrine rhythms probably are profoundly involved in aging. After examining the circadian rhythm of catecholamines, Prinz et al. (1979) postulated that the typical sleep changes found in the elderly may be related to increased sympathetic nervous system activity. Montalbetti et al. (1965) measured plasma cortisol and found a circadian rhythm of normal amplitude, but with an altered phase. The change in phase was thought to be a possible result of sleep disturbance in old age. Montalbetti and his associates also found that the cortisol rhythm was normal in the healthy elderly and elderly patients with cerebrovascular hemiplegia, but abnormal in the elderly blind (Colucci et al., 1975; D'Alessandro et al., 1974). Serio et al. (1970) found the phase of the circadian rhythm of cortisol to be delayed in older people, although unrelated to the presence or absence of sleep complaints. It seems probable that growth hormone secretion does not occur with a true circadian rhythm, but passively follows the appearance of Stage 3 and 4 sleep (SWS); and both SWS and growth hormone secretion are minimal in the elderly (Carlson et al., 1972; Finkelstein et al., 1972). Murri et al. (1977) confirmed the marked decrease in growth hormone in the elderly, but also found that sleep-associated prolactin secretion occurred and was similar to that of a normal young adult.

Psychiatric disorders, blindness, and organic disease of the CNS, conditions that are common in the elderly, have all been associated with circadian dyschronosis. Various forms of depression (including manic-depressive illness) have been associated with changes in the circadian rhythms of REM sleep, the overall sleep/

wake cycle, cortisol secretion, and other factors (Pflug and Tolle, 1971; Sachar et al., 1973a,b; Vogel et al., 1973).

Studies of Sleep/Wake Rhythms in Old Age Homes

Wessler et al. (1976) evaluated activity and sleep–wakefulness of institutionalized elderly patients. These investigators found a high-order circadian regularity and synchronization between individuals from day to day and concluded that the strict institutional regimen was probably beneficial. The observational study by Webb and Swinburne (1971) is one of the very few investigations to record the actual life-style and sleep/wake habits of all members of an aged community. The authors reported that the basic circadian patterning of sleep placement and amount was present despite the fact that the subjects spent almost one-half their time in bed and had broken nocturnal sleep and several daytime naps.

Sleep Disorders in the Elderly

As we have seen, subjective reports and polysomnographic studies have shown that the sleep of apparently healthy old people is, in several respects, quite different from that of younger people. The sleep of elderly females appears to undergo rather fewer age-related changes than that of elderly males, although females tend to report more changes and to be more dissatisfied about their sleep. Some subjective sleep complaints may be caused by an unwillingness to recognize and accept these apparently normal age-related changes, and other complaints may have their origin in a genuinely altered perception of the passage of time.

These subjective and objective changes are variously ascribed to normal "maturation" or to pathological deterioration. Nevertheless, recent work indicates that with or without symptoms, very many elderly people have significant and often unrecognized sleep/wake problems that are potentially lethal or, at the very least, seriously impair their quality of life. Some clue to the relevance of these changes may be found in the few reports of the sleep/ wake pathology of elderly people referred to sleep disorders clinics (see below), although it is not known to what extent this distribution of symptoms, signs, and pathology affects elderly people in the general population.

The evaluation and treatment of an elderly patient with a sleep disorder can be a problem for almost any physician. Physicians therefore do need to be aware of the nature and relevance of such sleep disorders, the implications of certain complaints, the various investigations that can be undertaken by the physician or a specialized diagnostic sleep disorders clinic, as well as the indications for undertaking screening tests on asymptomatic, but at-risk individuals.

The Symptoms

DISTURBED SLEEP

Although many older people complain about their sleep, relatively few appear to consult sleep specialists or even physicians. Complaints of nonspecific sleep disturbance and awakenings during the night, along with the use of sedative–hypnotic medications, appear to increase with age.

Several surveys with larger samples deserve special mention. In Great Britain, the McGhie and Russell (1962) survey of 2466 subjects aged 15 to "over 75" years, revealed that more older people claim to sleep fewer than 5 hours each night. Complaints of prolonged sleep latency were found to be approximately twice as prevalent in females in all age groups; moreover, these complaints were reported more often in females over 55 years than in younger women. Elderly subjects of both sexes reported "frequent night wakening" and "early morning awakening" more often than younger subjects, with as many as 15% of respondents aged 65 to 75 reporting arousal before 5:00 A.M.

The Karacan et al. (1976) study of 1645 adults (aged 16 and older) in Florida's Alachua County showed that 45% of the subjects reported trouble getting to sleep or staying asleep during the night. Positive responses were said to be "higher" in females and with increasing age. Pill-taking was also "higher" for females and "increased markedly" with age.

Hammond (1964) reported initial data from an ambitious prospective survey of 1,057,398 subjects over the age of 30, carried out by 68,116 volunteer workers of the American Cancer Society. The complaint of insomnia tended upward with age in both men and women, reaching a plateau at about 50. Overall, women complained more (31%) than men (16%). Kripke et al. (1979), including both Hammond and Garfinkel, re-examined these survey data with emphasis on sleep variables. For this report, the earlier data were re-analyzed along with six years of prospective follow-up data. The most salient feature was the highly significant relationship between stated nocturnal sleep time and mortality. Even men and women with no prior history of heart disease, high blood pressure, diabetes or stroke were more likely to die within six years if they reported that they usually slept more or less than 7 to 7.9 hours. These increased deaths were not associated with a reported complaint of insomnia or with sleeping pill use. Nevertheless, males and females who "often" took sleeping pills had a mortality rate 1.5 times higher than matched subjects who never used sleeping pills, and this appeared true for the elderly. Short sleep, insomnia, and sleeping pill use increased with age.

Although the term insomnia is widely used, there has never been agreement on its precise definition. Generally, it means disturbed sleep or the inability to sleep, but daytime consequences are also usually implied. In young insomniacs, sleep parameters often show little disturbance (Carskadon et al., 1976). In marked contrast is the extreme degree of objective disturbance that is often found in non-complaining elderly subjects. A recent study of non-complaining elderly individuals at Stanford disclosed that transient arousals of 10 seconds or less were very common and related well to daytime sleepiness (Carskadon et al., 1982). Such events are ignored in the standard scoring procedure of Rechtschaffen and Kales (1968), used by nearly all sleep centers in their clinical polysomnographic evaluations.

DAYTIME SLEEPINESS

Although many authors feel that daytime sleepiness and fatigue are common problems in the elderly (Laird, 1931; Meyer, 1971; Oswald, 1975), systematic data are extremely sparse. Nevertheless, the image of the nodding, napping, elderly person dozing all day long on a park bench has a pervasiveness that urges further investigation.

Daytime sleepiness has been discussed earlier in the text, and the line between normal extreme sleepiness and pathological sleepiness is not always clear. Generally, daytime sleepiness associated with a specific sleep disorder is more severe, and above all, persistent. Patients with pathological sleepiness often complain of fatigue and tiredness, weakness, blackouts, learning and memory problems, inappropriate sleep and sleep attacks, hallucinations, "foggy mind," lack of energy, and "no pep"; and such sleepiness is typically accentuated by inactivity, environmental warmth, and the use of alcohol (Broughton and Ghanem, 1976; Dement, 1976; Dement et al., 1978; Guilleminault et al., 1975). The diagnosis of pathological sleepiness in the elderly has been facilitated by the development of the Multiple Sleep Latency Test, which has become a part of the clinical routine in most sleep disorders clinics nationwide (Richardson et al., 1978; van den Hoed et al., 1981). This objective clinical test can be applied fairly simply to the elderly population, since it does not require skill, complex motor performance, sustained attention, or motivation on the part of the subject or patient. About one-half of the elderly patients seen at sleep disorders clinics are referred for the complaint of daytime sleepiness.

UNUSUAL NOCTURNAL BEHAVIOR

A common phenomenon in the elderly is nocturnal wandering or disorientation, sometimes known as the "sundown syndrome" (Prinz and Raskind, 1978). Other manifestations of abnormal nocturnal behavior include screaming, talking, moaning, scratching, and bruxism.

Sleep-related phenomena long considered entirely normal by the general public should be regarded as important symptoms of sleep pathology. Perhaps the most important of such phenomena is snoring. The presence of notable snoring almost always indicates some impairment of upper airway function during sleep (see below). Dozing off after a heavy meal can be relatively innocuous or it can be a clue to a serious nocturnal sleep disturbance.

Specific Sleep Disorder Diagnoses in the Elderly

In the past two years, elderly subjects evaluated at Sleep Disorders Clinics have been categorized according to the comprehensive nosology of sleep/wake disorders recently developed by the Association of Sleep Disorders Centers (1979). In reviewing preliminary data describing the prevalence of various disorders, we noted that (1) the nosology was developed primarily to account for the prevalence of sleep disorders in young and middle-aged adults and (2) these clinics may not see a representative population of elderly patients. On the other hand, there is no convincing *a priori* reason to suppose that these patients are not at least representative of elderly patients with chronic sleep problems.

Reynolds et al. (1979) found that insomnia associated with affective disorders (37%) and sleep apnea (18.5%) were the most common primary diagnoses in a series of 27 patients over 55 years of age. Coleman et al. (1981), drawing on a somewhat more general patient population, compared 83 patients over 60 years of age with 423 younger clinic patients. The category designated disorders of initiating and maintaining sleep (DIMS), or the insomnias, accounted for 49% of the elderly patients, whereas 47% were classified in the category designated disorders of excessive sleepiness (DOES). Four percent had some type of parasomnia. The most frequent primary diagnoses in the elderly, sleep apnea (39%) and sleep-related (nocturnal) myoclonus (18%),

were both substantially more common than in younger patients.

It must be noted, however, that these figures are potentially misleading because elderly people very frequently have multiple causes for their sleep/wake complaints and many etiological factors are intensely interactive. In the series of Coleman et al. (1981), 41% of the elderly patients were considered to have a clinically relevant secondary diagnosis, most often a psychiatric disorder, sleep-related (nocturnal) myoclonus, or restless legs. Twenty-eight percent had either a primary or secondary diagnosis of nocturnal myoclonus or restless legs, whereas 44% had sleep apnea. These diagnoses therefore occurred in as many as 68% of the elderly subjects. Also common among multiple diagnoses are insomnias caused by various medical, toxic, and environmental factors. In these conditions, the direct cause of the sleep/wake disorder is usually some nonspecific symptom such as chronic pain, pruritus, paraesthesiae, pyrexia, visceral tension, strangury, dyspnea, or abnormal movements. As a group, the elderly patients had more objective signs of sleep disturbance, with more wake after sleep onset, more frequent and longer arousals, and less Stage 4 sleep.

With our present knowledge, we can only guess that the elderly in the community and in old-age homes are most likely to suffer from

Sleep apnea (especially central apnea)
Sleep-related myoclonus (also known as periodic leg movement)
Restless legs syndrome
Persistent psychophysiological DIMS or DOES
Psychological DIMS—especially depression
Drug-dependant insomnia
Insomnia associated with degenerative diseases of the CNS
Medical conditions, especially those associated with chronic pain or discomfort
Circadian dyschronosis, especially advanced sleep phase, often occult or associated with an affective disorder

Several of these conditions can also be associated with severe daytime somnolence and napping.

For a full description of these disorders, the reader should refer to the full *Diagnostic Classification of Sleep and Arousal Disorders* (ASDC, 1979). The following elaborates on some of the more interesting or common disorders.

SLEEP APNEA SYNDROMES IN THE ELDERLY

Respiration in asymptomatic "normal" volunteers. In the elderly, the absence of a sleep/wake complaint does not mean the absence of sleep pathology. Nowhere is this more apparent than in the area of respiratory function. In several recent reviews (Orem, 1980; Phillipson, 1978; Sullivan and Issa, 1980), there is convincing evidence that respiratory regulation proceeds differently during sleep and wakefulness. This difference makes it possible to account for the co-existence in sleep disorders patients of *normal* breathing during wakefulness and *pathological* breathing during sleep.

The first observations on older individuals were made by Webb (1974) and Webb and Hiestand (1975), who measured oxygen consumption continuously in 20 normal volunteers aged 19 to 63. They found that respiration during sleep was very irregular in nine of eleven subjects 45 years old or older. Subsequently, Block et al. (1979) described sleep apneas, hypopneas,

and episodes of oxygen desaturation in normal subjects of whom seven males and one female were in their sixth or seventh decade. Carskadon and Dement (1981) conducted systematic observations on breathing during sleep in the elderly. In these studies, elderly volunteers were selected on the basis of having no complaint about their sleep and no serious health problem. They were, therefore, felt to be the group most likely to have good (undisturbed) sleep and normal respiration during sleep. Table 10-1 shows the results from 40 elderly subjects compared to 24 middle-aged subjects.

Since each apneic pause is terminated by an arousal, we may conclude that 37.5% of the elderly subjects experience five or more interruptions of their sleep per hour. These findings suggest that age-related respiratory impairment may account for a great deal of the well-known sleep fragmentation. Thirty percent had ten or more respiration disturbances per hour. Finally, there were no significant differences between males and females.

Ancoli-Israel et al. (1981a) have studied 24 healthy elderly volunteers who, on questioning, did have considerable complaints about their sleep. They also found that nine (or 37.5%) had sleep apnea syndrome, most commonly of the upper airway type. McGinty and Arand (1980) have reported work on elderly VA patients who were asymptomatic with regard to sleep. They found that one-half of a small

Table 10-1. Apneas during sleep in non-complaining healthy volunteers.

	Middle-aged	Elderly
Number	24 (12 M 12 F)	40 (18 M 22 F)
Mean age	49.9	73.8
Age range	48–60	62–86
Mean respiration disturbances/night	4.7	50.0
Range of respiration disturbances/night	0–12	0–216
Number with RDI > 5	0	15

Respiration Disturbance, apnea or hypopnea
Hypopnea, 50% reduction of breathing >10 seconds, terminating in
    arousal
Apnea, respiratory pause > 10 seconds
RDI, respiration disturbance index (number of respiration disturbances/
    hour of sleep)

sample had severe oxygen desaturation during sleep.

We note that none of the above data are from patients in sleep disorders centers. This fact raises the issues of "normal" sleep processes in the elderly and whether sleep matures or deteriorates with advancing years. It should be noted that most sleep disorders specialists regard 5 to 8 apneas per hour of sleep as the upper limit of normal. Application of this criterion leads one to conclude that at least one-third of all elderly individuals who are judged to be in good health when awake would receive a clinical diagnosis of sleep apnea syndrome.

Snoring in the elderly. The presence of snoring almost always indicates some degree of impairment of upper airway function and, in many cases, a very serious impairment. Lugaresi and his colleagues (1975) carried out pioneering observations of blood pressure during sleep in normal adult males who were heavy snorers. *All* subjects showed hemodynamic abnormalities during sleep. In a subsequent study, Lugaresi et al. (1978, 1980) concluded that lifelong nonapneic snoring may be a very important risk factor in the development of cardiovascular disease. A similar relationship to hypertension was recently reported by Pollak et al. (1978). Lugaresi and his colleagues also found that the prevalence of snoring increases with age. It seems that almost 60% of males and 45% of females in their sixties are habitual snorers.

Sleep apnea syndromes in patients referred to sleep centers. Of the three types of sleep apneas—upper airway, central, and mixed—the former is most often found in patients complaining of excessive daytime sleepiness. Other clinical symptoms include inordinately loud snoring, abnormal behavior, and choking attacks during sleep (which are mainly the result of the struggle to breathe), morning headache, and personality changes. Cardiac arrhythmias and pulmonary hypertension are common during the apneic episodes, and many patients have systemic hypertension. The anoxia, cardiac arrhythmias, and duration of ap-

neas tend to be worst during REM sleep. Central apnea is more often associated with multiple arousals from sleep and overt insomnia (Guilleminault et al., 1973, 1976).

Nocturnal oxygen desaturation in chronic obstructive lung disease. These patients also tend to show worsening of hypoxemia as the mechanism of control of respiration changes during REM sleep (Coccagna and Lugaresi, 1978; Flick and Block, 1977; Guilleminault et al., 1980; Hensley and Read, 1976; Wynne et al., 1979). These episodes of hypoxemia are accompanied by pulmonary and arterial hypertension and cardiac arrhythmias. Most patients have severe hypopnea, but some have predominantly upper airway sleep apnea. Evaluations of these patients have important implications for the use of nocturnal oxygen therapy.

SLEEP-RELATED NOCTURNAL MYOCLONUS (PERIODIC LEG MOVEMENT)

First described by Symonds in 1953, sleep-related myoclonus consists of repetitive movements of the lower extremities during sleep, including rapid partial dorsi-flexion of the foot, extension of the big toe, and partial flexion at the knee and hip (Guilleminault et al., 1975; Lugaresi et al., 1970). Periodicity and stereotypy are the most distinguishing feature of the movements. These movements often cause arousal and insomnia, and may also be a cause of excessive daytime somnolence (Coleman et al., 1980). A related and often severe disorder, restless legs syndrome (Ekbom, 1960), is also a frequent cause of insomnia.

ADDITIONAL DIAGNOSES OF INSOMNIA IN THE ELDERLY: PSYCHOPHYSIOLOGICAL INSOMNIA

The transient variety of psychophysiological insomnia is very common and generally associated with acute emotional conflicts or reactions. Persistent psychophysiological insomnia may result when the place of sleep or the attempt to sleep becomes associated with frustration and arousal. Conditioning factors arising from circumstances existing many years before will often have "trained" elderly people to sleep badly, and their long-established body image makes relaxation therapy or behavioral modification less effective. In the young, this type of insomnia is mostly associated with prolonged sleep latency, but in the elderly, awakenings during the night are common.

Psychiatric insomnia. Personality disorders may lead to poor sleep or to hypochondriacal complaints of poor sleep. Unipolar affective disorder commonly includes repeated awakenings and early-morning wakefulness, reduction of Stage 4 sleep, and short REM latency; and this reduction in REM latency may be more significant among the elderly (Kupfer, 1976).

Depression often occurs as part of the complex changes associated with retirement. One stress that may result in depression in late-middle–aged women has been referred to as the "empty nest syndrome" (Neugarten, 1970; Rickles, 1968), a condition that often coincides with the onset of menopause (Draper and Collum, 1977). Thus, biological and psychological factors can combine to produce depression in older women, and be typically associated with disturbed sleep. Cohen (1975) describes a "nocturnal neurosis" that he sees in about 50% of the elderly in medical consultations in midtown Manhattan.

Insomnia associated with use of drugs or alcohol. Misuse of drugs or alcohol or withdrawal from a wide variety of sedative/hypnotics and other CNS depressants can produce insomnia, as can the sustained use of stimulants (Clift, 1975; Mendelson, 1978). The multiple drugs used to treat nonsleep disorders in the aged can secondarily induce insomnia. As might be expected, this diagnosis often coexists with other sleep/wake diagnoses.

Insomnia due to other conditions. A wide variety of medical, toxic, and environmental conditions are associated with insomnia, and most of these are more likely to be encountered by the aged. Such patients are rarely referred to sleep disorders centers. Conditions of special relevance include

chronic pain (especially that due to arthritis), nocturia, nocturnal dyspnea, and chronic brain syndrome (Gerard et al., 1978).

OTHER DISORDERS OF EXCESSIVE SOMNOLENCE IN THE ELDERLY

Common causes of daytime somnolence in the elderly, sleep apnea syndromes, and sleep-related myoclonus have been discussed above.

Narcolepsy. Usually, narcolepsy begins in the second decade of life, although rarely onset may be as late as the sixth or the seventh decade; as far as is known, the syndrome does not remit. Although, as far as anyone knows, narcolepsy does not affect mortality, there may be a tendency for a patient who has had the illness many years to become "burned out": completely refractory to stimulants and almost lacking in initiative.

Hypersomnolence associated with use of central nervous system stimulants and depressants. Tolerance to or withdrawal from CNS stimulants and sustained use of CNS depressants can be associated with excessive daytime somnolence. Daytime carryover of long-acting hypnotics taken at bedtime is often overlooked in the elderly (Mendelson, 1978). The use of drugs for common nonsleep disorders may secondarily induce excessive somnolence. Such drugs include antihistamines, "major" and "minor" tranquilizers, methyl-DOPA, and tricyclic antidepressants, especially amitryptyline. Drug-induced daytime sedation from longacting hypnotics and anxiolytics may well be the most common cause of the problem.

Other conditions. Other medical, toxic, or environmental conditions are associated with disorders of excessive somnolence. Post-viral sleepiness and fatigue is well known, and in the elderly, chronic brain syndrome can also be associated with hypersomnolence.

DYSSOMNIAS ASSOCIATED WITH DISRUPTIONS OF THE 24-HOUR SLEEP/WAKE CYCLE

It has long been known that schedule changes, shift work, and transmeridian travel can lead to sleep disturbance, and it now seems likely that more obscure circadian rhythm abnormalities may be very significant among the elderly. The history of early morning arousal and evening drowsiness common among elderly individuals may well indicate the presence of an "advanced sleep phase syndrome." Disorders classified under this category are discussed in the preceding section on biological rhythms and sleep/wake functions.

DYSSOMNIAS ASSOCIATED WITH SLEEP, SLEEP STAGES, OR PARTIAL AROUSALS

There are a group of clinical conditions that are not disorders of the sleep/wake processes per se. They are intrusive phenomena either appearing exclusively in sleep or exacerbated by sleep. The nocturnal confusion and wandering associated with chronic brain syndrome is probably the most common problem in the elderly (Prinz and Raskind, 1978). Sleep-related cardiovascular symptoms, enuresis, gastroesophageal reflux, and sleep-related epileptic seizures are frequently seen in elderly persons. Asymptomatic polygraphic abnormalities are classified in this overall category and include such events as prolonged cardiac asystoles occurring only during REM sleep (Guilleminault et al., 1978). It is not known whether this condition occurs in the elderly.

Sedative/Hypnotics for Treating Insomnia in the Aged

An inappropriately large percentage of all sedative/hypnotics are administered to elderly people, yet the Institute of Medicine report (1979) and a subsequent thorough review of the scientific literature on sleep and aging (Miles and Dement, 1980), found only one report of a sleep-laboratory study of hypnotic efficacy in the elderly. However, there have been several studies in which the efficacy was assessed from subjective reports. Subject selection has usually been vague and based on patient complaints; and the patients may or may not have been using sleeping pills regularly. The studies were always short term (less than 4 weeks and almost always less than 2 weeks), but the drugs were usually compared with a placebo or each other in a double-blind procedure. General standards for the evaluation of hypnotic efficacy and safety have been discussed by Mendelson et al. (1981b).

Efficacy

Short-term subjective efficacy (in terms of changes in nocturnal sleep) of certain hypnotics has been reasonably demonstrated in the elderly and contrasted with other drugs that were not so effective. On the other hand, there is little subjective data on long-term efficacy, improvements in daytime alertness and well-being, or development of tolerance. There has been virtually no *objective* evidence of short-term or long-term efficacy, and it seems clear that this should be sought in terms of daytime functioning as well as nocturnal sleep.

Side Effects

Side effects of these medications have not been better studied. Subjective reports of side effects have frequently not been statistically significant; but drowsiness, ataxia, and incoordination, as well as such disinhibition reactions as disorientation, hallucinations, and restlessness appear to be more common in the elderly. Studies rarely addressed the issue of "day-after" effects on alertness and other functioning, and those that did obtained subjective information only. No study addressed the issue of the function of old people if aroused from drug-induced sleep by an emergency. No study dealt with acute drug withdrawal.

Alcohol and sleep deprivation appear to worsen sleep apnea (Guilleminault and Rosekind, 1981; Phillipson et al., 1980). It seems very likely that sleeping pills would also exacerbate the condition. Preliminary data (Miles and Dement, 1980; Mendelson et al., 1981a; Coburn et al., 1982) have confirmed this possibility, and the problem is now being actively investigated. The fact that sleeping pills are frequently prescribed in the elderly and that even apparently normal elderly people seem to have a very high incidence of occult central apnea (Carskadon and Dement, 1981) makes an inadvertent interaction highly probable. Moreover, elderly people tend to have a higher prevalence of those chronic cardiac and pulmonary problems known to be associated with respiratory impairment during sleep. Drug interactions appear likely to be important, since old people are more apt to be simultaneously taking different drugs for coexisting disorders, as well as more than one CNS depressant.

Indications

Previously published indications for use of sleeping pills in the elderly are unreliable because of (1) the difficulty in taking into account the "natural" change in sleep patterns with aging, (2) uncertainties as to the meaning of sleep/wake complaints in the elderly, (3) the possibility of occult sleep disorders, and (4) the dearth of information regarding the nature and severity of drug side effects. The Institute of Medicine report concluded that no benefit from the use of sleeping pills had ever been satisfactorily documented. These drugs probably are being given inappropriately in institutions such as nursing homes. Family physicians may well dispense sleeping pills to treat such symptoms as boredom, inactivity, depression, and agitated senility; and they may often be given inappropriately to patients who have a disorder known to be associated with sleep apnea or unknowingly to patients with a occult susceptibility to hypnotic-related sleep apnea.

Suitable indications might be (1) transient situational insomnia (including phase-shift and environmental factors), (2) persistant psychophysiological insomnia when there is little hope of retraining or effective psychotherapy, and (3) as adjunct therapy in chronic nocturnal discomfort. In all situations, the patient should be screened for drug contraindications and followed for evidence of daytime as well as nocturnal efficacy and side effects. Causes for insomnia for which there are other specific therapies should be sought, and, in general, those therapies should be preferred.

The dosage should be as small as possible and the administration intermittant insofar as permitted by rebound insomnia. The possible advantages of short-acting drugs should be explored. With these indications and precautions, it seems probable that in many situations, the benefits may outweigh the risks.

Despite the risks associated with hypnotic administration in the elderly, it is not feasible to carry out sleep-laboratory polysomnography on all patients for whom sleeping pills are to be prescribed. Polysomnography should be reserved for those people who (1) are especially at risk for sleep apnea or (2) present evidence of nocturnal myoclonus or some other condition for which an alternative treatment would clearly be indicated. On the other hand, it is now becoming possible to use low-cost portable monitors to screen patients for (1) total sleep time, sleep latency, and wake after sleep onset; (2) sleep "disturbance"; (3) sleep apnea; (4) ECG changes; and (5) abnormal movements (for example, nocturnal myoclonus) (Ancoli-Israel et al., 1981b, Miles et al. 1978; Kayed et al., 1979). We believe that such monitors can be used to screen elderly subjects (1) before administration of sleeping pills (to discover contraindications and confirm the diagnosis) and (2) after administration of hypnotics (to assess short- and long-term efficacy and side effects).

Conclusion

The nervous system undergoes many changes in the period between adulthood and senescence. It is not understood, however, whether any documented CNS changes underlie changes in sleep associated with aging. What accounts for the loss of respiratory drive during sleep? Why does periodic leg movement during sleep increase with age? These and many other questions remain for future investigators. Basic and clinical studies of sleep and aging have been relatively sparse, and it is only recently that a comprehensive examination of sleep-oriented function in the elderly has begun.

In practical terms, the following points should be highlighted:

(1) Sleep increasingly loses its continuity in older individuals; this contributes to daytime sleepiness and fatigue. However, attempts to provide symptomatic relief for sleep disturbance can make matters worse. The elderly are more sensitive to the daytime effects of long-acting hypnotics.

(2) Modern civilization carries with it a host of influences that adversely affect healthy sleep/wake schedules and circadian sleep tendencies. At present, we cannot detect changes in human biological clocks with aging, but we know that the sleep phase may become inappropriately advanced or delayed and that bed rest may contribute to this process. Principles of sleep hygiene, such as regular sleep schedule, avoidance of caffeine, and even chronotherapy, can provide some relief.

(3) There is a marked increase in sleep disorders with aging. It appears that the sleep of more than one-half the population over 65 is disturbed by sleep apnea, sleep-related myoclonus, or both. It is also likely that a very large number suffer from gastroesophageal reflux.

Major health concerns of elderly individuals almost always include sleep. In addition to subjective complaints, a complex panoply of changes in sleep parameters occur in both complaining and non-complaining older persons. Physicians, in particular, must be sensitive to these changes.

References

Agnew, H., Webb, W., and Williams, R. (1967). Sleep patterns in late middle aged males; an EEG study. Electroenceph. Clin. Neurophysiol. 23, 168–171.

Ancoli-Israel, S., Kripke, D., Mason, W., and Messin, S. (1981a). Comparisons of home sleep recordings and polysomnograms in older adults with sleep disorders. Sleep 4, 283–292.

Ancoli-Israel, S., Kripke, D., Mason, W., and Messin, S. (1981b). Sleep apnea and nocturnal myoclonus in a senior population. Sleep 4, 349–358.

Association of Sleep Disorders Centers. (1978). Certification Standards and Guidelines for Sleep Disorders Centers. Prepared by the Certification Committee.

Association of Sleep Disorders Centers. (1979). Diagnostic Classification of Sleep and Arousal Disorders. 1st Ed. Prepared by Sleep Disorders Classification Committee, H. Roffwarg, Chairman. Sleep 2, 1–137.

Block, J., Boysen, P., Wynne, J., and Hunt, L. (1979). Sleep apnea, hypopnea and oxygen desaturation in normal subjects. New Eng. J. Med. 300, 513–517.

Broughton, R. and Ghanem, Q. (1976). The impact of compound narcolepsy on the life of the patient. In C. Guilleminault, W. Dement, and Passouant, P., Eds. Narcolepsy. Spectrum Publications, New York, pp. 201–220.

Campbell, S. and Webb, W. (1980). Sleep length and sleep termination in an aging population. Sleep Res. 9,

Carlson, H., Gillin, J., Gordon, P., and Snyder, F. (1972). Absence of sleep-related growth hormone peaks in acromegalics and aged normal subjects. J. Clin. Endocrinol. Metab. 34, 1102–1105.

Carskadon, M., Brown, E., and Dement, W. (1982). Sleep fragmentation in the elderly: Relationship to daytime sleep tendency. Neurobiol. Aging 3, 321–327.

Carskadon, M. and Dement, W. (1979). Effects of total sleep loss on sleep tendency. Percept. Mot. Skills 48, 495–506.

Carskadon, M. and Dement, W. (1981). Respiration during sleep in the aged human. J. Gerontol. 36, 420–423.

Carskadon, M., Dement, W., Mitler, M., Guilleminault, C., Zarcone, V. and Spiegel, R. (1976). Self-report vs sleep laboratory findings in 122 drug-free subjects with complaints of chronic insomnia. Amer. J. Psychiatr. 133, 1382–1388.

Carskadon, M., van den Hoed, J., and Dement, W. (1981). Sleep and daytime sleepiness in the elderly. J. Geriatr. Psychiat. 13, 135–151.

Clift, A., Ed. (1975). Sleep disturbance and hypnotic drug dependence. Amsterdam, Excerpta Medica.

Coburn, S., Zeiger, D., Guilleminault, C., and Dement, W. (1982). Effects of a hypnotic (flurazepam 30 mg) on respiration and blood oxygen saturation during nocturnal sleep in ten, elderly, "normal" volunteers: A pilot study. Sleep Res. 11, 81.

Coccagna, G. and Lugaresi, E. (1978). Arterial blood gases and pulmonary and systemic arterial pressure during sleep in chronic obstructive pulmonary disease. Sleep 1, 117–124.

Cohen, C. (1975). Nocturnal neurosis of the elderly: Failure of agencies to cope with the problem. J. Amer. Geriatr. Soc. 24, 86–88.

Coleman, R., Miles, L., Guilleminault, C., Zarcone, V., van den Hoed, J., and Dement, W. (1981). Sleep-wake disorders in the elderly: A polysomnographic analysis. J. Amer. Geriatr. Soc. 29, 289–296.

Coleman, R., Pollak, C., and Weitzman, E. (1980). Periodic movements in sleep (nocturnal myoclonus): A relation to sleep-wake disorders. Ann. Neurol. 8(4), 416–421.

Colucci, C., D'Alessandro, B., Bellastella, A., and Montalbetti, N. (1975). Circadian rhythm of plasma cortisol in the aged (cosinor method). Gerontol. Clin. (Basel) 17, 89–95.

Conroy, R., Elliot, A., and Mills, J. (1970). Circadian excretory rhythms in night workers. Br. J. Ind. Med. 27, 356–363.

Czeisler, C., Richardson, G., Coleman, R., Zimmerman, J., Moore-Ede, M., Dement, W., and Weitzman, E. (1981). Chronotherapy: Resetting the circadian clocks of patients with delayed sleep phase syndrome. Sleep 4, 1–21.

D'Alessandro, B., Bellastella, A., Esposito, U., Colucci, C., and Montalbetti, N. (1974). Circadian rhythm of cortisol secretion in elderly and blind subjects. Br. Med. J. 2, 274.

Dement, W. (1976). Daytime sleepiness and sleep "attacks." In C. Guilleminault, W. Dement, and P. Passouant, Eds. Narcolepsy. Spectrum Publications, New York, pp. 17–42.

Dement, W., Carskadon, M., and Richardson, G. (1978). Excessive daytime sleepiness in the sleep apnea syndrome. In C. Guilleminault and W. Dement, Eds. Sleep Apnea Syndromes. Alan R. Liss, Inc., New York, pp. 23–46.

Draper, E., and Collum, J. (1977). Psychology of aging. Clin. Obstet. Gynecol. 20, 123–136.

Ekbom, K. (1960). Restless legs syndrome. Neurology 10, 868–873.

Feinberg, I., Fein, G., and Floyd, T. (1980). Period and amplitude analysis of NREM EEG in sleep: Repeatability of results in young adults. Electroenceph. Clin. Neurophysiol. 48, 212–221.

Feinberg, I., Koreska, R., and Heller, N. (1967). EEG sleep patterns as a function of normal and pathological aging in man. J. Psychiatr. Res. 5, 107–144.

Feinberg, I., March, J., Fein, G., Floyd, T., Walker, J., and Price, L. (1978). Period and amplitude analysis of 0.5 to 3 cycles per second activity in NREM sleep of young adults. Electroenceph. Clin. Neurophysiol. 44, 202–213.

Finkelstein, J., Roffwarg, H., Boyar, R., Kream, J., and Hellman, L. (1972). Age-related change in twenty-four hour spontaneous secretion of growth hormone. J. Clin. Endocrinol. Metab. 35, 665–670.

Flick, M. and Block, A. (1977). Continuous *in vivo* monitoring of arterial oxygenation in chronic obstructive lung disease. Ann. Int. Med. 86, 725–730.

Gerard, P., Collins, K., Dore, C., and Exton-Smith, A. (1978). Subjective characteristics of sleep in the elderly. Age Aging (Suppl.) 7, 55–63.

Guilleminault, C., Billiard, M., Montplaisir, J., and Dement, W. (1975). Altered states of consciousness in disorders of daytime sleepiness. J. Neurol. Sci. 26, 377–393.

Guilleminault, C., Cummiskey, J., and Motta, J. (1980). Chronic obstructive airflow disease and sleep studies. Amer. Rev. Resp. Dis. 122, 397–406.

Guilleminault, C., Eldridge, F., and Dement, W. (1973). Insomnia with sleep apnea: A new syndrome. Science 181, 856–858.

Guilleminault, C., Eldridge, F., Phillips, J., and Dement, W. (1976). Two occult causes of insomnia and their therapeutic problems. Arch. Gen. Psychiatr. 33, 1241–1245.

Guilleminault, C., Motta, J., Flagg, W., and Dement, W. (1978). Asystole and rapid eye movement sleep: A life-threatening disease related to phasic events? Sleep Res. 7, 231.

Guilleminault, C., Raynal, D., Weitzman, E., and Dement, W. (1975). Sleep-related myoclonus in patients complaining of insomnia. Trans. Amer. Neurol. Assoc. 100, 19–22.

Guilleminault, C. and Rosekind, M. (1981). The arousal threshold: Control of ventilation and sleep apnea. Clin. Resp. Physiol. 17, 341–349.

Halberg, F. and Nelson, W. (1976). Some aspects of chronobiology relating to the optimization of shift work. In Shift Work and Health, HEW Publication No (NIOSH), 76–203. U.S. Government Printing Office, Washington, D.C., pp. 13–47.

Hammond, E. (1964). Some preliminary findings on physical complaints from a prospective study of 1,064,004 men and women. Amer. J. Pub. Hlth. 54, 11–23.

Hensley, M. and Read, D. (1976). Intermittent obstruction of the upper airway during sleep causing profound hypoxemia: A neglected mechanism exacerbating chronic respiratory failure. Aust. N.Z. J. Med. 6, 481–486.

Institute of Medicine. (1979). Report of a Study: Sleeping Pills, Insomnia, and Medical Practice. National Academy of Science, Washington, D.C. 198 p.

Kales, A., Kales, J., Jacobson, A., Weissbach, R., Walter, R.D., and Wilson, T. (1966). All night EEG studies: Children and elderly. Electroencephgr. Clin. Neurophysiol. 21, 415.

Kales, A., Wilson, T., Kales, J., Jacobson, A., Paulson, M., Kollar, E. and Walter, R.D. (1967). Measurements of all-night sleep in normal elderly persons: Effects of aging. J. Amer. Geriatr. Soc. 15, 405–414.

Kamei, R., Hughes, L., Miles, L., and Dement, W. (1979). Advanced sleep phase syndrome studied in a time isolation facility. Chronobiologia 6, 115.

Karacan, I., Thornby, J., Anch, M., et al. (1976). Prevalence of sleep disturbance in a primarily urban Florida county. Soc. Sci. Med. 10, 239–244.

Kayed, K., Hesla, P.E., and Rosjo, O. (1979). The actioculographic monitor of sleep. Sleep 2(2), 253–260.

Kripke, D., Simons, R., Garfinkel, L., and Hammond, E. (1979). Short and long sleep and sleeping pills. Arch. Gen. Psychiatr. 36, 103.

Kupfer, D. (1976). REM latency: A psychobiologic marker for primary depressive disease. Biol. Psychiatr. 11, 159–174.

Laird, D. (1931). A survey of the sleep habits of 509 men of distinction. Amer. J. Med. 26, 271–274.

Lugaresi, E., Cirignotta, F., Coccagna, G., and Piana, C. (1980). Some epidemiological data on snoring and cardiocirculatory disturbances. Sleep 3, 221–224.

Lugaresi, E., Coccagna, G., and Cirignotta, F. (1978). Snoring and its clinical implications. In C. Guilleminault and W. Dement, Eds. Sleep Apnea Syndromes. Alan R. Liss Inc., New York, pp. 13–21.

Lugaresi, E., Coccagna, G., Farneti, P., Mantovani, M., and Cirignotta, F. (1975). Snoring. Electroencephalogr. Clin. Neurophysiol. 39, 59–64.

Lugaresi, E., Coccagna, G., Mantovani, M., Berti-Ceroni, G., Pazzaglia, P., and Tassinari, C. (1970). The evaluation of different types of myoclonus during sleep. Eur. Neurol. 4, 321–331.

McFarland, R. (1975). Air travel across time zones. Amer. Sci. 63, 23–30.

McGhie, A. and Russell, S. (1962). The subjective assessment of normal sleep patterns. J. Ment. Sci. 108, 642–654.

McGinty, D. and Arand, D. (1978). Data presented at 33rd Annual Meeting of the Gerontological Society of America, San Diego, November 1980.

Mendelson, W. (1978). The Use and Misuse of Sleeping Pills. Plenum Press, New York.

Mendelson, W., Garnett, D., and Gillin, J. (1981a). Flurazepam-induced sleep apnea syndrome in a patient with insomnia and mild sleep-related respiratory changes. J. Nerv. Dis. 169, 261–264.

Mendelson, W., Gillin, J., and Dement, W. (1981b). Hypnotic efficacy and safety. Sleep 4, 125–128.

Meyer, H. (1971). Sleep disorders in the elderly—a social medicine problem. Praxis, 60, 1041–1042.

Miles, L., Cutler, R., Drake, K., Rule, B., and Dement, W. (1978). Use of a temperature activity monitor to investigate chronobiological dysfunction in patients presenting to a sleep disorders clinic. Sleep Res. 7, 293.

Miles, L. and Dement, W. (1980). Sleep and aging. Sleep 3, 119–220.

Miles, L., Raynal, D., and Wilson, M. (1977). Blind man living in normal society has circadian rhythm of 24.9 hours. Science 198, 421–422.

Mills, J. and Hume, K. (1977). The circadian rhythm of sleep stages. Chronobiologia 4, 132.

Montalbetti, N., Bonini, P., and Ghiringhelli, F. (1965). I levelli nictemergli dei 17-idrossicorticosteroidi plasmatici nell angiosclerosi cerebrale senile. Giorn. Gerontolog. 13, 473–486.

Murri, L., Barreca, T., Gallamini, A., and Massetani, R. (1977). Prolactin and somatotropin levels during sleep in the aged. Chronobiologia 4(2), 135.

Neugarten, B. (1970). Dynamics of transition of middle age to old age: Adaptation and the life cycle. J. Geriatr. Psychiatr. 4, 71–87.

Orem, J. (1980). Neuronal mechanisms of respiration in REM sleep. Sleep 3, 251–267.

Oswald, I. (1975). Sleep difficulties. Br. Med. J. 1, 557–558.

Pfeiffer, E. and Davis, G. (1971). The use of leisure time in middle life. Gerontologist 11, 187–196.

Pflug, B. and Tolle, R. (1971). Disturbance of the 24-hr rhythm in endogenous depression by sleep deprivation. Intl. Pharmacopsychiatr. 6, 187–96.

Phillipson, E. (1978). Respiratory adaptations in sleep. Ann. Rev. Physiol. 40, 133–156.

Phillipson, E., Bowes, G., Sullivan, C. and Woolf, G. (1980). The influence of sleep fragmentation on arousal and ventilatory responses to respiratory stimuli. Sleep 3, 281–288.

Pollak, C., Brodlow, H., Spielman, A., and Weitzman, E. (1978). A pilot survey of the symptoms of hypersomnia-sleep apnea syndrome as possible risk factors for hypertension. 18th Annual Meeting of APSS, p. 289.

Preston, F. (1973). Further sleep problems in airline pilots on world-wide schedules. Aerosp. Med. 44, 775–782.

Prinz, P., Halter, J. Benedetti, C., and Raskin, M. (1979). Circadian variation of plasma catecholamines in young and old men: Relationship to rapid eye movement and slow wave sleep. J. Clin. Endocrinol. Metab. 49, 300–304.

Prinz, P., Obrist, W., and Wang, H. (1975). Sleep patterns in healthy elderly subjects: Individual differences as related to other neurological variables. Sleep Res. 4, 132.

Prinz, P. and Raskind, M. (1978). Aging and sleep disorders. In R. Williams and I. Karacan, Eds. Sleep Disorders: Diagnosis and Treatment. Wiley, New York, pp. 303–321.

Rechtschaffen, A. and Kales, A., Eds. (1968). A Manual of Standardized Terminology, Techniques, and Scoring System for Sleep Stages of Human Subjects. BIS/BRI, UCLA, Los Angeles.

Reynolds, C., Coble, P., Black, R., Holzer, B., Carroll, R., and Kupfer, D. (1979). Sleep disturbances in a series of elderly patients: Polysomnographic findings. J. Amer. Geriatr. Soc. 28, 164–170.

Richardson, G., Carskadon, M., Flagg, W., van den Hoed, J., Dement, W., and Mitler, M. (1978). Excessive daytime sleepiness in man: Multiple sleep latency measurement in narcoleptic and control subjects. Electroencephgr. Clin. Neurophysiol. 45, 621–627.

Rickles, N. (1968). The discarded generation— The woman past fifty. Geriatrics 23, 112–121.

Sachar, E., Halpern, F., Rosenfeld, R., Gallagher, T., and Hellman, L. (1973a). Plasma & urinary testosterone levels in depressed men. Arch. Gen. Psychiatr. 28, 15–18.

Sachar, E., Hellman, L., Roffwarg, H., Halpern, F., Fukushima, D., and Gallagher, T. (1973b). Disrupted 24-hour patterns of cortisol secretion in psychotic depression. Arch. Gen. Psychiatr. 28, 19–24.

Serio, M., Romano, M., DeMagistris, L., and Guisti, G. (1970). The circadian rhythm of plasma cortisol in subjects over 70 years of age. J. Gerontol. 25, 95–97.

Smith, J., Karacan, I., and Yang, M. (1977). Ontogeny of delta activity during human sleep. Electroencephalogr. Clin. Neurophysiol. 43, 229–237.

Solberger, A. (1965). Biological Rhythm Research. Elsevier, Amsterdam.

Spiegel, R. (1981). Sleep and sleeplessness in advanced age. In E. Weitzman, Ed. Advances in Sleep Research, Vol. 5. New York, Spectrum.

Sullivan, C. and Issa, F. (1980). Pathophysiological mechanisms in obstructive sleep apnea. Sleep 3, 235–246.

Symonds, C. (1953). Nocturnal myoclonus. J. Neurol. Neurosurg. Psychiatr. 16, 166–177.

Tune, G. (1968). Sleep and wakefulness in normal human adults. Br. Med. J. 2, 269–271.

Tune, G. (1969a). Sleep and wakefulness in 509 normal adults. Br. J. Med. Psychol. 42, 75–80.

Tune, G. (1969b). The influence of age and temperament on the adult human sleep-wakefulness pattern. Br. J. Psychol. 60, 431–441.

van den Hoed, J., Kraemer, H., Guilleminault, C., Zarcone, V., Miles, L., Dement, W., and Mitler, M. (1981). Disorders of excessive daytime somnolence: Polygraphic and clinical data for 100 patients. Sleep 4, 23–38.

Vogel, G., Thompson, F., Thurmond, F., and Rivers, E. (1973). The effect of REM deprivation on depression. Psychosomatics 14, 104–107.

Walsh, J., Stok, C., and Tepas, D. (1978). The EEG sleep of workers frequently changing shifts. Sleep Res. 7, 314.

Webb, P. (1974). Periodic breathing during sleep. J. Appl. Physiol. 37, 899–903.

Webb, P. and Hiestand, M. (1975). Sleep metabolism, and age. J. Appl. Physiol. 38, 257–262.

Webb, W. (1969). Twenty-four hour sleep cycling. In A. Kales, Ed. Sleep: Physiology and Pathology. Lippincott, Philadelphia, pp. 53–65.

Webb, W. and Agnew, H., Jr. (1971). Stage 4 sleep: Influence of time course variables. Science 174, 1354–1356.

Webb, W. and Swinburne, H. (1971). An observational study of sleep in the aged. Percept. Mot. Skills. 32, 895–898.

Weitzman, E., Czeisler, C., Coleman, R., Spielman, A., Zimmerman, J., and Dement, W. (1981). Delayed sleep phase syndrome: A chronobiological disorder with sleep-onset insomnia. Arch. Gen. Psychiat. 38, 737–746.

Weitzman, E., Kripke, D., and Goldmacker, D. (1970). Acute reversal of the sleep-waking cycle in man. Arch. Neurol. 22, 483–489.

Wessler, R., Rubin, M., and Sollberger, A. (1976). Circadian rhythm of activity and sleep-wakefulness in elderly institutionalized patients. J. Interdiscipl. Cycle Res. 7, 333–348.

Williams, R., Karacan, I., and Hursch, C. (1970). Electroencephalograph of Human Sleep: Clinical Applications. Wiley, New York, pp. 1–169.

Winget, C., Vernikos-Danellis, J., Cronin, S., Leach, C., Rambaut, P. and Mack, P. (1972). Circadian rhythm asynchrony in man during hypokinesis. J. Appl. Physiol. 33, 640–643.

Wynne, J., Block, J., Hemenway, J., Hunt, L., and Flick, M. (1979). Disordered breathing and oxygen desaturation during sleep in patients with chronic obstructive lung disease. Amer. J. Med. 66, 573–579.

III
Mental Status

11. Mental Status Examinations in Aging

DONNA COHEN   CARL EISDORFER
C. LOUISE HOLM

Mrs. M.: My husband was behaving irrationally off and on for perhaps two years. I lived in considerable fear and worry. He flew his own plane, and he skippered his own boat. And dear God, there were experiences that were very hazardous. I was afraid to go out on the boat with him. We would sail north into isolated areas where the tide was strong and the water was very cold. I had fallen in several times, but I blamed it on myself, at least for a while.

I tried to persuade him to fly commercially, but no, he had to take his own plane. I did not tell him I was afraid to fly with him. I would hire another plane and meet him. He made slight errors that were very frightening.

He is 75 and he has one leg, it takes quite a bit of physical ability for him to fly, but his coordination is not what it used to be.

Dr.: What were your feelings during this time?

Mrs. M.: Dreadful . . . dreadful. After all, I have been married 53 years now to a man I love dearly. He was once an extremely ingenious man. And now, he has just lost his knack at everything.

Cognitive disorders secondary to central nervous system dysfunction in the aged are a particularly important area of concern for neurologists and psychiatrists. The risk for a significant dementing disorder increases with advancing age, and it is estimated that at least 1 million Americans have a severe dementia with another 3 to 4 million manifesting a moderate to severe dementia (cf. the review of Schneck, et al., 1982). Mr. M., whose behavior is described in the opening dialogue, was diagnosed as having dementia of the Alzheimer type three years after his wife first observed significant disruptions at home and at work. Mrs. M. had seen a sequence of unusual behaviors in her husband long before she was convinced by her daughter to take Mr. M. to a physician for a comprehensive diagnostic evaluation. Among the most important components of such an evaluation is the mental status examination.

Introduction

The mental status examination is an approach employed to organize a diagnostic interview in order to identify strengths, weaknesses, and abnormalities in behavior as well as underlying ability or personality. There are, in addition, different types of instruments or tests that can aid in the assessment of mental status. Some focus solely upon cognitive functioning; others also evaluate such signs and symptoms of psychopathology as depression, anxiety, suspicion and paranoia, dangerous or bizarre behavior, somatic disturbances, and social maladjustment. Many mental status approaches are variations on common themes with comparable items, such as orientation to time, person, and place.

They differ in format as well as content and in the complexity of their questions. There is, however, one characteristic essential to all mental status examinations: clinical practicality. They must be relatively brief, convenient, require only a moderate level of cooperation from the individual being assessed, and consist of simple observations or tests.

This chapter will examine specific objectives of clinical mental status examinations, focusing upon dementia, and review a few of the tests used most widely today to evaluate cognitive dysfunction. A number of the instruments are presented in some detail. The chapter concludes with a discussion of methods that could develop and improve standards for the assessment of mental status.

Mental Status Evaluation

Mental status assessment should achieve several general objectives: These include evaluation of patients' degree of participation in the examination, as reflected in their level of consciousness, motivation, and attitude toward the examiner; the cognitive state of patients (as measured by simple tests to examine samples of different abilities); the quality and intensity of the patients' emotional state; any indication of unusual ideation or propensity for maladaptive behavior; and an appreciation of patients' personality style.

Conducting a complete mental status examination is not a trivial or easily mastered skill. In its complete form, it may take several hours and often challenges the most skilled clinician. Exploration of affect, belief systems, relevant issues in the patient's past and current life situation are all relevant to understanding the impaired individual. For the purposes of a practical approach to the evaluation of the patient with a dementing disorder, we will focus only upon one aspect of the mental status examination, the cognitive component.

Setting of the Evaluation

The examiner must be sensitive to the purpose of the mental status examination, which is frequently determined by the point at which the individual finds his way into the health delivery system (Gurland, 1980). When assessments are done to determine whether a patient must enter a specific setting or program in the mental health system, the approach may be different than when assessments are done to evaluate whether the individual is at risk for mental disorder and whether preventive steps are to be taken.

A mental status evaluation should be done in a way that does not threaten the individual or appear to cast doubt on his or her sanity. Frequently, a mental status examination is done when a person is in need of emergency treatment, has a fluctuating state of consciousness, is disoriented, or is showing lapses of memory and perhaps hallucinating. In such cases, the examination should be repeated after hospitalization, when the individual has stabilized.

The interview with an older person must show respect for the patient as an individual with certain rights. However, several areas of difficulty often arise when interviewing older patients. First, the patient may be infantilized by a child or a younger person who has assumed the role of parent surrogate. The older person may often be ignored, while the physician discusses the patient's condition with a son, a daughter, or even a grandchild. Second, the older person is often not psychologically oriented and does not have a positive attitude toward mental health professionals or questions of a psychological nature. This may be complicated by a feeling that the examination is designed to label them as crazy so as to institutionalize them. Consequently, it is difficult to create the setting for an honest interview. Finally, in the case of some patients, particularly inpatients or patients in long-term care, physical contact, speaking loudly and clearly, and making sure the patient fully understands the examiner are important. The wise clinician will endeavor to establish and maintain a high degree of rapport with the person being examined. It is also wise to ensure that the patient is cooperating with the examiner. Ascertaining the patient's belief as to the purpose of the examination and the implication(s) for outcome can be most helpful here.

Detecting and defining the nature of an abnormal condition is a major goal of a mental status assessment. Another objective is the assessment of change after treatment. In order to accomplish either of these goals, the mental status examination should be done in conjunction with a range of medical, psychological, and laboratory tests (Eisdorfer and Cohen, 1980), since a number of physical and psychiatric disorders cause cognitive dysfunction (Eisdorfer and Cohen, 1980; Libow, 1973).

Unfortunately, existing mental status examinations of cognitive status do not provide more than a gross estimate of generalized deficit in an individual. Our understanding of the dementing disorders of later life would be greatly improved by examinations that were more microanalytic in their identification and quantification of abnormal behavior (Eisdorfer and Cohen, 1982).

Commonly Used Mental Status Examinations

Typically, examinations of individuals with suspected dementia have included one or more of a variety of brief questionnaires to assess cognitive dysfunction. Several are reviewed below and in Tables 11-1 through 11-3.

Mental Status Questionnaire

The Mental Status Questionnaire (MSQ) (Kahn et al., 1960), is one of the earliest attempts to systematize the cognitive component of the mental status examination. It consists of ten questions, five that relate to orientation in space, person, and time and five that test general memory. The questions were selected from 31 originally used by Kahn and colleagues as those which most effectively discriminated individuals with "organicity." Several investigators have used some variant of this questionnaire for clinical research (e.g., Pfeiffer, 1975).

The MSQ was validated by Kahn and his colleagues in their original study as a tool for discriminating between dementias and functional disorders (Table 11-1). In Kahn's validation study, the MSQ was administered to a random sample of 1077 older persons residing in New York City homes for the aged, nursing homes, and state hospitals. Each person was interviewed by a psychiatrist within 1 month of completing the MSQ. The correlation between the psychiatrist's diagnosis (the validation criteria) and the performance on the MSQ was high: 94% of those making no errors on the MSQ were rated by the psychiatrist as cognitively intact or having mild chronic brain syndrome (CBS); 95% of those making 10 errors were rated as having moderate or severe CBS.

Cresswell and Lanyon (1981) studied the MSQ to examine its validity over the entire range of possible scores (0–10), not just the limits reported by Kahn et al. (1960). The subjects were 61 geriatric patients (average age, 70.5 years) who were consecutive admissions in a 5-month period to a county hospital. The validation criteria were consensus diagnoses of a psychiatrist and a clinical psychologist, who conducted independent evaluations. Four diagnostic dimensions were rated: "organicity," negative prognosis, depression, and global psychopathology. Scores on the MSQ correlated significantly ($r=0.87$, $p \leqslant .001$) with diagnoses of "organicity." Cresswell and Lanyon urge caution with regard to interpreting this high correlation, since results derived from this population of chronic, severely impaired older persons may not be generalizable to a less impaired population.

The MSQ has been shown to be reliable as well as valid. Wilson et al. (1973) gave the MSQ four times a week at 3-week intervals to 55 older patients judged to be stable. The scores of 75% of the patients changed by one point or less.

Fillenbaum's (1980) study also supports the validity of the MSQ for the purpose of discrimination between normal and demented patients. It can not, however, be used to determine the etiology of the dementia (e.g., depression vs. Alzheimer's disease). Other variations of the MSQ have used similar questions adding other features, for example, time to respond, in an effort to make the test more discriminating.

Table 11-1. Selected Validation Studies Using the Mental Status Questionnaire (MSQ)

Study	Sample	Validating criteria	Results	Comments
Kahn et al. (1960)	1077 individuals, aged 65 and over, residing in NYC state hospitals (169), proprietary nursing homes (426), or homes for the aged (482)	Psychiatric interview assessing 1. presence and degree of dementia 2. presence and degree of psychosis 3. certifiability of subject 4. degree of management problem (none, mild, moderate, severe)	1. Number of MSQ errors and severity of CBS were directly related: 10 errors—95% rated as having severe–moderate CBS 0 errors—94% rated as having no dementia or mild CBS 2. Number of MSQ errors and severity of psychosis were directly related: 10 errors—75% judged psychotic 0 errors—3% judged psychotic 3. The more MSQ errors, the more likely a subject to be judged "certifiable": 10 errors—89% judged "certifiable" 0 errors—5% judged "certifiable." 4. A linear relationship existed between severity of management problems and number of MSQ errors: 0 errors—94% presented no problems or mild management problems 10 errors—52% presented management problems	Original MSQ consisted of 31 questions; 10 were selected as most sensitive
Fillenbaum (1980)	83 community residents aged 65 or older	Diagnosis of presence or absence of non-reversible dementia was made by one of ten psychiatrists for subject on the basis of psychiatric examinations. Psychiatrists conducted own interview, but were required to report findings in a uniform format	MSQ has high specificity, low sensitivity. Using three errors as a cut-off point for dementia: 98% of normal subjects were identified correctly; 45% of subjects with dementia were identified correctly. Using two errors as cut-off point: 96% of normal subjects were correctly identified; 55% of subjects with dementia were correctly identified	Two items accounted for almost as much of the variance as did all 10: Date of birth; previous president
Cresswell and Lanyon (1981)	61 consecutive geriatric admissions to psychiatric ward of a county hospital over a period of 5 months	One psychiatrist and one psychologist independently rated each subject on four dimensions on the basis of individual interviews of 15–60 minutes and reviews of patient files: Organicity; negative prognosis; depression; global psychopathology	Correlation between raters' assessments were significant at 0.001 level: Organicity, −0.87; negative prognosis, −0.69; depression, 0.58; global psychopathology, −0.59	Four dimensions were judged to represent the most common diagnostic questions about psychogeriatric patients in a medical setting

Mini-Mental State Examination

The Mini-Mental State (MMS) examination consists of 11 questions divided into two types of tests (Folstein et al., 1975). The first section evaluates orientation and memory and requires vocal responses; the maximum score is 21. The second group of questions examines the ability to name objects, follow verbal and written commands, write a sentence spontaneously, and copy a complex polygon. These require the ability to read and write; the maximum score is 9. Thus, the total maximum score is 30.

Folstein and colleagues established the validity and the test-retest reliability of MMS in the evaluation of severity of cognitive impairment (Table 11-2). In the original study, the MMS was administered to three groups of subjects including 206 patients and 63 age- and sex-matched normals.

1. The first sample of 69 patients, tested shortly after admission to a private psychiatric hospital, were chosen as well-identified cases of non-reversible clinical dementia (29), affective disorders (10), depression with cognitive impairment (10), and depressive disorders (20).

2. The second patient sample were 137 consecutive admissions to the psychiatric hospital. Diagnoses, established by M.F. Folstein, included dementia (9), major depressive disorder (31), affective disorder, manic type (14), schizophrenia (24), personality disorder due to drug abuse (32), and neurosis (27).

3. The control sample were 63 normal subjects living in the community.

Scores on the MMS discriminated between the three diagnostic groups represented in the first sample: Patients with dementia (mean score, 9.7), depression with cognitive impairment (mean score, 19.0), and uncomplicated affective disorder, that is depression without cognitive impairment (mean score, 25.1). Thus, the MMS was consistent with the clinical impression of the presence and severity of cognitive impairment. The average score of the normal group was 27.6.

The MMS also appears to detect changes in the cognitive status of depressed patients after treatment. A total of 33 patients with depression and dementing disorders from sample 1 were tested before and after appropriate treatment. Those with dementia showed little change in their performance scores, as expected, whereas those with depression and cognitive dysfunction improved considerably.

The sample of 137 patients were evaluated to test the validity of the MMS in consecutive psychiatric admissions and to attempt to standardize the test. The mean MMS scores in each diagnostic category were as follows: clinical dementia, 12.2; major depressive disorder, 26.8; and neuroses, 27.6. Thus, in this group, the means were similar across diagnostic categories, except in the case of dementia.

Folstein and his colleagues demonstrated that the MMS was reliable on 24-hour or 28-day retest by single or multiple examiners. The Pearson correlation coefficient for scores on a 24-hour retest was 0.89 by a single examiner and 0.83 by a different examiner. When patients chosen for their clinical stability were tested twice, an average of 28 days apart, the product moment correlation between the first and second test was 0.98.

Cognitive Capacity Screening Examination

The Cognitive Capacity Screening Examination (CCSE) is a brief mental status examination developed to diagnose "diffuse organic mental syndrome" (OMS) in busy medical wards (Jacobs et al., 1977). It consists of 30 questions testing orientation to place and time, serial sevens capacity, verbal short-term memory, abstraction, digit recall, and arithmetic. Some questions are formulated to require performance of an interposed task; this design enhances stress and reveals defects that might otherwise go undetected.

Jacobs and colleagues validated the CCSE using four different samples (Table 11-2). The average age of the first three samples was 65. One sample included 24 medical inpatients for whom psychiatric consultations were requested. Of these 24 inpatients, 18 were diagnosed by the consulting psychiatrist as having OMS. There

Table 11-2. Validation Study Using the Cognitive Capacity Screening Examination (CCSE) and the Mini-Mental Status Examination (MMS)

Study	Sample	Validation criteria	Results	Comments
MMS Folstein et al., (1975)	Sample 1:69 patients with depression or dementia Sample 2:137 consecutively admitted inpatients Sample 3:63 healthy community residents	Three dimensions assessed: diagnosis, response to treatment, correlation with WAIS scores	Sample 1: MMS scores correlated significantly ($p. < .001$) with psychiatric diagnosis in sample 1 (dementia vs. depression) Sample 2: MMS scores changed substantially with treatment of depressed patients Sample 3: MMS Scores correlated significantly with both WAIS verbal and performance IQ's ($p \leqslant 0.001$) in a subgroup of patients from samples 1 and 2	
CCSE Jacobs et al., (1977)	24 adult medical inpatients with psychiatric consultations. 25 psychiatric inpatients 61 consecutively admitted inpatients 25 hospital staff members (Average age of hospital samples, 65.0)	Presence and degree of organic dysfunction assessed: Sample 1: psychiatric interview Sample 2:chart review, some laboratory tests, and EEG evaluations Sample 3:admissions diagnosis, some laboratory tests, and EEG evaluations Sample 4:presumed mental health	Correlation of diagnosis of organic dysfunction with a CCSE score < 20: Sample 1: Significant correlation ($p < 0.01$) Sample 2: Of patients diagnosed, 1 of 5 scored below 20 Sample 3: 10 patients were given EEG's 6 of 7 patients with abnormal EEG's scored below 20 Sample 4: 1 of 25 controls scored below 20	False positives and false negatives are possible. In particular, the CCSE does not distinguish between mental retardation and dementia of late life CCSE does *not* identify focal lesions CCSE scores are contaminated by minimal education or poor understanding of English

was a statistically significant correlation (*p* ≤ 0.01) between a diagnosis of OMS and a score of less than 20 on the CCSE (maximum score = 30). A score of 19 or less, therefore, was chosen as the cut-off score indicating OMS.

The second sample was 25 psychiatric inpatients whose diagnoses were unknown to the examiner. Of these 25 inpatients, 22 scored 20 or over on the CCSE. The three patients who scored below 20 showed some evidence of cognitive dysfunction. Four or five patients who manifested psychiatric dysfunction due to a physiological abnormality scored 25 or better on the CCSE.

In the third sample of 61 consecutively admitted medical patients, 23 patients scored 19 or below. Ten of sixty-one patients had EEG's during their stay, and six of the seven showing abnormal EEG's scored 19 or below. The fourth sample consisted of 25 hospital staff members. Only one individual in this group scored below 20, and this individual, a housekeeper, spoke English poorly.

Jacobs and his colleagues concluded that the CCSE is useful in detecting the presence of OMS. They caution that the test does not differentiate between organic dysfunction and mental retardation and that both false positives and false negatives are possible. The danger of false negatives has been emphasized by a recent validation study (Kaufman et al., 1979). In this study, scores on the CCSE were compared with clinical evaluations of 59 patients on a neurology service. Abnormal neurological signs were present in 90% of those patients identified by the CCSE as having a cognitive deficit. However, some cases of dementia, aphasia, and agnosia and nine cases of cognitive deficit associated with major cerebral disease went undetected by CCSE scores. Thus, false negative results were reported in about 15% and questionable negative results in about 10% of the patients.

The inter-rater reliability of the CCSE has been reported by Jacobs et al. (1977). Three independent examiners administered the questionnaire consecutively to six patients, three of whom had a diagnosis of OMS, and identical scores were achieved.

Clifton Assessment Schedule

The Clifton Assessment Schedule (CAS) is a brief mental status examination originally devised to evaluate chronic psychiatric patients (Pattie and Gilleard, 1975). Pattie and Gilleard (1976) validated it for a geriatric population. The three subtests of the CAS assess orientation, mental abilities, and psychomotor abilities. The Information and Orientation subtest has twelve questions and the Mental Abilities subtest has four; the psychomotor performance test is the Gibson Spiral Maze.

The CAS has been validated twice by Pattie and Gilleard (1975, 1976), but no reliability has been reported. The 1975 validation study tested 100 consecutive admissions (mean age, 71.4 years) to the acute ward of a psychiatric hospital. Scores on all three subtests showed a significant correlation with a psychiatric diagnosis of either a functional disorder or a dementing disorder. The information and orientation subtest discriminated most effectively between the two groups. Ninety-two percent of the patients were correctly classified using a cut-off score of 7 (out of 12) points.

In the 1976 validation study, the same authors studied a sample of another 80 consecutive admissions, 60 years old and older, to acute wards of the psychiatric hospital. Again, all the Clifton subtests differentiated between the organic and functional groups, and the Information/Orientation subtest was the best discriminator of psychiatric diagnosis.

The relationship of patients' CAS scores to discharge home, placement within the hospital, and mortality was also investigated in the Pattie and Gilleard studies (1975, 1976). In both studies, scores on all three CAS subtests were significantly related (*p* ≤ 0.001) to discharge home at 3-month follow-up. It should be noted that age was also significantly related (*p* ≤ 0.01) to discharge. The relationship of CAS subtests scores to placement within the hospital and mortality was less clearly defined.

The association between CAS scores to placement within the hospital was analyzed somewhat differently in the 1975 and 1976 studies (Table 11-3); the relationship

Table 11-3. Validation Studies Using the Clifton Assessment Schedule (CAS)

Study	Sample	Validation Criteria	Results	Comments
Pattie and Gilleard (1975)	100 consecutive in-patient admissions to acute wards of British psychiatric hospital (mean age, 71.4)	1. Psychiatric diagnosis of functional disorder or dementia 2. Three-month outcome	1. Significant correlation between scores on all three subtests and organicity ($p < 0.001$) 2. Significant correlation between three subtest scores and discharge ($p < 0.001$)	
Pattie and Gilleard (1976)	80 consecutive in-patient admissions to acute wards of British psychiatric hospital (over age 65)	1. Psychiatric diagnosis of functional disorder or dementia 2. Three-month outcome	1. Significant correlation between scores on all three CAS subtests and organicity ($p < 0.01$) 2. Significant correlation between scores on all three subtests and discharge ($p < 0.001$)	The Information/Orientation subtest is the most effective discriminator of organicity. More than 90% of the patients in this study were correctly classified using the cut-off score established in the 1975 study

of scores to mortality was examined only in the 1976 study. The placement of 92 of the 100 consecutive admissions into the psycho-geriatric or non-psychiatric wards (1975) was found to be significantly related ($p \le 0.01$) only to Mental Ability subtest scores. In 1976, the relationship of CAS subtest scores to placement and mortality was investigated not by giving the CAS to new admissions, but rather to patients who were already in non-psycho-geriatric and psycho-geriatric wards. There is no methodical discussion of the statistical significance of the findings. The patients in the non-geriatric wards were younger (although still averaging 65 years of age) and had higher scores on all the CAS subtests than the patients in the geriatric wards. The relationship of mortality to CAS scores was analyzed only for patients on two psycho-geriatric wards, one for men and one for women. Performance scores on all CAS subtests were significantly lower for men who died, but the relationship between mortality and CAS scores was not significant in women.

Cognitive Testing and the Management of Dementia

A brief mental status examination serves to demonstrate the presence of cognitive impairment. Once a diagnosis, after a series of medical examinations, has been established, a comprehensive evaluation of intellectual skills throughout the course of dementia is necessary to provide a framework to help understand and manage the patient. How quickly can the person do simple tasks such as turn off a light? How quickly does the patient respond in more complex situations when several instructions are given? Are long sentences, short phrases, or even simple words difficult to say? Does the patient understand and express anger, sadness, and happiness? Is concentration on more than one thing at a time possible? How distractible is the patient? Can the patient perform several consecutive actions or must step-by-step guidance be given? Can a daily schedule, a meal, or a trip to the store be organized? Can new information be learned by rehearsing it over and over? Can the patient

Table 11-4. Areas of intellectual functioning that should be evaluated during the course of dementia.

Speed

Motivation

Language

Nonverbal communication (anger, sadness, hostility, happiness)

General cognitive processes (learning, thinking, reasoning, problem-solving)

Attention

Memory

Focal cognitive skills (reading, writing, mathematics, fluency)

Metacognition (insight into own problems)

remember what was learned? What cues are needed? Is reading and writing for even short periods possible? Is the patient able to do arithmetic, write checks, handle money? Does the patient have any insight into the nature of the disease? Can the patient make plans for the future?

A wide range of abilities (Table 11-4) should be evaluated to establish a profile of deficits. These areas include time to perform simple and complex actions; the presence of aphasia, and proficiency in the use of language; the ability to use and respond to nonverbal cues; speed and accuracy in organizing, rehearsing, and retrieving learned information; the ability to focus and divide attention; the ability to remember and manipulate new information; the ability to read, write, and perform arithmetic tasks and other cognitive skills; and insight into the extent of cognitive dysfunction. These are typically best done by the judicious involvement of clinical neuropsychological laboratory tests that can aid in the management of the patient (Eisdorfer and Cohen, in press).

The Importance of Cognitive Assessment and Remediation

Cognitive tests provide an important assessment of the individual's strengths and weaknesses, as well as a basis for improved differential diagnosis and the assessment of change in performance. Cognitive skills do not deteriorate uniformly in patients with early dementia. Retained skills, such as semantic, auditory or attentional, may serve as strengths in the face of progressive cognitive impairment. Insight of the clinician into the skills an individual retains during the progression of the illness can provide guidelines for cognitive retraining and also provide the family or caregivers with a realistic base line for performance at home or in the institution, respectively.

Mental status evaluation at regular intervals focuses on the changing abilities of the patient and determines changes in management strategies. For example, in the early stages of dementia, if perceptual motor skills are relatively intact, limited driving to familiar locations may be permitted. When these abilities deteriorate significantly, other options should be explored to provide activities for the patient. Recreational activities, such as cycling, which provides enormous pleasure to people of all ages, should be encouraged if functional skills are present. Cognitively impaired individuals can continue to be active in a wide range of activities, including sports, shopping, and helping around the home, and they can play an active and valued role in the family, at least until the later stages of dementia. Unfortunately, many families and their physicians encourage dependency, reinforce helplessness in their impaired relatives, and often help create the one-person nursing home.

In general, physical exercise and activities should be structured for the patient and the family as part of a daily routine, even if it is as simple as running, walking, or gardening. Knowledge of the patient's strengths as well as weaknesses provides a basis for working with the family to find meaningful roles for the impaired relative throughout the course of the illness. Although memory and attentional dysfunctions often make the successful completion of such household chores as cooking, cleaning, and shopping impossible, individuals are often capable of successfully performing some part of these tasks. Accurate evaluations can provide the framework to recommend life and work roles for the patient. An older impaired adult may not be capable of doing the weekly shopping, but may derive enormous satisfaction

from running a simple errand for the day, for example, buying a loaf of bread or a quart of milk for the evening meal. In general, the physical environment and life roles should be structured to reward patients for successful performance rather than remind them of their disabilities. To go one step further, research is needed to design cognitively enhancing environments for the impaired aged, that is, to implement physical and social alterations that motivate the individual, stimulate ordered behavior, and provide incentives for using whatever capacities are intact or less impaired.

In addition to cognitive skills, several factors must be evaluated in planning the management of the patient because of their effect on his or her adaptive style (Table 11-5). A careful probing interview should be conducted with the patient and caregivers on a regular basis to monitor a range of environmental, psychosocial, family, and patient factors. The degree of dementia, the involvement of the family support system, past life experiences, and current preferences of the dementia patient are only a few of the factors that must be considered. A series of appropriate rewards must be identified that will moti-

Table 11-5. Factors That Limit Performance and Adaptation of Cognitively Impaired Individuals

Disease Factors:
Duration and severity of dementia
General health

Environmental Factors:
Clinical and community services
Living situation and demands of environment (cognitive enhancing aspects of environment; ability to control and influence environment)
Recent life events (deaths, economic changes, moves)
Family beliefs, attitudes, needs, and preferences
Medications

Patient Factors:
Functional capacity (ability to do things around the house)
Patient's beliefs, attitudes, needs, and preferences
Life history (education, work and leisure experience, life roles)
Affect (Depression, anxiety, paranoia, anger, and hostility)
Social skills (ability to relate to family and friends)

vate the patient to participate, and the program must be individually tailored to the patient. A detailed interview will provide information about the patient's family and personal history, work experience, leisure activities, achievements, and goals. The patient's physical and psychosocial environment must be carefully explored to determine what aspects of the environment help or hinder the patient's performance.

The co-existence of physical and psychological problems is the major factor in reducing performance in the demented patient. Sharp changes in mental capacity are often symptomatic of pathology in other somatic or biological systems. A more comprehensive evaluation and careful follow-up is warranted.

Depression should be assessed in a mental status evaluation. Since depression is among the treatable conditions contributing to cognitive loss in the elderly, this seems of particular importance, and it is an essential element of the differential diagnosis of dementia. In addition, the feelings of isolation, loss of capacity, and loss of jobs or social roles that are associated with the primary dementing disorder may all lead to a coincident (or secondary) depression. In more agitated or apathetic patients, a dysphoric mood, a slowed reaction time, a history of depression (or bipolar illness), or appetite or sleep changes should all alert the clinician to investigate the possibility of depression.

Improved Mental Status Examinations

The individual with dementia has deficits in areas of memory, learning, attention, communication, reasoning, as well as in a range of cognitive skills. In many instances, these intellectual changes are quite subtle at first, but become debilitating with time. However, despite a clinical expectation for generalized decline, there is no evidence that all cognitive skills deteriorate at the same rate in all patients. In a recent longitudinal study, Cohen and Eisdorfer (1980) found that performance in tasks requiring selective attention deteriorated more quickly than performance on memory tasks over a 1-year period in a

group of mildly impaired Alzheimer patients. It is necessary to identify the pattern and rate of cognitive fallout throughout the course of dementia. In the early and middle phase of the disease, many patients retain a wide repertoire of behavior at their pre-disease level, despite obvious deficits in specific (focal) areas. It is important, therefore, to examine an individual's strengths and weaknesses because these may provide important clues to a patient's adaptive capacity and limitations. Unfortunately, the brief mental status examinations currently used in clinical practice only identify generalized cognitive dysfunction. They do little to help us understand the patient.

The natural histories of the various types of dementia are not yet well documented. Often the patient's capacity for self-care and ability to adapt to the demands of the physical and social environment deteriorate slowly and relentlessly. Recent data suggest that although multi-infarct dementias are also progressive, there appears to be an exaggerated downward and stepwise deterioration as well as some transient periods of recovery (Hachinski et al., 1974). It has been reported that many patients with dementia of the Alzheimer type also display smaller, but noticeable stepwise degenerative changes in the middle and later stages of the illness.

Without objective, quantitative, psychological biomedical markers, it is not possible, at least at this time, to determine the shape and magnitude of the mathematical funtion that best fits the change in these two major classes of dementing disorder. Clinically, large individual differences are observed in the rate and course of change during the dementing process (Eisdorfer and Cohen, 1980).

Conclusion

Mental status evaluations that emphasize cognitive function and identify cognitive dysfunction can be used to establish the parameters for patient management through psychotherapy, pharmacotherapy, and cognitive enhancement. For patients in the early and middle stages of dementia, individualized and group training programs can help them work with less impaired or intact cognitive functions to compensate for major cognitive deficits. These require a set of cognitive shaping exercises so that easy and difficult tasks are ordered in hierarchy (Cohen, 1982). Cognitively impaired individuals can continue to be active in a wide range of activities, including sports, shopping, and limited work assignments, and they can play an active and valued role in the family, at least until the later stages of dementia. Unfortunately, many families and their physicians encourage dependency, reinforce helplessness in their impaired relatives, and often help create the one-person nursing home.

References

Cohen, D. (1982). Psychological issues in the diagnosis and treatment of patients with dementing disorders. In Psychopharmacology and Aging, C. Eisdofer and E. Fann Eds. Plenum Press, New York.

Cohen, D. and Eisdorfer, C. (in press). The Cognitive Evaluation Battery. Springer, New York.

Cresswell, C.L. and Lanyon, R.I. (1981). Validation of a screening battery for psychogeriatric assessment. J. Gerontol. 4, 435–440.

Eisdorfer, C. and Cohen, D. (1980). Diagnostic criteria for primary neuronal degeneration of the Alzheimer's type. J. Fam. Pract. 11, 553–557.

Eisdorfer, C. and Cohen, D. (1982). Mental Health Care of the Aging: A Multi-Disciplinary Curriculum for Professional Training. New York, Springer.

Fillenbaum, G.G. (1980). Comparison of two brief tests of organic brain impairment, the MSQ and the Short Portable MSQ. J. Amer. Geriatr. Soc. 8, 381–384.

Folstein, M.F., Folstein, S.E., and McHugh, P.R. (1975). "Mini-Mental State" a practical method for grading the cognitive state of patients for the clinician. J. Psychiatr. Res. 12, 189–198.

Gurland, B.J. (1980). The assessment of the mental health status of older adults. In Handbook of Mental Health and Aging, V.E. Birren and R.B. Sloane Eds. Prentice-Hall, Englewood Cliffs, N.J.

Hachinski, V., Lassen, N.A., and Marshall, J. (1974). Multi-infarct dementia. Lancet, ii, 207–209.

Jacobs, J.W., Bernhard, M.R., Delgado, A., and Strain, J.J. (1977). Screening for organic mental syndromes in the medically ill. Ann. Int. Med. 86, 40–46.

Kahn, R.L., Goldfarb, A.I., Pollack, M., and Peck, A. (1960). Brief objective measures for the determination of mental status in the aged. Amer. J. Psychiat. 117, 326–328.

Kaufman, D.M., Weinberger, M., Strain, J.J., and Jacobs, J.W. (1979). Detection of cognitive deficits by a brief mental status examination. Gen. Hosp. Psychiat. Vol. 1, 247–255.

Libow, L.W. (1973). "Pseudosenility": Acute and reversible organic brain syndromes. J. Amer. Geriatr. Soc. 21, 112.

Pattie, A.H. and Gilleard, C.J. (1975). A brief psychogeriatric assessment schedule—validation against psychiatric diagnosis and discharge from hospital. Br. J. Psychiat. 127, 289–293.

Pattie, A.H. and Gilleard, C.J. (1976). The Clifton Assessment Schedule—further validation of a psychogeriatric assessment schedule. Br. J. Psychiat. 129, 68–72.

Pfeiffer, E. (1975). A Short Portable Mental Status Questionnaire for the assessment of organic brain deficit in elderly patients. J. Amer. Geriatr. Soc. 28, 433–441.

Pfeiffer, R.I., Kurosaki, T.T., Harrah, C.H., Jr., Chance, J.M., Bates, D., Detels, R., Filos, S., and Butzke, C. (1981). A survey diagnostic tool for senile dementia. Amer. J. Epidemiol. 114, 515–527.

Schneck, M.K., Reisberg, B., and Ferris, S.H. (1982). An overview of current concepts of Alzheimer's disease. Amer. J. Psychiat. 139, 165–173.

12. Neuropsychology of Normal Aging

GAIL HOCHANADEL

EDITH KAPLAN

The clinical neuropsychologist is frequently called upon to distinguish cognitive changes related to normal aging from those signaling the onset of central nervous system pathology. The paucity and, in some instances, lack of norms for older adults on many tests and neuropsychological measures contribute to the difficulty of differential diagnosis. Existing norms are problematic. Cross-sectional analyses tend to exaggerate age differences because of cohort effects, whereas longitudinal analyses minimize age differences because of selective subject attrition.

Many of the early investigations in which attempts were made to delineate the cognitive changes associated with the normal aging process were limited in focus and level of analysis by a number of factors. On the one hand, the *Zeitgeist* in North American psychology fostered an actuarial approach to the assessment of cognitive functioning. On the other, the lack of sophistication among psychologists regarding functional cerebral organization led to a simplistic view of hemispheric specialization: the left hemisphere is verbal, the right hemisphere non-verbal. Furthermore, the dearth of noninvasive neuroradiological techniques precluded direct, *in vivo* investigations of normative functioning in the aging brain. These limitations notwithstanding, it is useful to consider the early investigations, as they raised questions that led to issues currently being addressed in neuropsychological research on normal aging.

Classical Aging Pattern

Both longitudinal and cross-sectional studies (Birren and Schaie, 1977; Hulicka, 1978) have provided evidence of a tendency for intellectual function to decline beginning in the seventh or the eighth decade, with a more pronounced decline beginning in the ninth decade. However, not all cognitive functions appear to deteriorate. Some intellectual abilities become impaired, while others remain intact or, in fact, improve throughout the life-span. A number of studies (Wechsler, 1958; Eisdorfer et al., 1959) described a pattern in which scores on the Verbal subtests of the Wechsler Adult Intelligence Scale (WAIS) remained relatively stable with increasing age, whereas scores on the Performance subtests, which rely primarily on nonverbal, visuospatial skills, declined. Because the Performance subtests were timed tasks, most of which require a motor response, it was suggested that the difference might be due to reduced motor speed in elderly subjects. However, it has been repeatedly demonstrated that the decline remains evident even after the factor of response speed is eliminated (Doppelt and Wallace, 1955; Klodin, 1975; Storandt, 1977). This pattern of preservation of verbal abilities with decline in nonverbal abilities has come to be referred to as the "classical aging pattern" and has also been found using other instruments designed to assess general intellectual functioning, such as the Primary Mental Abilities Test (Hulicka, 1978).

One explanation for this finding has been that the verbal tasks rely primarily on the use of previously stored information that is manipulated in familiar ways, whereas the nonverbal performance tasks require the manipulation of novel material in unfamiliar and more complex ways (Birren et al., 1963; Botwinick, 1977; Schonfield and Robertson, 1966). Cattell (1963) referred to this as the difference between "crystallized" intelligence, which reflects cultural assimilation throughout the life-span, and "fluid" intelligence, which purportedly reflects neurophysiological status and which selectively declines with aging (Horn and Cattell, 1967). Age-related impairments have been found in a variety of other visuospatial tasks, including the Bender-Gestalt Visual Motor Test and Archimedes Spiral Test (Gilbert and Levee, 1965), the Embedded Figures Test (Axelrod and Cohen, 1961), Ambiguous Figures (Botwinick et al., 1959; Heath and Orbach, 1963), Incomplete Figures (Danziger and Salthouse, 1978), figure drawings (Plutchik et al., 1978), spatial rotation (Cerella et al., 1981; Krauss et al., 1980), and spatial perspective-taking (Zaks and Labouvie-Vief, 1980; Ohta et al., 1981).

Hemispheric Differences

The development of neuropsychological assessment techniques has led to attempts to delineate the brain-behavior relationships associated with normal aging. There is now evidence that suggests that differential patterns of change in the brain are related to the aging process.

One of the first methods of investigation into this problem was to compare patterns of scores on a number of measures achieved by healthy elderly subjects with those obtained by patients with documented brain damage. In this way, similarities in cognitive impairment were correlated and associations with brain areas or systems were inferred. In studies using the WAIS and the Halstead-Reitan Neuropsychological Test Battery (Overall and Gorham, 1972; Goldstein and Shelly, 1975), the performance of non-brain damaged elderly subjects was found to differ from that of neurological patients diagnosed as having "diffuse" brain damage. This suggests that the changes that occur with normal aging do not result in a generalized deterioration in brain function. In fact, although the older subjects in general scored less well on factors of "nonverbal memory" and "psychomotor problem-solving," the older non-brain-damaged group scored even better than the younger non-brain-damaged group on the "language" abilities factor (Goldstein and Shelly, 1975). Schaie and Schaie (1977) also found that the pattern of older subjects' scores on the WAIS resembled that of patients with acute or chronic right hemispheric brain damage. Again, this pattern consisted of generally lowered scores on the Performance subtests relative to the Verbal subtests, the "classical aging pattern" described in earlier research. At the time, an alternative explanation in terms of brain function was offered, that is, that the right hemisphere is affected to a greater degree by the aging process than the left hemisphere, which results in a decline of visuoperceptual and visuoconstructional abilities relative to verbal abilities (Levy-Agresti and Sperry, 1968).

This hypothesis has gained further attention and support in recent years from a number of studies that compared the performance of young and elderly adults on a variety of neuropsychological measures. For example, Klisz (1978) reanalyzed the Halstead-Reitan Battery results reported earlier by Reed and Reitan (1963) for middle-aged and older normal subjects and found that the subtests that best discriminated between the two groups were those on which low scores are considered to be indicative of right hemisphere damage as opposed to left hemisphere or diffuse brain damage.

Goldstein and Shelly (1981) studied a heterogeneous group of 1247 neurological, psychiatric, and general medical Veterans Administration patients, divided into six age groups (20–70) as well as a subgroup of normal (non-neurologically impaired) patients (aged 20–60). They analyzed the patients' performance on a battery of tests, including a modified version of the Halstead-Reitan Battery, the WAIS, and some additional procedures utilizing a lateralization "key" developed by Russell et al. (1970). This "key" is a taxonomic decision rule system in which points are assigned as indicating left or right hemisphere or "diffuse" (i.e., bilateral) brain dysfunction based on score patterns. This system has reportedly been shown to predict lateralization of brain damage beyond the chance level when cross-validated against direct neurological evidence (Shelly and Goldstein, 1977). For example, a left hemisphere decision rule is "Performance on the Aphasia Test much lower than on the Spatial Relations Test," whereas a right hemisphere decision rule would be the reverse. Although they found a significant age effect for right hemisphere points, they also found a somewhat less powerful effect for left hemisphere points. The left hemisphere age effect was accounted for on the basis of reduced sensory perception on the right side of the body relative to the left. The right hemisphere age effect was accounted for on the basis of an increased tendency to suppress on the left side under double simultaneous stimulation and poorer performance with the left hand relative to the right hand on the Tactual Performance Test (TPT). This task requires a blindfolded subject to fit geometric forms into their respective positions on a board, first with the right, and then with the left hand. There is usually an improvement from the first to the second trial. Poorer performance with the left hand relative to the right represents a reversal of the expected normal pattern and is usually interpreted as a sign of right hemisphere dysfunction. This reversal of performance on the TPT with aging has been noted by a number of researchers. Price et al. (1980) reported this TPT reversal pattern in a group of high-level

functioning, retired school teachers. Their data suggest that the reversal was a result of decreased ability to organize and synthesize spatial relations, rather than a psychomotor slowing of the left hand or memory deficits per se.

Goldstein and Braun (1974) reported that more than 75% of normal subjects aged 70 to 79 showed a TPT reversal compared to less than 19% of subjects aged 30 to 40. They suggest that this finding may reflect a degeneration of interhemispheric fibers rather than a differential degradation of the cortical hemispheres themselves. However, this hypothesis is not tenable, since right hemisphere superiority for tactual recognition of forms and patterns and tactual perception of directionality in space has been demonstrated in commissurotomized patients (Milner and Taylow, 1972; Kuma, 1977), in patients with unilateral brain injury (Carmon and Benton, 1969; Fontenot and Benton, 1971), and in normal, right-handed subjects (Benton et al., 1973; Gardner et al., 1977; Dodds, 1978).

Other researchers have offered alternative interpretations for data thought to be suggestive of right hemisphere dysfunction in aging. For example, Benton et al. (1981) studied the performance of 162 healthy, well-educated volunteers ranging in age from 65 to 84 years on nine measures including temporal orientation (date, day of week, and time of day), Digit Span, Digit Sequence Learning (Digit Supraspan), Controlled Word Association (FAS), Logical Memory and Associate Learning from the Wechsler Memory Scale, Benton Visual Retention Test, Facial Recognition, and Judgment of Line Orientation. They calculated the frequency (percentage) of defective performances for the four age groups (65–69, 70–74, 75–79, and 80–84) based on a predetermined criterion, viz., a score below that achieved by 94 to 97% of the normative sample for the particular task. Using this approach, Benton et al. found that the tasks most sensitive to aging effects were tests of short-term visual memory (Benton Visual Retention Test), serial digit leaning (Digit Supraspan), and facial recognition and that, overall, there was a higher proportion of defective performances on the nonverbal tasks than on the verbal tasks. Based on the finding that the subjects did not produce as many defective scores on the line orientation judgment task (which the authors cite as the task most closely associated with the integrity of the right hemisphere), as on some of the other nonverbal tasks, they concluded that their results offer "little support" for the hypothesis that there is a relatively greater decline in right hemisphere function with increasing age. The lack of correspondence of performance on the line orientation test with the overall defective performance on the other nonverbal tasks, however, may be attributable to the different task demands. The line orientation task requires the matching of an always-present target to an array of lines, whereas the visuospaial tasks that were found to be most sensitive to aging involved a memory component, which adds to their complexity and places greater demands on right hemisphere processing. This has been noted to be the case for patients with frank right hemisphere lesions.

DeRenzi et al. (1977) found that spatial span scores (Corsi blocks) did not differentiate between side of lesion, whereas the introduction of a brief delay (placing a load on short-term memory) resulted in a significantly greater impairment for patients with right hemisphere lesions. Further, visual inspection of the data presented by Benton et al. (1981) reveals that defective performances on the line orientation task increase after the age of 75, which may suggest a differential age sensitivity to visuospatial task complexity. Finally, Benton et al. observed that the 80- to 84-year-old group showed a greater number of defective scores overall and on a wider range of tests, including verbal tasks, i.e., Logical Memory and Controlled Word Association, than the younger age groups. This suggested that a generalized decline in cognitive functioning does occur, but much later in the life-span.

Bigler et al. (1981) administered a battery including the WAIS and other tests (Wechsler Memory Scale, Category Test,

Trailmaking A&B, Reitan-Indiana Aphasia Screening Test, Reitan-Klove Sensory Perceptual Examination, and a motor examination, which included finger oscillation and grip strength) to a sample of healthy patients aged 16 to 75 who were referred to a neurological clinic for a "routine" examination. They reported significantly lower scores obtained by the oldest group for WAIS Performance total raw scores, but not for the Performance IQ, which was presumably related to the biasing of the age correction factor. This differs from previous studies, which, in general, have shown the age correction factor to be too small for older subjects. In particular, Digit Symbol was the only WAIS subtest on which the oldest group performed significantly worse than the younger group. They were also significantly slower on the Trailmaking tests. This led the authors to attribute these findings to psychomotor slowing, since they also found a trend, though nonsignificant, for bilaterally lowered finger oscillation scores in the older group. However, an apparent problem lies in the age groupings of the subjects, particularly for the oldest group (51–75), since previous studies have shown that the cognitive declines do not become apparent until at least the seventh or the eighth decade. By including younger adults in this group, significant findings may have been obscured for the older subjects, since there appears to be a trend, at least by visual inspection of the group means, for declining performance with age on the Block Design, Picture Arrangement, and Object Assembly subtests of the WAIS; this trend is consistent with the findings in previous studies.

Bak and Greene (1980) administered selected subtests of the Halstead-Reitan Battery, WAIS, and Wechsler Memory Scale to a sample of healthy adults and found that the younger group (mean age 55.6) performed better than the older group (mean age 74.9) on a number of these tests. Notably, the subtests on which the younger adults outperformed the older adults included nonverbal tasks, which rely heavily on visual attention and perception, visual recall, constructional ability, and manual speed (Visual Reproductions, Block Design, Digit Symbol, Trailmaking A&B, Tactual Performance Test, and a Finger Tapping Test). On the other hand, the older adults performed as well as the younger subjects on primarily verbal subtests (Speech Sounds Perception, Logical Memory, Associate Learning, Information, and Arithmetic). Bak and Greene, however, were reluctant to interpret their results as support for a differential decline of the right hemisphere, cautioning against generalizing from brain-behavior relationships noted in patients with frank brain damage to groups of normal individuals. They cite as evidence Elias's (1979) review of information-processing studies in normal subjects, in which Elias concluded that hemispheric asymmetries are not related to the processing of verbal and nonverbal stimuli per se, but rather to the strategies used to process the information.

"Qualitative" versus "Quantitative" Analyses

The studies reviewed thus far have all focused on elderly subjects' performance in terms of scores achieved on various measures. A focus on achievement alone, i.e., success or failure on given items of a test, however, may be misleading. Werner (1937) demonstrated that an individual may succeed or fail for a variety of reasons; an identical outcome may be achieved in different ways. Impairment in function may be evident in the strategy that an individual employs even though the final product may be correct.

A number of researchers (Ben-Yishay et al., 1971; Satz and Fletcher, 1981; Spiers, 1981, 1982; Kaplan, 1982) have pointed out that so-called "qualitative" observations, observations pertaining to the mode of approach and the characteristics of the process by which an individual produces a solution to a task, can be operationally defined and quantified and have high inter- and intra-rater reliability. This level of data analysis utilizes information that is otherwise disregarded in the more traditional quantitative psychometric approaches.

Ben-Yishay et al. (1971) employed an error analysis and strategy description approach to WAIS Block Design performance. They analyzed the style of performance (types of maneuvers produced en route to solution), constructional deviations, and activity rates for normal elderly subjects and right and left hemiplegic elderly patients. They reported high inter- and intra-rater reliability (.97 to .99) for their operationally defined categories of analysis. They found that right and left hemiplegics were equally impaired in terms of overall competence, that is, the number of designs correctly completed within the time limits. They differed, however, in terms of the frequency of types of errors. The left hemiplegics produced a significantly greater number of multiple constructional deviations (broken configurations such as the loss of the basic 2×2 or 3×3 square matrix) than did the right hemiplegics and elderly normals. The normal elderly group also produced more constructional deviations than the right hemiplegic group (72% of normal elderly vs. 62% of hemiplegics).

In another WAIS Block Design study of non-elderly, adult brain-damaged patients with a single focal brain lesion verified by CT scan, Kaplan et al. (1981) also found constructional deviations, which were a major feature of the performance of the right hemisphere lesion group, to be virtually absent in the left hemisphere lesion group. This differs from the finding of Ben-Yishay et al. (62% of right hemiplegics, i.e., presumed left hemisphere-lesioned patients with constructional deviations). The apparent discrepancy may be attributed to either differences in the mean ages of the groups (more elderly patients in the Ben-Yishay et al. study), and/or the criteria used to localize side of lesion. In the Ben-Yishay et al. study, patients were assigned to either the right or left hemisphere lesion group, based on the side of the hemiplegia. In addition, Kaplan's method for tracking performance from initiation to completion of the design revealed differences between strategies and errors produced by the two lesion groups. Patients preferentially started their designs in the hemi-attentional field ipsilateral to the lesion (i.e., the visual field contralateral to the non-compromised hemisphere) and made significantly more errors on those blocks in the hemi-attentional field contralateral to the lesioned hemisphere. These findings, together with those of Ben-Yishay et al., indicate that an impaired score on Block Design, per se, does not provide sufficient information for inferring lateralization of dysfunction. Further, the qualitative evidence from patients with lateralized lesions suggests that unimpaired performance depends upon the integrity of both cerebral hemispheres.

In another study, an analysis of the strategies used in correctly completed Wechsler Memory Scale Visual Reproductions (immediate recall) revealed a significant sex difference that otherwise would have been obscured (Albert and Kaplan, 1980). Women predominantly used an organized strategy, typical of young healthy adults, regardless of age, whereas men after the age of 65 tended to use a less well-integrated, more segmented approach.

A "qualitative" analysis has also been used for the Vocabulary subtest of the WAIS (Botwinick and Storandt, 1974). Although subjects were matched for their standardly derived scores, older subjects showed a decline in their use of high-level synonyms. Therefore, the common finding that verbal skills on the WAIS are preserved may be an artifact of the scoring system. This brings into question the validity of the "classical aging pattern."

"Frontal Systems" Effects

Nauta (1971), has demonstrated that the frontal lobes have reciprocal connections with the other major association cortices, limbic system, and subcortical structures in the thalamus and reticular formation. This frontal system is integrally involved in the mediation of arousal, vigilance, selective attention, ability to screen out irrelevant stimuli, the planning and initiation of complex activity, and the monitoring and adjustment of behavior through feedback (Luria, 1973). Certainly, the research on aging suggests degradation of these functions.

One of the most consistent findings of experimental research on aging has been that older subjects are impaired for tasks

that require the division of attention (Craik, 1977; Craik and Simon, 1980; Brinley and Fichter, 1970; Craik, 1973; Broadbent and Gregory, 1965; McGhie et al., 1965). Elderly subjects also are more easily distracted by extraneous stimuli and irrelevant cues on a variety of tasks. This deficit in selective attention has been demonstrated for simple stimulus (Layton, 1975), visual attention (Rabbitt, 1965; Jordan and Rabbitt, 1977), perceptual discrimination (Howell, 1972), perceptual grouping and visual scanning (Farkas and Hoyer, 1980), multiple recognition learning (Kausler and Klein, 1978), hidden-word identification (Schneider et al., 1977), and problem-solving (Hoyer et al., 1979).

Another approach to neuropsychological research on aging has been to administer tests that have been shown to correlate with more circumscribed brain lesions. For example, Farver (1975) administered the Boston Parietal Lobe Battery (Goodglass and Kaplan, 1972) and the Hooper Visual Organization Test (Lezak, 1976), a mental object assembly task, to a population of non-hospitalized elderly subjects. She found no impairments on the subtests of right-left orientation, verbal finger localization, and arithmetic, functions that have been associated with the integrity of the left parietal lobe (Critchley, 1966; Gerstmann, 1971; Strub and Geschwind, 1974). However, Farver did find age-related changes on recall of stick constructions, three-dimensional block constructions, clock setting, visual finger identification, and the Hooper Visual Organization Test, which all have a major visuospatial component and have been associated with right hemispheric dysfunction. This pattern of spared and impaired performances led Farver to conclude that right parietal functions decline with age, whereas left parietal functions do not. However, the conspicuous absence of right parietal signs (e.g., left hemi-inattention) on such visuospatial tasks as drawing familiar objects to command or to copy, and the absence of failures in map localization, suggested the need for a reanalysis of the errors on the "right parietal" tasks (Albert and Kaplan, 1980). Consequently, it was determined that the errors primarily consisted of failure to reverse right-left on the examiner facing the subject (echopraxia), perseveration, segmentation, that is, a focus on features or fragments with a consequent inability to integrate component parts into a whole (on the Hooper Visual Organization Test), features commonly observed in patients with right frontal system dysfunction (Luria, 1973), rather than right parietal involvement.

Preliminary results of a Dementia Screening Test developed by Albert and Kaplan (1977) and administered to 2242 subjects in the Framingham Heart Study* provide evidence for age-related impairments resembling deficits that are characteristic of patients with right frontal system pathology. Utilizing a descriptive analysis developed by Kaplan for the evaluation of Wechsler Memory Scale Visual Reproductions, Veroff (1980) reported an increase in prevalence of segmentation and perseveration, features that have been described as pathognomonic of frontal lobe dysfunction.

Memory and Learning

One of the most common complaints among the elderly is of forgetfulness (Abrams, 1978). In a survey of a general community, more than one-half of the persons over age 60 reported noticeable memory problems (Lowenthal et al., 1967). Specifically, they described a decline in memory for recent events and information, with relative preservation of remote memory.

Research tends to support this observation. A number of studies using a variety of paradigms and sampling techniques have demonstrated learning deficits among elderly subjects once the amount of information exceeded their primary memory span (Craik, 1977). A widely held explanation for this deficit is that the elderly are deficient in their depth of processing of information. It has been demonstrated that older subjects are less efficient and

less likely to spontaneously utilize organizational, semantic encoding strategies (Hulicka and Grossman, 1967; Eysenck, 1974; Canestrari, 1968; Erber et al., 1980; Pezdek, 1980; Puglisi, 1980; Howard et al., 1981) and utilize less active and less efficient rehearsal strategies (Sanders et al., 1980).

Pezdek (1980) examined life-span differences in semantic integration of pictures and sentences in memory. Of the four groups studied (third graders, sixth graders, high school students, and adults over the age of 60) only the sixth graders and high school students were found to employ semantic integration strategies spontaneously. The third graders and older adults showed no evidence of deeper processing of more semantic information. This suggests that the spontaneous use of strategies for effective memory processing develops within the life-span, but that with aging, there is a reversion to developmentally less differentiated, more superficial modes of processing, that is, a pull to the formal or perceptually prominent features of the stimulus. This "stimulus boundedness" is also a feature characteristically seen in the performance of patients with frontal lobe dysfunction (Goodglass and Kaplan, 1979).

Some researchers have reported that this encoding deficiency in the elderly can be compensated for, in some instances, by providing organizational categories or having the older subjects verbalize their own strategies (Crovitz, 1966; Hulicka and Grossman, 1967; Hultsch, 1969, 1971, 1975; Rabbitt et al., 1969; Canestrari, 1968; Treat and Reese, 1976).

In addition to impaired encoding, deficits in the retrieval of information have also been demonstrated in the elderly, particularly when older subjects are required to initiate spontaneous retrieval strategies in recall (Ceci and Tabor, 1981) as opposed to recognition (Schonfeld and Robertson, 1966), although deficits in recognition have also been reported (Botwinick and Storandt, 1974; Erber, 1974; Wickelgren, 1975). For comprehensive reviews of the literature on memory in the elderly, the reader is referred to Craik (1977) and Poon et al. (1980).

---

*This normative aging study component was directed by Drs. Martin Albert and Edith Kaplan in association with P. Wolf, A. Veroff, W. Rosen, T. Dawber, W. Kannel, and P. MacNamara.

Problem-Solving

A decline in problem-solving and concept formation ability in the elderly has been demonstrated on a variety of tasks (Arenberg, 1968; Rabbitt, 1977; Giambra and Arenberg, 1980; Bigler et al., 1981). Typically, these complex, multi-factorial tasks variously require the maintenance of focused attention; short-term memory; the ability to generate hypotheses; planning for contingencies; modifying responses on the basis of feedback; and initiating, sustaining, and shifting response sets. It is, therefore, not surprising that the elderly have difficulty on these tasks, since deficits in any one or more of the above component functions is likely to impair performance. Older adults appear to have reduced efficiency of information-seeking strategies, which tend to be haphazard and redundant (Jerome, 1962; Denney and Denney, 1974), and reduced response set flexibility, since they tend to perseverate (Heglin, 1956; Wetherick, 1965; Offenbach, 1974). These deficits in elderly normals are strikingly similar to those described in patients with frontal pathology (Luria, 1973).

Verbal Fluency

Verbal fluency is most profoundly impaired in patients with lesions in the language zone of the left hemisphere, in non-aphasic patients with lesions in the frontal region, particularly in the left hemisphere, anterior to Broca's area (Benton, 1968; Milner, 1974), and in the elderly (Veroff, 1980; Rosen, 1980).

Subjects in the Framingham Heart Study were given the Controlled Word Association Test of the Multilingual Aphasia Examination (Benton and Hamsher, 1977). On this task, the subject is required to produce as many words as possible (exclusive of proper nouns, numbers, and same word with different suffixes) for the letters "F," "A," and "S" (1-minute/letter). The performance of 732 men and women with a ninth to twelfth grade education, who ranged in age from 55 to 89, showed a marked age-related decline in the number of acceptable words produced. Errors con-

sisted of perseverations and loss of category set, such as introducing words beginning with "F" when "A" words were required. In addition, males performed more poorly than females (Veroff, 1980).

Rosen (1980) administered the same test using the letters "C," "F," "L" and a more restricted category, the Animal Naming subtest of the Boston Diagnostic Aphasia Examination (Goodglass and Kaplan, 1972), to three groups of mid-80-year-old nursing home residents ("normal" elderly and elderly with mild and moderate to severe dementia of the Alzheimer type). Only the normal elderly were helped by the greater structure of a more restricted category, and they produced significantly more animal words than words beginning with a given letter. Two sequential strategies were noted for the letter words, semantic (e.g. cantaloupe, caramels, crackers, etc., for the letter C) and phonemic (e.g. clear, clean, class, etc.). Clinically, we have noted that patients with frontal system pathology tend to produce a limited number of words and use a phonemic strategy. Dominated by phonemic features, they may produce such errors as "phone" while generating words for the letter "F."

Electrophysiological Evidence

Although early EEG data indicated a slowing of activity over the left temporal region in the elderly (Obrist and Busse, 1960), recent electrophysiological evidence supports neuropsychological data that suggest an age-related degradation in the frontal system. Specifically, a reduction in the amplitude of some components of evoked potentials that appear over frontal areas has been shown in the elderly (Tecce, 1978; Michalewski et al., 1980; Pfefferbaum et al., 1980; Ford and Pfefferbaum, 1980). Ford and Pfefferbaum (1980) have reported preliminary results of a study correlating event-related potentials (ERP) with CT findings, which suggests the presence of structural changes associated with electrophysiological changes in the frontal areas. A more comprehensive review of electrophysiological correlates of aging is presented elsewhere in this volume.

Clinical and Methodological Issues

A variety of factors affect the findings in aging research. Biases may be introduced by differences between cross-sectional and longitudinal sampling as well as inconsistencies regarding the assignment of subjects to age groups. Efforts to ensure a representative sample of the normal population result, on the one hand, in a too careful screening for the healthy sample. This may result in an extraordinary group that is considerably superior to a more typical peer group with common systemic disease. On the other hand, a less careful screening may result in the inclusion of individuals with cardiovascular disease, diabetes, and/or psychiatric disorders (particularly depression), which are known to affect cognitive functions. Differences with regard to reduced peripheral sensory acuity are not always identified and compensated for. Significant variables that have been commonly neglected, such as a history of developmental learning disability and alcohol and drug abuse, may similarly distort age effects. An individual's handedness has more recently been considered a relevant variable. However, on given tasks, the individual's hand preference has been found to be less important than familial handedness (Healey, 1981). Also, individual differences with regard to native talents, for example, artistic, musical, literary, over and above educational, occupational, and cultural experience are not always considered.

Finally, since most standard tests of cognitive function were constructed for younger subjects and are not as cognitively relevant to the tasks of daily living for the elderly, their face validity must be questioned. Further, specific items rich in detail that may be suitable for the younger adult handicap the elderly subject who is more susceptible to distraction by irrelevant information.

Guidelines for a Neuropsychological Evaluation of the Elderly

The variables identified above are as relevant for the clinician as they are for the researcher. The importance of an approach to test administration and analysis of behavior that focuses on the process by which a performance is achieved, that is, analysis of errors and description of strategies, should be underscored. This approach has been most eloquently articulated by Luria and Majovski (1977, p. 964).

Qualification of a symptom is never construed as the mechanistic application of a standardized test battery with formal quantitative interpretation of the results. In contradistinction, it is a clinically creative effort requiring from the neuropsychologist both critical thinking and readiness to reject initial hypotheses if they conflict with new data obtained or if there is confounding of the results.

This clinical approach is particularly suited to the examination of elderly individuals. It permits the flexibility necessary to respond to the variability in stamina, motivation, and susceptibility to stress and anxiety so commonly encountered in this population.

The selection of specific tests should sample functions associated with lateralized cortical regions (frontal, temporal, parietal, occipital), as well as those related to subcortical structures. The neuropsychological evaluation should provide a profile of intact and impaired functions, which could be compared with profiles obtained in younger adults and those of brain-damaged patients (below age 60) with verified structural lesions (for a description of recommended tasks, see Albert and Kaplan, 1980).

Advancing neurotechnology holds the promise that it may soon be possible to closely observe the dynamic interaction of structure and function in the central nervous system. With the development of more sensitive and relevant tasks, operationally defined error analyses and strategy descriptions, and consideration given to significant subject variables, adequate normative data may be obtained. Such a data base will serve clinicians in their efforts to evaluate the significance of cognitive changes in older individuals and should further our understanding of the neurobehavioral consequences of aging.

Acknowledgment

We wish to express our gratitude to Paul A. Spiers for his thoughtful reading, helpful suggestions, and assistance in the preparation of this chapter.

References

Abrams, M. (1978). Beyond three score and ten: A first report on a survey of the elderly. Age Concern Publications, Mitcham, Surrey.

Albert, M.L. and Kaplan, E. (1977). Dementia Screening Battery, unpublished test. Boston V.A. Hospital.

Albert, M.S. and Kaplan, E. (1980). Organic implications of neuropsychological deficits in the elderly. In New Directions in Memory and Aging, L. Poon, J. Fozard, L. Cermak, D. Arenberg, and L.J. Thompson, Eds. Erlbaum, Hillsdale, N.J.

Arenberg, D. (1968). Concept problem solving in young and old adults. J. Gerontol. 23, 279–282.

Axelrod, S. and Cohen, L.D. (1961). Senescence and embedded figure performances in vision and touch. Perceptual Motor Skills 12, 283–288.

Bak, J. and Greene, R. (1980). Changes in neuropsychological functioning in an aging population. J. Consullt. Clin. Psychol. 48(3), 395–399.

Benton, A.L. (1968). Differential behavioral effects in frontal lobe disease. Neuropsychologia 6, 53–60.

Benton, A.L. (1973). The measurement of aphasic disorders In Aspects patologicos del lengage, A. Caceres Valasquez, Ed. Lima, Centro Neuropsyicologico.

Benton, A.L., Eslinger, P., and Damasio, A. (1981). Normative observations on neuropsychological test performances in old age. J. Clin. Neuropsychol. 3 (1), 33–42.

Benton, A.L. and Hamsher, K. (1977). Multilingual Aphasia Examination. University of Iowa, Iowa City.

Benton, A.L., Levin, H., and Varney, N. (1973). Tactile perception of direction in normal subjects. Neurology 23, 1248–1250.

Ben-Yishay, Y., Diller, L., Mendleberg, I., Gordon, D., and Gerstman, L. (1971). Similarities and differences in block design performance between older normal and brain injured persons: a task analysis. J. Abn. Psychol. 78, 17–25.

Bigler, E., Steinman, D., and Newton, J. (1981). Clinical assessment of cognitive deficit in neurologic disorder 1: Effects of age and degenerative disease. Clin. Neuropsychol. 3, 5–13.

Birren, J., Botwinick, J., Weiss, A., and Morrison, D. (1963). Interrelations of mental and perceptual tests given to healthy elderly men. In Human Aging: A Biological and Behavioral Study, J.E. Birren, R.N. Butter, S.W. Greenhouse, L. Sokoleff, and M. Yarrow, Eds. Government Printing Office, Washington, D.C.

Birren, J. and Schaie, K. (1977). Handbook of the Psychology of Aging. Van Nostrand Reinhold, New York.

Botwinick, J. (1977). Intellectual abilities. In Handbook of the Psychology of Aging, J.E. Birren and K.W. Schaie, Eds. Van Nostrand Reinhold, New York.

Botwinick, J., Robbin, J.S., and Brinley, J.F. (1959). Reorganization of perceptions with age. J. Gerontol. 14, 85–88.

Botwinick, J. and Storandt, M. (1974). Vocabulary ability in later life. J. Gen. Psychol. 125, 303–308.

Brinley, J. and Fichter, J. (1970). Performance deficits in the elderly in relation to memory load and set. J. Gerontol. 25, 30–35.

Broadbent, D.E. and Gregory, M. (1965). Some confirmatory results on age differences in memory for simultaneous stimulation. Br. J. Psychol. 56, 77–80.

Canestrari, R.E. (1968). Age changes in acquisition. In Human Aging and Behavior, G.A. Talland, Ed. Academic Press, New York.

Carmon, A. and Benton, A. (1969). Tactile perception of direction and number in patients with unilateral cerebral disease. Neurology 19, 525–532.

Cattell, R.B. (1963). Theory of fluid and crystallized intelligence: A critical experiment. J. Ed. Psychol. 54, 1–22.

Ceci, S. and Tabor, L. (1981). Flexibility and memory: Are the elderly really less flexible. Exp. Aging Res. 7 (2), 147–158.

Cerella, J., Poon, J., and Flozard, J. (1981). Mental rotation and age reconsidered. J. Gerontol. 35 (5), 620–624.

Craik, F.I.M. (1973). Signal detection analysis of age differences in divided attention. Paper presented at the meeting of the American Psychological Association, Montreal.

Craik, F.I.M. (1977). Age differences in human memory. In Handbook of the Psychology of Aging, J.E. Birren, and K.W. Schaie, Eds. Van Nostrand Reinhold, New York.

Craik, F.I.M. and Simon, E. (1980). The roles of attention and depth of processing in understanding age differences in memory. In New Directions in Aging and Memory, L.W. Poon, J.L. Fozard, L.S. Cermak, and L.W. Thompson, Eds. Erlbaum, Hillsdale, N.J.

Critchley, M. (1966). The Parietal Lobes. Arnold, London.

Crovitz, B. (1966). Recovering a learning deficit in the aged. J. Gerontol. 21, 236–238.

Danziger, W. and Salthouse, T. (1978). Age and the perception of incomplete figures. Exp. Aging. Res. 4 (1), 67–80.

Denney, N.W. and Denney, D.R. (1974). Modeling effects on questioning strategies of the elderly. Develop. Psychol. 10, 458.

DeRenzi, E., Faglione, P., and Previdi, P., (1977). Spatial memory and hemispheric locus of lesion. Cortex 13, 424–433.

Dodds, A.G. (1978). Hemispheric differences in tactuospatial processing. Neuropsychologia 16, 247–254.

Doppelt, J. and Wallace,W. (1955). Standardization of the Wechsler Adult Intelligence Scale for older persons. J. Abn. Soc. Psychol. 51, 312–330.

Eisdorfer, C., Busse, E., and Cohen, L. (1959). The WAIS performance of an aged sample: The relationship between verbal and performance I.Q.s. J. Gerontol. 14, 197–201.

Elias, J. (1979). Age, sex and hemisphere asymmetry differences induced by a concurrent memory processing task. Exp. Aging Res. 5(3), 217–237.

Erber, J.T. (1974). Age differences in recognition memory. J. Gerontol. 29, 177–181.

Erber, J., Herman, T., and Botwinick, J. (1980). Age differences in memory as a function of depth of processing. Exp. Aging Res. 6(4), 341–348.

Eysenck, M.W. (1974). Age difference in incidental learning. Develop. Psychol. 10, 936–941.

Farkas, M. and Hoyer, W. (1980). Processing consequences of perceptual grouping in selective attention. J. Gerontol. 35(2), 207–216.

Farver, P. (1975). Performance of normal older adults on a test battery designed to measure parietal lobe functions. Unpublished masters thesis, Boston University.

Fontenot, D.J. and Benton, A.L. (1971). Tactile perception of direction in relation to hemispheric locus of lesion. Neuropsychologia 9, 83–88.

Ford, J. and Pfefferbaum, A. (1980). The utility of brain potentials in determining age-related changes in central nervous system and cognitive functioning. In Aging in the 1980's, L.W. Poon, Ed. American Psychological Association, Washington, D.C.

Gardner, E.B., English, A.G., Flannery, B.M., Hartnett, M.B., McCormick, J.K., and Wilhelmy, B.B. (1977). Shape recognition accuracy and response latency in a bilateral tactile task. Neurospsychologia 15, 607–616.

Gerstmann, J. (1971). On the symptomatology of cerebral lesions in the transitional area of the lower parietal and middle occipital convolutions. In M.D. Wilkins and I.A. Brody, Gerstmann's Syndrome. Arch. Neurol. Vol. 24, 475–476.

Giambra, L. and Arenberg, D. (1980). Problem solving, concept learning and aging. In Aging in the 1980's, L. Poon, Ed. American Psychological Association, Washington, D.C., pp. 253–259.

Gilbert, J.C. and Levee, D.F. (1965). Age differences on the Bender Visual-Motor Gestalt Test and Archimedes Spiral Test. Gerontology 2, 196–198.

Goldstein, G. and Braun, L. (1974). Reversal of expected transfer as a function of increased age. Percept. Motor Skills 38, 1139–1145.

Goldstein, G. and Shelly, C. (1981). Does the right hemisphere age more rapidly than the left? J. Clin. Neuropsychol. 3(1), 67–78.

Goldstein, S. and Shelly, C. (1975). Similarities and differences between psychological deficits in aging and brain damage. J. Gerontol. 30, 448–455.

Goodglass, H. and Kaplan, E. (1972). The Assessment of Aphasia and Related Disorders. Lea and Febiger, Philadelphia.

Goodglass, H. and Kaplan, E. (1979). Assessment of cognitive deficits in the brain injured patient. In Handbook of Neurobiology, Vol. 2, Neuropsychology, M.S. Gazzaniga, Ed. Plenum Press, New York.

Healey, J.M. (1981). Individual differences in the patterning and degree of cerebral lateralization of cognitive functioning. Unpublished doctoral dissertation, City University of New York.

Heath, H.A. and Orbach, J. (1963). Reversibility of the necker-cube: IV. Responses of elderly people. Percep. Motor Skills 17, 625–626.

Heglin, H.J. (1956). Problem solving set in different age groups. J. Gerontol. 11, 310–317.

Horn, J.L. and Cattell, R. (1967). Age differences in fluid and crystallized intelligence. Acta Psychol. 26, 107–129.

Howard, D., McAndrews, M., and Lasaga, M. (1981). Semantic priming of lexical decisions in young and old adults. J. Gerontol. 36(6), 707–714.

Howell, S.C. (1972). Familiarity and complexity in perceptual recognition. J. Gerontol. 27, 364–371.

Hoyer, W.J., Rebok, G.W., and Sved, S.M. (1979). Effects of varying irrelevant information on adult age differences in problem solving. J. Gerontol. 14, 553–560.

Hulicka, I. (1978). Cognitive Functioning in Late Adulthood, American Psychological Association Master Lecture Series. American Psychological Association, Washington, D.C.

Hulicka, I.M. and Grossman, J.L. (1967). Age group comparisons for the use of mediators in paired associate learning. J. Gerontol. 22, 46–51.

Hultsch, D.F. (1969). Adult age differences in the organization of free recall. Develop. Psychol. 1, 673–678.

Hultsch, D.F. (1971). Adult age differences in free classification and free recall. Develop. Psychol. 4, 338–342.

Hultsch, D.F. (1975). Adult age differences in retrieval: Trace dependent and cue dependent forgetting. Develop. Psychol. 11, 197–201.

Jerome, E.A. (1962). Decay of heuristic processes in the aged. In Social and Psychological Aspects of Aging, C. Tibbets and W. Donahuc, Eds. Columbia University Press, New York, pp. 802–823.

Jordan, T.C. and Rabbitt, P.M.A. (1977). Response times to stimuli of increasing complexity as a function of aging. Br. J. Psychol. 68, 189–201.

Kaplan, E. (1982). Process and achievement revisited. In Toward a Holistic Developmental Psychology, S. Wapner and B. Kaplan, Eds. Erlbaum, Hillsdale, N.J.

Kaplan, E., Palmer, E.P., Weinstein, C., Baker, E., and Weintraub, S. (1981). Block design: A brain-behavior based analysis. Paper presented at International Neuropsychological Society, Bergen, Norway.

Kausler, D.H. and Klein, D.M. (1978). Age differences in processing relevant versus irrelevant simuli in multiple-item recognition learning. J. Gerontol. 33, 87–93.

Klisz, D. (1978). Neuropsychological evaluation of older persons. In The Clinical Psychology of Aging, M. Storandt, E. Siegler and M. Elias, Eds. Plenum Press, New York.

Klodin, V. (1975). Verbal facilitation of perceptual-intergrative performance in relation to age. Unpublished doctoral dissertation, Washington University, St. Louis.

Krauss, I., Quayhagen, M., and Schaie, K. (1980). Spatial rotation in the elderly: Performance factors. J. Gerontol. 35(3), 199–206.

Kumar, S. (1977). Short-term memory for a non-verbal tactual task after cerebral commissurotomy. Cortex 13, 55–61.

Layton, B. (1975). Perceptual noise and aging. Psychol. Bull. 82, 875–883.

Levy-Agresti, J. and Sperry, R.W. (1968). Differential perception capacities in major and minor hemispheres. Proc. Nl. Acad. Sci. USA 61, 1151.

Lezak, M.D. (1976). Neuropsychological Assessment. Oxford United Press, New York.

Lowenthal, M.F., Berkman, P., and Associates. (1967). Aging and Mental Disorder in San Francisco. San Francisco, Jossey-Bass.

Luria, A.R. (1973). The Working Brain. Penguin Press, London.

Luria, A.R. and Majovski, L.V. (1977). Basic approaches used in American and Soviet clinical neuropsychology. Am. Psychol. 32, 959–968.

McGhie, A., Chapman, T., and Lawson, T. (1965). Changes in immediate memory with age. Br. J. Psychol. 56, 69–75.

Michalewski, H., Thompson, L., Smith, D., Patterson, J., Bowman, T., Litzelman, D., and Brent, G. (1980). Age differences in the contingent negative variation (CNV): Reduced frontal activity in the elderly. J. Gerontol. 35(4), 542–549.

Milner, B. (1964). Some effects of frontal lobectomy in man. In The Frontal Granular Cortex and Behavior, J.M. Warren and K. Akert, Eds. McGraw-Hill, New York.

Milner, B. and Taylor, L. (1972). Right hemisphere superiority in tactile pattern recognition after cerebral commissurotomy: Evidence for nonverbal memory. Neuropsychologia 10, 1–15.

Nauta, W.J.H. (1971). Neural associations of the frontal cortex. Acta Neurobiol. Exp., 32, 125–140.

Obrist, W.D. and Busse, E.W. (1960). Temporal lobe EEG abnormalities in normal senescence. Electroencephalogr. Clin. Neurophysiol. 12, 244.

Offenbach, S.I. (1974). A developmental study of hypothesis testing and cue selection strategies. Develop. Psychol. 10, 484–490.

Ohta, R., Walsh, D., and Krauss, I. (1981). Spatial perspective-taking ability in young and elderly adults. Exp. Aging Res. 7, 45–63.

Overall, J.E. and Gorham, D.R. (1972). Organicity versus old age in objective and projective test performance. J. Consult. Clin. Psychol. 39, 98–105.

Pezdek, K. (1980). Life-span differences in semantic integration of pictures and sentences in memory. Child Develop. 51, 720–729.

Pfefferbaum, A., Ford, J., Roth, W., and Kopell, B. (1980). Age-related changes in auditory event-related potentials. Electroencephalogr. Clin. Neurophysiol. 49, 266–276.

Plutchik, R., Conte, H.R., Weiner, M.B., and Teresi, J. (1978). Studies of body image. IV. Figure drawings in normal and abnormal geriatric and nongeriatric groups. J. Gerontol. 33, 68–75.

Poon, L., Fozard, J., Cermak, L., Arenberg, D., and Thompson, L. (1980). New Directions in Memory and Aging. Erlbaum, Hillsdale, N.J.

Price, L.J., Fein, G., and Feinberg, I. (1980). Neuropsychological assessment of cognitive function in the elderly. In Aging in the 1980's, Leonard W. Poon, Ed. American Psychological Association, Washington, D.C.

Puglisi, J. (1980). Semantic encoding in older adults as evidenced by release from proactive inhibition. J. Gerontol. 35(5), 743–745.

Rabbitt, P.M.A. (1965). An age-decrement in the ability to ignore irrelevent information. J. Gerontol. 20, 233–238.

Rabbitt, P. (1977). Changes in problem-solving ability in older age. In Handbook of the Psychology of Aging, J.E. Birren and K.W. Schaie, Eds. Van Rostrand, New York.

Rabbitt, P.M.A., Clancy, M.C., and Vyas, S.M. (1969). Proceedings of XVII International Congress of Gerontology, Washington, D.C.

Reed, H.B.C. and Reitan, R.M. (1963). A comparison of the effects of the normal aging process with the effects of organic brain damage on adaptive abilities. J. of Gerontol. 18, 177–189.

Rosen, W. (1980). Verbal fluency in aging and dementia. J. Clin. Neuropsychol. 2(2), 135–140.

Russell, E.W., Neuringer, C., and Goldstein, G. (1970). Assessment of Brain Damage: A Neuropsychological Key Approach. Wiley, New York.

Sanders, R., Murphy, M., Schmitt, F., and Walsh, K. (1980). Age differences in free recall rehearsal strategies. J. Gerontol. 35(4), 550–558.

Satz, P. and Fletcher, J. (1981). Emergent trends in neuropsychology: An overview. J. Consult. Clin. Psychol. 49, 851–865.

Schaie, K.W. and Schaie, T.P. (1977). Clinical assessment and aging. In Handbook of the Psychology of Aging, J.E. Birren and K.W. Schaie, Eds. Van Nostrand Reinhold, New York.

Schonfield, D. and Robertson, E. (1966). The coding and sorting of digits and symbols by an elderly sample. J. Gerontol. 23, 318–323.

Schneider, N.G., Gritz, E.R., and Jarvick, M.E. (1977). Age differences in simple paced tasks of attention and perception. Gerontology 23, 142–147.

Shelly, C.H. and Goldstein, G. (1977). A cross-validation of the Russell Leuringer and Goldstein neuropsychological keys. Paper presented at First European Conference, International Neuropsychological Society, Oxford, England.

Spiers, P.A. (1981). Have they come to praise Luria or to bury him? The Luria-Nebraska Battery controversy. J. Consult. Clin. Psychol. 49, 331–341.

Spiers, P.A. (1982). The Luria-Nebraska Neuropsychological Battery revisited: A theory in practice or just practicing? J. Consult Clin Psychol. 50, 301–306.

Storandt, M. (1977). Age, ability level, and method of administering and scoring the WAIS. J. Gerontol. 32, 175–178.

Strub, R. and Geschwind, N. (1974). Gerstmann syndrome without aphasia. Cortex 10, 375–387.

Tecce, J.J. (1978). Contingent negative variation and attention functions in the aged. In Event-Related Brain Potentials in Man, E. Caltaway, P. Tueting, and S.H. Koslow, Eds. Academic Press, New York.

Treat, N.J. and Reese, H.W. (1976). Age, pacing and imagery in paired-associate learning. Develop. Psychol. 12, 119–124.

Varney, N. and Benton, A.L. (1975). Tactile perception of direction in relation to handedness and familial handedness. Neuropsychologia 13, 449–454.

Veroff, A. (1980). The neuropsychology of aging: Qualitative analysis of visual reproductions. Psychol. Res. 41, 249–268.

Wechsler, D. (1958). The Measurement and Appraisal of Adult Intelligence, 4th Ed. Williams & Wilkins, Baltimore.

Werner, H. (1937). Process and achievement:

A basic problem of education and developmental psychology. Harvard Ed. Rev., May, 1937.

Wetherick, N.E. (1965). Changing an established concept: A comparison of the ability of young, middle aged and old subjects. Gerontologia 11, 82–95.

Wickelgren, W.A. (1975). Age and storage dynamics in continuous recognition memory. Develop. Psychol. 11, 165–169.

Zaks, P. and Labouvie-Vief, G. (1980). Spatial perspective taking and referential communication skills in the elderly: A training study. J. Gerontol. 35(2), 217–224.

13. Language in Aging

LORAINE K. OBLER

MARTIN L. ALBERT

With advanced age, even in the healthy person, problems of language communication may develop. More than before, we cannot remember someone's name or the precise word we are looking for. Sometimes we forget we have already told someone a story, and tell it again. If we become hard of hearing, our daily communication requires more effort, both for us and for those we deal with. If we have demonstrable brain damage we may become aphasic or demented, with increased difficulties in comprehension and production of speech.

Not every older person develops language disturbance, of course, perhaps not even minor anomias. But as the percentage of the population with language disturbances grows, neurologists must develop criteria for distinguishing the language changes of normal aging from those changes that indicate neurological illness. The clinical characterizations that follow are the result of our 6 years of study in the field of language in aging and dementia. There is currently no standard battery of tests for examining language in aging; we have included as an appendix the one we have developed, on which our clinical profiles are based.

Patterns of Language in Normal Aging

Naming, discourse, and comprehension should be evaluated. Most distressing of the signs of normal aging is difficulty in remembering the names of people. On the naming tasks we use clinically, it is common to see increase in performance through age sixty, and then a gradual decrease over the seventh decade, and a sharper decline among the group of seventy-year-olds (Goodglass, 1980). This is true for both low frequency verbs and nouns, although individuals will as a rule perform somewhat better with verbs than with nouns (Obler et al., 1981). With naming tasks in healthy individuals, one must consider premorbid ability. This includes educational level, previous occupation, and reading habits.

Response time for naming will increase with age; people may give a wrong word on their way to finding the correct word, but the healthy person will know when the correct response has been given. If the normal elderly person cannot find the correct word without help, s/he will respond quite quickly if the first sounds of the word are provided as a cue.

In discourse, we have found an increased elaborateness of language, especially written language, with increasing age after age 50 (Obler, 1980). The written sentences of healthy old people are more syntactically complex, and contain more modifiers than do those of 50-year-olds. Indeed it is not uncommon to see a 50-year-old writing sentences that are not fleshed out with simple modifiers, such as "the." In a 70-year-old, however, such a paragraph would be cause for concern.

Comprehension in the healthy elderly individual may decrease only in the event of hearing loss. Healthy hard-of-hearing subjects will know when they have not heard something well and will be able to make an intelligent guess about the meaning of a statement or question on the basis of the context. In noisy conditions, comprehension will break down for the presbycusic person, so clinicians should use as quiet a testing place as possible. (This will permit more accurate interpretation of the patient's comprehension abilities and, of course, prevent frustration.)

Clinical Features of Language Pathology in the Elderly

Subcortical Dementias

In the subcortical dementias, such as in patients with Parkinson's disease or progressive supranuclear palsy (PSP), conversation with the patient may be difficult because of the patient's dysarthria. When the examiner understands what it is that the patient is saying, however, s/he will note that the discourse is appropriate in content, but it may be somewhat brief due to the great effort in production. For the most part, responses will be informative, although in certain instances one word will have been substituted for another (semantic paraphasias), and there may be digression from the point. In PSP, phrasing of the words in a sentence may be markedly impaired; however, the sentence as a whole is meaningful. Questions will be answered appropriately and often with specific details.

Comprehension is well spared in these patients, as is repetition. In reciting automatic speech series, patients will start to mumble as they run through the series at an increasingly faster pace. If one stops them and obliges them to slow down, they will still speed up. Sometimes one can use externalized pacing, like tapping a rhythm loudly on the table, to enable the patient to produce the appropriate items.

These patients may have some difficulty with idioms and proverb interpretation.

Their responses are fairly concrete, even if they are well educated.

It is in the writing sample that we see the most language disturbance with these patients. Although they can produce materials of sentence length, the materials invariably evidence perseverations (that is, repetition of letters), omission of letters, and omission of certain word endings. As to reading aloud, these patients will have no linguistic difficulty beyond their dysarthria; but they may have reading comprehension disturbances with long passages.

Mild Alzheimer's Disease

Although one finds varying language patterns in this form of cortical dementia, as we have documented elsewhere (Auerbach et al., forthcoming), we shall speak here only of the predominant pattern, which accounts for about 75% of the patients we see.

In the early stages of Alzheimer's dementia, those patients who have a language disturbance will evidence it in their naming abilities, both on explicit naming tasks and also in discourse. These patients will have a substantial number of pauses in which they search for the correct word as they speak conversationally, or tell a story. They will sometimes substitute a word that is not quite the one they mean for the word they intend. Although they may often realize that they have not produced the intended word, and try to correct their error, they will not always do so. In telling a story, these patients may digress from their point, but, they will, as a rule, pull themselves back to it. Their discourse may be overly long and may dwell on topics that are not exactly appropriate to the questions asked. At this stage, however, the discourse is still informative, even if one cannot get prompt and precise answers to very specific questions.

In discourse, these patients may indicate that they are not sure of what they are saying, by incorporating "perhaps" or "maybe" or other indicators into their speech. We have found that younger dementing patients with naming problems cover their mouth with their hand, and so become unintelligible, in response to specific questions. These patients will as a rule answer two out of three of the questions: How old are you? When were you born? and What year is it now?

When asked to tell a tale, such as Little Red Riding Hood, these patients claim that they do not remember it. If you start them on it by saying "Once upon a time there was a little girl, and her name was Little Red Riding Hood," they may provide elements from another tale, for example telling you "and there were three bears." Some will recall the appropriate story, but rarely will a patient even in the early stages of Alzheimer's disease be able to tell a coherent tale with all the appropriate elements.

Naming, as we said above, is impaired in this group, and word list generation is also below the norm. These patients will have less facility than normal subjects in their ability to generate a list of animals and to name words starting with a certain letter. They are usually able to keep in set, however, and to return to it, if they give an item that is out of set. They may repeat one or two items and catch themselves doing it; they are unlikely to be able to continue providing items after one minute.

Comprehension in patients with early stage Alzheimer's dementia is still quite spared. If they are attending to the items, they will do quite well on single sentence questions, even those with complex syntax. When required to listen to a brief story and asked questions about it, however, they will get some, but not all answers correct.

On a repetition task, these patients will do quite well on phrases and sentences with high frequency words until one gives them overly long sentences. Their performances will generally break down much earlier, however, on items with low frequency words, like "The vat leaks" from the Boston Diagnostic Aphasia Examination (Goodglass and Kaplan, 1972). At this stage of the disease, patients will recognize that they have not correctly repeated the phrase and they will attempt to make meaningful sentences out of what it is they have heard. They may often ask the examiner to repeat a sentence before they will attempt to respond.

In reciting series of automatic speech, patients with early stage Alzheimer's disease will, as a rule, be able to initiate the activity on their own. However, for one or another of the series, they may run on after the end for a few items, or they may omit one or two items.

These patients have no trouble telling you the meaning of idioms, but when faced with proverbs they will employ words from the stimulus literally, and will provide incomplete responses that not infrequently are concrete. They will have some difficulty catching on to the opposites task, and may forget in the middle of the test what it was precisely that was wanted. However they will succeed with at least one-half the items if they are remided of the task when they err.

In the writing sample, these patients will be able to write a paragraph. In the course of that paragraph they may make one or two spelling errors, by deleting, adding, or perseverating on a letter. They may make one paragrammatic error, through incorrect word choice. In reading aloud they may stutter over a word, but will for the most part produce few errors. In reading for comprehension materials of any great difficulty or length, they will produce errors.

Mid-Stage Alzheimer's Disease

In the middle stages of the illness, the patient with Alzheimer's disease looks most like a Wernicke's aphasic. Discourse will often include a press of speech; it is empty of meaning and includes paragrammatisms and clang associations. The patient can no longer tell a coherent story, nor respond appropriately and consistently to questions requiring specific responses.

These patients make many errors on a naming task. In our testing they get 40% correct on the Action Naming Test (Obler and Albert, 1978) and 23% correct on the Boston Naming Test (Kaplan et al., 1976). Their errors include distant circumlocutions, both semantic and literal paraphasias, misperceptions, and incorporation of the correct response into sentences, without realizing that they have produced a correct response. Neither semantic nor sound cues are of much help when these patients cannot name an item. In mid-stage, Alzheimer's patients will have a great deal of difficulty with the word list generation task, although they will appear to understand what is required, since they may provide one or two correct responses. After that, however, they will perseverate or say that they cannot think of any other items.

In conversation with these patients, one gets the impression that they have not always comprehended the questions asked. They will appear to be answering a different question related to the one asked, probably having understood that a question was asked, and responding to one or two of the substantive words they picked up. On more structured comprehension tasks, these patients will do moderately well when the question is a single sentence. However, when obliged to listen to complex questions or to listen to paragraph length material and be questioned on it, these patients' responses will be random. Nonetheless they will still give a "yes" or a "no" to a yes–no question and some form of appropriate, though perhaps wrong, answer to a question requiring a substantive response.

In repetition tasks, these patients will have great difficulty with any low-frequency items and some difficulty with longer, high-frequency phrases beyond six words. Their errors may include nonsense words, as well as omissions and combinings of words within the target sentences.

With automatic speech, these patients are likely to need prompting in order to get started, and often may not complete a series, by omitting items either within the series or at its end.

Patients will appear not to understand when asked to explain an idiom. However they can sometimes be shown to appreciate the idiom if they are given a multiple choice response: "Does 'feeling blue' mean 'feeling happy' or 'feeling sad'?"

These patients will produce no more than one sentence on a writing sample, and may only be able to write their name. What they do write will contain spelling errors of omission or addition or repetition, and if they write a sentence its

grammar may be impaired. They may also write words that are not the ones we would expect they intend as targets, but they will not appreciate that they have made these errors. In reading even brief passages aloud, these patients will substitute one word for another or produce nonsense terms. Needless to say, they cannot read paragraph-length material and answer questions on it.

Late-Stage Alzheimer's Disease

By the final stage of the disease, Alzheimer's patients lose their press of speech and are frequently mute. They will often appear not to comprehend what is said to them. By the same token, they may initiate a word or phrase of speech when there is no one in the environment attending to them. There will be much repetition (palilalia) in what they do say, and clang associations are not infrequent in the limited discourse they produce. These patients are no longer amenable to structured testing.

Other Forms of Dementia

There is a small, but significant subgroup of demented patients who do not have marked language disturbance in the early stages of the disease, and probably do not go through the Wernicke-like period in the mid-stage of their disease. They are identified as patients with Alzheimer's disease by their memory loss and visuo-spatial malfunction early in the course of the disease. When tested in the middle stages of the disease they will produce less than normal speech in response to questions. That is, they do not speak much. On naming tasks, they will make errors only at the mid-stage, with low-frequency items. Rather than circumlocute, however, they will simply maintain that they do not know a word. As with the majority of patients with Alzheimer's dementia, they do not benefit greatly from sound cueing. These patients may have Pick's disease.

It is unclear to what extent patients with Pick's disease resemble patients with Alzheimer's dementia. In the work of Risberg and his colleagues (e.g., Gustafson et al.,

1978), Pick's disease is taken to implicate anterior areas, whereas Alzheimer's dementia involves posterior, more language-related areas of the left hemisphere. Holland (1981) has documented the progressive decline in written language in a patient with postmortem verified Pick's disease. Initially, the patient took to writing because he refused to speak. Over the course of several years, his writing deteriorated from fairly sound syntax and word choice and coherent exposition to single items, sometimes misspelled, with no obvious relations signaled among them.

Elderly Aphasics

Until recently, it was taken for granted that the standard aphasia syndromes occurred with no regard to age in the adult population over age 30. Studies in several institutions, however, have shown that populations of Wernicke's aphasics are significantly older than populations of Broca's aphasics, especially for males (Obler et al., 1978, Harasymiw et al., 1981, Miceli et al., 1981, Brown and Grober, in press). The Broca's aphasics have a mean age in the early 50's; the Wernicke's aphasics have a mean age in the early 60's. This fact confounds the difficulty in determining whether certain patients are Wernicke's aphasics or patients with Alzheimer's dementia.

Currently, the best way to distinguish Wernicke's aphasics from patients with Alzheimer's dementia is on non-linguistic grounds. Does the patient have a memory disturbance? Does the patient have severe visuospatial disorientation beyond that found with posterior left hemisphere lesions? Linguistically, we have two preliminary suggestions. One is that the patient with Wernicke's aphasia uses few and only simple conjunctions, such as "and" or "but," whereas the patient with Alzheimer's disease uses the logical conjunctions such as "although" or "because," illogically. The second potential discriminator can be found on the repetition task. Both patients with Wernicke's aphasia and patients with Alzheimer's dementia will perform less well on low-frequency items and on longer items. Their mode of re-

sponse, however, would seem to differ in that the Wernicke's aphasics provide more semantic substitutions for words (Obler et al., forthcoming), and make more errors on easy items.

Since there is an abundant literature on the linguistic symptoms of Wernicke's aphasia, we will not describe them here (Goodglass and Kaplan, 1972; Albert et al., 1981). It is important to mention, however, that there is some debate as to whether speech rehabilitation therapy is as effective in the older aphasics as it is in the younger aphasic. M. Sarno (1980) has treated this question convincingly. By eliminating all patients with evidence of any degree of dementia, she was able to demonstrate nonsignificant differences in response to aphasia therapy in younger and older aphasics.

Approaches to Therapy of Language and Communication Problems in the Elderly

The fact that M. Sarno (1980) had to eliminate demented patients from her study of therapy in elderly aphasics indicates that traditional modes of speech rehabilitation do not work with demented patients. Indeed, approaches to therapy of language and communication problems in the elderly are in their gestation stage. Cognitive therapies that have been proposed for older individuals focus on the problem of forgetting to do things rather than forgetting the names of things. Clinical approaches to dementia have focused on establishing diagnosis and on making life together as comfortable as possible for both the patients and their caretakers. From the patients we have counseled, we have learned of the practices families have developed in order to enhance communication with the dementing patient at a level that is rewarding for them. Some families read aloud to the patient. Others firmly encourage the patient to make notes as they think of whatever it is they wish to say. Others go to great lengths to search for topics of conversation that will not exclude demented patients, topics that allow them to participate.

Given these creative attempts, the development of such energetic organizations as the Alzheimer's Disease and Related Disorders Association, and the burgeoning interest in dementing patients by speech pathologists, we are optimistic that new modes of rehabilitation and therapy will be developed in the immediate future.

References

Albert, M., Goodglass, H., Helm, N., Rubens, A., and Alexander, M. (1981). Clinical Aspects of Dysphasia. Springer-Verlag, Vienna.

Auerbach, S., White, B., and Obler, L. Clinical subtypes in Alzheimer's disease, forthcoming.

Brown, J. and Grober, E. (1983). Age, sex and aphasia type. J. Nerv. Ment. Dis. 171, 431–434.

Goodglass, H. (1980). Naming disorders in aphasia and aging. In Language and Communications in the Elderly, L.K. Obler and M.L. Albert, Eds. D.C. Heath, Lexington, Mass.

Goodglass, H. and Kaplan, E. (1972). The Assessment of Aphasia and Related Disorders. Lea & Febiger, Philadelphia.

Harasymiw, S., Halper, A., and Sutherland, B. (1981). Sex, age, and aphasia type. Brain Lang. 12, 190–198.

Holland, A. (1981). Language deterioration in Pick's Disease, paper presented at Aphasia Research Center Psychology Colloquium.

Kaplan, E., Goodglass, H., and Weintraub, S. (1976). Boston Naming Test, experimental edition. VA Medical Center, Boston.

Miceli, G., Caltagirone, C., Gainotti, G., Masullo, C., Silveri, M.C., and Villa, G. (1981). Influence of age, sex, literacy and pathologic lesion on incidence, severity, and type of aphasia, Acta Neurol. Scand. 64, 370–382.

Obler, L. (1980). Narrative discourse styles in the elderly. In Language and Communication in the Elderly, L.K. Obler and M.L. Albert, Eds. D.C. Heath, Lexington, Mass.

Obler, L. and Albert, M. (1978). Action Naming Test, experimental edition. VA Medical Center, Boston.

Obler, L. and Albert, M. (1981). Language in the elderly aphasic and in the dementing patient. In Acquired Aphasia, M. Sarno, Ed. Academic Press, New York.

Obler, L., Albert, M., Goodglass, H., and Benson, D.F. (1978). Aphasia type and aging. Brain Lang. 6, 318–322.

Obler, L., Albert, M., and Goodglass, H. (1981). Word Finding Difficulties in Aging and Dementia, paper presented at Gerontological Society of America meetings, Toronto.

Obler, L., Albert, M., Helm-Estabrooks, N., and Nicholas, M. (1982). Repetition disturbance in Alzheimer's dementia and in the aphasias, forthcoming.

Sarno, M.T. (1980). Language rehabilitation outcome in the elderly aphasic patient. In Language and Communication in the Elderly, L.K. Obler and M.L. Albert, Eds. D.C. Heath, Lexington, Mass.

Wechsler, A.(1982). Presenile dementia presenting as aphasia. J. Neurol. Neurosurg. Psychiat. 40, 303–305.

APPENDIX. EXAMINATION OF LANGUAGE IN THE ELDERLY

Opening Conversation

Much information about language abilities can be gained from an introductory conversation in which the clinician asks the patients what problem brought them in. Clinicians must then ask themselves:

1. Is the response appropriate in content?

2. Is it appropriate in length, or too short or too long?

3. Does the patient keep to the point? If s/he digresses, can s/he come back to the point by him/herself? Can the examiner bring him/her back to the point?

4. Is the response informative, or is it empty?

5. Is the patient able to find the words s/he wants, or is there much use of indefinite words like "thing" or "something" or "whatchamacallit," or "this" and "that?" Does the patient substitute one word or phrase when in fact s/he means another one? If so, does s/he correct him/herself?

6. Are there nonsense words in what the patient says? Do the nonsense words rhyme?

7. Are there cases where the grammar is not quite right?

8. Does the patient stop talking appropriately, or does s/he run on and make it hard for the clinician to interrupt?

9. Does s/he mumble or cover her/his mouth with her/his hand?

10. Does the patient intersperse her/his speech with many indications of doubt, such as "perhaps" or "it depends?"

In addition to the question about what brings the patient in, one will ask specific questions relating to medical history: How old the patients are? When they were born? Have they have ever been hospitalized, and for what? In listening to the content of the responses, the clinician should also attend to the way the patient responds:

1. Does the patient answer questions appropriately, with a *yes* or *no* when that is called for, or with information when it is called for?
2. Does the patient respond to the question which was asked, or only to a related one, e.g., E: How about your eyes, how are they? C: Just got a new pair.
3. When asked for a numerical response, does the patient give some number? Is it the correct number?

At this point, it is important to ask if the patient ever knew and used a second language, so that one can avoid attributing later indications of language disturbance to brain damage, if in fact, they can be explained by a bilingual history. Also it is necessary to ascertain the patients' educational level and the degree of sophistication with which they were using language premorbidly: Did they read books? Did their job require articulate writing? Did they keep a household, but also read extensively?

Discourse

In addition to the questions related to medical history, one asks the patients to describe a standard picture, like the Cookie Theft Picture of the Boston Diag-

nostic Aphasia Battery, and to tell a well-known tale, such as Little Red Riding Hood.

One also determines

1. Whether or not the story is coherently told, that is, if elements are linked together in an appropriate order.
2. Whether or not the patient includes all appropriate elements.

Naming

For healthy people, one must use a naming battery such as the Boston Naming Test (Kaplan et al., 1976) for nouns and the Action Naming Test (Obler and Albert, 1978) for verbs. If patients have substantial naming disorders, as evidenced at the beginnings of those tests, one must explore naming abilities by means of the Boston Diagnostic Aphasia Examination items for body parts, colors, objects, and actions. If the patient is impaired on these items, the clinician can use objects around the room, and can perform actions her/himself, such as *sitting down, applauding, waving,* etc.

What one looks for in a naming examination is not just the number of responses correct, but also

1. Whether the patient takes longer than normal to respond on relatively common items.
2. Whether the patient responds to cues—both content and sound cues—when they cannot find the word otherwise.
3. Whether verbs are substantially easier to produce than nouns.

Word List Generation

The patient is asked to name as many animals as s/he can in a minute, and as many words beginning with the letter F. If there is suspicion of subcortical disease and the patient names ten items, steadily, over the course of 1 minute, then one should give the patient up to 3 minutes on this task. If even the animal listing task is too difficult, one may use Mattis's task of listing items one would find in a supermarket.

In analyzing the patient's response to this task, one notes, in addition to the numerical scores,

1. Whether the items are in the asked-for (appropriate) set or if the patient digresses (e.g., listing animals: horse, cow, whale, shark, sharkfin).
2. Whether the patient repeats items unwittingly.
3. Whether or not the patient is slow, but can continue listing new items.

Comprehension

In order to determine if a relatively healthy person has comprehension difficulties, one must use test sentences and questions like

1. Across the street I see my father's daughter. Is it a man or a woman I see?
2. The lion was killed by the tiger. Who died?
3. My mother asked my sister to mail a letter and she did. Who mailed the letter?

In order to test whether memory components enter into comprehension difficulties one may use paragraphs with questions, such as the complex ideational material of the Boston Diagnostic Aphasia Examination. In order to test whether attention is impaired in comprehension, one uses the Auditory A's test in which the patient is instructed to raise a hand each time s/he hears the letter A. Then a list of random letters is read to the patient. Attention is paid to whether there are false positives or false negatives, i.e., items missed or items incorrectly recognized. (Needless to say, suspected *hearing* difficulties should be ruled out by an audiological examination.)

Repetition

To test repetition, we use the sentence repetition task of the Boston Diagnostic Aphasia Examination. This provides both long and short phrases and sentences with high-frequency and low-frequency words. In addition to score, one looks at the sorts of errors made: Are they real words, but the wrong ones, nonsense words, words sharing sounds with the target words (i.e., phonemic paraphasias)? Are there omissions or additions to the given phrase? Is there a great discrepancy between the patient's ability on long versus short items?

On high-frequency versus low-frequency items?

Automatic Speech

For patients with suspected brain damage, it is important to ask for the days of the week, numbers from 1 to 21, months of the year, a well-known prayer, etc. The clinician must observe

1. Whether the patient can start the series on his/her own, or whether s/he can continue after a cue.
2. Whether the patient completes the task or continues on at the end (e.g., January, February, . . . December, January, February).
3. Whether items are omitted or added to the series.

At this point it is worthwhile to ask the patient to give you the months of the year backwards, and see how much difficulty this task causes.

Idioms and Proverbs

If the patient can explain the meaning of simple idioms, like "feeling blue" or "dropping someone a line," then clinicians may ask the meaning of proverbs. In addition to a gross measure of correctness, one must note

1. The literal repetition of the proverb or idiom, or components of it.
2. How abstract or concrete the response is.
3. How vague or clear the response is.

Opposites

On this task the patient is instructed to give the opposite of a word, "like comfortable—uncomfortable." Then a list of words is given, some of which require *un,* others *in* or forms of *in* (*il,* in *illegible,* for example). On this task one observes

1. Whether the patient can understand and remember the task over a number of items.
2. Whether the patient gives meaning opposites (e.g., *dishonest* for *legal* when *illegal* is correct) or synonyms.

3. Whether the patient perseverates on *un* or *not* responses to inappropriate items.

Writing Sample

Depending on the degree of severity of language impairment, one either asks patients to write what is going on in the picture shown earlier, to write a sentence about the weather, or to write their address and name. In a writing sample one looks for

1. Coherence of discourse
2. Inappropriate word selection
3. Letters added, omitted, or switched around in a word
4. Omission of word endings

Note: Many normal subjects, especially 50-year-old males, will use partial sentences on a picture-description task. That is, they may write:

Woman washing dishes. Boy on chair which is tipping over. Girl reaching for cookies. Sink spilling over.

Reading Passage or Sentence

Reading materials from the Boston Diagnostic Aphasia Examination may be used. The patient is asked to read both aloud and to him or herself for comprehension. The clinician looks for

1. Partial readings (some, but not all the words)
2. Incorrect readings of words
3. Lack of comprehension

14. Dementia in the Elderly

MICHAEL P. ALEXANDER

NORMAN GESCHWIND

The title of this chapter "Dementia in the Elderly" suggests that there is some unique aspect to dementia in older people that deserves consideration separate from dementia in general. We shall not attempt to review the entire topic of dementia, since numerous texts devoted to this problem have been published in the past few years (Wells, 1977; Nandy and Sherman, 1977; Gershon and Raskin, 1975; Miller, 1977; Katzman et al., 1977; Slade, 1981). We shall try, instead, to show that dementia in the elderly presents particular problems of diagnosis and management. Some questions arise immediately. Are the elderly at greater risk for diseases that cause dementia? Is the clinical picture different in the elderly than in younger people; that is, does age, as a contributory factor, override sex, education, culture, etc., in the manifestation of brain disease? Is treatment in the elderly different from that in the young? If the answer to any of these questions is "yes," then a special discussion of dementia in later life is justified. This chapter will first demonstrate that the answer to each of these questions is "yes." We shall then outline a scheme for diagnosis and consider six important causes of dementia in the elderly.

Every text on dementia struggles with the issue of definition (Wells, 1977). Dementia is one of those terms (confusion and speech are two others) that is defined differently in common usage and in medicine. In *Webster's New International Dictionary* (1981), dementia is defined as "a general mental deterioration due to organic or emotional factors"; sixteen subdefinitions follow, including six that describe subsyndromes of schizophrenia. Although a widespread definition is "general mental deterioration," it is not satisfactory. Since the various dementing syndromes show different patterns of deficit, general deterioration is difficult to measure and remains, in our view, an unacceptable concept. In fact, what one sees is deterioration in specific areas of behavioral function (memory, language, praxis, visuospatial capacity, reasoning, insight, or emotion).

Some definitions of dementia emphasize the pre-eminence of memory loss, but such a definition would neglect those diseases in which cognition is surely affected, but memory impairment absent or not prominent (Parkinson's desease, Pick's disease). Thus, patients with stable Korsakoff's disease would, by virtue of their memory impairment, be profoundly demented. Yet many neurologists customarily regard Korsakoff's disease as a circumscribed deficit (amnesia) and thus not truly a dementia.

Many definitions of dementia stress a deteriorating course. Accepting a deteriorating course as a criterion for dementia will, however, eliminate patients with severe multiple cognitive deficits after head injury, encephalitis, or anoxia. These patients may have, on any single examination, abnormalities compatible with a diagnosis of dementia, but the course may be stable or even improving. By custom, these patients may be considered demented, but because the source of cognitive impairment is so clear, these patients do not raise the same clinical problems as patients with progressive cognitive decline.

Let us suggest that, in fact, the term dementia does not have a sharp boundary. It refers to a loosely similar group of disabilities in which there is deterioration in one or more behavioral functions that leads to an incapacity for reasonably independent activity. A progressive dementia is a condition that can be expected to lead to such a state. By convention, transient states are often called by other names. Thus, we speak of an acute confusional state (such as may occur in Parkinsonism) as one type of dementia. The confusional states are dealt with in Chapter 15.

The Interaction of Aging and Dementia

Before reviewing the neurology of dementia, we shall consider some of the problems common to an aging population that might interact with, influence, or distort the clinical picture of dementing diseases.

Psychosocial Factors

It is surprising to observe how often families regard an aging relative's grossly abnormal behavior as a normal feature of aging or as an extension of the previous personality. Are there changes in personality in normal aging that are exaggerated in the demented elderly? The topic of personality in the aged is reviewed by Botwinick (1975); only a few limited comments are warranted here. First, elderly people commonly become cautious, requiring a higher certainty of success before engaging in an activity. In real-life situations, as well as in testing situations, they may elect the least risky solution or no solution at all (errors of omission) if not confident of success (Botwinick, 1973). Second, elderly patients are sometimes characterized as rigid, that is, unable to accept multiple solutions to a problem and unable to reject an initial hypothesis or opinion in order to reformulate answers to problems. Such a definition of rigidity clearly describes cognitive as well as behavioral traits. The purported trait of rigidity may actually be secondary to intellectual deficits seen in some normal elderly (Chown, 1961). Third, several investigators consider a reduction in social interactions to be a common consequence of aging (Cumming and Henry, 1961). There are numerous, health-related reasons for such disengagement, but even in the healthy elderly, it is common, and there is no clear relationship to the preservation of cognitive ability (Maddox and Eisdorfer, 1962). Whether interpreted as a social phenomenon, as manifestations of normal cognitive change, or as a combination of the two, these personality changes fall within the normal limits of expectation in an aging population. They are not necessarily evidence of a pathological personality change, as commonly observed in dementing illnesses. Insofar as these "normal" changes contribute to apathy, poor motivation, and limited, externally goal-directed behavior, however, they may accelerate the clinical appearance of pathological personality change.

Social changes concomitant with aging are numerous, and they may influence the clinical manifestations of dementia. The longer a human being survives, the more he or she can expect the death of friends and family (social isolation), loss of employment and income (financial isolation), loss of physical skills to declining capacity and to illness (physical isolation), and loss of mental activity secondary to all three forms of isolation. The clinical problem, as with personality change, is that of distinguishing between the type of social change that is compatible with normal aging and the types that are not. There is no definite evidence that the social factors contribute to the development of dementia (although this is possible), but they certainly influence the clinical manifestations of dementia. Social changes may contribute to decline in self-care, accelerate the development of depression, which also affects cognition, and make it too difficult to maintain an up-to-date knowledge of the world.

Depression

Although depression is often considered to result from purely psychosocial factors, we believe this view is too narrow. Depression is certainly an integral part of some dementing diseases [for example, Parkinson's disease (Mayeux et al., 1981) and Huntington's disease (McHugh and Folstein, 1975)], but it is not common in others [for example, Pick's disease (Cummings and Duchen, 1981)]. Furthermore, several drugs frequently cause depression (reserpine, propanolol, and methyldopa, for example). Some depressions, especially those in cyclic affective disorders, are probably the result of as yet unspecified "organic" pathology. Depressive illness due to organic causes is very common in the elderly, but so is functional (psychosocial) depression. Whatever the cause, depression must be considered in any discussion of dementia in the aged. It may present with progressive cognitive changes that are almost indistinguishable from changes caused by overt organic disease. More importantly, it is often treatable.

It is often difficult to distinguish depression from dementia in the elderly. Psychomotor retardation, impaired attention, and loss of initiative are typical manifestations of depression in the elderly (Wang, 1977), and they often lead to problems of memory loss, an inability to respond to complex stimuli, and an inability to solve novel problems. If overt affective change is not obvious, the depression may not be diagnosed. Kiloh (1961) described ten patients in whom a diagnosis of dementia was subsequently found to be in error: Eight of these patients had some type of depressive illness. Marsden and Harrison (1972) reported a study of 106 patients referred with a diagnosis of dementia: Fifteen patients were not demented; eight were depressed. Ron et al. (1979) reassessed 51 patients with an apparently firm diagnosis of dementia made in the au-

thor's hospital: Sixteen patients were not demented, and eight of these were primarily depressed. All these investigations emphasize similar conclusions: A prior history of depressive disease and powerful affective symptoms and signs at outset should alert the examiner to the possibility of primary depressive illness. Wells (1979) emphasized the same points in a study of ten patients with pseudodementia (six with depression).

The use of neuropsychological assessment in distinguishing depression from dementia has been controversial. Depressed patients often do very poorly on standardized tests, with particular difficulty on tests of memory (Gainotti et al., 1980), on nonverbal novel problem-solving (Kronful et al., 1973), and on tests requiring rapid answers. There may, however, be qualitative elements that assist in diagnosis. All the studies reviewed above have stressed that patients with depression presenting as dementia often complain of memory loss. In our experience most (but not all) patients with true dementing illnesses have no complaints about memory and often deny a problem when probed. Another distinguishing feature may be consistency of performance. Wells (1979) has noted that depressed patients are often inconsistent, missing easy questions, then answering difficult questions or giving different answers from day to day. Furthermore, depressed patients make minimal efforts, at times saying "I don't know," then replying correctly when encouraged.

The mechanism of cognitive impairment in depression is not known, but some studies have shed light on the neuropyschological processes in depression. Henry et al. (1973) found that the ability to learn and remember is inversely correlated with the severity of depression. Furthermore, depressed patients inadequately process and encode new material for memory; the processing failure is most acute when the patient must actively organize novel stimuli in order to recall them (Weingarten et al., 1981). These findings suggest a basic deficit in cognitive activation. Murphy and Weingarten (1973) demonstrated that drugs that activate depressed patients (such as L-dopa) can improve memory without improving mood. These findings support the idea that depressed patients have a true cognitive impairment, a dementia syndrome, based on impaired activation.

Others argue that there is not true pseudodementia, but that in some cases dementia and depression appear in parallel in the aged (Shraberg, 1978). We do not agree, since there is ample evidence that treatment of depression can promptly normalize neuropsychological deficits (Kronful et al., 1980) and rapidly alleviate clinical impairments (Wells, 1979). That the improvement may be long standing is incompatible with the suggestion that a dementing illness is proceeding in parallel with the depression (Kiloh, 1961). Depression can thus cause a fully reversible dementia in the elderly.

Cognitive Factors in Aging

The neuropsychology of aging is reviewed elsewhere in this text (Chapter 12) and has been reviewed in numerous other volumes (Weingarten et al., 1981). We wish to stress the point that changes compatible with normal aging should not be mistaken for dementia. Furthermore, one must be aware of possible interactions between these physiological changes and the pathological changes of dementia. The major categories of impairment in the normal elderly are in speed of performance, memory, and problem-solving.

As measured by simple reaction time or by speed on a continuous performance task, the elderly are slower (Botwinick, 1975). This slowness accounts for some of the deficient performance of elderly on purported intelligence tasks in which scores are improved when completion is speedy. Slowness, however, cannot account for all performance deficits. When tasks are sufficiently complex or novel (Horn, 1975), the normal elderly do less well than a younger population, even when they have unlimited time.

Forgetfulness is virtually a cliche in the elderly; memory deteriorates with normal aging. Botwinick and Storandt (1974) demonstrated a diminished capacity for focused concentration manifested as impaired short-term memory. Furthermore,

this memory loss most profoundly affects performance on short-term tasks of serial, supraspan learning. Interestingly, much of the impairment is alleviated by allowing elderly patients to set their own, slower pace for learning large numbers of items (Eisdorfer et al., 1963).

Problem-solving tasks are the most taxing tests of cognition for normal older people. Thus, the major component of the lowered Wechsler Adult Intelligence Scale scores after the 30's is the decline in scores on the Performance scale (Weschler, 1958).

Other characteristics of cognitive change have also been described. Tasks depending on old information and practiced operations are most resistant to aging. Relative preservation of verbal fluency is probably another example of the stability of overlearned capacities. On the other hand, intelligence dependent on flexibility and reason is most sensitive to aging. Mental competition and interference are most disruptive in the older person.

Changes in cognition in the normal elderly are clinically relevant for two reasons. First, it is often not easy to decide whether an elderly person is demented, particularly if he has had little formal education. This problem is magnified in the depressed older person; in this case, the combined effects of depression and normal aging may produce profound deficits in cognition. Ancillary testing does not always help. The CT scan shows an increase in cerebral atrophy with age, but there is no clear-cut correlation between it and cognitive function in the normal elderly (Earnest et al., 1979; Huckman et al., 1975). In a population study, the basic posterior background activity on the EEG slows with advancing age, but it slows even more in progressive dementia (Harner, 1975). For an individual, its diagnostic usefulness is low.

Some of the alleged differences in senile and presenile dementias may reflect the effects of the same disease upon people of different ages. Many investigators believe that dementing illnesses are not distinct pathophysiologically in the elderly (Tomlinson et al., 1970), but rather that the same illness manifests itself differently at different ages. There is strong precedent in clinical neurology for this general argument. Primary generalized epilepsy and Huntington's disease are disorders in which identical pathological processes in a young patient and in an older patient have strikingly different clinical appearances (Adams and Victor, 1977). Aphasia is another example; identical pathologies in the young patient and the old have profoundly different clinical effects (Brown and Hecaen, 1976). The effect of the many "normal" cognitive changes in the elderly on disease states of dementia may result in different clinical pictures of the same disease occurring at different ages.

The Effects of Systemic Illness

There are several reviews of the medical disorders that may cause dementia; we shall summarize some of the mechanisms by which medical disorders affect cognition in the elderly. Seventy-five percent of the elderly population are affected by one or more chronic medical illnesses (Wang, 1977). There is a close relationship between chronic medical illness and the development of dementia (Kay et al., 1964). Many such disorders disrupt brain function directly, for example, diabetes and hypoglycemia; hypertension and stroke; emphysema and hypoxic encephalopathy. Equally important, the drugs used to treat many medical conditions affect the brain adversely.

Medical illness may affect the brain in several ways. Probably the most common illnesses are the reversible metabolic impairments that occur with transient hepatic encephalopathy, hypothyroidism, hyponatremia, etc. Depending upon the rate of onset, the clinical problem will be either a confusional state or dementia. Permanent structural damage can also occur, for example, with hypoxic injury. Medical illnesses can also lead to direct structural damage, such as intracerebral hemorrhage secondary to hypertension. Compounding the specific effects of medical illness upon the brain are such secondary effects as hospitalization and loss of independence, physical inactivity, social isolation, and multiple medications.

The effect of medication is particularly noteworthy. The use of drugs is very high, and their effects are often magnified in elderly patients. There is a recent review of neuropsychiatric effects of drugs in the elderly (Levenson, 1979); we shall emphasize a few important problems. Antihypertensive agents often affect cognition significantly. Reserpine, the original antihypertensive, has depression and mental slowness as common side effects (Goodwin et al., 1972); it is no longer widely prescribed. In terms of its central nervous system (CNS) side effects, methyldopa is the most important current antihypertensive. Sedation is common and depression occurs in 10% of users (Hammond and Kiekendal, 1979). Slowly progressive cognitive changes are also seen and are made worse by the coincident use of antipsychotic agents (Thornton, 1976). In our clinical experience, methyldopa-induced cognitive change is an extremely common problem. Therefore, in hypertensive patients who have suffered a stroke, we routinely discontinue methyldopa and begin another agent. Propanolol is another antihypertensive with frequent adverse effects. Confusion and nightmares (Holland and Kaplan, 1976), hallucinations (Fleminger, 1978), and psychosis (Fraser, 1976) have all been reported. Most important, however, is the frequent occurrence of depression (Wall, 1967). Psychotropic agents often produce adverse cognitive effects in the elderly. Oversedation may be a problem with low doses of antipsychotic drugs, antidepressants, antianxiety drugs, and hypnotics. Confusional states are very common (35%) in elderly patients taking antidepressants (Hollister, 1979).

The possibility of interactions of diseases, drugs, normal aging, and depression should be evident at this point, but an example may help to focus the clinical problem. Consider the elderly patient with chronic hypertension who is taking a diuretic, methylodopa, and propanolol for blood pressure control. He is at risk for lacunar infarctions, perhaps initially subclinical, but eventually producing the substrate of multi-infarct dementia. He has or may develop cardiac and renal disease, which may alter cerebral circulation and drug metabolism, respectively. He takes two agents that act on the CNS, which may produce mental decline, depression, or both, particularly if underlying, even subclinical, cerebral disease is present. Since he is taking antihypertensives, he has been bothered by easy fatigability (Hammond and Kiekendal, 1979), and is unable to engage in his usual activities, including visiting his wife in her nursing home. Should he now have an episode of mild left hemiparesis and examination reveal mental slowness, impaired memory, poor reasoning, and a depressed affect, there would be no diagnostic algebra to easily compute the proportional contributions of aging, depression, inactivity, medication, reversible metabolic derangement, and structural cerebral disease.

Clinical Diagnosis of Dementia

The diagnosis of the cause of dementia follows the standard medical procedure: a careful history, a detailed clinical examination, including careful assessment of the mental status, and the proper use of indicated diagnostic tests.

History

Obtaining an adequate history will almost always require the assistance of a relative or a friend of the patient. Active and past medical and psychiatric illnesses may be relevant to the diagnosis. All medications being used should be tabulated, as well as illicit drug use and alcohol intake. The data may reveal the likely cause of cognitive changes: a past history of depression or of hypertension and methyldopa use or of past radical thyroidectomy, etc.

In the history of the dementing illness itself, one should note rate of onset, presence or absence of focal signs or symptoms, epilepsy, stroke, and family history of dementia.

Rapid onset (minutes to hours to a few days) of cognitive change is an important diagnostic criterion. Patients with rapid onset usually present with an acute confusional state. Rapid onset usually implies one of five disorders: stroke, metabolic disorder, exogenous intoxication, acute noncerebral illness, and sensory deprivation. These are discussed in Chapter 15. We wish to stress some cases in which these acute states do not clear, but rather become chronic confusional states.

Strokes in the distribution of one or both of the posterior cerebral arteries can lead to acute confusional states, but in some cases these become chronic, especially in those with right-sided or bilateral lesions (Medina et al., 1974). In left unilateral cases, an amnestic (Korsakoff) syndrome may last for months after clearing of delirium, and amnestic syndromes may be permanent after bilateral infarctions (Benson et al., 1974). Infarctions in the distribution of the right middle cerebral artery are an even more common cause of acute confusion, which again sometimes persists (Mesulam et al., 1976). These poststroke persistent confusional states raise the interesting possibility that even single-infarct dementia may occur.

Metabolic disorders (e.g., pulmonary insufficiency) or exogenous intoxications in the aged often lead to acute confusional states that, at times, do not clear. Acute noncerebral illness (e.g., a fractured hip) or sensory deprivation (e.g., the so-called "black-patch" psychosis following cataract surgery) in the aged often lead to an acute confusion that may not clear in some cases.

Why does acute confusion in the aged often not clear, despite disappearance of the original precipitant? It is probable that an acute episode leads to dementia in the form of a chronic confusion state when the patient's brain is already compromised by subclinical or early dementia. This explanation is, however, not adequate, since it does not explain two common outcomes of confusion: (1) In many cases the patient fails to return to the same level as before the acute episode and (2) some patients may remain confused for a long period after the episode at a stable level without further decline. Either of these events would suggest that susceptible brains may actually be permanently damaged by exposure to exogenous substances or by endogenous chemical responses. Damage by normally innocuous substances under certain conditions is not unknown, for example, the recent demonstration in rats of brain lesions after folic acid administration (Roberts et al., 1981).

Since the acute confusional state in the elderly may unpredictably fail to clear, leaving a chronic confusional state, it is essential that physicians caring for the elderly take all possible steps to prevent confusional states. There are obviously situations beyond control, but certain measures can be taken. Meticulous care must be used in the use of medications (prescription or over-the-counter). Hospitalization should only be recommended when essential. For elderly patients undergoing operations, which may result in some loss of sensory contact with the environment (ocular procedures, particularly), admission to the hospital should be 24 to 48 hours before the operation to allow the patient to become familar with surroundings, staff, and daily routine.

When the course of cognitive change is subacute (over days to weeks), the diagnostic probabilities change somewhat. Chronic exposure to CNS-active agents (barbituates, methyldopa, reserpine, tricyclic antidepressants, opiate analgesics, etc.) remains an important consideration. Systemic illnesses and metabolic disorders (anemia, renal failure, hypothyroidism, etc.) are also important. Although the mental changes develop slowly, making it more difficult to link them with medications or with systemic illness, these diagnoses should not be overlooked. With subacute mental changes, however, primary intracranial disease becomes more probable. One must consider subdural hematomas, Creutzfeld–Jacob disease, brain tumors, hydrocephalus, multi-infarct dementia, the subcortical degenerative diseases (Huntington's, Parkinson's, etc.), and the cortical degenerative diseases (Alzheimer's and Pick's).

When the course of mental decline is very gradual (over months to years), the focus of diagnosis changes more to the intrinsic cerebral diseases and particularly to the degenerative diseases and the multi-infarct states. Medical, pharmaceutical, and metabolic effects cannot be automatically disregarded, but they become less and less probable. The cerebral disorders will be reviewed below.

Examination

In *Principles of Neurology,* Adams and Victor (1977) outline a very useful clinical principle: many diseases that cause dementia produce abnormalities on physical examination and many others produce abnormalities on the neurological examination. Only in one category, the cortical degenerative diseases, are the physical and neurological examinations usually unrewarding. The reader is referred to Adams and Victor for a clinically helpful guide to the use of the examination in diagnosis of dementia. We only wish to stress a few points.

First, an acute confusional state or delirium presents a clinical problem of examination and diagnosis that is quite separate from the subacute or chronic dementias. Examination and diagnosis of confusional states are considered in Chapter 15 of this text. Second, the general medical examination must not be omitted in the assessment of dementia. Signs of hepatic dysfunction, of chronic anemia, of hypothyroidism, and of a hyperadrenocortical state are examples in which abnormal general physical findings can coexist with normal neurological examination. Third, the general neurological examination must be thorough. Many neurological diseases producing dementia commonly or invariably have abnormal signs on the routine neurological examination. Signs of rigidity and bradydinesia (Parkinson's disease), of choreoathetosis (Huntington's disease), of pseudobulbar paresis (progressive supranuclear palsy), of asymmetrical pyramidal and extrapyramidal signs (multi-infarct states), and of spastic ataxic gait (hydrocephalus) are examples of extremely useful neurological findings that may point to the correct diagnosis. The neurological diseases just mentioned may have very similar early behavioral and cognitive manifestations; accurate diagnosis depends upon the remainder of the neurological examination.

To establish the presence of dementia, a comprehensive mental status examination must be performed. The proper mental status examination is a subject of chapter-length importance itself and detailed elsewhere in this text (see Chapter 11) as well as in other sources (Strub and Black, 1977). We shall iterate a few principles. The examination must independently assess each sphere of cognitive function because different diseases have different patterns of disturbed functions. A minimal tabulation of the separate spheres to be examined is as follows:

1. State of arousal: position on wake–sleep continuum
2. Attention: concentration; freedom from distraction
3. Language: speech; language structure and content; auditory comprehension; repetition; naming; writing; reading
4. Praxis: facial; limb; real object use
5. Visuospatial capacity: drawing; copying; geography; topography; dressing
6. Memory: new learning; recent past memories; remote memory
7. Abstract reasoning: proverbs; similarities; multistep calculations
8. Emotion: affect (external expression); mood (internal feelings)
9. Personality: insight, inhibitions; interactions
10. Thought content: paranoia; delusions; hallucinations

It is our clinical impression that patients with intrinsic cerebral disease often have one of two different patterns of cognitive impairment. One pattern includes major deficits in new learning, recent past memories, naming, complex auditory comprehension, and visuospatial capacity (amnesia–aphasia–visuospatial). The other pattern includes deficits in new learning, abstract reasoning, emotion, and personality. A shorthand distinction between the two patterns is temporoparietal for the first and frontosubcortical for the second, drawing upon the *presumed* cerebral localizations of the impaired functions of the two patterns. This rather crude division corresponds to another rough, but useful classification, that is, "neat" and "sloppy" dementias. The "neat" dementias are those in which personality and social judgement are preserved, while language, memory, and visuospatial functions deteriorate. By contrast, the "sloppy" dementias are those in which personality and emotional changes occur early. Alzheimer's disease is one

classical example of the "neat" dementias in early stages, whereas general paresis is the classical "sloppy" dementia.

In our experience, the first pattern is highly suggestive of Alzheimer's disease and only rarely will another diagnosis be found, although patients with depressive pseudomentia may also fit this description. The second pattern is less suggestive of Alzheimer's disease and typically another diagnosis is made (multi-infarct state, Parkinson's disease, hydrocephalus, Pick's disease, or again, depression). The foregoing represents oversimplification, but as a rough first guide it is clinically useful. The differences between diseases are certainly more specific and complex, and as elaborated below, not all dementias are the same (Gainotti et al., 1980). Some diseases have profound effects upon memory (Alzheimer's, Huntington's), others on emotion (Parkinson's), and still others on personality (Huntington's, Pick's). Failure to have recognized the different patterns of dementia has reduced the validity and usefulness of many texts that list the neuropsychological changes of a unitary dementia; there is no such disorder.

Review of Major Dementias

The assessment of progressive intellectual deterioration is often considered unrewarding, since a common pessimistic opinion is that the patient will have some untreatable or unmodifiable disorder. There is, in fact, remarkably little information about the outcome of evaluations for dementia, but there is sufficient evidence to rebut the notion that all disorders are hopeless.

Marsden and Harrison (1972) reported the outcome in 106 patients referred by other neurologists and psychiatrists with a presumptive clinical diagnosis of dementia. Only 84 patients were unequivocally demented. Of these, 10% had a mass lesion, 10% multi-infarct dementia, 7% alcoholic dementia, 6% NPH, 10% other diagnoses, and 57% no diagnosis—the last presumably including the cases of Alzheimer's disease and other cortical degenerative diseases. Overall 20% of the cases had a potentially treatable disorder. Freemon (1976) reported the results of the evaluation of 60 consecutive, unscreened patients admitted for the possibility of dementia. The final diagnoses in the 60 patients included depression (1), NPH (7), subdural hematomas (2), drug effects (5), CNS syphilis (1), hepatic failure (1); that is, 30% of the cases had potentially treatable problems. There were five cases of multi-infarct dementia and eleven other specific, but untreatable disorders (Huntington's disease, alcoholic dementia, etc.). Finally, 26 patients (43%) had no specific diagnosis and presumably had one of the cortical degenerative diseases.

These studies suggest that among patients referred to neurologists for evaluation of possible dementia, one-half will show cortical degenerative processes. Multi-infarct dementia, depressive pseudodementia, and the effects of alcohol will be the next three most common diagnoses, NPH the most common potentially reversible neurological disorder. There will be small numbers of a variety of neurological diseases. Many patients with dementia secondary to drug effects, nutritional disorders, metabolic disease, and the overt effects of systemic disease will have been detected and treated without referral to a neurologist. Overall, about 25% of the patients will have a potentially treatable disorder: pyschiatric, such as depression; medical, such as hypothyroidism; or neurological, such as NPH. These approximations of clinical occurrence will not correspond to autopsy studies (Tomlinson et al., 1970; Go et al., 1978) for a number of reasons. Treatable cases definitely exist in sufficient number to warrant close evaluation of all cases of dementia.

Alzheimer's Disease

In this, the most common neurological disease that causes dementia (Kurtzke and Kurland, 1981), women are affected about twice as frequently as men. The tradition of dividing patients at an age boundary of 65 years into presenile and senile cases has, according to the most common current view, no certain clinical validity and no pathological validity (Tomlinson et al., 1970). One must, however, accept the fact that the issue of the existence of only one disease, of two diseases or of several diseases will be resolved only when the etiology is known. We shall follow the current mode (Katzman, 1976) of considering this a single disorder, Alzheimer's disease (AD). The prevalence of AD is not known with certainty, although various estimates suggest over 1,000,000 cases in the United States. Furthermore, both the incidence and prevalence of AD rise with increasing age (Kurtze and Kurland, 1981). Patients with AD have an age-adjusted survival time of 30% to 60% of that of their peers (Go et al., 1978; Coblentz et al., 1973); survival time is rougly proportional to the severity of dementia (Coblentz et al., 1973). The decreased survival in AD is responsible for the popularity of the phrase "the malignancy of Alzheimer's disease" (Katzman, 1976).

The clinical course in AD is not known with complete certainty, since studies of the changes in advancing dementia are often not confirmed as cases of AD, and autopsies of AD cases often yield scanty clinical information. Both our experience and the available literature, however, suggest a fairly typical course for most cases. Usually, the early changes are in memory (Go et al., 1978) and in mental efficiency (Lishman, 1978). If the patient is in a situation that demands high intellectual effort, these early effects may be quite apparent to others. This early awareness of mental change has two consequences. First, the patient may be sent for evaluation at a time when his mental deficits are quite subtle. Second, he may be aware of the problem and depressed or anxious in reaction to the uncertainty injected in his life. Diagnosis at this stage will require careful mental status testing and/or probing neuropsychological testing. Here, CT and the EEG are not likely to be helpful.

As the disease progresses, disturbances in memory and in higher level mental operations become more apparent. Appropriate concern and/or depression are likely to evolve into unfocused perplexity or apathy (Sjorgren et al., 1952). Visuospatial and topographical skills will deteriorate; the patient may get lost or be unable to locate familiar items around his house. Language is almost inevitably (in our experience) involved, first with word-finding problems that show up in empty and circumlocutory speech; second with comprehension problems at the level of complex material; third with linguistically abnormal sentence structures (see Chapter 13). In patients who live very routine, isolated, or intellectually undemanding lives, these changes can progress to a remarkable extent before the patient is brought to medical attention. These are the patients in whom trivial noncerebral illnesses (influenza, fever, etc.), new medications (sedatives, antihypertensives, etc.), or social changes (illness of a spouse, change in shopping routines, etc.) may precipitate a "pseudoacute" onset (Arie, 1973). On occasion, there is the apparent sudden onset of a gross thought disorder (senile psychosis), precipitated by the interaction of failing cognitive powers and one of the life changes mentioned above. If this acute disturbance is successfully treated, the underlying mental deterioration will be evident. In our experience, this pattern of AD is unique to the elderly population.

During the later stages, clear-cut abnormalities are seen in the EEG: slowing and loss of posterior alpha rhythms and bilateral polymorphous theta and delta activity (Harner, 1975). The CT scans may demonstrate increased ventricular size (Roberts and Caird, 1976) or enlarged cortical sulci (Earnest et al., 1979), but correlation between CT findings and degree of mental decline is low. Once the disease is clearly established, neuropsychological assessment will reveal a pattern of profound impairment in memory and in visuospatial tasks (Gainotti et al., 1980). Some basic neurological abnormalities also begin to appear in these later stages of cognitive decline. Symmetrical extrapyramidal motor defects (rigidity and flexed posture) (Pearce and Miller, 1973), seizures (Sim et al., 1966), and myoclonus (Mayeux et al., 1980) are the most common manifestations. A clinical diagnosis will have been made by this time in almost all patients.

The cause of AD is not known. There is evidence that genetic factors are important in all cases (Sjogren et al., 1952), but only a minority follow reliable genetic patterns, usually as an autosomal dominant disorder (Feldman et al., 1963). There is no evidence as yet that AD is a transmissible (? viral) disorder in most cases; even in the cases of alleged transmission of familial AD, the evidence is weak (Goudsmit et al., 1980). A primary disorder in intracellular microtubular function would account for the basic pathological abnormality (neurofibrillary tangles), the increased incidence of AD in adults with Down's syndrome (Olson and Shaw, 1969), and the increased incidence of aneuploidy in the lymphocytes of patients with AD (Cook et al., 1979). On the other hand, it is known that several diseases may have similar neurofibrillary changes without any known relationship to AD (Wisnieski et al., 1979).

The pathology of AD is well known, as is the approximate relationship of the pathological changes to clinical severity. We shall review the possible correlations between the neuropathological changes and severity of dementia. First, there is no qualitative abnormality unique to AD in comparative studies of normal elderly and demented elderly with AD (Blessed et al., 1968). Second, the pathological changes (neurofibrillary change, senile plaques, and granulovacuolar degeneration) are quantitatively markedly different; they are much more prominent in AD. Third, neuron counts in the cortex of elderly patients with AD compared to age-matched controls demonstrate a greater than 20% loss of neurons from the cortex of the patients with AD (Terry et al., 1981) and a greater than 50% loss of neurons in the hippocampus of these patients. There seems little doubt that the pathological changes are adequate to account for the severity of mental changes.

Some authors have interpreted the decline in mentation as a nonspecific, mass effect of neuronal loss in AD (Wells, 1977). We believe, however, that the effects are probably specific to the regions of cell loss. Neuronal loss is most marked in the hippocampus; the early and profound changes in memory may reflect this (Go et al., 1978). Neuronal loss is otherwise marked in neocortical association areas and in the cortical layer with the largest number of intercortical association connections (Terry et al., 1981); profound cognitive change without elemental neurological signs may reflect this. Subcortical structures in which neuronal loss occurs are (1) the medial amygdala (Herzog and Kemper, 1980), deficits in emotion and affect may result; and (2) the nucleus basalis of Meynert (Whitehouse et al., 1981), an anterior forebrain nucleus that sends cholinergic efferents to frontal and parietal neocortex. Degeneration of the nucleus basalis or of the septum could account in part for the loss of cholinergic synapses in AD (Davies and Maloney 1976; Drachman, 1977) and for the possible beneficial effect of cholinergic medications on memory in AD (Drachman and Sahakian, 1980; Peters and Levin, 1979).

The variety of clinical presentations of elderly patients with AD probably can be accounted for by an interaction between the patient's age, the patient's social and intellectual status, the presence of coexisting diseases, and the specific pattern of neuronal loss. The final picture will be very similar in all who survive.

Any discussion of treatment must still be sadly short. Numerous agents have been tried; none has as yet proven useful (McNamara and Appel, 1977). Current attempts to treat the known loss of cholinergic synapses in AD (Davies and Maloney, 1976) have utilized short-acting anticholinersterases, precursor loading with choline or lecithin, or both. None has been clearly and dramatically effective (Peters and Levin, 1979), but trials continue. Palliative management of these patients is often left to the family or the social worker, but should not be. Wells (1977) has eloquently summarized the many steps that may be taken to maximize intellectual and social function in patients with AD.

Multi-infarct Dementia

The term multi-infarct dementia (MID) is preferable to an often-used alternative, atherosclerotic dementia, for two reasons. First, the correlation between dementia and the diffuse large artery occlusive disease of atheroscelerosis is very low (Worm-Peterson and Pakkenberg, 1968). Second, in patients with this type of dementia the neuropathology is numerous, gross and microscopic infarctions (Tomlinson et al., 1970). Multi-infarct dementia, however, is not a single pathophysiological process. Some investigators have described as many as five distinct forms of dementia on a vascular basis (Bousser, 1977). Excluding certain types of disease, such as the diffuse vasculitides (periarteritis or lupus erythematosis) and hydrocephalus after intracerebral hemmorrhage, the neurological literature contains descriptions of three prominent patterns of dementia due to ischemic vascular disease.

Patients with multiple large cerebral infarctions are often demented. The thorough neuropathological studies of Tomlinson et al. (1970) confirmed the importance of gross cerebral infarction as a cause of dementia. It is not known how much the degree of dementia depends upon the total volume of necrotic brain (100 ml being an absolute indicator of dementia) and how much it depends upon the location of the infarctions (information not provided in detail). It seems probable that the location determines the quality of the cognitive deficits and that the volume serves as a marker of a threshold beyond which dementia is likely whatever the location and clinical features. Patients with this form of dementia virtually always have a definite history of major infarction. In fact, dementia is often the direct result of one major infarction imposed on previous, less damaging infarctions. The pathogenesis of major infarctions in these patients may either be multifocal embolic strokes or bilateral, large vessel thrombotic strokes.

Tomlinson et al. (1970) believed that small, deep infarctions were less important in causing dementia, since they are a relatively common finding in the normal elderly. Nevertheless most subsequent description of MID has focused on small lacunar infarctions. Fisher (1960) emphasized the steady decline in mentation as the number of lacunar infarctions increased. He also defined the importance of chronic hypertension in the pathogenesis of lacunar infarction (Fisher, 1965). The vascular pathology of these patients differs from that of the first group above. Rather than atherosclerotic obstruction of large vessels, most patients with lacunar infarctions had small lipid-laden plaques obstructing the small ($\leq$ 1 mm diameter) perforating branches of the middle cerebral or posterior cerebral arteries (Fisher, 1979). These patients usually have a history of stroke and of hypertension and unequivocal sensory–motor signs secondary to infarction in the basal ganglia, internal capsule, and/or thalamus. Many have pseudobulbar paresis, with dysphagia, dysarthria, and lability of emotional expression. This description seems to fit the patients with MID in the series of Marsden and Harrison (1972). These are the findings emphasized by Birkett (1972), and this is the type of patient with MID seen most often in our institutions.

The third clinical presentation of MID is subcortical arteriosclerotic encephalopathy (SAE), previously known as Binswanger's disease. (Olzewski, 1962). Several recent reports on this syndrome have clarified its clinical appearance and pathophysiology (Caplan and Schoene, 1978; Rosenberg et al., 1979; DeRueck et al., 1980; Loizou et al., 1981). Of 31 patients, 27 had a history of hypertension, 23 a definite history of stroke, and 19 a history of subacute, gradual mental deterioration often punctuated by additional stepwise decline. Twenty-nine of the patients had one or more motor signs (rigidity, spasticity, hemiparesis, bradykinesia, marche à petit pas, dysarthria, and dysphagia). The motor signs were almost always bilateral and generally asymmetrical; they are in all ways indistinguishable from the signs of lacunar infarctions. The pathology of SAE is a combination of lesions (Caplan and Schoene, 1978; DeRueck et al., 1980). The distinctive abnormalities in SAE are periventricular demyelination, which is maximal in the posterior frontal regions; scattered foci of demyelination within the cerebral convolutions; and patchy cystic necrosis along the walls of the ventricles. The vascular pathology, although not known precisely, is probably a simultaneous progression of atherosclerotic large vessel occlusive disease and hypertensive

perforator disease. Not unexpectedly, SAE is slmost universally associated with lacunar infarcts, although the opposite is not true.

Whatever the exact vascular pathology, the clinical presentations of MID are fairly similar, and many will be apparent from the descriptions above. The prevalence of cerebral infarction and, as a consequence, MID rises with increasing age, and particularly steeply after age 65; thus, MID is seen in the same age groups as AD (Arie, 1973). Unlike AD, men are more commonly affected in MID. The clinical characteristics of MID were outlined by Mayer-Gross et al. (1969). Subsequently modified by Hachinski et al. (1975), they were used to create a scale to identify cases of MID. This scale separated (Weingarten et al., 1981) demented patients into two groups (presumably AD and MID), without overlap. There was no difference in the severity of dementia in the two groups, but no information was provided on whether they differed in type of dementia. Eight items on the scale seemed to separate the groups best. Subsequently, other workers (Rosen et al., 1980) have demonstrated that the scale does predict pathology and that six items best identify MID: abrupt onset of dementia, stepwise deterioration, history of stroke, focal neurological signs, focal neurological symptoms, and history of hypertension.

The forms of MID often occur simultaneously; in particular, SAE is almost always seen with associated lacunar infarcts. As a result, it is difficult to establish a clinical picture of the types of dementia in MID that does not blur distinctions between lacunar state, cortical infarctions and SAE. Only a few conclusions seem warranted. First, focal deficits (aphasia, apraxia, etc.) are common in cases with cortical infarcts. Second, memory function may be relatively well preserved in MID (Gainotti et al., 1980; Caplan and Schoene, 1978). Third, in many patients with mild MID, the deficits may only be subtle changes in motivation, abstraction and higher level cognition. (Caplan and Schoene, 1978).

Treatment of MID is almost as limited as that for AD. There is no specific treatment for the cognitive abnormalities, once they develop. Treatment consists of proper management of the underlying vascular abnormality. This is a controversial area we shall not discuss in detail. In patients with lacunar disease or SAE, proper control of blood pressure is the most important step. In patients with infarction due to large vessel thromboembolic disease, treatment is the same as for patients with transient ischemic attacks or completed strokes, whichever is more appropriate for the individual case. It is our reading of the neurological literature that there is little reason to recommend any of the currently popular treatments. The other important step in these patients is to remember the increased susceptibility patients with MID often have to their antihypertensive medication. The physician must achieve a balance between blood pressure control and the pernicious CNS side effects of many medications (methyldopa, propalonol, resepine, and perhaps clonidine).

Normal Pressure Hydrocephalus

When first reported (Adams et al., 1965), this disorder offered the promise of a common, previously unrecognized and reversible cause of dementia. Its subsequent history has not fulfilled this promise. There are excellent reviews of this disorder: the reader is referred to Katzman (1977) for a complete consideration. We wish to stress only a few elements.

The majority of the cases in the literature are secondary to some known process; at the time of Katzman's extensive review in 1977, only 34% of the reported cases were idiopathic. The most common causes of secondary hydrocephalus are subarachnoid hemorrhage (an early or late complication) and trauma (Kazman, 1977; Wood et al., 1974). Many cases of secondary hydrocephalus are obstructive (noncommunicating), caused by tumors, aqueductal stenosis, or ependymitis (Messert and Baker, 1966); clinically there is nothing to distinguish the hydrocephalus of such secondary cases from idiopathic cases. Acute hydrocephalus with increased intratranial pressure presents as akinetic mutism (Katzman, 1977); subacute or chronic hydrocephalus produces progressive gait disorder, incontinence, and mental changes (Adams et al., 1965). These changes are the same in cases of hydrocephalus secondary to a known cause or in idiopathic cases. In the patients with secondary hydrocephalus, there may be additional neurological abnormalities as a result of the primary process (trauma, infection, tumor, etc.).

The major diagnostic problem, and the reason for including a discussion of hydrocephalus in this chapter, is the idiopathic case. That there are such cases is amply demonstrated by patients 1 and 2 in the report of Adams et al. (1965). That such cases are relatively infrequent is clear in the studies of Marsden and Harrison (1972) (6 out of 84 patients), Katzman (1977) (3 out of 56), and Freemon (1976) (7 out of 60). There is agreement about some of the clinical features of idiopathic hydrocephalus. Both sexes are affected; it occurs across all adult age ranges. The prominent gait disorder is variously described as spastic and apractic (Messert and Baker, 1966), shuffling and retropulsive (Adams et al., 1965), or Parkinsonian (Synert et al., 1973). An increase in tone, with elements of both spasticity and rigidity, may be found. The mental status changes are not as well characterized. Overall the dementia is relatively mild (Gainotti et al., 1980), often dominated by deficits in performance style—apathy, slowness, perseveration (Ojemann et al., 1969; Benson et al., 1970)—as much as by deficits in performance content. Memory may be the most impaired cognitive function in progressive hydrocephalus (Katzman, 1977; Ojemann et al., 1969). Urinary incontinence is of no diagnostic specificity. It is our impression that incontinence is prominent in NPH because of the combination of the motor impairment (the periventricular course of fibers for voluntary control of micturition) and apathy and psychomotor retardation.

The problem of establishing characteristic clinical signs for NPH is paralleled by the problem of establishing reliable laboratory criteria. It is safe to conclude that no suggested diagnostic measure is sufficiently valid to be relied upon. Many pneumoencephalogram, cisternogram, EEG, saline infusion, and CT criteria have had their proponents, but no single test has had sustained value in predicting therapeutic response (Coblentz et al., 1973; Shenkin et al., 1970; Messert and Wanamaker, 1974).

The response to treatment by placement of a ventricular shunt can be summarized briefly: (1) There is no pathognomonic criterion that predicts response. (2) Patients with a known etiology respond better (65% improve) than do patients with an unknown etiology (40% improve) (Katzman, 1977; Messert and Wanamaker, 1974), but the response may be blunted by the primary process (e.g., trauma). (3) The clinical criteria outlined above probably predict improvement better than any diagnostic test (Jacobs et al., 1976). (4) The major morbidity and mortality of shunts in this group are at least 10% (Wood et al., 1974).

Our understanding of this disorder is incomplete. It is probable that several disorders are unwittingly grouped as idiopathic hydrocephalus; some of these disorders will respond to shunting and some will not. The uncertain outcome of a diagnosis of NPH is no better typified than in the two series of patients with dementia described above. In the eighty-four cases of Marsden and Harrison (1972), five patients received a *final* diagnosis of NPH; four were unchanged after shunting. In the series of Freemon (1976) seven patients were given a *final* diagnosis of NPH; only one patient was substantially improved after shunting. Two good results and one postoperative death out of twelve patients with a *firm* diagnosis made at major medical centers does not suggest that this syndrome is truly understood or adequately recognized.

Currently, our recommendations are as follows. The clinical criteria identify the patients in whom further pursuit of diagnosis of NPH is worthwhile. If no alternative clinical diagnosis explains the findings (MID, Parkinson's disease, subdural hematomas, general paresis, chronic portosystemic encephalopathy), if the patient has large ventricles with normal or only mildly enlarged cortical sulci on CT scan, if neuropsychological testing does not demonstrate strikingly out-of-proportion focal

deficits (aphasia, apraxia, etc.), and if the patient and his family will accept the 10% risk of significant operative morbidity, we recommend shunting.

Thus, AD, MID, NPH, and depression are the major illnesses of the elderly that may present as progressive mental decline. We shall now review two other important causes of dementia in the elderly: one a cortical degenerative disease and one a subcortical degenerative disease.

Pick's Disease

The prevalence of Pick's disease is not known with certainty, but it is probably about one-tenth as common as AD (Stengel, 1943). It is more common in women. Most cases are sporadic, although 20% are familial, apparently inherited in an autosomal dominant pattern (Sjogren et al., 1952). It is most common between the ages of 40 and 60. The original case described by Pick was 71, but onset after age 65 is uncommon.

Because most textbooks state that there are no distinguishing features between AD and Pick's disease, it is probable that most series of AD without pathological confirmation include cases of Pick's disease and that some of the uncommon features of AD are actually features of Pick's disease. It is our belief that the two disorders can, in fact, usually be distinguished clinically. In pathologically confirmed Pick's disease, a few observations are consistently made. First, changes in personality and behavior herald the disorder and may be quite marked even when cognition is minimally impaired (Lishman, 1978; Stengel, 1943; Robertson et al., 1958). The changes in behavior include emotional blunting, apathy, paranoia, irritability, and inappropriate social behavior. Cummings and Duchen (1981) reported the early appearance of elements of the Kluver–Bucy syndrome: hyperorality, loss of affect, hypermetamorphosis, hypersexuality, and agnosia. Second, language deficits are often the first definite cognitive change. These language deficits may be simple anomia, circumlocution, and verbal paraphasia, but a number of unusual impairments have been described in Pick's disease. These include the repetitive use of the same verbal paraphasic substitution as an all-purpose response to word-finding deficits; the tendency to repeat a stereotyped greeting, sentence, or even story (Stengel, 1943); echolalia (Cummings and Duchen, 1981; Stengel, 1943); and a comprehension defect marked by the failure to comprehend single words in context even when the words can be repeated and spelled. Third, a more widespread cognitive impairment eventually supervenes, but memory and visuospatial functions may be relatively well preserved until late in the course; it is the sparing of these functions that most clearly separates this disorder from Alzheimer's disease. Fourth, the elementary neurological examination remains normal until late in the course, when symmetrical extrapyramidal abnormalities emerge.

The neuropathology of Pick's disease is as unrevealing of a primary cause as is the pathology of AD. The prominent cerebral atrophy has a characteristically intensely lobar distribution, with anterior frontal and temporal involvement (Cummings and Duchen, 1981). Microscopically there are neuronal loss, Pick bodies and "inflated" neurons, marked astrocytic gliosis in the involved cortical regions, and loss of myelin. The amygdala is profoundly involved (Cummings and Duchen, 1981). In AD, the corticomedial segments of the amygdala reveal neuronal loss, but in Pick's disease, the entire nucleus is profoundly involved. The early appearance of the Kluver–Bucy syndrome may be a result of the amygdaloid involvement.

There is no known treatment.

Parkinson's Disease

In several long-term studies of Parkinson's disease (PD), the average age at onset was in the mid-50's, but with many cases first seen after age 65 (Sweet and McDowell, 1975). According to Kurtze and Kurland (1981), population studies suggest a steadily increasing prevalence to at least age 75, when the prevalence is 2%. Parkinson's disease is an important cause of morbidity in the elderly. The cause is unknown.

Numerous illnesses masquerade as idiopathic PD, but postencephalitic Parkinsonism and so-called atherosclerotic Parkinsonism are the most common (Pollock and Hornabrook, 1966). The diagnostic criteria for postencephalitic cases are well reviewed by Pollock and Hornabrook (1966), and the criteria for atherosclerotic cases are the same as for MID. In fact, lacunar state–MID often cannot be clinically distinguished from atherosclerotic Parkinsonism. The clinical signs of PD are bradykinesia, rigidity, resting tremor, and postural changes (Adams and Victor, 1977). These motor signs, which may appear in any combination, are usually bilateral, but not necessarily symmetrical, from the outset. A more detailed review of the clinical findings and of the neuropathology of PD is found in all standard textbooks of neurology.

The prevalence and nature of dementia in PD is difficult to summarize. The literature on this aspect of PD is very uneven, but a few observations seem consistent. Dementia in PD occurs at a higher level than in the normal population (Pollock and Hornabrook, 1966; Markham et al., 1974). It varies from 8% to 56% in various studies presumably because different diagnostic criteria were used. Using only populations studied before the introduction of L-DOPA, Markham et al. (1974) found 26% of patients with PD to be demented. Loranger et al. (1972) evaluated 63 patients before treatment with L-DOPA. Using portions of the Weschler Adult Intelligence Scale, they made several interesting observations: 57% of the patients had an over 20-point difference between the verbal and performance tasks (the verbal was higher). Comparison with the performance of patients with depression (without PD) suggested that depression alone could not account for the findings in PD. The use of one performance task and one verbal task that did not depend on motor skills revealed the same deteriorated performance when compared to depressed patients and to normals. Finally, PD patients, compared to carefully age-matched controls, were still significantly worse. There was no correlation between intellectual decline and age of onset, age at testing, or duration of disease.

In most subsequent studies of dementia in PD, similar conclusions have been drawn. The incidence of mental impairment in PD is increased, although there is disagreement about the relationship to duration of disease (Mayeux et al., 1981; Garron et al., 1972; Lesser et al., 1979). Most investigators have not found a clear relationship between severity of depression and severity of dementia, but one recent careful report did find such a relationship (Mayeux et al., 1981). Most investigators found no correlation with age, but in the largest series, there was a strong correlation between increasing age and dementia in PD (Lieberman et al., 1979).

Other aspects of dementia in PD are unresolved. First, several investigators have suggested that dementia occurs in PD because of the coincident occurrence of AD or because of some as yet not understood interrelationship of PD and AD (Alvord et al., 1974; Sroka et al., 1981, Boller et al., 1980). Because the instruments used to assess dementia in these studies were very primitive and because the significance of unquantified Alzheimer's type changes in the brains of elderly patients with PD is not known, this alleged coincidental occurrence has not been critically assessed. It is an intriguing possibility that PD and AD are related in some manner because of the known relationship between Alzheimer's type neurofibrillary changes and Parkinsonism with dementia in a disease unique to the island of Guam. In idiopoathic PD, however, the significance of neurofibrillary tangles as more than a coincidental occurrence in two common diseases cannot be determined.

The second unresolved issue is the clinical nature of the mental deterioration in PD. Unfortunately, very few of the population surveys are helpful because the neuropsychological tools used are necessarily imprecise (Mayeux et al., 1981; Sroka et al., 1981; Boller et al., 1980). The findings of Loranger et al. (1972) are reviewed above. Two other conclusions are possible from the available data. Disorders of language, praxis, and visuoper-

ceptual capacity are almost never seen (Mageux et al., 1981; Gainotti et al., 1980; Boller et al., 1980). The cognitive deficits are mild when compared to other dementing diseases (Gainotti et al., 1980), but recent memory (Gainotti et al., 1980) and complex abstract reasoning (Boller et al., 1980) are the most common areas of impairment. Speed of performance is reduced, but does not account for the cognitive deficits (Loranger et al., 1972; Garron et al., 1972). The third unresolved issue is the response of dementia to treatment. All possible responses have been reported. Loranger et al. retested several of their patients after several months of L-DOPA therapy and found an improvement in 50% of the patients (Loranger et al., 1972). The longitudinal treatment studies have found a steady increase in the prevalence of dementia in a stable population of patients with PD despite maximal drug treatment (Sweet and McDowell, 1975; Markham et al., 1974). Furthermore, one of the most common side effects of treatment with dopaminergic agents is confusion, found in 25% (Mayeux et al., 1981) to 50% (Sweet and McDowell, 1975) of patients. Demented patients are most likely to become confused from medications and at the lowest doses (Sweet and McDowell, 1975). Yet there is no doubt that in some cases, chronic confusion improves with L-DOPA. Whether this is a direct effect or an indirect result of increased activity and consequent reduction of sensory deprivation or both is not clear.

Finally, in the consideration of PD, one must recall the high frequency of depression, variously 30% (Lieberman et al., 1979) to 76% (Markham et al., 1974). Depression does not account for the dementia, but it surely interacts with dementia. Depression in PD is inconsistent. Although it is not directly related to the severity of motor impairment (Mayeux et al., 1981), it may or may not improve with treatment of the motor impairment. However, it often responds independently to tricyclic antidepressants (Markham et al., 1974).

There is much to learn about mental changes in PD. We believe it safe to conclude (1) that mental decline in PD is common, (2) that it is not simply the interaction of PD and AD, (3) that it is qualitatively different from that of AD, MID, and Pick's disease, and (4) that it best fits the designation "subcortical dementia," in which the abnormalities are slow performance, mildly impaired memory, impaired higher level reasoning, and associated affective abnormality (depression) (Albert et al., 1974).

Alcoholism

Finally, a full review of the important neurological disorders that cause dementia must include a few observations about the effects of alcohol abuse. In the tabulations of the etiology of dementia mentioned previously (Marsden and Harrison, 1972; Freemon, 1976), alcoholic dementia was the final diagnosis in approximately 7% of the patients, a more common diagnosis than all other medical diseases combined. Clinical details are not provided; thus, the exact nature of mental decline in these patients is not known. Our understanding of the characteristics of alcoholic cognitive impairment comes from other sources. First, investigation of memory function and information processing in Korsakoff's disease, alcoholic controls, and nonalcoholic controls has generated a large body of incidental data about mental functions in chronic alcoholics without overt cerebral dysfunction (Butters and Cermak, 1976). These studies have shown that chronic alcoholics without overt cerebral dysfunction still have constant, reproducible neuropsychological deficits in at least three areas: short-term memory on a task with proactive interference (Cermak and Butters, 1973); depth and stability of information processing (Oscar-Berman, 1973), and visuoperceptive processing (Butters and Cermak, 1976).

A second level of knowledge about mental deficits in alcoholics comes from the study of patients with Korsakoff's syndrome. Korsakoff's syndrome is a profound deficit in the ability to form new memories, associated with a variable deficit in recall of old memories despite a clear sensorium (Butters, 1979). Further careful examination reveals a flattening of drives, unconcern about incapacities, and profound apathy (Victor et al., 1971). Nonetheless, by many definitions, Korsakoff's syndrome would not qualify as a dementia; rather, it would be considered a restricted deficit of memory. Traditional teaching held that Korsakoff's syndrome has an abrupt onset in a setting of confusion, ophthalmoplegia, nystagmus, and ataxia (Wernicke's encephalopathy) and that the primary etiology of both disorders was thiamine deficiency in nutritionally deprived alcoholics (Victor et al., 1971). There seems no doubt that the tradition is correct for Wernicke's encephalopathy. For Korsakoff's disease, the issue of etiology is more complicated.

Nonalcoholic patients with thiamine deficiency and Wernicke's encephalopathy do not develop a lasting amnestic state if treated with thiamine (Lishman, 1981); most alcoholics, even if treated, do. Many alcoholic patients in our hospital have a definite history of gradual memory decline culminating in Korsakoff's disease without ever suffering an acute thiamine deficient Wernicke's state; the literature confirms the existence of these gradual-onset Korsakoff cases (Cutting, 1978). The neuropathology of alcoholic Korsakoff's disease almost certainly includes cortical atrophy in addition to the often-described diencephalic lesions (Victor et al., 1971; Lishman, 1981). This cortical atrophy can be demonstrated at gross brain dissection (Courville, 1956) or by CT scan (Lishman et al., 1980). Understanding the nature of mental impairment in alcoholics is made even more complex by the recognition of another group of patients with alcoholic dementia (Lishman, 1981). These patients are chronic alcoholics with a gradual decline in cognition (average history is over one year). When evaluated, they show deficits across a wider range of cognitive functions than patients with Korsakoff's disease; this is reflected in depressed scores on both the verbal and performance scales of the Wechsler Adult Intelligence Scale (Cutting, 1978). Many alcoholics with gradual mental decline, with the diagnosis of Korsakoff's syndrome, may actually have this more profound impairment of cognition with associated cortical atrophy (Lishman, 1981). If alcoholics in this last group discontinue alcohol abuse, they may show considerable cognitive recovery sufficient to make some investigators reluctant to refer to this syndrome as alcoholic dementia. Cutting (1978), for instance, has suggested "accelerated psychological deterioration" as an alternative term. We see no problem with the term alcoholic dementia; it should not carry the connotation of irreversibility any more than NPH dementia does.

Assessment of cognition in alcoholics is always plagued by the multiple potential etiologies of mental deficits. The disorders described above are presumably related to thiamine deficiency and to the direct toxic effects of alcohol. Alcoholics also suffer from other vitamin dificiencies, including niacin deficiency (pellegra), which may be a much overlooked cause of dementia in these patients (Lishman, 1981). Alcoholics have high incidences of systemic illnessess that can affect cognition (cirrhosis, cardiomyopathy, etc.). Alcoholics are susceptible to repeated head injuries, and these carry cognitive consequences of their own (Alexander, 1982). There are uncommon cerebral degenerations in alcoholics in which the exact mechanism of brain damage is unknown and the clinical manifestations not defined. Marchiafava–Bignami disease, for instance, is a pathological diagnosis of atrophy of the central fibers of the corpus callosum throughout its extent (Victor, 1979). Most cases have prominent acute mental changes, but these cannot be separated from the coincident effects of intoxication, withdrawal, or systemic illness. In many cases, no clinical disorder is recognized, and the postmortem findings are unexpected. Victor (1979) describes as a clinical appearance of Marchiafava–Bignami disease a picture of slow evolution of behavioral and emotional disturbances over months to years. These disturbances might stabilize or improve.

It is our impression that Marchiafava–Bignami disease probably presents as a subacute or chronic behavioral disorder that may be unidentifiable because of other coincident cerebral disease. It may be an example of a specific dementia of alcoholism, which will eventually be clinically distinguishable from other pathological mechanisms of dementia in alcoholics.

In addition to the specific degenerative processes associated with alcoholism and the medical illnesses of alcoholism with cognitive consequences, the impact of repeated intoxications on mental functioning must not be overlooked. We suspect that many patients with history of subacute behavior change, forgetfulness, and unreliability are presenting with the cumulative effect of numerous episodes of transiently impaired function while acutely intoxicated. A short period of abstinence may clarify this problem. In our experience, this problem of repeated intoxications as a cause of apparent cognitive decline is particularly likely to be overlooked in successful, middle to upper-class patients.

In summary, the mental disorders of alcoholism probably represent several different processes. Some of these are distinct, clinically homogeneous disorders, such as acute Korsakoff's syndrome emerging out of Wernicke's encephalopathy. Others are pathologically distinct, but clinically heterogeneous, such as Marchiafava–Bignami disease. There is also a direct and cumulative toxic effect of alcohol on the brain that may produce a steadily progressive picture of cognitive decline: alcohol dementia. Finally, there is the impossible task of calculating the massed effects of poor nutrition, mixed subclinical vitamin deficiencies, direct toxic effect, and minor head injuries.

Conclusions

In this chapter several issues were faced. Dementia was defined in an operational manner to allow flexibility in its application. The numerous, almost unavoidable consequences of normal aging were reviewed in the sense of how they influence and alter dementing diseases. The diagnostic dilemma of depression in the elderly was emphasized. A series of basic principles of clinical assessment was outlined: history, physical examination, neurological examination, mental status evaluation, classification of dementia type, and diagnosis. Finally, the six most important neurological etiologies were reviewed in some detail.

Throughout, we have attempted to keep in perspective the interactions of aging and disease, since the elderly population are at greater risk for dementing disease. Common dementing diseases may have unique clinical presentations in the elderly. The factor of age alone is of tremendous significance in the clinical picture of these diseases. In every regard, the title "Dementia in the Elderly" seems justified.

References

Adams, R.D., Fisher, D.M., Hakim, S., Ojemann, R.G., and Sweet, W.H. (1965). Symptomatic occult hydrocephalus with normal cerebrospinal fluid pressure. N. Eng. J. Med. 272, 117–126.

Adams, R.D. and Victor, M. (1977). Principles of Neurology. McGraw-Hill, New York.

Albert, M.L., Feldman, R.G., and Willis, A.L. (1974). The subcortical dementia of progressive supranuclear palsy. J. Neurol. Neurosurg. Psychiat. 37, 121–130.

Alexander, M.P. (1982). Traumatic brain injury. In Psychiatric Aspects of Neurologic Disease, Vol. II. D.F. Benson and D. Blumer, Eds. Grune & Stratton, New York.

Alvord, E.C., Forno, L.S., Kusske, J.A. et al. (1974). The pathology of Parkinsonism: A comparison of degenerations in cerebral cortex and brain stem. Adv. Neurol. 5, 175–193.

Arie, T. (1973). Dementia in the elderly: Diagnosis and assessment. Br. Med. J. 4, 540–543.

Benson, D.F., LeMay, M., Patten, D.H. and Rubens, A.B. (1970). Diagnosis of normal pressure hydrocephalus. N. Eng. J. Med. 283, 609–615.

Benson, D.R., Marsden, C.D., and Meadows, J.C. (1974). The amnesic syndrome of posterior cerebral artery occlusion. Acta Neurol. Scand. 50, 133–145.

Birkett, D.P. (1972). The psychiatric differentiation of senility and arteriosclerosis. Br. J. Psychiat. 120, 321–325.

Blessed, G., Tomlinson, B.E., and Roth, M. (1968). The association between quantitative measures of dementia and of senile change in cerebral gray matter of elderly subjects. Br. J. Psychiat, 114, 797–811.

Boller, F., Mizutani, T., Roessmann, U., and Gambetti P. (1980). Parkinson disease, dementia, and Alzheimer disease: Clinicopathological correlations. Ann. Neurol, 7, 329–335.

Botwinick, J. (1973). Aging and Behavior. Springer, New York.

Botwinick, J. (1975). Behavioral processes in aging. In Genesis and Treatment of Psychologic Disorders in the Elderly, Vol. 2. S. Gershon and I. Sherwin, Eds. Raven Press, New York, pp. 1–18.

Botwinick, J. and Storandt, M. (1974). Memory, Related Functions and Age. C. Thomas, Springfield, Ill.

Bousser, M.G. (1977). Les conceptions actuelles des demences arteriopathiques. Encephal. 3, 357–372.

Brown, J.W. and Hecaen, H. (1976). Lateralization and language representation. Neurol. 26, 183–189.

Butters, N. (1979). Amnesic disorders. Clinical Neuropsychology, K.M. Heilman and E. Valenstein, Eds. Oxford University Press, New York, pp. 439–474.

Butters, N. and Cermak, L.S. (1976). Neuropsychological studies of alcoholic patients. In Empirical Studies of Alcoholism, G. Goldstein and C. Neuringer, Eds. Ballinger, Cambridge, Mass., pp. 153–193.

Caplan, L.R. and Schoene, W.C. (1978). Clinical features of subcortical arteriosclerotic encephalopathy (Binswanger's disease). Neurol. 28, 1206–1215.

Cermak, L.S. and Butters, N. (1973). Information processing deficits of alcoholic Korsakoff patients. Quart. J. Stud. Alcohol. 34, 1110–1132.

Chown, S.M. (1961). Age and rigidities. J. Gerontol. 16, 353–362.

Coblentz, J.M., Mattis, S., Zingesser, L.H., Kasoff, S.S., Wisniewski, H.M., and Katzman, R. (1973). Presenile dementia. Arch. Neurol. 29, 299–308.

Cook, R.H., Ward, B.E., and Austin, J.H. (1979). Studies in aging of the brain. IV. Familial Alzheimer's disease: Relation to transmissible dementia, aneuploidy and microtubular defects. Neurol. 129, 1402–1412.

Courville, C.B. (1956). The Effects of Alcohol on the Nervous System of Man. San Lucas Press, Los Angeles.

Cummings, J.L. and Duchen, L.W. (1981). The Kluver-Bucy syndrome in Pick's disease: Clinical and pathological correlations. Neurol. 31, 1415–1422.

Cumming, E. and Henry, W. (1961). Growing Old: The Process of Disengagment. Basic Books, New York.

Cutting, J. (1978). The relationship between Korsakoff's syndrome and "alcoholic dementia." Br. J. Psychiat. 132, 240–251.

Davies, P. and Maloney, A.J.F. (1976). Selective loss of central cholinergic neurons in Alzheimer's disease. Lancet ii, 1403.

DeRueck, J., Crevits, L., DeCoster, W., Sieben, G., and Vander Eecken, H. (1980). Pathogenesis of Binswanger's chronic progressive subcortical encephalopathy. Neurology 30, 920–928.

Drachman, D.A. and Sahakian, B.J. (1980). Memory and cognitive function in the elderly. Arch. Neurol. 37, 674–675.

Earnest, M.P., Heaton, R.K., Wilkinson, R.E., and Manke, WF. (1979). Cortical atrophy, ventricular enlargement and intellectual impairment in the aged. Neurology 29, 1138–1143.

Eisdorfer, C., Axelrod, S., and Wilkie, F. (1963). Stimulus exposure time as a factor in serial learning in an aged sample. J. Ab. Soc. Psychol. 67, 599–600.

Feldman, R.G., Chandler, K.A., Levy, L.L., and Glaser, G.H. (1963). Familial Alzheimer's disease. Neurol. 13, 811–824.

Fisher, C.M. (1960). Dementia in cerebrovascular disease. Trans. Amer. Neurol. Assoc. 85, 147–152.

Fisher, C.M. (1965). Lacunes: Small deep cerebral infarcts. Neurology 15, 774–784.

Fisher, C.M. (1979). Capsular infarcts. Arch. Neurol. 36, 65–73.

Fleminger, R. (1978). Visual hallucinations and illusions with propanolol. Br. J. Med. 1, 1182.

Fraser, H.S. and Carr, A.C. (1976). Propanolol psychosis. Br. Med. J. 129, 508–509.

Freemon, F.R. (1976). Evaluation of patients with progressive intellectual deterioration. Arch. Neurol. 33, 658–659.

Gainotti, G., Caltagirone, C., Masullo, C., and Miceli, G. (1980). Patterns of neuropsychologic impairment in various diagnostic groups of dementia. In Aging of the Brain and Dementia, Aging, Vol. 13.

Garron, D.C., Klawans, H.L., and Narin, F. (1972). Intellectual functioning of person with idiopathic parkinsonism. J. Nerv. Ment. Dis. 154, 445–452.

Gershon, S. and Raskin, A. (Eds.). (1975). Aging, Vol. 2. Genesis and Treatment of Psychologic Disorders in the Elderly. Raven Press, New York.

Go, R.C.P., Todorov, A.B., Elston, R.C., and Constantinidis, J. (1978). The malignancy of dementias. Ann. Neurol. 3, 559–561.

Goodwin, F.K., Ebert, M.G., and Bunney, W.E. Jr. (1972). Mental effects of reserpine in man: A Review. In Psychiatric Complications of Medical Drugs, R.I. Shade, Ed. Raven Press, New York, pp. 73–102.

Goudsmit, J., Morrow, C.H., Asher, D.M., Yanagihara, R.T. et al. (1980). Evidence for and against transmissibility of Alzheimer disease. Neurology 30, 945–950.

Hachinski, V.C. Iliff, L.D., Zilhka, E. et al. (1975). Cerebral blood flow in dementia. Arch. Neurol. 32, 632–637.

Hammond, J.J. and Kiekendal, W.M. (1979). Antihypertensive agents. In Neuropsychiatric Side Effects of Drugs in the Elderly, A.J. Levenson, Ed. Raven Press, New York, pp. 49–68.

Harner, R.N. (1975). EEG evaluation of the patient with dementia. In Psychiatric Aspects of Neurologic Disease, D.F. Benson and D. Blumer, Eds. Grune & Stratton, New York, pp. 63–82.

Henry, G.M., Weingarten, H., and Murphy, D.L. (1973). Influence of affective states and psycholactive drugs on verbal learning and memory. Amer. J. Psychiat. 130, 966–971.

Herzog, A.G. and Kemper, T.L. (1980). Amygdaloid changes in aging and dementia. Arch. Neurol. 37, 625–629.

Holland, D.B. and Kaplan, W.M. (1976). Propanolol in the treatment of hypertension. N. Eng. J. Med. 297, 930–936.

Hollister, L.E. (1979). Psychotherapeutic Drugs, in Neuropsychiatric Side Effects of Drugs in the Elderly, A.J. Levenson, Ed. Raven Press, New York, pp. 79–88.

Horn, J.L. (1975). Aging and Intelligence. In Aging, Vol. 2, Genesis and Treatment of Psychologic Disorders in the Elderly, S. Gershon and I. Sherwin, Eds. Raven Press, New York, pp. 19–44.

Huckman, M.S., Fox, J., and Topel, J. (1975). The validity of criteria for the evaluation of cerebral atrophy by computed tomography. Radiol. 116, 85–92.

Jacobs, L., Conti, D., Kinkel, W.R., and Manning, E.J. (1976). Normal pressure hydrocephalus. J. Amer. Med. Assoc. 235, 510–512.

Katzman, R. (1976). The prevalence and malignancy of Alzheimer's disease. Arch. Neurol. 33, 217–218.

Katzman, R. (1977). Normal pressure hydrocephalus. In Dementia, C.E. Wells, Ed. F.A. David, Philadelphia, pp. 69–92.

Katzman, R., Terry, R.D., and Bick, E.L. (Eds.). (1978). Alzheimer's Disease: Senile Dementia and Related Disorders. Raven Press, New York.

Kay, D.W.K., Beamish, P., and Roth, M. (1964). Old age mental disorders in Newcastle-upon-Tyne. Part II: A study of possible social and medical causes. Br. J. Psychiat. 110, 668–682.

Kiloh, L.G. (1961). Pseudodementia. Acta Psychiat. Scand. 37, 336–351.

Kronful, Z., Hamsher Kde, S., Digre, K., and Waziri, R. (1978). Depression and hemispheric function: Changes associated with unilateral ECT. Br. J. Psychiat. 132, 560–567.

Kurtzke, J.F. and Kurland, L.T. (1981). The Epidemiology of Neurologic Disease. In Clinical Neurology, Vol. 3, Ch. 48, A.B. Baker and L.J. Baker, Eds. Harper & Row, Hagerstown, Md.

Lesser, R.P., Fahn, S., Snider, S.R. et al. (1979). Analysis of the clinical problems in parkinsonism and the complications of long term levodopa therapy. Neurology 29, 1253–1260.

Levenson, A.J. (Ed.). (1979). Neuropsychiatric Side Effects of Drugs in the Elderly. Raven Press, New York.

Lieberman, A., Dziatolowski, M., Kupersmith, M. et al. (1979). Dementia in Parkinson's disease. Ann. Neurol. 6, 355–359.

Lishman, W.A. (1978). Organic Psychiatry. Blackwell Scientific Publishing, Oxford.

Lishman, W.A. (1981). Cerebral disorder in alcoholosm, Brain 104, 1–20.

Lishman, W.A., Ron, M.A., and Acker, W. (1980). Computed tomography and psychometric assessment of alcoholic patients. In Addiction and Brain Damage, D. Richter, Ed. Croom Helm, London, pp. 215–227.

Loizou, L.A., Kendal, B.E., and Marshall, J. (1981). Subcortical arteriosclerotic encephalopathy: a clinical and radiological investigation. J. Neurol. Neurosurg., Psychiat. 44, 294–304.

Loranger, A.W., Goodell, E., McDowell, F.H., Lee, J.E., and Sweet, R.D. (1972). Intellectual impairment in Parkinson's syndrome. Brain 95, 405–412.

McHugh, P.R. and Folstein, M.F. (1975). Psychiatric syndromes of Huntington's chorea: A clinical and phenomenologic study. In Psychiatric Aspects of Neurologic Disease, D.F. Benson and D. Blumer, Eds. Grune & Stratton, New York, pp. 267–285.

McNamara, F.O. and Appel, S.H. (1977). Biochemical approaches to dementia. In Dementia, C.E. Wells Ed. F.A. Davis, Philadelphis, pp. 155–168.

Maddox, G. and Eisdorfer, C. (1962). Some correlates of activity and morale among the elderly. Sociol. Proc. 40, 228–238.

Markham, C.H., Treciokas, L.J., and Diamond, S.G. (1974). Parkinson's disease and levodopa. West. J. Med. 121, 188–206.

Marsden, C.D. and Harrison, M.J.G. (1972). Outcome of investigation of patients with presentile dementia. Br. Med. J. 2, 249–252.

Mayer-Gross, W., Slater, E., and Roth, M. (1969). Clinical Psychiatry, 3rd Ed. Bailliere, Tindall and Carssell, London.

Mayeux, R., Hunter, S., and Fahn S. (1980). More on myoclonus in Alzheimer disease. Ann. Neurol. 8, 200.

Mayeux, R., Stern, Y., Rosen, J., and Leventhal, J. (1981). Depression, intellectual impairment and Parkinson disease. Neurology 31, 645–650.

Medina, J.L., Rubino, F.A., and Ross, E. (1976). Agitated delirium caused by infarction of the hippocampal formation and fusiform and lingual gyri. Neurology 24, 1181–1183.

Messert, B. and Baker, N.H. (1966). Syndrome of progressive spastic ataxia and apraxia associated with occult hydrocephalus. Neurology 16, 440–452.

Messert, B. and Wanamaker, B.B. (1974). Reappraisal of the adult hydrocephalus syndrome. Neurology 24, 224–231.

Mesulam, M.-M., Waxman, S.G., Geschwind, N., and Sabin, T., (1976). Acute confusional state with right middle cerebral artery infarction. J. Neurol. Neurosurg. Psychiat. 39, 84–89.

Miller, E. (1977). Abnormal Aging. Wiley, London.

Murphy, D.L. and Weingarten, H. (1976). Catecholomines and memory: Enhanced verbal learning during L-dopa administration. Psychopharmacol. Bull. 27, 319–326.

Nandy, K. and Sherwin, I. (Eds.). (1977) The Aging Brain and Senile Dementia. Plenum Press, New York.

Ojemann, G.A., Fisher, C.M., Adams, R.D., Sweet, W.H., and New, P.F.J. (1969). Further experience with normal pressure hydrocephalus. J. Neurosurg. 31, 279–294.

Olson, M.I. and Shaw, C.-M. (1969). Presenile dementia in mongolism. Brain 92, 147–156.

Olzewski, J. (1962). Subcortical arteriosclerotic encephalopathy: Review of the literature on the so-called Binswanger's disease and presentation of two cases. Wld. Neurol. 3, 559–575.

Oscar-Berman, M. (1973). Hypothesis testing and focusing behavior during concept formation by amnesic Korsakoff's patients. Neuropsychol. 11, 191–198.

Pearce, J. and Miller, E. (1973). Clinical Aspects of Dementia. Bailliere Tindall, London.

Peters, B.H. and Levin, H.S. (1979). Effects of physotigmine and lecithin on memory in Alzheimer disease. Ann Neurol. 6, 219–221.

Pollock, M. and Hornabrook, R.W. (1966). The prevalence, natural history and dementia of Parkinson's disease. Brain 89, 429–448.

Roberts, M.A., and Caird, F.I. (1976). Computerized tomography and intellectual impairment in the elderly. J. Neurol. Neurosurg. Psychiat. 39, 986–989.

Roberts, P.J., Foster, G.A., Thomas, E.M. (1981). Neurotoxic action of methyltetrahydrofolate in rat cerebellum unrelated to the direct activation of kainate receptors. Nature 293, 654–655.

Robertson, E.E., LeRoux, A., and Brown, J.H. (1958). The clinical differentiation of Pick's disease. J. Ment. Sci. 104, 1000–1024.

Ron, M.A., Toone, B.K., Garralda, M.E., and Lishman, W.A. (1979). Diagnostic accuracy in presenile dementia. Br. J. Psychiat. 134, 161–168.

Rosen, W.G., Terry R.D., Fuld, P.A., Katzman, R., and Peck, A. (1980). Pathological verification of ischemic score in differentiation of dementias. Ann. Neurol. 7, 486–488.

Rosenberg, G.A., Kornfeld, N., Stovring, J., and Bicknell, J.M. (1979). Subcortical arteriosclerotic encephalopathy (Binswanger): Computed tomography. Neurology 29, 1102–1106.

Shenkin, H.A., Greenberg, J., Bouzarth, W.F., Gutterman, P., and Morales, J.O. (1970). Ventricular shunting for relief of senile symptoms. J. Amer. Med. Assoc. 283, 609–615.

Shraberg, D. (1978). The myth of pseudodementia: Depression and the aging brain. Amer. J. Psychiat. 135, 601–603.

Sim, M., Turner, E., and Smith, W.T. Cerebral biopsy in the investigation of presenile dementia: I. Clinical aspects. Br. J. Psychiat. 112, 119–125.

Sjogren, T., Sjogren, H., and Lindgren, A.G.H. (1952). Morbus Alzheimer and morbus Pick. Acta Psychiat. Neurol. Scand. (Suppl. 82) 1–152.

Slade, W.R., Jr. (Ed.). (1981). Geriatric Neurology: Selected Topics. Futura Publishing Company, Mount Kisco, N.Y.

Sroka, H., Elizan, T.S., Yahr, M.D., Burger, A., and Mendoza, M.R. (1981). Organic mental syndrome and confusional states in Parkinson's disease. Arch. Neurol. 38, 339–342.

Stengel, E. (1943). A study on the symptomatology and differential diagnosis of Alzheimer disease and Pick's disease. J. Ment. Sci. 89, 1–20.

Strub, R.L. and Black, W. (1977). The Mental States Examination in Neurology. F.A. Davis, Philadelphia.

Sweet, R.D. and McDowell, F.H. (1975). Five years' treatment of Parkinson's disease with levodopa. Ann. Int. Med. 83, 456–463.

Sypert, G.W., Leffmann, H., and Ojemann, G.A. (1973). Occult NPH manifested by Parkinson's dementia complex. Neurology 23, 234–238.

Terry, R.D., Peck, A., De Teresa, R., Schecter, R., and Horoupian, D.S. (1981). Some morphometric aspects of the brain in SDAT. Ann. Neurol. 10, 184–192.

Thornton, W.E. (1976). Dementia induced by methyldopa with haloperidol. N. Eng. J. Med. 294, 1222.

Tomlinson, B.E., Blessed, G., and Roth, M. (1970). Observations on the brains of demented old people. J. Neurol. Sci. 11, 205–242.

Victor, M. (1979). Neurologic Disorders Due to Alcoholism and Malnutrition. In Clinical Neurology, Vol. 2, Ch. 22, A.B. Baker and L.H. Baker, Eds. Harper & Row, Hagerstown, Md.

Victor, M., Adams, R.D., and Colling, G.H. (1971). The Wernicke-Korsakoff Syndrome. F.A. Davis, Philadelphia.

Waal, H.J. (1967). Propanolol induced depression. Br. Med. J. 2, 50.

Wang, H.S. (1977). Dementia in old age. In Dementia, C.E. Wells, Ed. F.A. Davis, Philadelphia, pp. 15–26.

Webster's New International Dictionary (1981). 3rd Ed. P.B. Grove, Ed. G & C Merriam, Springfield, Mass.

Weingarten, H. Cohen P.M., Murphy, D.L., Martello, J., and Gerdt, C. (1981). Cognitive processes in dementia. Arch. Gen. Psychiat. 38, 42–47.

Wells, C.E. (1970). Pseudodementia. Amer. J. Psychiat. 136, 895–900.

Wells, C.E. (Ed.). (1977). Dementia. F.A. Davis, Philadelphia.

Weschler, D. (1958). The Measurement and Appraisal of Adult Intelligence 4th Ed. Williams & Wilkins, Baltimore, Md.

Whitehouse, P.J., Price, D.L., Clark, A.W.,

Coyle, J.T., and DeLong, M.R. (1981). Alzheimer disease: Evidence for selective loss of cholinergic neurons in the nucleus basalis. Ann. Neurol. 10, 122–126.

Wisniewski, K., Jervis, G.A., Moretz, R.C., and Wisniewski, H.M. (1979). Alzheimer neurofibrillary tangles in diseases other than senile and presenile dementia. Ann. Neurol. 5, 288–294.

Wood, J.H., Bartlet, D., James, A.E., and Udvanhelyi, G.B. (1974). Normal pressure hydrocephalus: Diagnosis and patient selection for shunt surgery. Neurology 24, 517–526.

Worm-Petersen, J. and Pakkenberg, H. (1968). Atherosclerosis of cerebral arteries, pathological and clinical correlations. J. Gerontol. 23, 445–449.

15. Acute Confusional States (Delirium) in the Elderly

Z.J. LIPOWSKI

Disorders of cognition are the most often encountered forms of psychopathology among the elderly in clinical settings. Delirium (acute confusional states) and dementia constitute the most common and important cognitive disorders. Confusion, a popular, if vague, designation for some of the manifestations of cognitive dysfunction, has been called "the very stuff of geriatric medicine" (Brocklehurst and Hanley, 1976) on account of its frequent occurrence in physically ill, elderly patients. Confusion often replaces pain or fever as the main presenting symptom of a physical illness in an old person (Report of the Royal College of Physicians, 1981). Along with incontinence, postural instability, and immobility, it represents one of the most frequent reasons for referral of patients to geriatricians (Brocklehurst, 1977). In addition to its diagnostic importance as a psychopathological manifestation of a large spectrum of organic diseases in the brain and elsewhere in the body, a confusional state increases the burden of illness for the patient and his or her family and creates serious management problems for physicians and nurses.

Despite its generally acknowledged importance, delirium, or confusional states, has attracted too little attention on the part of clinical investigators. As a result of such neglect, its incidence, pathogenesis, and pathophysiology are largely unknown. Furthermore, inconsistent, muddled, and overlapping terminology has hampered communication and no doubt contributed to the relatively undeveloped state of this area of medicine. The current resurgence of interest in mental disorders in the elderly may serve to attract attention to delirium and stimulate much-needed research on all its aspects.

Terminology and Definition

There is no universally accepted terminology of mental disorders in the elderly at present. Disorders discussed in this chapter have been variously referred to as acute confusional states, delirium, acute brain syndromes, and acute brain failure. "Confusion" is used very loosely by physicians and nurses and cannot be regarded as a scientific or a diagnostic term (Wolanin and Phillips, 1981; Adams, 1977). Yet despite its obvious disadvantages, the designation "acute confusional states" is used throughout the geriatric literature and is now established usage. It will be used as a synonym for "delirium," although delirium is preferred because it has been in use longer, it is shorter, and it involves explicit diagnostic criteria (DSM-III, 1980).

Definition. Delirium (acute confusional state) is a transient organic brain syndrome of acute onset characterized by concurrent disorders of attention, perception, thinking, memory, psychomotor behavior, and the sleep–waking cycle.

Incidence

Little is known about the incidence of delirium in the elderly, but it is usually stated to be high (Report of the Royal College of Physicians, 1981). The lack of precise diagnostic criteria, the inconsistent use of terms, and the varying methods of case finding have generally marred studies in this area, and thus, findings should be interpreted cautiously. Futhermore, the incidence figures reported may reflect the type of clinical setting in which they were collected, that is, a psychiatric hospital or a psychiatric ward in a general hospital, a general medical ward, a neurological hospital, or a geriatric unit.

Kral (1975) asserts that 7 to 10% of elderly patients admitted to mental hospitals or psychogeriatric units suffer from delirium; he believes, however, that the incidence of such states is likely to be much higher in general hospitals. Kral, however, offers no data to support his assertion. One of the few carefully designed studies focused on patients, aged 60 years or over, admitted to psychiatric wards of a general hospital (Simon and Cahan, 1963). The investigators diagnosed acute brain syndrome (delirium), alone or associated with the chronic syndrome, in 46% of the patients, 13% of whom displayed the acute syndrome only. A similar incidence, about 40%, was reported from a neurological hospital (Robinson, 1956). A much lower incidence has been reported from general medical wards. Bergmann and Eastham (1974) identified an acute confusional state in about 15% of elderly patients admitted to a medical unit. Seymour et al. (1980) found a similiar incidence among patients aged 70 years or over who were admitted as emergencies to a medical ward. By contrast, Bedford (1959) reported that 80% of 5000 patients over the age 65 admitted to the Oxford Geriatric Unit suffered from delirium. A subsequent study of admissions to 21 geriatric units in Britain found a much lower incidence,

(about 13%) (Hodkinson, 1973). In that study, however, patients were diagnosed as having a confusional state only if they had been mentally intact three months before admission and had a history of confusion of less than two weeks. These criteria of case finding obviously excluded patients with dementia and superimposed delirium.

Although the studies mentioned above do not allow firm conclusions to be drawn, they do indicate that, depending on the type of clinical facility, between 10 and 40% of patients over the age of 65 are likely to have delirium at the time of admission to a hospital. A large proportion, if not the majority, of such patients will have evidence of pre-existing dementia. There is an obvious need for epidemiological studies using standardized case-finding methods and explicit diagnostic criteria.

Clinical Features

The essential features of delirium include cognitive impairment, disturbances of attention and of the sleep–waking cycle, abnormal psychomotor behavior, relatively rapid onset, and a fluctuating course, of usually brief duration (Lipowski, 1980a,b: DSM-III, 1980).

Disorder of Cognition

A patient with delirium displays reduced ability to extract, process, retain, and retrieve information about his or her environment, body, and self. As a result, his or her awareness of the environment is impaired, and consequently, he or she is less able to plan, initiate, and sustain goal-directed behavior. This cardinal feature of delirium may be called a global disorder of cognition, in the sense that all the major cognitive functions, namely, perception, thinking, and memory, are concurrently impaired. The cognitive disorder may vary in degree from a mild confusion commonly experienced during any febrile illness to virtual cessation of cognitive activity.

Perception, or the process of extracting information about one's body and external environment, may be disordered in several respects. Probably the most common disturbances are defective perceptual discrimination and inability to integrate incoming percepts. In the prodromal phase of delirium, the patient often complains of hypersensitivity to light and sound. In a fully developed delirium, a variety of perceptual abnormalities may occur; these include illusions, hallucinations, distortions of body image, and impairment of the subjective sense of the passage of time. Various distortions of both perceived and hallucinated objects may be experienced, as exemplified by polyopsia, metamorphopsia (macropsia or micropsia), and dysmorphopsia (alteration or distortion of the shape of objects).

Illusions and hallucinations are a common, but by no means invariable or diagnostic feature of delirium. Illusions or improper identification and labeling of sensory stimuli may range from simple to elaborate. Commonly, the patient misinterprets some aspects of his or her surroundings, for example, misidentifying the pattern of the wallpaper for insects or folds in the bedcover for snakes. Hallucinations, that is, experiences of perceptual vividness in the absence of appropriate sensory stimuli, occur, according to different reports, in 40 to 75% of cases. Many delirious patients hallucinate only at night (Frieske and Wilson, 1966). Although hallucinations of any type, visual, auditory, tactile, kinesthetic, proprioceptive, olfactory, and gustatory, may be experienced, visual ones alone or combined with auditory predominate (Lipowski, 1980a).

Visual hallucinations in delirium are interpreted by most patients as real and are typically experienced as bright, colored, three-dimensional pictures of people or non-human objects of natural size and in motion. Less often, patients report Lilliputian hallucinations consisting of diminutive people or objects. Some patients hallucinate only when they close their eyes. Both the form and the content of visual hallucinations are highly variable. The contents may vary in complexity, symbolic elaboration, and degree of personal significance. They may range from simple visions of black or colored spots, stars, geometric figures, and the like to whole scenes involving people, animals, monsters, mythological figures, and inanimate objects stationary or in motion. Patients suffering from pulmonary and cardiac diseases reportedly tend to hallucinate white, black, or gray stationary figures (Head, 1901). By contrast, in alcohol withdrawal delirium, patients typically have hallucinations of many small animals or insects in vivid color and constant motion. Patients' reactions to the hallucinations may range from amused detachment to panic or rage. In one study, most patients were observed to hit at or run away from the hallucinations (Frieske and Wilson, 1966).

Auditory hallucinations are just as variable as the visual ones. They may be relatively simple, such as the sound of a fire alarm or police siren, or elaborate, involving entire conversations, screams for help, music, singing, and so forth. It is uncommon for delirious patients to report hearing voices repeating their (patients') thoughts or continually commenting on their actions. Such hallucinations are far more common in schizophrenia. Tactile hallucinations are the third commonest type of misperception of delirium and occur probably in 10 to 20% of cases. They are difficult to distinguish from paresthesiae. Kinesthetic hallucinations, that is, experiences of floating in the air or flying or other types of motion, are occasionally encountered. Olfactory and gustatory hallucinations are quite uncommon in delirium.

Since illusions and hallucinations are subjective experiences, one has to rely on the patient's report, and to a lesser extent, on observation of suggestive behavior, such as talking to invisible persons, to ascertain their presence. Some patients retain insight into the unreality of their experiences, are ashamed of or frightened by them, and deny having them. Furthermore, it is by no means easy to distinguish these misperceptions from delusions or false beliefs, vivid imagery, and dreams. A patient may also find it difficult to tell dreams from hallucinations, for instance. Indeed, he or she may wake up from a dream and continue to dream, or rather hallucinate, on the same theme while awake. Such blurring of the boundaries between internally derived imagery and veridical perceptions is common in delirium, and constitutes one aspect of the impaired reality testing.

Thinking is invariably disordered. There is typically some degree of disorganization of thought processes, often coupled with a tendency to uncontrolled dream-like or oneiric thinking. The patient's thoughts tend to be fragmented, disjointed, and difficult to control. His or her usual capacity to think selectively and logically for the purpose of grasping the situation, making judgments, problem-solving, and planning is compromised to some extent. Thinking may slow down markedly and be laborious, impoverished or, conversely, be abnormally accelerated and incoherent, filled with irrelevant and unbidden images, words, and fantasies. The capacity for abstract thinking and concept formation is impaired, and thus the patient has difficulty in defining words, finding synonyms, interpreting proverbs, and grasping the meaning of incoming information. The patient may be preoccupied with his or her reverie, alternatively neglecting external stimuli or incorporating them indiscriminately into the "day-dream." These features of delirious mentation were likely the reason why many eighteenth-century writers believed that delirium represented a waking dream, one arising from diseased sleep (Lipowski, 1980a).

As the delirious patient's ability to reason and to match incoming information against previously acquired knowledge is reduced, he or she readily develops delusions, that is, false beliefs incongruous with his or her intelligence and education. In delirium, the delusions are typically fleeting, unsystematized, and readily elicited and modified by environmental stimuli. Delusions of persecution are the commonest type, and the patient may believe that he or she is abducted, plotted against, imprisoned, tortured, about to be killed, or otherwise harassed or imperilled. Such delusions may also concern the patient's family or friends. One of my patients insisted that his daughter was being raped outside his room and tried to run to her rescue. It is impossible, in practice, to distinguish delusions from hallucinations and confabulations. All three are common phenomena in delirium, reflect disordered information processing, and constitute what Hughlings Jackson (1932) called "positive symptoms" or release phenomena accompanying loss of function of the highest nervous centers.

Memory is always impaired in delirium. Registration, retention, and retrieval of memories all appear to be faulty to some extent. Immediate recall is impaired, probably as a result of reduced attention. Recent memory is typically more affected than remote memory. Ability to learn new material is defective. The patient may use confabulations to fill memory gaps. There is some degree of both retrograde and anterograde amnesia. After recovery, the patient typically exhibits partial or complete amnesia for the delirious experience.

Spatiotemporal orientation is invariably defective in some degree. Normal orientation, that is, the ability to state correctly one's position in time and place and to identify familiar persons, depends on intact cognitive function. Abnormal orientation, or disorientation, may occur in reference to time, place, space, and other people. Orientation for time is the ability to state correctly the day of the week, the date, and time of day. Orientation for place is correct identification of where one is situated. Orientation for space is the ability to follow some familiar route and appreciate the topographical relationships of the place one is in. Orientation for person is the ability to identify correctly one's own name and those of familiar people.

In delirium, disorientation for time is required for diagnosis. It is the first type of disorientation to appear and the last to clear up. It has been proposed that one should suspect temporal disorientation in a person with some college training who misstates the date by more than one day, and in an individual with a high school education who misses the date by more than three days (Natelson et al., 1979). Of course, in more severe delirium, one encounters more marked errors in temporal orientation and the patient, when challenged, is not able to correct them.

Disorientation for place and person is

likely to be exhibited by the more severely delirious patient. He or she characteristically tends to misidentify the unfamiliar place and unfamiliar people for familiar ones (Levin, 1945). Thus, a nurse may be mistaken for the wife and the hospital for home or a hotel or another hospital more familiar to the patient. In severe delirium, the patient may fail to recognize the next of kin. Spatial disorientation may be manifested by difficulty in finding one's own room or getting lost in familiar surroundings. Loss of awareness of one's identity is exceedingly rare in delirium, if it ever occurs.

Disorder of Wakefulness and Attention

Organized mental activity requires optimal levels of wakefulness and attention. Attention refers to the ability to direct mental processes and to respond to stimuli in a selective, focused, and sustained manner. Alertness is that aspect of attention that involves readiness to receive and respond to stimuli, or the ability to mobilize and focus attention. Vigilance implies capacity for sustained attention. (Some authors use the terms "alertness" and "vigilance" synonymously, but the clinical study of delirium suggests the need to distinguish between them.) Both alertness and vigilance require full wakefulness. A normally awake person is able to mobilize, focus, sustain, and shift attention in response to internal or external stimuli and at will. In delirium, attention is disordered in some or all of its aspects, and this may be postulated to result from a disturbance of wakefulness and of the brain structures subserving it (Lipowski, 1980a,b).

A delirious patient may exhibit abnormally reduced or heightened alertness, but his or her ability to focus, sustain, and shift attention selectively and voluntarily is impaired. The patient tends to be readily distracted by irrelevant stimuli, that is, to be distractible, and is likely to display unpredictable spontaneous fluctuations of attention. As he or she responds to stimuli either sluggishly or erratically and indiscriminately, his or her ability to acquire, process, and grasp information is reduced. It is difficult to communicate with the patient, and it may be impossible to examine his or her mental status thoroughly. Furthermore, the attention disorder tends to fluctuate unpredictably over the course of a day, or even from moment to moment, making contact with the patient precarious.

Disturbance of attention is viewed by some writers as the primary deficit in delirium, one responsible for the disorganization of cognitive processes (Hernandez-Peon, 1966). Since the influential work of Bonhoeffer at the beginning of this century (Bleuler, 1975), however, the disorder of attention has been regarded as one of the key manifestations of the so-called clouding of consciousness, which, in turn, has been proposed as the core feature of delirium. This concept implies a quantitative view of consciousness as a continuum of states of awareness of self and environment, and a capacity to respond to stimuli, ranging from normal waking awareness to stupor and coma. Clouding, in this view, would correspond to that part of the spectrum that extends from mild confusion to stupor. In addition to disordered attention, clouding of consciousness is manifested by global cognitive impairment, as discussed earlier. In this writer's view, this still widely used term is redundant and ambiguous, and should be dropped. If used at all, it should serve only as a designation for the essential features of delirium described here and without any implication that it has explanatory significance or that it conveys additional information.

Closely associated with the disorder of attention is the disturbance of wakefulness and the sleep–waking cycle, a feature of delirium reported by countless observers since Hippocrates, but insufficiently stressed in textbook accounts of the syndrome (Lipowski, 1980a,b). Some degree of disorganization of the normal sleep–waking cycle is the rule. The patient may exhibit drowsiness during the day, and insomnia at night. The sleep–waking cycle may at times be reversed, or sleep loss may be almost total. Both observers and patients have referred to delirium as a twilight state between sleep and full wakefulness. The syndrome may be ushered in by insomnia and vivid dreams or nightmares passing over into nocturnal hallucinations and confusion. Characteristically, delirium tends to be most severe at night and may be largely confined to the night-time.

Disorder of Psychomotor Behavior

In addition to disorders of cognition, wakefulness, and attention, abnormal psychomotor behavior is an essential feature of delirium. In clinical practice, "psychomotor behavior" refers to observable voluntary and involuntary verbal and nonverbal behavior of the patient. It encompasses such behavioral features as the types and speed of movements, the form and flow of speech, nonverbal vocalizations, reaction time of motor responses, and characteristics of handwriting.

The patient may be predominantly hypoactive or hyperactive or may shift unpredictably between these extremes. The hypoactive patient appears inert and lethargic, speaks slowly and hesitantly, does not initiate movements readily, and is generally sluggish in his or her total motor behavior. Occasionally, the patient may manifest catalepsy or catatonia. By contrast, the hyperactive patient, epitomized by a victim of delirium tremens, appears excited and in almost constant motion. His or her reaction time is short, spontaneous movements abound, and all motor responses tend to be excessive in amount and speed. He or she may display tremor, choreiform movements, a variety of semi-purposive motions, and some relatively complex and goal-directed, but erratic and poorly sustained motor behavior. Such vocalizations as laughing, wailing, calling for help, or cursing may be observed. Groping, flapping aimlessly, tossing about, and picking at the bedclothes are all examples of common semi-purposive movements. More complex behavior is exemplified by dressing or undressing, getting out of bed, striking at people, or frantically exploring the surroundings. An occasional patient may mimic his or her customary activities, or occupation, as when a barman goes through the motions of filling a glass. A hyperactive patient tends to speak fast and under pressure and may lapse into loud or muttered, yet incoherent gibberish. Persev-

eration of psychomotor behavior is observed at times.

Chedru and Geschwind (1972a,b) studied speech and writing in acute confusional states. They found such abnormalities of speech as hesitation, repetitions, circumlocution, poorly organized structure, and verbal paraphasias. Most of their patients exhibited dysgraphia in the form of poorly drawn letters, neographisms, spelling errors, and improper spatial alignment of letters.

Associated Features

Several associated, inconsistent features may be displayed by delirious patients and contribute to the variability of the clinical picture. A whole range of emotional disturbances may be experienced and expressed; these include fear, excitement, depression, apathy, irritability, rage, or euphoria. Fear, rage, or both are often accompanied by their usual autonomic nervous system concomitants such as tachycardia, a flushed face, sweating, dilated pupils, and elevated blood pressure. Furthermore, the patient's facial expression, gestures, and other observable behavioral features tend to reflect the patient's dominant emotional state. Fear is common in delirium, but so are apathy and depression. Both fear and rage may represent emotional responses to the patient's threatening hallucinations and associated persecutory delusions. These psychotic symptoms are typically observed in the hyperalert and hyperactive patient. A patient's emotional state may vary during the same day, or even the same hour, and may shift from fear to apathy, for example, without obvious reasons. Such emotional lability is probably more common than a relatively stable affective state. A fearful patient may sustain injury in the course of attempted escape, whereas an angry and aggressive patient may assault people around him or her, having taken them for enemies. Medicolegal complications may result.

Course and Prognosis

The onset of delirium is typically rapid, a matter of hours or a few days. At first the patient may go through a *prodromal phase,* marked by such symptoms as difficulty in concentration and coherent thinking, somnolence, irritability, restlessness, anxiety, hypersensitivity to light and sound, insomnia, vivid dreams, and transient illusions and hallucinations. Full-blown delirium may first become manifest at night. The patient wakes up, often from a disturbing dream, and experiences frightening confusion about his or her whereabouts and situation. A hospitalized patient is apt to get out of bed and may try to leave the ward. During the day, the mildly delirious patient tends to be better oriented and may try to conceal cognitive deficits. As the delirium grows more severe, the patient becomes more consistently inattentive, disoriented, and either unusually quiet and somnolent or increasingly restless, excited, and noisy. Illusions and hallucinations are apt to become more prominent, and absorb the patient's attention, and concurrently his or her contact with the surroundings and ability to communicate adequately deteriorate. A severely delirious patient may gradually sink into stupor or move persistently and purposelessly to the point of exhaustion. Goal-directed actions are difficult or impossible. Incontinence of urine and feces is common at this stage, especially in the elderly. The patient is now fully disoriented, with his or her cognitive functions totally disorganized. From this point, the patient gradually returns to normal or progresses to coma and death. Many patients recover uneventfully, provided that the underlying illness is not fatal and is treated adequately. The usual duration of delirium averages one to two weeks, but occasionally it may last as long as a month. Episodes of nocturnal delirium may recur for weeks if the underlying organic factor persists. In a minority of cases, delirium may be followed by dementia, which may or may not be reversible.

The natural history and prognosis of delirium in the elderly have not been adequately investigated. Since an acute confusional state in an older person, as a rule, signals the onset or exacerbation of a physical illness, which may be life-threatening or terminal, the prognosis is guarded. By definition, delirium is a transient mental disorder, and its outcome should be full resolution and return to the premorbid psychological state. Depending on the underlying condition, however, delirium may be followed by coma and death or by a different and more protracted, or even permanent, organic brain syndrome.

Bedford (1959) reported that of 4000 patients aged 65 years or older who exhibited symptoms of confusional state on admission to hospital, fully 33% died within a month. Of those who recovered, 80% did so in less than a month, the majority of them within two weeks. In 18% of the cases, mental confusion lasted longer than a month; in about 5%, it lingered on for more than six months. Bedford emphasized that, compared to young patients, recovery after confusional states in the elderly may be slow and even incomplete, implying that in some cases dementia will ensue. Furthermore, he rightly stresses that elderly delirious patients demand the "application of the utmost vigilance and energetic treatment" so that they may recover fully and promptly.

Flint and Richards (1956) studied 242 confused patients over 60, admitted to a general medical unit. The mortality rate for this group was 76%, many dying within a few days of admission. The authors point out that the very high mortality rate in their series might have been the result of an undue delay in admission and the consequent advanced deterioration of the patients. In the multi-center study carried out in Britain, of the 186 elderly patients with acute confusional states, 25% died within a month (Hodkinson, 1973). In the San Francisco study, a similar percentage died within a month of admission (Epstein and Simon, 1967).

Insofar as one may generalize from these few studies, the prognosis of the elderly delirious patients is grave, with 20 to 30% mortality within a month of admission to hospital. These findings underscore the importance of early diagnosis, adequate investigation, and vigorous treatment of the underlying organic disease. Many delirious elderly patients had suffered from dementia, and when their delirium cleared up, they return to their previous, relatively stable demented state. On the other hand, transition from a pure delirium to dementia is claimed to be very rare, even in cases of recurrent or subacute confusional state arisng from progressive systemic disease (Roth, 1976).

Etiology

Associated Physical Conditions

Several studies on the physical illnesses and factors most often associated with, and presumably etiologically related to, delirium in the elderly are informative. Kay and Roth (1955) found a high incidence of "toxic-infective" conditions as well as cardiac, respiratory, and genitourinary disorders among elderly patients presenting with acute confusional states. Flint and Richards (1956) studied 242 elderly confused patients and found multiple etiological factors. In about 50% of their patients, confusion was attributed to a systemic disease, in 30%, cerebral disease; but in 20%, no specific organic factor could be identified. Heart failure, pulmonary disease, and uremia were by far the most common extracerebral diseases thought to be etiologically related to confusion. In the multi-center British study (Hodkinson, 1973), pneumonia, cardiac failure, urinary infection, carcinomatosis, and hypokalemia were identified as the most common organic factors precipitating delirium. Pre-existing dementia, defective hearing and vision, and Parkinsonism were given as important predisposing factors. Simon et al. (1970) found malnutrition, cardiac failure, alcoholism, and cerebrovascular accidents to be the disorders most commonly associated with acute brain syndromes in their elderly patients. Seymour et al. (1980) called attention to dehydration and/or sodium depletion as important etiological factors.

The above studies, despite their inconsistencies related to different settings in which they were carried out and to differences in methods of case identification, indicate that cardiac, pulmonary, and urogenital diseases are especially associated with delirium in the elderly. One should add adverse effects of drugs to this list, even though the above studies do not stress them (Report of the Royal College of Physicians, 1981).

Predisposing Factors

Age itself is a predisposing factor to delirium; it is claimed that delirium is four times more frequent in persons over 40 years of age than in younger persons (Doty, 1946). It is generally agreed that the elderly are especially apt to develop delirium in response to a wide range of etiological factors. As discussed earlier, these include systemic and, to a lesser extent, primary cerebral disease, intoxication with drugs, and withdrawal of alcohol or sedative–hypnotic drugs from individuals addicted to them. The high incidence of delirium in the elderly is likely to reflect such factors as impairment of cerebral circulation and, hence, increased vulnerability to hypoxia; a high prevalence and incidence of chronic systemic diseases (cardiovascular, respiratory, and metabolic); and increased frequency of episodes of illness, especially respiratory and urinary infections.

The aging organism is generally more susceptible to disease. The aging brain is more vulnerable to the adverse effects of hypoxia, fluid and electrolyte imbalance, deficiencies of hormones and vitamins, medications, and bacterial toxins. The homeostatic and immune mechanisms of the elderly are generally less efficient than those of younger people, and homeostasis is readily and seriously deranged by a whole spectrum of physicochemical, biological, and psychosocial stressors. The function of the aging brain may be already manifestly impaired or precariously compensated, and even relatively minor derangement of homeostasis, or such factors as sensory or sleep deprivation, social isolation, an unfamiliar environment, or the psychological stress of bereavement, may combine to precipitate acute brain failure, manifested by delirium.

Pre-existing brain damage or degenerative changes, addiction to alcohol, malnutrition, and impairment of vision and

Table 15-1. Etiological Factors in Delirium in the Elderly.

1. Drugs: Sedatives–hypnotics; anticholinergics, including phenothiazines, tricyclic antidepressants, and antihistamines; narcotics; diuretics; digitalis; anti-Parkinsonism drugs; antihypertensives; chlorpropramide; cimetidine
2. Alcohol and Drug Withdrawal
3. Cardiac Disease: Cardiac failure, myocardial infarction, cardiac arrhythmia, endocarditis
4. Infection: Especially pulmonary and urinary infection; bacteremia, septicemia, meningitis, encephalitis
5. Metabolic Disorders: Electrolyte, fluid, and acid–base imbalance; hepatic, renal, and respiratory failure; hypoglycemia, hyperglycemia; hypothyroidism, thyrotoxicosis; hypothermia, hyperthermia; vitamin B complex deficiency
6. Cerebrovascular Disorders: Stroke; transient ischemic attack; subdural hematoma; temporal arteritis; cerebral vasculitis
7. Neoplasm: Intracranial, extracranial (especially bronchogenic carcinoma)
8. Trauma: Head injury, burns, hip fracture, surgery
9. Epilepsy

hearing all predispose an elderly person to delirium.

Specific Etiological Factors

Table 15-1 lists the most common and important etiological factors associated with delirium in the elderly (Lipowski, 1980a). It is far from complete; for a more comprehensive listing, see Lipowski (1980a). Brief comments on the chief etiological factors follow.

Adverse Drug Reactions

The elderly are especially prone to adverse drug reactions, which are said to be about two and one-half times more common in patients over 60 than in those under 60 (Editorial, 1978). In a recent study of 2000 patients consecutively admitted to geriatric medicine units in Great Britain, 81.3% were found to be receiving prescribed drugs at the time of admission, and 15.3% of the recipients suffered from adverse reactions (Williamson and Chopin, 1980). Diuretics were the most often prescribed drugs and, hence, caused the largest number of adverse reactions (37.4%). Antihypertensive, psychotropic, and anti-Parkinsonian drugs had the highest risk of inducing such reactions and were particularly likely to result in hospitalization. Considering that a large proportion of the elderly population receives drugs, the prevalence and incidence of adverse reaction to them are liable to be high. Furthermore, about 25% of elderly patients are reported to receive four to six drugs simultaneously (Williamson and Chopin, 1980), and such "polypharmacy" increases the probability that adverse reactions will occur as a result of drug interactions (Lamy, 1980). Confusion is a common manifestation of drug toxicity in elderly patients (Levenson, 1979), and therapeutic-drug intoxication is claimed to be one of the most frequent causes of delirium in that patient population (Senility Reconsidered, 1980). Although epidemiological data are lacking, these claims are plausible in view of clinical reports that the drugs most frequently prescribed for the elderly, that is, diuretics, psychotropic agents, analgesics, hypnotic–sedatives, and digitalis, are all liable to induce delirium. In addition, many other drugs, only some of which are listed in Table 15-1, may be deliriogenic.

Several factors related to various aspects of the aging process appear to be implicated in adverse drug reactions, including delirium, in the elderly (Vestal, 1978):

1. Impaired hepatic detoxification, especially oxidation, resulting in slower biotransformation of some drugs and probably increased risk for delirium after intake of tricyclic antidepressants, benzodiazepines, anticonvulsants, and oral hypoglycemic agents
2. Reduced renal excretion due to decreased glomerular filtration rate, reduced renal blood flow, and altered

tubular function. Slower excretion prolongs the half-life of such drugs as digoxin, streptomycin, gentamicin, penicillin, and phenobarbitone

3. Reduction of protein binding of drugs due to reduced serum albumin; hence, more free drug is available for distribution to body tissues. As a result, the effects of narcotics, tolbutamide, and other drugs may be enhanced
4. Reduced total body water and, hence, higher concentration of drugs distributed in body fluids
5. Tendency to postural hypotension, hypothermia, and hyperthermia as a result of defective homeostatic protective mechanisms
6. Multiple drug use
7. Increased receptor organ sensitivity
8. Poor compliance in taking drugs as prescribed, compounded by confusion

Diuretics, the most frequently prescribed class of drugs for the elderly, may cause hypokalemia, hyperkalemia, hyponatremia, dehydration, hypercalcemia, and hypotension, all of which can contribute to the onset of delirium.

Psychotropic drugs are widely prescribed for the elderly, who reportedly receive 25% of all prescriptions for these agents (Prien, 1980). Benzodiazepines, especially diazepam, chlordiazepoxide, and flurazepam, head the list. All three of these psychotropic drugs depress the central nervous system in the elderly to a greater extent than in the younger patient. Diazepam and chlordiazepoxide are demethylated in the liver, and since liver function decreases with age, their metabolism and elimination are retarded in the elderly, resulting in accumulation of the drug and increased sedation. Diazepam, reported to have a half-life in hours as long as the patient's age in years, is particularly liable to elicit confusion in the elderly and should not be prescribed (Bliss, 1981). Oxazepam, by contrast, does not undergo demethylation and its elimination is not delayed; thus, it is a preferred anxiolytic for the elderly (Salzman, 1979).

Tricyclic antidepressants readily cause delirium in the elderly, who display increased sensitivity to the anticholinergic effects of these agents, possibly due to a decrease in the cholinergic activity of the aging brain (Salzman, 1979). Amitriptyline's anticholinergic side effects are particularly prominent and other tricyclics, such as desipramine or doxepin, should be used instead to reduce the risk of delirium. Phenothiazines, antihistamines, and various hypnotics containing scopolamine are anticholingeric and may induce delirium. The risk is increased by combining these drugs, a not uncommon practice. Thioridazine is a phenothiazine drug often used to sedate elderly patients, yet it has a high degree of anticholinergic activity. Lithium is liable to precipitate delirium in the elderly even if administered in relatively small doses although serum levels remain therapeutic. Its half-life in the older age group is 36 to 48 hours, in contrast to about 24 hours in the younger adult (Foster et al., 1977).

Anti-Parkinsonian drugs, that is, anticholinergic agents, levodopa, amantadine, bromocriptine, and lergotrile, may all cause delirium (Levenson, 1979; Lieberman et al., 1979; Ing et al., 1979; Sroka et al., 1981). Cimetidine-induced delirium in the elderly has attracted attention lately (McGuigan, 1981). Impaired renal function, coupled with blocking H2-receptors in the brain, has been suggested as the pathogenetic mechanism.

Limitations of space preclude a detailed discussion of drug-induced delirium (for more information see the monographs by Levenson, 1979, and Lipowski, 1980a).

Alcohol and Drug Withdrawal

Alcohol abuse in the elderly is quite prevalent (Wattis, 1981). A long history of excessive drinking and vulnerability to associated vitamin deficiencies are factors that increase the risk of delirium in the elderly. Dependence on any of the sedative–hypnotic drugs may result in delirium when that drug is rapidly withdrawn.

Cardiovascular Disorders

Circulatory diseases account for between 25 and 33% of the medical problems or medical diagnoses in the elderly (Sivertson, 1978), with cardiovascular disorders constituting one of the most important classes of etiological factors in delirium (Schuckit, 1977). Mental confusion may be induced by, and be a prominent manifestation of, myocardial infarction, heart failure, disorders of heart rhythm, aortic stenosis, hypertensive encephalopathy, and subacute bacterial endocarditis. All these conditions may result in cerebral ischemia–anoxia and, hence, delirium.

Myocardial infarction in an elderly patient may be painless and is said to present with acute confusional state in about 11% of the cases (Caird et al., 1976). A sudden onset of delirium in an elderly patient should always raise the possibility of myocardial infarction. Cardiac arrhythmias may present with sudden and transient episodes of confusion (Busse, 1979). Antiarrhythmic drugs, including digoxin, lidocaine, procainamide, quinidine, and phenytoin, may precipitate delirium (Lipowski, 1980a). Electrocardiographic monitoring is advisable in elderly patients presenting with unexplained, sudden delirious episodes. Congestive heart failure, a common problem in geriatrics, may give rise to hypoxemia and recurrent delirium associated with a reduction in cerebral perfusion and oxygen consumption (Eisenberg et al., 1960). Subacute and acute bacterial endocarditis lead to delirium in about 50% of the cases (Caird et al., 1976). Orthostatic hypotension tends to occur more in older than young patients and may be induced by many drugs, especially antihypertensive agents, tricyclic antidepressants, and antipsychotic medications, with resulting confusion. Hypertensive encephalopathy usually leads to delirium (Ram, 1978).

Infections

Any infection, but especially one involving the respiratory or urinary tract, may precipitate delirium in the elderly. Confusion may be the only presenting feature of bronchopneumonia, for example. Most infections tend to be more severe in older patients (Phair, 1979). Pneumonia, cholecystitis, urinary tract infection, diverticulitis, septicemia, bacteremia, and tuberculo-

sis may all give rise to delirium. Postulated pathogenetic mechanisms include such direct toxic effects on the brain as necrosis, inflammation, or edema, in case of intracranial infections; cerebral hypoxia and abnormalities of electrolyte, fluid, and acid–base balance in systemic infections; and the deleterious effects of fever on cerebral metabolism and sleep (Lipowski, 1980a).

Metabolic Disorders (Encephalopathies)

These are among the most common causes of delirium in all age groups. Electrolyte imbalance (Lindeman and Klinger, 1980) and dehydration/volume depletion (Seymour et al., 1980) are especially important deliriogenic factors in the elderly and may be induced by a wide range of drugs and by hepatic and renal disease, infection, neoplasm, surgery, and burns (Lipowski, 1980a; Coakley, 1981). Respiratory failure, acute or chronic, accounts for some 20% of cases of confusional states in the hospitalized elderly (Flint and Richards, 1956; Hodkinson, 1973). The ventilaotry response of normal elderly persons to hypoxemia and hypercapnia is diminished, and there is a general reduction in lung volume, ventilatory capacity and arterial oxygen tension (Coakley, 1981). Thus acute respiratory disease readily results in hypoxemia, which can manifest itself clinically as confusion. The latter is a common feature of pneumonia, acute-superimposed on-chronic respiratory failure, and pulmonary embolism.

Uremia, often due to prostatic hypertrophy and concurrent urinary tract infection, accounted for about 10% of delirium in one study of elderly patients (Flint and Richards, 1956). Hepatic failure is a less common cause of delirium in the elderly. Diabetes mellitus can lead to delirium as a result of ketoacidosis, non-ketotic hyperosmolar precoma, lactic acidosis, or hypoglycemia (Coakley, 1981; Podolsky, 1979). Thyroid disease, both hypothyroidism and thyrotoxicosis, may lead to a confusional state and be misdiagnosed because of an atypical presentation of thyroid dysfunction (Skillman and Falko, 1981). Hypercalcemia and hypocalcemia are common in the elderly and may give rise to delirium (Singer et al., 1977; Lipowski, 1980a). Vitamin deficiencies, especially of nicotinic acid, thiamin, vitamin B_{12}, and folate, are not uncommon in the elderly population (Beauchene and Davis, 1979) and may contribute to the incidence of delirium (Mitra, 1971; Shorvon et al., 1980). Hypothermia and heat stroke can both cause confusional states. A survey carried out in London showed that 3.6% of all patients over the age of 65 admitted to two general hospitals were hypothermic (Coakley, 1981). In mild hypothermia, with deep-body temperature between 32 and 35 °C, the patient is frequently confused. The elderly are particularly susceptible to heat stress and are at higher risk for development of heat stroke in hot and humid weather. Delirium is a common manifestation (Levine, 1969). Anemia is believed to cause mental confusion only when the hematocrit is 40% or less (Flint and Richards, 1956).

Cerebrovascular disorders

Strokes were believed to account for 10% of acute confusional states in the elderly in one series (Simon et al., 1970) and for about 30% in another (Flint and Richards, 1956). By contrast, a more recent British study failed to find any association between these states and stroke, and attributed this discrepancy to "methodological differences" (Hodkinson, 1973). Confusion may, on occasion, be the only presenting symptom of transient ischemic attack (TIA) (McDowell, 1980), but it is more likely to be present in patients suspected of having a TIA, but whose final diagnosis is not TIA (Futty et al., 1977). Delirium may be associated with stroke. Infarctions in the distribution of anterior, middle, and posterior cerebral arteries have been observed to precipitate agitated delirium (Horenstein et al., 1967; Medina et al., 1974, 1977; Mesulam et al., 1976). Confusion may accompany subarachnoid hemorrhage and cerebral embolism. Other intracranial vascular disorders associated with delirium include chronic subdural hematoma (Raskind et al., 1972) and the whole spectrum of noninfectious cerebral arteri-

tis, especially systemic lupus erythematosus (Dimant et al., 1979) and temporal arteritis (Paulley and Hughes, 1960).

Neoplasm

The highest incidence of brain tumors occurs in individuals aged 60 to 70 years (Schoenberg et al., 1978). A confusional state is likely to occur in 20 to 25% of the brain tumor cases, especially when the tumor is fast growing and associated with raised intracranial pressure. Tumors involving the occipital, temporal, and frontal lobes; the corpus callosum; the brain stem; and the region of the third ventricle appear to be particularly likely to give rise to delirium (Lipowski, 1980a).

Extracranial neoplasm may result in a confusional state through a variety of mechanisms, such as metastases to the brain, infiltration of the meninges, infection, disordered metabolic or endocrine function, malnutrition, and cardiovascular insufficiency. Carcinoma of the lung has been found to cause disturbances of consciousness in about 40% of cases—one-half due to cerebral metastases and one-half due to such factors as cardiovascular insufficiency, respiratory failure, and hypercalcemia (Schmid-Wermser et al., 1974). The effects of remote neoplasm, such as multifocal leukoencephalopathy, diffuse polioencephalopathy, and limbic encephalitis, may feature delirium at some stage. The hypercalcemia associated with malignant neoplasms of the lung, kidney, ovary, pancreas, and the reticuloendothelial system often presents with confusional state (Weizman et al., 1979).

Trauma

Head injury in an elderly person may be followed by coma of only short duration, but the subsequent confusion, with post-traumatic amnesia, may last for several weeks (von Wowern, 1966). Delirium may be associated with both intracranial and extracranial complications of head trauma. Traumatic hip fracture in the elderly is often complicated by acute confusional states (Williams et al., 1979). Burns are common in older patients (Slater et al.,

1981) and may cause delirium as a result of hypoxia, hypovolemia, hyponatremia, infection, and acidosis (Lipowski, 1980a). Delirium is a common postoperative complication in the elderly surgical patient (Millar, 1981). Postoperative hypoxemia, dehydration, electrolyte imbalance, infection, and narcotic and sedative drug intake may all precipitate delirium (Mesulam and Geschwind, 1976). The elderly are especially prone to develop postoperative infections, especially pulmonary ones. Bacteremia, resulting from urinary infections induced by catheterization or from intravenous catheters, may present only with delirium (Polly and Sanders, 1977).

Pathogenesis and Pathophysiology

The pathogenetic mechanisms leading to delirium have not been elucidated. The preceding section makes it clear that a wide range of etiological factors, acting singly or in combination, may give rise to the syndrome. These include intracranial and systemic diseases, exogenous poisons, and withdrawal from alcohol and hypnotic–sedative drugs in individuals addicted to them. It is unlikely that all these factors lead to delirium through the same pathway. Engel and Romano (1959) postulate that a general reduction of cerebral metabolism underlies all cases of delirium and is reflected in a concurrent clouding of consciousness and a slowing of the EEG background activity. Although this mechanism may represent the final common path for most cases of delirium, it does not apply to delirium tremens, for example, in which the EEG is not slowed (Allahyari et al., 1976).

Delirium may be induced by focal brain lesions. Infarctions in the most ventral and medial aspects of the occipital and temporal lobes (lingual and fusiform gyri) or the posterior parietal or the prefrontal regions of the right hemisphere may be associated with the syndrome (Mesulam, 1979). The pathogenetic significance of these anatomical locations is unknown. In the vast majority of cases, delirium accompanies disorders of cerebral metabolism involving the brain as a whole. The putative pathophysiological mechanisms include interference with the supply, uptake, or utilization of substrates for oxidative metabolism; disruption of synaptic transmission; impairment of synthesis of neurotransmitters, especially acetylcholine, or the presence of false neurotransmitters; disturbances in the normal ionic passage through excitable membranes; and alterations in electrolyte concentration, water content, osmolality, and pH in the internal milieu (Lipowski, 1980a).

It is probable that age-related degenerative changes in the brain and reduced acetylcholine synthesis predispose the elderly to delirium. Anticholinergic agents readily induce delirium in the elderly, which suggests that suppression of central cholinergic activity may constitute a major pathogenetic factor. Investigators using experimental models of anticholinergic delirium have proposed that derangement of the central cholinergic and adrenergic mechanisms affecting the medial ascending reticular activating system as well as the medial thalamic diffuse projection systems underlies delirium and produces its clinical manifestations (Itil and Fink, 1966). A preponderance of cortical inhibition would be reflected by EEG slowing and the concomitant clouding of consciousness and reduction in psychomotor activity. By contrast, a preponderance of facilitatory influences on the cerebral cortex by the medial thalamic diffuse projection systems would elicit fast activity in the EEG and increased psychomotor activity. It is of interest that physostigmine has been reported to reverse not only anticholinergic delirium (Lipowski, 1980a), but also that due to alcohol (Daunderer, 1978), amantadine (Berkowitz, 1979), and cimetidine (Mogelnicki et al., 1979), as well as delirium tremems (Powers et al., 1981). Increased central noradrenergic activity in delirium tremens could account for the marked psychomotor and sympathetic nervous system hyperactivity (Hawley et al., 1981).

Evidence from experimental and clinical studies suggests that delirium may be the outcome of several pathogenetic mechanisms involving both the cerebral cortex and the subcortical structures where integrated function is essential for normal sleep–

waking cycle, directed attention, and information reception, processing, and retrieval. An imbalance of the cerebral neurotransmitters, notably, acetylcholine and norepinephrine, coupled with a diffuse disturbance of functional brain metabolism, appears to be the most important pathogenetic mechanism. Future studies with positron emission tomography may clarify the nature and distribution of the pathophysiological changes in delirium due to different causes and elucidate the physiological correlates of such clinical features as hypo- and hyperactivity and hallucinations.

Diagnosis

The diagnosis of delirium involves two aspects: recognition of the clinical features of the syndrome and identification of the causative factor or factors (Lipowski, 1980a,b).

Clinical Diagnosis

The essential features of delirium described earlier lead to a clinical diagnosis in a patient of any age. These features may, however, be somewhat modified in the elderly, especially in a demented elderly individual. The more flamboyant symptoms, such as hallucinations, delusions, hyperactivity, and fear, which are often seen in the younger patient, may be absent. The elderly delirious patient may, by contrast, only display hypoactivity, lethargy, depression or indifference, bewilderment, exhaustion, disorientation for time and place, a fluctuating level of awareness with lucid intervals, and a typical nocturnal exacerbation of all symptoms. Diagnostic criteria for delirium in DSM-III (1980) are as follows:

1. Clouding of consciousness (reduced clarity of awareness of the environment), with a reduced capacity to shift, focus, and sustain attention to environmental stimuli
2. At least two of the following:
    (a) Perceptual disturbance: misinterpretations, illusions, or hallucinations

(b) Speech that is at times incoherent
(c) Disturbance of sleep–wakefulness cycle, with insomnia or daytime drowsiness
(d) Increased or decreased psychomotor activity
3. Disorientation and memory impairment (if testable)
4. Clinical features that develop over a short period of time (usually hours to days) and tend to fluctuate over the course of a day
5. Evidence, from the history, physical examination, or laboratory tests of a specific organic factor judged to be etiologically related to the disturbance

Assessment of Cognitive Function and Attention

A delirious patient is as a rule too ill, too distractible, too easily tired, and too uncooperative to permit extensive psychological testing, but assessment of cognitive functions and attention can be carried out at the bedside as part of the routine mental status examination. Several brief scales that allow quantification of cognitive impairment have been proposed (Jacob et al., 1977; Folstein et al., 1975; Pfeiffer, 1975). The following tests should be routine (Lipowski, 1980a):

1. Orientation: date, day of the week, time of day; ability to name the place (hospital, city) the patient is in; ability to identify familiar persons by name, occupation, or both
2. Recent memory: ability to give account of dates, reasons, and circumstances related to current illness, hospitalization, and other pertinent and verifiable facts; recall of three words and three objects after five minutes; digit span
3. Attention: serial sevens or threes, depending on the patient's education (serial sevens are useless in patients with less than 6 years of school) and degree of impairment
4. Abstract thinking: definitions of words; interpretation of proverbs; appreciation of similarities or shared attributes of and differences between concepts
5. Dynamics of thinking: word fluency

test, i.e., asking the patient to say as many single words within one minute as possible, the norm being about 30 words a minute

Laboratory Investigations

The DSM-III requires, as one of the diagnostic criteria for delirium, evidence from the history, physical examination, or laboratory tests of a specific organic factor thought to be etiologically related to the clinical syndrome. If, for example, the history reveals recent ingestion by the patient of a substance known to be deliriogenic, or the physical examination shows evidence of pneumonia or congestive heart failure, one may tentatively infer that the factor is etiologically related to the patient's delirium. In some cases, however, the cause of the delirium is not revealed by either the history or the physical examination. Laboratory investigation serves to help establish the nature of the causative factor or factors. Furthermore, a special investigation of cerebral function may be required to determine if a brain disorder is present and, thus, to confirm that the patient is suffering from delirium rather than from a functional psychiatric disorder that imitates some of the essential features of delirium. Although there is no single laboratory test that would definitively confirm the presence of delirium, the EEG is a useful aid.

The following list of laboratory investigations will serve as a guide, to be used with discernment and good clinical thinking, to help establish the cause of delirium in a given patient:

1. Blood chemistries: sodium, potassium, bicarbonate, chloride, calcium, phosphate, magnesium, blood urea nitrogen, liver function tests, arterial blood gases, ammonia, B_{12} and folate, thyroid function tests, cortisol levels, blood levels of drugs such as digoxin, heavy metals, alcohol
2. Drug screen
3. Hemogram
4. Blood culture
5. Urinalysis
6. Lupus erythematosus cell preparation and anti-nuclear antibody levels
7. Serology
8. Electrocardiogram
9. X-ray of chest, skull
10. Cerebrospinal fluid examination, including serology, culture, protein electrophoresis, glutamine
11. Electroencephalogram
12. Computerized tomography scan

It must be stressed that, in most cases, only the more routine of the above tests should be carried out, depending on the clinical findings and history. The rationale for and the cost of the more elaborate tests must be taken into account. In an occasional case, however, a recurrent or persistent delirium may tax the clinician's diagnostic acumen and demand an extensive laboratory investigation. Since the EEG is particularly useful in the diagnosis of delirium, it calls for a special discussion.

The Electroencephalogram in Delirium

Romano and Engel (1944) carried out classic studies of the EEG in delirium due to a wide range of metabolic, toxic, infectious, and other factors. All their patients exhibited bilateral, diffuse slowing of the EEG background activity, which was positively correlated with the degree of cognitive impairment. The more severe the reduction in the level of alertness, the slower the EEG background activity. As the patient's cognitive function improved, the EEG background frequency accelerated. The investigators concluded that the EEG was the most sensitive and reliable indicator of the functional metabolism of the brain and of cerebral insufficiency underlying clinical delirium (Engel and Romano, 1959).

More recently, Obrecht et al. (1979) reported EEG findings in 95 patients with an acute confusional state, 83 of whom had EEG abnormalities. In most patients with intracranial or extracranial pathology, the EEG's were abnormal, and usually markedly so. Almost one-half of the patients with primary intracerebral disease showed such abnormalities as asymmetry of delta activity and paroxysmal discharges, features that were rarely seen in patients with extracranial pathology. The authors concluded that the EEG was a valuable aid to the diagnosis of confusional states, helping to exclude functional psychiatric disorders and to determine whether confusion was primarily due to intracranial or systemic causes.

Pro and Wells (1977) found evidence that the EEG is useful in the differential diagnosis of delirium. They point out, however, that although patients showing reduced levels of awareness and arousal had an abnormally slow EEG, low voltage fast activity was more likely to predominate in the markedly fearful and agitated patient. In either case, a single EEG recording may be within normal limits and only serial recordings are liable to disclose abnormalities.

Thus, the EEG is a useful aid in the differential diagnosis of delirium, especially if serial recordings are carried out. The EEG abnormalities are nonspecific, and usually consist of slow background activity, in the theta or delta range, with or without superimposed fast activity. These changes are, like delirium itself, reversible. There is no need to use the EEG as a routine diagnostic test in delirium, but it may be utilized if a focal cerebral lesion, or a nonorganic psychiatric syndrome showing some features of delirium, is suspected.

Differential Diagnosis

In a typical case, the diagnosis of delirium is easy. A global cognitive–attentional disorder of acute onset, fluctuating in severity, featuring visual hallucinations, accompanied by a disturbed sleep–waking cycle and either restless or sluggish behavior, is almost certainly delirium. When such a syndrome develops in the presence of a known physical illness, or after accidental injury or surgery, a causal relationship may be assumed, and the diagnosis is practically definitive. In the elderly patient, however, the diagnosis may not be so easy for several reasons. First, the patient may already suffer from a dementia, on which delirium is superimposed, which blurs some clinical features of delirium. Its more striking characteristics, such as complex hallucinations, dream-like mentation, and persecutory delusions, are

liable to be absent, and the patient displays only dull confusion, bewilderment, apathy interrupted by noisy restlessness, incontinence of urine, and scattered hallucinations and delusions. Second, confusion may be a feature of the so-called functional, and especially the affective psychiatric disorders in the elderly. Third, a reliable history of the mode of onset and the duration of the disorder is often lacking. Fourth, in some 10 to 20% of the elderly with acute confusion, no physical illness or other organic factor known to affect brain function is found. And fifth, an abnormal EEG is of relatively little specific diagnostic value in delirium, since diffuse slowing is often encountered in non-delirious elderly individuals (Busse and Wang, 1965; Müller and Schwartz, 1978).

Thus, compared to the diagnosis in people under 65 years of age, the diagnosis of delirium in the elderly can be difficult. One needs to distinguish delirium, an organic brain syndrome, from other such syndromes as well as from nonorganic psychiatric disorders featuring confusion. For practical purposes, this implies distinguishing delirium from dementia and from an affective disorder. (See Chapters on Dementia and Geriatric Psychiatry.)

A common condition in dementing illnesses is nocturnal confusion or delirium, or the "sundown syndrome," marked by disorientation, wandering, and generally irrational behavior. Two main hypotheses have been advanced to account for the occurrence of nocturnal confusion: sensory deprivation during the night and disturbed sleep. Cameron (1941) showed that in patients with senile dementia delirium could be induced experimentally by placing them in a dark room during the day. He suggested that the removal of visual cues precipitated the delirium. Feinberg et al. (1965) proposed that nocturnal delirium in patients with dementing illnesses was a consequence of disordered sleep. These investigators observed that the demented elderly had a tendency to awaken abruptly from dream periods (REM sleep) and to display agitated delirium for five to ten minutes. They hypothesized that some cases of nocturnal delirium could be due to an abrupt transition from dreaming sleep to wakefulness, and the consequent intrusion of dreams into the waking state. This interesting hypothesis has not been proven. At this time, it is not even clear whether nocturnal confusion of demented patients is descriptively identical with delirium, as defined here. The need for more sleep studies of these patients as well as of those exhibiting delirium is compelling.

Some writers claim that delirium in the elderly may be due not only to physical illness or drugs, but also to such psychosocial stressors as bereavement or transfer to an unfamiliar environment (Kral, 1975; Wolanin, 1981). These authors fail to make clear, however, whether such factors are deliriogenic only in the demented or also in the normal elderly individuals. This important issue remains unresolved.

Delirium versus Functional Mental Disorders

In 10 to 20% of elderly patients exhibiting delirium, an organic causative factor could not be identified (Flint and Richards, 1956; Kay and Roth, 1955). Furthermore, Roth (1955) found that 12% of the acute depressed or manic elderly patients displayed clouding of consciousness. Kral (1975) observed that delirium could be precipitated in the elderly by endogenous or reactive depressions, for example, depression following the loss of a spouse.

It is not known at this time whether the confusional states allegedly precipitated by various psychological stressors or those associated with acute depressive or manic disorders differ clinically from delirium caused by known organic factors. As a general rule, if a patient exhibits symptoms suggestive of delirium, an attempt to identify the causative organic factors should be made. One should never assume a priori that the patient's symptoms are due to psychological stress of life change alone. Such an assumption could result in a failure to diagnose and treat a potentially reversible physical condition. If the history, physical examination, and routine laboratory tests fail to detect evidence of organic pathology, and if, in addition, the patient displays marked manic or depres-

sive symptoms, or if the doctor elicits a history of recent life change, an affective disorder or a brief reactive psychosis (DSM-III, 1980) rather than delirium is likely. A normal EEG would support such a diagnosis. An abnormal dexamethasone suppression test could confirm the diagnosis of depressive illness (Kalin et al., 1981).

Management

The management of a delirious patient involves two simultaneous approaches: identification and treatment of the underlying cause (or causes) and general symptomatic and supportive measures (Lipowski, 1980a; Bayne, 1978).

Treatment of the underlying pathology. This should involve careful scrutiny of all drugs taken by the patient, and elimination of those likely to be deliriogenic, as long as their intake is not essential for the patient's health. Sometimes, reducing the dose may be sufficient. It should be kept in mind that there may be more than one etiological factor, for example, concomitant hypoxia, electrolyte imbalance, and drug toxicity.

Maintenance of fluid and electrolyte balance and nutrition. Dehydration, hypo- or hypernatremia, malnutrition, and subclinical vitamin deficiency are common in elderly delirious patients and must be corrected.

Provision of an optimum sensory environment. Deficient or excessive sensory stimulation is likely to exacerbate delirium and should be guarded against. It is best to keep the patient in a quiet, well-lighted room and to leave a dim light on at night. The patient should not be exposed to the noise and shifting sights of a busy public ward, with all its unfamiliar stimuli that he or she is likely to misinterpret and build his or her hallucinations and delusions around. A radio or television set may help provide sensory stimulation, but the patient should not be exposed to loud sound and violent or monotonous shows. Familiarity of the environment is important in calming and orienting the patient. A few personal photographs or possessions may reassure the patient. Family members the patient likes should be allowed to stay with him or her beyond routine visiting hours and help feed and orient him or her. A clock and a calendar should be visible to the patient.

It is a advisable to tell the patient (and his or her family members) that he or she is suffering from delirium, a transient mental disorder due to a physical illness or to drugs. Such an explanation will help allay fear of permanent insanity.

Nursing care. The nurse has a key role to play in the patient's management. She is often the first person to observe early signs of delirium, especially at night. Her main functions are to report and record the patient's behavior and level of orientation; to provide ongoing emotional support for the confused and frightened patient; and to orient the patient systematically as to time, place, person, and reason for being in the hospital.

Ensuring sleep and sedation. A delirious patient usually suffers from insomnia and disturbed sleep. It is essential to correct this, since sleep loss and intrusion of dreaming into wakefulness may aggravate delirium. Rather than prescribe a hypnotic, which could increase the confusion, it is preferable to administer an antipsychotic drug. *Haloperidol* is the drug of choice, since it is effective in calming an agitated and hallucinating patient and relatively free of serious side effects (Lipowski, 1980a). The drug can be used as drops or tablets, or parenterally. It is desirable to use an initial test dose of 0.5 mg. If the patient is severely agitated, an initial dose of 3 to 5 mg may be given intramuscularly and repeated after 30 minutes if no response has occurred. For milder delirium, one may use a haloperidol liquid concentrate in doses of 0.5 to 3 mg twice daily, with the second dose being given in the early evening; a third dose may be given, if necessary, to ensure sound sleep. The elderly are especially prone to the extrapyramidal side effects of haloperidol and may require benztropine mesylate, 2 mg orally, at bedtime to counteract them. The purpose of haloperidol administration is to help prevent injury to the patient or other people due to his or her agitation, fear, combativeness, attempts to escape, etc. An inadequately sedated and markedly fearful or agitated delirious patient is at high risk of injury, with its potentially serious medical and medicolegal consequences. Ideally, the patient should be alert yet calm during the day and sleep soundly at night. The early recognition of delirium and adequate treatment of its cause, coupled with the general measures discussed earlier, may make sedation unnecessary.

References

Adams, G. (1977). Essentials of Geriatric Medicine. Oxford University Press, Oxford.

Allahyari, H., Deisenhammer, E., and Weiser, G. (1976). EEG examination during delirium tremens. Psychiatr. Clin. 9, 21–31.

Bayne, J.R.D. (1978). Management of confusion in elderly persons. Can. Med. Assoc. J. 118, 139–141.

Beauchene, R.E. and Davis, T.A. (1979). The nutritional status of the aged in the USA Age 2, 23–28.

Bedford, P.D. (1959). General medical aspects of confusional states in elderly people. Brit. Med. J. 2, 185–188.

Bergmann, K. and Eastham, E.J. (1974). Psychogeriatic ascertainment and assessment for treatment in an acute medical ward setting. Age and Ageing 3, 174–188.

Berkowitz, C.D. (1979). Treatment of acute amantadine toxicity with physostigmine. J. Pediatr. Vol. 95, 144–145.

Bleuler, M. (1975). Acute mental concomitants of physical disease. In Psychiatric Aspects of Neurological Disease. D.F. Benson and D. Blumer, Eds. Grune & Stratton, New York, pp. 37–61.

Bliss, M.R. (1981). Prescribing for the elderly. Br. Med. J. 283, 203–206.

Brocklehurst, J.C. (1977). Psychogeriatric care as a specialized discipline in medicine. Bull. N.Y. Acad. Med. 53, 702–709.

Brocklehurst, J.C. and Hanley, T. (1976). Geriatric Medicine for Students. Churchill Livingstone, Edinburgh.

Busse, E.W. (Ed.) (1979). Cerebral Manifestations of Episodic Cardiac Dysrhythmias. Excerpta Medica, Amsterdam.

Busse, E.W. and Wang, H.S. (1965). The value of electroencephalography in geriatrics. Geriatrics 20, 906–924.

Caird, F.I., Dall, J.L.C., and Kennedy, R.D. (1976). Cardiology in Old Age. Plenum Press, New York.

Cameron, D.E. (1941). Studies in senile nocturnal delirium. Psychiat. Quart. 15, 47–53.

Chedru, F. and Geschwind, N. (1972a). Disorders of higher cortical functions in acute confusional states. Cortex 8, 395–411.

Chedru, F. and Geschwind, N. (1972b). Writing disturbances in acute confusional states. Neuropsychologia 10, 343–353.

Coakley, D. (Ed) (1981). Acute Geriatric Medicine. Croom Helm, London.

Daunderer, M. (1978). Acute Alkohol-Intoxikation: Physostigmin als Antidot gegen Aethanol. Fortschr. Med. 96, 1311–1312.

Dimant, J., Ginzler, E.M., Schlesinger M. et al. (1979). Systemic lupus erythematosus in the older age group: Computer analysis. J. Amer. Ger. Soc. 27, 58–61.

Doty, E.J. (1946). The incidence and treatment of delirious reactions in later life. Geriatrics 1, 21–26.

DSM-III (1980). Diagnostic and Statistical Manual of Mental Disorders. 3rd Ed. American Psychiatric Association, Washington, D.C.

Editorial: Medication in the Elderly. J. Irish Med. Assoc. 71, 136–137.

Eisenberg, S., Madison, L., and Sensebach, W. (1960). Cerebral hemodynamic and metabolic studies in patients with congestive heart failure. II. Observations in confused subjects. Circulation 21, 704–709.

Engel, G.L. and Romano, J. (1959). Delirium, a syndrome of cerebral insufficiency. J. Chron. Dis. 9, 260–277.

Epstein, J.L. and Simon, A. (1967). Organic brain syndrome in the elderly. Geriatrics 22, 145–150.

Feinberg, I., Kovesko, R.L., and Schaffner, I.R. (1965). Sleep electroencephalographic and eye-movement patterns in patients with chronic brain syndrome. J. Psychiatr. Res. 3, 11–26.

Flint, F.J. and Richards, S.M. (1956). Organic basis of confusional states in the elderly. Br. Med. J. 2, 1537–1539.

Folstein, M.F., Folstein, S.E., and McHugh, P.R. (1975). "Mini-mental state." J. Psychiatr. Res. 12, 189–198.

Foster, J.R., Gershell, W.J., and Goldfarb, A.I. (1977). Lithium treatment in the elderly. J. Gerontol. 32, 299–302.

Frieske, D.A. and Wilson, W.P. (1966). Formal qualties of hallucinations: A comparative study of the visual hallucinations in patients with schizophrenic, organic and affective psychoses. In Psychopathology of Schizophrenia. P.H. Hoch and J. Zubin, Eds. Grune & Stratton, New York, pp. 49–62.

Futty, D.E., Conneally, P.M., Dyken, M.L. et al. (1977). Cooperative study of hospital frequency and character of transient ischemic attacks. V. Symptom analysis. J.A.M.A. 238, 2386–2390.

Hawley, R.J., Major, L.F., Schulman, E.A., and Lake, C.R. (1981). CSF levels of norepinephrine during alcohol withdrawal. Arch. Neurol. 38, 289–292.

Head, H. (1901). Certain mental changes that accompany visceral disease. Brain 24. 344–356.

Hernandez-Peon, R. (1966). Physiological mechanisms in attention. In Frontiers of Physiological Psychology. R.W. Russell, Ed. Academic Press, New York, pp. 121–147.

Hodkinson, H.M. (1973). Mental impairment in the elderly. J. Roy. Coll. Physicians (London) 7, 305–317.

Horenstein, S., Chamberlain, W., and Conomy, J. (1967). Infarction of the fusiform and calcarine regions: Agitated delirium and hemianopia. Trans. Amer. Neurol. Assoc. 92, 85–89.

Ing, T.S., Daugindas, J.T., Soung, L.S. et al. (1979). Toxic effects of amantadine in patients with renal failure. Can. Med. Assoc. J. 120, 695–697.

Itil, T. and Fink, M. (1966). Anticholinergic drug-induced delirium: Experimental modification, quantitative EEG and behavioral correlations. J. Nerv. Ment. Dis. 143, 492–507.

Jackson, J.H. (1932). Selected Writings. J. Taylor, Ed. Hodder and Stoughton, London.

Jacob, J.W., Bernhad, M.R., Delgado, A. et al. (1977). Screening for organic mental syndromes in the medically ill. Ann. Intern. Med. 86, 40–46.

Kalin, N.H., Risch, S.C., Janowsky, D.S., and Murphy, D.L. (1981). Use of dexamethasone suppression test in clinical psychiatry. J. Clin. Psychompharm. 1, 64–69.

Kay, D.W.K. and Roth, M. (1955). Physical accompaniments of mental disorder in old age. Lancet ii, 740–745.

Kral, V.A. (1975). Confusional states. In Modern Perspectives in the Psychiatry of Old Age, J.G. Howells, Ed. Brunner/Mazel, New York, pp. 356–362.

Lamy, P.P. (1980). Prescribing for the Elderly. Publishing Sciences Group, Littleton, MA.

Levenson, A.J. (Ed.) (1979). Neuropsychiatric Side Effects of Drugs in the Elderly. Raven Press, New York.

Levin, M. (1945). Delirious disorientation: The law of the unfamiliar mistaken for the familiar. J. Ment. Sci. 91, 447–450.

Levine, J.A. (1969). Heat stroke in the aged. Amer. J. Med. 47, 251–258.

Lieberman, A.N., Kupersmith, M., Gopinathan, G. et al. (1979). Bromocriptine in Parkinson disease: Further studies. Neurology 29, 363–369.

Lindeman, R.D., and Klingler, E.L. (1981). Combating sodium and potassium imbalance in older patients. Geriatrics 36, 97–106.

Lipowski, Z.J. (1980a). Delirium. Acute Brain Failure in Man. C.C. Thomas, Springfield, Ill.

Lipowski, Z.J. (1980b). Delirium updated. Compreh. Psychiat. 21, 190–196.

McDowell, F.H. (1980). Transient cerebral ischemia: Diagnostic considerations. Progr. Cardiovasc. Dis. 22, 309–324.

McGuigan, J.E. (1981). A consideration of the adverse effects of cimetidine. Gastroenterology 80, 181–192.

Medina, J.L., Chokroverty, S., and Rubino, F.A. (1977). Syndrome of agitated delirium and visual impairment: A manifestation of medial tempora-occipital infarction. J. Neurol. Neurosurg. Psychiat. 40, 861–864.

Medina, J.L., Rubino, F.A., and Ross, E. (1974). Agitated delirium caused by infarctions of the hippocampal formation and fusiform and lingual gyri. Neurology 24, 1181–1183.

Mesulam, M.M. (1979). Acute behavioral derangements without hemiplegia in cerebrovascular accidents. Primary Care 6, 813–826.

Mesulam, M.M. and Geschwind, N. (1976). Disordered mental states in the postoperative period. Urol Clin. NA 3, 199–215.

Millar, H.R. (1981). Psychiatric morbidity in elderly surgical patients. Br. J. Psychiat. 138, 17–20.

Mitra, M.L. (1971). Confusional states in relation to vitamin deficiencies in the elderly. J. Amer. Geriatr. Soc. 19, 536–545.

Mogelnicki, S.R., Waller, J.L., and Finlayson, D.C. (1979). Physostigmine reversal of cimetidine-induced mental confusion. J.A.M.A. 241, 826–827.

Müller, H.F. and Schwartz, G. (1978). Electroencephalogram and autopsy findings in geropsychiatry. J. Gerontol. 33, 504–513.

Natelson, B.H. Haupt, E.J., Fleischer, E.J., and Grey, L. (1979). Temporal orientation and education. Arch. Neurol. 36, 444–446.

Obrecht, R., Okhomina, F.O.A., and Scott, D.F. (1979). Value of EEG in acute confusional states. J. Neurol. Neurosurg. Psychiatr. 42, 75–77.

Paulley, J.W. and Hughes, J.P. (1960). Giant-cell arteritis, or arteritis of the aged. Br. Med. J . 4, 1562–1567.

Pfeiffer, E. (1975). A short protable mental status questionnaire for the assessment of organic brain deficit in elderly patients. J. Amer. Geriatr. Soc. 23, 433–441.

Phair, J.P. (1979). Aging and infection: A review. J. Chron. Dis. 32, 535–540.

Podolsky, S. (1978). Hyperosmolar nonketotic coma in the elderly diabetic. Med. Clin. NA 62, 815–828.

Polly, S.M. and Sanders, W.E. (1977). Surgical infections in the elderly: Prevention, diagnosis, and treatment. Geriatrics 32, 88–97.

Powers, J.S., Decorkey, D., and Kahrilas, P.J. (1981). Physostigmine for treatment of delirium tremens. J. Clin. Pharmacol. 21, 57–60.

Prien, R.F. (1980). Problems and practices in geriatric psychopharmacology. Psychosomatics 21, 213–223.

Pro, J.D. and Wells, C.E. (1977). The use of the electroencephalogram in the diagnosis of delirium. Dis. Nerv. Syst. 38, 804–808.

Ram, C.V.S. (1978). Hypertensive encephalopathy. Arch. Intern. Med. 138, 1851–1853.

Raskind, R., Glover, M.B., and Weiss, S.R. (1972). Chronic subdural hematoma in the elderly: A challenge to diagnosis and treatment. J. Amer. Geriatr. Soc. 20, 330–334.

Report of the Royal College of Physicians by the College Committee on Geriatrics: Organic mental impairment in the elderly. (1981). J. Roy. Coll. Physicians (London) 15, 141–167.

Robinson, G.W. (1956). The toxic delirious reactions of old age. In Mental Disorders in Later Life. O.J. Kaplan, Ed. Stanford University Press, Stanford, pp. 227–225.

Romano, J. and Engel, G.L. (1944). Delirium. 1. Electroencephalographic data. AMA Arch. Neurol. Psychiat. 51, 356–377.

Roth, M. (1955). The natural history of mental disorder in old age. J. Ment. Sci. 101, 281–301.

Roth, M. (1976). The psychiatric disorders of later life. Psychiat. Ann. 6, 417–445.

Salzman, C. (1979). Update on geriatric psychopharmacology. Geriatrics 34, 87–90.

Schmid-Wermser, I, Nagel, G.A., and Schmid, A.H. (1974). Zur klinischen Diagnose von Hirnmetastasen beim Bronchuskarzinom. Schweiz. Med. Wschr. 104, 464–468.

Schoenberg, B.C., Christine, B.W., and Whisnant, J.P. (1978). The resolution of discrepancies in the reported incidence of primary brain tumors. Neurology 28, 817–823.

Schuckit, M.A. (1977). The high rate of psychiatric disorders in elderly cardiac patients. Angiology 28, 235–247.

Senility reconsidered. (1980). J.A.M.A. 244, 259–263.

Seymour, D.G., Henschke, P.J., Cape, R.D.T., and Campbell, A.J. (1980). Acute confusional states and dementia in the elderly: The role of dehydration/volume depletion, physical illness and age. Age and Ageing 9, 137–146.

Shorvon, S.D., Carney, M.W.P., Chanarin, I., and Reynolds, E.H. (1980). The neuropsychiatry of megaloblastic anaemia. Br. Med. J. 281, 1036–1043.

Simon, A. and Cahan, R.B. (1963). The acute brain syndrome in geriatric patients. Psychiat. Res. Rep. 16, 8–21.

Simon, A., Lowenthal, M.F., and Epstein, L.J. (1970). Crisis and Intervention. Jossey-Bass, Inc., San Francisco.

Singer, F.R., Bethune, J.R., and Massry, S.G. (1977). Hypercalcemia and hypocalcemia. Clin. Nephrol. 7, 154–162.

Siverton, S.E. (1978). Common problems of ambulatory geriatric patients. Postgrad. Med. 64, 83–89.

Skillman, T.G. and Falko, J.M. (1981). Recognizing thyroid disease in the elderly: Current considerations. Geriatrics 36, 63–73.

Sroka, H., Elizan, T.S., Yahr, M.D., et al. (1981). Organic mental syndrome and confusional states in Parkinson's disease. Arch. Neurol. 38, 339–342.

Vestal, R.E. (1978). Drug use in the elderly: A review of problems and special considerations. Drugs 16, 358–382.

Wattis, J.P. (1981). Alcohol problems in the elderly. J. Amer. Geriatr. Soc. 29, 131–134.

Weizman, A., Eldar, M., Shoenfeld, Y. et al. (1979). Hypercalcaemia-induced psychopathology in malignant diseases. Br. J. Psychiat. 135, 363–366.

Williams, M.A., Holloway, J.R., Winn, M.C. et al. (1979). Nursing activities and acute confusional states. Nurs. Res. 28, 25–35.

Williamson, J. and Chopin, J.M. (1980). Adverse reactions to prescribed drugs in the elderly: A multicentre investigation. Age and Ageing 9, 73–80.

Wolanin, M.O. and Phillips, L.R.F. (1981). Confusion. Mosby, St. Louis.

Wowern, F., von (1966). Posttraumatic amnesia and confusion as an index of severity in head injury. Acta Neurol. Scand. 42, 373–378.

16. Psychiatric Syndromes of Old Age

B. GURIAN

S.H. AUERBACH

The psychiatric syndromes encountered in the elderly present the clinician with a challenge that often requires the skill and background of the neurologist as well as the psychiatrist. These syndromes are often marked by changes in behavior, mood, and cognition. The distinction between psychopathology and neuropathology is not always apparent. This presents a special problem in the elderly population in whom psychopathology and neuropathology may coexist.

The problem of distinguishing psychopathology from neuropathology can be seen in the historical roots of what is known as "modern psychiatry." In 1806, Pinel (1806), in *A Treatus on Insanity,* described senile deterioration as "childishness" of old age and categorized it with other psychiatric illness. The inability to recognize changes due to normal aging proved to be a problem for the early psychiatrists. In *Pathology of Mind,* published in 1879, Maudsley proposed that "senile insanity" was the predictable conclusion of a progression of mental impairment that was part of the natural aging process. He did, however, recognize a relationship between the cerebral atrophy seen at postmortem and the clinical condition of memory impairment in old age. Rothschild reviewed many of these historical issues in *Mental Disorders in Later Life* in 1956. Although he recognized

the role of neuropathology in the development of cognitive impairment, he stressed the important role of such other factors as the individual's response to life stress and environmental factors and the individual's genetic predisposition. Rothchild's major contribution, therefore, was again to highlight psychiatric issues in the study of behavioral changes in the elderly.

The problem of distinguishing psychopathology from neuropathology in the elderly still confronts the contemporary clinician. Psychiatric disorders may present with symptoms suggestive of neurological disease; neurological disorders may present with symptoms suggestive of psychiatric disease.

The need for a comprehensive neurobehavioral approach to the psychiatric syndromes of old age is obvious. The elements for such an approach can be found in many discussions of the "pseudo-dementias," in which there is both an acknowledgment of the cognitive impairments found in psychiatric disorders, and a recognition of the changes in affect and mood encountered in many neurologically based dementing illnesses. Such discussions point up the need to establish a neurobehavioral approach. One problem is that neurological disorders not uncommonly present with changes in affective behavior, in mood, or in specific areas of cognition. There are even more difficult problems when one considers that patients with neurological disease may develop reactive syndromes secondary to the primary disease.

The example of the elderly patient with a complaint of memory loss can serve to illustrate some of these problems. Such a patient may prove to be merely depressed or to have early Alzheimer's disease. On the other hand, the patient may be an alcoholic, with an amnestic disorder, who has become depressed, or the patient may have an amnestic syndrome from a focal ischemic event and be depressed as a reaction to this disability. Another possibility is a patient with a right hemisphere lesion, who presents with symptoms that mimic depressive illness because of restriction of affect and an impairment of memory for non-verbal information. Such a patient may or may not have a change in mood. In this case, the clinician would have only the verbal report of the patient of a depressive mood change, since affective behavior would be limited by the neurological illness.

A comprehensive approach to psychiatric syndromes must therefore include the perspectives of the psychiatrist and the neurologist. In this chapter, we focus on the interface between these perspectives. First we present the psychiatric viewpoint, to acquaint the clinician with common descriptive systems and major features of these syndromes. A method for analyzing the behavioral changes of old age will then be presented, which will help the clinician to distinguish neurobehavioral from psychiatric components of these syndromes.

Other chapters in this text have discussed the neuropsychology of normal aging (12), dementia in the elderly (14), acute confusional states in the elderly (15), and language in aging (13). These chapters should be reviewed by the reader.

The Psychiatric Syndromes

The nosology of the psychiatric syndromes of old age has tended to be controversial and complicated. Nevertheless, certain important concepts emerge from a review of its historical development.

The earliest modern accounts of mental disorders of later life are generally attributed to Kraeplin (1915) and Bleuler (1916), who studied presenile, senile, and arteriosclerotic psychoses. Roth (1955) noted the limitations of this approach and expanded it to include functional disorders. He outlined five distinct categories of mental illnesses in late life, derived solely from clinical description, and applied this classification system in a review of the case records of 450 patients. Only categories 1 and 2 are "functional" illnesses; categories 3, 4, and 5 are organic mental disorders.

1. Affective psychosis: A sustained manic or depressive symptom complex
2. Late paraphrenia: A paranoid delusion or paranoid system in a person who otherwise functions well in daily activities
3. Arteriosclerotic psychosis: A dementia with either focal neurological signs or a fluctuating course and rapid deterioration
4. Senile psychosis: A more gradual failure of recent memory, with progressive disorganization of cognitive functioning and personality
5. Acute confusion: An alteration of level of consciousness not easily related to a precipitant

The value of this classification system has been demonstrated by Blessed and Wilson (1982), who reviewed 320 patients, aged 65 and over, admitted to St. Nicholas Hospital, Newcastle-upon-Tyne, during 1976. They were able to classify 90% of these patients using the system described by Roth more than 20 years earlier.

The 1965 revision of the *Manual of the International Statistical Classification of Disease, Injuries, and Causes of Death* (1967) included categories of organic syndromes, arteriosclerotic dementia, delirious states (acute confusion), and two additional categories: (1) functional psychosyndromes, which is synonymous with paraphrenia or late-onset schizophrenia, and (2) involutional melancholia, which can be described as a late-onset psychiatric depression comparable to agitated involutional depression, described later in this chapter. This classification implies that the syndromes were considered on the basis of clinical description, as well as presumed etiology.

Another issue in classification is whether to consider disorders as they are modified by the aging process or to consider only those disorders that occur primarily in late life. The World Health Organization (1972) held a seminar on psychiatric diagnosis, classification, and statistics in Moscow in 1968. The participants recommended that "a multi-axial classification, similar to that for psychiatric disorders in childhood, be developed and tested in psychogeriatrics." A problem considered in the seminar was "whether a classification of mental disorders of old age should include pre-existing disorders as modified and influenced by aging, or should take into account mainly those disorders particularly linked with old age that occur only during that period of life." It was decided that an international classification of disease should provide a separate category for diseases that primarily occur late in life.

Bergmann, however, in his chapter on nosology in *Modern Perspectives in the Psychiatry of Old Age* (1975), stated "there are no clinical descriptions of functional psycho-syndromes which refer exclusively to the senium. The process of aging influences functional psycho-syndromes in respect to their clinical picture in course, genetic family history, and association with exogenous stresses. Understanding of these differences is important in the use of nosological descriptions of functional psychiatric disorders in old age."

The World Health Organization (1972) suggested nine major categories of mental illness in late life:

1. Atrophic senile psychosis
   a. (mild) psychoorganic syndrome
   b. moderate senile dementia
   c. severe senile dementia
2. Arteriosclerotic psychoses and other cerebrovascular diseases
   a. mild psychoorganic syndrome
   b. moderate psychoorganic syndrome
3. Acute confusional state
4. Presenile dementia
   a. Alzheimer [disease]
   b. Pick's disease

5. Affective psychosis
   a. late depression
   b. late mania
6. Schizophrenia
   late schizophrenia
7. Paranoid syndrome (paraphrenia)
8. Neurosis (acute psychogenic reaction reactive development)
9. Changes of personality occurring in old age

Note was made in the World Health Organization report that "much neurotic illness—and even more serious mental illness—appears to pass unrecognized, possibly because in old age attention tends to be focused on physical illness, or because apathy, depression or hypochondriasis are regarded as inevitable accompaniments of aging."

In the *Handbook of Geriatric Psychiatry* (1980), the psychiatric disorders of late life were categorized as (1) the organic mental disorders, (2) paranoia and schzophrenic disorders in later life, (3) affective disorders, (4) anxiety and dissociative and personality disorders, (5) adjustment disorders of late life, and (6) disorders related to biological functioning.

It should be noted that lists of "organic" and "functional" illnesses are included in the more recent classifications of mental illnesses in late life. The distinction between "organic" and "functional" is a curious one. Indeed, progress in modern psychiatry can be measured, in part, by discoveries of biological correlates for disorders previously considered to be "functional." Nevertheless, Wells (1982) has argued that organic and functional are still valuable distinctions. Even if they are no longer accurate literal descriptions, they still provide a useful guide for management. We concur with this argument, but urge the reader to keep in mind that these labels may not always retain their semantic purity.

The following classification has been adopted because it can be applied to a geropsychiatric practice. The emphasis is placed primarily on the clinical problems manifested in late life, disorders that present primarily in late life as well as disorders that present at all stages of life, including the senium. This classification will be followed in our discussion of major syndromes.

1. The dementias
2. The psychoses
    a. schizophrenia
    b. manic-depressive illness
    c. acute psychotic depression
    d. agitated involutional psychotic depression
    e. the paranoid state
    f. paraphrenia
3. The neuroses
    a. anxiety neurosis
    b. depressive neurosis
    c. a mixture of anxiety and depressive neurosis
    d. hypochrondriasis
4. The character disorders
5. The situational disturbances of late life

The recent Diagnostic and Statistic Manual of Mental Disorders (DSM-III) (1980) offers a contemporarty classification system. Unfortunately, it does not concisely address the issues of the elderly psychiatric population. We prefer the above system, but, when possible, we will refer to the classification within the DSM-III, (1980).

The clinical presentation of schizophrenia, manic-depressive psychosis, and acute psychotic depression in the elderly differs little from the presentation in younger persons. Schizophrenia and manic-depressive psychosis characteristically appear earlier in life and have a long, often fluctuating course. An acute psychotic depression, however, can occur for the first time at any age, including old age. In all these illnesses, the predominant feature is the disorder of the thought process. Mania and depression are, of course, also disorders of affect.

Schizophrenia of late life deserves a special note. In most studies of schizophrenia in late life the patients actually have an earlier onset schizophrenia (Mensh, 1979). The issue of late onset schizophrenia has been addressed primarily by the British, but with the emphasis on paraphrenia. The clinician should be wary of the diagnosis of late onset schizophrenia. In general, these patients will have either a dementia, chronic schizophrenia with an earlier onset, or paraphrenia, as described below.

Bridge et al. (1978) have reviewed the issue of how schizophrenia changes with age. There is evidence to suggest that schizophrenic patients show no further deterioration after an average of about five years (Bleuler, 1974). Bridge et al. (1978) also noted that paranoia, hyperactivity, and delusion may be reduced with advancing years. Schizophrenia may indeed "burn out" in old age.

The therapeutic approach (as with all forms of psychopathology) begins with the establishment of a meaningful working relationship, or alliance, between therapist and patient, and the circumspect use of adjunctive somatic therapies. The antipsychotic drugs should be selected on the basis of all their known effects, the patient's ability to metabolize and excrete them, and their interactions with other drugs being given the patient. The chemotherapeutic agent most appropriate for manic-depressive illness in the aged is a salt of lithium, usually the carbonate. In all psychotic depressions, once the neuroleptic has begun to help with the thought disorder, antidepressant medication may be indicated.

Agitated involutional psychotic depression (involutional melancholia or involutional psychosis) is listed in DSM-III under "major affective disorders" as a "major depressive episode." The patient may lose interest, and no longer take pleasure in all usual activities. There are appetite and sleep disturbances; psychomotor agitation (pacing, hairpulling, scratching, handwringing); feelings of worthlessness and guilt; a sense of bodily decay; and suicidal thoughts or attempts. The sense of guilt may be delusional, a common delusion is that the patient is being persecuted because of a terrible sin.

Agitated involutional psychotic depression remains one of the few real psychiatric emergencies in that it may progress rapidly to a life-threatening agitation, with self-destructive behavior, leaving little time for the therapist to establish an alliance, and little time for antidepressant medication to reach therapeutic levels. Hospitalization and an early decision to use electroconvulsive therapy may be life-saving.

The "paranoid state" must be distinguished from "schizophreniform disorders." "The paranoid state" is listed in DSM-III as "paranoia" under "paranoid disorders." Characteristically, a rigid, and often unshakable delusional system slowly develops within the context of an otherwise clear and orderly thought process. The patient's emotions and behavior are appropriate to the content of the delusion. There usually are no hallucinations, incoherence, or marked loosening of associations, as in schizophrenia.

In evaluating reports of a hostile world, "out to get the patient," the clinician should evaluate independently any "delusions," since some of the time the patient's perceptions may be accurate. One of society's current misfortunes is that the elderly *are* scapegoated, abused, and victimized, not only by strangers on the street, but also in insidious ways by family members and caregivers.

The term "paraphrenia," although well established in the British literature (Kay and Roth, 1961; Post, 1965), has only recently appeared in the American literature (Bridge and Wyatt, 1980a,b). Paraphrenia is a psychosis of late life, with the age of onset usually after age 60. It is marked by delusions, which are usually persecutory and bizarre, and sometimes hallucinations. The disorder is not otherwise associated with a disorder of affect in mood or cognition. Raskind (1982) has argued that the terms "paranoid disorder" and "schizophrenia," as defined in the DSM-III, do not accurately describe the paraphrenic patient. The bizarre delusions and the presence of hallucinations are excluded by the definition of the "paranoid disorder." Late onset and otherwise intact social functioning distinguish paraphrenia from schizophrenia, which is a disorder with onset before age 45, associated with a deterioration of personality, loosening of associations, affective incongruity, and blunting, or loss of volition.

Two aspects of paraphrenia must be considered. The first is an increased incidence of sensory deficits, particularly deafness, as noted by Kay and Roth (1961). The shortcomings of this study have been noted (Raskind, 1982), and some doubt cast upon the suggestion that sensory loss might be a contributing factor. Other studies (Cooper et al., 1974; Kay et al., 1976), however, suggest that a social hearing impairment may be associated with psychosis, particularly of the paranoid type. The second aspect is whether a more generalized dementia is present. Paranoia can accompany dementia, but we do not consider this to be paraphrenia. Roth (1955) and Blessed and Wilson (1982) stressed the difference between paraphrenia and dementia; and Raskind (1982) observed that the rate of dementia in paraphrenics is no higher than the rate in the general population.

Anxiety is probably present in all neuroses, and in some patients it may be the predominant symptom. Neurotic or reactive depression (dysthymic reaction, DSM-III) is common among the elderly, in whom losses have been compounded over a lifetime; the stressful effects of the compression of many losses in a short time is also significant. Clinical depression is not on a continuum with existential sadness; it is not neurotic to grieve. If the response to loss is functionally debilitating and unresolved over a reasonable time, it can then be said that there is a qualitative change in adaptation to stress. Psychotherapy, support, and the judicious use of minor tranquilizers may be indicated.

Hypochondriasis used to be understood as a depressive equivalent or a hypochondriacal neurosis. In DSM-III, it is classified as one of the somataform disorders. Physical symptoms are linked to psychological conflicts and are not under voluntary control. The patient is preoccupied with the fear of having a serious disease and this pervades and impairs usual social functioning, even though a thorough physical examination does not support the presence of any physical disorder. Such reassurance from the physician immediately places him or her among the alien nonbelievers and renders him or her useless. It is only through the slow, careful, sensitive building of trust that the hypochondriacal patient may stop doctor-shopping and begin to look at other, less bearable sources of pain in their lives.

The situational disturbances of late life are now grouped under "adjustment disorders", classified by specific type of concomitant symptomatology rather than age of onset. Thus, one may have an adjustment disorder with depression, anxiety, or a conduct disturbance.

A Systematic Approach to the Psychiatric Syndromes of Old Age

The clinician needs a systematic method to analyze the behavioral changes encountered in old age. The method must be as systematic as the one used in any specialized examination. Many of the issues raised by the clinician relate to the brain–behavior relationships of the aging individual, and, therefore, the approach must be broad enough to take into consideration the many neurological and psychiatric issues.

There are many aspects to a comprehensive examination in psychiatic disorders. The clinician should never overlook the critical importance of a good medical history and physical examination. The history identifies the natural course of a disease, the physical examination the relevent medical and neurological diseases. Most of these aspects, however, have been addressed elsewhere in this text; we will therefore restrict our discussion to three areas of special concern in the mental status: (1) affective or overt behavioral components, (2) components of mood or inner feeling and, (3) cognitive components.

Affective Behavior

We use the term "affect" to mean all the components that contribute to the motor expression of behavior. Five areas are noted: (1) affective state, (2) activity level, (3) range of affect, (4) rate of change, and, (5) degree of association/dissociation between affect and mood state.

THE AFFECTIVE STATE

This is reflected in the facial expression, the use of gestures, and the prosody of speech. Each component is used to assign a patient on the multi-dimensional scale that encompasses appearances associated with happiness, sadness, fear, anger, etc.

Although facial expression, gestural expression, and prosody should be noted separately, they usually parallel one another in the psychiatric population; they may be influenced by either neurological or psychiatric disease.

LEVELS OF ACTIVITY

These levels can be reflected in motor activity as well as in speech. Bradykinesia is commonly seen with depressive disorders (psychomotor retardation) and such fronto-subcortical diseases as Parkinson's or lacunar states. Hyperacitivity is a cardinal feature of manic disorders, but is also seen in some confusional disorders, as well as in patients with frontal lobe lesions.

RANGE OF AFFECT; RATE OF CHANGE

In affective disorders, the range may be restricted to either end of the spectrum. Restriction may become apparent in almost any of the bradykinetic disorders. Not uncommonly, patients with right hemisphere pathology will also have a restricted affect and appear sad. The *rate of change* in facial expression may become exaggerated in patients with pseudobulbar state in which fluctuations are extreme. Patients with frontal lobe disease may also present with fluctuations in affect without many of the other neurological signs of a pseudobulbar palsy. These patients may rapidly swing between the extremes of "anger," "happiness," etc.

THE DEGREE OF DISSOCIATION
FROM MOOD STATE

This part of the evaluation actually requires a simultaneous assessment of both affect and mood state. Not all patients who are bradykinetic with an apparent restriction in affect are sad. Some may be happy. The frequent, wide fluctuations in affect in patients with pseudobulbar palsy do not reflect their true mood. Finally, some patients, particularly those with lesions of the nondominant hemisphere, may lose the ability to translate mood state into affect. The latter has been referred to as an "aprosodic" disorder by Ross (1981) and will be discussed in more detail below.

Mood

The assessment of mood or inner feeling state requires great care. As noted above, mood may not always be reflected in affective behaviors, and special care must be taken to elicit the mood state of a patient. For instance, the patient with a pseudobulbar affective disorder may be able to verbalize sad feelings clearly, during recurrent bouts of exaggerated laughter.

Cognitive Components

Psychiatric syndromes are usually associated with changes in the way patients thinks about themselves and their environment. The causal relationship between psychiatric disorder and thought pattern is of considerable interest, but is beyond the scope of this discussion. Rather, we will address four issues that are of particular concern to the clinician dealing with the elderly population. We shall discuss (1) the pseudo-dementias, (2) non-linguistic disorders of communication and their potential relation to psychiatric disorders, and (3) paranoia.

Thought disorders are considered to be a major component of schizophrenia. The cognitive deficits seen in schizophrenia have been recently reviewed (Siedman, 1983). It is also likely that schizophrenia of late onset does not exist as a distinct entity. Therefore, this topic will not be discussed.

THE PSEUDO-DEMENTIAS

Kileh (1961) introduced the term "pseudo-dementia" to describe a group of patients with probable functional disorders who were suspected of being demented. In this group were patients with depression, mania, and presumed malingering. Although recent use of the term has often been restricted to patients with depressive illness, we feel that the original broader use of the term should be retained. Pseudo-dementia will therefore be defined here as the cognitive changes associated with functional disorders. If one accepts this definition, then two types of pseudo-dementia can be postulated. The first type is associated with patients who fail to perform appropriately on examinations because of factors other than those that can be attributed to true disorders of cognition. This group includes malingerers, patients who react adversely to an examiner, and patients who are simply preoccupied with other matters. It is often difficult to examine these patients, and under such circumstances, there may be some uncertainty as to whether there is a mental deterioration compatible with the dementia.

The second type of pseudo-dementia refers to an observed mental deterioration that appears to be quite consistent with a true dementia. Madden et al. (1979) reviewed 300 patients, 45 or over, who had been hospitalized with this disorder. They defined pseudo-dementia as a nondementing psychosis, characterized by deficits in orientation, retention, recent memory, calculations, and judgment. In terms of the definitions presented in the chapter on dementia, however, we prefer to call this a true dementia syndrome, which is potentially reversible.

The dementia syndrome of depression (Folstern and McHugh, 1978) is of particular importance to the clinician, and its recognition has implications for diagnosis and management. Depression is a relatively common problem in old age, and a depressive state has long been recognized as one of the most common defense mechanisms in the elderly (Ross, 1954). Williams and Jaco (11) noted that "a functional illness characterized by a depressive mood is as typical as or more typical in this age period than . . . an organic brain syndrome." About one-third of patients over 60 have depressive symptoms (Dovenmushe et al., 1970), and depressive illness is responsible for up to 45% of the psychiatric admissions of the over-65 group (Myers et al., 1963). All clinicians should be alert to the symptoms; depressive illness is often undetected by the non-psychiatric physician (Kline, 1976).

The association of cognitive deficits with depressive illness in the elderly is becoming generally accepted (see Chapter 14). Zung (1980) has suggested that the specific deficit in ability to learn can be viewed as a disturbance of the reticular activating system and its capacity to screen incoming sensory signals efficiently.

A practical clinical question emerges at this point: What cognitive changes might the clinician anticipate in the depressed elderly? The two primary features seem to be mental slowing and a disorder of mental control function. The latter term refers to the ability to sustain attention, to shift attention appropriately, and to inhibit inappropriate associations or shifts of attention. These components are ultimately involved in the ability to organize novel stimuli and therefore are reflected in the ability to learn and to solve complex problems. This pattern of deficits can be seen as deriving from the underlying disorder postulated by Zung (1980).

These observations can be applied in the clinical examination. Depression in the elderly resembles a fronto-subcortical pattern of dementia. The patient has an otherwise normal neurological examination and a history consistent with an affective disorder. He or she may have difficulties sustaining attention to complex tasks, organizing and solving complex problems, and performing various visuo-spatial tasks. Memory complaint is not uncommon, but the complaint often exceeds the impairment. The memory problem is noted largely in the ability to organize tasks—a problem that seems to span all aspects of the mental status examination.

A 70-year-old depressed man was seen because of a memory complaint. He illustrated his problem by noting that he was unable to recall the names of his 12 grandchildren. Indeed, when he attempted to list their names, he generated a haphazard list and was unable to complete it. He was then asked a series of structured questions: How many children do you have? Which one is the oldest? How many children does your eldest child have? What are the names of the children of this eldest child? How many children does your second oldest child have? . . . The sequence was continued until the patient listed the names of his 12 grandchildren.

The above example demonstrates why many depressed elderly are thought to have "apparent" memory problems. Thus, the patient above, when provided with the appropriate structure and organization, was able to proceed. Psychomotor retardation certainly complicates the disorder of mental control, as defined above. As a consequence, the performance of these patients, as in other fronto-subcortical dementias, is sensitive to time-limiting factors.

Certain implications for the clinical management of the elderly depressed emerge from the above discussion. Structure becomes essential. In order to address the psychosocial factors that contribute to the depression, the patient must be presented with a highly organized, structured program. This is the basis of the successful cognitive therapy for depression introduced by Beck and his colleagues (1979). It is of interest to note that we have implied that both the mood changes and the cognitive changes seen in this population are rooted in a common pathology. The evolution of a cognitive theory of depression may differ somewhat from this presentation. Nevertheless, the conclusions seen to coincide.

Finally, the reader must keep in mind that the elderly patient may present with an "atypical depression" manifested by somatic complaints, cognitive impairment, and a *paucity* of apparent mood changes. The clinician should be alert to this possibility so that a potentially reversible process may be treated.

Depressive illness is generally more common than manic disorders, especially in old age (Zung, 1980; Jamison, 1979). Manic disorders are generally characterized by a change in mood (euphoria), behavior (press of speech, general increased psychomotor activity), and cognition (flight of ideas, grandiosity, possible further disorganization of cognitive state with delusions). In a review of reported clinical observations, Jamison (1979) listed three features that are distinctive for mania in the elderly population, as follows.

1. *Confusion:* Delirium can be the presenting symptom of mania, especially in the elderly. Although recognized as early as 1849 by Bell and again by Kraeplin in 1921, delirious mania may often be overlooked. Swartz et al.

(1982) have suggested that many cases may be attributed to drug toxicity

2. *Paranoia:* Paranoid features may be more apparent than in a younger population

3. *Mixed affect or lability of affect:* "Miserable mania" may arise with the development of a concomitant depression. In such cases, morbid thought content may be added to the constellation of symptoms

The point to remember is that mania in the elderly is often atypical (Busse and Pfeiffer, 1975) and may be diagnosed as a dementia if the appropriate history is unavailable.

THE ROLE OF DISORDERS OF NON-LINGUISTIC COMMUNICATION

In recent years, increasing attention has been paid to the non-linguistic components of communication. Ross (1981) used the term "aprosodia" to describe an acquired disorder of the affective components of communication (affective prosody and emotional gesturing); Weintraub et al. (1981) further stressed that aprosodic patients may have more general disorders of prosody. These disorders are generally associated with lesions of the right hemisphere and may diminish the ability to translate mood and inner feeling into their appropriate affective components or the ability to comprehend the significance of the gestures, vocal inflections, and facial expressions used by others in the course of communication.

A knowledge of such disorders is of considerable importance in the clinical evaluation of patients with possible psychiatric disorders. Thus, it is possible that a lesion in the right hemisphere may impair a patient's ability to translate a mood state into its affective components. This may lead to a disruption in the patient's normal social interactions that, in turn, may heighten levels of stress. The potential contribution to a reactive syndrome seems clear. The clinician must therefore take special care to look for a possible dissociation between affect and mood.

Another type of disorder may be found in the patient who loses the ability to comprehend the information derived from facial expression, vocal intention, or other physical actions. In everyday life, many of our actions and words are ambiguous and can only be clarified by an interpretation of the non-linguistic elements. For instance, the statement, "I really like this book" can be spoken to convey either that you like or do not like the book. Similarly, an accurate interpretation of facial expression conveys considerable information in daily communication. Some patients with right hemisphere lesions lose this ability.

An inability to comprehend the non-linguistic aspects of communication can disrupt social interaction. Furthermore, the patient is isolated from a type of communication that is readily available to others. The ambiguity that results and the sense that others have a "secret" form of communication may lead to a paranoid disorder.

A patient was admitted to a psychiatric unit with the diagnosis paranoid schizophrenia. The patient had a large right frontal lobe lesion from a shrapnel injury ten years earlier which left him with a left central facial paresis and a minimal left hemiparesis. He had considerable difficulties in social interactions because of his inability to understand the "intended" information presented in daily interactions. He also had developed a feeling that people around him were able to communicate with each other without his knowledge. Over the years he began to develop a delusional system that incorporated this interpretation. When examined, years after his injury, he had a severe inability to express and interpret the non-linguistic aspects of languages.

This brief clinical history illustrates the case of a young person with a right frontal injury that resulted in minimal neurological signs. It is probable that a similar problem is even more likely to occur in an elderly population with medical illness and sensory deprivation.

Little is known about the natural history of disorders of non-linguistic communication (Weintraub et al., 1981). It is hoped that education will prevent many of the secondary psychiatric complications.

PARANOIA

Paranoia, at least in its milder forms, is not uncommonly found in old age. Symptoms may range from mild vague suspiciousness to a strong belief in the reality of a delusional system. We feel it best to consider a gradient of intensity of paranoid ideation, ranging from suspiciousness to paranoid delusions that may be transient, as in cases of confusional syndromes or toxic–metabolic states. Transient paranoid symptoms may also occur within the context of social isolation with or without some elements of sensory deprivation. Hallucinations may also be a part of this transient syndrome. The latter syndrome may respond to appropriate intervention (Eisdorfer, 1980).

The few points that are repeated in most reviews of the literature (Eisdorfer, 1980; Mensh, 1979) should be emphasized here. Paranoid ideas in the elderly are usually based in "reality." For instance, a patient may be concerned that his family is plotting to place him in a nursing home or that a landlord is planning to evict him so that the rent can be increased. Sensory deprivation is not uncommonly associated with the development of paranoia in the elderly and should be considered carefully in any patient, particularly the elderly. Loss and social isolation (Cumming and Henry, 1961) may also be factors in the development of paranoid symptoms. The psychosocial and cognitive changes commonly associated with normal aging probably play an important role in the development of paranoia in the elderly. The elderly appear to be more cautious in problem-solving (Botwinick, 1973). The cognitive changes of normal aging appear to result in difficulties with certain short-term memory tasks (Ross, 1954) and complex problem-solving (Horn, 1975) with a sensitivity to speed factors (Botwinick, 1975). The contribution of these factors to the evolution of paranoid ideas in an elderly patient without other evidence of neuropathology or psychopathology should be apparent.

Paranoid symptoms may also emerge in the context of an underlying dementia. Generally, the diagnosis of dementia becomes apparent during detailed examination. Raskind (1982) found the most common delusions to be of theft, with premorbid traits of compulsivity, suspiciousness, and litigiousness contributing to the development of delusions of theft with dementia. Because delusions of theft probably only affect a minority of the elderly demented, however, complaints of theft by the dementing patient should always be given due consideration (Raskind, 1982).

Several years ago, a 70-year-old woman who had falsified her age and continued to work in a Boston department store as a super salesperson, was seen in treatment. She went to work and came home each day, on public transportation, entered her apartment, and covered the windows and doors with blankets because she was convinced that airplanes passing over her home were directing radiation at her during the night. She would arise each morning, uncover the doors and windows, and go to work. She was treated for over a year with individual psychotherapy and a wide variety of anitpsychotic drugs without relief of the target symptom.

Paranoia is an interesting, but difficult, entity to treat as is seen in the above case history.

References

Beck, A.T., Rush, A.J., Shaw, B.F., and Emery, G.E. (1979). Cognitive Theory of Depression. Guilford Press, New York.

Bell, I.V. (1849). On a form of disease resembling some advanced stages of mania and fever. Am. J. Insanity 6, 97–127.

Bergmann, K. (1975). Nosology. In Modern Perspectives in the Psychiatry of Old Age. J. Howells, Ed. Brunner-Mazel Inc., New York. [Pinel, P.H. (1806) A treatise on Insanity. D.D., Sheffield, Trans. Ch. 7, p. 70.]

Blessed, G. and Wilson, I.D. (1982). The contemporary natural history of mental disorder in old age. Br. J. Psychiat 141, 59–67.

Bleuler, E. (1916). Lehrbuch der Psychiatrie. Julius Springer, Berlin.

Bleuler, M. (1974). The long term course of the schizophrenic psychoses. Psychol. Med. 4, 244–254.

Botwinick, J. (1973). Aging and Behavior. Springer, New york.

Botwinick, J. (1975). Behavioral process In Aging Vol. 2 Genesis and Treatment of Psychological Disorder in the Elderly, S. Gershen and I. Sherwin, Eds. Raven Press, New York, pp. 1–18.

Botwinick, J. and Storandt, M. (1974). Memory, Related Functions and Age. C.C. Thomas, Springfield, Ill.

Bridge, T.P., Connon, H.E., and Wyatt, R.J. (1978). Burned-out schizophrenia. Evidence for age effects on schizophrenia symptomatology. J. Gerontol. 3, 835–839.

Bridge, T.P. and Wyatt, R.J. (1980a). Paraphrenia: Paranoid states of late life. I. European Research. J. Amer. Geriatr. Soc. 28, 193–200.

Bridge, T.P. and Wyatt, R.J. (1980b). Paraphrenia: Paranoid states of late life. II. American Research. J. Amer. Geriatr. Soc. 28, 201–205.

Busse, E. and Blazer, D. (Eds.) (1980). Handbook of Geriatric Psychiatry, Van Nostrand Reinhold, New York.

Busse, E.W. and Pfeiffer, E. (1975). Behaviors and Adaptation in Later Life, Little Brown, Boston.

Chown, S. (1961). Age and realities. J. Gerontol. 16, 353–362.

Cooper, A. Garside, R.F., and Kay D.W.K. (1976). A comparison of deaf and non-deaf patients with paranoid and affective psychoses. Br. J. Psychiatr. 129, 532.

Cooper, A. Kay, D.W.K., Curry, A.K. Garside, R.F., and Roth, M. (1974). Hearing loss in paranoid and affective psychoses of the elderly. Lancet ii, 851–854.

Cumming, F. and Henry H. (1961). Growing Old: The Process of Discontentment. Basic Books, New York.

Diagnostic and statistical Manual of Mental Disorders, Third Edition (1980). Amer., Psychiatr. Assocn. Washington, D.C.

Dovenmushe, R.H., Reckless, J.B., and Newman, G. (1970). Depression reactions in the elderly. In Normal Aging. Duke University Press, Durham, N. Ca., pp. 90–97.

Eisdorfer, C.E. (1980). Paranoia and schizophrenic disorders in later life. In Handbook of Geriatric Psychiatry. E.W. Busse and D.G. Blazer, Eds. van Nostand Reinhold, New York, pp. 329–337.

Folstern, M.F. and McHugh, P.R. (1978). Dementia syndrome of depression. In Alzheimer's Disease: Senile dementia and Related Disorders, Vol. 7, Aging. R. Katzman, R.D. Terry, and K.L. Bick, Eds. Raven Press, New York, pp. 87–93.

Gerner, R.H. (1979). Depression in the elderly. In Psychopathology of Aging, O. Kaplan, Ed. Academic Press, New York, pp. 97–148.

Horn, J.L. (1975). Aging and intelligence. In

Aging Vol. 2, Genesis and Treatment of Psychologic Disorders in the Elderly. S. Gershen and I. Sherwin, Eds. Raven Press, New York, pp. 19–44.

International Classification of Disease. (1967). Manual of The International Statistical Classification of Diseases, Injuries, & Causes of Death, 1965 revision, Geneva, World Health Organization.

Jamison, K.J. (1979). Manic-depressive illness in the elderly. In Psychopathology of Aging, O. Kaplan, Ed. Academic Press, New York, pp. 79–95.

Kay, D.W.K., Cooper, A., Garside, R.F., and Roth, M. (1976). The differentiation of paranoid from affective psychoses by patients' premorbid characteristics. Br. J. Psychiatr. 129, 207.

Kay, D.W.K. and Roth M. (1961). Environmental and heriditary factors in the schizophrenia of old age (late paraphrenia) and their bearing on the general problem of causation in schizophrenia. J. Ment. Sci. 107, 649–686.

Kileh, L.G. (1961). Pseudodementia. Acta Psychiat. Scand. 37, 336–351.

Kline, N. (1976). Incidence prevalence and recognition of depressive illness. Dis. Nerv. Syst. 37, 10.

Kraeplin, E. (1915). Lehrbuch der Psychiatrie, 8th Ed. Barth, Leipzig.

Kraeplin, E. (1921). Manic-Depressive Insanity and Paranoia. H & S Livingston, Edinburgh, pp. 70–74.

Madden, J., Luhan, J., Kaplan, L., and Manfredi, H. (1952). Nondementing psychoses in older persons. J.A.M.A. 150, 1567–1572.

Maudsley, H. (1879). Senile insanity. In Pathology of Mind. McMillan, London.

Mensh, I.N. The older schizophrenic. In Psychopathology of Aging. O. Kaplan, Ed. Academic Press, New York, pp. 149–165.

Myers, J., Sheldon, D., and Robinson, S.S. (1963). A study of 138 elderly first admissions. Amer. J. Psychiatr. 120, 244–249.

Pinel, P.H., (1806). A Treatise on Insanity. D. Davis, trans. Sheffield.

Post, F. (1965). The Clinical Psychiatry of Late Life. Pergamon Press, Oxford.

Raskind, M. (1982). Paranoid syndromes in the elderly. In Treatment of Psychopathology in the Aging. C. Eisdorfer and W.E. Fann, Eds. Springer, New York, pp. 184–191.

Ross, E. (1981). The aprosodias. Arch. Neurol. 38, 561–569.

Ross, M. (1954). Some psychiatric aspects of

senescence: A review of the literature. Psychiatr. Quat. 28, 93–112.

Roth, M. (1955). The Natural History of Mental Disorders Arising in the Senium. J. Ment. Sci. 101, 281–301.

Rothschild, D. (1956). Senile psychosis and psychosis with cerebral arteriosclerosis. In Mental Disorders in Later Life, Ch. 11, O.J. Capland, Ed. Stanford University Press, Stanford, p. 289.

Seidman, L.J. (1983). Schizophrenia and brain dysfunction: An interpretation of recent neurodiagnostic findings. Psychol. Bull. 1983, (in press).

Swartz, M.S., Henschen, G.M., Carenar, J.O., and Hammett, E.B. (1982). A case of intermittent mania. Amer. J. Psychiatr. 139,137–138.

Weintraub, S., Mesualm, M-M., and Kramer, L. (1981). Disturbances in prosody. Arch. Neurol. 38, 742–744.

Wells, C.E., (1982) Pseudodementia and the recognition of organicity. In Psychiatric Aspects of Neurological Disease, Vol. II, D.F. Benson and D. Blumer, Eds. Grune & Stratten. New York, pp. 167–178.

Williams, W. and Jaco, E.G. (1958). An evaluation of functional psychoses in old age. Amer. J. Psychiatr. 116, 910–116.

World Health Organization. (1972) Psycho-Geriatrics. Report of the World Health Organization Scientific Group, Technical Report Series # 507.

Zung, W.W.K. (1980). Affective disorders. In Handbook of Geriatric Psychiatry Ch. 15, E.W. Busse and D.G. Blazer, Eds. Van Nostrand Reinhold, New York.

IV
Special Senses

17. The Neuro-ophthalmology of Aging

MICHAEL M. COHEN
SIMMONS LESSELL

It is generally accepted that the efficency of the visual system declines with aging. Certainly, anyone who is reading these lines through a presbyopic correction would have to agree. It would be most profitable to address two questions concerning this phenomenon. First, can we identify the "weak links" in the system? Visual acuity, for example, declines with senescence. But is this loss of acuity the consequence of a degraded image (due to a small pupil, alterations in the lens, or deterioration in the receptors), impairment of conduction in the myelinated visual pathway, or a breakdown in information-processing in the brain? This question poses important theoretical as well as practical considerations. If the "weak link" can be identified, it may be possible either to repair it or, more likely, to develop strategies to circumvent it.

The second question is practical. How much dysfunction can be anticipated in the aging patient and at what age does it commence? In other words, where does one draw the line between the normal aging process and an intrusive pathological state? For many of the visual and ocular motor subsystems, data are available to define normal according to the patient's age.* For

others it is not. Clearly, the most valuable data are those obtained from large-scale, decade-by-decade surveys of the population. Although some information can be obtained by comparing a group of youthful subjects to their aged counterparts, onset and rate of decline cannot be determined. For those systems in which decade-by-decade surveys are available, it is frequently surprising how early the first changes appear.

In the initial section of this chapter, we will review data concerning the aging visual and oculomotor systems. Then we will turn to some disease processes that are most typical of the aging patient.

Aging Neuro-ophthalmic Systems

Visual Acuity

Visual Acuity is probably the most studied visual parameter in aging (Anderson and Palmore, 1974; U.S. National Health Survey, 1960–1962; Richards, 1977; Slatoper, 1959). A modest decline in acuity prior to age 60 has been documented, followed by a rapid decline, in many patients, from 60 to 80 years of age. This is

---

*Dr. Irene Loewenfeld (1979) has chided us for using the terms *physiological* and *normal* interchangeably.

Physiological should be reserved for the robust and vigorous function typical of the healthy young individual. This should be differentiated semantically from *normal according to the patient's age.*

Special Senses

Table 17-1. Corrected Best Distance Vision in the Better Eye (Initial Examination).

	Age Group (%)			
	60–69 years	70–79 years	80+ years	Total N
20/20 or better	57	27	14	40
20/25	25	29	23	26
20/30–20/40	10	30	27	20
20/50 or worse	8	14	36	14
N	101	90	22	213

illustrated in Table 17-1, which shows cross-sectional data from the Duke Longitudinal Study on Aging (Anderson and Palmore, 1974).

Significant eye disease, such as cataracts, glaucoma, macular degeneration, and diabetic retinopathy, were encountered in only a few patients. Note that, by 80 years of age, only 14% of the initial study group had a corrected visual acuity of 20/20 or better. A similar decline was noted in the 10-year longitudinal study of 93 of these patients. The incidence of visual acuity of 20/50 or worse (in the better eye) increased by 13% in the 60 to 69 group (now 70 to 79) and by 32% in the 70 to 79 group (now 80 to 89) (Figure 17-1). Once again, there was evidence of specific eye pathology in only a few patients.

Although none of the studies was ideally designed, it is clear that visual acuity declines with age in the absence of specific, recognizable eye disease. In order to assess the implications of this, we must understand precisely what is tested when we measure visual acuity.

Visual acuity, as commonly tested with a Snellen chart, is a measure of visual discrimination of fine details with high contrast. Since fine details can only be discriminated by the macula, visual acuity tests only macular function. Moreover, only the very center of the macula (20' in visual field diameter) is capable of such fine discrimination (Frisen 1980). The standard eye chart thus measures the function of only about 2000 slender cones closely packed in the fovea. These cones, and their connection with the remainder of the visual system, provide the neural substrate for all fine discriminative visual tasks, such as reading.

Unfortunately, visual acuity as generally measured cannot altogether be relied upon as a measure of central vision. This is not a theoretical, but rather a practical problem. As with many older procedures developed before the current "high tech" era, we have failed to maintain strict standards. Conventional visual acuity testing provides a precise measure of central vision only if performed under standardized conditions, that is, equipment; illumination; criteria; etc. (Frisen, 1980).

Because the macular system is so precise, it has always been assumed that the decline in visual acuity with age is due to changes in the optical system of the aging eye. Changes in the pupil and the lens are most frequently cited. It is true that as the pupillary aperture decreases with age, there will be diminished illumination of the retina, as well as some diffraction of the optical image. It is also true that in normal aging of the eye, there are opacification of and color changes in the lens. However, the assumption that age-related decline in acuity is entirely optical in origin has recently been challenged on theoretical grounds (Weale, 1975). The eye, as an optical system, is responsible for only a small portion of visual loss in aging, which may amount to an 80% decline by the ninth decade.

Contrast sensitivity measurement is an additional means of analyzing central vision. (See Bodis-Wollner and Camisa, 1980 for a comprehensive review of contrast sensitivity.) In one sense, conventional visual acuity is a special case of contrast sensitivity wherein the subject is asked to resolve objects of different sizes (spatial frequencies) under conditions of high contrast (black on white). However, two implicit assumptions are made: (1) the ability of the eye to resolve the smallest letter also demonstrates its ability to resolve larger objects just as well and (2) contrast is not of primary importance. These assumptions are valid when applied to an acitivity such as reading—since letters are small objects in high contrast—but not when applied to activities that involve the resolution of larger objects, such as

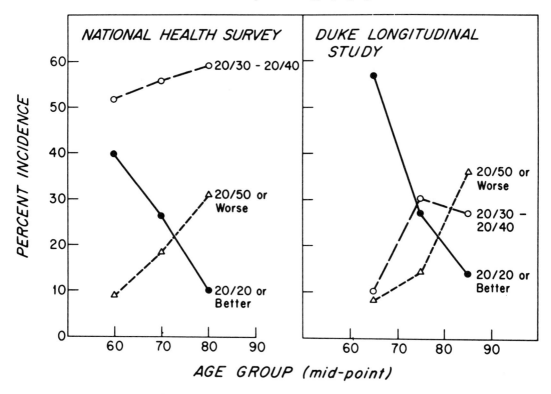

Figure 17-1. Individuals (%) with different visual acuity levels (Snellen values) in three age groups. (U.S. National Health Survey, 1968.)

faces. In fact, except for reading, most everyday activities do not depend upon our ability to resolve fine details of high contrast (Leibowitz et al., 1980).

Contrast sensitivity measurements employ sinusoidal gratings of variable size (spatial frequency) and variable contrast (Figure 17-2). By plotting these two variables, a curve is generated which describes the ability of an individual to see various sized objects at various levels of contrast.

Numerous investigators have shown that a patient with neural lesions, but with normal visual acuity, may have diminished ability to see larger objects (Bodis-Wollner, 1972; Arden, 1978; Regan et al., 1977). That is, the visual system seems to possess subsystems responsible for detecting various spatial frequencies.

In a recent series of well-controlled experiments designed to evaluate contrast sensitivity in aged patients, a selective loss

was demonstrated (Sekuler and Hutman, 1980; Hutman and Sekuler, 1980). The younger patients (mean age, 18.5 years) had a corrected acuity of 20/20, whereas in the older group (mean age, 73.2 years), the corrected acuity averaged 20/24. There was reduced sensitivity of the older individuals, primarily to low spatial frequencies. The young subjects were three times as sensitive to low frequencies. At high frequencies, the groups were almost identical. Since the older individuals were selected for normal or near-normal acuity, it is not surprising that high spatial frequencies were preserved. However, since optical factors tend to affect high more than low spatial frequencies (Bodis-Wollner and Camisa, 1980), these results suggest that there is a neural and not an optical cause for a major part of the age-related visual decline. Perhaps the subsystem for low spatial frequencies ages

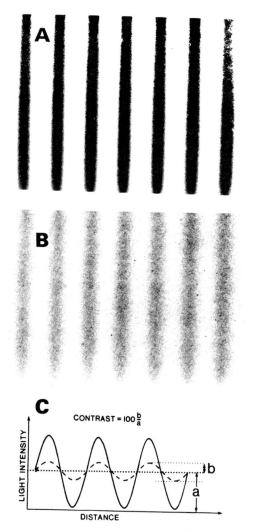

Figure 17-2. A (high contrast; ~ 50%) and B (low contrast; ~ 10%) sine-wave grating used to test patients' vision. C shows the variation of light intensity across the screen for a grating of almost 100 % contrast (continuous line) and for one of roughly 20% contrast (dashed line). The mean brightness (dotted line) is the same for both gratings, independent of contrast. Percentage contrast equals 100% (1_{max} -1_{min}/ 21 mean) equals 100b/a. (From Regan et al., 1977.)

example, in order to see "a pedestrian . . . on a dimly illuminated road, the limiting visual capacity may not be acuity but rather the ability to appreciate a small contrast difference between a large object and its background (Leibowitz et al., 1980).

There has been no large, decade-by-decade population study of both visual acuity and contrast sensitivity. One of the problems with visual acuity testing is that most chart systems do not have sufficient gradations to test vision better than 20/20, a Snellen acuity that is actually at the lower limit of "normal." A recent study indicates that 20/20 vision requires no more than 44% functional acuity channels (Feisen and Feisen, 1979). We would predict that a large population study would demonstrate that age-related visual loss commences much earlier than is generally supposed.

If, as seems likely, much of the age-related visual decline is neural rather than optical, are there age-related changes in the visual system? The only proper response is that we are confronted with an *embarras de richesses*. The major problem confronting the investigator is to decide which of the many changes is likely to be primary.

The retina is a logical starting point. A variety of fundoscopic and histological changes occur with age, independent of recognizable pathology (Prince, 1965; Fozard et al., 1977). Most of these changes affect the peripheral retina, however, and not the macular region. Electroretinography (ERG) has been performed in aged populations (Fozard et al., 1977), and there are mild but definite changes in both the A and B waves. Since ERG measures pre-ganglion cell electrical activity, there is some evidence to implicate the photoreceptors.

In a study of 16 subjects ranging in age from 40 to 90 years, a variety of morphological alterations were noted in the ganglion cells (Vrabec, 1965). The earliest changes included enlargement and tortuosity of the ganglion dendrites; there were also fewer ganglion dendrites in the neuropil. The ganglion cell body was increasingly packed with argyrophilic granules or lipofuscin.

The ganglion cell axons (nerve fiber

more rapidly than that for high frequencies and that acuity declines only where there is also a loss of the high frequency system.

Thus, in the elderly, standard tests of visual acuity will overestimate functional vision in low frequency conditions. For layer, optic disc tissue, and optic nerves) and associated structures also change unequivocally with age (Vrabec, 1977; Dolman et al., 1980). The following changes were noted:

1. The leptomeninges, including the optic nerve septae, become broader and occupy more of the cross-sectional area of the nerve
2. After the seventh decade, the nerve appears paler with myelin stains. This seems to be the result of depletion in the number of fibers, rather than of thinning of the individual sheaths
3. There is a progressive accumulation of lipofuscin granules and corpora amylacea
4. After the seventh decade, there is a loss of axons, with swollen axons at the level of the cribriform plate. Swollen axons increase in frequency from the seventh decade (3/15 specimens) through the eighth (5/15), ninth and tenth (8/15) decades (Dolman et al., 1980)

There are a number of explanations for these findings. Ganglion cell senescence might be the primary event leading to secondary axonal degeneration, and the cribriform portion of the optic nerve may display the most overt changes because it represents the "locus minoris resistentiae." Alternatively, the cribriform optic nerve may sustain the initial damage. Pathophysiological processes that have been proposed include compression by the thickened meninges, progressive ischemia, and age-related axonal "dystrophy."

Numerous studies have now demonstrated age-related increases in latency in components of the visual evoked response (VER) (Glaser and Laflamme, 1979; Celesia and Daly, 1977; Asselman et al., 1975). The amplitude may (Glaser and Laflamme, 1979) or may not (Celesia and Daly, 1977) decrease with age. Although it would be useful to ascribe the prolonged latency to an age-related optic neuropathy—and the most dramatic abnormalities in VER latency are generally caused by lesions in the optic nerves—it is still not known precisely which of the components can be correlated with an anterior and which with the posterior visual system.

Although there are no convincing data concerning senescent alterations in the lateral geniculate body or radiations, the visual cortex has been extensively studied (Strehler, 1976; Devaney and Johnson, 1980; Scheibel et al., 1975; Wisniewski and Terry, 1976; McGeer and McGeer, 1976). The number of neurons in the macular projection area of the visual cortex is significantly reduced with aging. In one study (Devaney and Johnson, 1980), the neuronal density dropped from about 40 million neurons/gram at age 20 to 20 million neurons/gram at age 80. This represents a loss of one-half of the cells that process information for many aspects of vision, including visual acuity. Despite the well-recognized redundancy in most human neural systems, it would be surprising if a 50% reduction did not have some effect on visual acuity. In addition to the neuronal drop-out, loss of dendritic spines and synaptic contacts from cells in the visual cortex have been documented (Scheibel et al., 1975). Neurochemical evidence of cell loss or dysfunction in the primary and association visual cortices is also available (McGeer and McGeer, 1976).

Visual Fields

The data regarding aging and the visual field is in one sense more useful than the visual acuity data, in that we have decade-by-decade studies. Diminution in the visual fields with age has now been conclusively documented on the tangent screen (Harrington, 1976), the arc perimeter (Wolf, 1967; Fisher, 1968), and the Goldmann perimeter (Drance et al., 1967a,b; Shutt et al., 1967). In fact, the instruction manual that accompanies the Goldmann perimeter addresses this age-related decline.

In older individuals, the most central isopters (I_1* on the Goldmann perimeter and 1/2000 with the tangent screen) are apt to be reduced in size and to fall within the blind spot (Harrington, 1976; Shutt et al.,

---

*The I_1, I_2, and I_4 test stimuli are 0.25 mm² spots of white light with relative intensities of .0315, .1, and 1.00.

1967). In one study (Shutt et al., 1967) with the Goldman perimeter, this occurred with increasing incidence as follows: under age 40, 7.4%; 40 to 49, 22.8%; 50 to 59, 37.5%; 60 or over, 76.7%.

In an arc perimeter study of the peripheral isopters with a 1 mm^2 target, there was a continual decline in the size of the field from youth (age 16) to old age (age 96) (Wolf, 1967). However, the extent of the decline was minimal prior to age 60 and marked after age 60. Contrasting results were found in a study of 134 subjects from the second through the eighth decade (Drance et al., 1967a). The protocol consisted of blind spot delineation with the I$_2$ stimulus, followed by I$_2$ field, I$_4$ field, and finally static perimetry along the 90- to 270-degree meridia. The area of the blind spot increased linearly with age, although this increase was small. Both the central (I$_2$) and peripheral (I$_4$) isopters displayed a *linear* decline with age, beginning in the youngest age groups, and progressing through senescence. The area of the I$_4$ field (total area minus the area of the blind spot) declined from approximately 13000 mm^2 (age 10) to 8500 mm^2 (age 80). The I$_2$ field similarly declined from about 3500 mm^2 to 1500 mm^2.

The explanation for the decline is not clear. The small pupil is frequently invoked, but in the preceding study, the pupils were dilated with drops to 6 millimeters in over 86% of the subjects. Progressive opacification of the lens may account for some of the diminution, but probably not a significant amount (Wolf, 1967). The effect of lid position was found to be minimal (Drance et al., 1967a). Lastly, we are confronted with the proposition that senescence in the visual system begins at an earlier age than we generally suppose.

Color Vision

The progressive yellowing of the lens with age has predictable consequences for color sense; there is a differential loss of sensitivity to the shorter (blue) wavelengths with age (Said and Weale, 1959). However, there is also some loss of sensitivity over the entire spectrum (Gilbert, 1957) by the fourth decade. Since, in some subjects, the two eyes may differ significantly in spectral sensitivity, at least some of the deficiency may be optical (lenticular). However, when young and elderly aphakic subjects are tested, changes in spectral sensitivity are still present; thus, changes in the lens do not *completely* account for the changes in color vision with age (Ordy and Brizzee, 1979).

Lenticular yellowing also affects the ophthalmoscopic appreciation of disc color. If the lens of an elderly patient is viewed through a slit lamp, the reflection from the anterior surface is bluish-white, while the reflection from the posterior surface is yellow. With an ophthalmoscope, light must pass through the lens twice, blue light being scattered each time. The senescent yellowing of the lens and the preferential scattering of blue light causes the aging lens to act as a "minus blue filter." The practical consequence is that the predominantly longer wavelengths impart a red color to the disc, which may obscure disc pallor. Conversely, if the aged lens is extracted, the augmented transmission of the shorter blue wavelengths frequently produces the appearance of pallor.

The Pupil

A recent comprehensive study provides us with a theoretical as well as a quantitative understanding of the pupillary changes related to age (Loewenfeld, 1979). This well-controlled study includes thousands of normal subjects from the first to the ninth decade. It could be argued that we are now on more solid ground in discussing the effect of aging on the pupillary system than on any other system in neuro-ophthalmology.

It has been appreciated for some time that the pupils tend to become smaller with age, but the time of onset and the extent were controversial. Figure 17-3 illustrates the data from 1471 subjects. The so-called "senile miosis" actually begins at high school age. The average pupillary diameter (in darkness) declines from about 7 mm to about 4.25 mm. If the latter figure appears unusually large, that is because clinical examinations of patients are not conducted in the dark, which is the only

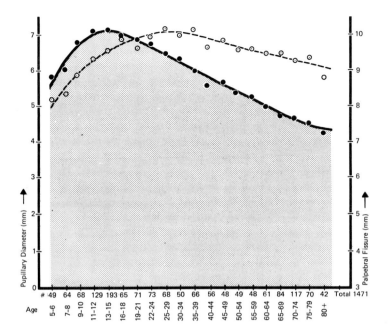

Figure 17-3. Pupil diameter (mm)(●) and width of palpebral fissure (mm)(○) in 1471 subjects (averages/age group) were chosen at random. Right-eye and left-eye measurements were averaged. Averaged age groups and number of subjects per group below the abscissa. Smaller age steps were taken for children because of the relatively rapid growth period. (From Loewenfeld, 1979.)

way to compare base-line pupillary size. Examining patients in "ambient" light creates another testing artifact—it produces spurious poor pupillary light responses. The explanation will shortly be apparent.

Why is the pupil reduced in size? Senile iris degeneration is most often held the reason. However, although pupillary decline begins during the second decade, senile iris degeneration rarely begins before age 40, and additionally, the pupils of old people respond well to both adrenergic and cholinergic drugs. This would not be possible if the iris musculature were significantly damaged. The evidence suggests that iris degeneration contributes to senile miosis only after age 60, and even then the contribution is minor. The following features are compatible with the minor muscle "stiffness" or iris degeneration:

1. There is a longer latency to the pupillary light reflex in the elderly
2. The maximum attainable speed of the reflex declines
3. Elderly pupils cannot be driven as rapidly or as well by rapid oscillations

A second popular theory contends that an age-related decline in the sympathetic nervous system deprives the dilator muscle of its "tone." The sphincter muscle, no longer effectively opposed, would then contract (Schafer and Weale, 1970). There are several objections to this theory. First, the degree of contraction is greater than that seen with the most complete sympathetic paralysis. Second, and equally telling, there is no other (i.e., sudomotor or vasomotor) evidence of sympathetic involvement.

The hypothesis we find most acceptable implicates the central rather than the peripheral nervous system (Loewenfeld, 1979). This postulates a progressive, age-related weakening in the central inhibition of the pupillary reflex. It is well known that intense arousal, especially in young children, can entirely "override" the light reflex and produce large unreactive pupils—and occasionally lead to an inappropriate neurological evaluation. On the other hand, with fatigue and in sleep, there is a gradual loss of central inhibition of the oculomotor complex. This explains the miosis that is invariably associated with sleep, despite the obvious decrease in light following lid closure. The hypothesis is that, with aging, pupillary "fatigue" signs become permanent.

Aged patients not only have small pupils, but also (because of weak central inhibition) they may react poorly to light. This seeming paradox is resolved if we consider that, all else being equal, a miotic pupil will responsd to less additional light than a large pupil. This strictly mechanical limitation has been called "the law of initial values." Thus, elderly pupils will be small—and their light reaction seemingly poor—if they are not examined in darkness because they are already overresponding to the ambient light.

These observations of the pupillary changes in aging force us to reappraise the concept of "diabetic" pupils. Such pupils are said to be small and sluggishly reactive because of the presence of diabetes. When age is taken into consideration, however, diabetic miosis is not nearly as abnormal. One hundred and seventy-five diabetics were examined and compared with the appropriate age groups in the population survey (Loewenfeld, 1979). Although 105 of the diabetic patients had smaller pupils than the norm, only a few had marked miosis, and 66 diabetics had larger pupils.

The pupillary near reflex declines somewhat with age, but, as with the light reflex, the apparent decline is greater than the actual decline—and for precisely the same reason. The elderly pupil partially constricts in response to even the small amount of ambient light necessary to observe the result of the near reflex. It is, again, not surprising that the near reflex appears to be more impaired than it actually is.

The Corneal Reflex

Testing for corneal reflex integrity is an important part of both the neurological and neuro-ophthalmologic examinations. Since the reflex (and related sensory function of the ophthalmic division of the trigeminal nerve) is sometimes of crucial importance in neuroanatomical localization of pathology, it is surprising that it has received scant attention. A recent electrophysiological study demonstrated that the corneal reflex latency may be a sensitive test for subtle trigeminal nerve lesions (Ongerboer de Visser et al., 1977). This same study also documented the increase in corneal reflex latency with age. The mean latency increased from 44.3 milliseconds in 10- to 40-year-old subjects to 51.4 milliseconds in subjects 61 to 80 years old.

It is important to know whether the reflex is delayed because of a "decay" in the afferent or in the efferent signal. More importantly for the clinician, it is important to know if corneal sensation declines with age.

Several studies suggest that corneal sensitivity does decline with age (Boberg-Ans, 1956; Jalavisto et al., 1951). In a recent study (Millodot, 1977), corneal touch threshold (CTT) was measured in 205 healthy subjects representing the first through the ninth decade. The CTT increased (and corneal sensitivity declined) throughout life, although the decline was more rapid after the fifth decade. By the ninth decade, corneal sensitivity was only one-half to two-thirds as great as in the second and the third decade.

One clinical study cautions that the corneal reflex may be entirely absent in elderly normal patients (Rai and Elias-Jones, 1979).

Accommodation

The age-related decline in the amplitude of accommodation of the human eye is illustrated in Figure 17-4. The data represent the values of five investigators obtained from over 5000 eyes. It is safe to say that the decrease in accomodation is the most predictable age-related decline of the visual system. By age 40 to 55, a presbyopic correction will be necessary for accurate near vision. The practical importance is that if an elderly patient's vision is to be accurately tested with a near card, his presbyopic correction or a substitute must be in place, since, in the neurological or neuro-ophthalmic evaluation of vision, the only concern is the *best corrected visual acuity*. Uncorrected visual acuity (near or distance) is only of interest to the ophthalmologist, optometrist, and the patient.

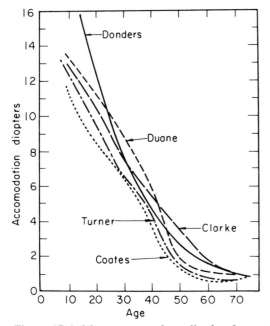

Figure 17-4. Mean curves of amplitude of accommodation (diopters) versus age. The amplitude of accommodation in diopters is the difference between the near and far distances (stated in reciprocal meters) at which the eye will bring an image to a sharp focus on the retina. (From Ordy et al., 1979.)

Ocular Motor System

The ocular motor system also undergoes a progressive loss of vigor with age. Clinically, this has been suspected for some time, but it was not quantified until recently.

A commonly appreciated clinical manifestation is the reduction in accommodative convergence. As we have seen, the amplitude of accommodation declines with age. Convergence, which accompanies accommodation and pupillary miosis in the so-called near reflex, also declines (Schafer and Weale, 1970), but has never been studied in a large population.

In testing convergence, the test must be performed correctly in order to avoid spuriously negative results. Convergence is a voluntary act, which is visually initiated, and the patient must be able to focus on the near object used as a stimulus. Therefore, the patient should be tested with his/her presbyopic correction.

Senile ptosis is a slowly progressive, mainly symmetric disorder, not accompanied by extraocular muscle paralysis. Most authors ascribe it to an involution of the levator palpebrae superioris, the levator aponeurosis, or Mueller's muscle or to atrophy of orbital fat, or a combination of these factors (Duke-Elder and MacFaul, 1974; Beard, 1976).

The palpebral fissure decreases a few millimeters after age 60 (Fox, 1966), but a large population study was required to document its onset (Loewenfeld, 1979). The trend actually begins in the middle 30s, and the similarity to the pupillary curve is intriguing. As Figure 17-3 illustrates, the lid curve is shifted somewhat to the right. The average narrowing of the fissure (and it is fair to assume that this represents ptosis and not elevation of the lower lid) is only 1 millimeter, but since this is a numerical average, larger declines are to be expected.

A progressive, symmetric restriction in upgaze also accompanies aging. The extent of ocular elevation has recently been measured in 367 patients of different age groups and is shown as follows (Chamberlain, 1970).

Age (years)	Ocular elevation (°)
5–14	40.1
15–24	37.3
25–34	36.0
35–44	32.9
45–54	30.4
55–64	26.5
65–74	21.9
75–84	16.8
85–94	16.1

There was no limitation in lateral gaze or downgaze and there were no other oculomotor disturbances. Chamberlain (1970) speculates, and others (Daroff, 1975) have agreed, that the restriction in upgaze may be due to "disuse." That is, most older people of average height have little need to elevate their eyes in extreme upward gaze and consequently there is disuse atrophy. The study also presents measurements on four individuals, aged 45 to 54, with severe kyphosis (Chamberlain, 1970). They had

better than expected elevation (35° instead
of 30°). It is proposed that these individuals would have a greater requirement for
upgaze owing to their physical limitations.
If we review the above data, we find that
the trend begins in the second decade. An
individual would attain his full height by
the end of the second decade—and have
less of a need to look up to people.
However, the age of onset and overall
extent of the upgaze decline are similar to
the age of onset and extent of "senile"
miosis and "senile" ptosis. This similarity
raises the possibility that all three might
result from supranuclear, central nervous
system processes. Speculation aside, the
crucial clinical point is that restriction of
upgaze may also be seen with various
lesions of the mesencephalon. This, however, is invariably accompanied by other
mesencephalic eye signs, such as lid retraction, convergence–retraction, nystagmus,
skew deviation, abnormal pupils, and
downgaze paralysis. An isolated upgaze
limitation that does not greatly exceed the
above norms should be accepted as an
age-related phenomenon.

Restriction of horizontal gaze with age
has rarely been studied in this way, but to
at least one investigator there is the "impression that as folks grow older it also
becomes increasingly difficult for them to
bring the eyes into full positions of abduction and adduction" (Von Noorden, 1970).
This impression is supported by a single
early study (Holland, cited by Miller,
1975).

Whether or not the range of horizontal
eye movements is reduced, there is now
clear evidence of reduced *efficiency* of the
pursuit, saccadic, and opticokinetic (OKN)
systems in the elderly (Sharpe and Sylvester, 1978; Spooner et al., 1980; Kuechenmeister et al., 1977). One study evaluated the effect of aging on the smooth
pursuit system (Sharpe and Sylvester,
1978). Fifteen young volunteers (19 to 32
years old, mean age 23) and 10 elderly
volunteers (65 to 77 years old, mean age 72)
served as subjects. There were significant
differences in all the parameters studied,
including (1) mean pursuit velocity, (2)
maximum individual pursuit velocities, (3)
pursuit latency, and (4) number of intrusive

saccades per second. The basic defect is a
reduction in the gain of the system (eye
velocity ÷ target velocity) with age. In the
young subjects, gain exceeded 0.96 with
target velocities up to 30°/second, but in the
elderly, the highest mean gain was 0.94 with
a 5°/second target velocity. At a target
velocity of 10°/second, the elderly group
could no longer keep up and there was an
increasing imposition of saccades. The
younger subjects could maintain smooth
pursuit until the target velocity exceeded
30°/second—and some subjects could continue to do so at even higher target velocities. Even at very slow target velocities
(5°/second), the smooth pursuit latencies
were significantly prolonged in the elderly.

This study has important clinical implications. Defective pursuit (evidenced clinically by saccadic tracking) is a frequent
sign of cerebral, cerebellar, or brain-stem
dysfunction. If we are to analyze the
pursuit system clinically, it is clear that age
must be considered an additional variable.
We must also keep in mind that elderly
patients begin to fail with target velocities
above 5°/second, whereas younger patients
do well until 30°/second. A common clinical error is to test the pursuit system only
at high velocity.

A second study confirmed the impairment of smooth pursuit and documented a
concomitant decline in the saccadic and
OKN slow component velocity (Spooner
et al., 1980). Of interest, the study was
initiated to examine whether or not vertebrobasilar insufficiency (VBI) produced
subclinical abnormalities in the electronystagmography recording of eye tracking. Indeed, when the patients with VBI
(mean age 67 years) were compared with
a control population (mean age 42 years),
there were abnormalities on each portion
of the eye tracking test battery. But in an
elderly normal population (mean age 65
years), there were similar eye tracking
abnormalities. These included (1) slowed
smooth pursuit, (2) diminished maximum
saccadic velocity (3) increased saccadic
latency, and (4) diminished slow phase
velocity of OKN. As the authors point
out, it would be important to know
whether there is a critical cut-off age or
whether ocular motor function is linearly

related to age (which we suspect is the case).

Are the vitiations of the ocular motor system primarily supranuclear, nuclear, or infranuclear? There are, unfortunately, too few data to answer this question with any degree of certainty, although sporadic data are available.

In global terms, if we compare age-related cell loss in the cortex, with that in the brain stem there is a gross discrepancy (Brody, 1976). Although there is marked variation from region to region, cortical cellular fall-out is a common phenomenon. We have already remarked on the 50% reduction in the neuronal population of the macular area of the striate cortex. In contrast, only the locus ceruleus, among the brain-stem nuclei so far studied, showed a diminished number of cells with aging. Total cell counts of both the abducens (Vijayashankar and Brody, 1977) and trochlear (Vijayashankar and Brody, 1973) nuclei have failed to demonstrate any significant age-related depopulation. To our knowledge, the oculomotor complex and the cells of the paramedian pontine reticular formation have not been examined. Since the oculomotor abnormalities of aging are invariably symmetrical, on clinical grounds, a supranuclear defect (including the paramedian pontine reticular formation) would be expected.

What about the extraocular muscles themselves? They have been studied (Miller, 1975; Muhlendyck and Ali, 1978) and age-related changes are present from early adulthood. These consist of increasing fibrosis, *ringbinden,* nemalin bodies, ribosomal accumulations, and fragmentation and dissolution of the myofibrils. Older subjects, additionally, will display vacant sarcoplasm, leptomeric bodies, mitochondrial hypertrophy, pleomorphism, and inclusions. Whether these changes indicate primary muscle sensecence or are secondary to a disruption in neural influence is unknown (Daroff, 1975).

Since we are still uncertain about the pathogenesis of the so-called "myogenic" changes in skeletal muscle (which is easy to obtain), the pathogenesis of changes in extraocular muscle (which is difficult to obtain) is understandable.

Neuro-ophthalmic Disorders in the Elderly

This section will focus on those neuro-ophthalmic disorders that occur with increased frequency in, or are restricted to, the elderly. Perforce, this will eliminate from discussion diseases that display little or no age preference. The organization will be syndromatic and will emphasize those disorders that present either diagnostic or therapeutic challenges.

Acute Monocular Blindness

Sudden, spontaneous, painless loss of vision presents the clinician with a manageable diagnostic challenge. It is manageable because the major differential diagnoses are limited and almost invariably distinguishable by a thorough history and physical examination. The following diagnoses should be considered:

1. Retinal detachment
2. Disciform hemorrhage of the retina
3. Vitreous hemmorrhage
4. Central retinal vein occlusion
5. Central retinal artery occlusion
6. Ischemic optic neuropathy

Retinal detachment usually results from traction by the vitreous humor on a torn retina. Often premonitory flashes of light or a shower of floaters precede the detachment. The patient may notice a shadow in the peripheral field before the loss of central vision. Retinal detachment is readily diagnosed by ophthalmoscopic examination if the pupil is dilated (Lessel, 1967). Figure 17-5 illustrates the extent of the retina visible with a direct ophthalmoscope through an undilated and a dilated pupil.

Disciform hemorrhage of the retina is generally the result of bleeding from neovascular tufts deep to the retina in the region of the macula. They commonly occur in middle or later life and are usually ascribed to "senile macula degeneration." The hemorrhage appears as a dark red blot in the macular region. Again, recognition of this disorder is considerably enhanced if the pupil is dilated.

A large *vitreous hemorrhage* may be inferred from the inability to visualize the

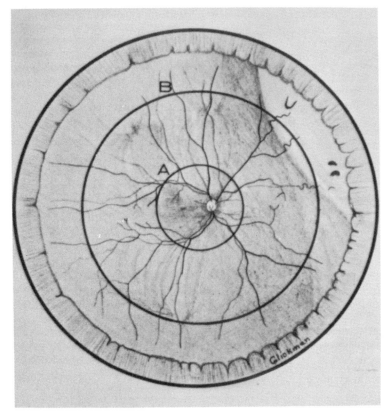

Figure 17-5. Retinal detachment in the superior nasal periphery of the right eye. Lines A and B, extent of the retina visible with the direct ophthalmoscope through an undilated and a dilated pupil, respectively. The retinal periphery must be visualized with the indirect binocular ophthalmoscope for recognition of the lesion. (From Lessell, S 1967.)

retina or disc despite a clear cornea, anterior chamber, and lens. Bleeding from retinal neovascularization in patients with diabetic retinopathy is a common cause of hemorrhage, although retinal tears, local trauma, subarachnoid hemorrhage, and bleeding diatheses should also be considered.

Central retinal vein occlusion (Hayreh, 1977; McGrath et al., 1978; Editorial, 1976; Kearns and Hollenhorst, 1963; Neupert et al., 1976) in elderly patients usually results from compression of the vein by an adjacent, arteriosclerotic central retinal artery. These two vessels share a common sheath as they traverse the optic nerve. Diabetes, glaucoma, hyperviscosity states, or other disorders that reduce blood flow from the retina can predispose to its occurrence (McGrath et al., 1978). The *sturm und drang* appearance of the fundus is characteristic. There is disc edema, tortuosity and engorgement of the retinal veins, and hemorrhages throughout the retina (Figure 17-6). Central retinal vein occlusion usually has no neurological sig-

nificance. It has been suggested that carotid artery stenosis or occlusion may be a predisposing factor (Kearns and Hollenhorst, 1963; Neupert et al., 1976), although the objection has been raised that the arteriosclerosis of the central retinal artery and the atherosclerosis of the carotid artery are concomitant, but causally unrelated manifestations of widespread vascular disease (Hayreh, 1977). Unless there are other signs of carotid artery disease, neurological and neurovascular evaluation are unwarranted.

The same cannot be said about *central retinal artery occlusion,* which has important ocular, systemic, and neurological implications. The pathophysiology of the occlusion is generally either vaso-obliterative or embolic, although poor perfusion pressure (due to elevated intraocular pressure or decreased systemic blood pressure) and arterial spasm are sometimes invoked (Gold, 1977). Whether the occlusion is thrombotic or embolic, the ophthalmoscopic picture is similar. There is segmentation of the blood column and the

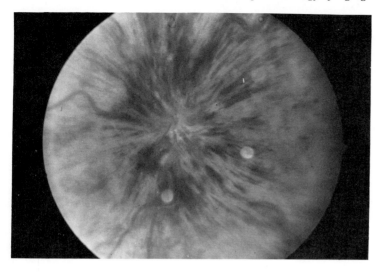

Figure 17-6. Appearance of optic fundus after occlusion of the central retinal vein. Note the profusion of superficial retinal hemorrhages oriented radially on the optic disc.

retina soon becomes milky with a cherry-red spot at the macula (Figure 17-7). If seen shortly after occlusion, these changes may be subtle. Over several weeks, all these signs may disappear as the disc becomes progressively more pale and atrophic.

The peak incidence of central retinal artery occlusion is in the seventh decade (Lorentzen, 1969). In a recent study of 54 patients, 44 were over 40 years of age (Appen et al., 1975). In this group there were eight with strokes, five with ipsilateral carotid occlusion, six with visible retinal emboli, ten with cardiac valvular disease, and eleven with hypertension. Another

study of 30 cases of central retinal artery occlusion confirmed the frequent association with cerebrovascular disease (Tomsak et al., 1979). Carotid angiography was performed in 13 patients, and 10 patients (76%) had significant ipsilateral carotid artery disease. It is clear from these and other studies that unless a cardiac source is readily apparent, or unless arteritis is suspected, investigation of the carotid artery is indicated. If a thorough systemic and neurological investigation proves negative, it can be assumed that the vascular disease is intrinsic to the central retinal artery. Hypertensive arteriosclerosis is undoubtedly causative in many cases. However, other

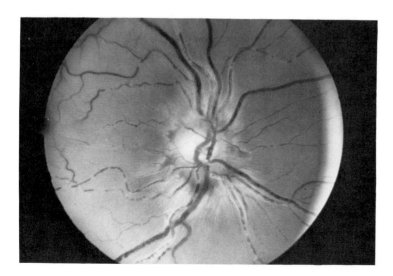

Figure 17-7. Appearance of the optic fundus several hours after obstruction of the central retinal artery. The disc looks normal, but the retina is milky and the blood column is discontinuous in the arteries.

causes of vasculopathy should be considered. Since, as we will see, giant cell arteritis may present as a central retinal artery occlusion, an erythrocyte sedimentation rate must be included in the systemic evaluation.

Ischemic optic neuropathy is the term used to designate infarction of the optic nerve head (Hayreh, 1974a,b; Eagling et al., 1974; Ellenberger et al., 1973; Boghen and Glaser, 1975). It results from occlusion of the posterior ciliary arteries, which are, like the central retinal artery, derived from the ophthalmic artery (and ultimately the carotid artery). The central retinal artery and posterior ciliary arteries are usually reciprocal in their vascular territories. The former supplies the retina (but not the optic disc), the latter primarily the optic disc. The ophthalmoscopic pictures of these two vascular occlusion syndromes are also reciprocals. In central retinal artery occlusion, the retina becomes edematous, while the disc is normal until optic atrophy develops. In ischemic optic neuropathy, the retina is normal, but the disc becomes edematous (Figure 17-8). The disc edema is generally pale and may involve the entire disc or only a section. There may also be a few small hemorrhages and microinfarcts in the peripapillary nerve fiber layer (cotton wool spots). The visual loss may be complete or partial; when partial, it is often possible to identify an altitudinal field defect, especially in the lower one-half of the field.

Ischemic optic neuropathy affects the elderly in one of two clinical contexts. Most frequently, it occurs in isolation. There is a background of hypertension or diabetes in over 50% of the cases, and it is presumed that, in these patients, occlusion occurs directly in the posterior ciliary arteries. Autopsy confirms that these vessels do undergo athero- and arteriosclerosis (Ellenberger and Netsky, 1968). On rare occasions, there may be an association with either embolic or occlusive carotid artery disease (Eagling et al., 1974; Lieberman et al., 1978). However, this is so uncommon that, in the absence of other signs of vascular disease, evaluation of the carotid system is not justified. Systemic evaluation should include an erythrocyte sedimentation rate (ESR), complete blood count (CBC), platelet count, serum protein electrophoresis, 2-hour post-prandial blood sugar, a serological test for syphilis, antinuclear antibody (ANA), and skull X-rays with optic canal views. If these studies are unremarkable, no further evaluation is necessary. Unfortunately, there is no effective therapy (Eagling et al., 1974; Bogen and Glaser, 1975), although steroids have been advocated by some (Hayreh, 1974b). It is important to be aware that approximately 40% of patients will suffer an attack in the other eye (Bogen

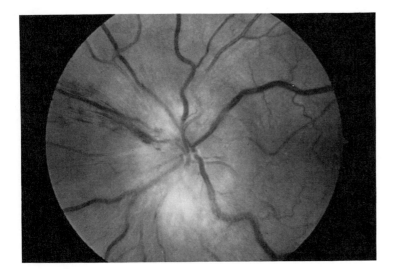

Figure 17-8. Appearance of the optic fundus of a patient with acute ischemic optic neuropathy. There is edema of the optic disc and several flame-shaped hemorrhages.

and Glaser, 1975). If the patient is first observed after the second attack, the physician is liable to make the erroneous diagnosis of Foster Kennedy syndrome, since there is optic atrophy of the initially affected disc and edema of the currently affected one (Schatz and Smith, 1967). The key is that vision is reduced in the edematous eye. This would not be expected to occur in papilledema.

Since ischemic optic neuropathy may be the initial sign of giant cell arteritis, every patient with ischemic optic neuropathy requires immediate evaluation to either confirm or rule out arteritis. There are some minor differences in the presentation. The "arteritic" variety of ischemic optic neuropathy tends to occur in a *slightly* older age group (over 60) than does the "arteriosclerotic" variety (under 60), but there is so much overlap that this kind of epidemiological data is of little help in the individual patient. In addition, the visual impairment (acuity and field) is usually more pronounced in the arteritic group. Whereas in the arteriosclerotic variety there is invariably disc edema, there are instances of retrobulbar involvement—and hence an initially normal disc—in the arteritic form. The arteritic form, when unaccompanied by other systemic symptoms and signs of giant cell arteritis, is referred to as "occult" temporal (or giant cell) arteritis (Semmons and Cogan, 1962; Cullen, 1967).

Giant Cell Arteritis

Giant cell (temporal) arteritis rarely appears before age 50. In subsequent decades, both age-related incidence and prevalence increase dramatically. Between ages 60 to 69, the prevalence is about 33/100,000; over age 80 this increases to 844/100,000 (Hauser et al., 1971). When dealing with such a prevalent disease, even the uncommon modes of presentation are important.

The varied systemic and neurological modes of presentation of giant cell arteritis have been thoroughly reviewed (Hauser et al., 1971; Hollenhorst et al., 1960; Huston et al., 1978). These include (1) the classic syndrome of headache, scalp tenderness,

malaise, weight loss, and low-grade fever, (2) the polymyalgia rheumatica syndrome; (3) facial neuralgia, jaw claudication, or dysphagia; (4) confusion or dementia; (5) vertigo, deafness, and ear pain; (6) coronary artery disease; (7) stroke (primarily vertebrobasilar); (8) fever of unknown origin; (9) polyarteritis; and (10) aortic arch syndrome. The neuro-ophthalmic syndromes are likewise varied and include (1) ischemic optic neuropathy (papillopathy); (2) amaurosis fugax preceding (1) (by hours or days at most); (3) retrobulbar optic neuropathy; (4) central retinal artery occlusion; (5) ocular ischemia, iritis, and conjunctivitis; (6) pupillary abnormalities—fixed dilated pupil or "tonic" pupil; (7) ocular motor palsies and diplopia; (8) scintillating scotomata; (9) formed visual hallucinations; and (10) cortical blindness. Order can be imposed on this seeming potpourri of neuro-ophthalmic signs by considering the sites of predilection of giant cell arteritis in the cranial vascular tree. The following table lists the prevalence of "severe" involvement, by percentage, for various arteries (Wilkinson and Russel, 1972):

Artery	Prevalence (%)
Superficial temporal	100
Vertebral	100
Ophthalmic	76
Posterior ciliary	75
External carotid	47
Internal carotid (petrous and cavernous)	38
Proximal central retinal	60
Distal central retinal	26

The frequent involvement of the posterior ciliary artery (75%) correlates with the high incidence of ischemic optic neuropathy. Despite an almost as frequent involvement of the proximal central retinal artery (60%), clinical central retinal artery occlusion is much less common than ischemic optic neuropathy. Doubtless, this discrepancy reflects in part the smaller lumenal size of the posterior ciliary arteries. Ocular ischemia, pupillary abnormalities, and some of the ocular motor palsies are due to extensive involvement of the orbital branches of the ophthalmic artery. A recent autopsy study (Barricks et al., 1977) documents the severe involvement of virtually all the orbital branches of the ophthalmic artery. The patient had bilateral ischemic optic neuropathy, bilateral central retinal artery occlusion, bilateral ischemic pupillopathy, and bilateral ophthalmoplegia. In this case, the ophthalmoplegia was due to extraocular muscle ischemia, but third and sixth cranial nerve involvement has been previously reported. Ischemia of the cavernous portions of the nerves and fasicular involvement due to brain-stem infarction undoubtedly account for other cases of ocular motor palsy. In one series (Hollenhorst et al., 1960), 12% of the patients complained of diplopia.

The occurrence of positive (scintillating scotoma, formed visual hallucinations) and negative (cortical blindness) visual phenomena correlates with the extremely frequent involvement of the vertebral arteries. If both vertebral arteries are affected simultaneously—and this is not uncommon—the occipital lobe may bear the brunt of the vascular embarrassment, since it is the most distal vascular bed.

The hallmark of giant cell arteritis, an elevated ESR, is present in almost all patients. Overreliance should not be placed on the ESR, however, since the literature is full of otherwise typical cases of giant cell arteritis that were diagnostic dilemmas due to a rigid insistance on an elevated ESR (Eagling et al., 1974; Kansu et al., 1977; Weintraub, 1978). The ESR tends to rise somewhat with age (Hayes and Stinson, 1976; Sparrow et al., 1980; Sharland, 1980), although the degree and significance of the elevation is debatable. Certainly a value above 30 to 40 mm/hour (Westergren or Wintrobe) requires explanation. Conversely, such anti-inflammatory drugs as indocin and aspirin may artificially lower the ESR. There is a constellation of other laboratory abnormalities that may aid in the diagnosis, including anemia, leukocytosis, thrombocytosis, elevation of alpha-2-globulin and beta-globulins, and elevated fibrinogen level.

The diagnosis should be established in every case with a superficial temporal artery biopsy. Since the therapy, high-dose corticosteroids, is not without hazards, a firm diagnosis is required. The problem of "skip areas" can be minimized by insisting on a long biopsy (3 to 7 cm) (Klein et al., 1976). If the initial biopsy is negative and suspicion is high, the contralateral artery should also be biopsied (Sorenson and Lorenzen, 1977). Even a negative biopsy does not rule out the diagnosis (Bogen and Glaser, 1975; Hollenhorst et al., 1960; Rush and Kramer, 1979).

If there are visual symptoms, such as amaurosis fugax or ischemic optic neuropathy, intravenous corticosteroids, followed by high-dose oral corticosteroids, should be started immediately. The temporal artery biopsy should be obtained as soon as possible following the institution of steroid therapy. Giant cell arteritis requires daily steroids. An alternate-day regimen is not adequate (Hunder et al., 1975).

Amaurosis Fugax

Amaurosis fugax (AF) (Marshall and Meadows, 1968; Wilson and Russell, 1977; Eadie et al., 1968; Hooshmand et al., 1974; Mungas and Baker, 1977) may be defined as monocular loss of vision of brief duration. The visual loss may be partial (e.g., loss of the upper or lower half of the visual field) or complete and may be relative or absolute within the defective field of vision. The loss of vision usually lasts several minutes. Attacks may occur several times a day or only a few times a year. Usually loss of vision is not accompanied by symptoms of transient hemispheric dysfunction, although the patient may have transient hemispheric ischemia as separate incidents.

Management of stroke and transient ischemic attacks are covered in Chapter 26. The major difficulty, however, lies less in the realm of management—most neurologists are aware of the significance of AF—but rather in the recognition of what constitutes an attack of AF. The following guidelines are offered:

1. Since AF is, by definition, monocular, it must be distinguished from transient

visual field loss. Even intelligent patients will frequently confuse the two. If the patient reports that he alternately closed each eye during an attack and only one eye was faulty, this represents prima faciie evidence of AF.

2. Although a "curtain" that ascends or descends (or both) to obscure the visual field is the hallmark of AF, it is only present in one-half the cases (Wilson and Russell, 1977). The curtain is sometimes reported as having been drawn across the field in a horizontal direction. Other patients merely describe a cloud, shadow, or shutter effect.

3. The visual loss need not be complete. Rather there may be a "graying-out" of vision.

4. As defined, AF is a *negative* visual phenomenon. Although such transient *positive* visual phenomena as phosphenes occur in patients with carotid vascular disease (and may accompany loss of vision in AF), they themselves do not represent true AF.

A recent prospective study of AF indicates that age is the best predictor of finding an operable lesion (Wilson and Russell, 1977). Sixty-seven patients were subjected to arteriography; 42 patients were 50 years of age or older and 15 were younger. In the older age group, twenty-one (50%) had an operable lesion. This was true of only three (20%) of the younger patients. Other predictive factors analyzed in the study included a history of transient cerebral ischemic attacks, intermittent claudication, blood pressure over 150/90 mm Hg, and carotid bruit. Every patient who had all four had an operable lesion. If three factors were present, the chances of an operable lesion were greater than 85%. The authors conclude that all patients over 50 with typical AF be studied, but that in the younger patients, angiography should be reserved for those with multiple risk factors.

A previous report documented the benign course of 12 young patients with otherwise typical AF (aged 14 to 51 years, mean age 29.5) (Eadie et al., 1968). Eight of these patients were studied with angiography and no lesions were found. The etiology of AF in the younger age group is not known, although retinal migraine is often proposed. The importance of this benign subgroup is twofold. First, young patients without other neurovascular stigmata do not generally require extensive evaluation. Second, the same obscure mechanism that is behind benign AF in the younger patients may also be operant in some of the older patients (see "migraine-like symptoms in the elderly," below). After all, in a significant number of elderly patients, the precise cause of AF is not known.

Ischemic Chiasmal Syndrome

The common causes of the chiasmal syndrome (including pituitary adenoma, craniopharyngioma, and supraseller meningioma) are well represented in the elderly (Hankinson et al., 1976) (Figure 17-9).

An additional consideration in patients

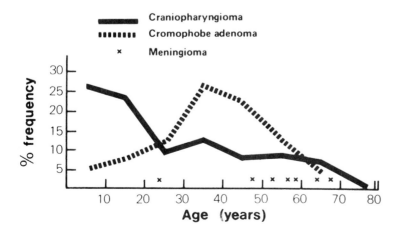

Figure 17-9. The three most common tumors in the pituitary and parapituitary region, by age, based on a retrospective study of sixty pituitary adenomas, seven severe suprasellar meningiomas, and one hundred and sixty craniopharyngiomas. (From Hankinson and Banna, 1976.)

with severe atherosclerotic vascular disease (or arteritis, on rare occasions) is the *ischemic chiasmal syndrome* (Hilton and Hoyt, 1966; Lee et al., 1975). The chiasm is usually immune to the effects of ischemic cerebrovascular disease because of its rich vascular supply, which includes a contribution from the following arteries: ophthalmic, anterior cerebral, anterior communicating, internal carotid (lateral chiasmal branches), superior hypophyseal, middle cerebral, posterior communicating, and anterior choroidal. Occlusion of a limited number of these arteries is insufficient to embarrass the vascular supply to the chiasm and proximal optic nerves. When these vessels (especially the internal carotid and anterior cerebral) are markedly atherosclerotic, ischemia and infarction may occur. A number of mechanisms have been proposed:

1. In rare instances, severe atherosclerosis of the supraclinoid carotid (so-called dolichoectasia or "fusiform aneurysm") may compress the lateral aspect of the chiasm, producing unilateral or bilateral nasal field defects (Thompson, 1979; Glaser, 1978).

2. Since the proximal optic nerves lie between the supraclinoid carotid and the anterior cerebral arteries, dolichoectasia of these vessels may mechanically "grove" the proximal optic nerve (Lindenberg et al., 1973), especially the medial portions. This would produce a slowly progressive, unilateral or bilateral visual loss with either an optic nerve or a chiasmal pattern.

3. Alternatively, the dolichoectasia may so distort the anterior cerebral arteries that small branches from both the anterior cerebral and anterior communicating arteries would be stretched, producing secondary ischemia (Hilton and Hoyt, 1966).

The diagnosis of ischemic chiasmal syndrome is suggested when skull X-rays or CT scan demonstrate carotid calcification. Angiography is generally required to make the diagnosis. It should be remembered that the ischemic chiasmal syndrome is, for the most part, a diagnosis of exclusion. A "mass lesion" must first be categorically ruled out.

Isolated Post-geniculate Field Defects in the Elderly

Isolated visual field defects are common in the elderly, although their significance and management are rarely addressed.

In an early study (Smith, 1962) of 100 patients (11 to 96 years old) with homonymous hemianopia—many of whom had additional neurological signs—there was a nearly equal incidence of vascular disease (43%) and tumor (38%). The location of the lesions was occipital, 39%; parietal, 33%; and temporal, 24%. Only exceptionally was the optic tract or the lateral geniculate body involved. In many cases, the location of the lesion was presumptive.

A more recent study of 104 patients with homonymous hemianopia is more germane to our discussion (Trobe et al., 1973). Only patients with *isolated* homonymous hemianopia were included. Over 70% of patients were older than 50 years of age.

In 92 out of 104 cases (89%), the cause was presumed to be vascular disease, usually posterior cerebral artery occlusion. The remaining 12 cases had a variety of lesions: pituitary adenoma, occipital tumor, occipital porencephaly, temporal lobe abscess, carotid aneurysm, multiple sclerosis, congenital lesion, and traumatic encephalopathy. The clinical course of these patients is worthy of note. The three tumors all showed progressive visual field loss or other CNS signs. In contrast, only four of the ninety-two vascular cases developed other neurological manifestations. Thus, the neurological prognosis for an isolated homonymous hemianopia in the elderly is good.

Both these studies were performed before computerized tomography (CT) was available. A recent CT study confirmed the high incidence of posterior cerebral artery (PCA) occlusion as a cause of isolated homonymous hemianopia (McAuley and Russell, 1979). The site of occlusion is most often the proximal segment of the posterior cerebral artery (PCA) (Goto et al., 1979). This is not surprising, since the proximal portion of PCA is one of the most common sites of intracranial atherosclerosis (Goldberg, 1981).

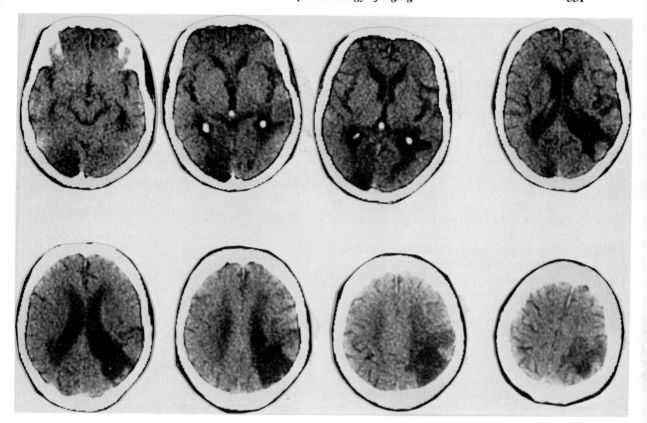

Figure 17-10. A CT scan of a right parieto-occipital wedge-shaped infarction (chronic) and a left occipital lobe infarction (subacute).

Although not as common as PCA distribution infarction, wedge-shaped parieto-occipital infarcts also account for some cases of isolated homonymous hemianopia. Figure 17-10 demonstrates both of these lesions in the same patient. On the right, there is an old parieto-occipital infarct; on the left, a more recent infarction in the PCA distribution. The latter produced total blindness in this 64-year-old man who had a previous left homonymous hemianopia. Whereas the occipital infarction is most often due to intrinsic PCA disease (usually thrombosis, but occasionally emboli), the parieto-occipital "wedge-shaped" infarct is in the distribution of the distal parietal branches of the middle cerebral artery (MCA) and represents either infarction in a distal vascular bed of the carotid artery (due to stenosis or occlusion) or emboli within the carotid–middle cerebral artery distribution.

It should be possible to differentiate these lesions clinically, by testing for opt-cokinetic nystagmus (OKN). With pure occipital infarction, OKN will be normal; whereas with parieto-occipital infarction, OKN will be normal as the stripes are rotated toward the side of the lesion. Ultimately, the lesions can be distinguished with CT.

Management depends on the site of infarction. Thus, PCA infarction carries a favorable prognosis and does not require intervention, but parieto-occipital infarction *may* represent the first evidence of carotid vascular disease, so further evaluation should be considered.

Neglected Syndromes of the Posterior Cerebral Artery

The vascular syndromes of the anterior and cerebral artery and the MCA have received great attention in the last few decades. However, except for the thalamic syndrome, the classical midbrain syndromes, and the occurrence of homonymous field defects, the PCA has been relatively neglected by neurologists. Many of the syndromes are quite distinctive.

GENICULOCALCARINE BLINDNESS

The most common cause of geniculocalcarine blindness is bilateral PCA infarction, although a diverse group of disorders must also be considered (Lessell, 1975) (Table 17-2). Unfortunately, patients with geniculocalcarine blindness sometimes confuse the clinician. Problems in recognition may include the following:

1. Coexistent anterior visual pathway lesions may mask the geniculocalcarine lesions that are the actual cause of the patient's defective vision.

2. Unilateral or asymmetric anterior visual pathway lesions may produce unequal visual acuities—never the case with geniculocalcarine lesions—so that the physician does not consider a geniculocalcarine lesion.

3. Hysterical blindness may be difficult to differentiate from geniculocalcarine blindness.

4. Coexistent motor, intellectual, psychiatric, and language disorders may interfere with recognition.

Table 17-2. Causes of Geniculocalcarine Blindness

Bilateral PCA or, uncommonly, distal MCA occlusion

Anoxia

Trauma

Ictal/postictal

Migraine

Congenital malformations or hydrocephalus

Schilder's disease

Subacute sclerosing panencephalitis

Tumor

Toxic (ethanol, ? methanol, lead, mercury)

Postcerebral angiography

Jakob–Creutzfeldt disease

Post pump oxygenator

5. Patients with geniculocalcarine blindness may deny that they are blind (Anton's syndrome). Although Anton's syndrome is classically associated with geniculocalcarine blindness, it is not generally recognized that it may be associated with *any* disorder that causes blindness. There are two prerequisites for the syndrome: blindness and a disorder that alters the mental status, for example, an acute confusional state. Both requisites are simultaneously fulfilled with bilateral occipital lobe infarctions. Alternatively, two distinct disorders (e.g., glaucoma and metabolic encephalopathy) may be responsible.

ALEXIA WITHOUT AGRAPHIA

Occlusion of the left PCA may produce the syndrome of alexia without agraphia. Patients are unable to understand written words, but are quite capable of recognizing words that are spelled to them; they can also spell words upon request. Thus, they have become functionally illiterate, despite the fact that their intellect is intact. The explanation is that the left occipital lobe infarction has produced a right homonymous hemianopia, while concomitant infarction of the splenium of the corpus callosum (supplied by the posterior pericallosal artery, a branch of the parieto-occipital artery) keeps visual information from the intact right occipital lobe from reaching the left angular gyrus.

HEMIPLEGIC SYNDROME OF THE POSTERIOR CEREBRAL ARTERY

This syndrome includes the combination of alexia without agraphia *plus* right hemiplegia and right hemisensory loss (Benson and Tomlinson, 1971). It is due to a more proximal occlusion involving the peduncular branches of PCA (hemiplegia) as well as the branches to the thalamus (hemisensory loss).

AMNESIC SYNDROME OF POSTERIOR CEREBRAL ARTERY

Ten patients who suffered the acute onset of amnesia associated with either unilateral or bilateral visual field defects were recently studied (Benson et al., 1974). Since the temporal branch of the PCA supplies mesial temporal structures (including the hippocampus), infarction in this distribution is responsible for the amnesia. Either left-sided or bilateral lesions are required to produce the amnesia, which is indistinguishable from that associated with Korsakoff syndrome.

EYE PAIN AND HOMONYMOUS HEMIANOPIA

It is not generally recognized that occlusion of the PCA may produce referred pain to the ipsilateral eye (Knox and Cogan, 1962). In our experience, the combination of eye pain (which may be intense) and contralateral homonymous hemianopia is invariably perplexing to those unfamiliar with the syndrome.

Migraine-like Symptoms in the Elderly

When an adolescent or young adult describes a fortification spectrum, or a related visual phenomenon, preceding a headache, we do not hesitate to diagnose "classic migraine." If the headache is absent, but the visual phenomenon is reminiscent of migraine, most of us are willing to make the diagnosis of "ophthalmic migraine." But what are we to do with a patient who begins to experience classic migraine in middle or old age? Worse yet, what of the elderly patient who presents only with visual symptoms identical to those in ophthalmic migraine?

This is by no means an uncommon problem. Rather, it is a frequent cause for neuro-ophthalmic referral in the elderly. One neuro-ophthalmologist readily collected 43 such patients with ophthalmic migraine in 19 months, and 18 of these patients were over age 50 (Hedges, 1972).

Unfortunately, there is no unanimity regarding either classification or management of these migraine-like phenomena in the elderly. Some have considered the *de novo* occurrence of migraine in a patient over age 40 and with a negative family history of migraine as evidence of atherosclerotic vertebrobasilar disease (Smith, 1972). We strongly disagree with this. We have followed numerous patients with late-onset classic migraine or ophthalmic migraine and their course is generally

benign. These patients also differ from the typical patient with atherosclerotic vertebrobasilar disease by the absence of other symptoms and signs referrable to the posterior circulation. For the most part, we do not subject these patients to a full evaluation, although we do obtain a CBC, platelet count, ESR, and ANA examination. Systemic lupus erythematosus may produce typical migraine-like visual phenomena (Brandt and Lessell, 1978). There is evidence that platelet aggregability may be altered in some of these patients (Raymond et al., 1980). Many respond to aspirin, other antiplatelet aggregation medications, or coumadin.

C.M. Fisher (1979) has gone even further. He concurs that isolated migrainous scintillations are common in the elderly—and, by implication, he does not evaluate these patients. He has recently collected 120 patients who have unexplained transient ischemic attacks in association with normal cerebral angiograms. Because of the similarity to the symptoms of classic migraine he has chosen to call the condition "late-life migraine accompaniments," from the French *migraine accompagnée*, which signifies the symptoms of the aura or prodrome phase. Table 17-3 lists the classification of these 120 patients. Note that patients with only scintillating scotoma have been excluded.

Undoubtedly, this will trouble most migraine purists. However, since there are no specific diagnostic criteria or laboratory tests for migraine, it is really a question of whether one is a "lumper" or a "splitter." Whatever one chooses to call these patients, their existence is invaluable for ultimately unraveling the biology of the migraine syndrome and in managing elderly patients with migraine-like symptoms.

Cerebrovascular Disease: Carotid versus Vertebrobasilar Systems

The current management of cerebrovascular disease depends upon the ability to ascertain whether the patient's disease is within the carotid system, the vertebrobasilar system, or both. Neuro-ophthalmic symptoms and signs are frequent in both

Table 17-3. Fisher's Classification of 120 Patients with Migraine Accompaniments.

Visual (excluding isolated scintillating scotoma)	
Blindness	14
Homonymous hemianopia	5
Blurred or hazy vision, difficulty focusing	6
Visual* and paresthesias	18
Visual* and speech disorders (dysarthria or aphasia)	7
Visual* and brain-stem symptoms	14
Visual*, paresthesias, and speech disturbance	7
Visual*, paresthesias, speech disturbance, and paresis	7
Nonvisual accompaniments only	25
Recurrence of old stroke deficit	9
Miscellaneous	8
	120

*Within these categories, the visual symptoms may be scintillating scotoma, transient homonymous hemianopia, blindness, or other visual phenomena.

systems and sufficiently distinctive to assist in clinical diagnosis (Hollenhorst, 1959; Minor et al., 1959). Table 17-4 documents the symptoms and signs in 124 patients with carotid disease. Note that homonymous hemianopia does occur with carotid disease. It results from ischemia or infarction of the optic tract or lateral geniculate body (both rare), distal geniculo-calcarine radiations (see above), or the occipital lobe, if the PCA maintains its "fetal" origin from the internal carotid.

In contrast are the neuro-ophthalmic findings in vertebrobasilar disease (Table 17-5) (Minor et al., 1959). Whereas in carotid disease neuro-ophthalmic symptoms and signs tend to occur singly, multiple findings are common in vertebrobasilar disease. The concurrence of homonymous hemianopia and an ocular motor defect was particularly noteworthy in this study. Careful attention to subtle ocular motor defects is especially important in patients with allegedly isolated homonymous hemianopia. As we have seen, a truly isolated field defect carries a generally favorable prognosis, since in most cases the disease is intrinsic to the PCA. The combination of brain-stem and occipital lobe deficits usually implies vertebral and/or basilar disease. The management may be different and the prognosis worse.

Table 17-4. Ocular Signs and Symptoms in 124 Patients with Carotid Occlusive Disease.

	No.	%
Amaurosis fugax	50	40
Visual defects		
Central retinal artery occlusion	14	11
Central retinal artery occlusion plus		
contralateral homonymous hemianopia	6	5
Homonymous hemianopia		
Transient	3	2
Permanent	8	6
Unilateral retinopathy	15	12
Unequal retinal hypertensive vascular changes	10	8
Pupil smaller on affected side	2	1

Table 17-5. Ocular Findings in 183 Patients with Vertebrobasilar Disease.

	Incidence
Episodes of blurred vision	73
Diplopia	50
Bilateral homonymous hemianopia	26
Unilateral homonymous hemianopia	21
Nystagmus (without internuclear ophthalmoplegia)	18
Transient homonymous hemianopia	15
Internuclear ophthalmoplegia Unilateral (6) Bilateral (3) One-and-a-half syndrome (4) Plus other (2)	15
Paresis of conjugate gaze	10
Ptosis	8
Distorted vision (especially, scintillating scotoma)	8
Conjugate deviation	2

Isolated Extraocular Muscle Palsies

Elderly patients with isolated extraocular muscle palsies are commonly seen in neuro-ophthalmic practice. Although trauma, tumor, and aneurysm remain considerations, microvascular disease becomes an increasingly important consideration in the differential diagnosis of the elderly (Table 17-6).

Microvascular cranial nerve infarction is readily accepted as a cause of third, fourth, or sixth nerve palsies in the clinical setting of diabetes and hypertensive cerebrovascular disease. Pupil-sparing third nerve palsy, for example, is a well-recognized syndrome in diabetes (Goldstein and Cogan, 1960). However, in the absence of an obvious cause for small-vessel disease and especially when the fourth or the sixth nerve is involved, the level of consternation on the part of the clinician is often high. The following caveats are offered:

1. No matter how scrupulously these patients are evaluated, a sizable minority (about 20 to 25%) cannot be diagnosed (*cryptogenic*). This is particularly true of the elderly population. Undoubtedly, many of these patients have sustained a microvascular infarct, although this diagnosis must often remain presumptive. The majority will improve or recover in three months.

Table 17-6. Isolated Extraocular Muscle Palsies.

	Total	Trauma	Tumor	Diabetes or vascular	Aneurysm	Cryptogenic	Other
Isolated 3rd nerve (Rucker, 1966)	274	34	50	47	50	55	38
Isolated 4th nerve (Rucker, 1966)	84	23	7	13	0	23	13
Isolated 4th nerve (Rougier et al., 1973)	40	26	2	0	1	8	3
Isolated 6th nerve (Rucker, 1966)	515	55	159	46	15	112	128
Isolated 6th nerve (Shrader and Schlezinger, 1960)	104	3	7	38	0	25	31

2. *Non-neural* causes are usually neglected. This is due in part to semantic carelessness. If there is a defect in the abduction of one eye, for example, it is incorrect to assume that there is a "sixth nerve palsy." Rather, the rubric under which the patient is evaluated should be "abduction palsy." The abduction palsy may indeed be due to a lesion in the sixth nerve; or the fault may lie in the neuromuscular junction, the muscle, or the orbit. Although a detailed exposition of the non-neural causes of extra-ocular muscle palsies is beyond the scope of this chapter, three diseases merit consideration, since they frequently masquerade as isolated extraocular muscle palsies in elderly patients: myasthenia, Graves' ophthalmopathy, and orbital pseudotumor.

Ocular myasthenia occurs in all age groups. Women are more commonly affected in the early decades, whereas men predominate among the elderly (Osserman and Genkins, 1971) (Figure 17-11). Between 15 to 59% of cases present with *only* ocular signs (Daroff, 1980). Ocular myasthenia may mimic any isolated muscle palsy. Indeed, myasthenia is unequaled as a mimic of other neurological and neuro-ophthalmic disorders. *Any puzzling ocular motor distrubance (with normal pupils) should raise the question of myasthenia and prompt a Tensilon test.* The varied ocular signs of myasthenia include

> Ptosis
> Isolated muscle palsies
> Various combinations of muscle palsies
> Lid twitch sign (of Cogan)
> Paradoxical lid retraction
> Pseudogaze palsy
> Pseudointernuclear ophthalmoplegia
> Myasthenic nystagmus
> Orbicularis oculi weakness
> Fixed chronic ophthalmoplegia

The peak incidence of *Grave's ophthalmopathy* is the fourth and fifth decades, but cases in the sixth through the eighth decade are not uncommon. Like myasthenia, Graves' ranks high on the list of initially missed diagnoses. In subtle cases, when the typical "congestive" orbital signs are absent, the presentation may be that of an apparently isolated extraocular muscle

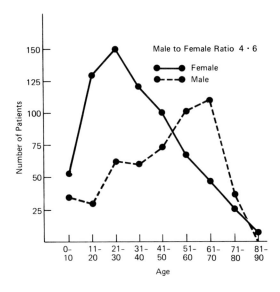

Figure 17-11. Onset of myasthenia gravis in 1,227 patients by age and sex. (From Osserman, K.E., Genkins, G., Studies in Myasthenia gravis: Review of a twenty-year experience in over 1200 patients. Mt. Sinai J. Med. 38:497–537, 1971.)

palsy. The single most common pattern is a unilateral elevator palsy, which resembles superior rectus palsy. The actual problem is infiltration of the inferior rectus, which restricts upward mobility. Forced duction testing (which usually must be performed by an ophthalmologist) reveals that the globe is tethered by the taut, unyielding inferior rectus muscle. Similar infiltration of the medial rectus produces weakness of abduction, prompting a misdiagnosis of sixth nerve palsy. The third most common "syndrome" is isolated downgaze limitation due to involvement of the superior rectus. As in myasthenia, combinations of restricted muscles may result in puzzling ocular motility patterns. Once the diagnosis is suspected, it can be verified by CT or orbital ultrasound. It should be recalled that Graves' ophthalmopathy is commonly present without clinical evidence of endocrinopathy.

Orbital pseudotumor is a nonspecific

inflammation of the orbital tissues (Blodi and Gass, 1968; Henderson, 1973). There is no age preference and there are well-documented cases from infancy to senescence. Typically, there is painful ophthalmoplegia with overt signs of orbital involvement (proptosis, chemosis, etc.), but as in Graves', the orbital signs may be subtle. The diagnosis can usually be confirmed with CT or ultrasound. There is an increasing suspicion that orbital pseudotumor and Tolosa–Hunt syndrome represent the same process with a different locus of involvement. Whereas in orbital pseudotumor the inflammation occurs in the orbital tissues, in Tolosa–Hunt, it occurs in the superior orbital fissure or anterior cavernous sinus.

3. Certain *neural* causes of isolated extraocular muscle palsies are characteristic of the elderly population.

Although *nasopharyngeal tumors* can occur at any age, the highest incidence is in the seventh and the eighth decade, with a male predilection. The tumor begins in the nasopharyngeal roof near the ostium of the Eustachian tube, and thus the earliest signs may be aural (pain, popping sensation, serous otitis). The diagnosis is almost invariably missed at this stage. Tumor extension next involves the basal foramina of the middle fossa. Any of the cranial nerves may be involved including the abducens, oculomotor, or trochlear, in that order of frequency (Godtfredsen and Lederman, 1965). The diagnosis may be difficult to establish. In our experience, X-rays of the base, CT, and cerebrospinal fluid (CSF) examination are frequently negative even when multiple cranial nerves are involved. On occasion, blind biopsy of the nasopharynx may be positive, even in the absence of visible tumor on otolaryngological examination.

In *meningeal carcinomatosis,* cranial nerve involvement may be the first evidence of an occult carcinoma. Reviews (Olson et al., 1974; Little et al., 1974) indicate that ocular motor involvement is strikingly common. It is worth stressing that multiple examinations of the CSF may be necessary to document the malignant cells. Cranial nerve involvement is usually a late manifestation of systemic cancer.

Cavernous sinus fistulas represent abnormal communications between the carotid artery system and the cavernous sinus. There are three types of communications (Peeters and Kroger, 1979). Direct communications between the carotid artery and the cavernous sinus (so-called carotid cavernous fistulas) are readily recognized. There is an apoplectic onset of pain, pulsating exophthalmos, orbital bruits (both objective and subjective), ophthalmoplegia of varying degree, arteriolization of the conjunctival veins, and signs of increased orbital venous pressure. The majority are due either to trauma or aneurysm. In the other two types, communication is between meningeal branches of either the internal or external carotid artery and the cavernous sinus (so-called dural cavernous sinus fistulas). The signs and symptoms in the latter two types are muted, since the flow is not as great. Bruit, in particular, may be absent, which hinders diagnosis. Diplopia is usually secondary to a sixth nerve palsy. Dural cavernous sinus fistulas most often occur in women over the age of 50.

Aneurysms and meningiomas of the cavernous sinus may be truly elusive. In clinical and radiological reports of 20 patients, an initially correct diagnosis was never made (Trobe et al., 1980; Post et al., 1978). Incorrect diagnoses included "orbital tumor, Graves', myasthenia, brain-stem disorder, and diabetic or atherosclerotic cranial neuropathy." As in the fistulas, the sixth nerve is usually affected first and "idiopathic sixth nerve palsy" is a frequent misdiagnosis. Peak incidence is in the sixth through the eighth decade. Women are affected more often than men.

The evaluation of an isolated ocular motor palsy in an elderly patient should include the following (if appropriate):

1. FBS and 2-hour postprandial blood sugar
2. ESR
3. Fluorescent Treponemal Antibody-absorbed (FTA–ABS)
4. CT
5. Forced duction test
6. Tensilon test
7. CSF examination

Bilateral Ophthalmoplegia in the Elderly

Only a handful of diseases produce bilateral ophthalmoplegia in the elderly population. Nevertheless, we have been struck by the frequency with which these diseases puzzle the clinician. The initial step, which is often omitted, is to determine whether the disease is supranuclear or infranuclear. This can readily be accomplished by demonstrating residual eye movement with oculocephalic or caloric stimulation. If either procedure is positive and if the patient is unable to voluntarily move his eyes, the process is supranuclear. A negative response all but guarantees that the process is infranuclear.

The Steele–Richardson–Olszewski syndrome, or progressive supranuclear palsy, is a degenerative disease of middle and late life (Pfaffenbach et al., 1972). It is characterized by progressive limitation of eye movements, pseudobulbar palsy, dysarthria, axial rigidity, corticospinal tract signs, and dementia. The evolution of the bilateral ophthalmoplegia is stereotyped and assists in the diagnosis. Vertical saccades are lost first. Limitation of downward gaze (saccades and pursuit) often occurs next. Then, other vertical and horizontal eye movements are impaired. At this stage, there are square-wave jerks—1 to 3 degree conjugate saccades occurring to either side of fixation (Troost and Daroff, 1977). The oculocephalic reflex elicits a full range of movement in all directions, but may be difficult to obtain vertically due to neck rigidity. Caloric stimulation produces tonic deviation without nystagmus. Eventually, there is "global" paralysis of gaze. In the terminal stages, there may be brain-stem nuclear involvement as well, with loss of reflex eye movements.

We prefer the eponymic designation, since a host of other diseases may produce "progressive supranuclear palsy" (Finelli et al., 1977):

Huntington's disease
Wilson's disease
Hereditary spinocerebellar degenerations
Ataxia telangiectasia
Whipple's disease
Lipid storage diseases
Progressive multifocal leukoencephalopathy
Lesions at the mesodiencephalic junction

Parkinson's disease produces a variety of ocular signs involving both the eyes and the eyelids (Corin et al., 1972; Smith, 1966; Loeffler et al., 1966). In a study of 70 patients, 75% had some ocular motor impairment (Corin et al., 1972). The most frequent abnormality is a limitation of conjugate upward gaze, but since, as we have seen, this is an inevitable consequence of aging, the limitation must be extreme before it is clinically significant. As in Steele–Richardson–Olszewski disease, there are hypometric saccades and "cogwheel" pursuit. The degree of ocular motor involvement—which roughly parallels the extrapyramidal dysfunction—varies from mild impairment to almost complete supranuclear ophthalmoplegia. Usually the clinical (and pathological) signs of Parkinson's disease and Steele–Richardson–Olszewski disease are sufficiently distinctive to allow differentiation. Occasionally, however, patients with otherwise typical Parkinson's disease have such severe gaze disturbances that it is difficult to know which designation is more appropriate. About two-thirds of Parkinsonian patients also have eyelid abnormalities, consisting of upper lid retraction (which sometimes prompts a diagnosis of Graves'), ptosis, or blepharospasm. Other common eye signs include eyelid tremor, "apraxia" of eyelid opening, infrequent blinking, motor impersistance, and a positive glabellar reflex.

Lesions at a subthalamic or an upper brain-stem level (usually stroke) can interrupt both the saccadic and the pursuit subsystems that converge at this point. Designated as the Roth–Bielschowsky syndrome (Hoyt and Daroff, 1971), this supranuclear gaze paralysis should be easily recognized, since its onset is apoplectic.

Few disorders typically produce bilateral, infranuclear ophthalmoplegia. Myasthenia and Graves' ophthalmopathy have already been discussed.

Chronic progressive external ophthalmoplegia (CPEO) (Lessell, 1975; Drach-

Table 17-7. Findings that May Be Associated with Chronic Progressive External Ophthalmoplegia.

Dysphonia	Elevated CSF protein
Dysphagia	Corneal opacities
Facial muscle weakness	Optic atrophy
Neck muscle weakness	Atypical pigmentary retinopathy
Limb muscle weakness	Retinitis pigmentosa (classical)
Sphincter weakness	Proptosis
Lower motor neuron lesions	Cardiomyopathy
Ataxia	Cardiac conduction defects
Dystonia	Hypogonadism
Peripheral neuropathy	Early menopause
Corticospinal tract signs	Small stature
Dementia	Delayed sexual maturation
Seizures	Curare sensitivity
EEG slowing	Succinylcholine sensitivity

man, 1968) is an insidiously progressive disorder that produces bilateral, symmetric ophthalmoplegia and ptosis, in addition to a host of other abnormalities (see below). It is not a disease entity, per se, but rather a collection of diseases in which the primary or exclusive manifestation is progressive (infranuclear) external ophthalmoplegia. From this collection, a number of specific disorders can be identified. A few neuromuscular diseases (Lessell, 1975), such as myotonic dystrophy and fascioscapulohumeral dystrophy, may exhibit progressive ophthalmpoplegia, but they are distinct pathological entities. The Kearns–Sayre syndrome, characterized by early and sporadic onset and the clinical triad of progressive external ophthalmoplegia, pigmentary degeneration of the retina, and heart block, can also stand by itself (Berenberg et al., 1977). However, once one has "split" away these relatively distinct disorders, there remains a group of patients in whom the most prominant finding is CPEO. In addition to the ophthalmoplegia, most patients will have one or more of the associated findings listed in Table 17-7 (Lessell, 1975).

In most instances, the first symptoms of CPEO appear by the fourth decade, but not uncommonly the patient will defer seeking medical attention until much later. A positive family history is obtained in about one-half of the cases.

Ptosis usually precedes the onset of ophthalmoplegia; both tend to be symmetric. Because of the ptosis, as well as the relative symmetry, most patients tolerate the ophthalmoplegia remarkably well.

There is one other variety of CPEO that can be "split" away—oculopharyngeal dystrophy. The onset of this variety—which predominantly affects the eyelids and pharyngeal muscles—is usually late. The extraocular muscles are spared relatively (although never entirely normal), which has prompted the description "palpebropharyngeal dystrophy."

Unless there is incontrovertible evidence of familial involvement, a Tensilon test should be performed. The evaluation of all patients with CPEO should include an EKG, fluoroscopy with a barium swallow, EMG and nerve conduction times, muscle biopsy, and serum muscle enzymes.

References

Anderson, B. and Palmore, E. (1974). Longitudinal evaluation of ocular function, In Normal Aging II, Reports from the Duke Longitudinal Studies, 1970–1973, E. Palmore, Ed. Duke University Press, Durham, N.C., pp. 24–32.

Appen, R.E., Wray, S.H., and Cogan, D.G. (1975). Central retinal artery occlusion. Amer. J. Ophthalmol. 79, 374–381.

Arden, G.B. (1978). The importance of measuring contrast sensitivity in cases of visual disturbance. Br. J. Ophthalmol. 62, 198–209.

Asselman, P., Chadwick, D.W., and Marsden, C.D. (1975). Visual evoked responses in the diagnosis and management of patients suspected of multiple sclerosis. Brain 98, 261–282.

Barricks, M.E., Traviesa, D.B., Glaser, J.S., and Levy, I.S. (1977). Ophthalmoplegia in cranial arteritis. Brain 100, 209–221.

Beard, C. (1976). Ptosis, 2nd Ed. Mosby, St. Louis, p. 57.

Benson, D.F., Marsden, C.D., and Meadows, J.C. (1974). The amnesic syndrome of posterior, cerebral occlusion. Acta Neurol. Scand. 50, 133–145.

Benson, D.F. and Tomlinson, E.B. (1971). Hemiplegic syndrome of the posterior cerebral artery. Stroke 2, 559–564.

Berenberg, R.A., Pellock, J.M., Dimauro, S. et al. (1977). Lumping or splitting? "Ophthalmoplegia-plus" or Kearns-Sayre syndrome? Ann. Neurol. 1, 37–54.

Blodi, F.C. and Gass, J.D. (1968). Inflammatory pseudotumor of the orbit Br. J. Ophthalmol. 52, 79–93.

Boberg-Ans, J. (1956). On corneal sensitivity. Acta Ophthalmol. 34, 149–162.

Bodis-Wollner, I. (1972). Visual acuity and contrast sensitivity in patients with cerebral lesions. Science 178, 769–771.

Bodis-Wollner, I. and Camisa, J.M. (1980)., Contrast sensitivity measurement in clinical diagnosis. In Neuro-ophthalmology, Vol. 1/1980, S. Lessell and J.T.W. Van Dalen, Eds. Excerpta Medica, Amsterdam pp. 373–401.

Boghen, D.R. and Glaser, J.S. (1975). Ischaemic optic neuropathy—the clinical profile and natural history. Brain 98, 689–708.

Brandt, K. and Lessell, S. (1978). Migrainous phenomena in systemic lupus erythematosus. Arthritis Rheum. 21, 7–16.

Brody, H. (1976). An examination of cerebral cortex and brainstem aging. In Neurobiology of Aging, R.D. Terry and S. Gershon, Eds. Raven Press, New York, pp. 177–181.

Celesia, G.G. and Daly, R.F. (1977). Effects of aging on visual evoked responses. Arch. Neurol. 34, 403–407.

Chamberlain, W. (1970). Restriction in upward gaze with advancing age. Trans. Amer. Ophthalmol. Soc. 68, 235–244.

Corin, M.S., Elizan, T.S., and Bender, M.B. (1972). Oculomotor function in patients with Parkinson's disease. J. Neurol. Sci. 15, 251–265.

Cullen, J.F. (1967). Occult temporal arteritis. Br. J. Ophthalmol. 51, 513–525.

Daroff, R.B. (1975). Summary of clinical presentations. In Basic Mechanisms of Ocular Motility and Their Clinical Implications. G. Lennerstrand and P. Bach-y-Rita, Eds. Pengamon Press, Oxford, pp. 436–443.

Daroff, R.B. (1980). Ocular myasthenia: diagnosis and therapy. In Neuro-ophthalmology, Vol. 10, J.S. Glaser, Ed. Mosby, St. Louis, pp. 62–71.

Devaney, K.O. and Johnson, H.A. (1980). Neuron loss in the aging visual cortex of man. J. Gerontol. 35, 836–841.

Dolman, C.L., McCormick, A.Q., and Drance, S.M. (1980). Aging of the optic nerve. Arch. Ophthalmol. 98, 2053–2058.

Drachman, D. (1968). Ophthalmoplegia-plus. The neurodegenerative disorders associated with progressive external ophthalmoplegia. Arch. Neurol. 18, 654–674.

Drance, S.M., Berry, V., and Hughes, A. (1967a). Studies on the effects of age on the central and peripheral isopters of the visual field in normal subjects. Amer. J. Ophthalmol. 63, 1667–1672.

Drance, S.M., Berry, V., and Hughes, A. (1967b). The effects of age on the central isopter of the normal visual field, Canad. J. Ophthal. 2, 79–82.

Duke-Elder, S. and MacFaul, P.A. (1974). In The clinical types of ptosis. S. Duke-Elder, Ed. System of Ophthalmology, Vol. 13, Part 1. Mosby, St. Louis, p. 552.

Eadie, M.J., Sutherland, J.M., and Tyrer, J.H. (1968). Recurrent monocular blindness of uncertain cause. Lancet i, 319–321.

Eagling, E.M., Sanders, M.D., and Miller, S.J. (1974). Ischaemic papillopathy. Clinical and fluorescein angiographic review of forty cases. Br. J. Ophthal. 58, 990–1008.

Editorial comment (Hedges, 1972)

Editorial: Retinal venous obstruction. Br. J. Ophthal. 60, 395–396.

Ellenberger, C., Keltner, J.L., and Burde, R.M. (1973). Acute optic neuropathy in older patients. Arch. Neurol. 28, 182–185.

Ellenberger, C. and Netsky, M.G. (1968). Infarction in the optic nerve. J. Neurol. Neurosurg. Psychiat. 31, 605–611.

Feisen, L. and Frisen, M. (1979). Micropsia and visual acuity in macular edema. A study of the neuro-retinal basis of visual acuity. Albrecht von Graefes, Arch. Klin. Exp. Ophthalmol. 210, 69–77.

Finelli, P.F., McEntee, W.J., Lessell, S., Morgan, T.F., and Copetto, J. (1977). Whipple's disease with predominantly neuro-ophthalmic manifestations. Ann. Neurol. 3, 247–254.

Fisher, C.M. (1979). Transient migrainous accompaniments (TMA's) of late onset. Stroke 10, 96–97.

Fisher, R.F. (1968). The variations of the peripheral visual fields with age. Docum. Ophthal. 24, 41–67.

Fox, S.A. (1966). The palpebral fissue. Amer. J. Ophthalmol. 62, 73–78.

Fozard, J.L., Wolf, E., Bell, B. et al. (1977). Visual perception and communication. In Handbook of the Psychology of Aging, Ch. 20, J.E. Birren and K.W. Schaie, Eds. Van Nostrand, New York, pp. 497–534.

Frisen, L. (1980). The neurology of visual acuity. Brain 103, 639–670.

Gilbert, J.G. (1957). Age changes in color matching. J. Gerontol. 12, 210–215.

Glaser, J.S. (1978). Topical diagnosis: Prechiasmal visual pathways. In Clinical Ophthalmology, Vol. 2, Ch. 5, T.D. Duane, Ed. Harper & Row, Hagerstown, Md., pp. 1–72.

Glaser, J.S. and Laflamme, P. (1979). The visual evoked response: Methodology and application in optic nerve disease. In Topics in Neuro-ophthalmology, H.S. Thompson, Ed. Williams & Wilkins, Baltimore, pp. 199–218.

Godtfredsen, E. and Lederman, M. (1965). Diagnostic and prognostic signs and symptoms in malignant nasopharyngeal tumors. Amer. J. Ophthalmol. 59, 1063–1069.

Gold, D. (1977) Retinal arterial occlusion. Trans. Amer. Acad. Ophthalmol. Otol. 83, OP 392–408.

Goldberg, H. (1981). Personal communication.

Goldstein, J.E. and Cogan, D.G. (1960). Diabetic ophthalmoplegia with special reference to the pupil. Arch. Ophthalmol. 64, 592–600.

Goto, K., Tagawa, J., Uemura, K., Ishii, K., and Takahasi, S. (1979). Posterior cerebral artery occlusion: Clinical, Computed tomographic, and angiographic correlation. Radiology 132, 357–368.

Hankinson, J. and Banna, M. (1976). Pituitary and Parapituitary Tumors. Saunders, London, pp. 13–58.

Harrington, D.O. (1976). The Visual Fields: A Textbook and Atlas of Clinical Perimetry. Mosby, St. Louis, p. 102.

Hauser, W.A., Ferguson, R.H., Holley, K.E., and Kurland, L.T. (1971). Temporal arteritis in Rochester, Minnesota, 1951 to 1967. Mayo Clin. Proc. 46, 597–601.

Hayes, G.S. and Stinson, I.N. (1976). Erythrocyte sedimentation rate and age. Arch. Ophthalmol. 94, 939–940.

Hayreh, S.S. (1974a). Anterior ischaemic optic neuropathy. I. Terminology and pathogenesis. Br. J. Ophthal. 58, 955–963.

Hayreh, S.S. (1974b). Anterior ischaemic optic neuropathy. II. Fundus on ophthalmoscopy and fluorescein angiography. Br. J. Ophthal. 58, 964–980.

Hayreh, S.S. (1977). Central retinal vein occlusion: Differential diagnosis and management. Trans. Amer. Acad. Ophthalmol. Otol. 83, OP-379–391.

Hedges, T.R. (1972). Isolated ophthalmic migraine: Its frequency, mechanisms, and differential diagnosis. In Neuro-ophthalmology Vol. 6, Symposium of the Univ. of Miami and the Bascom Palmer Eye Institute, J.L. Smith, Ed. Mosby, St. Louis.

Henderson, J.W. (1973). Orbital Tumors. Saunders, Philadelphia, pp. 555–580.

Hilton, G.F. and Hoyt, W.F. (1966). An arteriosclerotic chiasmal syndrome. Bitemporal hemianopia associated with fusiform dilatation of the anterior cerebral arteries. J.A. M. A. 196, 1018–1020.

Holland, G., quoted by Miller, 1975.

Hollenhorst, R.W. (1959). Ocular manifestations of insufficiency or thrombosis of the internal carotid artery. Amer. J. Ophthalmol. 47, 753–767.

Hollenhorst, R.W., Brown, J.R., Wagener, H.P., and Shick, R.M. (1960). Neurologic aspects of temporal arteritis. Neurol. 10, 490–498.

Hooshmand, H., Vines, F.S., Lee, H.M., and Grindal, A. (1976). Amaurosis fugax: Diagnostic and therapeutic aspects. Stroke 5, 643–647.

Hoyt, W.F. and Daroff, R.B. (1971). Supranuclear disorders of ocular control systems in man. Clinical, anatomical, and physiological correlations-1969. In The Control of Eye Movements, P. Bach-y-Rita, C.C. Collins, and J.E. Hyde, Eds. Academic Press, New York, pp. 175–235.

Hunder, G.G., Sheps, S.G., Allen, G.L., and Joyce, J.W. (1975). Daily and alternate-day corticosteroid regimens in the treatment of giant cell arteritis. Ann. Int. Med. 82, 613–618.

Huston, K.A., Hunder, G.G., Lie, J.T., Kennedy, R.H., and Elveback, L.R. (1978). Temporal arteritis: A 25-year epidemiologic, clinical and pathologic study. Ann. Intern. Med. 88, 162–167.

Hutman, L.P. and Sekuler, R. (1980). Spatial vision and aging. II: Criterion effects. J. Gerontol. 35, 700–706.

Jalavisto, E., Orma, E., and Tawast, M. (1951). Aging and relationship between stimulus intensity and duration in corneal sensitivity. Acta Physiol. Scand. 23, 224–233.

Kansu, T., Corbett, J.J., Savino, P., and Schatz, N.J. (1977). Giant cell arteritis with normal sedimentation rate. Arch. Neurol. 34, 624–625.

Kearns, T.P. and Hollenhorst, R.W. (1963). Venous stasis retinopathy of occlusive disease of the carotid artery. Proc. Mayo Clin. 38, 305–312.

Klein, R.G., Cannbell, R.J., Hunder, G.G., and Carney, J.A. (1976). The existence and significance of skip lesion intemporal arteritis. Mayo Clin. Proc. 51, 504–510.

Knox, D.L. and Cogan, D.G. (1962). Eye pain and homonymous hemianopia. Amer. J. Ophthalmol. 54, 1091–1093.

Kuechenmeister, C.A., Linton, P.H., Mueller, T.V., and White, H.B. (1977). Eye tracking in relation to age, sex and illness. Arch. Gen. Psychiatr. 34, 578–579.

Lee, K.F., Schatz, N.J. and Savino, P.J. (1975). Ischemic chiasmal syndrome. In Neuro-ophthalmology, Vol. 8, Symposium of the Univ. of Miami and the Bascom Palmer Eye Institute. J.S. Glaxer and J.S. Smith, Eds. Mosby, St. Louis, pp. 115–130.

Leibowitz, H., Post, R., and Ginsburg, A. (1980). The role of fine detail in visually controlled behavior. Invest. Ophthalmol. Vis. Sci. 19, 846–848.

Lessel, S. (1967). Misinterpretation of signs of retinal detachment. New Eng. J. Med. 277, 1297–1299.

Lessell, S. (1975a). Higher disorders of visual function: Negative phenomena. In Neuro-ophthalmology, Vol. 8, Symposium of the Univ. of Miami and Bascom Palmer Eye Institute. J.S. Glaser and J.L. Smith, Eds. Mosby, St. Louis, pp. 1–26.

Lessell, S. (1975b). Chronic progressive external opthalmoplegia. In Neuro-ophthalmology, Vol. 7, Symposium of the Univ. of Miami and the Bascom Palmer Eye Institute. J.S. Glaser and J.L. Smith, Eds. Mosby, St. Louis, pp. 216–236.

Lieberman, M.F., Shahi, A., and Green, W.R. (1978). Embolic ischemic optic neuropathy. Amer. J. Ophthalmol. 86, 206–210.

Lindenberg, R., Walsh, F.B., and Sacks, J.G. (1973). Neuropathology of Vision. Lea and Febiger, Philadelphia.

Little, J.R., Dale, A.J., and Okazaki, H. (1974). Meningeal carcinomatosis. Arch. Neurol. 30, 138–143.

Loeffler, J.D., Slatt, B., and Hoyt, W.F. (1966). Motor abnormalities of the eyelids in Parkinson's disease. Arch. Ophthalmol. 76, 178–85.

Loewenfeld, I.E. (1979). Pupillary changes related to age. In Topics in Neuro-ophthalmology, H.S. Thompson, Ed. Williams & Wilkins, Baltimore, pp. 124–150.

Lorentzen, S.E. (1969). Occlusion of the central retinal artery: A follow-up. Acta Ophthalmol. 47, 690–703.

McAuley, D.L. and Russell, W.R. (1979). Correlation of CAT scan and visual field defects in vascular lesions of the posterior visual pathways. J. Neurol. Neurosurg. Psychiatr. 42, 298–311.

McGeer, E. and McGeer, P. (1976). Neurotransmitter metabolism in aging brain. In R.D. Terry and S. Gershon, Eds. Neurobiology of Aging, Raven Press, New York, pp. 389–403.

McGrath, M.A., Wechsler, F., Hunyor, A.B., and Penny, R. (1978). Systemic factors contributory to retinal vein occlusion. Arch. Intern. Med. 138, 216–220.

Marshall, J. and Meadows, S. (1968). The natural history of amaurosis fugax. Brain 91, 419–434.

Miller, J.E. (1975). Aging changes in extraocular muscle, In Basic Mechanisms of Ocular Motility and Their Clinical Implications, G. Lennerstrand and P. Bach-y-Rita, Eds. Pergamon Press, Oxford, p. 47.

Millodot, M. (1977). The influence of age on the sensitivity of the cornea. Invest. Ophthalmol. Vis. Sci. 16, 240–242.

Minor, R.H., Kearns, T.P., Millikan, C.H., Siekert, R.G., and Syre G.P. (1959). Ocular manifestations of occlusive disease of the vertebral-basilar arterial system. Arch. Ophthalmol. 62, 84–96.

Muhlendyck, H. and Ali, S.S. (1978). Histological and ultrastructural studies on the ringbands in human extraocular muscles. Albrecht Von Graefes Arch. Klin. Exptl. Ophthalmol. 208, 177–191.

Mungas, J.E. and Baker, W.H. (1977). Amaurosis fugax. Stroke 8, 232–235.

Neupert, J.R., Brubaker, R.F., Kearns, T.P., and Sundt, T.M. (1976). Rapid resolution of venous stasis retinopathy after carotid endarterectomy. Amer. J. Ophthalmol. 81, 600–602.

Olson, M.E., Chernik, N.L., and Posner, J.B. (1974). Infiltration of the leptomeninges by systemic cancer. Arch. Neurol. 30, 122–137.

Ongerboer de Visser, B.W., Melchelse, K., and Megens, P.H. (1977). Corneal reflex latency in trigeminal nerve lesions. Neurology 27, 1164–1167.

Ordy, J.M. and Brizzee, K.R. (1979). Functional and structural age differences in the visual system of man and non-human primate models. In Sensory Systems and Communication in the Elderly, Aging, Vol. 10, J.M. Ordy and K. Brizzee, Eds. Raven Press, New York.

Osserman, K.E. and Genkins, G. (1971). Studies in myasthenia gravis: Review of a twenty-year experience in over 1200 patients. Mt. Sinai J. Med. 38, 497–537.

Peeters, F.L. and Kroger, R. (1979). Dural and direct cavernous sinus fistulas. Amer. J. Roentgenol. 132, 599–606.

Pfaffenbach, D.D., Layton, D.D., and Kearns, T.P. (1972). Ocular manifestations in progressive supranuclear palsy. Amer. J. Ophthalmol. 74, 1179–1184.

Post, J.D., Glaser, J.S., and Trobe, J.D. (1978). The radiographic recognition of two clinically elusive mass lesions of the cavernous sinus: Meningiomas and aneurysms. Neuroradiology 16, 499–503.

Prince, J.H. (1965). Introduction to Aging and Pathology of the Retina. C.C. Thomas Springfield, Ill. pp. 11–12.

Rai, G.S. and Elias-Jones, A. (1979). The corneal reflex in elderly patients. J. Amer. Geriatr. Soc. 27, 317–318.

Raymond, L.A., Kramias, G., Glueck, H., and Miller, M.A. (1980). Significance of scintillating scotoma of late onset. Surv. Ophthalmol. 25, 107–113.

Regan, D., Silver, R., and Murray, T. (1977). Visual acuity and contrast sensitivity in multiple sclerosis—hidden visual loss. Brain, 100, 563–579.

Richards, O.W. (1977). Effects of luminance and contrast on visual acuity, ages 16 to 90 years. Amer. J. Optom. Phys. Opt. 54, 178–184.

Rougier, J., Girod, M., and Bongrand, M. (1973). Etiology of and recovery from trochlear nerve paralysis: Apropos of 40 cases. Bull. Soc. Ophthalmol. Fr. 73, 739–744.

Rucker, C.W. (1966). The causes of paralysis of the third, fourth, and sixth cranial nerves. Amer. J. Ophthalmol. 61, 1293–1298.

Rush, J.A. and Kramer, L.D. (1979). Biopsy—negative cranial arteritis with complete oculomotor nerve palsy. Ann. Ophthalmol. 11, 209–213.

Said, F.S. and Weale, R.A. (1959). The variation with age of the spectral transmissivity of the living human crystalline lens. Gerontologia 3, 213–231.

Schafer, W.D. and Weale, R.A. (1970). The influence of age and retinal illumination on the pupillary nerve reflex. Vision Res. 10, 179–191.

Schatz, N.J. and Smith, J.L. (1967). Nontumor causes of the Foster–Kennedy syndromes. J. Neurosurg. 27, 37–44.

Scheibel, M.E., Lindsay, R.D., Tomiyasu, V., and Scheibel, A.B. (1975). Progressive dendritic changes in aging human cortex. Exptl. Neurol. 47, 392–403.

Sekuler, R. and Hutman, L.P. (1980). Spatial vision and aging. I: Contrast sensitivity. J. Gerontol. 35, 692–699.

Semmons, R.J. and Cogan, D.G. (1962). Occult temporal arteritis. Arch. Ophthalmol. 68, 8–12.

Sharland, D.E. (1980). Erythrocyte sedimentation rate: The normal range in the elderly. J. Amer. Geriat. Soc. 28, 346–348.

Sharpe, J.A. and Sylvester, T.O. (1978). Effect of aging on horizontal smooth pursuit. Invest. Ophthalmol. Vis. Sci. 17, 465–468.

Shrader, E.C. and Schlezinger, N.S. (1960). Neuro-ophthalmic evaluation of abducens nerve paralysis. Arch. Ophthalmol. 63, 84–91.

Shutt, H.K.R., Boyd, T.A., and Slater, A.B. (1967). The relationship of the visual fields, optic disc appearance and age in non-glaucomatous and glaucomatous eyes. Canad. J. Ophthal. 2, 79–82.

Slatoper, F.J. (1959). Age norms of refraction and vision. Arch. Ophthalmol. 43, 466–481.

Smith, J.L. (1962). Homonymous hemianopia: A review of 100 cases. Amer. J. Ophthalmol. 54, 616–623.

Smith, J.L. (1966). Ocular signs of Parkinsonism. J. Neurosurg. 24, 284–285.

Sorenson, P.S. and Lorenzen, I. (1977). Giant-cell arteritis, temporal arteritis, and polymyalgia rheumatica. Acta Med. Scand. 201, 207–213.

Sparrow, D. Rowe, J.W., and Silbert, J.E. (1980). Cross-sectional and longitudinal changes in the erythrocyte sedimentation rate in men. J. Gerontol. 36, 180–184.

Spooner, J.W., Sakala, S.M., and Baloh, R.W. (1980). Effect of aging on eye tracking. Arch. Neurol. 37, 575–576.

Strehler, B.L. (1976). Introduction: Aging and the Human Brain. In Neurobiology of Aging, R.D. Terry and S. Gershon, Eds. Raven Press, New York, pp. 1–22.

Thompson, H.S. (1979). Binasal field loss. In Topics in Neuro-ophthalmology, H.S. Thompson, Ed. Williams & Wilkins, Baltimore, pp. 82–85.

Tomsak, R.L., Hanson, M., and Gutman, F.A. (1979). Carotid artery disease and central retinal artery occlusion. Cleveland Clin. Quart. 46, 7–11.

Trobe, J.D., Glaser, J.S., and Post, J.D. (1978). Meningiomas and aneurysms of the cavernous sinus. Arch. Ophthalmol. 96, 457–467.

Trobe, J.D., Lorber, M.L., and Schlezinger, N.S. (1973). Isolated homonymous hemianopias: A review of 104 cases. Arch. Ophthalmol. 89, 377–381.

Troost, B.T. and Daroff, R.B. (1977). The ocular motor defects in progressive supranuclear palsy. Ann. Neurol. 2, 397–403.

United States National Health Survey (1968). Monocular–binocular visual acuity of adults. Public Health Service Pub. No. 100–Series 11, No. 30. 1960–1962.

Vijayashankar, N. and Brody, H. (1973). The neuronal population of the nuclei of the trochlear nerve and the locus coeruleus in the human. Anat. Rec. 172, 421–422.

Vijayashankar, N. and Brody, H. (1977). A study of aging in the human abducens nucleus. J. Comp. Neurol. 173, 433–437.

von Noorden. Discussion of the study of W. Chamberlain op. cit. p. 243–244.

Vrabec, F. (1965). Senile changes in the ganglion cells of the human retina. Br. J. Ophthalmol. 49, 561–72.

Vrabec, F. (1977). Age changes of the human optic nerve head: A neurohistologic study. Albrecht Von Graefes Arch. Klin. Exptl. Ophthalmol. 202, 231–236.

Weale, R.A. (1975). Senile changes in visual acuity. Trans. Ophthal. Soc. U.K. 95, 36–38.

Weintraub, M.I. (1978). Temporal arteritis. Arch. Neurol. 35, 183.

Wilkinson, I.M. and Russell, R.W. (1972). Arteries of the head and neck in giant-cell arteritis. Arch. Neurol. 27, 378–391.

Wilson, L.A. and Russell, R.W. (1977). Amaurosis fugax and carotid artery disease: Indications for angiography. Br. Med. J. 2, 435–437.

Wisniewski, H.M. and Terry, R.D. (1976). Neuropathology of aging brain. In Neurobiology of Aging, R.D. Terry and S. Gershon, Eds. Raven Press, New York, pp.215–280.

Wolf, E. (1967). Studies on the shrinkage of the visual field with age. Highway Res. Rec. 167, 1–7.

18. Neurotology of Aging: Vestibular System

ROBERT W. BALOH

Pathophysiology of Vestibular Symptoms and Signs

The vestibular end organs transduce the forces associated with head acceleration into a biological signal to the brain so that a subjective awareness of head position in space (orientation) is developed and motor reflexes for postural and ocular stability are elicited. The macules of the utricle and sacule sense linear acceleration and the cristae of the semicircular canals angular acceleration. At rest, the afferent nerves from the macules and cristae maintain a balanced tonic rate of firing into the vestibular nuclei. This tonic activity and its modulation with head movements is passed on to cortical, brainstem and spinal centers to elicit the appropriate vestibulo-ocular and vestibulo-spinal reflexes (Baloh and Honrubia, 1979).

Loss of base-line activity originating from one labyrinth typically leads to an illusion of movement, nystagmus, and imbalance. Damage to a single semicircular canal or to its afferent nerve produces a slow conjugate deviation of the eyes toward the damaged side, interrupted by quick corrective movements in the opposite direction (vestibular nystagmus) because of asymmetry in tonic vestibulo-ocular activity. The patient also experiences an illusion of rotation (vertigo) in the plane of the damaged canal. More commonly, lesions involve all the end organs or the nerves of one labyrinth to produce nystagmus and vertigo in a plane determined by the balance of afferent signals from the contralateral intact labyrinth (usually near the horizontal, since the vertical signals partially cancel out). If a patient with such a lesion attempts to fixate on an object, it will appear blurred and seem to be moving in the opposite direction of the slow phase of his spontaneous nystagmus (away from the side of the lesion). This illusion of movement occurs because the brain lacks eye proprioceptive information and interprets the target displacement on the retina as object movement rather than eye movement. By contrast, if the patient closes his eyes, the surround seems to spin toward the side of the lesion due to an imbalance of tonic vestibular signals arriving at the subjective sensation centers of the cortex. Finally, the asymmetry of vestibulo-spinal activity leads to postural and gait imbalance with the patient tending to fall toward the side of the lesion.

Patients who lose vestibular function bilaterally in a symmetrical fashion (for example, secondary to ototoxic drugs) do not develop vertigo or nystagmus, since their tonic vestibular activity remains in balance. However, they do complain of unsteadiness and visual distortion due to the loss of vestibulo-spinal and vestibulo-ocular reflex activity, respectively. Characteristically, when walking, such patients are unable to fixate on objects because the surrounds are bouncing up and down (oscillopsia). In order to see the faces of passers-by, they learn to stop and hold their heads still. Their imbalance is typically worse at night when they are less able to use vision to compensate for the loss of vestibulo-spinal function.

The severity of symptoms and signs following vestibular lesions depends on (1) the extent of the lesion, (2) the rapidity with which the functional loss occurs, and (3) the age of the patient. If a patient slowly loses vestibular function on one side only over a period of months to years (for example, with an acoustic neuroma), symptoms and signs may be absent. On the other hand, a sudden unilateral loss of labyrinthine function is a dramatic event. The patient complains of severe vertigo and nausea and is pale and perspiring and usually vomits repeatedly. He prefers to lie quietly in a dark room, but can walk if forced to (falling toward the side of the lesion). A brisk spontaneous nystagmus interferes with vision. These symptoms and signs are usually transient and the process of compensation begins immediately. Within one week of the lesion, a young patient can walk without difficulty and, with fixation, can inhibit the spontaneous nystagmus. Within one month, most young patients return to work with few, if any, residual symptoms. By contrast, elderly patients compensate for a unilateral loss of vestibular function much more slowly (weeks to months) and may never return to their prior level of function. Similarly, gradual bilateral loss of vestibular function in a young patient may be difficult to identify, since the patient learns to use other sensory information to compensate for the vestibular loss. An elderly patient, however, may be incapacitated by such a lesion, particularly if other sensory deficits are present (such as peripheral neuropathy and impaired vision).

Clinical History

As indicated in the previous section, the characteristic symptoms of vestibular system disease are vertigo, imbalance, and visual distortion. Although the presence of vertigo indicates a lesion within the vestibular system (including visual-vestibular and nuchal-vestibular pathways), its absence does not rule out a vestibular lesion. Other less specific descriptions of the dizzy sensation associated with vestibular dysfunction include giddiness, swimming in the head, floating, and "drunkenness." Rarely, a patient will complain of an illusion of linear movement; this suggests the isolated involvement of a macule or its central connections. Dizziness caused by vestibular lesions is usually worsened by rapid head movements, since the new stimulus is sensed by the intact labyrinth and existing asymmetries are accentuated. Episodes may be precipitated by turning over in bed, sitting up from the lying position, extending the neck to look up, or bending over and straightening up. Symptoms of autonomic dysfunction (for example, sweating, nausea, vomiting) nearly always accompany the vertigo of vestibular lesions, but, occasionally, these vegetative symptoms are the only manifestation of such a lesion.

The description of vestibular symptoms alone does not differentiate peripheral from central lesions. For this one must rely on the associated symptoms (Table 18-1). Lesions of the labyrinth usually produce hearing loss, tinnitus, and a sensation of pressure, fullness, or pain in the ear. Involvement of the eighth nerve also produces hearing loss and tinnitus, but not the latter symptoms. If the lesion is in the internal auditory canal, there may be associated ipsilateral facial weakness; if it is in the cerebellopontine angle, ipsilateral facial numbness and weakness and ipsilateral extremity ataxia commonly occur.

Because of the close approximation of other neuronal centers and fiber tracts it is unusual to find lesions in the brainstem and cerebellum that cause isolated vestibular symptoms. Lesions of the brainstem are invariably associated with other cranial nerve and long tract symptoms. For example, with transient vertebrobasilar insufficiency, vertigo is associated with other brainstem and occipital lobe symptoms, such as diplopia, hemianoptic field

Table 18-1. Symptoms Commonly Associated with Lesions at Different Neuroanatomical Sites.

Labyrinth	Brainstem
Hearing loss	Diplopia
Tinnitus	Visual hallucinations (unformed)
Pressure	Dysarthria
Pain in the ear	Drop attacks
	Extremity weakness and numbness
Internal Auditory Canal	
Hearing loss	Cerebellum
Tinnitus	Imbalance
Facial weakness	Incoordination
Cerebellopontine Angle	Temporal Lobe
Hearing loss	Absence spells
Tinnitus	Visual hallucinations (formed)
Facial weakness and numbness	Visual illusions
Extremity incoordination	Olfactory or gustatory hallucinations

defects, drop attacks, weakness, numbness, dysarthria, and ataxia. Lesions of the cerebellum (for example, infarction or hemorrhage) may be relatively silent, but are always associated with extremity and truncal ataxia in addition to vertigo. Hearing loss for pure tones is unusual with brainstem lesions, even in the late stages.

Vertigo can occur as part of the aura of temporal lobe seizures. The cortical projections of the vestibular system are activated by a focal discharge within the temporal lobe. Such vertigo is nearly always associated with other typical aura symptoms, such as an abnormal taste or smell and a distortion of the visual world (hallucinations and illusions). Occasionally, however, vertigo is the only manifestation of the aura. In such cases, the association with typical "absence" spells should lead to the correct diagnosis.

Examination of the Vestibular System

The examination of a patient complaining of vestibular symptoms should emphasize the head and neck and include a neurological evaluation. The former should include careful inspection of the carotid and vertebral arteries and visualization of the external auditory canal and tympanic membrane, the latter should focus on the cranial nerves, gait, and coordination. Evaluation of the vestibulo-spinal and vestibulo-ocular reflexes can provide a quick bedside assessment of vestibular function.

Tests of Vestibulo-spinal Function

As a general rule, tests of the vestibulo-spinal reflexes lack specificity and sensitivity. Because of the overlap in function it is difficult to distinguish vestibular signs from signs resulting from lesions of the proprioceptive and cerebellar pathways.

Past pointing refers to a reactive deviation of the extremities caused by an imbalance in the vestibular system. One tests it by having the patient place his extended index finger on that of the examiner, close his eyes, raise the extended arm and index finger to a vertical position and attempt to return his index finger to the examiner's. Consistent deviation to one side is past pointing. As with all tests of vestibulo-spinal function, extralabyrinthine influences should be eliminated as much as possible by having the patient seated with eyes closed and arm and index finger extended throughout the test. The standard finger-to-nose test will not identify past pointing, since joint and muscle proprioceptive signals permit accurate localization even when vestibular function is lost. Patients with acute peripheral vestibular damage past point toward the side of loss, but compensation usually corrects the past pointing and can even produce a drift to the other side.

For the Romberg test, the patient stands

with feet together, arms folded against the chest and eyes closed. Patients with acute unilateral labyrinthine lesions sway and fall toward the damaged side. Like the past pointing test, however, the Romberg test is not a good indicator of chronic unilateral vestibular impairment and sometimes the patient will fall toward the intact side. When performed with eyes open, tandem walking or heel-to-toe walking is primarily a test of cerebellar function, since vision compensates for chronic vestibular and proprioceptive deficits. Acute vestibular lesions, however, may impair tandem walking even with the eyes open. Tandem walking with eyes closed provides a good test of vestibular function as long as cerebellar and proprioceptive function are intact. As with other tests of vestibulo-spinal function, however, the direction of falling in patients with chronic lesions is not a reliable indicator of the side of the lesion. So-called stepping or marching tests have the same limitation as the tandem walking test.

Tests of Vestibulo-ocular Function

The normal function of the vestibulo-ocular reflex (VOR) is illustrated by the animal experiment shown in Figure 18-1. The rabbit is ideally suited for demonstrating VOR function, since it rarely makes spontaneous eye movements. If the head is rotated back and forth over a small angle in a sinusoidal fashion, the eyes oscillate in a smooth sinusoidal fashion 180° out of phase with the head. The eyes thus remain stationary in space, ensuring stable vision. As the angle of head rotation increases, the smooth compensatory eye movement is broken up by a series of fast resetting movements (producing nystagmus). If these resetting movements did not occur, the eyes would become pinned in the end of the orbit and the reflex would be non-functional. Because of the fast components the VOR has an unlimited range of function. The eye velocity during the slow phase continues to be equal and opposite to that of the head if the VOR is working

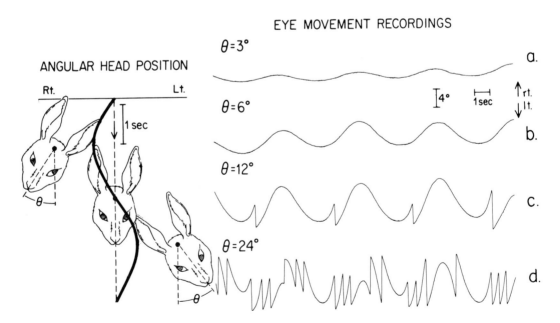

EYE MOVEMENT RECORDINGS

ANGULAR HEAD POSITION

Figure 18-1. Horizontal compensatory eye movements in the rabbit induced by rotating the head back and forth in a sinusoidal fashion (0.2 Hz) at four different peak angular displacements (Θ). (From Baloh and Honrubia, 1979.)

perfectly. As we will see later, measurement of slow phase eye velocity during caloric and rotatory testing can be a sensitive functional test of the VOR.

Clinical testing of the VOR usually focuses on an assessment of physiological and pathological nystagmus. Physiological vestibular nystagmus can be induced by either rotatory or caloric stimulation, whereas pathological vestibular nystagmus either occurs spontaneously or after a change in position.

Physiological Vestibular Nystagmus

ROTARY-INDUCED VESTIBULAR NYSTAGMUS

In an alert human, rotating the head back and forth in the horizontal plane, as we did with the rabbit in Figure 18-1, induces compensatory horizontal eye movements that depend on both the fixation pursuit and vestibular systems. Because of the combined visual-vestibular effect, a patient with complete loss of vestibular function and normal pursuit may still have normal compensatory eye movements on this test. This so-called doll's eye maneuver is a useful bedside test of vestibular function in a comatose patient, however, since such patients cannot generate pursuit or corrective fast components. In this setting, slow conjugate compensatory eye movements indicate normally functioning vestibulo-ocular pathways.

CALORIC-INDUCED VESTIBULAR NYSTAGMUS

The caloric test uses a nonphysiological stimulus to induce endolymphatic flow in the horizontal semicircular canal and, thus, horizontal nystagmus by creating a temperature gradient from one side of the canal to the other. With the warm caloric stimulus illustrated in Figure 18-2, the column of endolymph nearest the middle ear rises because of its decreased density. This causes the cupula to deviate toward the utricle (ampullopetal flow) and produces horizontal nystagmus with the fast phase directed toward the stimulated ear. A cold stimulus produces the opposite effect causing ampullofugal endolymph flow and nystagmus directed away from the stimulated ear (cold opposite, warm

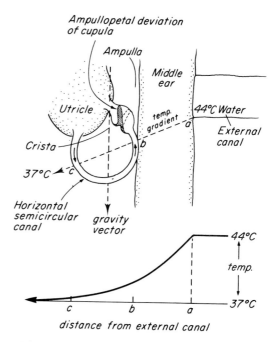

Figure 18-2. Caloric stimulation of the horizontal semicircular canal with 44 °C water. (From Baloh and Honrubia, 1979.)

same—COWS). Because of its ready availability, iced water (approximately 0 °C) is usually used for bedside caloric testing. To bring the horizontal canal into the vertical plane, the patient lies in the supine position with the head tilted 30° forward. Infusion of 10 cubic centimeters of iced water induces a burst of nystagmus usually lasting from one to three minutes. In a comatose patient, only a slow tonic deviation toward the side of stimulation is observed. In normal subjects, the duration and speed of induced nystagmus varies greatly depending on the size of the external canal, the thickness of the temporal bone, the circulation to the temporal bone, and the subject's ability to use fixation to suppress the nystagmus (all age-dependent factors). In a patient of any age, however, the responses tend to be symmetrical. A greater than 20% asymmetry in nystagmus duration suggests a lesion on the side of the decreased response. This should always be confirmed, however, with standard bithermal caloric testing and electronystagmography (see below).

Pathological Vestibular Nystagmus

SPONTANEOUS VESTIBULAR NYSTAGMUS

As described earlier, spontaneous vestibular nystagmus results from an imbalance in tonic vestibulo-ocular signals. The nystagmus is usually horizontal with a torsional component. The slow phase is directed toward the side of the lesion and the fast phase toward the intact side. Gaze in the direction of the fast component increases the frequency and amplitude, whereas gaze in the opposite direction has the reverse effect (Alexander's law). Vestibular nystagmus resulting from lesions of the labyrinth or the eighth nerve (that is, peripheral lesions) is strongly inhibited by fixation. Unless the patient is seen within a few days of the acute episode, spontaneous nystagmus will not be present when fixation is permitted (that is, on routine examination). In this instance, Frenzel glasses (+30 lenses) are particularly useful for abolishing fixation and uncovering spontaneous vestibular nystagmus. Acquired persistent spontaneous nystagmus not inhibited by fixation (fixation nystagmus) indicates a lesion in the brainstem and/or cerebellum. Fixation nystagmus is often purely horizontal or vertical, since horizontal and vertical vestibular ocular pathways separate, beginning at the vestibular nuclei.

POSITIONAL NYSTAGMUS

Two general types of positional nystagmus can be identified on the basis of nystagmus regularity: static and paroxysmal. Static positional nystagmus is induced by slowly placing the patient into the supine, right lateral and left lateral positions. This type of positional nystagmus persists as long as the position is held. Paroxysmal positional nystagmus, on the other hand, is induced by a rapid change from erect sitting to supine, head-hanging left, center, or right position. It is initially high in frequency, but rapidly dissipates within one-half to one minute.

Static positional nystagmus is usually not associated with vertigo and is seldom seen without the aid of Frenzel glasses to inhibit fixation. It may be undirectional in all positions or direction-changing in different positions. Direction-changing and direction-fixed static positional nystagmus occur with both peripheral and central vestibular disorders (Harrison and Ozsahinoglu, 1975). Their presence only indicates a dysfunction in the vestibular system without localizing it; thus, they have the same significance as vestibular nystagmus. As with vestibular nystagmus, however, lack of suppression with fixation and signs of associated brain-stem dysfunction suggest a central lesion.

The most common variety of paroxysmal positional nystagmus (so-called benign paroxysmal positional nystagmus) usually has a three- to ten-second latency before onset and rarely lasts longer than fifteen seconds. The nystagmus is always torsional and is prominent in only one head-hanging position. A burst of nystagmus in the reverse direction usually occurs when the patient moves back to the sitting position. Another key feature is that the patient experiences severe vertigo with the initial positioning, but with repeated positioning the vertigo and nystagmus rapidly disappear (that is, fatigability).

Benign paroxysmal positional nystagmus is a sign of vestibular end organ disease (Dix and Hallpike, 1951; Baloh et al., 1979). It can be the only finding in an otherwise healthy individual, particularly if elderly, or it may be associated with such other signs of peripheral vestibular damage as vestibular nystagmus and unilateral caloric hypoexcitability. When an abnormality is identified on caloric testing, the nystagmus will invariably occur when the patient is positioned with the damaged ear down. Benign paroxysmal positional nystagmus is a common sequela of head injury, viral labyrinthitis, and occlusion of the vasculature to the inner ear. In the majority of cases, however, it occurs as an isolated symptom of unknown cause.

Paroxysmal positional nystagmus can also result from brainstem and cerebellar lesions (Hallpike, 1962). This type does not decrease in amplitude or duration with repeated positioning, it does not have a clear latency, and it usually lasts longer than 30 seconds. The direction is unpredictable and may be different in each position. It is often purely vertical with the fast phase directed downward (toward the cheeks).

Electronystagmography

The pigmented layer of the retina maintains a negative potential with regard to the surrounding tissue by means of active ion transport. Because of the sclera's insulating properties the cornea is positive relative to the retina. An electrode placed in the vicinity of the eye becomes more positive when the cornea rotates toward it and less positive when it rotates away from it. Electronystagmography (ENG) recordings are usually made with a three electrode system using differential amplifiers. Two (active) electrodes are placed on each side of the eye and a reference (ground) electrode somewhere remote from the eyes (usually on the forehead). The two active electrodes measure a potential change of equal amplitude, but opposite direction. The difference in potential between these electrodes is amplified and

used to displace a pen-writing recorder or similar device to produce a permanent record. Since the differential amplifiers monitor the difference in voltage between the two active electrodes, remote signals (electrocardiographic or electroencephalographic, for example) arrive at the electrodes with approximately equal amplitude and phase and cancel out.

With ENG, one can quantify the slow component velocity, frequency, and amplitude of spontaneous or induced vestibular nystagmus and the changes in these measurements brought about by loss of fixation (either with eyes closed or eyes open in darkness) (Baloh, 1976). The effect of change in eye position and fixation on spontaneous vestibular nystagmus is illustrated with the ENG recordings in Figure 18-3. The patient was tested three days after and again two weeks after a left labyrinthectomy. On the initial recording, spontaneous nystagmus to the right is present with fixation, although it is much more prominent without fixation. On the subsequent recording, nystagmus only oc-

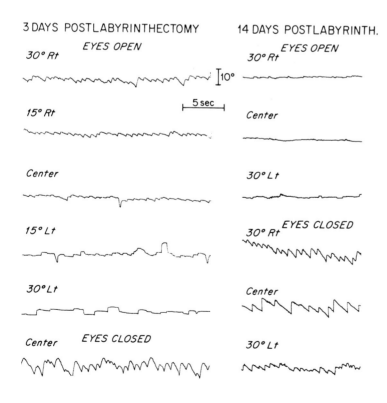

Figure 18-3. An ENG recording (bitemporal horizontal) of spontaneous vestibular nystagmus taken 3 days and 14 days after the patient underwent a left labyrinthectomy. By convention, upward pen deflection, eye movement to the right; downward pen deflection, eye movement to the left. (From Baloh, 1976.)

curs when eye closure removes fixation. This pattern is typical of an acute peripheral vestibulopathy of any cause. As a general rule, nystagmus with fixation (nystagmus seen on routine neurological examination) disappears within one to two weeks after the occurrence of an acute peripheral vestibular lesion. By contrast, vestibular nystagmus can be recorded, with eyes closed, for up to five to ten years after an acute peripheral vestibular lesion. In some patients, vestibular nystagmus emerges only when they are mentally altered (for example, when performing serial seven subtractions from one hundred).

Bithermal Caloric Testing

With bithermal caloric testing, each ear is irrigated for a fixed time (30 or 40 seconds) by a constant flow rate of water that is 7° below body temperature (30 °C) and 7° above body temperature (44 °C). The peak slow phase velocity after each stimulus is measured with ENG and the four values are compared with two standard formulas. The vestibular paresis formula

$$\frac{(R30° + R44°) - (L30° + L44°)}{R30° + R44° + L44° + R30°} \times 100$$

compares the right-sided responses with the left-sided responses and the directional preponderance formula

$$\frac{(L30° + R44°) - (L44° + R30°)}{L30° + R44° + L44° + R30°} \times 100$$

compares nystagmus to the right with nystagmus to the left in the same subject. In both these formulas, the difference in response is reported as a percentage of the total response. This is important because the absolute magnitude of caloric response depends on several factors, including age (Bruner and Norris, 1971; Mulch and Peterman, 1979). Dividing by the total response normalizes the measurements to remove the large variability in absolute magnitude of normal caloric responses. In our laboratory, the upper normal value for vestibular paresis is 22%, whereas that for directional preponderance is 28%. These values do not vary with age.

Typical responses to the standard bithermal caloric test in a patient with a left

labyrinthine lesion (posttraumatic) are shown in Figure 18-4. After each stimulus, the slow phase velocity reaches a peak within thirty to sixty seconds and then decays over the next one to two minutes. Inserting the peak slow phase velocity after each stimulus into the vestibular paresis formula

$$\frac{(3 + 3) - (7 + 25)}{3 + 3 + 7 + 25} \times 100$$

and into the directional preponderance formula

$$\frac{(3 + 25) - (7 + 3)}{3 + 25 + 7 + 3} \times 100$$

yields a 68% left vestibular paresis and a 47% right directional preponderance. Both values are outside the normal range and are consistent with an acute unilateral peripheral vestibular lesion (labyrinth and/or eighth nerve including the root entry zone in the brainstem). As a general rule, a significant vestibular paresis on bithermal caloric testing indicates a peripheral vestibular lesion, whereas a significant directional preponderance is nonlocalizing (that is, it can occur with peripheral and with central lesions). The latter is often associated with spontaneous nystagmus, in which case the velocity of the slow components of the spontaneous nystagmus adds to that of caloric-induced nystagmus in the same direction and subtracts from that of caloric-induced nystagmus in the opposite direction (Coats, 1966). The patient whose caloric data is illustrated in Figure 18-4 had a spontaneous vestibular nystagmus beating to the right (consistent with the right directional preponderance).

Rotatory Testing

Rotatory tests of the VOR are not widely used as part of the routine vestibular examination for two reasons: (1) rotatory stimuli affect both labyrinths simultaneously, compared to the selective stimulation of one labyrinth possible with caloric tests, and (2) expensive bulky equipment is required in order to generate precise rotatory stimuli. Rotatory tests do have several advantages, however. Multiple graded

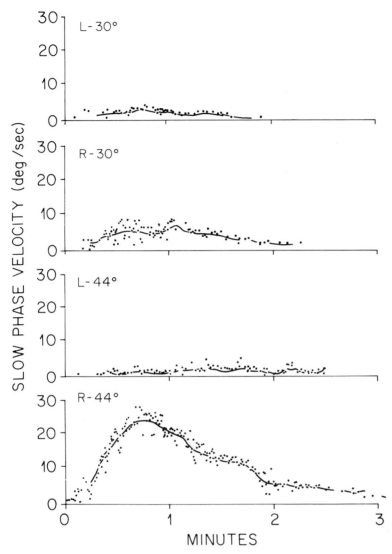

Figure 18-4. Bithermal caloric test performed on a patient with a left post-traumatic labyrinthopathy. Each dot represents the average velocity of one nystagmus slow phase.

stimuli can be applied in a relatively short period of time, and rotatory testing is usually less bothersome to patients than caloric testing. Unlike caloric testing, a rotatory stimulus to the semicircular canals is unrelated to physical features of the external ear or temporal bone, so that a more exact relationship between stimulus and response is possible.

The results of sinusoidal rotatory testing in the patient with a left peripheral vestibular lesion (the patient whose caloric data was illustrated in Figure 18-4) are shown in Figure 18-5. As with the rabbit in Figure 18-1, the patient was rotated back

and forth in the plane of the horizontal semicircular canals. His eyes were opened in complete darkness and he performed mental arithmetic to maintain alertness. The ENG recording of induced nystagmus was similar to the bottom trace in Figure 18-1. Fast components were removed and the slow phase velocity was sampled every 25 milliseconds to generate the plot shown in Figure 18-5. Two measurements are typically derived from these plots: the gain (peak slow phase eye velocity/peak chair velocity) in each direction and the phase relationship between the eye and chair velocities. In normal subjects at 0.05

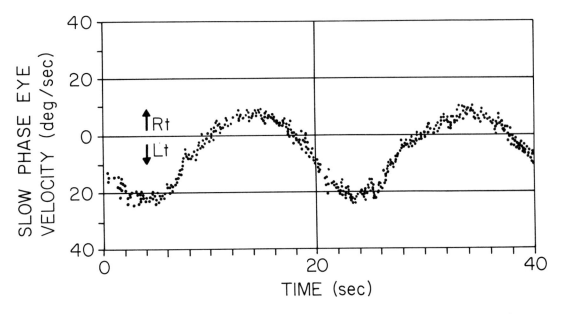

Figure 18-5. Sinusoidal rotatory test (0.05 Hz, peak velocity 30°/sec) performed on the same patient whose caloric data is illustrated in Figure 18-4. Fast components were removed from the ENG trace and the velocity of the remaining slow components was sampled every 25 msec. The peak velocity of slow phases to the left is approximately three times that of slow phases to the right.

Hertz, the gain is symmetrical (mean 0.5 ± 0.15) and there is a slight phase advance of the eye velocity relative to the chair velocity (10° ± 4°). In the patient whose data is illustrated in Figure 18-5, rotation toward the side of the lesion (to the left) resulted in a lower peak slow phase velocity than did rotation toward the intact side and the phase advance of the eye velocity relative to the chair velocity was increased. These are typical findings with an acute unilateral peripheral vestibular lesion. With compensation, however, both measurements may return to normal (Jenkins et al., 1979).

Rotatory testing is very useful for evaluating patients with bilateral peripheral vestibular lesions (for example, ototoxic drug exposure), since both labyrinths are stimulated simultaneously and the degree of remaining function is accurately quantified. Because the variance associated with normal rotatory responses is less than that associated with caloric responses, dimin-

ished function is identified earlier (Baloh et al., 1979a). Artifactually diminished caloric responses occasionally occur in patients with angular, narrow external canals or with thickened temporal bones. Since a rotatory stimulus is unrelated to these factors, rotatory-induced nystagmus is normal in such patients. Patients with absent caloric responses may have decreased, but measurable, rotatory-induced nystagmus, particularly at higher stimulus velocities. The ability to identify remaining vestibular function, even if minimal, is an important advantage of rotatory testing, particularly when the physician is contemplating ablative surgery or is monitoring the effects of ototoxic drugs.

Patients with peripheral vestibular lesions, like normal subjects, can suppress physiological vestibular nystagmus when they are rotated with a fixation point. By contrast, patients with central vestibular lesions (particularly lesions of the vestibulocerebellum) often cannot suppress physiological vestibular nystagmus with fixation (Baloh et al., 1981). Rotatory stimuli are ideally suited for evaluating fixation suppression, since the same precise stimulus can be presented on repeated occasions with and without fixation. Abnormalities in fixation suppression of vestibular nystagmus are highly correlated with abnormalities in smooth pursuit (Dichgans et al., 1978) (see below).

Tests of Visual–Ocular Control

Along with the VOR, two visually controlled ocular stabilizing systems produce versional eye movements, the saccadic and smooth pursuit. The saccade system responds to a retinal position error to bring a peripheral target to the fovea in the shortest possible time. The smooth pursuit system maintains gaze on a moving target by generating a continuous match of eye and target velocity. Optokinetic nystagmus is generally considered to be a form of smooth pursuit in which the eye tracking motion is periodically interrupted by corrective saccades in the opposite direction

to relocate the gaze on new targets coming into the visual field.

With ENG, the peak velocity, accuracy, and delay time of saccades; smooth pursuit velocity; and optokinetic slow component velocity can be accurately measured and compared with normative data (Baloh et al., 1977). Since each of these values are age dependent, it is critical that age-matched normal controls are used (Spooner et al., 1980). Table 18-2 summarizes the types of saccade, smooth pursuit, and optokinetic abnormalities commonly associated with focal lesions of the nervous system. With one exception, peripheral vestibular lesions do not impair visual ocular control. After an acute unilateral labyrinthine or vestibular nerve lesion, smooth pursuit and optokinetic slow phase velocity will be transiently decreased to the contralateral side (that is, in the direction of the spontaneous nystagmus).

Computerized X-Ray Tomography

Computerized X-ray tomography (CT scanning) has produced a new era of

Table 18-2. Summary of Visual Ocular Control Abnormalities Produced by Focal Neurological Lesions.

Location of Lesion	Saccades	Smooth Pursuit	Optokinetic Nystagmus
Unilateral peripheral vestibular	Normal	Transient contralateral impairment	Transient contralateral decreased SCV*
Cerebello-pontine angle	Ipsilateral dysmetria**	Progressive ipsilateral or bilateral impairment	Progressive ipsilateral or bilateral decreased SCV
Diffuse cerebellar	Bilateral dysmetria	Bilateral impairment	Bilateral decreased SCV
Intrinsic brainstem	Decreased maximum velocity, increased delay time	Ipsilateral or bilateral impairment	Ipsilateral or bilateral decreased SCV, disconjugate
Basal ganglia	Hypometria,*** increased delay time (bilateral)	Bilateral impairment	Bilateral decreased SCV
Frontoparietal cortex	Contralateral hypometria	Normal	Normal
Parieto-occipital cortex	Normal	Ipsilateral impairment	Ipsilateral decreased SCV

*Slow component velocity.
**Under- and overshoots.
***Undershoots only.

noninvasive radiological diagnosis. To date, its main value with regard to the diagnosis of vestibular system disease has been an improvement in our ability to image lesions within the brain parenchyma. Infarction, hemorrhage, tumors, and atrophy can usually be identified without invasive procedures.

So far, CT scanning has not been particularly useful for imaging lesions within the temporal bone. For example, an acoustic neuroma must be greater than 2 centimeters in diameter to be reliably identified with first generation CT scanners (Thomsen et al., 1977). With newly developed scanners, however, one can often trace the vestibular and auditory nerves into the internal auditory canal and identify localized swelling. With continued advances in technology, our ability to image lesions within the temporal bone should continue to improve.

Differential Diagnosis of Common Vestibular Disorders in the Elderly

Infection

BACTERIA

Invasion of the labyrinth by bacteria is an infrequent occurrence since the introduction of antibiotics. With otitis media, bacteria can enter the inner ear through the oval or round windows or by eroding the bony walls. Patients with bacterial meningitis may develop labyrinthitis when bacteria enter the perilymphatic space from the cerebrospinal fluid via the cochlear aqueduct or internal auditory canal. Although usually a benign disorder, otitis externa can produce a life-threatening disease called malignant external otitis in elderly diabetic patients. *Pseudomonas aeruginosa* invades the junction of the cartilaginous and osseous portions of the external auditory canal and spreads to the temporo-occipital bones. The most common neurological sequela is involvement of the facial nerve in the Fallopian canal or at the stylomastoid foramen. Occasionally, multiple cranial nerves are compressed extradurally, and, in rare cases, the infection spreads across the dura to produce a purulent meningitis. Prolonged treatment with effective antibiotics has improved the previously poor prognosis in this condition (Fadan, 1975).

VIRAL

One of the most common clinical vestibular syndromes at any age is the acute onset of severe vertigo, nausea, and vomiting unassociated with auditory or neurological symptoms. Most of these patients gradually improve over one or two weeks, but some develop recurrent episodes. Laboratory studies usually reveal spontaneous vestibular nystagmus, unilateral caloric hypoexcitability, and normal hearing. A large percentage of such patients report an upper respiratory tract illness one to two weeks before the onset of vertigo. This syndrome frequently occurs in epidemics (epidemic vertigo), may affect several members of the same family, and erupts more commonly in the spring and early summer. All these factors suggest a viral origin, but attempts to isolate an agent have been unsuccessful, except for occasional findings of a herpes zoster infection. Pathological studies showing atrophy of one or more vestibular nerve trunks with or without atrophy of their associated sense organs support a vestibular nerve site and probable viral etiology for this syndrome (Schuknecht and Kitamura, 1981).

FUNGUS

Mucormycosis of the mastoid bone has become an increasingly common clinical problem, particularly in the elderly. It occurs in patients who are chronically ill (often with diabetes or malignancy) and who are receiving chemotherapy or broad-spectrum antibiotics (Hutter, 1959; Meyer et al., 1972). The organism enters the sinuses through the nose and penetrates the muscular walls of arteries to produce thrombosis and infarction of tissue. The infection may then spread to the petrous apices, the middle and inner ears, and into the intracranial cavity. Thrombosis of the major cerebral arteries often develops despite treatment with Amphotericin.

Vascular Disorders

TRANSIENT ISCHEMIA

Vertebrobasilar insufficiency is a common cause of vertigo in the elderly (Williams and Wilson, 1962). Whether the vertigo originates from ischemia of the labyrinth, brainstem, or both structures is not always clear, since the blood supply to the labyrinth, eighth nerve, and brainstem comes from the vertebral arteries. The vertigo is abrupt in onset, usually lasting several minutes and is frequently associated with nausea and vomiting. The key to the diagnosis is to find associated symptoms resulting from ischemia in the remaining territory supplied by the posterior circulation. These include, in order of frequency, visual hallucinations, drop attacks and weakness, visceral sensations, visual field defects, diplopia, and headaches. These symptoms occur in episodes, either in combination with the vertigo or alone. Vertigo may be an isolated initial symptom of vertebral basilar insufficiency, but repeated episodes of vertigo without other symptoms suggest another diagnosis (Fisher, 1960).

INFARCTION

Since the labyrinthine artery divides into a cochlear and vestibular branch, there is an anatomical substrate for isolated infarction of either the auditory or the vestibular labyrinth. The former would result in sudden unilateral deafness; the latter would produce an acute vestibular syndrome. How often such vascular events occur is disputed, primarily due to lack of pathological confirmation. This diagnosis must be kept in mind, however, in elderly subjects with known atherosclerotic vascular disease, particularly if they have a prior history of vascular occlusion.

Vertigo is a common symptom with infarction of the lateral brain stem and/or cerebellum. The zone of infarction producing the lateral medullary (Wallenberg's) syndrome consists of a wedge of the dorsolateral medulla just posterior to the inferior olive, which is supplied by the posterior inferior cerebellar artery. It usually occurs from occlusion of the ipsilateral vertebral artery and infrequently from occlusion of the posterior inferior cerebellar artery (Fisher et al., 1961). Characteristic symptoms include vertigo, nausea, vomiting, intractable hiccuping, ipsilateral ataxia, ipsilateral facial pain, diplopia, dysphagia, and dysphonia. The diagnosis is confirmed by the neurological examination, which localizes all findings to the appropriate area in the lateral medulla. Ischemia in the distribution of the anteroinferior cerebellar artery usually results in infarction of the dorsolateral pontomedullary region and the inferolateral cerebellum. Since the labyrinthine artery arises from the anteroinferior cerebellar artery approximately 80% of the time, infarction of the membranous labyrinth is a common accompaniment. Severe vertigo, nausea, and vomiting are the initial and most prominent symptoms. Other associated symptoms include unilateral hearing loss, tinnitus, facial paralysis, and cerebellar asynergy. As with Wallenberg's syndrome, the diagnosis of the lateral pontomedullary syndrome depends on the highly localizing findings on neurological examination.

In some instances, occlusion of the vertebral artery, the postcroinferior cerebellar artery, or the anteroinferior cerebellar artery results in infarction confined to the posteroinferior cerebellar hemisphere without accompanying brainstem involvement. The initial symptoms are severe vertigo, vomiting, and ataxia, and since typical brainstem signs do not occur, a diagnosis of an acute peripheral labyrinthine disorder might be mistakenly make. The key differential point is the finding, on examination, of prominent ipsilateral cerebellar signs, particularly ipsilateral extremity and gait ataxia and gaze evoked nystagmus. After a latent interval of 24 to 96 hours, some patients develop progressive brainstem dysfunction due to compression by a swollen cerebellum. A relentless progression to quadriplegia, coma, and death follows unless the compression is surgically relieved (Sypert and Alvord, 1975).

Tumors

CARCINOMA

Epidermoid carcinomas arise from epidermal cells of the auricle, external auditory canal, or the middle ear and mastoid. The prognosis is good for tumors confined to the auricle and external canal, but not for those invading the middle ear and mastoid. The latter are frequently associated with prominent labyrinthine symptoms, which typically include vertigo, hearing loss, pain, otorrhea, mastoid swelling, and facial paralysis. The tumor is frequently visible in the external canal and erosion of the temporal bone is apparent on X-ray examination. To treat invasion of the middle ear and mastoid, a subtotal resection of the temporal bone is required if the entire tumor is to be removed.

Metastatic involvement of the temporal bone is common with several different tumor types, but apparently because of the enchondral layer's resistance, neoplasms rarely invade the bony labyrinth. The most common site of origin for metastatic tumors in order of frequency are breast, kidney, lung, stomach, larynx, prostate, and thyroid gland (Schuknecht et al., 1968). The internal auditory canal is a frequent site of metastatic tumor growth. From this site, tumor cells destroy the seventh and eighth nerves and extend into the inner ear or into the cerebellopontine angle. Irregular destruction of bone by the rapidly growing tumor is usually apparent on X-ray examination. Metastatic tumors from the breast and prostate commonly induce new bone formation.

BENIGN TUMORS

Vestibular schwannomas (acoustic neuromas) account for approximately 10% of intracranial tumors and over 75% of cerebellopontine angle tumors. About 50% are diagnosed in the fifth and the sixth decade of life, but the diagnosis is rare beyond the age of 70 (Mathew et al., 1978). By far the most common symptoms associated with vestibular schwannomas are slowly progressive hearing loss and tinnitus from compression of the cochlear nerve. Vertigo occurs in less than 20% of patients, but approximately 50% complain of imbalance or dysequilibrium. Large tumors extending into the cerebellopontine angle can be identified by CT, but posterior fossa myelography is needed to identify small tumors confined to the meatus.

Aminoglycoside Ototoxicity

The ototoxicity of the aminoglycosides results from hair cell damage in the inner ear (Rudnick et al., 1980). Unlike other antibiotics, the aminoglycosides are concentrated in the perilymph and endolymph, which increases their ototoxic potential. Of the common aminoglycosides, streptomycin primarily damages the hair cells of the cristae, with relative sparing of the hair cells of the macules and cochlea. Because of this highly selective effect on the vestibular end organ, streptomycin has been used to produce a chemical vestibulectomy in patients with Meniére's syndrome.

Patients with aminoglycoside ototoxicity rarely complain of vertigo, but consistently report unsteadiness of gait, particularly at night or in a darkened room. Serial rotatory or caloric tests are useful for monitoring vestibular responsiveness during drug administration. Aminoglycosides should be used with great caution in the elderly and particularly in patients with renal failure.

Syndromes of Unknown or Multiple Causes

BENIGN PAROXYSMAL POSITIONAL VERTIGO

Patients with this disorder develop brief episodes of vertigo (<30 seconds) with position change typically when turning over in bed, bending over, and straightening up or extending the neck to look up. As indicated earlier, benign paroxysmal positional vertigo can result from head injury, viral labyrinthitis, and vascular occlusion or it may occur as an isolated symptom of unknown cause. The latter is particularly common in the elderly. This syndrome is important to recognize, since in the vast majority of patients, the symptoms spontaneously remit within six months of onset. The diagnosis rests on finding characteristic paroxysmal positional nystagmus after a rapid change from the sitting to the head-hanging position (see positional nystagmus).

In studies of the temporal bones of a few patients with typical benign paroxysmal positional nystagmus, basophilic deposits on the cupulae of the posterior canals have been observed (Schuknecht, 1969). These deposits were present only on one side, the side that was undermost when paroxysmal positional nystagmus and vertigo were induced. They are apparently otoconia released from a degenerating utricular macule. The otoconia settle on the cupula of the posterior canal (situated directly under the utricular macule), making it heavier than the surrounding endolymph. When the patient moves from the sitting to a head-hanging position (the provocative test for paroxysmal positional nystagmus), the posterior canal moves from an inferior to superior position, a utriculofugal displacement of the cupula occurs, and a burst of nystagmus is produced. The latency before nystagmus onset could be due to the period of time required for the otoconial mass to be displaced, and fatigability may be caused by the dispersing of particles in the endolymph. Consistent with this theory, the burst of rotatory paroxysmal positional nystagmus is in the plane of the posterior canal of the "down" ear, with the fast component directed upward (toward the forehead) as would be predicted from ampullofugal stimulation of the posterior canal (Baloh et al., 1979b). Additional support for this theory comes from reports showing the disappearance of fatigable paroxysmal positional nystagmus after the ampullary nerve has been sectioned from the posterior canal on the diseased side (Gacek, 1974).

DYSEQUILIBRIUM OF THE AGED

As with all other sensory systems, the vestibular system undergoes numerous changes with aging. There is a gradual loss of sensory cells and primary afferent neurons accompanied by a loss of otoconia from the macules (particularly in the saccule) and an accumulation of lipofucsin granules in the remaining sensory, ganglion, and supporting cells (Ishii et al., 1967; Johnson and Hawkins, 1972). Unlike the other sensory systems, however, the functional significance of these degenerative changes is not clear. Because the functional role of the vestibular system overlaps that of the proprioceptive and visual systems a gradual loss of vestibular

function with aging could easily be masked. By contrast, degenerative changes with aging in the nearby auditory system have clear clinical effects (for example, presbycusis).

Surprisingly, function studies of the vestibulo-ocular reflex (caloric and rotatory tests) do not show a gradual decline in response with aging, but rather show a hyperresponsiveness, particularly between the ages of 40 to 70 (Bruner and Norris, 1971; Mulch and Petermann, 1979). Apparently two separate phenomena occur with aging—loss of central inhibitory control and loss of end organ function. The former, which is dominate at middle age, accounts for increased responses up to the age of 70; the latter, which finally becomes more important after the age of 70, accounts for a gradual decrease in responses.

Based on the earlier discussion of the pathophysiology of vestibular symptoms and signs, a gradual symmetrical loss of vestibular end organ function would not be expected to produce prominent symptoms. Since the balance between the two sides is unchanged, vertigo and nystagmus would not result. Postural and gait imbalance might occur, but the central nervous system usually compensates for such a loss by using other sensory information. However, since parallel degenerative changes occur in other sensory systems and within the central nervous system itself, degenerative changes in the vestibular end organs with aging almost certainly have significant effects upon postural and gait stability (that is, multisensory dizziness).

Treatment of Vertigo

Treatment of vertigo can be divided into two general categories: specific and symptomatic (Baloh, 1981). Specific therapies include, for example, antibiotics for bacterial labyrinthitis; anticoagulants, for vertebrobasilar insufficiency; and surgery, for a tumor within the temporal bone. Obviously, whenever possible, treatment should be directed at the underlying disorder. In the majority of cases, however, specific therapy is not available and the clinician must rely on symptomatic treatment.

Of the large number of antivertiginous

Table 18-3. Antihistamines used to treat vertigo.

Drug	Dosage	Sedation	Dryness of Mucous Membranes
Meclizine	25 mg orally q 4–6 h	+	+
Cyclizine	50 mg orally or intra-muscularly q 4–6 h or 100 mg suppository q 8 h	+	++
Dimenhydrinate	50 mg orally or intra-muscularly q 4–6 hr or 100 mg suppository q 8 hr	+	+
Promethazine	25 or 50 mg orally or intramuscularly or suppository q 4–6 h	+++	++

medications available, the antihistamines are most useful for treating elderly patients because they have the fewest undesirable side effects. The commonly used antihistamines, their main side effects, and the recommended dosage are listed in Table 18-3. All produce sedation and dryness of the mucous membranes to varying degrees. As a general rule, the usefulness of each of these drugs has been determined by empirical observation and, in any given individual, it is difficult to predict which drug will be most effective. A patient may respond to one drug, but not to other drugs in the same class.

The strategy concerning which drug to use is usually based on the severity and time-course of the symptoms. An episode of prolonged severe vertigo is one of the most distressing symptoms one can experience. The patient prefers to lie still with eyes closed in a quiet, dark room. In this setting, the sedation produced by promethazine is a desirable effect. The drug can be given via suppository if the patient is unable to tolerate oral medication.

Chronic recurrent vertitgo is a different therapeutic problem, since the patient is usually trying to carry on normal activity and sedation is undesirable. Meclizine, cyclizine, and dimenhydrinate are all effective for treating recurrent episodes of mild to moderate vertigo. These drugs are also useful for prophylaxis of motion sickness.

Treatment of positional vertigo is a particularly difficult therapeutic problem, since the episodes of vertigo are very severe, but usually last only a few seconds. In order to suppress these brief bouts completely, the patient would have to be heavily sedated throughout the day, which is usually unacceptable. As indicated earlier, the most common positional vertigo, benign paroxysmal positional vertigo, has the characteristic features of short duration (usually 15 seconds or less) and decreasing severity with repeated positional changes. More than 90% of patients have a spontaneous remission within six months, although the vertigo recurs in a small percentage of patients. Once the diagnosis is clear, a simple explanation of the nature of the disorder and its good prognosis provides a great deal of relief for the patient. Preliminary studies indicate that having the patient make repeated positional changes from the sitting to the lateral position several times a day causes the episodic vertigo to remit faster than if the patient avoids positional changes (Brandt and Daroff, 1980).

References

Baloh, R.W. (1976). Pathologic nystagmus: A classification based on electro-oculographic recordings. Bull. L. A. Neurol. Soc. 41, 120.

Baloh, R.W. (1981). Episodic vertigo. In Current Therapy. HF Conn, Ed. Saunders, Philadelphia, pp. 793–796.

Baloh, R.W. and Honrubia, V. (1979). Clinical Neurophysiology of the Vestibular System. F. A. Davis, Philadelphia.

Baloh, R.W., Honrubia, V., and Sills, A.

(1977). Eye-tracking and optokinetic nystagmus. Results of quantitative testing in patients with well-defined nervous system lesions. Ann. Otol. Rhinol. Laryngol. 86, 108.

Baloh, R.W., Sakala, S. and Hunrubia, V. (1979b). Benign paroxysmal positional nystagmus. Amer. J. Otolaryngol. 1, 1–5.

Baloh, R.W., Sills, A.W., and Honrubia, V. (1979a). Impulsive and sinusoidal rotatory testing. A comparison with results of caloric testing. Laryngoscope 89, 646–654.

Baloh, R.W., Yee, R.D., Kimm, J., and Honrubia, V. (1981). Vestibulo-ocular reflex in patients with lesions involving the vestibulo-cerebellum. Exptl. Neurol. 72, 141.

Brandt, T. and Daroff, R.B. (1980). Physical therapy for benign paroxysmal positional vertigo. Arch. Otolaryngol. 106, 484–485.

Bruner, A. and Norris, T.W. (1971). Age related changes in caloric nystagmus. Acta Otolaryngol. (Stockholm) Suppl. 282.

Coates, A.C. (1966). Directional preponderance and spontaneous nystagmus. Ann. Otol. Rhinol. Laryngol. 75, 1135.

Dichgans, J., Reutern, G.M. von, and Rommelt, V. (1978). Impaired suppression of vestibular nystagmus by fixation in cerebellar and non-cerebellar patients. Archiv. f. Psychiatr. Nervenkrankhe. 226, 183–199.

Dix, M.R. and Hallpike, C.S. (1951). The pathology, symptomatology, and diagnosis of certain disorders of the vestibular system. Ann. Otol. Rhinol. Laryngol. 61, 987.

Fadan, A. (1975). Neurological sequela of malignant external otitis. Arch. Neurol. 32, 204.

Fisher, C.M. (1960). Vertigo in cerebrovascular disease. Arch. Otolaryngol. 85, 855.

Fisher, C.M., Karnes, W. E., and Kubik, C. S. (1961). Lateral medullary infarction—the pattern of vascular occlusion. J. Neuropathol. Exptl. Neurol. 20, 323.

Gacek, R. (1974). Transection of the posterior ampullary nerve for relief of benign paroxysmal positional vertigo. Ann. Otol. Rhinol. Laryngol. 83, 569.

Hallpike, C.S. (1975). Vertigo of central origin. Proc. Roy. Soc. Med. 55, 364.

Harrison, M.S. and Ozsahinoglu, C. (1975). Positional vertigo. Arch. Otolaryngol. 101, 675.

Hutter, R.V.P. (1959). Phycomycetous infection (mucormycosis) in cancer patients: A complication of therapy. Cancer 12, 330–350.

Ishii, T., Murakami, Y., Kimura, R., and Balogh, K. (1967). Electron microscopic and histochemical identification of lipofuscin in the human inner ear. Acta Otolaryngol. 64, 17.

Jenkins, H., Lau, C.G.Y., Baloh, R.W., and Honrubia, V. (1979). Implications of Ewald's second law for diagnosis of unilateral labyrinthine paralysis. Otolaryngol. Head Neck Surg. 87, 459–462.

Johnson, L. and Hawkins, J. (1972). Sensory and neural degeneration with aging, as seen in microdissections of the human inner ear. Ann. Otol. Rhinol. Laryngol. 81, 179.

Mathew, G.D., Facer, G.W., Suh, K.W., Houser, O.W., and O'Brien, P.C. (1978). Symptoms findings and methods of diagnosis in patients with acoustic neuroma. Laryngoscope 88, 1893–1903.

Meyer, R.D., Rosen, P., and Armstrong, D. (1972). Phycomycosis complicating leukemia and lymphoma. Ann. Intern. Med. 77, 871–879.

Mulch, G. and Peterman, W. (1979). Influence of age on results of vestibular function tests. Ann. Otol. Rhinol. Laryngol. 88 (Suppl. 56).

Rudnick, M.D., Ginsberg, I.A., and Huber, P.S. (1980). Aminoglycoside ototoxicity following middle ear injection. Ann. Otol. Rhinol. Laryngol. 89 (Suppl. 77).

Schuknecht, H. (1969). Cupulolithiasis. Arch. Otolaryngol. 90, 765.

Schuknecht, H., Allam, A., and Murakami, Y. (1968). Pathology of secondary malignant tumors of the temporal bone. Ann. Otol. Rhinol. Laryngol. 77, 5.

Schuknecht, H. F. and Kitamura, K. (1981). Vestibular neuritis. Ann. Otol. Rhinol. and Laryngol. 90 (Suppl. 78).

Spooner, J., Sakala, S., and Baloh, R. W. (1980). Effect of aging on eye tracking. Arch. Neurol. 37, 575–576.

Sypert, G.W. and Alvord, E.C. (1975). Cerebellar infarction. Arch. Neurol. 32, 357.

Thomsen, J., Gyldensted, C., and Lester, J. (1977). Computer tomography of cerebellopontine angle lesions. Arch. Otolaryngol. 103, 65.

Williams, D. and Wilson, T.G. (1962). The diagnosis of the major and minor syndromes of basilar insufficiency. Brain 85, 741.

19. Neurotology of Aging: The Auditory System

DEBORAH HAYES

JAMES JERGER

In the auditory system, presbyacusis is the inevitable consequence of aging. It is the most common cause of hearing loss in adults. The prevalence of significant, bilateral hearing loss in individuals age 65 years or older is 133/1000 persons (U.S. Public Health Service, 1967). In fact, over one-half of all Americans who suffer significant hearing loss are 65 years old or older.

Presbyacusis, as a clinical entity, has two distinct components, one related to changes in the auditory periphery, the other to changes in the central auditory system. The peripheral component is limited to age-related changes in the outer, middle, and inner ear. It is primarily revealed by changes in hearing sensitivity. The central component reflects age-related changes in the auditory pathways of the central nervous system. Its principal manifestation is loss in the ability to understand speech, especially under difficult listening conditions. The interaction of peripheral and central components makes presbyacusis an exceedingly complex clinical problem.

It is well documented that age-related changes in the auditory system may be demonstrated both by histopathological

Preparation of this chapter was supported in part by Public Health Service Research Grant NS-10940 from the National Institute of Neurological and Communicative Disorders and Stroke.

and behavioral means as early as the fourth decade. The handicapping result of presbyacusis, however, is not typically evident until the seventh decade. The typical complaint of the presbyacusic patient is, "I can hear, but I can't understand." In most cases, rehabilitation of the presbyacusic patient is limited to amplification.

The Peripheral Component

The peripheral component of presbyacusis represents changes in the outer, middle, and inner ear related to aging.

Anatomical Effects

In the outer ear, age-related changes include an increase in pinna size and atrophic changes in the supporting walls of the external auditory meatus (Hinchcliffe, 1962a).

Etholm and Belal (1974) described arthritic changes in the middle ear of the incudomalleal and incudostapedial joints. These changes include calcification of the articular cartilage and obliteration of the joint space, which increased in severity with increasing age.

In the inner ear, a variety of age-related changes are evident. These include (1) primary degeneration of hair and supporting cells, (2) primary degeneration of nerve cells and fibers, (3) atrophy of the stria vascularis, (4) alteration and acellularity of the spiral ligament, (5) accumulation of lipofuscin and other cellular debris, and (6) thickening of the basilar membrane (Saxen, 1952; Schuknecht, 1955, 1964; Jorgensen, 1961; Hinchcliffe, 1962a; Hansen and Reske-Nielsen, 1965; Bredberg, 1967; Ishii et al., 1967; Wright and Schuknecht, 1972; Spoendlin, 1975; Nadol, 1979, 1981).

Structural changes in the peripheral auditory system accompanying aging are pervasive and especially evident in the histopathological evaluation of cochlear tissue. Specific effects of these changes on auditory behavior, however, are largely unknown.

Behavioral Effects

Behavioral effects of aging on the peripheral auditory system are primarily revealed by a slowly progressive, bilateral sensorineural hearing loss affecting high-frequency sensitivity first, and later involving the entire spectrum. Hearing loss for "ultra-audiometric" frequencies (that is, 10 kHz and above) begins at about age 20 (Hinchcliffe, 1962a; Osterhammel and Osterhammel, 1979; Osterhammel, 1980). Hearing loss in the "speech" region (500 to 4 kHz) is frequently evident in the age range 60 to 70 years.

The bulk of peripheral presbyacusic sensitivity loss is related to cochlear effects. There is no compelling evidence of a significant conductive (outer ear or middle ear) component to age-related hearing loss. Although several investigators (Glorig and Davis, 1961; Nixon et al., 1964; Milne, 1977) have reported a substantial conductive component to the hearing loss related to age, lack of adequate control for collapsing ear canals may have affected their results. Collapsing ear canals result from closure (collapse) of the external auditory meatus by pressure of the earphone and the earphone cushion during audiometric testing. The behavioral result is an artificial elevation in air-conduction sensitivity, especially for high-frequency (1 kHz and above) signals. Bone-conduction sensitivity is not affected. The resulting audiogram shows an air–bone gap (conductive component), which is an iatrogenic product of the audiometric test. Collapsing ear canals are especially prevalent in the elderly. Schow and Goldbaum (1981) estimate that over 40% of elderly nursing home residents have collapsing ear canals, which result in a 15 dB or greater elevation in hearing sensitivity during audiometric testing. Current methods of evaluation, including acoustic immittance measures and the use of circumaural earphone cushions, provide an effective control for the spurious effect of collapsing ear canals on the pure-tone audiogram.

Numerous attempts have been made to define the "average" pure-tone audiogram of presbyacusis. Bunch (1929, 1931) was among the first to quantify loss in hearing sensitivity related to age. His pioneering work revealed little age-related effect on pure-tone sensitivity for signals of 500 Hz and below, but systematic decrease in sensitivity with increase in age (20 to 69 years) for pure tones of 1 kHz and above. Subsequent investigators have confirmed and extended Bunch's work (Pestalozza and Shore, 1955; Sataloff and Menduke, 1957; Hinchcliffe, 1959, 1962a; Goetzinger et al., 1961; Corso, 1963; Sataloff et al., 1965; Konig, 1969; Jerger, 1973; Osterhammel and Osterhammel, 1979; Osterhammel, 1980; Møller, 1981). Not unexpectedly, there are differences in the "average audiogram" among the various investigations related to differences in sampling methods, screening criteria, and other experimental variables. Nevertheless, Bunch's observations have been substantially confirmed.

Figure 19-1 shows the average pure-tone audiogram by age–decade for subjects screened for significant otological history and noise exposure (from Osterhammel and Osterhammel, 1979; $N = 286$). Figure 19-1a shows the average audiogram for women; Figure 19-1b the average audiogram for men. Note that, for both women and men, average loss at 500 Hz varies less than 20 dB over the age range 10 to 79 years, but average loss at 4 kHz increases by more than 40 dB in this same age range. The figures clearly demonstrate increase in loss with increase in frequency and age for

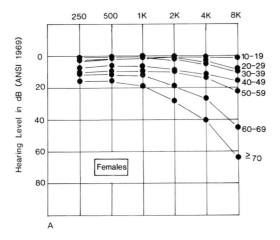
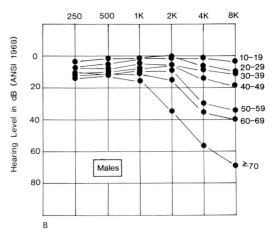
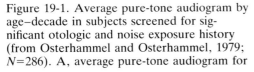

A

B

Figure 19-1. Average pure-tone audiogram by age–decade in subjects screened for significant otologic and noise exposure history (from Osterhammel and Osterhammel, 1979; *N*=286). A, average pure-tone audiogram for women; B, average pure-tone audiogram for men. For both men and women, sensitivity loss increases with increase in age and frequency. Men show a greater high-frequency sensitivity loss than women.

both sexes. Men demonstrate greater loss in high-frequency (2 to 4 kHz) sensitivity than women. This sex difference may be related to differences in total life-long noise exposure for men and women.

Other investigators have noted an apparent age-related sex-effect on low-frequency (1 kHz and below) sensitivity (Goetzinger et al., 1961; Corso, 1963; Hayes and Jerger, 1979a). They noted that women were less sensitive in the low-frequency range than men. Hayes and Jerger (1979a, b) attributed increased low-frequency sensitivity loss in women to central rather than peripheral effects. Recently, Jerger and Jerger (1980) documented low-frequency sensitivity loss in a patient with surgically confimed central auditory pathway dysfunction. In addition, Hansen and Reske-Nielsen (1965) correlated a histopathological finding of cochlear tissue with premortem behavioral audiograms and were unable to demonstrate a cochlear origin of low-frequency hearing loss in elderly subjects. They concluded that hearing loss for low frequencies was a purely central phenomenon. It may be that sex effects observed on the pure-tone audiogram

reflect a difference in the ratio of peripheral to central aging in men and women.

In summary, the majority of the loss in pure-tone sensitivity accompanying aging is characterized by a slowly progressive, bilateral sensorineural loss affecting high frequencies more than low frequencies, and typically greater in men than in women. Loss in high-frequency sensitivity is most parsimoniously attributed to peripheral (that is, cochlear) effects, whereas loss in low-frequency sensitivity is the likely result of central (that is, brainstem and temporal lobe) effects. There appears to be an important sex effect in the expression of peripheral versus central effects in the pure-tone audiogram.

Sensorineural hearing loss, in any age individual, is usually accompanied by loss in speech understanding ability. In other words, in addition to a peripheral effect on pure-tone sensitivity, there is also a peripheral effect on speech understanding ability. In the elderly, however, this effect is disproportionate to the degree of hearing loss (Gaeth, 1948; Pestalozza and Shore, 1955; Calearo and Lazzaroni, 1957; Blumenfeld et al., 1969; Bergman, 1971; Bergman et al., 1973; Jerger and Hayes,

1977). The discrepancy between expected and observed decrease in speech understanding ability is thought to reflect the central component of presbyacusis.

The Central Component

The central component of presbyacusis reflects changes in auditory structures and pathways in the brainstem and cortex. Both histopathological and behavioral studies suggest that age-related changes in the central auditory system occur as early as the fourth decade (Brody, 1955; Bergman, 1971; Bergman et al., 1973).

Anatomical Effects

The histopathological changes include loss of neuronal population and accumulation of lipofuscin throughout the central auditory system. Fisch et al. (1972) described degenerative changes of arterial vessels of the internal auditory meatus with age. Konigsmark and Murphey (1970) evaluated age-related changes in the ventral cochlear nucleus of the brainstem auditory pathways. Brody (1955) reported a reduction of more than one-half the cells of the superior temporal gyrus over the age range from 20 to 79 years. Kirikae et al. (1964) and Kirikae (1969) related histopathological changes in central auditory pathways to behavioral manifestations of presbyacusis.

Behavioral Effects

The effects of the central component of presbyacusis may be observed on all aspects of auditory behavior, from sensitivity to pure-tone signals to success of hearing aid fitting. The principal effect, as noted, is loss of the ability to understand speech, especially under difficult listening conditions.

The effect of age on the ability to understand speech was first described by Gaeth (1948). He observed a disproportionate loss in intelligibility for "common" words in hearing-impaired subjects age 60 years and older. He noted that the phenomenon was most prevalent in subjects with moderate-to-severe hearing losses, but that it was also associated with age.

Gaeth's pioneering work first suggested the complex interaction between age, hearing loss, and speech understanding ability.

Numerous investigators have confirmed Gaeth's initial observations (Pestalozza and Shore, 1955; Goetzinger et al., 1961; Konig, 1969; Jerger, 1973; Jerger and Hayes, 1977). Results of a study by Pestalozza and Shore (1955), for example, showed that performance of monosyllabic phonemically balanced (PB) words (the common material for tests of word recognition) for subjects age 60 years and older was 20 to 40% poorer than performance for subjects age 50 years and younger, in spite of control for degree of sensitivity loss. Pestalozza and Shore concluded that this phenomenon was best explained on the basis of "non-peripheral," that is, central, effects.

Jerger (1973) examined word recognition scores in 4095 ears of 2162 patients with sensorineural hearing impairment, ranging in age from 6 to 89 years. He reported an average maximum PB score (PB $_{max}$) as a function of age–decade with hearing loss held constant. His data are summarized in Figure 19-2. The PB$_{max}$ decreases as age increases. The age effect is especially pronounced in the older age-decades (60 to 69, 70 to 79, and 80 to 89 years). Jerger determined the general shape of the functional relationship between word recognition score and age. The exponential expression of this relationship agreed reasonably well with general equations expressing the relationship between changes in sensory thresholds and age (Hinchcliffe, 1962b).

The effects of central auditory aging on speech understanding ability can also be observed on materials other than single words. Jerger and Hayes (1977) compared performance for a word recognition task and for a sentence identification task in 204 subjects categorized by age–decade. The word recognition task (PB) was presented under quiet conditions; the sentence identification task was presented in ipsilateral speech competition (synthetic sentence identification or SSI). Figure 19-3 shows the results of that investigation (for

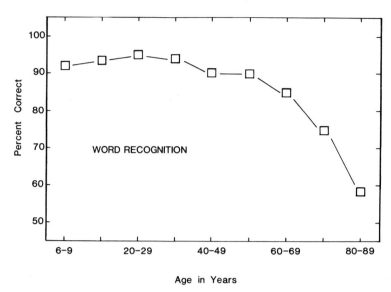

Figure 19-2. Average maximum word recognition score by age decade for hearing-impaired subjects (from Jerger, 1973; *N*=2162 patients, 4095 ears). Word recognition ability decreases dramatically in age decades 60–69 years, 70–79 years, and 80–89 years.

left ears only). Although average performance for both sets of materials decreases with increases in age, performance for the sentence identification task decreases to a greater extent than performance for the word recognition task. In addition, performance for sentences begins to decrease at about age 30 to 39 years, with an accelerated decline to about age 60 to 69. Performance for words, on the other hand, does not show systematic decrement until age 50 to 59. Apparently, undistorted PB words are not sufficiently stressful to re-

veal the effects of central aging on speech understanding ability until it is fairly pronounced. Jerger and Hayes attributed the discrepancy in performance for word recognition and sentence identification to the "central aging effect." They noted that the effect was similar in both magnitude and direction (performance for sentences poorer than performance for words) to the effect observed in younger subjects with documented central auditory dysfunction (Jerger and Jerger, 1975). In addition, they reported that peripheral hearing loss

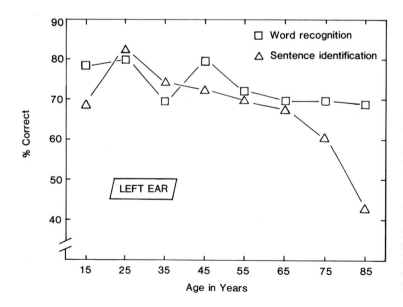

Figure 19-3. Average maximum word recognition and sentence identification scores by age decade for hearing-impaired subjects (from Jerger and Hayes, 1977; *N*=204, left ears only). Both words and sentences show decrease in maximum performance score with increase in age. Performance for sentences decreases more than performance for words.

did not account for the discrepancy between performance for sentences and performance for words. Sentence identification poorer than word recognition is a uniquely central effect.

More recently, Shirinian and Arnst (1982) further investigated the various patterns of word and sentence performance associated with age. They described an additional age-related effect; decreased performance for sentence identification relative to word recognition, but only at high speech intensity levels. This phenomenon, termed "rollover," had been described previously in young subjects with documented eighth nerve and central auditory pathway dysfunction (Jerger et al., 1980). The rollover phenomenon has been observed in elderly subjects on speech materials other than sentences (Gang, 1976). Its presence suggests that simple speech amplification will not necessarily improve the speech understanding problems of the elderly.

Shirinian and Arnst made two additional important observations. First, they confirmed that the central PB–SSI pattern was not related merely to peripheral hearing loss. They observed the central age-related effect in elderly subjects with normal pure-tone audiograms. Second, Shirinian and Arnst observed greater central auditory aging in women than in men. This finding again suggests a sex effect in the ratio of peripheral versus central age-related changes.

Investigations of performance on undistorted speech materials effectively rule out a peripheral basis for the disproportionate speech understanding problems of the elderly. For relatively difficult speech materials (for example, sentences in speech competition), performance decrements may appear as early as the fourth decade (Bergman, 1971; Jerger and Hayes, 1977; Orchik and Burgess, 1977). For easier speech understanding tasks (words in quiet), performance is typically unaffected until about age 60 to 69. It is not surprising that many elderly, hearing-impaired patients complain of difficulty in understanding speech, especially under noisy conditions.

In addition to effects on the pure-tone audiogram and speech understanding ability, the central component of presbyacusis profoundly affects successful auditory rehabilitation of the elderly patient. It is commonly recognized that, of any patient population, the elderly derive the least benefit from amplification. The discrepancy between apparent potential and actual benefit from hearing aid use is usually attributed to central effects (Niemeyer, 1968; Jerger and Hayes, 1976).

In a retrospective study of performance with a hearing aid in subjects 60 years old and older, Hayes and Jerger (1979b) divided these subjects into three groups, based on results of tests of speech understanding ability (word recognition versus sentence identification). One group showed no evidence of central auditory aging—they exhibited a primarily peripheral auditory deficit (sentence identification equal to or better than word recognition). The second group showed mixed peripheral and central effects—sentence identification was poorer than word recognition by 4 to 20%. The third group showed evidence of pronounced central effects—sentence identification was poorer than word recognition by more than 20%. Hayes and Jerger then studied the relationship between degree of hearing loss, presence and magnitude of the central age-related component, and performance with a hearing aid. This relationship revealed that elderly subjects with only mild hearing loss, but pronounced central auditory aging, perform substantially poorer with a hearing aid than elderly subjects with moderate hearing loss, but no central component. In other words, the presence of a central aging effect limits performance with a hearing aid to a greater extent than the degree of peripheral hearing loss.

McCandless and Parkin (1979) examined the relationship between satisfaction with hearing aid use and site of lesion. They found that as the site of lesion moved from peripheral to central, subject satisfaction with hearing aid use declined. In subjects with purely peripheral, conductive hearing loss, satisfaction with hearing aid use was as high as 84%. In subjects with a central site, satisfactory hearing aid use declined to less than 15%.

Although these results are not surprising

to any clinician whose practice includes presbyacusic patients, it is sobering to note the extent to which central auditory involvement can limit successful auditory rehabilitation. The traditional approach for predicting successful use of a hearing aid, based on degree of peripheral hearing loss and word recognition score, may be entirely inappropriate in elderly subjects. Techniques yielding better definition of central auditory function may more accurately predict potential for hearing aid use.

Clinical Audiometric Evaluation of the Presbyacusic Patient

Clinical audiometric evaluation of the presbyacusic patient may require two distinct stages. In the first stage, the patient is evaluated by standard audiometric tests to determine both the overall degree of hearing loss and the magnitude and type of the speech understanding deficit. If there is sufficient hearing loss, and the patient is motivated for hearing aid use, the second stage of evaluation is recommended. In this stage, the patient's potential for hearing aid use is evaluated and specific recommendations for auditory rehabilitation are made.

Basic Audiometric Evaluation

The minimum audiometric test battery necessary for adequate evaluation of the elderly patient includes three measures: (1) acoustic immittance measurement of middle ear function, (2) pure-tone audiometry, and (3) diagnostic speech audiometry. Each one serves a specific purpose in defining the peripheral and central components of presbyacusis.

Acoustic Immittance Measures

Acoustic immittance measures are especially suited for evaluation of middle ear, cochlear, and eighth nerve function. The acoustic immittance test battery consists of three components: (1) tympanometry, a dynamic measure of the immittance properties of the middle ear in the plane of the tympanic membrane; (2) static immittance, an estimate of the immittance properties of

the middle ear "at rest"; and (3) acoustic reflex measures, evaluation of the reflexive contraction of the stapedius muscle to loud sounds. All three components are measured by sealing a small acoustic probe, which delivers a constant sound pressure level (SPL) probe tone, in the external auditory meatus and measuring the amount of sound energy that is reflected back from the tympanic membrane.

Tympanometry is performed by varying the air pressure in the external auditory meatus and measuring the change in the acoustic immittance properties of the middle ear. Typically, a strip chart automatically records change in SPL of the acoustic probe sealed in the meatus as air pressure is varied from $+200$ to -200 mm H_2O (relative to atmospheric pressure). The resulting graph, the tympanogram indirectly measures the acoustic transmission properties of the middle ear. In the normal subject, maximum transmission occurs when air pressure in the sealed external auditory meatus is equal to atmospheric pressure (0 mm H_2O), and the tympanogram shows a "peak" of maximum compliance at 0 mm H_2O. In the presence of a middle ear disorder, which alters the physics of the system, the tympanogram typically assumes one of three clinically distinct tympanometric shapes. In the case of presbyacusis, the tympanogram is usually normal, showing maximum sound transmission (maximum compliance) at 0 mm H_2O.

Static immittance measures are made by comparing transmission properties of the middle ear system at a point of reduced compliance ($+200$ mm H_2O) with transmission properties of the system at rest (0 mm H_2O). This measure attempts to quantify the immittance properties of the middle ear system. Although static immittance measures are a useful adjunct to tympanometry and acoustic reflex measures, they are of limited value alone, due to the considerable overlap of normal and pathological ranges. In presbyacusis, static immittance is typically within the normal range. Some investigators have reported a slight decrease in static immittance with increase in age (Jerger et al., 1972; Hall, 1979). Their data support the histopathological evidence of reduced middle ear compliance with age (Etholm and Belal, 1974). However, the effect is slight and, on the average, static immittance measures from elderly subjects fall within the normal range.

Measurement of the acoustic reflex, the contraction of the stapedius muscle in response to a relatively loud sound, is probably the most powerful diagnostic component of acoustic immittance battery. When the stapedius contracts it alters the acoustic immittance properties of the middle ear. In clinical measurements, a sound is introduced into the ear and the change in SPL of the probe tone is monitored. If the sound has produced the acoustic reflex, the change in acoustic immittance will be observed as a change in SPL of the probe tone (needle deflection) on the monitor. The acoustic reflex may be elicited by both pure-tone and noise signals.

In order to elicit the acoustic reflex, a number of conditions must be met. First, the sound must be sufficiently intense. In subjects with normal hearing, the average threshold of the acoustic reflex for pure tones is 85 dB hearing level (HL) (Jerger et al., 1972). The threshold for noise is usually lower. Cochlear hearing loss does not substantially affect the acoustic reflex threshold for pure tones until it exceeds 50 to 60 dB HL (Silman and Gelfand, 1981). Cochlear hearing loss elevates the reflex threshold level for noise (Jerger et al., 1974). In fact, the relationship between the threshold for noise and the threshold for pure tones fairly accurately predicts hearing loss, at least in children and young adults.

Second, the afferent limb of the reflex arc, eighth nerve, and brain-stem auditory pathways must be intact. A principal effect of retrocochlear disorder is to abolish or significantly alter the acoustic reflex.

Third, the efferent limb of the reflex arc, seventh nerve, and middle ear structures must be functional. Seventh nerve dysfunction or a middle ear disorder, of even a minor degree, on the recording side may compromise detection of the change of acoustic immittance during the acoustic reflex.

In clinical practice, two reflex measures of diagnostic significance are evaluated. These are (1) the absolute reflex threshold level for a variety of pure-tone and noise signals presented both ipsilaterally and contralaterally and (2) the supra-threshold reflex decay. Threshold measures are considered abnormal if they fall outside the normal range (70 to 100 dB HL for pure tones). Reflex decay is abnormal if the reflex response to a continuous, supra-threshold (+10 dB) pure tone declines to less than one-half the initial value within 5 seconds (Anderson et al., 1969). An abnormality of either of these two clinical measures suggests eighth nerve or brain-stem auditory pathway dysfunction.

The effect of age on the acoustic reflex is complex. Age-related threshold changes depend on the type of reflex-eliciting signal (pure tone or noise). In general, it has been shown that the relationship between the acoustic reflex threshold for pure-tone and noise changes with age, such that the thresholds for the two types of signals tend to converge (Handler and Margolis, 1977; Jerger and Brown, personal communication; Jerger et al., 1978a,b; Silman, 1979). The significance of this finding relates to prediction of hearing loss from the acoustic reflex. Age-related effects on reflex decay are less well documented. The increased prevalence of reflex decay with increased age is not unexpected, however, in view of the documented age-related effects on the eighth nerve and brain-stem auditory pathways (Konigsmark and Murphey, 1970; Fisch et al., 1972).

Thus, the principal uses of acoustic immittance measurements in the evaluation of presbyacusis are (1) to differentiate normal from abnormal middle ear function and (2) to test the integrity of eighth nerve and brain-stem auditory pathways.

Pure-Tone Audiometry

The second major component of the audiometric evaluation is pure-tone audiometry. Pure-tone audiometry is simply the measurement of hearing threshold for pure-tone signals delivered monaurally. Test signals may be delivered by both air conduction (earphones) and bone conduction (bone vibrator). The threshold for air conduction signals yields a measure of overall degree of loss; a difference in the threshold for air conduction versus bone conduction signals (air–bone gap) suggests the presence of a conductive component (acoustic immittance measures are, of course, a far more sensitive indicator of middle ear disorder). In any subject, but especially in the elderly subject, care must be taken to avoid collapsing the ear canals, which artifically elevates the threshold to air conduction signals and, consequently, produces a spurious air–bone gap.

In clinical practice, pure tones at octave intervals from 250 to 8 k Hz are employed as test signals. The patient's threshold, measured in dB hearing level (HL) in reference to "average normal hearing", is plotted by frequency; the resulting graph is the pure-tone audiogram. A single value expresses the overall degree of hearing loss. By clinical convention, this value is the average sensitivity for pure-tone signals of 500 and 1 k and 2 kHz (pure-tone average or PTA).

The principal use of pure-tone audiometry in the evaluation of the elderly patient is quantification of the overall degree of hearing loss. In general, the subjective handicap of hearing loss is most closely related to overall degree of loss (Jerger et al., 1968; Noble and Atherly, 1970) and varies as a function of age (Merluzzi and Hinchcliffe, 1973). The pure-tone audiogram is used to estimate the difficulty the patient will experience in everyday life due to peripheral auditory effects. Speech audiometry is used to evaluate the extent to which the hearing handicap is compounded by central auditory aging.

Speech Audiometry

The primary role of speech audiometry in clinical evaluation is to define the presence and magnitude of central auditory effects (Jerger and Hayes, 1977; Jerger et al., 1980). In the case of confounding peripheral hearing loss (the usual case in presbyacusis), it is necessary to evaluate speech understanding ability with a variety of speech materials. One set of materials should be maximally sensitive to the effect of peripheral sensitivity loss; a second set should be maximally sensitive to central auditory dysfunction, but relatively unaffected by peripheral effects. Comparison of performance for the two sets of materials differentiate peripheral from central speech understanding deficits.

Of course, no speech understanding task measures purely peripheral effects. Word recognition tasks, however, are less compromised by central effects than are other clinically useful tests. Peripheral effects on speech understanding ability are commonly evaluated by PB word recognition. In this test, lists of 25 or 50 open-set, monosyllabic words are drawn from general American English and "balanced" to match the phonemic content of the language. The patient's task is to repeat each word as it is presented. These materials are only minimally affected by central auditory dysfunction, but are maximally sensitive to peripheral effects (Speaks et al., 1970; Jerger and Hayes, 1977; Hayes and Jerger, 1979a,b; Shirinian and Arnst, 1982). They provide an effective control for peripheral effects on the speech understanding problems related to aging.

A useful material for evaluation of central effects is synthetic sentences in the presence of ipsilateral speech competition (SSI). These materials consist of a closed message set of 10 "synthetic" (that is, grammatically correct, nonsense) sentences presented at 10-second intervals during an unrelated continuous discourse. The continuous discourse speech competition is usually presented at the same intensity level as the primary sentences (0 dB message-to-competition ratio, or 0 dB), but may be presented at any MCR. In some elderly subjects, +10 dB MCR (sentences 10 dB more intense than competition) is employed to define more adequately the central speech understanding deficit. At any MCR, the subject's task is to identify each sentence as it is presented from the list of 10 alternatives. Performance for this sentence identification task is less affected by peripheral hearing loss than is performance for the word recognition task, but it is uniquely sensitive to central effects (Jerger and Hayes, 1977; Jerger et al., 1980; Shirinian and Arnst, 1982).

In clinical practice, performance for both speech materials is evaluated at several speech intensity levels. Usually three to four levels are sufficient to describe the patient's complete performance–intensity (PI) function. The PI function is used to evaluate the presence of rollover.

Comparison of performance for the two sets of materials estimates both peripheral and central effects on speech understanding ability. In the case of purely peripheral effects, three distinct patterns of PB–SSI performance emerge, depending on the configuration of the pure-tone audiogram (Jerger and Hayes, 1977). In subjects with flat audiometric configurations (that is, equal sensitivity for pure tones in the range 500 to 4 k Hz), performance for the two sets of materials is nearly equivalent ($SSI_{max} = PB_{max}$). In subjects with sloping pure-tone audiograms (that is, sensitivity for 2 k and 4 k Hz substantially poorer than sensitivity for 500 and 1 k Hz), performance for sentences is better than performance for words ($SSI_{max} > PB_{max}$). The magnitude of the discrepancy depends on the steepness of the audiometric slope. Finally, in subjects with rising audiometric contours (that is, sensitivity for 500 Hz poorer than sensitivity for 1k and 2k Hz), performance for words is better than performance for sentences ($PB_{max} > SSI_{max}$). The effect is slight, however, and the magnitude of the discrepancy does not exceed 20%. Rollover, as defined as paradoxical decrease in speech understanding ability with increase in speech level, is not observed in any pattern of peripheral effect.

In the case of purely central effects, two patterns of speech understanding performance emerge. First, performance for words is better than performance for sentences ($PB_{max} > SSI_{max}$). The effect typically exceeds 20%. Second, performance for both sets of materials decreases as speech intensity increases, the "rollover" phenomenon. Both patterns may be observed in subjects with completely normal pure-tone audiograms.

Presbyacusis may be considered a special case of the central effect confounded by peripheral sensitivity loss. Any number of patterns may emerge, depending on the magnitude of the peripheral versus the central component. For example, some elderly subjects may show a speech understanding pattern consistent with both the degree and contour of the pure-tone audiogram. This result primarily demonstrates peripheral presbyacusis. Other subjects may exhibit normal performance for words, but somewhat reduced performance for sentences in competition. This result may be attributed to mixed peripheral and central presbyacusis. Finally, some elderly subjects may perform exceedingly poorly for sentences, but relatively well for words. These subjects exhibit pronounced central presbyacusis. In general, we expect the pattern of presbyacusis to be symmetrical in both ears. It is not unusual, however, to find patterns of peripheral and mixed presbyacusis or central and mixed presbyacusis in the same subject.

In our experience, the pattern of presbyacusis (primarily peripheral, mixed, or primarily central) exhibited by individual elderly subjects provides a useful index for estimating potential for hearing aid use and auditory rehabilitation. Regardless of the specific presbyacusic pattern, however, the elderly, hearing-impaired subject should be evaluated for amplification if he/she is motivated for hearing aid use. In general, although the degree of central auditory aging may limit the benefit of amplification, it does not necessarily preclude successful hearing aid use.

Hearing Aid Evaluation

Perhaps no aspect of clinical audiometry evokes as much controversy as hearing aid evaluation. There are numerous philosophies underlying a myriad of techniques employed in clinical practice today. Some investigators argue that hearing aid performance is most reasonably assessed by formal tests of speech understanding ability. Others assert that techniques employing more easily calibrated signals (pure tones and noise) provide better estimates of suitable amplification for individual subjects. Still others eschew formal testing altogether and recommend amplification based on patient preference on informal listening trials. Regardless of the approach, however, the goal of any hearing aid evaluation is to arrive at a set of realistic rehabilitative recommendations for the hearing-impaired individual.

By traditional speech audiometric techniques, the patient is evaluated both unaided and with various hearing aid arrangements in a calibrated sound field. Performance may be evaluated in a number of listening conditions (that is, in quiet, in the presence of either noise or speech competition) at various levels of listening difficulty. The hearing aid that provides the most benefit (that is, improvement in speech understanding performance) is recommended. These techniques attempt to estimate patient potential in realistic, everyday listening conditions. An integral part of the evaluation is patient and family counseling of realistic expectations of hearing aid use.

By prescriptive evaluative techniques, the electro-acoustic characteristics of the ideal hearing aid for each patient are determined from a set of measurements of threshold detection and comfort and discomfort levels. Normally, non-speech (that is, pure tones and noise) signals are employed as test materials. The patient may or may not be tested with a specific instrument before it is recommended. By these techniques, the electro-acoustic characteristics that theoretically maximize speech understanding ability are stressed.

The presbyacusis patient may represent a special problem for either evaluative approach. He may not have the stamina required for the lengthy evaluation process. He may not be sufficiently motivated for successful adjustment to hearing aid use. Finally, he may not be able to master adequately the instrument's controls and adjustments, especially if additional physical limitations, such as arthritis or poor vision, are present.

Nevertheless, even if the elderly, hearing-impaired patient cannot be successfully rehabilitated by traditional means of amplification, he can be helped substantially by realistic patient and family counseling. In many cases, the elderly, hearing-impaired patient and his family can be taught to maximize speech communication by minimizing difficult listening conditions. In addition, nonwearable aids, such as amplifier controls on the telephone or chair-side television and radio receivers, may fill the need of many presbyacusic patients. In short, although not all presbyacusic patients are candidates for hearing aid use, all are candidates for auditory rehabilitation by counseling and supplemental communication aids.

Illustrative Cases

The following three cases highlight the various patterns of presbyacusis as demonstrated by speech audiometry. Each patient received a complete audiometric and hearing aid evaluation and each received a hearing aid as the principal means of auditory rehabilitation. The differing experiences of the three patients demonstrates the importance of peripheral versus central age-related components, and realistic counseling, to rehabilitative success in presbyacusis.

Case I

Case I (S.P.), an 86-year-old woman with a 20-year history of gradually progressive, bilateral hearing loss, is socially active and participates in community and church affairs. She is chairman of a women's auxiliary group and volunteers at a hospital gift shop several days a week. Recently, S.P. noted increasing difficulty in everyday communication, especially at meetings. She lives with her daughter and son-in-law and describes only minimal communication problems at home. Her general physician referred her to an otologist for evaluation of her hearing problem; the otologist referred her to the Audiology Service for audiometric and hearing aid evaluation.

The results of the basic audiometric evaluation are shown in Figure 19-5 (see Figure 19-4 for key to symbols). The pure-tone audiogram (upper half) shows a mild-to-moderate, bilaterally symmetrical sensorineural hearing loss (RE PTA = 45 dB HL; LE PTA = 46 dB HL). Acoustic reflex thresholds to pure-tone

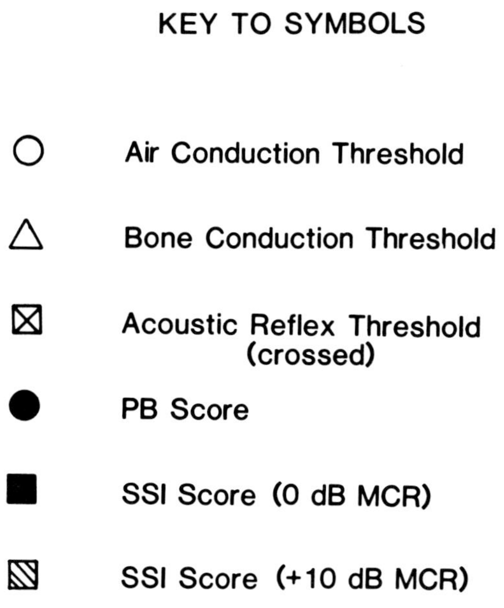

KEY TO SYMBOLS

○   Air Conduction Threshold

△   Bone Conduction Threshold

⊠   Acoustic Reflex Threshold
(crossed)

●   PB Score

■   SSI Score (0 dB MCR)

◨   SSI Score (+10 dB MCR)

Figure 19-4. Key to symbols employed in Figures 19-5, 19-6, and 19-7.

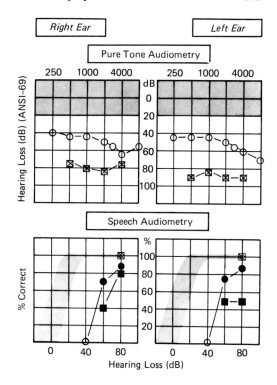

Figure 19-5. Results of basic audiometric evaluation of case I, an 86-year-old woman. Pure-tone audiometry shows mild-to-moderate, bilaterally symmetrical sensitivity loss. Acoustic reflex thresholds are present at normal levels. Speech audiometry reveals "peripheral" presbyacusis in the right ear (performance for words and sentences is nearly equivalent) and "mixed" presbyacusis in the left ear (performance for sentences 4 to 20% poorer than performance for words). This patient is a successful hearing aid user.

signals are within the normal range (70 to 100 dB HL). This relationship of elevated behavioral threshold, but normal acoustic reflex threshold, is consistent with cochlear dysfunction.

Speech audiometry reveals peripheral presbyacusis in the right ear and mixed presbyacusis in the left ear. In the right ear, performance for a word recognition (PB) task and a sentence identification (SSI-0 dB MCR) task are nearly equivalent ($PB_{max} = 84\%$; $SSI_{max} = 80\%$). In the left ear, however, sentence identification is substantially poorer than word recognition ($PB_{max} = 88\%$; $SSI_{max} = 50\%$). In an easier sentence identification task (SSI +10 dB MCR), her performance is 100% in both ears.

The patient was evaluated for hearing aid use by speech audiometric techniques. She obtained substantial (70 to 90%) improvement in speech understanding ability, especially in difficult listening conditions. A hearing aid was recommended for her right ear, the ear with peripheral presbyacusis.

Six months after purchasing the hearing aid, S.P. considers herself a successful hearing aid user. She wears the aid six to eight hours daily, and reports definite improvement in communication at meetings and the theater. S.P. says her hearing aid has "put me back in tune. . . ."

Case I represents successful auditory rehabilitation of the presbyacusic patient. Her pure-tone audiogram is quite typical of elderly women; her speech understanding performance for both words and sentences, consistent with combined peripheral and mixed presbyacusis, is quite good in spite of her advanced age. In addition, S.P. is an active, well-motivated hearing aid candidate. Her demanding life-style, motivation, and pattern of presbyacusis contribute to her successful adjustment to hearing aid use.

Case II

Case II (H.J.), an 81-year-old retired physician, has noted a gradually progressive, bilateral hearing loss, somewhat greater in his right ear, for more than 20 years. He is active in the local medical society. He tried a hearing aid previously, but received only limited help for his chief complaint, difficulty hearing in crowded meetings. The patient and his wife live alone. Although H.J. does not notice a problem communicating at home, his wife does. He came to the Audiology Service for hearing aid evaluation.

The results of the basic audiometric evaluation are shown in Figure 19-6. The pure-tone audiogram shows a moderate-to-severe, steeply sloping sensorineural

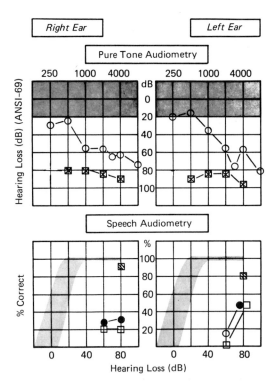

Figure 19-6. Results of basic audiometric evaluation of case II, an 81-year-old man. Pure-tone audiometry shows a moderate-to-severe, steeply sloping sensorineural hearing loss in both ears. Acoustic reflex thresholds are within the normal range. Speech audiometry is consistent with "mixed" presbyacusis bilaterally. Case II is a successful, part-time hearing aid user.

loss in both ears, with a somewhat greater loss in the right ear (RE PTA = 44 dB HL; LE PTA = 36 dB HL). Acoustic reflex threshold levels are within the normal range (70 to 100 dB HL).

Speech audiometry is consistent with mixed presbyacusis. Performance for words is better than performance for sentences by 12% in the right ear (PB $_{max}$ = 32%; SSI $_{max}$ = 20%) and by 8% in the left ear (PB $_{max}$ = 48%; SSI $_{max}$ = 40%). In addition, performance for both sets of materials, but especially performance for sentences, is poorer than expected for the pure-tone audiogram. Performance for an easier sentence task (SSI +10 dB MCR) is good (80 to 90%) bilaterally.

The patient was evaluated for hearing aid use by speech audiometric techniques. He was evaluated with his own, unsatisfactory, hearing aid and several more suitable models. His own hearing aid had been fitted to his right ear; he received substantially more benefit from a different model fitted to his left ear. He subsequently purchased a hearing aid for his left ear.

Four months after purchasing his hearing aid, H.J. gave a favorable report. He considers the current hearing aid much more helpful than his previous model, especially in difficult listening conditions. He is experiencing some difficulty with earmold adjustment and returns for frequent follow-up service, but he rates his current hearing aid experience as "good." He uses his hearing aid approximately four hours a day.

As a successful, part-time hearing aid user, H.J. finds amplification useful in selected listening conditions, but not in all communication situations. Although a younger patient with a similar pure-tone audiogram, but better overall speech understanding performance, might require full-time hearing aid use, H.J.'s life-style, motivation, and pattern of presbyacusis, limit his need for, and benefit from, amplification. Nevertheless, H.J. is considered a rehabilitative success.

Case III

Case III (O.O.) is an 83-year-old retired high school teacher. She has noticed a gradual hearing loss in both ears for many years. Although she has considered hearing aid use, she never tried amplification. The patient lives by herself and is not active socially. Her major communication complaint is difficulty in hearing television programs.

The result of O.O.'s basic audiometric evaluation are shown in Figure 19-7. The pure-tone audiogram shows a moderate, relatively flat configuration in both ears (RE PTA = 50 dB HL; LE PTA = 52 dB HL). Air-conduction and bone-conduction thresholds show no demonstrable air–bone gap. In spite of normal tympanometric and static immittance results, acoustic reflexes are absent, with sound presented

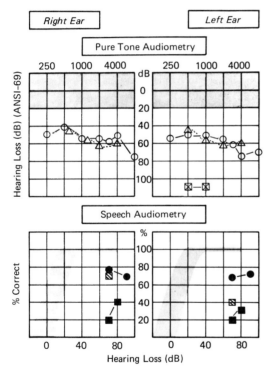

Figure 19-7. Results of basic audiometric evaluation of case III, an 83-year-old woman. Pure-tone audiometry shows a moderate, relatively flat sensorineural hearing loss bilaterally. Acoustic reflex threshold levels are elevated. Speech audiometry reveals "central" presbyacusis (performance for sentences more than 20% poorer than performance for words). This patient is experiencing difficulty with hearing aid use.

to the right ear, and elevated, with sound presented to the left ear (110 dB HL). In the absence of a middle ear disorder, this result suggests brain-stem auditory pathway dysfunction.

The results of speech audiometry are consistent with central presbyacusis. Performance for words (PB) is good in both ears (RE PB $_{max}$ = 76%; LE PB $_{max}$ = 72%). Performance for sentences (SSI-0 dB MCR) is substantially poorer (RE SSI $_{max}$ = 40%; LE SSI $_{max}$ = 30%). Performance for an easier sentence identification task (SSI +10 dB MCR) is only somewhat better (RE SSI +10 dB = 70%; LE SSI +10 dB = 40%). Her exceedingly poorer performance of sentence identification tasks reveals a pronounced, central age-related component.

The patient was evaluated for hearing aid use by speech audiometric techniques. She demonstrated excellent speech understanding improvement in easy listening conditions (90 to 100%), but only limited improvement in more difficult listening conditions (40%). A hearing aid was recommended for use in her right ear.

Adjustment to the hearing aid has been difficult for O.O. She complains of only occasional benefit, "sometimes it helps, but sometimes it doesn't. . . ." She has had numerous hours of follow-up counseling and services. Although O.O. is motivated to continue hearing aid use, she is disappointed with the limitations of amplification. She uses her hearing aid approximately 4 to 6 hours daily.

Among presbyacusic patients, O.O.'s experience is not uncommon. There is frequently a considerable discrepancy between apparent potential for, and actual benefit from, hearing aid use. Based on tests of pure-tone sensitivity and word recognition ability, O.O. appears to be an ideal hearing aid candidate. She exhibits sufficient hearing loss to warrant amplification, and word recognition ability is quite good. However, performance for the more difficult, sentence identification task reveals a substantial age-related central component. This central component affects the potential for satisfactory hearing aid use, especially in difficult listening conditions. If amplification is recommended, the central presbyacusic patient typically requires considerably more counseling and follow-up services than either peripheral or mixed presbyacusic patients. Nevertheless, with repeated and realistic counseling, and professional dedication to successful rehabilitation, even patients with pronounced central auditory aging can benefit from amplification.

Summary

These three cases illustrate the diverse nature of presbyacusis. Although the pure-tone audiograms demonstrate the characteristic, age-related mild-to-moderate, bilaterally symmetrical sensorineural loss, speech audiometry reveals the wide range of peripheral and central effects. Case I demonstrates primarily peripheral presbyacusis and an expectedly successful auditory rehabilitation. Case II illustrates mixed presbyacusis with satisfactory, part-time hearing aid use. Finally, case III shows the effects of central presbyacusis on auditory rehabilitation. Satisfactory hearing aid use may be achieved with intensive counseling and follow-up services.

Presbyacusis may be expected to affect most elderly individuals in one form or another. It is imperative that continuing efforts are made to reduce the isolation and frustration of the patient with the devastating handicap of age-related hearing loss.

References

Anderson, H., Barr, B., and Wedenberg, E. (1969). Intra-aural reflexes in retrocochlear lesions. Nobel Symposium 10: Disorders of the Skull Base Region. Almqvist and Wiksell, Stockholm.

Bergman, M. (1971). Hearing and aging. Audiol. 10, 164–171.

Bergman, M., Blumfield, V., Cascardo, D., Dash, B., Levitt, H., and Marguiles, M. (1973). Age-related decrement in hearing for speech: sampling and longitudinal studies. J. Gerontol. 31, 533–538.

Blumenfeld, V., Bergman, M., and Millner, E. (1969). Speech discrimination in an aging population. J. Speech Hear. Res. 12, 210–217.

Bredberg, D. (1967). The human cochlea during development and aging. J. Laryngol. 84, 439–458.

Brody, H. (1955). Organization of the cerebral cortex. Study of aging in human cerebral cortex. J. Comp. Neurol. 102, 511–556.

Bunch, C.C. (1929). Age variations in auditory acuity. Arch. Otolaryngol. 9, 625–636.

Bunch, C.C. (1931). Further observations on age variations in auditory acuity. Arch. Otolaryngol. 13, 170–180.

Calearo, C. and Lazzaroni, A. (1957). Speech intelligibility in relation to the speech of the message. Laryngoscope 67, 410–419.

Corso, J.F. (1963). Age and sex differences in pure tone thresholds. Arch. Otolaryngol. 77, 385–405.

Etholm, B. and Belal, A. (1974). Senile changes in the middle ear joints. Ann. Otol. Rhinol. Laryngol. 83, 49–54.

Fisch, U., Dubozi, M., and Grieg, D. (1972). Degenerative changes of arterial vessels of the internal auditory meatus during the process of aging. Acta Otolaryngol. 73, 259–264.

Gaeth, J. (1948). A study of phonemic regression in relation to hearing loss. Unpublished doctoral dissertation. Northwestern University.

Gang, R. (1976). The effects of age on the diagnostic utility of the rollover phenomenon. J. Speech Hear. Disorders. 41, 63–69.

Glorig, A. and Davis, H. (1961). Age, noise and hearing loss. Trans. Amer. Otol. Soc. 49, 262–280.

Goetzinger, C., Proud, G., Dirks, D., and Embrey, J. (1961). A study of hearing in advanced age. Arch. Otolaryngol. 73, 662–674.

Hall, J. (1979). Effects of age and sex on static compliance. Arch. Otolaryngol. 105, 153–156.

Handler, S. and Margolis, R. (1977). Prediction of hearing loss from stapedius reflex thresholds in patients with sensori-neural impairment. Trans. AAOO. 84, 425–431.

Hansen, C.C. and Reske-Nielsen, E. (1965). Pathological studies in presbycusis. Arch. Otolaryngol. 82, 115–132.

Hayes, D. and Jerger, J. (1979a). Low-frequency hearing loss in presbycusis—a central interpretation. Arch. Otolaryngol. 105, 9–12.

Hayes, D. and Jerger, J. (1979b). Aging and the use of hearing aids. Scand. Audiol. 8, 33–40.

Hinchcliffe, R. (1959). The threshold of hearing as a function of age. Acustica 9, 303–308.

Hinchcliffe, R. (1962a). The anatomical locus

of presbycusis. J. Speech Hear. Dis. 27, 301–310.

Hinchcliffe, R. (1962b). Aging and sensory thresholds. J. Gerontol. 17, 45–50.

Ishii, T., Murakami, Y., Kimura, R.S., and Balogh, K. (1967). Electron microscopic and histochemical identification of lipofuscin in the human inner ear. Acta Otolaryngol. 64, 17–29.

Jerger, J. (1973). Audiological findings in aging. Adv. Oto-Rhino-Laryngol. (Basel) 20, 115–124.

Jerger, J. and Brown, D. (1982). Personal communication.

Jerger, J., Burney, P., Mauldin, L., and Crump, B. (1974). Predicting hearing loss from the acoustic reflex. J. Speech Hear. Disorders 39, 11–22.

Jerger, J. and Hayes, D. (1976). Hearing aid evaluation: Clinical experience with a new philosophy. Arch. Otolaryngol. 102, 214–225.

Jerger, J. and Hayes, D. (1977). Diagnostic speech audiometry. Arch. Otolaryngol. 103, 216–222.

Jerger, J., Hayes, D., and Anthony, L. (1978b). Effect of age on prediction of sensori-neural hearing level from the acoustic reflex. Arch. Otolaryngol. 104, 393–394.

Jerger, J., Hayes, D., Mauldin, L., and Anthony, L. (1978a). Factors influencing prediction of hearing level from the acoustic reflex. Monographs in Comtemporary Audiology, Vol. 1, (1).

Jerger, J. and Jerger, S. (1975). Clinical validity of central auditory tests. Scand. Audiol. 4, 147–163.

Jerger, J., Jerger, S., and Mauldin, L. (1972). Studies in impedance audiometry. I. Normal and sensori-neural ears. Arch. Otolaryngol. 96, 513–523.

Jerger, J., Neely, J., and Jerger, S. (1980). Speech, impedance and auditory brainstem response audiometry in brainstem tumors. Importance of a multiple-test strategy. Arch. Otolaryngol. 106, 218–223.

Jerger, J., Speaks, C., and Trammell, J. (1968). A new approach to speech audiometry. J. Speech Hear. Dis. 53, 318–328.

Jerger, S. and Jerger, J. (1980). Low-frequency hearing loss in central auditory disorders. Amer. J. Otol. 2, 1–4.

Jorgensen, M. (1961). Changes of aging in inner ear. Arch. Otolaryngol. 74, 164–170.

Kirikae, I. (1969). Auditory function in advanced age with reference to histological changes in the central auditory system. Intl. Audiol. 8, 221–230.

Kirikae, I., Sato, T., and Shitara, T. (1964). A study of hearing in advanced age. Laryngoscope 74, 205–220.

Konig, E. (1969). Audiological tests in presbycusis. Intl. Audiol. 8, 240–259.

Konigsmark, B.W. and Murphey, E.A. (1970). Volume of the ventral cochlear nucleus in man: Its relationship to neuronal population and age. J. Neuropathol. Exptl. Neurol. 31, 304–316.

McCandless, G. and Parkin, J. (1979). Hearing aid performance relative to site of lesion. Otolaryngol. Head Neck Surg. 87, 871–875.

Merluzzi, F. and Hinchcliffe, R. (1973). Threshold of subjective auditory handicap. Audiol. 12, 65–69.

Milne, J.S. (1977). The air-bone gap in older people. Br. J. Audiol. 11, 1–6.

Møller, M. (1981). Hearing in 70 and 75 year old people: Results from a cross-sectional and longitudinal population study. Amer. J. Otolaryngol. 2, 22–29.

Nadol, J. (1979). Electron microscope findings in presbycusic degeneration of the basal turn of the human cochlea. Otolaryngol. Head Neck Surg. 87, 818–836.

Nadol, J. (1981). The aging peripheral hearing mechanism. In Aging Communication Processes and Disorders, D. Beasley and G. Davis, Eds. Grune & Stratton, New York, 63–85.

Niemeyer, W. (1968). Problems of auditory prosthetics in age. Electromedia 4, 114–117.

Nixon, J.C., Glorig, A., and High, W.S. (1964). Changes in air and bone conduction thresholds as a function of age. J. Laryngol. 76, 288–298.

Noble, W. and Atherly, G. (1970). The hearing measure scale: A questionnaire for the assessment of auditory disability. J. Aud. Res. 10, 229–250.

Orchik, D. and Burgess, J. (1977). Synthetic sentence identification as a function of age of the listener. J. Amer. Audiol. Soc., 3, 42–46.

Osterhammel, D. (1980). High-frequency audiometry: Clinical aspects. Scand. Audiol. 9, 249–256.

Osterhammel, D. and Osterhammel, P. (1979). High-frequency and audiometry: Age and sex variations. Scand. Audiol. 8, 73–81.

Pestalozza, G. and Shore, I. (1955). Clinical evaluation of presbycusis on basis of different tests of auditory function. Laryngoscope, 65, 1136–1163.

Saxen, A. (1952). Inner ear in presbycusis. Acta Otolaryngol. 41, 213–227.

Sataloff, J. and Menduke, H. (1957). Presbycusis. Arch. Otolaryngol. 66, 271–274.

Sataloff, J., Vassalo, L., and Menduke, M. (1965). Presbycusis air and bone conduction thresholds. Laryngoscope 75, 889–901.

Schow, R. and Goldbaum, D. (1980). Collapsed ear canals in the elderly nursing home population. J. Speech Hear. Dis. 45, 259–267.

Schuknecht, H. (1955). Presbycusis. Laryngoscope 65, 202–210.

Schuknecht, H. (1964). Further observations on the pathology of presbycusis. Arch. Otolaryngol. 80, 369–382.

Shirinian, M. and Arnst, D. (1982). Patterns in performance-intensity functions for phonetically balanced word lists and synthetic sentences in aged listeners. Arch. Otolaryngol. 108, 15–20.

Silman, S. (1979). The effects of aging on the stapedius reflex thresholds. J. Acoust. Soc. Amer. 66, 735–738.

Silman, S. and Gelfand, S. (1981). The relationship between magnitude of hearing loss and acoustic reflex threshold levels. J. Speech Hear. Dis. 46, 312–216.

Speaks, C., Jerger, J., and Trammell, J. (1970). Comparison of sentence identification and conventional speech discrimination scores. J. Speech Hear. Res. 13, 755–767.

Spoendlin, H. (1975). Retrograde degeneration of the cochlear nerve. Acta Otolaryngol. 79, 266–275.

U.S. Public Health Service, National Center for Health Statistics. (1967). Characteristics of persons with impaired hearing. Vital and Health Statistics. U.S. Dept. of H.E.W., Washington, D.C.

Wright, J. and Schuknecht, H. (1972). Atrophy of the spiral ligament. Arch. Otolaryngol. 96, 16–21.

V
Motor System and Sensation

20. Aging and Human Locomotion

RAYMOND D. ADAMS

Upright stance and bipedal locomotion are distinctive attributes of the human species. The neural sequences on which they depend are as basic as a spinal reflex, but because of their complexity, they are more properly considered as instinctive. They evolve early in life in conformity to a predictable timetable. Every child walks between the age of 9 and 18 months, no matter the circumstances under which he is reared. Locomotion of the more elementary types then becomes perfected in the following years, after which it gradually is adapted to all the feats of skill involved in work and sports.

There is a tendency to think of locomotion as being present or absent in a kind of all-or-none fashion. Of course, every sensible person is most aware of the dreadful consequences of a disease, such as a spinal injury, that leaves a patient permanently paraplegic. Unappreciated are the more subtle alterations of locomotion that occur from early adult life to the end of the senium and which appear to be related to aging rather than to disease. It is these aging effects that will be described here.

But first, to be more specific about types and degrees of gait change seen clinically, a few remarks about the normal adult gait and the possible ways in which it deteriorates are in order.

Normal Locomotion in the Young Adult

One seldom is forced to think about the normal gait, for it is so natural as to be taken for granted. Yet, it should be observed carefully if slight deviations are to be appreciated. Adams and Victor (1981) describe the normal gait as follows:

The body is erect, the head straight, the arms hanging loosely and gracefully at the sides, each moving rhythmically forward with the opposite leg. The feet are slightly everted and the steps are of moderate length and approximately equal, the internal malleoli of the tibias almost touching and each foot being placed almost in line with the other. With each step there is a coordinated flexion of hip and knee, dorsiflexion of the foot and a barely perceptible elevation of the hip so that the foot clears the ground. The heel strikes the ground first and inspection of the shoes will show that this part is most subject to wear. The muscles of greatest importance in maintaining the erect posture are the erector spinae and the extensors of the knee and hip.

Upon close analysis the normal gait can be reduced to the following elements: 1) antigravity support of the body, 2) stepping, 3) an adequate degree of equilibrium, and 4) a means of propulsion. *Support* is provided by antigravity reflexes which keep the knees, hips, and back in a position of firm extension but modifiable by the position of head and neck. These reflexes depend on the integrity of the spinal cord and brainstem (transection of the neuraxis between the red and vestibular nuclei leads to exaggeration of these antigravity reflexes—decerebrate rigidity). *Stepping* is a basic pattern of movements usually alternating, and present at birth. It is integrated at the midbrain and spinal levels. Its appropriate stimuli are contact of the sole with a flat surface and inclination of the body forward and alternately from side to side. *Equilibrium* involves the maintenance of balance at right angles to the direction of movement. The center of gravity during the continuously unstable equilibrium which prevails in walking must shift from side to side within narrow limits as the weight is borne first on one foot and then on the other. Involved here are the proprioceptive sensory mechanisms, the labyrinths, vision and reflexes under their control, especially via the cerebellum. *Propulsion* is provided by leaning forward and slightly to one side and permitting the body to fall a certain distance before being checked by the support of the leg. Here both forward and alternating lateral movements must occur. But in running, where at one movement both feet are off the ground, a forward thrust or drive of the hind leg is also needed.

Of course, gaits vary enormously as do the natural postures of the body. One can virtually identify people by their manner of walking. Locomotion involves more than walking. In such varied functions as standing, sitting, arising from a chair, turning around, etc., many motor sequences of different types are required.

Once walking and running are achieved, the normal locomotory performances are available to be adapted to a number of acquired skills, such as hopping, skipping, jumping over a barrier, kicking a ball, dancing, riding a bike, playing an organ, etc. None can be acquired until a certain level of maturation of the nervous system has occurred. The mentally retarded often cannot learn these skills, and their locomotion is delayed, primitive, and undifferentiated. In sum, the entire sequence of human locomotory activities is surely programmed by the nervous system. The most elementary ones are inherited; many of the more refined skills are learned, but always the limits of perfection are set by the neural organization.

Locomotory Changes with Age

Many sources of biological data (anatomical and physiological) inform us that aging begins in early adult life and continues until death. Loss of neurons appears to be the basic process, but little is known about the factors that control neuronal death. In the beginning, such physiological changes are slight and subtle and have no presently definable morphological equivalency.

One turns to the accomplished athlete for evidence of the earliest alterations. There is a recognized decline in performance in almost every athletic skill during the fourth decade of life. Only the long-distance runner maintains his capacity during this period. The deficits during the fourth decade are difficult to ascertain. The older player may perform one set of tennis well, but be unable to sustain performance in a long, intensely contested match. Consistency and accuracy of shot-making, as well as agility and stamina, lessen. Older baseball, football, and basketball players experience increasing difficulty in conditioning themselves, especially their legs, and of course, this may involve muscles and joints as well as the fine nervous control of movements. In baseball players, the legs are known to give out before the arms; in fact, eye–hand coordination may be so well preserved that the player continues to play as a "designated hitter" with a younger substitute "running the bases" for him. In the average 30- to 40-year-old individual who has never brought his locomotion and motor skills to this level of perfection, these changes would not be detectable in his daily life.

By the fifth and sixth decade, there is no doubt as to the decline in agility and athletic prowess. One runs more slowly and the normal stamina of the younger person is lacking. On sudden turning, poor balance may cause an unexpected lurch. On the stairs, an occasional misstep results in the toe catching the riser. Many individuals begin to feel more confident touching the banister. In climbing over rocks and logs, the feet "become tangled." A drink or two may occasion a fall on a slick dance floor, to everybody's embarrassment.

These small disabilities have no readily affirmed anatomical or physiological basis. It is noteworthy that positional vertigo occurs with increasing frequency, and labyrinthine function generally becomes less effective during this period of life. Minor postural fluctuations of blood pressure are not unusual, especially in the ill or sedentary person. Arthritis of hips and knees has a way of weakening the legs and interfering with squatting and kneeling.

By the seventh decade, denervation atrophy of the leg muscles is reflected in diminished ankle jerks, and a mild sensory ataxia is added. These latter motor and sensory changes have been traced to a loss of anterior horn cells in the spinal cord and of nerve cells in the dorsal root ganglia, as shown by Tomlinson, et al. (1969) and Morrison (1959). Subtle cerebellar deficits are often associated, but are difficult to separate from the effects of sensory deprivation.

The Senile Gait

All the aforementioned changes are slight and gradual and should not be the source of medical complaint. They more or less parallel similar slight changes in memory and other mental functions, which again are accepted as "normal for age." However, there is a small number of individuals whose gait begins to fail in the eighth and ninth decades of life out of proportion to other neurological deficits. This is the only gait disorder that is thus far ascribed to age alone, an interpretation which, as we shall see, is only tentative. The step shortens gradually until the heel of one foot does not pass the toe of the other and the foot is no longer lifted from the floor. The gait is thus reduced to a shuffle. The base is slightly widened. Turning becomes difficult and requires a series of five to ten steps rather than the normal swift pivot. Upon arising, the first step may be impossible for a few moments, unless the patient is taken by the arm and started. Marching to a military chant may facilitate walking, especially in the old soldier. More often than not, taking the patient by the arm or having him take the examiner's arm does not significantly lengthen the step, and if the examiner walks fast the patient drags behind. Walking a line tandem is impossible. The arms are held at the sides and swing only a few inches, if at all. A variable resistance is encountered on attempting to passively flex and extend the arms and legs. It is as if the patient is incapable of relaxing the limbs voluntarily. Kleist (1927) referred to this condition as gegenhalten and Dupré (1910) used a more general term, "paratonic rigidity." Grasping and sucking reflexes

appear to be released in some cases. The posture of the trunk is variably flexed and the eyes are fixed straight ahead. The arm movements are relatively normal. Running is impossible.

For a time, the patient ascribes his walking difficulty to a lack of self-confidence or a fear of falling, and indeed he should be apprehensive, for hurtful falls are frequent. He beseeches the examiner to refer him to a rehabilitation center or to a psychotherapist.

As locomotion continues to fail, the patient reaches a stage at which he cannot walk unassisted, and later he can only stand. Sitting down becomes hazardous. The patient approaches a chair, turns, sidling cautiously toward it, but is unable to place his buttocks on the seat. He may land on the edge or side and fall off. Later, he is reduced to bed and chair existence and finally to bed. The ultimate in gait dissolution is to be curled up in bed, the legs flexed and relatively useless and only the hands, face, and tongue mobile. This is the state termed "cerebral paraplegia in flexion" by Yakovlev (1954) who thinks of it as a reversion to the fetal position that begins and presumably ends life. In this advanced bed-fast stage of the locomotory disorder, the patient is nearly always profoundly demented.

At a stage when the patient is walking with "le march à petits pas," but is unable to move the legs freely while lying down, neurologists have tended to refer to the condition as "apraxia of gait." But if by apraxia we mean loss of learned motor skills in the absence of paresis, ataxia, or extrapyramidal or sensory deficit, the term is obviously inappropriate for, as was stated above, one does not learn to walk. If an ataxic element presents, the term "frontal lobe ataxia" is a common designation, but again without other signs of ataxia or intention tremor.

Implicit in both these terms is the postulation of a bifrontal lesion, but here speculation outruns anatomy. In isolated instances of complete bilateral prefrontal lobotomy for tumor, such as the case reported by Brickner (1936), gait was not affected. Only when the primary and secondary motor areas are included in the lesion is mobility disturbed, and then in a different way—that of a spastic hemiparesis or quadriparesis with the Wernick–Mann postural set of flexed arm and extended leg. In the anatomical studies of Yakovlev (1954), the five autopsied cases were all young degenerate epileptics; and, as Yakovlev himself pointed out, the material had been in formalin so long before sectioning that detailed cytological studies were virtually impossible. The author had an opportunity to review the sections of these cases some years ago and agrees that the Nissl stains were uninterpretable. Myelin stains revealed widespread cerebral atrophy, frontal more than other parts, and also an atrophy of the lateral parts of the globus pallidi. In addition, the tracts of the brain stem and thalami were affected widely. Only the cerebellum was relatively spared. The diffuse topography of the lesions was not surprising for the patients had been both amented and demented. Moreover, as was pointed out by Yakovlev (1954) in his description of the senile population with cerebral paraplegia in flexion, a severe dementia and apathy were concomitant phenomena. The only tentative conclusion that can be drawn is that the senile gait disorder must represent a combination of frontal lobe and basal ganglia degeneration and that no case to date has had an adequate postmortem examination, particularly the type of case in which the senile gait was not accompanied by dementia. Also, the idea that the small-stepped gait is a pure effect of aging is open to question. Equally plausible is the possibility that it is an age-linked disease of multiple etiologies.

A more detailed neurological examination of such patients shows the basic disorder to be one of steppage and equilibrium and only later do support and propulsion fail. Certain parts of the nervous system are more or less exonerated. As a rule, the tendon reflexes are not hyperactive, there is no Babinski sign, and the leg muscles are not weakened. Thus, one must assume that the corticospinal tracts are intact. Yakovlev (1954) points out that reflexes of defense, if present, differ from the spinal flexor automatisms the French called *contracture tendin-réflèxe* with pyramidal signs. Instead, the primary modalities of sensation are preserved, Babinski signs are absent, and the stimulus that evokes flexion is contact of the more proximal parts of the lower extremities. To this Babinski (1934) gave the term *contracture cutanéo-réflèxe*. Rigidity is of the paratonic type and not that of Parkinsonism and the latter is excluded by the lack of tremor and bradykinesia. There is no ataxia.

Age-Linked Diseases in which Disorder of Locomotion is a Prominent Feature

Other abnormalities in gait in late life are associated with the following diseases: multi-infarct dementia; normal pressure hydrocephalus; Parkinson's disease with dementia; agitated depression with neuroleptic drug effects; and the Steele–Richardson syndrome. Since these diseases have a predilection for the senium, they must be distinguished from aging.

It is rather interesting that in the most frequent of the degenerative diseases of late life, namely Alzheimer-senile dementia, early gait disorder is a rarity. In nearly every case, memory failure, language and calculation disorders, and impaired thinking are the initial abnormalities. Only in far advanced cases, usually to be found in institutions for the infirm, does locomotion deteriorate. Some patients will then become unable to walk, will curl up in bed, and become virtually paraplegic.

In contrast, multi-infarct diseases of the nervous system may produce hemiparetic or quadriparetic signs and there may also be cerebellar deficits. In some instances, patients with bilateral pyramidal signs may show rigidity and tremor. Critchley (1929) called this *arteriosclerotic Parkinson's syndrome*. However, in our pathological material, such patients have been proven to be examples of paralysis agitans with unrelated vascular disease. The vascular lesions have not affected the substantia nigra or nigro-striatal connections. In other cases, a review of the clinical findings reveals evidence of corticospinal and corticobulbar signs that may have been misinterpreted as Parkinson's disease.

Our clinical experience of normal pressure hydrocephalus, in which gait disorder has proven to be one of the earliest findings, have been of interest. In nearly all cases in which a ventriculo-atrial or ventriculo-peritoneal shunt was successful in relieving the clinical symptoms, gait disorder has preceded mental changes. The abnormality of gait begins as a slight insecurity of balance. The patient is inclined to touch the wall or articles of furniture for assurance as he walks, or he seeks the arm of a companion. The movements of the legs become rather stiff, the steps shorten slightly, and the base widens. The possibility of Parkinson's disease may be suggested, but there is no tremor, rigidity, or slowness of alternating movements. Because of an inability to walk a line tandem the possibility of a cerebellar ataxia is raised, but again, there is no intention tremor, ataxia of leg movements, or irregular slowing of alternating movements, the more convincing signs of cerebellar deficit. In some obscure way, the sequences of movement necessary to maintain equipoise under the constantly changing conditions of walking, turning, and standing are inadequate. A given group of muscles, when called upon to adjust posture or equilibrium, does not act at the proper moment. Sometimes there are tonic foot responses, suggesting a premotor disorder, but this has never been confirmed pathologically. "Drop attacks" are observed in some cases, and once on the floor, the fully conscious patient may be unable to arise for several minutes unless aided. Further progression of the hydrocephalus may result, finally, in inability to walk, to stand, and even to sit, and these motor deficits regress in reverse order after shunting. The anatomical basis of the gait disorder of normal pressure hydrocephalus has not been established. There are elements of premotor involvement, as the commonly associated sphincteric incontinence indicates. We favor the notion that it is mainly a disorder of frontal lobe connections with basal ganglia.

The severely demented patient who is receiving neuroleptic drugs for depression and agitation may pose a number of special problems in gait analysis. First, some of these patients have Parkinson's disease and have become demented or depressed. But usually, the signs of Parkinson's disease are unmistakable, if a careful examination is made, and by history they will have preceded the depression or dementia. Some such patients have a severe retarded depression and will sit immobile in a slightly flexed position so that even an experienced neurologist may diagnose Parkinson's disease. Locomotion and posture become normal as the depression responds to therapy. Chlorpromazine and other neuroleptic drugs frequently induce some of the symptoms of Parkinson's disease. The gait becomes stiff, the steps are shorter, the natural grace of body movements disappears and the arms swing little if at all. A fine tremor may be added, particularly if lithium is used as therapy.

In Steele–Richardson disease, we have observed a number of changes in gait and equilibrium, appearing sometimes before the more characteristic supranuclear paralysis of vertical gaze and dystonia of cervical musculature. In some instances, the gait becomes mincing and short-stepped in a manner suggestive of Parkinson's disease. In others there is a curious "toppling." The patient moves suddenly, lurches as though off balance, and crashes to the floor. In all probability, there is an impairment of the vestibular control of balance, yet the patient does not complain of vertigo and there is no evidence of cerebellar ataxia. A similar "toppling" is sometimes observed in other diseases causing lesions at the brain-stem level.

Summary

In sum, the author would emphasize the wide variety of disturbances of locomotion that are to be observed in the senile patient. Some are relatively stereotyped and characteristic of, though not specific to, the aging process per se and may occur as isolated phenomena. The relationship of the short-stepped gait of the aged to the subtle and progressive changes in motility that begin to appear in middle age and continue into the senium is unclear. Finally, it is pointed out that many age-linked diseases of late life de-range locomotion in characteristic ways. Knowledge of the type and significance of these gait disorders is of value in diagnostic medicine.

References

Adams, R.D. and Victor, M. (1981). Principles of Neurology. Ch. 5, 2nd Ed. McGraw-Hill, New York.

Babinski, J. (1934). Sur une forme de paraplégie spasmodique consécutive à une lésion organique et sans dégénération du système pyramidal, Mem Soc., Med. Hop. Parks, 1899, cited in Oevre Scientifique, Masson et Cie, Paris, p. 315.

Brickner, R.M. (1936). The Intellectual Functions of the Frontal Lobes. MacMillan, New York.

Critchley, M. (1929). Arteriosclerotic parkinsonism. Brain, 52, 23, 1929.

Dupré, E. (1910). Débilite mentale et débilite motrice associée. Abstr. Rev. Neurol. 2, 54.

Kleist, K. (1927). Gegenhalten (Motorischer Negativismus) Zwangsgreifen und Thalamus Opticus. Monatschr Psychiat Neurol. 65, 317.

Martin, J.P. (1963). The basal ganglia and locomotion, Ann. Roy. Coll. Surg. (Engl.) 22, 219.

Morrison, L.R. (1959). The Effect of Advancing Age Upon the Human Spinal Cord. Harvard University Press, Cambridge, Mass.

Tomlinson, B.E., Walton, J.N., and Rebeiz, J.J. (1969). The effects of ageing and of cachexia upon skeletal muscle. A histopathologic study. J. Neurol. Sci. 9, 321.

Yakovlev, P.I. (1954). Paraplegia flexion of cerebral origin. J. Neuropathol. Exptl. Neurol. 13, 267.

21. Movement Disorders in the Elderly

HAROLD L. KLAWANS

CAROLINE M. TANNER

The term "movement disorders" includes a variety of syndromes that involve abnormalities in the control of movement and the production of abnormal involuntary movements. Movement disorders in the elderly may be of diverse etiologies, but most commonly they are related to isolated central nervous system degenerative processes or to metabolic disorders of the nervous system associated with systemic illnesses. Less common etiologies include cerebrovascular disease, neoplasm, and infection. In general, the diagnosis and management of these disorders depends more on the clinical acumen of the physician than on any specific test or set of tests. In the first part of this chapter, the individual clinical manifestations of specific disorders of movement, their differentiation, and those etiologies most common in the senium will be presented. In the second part, specific diseases or clinical syndromes will be discussed, with the emphasis on diagnosis and management.

Tremor

A tremor is a rhythmic form of abnormal involuntary movement in which an alternating involvement of the agonists and

This work was supported in part by the United Parkinson Foundation and the Boothroyd Foundation, Chicago, IL.

antagonists at any one joint results in a regular patterned movement. Tremors may be conveniently classified as those maximal at rest (resting tremors), those maximal with maintenance of a specific posture (postural tremors), and those maximal at the end of purposeful motor acts (intention tremors). Although many tremors may show more than one of these characteristics, in general, one will predominate. The correct clinical description of a particular tremor is critical to effective diagnosis and management of the underlying disorder (Table 21-1).

REST TREMOR

The tremor of parkinsonism is a rest tremor, that is, it occurs at rest and disappears on purposeful movement (Parkinson, 1817). It usually is aborted by the initiation of any willed act, but may reappear a few moments later, despite continuation of the action. In most cases, however, the tremor is less prominent on action than it is during rest and is characteristically absent during sleep.

Usually the tremor is insidious in onset. Invariably it affects the distal parts of the extremity earlier and to a greater extent than the proximal parts. It is most prominent in the fingers, often less prominent in the wrists, and involves the forearm or upper arm only infrequently. The rate of

Table 21-1. Classification of Tremors.

Type	Characteristics
Resting tremor of Parkinson's disease	Rhythmic oscillatory movement in relaxed limbs. Decreased by intention
Postural or essential tremor	Rhythmic movements of distal upper extremities during maintenance of a posture
Intention tremor	Rhythmic involuntary movement of fingers superimposed on purposeful action

the tremor averages about three to five oscillations per second. A number of descriptive terms, such as pill-rolling or cigarette-rolling, have been used to describe these movements, but the rotary component is often lacking, so that the term to-and-fro is more appropriate. The tremor can also involve the leg, where again it is usually more marked distally in the foot than it is proximally in the hip. The head, jaw, and pectoral structures can also become involved.

Although manifestations of Parkinsonism almost always involve the entire body, the symptoms can be markedly asymmetrical. This is especially true of the tremor, which frequently begins in one arm or one leg and can remain predominantly unilateral for several years.

Resting tremor is the hallmark of parkinsonism of any etiology. It may also be seen in more diffuse degenerative disorders with associated parkinsonian symptoms, such as the Shy–Drager syndrome, olivopontocerebellar degeneration, Wilson's disease, and progressive supranuclear palsy. Drug-induced parkinsonism is clinically identical to idiopathic parkinsonism.

POSTURAL TREMOR

Postural tremor is the term used to describe the abnormal movement that is most prominent in limbs maintaining a static posture against gravity. Postural tremor is most frequently seen in the complex of benign essential–familial–senile tremor and is considered to be the sole manifestation of a benign monosymptomatic disorder of the central nervous system

(Critchley, 1949). Essential tremor generally involves the distal parts of the upper extremities and is relatively rhythmic at a varying frequency of 4 to 12 Hz. Although usually unilateral in onset, the movement almost always becomes bilateral and symmetrical. Essential tremor can start at any age, but is most frequent in the sixth and the seventh decade. The patient may or may not have a family history of the disorder. The tremor is often exacerbated when the involved extremity is used in tasks requiring precision, such as writing. Like other involuntary movement disorders, postural tremor is aggravated by emotional stress and fatigue.

The patient with essential tremor may have involuntary movements of the head and neck, called titubation. When the patient attempts to maintain normal head posture, involuntary rhythmic movements may occur in either a vertical ("yes-yes" pattern) or a horizontal ("no-no" pattern) plane. This may be the sole manifestation of the disorder or it may coexist with tremor of the extremities.

To test for the presence of postural tremor, the physician should instruct the patient to extend the arms in the outstretched position. In postural tremor, the tremor is absent at rest (for example, hands relaxed in the lap), marked on maintaining the posture with the arms and fingers extended, decreased to some extent by movement (for example, bringing the finger in to touch the nose), but it will reappear on maintaining another posture, such as holding the finger in front of the nose. Watching the patient write is also frequently helpful. In parkinsonism, the initiation of writing ameliorates the tremor. In benign essential tremor, attempting to maintain the hand posture for handwriting exacerbates the tremor. In the former, the handwriting itself is small and cramped, with a fine tremor, if any. In the latter it is large and messy, with an obvious marked tremor. Postural tremor may also be seen in patients treated with lithium carbonate, the tricyclic antidepressants, or various sympathetic drugs; in patients undergoing alcohol withdrawal; and in patients with thyrotoxicosis.

INTENTION TREMOR

A rhythmic involuntary movement superimposed on purposeful action, intention tremor is maximal when approaching the goal of the movement. The intentional component of the tremor is most obvious at the termination of purposeful movement, so that a patient asked to touch the examiner's finger with outstretched arm and index finger will be unable to maintain a stable end-point posture, although tremor during the actual movement may have been much less marked. An identical tremor is often seen in patients with cerebellar disease or multiple sclerosis (Brown, 1981). It is often present in association with postural tremor and, thus, is a characteristic component of benign essential tremor. Patients with parkinson-

ism will occasionally display both resting and intention tremors, especially during periods of stress.

Abnormalities of Tone

Tone is defined as the resistance present in a resting muscle. Tone is assessed on physical examination by moving a specific joint through the full range of motion, while the patient maintains those muscles at rest (Fig. 21-1). In practice, it is difficult for many persons to avoid involuntarily assisting the examiner. Such techniques as distraction with idle conversation and random, unpredictable directions of motion further assure that the muscle groups tested are at rest. Tone may be normal, increased, or decreased in movement disorders.

Hypertonicity

RIGIDITY

Rigidity is a form of increased resistance to passive movement (Wilson, 1925). If rigidity is diffusely present, it is felt best in the arm, especially at the wrist and over the biceps. Rigidity is present in both agonists and antagonists and is present throughout the entire range of motion. When it is of similar intensity throughout the range of motion, it is often called lead-pipe rigidity. In other instances, however, the hyper-

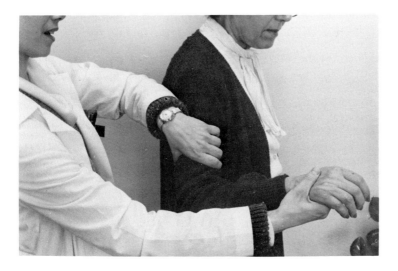

Figure 21-1. Technique for evaluating resistance to passive movement. The examiner simultaneous moves both the wrist and elbow joint, while palpating the biceps and the wrist.

tonic muscle, when passively stretched, exhibits an irregular jerkiness as if it were being pulled out over a ratchet. This results in an alternating series of jerks referred to as cogwheel rigidity. Although rigidity of the lead-pipe variety may be appreciated in a variety of disorders involving the extrapyramidal system, cogwheel rigidity is a major symptom of parkinsonism. Rigidity must be differentiated from two other types of increased tone: spasticity and gegenhalten.

SPASTICITY

Spasticity is the type of increased muscle tone seen in lesions of the pyramidal tract (Young and Delwaide, 1981). In spasticity, agonists and antagonists are not involved equally. The increased tone of spasticity is most marked in the flexors of the arm and the extensors of the leg and is not equal in the flexors or extensors of each extremity. In spasticity, the tone suddenly gives out following an initial resistance to sudden passive movements. This clasp-knife phenomenon is seen only in spasticity and helps to differentiate it from rigidity.

GEGENHALTEN

A manifestation of diffuse frontal lobe disease, gegenhalten is a form of increased resistance to passive movement in which the degree of resistance parallels the degree of effort on the part of the examiner. The harder the examiner pushes, the more the patient resists. This is not seen in rigidity or spasticity.

The presence of either spasticity or gegenhalten implies an involvement of the brain greater than that which occurs in pure idiopathic parkinsonism. Spasticity implies disease of the pyramidal system, whereas gegenhalten implies frontal lobe disease. The latter is often associated with akinesia, dementia, and primitive reflexes such as grasp and snout. It is important to differentiate parkinsonism due to localized dysfunction of the substantia nigra from these more diffuse diseases, since only the former is likely to respond to treatment with levodopa or dopaminergic agonists.

Hypotonicity

Diminished resting tone may occur in patients with two general classes of disorder—those with chorea and those with cerebellar hemispheral disease. Passive motion at the joint is accomplished with great facility. In patients with cerebellar disorders, especially, the ability to "check" a reflex rebound of a suddenly released limb, when the patient is actively resisting the examiner, may be absent.

Akinesia

The terms akinesia and bradykinesia refer to three related goups of symptoms. These are (1) a marked poverty of spontaneous movements, (2) a loss of normal associated movements, and (3) slowness in the initiation and execution of all voluntary movements (Klawans and Cohen, 1970). The manifestations of akinesia include the "masked" parkinsonian facies that demonstrates a marked poverty of movement, both volitional and emotional. The facial features are flattened and the face is smoother than normal. When this is combined with the characteristic lack of facial movement, a frozen or wooden expression results. Whatever emotional responses are possible are slow in developing, but can become prolonged, resulting in a frozen smile. The term reptilian stare describes the characteristic lack of blinking and wide palpebral fissures superimposed on the motionless facial background in parkinsonism.

Patients often sit immobile, seldom crossing their legs, folding their arms, or displaying any of the wide variety of spontaneous movements seen in normal individuals at rest. They have a great deal of difficulty initiating gross movements. The simple task of getting up from a chair is often difficult. This is especially true of a low, soft chair. Patients may have to make a great effort with their arms, and rock back and forth several times, in order to rise from a deep chair. Patients may be unable to initiate this movement at a stage in the disease when they are still able to work and to carry out most of their daily activities.

Characteristically, many associated movements are affected. The most important of these is the swinging of arms on walking or running. These are frequently diminished early in the course of parkinsonism, and may also be decreased in other disorders of the basal ganglia and their associated structures, such as dystonias. In general, extensive bradykinetic symptoms are uncommon in non-parkinsonian patients, although fine coordinated movements may be diminished in some patients with dystonic disorders.

It is important to differentiate the akinesia of parkinsonism from the loss of willed activity in depression, since inappropriate diagnosis of the parkinsonian patient as depressed delays effective therapy.

Disorders of Posture and Balance

Patients with movement disorders may suffer from two general types of balance disorder, striatally mediated loss of postural reflexes and cerebellar gait ataxia. Although these disorders may coexist, it is often possible to make clear clinical distinctions of significant diagnostic value.

LOSS OF POSTURAL REFLEXES

Until recently, the disorders of postural fixation, equilibrium, and righting reactions that are commonly seen in parkinsonism have been largely ignored (Klawans and Cohen, 1970). The term "postural fixation" means support of part of the body for the purpose of maintaining a posture, not for the purpose of carrying out a specific act with that part of the body. An example of this is the support given to the arm at the shoulder during the use of the hand. In patients with Parkinson's disease, postural fixation of the head is often abnormal. A patient's head may fall forward while the patient is in an upright position. This falling forward of the head is reminiscent of the way a normal person's head falls as he becomes drowsy. In parkinsonism, it occurs while the patient is wide awake. The lapses of postural fixation can occur despite significant amounts of rigidity. Parkinsonian patients may also have difficulty in postural fixation of their trunk, so that they

are unable to maintain an upright position while seated or, rarely, be unable to maintain an upright position of the trunk while standing or walking; the result is the stooped parkinsonian posture. It is not uncommon for this postural abnormality to be asymmetrical, so that the patient may sit or stand leaning to one side. These patients may also demonstrate difficulty in maintaining the posture of either their arms or their legs.

A large number of patients have signs that demonstrate their lack of normal reflex reactions. A patient with Parkinson's disease frequently is able to walk quite well and support the body against the normal forces of gravity; however, if other forces are added, there is a great deal of difficulty in opposing them. The patient is easily displaced by pushing. A single shove on the chest may produce a series of backward steps or a retropulsion the patient cannot prevent. In more severely involved individuals, a similar push may result in the patient falling. This occurs whether or not the patient is expecting to be pushed. It is a common experience that, even in a patient expecting the push, a minimal effort on the part of the examiner will produce profound retropulsion (Figure 21-2). When pushed from behind, an analogous propulsion may occur. Loss of postural reflexes resulting in sudden episodes of falling can be the initial complaint of parkinsonism, and if this is not associated with other signs of the disease, there may be great difficulty in diagnosis and thus, treatment. Over the last decade, we have observed numerous patients in whom loss of postural reflexes was the presenting complaint of a parkinsonian state. These were all patients over the age of 60 whose only symptom was falling. Recognition of parkinsonism as a cause of falling in this age group is important, so that correct and effective therapy can be initiated.

CEREBELLAR GAIT ATAXIA

A second abnormality of balance may be observed in patients with disease of the cerebellar vermis (Brown, 1981). These patients are unable to stand or walk without maintaining a wide distance between their feet (broad-based gait). If

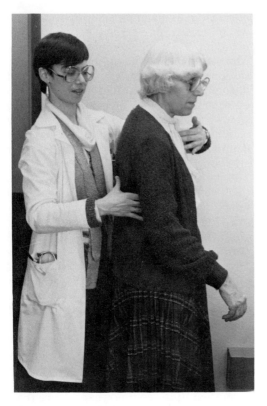

Figure 21-2. Technique for safely evaluating postural reflexes with the examiner stationed behind the patient, to catch the patient if necessary, and reaching around to apply pressure.

involvement is more severe, patients will be unable to maintain a sitting posture without the additional support of their arms. Patients with postural and balance problems of cerebellar origin may be distinguished from patients with striatal disease by their absolute inability to maintain a tandem stance (that is, one heel directly touching the toe of the other foot as if the patient were standing on a tightrope). By contrast, parkinsonian patients with significant retropulsion after a minimal postural threat can maintain such a stance.

Choreatic Disorders

CHOREA

The word chorea is derived from the Greek word for "dance" and was origi-

nally applied to the dance-like gait and continual limb movements seen in acute infectious chorea (Klawans and Cohen, 1970). The exact meaning of the term has changed significantly; "chorea" is now used to describe an entire class of abnormal spontaneous movements. A choreatic movement is a single, isolated muscle action, producing a short, rapid, uncoordinated jerk of the face, trunk, or extremities. The movements affecting the limbs are most often distal, although proximal musculature may be involved. Two or more successive or simultaneous choreiform movements can produce complex movement patterns, and when superimposed on normal walking, they result in a dance-like gait. Often, a patient attempts to conceal the abnormal movement by a volitional action, such as crossing the legs to conceal a spontaneous movement of the lower leg.

The usual causes of chorea in the elderly are shown in Table 21-2. These disorders will be discussed in more depth in the second part of this chapter.

CHOREOATHETOSIS

Athetosis refers to slow, writhing, involuntary movements at one or more joints and often involves entire body parts. Finer choreiform movements are commonly superimposed on the slower and grosser athetoid movements, so that the final clinical picture is best described as choreoathetosis. In general, those clinical syndromes resulting in chorea also produce choreoathetosis.

HEMIBALLISMUS

Hemiballismus (Klawans et al., 1976) is an uncommon, involuntary movement dis-

Table 21-2. Cause of Chorea in the Elderly.

Spontaneous oral masticatory syndrome of the elderly

Senile chorea

Neuroleptic-induced tardive dyskinesia

Huntington's disease

Other drug-induced choreas: Central stimulants; phenytoin

Acquired hepatocerebral degeneration

order characterized by wild, flailing movements of the extremities on one side of the body; they are most marked in the arm. This disorder generally presents with violent, flinging movements of the upper extremity that resemble a severe form of choreoathetosis. The movements are constant, exacerbated by stress, ameliorated by relaxation, and usually absent in sleep. The etiology of hemiballismus is most commonly vascular, although ballistic movements may rarely be seen as one component of a generalized choreiform disorder. Diagnosis and management will be discussed in more detail below.

Dystonias

Characteristically, dystonic movements are relatively slow and long sustained (Klawans and Weiner, 1981a). The maintenance of an abnormal or altered posture involving either a single focal part of the body or a diffuse region is the *sine qua non* of dystonia. Frequently, spasmodic or jerky movements are superimposed on this sustained postural abnormality. Dystonia can either be generalized or partial, but generalized dystonia is exceptionally rare in the elderly. The more common forms of partial or segmental dystonia are listed in Table 21-2 and will be discussed later in this chapter.

Myoclonus

Myoclonus is a brief, lightning-like jerk of a group of muscle fibers, an entire muscle, or groups of muscles, and is abrupt and involuntary. Myoclonic movements may be single or repetitive, but they are generally nonrhythmic and asymmetrical. Some myoclonic disorders may have a particular situational character, including those produced by particular stimuli or those present during early sleep, whereas others may show no apparent relationship.

Myoclonus may be caused by a variety of disorders affecting multiple levels of the neuraxis (Kinsbourne and Rosenfeld, 1975). In the elderly population, myoclonus is most commonly seen in degenerative disorders, toxic states, and as part of a benign, life-long disorder.

Tics

Tics (Friedhoff and Chase, 1982) are brief, seemingly purposeful involuntary movements of muscle groups functioning in a normal relationship to one another. They are repetitive, nonrhythmic, and stereotypic. In the elderly population, tics may be seen as either the manifestation of a life-long disorder (Tourette syndrome) or as simple movements of adult onset.

Parkinson's Disease

Parkinson's disease is a symptom complex made up of four separate classes of manifestations: resting tremor, cogwheel rigidity, akinesia, and loss of postural reflexes (Klawans and Cohen, 1970).

Parkinsonism begins insidiously, and it is difficult for many patients to date the exact onset of their disease. Loss of dexterity for skilled movements or mild stiffness in one hand may precede the onset of noticeable tremor by many years. The patient may well accept a decrease in his ability to carry out specific fine movements, a slowly progressive change in the gait, or a mild degree of fatigue in one or both arms or legs, and not seek medical attention. It is not unusual for an examining physician to be able to push back the date of onset of the disease by several years as a result of careful questioning as to when any degree of stiffness, rigidity, or loss of dexterity was noted by the patient.

The disease is progressive in virtually all patients. The degree and rate of progression, however, are not only variable from patient to patient, but are variable with time in any single patient. Many patients progress quite slowly and then have exacerbations during which there is a marked progression of symptoms. The end result of many years of this disease is severe disability, due in most part to the progression of akinesia and postural instability. All too often, the patient becomes bedridden and unable to care for himself.

In most patients, speech is also disturbed. The voice becomes monotonous. Normal speed is lost, syllables become slurred, and sentences tend to fade into a mutter. There is often an inability to speak freely at all, and the patient may stop in the middle of a sentence. This is similar to the freezing phenomena seen in other activities, such as walking. In severe instances, the victim is no longer able to communicate by speaking. As the patient becomes more and more disabled by his motor difficulty in communication, the question often arises as to whether the patient has been affected mentally. This question is often surprisingly difficult to answer objectively.

With the great difficulty in communication between the patient and the examiner, it it both frustrating and time-consuming, for both the patient and the examiner, to evaluate the patient's mental function adequately. Many of the objective tests of mental function have a built-in time bias, so that marked akinesia may prejudice the result of the objective testing. Previously, this may not have been a serious problem in that such severe akinesia was usually refractory to all forms of treatment. However, since this may no longer be true, this problem is serious. Many neurologists believe that there is greater prevalence of cerebral atrophy in patients with Parkinson's disease, as measured by pneumoencephalography and CT scan, than one would expect in a normal group of individuals of the same age. Pathologically, senile degenerative changes of the brain are present in a large number of patients with Parkinson's disease. The incidence, however, of mental changes in Parkinson's disease is not known. Nor is there any reliable information on how frequently these cerebral manifestations become prominent at a time in the patient's clinical course when he is not severely disabled because of limited motor function.

There have been relatively few longitudinal studies of the rate of progression and the mortality associated with Parkinson's disease. Based on the history of the syndrome of parkinsonism in 802 patients, Hoehn and Yahr (1968) found that approximately one-fourth of the patients with idiopathic parkinsonism were either severely disabled or dead within five years after the onset of the disease. By 10 years, two-thirds of the patients were severely disabled or dead, and by 14 years, more than three-fourths were classified as endstage, or they had died. There is no question that parkinsonism does shorten life expectancy substantially, regardless of the age at time of onset. Levodopa and related agents have increased the life expectancy in patients with Parkinson's disease, but, as a result, an increased incidence of dementia has been found in afflicted patients.

Most neurology texts describe three major types of parkinsonism: postencephalitic, idiopathic, and arteriosclerotic. This has resulted in the unfortunate practice of stating that a patient has postencephalitic parkinsonism if he had any form of encephalitis as part of the world-wide epidemic of 1917–1926, arteriosclerotic parkinsonism if his symptoms appear at an elderly age, and idiopathic parkinsonism if he has no history of encephalitis and is not elderly. Although postencephalitic parkinsonism was once common, new cases rarely, if ever, occur today, and there is no evidence that arteriosclerosis is causally related to parkinsonism. In general, all parkinsonism seen today is a manifestation of degenerative disease of the brain.

The underlying pathology of Parkinson's disease is a neuronal degeneration of the zona compacta of the substantia nigra. A variety of other pathological changes also occur in patients with parkinsonism, including atrophy of the cerebral cortex.

Other degenerative diseases of the central nervous system frequently include the signs and symptoms of parkinsonism and should therefore be included in the differential diagnosis of Parkinson's disease. These clinical syndromes will be discussed more fully later in this chapter, but important differential points will be presented now. The Shy–Drager syndrome commonly presents with features of Parkinson's disease, and is prominently associated with idiopathic orthostatic hypertension and other features of autonomic dysfunction, such as incontinence and impotence. Olivopontocerebellar degeneration (OPC), which can include extrapyramidal symptoms, including tremor, rigidity, and akinesia, most often presents with cerebellar ataxia and is often also accompanied by pyramidal signs. Progressive supranuclear palsy (PSP) must be considered in the differential diagnosis of parkinsonism; however, in PSP, retroflexion of the neck and paresis of downward gaze are features that distinguish this degenerative CNS disease from Parkinson's disease. Occasionally, confusion may arise in differentiating the patient with dementia who has gegenhalten from the patient with parkinsonian rigidity. Patients with normal pressure hydrocephalus (NPH) have been reported to manifest various parkinsonian features. The diagnosis of NPH is made clinically by demonstrating the triad of dementia, gait apraxia, and incontinence.

BIOCHEMISTRY AND PHARMACOLOGY OF PARKINSON'S DISEASE

The axons of the neurons in the substantia nigra reach the ipsilateral striatum where they synapse with a large number of neurons. Dopamine is the transmitter at each of these synapses. In Parkinson's disease, the degeneration of substantia nigra cells results in a loss of dopaminergic input into the striatum. Two premises form the basis for the presently accepted theory of the pharmacology of parkinsonism (Klawans, 1968). The first is that acetylcholine and dopamine have antagonistic effects on striatal neurons and that normal striatal function depends upon the balance between these two neurotransmitters. The second is that a shift of this balance in favor of acetylcholine tends to produce the symptoms of parkinsonism. Before the introduction of levodopa therapy, treatment of parkinsonism had focused on antagonizing the relatively overactive cholinergic input to the striatum. The various side effects of anticholinergic agents (including memory loss, sedation, pupillary dilation, decreased ocular accommodation, dry mouth, diminished sweating with possible hyperthermia, tachycardia, gastrointestinal hypomotility, and urinary retention) have been attributed to the ability of these agents to antagonize the activity of acetylcholine at acetylcholine receptors in the CNS and the peripheral autonomic nervous system.

The use of levodopa in the treatment of parkinsonism is associated with a much wider variety of side effects, which occur in a remarkably high percentage of all patients receiving this agent. It is possible to analyze these side effects in terms of the effect of levodopa administration on the function of various types of receptor sites. This approach results in a greater understanding of the pathophysiology of the various side effects and may lead to more fruitful methods of prevention and treatment. In order to understand the various mechanisms that underlie the side effects of levodopa, certain aspects of the biochemistry and physiology of levodopa must be reviewed.

Dopamine itself cannot be used to replace the nigrostriatal dopamine deficiency of parkinsonism, since dopamine does not cross the blood-brain barrier. Levodopa, the immediate precurser of dopamine, although pharmacologically inert, does cross the blood-brain barrier and is then converted to dopamine by the activity of the enzyme dopa decarboxylase.

The various side effects of levodopa can be divided physiologically into three classes (Klawans and Bergen, 1975):

Peripherally mediated side effects. These are thought to be caused by active amines formed outside the CNS. They include anorexia, nausea, vomiting, weight loss, and, rarely, cardiac arrhythmias. Such side effects are greatly diminished by giving levodopa with a peripheral dopa decarboxylase inhibitor (for example, carbidopa), which prevents the formation of active amines outside the CNS. Because of the efficacy of these agents in limiting peripheral side effects, they have replaced levodopa itself.

Mixed central and peripheral side effects. Both central and peripheral mechanisms are felt to be of physiological significance in the pathophysiology of one side effect, hypotension. This is partly ameliorated by coadministration of a dopa decarboxylase inhibitor.

Centrally mediated side effects. These are thought to be caused by the activity of levodopa within the CNS. They increase with duration of levodopa therapy, and after several years of therapy, frequently limit the dosage and efficacy of levodopa. These side effects are not decreased by decarboxylase inhibitors and include (1) choreatic movements (levodopa-induced dyskinesias); (2) myoclonus; (3) pyschiatric side effects, such as nightmares, altered dream states, visual hallucinations, and paranoid psychosis; (4) daytime sleepiness and fragmentation of nocturnal sleep; and (5) sudden intermittent loss of drug effect or the on/off phenomenon.

Since these central side effects are all related to duration of therapy and dose of levodopa, only patients with significant disability should be placed on it. In patients with mild parkinsonism, treatment should be initiated with either an anticholinergic agent or amantadine. When levodopa therapy is initiated, starting doses should be low. Throughout the course of treatment, only the lowest levodopa dosage to produce therapeutic efficacy should be employed.

Other Diseases with Parkinsonian Features

Progressive supranuclear palsy (PSP, or Steele–Richardson–Olzsewski syndrome) is a late onset degenerative disease of the brain, which includes supranuclear ophthalmoplegia affecting chiefly vertical gaze, pseudobulbar palsy, dysarthria, dystonic rigidity of the neck and upper trunk, mild dementia, and other cerebellar and pyramidal symptoms (Klawans and Ringel, 1971). The disease usually begins in the sixth decade and is rapidly progressive, resulting in a marked incapacity of the patient in two to three years. Terminally, these patients demonstrate marked rigidity of axial musculature and an inability to sit up or to roll over in bed. The patients usually die of intercurrent illness within four to six years of the onset of symptoms. In some respects, these patients resemble patients with parkinsonism because of their masked facies, marked akinesia, and gait difficulties, as well as very poor postural stability; however, patients with PSP have distinct features not seen in parkinsonism. The most obvious are a peculiar erect posture with backward retraction of the neck and a marked ophthalmoplegia, especially of the vertical gaze. Also present are varying degrees of pseudobulbar palsy and pyramidal motor findings.

The diagnosis of PSP is clinical. Symptoms of parkinsonism in an elderly patient with retrocollis and paresis of vertical gaze (especially downward gaze) invariably support the diagnosis of PSP. As regards response to therapy, PSP is analogous to OPC; that is, the parkinsonian features of these degenerative diseases, such as bradykinesia, poor postural reflexes, and rigidity, will respond to levodopa therapy, whereas the vertical gaze palsy, dystonic neck rigidity, and pseudobulbar signs of PSP will not.

Because the many signs of PSP are not responsive to dopamine depletion, as are the parkinsonian features, the overall efficacy of levodopa is poor, although the occasional PSP patient in whom parkinsonian features are predominant may do well on levodopa. Patients with PSP are usually not disabled by their parkinsonian features and little useful improvement with levodopa is noted, despite some decrease in rigidity and akinesia. They usually complain of increasing helplessness in standing, sitting, turning, and walking. This appears to be a result of the unique combination of an inability to look down, plus an extremely rigid extensor posturing of the neck. Both these features accentuate their postural instability and make any simple task difficult if it requires looking downward.

The *Shy–Drager syndrome,* a degenerative disorder of both the central and the autonomic nervous system, is characterized by primary or idiopathic hypotension, occasional urinary and fecal incontinence, impotence, and parkinsonism or other motor features, especially ataxia (Shy and Drager, 1960). The clinical manifestations vary according to the degree of pathological involvement within the intermediolateral cell column of the spinal cord and the substantia nigra. Onset of the Shy–Drager syndrome is most often between the fifth and the seventh decade of life, and there appears to be a slight predominance of this disorder in males.

Although initially felt to be a disease presenting as orthostatic hypotension, the Shy–Drager syndrome is now known to present in various ways. Symptoms of parkinsonism may be the early prominent features. Incontinence, ocular palsies, iris atrophy, and weakness with fasciculations have all been described both early and late in the disease.

Olivopontocerebellar degeneration is the commonest form of hereditary cerebellar degeneration beginning in middle or late adult life (Klawans and Zeitlin, 1971). Patients manifest both parkinsonian features and ataxia. Both are slowly progressive and only the former responds to anti-parkinsonian medication.

Striatonigral degeneration, a degenerative disease of the CNS of unknown etiology, is characterized clinically by parkinsonism and pathologically by degeneration of both the substantia nigra and the putamen (Adams et al., 1964). Striatonigral degeneration, reported to be familial in many instances, afflicts a younger population (third and fourth decade of life) than does idiopathic Parkinson's disease. Spasticity and dysarthria appear to be more common in patients with striatonigral degeneration.

Biochemically, striatonigral degeneration differs from Parkinson's disease in that concentrations of dopamine within the neostriatum have been reported to be either normal or only minimally depressed. In a recent review of therapy in patients with pathologically proven striatonigral degeneration, six of ten patients showed no response at all to levodopa, whereas four improved, but only transiently.

Other Diseases with Tremor

Senile tremor or *benign essential tremor,* a disorder of adult onset, is characterized solely by tremor of the head and neck (titubation) and the extremities. This tremor is most prominent with the maintenance of a sustained posture; its clinical differentiation is described above. Although postural tremor may be present in other neurological disorders, including Parkinson's disease, the presence of this tremor as an isolated finding does not imply progression to a more extensive neurological disease. Tremors of this type are commonly familial.

Essential tremor may be so severe as to interfere with function. If treatment is necessary, such beta adrenergic blocking agents as propranolol (40–240 mg/day) are effective if there are no contraindications to such therapy (Sweet et al., 1974). Not infrequently, a patient will state that one or two ounces of an alcoholic beverage ameliorates the tremor. If evidence of alcohol abuse is not present, the intermittent use of alcohol may provide a safer alternative for patients who cannot tolerate beta adrenergic blockers.

Cerebellar syndromes, which include tremor and gait difficulty, are also seen in the senium. Detailed discussion of these disorders is beyond the scope of this chapter, but syndromes important to differential diagnosis in this age group will be mentioned. Cerebellar disorders may be simplistically divided into two groups of symptoms with specific anatomical correlates (Brown, 1981). The first of these is the "hemispheral syndrome" in which intention tremor predominates in both extremities ipsilateral to the cerebellar lesion. The second is the "midline syndrome," in which gait ataxia is the prominent feature. In both symptom complexes, the degree of associated nystagmus, dysarthria, and hypotonicity may vary. Both olivopontocerebellar degeneration and the Shy–Drager syndrome have been discussed above. Other common causes of cerebellar diseases in the elderly include cerebrovascular disease and metastatic brain disease, but both etiologies are most likely to cause unilateral signs and symptoms of cerebellar hemispheral dysfunction ipsilateral to the lesioned side. More prominent cerebellar gait disorders may be observed in chronic alcoholics, often with associated amnesia and disordered ocular motility (Wernicke's syndrome), a nutritional disorder that may be partially reversed by thiamine supplementation. Similar gait dysfunction without cognitive change may be rarely seen in association with occult neoplasm (most commonly of the lung and ovary).

Choreiform Disorders

Huntington's disease is the best understood of all choreatic disorders. It usually begins before age 40, and its manifestations include chorea and personality change, varying from irritability or depression to psychosis and dementia. Inherited as a dominant disease with complete penetrance, it is an inexorably progressive disorder, which only rarely begins after age 60 (Klawans and Cohen, 1970).

Senile chorea is a syndrome of generalized and symmetrical choreiform movements of gradual onset and progression in patients of advanced age with no evidence of mental deterioration (Weiner and Klawans, 1973a). This entity has been repeatedly described as a clinical syndrome distinguishable from other choreic entities. Since a common error in diagnosis is to confuse senile chorea with Huntington's chorea, MacDonald Critchley established the following diagnostic criteria: "excluded from the diagnostic category of senile chorea should be all cases with a family history of either chorea or insanity in which the chorea appeared in middle age, persisted into old age, or had an apoplectic onset. If these criteria are applied, senile chorea, although rare, is a distinct clinical entity."

Senile chorea is associated with some degeneration of the pallidum and corpus dentatum, but more particularly, with degeneration of the striatal cells.

The *spontaneous oral masticatory syndrome,* a syndrome of spontaneous lingual–facial–buccal movements in the elderly, consists of repetitive, uncontrolled, unintentional movements of the tongue, lower facial (oral or buccal) muscles, and the jaw or masticatory muscles (Weiner and Klawans, 1973a). The slow complex movements of the tongue and lips range from gentle lateral lingual motions to rapid complete protrusion of the whole tongue. When the mouth is opened, the tongue may be seen to writhe. There also may be repetitive sucking and smacking movements of the lips, as well as closure of the eyes and changing facial expressions. The term *spontaneous* usually means that these movements are unintentional, but, more significantly, it implies that they are not related to long-term neuroleptic treatment.

The occurrence of spontaneous lingual–facial–buccal dyskinesias in older persons who do not exhibit any readily identifiable extrapyramidal syndrome or have not been receiving any drug therapy is fairly common, much more so than the occurrence of senile chorea. Lingual–facial–buccal dyskinesias resemble the movements seen in all choreic disorders; in this respect, they resemble the facial movements of senile chorea. It has been suggested that lingual–facial–buccal dyskinesia in the elderly may be the earliest manifestation of senile chorea and may represent the minimal, but most frequent manifestation of degeneration of the striatum in the elderly. This implies that the region of the striatum topographically related to the face is most likely to produce the abnormal movements associated with the degeneration seen in aged patients.

The current concept of the pathophysiology of spontaneous lingual–facial–buccal dyskinesia in the elderly suggests an altered responsiveness of striatal dopamine receptor sites, so that this disturbance of movement is in fact the species-specific form of stereotyped behavior for man. Lingual–facial–buccal dyskinesia would therefore be a disorder of the corpus striatum and a disease of the basal ganglia. However, as opposed to the analogous, amphetamine-induced stereotyped behavior in animals, stereotyped behavior in man is not related to an increased concentration of dopamine within the striatum, but, as in other choreic syndromes, to an altered responsiveness of the neuron that responds to dopamine.

Spontaneous lingual–facial–buccal dyskinesias and senile chorea represent the extremes of clinical expression of the same disease process. Lingual–facial–buccal dyskinesia represents the early stage of the disease, for which, as yet, no specific histopathological pattern has been demonstrated. Senile chorea is the full clinical manifestation of the motor disturbance, associated with a progressive degenerative process in the corpus striatum. The etiology of this degenerative process is unknown.

Most cases of lingual–facial–buccal dyskinesia and senile chorea do not interfere with daily life and require no treatment. If symptoms are disabling, treatment with either dopamine-depleting agents, such as reserpine or tetrabenazine, or dopamine receptor site blockers, such as the pheno-thiazines or butyrophenones, may be cautiously instituted. (Weiner and Klawans, 1973b). Since both groups of drugs have significant side effects, particularly in the elderly population, they should be administered only when choreiform symptoms are disabling.

Tardive dyskinesia (Klawans, 1973) is a well-recognized side effect of long-term neuroleptic therapy. The most prominent manifestation is lingual–facial–buccal dyskinesia. Limb and truncal chorea may accompany the facial movements. The syndrome is most often seen in chronic schizophrenic patients ranging in age from 50 to 70 years. It must be stressed, however, that all age groups are susceptible and that the movement disorder is known to occur in nonpsychiatric patients receiving phenothiazines or butyrophenones as antiemetics. Tardive dyskinesia occurs late in the course of neuroleptic therapy, often after the drug dosage is decreased or therapy discontinued. The involuntary movements may persist for months to years after neuroleptic therapy has been discontinued, and response to any type of therapy is poor.

The choreiform movements of tardive dyskinesia are not unique to this neuroleptic-induced syndrome, but are clinically identical to Huntington's disease, levodopa-induced dyskinesias in Parkinson disease, and senile chorea. Differentiation of these disorders requires, therefore, accurate history taking, in addition to physical examination.

Neither the pathophysiology nor the pathogenesis of chorea has yet been fully elucidated. There is evidence, however, that dopamine, acting at striatal dopaminergic receptor sites, may be closely related to the inititation of these choreiform movements in several clinical settings. Drugs that alter the availability of dopamine at dopaminergic receptor sites alter choreiform symptomatology. Huntington's disease is relieved by drugs that decrease the activity of dopamine at striatal dopamine receptors, whereas levodopa, which markedly increases available dopamine, exacerbates the symptomatology of Huntington's disease.

Tardive dyskinesia is also thought to be related to dopaminergic mechanisms. The neuroleptic agents believed to be responsible for the production of tardive dyskinesia are known to block the access of dopamine to striatal dopaminergic receptor sites and, as a result, acutely produce the symptoms of parkinsonism. It has been proposed that the neuroleptic blockade of dopamine receptors may be the equivalent of a "chemical denervation" of those dopamine-sensitive cells. When dopamine access to the receptor is restored by the diminution or the removal of the chemical barrier, an abnormal cellular responsiveness to endogenous dopamine results in the abnormal clinical features of tardive dyskinesia. Although lingual–facial–buccal dyskinesia is the most prominent choreic movement seen in tardive dyskinesia, limb, truncal, and respiratory dyskinesias have also been noted.

Treatment of tardive dyskinesia is directed at prevention by intermittent drug holidays or by early recognition. If recognized in its initial stage, tardive dyskinesia may abate with discontinuation of the neuroleptic. Depletion of dopamine by reserpine or tetrabenazine has been shown to diminish these involuntary movements. Increasing the neuroleptic dose will decrease or abolish these dyskinesias, but this is only a temporary measure because eventually the patient will "break through" again. The only role for neuroleptics in the management of patients with tardive dyskinesia is during treatment of the underlying psychosis. These agents should never be used to treat tardive dyskinesia, as they would continue to produce the pathogenetic alteration that causes this disorder. Reserpine is the most effective treatment now available.

Although *Wilson's disease* does not begin after the age of 50, another disorder, including both hepatic and central nervous system dysfunction, may occur in the elderly. *Acquired hepatocerebral degeneration* (AHCD) is usually manifested by progressive symptoms, including dementia, ataxia, rigidity, tremor,and choreoathetotic movements (Klawans, 1973). This syndrome is almost invariably associated with prolonged portal-systemic shunting of blood either secondary to cirrhosis itself or to surgical procedures performed to relieve portal hypertension. A characteristic pathological picture in the CNS, including both neuronal degeneration in specific regions and widespread astrocytosis, is seen in such patients. Classic hepatic encephalopathy with asterixis is the most frequent and well-known neurological complication of chronic liver disease and is seen intermittently in about 80% of all patients with AHCD.

Choreoathetotic movements, especially of the tongue, face, and mouth, have been described frequently in AHCD. These movements bear no constant relationship to the presence of hepatic coma or to the degree of hepatic encephalopathy as determined by level of consciousness. Once they occur, these movements are usually persistent and unresponsive to all therapeutic measures. The movements that occur in AHCD are identical to the dyskinesias seen in patients with Huntington's disease and tardive dyskinesia. The choreatic movements seen in AHCD are felt to be due to pathological changes within the striatum, but their pathogenesis has not been established.

A number of other rare causes of chorea are also known. These include hyperthyroidism, chronic ingestion of such central stimulants as amphetamine or methylphenidate, and phenytoin intoxication. They are all rare in the elderly.

Hemiballismus is a rare hypermotility disorder in which movements are more violent, disabling, and potentially harmful than the more usual choreiform or choreoathetoid movements (Klawans et al., 1976). The most common etiology is vascular, with damage to either the subthalamic nucleus (corpus Luysii) or its related tracts. Although hemorrhage and infarction in the subthalamic nucleus are the most common causative processes, demyelination within the adjacent white matter tracts (as in multiple sclerosis) may also be related to the production of hemiballismus. Hemiballismus is present in the extremities contralateral to the involved subthalamic nucleus.

Hemiballismus has, until recently, carried a grave prognosis; however, recent advances in neuropharmacology have furthered our knowledge of the pathophysiology of this disorder, and hence has led to a rational therapeutic approach. Patients with hemiballismus have been shown to have markedly increased levels of homovanillic acid in their cerebrospinal fluid, suggesting that overproduction of dopamine may be related to the production of this movement disorder. Treatment with dopamine receptor site antagonists, such as haloperidol, has been shown to be particularly efficacious and has improved the prognosis of hemiballismus patients; however, there may be a spontaneous remission of the movements, or the patient may develop more subtle choreiform movements or require life-long therapy.

Surgery is rarely necessary since the advent of haloperidol therapy.

Dystonic Disorders

Dystonias in the elderly are almost invariably partial dystonias, that is, those involving isolated body parts (Klawans and Weiner, 1981a). Of these, the most common disorder with onset in late life is *Meige syndrome*. This syndrome appears to be a variant of adult-onset torsion dystonia and consists of oromandibular dystonia in conjunction with blepharospasm. These dystonic facial movements are distinct from lingual–facial–buccal dyskinesias and are characterized by prolonged contraction of the muscles of the mouth and jaw. The dystonic movements may last a minute or two and are often repetitive, but irregular in timing. Peak age of onset of Meige syndrome is the sixth decade. The syndrome may present as blepharospasm alone, with the dystonic movements of the orofacial musculature following at a variable interval. Patients with this disorder often have some degree of dysphagia, resulting from involvement of hypopharyngeal musculature, or may suffer associated hoarseness or spastic dysphonia if the laryngeal muscles are involved. Although involvement may be limited to the above muscle groups, the adult-onset dystonias may follow a slowly progressive course. In this latter situation, spasmodic torticollis and writer's cramp may also be seen in the elderly population, either as isolated signs or in combination with other dystonias, especially those affecting brachial musculature.

Spasmodic torticollis may be defined as an abnormal involuntary contraction of neck muscles resulting in a relatively sustained movement or posture of the head. The muscles most commonly involved in spasmodic torticollis are the sternocleidomastoids and the trapezii. Although a unilateral pattern is often seen, bilateral involuntary movements of the neck are present in most patients with spasmodic torticollis. The onset of spasmodic torticollis is rare after the age of 65 or 70, being most common in the third to the fifth decade.

The abnormal involuntary movements of spasmodic torticollis may be modified by slight gestures (*geste antagonistique*), such as the placement of the index finger on the chin. Although modification by such minimal gestures was initially felt to support a psychogenic basis for the production of spasmodic torticollis, it is now known that such minor voluntary movements alter afferent postural impulses and thus ameliorate the abnormal involuntary movement.

A posterior flexion on the head upon the neck, *retrocollis* is secondary to increased tonus of the posterior neck muscles. It is a rare isolated dystonia, most often seen as a part of a spasmodic torticollis. This movement disorder is more commonly seen in acute, neuroleptic-induced dystonias, a disorder more frequent in young adults.

Writer's cramp is a familiar segmental dystonia caused by spasms of the muscles of the forearm and hand. Since writer's cramp is usually provoked by the performance of fine movements of the distal upper extremity, it is considered to be a form of action dystonia. Frequently, the patient will complain of pain in the forearm and hand in connection with writing or using hand utensils. As is the case with most dystonias, writer's cramp has in the past been felt to be of psychogenic origin, since it is frequently occupationally related and may lead to significant disability on the job. Neurological evaluation of the patient with writer's cramp may, at times, reveal increased muscle tone in asymptomatic extremities; occasionally, subtle torsion spasms of the face, neck, or lower extremity may be seen.

Other than idiopathic dystonias, the only common cause of dystonia in adults is the acute administration of neuroleptics. These acute, neuroleptic-induced dystonias are much more common in young adults receiving their first neuroleptic therapy and are frequently accompanied by prominent agitation. The only neuroleptic-induced dystonias not also seen commonly as a naturally occurring dystonia are oculogyric crises. These sudden, conjugate marked deviations of both eyes in a single direction, usually upward, can be both painful and frightening. All drug-induced dystonias begin acutely and are self-limited.

Acute, neuroleptic-induced dystonias respond to drug withdrawal. Signs may be dramatically reversed by the administration of an anticholinergic agent or an agent, such as benadryl, with anticholinergic properties.

The treatment of idiopathic partial dystonias is more problematic, although many investigators have had success in at least some patients using anticholinergic agents and/or baclofen.

Myoclonic Disorders

Myoclonus in the elderly may occur in a variety of clinical contexts, ranging from benign life-long disorders to severe toxic or degenerative processes (Klawans and Weiner, 1981b). Experimental studies of myoclonus have shown that segmental myoclonic movements may be produced by stimulation at any point along the neuraxis from spinal cord to motor cortex. Cortical spikes may or may not be associated with contralateral myoclonic movements. Myoclonus may be most obvious with volition (action myoclonus) or may occur solely during drowsiness. This part will briefly identify those disease entities that affect the elderly and include prominent myoclonic components.

Benign nocturnal myoclonus, a disorder generally of early adult onset, is characterized by myoclonic movements of the lower extremities, or the entire body, that occur as the patient is drifting off to sleep. The movements are generally sufficient to awaken the patient. The disorder is often familial and is not generally associated with more extensive neurological disease.

Benign familial myoclonus, a less common disorder of adult onset, is characterized by segmental, frequent, but arrhythmic myoclonic movements. The disorder is not progressive. Some cases have been found to respond to the central serotonin antagonist methysergide, whereas other cases appear to respond to such serotonergic agents as clonazepam or the precursor tryptophan with added carbidopa.

Palatal myoclonus is the rhythmic contraction of palatal and sometimes laryngeal and diaphragmatic musculature. It occurs most commonly after infectious or vascular damage to brain-stem structures. Palatal myoclonus differs from other myoclonic disorders both by its persistence during sleep and its rhythmicity. There is no clearly efficacious therapy.

Post-anoxic myoclonus, which may be seen in patients who have recovered from prolonged anoxic episodes, is often of the action type. It may be treated with clonazepam or tryptophan plus carbidopa in some cases, which suggests lowered central serotonergic activity.

Uremic encephalopathy and other severe metabolic disturbances may also include myoclonic movements. These are often sensitive to environmental stimuli, such as sudden noises, lights, or touches (stimulus-sensitive myoclonus). They may be intermittent or frequent and nearly rhythmic in character. Correction of the underlying metabolic disorder will improve myoclonic symptoms. Treatment with agents altering serotonin metabolism is not generally of much benefit.

Jakob-Creutzfeldt disease or *subacute spongiform encephalopathy,* a rapidly progressive disorder of late middle age, is characterized by dementia, myoclonus, and ataxia. The myoclonus is stimulus-sensitive. Initially it can be unilateral, but it invariably involves the entire body and is associated with a characteristic EEG pattern of periodic spikes, with loss of normal background activity. The disorder is believed to be the result of a transmissable agent (a slow virus infection) and is invariably fatal.

Tics

Tourette syndrome is a life-long disorder, with onset between the ages of 2 and 15 (Friedhoff and Chase, 1982). It is characterized by multiple simple and complex motor and vocal tics, which change in character and frequency over time. These movements disappear during sleep and orgasm and diminish with concentration. In a few cases, childhood tics may apparently resolve and then recur in late life. Tourette syndrome appears to involve a disorder of central dopaminergic neurons; if symptoms are disabling, they may be treated with dopamine receptor site blockers.

Simple tics may occur in the elderly as one or two isolated movements. These involuntary movements do not require treatment and are not associated with other neurological disorders.

References

Adams, R.D., Van Bogart, L., and Vander Eecken, H. (1964). Striatonigral degeneration. J. Neuropathol. Exptl. Neurol. 23, 584–589.

Brown, J.R. (1981). Diseases of the cerebellum. In Clinical Neurology, Ch. 29, A.B. Baker and L.H. Baker, Eds. Harper & Row, Philadelphia, pp. 1–38.

Critchley, M. (1949). Observations on essential (heredofamilial) tremor. Brain 72, 113–139.

Friedhoff, A.S. and Chase, T.N. (Eds.) (1982). Advances in Neurology, Vol. 35, Gilles de la Tourette Syndrome. Raven Press, New York.

Hoehn, M.M. and Yahr, M.D. (1967). Parkinsonism: Onset, progression and mortality. Neurology 17, 427–442.

Kinsbourne, M. and Rosenfeld, D. (1975). Nonprogressive myoclonus. In Myoclonic Seizures, M.H. Charlton, Ed. Roche Medical Monograph Series, Excerpta Medica, Amsterdam, pp. 30–59.

Klawans, H.L. (1968). The pharmacology of parkinsonism. Dis. Nerv. Syst. 29, 805–816.

Klawans, H.L. (1973). The Pharmacology of Extrapyramidal Movement Disorders. S. Karger, Basel.

Klawans, H.L. and Bergen, D. (1975). The side effects of levodopa. In The Clinical Uses of L-Dopa, G. Stern, Ed. Medical and Technical Publishing Co., Oxford, pp. 73–105.

Klawans, H.L. and Cohen, M.M. (1970). Diseases of the extrapyramidal system. Disease a Month (January), 1–52.

Klawans, H.L., Moses, H., Nausieda, P.A., Bergen, D., and Weiner, W.J. (1976). Treatment and prognosis of hemiballismus. New Eng. J. Med. 295, 1348–1350.

Klawans, H.L. and Ringel, S. (1971). Observations on the efficacy of L-dopa in progressive supranuclear palsy. Eur. Neurol. 5, 107–116.

Klawans, H.L. and Weiner, W.J. (1981a). Textbook of Clinical Neuropharmacology, Ch. 5, Dystonia. Raven Press, New York, pp. 75–81.

Klawans, H.L. and Weiner, W.J. (1981b). Textbook of Clinical Neuropharmacology, Ch. 15, Myoclonus. Raven Press, New York, pp. 129–138.

Klawans, H.L. and Zeitlin, E., (1971). L-Dopa in parkinsonism associated with cerebellar dysfunction (probably olivopontocerebellar degeneration). J. Neurol. Neurosurg. Psychiatr. 23, 14–19.

Parkinson, J. (1817). An Essay on the Shaking Palsy. Sherwood, Neely and Jones, London.

Shy, G.M. and Drager, G.A. (1960). A neurological syndrome associated with orthostatic hypotension. A clinical-pathological study. Arch. Neurol. 2, 511–518.

Sweet, F.D., Blumberg, J., Lee, J.E., and McDowell, F.H. (1974). Propranolol treatment of essential tremor. Neurology (Minneap.) 24, 64–67.

Weiner, W.J. and Klawans, H.L. (1973a). Lingual-facial-buccal movements in the elderly. II. Pathogenesis and relationship to senile chorea. J. Amer. Geriatr. Soc. 21, 318–320.

Weiner, W.J. and Klawans, H.L. (1973b). Lingual-facial-buccal movements in the elderly. I. Pathophysiology and treatment. J. Amer. Geriatr. Soc. 21, 314–317.

Wilson, S.A.K. (1925). Disorders of motility and of muscle tone, with special reference to the corpus striatum. Lancet ii, 1, 53, 169, 215.

Young, R.R. and Delwaide, P.J. (1981). Spasticity. N. Eng. J. Med. 304, 28–33, 96–99.

22. Aging of the Neuromuscular System

THEODORE L. MUNSAT

The Motor Unit as a Tissue

The quality of life in old age is intimately related to the ability to perform physical activities. Its reduction diminishes the very essence of the individual as a functioning human being. It is through physical activity, and more specifically, the capacity of the neuromuscular system, that one expresses emotion, communicates with friends and relatives, takes in nourishment, wards off threats from the environment, and performs all those acts that make us feel alive.

With aging, neuromuscular performance is reduced. At first slowly and then with greater rapidity, muscle bulk is lost, the speed of movement and muscular contraction slows, and strength decreases. Although CNS factors undoubtedly play a role in these changes, there is evidence that the motor unit itself undergoes significant involutional change. This presentation will review the somewhat scanty and, at times, contradictory evidence documenting age-related changes in the motor unit. An attempt will be made to synthesize this information into workable hypotheses, but the reader should be aware that much work remains to be carried out before we fully understand the pathogenesis and etiology of these changes. The important question of whether these changes are preventable or reversible will be discussed.

The motor unit (MU) is the basic functional element of contracting muscle. It is composed of a single alpha motoneuron, whose cell body lies in the spinal cord or brain stem, and all the muscle fibers it innervates. Although the two cell types differ quite radically in structure, metabolism, and function, it is useful to consider the MU as a single tissue. In recent years, experimental and clinical evidence has shown that the alpha motoneuron has profound "trophic" effects on the muscle fiber. In the most extreme case, when the nerve is sectioned, the muscle fibers atrophy and eventually disappear. A less dramatic, but nonetheless important change occurs when the nerve remains structurally intact, but becomes metabolically impaired. It has been postulated, for example, that certain diseases of muscle may, in fact, be caused by defective neuronal control. Conversely, excessive discharge of the nerve can produce dramatic enlargement and enhanced metabolic capacity in the muscle fibers stimulated. That the muscle fiber, in turn, may affect the alpha motoneuron is a more recent concept, but one that merits serious consideration.

Muscle and nerve do have certain common attributes. They are both electrically excitable and they both respond to many pharmacological agents in a similar manner. They are the most metabolically active cells in the body. In addition, they are both postmitotic cells and might be expected to show the involutional effects of aging prominently. Although capable of regeneration after injury, there is evidence to suggest that both muscle and nerve regenerate less well in the aged. The interdependence of alpha motoneuron and skeletal muscle fiber is important to keep in mind in trying to understand age-related effects on the MU. This will be discussed in more detail below.

Normal Structure and Function

Although it is beyond the scope of this section to review in any detail the normal anatomy, physiology, and energy requirements of the MU, a brief review, focusing on those aspects pertinent to aging, will be of help.

The MU is the final common pathway of willed and involuntary motor activity, controlled by pathways collectively known as the pyramidal and extrapyramidal systems. The number of muscle fibers innervated by a single anterior horn cell varies from a few hundred, in muscles requiring fine control, to several thousand in such large bulk muscles as the quadriceps. The muscle fibers of a single MU are interspersed with those of several others and are distributed over a relatively large area. In the cat gastrocnemius, for example, a single motor unit is distributed over approximately one-third of the cross-sectional area of the whole muscle. Muscle units discharge synchronously. That is, a single nerve action potential will discharge all the muscle fibers in that unit. Muscle units are fiber-type uniform. All the muscle fibers in the same MU are the same, histochemically and have similar physiological and biochemical characteristics.

The soma of the alpha motoneuron measures some 70 μ in diameter. Its peripheral extension, the axon, however, may extend to a length of 1 m before it reaches the muscle fibers it innervates. Since the protein-generating machinery (endoplasmic recticulum, Nissl substance) is located at some distance from the metabolically active terminal of the cell, a mechanism for the transport of enzymes, macromolecules, and other essential elements is necessary. Considerable metabolic activity occurs at the neuromuscular junction where acetylcholine is released, enzymatically degraded, taken back up by the nerve terminals, and then resynthesized and repackaged. All the enzymes and metabolic substrates necessary for most of this activity is processed "upstream" in the cell body. The synthesized materials are then transported along the axon by a system of axoplasmic transport. Both fast (400 mm/day) and slow (1–3 mm/day) rates have been identified. Slow axoplasmic transport may be reduced in aging. Interference with this transport mechanism affects the functioning of the MU. Interference with axoplasmic transport occurs in such "dying-back" neuropathies as diabetic neuropathy and may be a factor in muscle fiber alterations attributed to "trophic factor" impairment.

The adult skeletal muscle fiber is a syncytium measuring approximately 50 μ in diameter and extending from the proximal to the distal insertion of the muscle (Figure 22-1). Individual muscle fibers are organized in fascicles surrounded by connective tissue and each fascicle contains fibers from many MU. The muscle fiber, in turn, is composed of 50 to 100 myofibrils, each separated from adjacent myofibrils by three membranous subcellular structures: the transverse tubular system, which conducts the electrical impulse from the surface to the inside of the fiber; the sarcoplasmic reticulum, which is responsible for storing, releasing, and pumping calcium; and mitrochondria, which are the site of oxidative cellular metabolism. The myofibril, in turn, is composed of overlapping contractile elements (myofilaments) of two types: thick myofilaments composed of club-shaped myosin molecules and thin myofilaments composed of helically arranged globular–actin molecules. In addition to its function as a contractile protein, the head of the myosin molecule exhibits adenosine triphosphatase (ATPase) activity, a critical function that determines the speed of contraction. The actin filaments are firmly anchored to the Z-bands, which are composed of a 10 S

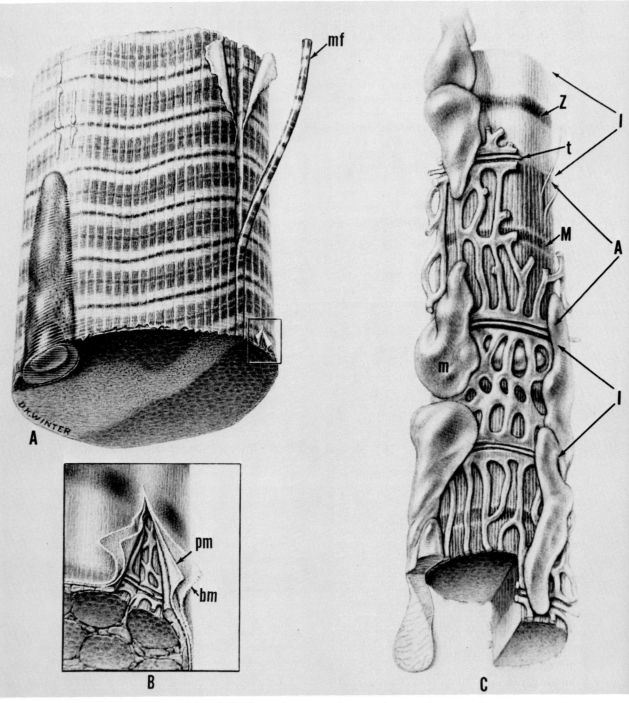

Figure 22-1. Structure of the skeletal muscle fiber. A. Microscopic view of repeating sarcomeres and a myofiber nucleus. A single myofilament (mf) has been teased out and enlarged in C. B. The relationship between the basement membrane (bm), the plasma membrane (pm), and the underlying myofibrils and sarcotubular systems. C. Ultrastructure of the three major membranous elements: sarcoplasmic reticulum (s), which functions as a calcium pump; the transverse tubular system (t), which conducts the electrical impulse from the surface into the myofiber; and the mitochondria (mi), which are involved with oxidative metabolism. (From H. Price and R.L. Van de Velde, 1981.)

alpha actinin and form the boundaries of the sarcomere, the basic repeating unit of the myofiber. Troponin and tropomyosin, two proteins involved in the regulation of the contractile process, are located at intervals along the thin filaments. Contraction takes place by the sliding of thick upon thin filaments, with further interdigitation of the overlapping filaments and closer approximation of the Z-bands.

The energy required for muscle contraction derives from two substrates—glycogen and lipid. Protein is utilized as an energy source only under conditions of starvation or in certain pathological states. Glycogen, stored as macromolecules in small clumps between myofibrils, is the main energy source for high intensity, short-duration tasks, such as lifting or pushing a heavy object for a short distance. It is of interest that intramuscular stores of glycogen are the main source of this energy, since hepatic stores are not readily available. When intramuscular stores of glycogen are depleted, the body must shift to aerobic metabolism and the oxidation of lipid. Long- and medium-chain fatty acids are the other main source of energy for contracting muscle. Energy-producing reactions take place primarily within the mitochondria and require oxygen. This aerobic metabolism provides most of the energy for low intensity, longer-duration work. For example, lipid is primarily utilized for energy at rest and during such activities as long distance running.

In lower animals, the muscles used primarily for aerobic, long-duration, low-intensity work are dark, or red, because of their high myoglobin content and abundant capillary network. Physiologically, these muscles contract slowly and are relatively nonfatigable. Conversely, muscles utilizing glycogen as an energy source have a short-duration, high-torque output and are white. These muscles (and fibers) contract rapidly and are easily fatigable.

In the human, no single muscle is entirely dark or light. Rather, each muscle is a random mixture of both fiber types. A number of histochemical reactions can be used to identify the various metabolic and physiological characteristics of muscle fibers, but the reaction that most clearly

and usefully identifies them is myosin ATPase. On this basis, muscle fibers are termed type 1 if they are ATPase light and type 2 if they are ATPase dark. Type 1 fibers thus have a high aerobic capacity and are capable of low-intensity, long-duration activity without fatigue, whereas type 2 fibers have a high glycogen content and are capable of high-torque output, but fatigue rapidly. This scheme is, of necessity, simplistic, since all muscle fibers do not fit easily into one of these two major catagories, but it serves us as a basis to better understand some of the more important age-related changes in the MU.

Problems in Muscle Unit Research

Laboratory and clinical observations of changes in the MU with aging are limited because of inherent problems and methodological inadequacies. It is important to understand this when one tries to critically evaluate and analyze reports in the literature. Certain problems pertain only to humans, others to both humans and laboratory animals.

In the human, MU accessibility is more of a problem than one might think. Although muscle biopsies are easily obtained from most muscles, it is very difficult to obtain intact whole muscle fibers, which are preferred for contraction dynamics studies. Other muscles, of clinical and pathological importance, are not accessible. Although nerve biopsies in humans are now carried out more frequently and provide much useful information, these biopsies are limited to only a few nerves for reasons of safety. Discomfort at the biopsy site is still a problem. Because of the spotty nature of many processes affecting the MU, and the relatively small amount of tissue obtained at any one biopsy, sampling error is a major problem. This shortcoming is a major issue in all neuromuscular research. Multiple needle biopsies of muscle help, but the small amount of tissue obtained still poses problems.

Although the structural and biochemical differences between various nerves and muscles in the same human have not been clearly identified, muscles and nerves react quite differently to different pathological processes and it is clear that they have

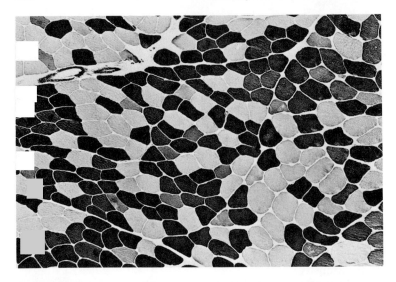

Figure 22-2. Muscle fiber types. A. Normal human muscle biopsy stained for myofibrillar ATPase (pH 9.5). The dark type 2 fibers are fast twitch, and easily fatigable. The lighter type 1 fibers are slow twitch, and fatigue resistant. A random mixture of equally represented fibers is normal. B. With aging there is selective atrophy and possibly loss of type 2 fibers. This type 2 fiber atrophy is seen in a number of other conditions, including steroid-induced myopathy and any form of disuse. It can be reversed by exercise or electrical stimulation.

different metabolic susceptibilities. In animals, muscles vary quite dramatically from one part of the body to another. In fact, muscle tissue obtained from one part of a single muscle often differs significantly from tissue from another part. This adds to the sampling error and makes it most important to control this variable (Gutmann and Hanzlikova, 1976).

Considerable species variation makes it hazardous to extrapolate between animal species and from animals to humans (Ingram et al., 1981). Other variables that are often poorly controlled include exercise and activity patterns (which can dramatically alter neuromuscular function), sex

and racial differences, nutritional status, and changes in the circulatory and endocrine systems. In the human, it is extremely difficult to assess and quantify neuromuscular capability accurately because motivation varies.

Nerve–Muscle Interaction

Trophic Effects

That muscle depends upon its nerve supply for maintenance has been known since ancient times. When the integrity of a muscle's nerve supply is compromised, the muscle becomes flaccid, underresponsive to both voluntary and involuntary signals, and its bulk is reduced. However, the full nature of this dependence of muscle upon its innervation was not systematically explored until the landmark studies of Buller et al. in 1960. Their initial experiments consisted of transecting nerves to red and white muscles, transposing them, and allowing them to reinnervate the now "foreign" muscle. They observed that the white muscles became red and the red whiter. Subsequent experiments showed that this myofiber conversion involved a wide range of structural, physiological, and biochemical changes (Guth, 1968). Thus, it was hypothesized that the physiological and biochemical characteristics of muscle were mutable and dependent upon the alpha motoneuron.

Subsequently, experiments by McComas et al. (1971) in England suggested that certain diseases of muscle, such as Duchenne muscular dystrophy, which were traditionally thought to be due to primary defects of the muscle fiber, were more likely to be caused by defective innervation and thus impaired neuronal control. However, since classic evidence of denervation was lacking (fibrillation and sharp waves on EMG; group atrophy and fiber type grouping on biopsy), it was proposed that the changes were caused by "functional" denervation, that is, a defect in the trophic control mechanism.

These clinical and animal observations suggested to some that the muscle fiber was rather easily altered by neuronal control mechanisms. The nature of this trophic function remains uncertain. Three main hypotheses have been advanced: (1) The programmed release of acetylcholine, the normal transmitter at the skeletal neuromuscular junction, is sufficient to maintain the integrity of the myofiber. (2) As yet unidentified trophic substances, presumably proteins manufactured in the soma, are responsible for this effect. These substances are moved to the motor nerve terminal by axoplasmic transport, released at the junction, and in some manner enter the muscle fiber. (3) Muscle fiber is maintained by its regular contraction against resistance. If work is regularly performed, the fiber will be maintained. The nerve merely serves to relay the signal for contraction. Drachman (1974) has proposed that all three mechanisms occur, but to differing degrees in different situations.

These trophic relationships have usually been considered a one-way street, that is, the trophic action of nerve on muscle. However, recent evidence suggests that the muscle fiber may also act on the alpha motoneuron. Cultured skeletal muscle releases a substance that enhances the synthesis of choline acetyltransferase by spinal cord neurons (Giller et al., 1977). Similar studies suggest that skeletal muscle contains a humoral factor that enhances the growth and activity of motoneurons. Murphy et al. (1977) have suggested that this substance might be similar to nerve growth factor. One might thus speculate that neuronal changes can occur when skeletal muscle is either damaged or atrophies because of inactivity. This might explain the several cases in which MU dysfunction seems to be related to changes on both sides of the neuromuscular junction, such as is seen in myotonic muscular dystrophy, or possibly with aging, as has been suggested by Gutmann and Hanzlikova (1972).

Use and Disuse

A detailed analysis of the effects of use and disuse on the MU are beyond the scope of this section. However, these concepts are crucial to the understanding of age-related MU changes and whether age-related changes are reversible. If a nerve is transected by surgery or trauma, the muscle it innervates shows all the effects of denervation, including a widening of the chemosensitive receptor zone, a lowering of the resting membrane potential, an enhanced sensitivity to depolarizing agents, loss of histochemical specificity, and loss of bulk (Guth, 1968). However, when muscle is denervated it also becomes inactive. Which changes are then the result of loss of neuronal control (trophic effect) and which the result of inactivity or disuse? This is a critical question from a therapeutic point of view. Those changes resulting from inactivity are more likely reversible and preventable.

When a limb is inactivated, with its nerve supply intact, by casting, skeletal pinning, or tenotomy, changes similar to those seen in structural denervation are observed. These include weakness, atrophy (particularly of type 2 fibers), physiological speeding, and lowered oxidative capacity. In addition, if denervated muscle is stimulated directly in a manner that simulates normal activity, many of the features associated with denervation can be avoided (Drachman and Witzke, 1972). In fact, directly stimulated denervated muscle can be converted from one fiber type to another without a neuronal connection. In stimulation studies in humans, Munsat et al. (1976) have demonstrated that the maintenance of muscle fiber integrity and the capacity of fibers to convert from one type to another does not depend only upon neuronal stimulation or contraction. Work must be done by the contracting muscle. Isotonic contraction without work is not sufficient to prevent retrogressive changes. Thus, denervation and disuse have many common features. It would appear that disuse and the absence of a regular work pattern are the features common to both these processes, resulting in a reduction in MU performance.

Degeneration and Regeneration

NERVE

Peripheral nerves have a great capacity to repair and regenerate after injury. The degree and completeness to which this occurs depends on many factors, but particularly on the pathological process that caused the damage. In neuropathies that are primarily a result of demyelination, remyelination is accomplished by activated Schwann cells. In axonal damage, regrowth of the axon occurs along the intact Schwann cell sheath. In both these situations, axonal sprouting may be quite active so that reinnervation produces a larger MU. Newly reinnervated muscle fiber is converted to the fiber type of the parent MU. This results in fiber type grouping, whereby the muscle loses its characteristic random distribution of fiber types and has small or large groups of fibers with the same histochemical reactivity. Experimental evidence suggests that the ability of motorneurons to sprout and reinnervate denervated muscle is impaired in the aged (Pestronk et al., 1980; Gutmann et al., 1942; Black and Lasek, 1972). Both nerve terminal and axonal sprouting are reduced in respose to neuromuscular junction blockade and nerve crush lesions (Pestronk et al., 1980).

MUSCLE

It is now well established that, contrary to previous thought, muscle has a remarkable capacity to regenerate after injury. After mechanical damage, regenerative activity begins within 48 hours and is complete within a few weeks. If an entire fiber is damaged, it is unlikely that repair will occur, since muscle fibers are postmitotic cells and do not replicate. However, repair of focal damage to a fiber takes place quite readily. Two forms of regeneration are recognized—"continuous" and "discontinuous." In the former, regeneration takes place by "budding" from the intact ends of the damaged segment. Newly formed myoblasts accumulate in the damaged zone and then fuse to reconstitute the fiber. In "discontinuous" regeneration, the segment to be replaced is formed by the fusion of myoblasts outside the fiber. The origin of these newly formed myoblasts, in either case, is probably from the so-called satellite cell, a dormant primitive cell lying betwen the plasma and the basement membranes and capable of developing into a myoblast. Regenerating muscle fibers can be identified by their large, vesicular nuclei, which contain prominent nucleoli and large amounts of sarcoplasmic RNA.

Recent studies suggest that regeneration in aged muscle is impaired (Snow, 1977; Zacks and Sheff, 1982).

Age-Related Changes

Muscle Mass

One of the more obvious, common changes in the MU accompanying aging is reduction in bulk. The muscle contours become blunted and rounded, and the total muscle mass decreases from 43 to 25% in senescence (Serratrice et al., 1968). Although direct muscle fiber counts have not been made in humans, the decrease in bulk is more likely due to atrophy of individual fibers rather than to a reduction in the total number of fibers. Muscle fiber atrophy, particularly of type II fibers, is one of the best documented comcomitants of aging (Rebeiz et al., 1972; Jennekins et al., 1971). Using computed tomography Haggmark et al. (1978) were able to correlate fiber atrophy and decrease in bulk.

The Muscle Fiber

SIZE AND NUMBER

In rodents, the total number of muscle fibers are reduced with age. For example, total counts in the extensor digitorum longus (a fast muscle) in young and old rats are 3519 and 2990 respectively, significant at $p < 0.05$ (Caccia et al., 1979). Similar values in soleus (a slow muscle) are 2966 and 2152, also significant at $p < 0.05$. It is of great interest, however, that the number of muscle fibers lost is higher than one would expect relative to the reduction of alpha motoneurons (Gutmann et al., 1968).

All carefully performed studies in both humans and animals reveal a progressive reduction in muscle fiber size with aging (Rebeiz et al., 1972; Serratrice et al., 1968; Tomlinson et al., 1969). Atrophic changes have been variously reported as being generalized to all fibers, or scattered. In studies utilizing histochemical techniques, the atrophy predominantly involves type 2 fibers, those fibers that are fast twitch and anaerobic in metabolic activity. This is true in both animal (Caccia et al., 1979) and human (Jennekins et al., 1971; Orlander et al., 1978; Tomonaga, 1977) tissue and in both fast and slow muscles (Caccia et al., 1979). Type 2 atrophy is more prominent in females and in type 2b subgroup (Aniansson et al., 1978). The percentage of type 2 fibers and the cross-sectional areas are both reduced (Larsson, 1978; Scelsi et al., 1980; Orlander et al., 1978), indicating

preferential loss and atrophy of type 2 fibers. Type 1 fibers are not totally spared, although a more modest reduction in size is observed (Jennekins et al., 1971). The degree of atrophy in type 2 fibers does not fully account for the observed loss of strength. This suggests that factors other than simple loss of tissue mass are involved.

MORPHOLOGICAL ALTERATIONS

A wide range of morphological alterations in both type 1 and type 2 fibers have been reported with aging. Changes characteristic of myopathies usually seen in childhood, which possibly represent a retrogressive change, have been reported by Tomonaga (1977). He also observed proliferation of Z-band material into rod shaped or nemaline bodies and an accumulation of subsarcolemal aggregates, which stained red with Gomori trichrome (ragged red fibers). He observed increased numbers of sarcolemal nuclei and nonspecific degenerative features. Jennekins et al. (1971) and Serratrice et al. (1968) also reported various myopathic features, such as necrosis, intracellular nuclei, and random fiber size. However, in the former study, several of the patients, aged 65 to 92, had significant medical problems, and in the latter most of the subjects had proximal muscle weakness consistent with a myopathy and not normal aging. Other nonquantitated and nonspecific changes, such as lipid, lipofuscin, and lysosomal accumulations, have been observed (Tomonaga, 1977; Scelsi et al., 1980).

In reviewing these changes, which traditionally are considered "myopathic," one is less impressed with their significance than with their nonspecificity and the relatively few fibers involved. In all these studies, one cannot be certain that the patients were indeed free of illness that could affect muscle or that the biopsy was taken from a truly representative area of the body and not a traumatized or disused area.

Of greater interest are changes suggestive of denervation. In several studies, some aspects of the muscle biopsy in normal aged were more traditionally associated with neuromuscular diseases due to interference with innervation. Scelsi et al. (1980) biopsied the vastus lateralis in 45 healthy sedentary men and women, aged 65 to 89 years, and observed fibers with rings (targetoid) and some degree of fiber type grouping. Tomlinson et al. (1969) observed denervation and reinnervation that did not correlate directly with aging. However this postmortem study is somewhat faulted in that many of the subjects had such medical illness as diabetes mellitus or bronchial carcinoma, which could cause denervation. Jennekens et al. (1971) observed neuropathic changes in eight patients autopsied between ages 65 and 92. Although these subjects had associated illnesses, none was directly capable of producing neuropathy. Changes of denervation were much more impressive than myopathic changes and involved ringed fibers, target fibers (three or more zones), central cores, and fiber type grouping.

We can conclude from these studies, as well as from our own observations, that myopathic and neuropathic changes are found in aged muscle. However, the changes are modest, at best, and no consistent pattern is observed. If anything, changes suggestive of denervation are the most common, although it is difficult to be certain whether these are solely age-linked or are secondary to other associated illness, such as diabetes, osteoarthritic nerve root compression, or disuse.

ULTRASTRUCTURE

Mitochondrial volume decreases with age, according to Orlander et al. (1978); it remains unchanged according to deCoster et al. (1981). There are significant age-related reductions in the surface density and volume of sarcoplasmic reticulum and transverse tubular system (deCoster et al., 1981). This disagrees with the observations of Fujisawa (1974), who reported proliferation and dilation of these structures.

Disorganization of myofibrillar architecture, Z-band "streaming," and minor rod-body formation may be seen in aging muscle (Scelsi et al., 1980), but less commonly, one observes myelin figures, mitochondrial inclusions, and tubular aggre-

gates (Tomonaga, 1977). Capillary basement membranes may be widened and replicated (Scelsi, 1980). In a biopsy study of eight subjects, aged 70 to 83, with no evidence of nerve or muscle disease by EMG or other laboratory tests, Shafiq et al. (1978) observed only modest changes in scattered fibers. The changes included cytoplasmic bodies, minor focal degenerative features, and increased numbers of lipofuscin granules.

Muscle satellite cells are small mononucleated cells of a primitive nature, which can transform into myoblasts under appropriate stimulation. They are located between the basement membrane and the sarcolemma. Under the light microscope, they cannot be differentiated from sarcolemma nuclei. In a recent study of mice between eight and thirty months of age, no major change in the cytological features of satellite cells in soleus and gastrocnemius muscles was observed (Snow, 1977). However, certain morphological changes suggest that myosatellite cells in senile muscle might be metabolically less active. These changes include heterochromatin, an absence of nucleoli, reduction of the cytoplasm, reduction in rough endoplasmic reticulum, and poorly developed Golgi apparatus. The basement membrane in older animals is considerably thickened. In addition there is a reduction of the proportion of satellite nuclei in each myofiber from 4.6% at eight to ten months to 2.4% at twenty nine to thirty months, despite the fact that the total number of myonuclei increased from 387 to 498. It was suggested that the observed decrease in satellite cells was a result of their passage into the interstitial space when external lamina material was deposited around the cell.

The significance of these changes has not been determined, but these observations suggest that aged muscle may have a reduced capacity to regenerate after injury.

ELECTROPHYSIOLOGY

Using the electrophysiological technique of MU counting pioneered by McComas et al. (1971), Caccia et al. (1979) determined that the number of MU in rat soleus dropped from a mean of twenty nine in young animals to seven in old. The values in mouse soleus were twenty eight and eighteen respectively. A similar reduction has been observed in human muscle (Campbell et al., 1973). However, the accuracy of this technique has been disputed. The increase of MU fiber density in human extensor digitorum communis (Stalberg and Thiele, 1975) suggests reinnervation.

Larssen et al. (1979) studied the patellar reflex time of healthy males with white-collar jobs age 25 to 65. He observed a prolongation of the total reflex time, but this was due almost entirely to a delay in the motor time component. The reflex latency, representing the neuronal component, was unchanged. Gutmann et al. (1971) have observed a prolongation of contraction time, latency, twitch tension rate, and relaxation time.

In the rodent soleus, twitch tension remains unchanged with aging, but contraction and half relaxation times are slowed and latency is increased (Caccia et al., 1979, Gutmann and Hanzlikova, 1972). This would be consistent with the observed reduction in volume of the physiologically fast twitch muscle fibers.

Frolkis et al. (1976) carried out detailed electrophysiological studies of age-related changes in rodents. The resting membrane potential changed little with age until very old animals (36 months) were studied, at which time they decreased approximately 10%. Stimulated current flows showed more impressive changes, with a linear reduction with increasing longevity. In rat diaphragm, Smith (1979) observed a 3.6mV drop in resting membrane potential in senescent animals.

Acetylcholine sensitivity has been reported as reduced (Frolkis et al., 1976) and unchanged (Gutmann and Hanzlikova, 1972).

BIOENERGETICS OF AGING

The muscle fiber is so constructed and constituted that it can carry out work in an energy-efficient manner. Its energy turnover is greater than any other cell, and it can rapidly increase this energy turnover under stress. It also has a unique capacity

to undergo a variety of structural and metabolic changes in response to repeated work demands, that is, exercise. This then allows the organism to subsequently perform the same work in a more efficient manner. With aging, a number of as yet poorly defined changes occur, which reduce this capacity to perform work effectively and which may also reduce the capacity to exercise with the usual metabolic adjustments. This section will review some of the more important aspects of metabolism, or bioenergetics, of aging muscle. It should be emphasized that the energy supply of the muscle fiber, and its performance capacity, depends on a number of external factors. These factors include external oxygen supply, the diffusing capacity of the lungs, the transport and storage capabilities of the blood, the functional performance of the cardiovascular system, and the availability of carbohydrate and lipid energy substrates.

In vivo studies. With aging, the plasma resting values for lactic acid (LA), pyruvic acid (PA), serum creatine phosphokinase (CPK), serum electrolytes, extracellular water, and most energy substrate levels do not change significantly (Moller et al., 1979). A modest increase in plasma tyrosine, histidine, valine, lysine, and total essential amino acids have been observed (Moller et al., 1979).

Muscle metabolism during exercise has been studied in a variety of ways. Most commonly, aerobic functions (those requiring oxygen utilization and carried out by mitochondria) are evaluated by measuring the amount of oxygen metabolized in a given period of time during a specified amount of work. The best single physiological indicator of one's capacity to maintain moderate or heavy work is the measurement of oxygen utilization during a maximal work effort—the V_{O_2max}. Most typically, the V_{O_2max} is measured during bicycle or treadmill exercise. The value is usually achieved during the second or third minute of exhaustive work. All authors agree that V_{O_2max} decreases with age. Suominen et al. (1977b) have observed a 1% decrease per year after age 25, Astrand (1960) has observed a similar reduction of 30% between ages 35 to 63. For example, decreases from 50 ml/g/a minute at age 18 to V_{O_2max} 26 at age 75 (Astrand, 1960). However, the standard deviations are wide, suggesting other modifying factors that undoubtedly include genetic influences, prior exercise history, and nutrition.

The efficiency and integrity of anaerobic metabolism can be estimated by determining the degree of LA (and less so, PA) generation during exercise. Conditioned muscle produces relatively less LA during a given amount of exercise than unconditioned muscle. Tzankoff and Norris (1979) studied 180 men of the Baltimore Longitudinal Study, aged 20 to 80, and evaluated LA generation after continuous, multistage treadmill exercise. They found that older subjects generated higher maximal levels of LA after exercise and that recovery to normal levels was delayed. This was interpreted as an impairment of diffusion of LA out of the myofiber. However, a similar change could be the result of defective oxidative metabolism, with a greater reliance on anerobic energy generation. Thus, post exercise LA peaks later in the aged and this should be taken into consideration in single, postexercise sampling. In contrast, Wahren et al. (1974) found no difference in LA generation when they studied blood flow response after leg exercise. They observed, as expected, that blood flow rose less in the aged, but that arterial–venous differences were greater. The two effects balanced, resulting in no significant difference in blood LA levels after exercise.

In an attempt to define glucose utilization and insulin responses, Kalant et al. (1980) studied 35 healthy subjects aged 22 to 73, using a glucose-clamp technique. Blood glucose utilization by forearm muscle was found to be proportional to insulin concentration. Whole-body glucose utilization, forearm muscle glucose utilization, and insulin response to hyperglycemia were not affected by age.

In-vitro studies. Bioenergetic studies on muscle samples from both animals and humans are subject to difficulties controlling such variables as sampling error, preparation techniques, exercise history, and nutri-

tional aspects. The literature is sparse, incomplete, and at times contradictory.

Humans. Moller et al. (1980) observed only modest decreases in high energy metabolites (ADP, ATP, and phosphocreatine) in the aged. Intramuscular levels of PFK and LDH showed little change (Orlander et al., 1978). Other intrasarcoplasmic enzymes necessary for glycolysis and gluconeogenesis were reduced, however (Schlenska and Kleine, 1980). In a biopsy study of 12 untrained subjects in good health, these authors observed a significant decrease of 6-phosphofructokinase, triosephospate dehydrogenase, and phosphoenolpyruvate carboxykinase activity, whereas increases were found for hexose diphosphatase and 3-hydroxyacyl-CoA diphosphatase. Other glycolytic enzymes were unchanged, as was lysosomal acid phosphatase. Enzymes involved with mitochondrial gluconeogenesis (pryruvate carboxylase, malic dehydrogenase) and GOT and GPT were only minimally reduced. These changes were not explicable by the change in fiber type composition alone and suggested a specific disturbance in cytoplasmic glycolysis and gluconeogenesis. Fatty acid patterns and cholesterol are unchanged in the aged (Thomas et al., 1978).

Animals. Animal studies of enzymatic alterations with aging have shown that different muscles demonstrate varying changes in various enzymes. Bass et al. (1975) studied three different rodent muscle types—fast (EDL), slow (soleus), and special (diaphragm). In EDL, a significant reduction in the glycolytic enzymes triosephosphate dehydrogenase, LDH, and GPDH was found, whereas little change in the oxidative enzymes MDH and citrate synethase occurred. This would be consistent with histochemical studies showing a reduction in the size and number of type 2 fibers. In soleus, glycolytic and oxidative enzyme activity was reduced. Activity of the mitochondrial enzymes MDH and CS was reduced, the former to a much greater degree. Only minor changes were seen in enzyme levels in the diaphragm. The loss of glycolytic enzymes in fast muscle and the loss of oxidative activity in slow muscle might be interpreted as representing a dedifferentiation of enzyme patterns, that is, a return to a more fetal pattern. The necessity of interpreting enzyme changes in animal studies relative to the muscle sampled is clear.

The small changes in oxidative enzyme activity and the significant reduction in oxygen utilization (see below) do not explain the reduction in work capacity that occurs with aging. These changes, however, could be explained by a defect in the contractile system. Unfortunately, few studies have been performed in this area. The contracture response of aged human muscle, obtained at biopsy, to caffeine and 2% halothane is normal (Gronert, 1980). However, at age 79, the amino acids that cross-link actin and myosin are 31% less than early in life. This reduction is linear with time (Fujii and Kurosu, 1979). Gershon and Gershon (1973) have demonstrated age-related molecular alterations in intrasorcoplasmic enzymes that cross-react antigenically with "young" enzymes; this could be the basis of functional impairment.

Neuromuscular Junction

Morphological studies of distal motor nerves with intravital methylene blue techniques reveal increasingly complex terminal branchings and an occasional spherical axonal swelling (Harriman et al., 1970; Gutmann and Hanzlikova, 1965). However, quantitative studies of the numbers of terminal motor nerve branchings fail to reveal the increased terminal innervation ratio one would expect with denervation (Coers et al., 1973). Acetylcholine esterase reaction product is reduced in amount and the contours of the subneural apparatus are disordered (Gutmann and Hanzlikova, 1965). Marchi et al. (1980) also found decreased choline uptake by aged nerve terminals.

In electrophysiological studies of the neuromuscular junction, a 1.75-fold increase in miniature end-plate potential discharge in aged rats is observed but there is no difference in facilitation or post-tetanic potentiation (Smith, 1979). In contrast, Gutmann et al. (1971) found spontaneous transmitter release to be reduced.

After curare administration, repetitive nerve stimulation produced a proportionately greater depression of synaptic function (Smith, 1979). Synaptic failure in aged rodents occurs at lower frequencies of stimulation and after shorter stimulation periods and may be related to the observed morphological changes.

Peripheral Nerve

A number of age-related changes in the peripheral nervous system have been documented. The exact character and pathogenesis of these changes is uncertain, but, in general, they suggest a degenerative process that affects both axonal and Schwann cell function. Clinically, senescence is accompanied by reduced vibratory perception in the distal legs, which is assumed to be related to changes in the peripheral nervous system. Whether loss of ankle reflexes is a concomitant of normal aging is uncertain. When sensory perception is studied quantitatively, a progressive impairment of touch-pressure perception, which approaches a fourfold reduction in males over age 40, can be shown (Dyck et al., 1972).

Accurate, quantitative anterior horn cell counts have not yet been carried out in humans, but a reduction in numbers can be assumed from the reduction in motor fibers in the anterior roots and peripheral motor nerves. Using a sectional "squash" technique in rodents, Wright and Spink (1959) observed that the number of large anterior horn cells remained constant from 6 to 50 weeks, but were reduced by approximately 15% at 110 weeks. Unfortunately, they did not examine older animals. Although there is considerable variation within each decade, axonal counts reveal a significant decrease in both anterior and posterior roots beginning after age 30 (Kawamura et al., 1977). By age 89, a 32% reduction in anterior root axons is observed (Corbin and Gardner, 1937; Gardner, 1940), accompanied by an increase in connective tissue. In the remaining anterior spinal roots, demyelination and remyelination is very prominent, but could be secondary to axonopathy (Spencer and Ochoa, in press).

The most prominent morphological change in anterior horn cells is the accumulation of lipofuscin, which begins in the third decade. There is considerable variation in the degree of lipofuscin accumulation between individual cells. However, after age 60, all anterior horn cells contain this "aging" material, and in some cells, the accumulation is so great that it displaces subcellular organelles (Prineas and Spencer, 1975). It is of considerable interest that neurofibrillary tangles, which are the hallmark of aging in cortical neurons, are rare in anterior horn cells.

Peripheral nerve motor conduction velocities decrease progressively with advancing age (Kaeser, 1970; Norris et al., 1953; Mulder et al., 1961). Conduction velocities at birth, when myelination is incomplete, are approximately one-half those of adulthood. In the seventh decade of life, motor conduction velocities are 3 to 4 M/second slower than in early adulthood. Sensory nerve conduction velocities begin slowing after the second decade. In the ulnar nerve, there is a reduction of 1 M/sec a decade from age 20 to 55 and 3 M/sec a decade after this age (Buchtal and Rosenfalck, 1966). Velocity impairment is accompanied by a decrease in the amplitude of the evoked sensory potential.

Age-related changes in axoplasmic transport have been reported by several authors. Although protein content and cholinesterase activity increase in aged rats, the rate of fast axoplasmic flow slows (McMartin and O'Connor, 1979). Electrophysiological determinations of functioning motor units (Campbell et al., 1973; Brown, 1972) in human muscle has revealed rather significant reductions in late life (Figure 22-3). In the extensor hallucis brevis, the indirect isometric twitch was found to be 310±88g, below the age of 59, and 210±131g, above this age. The mean number of "functioning" MU's in 66 patients, aged 3 to 58, was 197. After age 60, MU counts were reduced by an average of 60%. In the eighth and the ninth decade, otherwise normal individuals were often found to have only a few functioning MU's in this muscle. Furthermore, the remaining MU territories were enlarged, a finding suggestive of reinervation. Although the reliability of this technique has been questioned, these findings are somewhat inexactly correlated with the reduced axonal counts in anterior roots. It has been further suggested that MU's in late life may be morphologically intact, but functionally inactive, which would account for this discrepancy in the anatomical and physiological studies.

A number of morphological changes have been observed in aged peripheral nerves that could account for some of the physiological changes. In careful histometric studies of motor nerves, there is a significant reduction in both large and small myelinated fibers, as well as unmyelinated fibers, with aging (Stevens et al., 1973; Dyck, 1975). The remaining axons in both motor and sensory nerves demonstrate a variety of pathological alterations (Van Steenis and Kroes, 1971). The linear relationship between fiber diameter and internodal length is lost, suggesting that demyelination and remyelination have occurred (Lascelles and Thomas, 1966). Evidence of segmental demyelination and remyelination is particularly strong in anterior roots (Griffiths and Duncan, 1975). Myelin ovoids suggestive of axonal degeneration, irregularities in the myelin sheath, and segmental demyelination are seen with increasing frequency with advancing age (Dyck, 1975). Retrogressive degenerative changes are observed in unmyelinated axons as well (Ochoa and Mair, 1969). These changes are not completely characteristic of any of the better documented mechanisms of neuronal damage. In a recent review, Spencer and Ochoa (in press) discuss in detail several proposed causes of these retrogressive changes in peripheral nerve including ischemia, repeated minor trauma, a dying-back axonopathy, and lipofuscin accumulation in anterior horn cells.

Strength and Endurance

Having reviewed those morphological, biochemical, and metabolic changes that are presumably a concomitant of normal aging, we might then inquire as to the functional and performance changes that accompany them. Is there, in fact, a

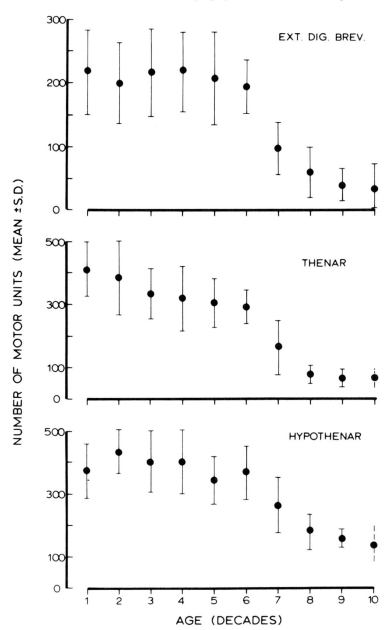

Figure 22-3. Values for MU counts in three different muscles as determined by the electrophysiological technique of McComas (1977). Between 55–60 years of age, there is rapid reduction in functioning MU at a time when muscle strength and anterior horn cell axonal counts are decreasing.

reduction in strength and endurance that can be attributed to a "normal" aging process? As in the study of age-related changes in other areas of the body, the very large number of variables that are difficult to control makes it difficult to answer this question. In addition, CNS changes that result in defects of coordination may be difficult to separate from MU changes (Shock and Norris, 1970).

An occasional study has reported that strength does not decline with age (Petrofsky and Lind 1975), but the vast majority of observations dealing with this subject report a clear, age-related decline in both static (isometric) and dynamic (isotonic) strength. In general, although strength in males is greater than females in all age groups, the rate of age-related loss is similar in both sexes. Aniansson et al.

(1978) have observed that maximum hand grip and quadriceps strength both deteriorate approximately 40% from the third to the seventh decade in both sexes. Thus, rates of deterioration are not only similar between the sexes, but also the strength loss seems to take place at the same rate in different muscles.

Larsson et al. (1979) have shown that both static and dynamic strength, at all contraction velocities tested, increase from the second to the third decade, plateau to the fourth, and then decline. In testing 114 males between ages 11 to 70 on a Cybex isokinetic dynamometer, they observed mean torque values of approximately 75 at age 11, 125 at age 15, 200 at age 25, 200 at age 35 and 45, 175 at age 55, and 150 at age 65. Bosco and Korni (1980) reported similar results in a study of vertical jumps.

The results of endurance testing are more difficult to interpret in terms of MU dysfunction, since pulmonary, cardiovascular, and metabolic–endocrine factors are involved. Endurance testing, depending on the testing situation used, is mainly a measure of aerobic (oxidative) capacity. An age-related decline in endurance testing has been shown by several investigators and would appear to be the result (in part) of MU factors. The changes are similar in both sexes (Profant et al., 1972). Although cardiovascular changes do limit exercise, evidence suggests that these factors are less important than MU changes (Bassey, 1978). Astrand et al. (1960) observed that aerobic work capacity decreases approximately 30% between ages 35 to 63, but the very wide standard deviations (S.D.) of his results suggest the possibility of other uncontrolled variables. He suggested that the wide S.D. might indicate a mutable (? reversible) process. A reduction of 43% over approximately the same time interval was observed in quadriceps muscle endurance testing (Aniansson et al., 1978). Endurance capacity at higher levels of work are more affected than at lower levels (Frolkis et al., 1976; Bassey, 1978). In another study, however, Larsson and Karlsson (1978) found no age-related change in either isometric or dynamic endurance.

The observed decline in strength and performance does not appear to be related to either fat-free mass (MacLennon et al., 1980) or measurable atrophy of the extremities. This agrees with other observations that reduction in function performance is not entirely related to reduction of functioning muscle mass and that other factors of a metabolic or biochemical nature may be involved. Motor performance deterioration is species-specific (Ingram et al., 1981).

Prevention and Reversibility

The potential for preventing age-related changes in the MU is theoretically greater than for age-related changes in other tissues. This assumption is justified because of the well-documented ability of muscle to respond to physiological stimulation by improving its functional capacity and even by correcting certain types of structural and chemical damage. In response to appropriate stimuli, muscle fiber can enlarge its size several-fold and increase its oxidative capacity, its ability to generate torque, its capacity to produce work, and its overall mechanical efficiency. The two main questions that then follow are (1) Are age-related functional changes in part a result of disuse? and (2) can activity prevent and/or reverse these regressive and functionally disturbing changes? Although information is still incomplete, and at times contradictory, the answer to both of these questions is a cautious and qualified "Yes."

Aging is associated with an evolving reduction of physical activity, and deconditioning occurs fairly rapidly (Bassey, 1978). Additionally, surveys demonstrate that actual activity in the elderly is less than what they themselves perceive (Sidney and Shepard, 1977). Is there evidence that a program of life-long exercise prevents age-related changes in the MU? Studies to date strongly suggest that such is indeed the case (Bortz, 1980; Kiessling, et al., 1974). It is clear that even modest exercise will dramatically prolong life for both male and female rodents (Retzlaff et al., 1966). However, the mechanism by which this benefit occurs is unclear and might well reflect cardiovascular conditioning rather than preservation of MU function. Grimby and Saltin (1966) physiologically analyzed 32 males, aged 42 to 68, who were well-trained, life-long, long distance runners and observed a significantly elevated capacity to perform aerobic work. In a 14-year study of 17 elderly males who had engaged in regular exercise for many years, Hollman (1965) observed that the V_{O_2max} decreased by only 10% as compared to a 31% decrease in sedentary controls. In a 10-year longitudinal study, no significant neuromuscular deterioration was observed when the subjects engaged in a regular exercise program (Gore, 1972). Dehn and Bruce (1972) observed that the V_{O_2max} declined threefold more rapidly in sedentary than in active subjects.

A number of other studies have addressed the question of whether age-related reduction in strength and work capacity can be reversed in late life. deVries (1970) put 112 relatively sedentary males, age 52–87, through a vigorous exercise program for 1 hour, three times a week. The exercise involved 15 to 20 minutes of calisthenics, 15 to 20 minutes of a brisk run-walk, and 15 to 20 minutes of isometric stretching or aquatics. Impressive changes occurred in oxygen transport capacity and the cardiovascular system. However, equally significant changes were observed in the neuromuscular unit. Arm strength improved by 6.4% at 6 weeks and 11.9% at 42 weeks. Work capacity was increased by 15.8% at the end of the 42-week testing period. Interestingly, it was observed that the trainability of aged muscle was not enhanced by a history of active physical acitivity in youth.

Suominen et al. (1977a) put 26 retired males and females, aged 69, through five 1-hour exercise periods each week for eight weeks. At the end of this training period, the V_{O_2max} had increased from 28.9 ml/g a minute to 32, for females from 27.9 to 31.3. They also observed an increase of muscle malate dehydrogenase activity, but not lactate dehydrogenase, consistent with the observed improvement in oxidative capacity. In a related study (Suominen et al., 1977b) utilizing submaximal bicycle exercise, they recorded an 11% increase in V_{O_2max} and increased tissue levels of the

oxidative enzyme succinate dehydrogenase. In this study, higher levels of glycogen, LDH, and a reduced, exercise-induced LA elevation suggested a simultaneous improvement in anerobic capacity after the training period. Although Saltin et al. (1969) observed a comparable rise in V_{O_2max} after 8 to 10 weeks of conditioning in 42 males aged 34 to 50, they did not observe any change in post exercise lactate elevation. Orlander et al. (1980) and Orlander and Aniansson (1980) found less impressive exercise-induced changes in the aged. Although the V_{O_2max} increased, there were no significant changes in the volume fractions of mitochondria or lipid, fiber type distribution or the enzymes PFK, LDH, citrate synthase, and cytochrome oxidase. This differed from younger subjects in whom an increase V_{O_2max} was accompanied by the expected morphological and biochemical changes. They suggest that, in aged muscle, other mechanisms may increase the V_{O_2max}.

The ability of exercised muscle to increase its oxidative capacity in response to exercise or indirect stimulation has been clearly demonstrated in both animals (Salmons and Henriksson, 1981) and humans (Munsat et al., 1976). After 10 to 13 weeks of training 46- to 62-year-old sedentary men, Kiessling et al. (1974) observed an 8% increase in V_{O_2max} and an 80% increase in cytochrome oxidase. It is reasonably certain that age does not limit this capacity. The response of anerobic substrates and enzymes, however, is less impressive, both in the normal young and the aged. The aerobic response to exercise can occur within a few weeks. Lower intensities of work may increase the V_{O_2max} without significantly altering tissue levels of oxidative enzymes (Orlander et al., 1980).

Sidney and Shephard (1978) subjected 14 men and 28 women, aged 60 to 83, to physical conditioning endurance training exercises. Measurements were made before and 7, 14, and 52 weeks after training was started. There was a final 24% improvement in V_{O_2max}, which compared quite favorably with a younger group. Most of the improvement occurred over the first seven weeks of training and in those subjects who engaged in more intensive and more frequent exercise. Improvement in the V_{O_2max} was more noticable with the treadmill exercise than with the bicycle. Orlander and Anianson (1980) studied five elderly men, aged 70 to 75, who engaged in a 12-week program of submaximal bicycle exercise. They observed a significant increase in aerobic capacity accompanied by an increase in mitochondrial oxidative capacity. However, the volume fractions of both mitochondria and lipid were unchanged, suggesting that the mechanism of improved oxidative capacity differs in the young and in the old. In the old, the improved capacity to oxidize substrate occurred without an increase in that mitochondrial volume. Moritani and deVries (1980) have shown that young and old have a similar capacity to improve strength with exercise. This improvement in strength corresponds to a reversal of age-related type 2 atrophy (Larsson, 1978).

Conclusion

Studies of age-related changes in the motor unit (MU) have the same problems as age-related studies of other organ systems. In the elderly, diets are often inadequate, medical illness is common, and inactivity is the rule. All these factors can affect the MU and are variables that are very difficult to control. However, a number of age-related changes have been reasonably well documented. The better-established and functionally more significant changes consist of reduced static and dynamic strength, smaller, and possibly fewer type 2 myofibers, a loss of alpha motoneurons, and a reduced oxidative capacity of exercising muscle. Several morphological observations are at variance with the physiological and functional changes. For example, although there is a significant loss of alpha motoneurons with aging, as determined by axon and MU count, there is little evidence of denervation or reinnervation on muscle biopsy or by electromyogram. Loss of strength in the aged is greater than expected relative to reduction of muscle fiber mass. These inconsistencies have not been explained.

The pathogenesis of age-related neuromuscular changes is uncertain. Although there is a movement to incriminate a reduction of neurotrophic factors on the muscle fiber, the evidence for the existence of such factors is very slim indeed. Of more current interest is the likelihood that the muscle fiber may have important trophic effects on the motoneuron. There is increasing support for the view that MU maintanence is a function of use and that age-related changes in the MU are, in great part, a result of disuse.

A growing body of evidence suggests that these MU changes are not an inevitable result of the aging process, but rather are preventable. The slogan "Use it or lose it" seems particularly applicable to the MU. Studies indicate that those who maintain a life of regular exercise avoid some of the functionally more disturbing losses of aging. However, considerably more evidence is needed to support this conclusion. A greater body of information documents the fact that age-related deterioration in neuromuscular function can be reversed with relatively little effort over a relatively short period of time. Whether reversal increases longevity is uncertain. However, its beneficial effect on quality of life is quite clear.

References

Aniansson, A., Grimby, G., Hedberg, M., Rundgren, A., and Sperling, L. (1978). Muscle function in old age. Scand. J. Rehab. Med. 6, 43–49.

Astrand, I. (1960). Aerobic work capacity in men and women with special reference to age. Acta Physiol. Scand. (Suppl. 169).

Bass, A., Gutmann, E., and Hanzlikova, V. (1975). Biochemical and histochemical changes in energy supply—enzyme pattern of muscles of the rat during old age. Gerontologia 21, 31–45.

Bassey, E.J. (1978). Age, inactivity and some physiological responses to exercise. Gerontology 24, 66–77.

Black, M.M. and Lasek, R.J. (1972). Slowing of the rate of axonal regeneration during growth and maturation. Exptl. Neurol. 63, 108–119.

Bortz, A.U. (1980). Effect of exercise on aging—effect of aging on exercise. J. Amer. Geriatr. Soc. 28 (2), 49–51.

Bosco, C. and Korni, P.V. (1980). Influence of aging on the mechanical behavior of leg extensor muscles. Eur. J. Appl. Physiol. 45, 20.

Brown, W.F. (1972). A method for estimating the number of motor units in thenar muscles and the changes in motor unit count with ageing. J. Neurol. Neurosurg. Psychiatr. 35, 845.

Buchtal, F. and Rosenfalck, A. (1966). Evoked action potentials and conduction velocity in human sensory nerves. Brain Res. 3, 1.

Buller, A.J., Eccles, J.C., and Eccles, R.M. (1960). Interactions between motoneurones and muscles in respect of the characteristic speeds of their responses. J. Physiol. 150, 417–439.

Caccia, M.R., Harris, J.B., and Johnson, M.A. (1979). Morphology and physiology of skeletal muscle in aging rodents. Muscle Nerve 3, 202–12.

Campbell, M.J., McComas, A.J., and Petito, F. (1973). Physiological changes in aging muscles. J. Neurol. Neurosurg. Psychiatr. 36, 174–182.

Coers, C., Telerman-Toppet, N., and Gerard, J.M. (1973). Terminal and innervation ratio in neuromuscular diseases. I. Methods and Controls. Arch. Neurol. 29, 210.

Corbin, K.B. and Gardner, E.D. (1937). Decrease in number of myelinated fibers in human spinal roots with age. Anat. Rec. 68, 63–74.

DeCoster, W., DeReuck, J., Sieben, G., and Vander Eecken, H. (1981). Early ultrastructural changes in aging rat gastrocnemius muscle: A stereologic study. Muscle Nerve 4, 111–116.

Dehn, M.M. and Bruce, R.A. (1972). Longitudinal variations in maximal oxygen intake with age and activity. J. Appl. Physiol. 33, 805–807.

deVries, H. (1970). Physiological effects of an exercise training regimen upon men aged 52–88. J. Gerontol. 25, 325.

Drachman, D.B. (1974). The role of acetylcholine as a neurotrophic transmitter. Ann. N.Y. Acad. Sci. 228, 160–175.

Drachman, D.B. and Witzke, F. (1972). Trophic regulation of acetylcholine sensitivity of muscle: Effect of electrical stimulation. Science 176, 514–516.

Dyck, P.J. (1975). Pathologic alterations of the peripheral nervous system of man. In Peripheral Neuropathy Vol. 1. P.J. Dyck, P.K. Thomas, and E.H. Lambert, Eds. Saunders, Philadelphia.

Dyck, P.J., Schultz, P.W., and O'Brien, P.C. (1972). Quantitation of touch-pressure sensation. Arch. Neurol. 26, 465.

Frolkis, V.V., Martynenko, O.A., and Zainostyan, V.P. (1976). Aging of the neuromuscular apparatus. Gerontology 22, 244–279.

Fujii, K. and Kurosu, H. (1979). Age-related changes in the reducible cross-links of connection from human skeletal muscle. Biochem. Biophys. Res. Comm. 89, 1026–32.

Fujisawa, K. (1974). Some observations on the skeletal musculature of aged rats: 1. Histological aspects. J. Neurol. Sci. 22, 353–366.

Gardner, E. (1940). Decrease in human neurons with age. Anat. Rec. 77, 529–536.

Gershon, H. and Gershon, D. (1973). Altered enzyme molecules in senescent organisms: Mouse muscle aldolase. Mech. Ageing Dev. 2, 33–41.

Giller, E.L., Neale, J.H., Bullock, P.N., Schrier, B.K., and Nelson, P.G. (1977). Choline acetyltransferase activity of spinal cord cell cultures increased by co-culture with muscle and by muscle-conditioned medium. J. Cell. Biol. 74, 16.

Gore, I.Y. (1972). Physical activity and aging, a survey of Soviet literature. Geront. Clin. 14, 65.

Griffiths, I.R. and Duncan, I.D. (1975). Age changes in the dorsal and ventral lumbar nerve roots of dogs. Acta Neuropathol. 32, 75.

Grimby, G. and Saltin, B. (1966). Physiological analysis of physically well-trained middle-aged and old athletes. Acta Med. Scand. 179, 513–526.

Gronert, G.A. (1980). Contracture responses and energy stores in quadriceps muscle from humans age 7–82 years. Hum. Biol. 52 (1), 43–51.

Guth, L. (1968). Trophic influence of nerve on muscle. Physiol. Rev. 48, 645–687.

Gutmann, E., Guttman, L., Medawar, P.B., and Young, J.Z. (1942). The rate of regeneration of nerve. J. Exptl. Biol. 19, 14–44.

Gutmann, E. and Hanzlikova, V. (1965). Age changes of motor end plates in muscle fibres of the rat. Gerontologia II, 12.

Gutmann, E. and Hanzlikova, V. (1972). Age changes in the neuromuscular system. Williams & Wilkins, Baltimore.

Gutmann, E. and Hanzlikova, V. (1976). Fast and slow motor units in aging. Gerontology 22, 280–300.

Gutmann, E., Hanzlikova, V., and Jakoubek, B. (1968). Changes in the neuromuscular system during old age. Exptl. Gerontol. 3, 141–146.

Gutmann, E., Hanzlikova, V., and Vyskoci, L.F. (1971). Age changes in cross-striated muscle of the rat. J. Physiol. Lond. 216, 331–343.

Haggmark, T., Jansson, E., and Suane, B. (1978). Cross-sectional area of the thigh muscle in man measured by computed tomography. Scand. J. Clin. Lab. Invest. 3 8, 355–360.

Harriman, D.G.F., Taverner, D., and Woolf, A.L. (1970). Ekbom's syndrome and burning paraesthesiae. A biopsy study by vital staining and electron microscopy of the intramuscular innervation, with a note on the age changes in motor nerve endings in distal muscles. Brain 93, 393.

Hollman, W. (1965). Korperliches training als prevention von Herz—Kreislauf—Krankheiten, Hippokrates, Stuttgart, p. 62.

Ingram, D.K., London, E.D., Reynold, M.A., Waller, S.B., and Goodrich, C.L. (1981). Differential effects of age on motor performance in two mouse strains. Neurobiol. Aging 2, 221–227.

Jennekens, F.G.I., Tomlinson, B.E., and Walton, J.N. (1971). Histochemical aspects of five limb muscles in old age: An autopsy study. J. Neurol. Sci. 14, 259–276.

Kaeser, H.E. (1970). Nerve conduction velocity measurements, In Handbook of Clinical Neurology Vol. 7. P.J. Vinken and A.W. Bruyn, Ed. North Holland: Amsterdam, p. 114.

Kalant, N., Leibovici, D., Leibovici, T., and Fukushima, N. (1980). Effect of age on glucose utilization and responsiveness to insulin in forearm muscle. J. Amer. Geriatr. Soc. 28 (7), 304–307.

Kawamura, Yl, Okazaki, H., O'Brien, P.C., and Dyck, P.J. (1977). Lumbar motoneurons of man: 1) Number and diameter histogram of alpha and gamma axons of ventrol root. J. Neuropath. Exptl. Neurol. 36, 853.

Kiessling, K.H., Pilstromm, L., Rylund, A., Saltin, B., and Piehl, K. (1974). Enzyme activities and morphometry in skeletal muscle of middle-aged men after training. Scand. J. Clin. Lab. Invest. 33, 63–69.

Larsson, L. (1978). Morphological and functional characteristics of the aging skeletal muscle in man. A cross-sectional study. Acta Phys. Scand. (Suppl.) 457, 1–36.

Larsson, L., Grimby, G., and Karlsson, J. (1979). Muscle strength and speed of movement in relation to age and muscle morphology. J. Appl. Physiol. 46, 451–456.

Larsson, L. and Karlsson, J. (1978). Isometric and dynamic endurance as a function of age and skeletal muscle characteristics. Acta Physiol. Scand. 104, 129–136.

Lascelles, R.G. and Thomas, P.K. (1966). Changes due to age in internodal length in the sural nerve in man. J. Neurol. Neurosurg. Psychiatr. 29, 40.

MacLennan, W.J., Hall, M.R., Timothy, J.I., and Robinson, M. (1980). Is weakness in old age due to muscle wasting. Age Ageing 9 (3). 188–192.

Marchi, M., Hoffman, D.W., and Giacobini, E. (1980). Ageing of the peripheral nervous system: Age dependent changes in cholinergic synapses. In Neural Regulatory Mechanisms during Aging. Alan R. Liss, Inc. New York.

McComas (1977). Neuromuscular Function and Disorders. Boston, Butterworths.

McComas, A.J., Fawcett, P.R.W., Campbell, M.J., and Sica, R.E.P. (1971). Electrophysiological estimation of the number of motor units within a human muscle. J. Neurol. Neurosurg. Psychiatr. 34, 121–131.

McMartin, D.N. and O'Connor, J.A. (1979). Effect of age on axoplasmic transport of cholinesterase in rat sciatic nerves. Mech. Ageing Dev. 10, 241–248.

Moller, P., Bergstrom, J., Erikson, S., Furst, P., and Hellstrom, K. (1979). Effect of aging on free amino acids and electrolytes in skeletal muscle. Clin. Sci. 56, 427–432.

Moller, P., Bergstrom, J., Furst, P., and Hellstrom, K. (1980). Effect of aging on energy-rich phosphagens in human skeletal muscles. Clin. Sci. 58, 6, 553–555.

Moritani, T. and deVries, H.A. (1980). Potential for gross muscle hypertrophy in older men. J. Gerontol. 35, 672–682.

Mulder, D.W., Lambert, E.H., Bastrom, J.A., and Sprague, R.G. (1961). The neuropathies associated with diabetes mellitus. Neurology 11, 275–284.

Munsat, T.L., McNeal, D., and Waters, R. (1976). Effects of nerve stimulation on human muscle. Neurology 33, 617.

Murphy, R.A., Singer, R.H., Saide, J., Pantagis, N.J., Blanchard, M.H., Byron, K.S., Arnason, B.G.W., and Young, M. (1977). Synthesis and secretion of a high molecular weight form of nerve growth factor by skeletal muscle cells in culture. Proc. Natl. Acad. Sci. 74, 4496.

Norris, A.H., Shock, N.W., and Wagman, I.H. (1953). Age changes in the maximum conduction velocity of motor fibers of human ulnar nerves. J. Appl Physiol. 5, 589–593.

Ochoa, J. and Mair, W.G.P. (1969). The normal sural nerve in man. II Changes in the axons and Schwann cells due to ageing. Acta Neuropathol. (Berl.) 13, 217.

Orlander, J. and Aniansson, A. (1980). Effect of physical training on skeletal muscle metabolism and ultrastructure in 70–75-year-old men. Acta Physiol. Scand. 109, 149–154.

Orlander, J., Kiessling, K.H., and Ekblom, B. (1980). Time course of adaptation to low intensity training in sedentary men: Dissociation of central and local effects. Acta Physiol. Scand. 108, 85–90.

Orlander, J., Kiessling, K.H., Larsson, L., Karlsson, J., and Aniansson, A. (1978). Skeletal muscle metabolism and ultrastructure in relation to age in sedentary men. Acta Physiol. Scand. 104, 249–261.

Pestronk, A., Drachman, D.B., and Griffin, J.W. (1980). Effects of aging on nerve sprouting and regeneration. Exptl. Neurol. 70, 65–82.

Petrofsky, J.S. and Lind, A.R. (1975). Aging, isometric strength and endurance and cardiovascular response to static effort. J. Appl. Physiol. 38, 91–95.

Price, H. and Van de Velde, R.L. (1981). Ultrastructure of the skeletal muscle fiber. In Disorders of Voluntary Muscle, J. Walton, Ed. Churchill-Livingston, New York.

Prineas, J. and Spencer, P.S. (1975). Pathology of the nerve cell body in disorders of the peripheral nervous system. In: Peripheral Neuropathy Vol. 1, P.J. Dyck, P.H. Thomas, and E.H. Lambert, Ed. Saunders. Philadelphia.

Profant, G.R., Early, R.G., Nilson, K.L., Kusum, V., and Bruce, R.A. (1972). Responses to maximal exercise in healthy middle-aged women. J. Appl. Physiol. 53, 595–599.

Rebeiz, J.J., Moore, M.J., Holden, E.M., and Adams, R.D. (1972). Variations in muscle status with age and systematic diseases. Acta Neuropathol. 22, 127–144.

Retzlaff, E., Fontaine, J., and Futura, W. (1966). Effect of daily exercise in life-span of albino rats. Geriatrics 21, 171.

Salmons, S. and Henriksson, J. (1981). The adaptive response of skeletal muscle to increased use. Muscle Nerve 4, 94–105.

Saltin, B., Hartley, L.H., Kilborn, A., and Astrand, I. (1969). Physical training in middle-aged and older men. II Oxygen uptake, heart rate and blood lactate concentration at submaximal and maximal exercise. Scand. J. Clin. Lab. Invest. 24, 323–334.

Scelsi, R., Marchetti, C. and Poggi, P. (1980). Histochemical and ultrastructural aspects of M. vastus lateralis in sedentary old people (age 65–89 years). Acta Neuropathol. (Berl.) 51 (2), 99–105.

Schlenska, G.K. and Kleine, T.O. (1980). Disorganization of glycolytic and gluconeogenic pathways in skeletal muscle of aged persons studied by histometric and enzymatic methods. Mech. Ageing Dev. 13 (2), 143–154.

Serratrice, G., Roux, H., and Aquaron, R. (1968). Proximal muscular weakness in elderly subjects. J. Neurol. Sci. 7, 275–299.

Shafiq, S.A., Lewis, S.G., Dimino, L.C., and Schultz, H.S. (1978). Microscopic study of skeletal muscle in elderly subjects. In Aging Vol. 6. G. Kaldon and W.J. DiBattista, Eds. Raven Press, New York.

Shock, N.W. and Norris, A.H. (1970). Neuromuscular coordination as a factor in age changes in muscular exercise. Med. Sport 4, 92–99.

Sidney, K.H. and Shepard, R.J. (1977). Activity patterns of elderly men and women. J. Gerontol. 32, 25–32.

Sidney, K.H. and Shephard, R.J. (1978). Frequency and intensity of exercise training for elderly subjects. Med. Sci. Sports 10, 125–131.

Smith, D.O. (1979). Reduced capabilites of synaptic transmission in aged rats. Exptl. Neurol. 66, 650–666.

Snow, M.H. (1977). The effects of aging on satellite cells in skeletal muscles of mice and rats. Cell Tiss. Res. 185, 399–408.

Spencer, P.S. and Ochoa, J. (in press). The mammalian peripheral nervous system in old age. In Aging and Cell Structure, J. Johnson, Ed. Raven Press, New York.

Stalberg, E. and Thiele, B. (1975). Motor unit fiber density in the extensor digitorium communis muscle. J. Neurol. Neurosurg. Psychiatr. 38, 874–880.

Stevens, J.C., Lafgren, E.P., and Dyck, P.J. (1973). Histometric evaluation of branches of peroneal nerve: Technique for combined biopsy of muscle nerve and cutaneous nerve. Brain Res. 52, 37–59.

Suominen, H., Heikkinen, E., Liesen, H., Michel, D., and Hollman, W. (1977b). Effects of 8 weeks endurance training on skeletal muscle metabolism in 56–70 year old sedentary men. Eur. J. Appl. Physiol. 37, 173–180.

Suominen, H., Heikkinen, E., and Parkatti, T. (1977a). Effect of eight weeks physical training on muscle and connective tissue of the m. vastus lateralis in 69 year old men and women. J. Gerontol. 32, 33–37.

Thomas, T.R., Londeree, B.R., Gerhardt, K.O., and Gehrke, (1978). Fatty acid pattern and cholesterol in skeletal muscle of men aged 22 to 73. Mech. Ageing Dev. 8, 429–434.

Tomlinson, B.E., Walton, J.N., and Rebeiz, J.J. (1969). The effects of aging and cachexia upon skeletal muscle. A histological study. J. Neurol. Sci. 9, 321–346.

Tomonaga, M. (1977). Histochemical and ultrastructural changes in senile human skeletal muscle. J. Amer. Geriatr. Soc. 25, 125–131.

Tzankoff, S.P. and Norris, A.H. (1979). Age-related differences in lactate distribution kinetics following maximal exercise. Eur. J. Appl. Physiol. 1, 35–40.

Van Steenis, G. and Kroes, R. (1971). Changes in the nervous system and musculature of old rats. Vet. Pathol. 8, 320.

Wahren, J., Saltin, B., Jorfeldt, L., and Pernow, B. (1974). Influence of age on the local circulatory adoption to leg exercise. J. Clin. Lab. Invest. 33, 79–86.

Wright, E. and Spink, J. (1959). A study of the loss of nerve cells in the central nervous system in relation to age. Gerontologia 3, 277–287.

Zacks, S.I. and Sheff, M.F. (1982). Age-related impeded regeneration of mouse minced anterior tibial muscle. Muscle Nerve 5, 152–161.

23. Peripheral Nerve Disorders in the Elderly

THOMAS D. SABIN

NAGAGOPAL VENNA

Clinical neurologists have long noted the loss of vibration sense and dampened ankle jerks that are the ubiquitous bedside physical findings in the aged (Critchley, 1931). This loss of vibration sense and reflexes is in the lower extremities, that is, in the distribution of the longest axons in the body and, therefore, points to the presence of a peripheral polyneuropathy.

Age-Linked, Structural Changes in the Peripheral Nervous System

Morphological changes in the nerve cells, roots, peripheral nerves, and specialized nerve terminals have been linked with the aging process. Counts of large- and intermediate-sized cells in the anterior gray columns of the lumbar area indicate that there is a drop-out of 5 to 8% of these cells per decade of adulthood (Kawamura and Dyck, 1977). A similar rate of age-linked cell loss for the loss of alpha and gamma motor neurons in the same lumbar segments has been demonstrated (Kawamura et al., 1977). Corbin and Gardner (1937) found a 32% loss of fibers in both the dorsal and ventral roots of T8 and T9 at age 90 years. The degeneration of the dorsal columns that occurs with aging very likely reflects the dissolution of the centrally directed axons of the dorsal root ganglion cells. The longer fibers comprising the gracile columns are most affected in this process (Morrison et al., 1959; Mufson and Stein, 1980).

The peripheral nerves also show a similar degree of drop-out with aging (Ochoa and Mair, 1969). The number of fibers and the spectrum of fiber diameter, as well as the internodal length of teased fibers of various diameters, have been determined for certain nerves from autopsy and biopsy materials (Stevens et al., 1973). Rexed (1944) studied cranial nerves and spinal nerve roots and found that the age-linked loss of nerves affected thick fibers more than thin fibers. In a study of the sciatic nerve of 100 subjects over the age of 60 and 10 younger subjects, Takahaski (1966) not only confirmed that the loss of myelinated fibers from the sciatic nerve increased with age, but also showed that this loss selectively affected the thickly myelinated fibers, with relative preservation of the thin fibers. These changes correlated well with absence of ankle reflexes in the subjects studied. The greater involvement of large myelinated fibers has not been documented in all studies, and it is possible that the anatomical site of the nerve is important. O'Sullivan and Swallow (1968) and Swallow (1966) found disproportionate age-linked loss of large fibers in the anterior tibial nerve and sural nerve, but not in the superficial radial nerve. The vulnerability to this loss may be related to nerve fiber length. The area of the nerve fascicles appears to remain constant with age, but the connective tissue component of the fascicle presumably increases as the number of nerve fibers decreases.

Aging is also associated with a gradual shortening of the mean internodal length. In the study by Stevens et al. (1973), the mean internodal length at age 46 was 1135 μ as compared to 774 μ at age 70. This shortening could reflect the selective dropout of large fibers. Since the shortening is associated with a clear increase in the variability of internodal length, demyelination and remyelination must also have occurred. Lascalles and Thomas (1966) studied human sural nerves and found not only irregularities in internodal lengths indicating remyelination, but also axons with uniformly short internodes, suggesting axonal regeneration after Wallerian degeneration. Vizoso (1950) found abnormally long internodal lengths on some nerve fibers from aged subjects and thought that this finding might reflect a thinning of such fibers without actual degeneration.

Chronic trauma and vascular disease have been suggested as causes of segmental demyelination that might be cumulative with advancing age. The effects of chronic trauma producing similar changes have been studied in aging animals (Grover-Johnson and Spencer, 1981). The alterations in the myelin sheath thought to be characteristic of primary demyelination have, however, been rarely observed in cases of primary axonal degeneration (Dyck et al., 1971).

Striking age-related changes have also been demonstrated in intramuscular nerve terminals (Harriman et al., 1970). Preterminal nerve endings, stained vitally with methylene blue, showed marked sprouting after emergence from the nerve bundle. The sprouts often produced multiple endplates on a single muscle fiber. The endplates were larger and more complex in appearance than normal endplates. The intramuscular nerve bundle and subterminal nerve fibers in the aged patients also contained numerous spherical axonal swellings, which resembled corpora amylacea.

Quantitative studies of Meissner's corpuscles have shown that they decrease in concentration with age (Bolton et al., 1966). During the growing years, the decrease may be due to an increase in the size of the digit, but the decrease continues beyond this phase, and in old age, the corpuscles become sparse, irregular in horizontal distribution, and highly variable in size and shape. In the age group 31 to 50 (mean 38.2), there were 15.7 Meissner's corpuscles per square millimeter at the tip of the little finger (S.D. 8.8) as compared to 8.4 (S.D. 3.3) in the 71 to 84 age group. In Ridley's 1968 study, the total number of Meissner's corpuscles in a 3 mm punch biopsy of skin was divided by the number of epidermal ridges (Meissner index). A decline occurred in this index from 0.930 in the first decade to 0.228 in the eighth decade.

Physiological Findings in the Neuropathy of Aging

Physiological age-linked alterations in the peripheral nervous system have also been extensively documented. A gradual decline in maximal nerve conduction velocity with age has been described in repeated studies (Norris et al., 1953; Lafratta and Canestiari, 1966; Downie and Newell, 1961). Mayer (1963) measured sensory conduction velocities in relation to age in the posterior tibial and common peroneal nerves and found a decline after the age of 50 years. The sensory conduction was 48.9 ± 2.6 m/second for the posterior tibial nerve in the 51 to 80 year group, as compared to 49.0 ± 3.8 m/second in the 36 to 50 year group. The common peroneal nerve sensory conduction in the 51 to 80 year group was 46.1 ± 4.0 m/second, as compared to the 50.4 ± 1.0 m/second for the 36 to 50 year group. The H-reflex from the popliteal fossa was prolonged after the age of 50 years, with values of 28.2 ± 1.5 m/second. Behse and Buchthal (1971) studied sensory conduction along the proximal and distal segments of the superficial peroneal, sural, and posterior tibial nerves of 71 subjects and correlated the results with age. They demonstrated slowing of conduction with increasing age in both the proximal and distal segments of these nerves. A maximum conduction velocity of 56.5 m/second in subjects age 15 to 30 years compared to 53.1 m/second in subjects age 40 to 65 years in the proximal segments. In the distal segments, maximum conduction velocity was 46.1 m/second in the younger group and 42.5 m/second in the older group. LaFratta and Zalis (1973) measured sural nerve conduction in 52 subjects without neurological disease and demonstrated slowing of the conduction velocity with increasing age at this site as well. In an elegant study, Dorfman and Bosley (1979) measured not only motor and sensory conduction in peripheral nerves, but also F-response from median and tibial nerves and related them to age. The F-wave latencies increased with age at a yearly rate of 0.04 msec/m in the median nerve, and at a yearly rate of 0.12 msec/m in the tibial nerve. The median nerve motor conduction yearly rate decreased by 0.15 m/second, whereas sensory conduction decreased by 0.16 m/second. Slowing of maximal conduction velocities could be due to a shorter average internodal length following demyelination and remyelination or a selective drop-out of the faster conducting fibers from the peripheral nerves.

Brown (1972) estimated the number of motor units in the median innervated thenar muscles, using an incremental nerve stimulation technique. There was an age-related fall in the number of motor units, which accelerated at mid-life. Some elderly subjects with clinically normal strength had only 50% of the number of motor units present in youth.

Summary of the Anatomical and Physiological Changes

The available morphological and physiological data adequately document significant age-linked changes in the peripheral nervous system. There is a loss of 5 to 8% of nerve fibers a decade after age 40, and a progressive slowing of maximal sensory and motor conduction velocities at a yearly rate of 0.12 to 0.16 m/second. There is also an increasing number of abnormalities in myelination with increasing age. Longer

fibers and larger fibers are most affected. Although some of the changes, especially the alterations in myelination, might be due to cumulative effects of trauma or vascular disease or both, primary degeneration of nerve cells and axons is also occurring. Clinical deficits in the distribution of the longest nerve fibers may appear in both primary "dying back" axonal disorders or with randomly scattered demyelination; the longest fibers have the greatest statistical chance of accumulating lesions (Sabin et al., 1978).

Clinical Importance of the Neuropathy of Aging

Clinical implications of the neuropathy of aging have not been fully explored. The bedside finding of diminished vibratory sensation has been extensively documented, however; the sensory threshold increases the more distal the stimulation site (Pearson, 1928; Rosenberg, 1958; Steinberg and Graber, 1963; Goldberg and Lindblom, 1979).

Loss of large fibers from the distal lower extremities may contribute to senile gait disorder (Sabin, 1982). Loss of IA afferents from muscle spindles might deprive the elderly individual of the sense of "movement," even though the sense of "position" is relatively unimpaired (Craske, 1977). This speculation might be carried one step further to explain the common tendency of patients with senile gait disorders to fall backward. If loss of IA fibers is related to axonal length, then the anterior tibial compartment would lose this innervation before the gastrocnemius–soleus group because the nerve fibers to the anterior compartment are about 10 cm longer than those coursing to the posterior compartment of the leg (Sunderland, 1978). Simultaneous contraction of both compartments under these circumstances of selective denervation would result in a volley of IA afferents arising only from the gastrocnemius–soleus muscles. This situation would be similar to the effects of placing a vibrator over the gastrocnemius–soleus groups of both legs in a healthy young adult. The individual will tend to fall over backward if his eyes are closed (Eklund, 1969). The vibrator repeatedly distorts and restores the nuclear bag portion of muscle spindles, with a consequent volley of activity in the IA afferents. This volley simulates that which would occur with continuous stretch of these muscles and induces a reflex contraction in the vibrated muscles and a constant error in perceived position of the limb (Goodwin et al., 1972). This postulate applied to senile gait disorder would then explain not only the tendency to fall backward, but also the frequent complaint of "fearfulness and dizziness" that might reflect a marked distortion in the sense of movement in the lower extremities, that is, a "spindle vertigo."

The neuropathy of aging might play a role in other age-related disturbances, which are generally viewed as a decline in "higher cortical functions," such as sensory discrimination and motor learning tasks. Peripheral mechanisms have been involved in essential (senile) tremor and primary writing tremor (Shahani and Young, 1978; Rothwell et al., 1979).

Although increased cardiac vagal tone and constipation in old age are common clinical phenomena, anatomical and physiological changes in the autonomic peripheral nerves have not been clearly documented. Age-related autonomic neuropathy might have important implications in the understanding of these disorders and of others, such as labile blood pressure (Gribben et al., 1969), liability to arrhythmias (Nielsen, 1969), poor temperature regulation, and sexual dysfunction. Precise delineation of an autonomic neuropathy of aging would also contribute significantly to gerontological pharmacology.

Polyneuropathies in the Aged

Polyneuropathy is common in the elderly. Despite diverse causes, the clinical expression is often the same. Evidence of altered, sensory, motor, reflex, autonomic, and trophic functions appears symmetrically in distal parts of limbs, in various combinations and degrees of severity. Common symptoms are tingling and numbness, but the sensation of burning, coldness, crawling, and an exquisite sensitivity of the skin to touch may also occur, often with annoy-

ing persistence. Deep aching, cramp-like, or lancinating pain, which is typically worse at night, may occur in the limbs. When deep sensibility is impaired, patients experience a heaviness in the limbs, a feeling of walking on "cotton," and an unsteadiness of gait. When this loss of sensation is combined with poor vision, the patient may fall, especially in the dark. Diminution or loss of touch, pain, temperature, position, and vibration sensations and sometimes decreased sweating occur in stocking and later in glove distribution. In advanced cases, hypesthesia extends to the wall of the abdomen and chest on either side of anterior midline in the shape of a long teardrop. This zone represents the distal-most territory of the intercostal nerves (Sabin, 1971). Irregular "pseudoathetoid" movements of the fingers of outstretched hands is due to loss of proprioception. Ankle reflexes are lost early, followed by reflexes at the knees and later in the upper limbs. An unusual variation is loss of pain and temperature in stocking and glove distribution, accompanied by visceral autonomic dysfunction, while proprioception, touch, and tendon reflexes are intact (Brown et al., 1976). This reflects a selective involvement of small diameter fibers. When pain sense is lost in the feet, the patient becomes vulnerable to recurrent painless trauma, with trophic ulcers. Motor impairment can vary from extensive to inconspicuous. Loss of fullness of the extensor digitorum brevis over the outer aspect of the dorsum of the foot is an early sign. Wasting and weakness of the intrinsic muscles of the feet produce the claw-toe deformity and may spread to the calves and the hands.

Polyneuropathy In Diabetes Mellitus

Maturity-onset diabetes mellitus is by far the most common cause of polyneuropathy in the elderly. Peripheral nerves show a nonspecific segmental destruction of the myelin and a dwindling of axons, affecting all fiber sizes. Small diameter fibers (subserving pain, temperature, and autonomic functions) rarely are selectively injured (Brown et al., 1976). The longstanding debate as to whether demyelination (implying Schwann cell dysfunction) or axonal loss (reflecting neuronal injury) is the primary abnormality remains unresolved. Small blood vessels occluded by platelet–fibrin plugs in the nerve trunks have attracted renewed attention, since platelet function and coagulation abnormalities have recently been demonstrated in diabetes (Timperley et al., 1976). Recent biochemical analyses of diabetic nerves reveal many changes, such as elevated levels of sorbitol, fructose, and cholesterol esters, and a marked reduction of phospholipids, cerebrosides, and cholesterol; the significance of these findings is uncertain (Dyck et al., 1980).

Neuropathy may be the presenting feature of diabetes in the elderly because the derangement in glucose metabolism is often mild enough to escape detection. The polyneuropathy is typically sensory and autonomic and develops in a distal symmetrical pattern. The onset is most often insidious, but the neuropathy is occasionally precipitated by the stress of an acute cardiac or cerebral infarction, surgery, sepsis, or a period of poor control of blood sugar. Sudden onset of neuropathy is rarely seen when treatment with insulin or oral hypoglycemic drugs is initiated. Limb pains may be intractable and most distressing. In a recent study (Turkington, 1980), many such patients were found to have significant depression, and pain and depression resolved within three months of treatment with tricyclics. Some patients with painful neuropathy have visceral autonomic involvement and selective loss of pinprick and temperature, although touch, propriception, and tendon reflexes are retained. An extreme manifestation of painful diabetic polyneuropathy is the syndrome of diabetic neuropathic cachexia (Ellenberg, 1974). Middle-aged or elderly men with mild diabetic polyneuropathy experience pain in the limbs, anorexia, depression, insomnia, and profound weight loss. Tests for malignancy and other wasting diseases are negative, and the syndrome resolves completely, except for diabetes and neuropathy, in about a year. Pathogenesis of this remarkable condition is not understood, although hypothalamic dysfunction has been postulated.

Recurrent trauma to insensitive feet causes calluses over the distal foot, which may ultimately break down to painless punched-out "trophic" ulcer. This sets the stage for serious necrotizing bacterial infection of deep fascial spaces of the foot and osteomyelitis. In about one out of one thousand patients, mostly over the age of 50 and with diabetes of over 15 years duration, insidious, painless destruction of mid-tarsal, metatarso-phalangeal and less commonly, ankle, joints results in striking deformities of the foot; these are known as Charcot neuroarthropathy. Synovitis and arthritis are associated with deposition of calcium-pyrophosphate crystals in the insensitive joint surface prior to the destructive phase of Charcot neuroarthropathy. Autonomic neuropathy affecting the viscera and the limbs is now recognized as a common accompaniment of the polyneuropathy. Impotence; painless urinary retention; intermittent, often nocturnal diarrhea; gastroparesis; postural hypotension; and anhydrosis are some of its myriad manifestations. Cerebrospinal fluid protein is regularly increased, sometimes as high as 200 mg/100 ml. The polyneuropathy tends to persist indefinitely once it becomes clinically manifest and, in a substantial number of patients, it causes long-term severe disability, chiefly because of pain and sensory loss. A recent prospective study indicates that the advent of autonomic neuropathy is ominous. The mortality rate at 5 years was an alarming 50%, with one-half of the deaths directly or indirectly attributed to autonomic dysfunction (Ewing et al., 1980). Some reports have highlighted unexpected cardiorespiratory arrests in such patients in relation to chest infection or respiratory depressant drugs (Page and Watkins, 1978).

The mainstay of treatment for diabetic neuropathy continues to be the symptomatic management of insensitivity, pain, and autonomic disturbance. Treatment of diabetes itself seems to have little effect on clinically established polyneuropathy. However, recent preliminary studies hold some hope for the future. Patients with recently diagnosed diabetes and subclinical polyneuropathy showed significant improvement in motor nerve conduction velocities or correction of abnormal perception of vibration during ischemia with insulin or sulfonylurea therapy (Ward et al., 1971; Terkildsen and Christensen, 1971). This effect was noted within a few weeks and continued up to six months. Control of hyperglycemia appears to mediate this effect. In patients over 50 years old with maturity onset diabetes, the degree of fasting hyperglycemia is inversely related to the severity of motor nerve conduction velocity slowing (Graf et al., 1979). The improvement in conduction velocities with treatment is proportional to the degree of control of the hyperglycemia (Porte et al., 1981). Improved methods for control of hyperglycemia may sustain this beneficial effect. In experimental diabetic neuropathy of animals, it has already been established that prolonged motor conduction velocities can be reliably prevented or reversed by rigorous control of hyperglycemia with insulin. The discovery that blood glucose in diabetes is nonenzymatically (glycosylation) linked to hemoglobin, lens crystallin, and the basic myelin protein of nerves suggests a new mechanism by which hyperglycemia might interfere with peripheral nerve function (Bunn, 1981). If this abnormal glucose binding is significant in the pathogenesis of diabetic neuropathy, then it would be theoretically possible to prevent disabling neuropathy by early and persistent maintenance of euglycemia. The use of continuous preprogrammed subcutaneous insulin infusion has made near normoglycemia feasible for as long as several months. The artificial pancreas and pancreatic beta cell transplantation would be expected to avert diabetic complications as well as to control glucose blood levels.

Another metabolic manipulation involves the polyalcohol myoinositol (Winegrad and Greene, 1976). The peripheral nerves in acute experimental diabetes are depleted of myoinositol and when the animal's diet is fortified with 1% myoinositol, neuropathy is prevented or improved despite persistent hyperglycemia. In two human trials of oral myoinositol therapy (Salway et al., 1978; Clements et al., 1979) lasting up to 4 months, improvement in symptoms and sensory nerve conduction velocity was noted, although this result was not found in another study (Gregerson et al., 1978). Although myoinositol is normally concentrated in peripheral nerves and is known to be incorporated into inositol-phospholipids of the axolemmal membrane, its physiological role is not clear. The fact that a 3% myoniositol diet in experimental animals is actually *detrimental* to nerve conduction and that an *excess* of myoinositol is implicated in uremic polyneupathy should point to caution in its use.

Accumulation of another polyalcohol, *sorbitol,* in the peripheral nerves in experimental diabetes is well documented (Gabbay, 1969). Sorbitol is formed from glucose and accumulates chiefly in the Schwann cells. In excess, it is believed to produce Schwann cell dysfunction. When neuropathy is reversed by insulin, the nerve content of sorbitol gradually falls. Furthermore, if the formation of sorbitol is prevented by the aldose-reductase inhibitor arlestatin, motor nerve conduction velocities improve. Accumulation of sorbitol has been postulated to cause osmotic swelling in Schwann cells and, thus, to impair nerve function. Arlestatin was administered intravenously to a few patients for a few days (Culebras et al., 1981), but no objective improvement could be demonstrated, although it was well tolerated. In a recent, longer, double-blind crossover study, another aldose-reductase inhibitor, Sorbinil, was used in patients with subclinical polyneuropathy, and a significant improvement of motor nerve conduction velocities demonstrated (Judzewitsch and Jaspin, 1983).

These metabolic manipulations do not appear very promising in themselves, but they indicate the promise of research into basic mechanisms of nerve injury in diabetes. The recent discovery of *chronic* diabetes and polyneuropathy in Chinese hamsters and certain strains of mice adds valuable animal models for such studies.

Polyneuropathy in Uremia

Chronic renal failure in the elderly usually results from renal arteriosclerosis or pyelonephritis or both. When maintenance hemodialysis became commonplace about 15 years ago and patients with end-stage renal disease survived for many years, polyneuropathy emerged as a crippling complication of this syndrome. Recently, however, more efficient, more frequent, and earlier dialysis has already diminished its impact. The neuropathy is distal, symmetrical, and sensorimotor and is characterized by an axonal degeneration of large diameter fibers. There is a severe, symptomatic chronic uremia (creatine clearance of < 10 ml/minute and serum creatinine of > 10 mg%) when neuropathy appears, often with prominent pain and various dysesthetic sensations in the legs and feet. Many patients also experience distressing deep discomfort in the legs while inactively lying in bed or waiting for dialysis, which is temporarily relieved by moving the legs or walking. This restless-leg syndrome has not been proven to be neuropathic. The neuropathy may progress to severe sensory loss and even paralysis of all limbs. Autonomic neuropathy is mild, but may cause postural hypotension in relation to dialysis or impotence. Cerebrospinal fluid (CSF) protein may be increased up to 200 mg%.

This is one of the few chronic metabolic polyneuropathies that regularly improves with treatment of the underlying disease. Maintenance hemodialysis or peritoneal dialysis, at home or in the hospital, halts the neuropathy and improves sensation and later strength, although this takes many months. Despite clinical improvement, nerve conduction velocities remain abnormal. Severe established neuropathy often responds poorly to dialysis and, on occasion, rapid deterioration occurs in the first weeks of dialysis (Jebsen et al., 1967). Hemodialysis, though well tolerated the first three years, later causes serious complications in the elderly. Long-term peritoneal dialysis at home is now safer and more practical for the elderly (Tenckhoff and Curtis, 1970). In fact, the success of peritoneal dialysis in ameliorating neuropathy even when chemical control of uremia is not good has led to the concept of "middle molecules" that accumulate in uremia that are injurious to peripheral nerves. These putative toxins, with molecular weights of 300 to 1500, may readily permeate peritoneal membranes, but are less efficiently removed by conventional hemodialysers. The identity and significance of these substances is still not established. Many other dialysable uremic "toxins" have been studied. The polyalcohol myoinositol accumulates in uremia and is shown to cause polyneuropathy in experimental animals. Paradoxically, it is the *deficiency* of this substance that is postulated to be involved in the development of the neuropathy of diabetes. An inhibitor of transketolase, a thiamine-dependent enzyme of normal peripheral nerves, has been detected in uremia as well as many other polypetides, but no single substance has been consistently correlated with polyneuropathy. The efficiency of the currently popular, continuous, *ambulatory* peritoneal dialysis in the prevention and treatment of neuropathy has not yet been established.

The most effective treatment for uremic polyneuropathy is renal transplantation. This has successfully been done in many elderly patients. Even severe neuropathy shows dramatic improvement, often beginning within weeks (Bolton et al., 1971). Autonomic as well as sensorimotor features improve. This improvement has been correlated with a fall in plasma myoinositol concentration to normal (Oh et al., 1978). When neuropathy recurs after late failure of the transplant, retransplantation again improves the neuropathy (Bolton, 1976). When a few patients underwent bilateral nephrectomy for uncontrollable hypertension due to chronic renal failure, a remarkable recovery from neuropathy was observed (Popovtzer et al., 1969). On the other hand, neuropathy may at times develop in nephrectomized patients who are maintained by dialysis. The greatest impact of modern treatment has undoubtedly been in the *prevention* of clinical polyneuropathy by the institution of effective dialysis early in the course of chronic renal failure.

Polyneuropathy Associated with Malignancy

In middle-aged and elderly patients, disabling polyneuropathy may develop over a few months as a rare, remote effect of cancer. Characteristically, it is combined with a sprinkling of such neurological signs as proximal myopathy, myasthenic syndrome, or cerebellar ataxia. The CSF protein is often elevated to 200 mg%. The neuropathy may precede other evidence of malignancy by several months or even a few years. In the more common, mixed sensorimotor form, only nonspecific axonal degeneration and demyelination of peripheral nerves is found. In the rare, purely sensory neuropathy, the dorsal root ganglia show extensive loss of neurons and inflammatory cell infiltration, with secondary degeneration in the dorsal columns and posterior nerve roots. The pathogenesis of these syndromes is unknown. Virus particles have been sought, but not detected in the ganglion cells, and immunological mechanisms, although suspected, have not been demonstrated.

The clinical picture of the sensimotor polyneuropathy is nonspecific. Carcinoma of the lung is the most common associated tumor, although sensimotor polyneuropathy has been described with carcinoma of the breast, stomach, colon, bladder, kidney, uterus, and even reticulum cell sarcoma. The severe neuropathic disability usually persists indefinitely, despite treatment of the associated cancer. However, near-complete recovery was reported following removal of a renal carcinoma (Swan and Wharton, 1963) and improvement occurred after treating a few cases of carcinoma of the lung. In some instances, improvement of neuropathy coincided with corticosteroid administration (Croft et al., 1967). Spontaneous regression of neuropathy, with or without relapses, is rare.

Ganglioneuritis, which is much rarer, has a more distinctive clinical picture; it often begins asymmetrically in upper extremities, but eventually affects all limbs (Denny-Brown, 1948). Pain, paresthesias, and dysesthesias are accompanied by a striking loss of joint position, vibration, touch, pin, and temperature sensations. Ataxia of gait and limbs with continuous irregular pseudoathetoid movements, which are most noticeable in the fingers, reflect a severe loss of proprioception. In contrast to the dense sensory impairment, there is little clinical or electrophysiological evidence of motor neuropathy. Most cases are associated with small cell carcinoma of the lung, but it has been recorded with cancer of the esophagus and cecum. Unfortunately, the neuropathy progresses relentlessly despite treatment of the associated cancer. The gloomy prospect of finding a malignant neoplasm when an elderly person presents with this rare form of neuropathy is brightened by a recent report in which no cancer was detected in otherwise typical cases of the neuropathy after an average follow-up of 7 years (Kaufman et al., 1981).

Plasma Cell Dyscrasias with Polyneuropathy

The use of immunological tests has led to the increasing recognition of a spectrum of plasma cell dyscrasias, associated with polyneuropathy, that affect chiefly middle-aged and elderly patients. These are of special interest because the dyscrasia itself may be occult and the polyneuropathy is sometimes reversible, and because it raises the question of immunopathogenesis of neural damage.

Chronic polyneuropathy occurs in typical multiple myeloma; its osteosclerotic variant, solitary myeloma; Waldenström macroglubulinemia; and benign monoclonal gammopathy. Nerves show nonspecific axonal degeneration of segmental demyelination and are occasionally infiltrated by myeloma cells or lymphocytes. Immunoflourescent studies (Propp et al., 1975; Dalakas and Engel, 1981) have revealed monoclonal immunoglobulins, identical to those in the circulation, attached to myelin sheaths in multiple myeloma, Waldenström macroglobulinemia, and benign monoclonal gammopathy. Similarly distributed IgG was found in a case of osteosclerotic multiple myeloma without circulating monoclona immunoglobulins. Although it is tempting to implicate these immunoglobulins or their fragments in the production of nerve damage, such a mechanism has not been proven.

Clinically, there is a preponderance of cases among middle-aged and elderly men.

The neuropathy is sensorimotor, distal, and symmetrical and may be mild, or severe enough to cause quadriplegia (Kelly et al., 1981). Autonomic dysfunction is absent. It may precede other clinical manifestation by a year or two. In multiple myeloma, bone pain, anemia, renal insufficiency, weight loss, and infection tend to overshadow peripheral nerve damage. In patients with Waldenström macroglobulinemia, there is eventually an enlargement of the lymph nodes, liver, and spleen; a bleeding tendency; and serum hyperviscosity. In contrast, polyneuropathy, sometimes with papilledema, is frequently the outstanding feature of osteosclerotic multiple myeloma, solitary myeloma, and benign monoclonal gammopathy. An exception is the recently described syndrome of osteosclerotic myeloma (single or multiple), accompanied by an extraordinary array of multisystem involvement as well as polyneuropathy (Iwashita et al., 1977). The skin shows diffuse dark pigmentation and excessive hair, white nails, finger clubbing, and leg edema occur. Hypogonadism, diabetes mellitus, hypothyroidism, and hepatosplenomegaly complete the picture.

The CSF protein is increased up to 200mg% in multiple myeloma, Waldenström macroglobulinemia, and benign monoclonal gammopathy. Elevation up to 1000 mg% may occur in the osteosclerotic variant of multiple myeloma. Skeletal survey is a key investigation and reveals the lytic lesions of multiple myeloma or the dense lesions in osteosclerotic myeloma. A diligent search is needed to detect the solitary lytic or sclerotic bone lesion. Biopsy of the lesion confirms the diagnosis. Unique radiological changes in the spine have been described in cases associated with dermoendocrinopathy (Bardwich et al., 1980). Serum protein electrophoresis readily reveals a large monoclonal spike in multiple myeloma and Waldenström macroglobulinemia. However, immunoelectrophoresis of serum and 24-hour urine is needed to demonstrate the low concentrations of monoclonal immunoglobulins in cases of rare, light-chain multiple myeloma, osteosclerotic myeloma variants, and benign monoclonal gammopathy.

Conventional treatment is disappointing in neuropathy-associated multiple myeloma. However, local radiotherapy or excision of solitary myeloma produces a remarkable regression of the neuropathy (Morley and Schweiger, 1967). Further, in cases with multisystem involvement, the skin and endocrine abnormalities may also be strikingly ameliorated. Treatment with chlorambucil and plasmaphoresis has improved the neuropathy of Waldenström macroglobulinemia (Iwashita et al., 1974). Cytotoxic drugs have produced mild to marked improvement in the peripheral neuropathy of benign monoclonal gammopathy (Dalakas and Engel, 1981).

Polyneuropathy with Nonhereditary Amyloidosis

This neuropathy is being increasingly identified. A few cases are due to multiple myeloma or Waldenström macroglobulinemia, but the majority are due to primary systemic amyloidosis (Kelly et al., 1979). The occurrence of monoclonal immunoglobulins in most patients with primary systemic amyloidosis and the immunoglobulin light-chain make-up of amyloid make it likely that amyloid neuropathy is a part of the spectrum of neuropathies associated with plasma cell dyscrasia.

Peripheral nerves show amyloid chiefly in the walls of capillaries and arterioles of the endoneurium and perineurim, but occasionally there is nodular or diffuse infiltration of the interstitium. A selective loss of unmyelinated and thinly myelinated fibers of nociceptive and autonomic function often occurs. Dorsal roots and autonomic ganglia and the connective tissue of carpal tunnels may show amyloid deposits. The symmetrical polyneuropathy syndrome is not likely to be due simply to the mechanical effects of amyloid in the nerves. Nerve damage and amyloid deposits are probably different expressions of a common immunopathological mechanism.

Men in the sixth and the seventh decade are most often affected. Deep and persistent pains and dysesthesias are prominent in the limbs. Pain and temperature sense are decreased or lost in a stocking–glove distribution, while touch, proprioception,

and tendon reflexes are intact. This dissociation of sensory loss, however, is not
invariable. In chronic cases, trophic ulcers
and even Charcot neuroarthropathy may
develop in the feet and ankles. Autonomic
dysfunction is manifested by postural hypotension, impotence, and bowel and
bladder disturbances. A clinical clue to
amyloid neuropathy is presentation with
unilateral or bilateral carpal tunnel syndromes. In primary systemic amyloidosis,
multisystem involvement usually presents
with a nephrotic syndrome and cardiac
failure.

Cerebrospinal fluid protein is increased
up to 300 mg%; the skeletal X-ray survey
is negative and bone marrow biopsy
shows a plasmacytosis of less than 15%.
Immunoelectrophoresis of the blood and
urine reveals monoclonal immunoglobulins in almost all cases, although low in
concentration.

Conventional treatment of underlying
multiple myeloma and Waldenström macroglobulinemia or the experimental treatment of primary systemic amyloidosis with
cytotoxic drugs or colchicine unfortunately
have not stopped the progression of this
severe polyneuropathy.

Chronic Vascular Insufficiency and Polyneuropathy

Chronic occlusion of the ileo-femoral-popliteal arterial tree due to artherosclerosis is
common in the elderly. Polyneuropathy
does result from this, but its clinical and
pathological boundaries have not been
defined clearly (Eames and Lange, 1967).
Certain features, however, make the diagnosis of chronic ischemic polyneuropathy
probable. Ischemia in the legs is evident in
the form of intermittent claudication and
rest pain by the time neuropathy appears.
Rest pain, confined to the toes, is a
continuous, burning sensation that is
worse at night. Pulses are diminished or
absent. The skin may be cold, pale, and
dry, with a loss of hair and lusterless nails.
Cyanosis or gangrene may occur. The
neuropathy is chiefly sensory and limited
to the feet and legs. Tingling and numbness are common and may increase with
exercise and subside with rest. Episodes of

severe pain may be precipitated by cold,
heat, or even touch, and sometimes spontaneous lightning-like pains occur in the
feet. There is a partial patchy decrease of
sensation to touch and pain, in an asymmetrical stocking distribution. Position
and vibration sense may be diminished
over the feet. Foot-drop from peroneal
nerve palsy may be an occasional added
feature. The nerves show distal segmental
demyelination, remyelination, and axonal
degeneration combined with fibrosis.
Small arteries of the epinerium are often
obliterated by a thickened intima and
degeneration of fibrosis of the media.

The effect of an ileo-femoral-popliteal
by-pass on neuropathic symptoms has not
systematically been studied. Paresthesias
and pain may persist for months, although
claudication and ischemic rest pain resolve
quickly in the postoperative period. The
response of neuropathic symptoms to such
antiplatelet agents as aspirin, with or
without bypass, has not been studied.

Mononeuropathies Commonly Encountered in the Elderly

Herpes Zoster and Post-herpetic Neuralgia

The herpes zoster virus invades a nerve
and produces a vesicular eruption within
the cutaneous dermatomal distribution of
the affected root or roots. The acute
disease is painful, and the pain may precede the skin eruption. About 10% of all
patients develop a persistent dysesthetic
state known as post-herpetic neuralgia.
This is often an excruciatingly painful
state, characterized by paroxysms of stab-
bing pains superimposed on a continuous
burning sensation in the affected root
distribution. Examination reveals the scars
left by the eruption and areas of variable
threshold to sensory testing. The pinprick
threshold may be elevated to a single
stimulus, but temporal summation may
cause a diffuse, highly unpleasant pain.
Some areas may be hyperesthetic to even
light touch or the friction of clothing. The
pain may then become the focus of the
patient's life, and dramatic personality
changes with insomnia, depression, and
irritability and even suicide may ensue.

The chance of developing post-herpetic neuralgia increases with advancing age, and nearly one-half the patients over 60 will develop some degree of post-herpetic neuralgia, especially those with ophthalmic or thoracic zoster.

In one controlled study of patients over the age of 60, the incidence of post-herpetic neuralgia was reduced from 73% to 30% by steroid treatment during the acute phase of the disease (Eaglestein et al., 1970). We would recommend a three-week course of steroids in otherwise healthy elderly patients with acute zoster. In elderly patients with severe diabetes, tuberculosis, peptic ulcers, compromised immunity, or other conditions for which steroids should not be used, local epidural blocks of the involved root (Perkins and Hanlon, 1978) or stellate ganglion block for herpes zoster ophthalmicus (Laflamme et al., 1979) appear to not only control the pain of the acute disease, but also to reduce the incidence of post-herpetic neuralgia. In another study, amantadine HCl, 200 mg/day for 4 weeks, significantly decreased the neuralgia (Galbraith, 1973). An interesting new development is the use of L-DOPA: In a double-blind controlled study, the pain of herpes was substantially decreased. Its role in the prevention of post-herpetic neuralgia, however, should be studied.

Once established, post-herpetic neuralgia is extremely difficult to treat, and it does not take long to realize the futility of analgesic use. Occasional mild cases may be controlled by such local measures as tight dressings, ethyl chloride sprays, or vibrator stimulation within the affected area. An occasional patient, even with protracted severe post-herpetic neuralgia, will respond to transcutaneous nerve stimulation (Nathan and Wall, 1974). A series of 12 subcutaneous injections of steroids has been reported to provide excellent results in a high proportion of cases (Epstein, 1971).

Surgical procedures, aimed at sectioning the pain pathways, such as posterior rhizotomy and anteriolateral cordotomy have been disappointing. The anticonvulsants diphenylhydantoin and carbamazepine, which can be extremely effective in the treatment of other neuralgic pain, have also been disappointing in post-herpetic neuralgia.

The combination of a tricyclic antidepressant and a phenothiazine is the most effective remedy in the severest cases. Both these drugs have significant side effects, especially in the elderly, and must be used with caution. Combinations of a tricyclic with an anticonvulsant (diphenylhydantoin or carbamazepine) is worth trying prior to adding a phenothiazine. The tricyclic should be used for at least 4 to 6 weeks before it is judged not useful. A rare complication of herpes zoster in the elderly is the development of a disabling reflex sympathetic dystrophy. Cervical zoster may cause shoulder–hand syndrome, and less commonly, sacral zoster leads to a sympathetic dystrophy in the leg and foot. Recently, a patient responded well to propranolol (Visitsunthorn and Prete, 1981).

Diabetic Amyotrophy

This distinct clinical entity is quite rare compared to the commonplace distal symmetrical mostly sensory-autononic polyneuropathy of diabetes mellitus (Locke et al., 1963). Infarcts in nerves have been demonstrated, but there is not a full understanding of the pathogenesis of this condition at the present time. There is an astonishingly high rate of misdiagnosis of this condition, even in sophisticated medical settings. The name of the disorder indicates that paralysis is the essential feature, but this is misleading, since pain is usually the presenting problem. The typical patient is elderly, with recent onset or undiagnosed mild diabetes mellitus, who complains of intense, persistent, "aching," searing pains in the anterior thigh or hip region. The pain is difficult to describe and is often most eloquently expressed in the patient's face as he gestures with flowing movement of the hand just over the affected areas, but avoids touching them. As the pain intensifies over the next few weeks, the patient usually notes that it is most severe at night. The simultaneous development of weakness in the proximal muscles on the affected side is most pronounced in the iliopsoas and quadriceps muscles. The patient has difficulty in rising from a chair or climbing stairs, or he falls because his knee "buckles." These patients tend to lose large amounts of weight (10 to 80 lb.) and are often extensively investigated for malignancy.

On physical examination, there is atrophy and weakness in the femoral nerve distribution, and some spillover of involvement into the gluteal, obturator, or sciatic nerves is usually detectable. The knee jerk is absent, but the ankle jerk is most often present. This finding frequently leads to the incorrect diagnosis of an L4 radiculopathy secondary to a herniated intervertebral disc. There is usually no alteration in sensory threshold or tenderness despite the complaint of pain.

The disease can develop bilaterally, but the time of onset, the distribution and severity of the paralyses, and the pain are different on the two sides. The patient with bilateral femoral nerve paralysis is unable to stand. Diabetic amyotrophy, in contrast to the common slowly progressive diabetic sensory polyneuropathy, runs a self-limited course with a tendency for improvement within 3 to 18 months of onset. The diagnosis rests upon the history and physical findings. The electromyographer can confirm the pattern of denervation in the various affected muscles, but there are no specific diagnostic findings on electrophysiological studies. The suspicion of an L4 herniated disc can be laid to rest because (1) the degree of paralysis and atrophy of the quadriceps femoris and iliopsoas is greater than the destruction of a single root in these multi-root innervated muscles could produce; and (2) L4 makes little contribution to the iliopsoas (L 2 to 3), but destruction of L4 is necessary to abolish knee jerk.

The pathogenesis of diabetic amyotrophy is unknown, but some lines of evidence suggest a vascular etiology. Examination of the affected nerves by uninterrupted serial microscopic sections show multiple small areas of infarction that particularly affect the fascicles of the nerve, bridging from one position to another within the nerve (Raff et al., 1968). No vascular occlusions could be found to account for these apparent infarcts. Excruciatingly painful infarcts of the thigh muscle in elderly diabetics, without evidence of nerve damage, have been reported (Banker and Chester, 1973). It is possible that the nerves and muscles in the thigh are at some point in the "borderzone" circulation between arterial supplies and develop microinfarcts due to capillary occlusion with platelets and fibrin during times when the circulation is slowed. Several patients in our experience have had documented bouts of hypotension and one had occlusion of the iliac artery several weeks prior to the onset of an ipsilateral diabetic amyotrophy.

The treatment of diabetic amyotrophy is challenging. The first principle is to avoid patient addiction during the painful phase of this self-limited disease. The use of anticonvulsants is the first line. There is a low probability of achieving control of the pain (10 to 15%, but the response is gratifying in those few patients. We begin with diphenylhydantoin at 300 to 400 mg/day. If therapeutic levels fail to control the pain, then therapeutic levels of carbamazepine are given. If this fails, we discontinue the carbamazepine and use amitriptyline hydrochloride 50 to 100 mg/day. This drug should not be discontinued until 4 to 6 weeks of therapy at adequate doses have been proven fruitless. In intractable cases, fluphenazine hydrochloride, at 2.5 mg bid, may be added to the amitriptyline (Davis et al., 1977). The patient and physician must try to separate the neuromuscular pain from the pain in the hip, knee, or lumbar spine that often develops as a result of the altered musculoskeletal mechanics associated with the paralysis of the iliopsoas and femoral muscles. This pain can usually be controlled with the concomitant use of non-narcotic analgesics, especially aspirin.

Aspirin is moderately effective for control of the pain, and it also has the theoretical additional value of inhibiting platelet aggregation. If a vascular etiology of diabetic amyotrophy is correct, anti-aggregation drugs may prove effective in arresting the disease. Increased synthesis of prostaglandin-E–like material by platelets has been observed in diabetics, and anti-aggregating drugs have been reported to successfully treat diabetic necrobiosis (A. Eldor et al., 1978).

When paralysis is severe, the patient may benefit from bracing. There is danger of developing genu recurvatum because paralysis of the knee extensors requires the patient to lock the knee in hyperextension in order to bear weight without the knee buckling. This results in excessive stress on the ligaments and tendons of the knee joint. General supportive therapy and reassurance that the pain is not permanent will be greatly appreciated by those suffering this strange disorder.

Trigeminal Neuralgia

This disease commonly afflicts the elderly and middle-aged. The patient complains of paroxysms of excruciating lightening-like pain radiating into the gums, lips, or cheek on one side of the face. A trigger zone is usually present; slight stimulation of this area precipitates a salvo of pain. The trigger zone and the pain are most often in the maxillary or mandibular division of the trigeminal nerve. There are no other signs of neurological dysfunction present in true trigeminal neuralgia. If such signs as sensory loss or decreased corneal reflex are present, or if the patient is a young adult, an underlying disorder such as multiple sclerosis or fifth nerve compression should be suspected.

The response to carbamazepine is so specific and dramatic that prompt relief following the use of this agent is of diagnostic importance. The drug is used for several weeks to induce a remission and then slowly tapered. Side effects from this drug are common, and a few of them are severe. Several cases of fatal bone marrow suppression have occurred; thus, the use of the drug must be carefully monitored with laboratory studies especially in the first few months of its use. In some patients who cannot tolerate the drug or in some 20 to 40% of those who become refractory within 2 years, other modalities must be tried. Diphenylhydantoin, chlorphenesin and L-DOPA have been utilized with limited success.

Surgical treatment is usually required when carbamazepine therapy is unsatisfactory. Percutaneous radiofrequency gangliolysis is accomplished by placing an electrode via the foramen ovale into the Gasserian ganglion. A radiofrequency lesion causes selective damage to the smaller fibers subserving pain and touch sensation, so that sensory testing in the conscious patient allows preservation of protective touch sensation and reduces the problem of anesthesia dolorosa (Sweet, 1976). Ligh anesthesia, brief hospitalization (12 days), zero mortality, and 80% good results at the end of one year make this surgery available to even debilitated, aged patients.

Exploration of the posterior fossa and microscopic search for a tortuous arterial loop compressing the nerve root entry zone of the Gasserian ganglion is another modern surgical approach (Janetta, 1976). The artery is lifted off the ganglion, and the results are favorable in a high percent of cases (Voorhies and Patterson, 1981). The great advantages of these procedures is that the surgery does not produce any neurological deficit. However, a craniotomy with general anesthesia and more prolonged hospitalization make this procedure less suitable for the elderly infirm than the radiofrequency technique.

Compression Palsies

The elderly have an increased liability to entrapment neuropathies. These neuropathies are the result of a conspiracy of anatomy and activity. There are certain points along the pathway of nerves in which there is an increased vulnerability to repeated trauma or compression. This is a result of either the superficial location of the nerve, which exposes it to injury, or a result of the nerve coursing through a confining passageway comprised of various connective tissue structures. Specific activities, such as resting on the elbows (ulnar nerve), crossing the legs (peroneal nerve), or repeated wrist flexion–extension movements (median nerve), then serve to compress the vulnerable segment of nerve. Compression at one point along the course of a nerve fiber renders that nerve more vulnerable to a second locus of compression. This "double crush" effect explains the otherwise baffling clinical situations in which there is, for example, numbness in the hand with features of both cervical root compression of spondylosis and carpal tunnel syndrome. The diminished axoplasmic flow secondary to the proximal compression apparently reduces the margin of safety for a second more distal site of partial compression. This is a commonly encountered problem in the aged, and successful treatment demands that all points of compression along the path of an affected nerve be simultaneously treated. Another common example of this problem is seen when a cervical collar, worn for spondylosis with nerve root involvement, precipitates a thoracic outlet syndrome by direct compression of the brachial plexus by producing a tendency to lower the shoulders. Weight loss in senescence and prolonged periods of immobility are also precipitating factors for compression palsies. This is an important practical consideration in the patient with hemiplegia who, because of prolonged immobility, may have developed compression palsies, which when superimposed on the upper motor neuron lesion, interfere with optimal recovery of function in the affected limbs (Moskowitz and Porter, 1963).

The three most common compression neuropathies are the carpal tunnel syndrome, ulnar neuropathy due to compression at the elbow, and compression of the peroneal (lateral popliteal) nerve at the head of the fibula.

The *ulnar nerve* may be compressed either by external trauma where it is most superficial at the medial epicondyle or entrapped as it passes through the aponeurosis of the flexor carpi ulnaris in the cubital tunnel (Miller, 1979). The patient complains of tingling or numbness in the fifth and medial one-half of the fourth finger, and often of an aching sensation at the elbow. Prolonged elbow flexion makes the symptoms worse. Motor involvement leads to weakness and atrophy that is most obvious in the interossei, with clawing of the fourth and the fifth finger. The nerve is often tender, and a gentle tap at the site of compression may elicit tingling in the fingers. Segmental nerve conduction ve-

locities measurements will confirm slowing in the compressed segment. Conservative treatment consists in padding the elbows and instructing the patient to avoid resting on his elbows, strenuous elbow movements, and prolonged elbow flexion. When these simple measures fail, the nerve should be surgically transposed from the ulnar groove to be implanted in the flexor–pronator muscle mass in front of the elbow. If the ulnar neuropathy is due solely to entrapment by the flexor carpi ulnaris aponeurosis, then simple decompression without transposition may suffice. These procedures are done with local anesthesia and are well tolerated even in an elderly population.

The best-known entrapment syndrome is a result of compression of the *median nerve* in the carpal tunnel beneath the transverse carpal ligament at the wrist (Thompson and Kopell, 1959). The carpal tunnel syndrome is often bilateral and may be associated with such system disorders as hypothyroidism, acromegaly, connective tissue disease, amyloidosis, leprosy, or diabetes mellitus. The patient complains of bouts of tingling in the fingers. Aching or burning pain is often present at the wrist and hand, but may radiate proximally to the forearm, arm, or even the shoulder. The symptoms often awaken the patient from sleep. Repetitive wrist movements, as in typing and driving, may precipitate symptoms during the day. As the neuropathy worsens, the patient notes clumsiness in such activities as picking up small objects from a flat surface and complains that "things drop from my hand." A gentle tap on the nerve at the wrist or full passive flexion of the wrist for a minute often reproduces the symptoms. Sensation for touch and pin-prick is most likely to be blunted over the tips of the middle and index fingers. Wasting of the median innervated intrinsic hand muscles, a late feature, results in guttering of the thenar eminence and opposition of the thumb may be weak. Measurement of the distal motor latency is abnormal in 70% of cases, and sensory nerve conduction velocities, though more difficult to perform, are even more sensitive diagnostic indicators of the carpal tunnel syndrome. Conservative treatment is tried first in most instances. Some patients respond to having the wrist splinted in a neutral position, especially at night. An injection of methyl prednisolone acetate into the region of the carpal tunnel offers dramatic and lasting relief for another group of cases. Surgical therapy consists of sectioning the transverse carpal ligament under local anesthesia and good results can be expected for most patients.

The peroneal nerve is a third example of a common compression neuropathy that plagues the elderly. The nerve may be traumatized by sitting with one leg crossed over the other, compressing the nerve as it winds across the neck of the fibula. The edge of a chair or car seat can also compress the nerve at this site. The nerve may also be entrapped as it passes under the tendinous origin of the peroneus longus. Dorsiflexion and inversion of the foot increases compression at this site. The patient complains of stinging or aching pain in the upper-outer leg, often with radiation along the outer side of the dorsum of the foot. Patients complain that they often twist their ankle or that they trip easily because the toes get caught on the edge of carpets, curbings, or stairs. Wasting may be evident in the anterior tibial compartment and the nerve is often tender and slightly enlarged at the site of entrapment. Conservative treatment consists of instructions to avoid compressing the nerve. A small laterally placed wedge in the shoe so as to slightly evert the foot serves to decrease the tension on the nerve from the origin of the peroneus longus. Exploration of the fibular tunnel sometimes reveals a ganglion as the cause of the compression. Surgical results in decompressing the nerve are often gratifying. If foot-drop persists, a short leg brace will produce an easier and far safer gait for the elderly patient.

References

Banker, B.Q. and Chester C.S., (1973). Infarction of thigh muscle in the diabetic patient. Neurol. 23, 667–677.

Bardwich, P.A. and Zvaifler, N.J. (1980). Plasma cells dyscrasia with polyneuropathy, organomegaly and endocrinopathy, M-protein and skin changes: The POMS syndrome. Medecine 59, 311–321.

Behse, F. and Buchthal F., (1971). Normal sensory conduction in the nerves of the leg in man. J. Neurol. Neurosurg. Psychiat. 34, 404–414.

Bolton, C.F. (1976). Electrophysiological changes in uremic neuropathy after successful renal transplantation. Neurol. 26, 152.

Bolton, C.F., Baltzan, M.A., and Baltzan, R.B. (1971). Effects of renal transplantation on uremic polyneuropathy. New Eng. J. Med. 284, 1170–1175.

Bolton, C.F., Winkelmann, R.K., and Dyck, P.J. (1966). A quantitative study of Meissner's corpuscles in man. Neurol. 16, 1–9.

Brown, J.J., Martin, J.R., and Asbury, A.K. (1976). Painful diabetic neuropathy: A morphometric study. Arch. Neurol. 33, 164–171.

Brown, W.F. (1972). A method for estimating the number of motor units in thenar muscles and the changes in motor unit count with aging. J. Neurol. Neurosurg. Psychiat. 35(6), 845–852.

Bunn, H.F. (1981). Nonenzymatic glycosylation of protein; relevance to diabetes. Amer. J. Med. 70, 325–330.

Clements, R.S., Voureant, B., and Kuba, T. et al. (1979). Dietary myoinositol intake and peripheral nerve function in diabetic neuropathy. Metabolism 28, 477–483.

Corbin, K.B. and Gardner, E.D. (1937). Decrease in number of myelinated fibres in human spinal roots with age. Anat. Rec. 68, 63–74.

Craske, B. (1977). Perception of impossible limb positions induced by tendon vibration. Science 196, 71–73.

Critchley, M. (1931). The neurology of old age. Lancet i, 119–1127.

Croft, P.B., Urich, H., and Wilkinson, M. (1967). Peripheral neuropathy of the sensorimotor type associated with malignant disease. Brain 90, 31–66.

Culebras, A., Alio, J., and Herrera, J.L. et al. (1981). Effect of aldose reductase inhibitor on diabetic peripheral neuropathy. Arch. Neurol. 38, 133–134.

Dalakas, M.C. and Engel, K.W. (1981). Polyneuropathy with monoclonal gammopathy: Studies of 11 patients. Ann. Neurol. 10, 45–52.

Davis, J.L., Lewis, S.B., and Gerich, J.E. et al. (1977). Peripheral diabetic neuropathy treated with amitriptyline and fluphenazine. J.A.M.A. 238, 2291–2292.

Denny-Brown, D.E. (1948). Primary sensory neuropathy with muscular changes associated with carcinoma. J. Neurol. Neurosurg. Psychiat. 11, 73–87.

Dorfman, L.J. and Bosley, T.M. (1979). Age related changes in peripheral central nerve conduction in man. Neurol. 29, 38–44.

Downie, A.W. and Newell, D.J. (1961). Sensory nerve conduction in patients with diabetes mellitus and controls. Neurol. 11, 876–882.

Dyck, P.J., Johnson, W.J., Lambert, E.H., and O'Brien, P.C. (1971). Segmental demyelination secondary to axonal degeneration in uremic neuropathy. Proc. Mayo Clin. 46, 400–431.

Dyck, P.J., Sherman, W.R., and Hallcher, L.M. et al. (1980). Human diabetic endoneurial sorbitol, fructose and myoinositol related to sural nerve morphometry. Ann. Neurol. 8, 590–596.

Eaglestein, W.H., Katz, R.K., and Brown, J.A. (1970). The effects of early corticosteroid therapy on the skin eruption and pain of herpes zoster. J.A.M.A. 211, 1681.

Eames, R.A. and Lange, L.S. (1967). Clinical and pathological study of ischaemic neuropathy. J. Neurol. Neurosurg. Psychiat. 30, 215.

Eklund, G. (1969). Influence of muscle vibration on balance in man. Acta Soc. Med. 74, 113–117.

Eldor, A., Diaz, E.G., Naparstek, E. (1978). Treatment of diabetic necrobiosis with aspirin and dipyridamole. N. Eng. J. Med. 298, 1033.

Ellenberg, M. (1974). Diabetic neuropathic cachexia. Diabetes 23, 418–423.

Epstein, E. (1971). Triamcinalone-procaine in the treatment of Zoster and post-Zoster neuralgia. Calif. Med. 115, 6–10.

Ewing, D.J., Campbell, I.W., and Clarke, B.F. (1980). The natural history of diabetic autonomic neuropathy. Quart. J. Med. 59, 95–108.

Gabbay, K.H. (1969). Factors affecting the sorbitol pathways in diabetic nerve. Diabetes 21, 336.

Galbraith, A.W. (1973). Treatment of acute herpes zoster with amantadine hydrochloride (symmetrical). Br. Med. J. 4, 693–695.

Garland, H.T. and Taverner, D. (1953). Diabetic myelopathy. Br. Med. J. 1, 1405–1408.

Goldberg, J.M. and Lindblom, U. (1979). Standardised method of determining vibratory perception thresholds for diagnosis and screening in neurological investiga-tion. J. Neurol. Neurosurg. Psychiat. 42, 793–803.

Goodwin, G.M., McClosky, D.F., and Matthews, P.B.C. (1972). The contribution of muscle afferents to kinaesthesia shown by vibration induced illusions of movement and by the effects of paralysing joint afferents. Brain 95, 705–748.

Graf, R.J., Halter, J.B., and Halar, E. et al. (1979). Nerve conduction abnormalities in untreated maturity-onset diabetes: Relation to levels of plasma glucose and glycosylated hemoglobin. Ann. Int. Med. 90, 298–303.

Gregersen, G., Borsting, H., and Theil, P. et al. (1978). Myoinositol and function of peripheral nerves in human diabetes. Acta Neurol. Scand, 58, 241–248.

Gribbin, B., Pickering, T.G., and Sleight, P. (1969). Decrease in baroreflex sensitivity with increasing arterial pressure and with increasing age. Br. Heart J. 31(6), 792.

Grover-Johnson, N. and Spencer, P.S. (1981). Peripheral nerve abnormalities in aging rats. J. Neuropathol. Exptl. Neurol. 40, 155–165.

Harriman, D.G.F., Taverner, E.R., and Woolf, A.L. (1970). Ekbom's syndrome and burning parenthenae. Brain 93, 393–406.

Iwashita, H., Argyrakis, A., and Lowitzsch, K. et al. (1974). Polyneuropathy in Waldenström's macroglobulinemia. J. Neurol. Sci. 21, 341–354.

Iwashita, H., Ohnishi, A., and Mashiro, A. et al. (1977). Polyneuropathy skin hyperpigmentation, edema and hypertrichosis in localized osteoscleortic myeloma. Neurol. 27, 675–681.

Jannetta, P.J. (1976). Microsurgical approach to the trigeminal nerve for tic douloureux. Prog. Neurol. Surg. 7, 180–200.

Jebsen, R.H., Tenckhoff, H., and Honet, J.C. (1967). Natural history of uremic polyneuropathy and effects of dialysis. N. Eng. J. Med. 277, 327–333.

Judzewitsch, R.G., Jaspin, J.B., et al. (1983). Aldose reductase inhibition improves nerve conduction velocity in diabetic patients. N. Eng. J. Med. 308, 119–125.

Kaufman, M.D., Hopkins, L.C., and Hurwitz, B.J. (1981). Progressive sensory neuropathy in patients without carcinoma, a disorder with dinstinctive clinical and electrophysiological findings. Ann. Neurol. 9, 237–292.

Kawamuara, Y. and Dyck, P.J. (1977). Lumbar motoneurons of man. III. The number and diameter distribution of large and intermediate-diameter cytons by nuclear columns. J. Neuropathol. Exptl. Neurol. 36, 861–870.

Kawamura, Y., O'Brien, P., Okazaki, H., and Dyck, P.J. (1977). Lumbar motoneurons of man. II. The number and diameter distribution of alpha and gamma cytons. J. Neuropathol. Exptl. Neurol. 36, 860.

Kelly, J.J., Kyle, R.A., and Miles, J.M. et al. (1981). The spectrum of peripheral neuropathy in myeloma. Neurology 31, 24–31.

Kelly, J.J., Kyle, R.A., and O'Brien, P.C., et al. (1979). The natural history of peripheral neuropathy in primary systemic amyloidosis. Ann. Neurol. 6, 1–7.

Laflamme, M.Y., Labrecque, B., and Mignault, G. (1979). Zona ophthalmique: Traitement de la neuralgie zonateuse par infiltrations stellaires repetees. Canao J. Ophthal. 14, 99.

Lafratta, C.W. and Canestrari, R.E. (1966). A comparison of sensory and motor nerve conduction velocities as related to age. Arch. Phys. Med. Rehab. 47, 286–290.

Lafratta, C.W. and Zalis, A.W. (1973). Age effects on sural nerve conduction velocity. Arch. Phys. Med. Rehab. 54, 475–477.

Lascelles, R.G. and Thomas, P.K. (1966). Changes due to age in internodal length in the sural nerve of man. J. Neurol. Neurosurg. Psychiat. 29, 40–44.

Lassek, A.M. (1954). The pyramidal tract. C.C. Thomas, Springfield, Ill.

Locke, S., Lawrence, D.G., and Legg, M.A. (1963). Diabetic amyotrophy. Amer. J. Med. 34, 775–785.

Mayer, R.F. (1963). Nerve conduction studies in man. Neurol. 13, 1021–1030.

Miller, R.G. (1979). The cubital tunnel syndrome. Ann. Neurol. 6, 56–59.

Mufson, E.J. and Stein, D.G. (1980). Degeneration in the spinal cord of old rats. Exptl. Neurol. 70, 179–186.

Morley, J.B. and Schweiger, A.C. (1967). The relation between chronic polyneuropathy and osteosclerotic myeloma. J. Neurol. Neurosurg. Psychiat. 30, 432–441.

Morrison, R.L., Cobb, S., and Bauer, W. (1959). The effect of advancing age upon the human spinal cord. Harvard University Press, Cambridge.

Moskowitz, E. and Porter, J.J. (1963). Peripheral nerve lesions in the upper extremity in hemiplegic patients. New Eng. J. Med. 269, 776–778.

Nathan, P.W. and Wall, P.D. (1974). Treatment of post-herpetic neuralgia by prolonged electrical stimulation. Br. Med. J. 3, 645–647.

Neilsen, K.C. (1969). Possible relation between the degree of cardiac adrenergic innervation and the resistance to hypothermic ventricular fibrillation in young cats. Acta Physiol. Scand. 76(1), 1–9.

Neilson, V.K. (1973). Sensory and motor nerve conduction in the median nerve in normal subjects. Acta Med. Scand. 194, 435–443.

Norris, A.H., Shock, N.W., and Wagman, I.H. (1953). Age changes in the maximum conduction velocity in motor fibres of human ulnar nerves. J. Appl. Physiol. 5, 589–593.

Ochoa, J. and Mair, W.G.P. (1969). The normal sural nerve in man: II. changes in the axons and Schwann cells due to aging. Acta Neuropathol (Berl.) 13, 217–239.

Oh, S.J., Clements, R.S., and Lee, Y.W. et al. (1978). Rapid improvement in nerve conduction velocity following renal transplantation. Ann. Neurol. 4, 369–373.

O'Sullivan, D.J. and Swallow, M. (1968). The fibre size and content of the radial and sural nerve. J. Neurol. Neurosurg. Psychiat. 31, 464–470.

Page, M. and Watkins, P.J. (1978). Cardiorespiratory arrest and diabetic autonomic neuropathy. Lancet, i, 14–16.

Pearson, G.H.J. (1928). Effect of age on vibratory sensibility. Arch. Neurol. (Chicago) 20, 482–496.

Perkins, H.M. and Hanlon, P.R. (1978). Epidural infection of local anesthetic and steroid for relief of pain secondary to Herpes Zoster. Arch. Surg. 113, 253.

Popovtzer, M.M., Rosenbaum, B.J., Gordon, A., and Maxwell, M.H. (1969). Relief of uremic neuropathy after bilateral nephrectomy. N. Eng. J. Med. 281, 949–950.

Porte, D., Graf, R.J., and Halter, J.B. et al. (1981). Diabetic neuropathy and plasma glucose control. Amer. J. Med. 70, 195–200.

Propp, R.P., Means, E., and Deibel, R. et al. (1975). Waldenström's macroglobulinemia and neuropathy. Neurology 25, 980–988.

Raff, M.C., Sangalaug, V., and Asbury, A.K. (1968). Ischemic mononeuropathy multiplex associated with diabetes mellitus. Arch. Neurol. 18, 487–499.

Rexed, B. (1944). Contributions to the knowledge of postnatal development of peripheral nervous system of man. Acta Psychiat. Scand. (Suppl.) 33, 5–206.

Ridley, A. (1968). Silver staining of innervation of Meissner corpuscles in peripheral neuropathy. Brain 91, 539–552.

Rosenberg, G. (1958). Effect of age on peripheral vibratory perception. J. Amer. Geriat. Soc. 6, 471.

Rothwell, J.C., Traub, M.M., and Marsden, C.D. (1979). Primary writing tremor. J. Neurol. Neurosurg. Psychiat. 42, 1106–1114.

Sabin, T.D. (1971). The neurological features of lepromatous leprosy. Amer. Fam. Physician 4, 84–94.

Sabin, T.D. (1982). Biological aspects of falls: Mobility limitations in the elderly. J. Amer. Geriat. Soc. 30(1), pp. 51–58.

Sabin, T.D., Geschwind, N., and Waxman, S.G. (1978). Patterns of clinical deficits in perhipheral nerve disease. In S.G. Waxman, Ed. Physiology and Pathology of Axons. Raven Press, New York.

Salway, J.F., Finnegan, J.A., and Barnett, D. et al. (1978). Effect of myoinositol on peripheral nerve function in diabetes. Lancet ii, 1282–1284.

Scheibel, M.E., Tomiyasu, U., and Scheibel, A.B. (1977). The aging human betz cell. Exptl. Neurol. 56, 598–609.

Shahani, B.T. and Young, R.R. (1978). Action tremors: A clinical neurophysiological review. In J.E. Desmedt, Ed. Physiological Tremor, Pathological Tremors and Clonus. Karger, Basel, pp. 129–137.

Steinberg, F.U. and Graber, A.L. (1963). The effect of age and peripheral circulation on the perception of vibration. Arch. Phys. Med. Rehab. 44, 645–650.

Stevens, J.C., Lofgren, E.P., and Dyck, J.P. (1973). Histometric evaluation of branches of peroneal nerve. Brain Res. 52, 37–59.

Sunderland, S. (1978). Nerves and Nerve Injuries, 2nd Ed. Churchill-Livingstone; Edinburgh, pp. 927–930.

Swallow, M. (1966). Fibre size and content of the anterior tibial nerve of the foot. J. Neurol. Neurosurg. Psychiat. 29, 205–213.

Swan, C.H. and Wharton, B.A. (1963). Polyneuritis and renal carcinoma. Lancet ii, 383.

Sweet, W.H. (1976). Treatment of facial pain by percutaneous differential thermal trigeminal rhizotomy. Prog. Neurol. Surg. 7, 153–179.

Takahashi, J. (1966). A clinicopathologic study of the peripheral nervous system of the aged: Sciatic nerve and autonomic nervous system. Geriatrics 21, 123–133.

Tenckhoff, H. and Curtis, F.K. (1970). Experience with maintenance peritoneal dialysis in the home. Trans. Amer. Soc. Artif. Int. Organs 16, 90–95.

Terkildsen, A.B. and Christensen, N.J. (1971). Reversible nervous abnormalities in juvenile diabetics with recently diagnosed diabetes. Diabetologia 7, 113–117.

Thompson, W.A.L. and Kopell, H.P. (1959). Peripheral entrapment neuropathies of the upper extremity. New Eng. J. Med. 260, 1261–1265.

Timperley, W.R., Preston, F.E., and Duckworth, T. et al. (1976). Clinical and histological studies in diabetic neuropathy. Diabetologia 12, 237–243.

Turkington, R.W. (1980). Depression masquerading as diabetic neuropathy. J.A.M.A. 243, 1147–1150.

Vizoso, A.D. (1950). The relationship between internodal length and growth in human nerves. J. Anat. (London) 84, 342–353.

Visitsunthorn, U. and Prete, P. (1981). "Reflex sympathetic dystrophy of lower extremity"—a complication of herpes zoster with dramatic response to propranolol. West. J. Med. 135, 62–66.

Voorhies, R. and Patterson, R. (1981). Management of trigeminal neuralgia. J.A.M.A. 245, 2521–2523.

Ward, J.D., Fisher, D.J., and Barnes, C.G. et al. (1971). Improvement in nerve conduction following treatment in newly diagnosed diabetics. Lancet i, 428–430.

Waxman, S.G. and Sabin, T.D. (1981). Diabetic truncal polyneuropathy. Arch. Neurol. 38, 46–47.

Winegard, A.J. and Greene, D.A. (1976). Diabetic polyneuropathy: The importance of insulin deficiency, hyperglycemia and alterations in myoinositol metabolism in its pathogenesis. New Eng. J. Med. 295, 1416–1420.

VI
Common Neurological Disorders

24. Brain Tumors in the Elderly

J. GREGORY CAIRNCROSS

JEROME B. POSNER

Brain tumors occur in all age groups, including the elderly, but the nature of the tumor varies with the age of the patient. In childhood and adolescence, medulloblastomas, ependymomas, cystic cerebellar astrocytomas, low-grade astrocytomas of the cerebral hemispheres, and craniopharyngiomas predominate. In contrast, throughout adult life, malignant astrocytomas, meningiomas, metastatic brain tumors, low-grade supratentorial astrocytomas, and chromophobe adenomas are the common intracranial tumors. Brain tumors of the elderly are not substantially different from those of earlier adult life, except that low-grade astrocytomas become increasingly infrequent with advancing years. The symptoms and signs of intracranial tumor in the aged are also similar to those in other age groups. The development of computerized tomographic (CT) scanning has revolutionized the diagnosis of intracranial neoplasms in all age groups. This technical achievement has been especially helpful in the evaluation of elderly patients with neurological disease because of the considerable morbidity associated with cerebral angiography and pneumoencephalography in older patients. For the most part, the treatment of intracranial neoplasms is dictated by the histological type of the tumor, not the age of the patient. In general, this is also true of brain tumors in the elderly, although in certain situations the general health of the patient and the inherent toxicity of specific treatment modalities will influence therapeutic decisions. For example, a small right frontal meningioma producing focal motor seizures in an elderly individual with severe coronary artery disease and congestive heart failure might best be treated with anticonvulsants alone, rather than surgical removal. With certain brain tumor types, the age of the patient is of considerable prognostic importance, independent of treatment. This is especially true of malignant astrocytomas in the older patient.

We will begin our discussion of the occurrence and management of brain tumors in the elderly with a brief classification of intracranial tumors. The epidemiology of intracranial neoplasms, with special attention to observations in the aged, will follow. The symptoms and signs of intracranial tumors, diagnostic problems in the elderly, and treatment of the common tumor types in the older patient are then discussed.

Classification of Intracranial Tumors

Intracranial neoplasms can be divided into two large groups: primary and metastatic. Primary tumors have been further subdi-

Table 24-1. A Classification of Primary Intracranial Tumors.

A. Tumors of Neural Elements
  1. Medulloblastoma
  2. Neuroblastoma
  3. Ganglioneuroma
  4. Ganglioglioma
B. Tumors of Neuroglial Elements
  1. Astrocytoma
    Low-grade astrocytoma (histological grades I and II)
    Malignant astrocytoma (histological grades III and IV)
  2. Oligodendroglioma
  3. Ependymoma
C. Tumors of Meningeal Elements
  1. Meningioma
  2. Sarcoma
  3. Melanoma
D. Tumors of Perineural Elements
  1. Schwannoma
  2. Neurofibroma
E. Tumors of Lymphoreticular Elements
  1. Lymphoma
  2. Plasmacytoma
  3. Histiocytoma
F. Tumors of Vascular Elements
  1. Hemangioblastoma
  2. Sarcoma
G. Tumors of the Choroid Plexus
  1. Choroid plexus papilloma
H. Tumors of the Pineal Gland
  1. Pineocytoma
  2. Pineoblastoma
I. Tumors of Maldevelopment (arising from various cell types)
  1. Craniopharyngioma
  2. Dysgerminoma
  3. Teratoma
  4. Lipoma
  5. Dermoid; epidermoid
  6. Hamartoma
  7. Chordoma
J. Tumors of the Pituitary Gland
  1. Chromophobe adenoma
  2. Acidophilic adenoma
  3. Basophilic adenoma

Table 24-2. The Frequency of Primary Tumor Types.

Tumor Type	Percentage of Total (all ages)
Tumors of neuronal elements	4
Tumors of neuroglial elements	62
Tumors of meningeal elements	18
Tumors of perineural elements	2
Tumors of lymphoreticular elements	1
Tumors of vascular elements	2
Tumors of the choroid plexus	1
Tumors of the pineal gland	1
Tumors of maldevelopment	3
Tumors of the pituitary gland	5

Epidemiology of Intracranial Tumors

Using data gathered from the Connecticut Tumor Registry and the Rochester–Omstead Medical Records System, Schoenberg (1978), and more recently Annegers et al. (1981), have estimated the age-adjusted incidence rate for primary intracranial neoplasms at approximately 8 per 100,000 population. Considering only primary intracranial tumors diagnosed prior to death, the incidence rate can be seen to vary considerably from decade to decade. The incidence of primary brain tumors tends to increase gradually over the years, reaching a peak of approximately 25 per 100,000 population at age 70 (Schoenberg, 1978). Thereafter, there is a tendency for the incidence to decline. When all primary intracranial neoplasms are considered, including those diagnosed at autopsy, the Rochester–Omstead studies indicate that the incidence of primary brain tumor increases steadily throughout life with no sign of decline after age 70 (Annegers et al. 1981). In fact, the incidence at age 80 was approximiately 90 cases per 100,000 population. Further analysis by Schoenberg et al. (1978) indicates that the inclusion of patients with small asymptomatic meningiomas, diagnosed only at autopsy and unsuspected during life, account for the steadily increasing incidence rates with advancing years and the very high rates in the aged.

The discussion in the preceding para-

vided by Rubenstein (1972) and others on the basis of the presumed cell of origin. Table 24-1 lists the major primary intracranial tumors according to the cell type from which they are believed to have arisen. Data analyzed by Schoenberg et al. (1978) from the Connecticut Tumor Registry indicates that 80% of all primary intracranial tumors arise from neuroglial and meningeal elements. When patients under 15 years of age are excluded, this figure rises to 85%. The frequency of various histological tumor types, considering all age groups, are summarized in Table 24-2. Intracranial metastases have been classified by either the systemic tumor type (lung, breast, colon, etc.) or the location of the intracranial metastatic lesion (for example, leptomeningeal, parenchymal).

graph refers to the age-adjusted incidence rates for all primary intracranial neoplasms. The age-specific incidence rates by histological type show interesting differences and are briefly reviewed. Illustrations of the age-specific incidence rates for malignant astrocytoma, meningioma, low-grade astrocytoma, medulloblastoma, neurilemoma, chromophobe adenoma, and craniopharyngioma are found elsewhere (Schoenberg, 1978). Of particular note are the dramatic decrease in the incidence of malignant astrocytoma after age 65, the rare occurrence of medulloblastoma after the early adult years, and the steadily increasing incidence of both meningioma and chromophobe adenoma with advancing years. Malignant astrocytoma is an uncommon tumor in childhood and adolescence. The incidence increases dramatically through the younger adult years, reaching a peak at age 65. Thereafter, there is a dramatic decrease in the incidence of this primary tumor type such that it is considered an uncommon tumor after age 80. Like malignant astrocytoma, meningioma is an infrequent tumor in childhood and adolescence, but thereafter the incidence increases steadily with advancing years. This increase continues even at advanced ages. The curve for low-grade astrocytoma has two peaks: the first in childhood and early adolescence, due largely to the appearance of cystic cerebellar astrocytomas in this age group, the second in the mid-adult years between ages 40 and 60. The majority of these tumors are located in the cerebral hemispheres. After age 65, the incidence of low-grade astrocytoma decreases dramatically. Medulloblastoma is the most common primary intracranial neoplasm in childhood, but its incidence decreases dramatically after adolescence. In several studies, there is a second small peak for medulloblastoma in the mid-adult years, but its occurrence after age 65 is exceedingly rare. Neurilemoma is an uncommon tumor in childhood and adolescence; its incidence increases in the early adult years, reaching a peak between ages 50 and 60, with a sharp decline thereafter. Like meningioma, the incidence of chromophobe adenoma increases steadily

with advancing years and is rarely seen in childhood. Craniopharyngioma, on the other hand, is a tumor that occurs in childhood, adolescence, and throughout adult life. The incidence rate changes very little with age. There are several reports of craniopharyngioma occurring in the aged (Banna, 1976; Herishanu, 1970).

The overall incidence and the age-specific incidence of metastatic brain tumors is more difficult to estimate. Intracranial metastases are found in approximately 20% of cancer patients undergoing postmortem examination. Metastatic lesions are found in the extradural and subdural spaces, infiltrating the leptomeninges focally or diffusely, and in the brain parenchyma. Intracerebral (parenchymal) metastases are detected in 10 to 15% of autopsied cancer patients (Posner and Chernik, 1978). The experience at Memorial Sloan-Kettering Cancer Center would suggest that two-thirds to three-quarters of these lesions were symptomatic during life. The systemic tumors most commonly found in the brain are carcinoma of the lung and carcinoma of the breast. Since both tumors tend to disseminate widely and are among the most common malignancies in the adult population, it is not surprising that they constitute the majority of brain metastases in most large series (Cairncross et al., 1980; Zimm et al., 1981; Hendrickson, 1977). Independent of their incidence, there is a tendency for certain systemic tumors to metastasize frequently to the central nervous system (CNS). Melanoma and choriocarcinoma regularly spread to the brain. Autopsy studies reveal metastatic brain tumors in 50 to 75% of patients dying with these tumor types (Posner and Chernik, 1978; Walker, 1972). Carcinomas of the lung and breast are intermediate in this respect, with brain metastases being found at autopsy in 20 to 40% of patients dying as a result of disseminated tumor (Posner and Chernik, 1978). Carcinomas of the colon, pancreas, kidney, bladder, prostate, and cervix metastasize to the brain less often. Fewer than 10% of autopsies in patients dying with these tumor types show brain metastases (Posner and Chernik, 1978).

Brain metastases certainly develop in

Table 24-3. The Occurrence of Brain Metastases in Patients Age 65 or Older.

Tumor Type	Mean Age of All patients	Number of patients	Percentage of Patients 65 or older	Median Survival (weeks)	
				All patients	Patients 65 or older
Lung	57	72	26	12	10–12
Breast	55	38	16	13	8
Melanoma	56	26	12	10	10
Colon	61	11	36	8	6–10
Kidney	64	7	43	15	7
Testes	28	11	0	16	—
Multiple primaries	68	10	40	10	4–6
Unknown primary	53	10	10	12	20
Miscellaneous	56	16	38	13	8
Total	56	201	23	12	8–9

older patients with systemic cancer. Our own experience with 201 patients with brain metastases diagnosed and treated between January 1, 1977 and July 31, 1978 indicates that 23% of all patients were 65 years of age or older at the time their metastatic brain tumor was diagnosed (Cairncross et al., 1980). Table 24-3 lists, by tumor type, the percentage of patients over age 65 at the time of diagnosis, together with their median survival compared to that of the group as a whole.

In cancer patients, the relationship between age and the likelihood of developing brain metastases has been addressed by Aronson et al. (1964). In patients with carcinomas of the lung, breast, and colon, these tumors were more likely to metastasize to the brain in younger patients. Elderly patients with these tumor types developed a brain metastasis infrequently in comparison to young and middle-aged adults. Whether this observation reflects the fact that older patients with cancer live a shorter period of time and are therefore less likely to develop brain metastases or whether these tumors are less aggressive when they occur in older patients is open to speculation.

Two recent studies have analyzed the occurrence of brain tumors in the elderly population. In both studies, that of Twomey (1978) and that of Tomita and Raimondi (1981), malignant astrocytoma, meningioma, and brain metastasis taken together accounted for over 90% of all

intracranial neoplasms in patients 65 years of age or older. In a similar study by Moersch et al. (1941), malignant astrocytoma, meningioma, and cerebral metastasis accounted for only 70% of brain tumors in the elderly. In this review, more than 20% of all intracranial tumors in patients aged 60 or over were acoustic neuromas. Table 24-4 summarizes the results of these studies. Pennybacker (1968) reviewed the neurosurgical experience in 100 consecutive patients, aged 65 or older, evaluated at a large neurosurgical referral center. Fifty patients had neoplastic disease of the brain or spinal cord. Of these, 26 had primary intracranial tumors. In order of decreasing frequency, the histological types encountered were glioma (58%), meningioma (27%), neurilemoma (11%), and pituitary adenoma (4%). The number of metastatic brain tumors was not specified in this study. It is likely that all of these studies underestimate the incidence of metastatic brain tumors and that brain metastases are more common than primary brain tumors in the elderly. The underestimation occurs because most incidence studies are from neurosurgical centers and most metastatic brain tumors are not treated surgically.

Although epidemiological studies suggest a dramatic decrease in the incidence of benign and malignant glial tumors after age 65, in fact, in most series of elderly patients with brain tumors, this histological type remains the most common pri-

Table 24-4. Brain Tumors in the Elderly.

	Moersch et al. (1941)	Twomey (1978)	Tomita and Raimondi (1981)
Age of patients	≥60	≥65	≥65
Time period	1920–40	1970–77	1967–79
Number of patients	100	30	80
Percentage of major tumor types			
Astrocytoma	36	40	51
malignant	(35)	—	(48)
low-grade	(1)	—	(3)
Meningioma	25	13	18
Metastasis	11	43	24
Other	28	3	7

mary brain tumor. Meningiomas are the next most frequent primary tumor. Neurilemomas (acoustic neuroma) are the third most common primary intracranial neoplasm in the elderly, with other tumor types being exceedingly unusual.

The remainder of this chapter will deal with the diagnosis and treatment of intracranial tumors in the elderly. We will restrict our remarks to the three common brain tumors in patients age 65 or over, namely, malignant astrocytoma, brain metastasis, and meningioma. Neurilemoma, pituitary adenoma, craniopharyngioma, and other rare brain tumors in the elderly will not be discussed further, since if the patient's general medical condition permits it, the treatment of these tumor types, provided they are symptomatic, is surgical removal.

Diagnostic Considerations

Clinical Presentation

The onset of symptoms and signs in patients with intracranial neoplasms may be acute (appearing over minutes to hours), subacute (appearing over days to weeks), or insidious (appearing over months to years). In general, the mode of onset reflects the pathogenesis of specific symptoms and signs and the histology of the tumor. Intracranial neoplasms produce neurological dysfunction by a variety of mechanisms. The pathophysiology of symptoms and signs is summarized in Table 24-5.

In most instances, the sudden development of neurological symptoms and signs is indicative of seizure activity, hemorrhage into the tumor bed, or vascular compression with secondary ischemia. Tumor compression or invasion of normal tissue, edema formation, cerebral herniations, obstruction of cerebrospinal fluid (CSF) pathways with resulting hydrocephalus, and, in the case of malignant neoplasms, leptomeningeal spread produce symptoms and signs that have a subacute onset. Tumors that arise in relatively silent areas of the brain, such as the nondominant frontal lobe or nondominant temporal lobe, and that are histologically benign, account for the majority of intracranial neoplasms heralded by the insidious development of neurological dysfunction. The subacute onset of symptoms and signs is typical of both malignant astrocytoma and metastatic brain tumor. However, a significant number of patients with

Table 24-5. Pathophysiology of Neurological Symptoms and Signs in Patients with Intracranial Neoplasms.

1. Tumor destruction of normal brain
2. Edema
3. Brain shifts (i.e., cerebral herniations)
4. Seizure activity
5. Obstruction of CSF pathways (i.e., hydrocephalus)
6. Hemorrhage or cyst formation
7. Vascular compression or invasion (i.e., ischemia)
8. Leptomeningeal invasion

these tumor types present acutely. It is unusual for patients with metastatic brain tumor to develop neurological problems insidiously. It is not uncommon, on the other hand, for patients with malignant astrocytoma to give a history that suggests that the illness evolved over a period of several years. It appears that low-grade astrocytomas may undergo malignant degeneration, which accounts for the protracted period of minor symptoms followed by a period of rapid worsening. Meningiomas, unless they cause seizures, are rapidly growing, or are growing within the ventricular system where they lead to hydrocephalus, rarely present with acute or subacute symptoms. Rather, they grow slowly, gradually compressing and displacing underlying brain, with the appearance of symptoms and signs over a period of months to years. The pathogenesis and mode of onset of neurological symptoms and signs in elderly patients with intracranial neoplasms do not differ from those seen in children and younger adults. However, the physician must be cautious in the interpretation of neurological disorders in the elderly, lest acute symptoms and insidious symptoms be hastily and incorrectly attributed to vascular disease and senile dementia, respectively.

The symptoms and signs of intracranial tumor (headache, vomiting, mental status change, focal weakness, seizures, speech difficulty, ataxia, etc.) are well known and are features of intracranial mass lesions in patients of all ages. Nevertheless, symptoms in patients with intracranial tumor tend to vary, depending upon the age of the patient. For example, in children, headache, vomiting, papilledema, and ataxia are the common manifestations of intracranial tumor, principally because in this age group the majority of brain tumors occur in the posterior fossa. In adults, the common brain tumors are supratentorial, with the major symptoms and signs being somewhat different. Headache is less frequent, with vomiting, papilledema, and ataxia replaced by behavioral and intellectual changes, hemiparesis, and seizures. Further, with respect to symptoms, at least, there are subtle, but clinically important differences between young and middle-aged adults with brain tumors and their elderly counterparts. Table 24-6 lists the symptoms at diagnosis in patients with malignant astrocytoma and metastatic brain tumor, comparing two groups of patients of all ages with the elderly patients reported by Tomita and Raimondi (1981).

In patients with malignant astrocytoma, headache and seizure activity are less frequent, but motor weakness and mental change tend to be more prominent. Similarly, in patients with brain metastasis, headache is less common in the elderly, although other symptoms do not vary substantially with age. Hasting (1939), in describing the difficulties in differential diagnosis of brain tumor in older age groups, pointed to the fact that the three cardinal symptoms of brain tumor (headache, vomiting, and papilledema) were, in fact, uncommon findings with advancing age. Because the classic signs and symptoms of raised intracranial pressure in elderly patients with intracranial mass lesions are frequently absent, prompt and accurate diagnosis demands care and discernment on the part of the examining physician. This is especially true in patients

Table 24-6. Symptoms at Diagnosis in Patients with Malignant Astrocytoma and Brain Metastasis Comparing Elderly Patients with those of All Ages.

	Malignant Astrocytoma		Metastatic Brain Tumor	
	Walker et al. (1978)	Tomita and Raimondi (1981)	Cairncross et al. (1980)	Tomita and Raimondi (1981)
Motor weakness	45%	50%	21%	32%
Mental change	35%	47%	33%	32%
Headache	55%	32%	45%	32%
Seizure	36%	13%	20%	21%

with frontal brain tumors, in whom behavioral and motor changes are often easily dismissed as the psychomotor retardation of depression or senile dementia, common afflictions of the elderly.

Diagnostic Tests

As suggested above, intracranial neoplasms may be difficult to diagnose in the elderly because the signs and symptoms of raised intracranial pressure are frequently absent. Further, the signs and symptoms commonly associated with brain tumors in the aged are also those typical of progressive vascular insufficiency and senile dementia. The difficulties in bedside differential diagnosis are amplified by the reluctance of most clinicians to subject elderly patients to the hazards of invasive neurological tests. The morbidity associated with cerebral angiography and pneumoencephalography is considerable, and is enhanced in the elderly. The development of CT scanning has revolutionized the evaluation of patients with neurological disorders. The major risk of CT scanning is the risk of intravenous contrast infusion at any age. In patients with a history of allergy to iodinated contrast materials or of renal insufficiency, it may be necessary to limit the test to a non-contrast study. The CT scan is the ideal screening test for elderly patients with neurological symptoms compatible with an intracranial neoplasm. It is no longer necessary to shy away from investigations in elderly patients with neurological problems. It is certainly true that seizures in the adult population over age 70 are far more likely to be due to vascular disease than to tumor and that the evaluation of unselected elderly patients with dementia reveals a treatable cause in less than 5%; nevertheless, elderly patients with seizures and intellectual decline can now be quickly and safely evaluated by the CT scan.

Malignant astrocytoma, metastatic brain tumor, and meningioma are readily identified by CT scan. Multiple, contrast-enhancing mass lesions, which occasionally can only be demonstrated by double-dose contrast, are in most instances brain metastases. It is more difficult to predict the histological tumor type on the basis of the CT appearance for patients with solitary contrast-enhancing mass lesions; however, it is often possible for the neuroradiologist to distinguish meningioma from malignant astrocytoma and metastatic brain tumor on the basis of its intense contrast enhancement and relationship to the dura. The presence of ring enhancement and surrounding edema does not reliably distinguish among these three tumor types, although meningiomas generally enhance homogeneously. A metastasis arising from the dura may be indistinguishable radiologically from a meningioma. A history of systemic cancer or a chest X-ray with multiple pulmonary nodules in a patient with a solitary intracranial tumor would of course strongly point to a diagnosis of brain metastasis. Patients with breast cancer, however, have an increased incidence of intracranial meningioma, a point to be kept in mind when the CT appearance suggests this tumor type (Schoenberg et al., 1975).

To summarize, it may be difficult to diagnose intracranial tumor in an elderly patient, but it is now possible to screen older patients for treatable causes of neurological dysfunction by CT scanning. The common intracranial neoplasms in patients over age 65, namely, malignant astrocytoma, metastatic brain tumor, and meningioma, are readily visualized on CT scan. Although surgery may be necessary to establish the histological diagnosis, in many instances, the CT appearance is sufficiently characteristic to allow the neuroradiologist to make a confident diagnosis.

Treatment

General Considerations

Since the treatment of intracranial tumors is dictated by the tumor type, not the age of the patient, the overall health of the patient is a consideration in planning specific treatment. This is an especially important factor in the elderly, since coincident coronary artery disease, hypertension, diabetes, chronic obstructive pulmonary disease, venous insufficiency, and other common medical problems in later life may limit the therapeutic options for specific patients.

The treatment of brain tumors in patients of any age may include surgery, radiation therapy, chemotherapy, and adrenocorticosteroids. Before discussing the treatment of individual brain tumor types, we consider briefly the benefits and hazards of the major treatment modalities in the aged patient.

Intracranial surgery in elderly patients is surprisingly well tolerated. Considering all neurosurgical procedures, including those on the spine, Stewart et al. (1975) report a surgical mortality of only 5%. Pennybacker (1949) points out that elderly patients with benign intracranial tumors tolerate surgery well. There were no deaths in 34 patients over age 60 operated on for a variety of benign lesions. He was less enthusiastic about neurosurgery for malignant disease, either primary malignant tumors or brain metastases, but does not describe his experience with these tumor types in detail. Tomida and Raimondi (1981) had a 4% one-month mortality rate in 80 elderly patients with intracranial tumors. All deaths were secondary to bronchopneumonia in patients with malignant intracranial lesions. Fifty-six percent of their patients with motor weakness, mental changes, or impaired consciousness benefited from surgery; 21% continued to deteriorate or worsened suddenly following surgical intervention. They reported 27 postoperative systemic complications in 23 of 80 patients; 52% of these systemic complications were pulmonary, and the remainder a variety of disorders including hypotension, cardiac arrythmia, angina, thrombophlebitis, stroke, septicemia, urinary tract infection, GI bleeding, and inappropriate ADH secretion. Importantly, cardiac problems in this elderly group of patients constituted only 11% of postoperative problems, and none of these was fatal. The authors emphasized the postoperative mortality and morbidity in elderly patients undergoing intracranial surgery was largely the result of pneumonia, pulmonary embolus, and atelectasis, problems that could be largely circumvented by early and vigorous mobilization in the postoperative period. They con-

cluded that, from the medical point of view, craniotomy was not a major operation. Although the literature in this area is not extensive, the prevailing view appears to be that elderly patients in good general health should be considered surgical candidates. It is also true, however, that elderly patients tolerate minor degrees of damage to the brain at the time of surgery less well than do their younger counterparts. This plasticity of the younger brain is particularly evident following head injury. Pennybacker (1949) has encountered an analogous situation in posterior fossa surgery for acoustic neuromas. Cerebellar deficits following posterior fossa surgery in chidren invariably improved with time. To a lesser degree, this was also the case with young adults. However, in some elderly patients, an incapacitating and permanent ataxia followed the apparently successful removal of acoustic tumors. Pennybacker has suggested that small, minimally symptomatic tumors be observed rather than removed, and that larger symptomatic lesions be subtotally rather than totally resected, to minimize damage to the aged cerebellum. Similarly, traction on a frontal or temporal lobe or prolonged hypotension are less likely to be tolerated by the aged brain. With the understanding that the recuperative powers of the brain are lessened with advancing years and that early mobilization will be necessary to prevent postoperative pulmonary complications, a good outcome can be anticipated in most elderly patients undergoing intracranial tumor surgery.

Radiation therapy has been demonstrated to prolong survival and, in many instances, to improve or maintain the quality of life in patients with malignant brain tumors, either primary or metastatic. Data from the Brain Tumor Study Group (BTSG) have indicated that radiation therapy to the whole brain in patients with malignant glioma increases survival at least twofold over that following surgery alone (Walker et al., 1978). Similarly, the median survival in patients with metastatic brain tumor was increased from two to four months following whole-brain radiation therapy (Cairncross et al., 1980; Hazra et al., 1972). Since patients with

Table 24-7. Complications of Whole-Brain Radiation Therapy.

Neurological
  Acute encephalopathy
  Early-delayed encephalopathy
  Late-delayed encephalopathy (radiation necrosis)
  Dementia
  Visual loss (optic atrophy)
  Stroke syndromes
  Cerebral neoplasms

Nonneurological
  Ageusia (loss of taste)
  Xerophthalmia (dry eyes)
  Xerostomia (dry mouth)
  Hearing loss
  Acute perotitis
  Alopecia

brain metastases invariably have active systemic disease, which in itself may limit life, survival data alone may substantially underestimate the effectiveness of brain irradiation in controlling metastatic disease to the intracranial space (Cairncross and Posner, in press). Although of benefit in the treatment of patients with malignant brain tumors, brain irradiation is not without hazard. The complications of whole-brain radiation therapy, both neurological and nonneurological, are listed in Table 24-7.

A detailed discussion of radiation toxicity is beyond the scope of this chapter. In our experience, the three serious complications of whole-brain radiation therapy are late delayed encephalopathy (radiation necrosis), dementia, and blindness. There is little in the literature addressing the issue of irreversible damage to the brain and optic pathways following radiation therapy as related to age. It is not our impression that radiation necrosis of the brain and blindness are more frequent in the elderly population. We now routinely shield the optic nerves and optic chiasm in all patients receiving whole-brain radiation therapy with the hope of eliminating blindness as a complication. Work by Caveness (1980) in experimental animals has suggested that the age of the host plays a role in the occurrence and ultimate effect of radiation-induced cerebral necrosis. In his studies, cerebral edema and necrosis were more prominent in the younger animals. If

these results can be extrapolated to humans, elderly patients would be less likely to develop symptomatic cerebral necrosis than children or young adults. Eighteen months to two years following whole-brain radiation therapy, a significant number, perhaps 25%, of treated patients will develop a mild to moderate dementia. For the most part, this observation has been made in older patients with malignant astrocytoma who received 6000 rads. It is unclear whether the tendency for this syndrome to appear in the older patient reflects a unique susceptibility of the aged brain to radiation injury, or, perhaps more likely, to a decreased reserve in the aged brain. The data are inconclusive at this time, but they suggest that children with acute leukemia receiving prophylactic cranial irradiation and intrathecal chemotherapy develop a variety of learning disabilities consistent with brain injury (Ch'ien et al., 1980). If this is the case, then perhaps mild dementia is a universal complication of cranial irradiation in doses designed to eradicate tumor.

The value of chemotherapy in the treatment of patients with Hodgkin's disease and the acute leukemias is unquestioned. It has been more difficult to establish that chemotherapy is of benefit in patients with solid tumors. The role of chemotherapy in the management of patients with metastatic brain tumor and primary malignant brain tumor has been under intensive study. The best evidence in support of chemotherapy has come from the work in the BTSG, showing that the lipid-soluble nitrosourea BCNU, in conjunction with surgery and whole-brain radiation therapy, prolongs survival over that achieved by surgery and radiation alone (Walker et al., 1980). Although median survival is only slightly longer in the chemotherapy group, prolonged survivals (18 months to 3 year) are only seen in the patients receiving chemotherapy. It is also clear (again from the BTSG data) that elderly patients (over age 65) do considerably less well, as judged by survival, than younger patients receiving identical treatment. It is not entirely clear why. Speculations include delays in diagnosis in the elderly population, with early symptoms having been attributed to vascular disease or senile dementia, malignant brain tumors in the elderly are intrinsically more aggressive and respond to treatment less well, and alterations in immune function in the aged have a permissive effect on tumor growth. Our own experience would suggest that the poorer response of elderly patients is not simply due to a failure to tolerate chemotherapy, since, with few exceptions, our older patients have received as much BCNU as their younger counterparts. This is somewhat surprising, since one might expect bone marrow reserves to be diminished in the elderly. Unpublished data from the Radiation Therapy Oncology Group (RTOG) have suggested that chemotherapy has no role in the treatment of elderly patients with malignant glial tumors. The conclusion that elderly patients with malignant primary brain tumors should not receive chemotherapy is, in our view, premature. The value of chemotherapy in the treatment of metastatic brain tumors remains uncertain. The experience acquired to date in the chemotherapy of both primary and metastatic malignant brain tumors would suggest that elderly patients will tolerate chemotherapy and that the limiting factor is not age-related toxicity, but rather effective chemotherapeutic agents.

Adrenocorticosteroid hormones (steroids) have been used in the treatment of brain tumors for 25 years (Kofman et al., 1957). The steroids act by decreasing the edema that invariably surrounds malignant astrocytomas, metastatic brain tumors, and rapidly growing meningiomas. Prompt symptomatic improvement is observed in the majority of patients within 48 hours of treatment. The symptoms most likely to respond to steroid therapy are those that reflect generalized brain dysfunction due to cerebral edema, increased intracranial pressure, and brain shifts. Focal symptoms and signs appropriate to the location of the tumor respond less favorably. Therefore headache, alterations in consciousness, and signs and symptoms of cerebral herniation are more likely to resolve than seizures, hemiparesis, and aphasia. These differences are relative in that neurological symptoms of all types improve to some

degree with steroid use. The particular steroid preparation used does not appear to be crucial. Dexamethasone is widely used because of its minimal mineralocorticoid activity and because it may be less likely to cause steroid psychosis even in large doses (Fishman, 1975). The optimal steroid dose is unknown. The standard starting dose is the equivalent of 16 mg of dexamethasone a day in divided doses. Patients not improving may respond to higher doses (Lieberman et al., 1977). Graham and Caird (1978) have demonstrated that steroids are effective in the control of symptoms and signs of intracranial tumor in the elderly. In their series, six of eight patients with malignant astrocytoma and four of eight patients with metastatic brain tumor responded to dexamethasone in doses of 12 to 16 mg/day. They remark that this response rate was similar to that seen in their younger patients. It has also been our experience that response to steroids is independent of age. Although elderly patients respond to steroids, the incidence of both serious and minor side effects is increased. Beks et al. (1972) compared two large neurosurgical patient groups: one treated with steroids, the other not. The steroid-treated group had sixteen complications, the control group three. Graham and Caird (30) have reported steroid-related complications in five of twenty elderly brain tumor patients. Serious side effects were encountered in two patients: perforation of a colonic diverticulum and perforation of an unsuspected duodenal ulcer. In general, we have found that older patients tolerate high doses of steroids well for short periods of time. Clearly, the dose should be reduced to the minimum level required to control symptoms. This requires that definitive treatment (either surgery or radiation theapy) be given as soon as possible so that steroids can be tapered. Elderly patients are not immune to the complications of prolonged steroid use, although evidence that they are more susceptible because of their age is lacking. Severe oral candidiasis and herpes zoster are two complications of steroid use we have tended to see more often in elderly patients. To summarize, adrenocorticosteroids are effective in temporarily controlling the symptoms and signs of intracranial tumor in elderly patients, and following definitive treatment, steroids should be tapered and, if possible, discontinued in order to avoid the inevitable complications of their prolonged use.

Treatment of Specific Tumor Types

As discussed above, malignant astrocytoma, metastatic brain tumor, and meningioma taken together constitute 90% or more of all intracranial tumors in elderly patients. The optimal treatment of each tumor type will now be considered. The treatment recommended is largely dictated by the tumor type, with certain modifications for elderly patients.

MALIGNANT ASTROCYTOMA

In general, the treatment of malignant astrocytoma in elderly patients is disappointing. Irrespective of treatment, the survival time is short. As discussed, the RTOG data suggest that vigorous treatment offers no advantage over biopsy and supportive care in patients over age 65. These observations raise the important question about whether aggressive treatment should be offered to elderly patients with malignant astrocytoma. In our view, this issue is still unresolved. The issue is clearer in young and middle-aged adults, for whom there is now substantial evidence to support the view that optimal treatment for malignant astrocytoma consists of maximal surgical resection followed by whole-brain radiation therapy in a dose of 5500 to 6000 rads and systemic chemotherapy with BCNU. Studies are now underway to evaluate newer chemotherapeutic agents and multiple-drug therapy.

METASTATIC BRAIN TUMOR

The mainstays of treatment for patients with brain metastases are adrenocorticosteroid hormones and whole-brain radiation therapy. After completing brain irradiation, steroids are tapered and, where possible, discontinued. Approximately 75% of patients respond to treatment, as judged by neurological symptoms and signs, steroid requirements following ra-

diation therapy, and tumor regression on post-treatment CT scans (Cairncross et al., 1980). The median survival following the diagnosis of metastatic brain tumor is 3 to 4 months in most series, a discouraging observation due, in many instances, to advancing systemic disease in the setting of controlled intracranial tumor. In our opinion, there are few indications for surgery as the primary treatment of metastatic brain tumor. When the diagnosis is in question, particularly if there is no history of systemic cancer, then surgery is indicated. Patients with solitary metastatic tumors in "accessible and silent" areas of brain may be considered surgical candidates if the primary tumor is radioresistant. In our experience, metastases from melanoma, colon cancer, and kidney cancer respond poorly to radiation therapy. We emphasize that these tumors are less radiosensitive, not absolutely radioresistant, and we have observed responses to radiation therapy in these tumor types as well. Our own bias is to radiate these patients first and to consider surgery only if radiation therapy fails. As discussed previously, the role of systemic or intraarterial chemotherapy in patients with metastatic brain tumor is still under investigation and, at this time, does not have a place as a primary treatment modality.

MENINGIOMA

The treatment of symptomatic intracranial meningioma is surgical removal. Rapidly growing meningiomas may incite considerable edema in the underlying compressed brain. The edema is usually visible on CT scan and responds to steroids. Following removal of the tumor, steroids can be tapered and stopped. There is little argument that symptomatic meningiomas in young and middle-aged adults should be removed; symptoms are likely to worsen and surgical removal will only be more difficult with time. Since meningiomas are, for the most part, slowly growing tumors, the physician may have the option, in selected elderly patients, of avoiding surgery. This is a serious consideration when seizures are the only symptom of the intracranial tumor. Patients with altered mental status, raised intracranial pressure, hemiparesis, etc., should be considered for surgery, irrespective of their age, provided there are not medical contraindications. Elderly patients who require steroids to control their neurological symptoms should also be considered for surgery. Clearly, small incidental meningiomas in elderly patients discovered at the time of CT scanning for other reasons should not be removed. As discussed by Pennybacker (1949), the neurosurgeon may choose to subtotally remove large meningiomas or those in critical locations (especially in the posterior fossa); because the tumors are slowly growing, symptomatic recurrence is a less important concern and relief of symptoms for several years is an acceptable treatment.

References

Annegers, J.F., Schoenberg, B.S., and Okazaki, H. et al. (1981). Epidemiologic study of primary intracranial neoplasms. Arch. Neurol. 38, 217–219.

Aronson, S.M., Garcia, J.H., and Aronson, B.E. (1964). Metastatic neoplasms of the brain: Their frequency in relation to age. Cancer 17, 558–563.

Banna, M. (1976). Craniopharyngioma: A review article based on 160 cases. Br. J. Radiol. 49, 206–223.

Beks, J.W.F., Doorenbos, H., and Walstra, G.J.M. Clinical experiences with steroids in neurosurgical patients. In H.J. Reulen and K. Schurman, Eds. Steroids and Brain Edema, Springer-Verlag, Berlin, pp. 233–238.

Cairncross, J.G., Kim, J.H., and Posner, J.B. (1980). Radiation therapy for brain metastases. Ann. Neurol. 7, 529–541.

Cairncross, J.G. and Posner, J.B. (in press). The management of brain metastases. In M.E. Walker, Ed., Oncology of the Nervous System, Martinus-Nijhoff.

Caveness, W.F. (1980). Experimental observations: Delayed necrosis in normal monkey brain. In H. A. Gilbert, and A.R. Kagin, Eds. Radiation Damage to the Nervous System, Raven Press, New York, pp. 1–38.

Ch'ien, L.T., Aur, R.J.A., Stagner, S., et al. (1980). Longterm neurological implications of the somnolence syndrome in children with acute lymphocytic leukemia. Ann. Neurol. 8, 273–277.

Fishman, R.A. (1975). Brain edema. New Eng. J. Med. 293, 706–711.

Graham, K. and Caird, F.I. (1978). High-dose steroid therapy of intracranial tumor in the elderly. Age and Aging 7, 146–150.

Hastings, D.W. (1939). Difficulties in differential diagnosis of brain tumor in older age groups. J. Nerv. Ment. Dis. 89, 44–51.

Hazra, T., Mullins, G.M., and Lott, S. (1972). Management of cerebral metastases from bronchogenic carcinoma. Johns Hopkins Med. J. 130, 377–383.

Hendrickson, F.R. (1977). The optimum schedule for palliative radiotherapy for metastatic brain cancer. Int. J. Radiat. Oncol. Biol. Phys. 2, 165–168.

Herishanu, Y. (1970). Craniopharyngioma in aged patients. J. Amer. Geriat. Soc. 18, 261–263.

Kofman, S., Garvin, J.S., and Nagamani, D., et al. (1957). Treatment of cerebral metastases from breast carcinoma with prednisolone. J. Amer. Med. Assoc. 163, 1473–1476.

Leiberman, A., LeBrun, Y., Glass, P. et al. (1977). Use of high-dose corticosteroids in patients with inoperable brain tumors. J. Neurol. Neurosurg. Psychiat. 40, 678–682.

Moersch, F.P., Craig, W.M., and Kernohan, J.W. (1941). Tumors of the brain in aged patients. Arch. Neurol. Psychiat. 45, 235–245.

Pennybacker, J. (1949). Intracranial tumors in the aged. Edinburgh Med. J. 56, 590–600.

Pennybacker, J. (1968). The neurosurgery of old age. Cesk. Neurol. 31, 73–79.

Posner, J.B. and Chernik, N.L. (1978). Intracranial metastases from systemic cancer. Adv. Neurol. 19, 579–592.

Rubenstein, L.J. (1972). Tumors of the central nervous system. In H.I. Firminger, Ed. Atlas of Tumor Pathology, Series II, Fas. 6, Armed Forces Institute of Pathology, Washington, D.C.

Schoenberg, B.S. (1978). Epidemiology of primary nervous system neoplasms. Adv. Neurol. 19, 475–495.

Schoenberg, B.S., Christine, B.W., and Whisnant, J.P. (1975). Nervous system neoplasms and primary malignancies of other sites: The unique association between meningiomas and breast cancer. Neurology 25, 705–712.

Schoenberg, B.S., Christine, B.W., and Whisnant, J.P. (1978). The resolution of discrepancies in the reported incidence of primary brain tumors. Neurology 28, 817–823.

Stewart, I., Millac, P., and Shephard, R.H.

(1975). Neurosurgery in the older patient. Postgrad. Med. J. 51, 453–456.

Tomita, T. and Raimondi, A.J. (1981). Brain tumors in the elderly. J. Amer. Med. Assoc. 246, 53–55.

Twomey, C. (1978). Brain tumors in the elderly. Age Aging 7, 138–145.

Walker, M.D. (1972). Brain and peripheral nervous system tumors. In J.F. Holland and E. Frei, Eds. Cancer Medicine, Philadelphia, Lea & Febiger, pp. 1385–1407.

Walker, M.D., Alexander, E., and Hunt, W.E. et al. (1978). Evaluation of BCNU and/or radiotherapy in the treatment of anaplastic gliomas. J. Neurosurg. 49, 333–343.

Walker, M.D., Greene, S.B., and Byar, D.P. (1980). Randomized comparisons of radiotherapy and nitrosoureas for the treatment of malignant glioma after surgery. New Eng. J. Med. 303, 1323–1329.

Zimm, S., Wampler, G.L., Stablein, L., et al. (1981). Intracerebral metastases in solid tumor patients: Natural history and results of treatment. Cancer 48, 384–394.

25. Cerebrovascular Diseases in the Elderly: Epidemiology

PHILIP A. WOLF   WILLIAM B. KANNEL
JOEL VERTER

Stroke is the commonest serious neuro-logical disease of late adult life and the most devastating clinical manifestation of hypertension and atherosclerosis. It is not a chance or random occurrence as the term cerebrovascular *accident* implies, but is instead the predictable consequence of a chain of events set in motion many years before. The evolution of hypertension and other host and environmental precursors into clinical manifestations of cerebrovascular disease has been delineated by prospective epidemiological study of the general population. Prevention, not treatment of the clinical manifestations, is more likely to reduce the morbidity and mortality from stroke; and this requires correction of the precursors in stroke-prone individuals.

Evidence that such an approach is fruitful is emerging from controlled clinical trials and mortality data that suggest an accelerating decline in death rates from stroke.

Assessment of the incidence and identification of the precursors of stroke have been accomplished in prospective population studies, such as the Heart Disease Epidemiology Study at Framingham, Massachusetts. These studies provide data on the way clinical manifestations of cerebrovascular disease evolve and how stroke is related to the other cardiovascular conse-quences of aging, particularly coronary heart disease (CHD) and cardiac failure (CHF). The manifestations and precursors of stroke and CHD in the elderly are not the same as they are at younger ages. Assessment of these differences may disclose important clues to pathogenesis and thereby provide strategies for prevention.

Prevalence

The National Survey of Stroke estimates there were 1.7 million survivors of a stroke in the coterminous United States on Prevalence Day, July 1, 1976, a prevalence rate for all ages of 794 per 100,000. The prevalence rates per 100,000 ranged from 66 below age 45, to 998 for ages 45 to 64, to 5063 for those 65 and over (Table 25-1). The prevalence is substantially higher for blacks, particularly at younger ages (Baum and Robins, 1981).

Stroke is a major contributor to disability and is estimated to account for one-half the patients hospitalized for acute neurological disease. In the Framingham Study, 71% of survivors of stroke had impaired vocational capacity when assessed an average of 7 years after stroke (Gresham et al., 1975). Sixteen percent were institutionalized, 31% needed assistance in self-care, and 20% required assistance in ambulation. The estimated annual cost of care for

Table 25-1. Cerebrovascular Disease: Age-Specific Prevalence Rates/100,000 Population, Both Sexes.

	Rochester, Minnesota* 1970 (A)	United States** National Survey of Stroke, Average, 1976	United States** Health Interview Survey (HIS) 1977
AGE			
<35	10		
35–44	200		
45–54	440		
55–64	810		
65–74	3560		
75⁺	5970		
Age-adjusted (to U.S. 1970)	556	743	1238
Cases	(303)	(637)	Interviews (111,000)***

*Matsumoto et al., 1973; Modified from Kurtzke, 1976.
**Modified from Baum and Robins, 1981.
***From Division of Health Interview Statistics, 1977.

stroke in the United States in 1976 was more than 3 billion dollars (Baum and Robins, 1981). There are additional indirect costs, including loss of present and future earnings, amounting to more than twice this amount. The potential rewards of stroke prevention in health care and resources are enormous.

Incidence

It is estimated that about 400,000 stroke patients are discharged from acute care hospitals in the United States annually: three-fourths after an initial stroke and the remainder for a recurrence (Robins and

Baum, 1981). The reported incidence of stroke varies widely, depending on the source of the sample (hospitalized cases or general population), the sample's age composition, and whether initial and recurrent strokes are included (Kurtzke, 1976). The incidence of stroke is lower and occurs later in life than CHD, requiring larger cohorts followed for longer periods to achieve an equivalent number of cases for investigations (Kuller, 1978). Stroke incidence is strikingly related to age, with a more than doubling of incidence rates in each successive decade above age 55 (Table 25-2). Clearly, the increasing numbers of persons age 70 and over in the

Table 25-2. Average Annual Age-Specific Incidence Rates of Initial Strokes/100,000 Population in Two Community Surveys.*

Age	National Survey of Stroke 1976	Rochester, Minn. 1955–1959
<35	3	4
35–44	31	35
45–54	106	110
55–64	262	364
65–74	582	791
75–84	1383	(75⁺) 2156
85	1825	
All Ages	141	154
No. cases	(est. 594,000)	(993)
Size of population	211 million	43,000

*Adapted from Robins and Baum, 1981.

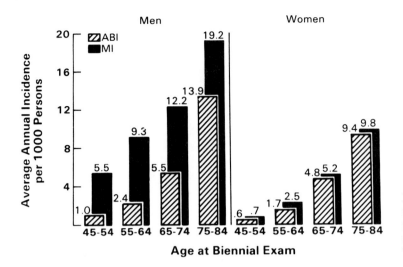

Figure 25-1. Incidence of myocardial versus brain infarction by age in each sex. 24-Year followup: The Framingham study.

population make stroke prevention a major public health necessity.

Analogous manifestations of CHD and cerebrovascular disease may be compared by examining age and sex specific incidence rates per 1000 of myocardial infarction (MI) and atherothrombotic brain infarction (ABI) (Figure 25-1). These Framingham Study data represent 24 years of follow-up of approximately 5000 men and women who were ages 30 to 62 at entry to the study in 1950. They represent a general population sample of adults resident in the town of Framingham in 1949 and who were free of cardiovascular disease at entry. Follow-up has been satisfactory, with 85% taking each examination and only 3% completely lost to follow-up after 24 years. In men, the age-adjusted (direct method), average, annual incidence rates for MI is 8.5 per 1000, three times the 2.7 per 1000 rate for ABI. For women, age-adjusted average annual incidence rates of MI and ABI are nearly identical, with rates of 2.4 and 2.1 per 1000, respectively. In both sexes, rates rise with age, but the 20-year lag in incidence experienced by women for MI is not present for ABI for which age-specific rates are similar. Overall, the incidence rate of ABI is about 30% greater in men than women, and this sex differential is most striking below age 65. Although stroke, generally, and ABI, specifically, occurs most frequently in the senium, 20% of ABIs occur in persons below age 65.

Frequency of Stroke by Type

Estimates of the prevalence of the different clinical varieties of cerebrovascular disease vary widely depending upon the source of the data. Hospital and neurology service data are subject to selective biases and are likely to overrepresent the more severe and troublesome stroke cases. By virtue of its frequently lethal outcome, intraparenchymal hemorrhage is overrepresented in postmortem series. General population survey data, although more representative, often suffer from small numbers of cases and lack the uniform and sophisticated clinical and laboratory evaluations needed to distinguish stroke types (Mohr et al., 1978). Distinctions by type of stroke—brain infarction due to occlusive disease of large arteries, lacunar infarction, cerebral embolism, intraparenchymal hemorrhage, and subarachnoid hemorrhage—are clearly necessary for an understanding of the epidemiology of the various manifestations of cerebrovascular disease that have different pathogenetic mechanisms. This critical issue is dealt with in detail by Drs. Kase and Mohr in Chapter 26.

In the Framingham Cohort, at the end of a 24-year follow-up, 344 initial cases of stroke occurred (Table 25-3). Atherothrombotic brain infarction is the commonest type, accounting for 60%, with transient ischemic attacks (TIA), unaccompanied by stroke, representing an ad-

Table 25-3. Frequency of Initial Stroke by Type, Men and Women, 45–84. 24-Year Follow-up: The Framingham Study.

	Number of Cases		Percent of All Strokes
	Men	Women	
Atherothrombotic brain infarction	100	107	60
Cerebral embolus	21	26	14
Intracerebral hemorrhage	9	6	4
Subarachnoid hemorrhage	14	18	9
Transient ischemic attack only	20	13	10
Stroke from other causes	5	5	3
Total	169	175	100

ditional 10%. Thus, two-thirds of stroke cases are due to ischemia and infarction secondary to occlusive disease of the small- and medium-sized arteries. Stroke due to cerebral embolus (CE), with a recognized embolic source, accounts for 14% of cases. Together, intraparenchymal hemorrhage (IH) and subarachnoid hemorrhage (SH) comprise 14% of the total. Subarachnoid hemorrhage, usually due to a pathologically confirmed ruptured berry aneurysm of the circle of Willis, is about twice as frequent as spontaneous IH. This two-to-one ratio of SH to IH is the inverse of the ratio found in most hospital registries (Mohr et al., 1978). Recent, community-based data from Rochester, Minnesota is in keeping with the Framingham findings (Garraway et al., 1979), whereas National Survey of Stroke data (Gross et al., 1981) and a population-based stroke study in south Alabama show a higher frequency of IH (Weinfield, 1981). The recent ability to discern small hemorrhages on CT scan will increase the number of diagnosable IH's, probably at the expense of the ABI category rather than the SH. The reasons for the variations in relative frequency between SH and IH is unclear and unlikely to be explained by diagnostic custom or in imprecision. It is of interest that the frequency of each type is quite similar in the two sexes (Table 25-3). This is in contrast to the frequency of the various clinical manifestation of CHD by sex, where a marked excess of MI and sudden death is seen in men and an excess of angina pectoris in women. Mortality data disclose a dramatic

variation in the relative frequency of stroke type over time and in different geographical areas, suggesting that they are unreliable for this purpose (Kuller, 1978). Crucial to the problem of determining relative frequency by stroke type is the difficulty of clinically distinguishing between (1) stroke due to embolism, particularly embolism without apparent source; (2) stroke due to occlusive disease of the larger vessels, segregating extracranial carotid and vertebral, from intracranial carotid, vertebral-basilar, and, less commonly, the other major cerebral arteries; and (3) stroke due to occlusion of small penetrating arteries with lacunar infarction. By using arteriography and CT scanning, a clearer picture of the relative frequency of stroke by type is emerging (Mohr et al., 1978). Interestingly, it now appears that only 10% of all strokes are due to occlusive disease in the surgically accessible extracranial portion of the internal carotid artery (Mohr, 1978).

Risk Factors

Major reduction in disability and death from stroke is more likely to come from prevention than from more effective medical or surgical treatment. Identification of the major risk factors for stroke and of the stroke-prone individual should facilitate preventive efforts. A universal finding in epidemiological studies is that the most important risk factor for stroke, infarction as well as hemorrhage, is hypertension. Impaired cardiac function, with evidence of congestive heart failure (CHF), prior

CHD, or electrocardiographic abnormalities are also powerful contributors to stroke incidence. Elevated blood lipids, cigarette smoking, diabetes, and obesity are less potent precursors for stroke than for CHD or peripheral vascular disease. An elevated blood hematocrit within the normal range has been shown to independently contribute to stroke risk.

Several factors implicated in stroke incidence at younger ages, such as cigarette smoking and elevated serum cholesterol, lose their impact with advancing age. These are risk factors that tend to identify candidates for CHD with greater efficiency than candidates for stroke, and even for CHD, their impact is greatest below age 65 (Kannel, 1978).

Cerebral embolism is chiefly a consequence of cardiac disease—valvular disease, myocardial infarction, and irregular cardiac rhythm (notably atrial fibrillation), or complications of cardiac surgery. Emboli arising from ulcerated lesions of the brachiocephalic arteries and paradoxical embolism are implicated in patients without an obvious embolic source.

Intraparenchymal hemorrhage is chiefly due to hypertension-induced Charcot–Bouchard microaneurysms, or as a complication of anticoagulant therapy. Spontaneous subarachnoid hemorrhage is chiefly secondary to congenital aneurysm of the circle of Willis, which may be associated with pre-existing hypertension.

Atherogenic Host Factors

Hypertension

Hypertension is the dominant precursor of stroke, generally, and is as strongly related to ABI as it is to IH (Figure 25-2).

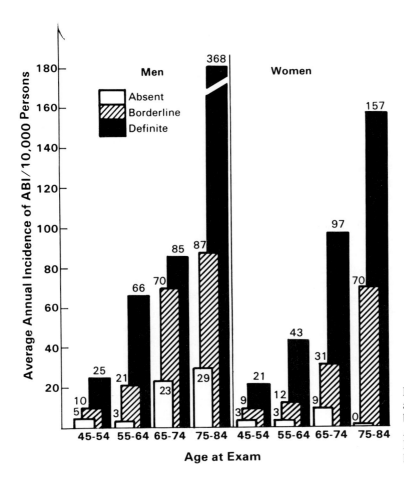

Figure 25-2. Hypertension and Risk of Atherothrombotic Brain Infarction by Age in Each Sex. 24-Year Follow-up: The Framingham Study.

Table 25-4. Risk of Atherothrombotic Brain Infarction According to Various Components of Blood Pressure. 24-Year Follow-up, Framingham Study: Men and Women 45 to 84.

Quintile of Component of Blood Pressure	Age-Adjusted Average Annual Incidence/1000							
	Systolic Pressure		Diastolic Pressure		Pulse Pressure		Mean Arterial Pressure	
	Men	Women	Men	Women	Men	Women	Men	Women
Q I	1.0	0.1	2.0	0.9	0.9	1.0	1.1	0.3
II	1.4	0.7	2.1	0.8	1.3	0.6	1.4	0.6
III	2.7	2.1	0.9	1.8	2.8	1.5	2.3	0.9
IV	5.7	2.6	3.2	2.5	2.5	2.3	2.9	2.0
V	8.8	7.0	5.7	5.4	6.8	3.9	5.4	4.6
Standardized multivariate regression coefficient	.634	.722	.506	.683	.535	.570	.604	.755
Z-Value ($Z=2.58=P<.01$)	6.24	8.08	4.44	7.27	5.06	5.82	5.77	8.36

Hypertension is not only the most powerful contributor to stroke incidence, it is also a highly prevalent abnormality, having an impact on a large portion of the population (Wolf, 1975). Risk of stroke is related to the height of the blood pressure, throughout its range (Kannel et al., 1970). For ABI, the incidence rises as the pressure rises, with an adverse impact among mild, moderate, and severe hypertensives. There is no critical value of pressure level, systolic or diastolic, below which stroke or ABI does not occur. For stroke generally, and for ABI specifically, the effect of hypertension continues with advancing age in either sex. These data strongly suggest that control of hypertension is no less important for stroke prevention in the eighth and the ninth decade than it is at younger ages.

An examination of various components of blood pressure, in relation to incidence of brain infarction, gives no indication that any feature of blood pressure is more closely linked than systolic pressure (Table 25-4). The average annual incidence of ABI, age adjusted, is shown according to systolic, diastolic, pulse pressure, and mean arterial pressure. Risk is examined according to quintile of the distribution of each; in order to place them on equal footing for the different ranges of values, standardized regression coefficients are given for each, as well as multivariate significance test values. All appear to favor systolic pressure, although there is no significant difference among these various trends.

Isolated Systolic Hypertension

With the disproportionate rise in systolic pressure that occurs with advancing age, isolated systolic hypertension becomes highly prevalent. However, it is far from innocuous.

Not only is systolic blood pressure as powerful a predictor of brain infarction as the diastolic component, but isolated elevations of systolic pressure are also important. Even in the elderly (65 to 84), there is at least a twofold increased risk of brain infarction among those with systolic pressures exceeding 160 mm Hg accompanied by diastolic pressures consistently below 95 mm Hg (Table 25-5).

Because hypertension is the predominant contributor to stroke incidence, the importance of isolated systolic hyperten-

Table 25-5. Risk of Brain Infarction in the Elderly with Isolated Systolic Hypertension. 24-Year Follow-up, Framingham Study.

Isolated systolic hypertension	Average Annual Incidence/1000			
	65–74		75–84	
	Men	Women	Men	Women
Absent	4.6	3.8	9.4	7.9
Present	11.0	8.3	30.7	12.0
Z-Value ($Z=1.96=P<.05$)	2.37	2.63	2.32	0.88

Isolated systolic hypertension = Systolic 160+ mm Hg/Diastolic <95 mm Hg

sion in the development of strokes was studied in the Framingham Cohort, taking into account the degree of associated arterial rigidity. The arterial rigidity was estimated from pulse wave recording using the degree of blunting of the pulse wave diastolic notch as a measure of loss of arterial elastic recoil. Although this is an imperfect measure of arterial rigidity, risk of cardiovascular disease was found to be related to the degree of blunting (Kannel et al., 1981). Also, the prevalence of isolated systolic hypertension and pulse pressure were found to be related. All three (pulse pressure, systolic hypertension, and pulse wave changes) and diastolic notch blunting increased with age.

Based on prospective data relating future stroke incidence to systolic pressure, diastolic pressure, age, and pulse wave configuration, isolated systolic hypertension was found to be an independent risk factor for the development of stroke, taking associated arterial rigidity into account. Subjects with isolated systolic hypertension were found to experience two to four times as many strokes as normotensive persons (Kannel et al., 1981). When taken alone, diastolic pressure is related to stroke incidence in the subject with systolic hypertension, but the diastolic component adds little to risk assessment. In men in this systolic hypertension subgroup, the diastolic pressure was actually misleading.

The findings strongly suggest that the increased risk of stroke associated with systolic hypertension probably is a direct result of the pressure rather than only a reflection of the underlying arterial rigidity. This suggests that treatment to lower the systolic pressure may well be efficacious in reducing the risk of stroke in systolic hypertension. A controlled trial to determine the indications, contraindications, best drugs, dosage, side effects, benefits, and hazards would seem long overdue.

Lipids

Elevated serum total cholesterol is positively related to the incidence of CHD. The association is equally strong for men and for women and for each of the clinical manifestations of CHD. The strength of the association, however, decreases above age 55, particularly in men (Gordon et al., 1977). When blood cholesterol is partitioned into its component parts of high, low, and very low density lipoproteins (HDL, LDL, and VLDL), a relationship with CHD above age 55 re-emerges. The HDL-cholesterol (HDL-C) is *inversely* related to CHD incidence, whereas the LDL-C is positively associated with CHD. The association of total cholesterol and lipoprotein–cholesterol fractions with stroke occurrence is far less clear or consistent. Serum total cholesterol above age 65 was *inversely* related to incidence of stroke, generally, and to ABI, specifically; this negative association was particularly striking in women (Table 25-6). This strong negative impact on stroke incidence persists even after other risk factors are taken into account, as shown by the significant multivariate logistic regression coefficients. For ABI, in particular, the inverse relationship is significant only in those aged 75 to 84 years. On the 11th biennial examination of the Heart Study cohort at Framingham, a complete fasting lipid profile was obtained on nearly 2500 men and women, aged 50 to 79, who were free of cerebrovascular disease. The sole strong relationship of the lipoprotein–cholesterol fraction to stroke incidence is the significant *negative* association of LDL-C with stroke in women. No significant protective effect of HDL-C on stroke was found, and there was no clear relationship of triglyceride level to stroke risk.

The inverse LDL-C relationship to stroke incidence has also been noted in studies of Japanese men living in Hawaii and in Japanese residents in Hisayama, Japan (Kagan et al., 1974). In these two instances, the inverse relationship was for hemorrhagic stroke only.

Diabetes

Diabetics are known to develop cardiovascular disease, including stroke, at an increased rate. Recent prospective data have begun to clarify the role of diabetes in morbidity and mortality from cardiovascular disease. In Framingham, peripheral arterial disease with intermittant claudica-

Table 25-6. Regression of Incidence of Stroke on Serum Total Cholesterol According to Age. 24-Year Follow-up, The Framingham Study.

Total Stroke	Number of Cases		Logistic Regression Coefficients	
Age	Men	Women	Men	Women
45–54	32	22	.0054	.0036
55–64	59	52	.0012	−.0022
65–74	59	77	−.0008	−.0089**
75–84	19	23	−.0234**	−.0181**
45–84	169	174		
Univariate (age 45–84)			−.0016	−.0035**
Multivariate (age 45–84)			−.0003	−.0057**
Atherothrombotic Brain Infarction				
45–54	16	14	.0084	.0041
55–64	33	31	.0013	.0028
65–74	36	45	−.0014	−.0069
75–84	15	17	−.0200*	−.0182**
45–84	100	107		
Univariate (age 45–84)			−.0017	−.0014
Multivariate (age 45–84)			−.0002	−.0037

Note: Estimated by the method of Walter-Duncan. Multivariate analysis includes serum cholesterol, systolic, blood pressure, cigarettes, glucose, ECG-LVH and age. Coefficients are not standardized.
*$p < .05$
**$p < .01$

tion occurs more than four times as often in diabetics as in nondiabetics, making it the greatest relative risk. Why the arteries to the legs are more susceptible than the coronary or brachiocephalic arteries to atherosclerosis in diabetics is unclear; however, neither the coronary nor the cerebral circulation is spared.

The relative impact of diabetes is substantial for ABI, more so in women than in men, and diabetes accounts for a greater proportion of brain than myocardial infarctions. Diabetes independently contributes to incidence of ABI in multivariate analysis when age, systolic blood pressure, serum total cholesterol, cigarette smoking, and left ventricular hypertrophy (LVH) by ECG, are accounted for. Overall, the risk of ABI is 2.6 times greater in men ($p < 01$), and 3.1 times greater in women ($p < 05$) among diabetics (Figure 25-3).

Environmental Factors

Despite sizable geographical variations and cultural trends in stroke mortality, there are few identified environmental factors that contribute substantially to stroke occurrence. Cigarette smoking and obesity have some influence on ABI incidence, whereas physical activity, diet, "softness" of water, coffee drinking, alcohol consumption, climate, and migration exert a doubtful effect.

Cigarette Smoking

Cigarette smoking is strongly related to the incidence of peripheral vascular disease and CHD in men. In both, the impact is substantial below age 65, with waning of effect in those above age 65. For CHD, cigarette smoking seems to exert its impact chiefly by precipitating MI and sudden death in predisposed persons rather than by promoting atherogenesis. The MI and sudden death rates revert to nonsmoker levels soon after discontinuance of the cigarette habit. In the Framingham cohort, the influence of cigarette smoking on ABI can only be examined in men, since few women in this cohort are smokers. As in

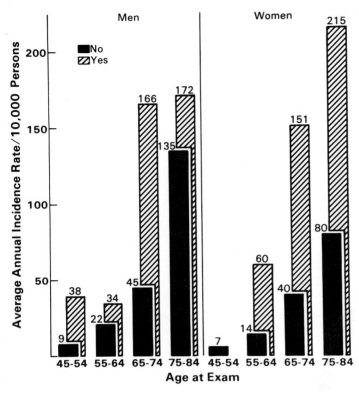

Figure 25-3. Diabetes and Incidence of Atherothrombotic Brain Infarction by Age in Each Sex. 24-Year-Follow-up: The Framingham Study.

MI, cigarette smoking is a risk factor for ABI only in men below age 65. The heightened risk reaches statistical significance for ABI in men 45 to 54 and increases with number of cigarettes smoked daily.

Other Host Factors

Impaired Cardiac Function

Cardiac impairment ranks third, following age and hypertension, as a risk factor for stroke, in general, and for ABI specifically. At any level of blood pressure, persons with cardiac disease, occult or overt, have more than twice the risk of stroke. Cardiac impairments include overt disease such as CHD and CHF, evidence of LVH by ECG and X-ray, and rhythm abnormalities, particularly atrial fibrillation (AF).

Although CHD is a frequent occurrence in persons who appear well, stroke and ABI develop on a background of established hypertension (70%), CHD (30%),

peripheral vascular disease (PVD) (30%), diabetes (15%), and overt CHF (15%). Brain and myocardial infarctions frequently coexist, and their coexistence increases with age (Kagan et al., 1976). Coronary heart disease is the major cause of death among stroke and ABI survivors, as it is in patients with TIA's or carotid bruits (Wolf et al., 1981; Toole et al., 1975).

Overt evidence of impaired cardiac function, prior CHD, and CHF are significantly related to stroke and ABI incidence (Table 25-7).

Probably a reflection of the impact of prolonged or severe hypertension, LVH by ECG increases in prevalence with age and blood pressure. The risk of brain infarction increased substantially in those who developed this ECG abnormality. This excess risk persists on adjustment for blood pressure and age. In contrast to ECG-LVH, generalized cardiac enlargement by X-ray was a less powerful predictor of ABI. Nonspecific ST and T wave abnormalities, intraventricular block, and

Table 25-7. Age-Adjusted Average Annual Incidence of ABI According to Antecedent Cardiac Abnormalities—CHD, CHF, LVH-ECG. 24-Year Follow-up. Framingham Study. Men and Women 45–84 Years.

Cardiac Risk Factor	CHD*		CHF*		LVH by ECG*	
	Men	Women	Men	Women	Men	Women
Absent	2.3	1.7	2.5	1.9	2.3	1.7
Present(definite)	5.7	5.5	6.2	8.1	10.2	13.3

*$P<.01$.

atrioventricular block were also associated with increased ABI incidence. Atrial fibrillation, even in the absence of rheumatic heart disease (RHD), was a powerful precursor of stroke—specifically of embolic stroke (Wolf et al., 1968; Bharucha et al., 1983). The major culprit was *chronic AF*, which increased in frequency with increasing age and blood pressure. When these variables were adjusted, it was found that patients with nonrheumatic AF developed strokes at more than five times the rate of those without this abnormality (Wolf et al., 1978a). When AF occurred in a setting of RHD, particularly mitral stenosis, stroke occurred 17 times more frequently. Clearly chronic, not paroxysmal or intermittent AF, is the chief culprit (Bharucha et al., 1981) and stroke occurring in the setting of chronic nonrheumatic AF is largely embolic (Hinton et al., 1977; Fairfax et al., 1976).

Atrial fibrillation is a particularly important precursor of stroke in the elderly, accounting for most cerebral emboli. Between 10 and 20% of all strokes occurring in an elderly population are in persons with AF (Fairfax et al., 1976; Bharucha et al., 1981). It is an easily recognized characteristic and prevention of cerebral emboli with anticoagulants can be undertaken. Recovery from the initial stroke is often quite good, making the prevention of a recurrence especially urgent.

Actuarial data clearly show an adverse impact of chronic nonrheumatic AF on survival, a finding that contradicts the prevailing notion that AF is often a benign accompaniment of aging (Wolf et al., 1981). Controlled clinical trials of anticoagulants and antiplatelet agents to prevent stroke in persons with chronic AF are long overdue.

Hematocrit

Data from Framingham (Kannel et al., 1972) have called attention to the relationship of high normal blood hemoglobin concentration (or high normal hematocrit level) to an increased incidence of cerebral infarction. Confirmation of this relationship has come from a Japanese autopsy study (Tohgi et al., 1978) and from several clinical and radiological studies of stroke patients (Pearson and Thomas, 1979; Harrison and Mitchell, 1966). Although it had long been recognized that pathologically elevated hematocrits predispose to stroke, the role of increased blood hemoglobin concentration in the upper normal range in promoting cerebral infarction was not recognized. Blood viscosity increases with increments of hemoglobin concentration within the normal range (Thomas et al., 1977), and this may reach pathological significance in narrowed, small penetrating arteries (Tohgi et al., 1978) and in high-grade stenosis of a major cerebral artery (Harrison and Mitchell, 1966). Reduction of high normal hematocrits by venesection has been shown to be associated with a reduction in blood viscosity, with a corresponding increase in cerebral blood flow.

Elevated blood pressure and cigarette smoking are associated with high normal blood hemoglobin concentrations (Figure 25-4). These associated variables account for much, but not all, the relationship to ABI incidence.

Race

Substantial racial differences in stroke morbidity and mortality rates have been reported. Japanese, in Japan, have high stroke death rates—higher than the death

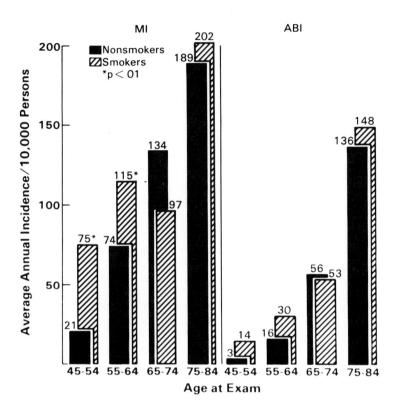

Figure 25-4. Incidence of Atherothrombotic Brain Infarction, according to blood hematocrit level, by age in each sex: the Framingham Study.

rates from heart disease. Intracerebral hemorrhage as the chief type of stroke among Japanese has been declining as the incidence of cerebral infarction rises. Autopsy studies derived from the prospective study of stroke in Hisayama, Japan, where the rate of postmortem examinations is high, now show hemorrhage to account for 30% of all strokes (Omae et al., 1976). Japan-born Japanese living in Hawaii and California have a correspondingly lower death rates from stroke (Worth et al., 1975). These data suggest that environmental factors (including diet) have a major influence on racial and ethnic patterns of disease.

Mortality data consistently show higher death rates from stroke among blacks in the United States. Incidence data, although consistent with these findings, are based upon crude case ascertainment and rather small numbers (Heyden et al., 1969). Blacks in the southeastern part of the United States have especially high

stroke death rates, as compared to whites of all ages and both sexes. The racial differences generally decrease with advancing age and have been diminishing over time (Miller and Kuller, 1973).

Hormonal Influences

Exogenous Estrogens, Castration, and the Menopause

The role of oral contraceptives in stroke applies to young women and is germane to a discussion of stroke in the elderly only insofar as it can shed light on the pathogenesis of stroke generally. There are several situations in which hormonal influences may be examined in relation to stroke incidence. The age of onset for stroke, generally, and for ABI, specifically (Figure 25-1), is about the same in women as in men—in contrast to the 20-year delay in MI incidence in women. Hysterectomy, by inducing surgical menopause, abolishes this protective effect for CHD, and this adverse impact of hysterectomy seems to hold even when one or both ovaries are left intact (Gordon et al., 1978). Two studies from Scandinavia suggest a several-fold higher probability of death from stroke in castrated females (Ask-Upmark, 1962). Since surgical menopause accounts for a high proportion of total menopause, as high as 30% in some U.S. populations, the cardiovascular consequences of this medical practice warrants careful scrutiny. On the other hand, a case control study of estrogen use and risk of stroke in post-menopausal women disclosed no significant relationship (Pfeffer and Van Den Noort, 1976). There was, however, a significant excess of estrogen takers among women 70 to 79 years who had sustained a nonembolic cerebral infarction (Pfeffer and Van Den Noort, 1976), which may have been related to heightened blood pressure from the estrogens. The rate of stroke occurrence is increased in men taking estrogens (in the form of stilbesterol) for prostatic cancer (Byar, 1973; Veterans Administration Cooperative Urological Research Group, 1967). Clearly, the relationship of exogenous and endogenous estrogens to risk of cardiovascular disease, including stroke, warrants further investigation.

Heredity

Stroke occurs with sufficient frequency in the general population such that chance familial aggregation is likely. Excess strokes occur in the family of stroke patients as compared to the spouse's family. The excess cases were limited to siblings, but risk in these blood relatives was only slighter greater than in unrelated persons (Alter and Kluznik, 1972; Heyden et al., 1969; Davidenkova et al., 1966; Slack and Evans, 1966; Gifford, 1966; Issaeva and Mikheeva, 1967; Gertler et al., 1968). A hereditary predisposition to stroke must take into account genetic susceptibility to hypertension and diabetes. These inherited stroke precursors might account for much of the excess of strokes in relatives of stroke patients.

The Stroke Risk Profile

Risk factor information can be efficiently synthesized into a composite risk estimate using multiple logistic equations. These describe the conditional probability of a cerebrovascular event for any given set of risk variables from their known coefficients of regression on incidence and constants for the intercept (Gordon et al., 1971). This allows a more logical selection of patients for preventive management and avoids underestimating the risk to persons with multiple marginal "abnormalities" according to categorical assessments of risk factors. It also avoids overreacting to those with only a single abnormality.

Risk estimates can be obtained with such formulations over a wide range, depending on the combined strength of the components. Using a set of components applicable to cardiovascular disease in general (systolic blood pressure, serum cholesterol, glucose tolerance, cigarette habit, and ECG-LVH), one-tenth of the asymptomatic population can be identified, from which about one-half of the ABIs will emerge. This segment of the population has a 40 to 47% chance of an ABI in eight years (Kannel et al., 1970).

Signs of Compromised Cerebral Circulation

The availability of medical treatment and effective surgery to restore flow through or around a narrowed or an occluded carotid artery has stimulated interest in the early detection of a compromised cerebral circulation prior to stroke occurrence. Technology is available to noninvasively detect such obstructions and to measure flow in the extracranial cerebral circulation.

Two clinical findings indicate that a compromised cerebral circulation may be present—an asymptomatic carotid bruit and TIAs.

Asymptomatic Carotid Bruits

The prognostic importance and management of persons with asymptomatic carotid bruits is uncertain, since it is not clear what proportion of strokes are heralded by carotid bruits or whether, when carotid bruit is present, the stroke is actually caused by the obstructive disease in the vessel involved. Carotid bruits may be associated with a greater incidence of strokes either because they are directly involved in the pathogenesis of the ictus or because they are a nonspecific indicator of generalized atherosclerosis, which often includes the intracerebral vessels. It is also not clear how often asymptomatic carotid bruits lead to transient ischemic cerebral attacks and whether those that do are specifically related to the subsequent occurrence of strokes. In the Framingham Study, beginning with the ninth biennial examination in 1966 and on all subsequent examinations, carotid bruits were routinely sought out by auscultation. Over eight years, carotid bruits appeared in 171 subjects, 66 in men and 105 in women, all of whom were initially asymptomatic and free of bruit. The incidence of bruits increased with age and was equal in men and women, rising from 3.5% at ages 45 to 54, to 7.0% at ages 67 to 79 (Wolf et al., 1981). The incidence was greater in subjects with hypertension and in subjects with CHD and diabetes. Transient ischemic attacks appeared in eight and strokes in twenty of the subjects, a stroke rate over twice that expected for age and sex. More often than not, however, the cerebral infarction occurred in a vascular territory different from that of the carotid bruit, and often in the posterior circulation. Also, all the strokes that occurred in these persons were not cerebral infarction due to large vessel atherosclerosis; ruptured aneurysm, emboli from the heart, or lacunar infarction was the mechanism of stroke in nearly one-half the cases. Interestingly, the incidence of myocardial infarction was also increased twofold in those with asymptomatic carotid bruit. General mortality was also increased; 1.7-fold in men, and 1.9-fold in women, with 79% of the deaths due to cardiovascular disease, including stroke.

Carotid bruit is clearly an indicator of increased stroke risk; in asymptomatic populations, however, the bruit is chiefly a nonfocal signal of advanced atherosclerotic disease and not necessarily an indica-

tor of local arterial stenosis that will precede ipsilateral cerebral infarction in the territory of the carotid with the bruit.

Transient Ischemic Attacks

Transient ischemic attacks are reversible focal neurological deficits, lasting minutes to 24 hours. Based on retrospective clinical data from patients who have sustained a stroke, TIA's are believed to frequently precede the development of brain infarction. However, best estimates indicate that only 10% of all strokes are actually preceded by TIA's (Whisnant, 1974; Mohr et al., 1978; Hass, 1977).

It is also estimated that atherothrombotic disease of the surgically accessible carotid artery accounts for less than 15% of strokes and that atherothrombotic disease of the large extracranial arteries, including the carotid, altogether underlies about 33% of all strokes (Mohr et al., 1978).

The incidence of TIA's is uncertain because of non-uniform definitions and case ascertainment. The best estimate is that the yearly incidence approaches one per 1000 in the elderly. Over 65% of patients who experienced TIA's before stroke had carotid artery disease. It is estimated that only 30% of patients with carotid territory TIA's have clinical signs of extracranial carotid disease on careful examination.

The risk of stroke is believed to be increased tenfold in those who experience TIA's. Fully 35% can expect a stroke within four years (Mohr et al., 1978). It is estimated that the risk of a stroke in persons with a well-defined TIA is approximately 7% per year (Hass, 1977). The risk of a stroke appears to be greater in the carotid than in the vertebrobasilar territories. If a stroke is to occur, it is likely to do so within a few months of onset of TIA's. Although the risk of a stroke is substantially increased, survival is little altered compared to persons the same age in the general population (Whisnant, 1974).

The prognosis for those with carotid territory TIA's without demonstrable vascular abnormality is almost as ominous as in those with stenotic occlusion, suggesting a nonfocal generalized condition or a source for local emoblism.

The risk of TIA's and the probability of their evolving into brain infarctions is best discerned from prospective study of a general population sample. In the Framingham cohort, ABI was preceded by TIA's in 12% of the cases. The average annual incidence of TIA's was similar in men and women. Incidence rose with age from four per 100,000 for those under age 40 at entry, to eight per 100,000 at age 40 to 49 at entry, to 14 per 100,000 at age 50 to 62 at entry. There were three to four times as many persons with neurological symptoms suggesting TIA's as there were persons who fulfilled minimal criteria and could be classified as definite TIA.

Stroke developed in about 40% of the persons with TIA. One-half of the brain infarctions that followed the TIA's occurred within three months of the onset of the TIA's and two-thirds within six months. In most cases, there were fewer than four TIA's preceding the stroke. It thus appears that 40% of subjects with TIA's will develop brain infarctions, and that if stroke is to occur it will happen soon after the TIA episodes begin. This suggests that the onset of TIA's constitutes an urgent situation requiring prompt medical or surgical intervention.

Survival and Recurrence Following Stroke

Survival following stroke clearly depends on the type of stroke. In the Framingham cohort, 30-day case fatality rates ranged from 15% for ABI and cerebral embolism to 46% and 83% for subarachnoid and intracerebral hemorrhage, respectively. Since ABI accounts for 60% of stroke cases, the overall, immediate, 30-day case fatality rate is approximately 20%. As expected, mortality is clearly related to age at stroke ranging, for ABI, from 8% below age 60 to 23% in men and women age 70 and older.

Long-term survival is strongly related to the presence of prestroke cardiac disease and, to a lesser extent, hypertension. In the absence of antecedent CHD, CHF, or hypertension, survival following stroke or

ABI closely approximates that of the rest of the cohort of the same age and sex.

Cumulative, age-adjusted, 5-year survival rates for brain infarction were reduced by prestroke cardiac disease (CHD or CHF or both) and hypertension prior to initial stroke from .85 to .35 in men and .70 to .56 in women. Hypertension alone reduced survival from .85 to .51 in men, but not in women. Not surprisingly, death following stroke is often due to cardiovascular disease (about 25%) and recurrent stroke (45%). Survival was lower in men. Stroke, specifically ABI, tends to recur, with 5-year cumulative recurrence rates of 40% for men and 20% for women. Recurrent strokes were frequently of the same type as the initial stroke. Recurrence was more common among persons with cardiac comorbidity and hypertension prior to the initial stroke, and this impact was more substantial in men than women.

The Declining Incidence of Stroke

Mortality trends in Western nations, including the United States, indicate a recent accelerated decline in stroke *mortality* (Acheson, 1960; Wylie, 1962; Borhani, 1965; Prineas, 1971; Metropolitan Life Insurance Co., 1975; Harborman et al., 1978; Levy, 1979). This decline seems real, despite recognized limitations imposed by practices in death certification and inaccuracies in death diagnoses (Florey et al., 1967; Israel and Klobba, 1969). *Morbidity* statistics on the actual incidence of strokes are sparse and the comparability of case ascertainment over time is questionable (Eisenberg et al., 1964; Aho and Fogelholm, 1974; Abu-Zeid et al., 1975; Christie, 1976; Hansen and Marquardsen, 1977). Study of trends in stroke incidence in the Framingham cohort, in which uniform criteria and case ascertainment had been maintained over three decades, confirm a decline in stroke incidence, but only in women (Wolf et al., 1978b).

Stroke is part of a larger problem of cardiovascular disease (CVD) and time trends must be examined from the perspective of overall mortality. Age-adjusted cardiovascular mortality rates in the United States have declined almost 32%

over the past 30 years. This decrease has accelerated over the past decade, accounting for two-thirds of the 30-year decline. Despite an aging population of increasing size, the total number of deaths attributed to CVD recently fell below 1 million for the first time in almost a decade. The decline in cardiovascular mortality occurred in both sexes, in non-whites as well as whites *and at all adult ages,* including 65 to 74, 75 to 84, and 85 and older.

In the period 1968 to 1976, mortality rates from coronary heart disease, the leading cause of death in the United States, declined 25%. For stroke, the decline was 32%. A downward trend in stroke mortality has been apparent for more than 50 years, but has accelerated in recent years (Soltero et al., 1978). The death rate for stroke has fallen more rapidly than that for other components of cardiovascular disease. In the 1940's and 1950's, stroke mortality in the United States declined at a rate of 1% per year. Since 1972, the rate of decline has been 5% per year (Levy, 1979).

The sizable geographical differences in reported stroke death rates in the United States have narrowed, and stroke death rates from all regions have fallen over the past 15 years (Soltero et al., 1978; Moriyama et al., 1971). The decline has been especially notable in non-whites, and the 48.5% fall in stroke mortality for non-white females (1960–1975) represents a dramatic change in the racial patterns of stroke mortality.

It is not possible to determine at present whether the declining mortality is due to a fall in the incidence rate or whether it is due to better treatment. It is not even clear whether the rates are declining for hospitalized or out-of-hospital deaths. It is likely, however, that the decline is real and not simply a result of changes in death certification practices. It is also likely that both primary prevention and better medical care have contributed to the decline.

Hypertension, a demonstrated contributor to stroke incidence and mortality, is being more effectively controlled; hence, the decline in stroke mortality is not unexpected (Levy, 1979). The Veterans Administration Cooperative Study on An-

tihypertensive Agents (1967, 1970) leaves little doubt that treatment of hypertension can prevent strokes. However, this cannot be accepted unequivocally, since stroke mortality was declining years before effective antihypertensive therapy became available. It is interesting that, in the Framingham Study, a decline in stroke incidence could be shown only for women, and that women have had more effective blood pressure treatment and control than men (Wolf et al., 1978). It is difficult to escape the conclusion that hypertension control efforts have contributed to stroke death rate declines. In the United States, from 1972 to 1977, age-adjusted death rates for hypertension-relation cardiovascular disease declined 20%, whereas unrelated cardiovascular disease declined 9%.

The incidence of stroke, nonfatal as well as fatal, is difficult to determine accurately. There are few defined populations in which stroke has been studied over a sufficiently long time to draw conclusions about temporal trends. To discern changes in incidence of specific stroke types, that is, thrombosis, embolism, intracerebral hemorrhage, or subarachnoid hemorrhage, a degree of diagnostic sophistication is required. Studies in Rochester, Minnesota, however, suggest a decline in stroke occurrence during the period 1945 to 1974 (Matsumoto et al., 1973).

Clinicians have noted that hypertensive encephalopathy, a fairly commonly encountered condition prior to 1950, is now a rarity (Wolff and Lindeman, 1966; Carter and Barham, 1970). Massive hypertensive intracerebral hemorrhage is also less frequently seen in hospital emergency rooms and on autopsy tables. In 1964, clinicians in Goteberg, Sweden noted a decline in the number of patients seen with hypertensive intracerebral hemorrhage, particularly below the age of 55 (Aurell and Hood, 1964). Patients with intracerebral hemorrhage turned out to be untreated hypertensives with markedly elevated blood pressures. In a comparison of autopsy records representing 97% of all hospital deaths, cerebral hemorrhage rates were lower below age 65 than in prior years. Median age at hemorrhage in 1961 was five years higher than the age in 1948.

This decline in intracerebral hemorrhage was also noted in studies in Rochester, Minnesota, where incidence rates fell by 34% when the 15-year period from 1961 to 1976 was compared to the period from 1945 to 1960. Median age at onset of hemorrhage also increased, from 67 years in 1945 to 1952 to 71 years in 1969 to 1976 (Garraway et al., 1979).

This decrement in intracerebral hemorrhage rates predates the advent of the computerized tomographic (CT) scan of the head. The CT scan has demonstrated that many more restricted hemorrhages occur than had been suspected. These strokes were previously thought to be infarcts, since the event was nonlethal, the deficit restricted, and the cerebrospinal fluid free of blood. Whether the rate of smaller hypertensive hemorrhages is also changing is yet to be determined.

Control of Hypertension and Stroke Prevention

On the basis of clinical observation among groups of patients with treated and untreated severe hypertension, clinicians have noted an improvement in outcome among the treated (Wolff and Lindeman, 1966; Carter and Barham, 1970). The Veterans Administration Cooperative Study, in a controlled clinical trial, demonstrated a highly significant benefit in stroke prevention and in survival among treated *severe* hypertensives whose pretreatment diastolic blood pressure levels were above 115 mm Hg. The degree of benefit correlated with levels of prerandomization blood pressure and with degree of blood pressure control (Taguchi and Freis, 1974). In the moderate hypertensives with pretreatment diastolic blood pressure between 104 and 115 mm Hg, there were one-fourth the number of strokes in the treated as in the placebo (control) group during the average 3.8-year follow-up period.

Control of moderate and severe hypertension to prevent or to reduce stroke occurrence has been repeatedly shown, with few exceptions (Beevers et al., 1978). In a recent, community-based, randomized controlled trial involving nearly 11,000 persons with high blood pressure,

including *mild* hypertension, the five-year mortality was significantly lower in the systemically treated and controlled antihypertensive treatment group than in those given standard care (Hypertension Detection and Follow-up Program Cooperative Group, 1979). In the group with mild hypertension (entry diastolic blood pressure 90 to 104), mortality was significantly reduced by 20% in the systematic treatment group. This benefit was due to a reduction in death from cardiovascular disease, including a 45% reduction in stroke and a 46% decrease in acute MI. In the systematic treatment group, control of blood pressure was consistently better at all ages, in blacks and whites and in both sexes. This hypertension control was matched by a corresponding reduction in mortality in the older age groups, in white men and in black men and black women. These findings have enormous potential significance for disease prevention, since about 70% of hypertensives in the United States fall in the mild hypertension category, with diastolic blood pressures averaging between 90 and 104 mm Hg. Sixty percent of the excess mortality attributable to hypertension occurs among persons in this blood pressure range.

Study of the effect of reduction of the blood pressure level in older persons with isolated systolic hypertension is being made in a controlled clinical trial, the Systolic Hypertension in the Elderly Program (SHEP).

Preventive Implications

The appearance of stroke or TIA should be regarded as a failure of prevention. Measures to diagnose and treat the stroke patient at this point are often too little and too late. In the case of cerebral infarction and cerebral hemorrhage, physicians must shift their attention from the allure of applying high technology instrumentation to the patient with advanced cerebrovascular disease to the more mundane day-to-day business of modifying risk factors for disease prevention in the presymptomatic candidate for stroke. This requires attending to what are often considered medical trivia—modest elevation of blood pressure; early signs of cardiac impairment; and the application of general hygenic measures to obesity, cigarette smoking, and physical inactivity to try to prevent cardiovascular disease.

Prospects for prevention of stroke would be greatly improved by the demonstration of correctable environmental determinants of its incidence. Unfortunately, there are few powerful environmental contributors to stroke mortality.

The accelerated decline in the incidence and mortality of cerebrovascular disease in recent years is a clear indication that stroke is not an inevitable consequence of aging or of genetic constitution. Diminution of stroke mortality has occurred at all ages, including the eighth and the ninth decade of life.

Each physician can identify "prime" candidates for stroke among his asymptomatic patients. Control of severe and moderately severe hypertension will definitely prevent stroke. Patients with these levels of blood pressure require vigorous and sustained therapy to maintain normotension. However, the greatest impact of elevated blood pressure on the public health is attributable to *mild* elevations of pressure because this abnormality is so common. Medical treatment of the 40% of the adult population of the United States known to have at least mild hypertension, (with diastolic pressure between 90 and 104 mm Hg), is an extraordinary therapeutic and financial endeavor. Antihypertensive drugs do have significant adverse effects limiting their acceptance. What is needed are hygenic measures that can be practiced by the individual to reduce the risk of cardiovascular disease, including stroke. Weight loss, reduction of salt in the diet, and giving up cigarette smoking are measures that can be advocated for most people. In addition, the practicing physician, on the basis of a few historical, clinical, and laboratory tests, can identify 10% of the population in whom the majority of strokes will occur. Utilizing a history of cigarette smoking, an ECG, a blood sugar, systolic blood pressure, and serum cholesterol, a cardiovascular risk profile can be determined for each person, and the risk of subsequent stroke, CHD, or peripheral arterial disease determined. It is to those hypertensives among persons comprising the population whose cardiovascular or stroke risk profiles fall in the uppermost decile that vigorous antihypertensive therapy should be applied.

The appearance of impaired cardiac function, overt (CHD and CHF) or occult (LVH by ECG, enlarged heart on X-ray, or intraventricular block) heralds a definite increment in risk of stroke and marks the person as definitely stroke-prone. Initiation of antihypertensive therapy, including a diuretic, prior to the appearance of frank cardiac failure might help prevent stroke. Overt signs of a compromised cerebral circulation (the appearance of a carotid bruit or TIA) should alert the physician to the extreme hazard his patient faces. As noted, 40% of patients with TIA's develop stroke, one-half within three months of TIA onset, and 10% of persons developing carotid bruit have a stroke within eight years of bruit appearance. These persons desperately need all the risk reduction measures at the physicians' disposal, and, particularly, control of elevated blood pressure. Physicians have been loathe to lower the blood pressure of patients following stroke or TIA for fear of precipitating a stroke. Reduction in blood pressure among hypertensives with prior stroke or TIA has been shown, in fact, to increase cerebral blood flow (Meyer et al., 1968).

It can be clearly stated that the benefits outweigh the hazards. *Control of blood pressure elevation is the single most effective means of stroke prevention.* Prevention of stroke recurrence also rests on antihypertensive therapy (Rabkin et al., 1978).

References

Abu-Zeid, H.A.H., Choi, N.W., and Nelson, N.A. (1975). Epidemiologic features of cerebrovascular disease in Manitoba: Incidence by age, sex and residence, with etiologic implications. Canad. Med. Assoc. J. 113, 379–384.

Acheson, R.M. (1960). Mortality from cerebrovascular accident and hypertension in the Republic of Ireland. Br. J. Prev. Soc. Med. 14, 139–147.

Aho, K. and Fogelheim, R. (1974). Incidence

and early prognosis of stroke in Espoo-Kaunianen Area, Finland, in 1972. Stroke 5, 658–661.

Alter, M. and Kluznik, J. (1972). Genetics of cerebrovascular accidents. Stroke 5, 258.

Ask-Upmark, E. (1962). Life and death without ovaries. Acta Med. Scand. 172, 129–135.

Aurell, M. and Hood, B. (1964). Cerebral hemorrhage in a population after a decade of active anti-hypertensive treatment. Acta Med. Scand. 176, 377–383.

Baum, H.M. and Robins, M. (1981). Survival and Prevalence, the National Survey of Stroke. Stroke. 12 (Suppl. 1), 59–68.

Beevers, D.G., Johnson, J., Devine, B.L. et al. (1978). Relation between prognosis and the blood pressures before and during treatment of hypertensive patients. Clin. Sci. Mol. Med. 55 (Suppl.), 333–336.

Bharucha, N.E., Wolf, P.A., Kannel, W.B., and McNamara, P.M. (1981). Epidemiological Study of Cerebral Embolism: The Framingham Study. Transactions of the American Neurological Association, pp. 357–358.

Bharucha, N.E., Wolf, P.A., Kannel, W.B. et al. (1983). Atrial Fibrillation, a Frequent Cause of Embolic Stroke: The Framingham Study. manuscript.

Borhani, N.O. (1965). Changes in geographic distribution of mortality from cerebrovascular disease. Amer. J. Pub. Hlth. 55, 673–681.

Byar, D.P. (1973). The Veterans Administration Cooperative Urological Research Group's Studies of Cancer of the Prostate. Cancer 32, 1126.

Carter, A. and Barham, A. (1970). Hypertensive therapy in stroke survivors. Lancet i, 485.

Christie, I. (1976). Stroke in Melbourne: A study of relationship between a teaching hospital and the community. Med. J. Aust. 1, 565–568.

Davidenkova, E.F., Babkova, A.V., Godinova, A.M. et al. (1966). A clinico-genetic study of patients with thrombosis of cerebral vessels. Klinichesk. Medits. (Moskva) 44, 27.

Eisenberg, H., Morrison, J.T., Sullivan, A. et al. (1964). CVA's: Incidence and survival rates in a defined population, Middlesex County, Connecticut, J.A.M.A. 189, 883–888.

Fairfax, A.J., Lambert, C.D., and Leatham, A. (1976). Systemic embolism in chronic sinoatrial disorder. New Eng. J. Med. 295, 190–192.

Florey, C.D.V., Senter, M.G., and Acheson, R.M. (1967). A study of the validity of the diagnosis of stroke in mortality data. I. Certificate Analysis. Yale J. Biol. Med. 40, 148–163.

Friedman, G.D., Loveland, D.B., and Ehrlich, S.P. (1968). Relationship of stroke to other cardiovascular disease. Circulation 38, 533–541.

Garraway, W., Whisnant, J.P., Whisnant, J.P., Furkin, A.J. et al. (1979). The declining incidence of stroke. New Eng. J. Med. 300, 449–452.

Gertler, M.M., Rusk, H.A., Whiter, H.H. et al. (1968). Ischemic cerebrovascular disease: The assessment of risk factors. Geriatrics 23, 135.

Gifford, A.J. (1966). An epidemiological study of cerebrovascular disease. Amer. J. Pub. Hlth. 58, 452.

Gordon, T., Castelli, W.P., Hjortland, M.C., et al. (1977). High density lipoprotein as a protective factor against coronary heart disease: The Framingham Study. Amer. J. Med. 62, 707–714.

Gordon, T., Kannel, W.B., Hjortland, M.C., and McNamara, P.M. (1978). Menopause and coronary heart disease: The Framingham Study. An. Int. Med. 89, 157–161.

Gordon, T., Sorlie, P., Kannel, W.B. (1971). An epidemiological investigation of cardiovascular disease. Coronary heart disease, atherothrombotic brain infarction, intermittent claudication. A multivariate analysis of some factors related to their incidence. In: The Framingham Study, 16 Year Follow-up. Government Printing Office, Washington, D.C.

Gresham, G.E., Fitzpatrick, T.E., Wolf, P.A., McNamara, P.M., Kannel, W.B., and Dawber, T.R. (1975). Residual disability in stroke survivors: The Framingham Study. New Eng. J. Med. 293, 954–956.

Gresham, G.E. and Phillips, T.F. (1979). Relative merits of three standard indexes in classifying ADL status in long-term survivors of stroke. Stroke 10, 96 (Abstr.).

Gresham, G.E., Phillips, T.F., Wolf, P.A., McNamara, P.M., Kannel, W.B., and Dawber, T.R. (1979). Epidemiologic profile of long-term stroke disability: The Framingham Study. Arch. Phys. Med. Rehab. 60, 487–491.

Gross, C.R., Case, D.S., Sher, C.L., and Mohr, J.P. (1981). Stroke Incidence in South Alabama presented at the Annual Meeting, Society for Epidemiological Research, June 20, 1981 (Abstr.).

Hansen, B.S. and Marquardson, J. (1977).

Incidence of stroke in Frederiksberg, Denmark. Stroke 8, 663–665.

Harborman, S., Capildeo, R., and Rose, F.C. (1978). The changing mortality of cerebrovascular disease. Quart. J. Med. 47, 71–88.

Harrison, M.J.G. and Mitchell, J.R.A. (1966). The influence of redblood cells on platelet adhesiveness. (1977). Lancet ii, 1164–1164.

Hass, W.K. Aspirin for the limping brain. Editorial. Stroke 8, 299.

Heyden, S., Heyman, A., and Camplong, L. (1969). Mortality patterns among parents of patients with atherosclerotic cerebrovascular disease. J. Chron. Dis. 22, 105.

Heyman, A., Karp, H.R., Heyden, S. et al. (1971). Cerebrovascular disease in the biracial population of Evans County, Georgia. Arch. Int. Med. 128, 949–955.

Hinton, R.C., Kistler, J.P., Fallon, J.T., et al. (1977). Influence of etiology of atrial fibrillation on incidence of systemic embolism. Amer. J. Cardio. 40, 509.

Hypertension Detection and Follow-up Program Cooperative Group (1979). Five-year findings of the Hypertension Detection and Follow-up Programs. I. Reduction in mortality of persons with high blood pressure, including mild hypertension. J.A.M.A. 242, 2562–2571.

Israel, R.A. and Klobba, A.J. (1969). A preliminary report on the eighth Russian ICDA on cause of death statistics. Amer. J. Pub. Health. 59, 1651–1660.

Issaeva, I.I. and Mikheeva, V.V. (1967). The role of hereditary factors in the evolution of apoplexy. Zh. Nevropathol. Psikhiatrii imeni S S Korsakova 67, 22.

Kagan, A., Harris, B.R., Winkelstein, W., et al. (1974). Epidemiologic studies of coronary heart disease and stroke in Japanese men living in Japan, Hawaii and California: Demographic, physical dietary and biochemical characteristics. J. Chron. Dis. 27, 345.

Kagan, A., Paffer, J.S., and Rhoads, G.C. (1980). Factors related to stroke incidence in Hawaiian Japanese men. The Honolulu Heart Study. Stroke 11, 14.

Kagan, W., Paffer, J., Rhoads, G.G. et al. (1976). Epidemiologic studies of coronary heart disease and stroke in Japanese men living in Japan, Hawaii and California: Prevalence of stroke. In P. Scheinberg, Ed. Cerebrovascular Diseases. Raven Press, New York, p. 267.

Kannel, W.B. (1978). Status of CHD Risk Factors. J. Nutr. Educ. 10(1), 10–14.

Kannel, W.B., Castelli, P., and Gordon, T. (1979). Cholesterol in the prediction of atherosclerotic disease. Ann. Int. Med. 90, 85–91.

Kannel, W.B., Castelli, W.P., Gordon, T., and McNamara, P.M. (1971). Serum cholesterol, lipoproteins and risk of coronary heart disease: The Framingham Study. Ann. Int. Med. 74, 1–12.

Kannel, W.B., Gordon, T., Wolf, P.A., et al. (1972). Hemoglobin and the risk of cerebral infarction: The Framingham Study. Stroke 3, 409–419.

Kannel, W.B., Wolf, P.A., McGee, D.L., et al. (1981). Systolic blood pressure, arterial rigidity and risk of stroke: The Framingham Study. J.A.M.A. 245(1), 1442–1445.

Kannel, W.B., Wolf, P.A., Verter, J. et al. (1970). Epidemiologic assessment of the role of blood pressure in stroke: The Framingham Study. J.A.M.A. 214, 301.

Kuller, L.H. (1978). Epidemiology of stroke. In B.S. Schoenberg, Ed. Advances in Neurology, Vol. 19: Neurological Epidemiology: Principles and Clinical Applications. Raven Press, New York, p. 281.

Kurtzke, J.F. (1976). Epidemiology of cerebrovascular disease. In Cerebrovascular Survey Report for Joint Council Subcommittee on Cerebrovascular Disease, National Institute of Neurological and Communicative Disorders and Stroke and National Heart and Lung Institute. Rochester, Minnesota: Whiting Press, Inc., p. 213.

Levy, R.I. (1979). Stroke decline: Implications and prospects. New Eng. J. Med. 300, 490–491.

Matsumoto, N., Whisnant, J.P., Kunand, L.T., and Okazaki, H. (1973). Natural history of stroke in Rochester, Minnesota, 1955 through 1969: An extension of a previous study, 1945 through 1954. Stroke 4, 20–29.

Metropolitan Life Insurance Company (1975). Recent trends in mortality from cerebrovascular disease. Stat. Bull. 56, 2–4.

Meyer, J.S., Sawada, T., Kitamura, A., et al. (1968). Cerebral blood flow after control of hypertension in stroke. Neurology 18, 772–781.

Miller, G.D. and Kuller, L.H. (1973). Amer. J. Epidemiol. 98, 233–242.

Mohr, J.P. (1978). Transient ischemic attacks and the prevention of strokes. Editorial. New Eng. J. Med. 299, 93.

Mohr, J.P., Caplan, L.R., Melski, J.W., et al. (1978). The Harvard Cooperative Stroke Registry: A prospective registry. Neurology 28, 754.

Moriyama, I.M., Krueger, D.E., and Stamer,

F. (1971). Cerebrovascular Diseases in the United States. Harvard University Press, Cambridge, Mass.

Omae, T., Takeshita, M., and Hirota, Y. (1976). The Hisayama Study and Joint Study on Cerebrovascular Diseases. Raven Press, New York, p. 255.

Pearson, T.C. and Thomas, D.J. (1979). Physiological pharmacological factors influencing blood viscosity and cerebral blood flow. In G. Tognomi and S. Geratini, Eds. Drug Treatment and Prevention in Cerebrovascular Disorders. Elsevier/North-Holland, Amsterdam, p. 33.

Pearson, T.C. and Wetherley-Mein, G. (1978). Vascular occlusive episodes and venous haematocrit in primary proliferative polycythaemia. Lancet ii, 1219–22.

Pfeffer, R.I. and Van Den Noort, S. (1976). Estrogen use and stroke risk in postmenopausal women. Amer. J. Epidemiol. 103, 445–456.

Prineas, R.J. (1971). Cerebrovascular disease occurrence in Aust. Med. J. Austra. 2, 509–515.

Rabkin, S.W., Mathewson, F.A.L., and Tate, R.B. (1978). The relation of blood pressure to stroke prognosis. Ann. Int. Med. 89, 15–20.

Robins, M. and Baum, H.M. (1981). Incidence, the National Survey of Stroke. Stroke 12 (Suppl. 1), 145–157.

Shurtleff, D. (1974). Some characteristics related to the incidence of cardiovascular disease and death: The Framingham Study, 18 year follow-up. In The Framingham Study, W.B. Kannel and T. Gordon, Eds. U.S. Government Printing Office, Washington, D.C.

Slack, J. and Evans, K.A. (1966). The increased risk of death from ischaemic heart disease in first degree relatives of 121 men and 96 women with ischaemic heart disease. J. Med. Genet. 3, 239.

Soltero, I., Kiu, K., Cooper, R., et al. (1978). Trends in mortality from cerebrovascular diseases in the United States, 1960 to 1975. Stroke 9, 549.

Taguchi, J. and Freis, E.D. (1974). Partial reduction of blood pressure and prevention of complications in hypertension. New Eng. J. Med. 291, 329.

Thomas, D.J., Marshal, J., Ross Russell, R.W. et al. (1977). Effect of haematocrit on cerebral blood-flow in man. Lancet ii, 941.

Tohgi, H., Yamanouchi, H., Murakami, M., et al. (1978). Importance of the haematocrit as a risk factor in cerebral infarction. Stroke 9, 369–374.

Toole, J.F., Janeway, R., Choe, K., et al. (1975). Transient ischemic attacks due to atherosclerosis, a prospective study of 160 patients. Arch. Neurol. 32, 5.

Veterans Administration Cooperative Study Group on Antihypertensive Agents. (1967). Effects of treatment on morbidity in hypertension. I. Results in patients with diastolic blood pressures averaging 115 through 129 mm Hg. J.A.M.A. 202, 116–122.

Veterans Administration Cooperative Study Group on Antihypertensive Agents. (1970). Effects of treatment of morbidity in hypertension. II. Results in patients with diastolic blood pressure averaging 90 through 114 mm Hg. J. Amer. Med. Assoc., 213, 1143.

Veterans Administration Cooperative Urological Research Group. (1967). Treatment and survival of patients with cancer of the prostrate. Surg. Gynecol. Obstet. 124, 1011–1017.

Weinfeld, F.D., Ed. (1981). The National Survey of Stroke. Stroke 12 (Suppl. 1).

Whisnant, J.P. (1974). Epidemiology of stroke: Emphasis on transient cerebral ischemia attacks and hypertension. Stroke 5, 68.

Wolf, P.A. (1975). Hypertension as a Risk Factor for Stroke. In Cerebral Vascular Diseases, J.P. Whisnant and B. Sandok, Eds. Grune & Stratton, New York, pp. 105–112.

Wolf, P.A., Dawber, T.R., Thomas, H.E., et al. (1978a). Epidemiologic assessment of chronic atrial fibrillation and risk of stroke: The Framingham Study. Neurology 28, 973–977.

Wolf, P.A., Dawber, T.R., Thomas, H.E. (1978b). The declining incidence of stroke: The Framingham Study. Stroke 9, 97 (Abstr.).

Wolf, P.A., Kannel, W.B., Sorlie, P. (1981). Asymptomatic carotid bruit and risk of stroke: The Framingham Study. J.A.M.A. 245(14), 1442–1445.

Wolf, P.A., Sacco, R.L., Kannel, W.B., et al. (1981). Survival and recurrence following stroke: The Framingham Study. Stroke 12, 120 (Abstr.).

Wolff, F.W. and Lindeman, R.D. (1966). Effects of treatment in hypertension results of a controlled study. J. Chron. Dis. 19, 227.

Worth, R.M., Kato, H., and Rhoads, G.G. (1975). Amer. J. Epidemiol. 102, 481–490.

Wylie, C.M. (1962). Cerebrovascular Accident Deaths in the United States and in England and Wales. J. Chronic. Dis. 15, 85.

26. Cerebrovascular Diseases in the Elderly: Clinical Syndromes

CARLOS S. KASE

J.P. MOHR

Cerebrovascular disorders occupy a prominent place among the diseases that afflict elderly populations. An increasing incidence of stroke with age has been a constant finding in population studies (Kurtzke, 1969; Matsumoto et al., 1973; Hansen and Marquardsen, 1977; Herman et al., 1980; Ueda et al., 1981). The figures from the recently completed South Alabama Population Study of Stroke (Gross et al., in press) are shown in Figure 26-1. The peak incidence was found in the seventh decade, and three-quarters of the strokes occurred in the group from 50 to 80 years of age. This increasing incidence with age was a feature that applied to all forms of stroke and occurred in both sexes and both racial groups (whites and blacks) studied (Figure 26-2).

When the figures on incidence of stroke *subtype* are analyzed in large groups of patients, some significant differences are seen. In the NINCDS-sponsored prospective collaborative National Pilot Stroke Data Bank project (Kunitz et al., in press), a total of 934 patients was studied over an 18-month period. The frequency distribution of stroke subtype by age is shown in Table 26-1. For the category of cerebral infarction (thrombosis, embolism, lacunes, and infarcts of unknown etiology), 85 to 90% of the cases occurred between the ages of 51 and 80, whereas the hemor-

rhagic varieties occurred most often in individuals one or two decades younger. As a result, cerebral infarcts were the most common stroke subtypes in older individuals, whereas subarachnoid and intracerebral hemorrhages were the most frequent in those younger than 50 years. Among the patients with cerebral infarcts, embolism occurred somewhat more frequently in the younger patients, whereas thrombosis or infarct of undetermined etiology predominated in those older than 60 years. The importance of the latter group (infarct of unknown cause) probably represents a relative lack of diagnostic effort (especially angiogram) in pursuing a definitive diag-

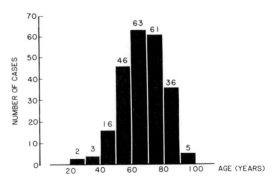

Figure 26-1. Age distribution of stroke cases in the South Alabama Population Study. (From Gross et al., in press.)

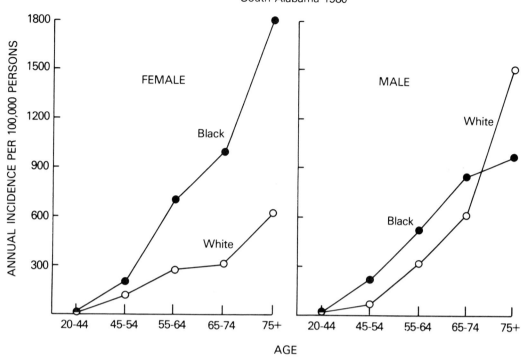

Figure 26-2. Stroke incidence by age, race, and sex in the South Alabama Population Study. (From Gross et al., in press.)

nosis in the elderly patient with acute stroke. Lacunar infarcts were the least common variety of infarct in all age groups.

From the above figures, it is apparent that cerebral infarction, thrombotic and embolic, is the most frequent stroke subtype in the elderly, intracranial hemorrhage being a condition that mostly affects the younger age groups in the adult population. The discussion that follows will stress those stroke subtypes that are more characteristic of elderly individuals.

Clinical Syndromes of Stroke Subtypes

Atherothrombosis

The pathological basis of this condition is progressive arterial stenosis with eventual occlusion, as a result of progressive build-up of atherosclerotic degeneration of the arterial wall. The initial lesion adopts the form of the so-called fatty streak (Geer et al., 1968), thought to be the precursor of the fibrous plaque that leads to the enlarging atheroma (National Heart and Lung Institute Task Force on Arteriosclerosis, 1971). Once this plaque develops, its further progression is determined by other poorly understood events, among them hemorrhage into the plaque. The rate of development of stenosis from atheroma is quite variable: at times, plaques appear not to change significantly in size over periods of years (Javid et al., 1970), whereas others have been found to evolve from moderate stenosis to virtual occlusion in periods as short as a few weeks (Mohr and Kase, 1983). The pathological changes appear to involve not merely an evolving atheroma, but also a thrombus superimposed upon it. In the setting of hemodynamically significant atherostenosis, plate-

Table 26-1. Age Distribution by Stroke Subtype NINCDS Stroke Data Bank Project* (N = 933): Stroke Subtype.

	Thrombosis	Embolus	Lacune	Unknown	ICH	SAH	Other	TOTAL
Age								
0–20	0	1 (0.5%)	0	1 (0.4%)	1 (1%)	0	0	3 (0.3%)
21–30	0	6 (3%)	0	3 (1.3%)	4 (4%)	12 (11.7%)	1 (4.3%)	26 (2.8%)
31–40	4 (2.3%)	10 (5.1%)	3 (3%)	5 (2.1%)	5 (5%)	18 (17.5%)	1 (4.3%)	46 (4.9%)
41–50	12 (6.9%)	15 (7.6%)	8 (8%)	18 (7.7%)	25 (24.8%)	26 (25.2%)	6 (26.1%)	110 (11.8%)
51–60	49 (28.3%)	51 (25.8%)	32 (32%)	39 (16.6%)	28 (27.7%)	15 (14.6%)	5 (21.7%)	219 (23.5%)
61–70	69 (39.9%)	52 (26.3%)	31 (31%)	86 (36.6%)	26 (25.7%)	26 (25.2%)	6 (26.1%)	296 (31.7%)
71–80	38 (22%)	48 (24.2%)	24 (24%)	64 (27.2%)	10 (9.9%)	4 (3.9%)	4 (17.4%)	192 (20.6%)
80+	1 (0.6%)	15 (7.6%)	2 (2%)	19 (8.1%)	2 (2%)	2 (1.9%)	0	41 (4.4%)
Total	173 (18.5%)	198 (21.2%)	100 (10.7%)	235 (25.2%)	101 (10.8%)	103 (11%)	23 (2.5%)	

*Kunitz et al., in press.

let–fibrin complexes have been shown superimposed on the atheroma, perhaps being the means by which the lumen is occluded by thrombus (Fisher, 1975). The role of arachidonic acid metabolites (thromboxane, prostacyclin) in both the genesis of atheroma and the initiation of the events that eventually lead to thrombotic arterial occlusion, is now under study (Moncada and Vane, 1978).

The atherothrombotic process characteristically affects arteries serving the brain at proximal, mostly extracranial sites. These sites, in order of frequency (Fisher et al., 1965a; Castaigne et al., 1970, 1973), are the cervical carotid bifurcation, proximal vertebral artery, carotid siphon, proximal one-third of the basilar, and, finally, the middle and posterior cerebral artery stems. Thus, the situation is one of a predominantly proximal arterial disease that leads to symptoms when the brain parenchyma, located at a considerable distance from the causative lesion, becomes involved.

The *clinical presentation* in cerebral atherothrombosis varies according to the vessel involved. However, some general features apply to these cases as a group. The first is the occurrence of transient ischemic attacks (TIA's). These may develop from atherostenosis of either extracranial or intracranial arteries, and present as brief episodes of reversible focal neurological deficit, classically defined as less than 24 hours duration. The pathogenesis is thought to relate to two possible mechanisms, distal insufficiency from critical reduction in blood flow distal to a point of severe stenosis, or embolism from physical disruption of an atheroma or other related particulate matter. Transient ischemic attacks due to the former mechanism are associated with a 50% frequency of atherostenosis of the corresponsing artery, and tend to last minutes rather than hours (Pessin et al., 1977); TIAs due to embolism are of longer duration, are less frequently correlated with focal atherostenosis, and are associated with angiographic evidence of intracranial embolic branch occlusions (Pessin et al., 1977). In patients with a completed stroke, a prior history of TIAs can be elicited in 50 to 60% of cases of internal carotid artery involvement (Duncan et al.,

1976), 65% of cases of middle cerebral artery occlusion (Hinton et al., 1979), and in 40 to 60% of cases of vertebrobasilar occlusive disease (Duncan et al., 1976).

A second general feature of thrombotic stroke is progression at onset. In arteriographically documented thrombotic occlusion of extracranial and intracranial arteries, the onset is sudden or on awakening in 70 to 80% of the cases (Pessin et al., 1979; Kunitz et al., in press), the rest being characterized by stepwise or smooth progression, and even by fluctuations. In addition, the early course (first 24 hours) in thrombotic stroke is characterized by continued worsening in as many as one-third of the patients (Kunitz et al., in press), a feature that distinguishes this form of infarction from embolism and, to a lesser extent, from lacunar strokes (see below).

A high frequency of certain risk factors is common in thrombotic stroke. There is a significant association with arterial hypertension (55 to 60% of the cases) and diabetes (25 to 30% of the cases) (Mohr et al., 1978a; Kunitz et al., in press). The association between this type of stroke and hypertension applies to both sexes and all age groups; this risk factor shows no tendency to lose significance with advancing age (Wolf et al., 1977).

Finally, thrombosis is characterized by a relative absence of associated symptoms at onset. Headache and vomiting occur with a low frequency at the onset of cerebral infarction, in particular in atherothrombotic disease: 12 to 18% and 10%, respectively (Mohr et al., 1978a; Kunitz et al., in press). Seizures at onset are seen in only 0.4 to 3% of the cases (Mohr et al., 1978a; Price et al., in press). These low figures contrast with the higher frequency of such symptoms in cases of hemorrhagic stroke.

The findings on neurological examination vary depending on the vessel affected. In the analysis of clinical syndromes that follows, those most commonly due to atherothrombosis will be dealt with in this section; those due to cerebral embolism, in the next section. The vessels classically involved in cases of atherothrombotic cerebral infarction are the extracranial internal carotid artery, the vertebral arteries, and the basilar artery.

INTERNAL CAROTID ARTERY

The classic case presents with a prior history of TIAs that can be either ocular (transient monocular blindness, TMB, amaurosis fugax) or hemispheral, since both structures—retina and cerebral hemisphere—receive their blood supply from branches of the ipsilateral internal carotid artery (ICA). Transient monocular blindness occurs as a sudden, unilateral, painless, total or partial ("blurring") loss of vision, which develops within seconds, typically as a "curtain" or "windowshade" that descends or ascends until it obscures the whole field of vision. In over 90% of the cases, these attacks last 15 minutes or less (Pessin et al., 1977). The transient hemispheric attacks present with a variety of symptoms, mostly reflecting ischemia in areas corresponding to the distribution of the middle cerebral artery; the most common manifestation is a combined sensory and motor unilateral deficit, followed, in decreasing order of frequency, by isolated motor, sensory, or aphasic deficits (Pessin et al., 1977). In 60% of the cases, these attacks last 15 minutes or less. The simultaneous occurrence of both types of TIA is extremely rare, but an alternation between the two types is common and carries a higher probability of tight ICA stenosis than either type alone (Pessin et al., 1977).

Following a variable number of TIAs, the completed stroke that results from ICA occlusion reflects infarction from either distal flow failure (Fisher, 1951) or embolization (Castaigne et al., 1970). The latter mechanism is probably the most common, since it accounts for virtually two-thirds of strokes from ICA atherothrombosis (Pessin et al., 1979). The clinical syndromes that result are identical to those due to embolism of cardiac origin; they will be discussed in the following section. The physical findings that specifically point to ICA occlusion as the cause of a stroke are those that reflect a "distal insufficiency" pattern of infarction and, in particular, elements of the neurovascular examination that indicate stenosis or occlusion of that extracranial artery. The "distal insufficiency" concept of ischemia

or infarction implies decreased vascular perfusion on those areas of the brain parenchyma located at the greatest distance from the site of stenosis or occlusion (Mohr, 1969, 1979). As a consequence, "stagnation thrombus" may develop from local circulatory failure at these distant sites (Fisher, 1957), and infarction follows. In the case of the ICA, areas at risk include the most distal segments of the cortical branches of the middle cerebral artery, in particular the superior parietal and posterior temporal-occipital area (Mohr, 1979). The clinical syndromes from cerebral infarction in this distribution are characterized by a prominent visual field defect, aphasia, or hemi-inattention features (from dominant or non-dominant hemisphere involvement, respectively) and variable degrees of contralateral sensorimotor deficit. The sensorimotor deficit should affect the proximal more than the distal segments of the upper limb, reflecting the location of the infarct along the upper portions of the frontoparietal convexity (Mohr, 1979). Although the above constellation of symptoms is commonly found—bilaterally—in cases of cardiac arrest and hypotension, with a bilateral distal field infarction, its unilateral occurrence from ICA atherothrombosis is difficult to document. In a clinico-angiographic study of acute cerebral infarction from ICA occlusion or tight stenosis, Pessin et al. (1979) found a possible mechanism of "low-flow" as the explanation for the infarcts in one-third of their cases. Angiography revealed a slowing of circulation throughout the entire middle cerebral artery distribution in those cases, as opposed to direct or indirect evidence of intracranial branch occlusion in cases diagnosed as embolic. The clinical differences between the two groups of patients were a higher frequency of preceding TIA's and less severe clinical deficits in those with a non-embolic mechanism. These authors could not distinguish between two groups of patients with clinically well-defined neurological findings to delineate a different topography of the infarcts. Thus, it is apparent that a "distal insufficiency" mechanism of reduced cerebral flow, although a possible explanation for recurrent stereotypic TIA's (Duncan et al., 1976), is hard to document as the source of cerebral infarction from ICA atherothrombosis, in which distal embolism appears to account for the great majority of events. As a result, the neurological examination findings in themselves have no distinctive elements to suggest extracranial ICA atherothrombosis as the cause of the stroke.

In addition to the high diagnostic value of TIA's in the same vascular territory, some features of the neurovascular examination may prove to be useful. Physical findings that suggest ICA stenosis or occlusion can be sought at the bedside; the most reliable are a locally generated bruit and abnormalities in the pattern of facial pulses. A local cervical bruit can be detected in approximately 70% of patients with a "tight" (>75% stenosis, or 2 mm or less residual lumen) ICA stenosis (Gautier et al., 1975). The site of maximal intensity of the bruit usually corresponds to the carotid bifurcation area (in front of the upper portion of

the thyroid cartilage); it can radiate into the ocular region, and its intensity usually decreases with the Valsalva maneuver. The latter point is useful in differentiating them from bruits originating in the external carotid artery (ECA), which do not change with this maneuver, but rather show a transient decrease in amplitude while facial branches of the ECA (facial and pre-auricular arteries) are being compressed (Lees and Kistler, 1978). The site of origin of the bruit and the severity of the local stenosis that causes it can be further delineated by noninvasive analysis of the intensity–frequency relationships of the sound by quantitative phonoangiography (Duncan et al., 1975a). This noninvasive method allows an estimation of the residual arterial lumen, within a 1.5 mm difference with the angiogram, in more than 90% of the cases (Duncan et al., 1975a), and in addition, it can distinguish ICA origin from ECA origin of the sound (Figure 26-3), as well as murmurs radiating from the cardiac area (Kistler et al., 1978).

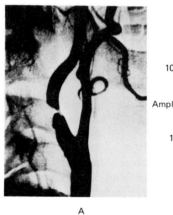

A

PHONOANGIOGRAPHIC DETECTION
OF INTERNAL CAROTID ARTERY
STENOSIS

Est. Lumen 0.7mm
Break Freq. 725Hz.

B

C

PHONOANGIOGRAPHIC DETECTION
OF EXTERNAL CAROTID ARTERY
STENOSIS

Est. Lumen 0.9 mm
Break Freq. 588 Hz.

D

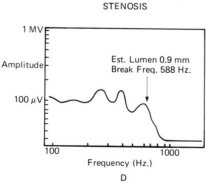

Figure 26-3. Phonoangiographic detection of stenosis of internal (A,B) and external (C,D) carotid artery. Shown in D is the pattern of "multiple peaks" preceding the break frequency which characterizes bruits originating in stenosis of the external carotid artery.

Another bedside test of value in the diagnosis of ICA atherothrombosis is facial pulse palpation. When ICA stenosis, or occlusion, occurs at its origin, collateral flow develops through anastomoses of the facial branches of the ECA into the distal orbital branches of the ophthalmic artery, which fills in a retrograde fashion into the intracranial ICA (Fisher, 1970; Caplan, 1973; Ackerman and Taveras, 1975). A common finding is an increase in the amplitude of the pulse in ECA branches (facial, pre-auricular, temporal arteries) on the side of the ICA disease, which reflects increased collateral flow (Fisher, 1970). A more sensitive sign is the demonstration, by facial palpation, of flow reversal in the frontal (Caplan, 1973) or supratrochlear (Ackerman and Taveras, 1975) arteries, a reliable indicator of hemodynamically significant stenosis or occlusion of the ICA. This pattern of abnormal collateral flow can be determined more precisely by the use of directional Doppler testing. The demonstration of reversal of flow in frontal or supratrochlear arteries is strong evidence of ipsilateral ICA disease, ranging from residual lumens of 1.5 mm to complete occlusion (Ackerman, 1979).

Definitive documentation of ICA stenosis or occlusion requires angiography. Symptomatic stenoses leading to either TIA's or infarction are usually "tight," with residual lumens of 2 mm or less, a degree of stenosis shown to be associated with hemodynamic changes (Brice et al., 1964). Occluded cervical ICAs can have a number of angiographic patterns, some indicating a pathogenetic mechanism for the occlusion: a sharp, pointed, tapering stenosis of the ICA, distal to which there is a thread-like luminal filling that may open distally into a normal size lumen—the "string sign" (Fisher et al., 1978)—is commonly seen in carotid dissection. In the atherosclerotic variety of ICA occlusion, on the other hand, several angiographic patterns have been recognized (Pessin et al., 1980): a sharp, pointed stump; amputation of the artery at its origin; a rounded, blunt stump. The old notion that the first pattern indicates recent occlusion, and the other two are

found in the chronic stage does not seem justified, since all three patterns were seen when arteriograms were performed within 6 days of onset (Pessin et al., 1980). Finally, the demonstration of the mechanism of stroke (embolic versus nonembolic) and the pattern of collateral circulation adds to the unique value of angiography in planning definitive therapy for ICA atherosclerotic disease.

VERTEBRAL ARTERIES

The unique anatomical features of this portion of the vertebrobasilar system determine many variations in the clinical syndromes that result from occlusive arterial disease. Each vertebral artery (VA) has a long extracranial course, with two intracranial branches, the posterior-inferior cerebellar artery (PICA) and the anterior spinal artery (ASA), shortly before they join at the ponto-medullary junction to form the basilar artery. The longer extracranial portion of these arteries is the most common site for atherosclerotic (Fisher et al., 1965) and traumatic occlusions (Heros, 1979; Sherman et al., 1981). However, symptoms from a VA occlusion are more likely to occur from intracranial than extracranial occlusions (Fisher et al., 1965), a situation opposite to that in the carotid system. This is presumably due to a secondary involvement of the VA branches (PICA, ASA) at their origin from the VA, whereas a more proximal (cervical) VA occlusion can be asymptomatic on account of a patent contralateral VA or development of an efficient cervical collateral circulation. The topography of atheromatous changes differ from that in the carotid system; in the VA, atherosclerotic plaques tend to occur at random throughout its length (Fisher et al., 1965), without sites of predilection, and ulceration is an uncommon phenomenon (Fisher et al., 1965). The severity of this atherosclerotic process in the VA progresses with age, as does the severity in other arterial systems (Fisher et al., 1965). Finally, occlusive disease of the VA is characteristically an atherothrombotic process, embolism being a rarity (Fisher et al., 1961; Escourolle et al., 1976).

The clinical syndromes that result from VA occlusive disease can be of two types, those due to the local effects of thrombotic VA occlusion and those due to a distal embolism into the basilar artery. The latter will be discussed among the basilar artery syndromes. The syndromes due to VA atherothrombotic occlusion are fairly stereotypic, and they involve infarction in either the medulla or the cerebellum.

Medullary infarction from VA occlusion most commonly affects its dorso-lateral portion, resulting in the classical syndrome of Wallenberg. The infarction lies in the vascular distribution of the PICA, and the structures affected include the inferior cerebellar peduncle, the nucleus and descending root of the trigeminal nerve, the lateral spinothalamic tract, vestibular nuclei, the nucleus ambiguus, and the descending sympathetic tract. The corresponding clinical features are ipsilateral cerebellar ataxia, hypesthesia for pain and temperature on the ipsilateral half of the face and contralateral trunk, and limbs, vertigo and nystagmus, ipsilateral palatal and vocal cord paresis with dysphagia and dysphonia, and Horner's syndrome. Variations in this combination of symptoms and signs are common, and they reflect minor differences in the size and location of the lateral medullary infarction (Currier, 1969; Hauw et al., 1976). The vascular lesion responsible for this infarction is usually a thrombotic occlusion of the intracranial VA (Fisher et al., 1961; Escourolle et al., 1976), commonly involving this artery at the site of origin of the PICA (Castaigne et al., 1970; Escourolle et al., 1976). An isolated occlusion—thrombotic is more common than embolic—of the corresponding PICA occurs less commonly, in only 12 to 13% of the cases (Fisher et al., 1961; Escourolle et al., 1976).

A second variety of medullary infarction occurs where the lesion is confined to its medial portion, a "medial medullary" infarction (Dejerine, 1914) (Figure 26-4). It is characterized by involvement of the pyramid, medial lemniscus and nucleus and/or exiting fibers of the hypoglossal nerve, with a resulting contralateral hemiplegia and hemisensory loss for proprioception, vibration and discriminative touch, and ipsilateral tongue paresis. A total of 18 cases has been reported in the literature (Kase et al., 1983), the vascular lesions corresponding to occlusions of the VA or ASA, and more commonly thrombotic than embolic. Bilateral medial medullary infarctions have been reported (Hauw et al., 1976; Kase et al., 1983; Mizutani et al., 1980), associated with a devastating quadriplegia, bilateral anesthesia, and respiratory paralysis.

Cerebellar infarction due to VA occlusion commonly affects the posterior aspect of the inferior surface of one cerebellar hemisphere (Sypert and Alvord, 1975), the area supplied by branches of the PICA. The vessel occluded is commonly the intracranial VA (50% of the cases), and in only 25% of the cases is the PICA itself the site of occlusion (Sypert and Alvord, 1975). An atherothrombotic process is responsible for three-quarters of the cases, embolism for the remaining one-quarter (Sypert and Alvord, 1975). An associated lateral medullary infarction was detected in 30% of the cases in the autopsy series of Sypert and Alvord (1975), indicating that cerebellar infarction occurs more commonly as an isolated event, rather than as part of an extensive infarct involving the entire vascular distribution of the PICA. As a result, cerebellar infarction can present clinically with a sudden onset of vertigo, instability, and nystagmus, which often leads to the erroneous diagnosis of "labyrinthitis" (Duncan et al., 1975b; Heros, 1982). In this setting, careful examination of coordination can sometimes detect a mild ipsilateral appendicular ataxia and suggest the correct diagnosis; an additional element of help in distinguishing acute cerebellar infarction from "labyrinthitis" is the presence of a direction-changing nystagmus in the former, whereas the nystagmus in a purely peripheral labyrinthine disorder is direction-fixed (Duncan et al., 1975b). Underscoring the importance of this differential diagnosis is the fact that cerebellar infarction can be followed by severe edema and brainstem compression, leading to respiratory paralysis, coma, and death (Lehrich et al., 1970; Momose and Lehrich, 1973; Sypert and Alvord, 1975). This course in cerebellar infarction, if

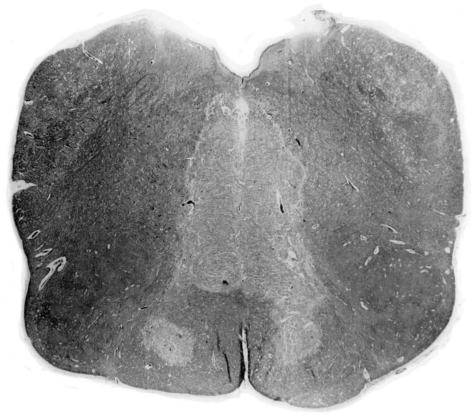

Figure 26-4. Medulla with bilateral symmetric infarction of the medial territory, in the distribution of the anterior spinal artery. H&E, ×5. (From Kase et al., in press.)

untreated, has an 80% mortality. The value of prompt surgical intervention for posterior fossa decompression and resection of necrotic cerebellar tissue has been amply documented (Scotti et al., 1980), at times in patients who had become comatose preoperatively from brainstem compression (Momose and Lehrich, 1973). On the other hand, cases of cerebellar infarction with a "benign" course undoubtedly occur, as the incidental CT or autopsy finding of an old cerebellar infarction is not rare (Sypert and Alvord, 1975; Duncan et al., 1975b). A prediction of clinical course cannot be made at the onset, and close clinical monitoring is always indicated for early detection of signs of brainstem compression (Scotti et al., 1980). Early CT indicators of a possible progressive course may be the presence of fourth

ventricular compression and developing hydrocephalus (Scotti et al., 1980).

BASILAR ARTERY

This artery and its branches carry the blood supply for most of the brainstem and cerebellum. It is a single midline trunk, the basilar artery (BA), from which a number of branches of varying diameters and lengths (the long circumferential, short circumferential, and midline penetrators) arise throughout its long course on the ventral surface of the pons and midbrain. Atheroma is characteristically present in the wall of the artery at the sites from which the circumferential and penetrating arteries arise (Fisher and Caplan, 1971). Here, a small focus of atheroma, insufficient to disturb overall BA flow, may sufficiently stenose the ostium of a penetrator as to cause a miniature version of the events that occur in the larger arteries from major stenosis (Fisher, 1977). With increasing atheroma in the BA, the same processes of hemodynamically significant stenosis and embolization may occur as occur in the carotid territory.

Occlusive BA disease has been described in all age groups, but its greater frequency is in the sixth, seventh, and eighth decades, when 95% of the cases occur (Archer and Horenstein, 1977). The arterial occlusion is thrombotic in nature in the majority of cases (93%) (Castaigne et al., 1973), although Kubik and Adams (1946) have reported embolism in nearly 40% of the cases. The distribution of these two types of occlusive process tends to follow a predictable pattern along the BA: following the usual sites of atheroma location (Fisher et al., 1965), thrombotic occlusions occur more often in the lower and middle thirds (Castaigne et al., 1973), whereas embolism is most commonly the cause of occlusions in distal segments of the artery (Kubik and Adams, 1946; Caplan, 1980). In the discussion that follows, the clinical syndromes of BA atherothrombosis will be analyzed, since this process occurs in elderly populations more often than embolism.

In the analysis of cases of basilar occlusion, a wide range of mechanisms and clinical outlooks has been documented (Kubik and Adams, 1946; Biemond, 1951; Archer and Horenstein, 1977; Caplan, 1979; Patrick et al., 1980; Jones et al., 1980). The clinical deficits range from coma and early death to mild deficits of a transient nature associated with a good functional prognosis. In the former, the setting is one of sudden onset of hemiplegia or quadriplegia with anesthesia of the limbs and trunk, associated with horizontal gaze palsies, ocular "bobbing," facial paralysis, and sensory deficit, commonly followed by coma and respiratory rhythm abnormalities. Almost invariably fatal, these are cases of complete occlusion of the BA, with poor or nonexistent angiographic collateral circulation to the brainstem (Figure 26-5). A less severe clinical presentation commonly occurs in basilar distribution infarction, in which the sud-

den onset of signs of brainstem ischemia is followed by a fluctuating course of the deficits. Jones et al. (1980) found this pattern in more than one-half their cases, and most of the clinical fluctuations occurred within 48 hours of onset. A similar temporal profile was observed by Patrick et al. (1980) in a series of 39 cases of infarction in the vertebrobasilar territory. The basis for this unstable state in the early stages of BA occlusion is unclear, but is likely to represent the hemodynamic changes resulting from the degree of BA occlusion and the development of collateral circulation (Caplan, 1979). During this period of hemodynamic instability, blood flow through the BA and branches can be critically influenced by variations in systemic blood pressure, cardiac arrhythmias, and positional changes (Caplan and Sergay, 1976; Sundt et al., 1978).

The correlation between the clinical presentation and the angiographic aspects of BA occlusion has been carefully analyzed in only a few instances (Moscow and Newton, 1973; Caplan and Rosenbaum, 1975; Caplan, 1979). Moscow and Newton (1973) reported major collaterals in six survivors with BA occlusion, whereas three patients who died showed an insufficient development of collateral flow. In Caplan's (1979) series of six cases, a benign clinical outcome was correlated with the presence of collaterals, non-sudden onset, and prior history of TIAs, the latter two features pointing to atherothrombosis rather than embolism as the mechanism of arterial occlusion. A point of major importance raised by the above studies is the recognition that cases of documented BA occlusion at times present with minor neurological signs at onset, and pursue a benign outcome. Such cases are important, since their presentation can be identical to that of occlusion of a "basilar branch" (Fisher and Caplan, 1971), a condition with a more "benign" pathology, in the form of non-stenosing atheroma of the wall of the BA. Such atheromatous deposits can occlude the ostium of a basilar branch as it arises from the main trunk, producing a small pontine infarction of lacunar type. The purely clinical differentiation of the latter from a minimally

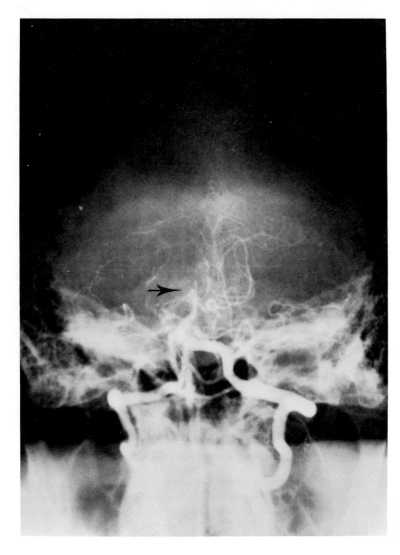

Figure 26-5. Angiographic documentation of complete occlusion of the basilar artery in its middle portion (arrow) with minimal evidence of collateral circulation.

symptomatic total occlusion of the BA may be impossible. This justifies the use of diagnostic angiography since it is conceivable (although not proven) that the two conditions have different prognoses, a more benign one being associated with basilar branch occlusions.

Embolism

Like atherothrombosis, the syndromes produced by embolism vary with the arterial territory affected. Some general differences between atherothrombotic and embolic infarcts include:

1. Whereas thrombosis occurs in rela-

tively predictable locations, embolism may occur into almost any conceivable trunk or branch or even in multiple branches of a given vessel.

2. Since embolism strikes without warning, the collateral circulation available to limit the size of the infarct is more circumscribed than that which develops in cases of progressive atherothrombus.

3. The embolic material varies from the usual fragment of bland mural thrombus (from the valves or walls of the heart or from the walls of great vessels) to thrombus–bacteria complexes (Jones et al., 1969), cholesterol fragments (Gore and Collins, 1960), microscopic aggregates of

tumor (Ghatak, 1975), bubbles of gas or fat following surgery or fractures (Peltier et al., 1974), and even foreign bodies (Kase et al., 1981a). Most of the embolic material is highly unstable, rapidly fragmenting, and, at times, surprisingly evanescent. This accounts for the high degree of variabiliy in the severity of the deficit in the early stages of embolic infarction, and the sometimes dramatic resolution of deficits within hours from onset. Such a course is unlikely to occur in atherothrombotic infarction.

4. As a result of the instability and migrating capacity of the occluding material, embolic infarcts are frequently of the hemorrhagic type (Fisher and Adams, 1951), whereas those resulting from atherothrombosis are pale or anemic.

Embolism accounts for at least 20 to 25% of strokes (Mohr et al., 1978a; Kunitz et al., in press). Its distribution by age groups differs only slightly from that of atherothrombosis, with a tendency for embolism to predominate in both extremes of life (individuals younger than 40 or older than 80), with a comparable frequency in ages 40 to 80 (Kunitz et al., in press). Some general clinical features apply to embolism as a group:

1. Sudden onset is the rule, and a deficit that is "maximal from the onset" is the landmark of this condition. This type of onset characterized 79% of the embolic cases in two large series of stroke patients (Mohr et al., 1978a; Kunitz et al., in press).

2. Early improvement, detected within 24 hours from onset, occurs in fully 40% of cases of embolism (Kunitz et al., in press), a frequency that surpasses that of all other stroke varieties.

3. The clinical syndromes of embolism result from arterial occlusion at many possible levels within a given arterial trunk, thus producing a wide variety of clinical presentations. These depend on the location of the occlusion at either the proximal or the distal segments of the artery; the latter produces a less serious syndrome than would result from the former.

In the discussion that follows, the clinical syndromes that result from occlusion of the three major supratentorial arteries, the middle cerebral, anterior cerebral and posterior cerebral, with special emphasis on those clinical presentations that are most suggestive of embolism, will be analyzed. Most of the analysis will concentrate on embolism to the middle cerebral artery and branches, since they represent the vessels most commonly affected (Lhermitte et al., 1968; Mohr et al., 1978a; Gacs et al., 1982; Kunitz et al., in press) (Table 26-2).

MIDDLE CEREBRAL ARTERY

The stem of the middle cerebral artery (MCA) gives off the small lenticulostriate arteries that penetrate the brain to supply the striatum (caudate nucleus and putamen), globus pallidus, most of the internal capsule, the external capsule, and the claustrum. The two divisions of the MCA supply the surface of the cerebrum. The *upper division* supplies the entire insula, most of the frontal lobe, and almost all the convex surface of the anterior half of the parietal lobe. The *lower division* branches at the posterior end of the Sylvian fissure to supply almost all the temporal lobe, the

Table 26-2. Vessel Affected in Cerebral Embolism. NINCDS Stroke Data Bank* (*N* = 148).

| Stem | Middle Cerebral Artery | | Anterior Cerebral Artery | Posterior Cerebral Artery | | Basilar |
	UD**	LD***		Stem	Branch	
55	48	20	1	10	3	11
(37%)	(32%)	(13%)	(0.6%)	(7%)	(2%)	(7%)

*From Kunitz et al., in press.
**UD, upper division.
***LD, lower division.

posterior half of the parietal lobe, and the adjacent lateral occipital region.

The MCA is the major intracranial arterial territory supplied by the internal carotid (Gacs et al., 1982). As a result, it is the main territory into which embolic particles are distributed. Blood is directed into the two divisions of the middle cerebral artery more or less equally, but within each division, the frequency of embolic occlusions appear to be determined by the angles at which the branches leave the main trunk of the individual division. In the upper division, the orbitofrontal branch is acutely angulated and only rarely embolized (Waddington and Ring, 1968; Gacs et al., 1982). More or less similar rates of embolic occlusion occur in the remaining branches of the upper division. In the lower division, the angular and parietal arteries account for the majority of occlusions, representing almost one-third of all intracranial embolic phenomena (Gacs, et al., 1982).

Occlusion of the main trunk represents between 20 and 34% of the embolic phenomena in the MCA territory (Mohr et al., 1978a; Gacs et al., 1982). The resulting infarction affects both the deep and the cortical surface territories of the MCA, involving the basal ganglia, internal capsule, and a large portion of the cerebral hemisphere. This extensive infarct causes contralateral hemiplegia, hemianesthesia, and homonymous hemianopia. Associated disturbances in behavior include aphasia and apraxia (if the dominant hemisphere is affected) or impaired awareness of the stroke (non-dominant hemisphere). To the extent that collateral flow (through borderzone vessels shared with the anterior or posterior cerebral arteries) rescues the endangered territory, the symptoms and signs are much less severe. In some cases, the collateral flow supplies blood all the way back to the site of the occlusion, and involvement is limited to the territory of the penetrating arteries, for which no significant collateral exists (Mohr, 1982); the deep infarct that occurs usually affects the basal ganglia and internal capsule, at times producing no more than a syndrome of pure hemiparesis, unaccompanied by sensory, visual, language, or behavior dis-

turbances. Ordinarily, however, the retrograde collateral is nowhere near this complete, and occlusion of the MCA stem can produce the most extensive deficit in language, behavior, and unilateral sensorimotor function encountered in clinical neurology. In lesions involving most of the gyri surrounding the Sylvian region in the dominant hemisphere, the initial disturbance of speech and comprehension is so profound it is characterized as "total aphasia," a term used since before the turn of the century (Brown, 1972; Mohr et al., 1978b). Apraxia in its major forms is also usually encountered in MCA territory infarcts involving the dominant hemisphere (Geschwind, 1965; Brown, 1972). The contralateral sensorimotor syndrome is quite profound, since the infarct affects both the cerebral gray matter of the sensorimotor cortex and the deeper basal ganglia and capsular white matter pathways. In a study of 20 cases with varying degrees of motor aphasia, Mohr et al. (1978b) found that the hemiplegia was at first complete in the trunk, face, and limbs on the affected side. Within weeks, however, some control reappeared in the trunk and axial portion of the limbs, which began to move against gravity. The contralateral sensory disturbance, present to the midline of the body, improved over weeks to a final picture in which sensation to pinprick seemed blunted only in the lower face, distal arm and hand, leg, and foot. The initial contralateral hemianopia faded when the visual radiation was spared, but when the syndrome was present beyond a few weeks, it usually reflected infarction large enough to involve the radiations deep in the parietotemporal regions (Naeser and Hayward, 1978; Mazzochi and Vignolo, 1979). Disturbances of consciousness are rare even in large MCA territory infarct (Mohr et al., 1978b), unless the infarct also involves the anterior cerebral artery territory.

The *major divisions of the MCA, or their branches,* are so rarely affected by thrombosis that their occlusion is usually attributed to embolism. In the *upper division,* occlusion usually produces contralateral hemiparesis and hemisensory syndromes, accompanied by aphasia when the dominant hemisphere is involved or by impaired awareness of the deficit when the right hemisphere is involved. Like the syndromes of language disturbance produced by occlusion of the MCA stem, upper division embolic syndromes usually begin as total aphasia. Months elapse before speech reappears. Such speech is hesitant and frequently interrupted by dyspraxia of the oropharynx, larynx, and respiratory apparatus. The dysphasia that accompanies large Sylvian lesions is most easily demonstrated with tasks involving small grammatical words, and in the construction of sentences involving few nouns. Spontaneously uttered sentences are condensed, miss many of the filler words, and take the form of telegraphic speech (Brown, 1972) or agrammatism (Brown, 1972; Mohr et al., 1978b; Naeser and Hayward, 1978). The same problems with grammar that are apparant in speaking and writing also impair comprehension of words heard and seen. This syndrome, also known by the eponym Broca aphasia is all but impossible to distinguish from the syndrome encountered in occlusion of the MCA stem, save for its somewhat lesser severity.

Dyspraxias also occur in the more focal syndromes and are easily demonstrated when the accompanying dysphasia is mild enough so that reliable testing can be carried out. The motor form ("limb-kinetic" or "innervatory" dyspraxia) occurs as part of the same syndrome of paresis produced by the cerebral lesion (Liepmann, 1915; Geschwind, 1975). Attempts to use the involved limbs reveal a disturbance in movement beyond that due simply to weakness. Geschwind (1975) has emphasized that the patient appears clumsy or unfamiliar with the movements called for. Although difficult to demonstrate, innervatory dyspraxia is a useful sign to elicit, since it is considered to reliably indicate that the lesion producing the hemiparesis involves the hemisphere surface, and presumably includes the premotor region and other association systems. Dyspraxias of this type are thought not to occur with lesions involving the internal capsule or with those lower in the nervous system (Geschwind, 1975).

The larger infarcts usually produce contralateral hemiparesis and hemisensory syndromes because the sensorimotor cortex is supplied by the upper MCA division. The hemiparesis in upper division syndromes may occur when the infarction spares the deeper territories of the MCA, in which case it is believed the prognosis for functional recovery may be better, although this point has not been clarified by clinical studies. The hemiparesis usually affects the face and arm more than the leg in such cases, since the arterial supply to the sensorimotor cortex of the leg arises mainly from the anterior cerebral artery territory, and the pathways through the white matter and the internal capsule have been spared in contrast to their involvement when the stem of the MCA has been occluded. The initial involvement of the face characteristically affects the forehead as well as the lower half, mimicking a peripheral facial nerve palsy; the movements of the forehead that diagnose the "central" facial paresis may not begin for several days following the acute stroke (Mohr et al., 1978b).

The arrangement of the individual branches of the upper division of the MCA leads to a wide variety of focal embolic syndromes. The smaller and the more superficial the injury, the shorter the disruption in speech and the less the associated dysphasia (Mohr et al., 1978b). A syndrome of *acute mutism* occurs when focal infarction is confined to any single gyrus of the insula or the upper banks of the opercular cortex (Roch-LeCours and Lhermitte, 1976; Mohr et al., 1978b; Mazzochi and Vignolo, 1979). This region spans the distance from the anterior inferior frontal region all the way to the anterior parietal lobe, but the effect has been best demonstrated by infarcts confined to the inferior extent of the motor strip, as demonstrated by Roch-LeCours and Lhermitte (1976). In such cases, speech may reappear within minutes to days. It consists initially of crude vowels (dysphonia) and poorly articulated consonants (dysarthria), but prominently featured is a disturbance in the skilled coordination (dyspraxia) of breathing and speaking, which produces a dysrhythmic

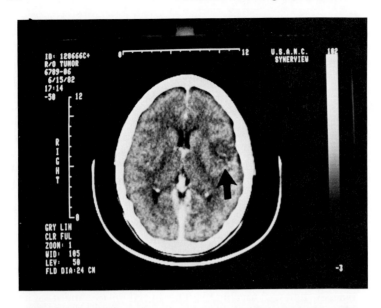

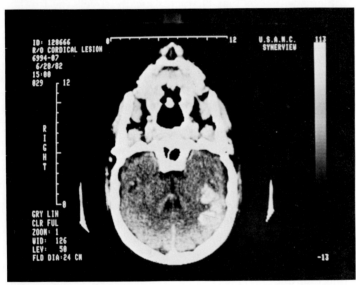

Figure 26-6. (A) CT scan showing area of infarction in the inferior portion of the frontal operculum or Broca area (arrow). (B) Coronal view of same infarct enhanced after contrast infusion.

articulation (dysprosody) with faulty intonation, stress, and phrasing of words and sentences, a syndrome known collectively as aphemia or *speech dyspraxia* (Mohr, 1973). When the lesion occurs in the inferior frontal region (Broca area) of the operculum (Figure 26-6), dyspraxia predominates (Mohr et al., 1978b). When the sensorimotor cortex itself is affected, dysarthria and dysphonia are more prominant (Roch-LeCours and Lhermitte, 1976; Damasio et al., 1979). Despite the speech disturbance, there is so little abnormality

in the language conveyed through the speech that a diagnosis of aphasia is not usually made. The more posteriorly placed infarcts, especially those that involve the anterior parietal operculum, have been postulated by Luria (1966) to interfere with afferent control of the positioning of the oropharynx. The mispronunciations made by the patient are easily mistaken for dysphasia. Since most of the errors represent a speech, but not a language disorder, the patient's language comprehension is often intact despite his distorted speech utterances, which in some cases are meaningless jargon. In many cases of branch occlusion affecting the upper division, an accompanying contralateral hemiparesis precludes much testing of writing, but if testable, little language disturbance is found. Since comprehension of words, heard or seen, is largely subserved by regions more posterior in the brain, it is usually intact. Whether this syndrome qualifies as "conduction aphasia" is still a subject of dispute, as are the anatomical boundaries for the condition (Damasio and Damasio, 1980).

Hemiparesis from branch occlusions usually affects the face and arm more than the leg. Hemianopia is usually not present at any time, but in the very earliest hours or days, a hemineglect to visual stimuli from the contralateral side of space may simulate it.

In addition to these deficits, "ideomotor dyspraxia" is frequently encountered (Brown, 1972; Geschwind, 1975). The lesion is believed to disrupt the connections between the region of the brain containing the "ideas" and the region involved in the execution of the movements (Heilman and Valenstein, 1979). The lesion should produce a disturbance analogous to the so-called conduction aphasia, with motor behavior that is intact when executed spontaneously, but faulty in response to verbal command. Accordingly, a disruption of the alleged pathways emanating from the posterior temporal region of the dominant hemisphere should produce ideomotor dyspraxia of the limbs of both sides of the body. For movements to be executed through the hemisphere non-dominant for language in response to dictated commands processed by the dominant hemisphere, the lesion could involve the presumed white matter pathways through the dominant hemisphere to its motor cortex, the motor cortex itself, or the white matter connecting through the corpus callosum to the motor cortex of the non-dominant hemisphere. Because there are so many presumed pathways involved, ideomotor dyspraxia is quite common. The syndrome most frequently involves the limbs served by the non-dominant hemisphere when the lesion affects the convex-

ity of the dominant hemisphere. Analysis of the co-existing right hemiparesis and the dysphasias, usually of the motor type, often occupy the physician to such an extent that the ideomotor dyspraxia of the non-dominant limbs goes unnoticed. The patient's dysphasia often confounds efforts made to demonstrate the presence of ideomotor dyspraxia. When dysphasia is mild, the dyspraxia is demonstrated when the patient fails to produce the movements on command that he can mimic or execute spontaneously at other times. The disturbances are most apparent for movements involving the distal end of the appendages (fingers, hand) and oropharynx, whereas the axial and trunk movements are often spared (Heilman and Valenstein, 1979). This form of ideomotor dyspraxia has been shown to remit within six weeks of onset, even with a well-established left opercular infarct (Mohr, 1973).

The *lower division* on the MCA gives off its several branches almost together, making many of them susceptible to involvement by the same arterial occlusion, even when a relatively small embolus is involved. This difference in anatomy accounts for the lower incidence of distinctive variations, clinically. The posterior portions of the brain are also more compact than the anterior. As a result, the larger infarctions and lesions due to tumors, abscesses, or other masses in posterior brain regions tend to share most of the same clinical features. Deeper lesions disrupt the visual radiations to give a contralateral hemianopia. When this sign is present with infarction, it usually signifies a large infarct that has penetrated from the surface all the way through the depths of the temporo-parietal white matter supplied by the involved artery. Hemianopia persisting beyond a week or so in such cases carries a poor prognosis for clinical recovery of the co-existing aphasia. The few, discretely focal infarctions that occur in the lower division are usually due to embolism (Mohr, 1980).

In the lower division syndromes, aphasia (Wernicke or "sensory" aphasia), without hemiparesis, is the usual picture of dominant hemisphere infarction, whereas non-dominant behavior disturbances may ap-

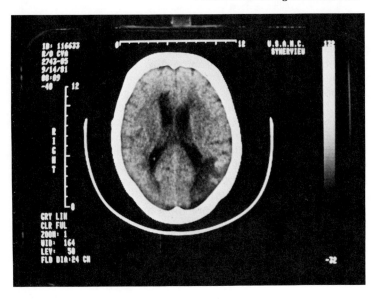

Figure 26-7. CT scan of infarction in the distribution of the lower division of the left middle cerebral artery.

pear alone when the opposite side is involved. In large, dominant hemisphere lesions (Figure 26-7), the effects on the patient are almost the reverse of the insular–opercular syndromes (Brown, 1972): speech is filled with grammatical words, but omissions or distortions affect the key words—the predicative elements—that contain the essence of the message. The patient speaks easily, engages in simple conversational exchanges, and even appears to be trying to communicate. But the partial phrases, disjointed clauses, and incomplete sentences convey little useful information (Kreindler and Fradis, 1968). When specific predicative words are required, the patient usually hesitates and blocks, and he either fails to utter the words (omissions) or he pronounces similar sounding words (literal paraphasias) or replaces them with other words having similar meanings (verbal paraphasias) (Kreindler and Fradis, 1968). A similar disturbance in language affects the patient's attempt to understand words heard or read. The extent of the language disturbance in milder cases may be revealed only in prolonged conversation.

Focal lesions limited to the posterior temporal lobe usually produce part of the syndrome of "sensory aphasia." Bogen and Bogen (1976) have demonstrated that dogma more than data, determines exactly how large an area of brain injury is needed for the full syndrome to develop, and re-emphasized that the boundaries of "Wernicke's area" are unclear (Naeser and Hayward, 1978). Speech and the language it conveys are only slightly disturbed, and reading for comprehension may pass for normal, but auditory language comprehension is grossly defective. Such cases were traditionally named "pure word deafness" (Brown, 1972; Mohr, 1980). However, the spoken language usually contains verbal paraphasias, and silent reading is disturbed for more complex materials. This syndrome might be better named "the auditory form of sensory aphasia" (Mohr, 1980). It has a good outlook for almost full clinical recovery within a few weeks. A similarly restricted dysphasia, this time predominantly involving reading and writing, occurs with a more posteriorly placed focal lesion that damages the posterior parietal and lateral occipital regions. Reading comprehension and writing are strikingly abnormal (Kreindler and Fradis, 1968). This syndrome has been traditionally known as "alexia with agraphia" (Mohr, 1980). However, spoken language and auditory comprehension are also disturbed, although not to the same degree as reading and writing. A better label for this syndrome might be "the visual form of sensory aphasia." Like its auditory counterpart, it also has a good outlook. The auditory and visual forms of Wernicke aphasia occur together in cases with larger lesions. Whether the major syndrome of sensory aphasia is a unified disturbance or a synergistic result of several separate deficits still remains unclear (Kreindler and Fradis, 1968; Bogen and Bogen, 1976).

ANTERIOR CEREBRAL ARTERY

This vessel is rarely the site of embolic occlusions, accounting for only 3 to 7% of cerebral embolism cases (Mohr et al., 1978a; Gacs et al., 1982). The stem of the anterior cerebral artery (ACA) gives rise to the "medial lenticulostriate arteries," which penetrate into the brain to supply the anterior limb of the internal capsule, the head of the caudate nucleus, and the putamen (Berman et al., 1980). The trunk courses forward, upward, and then backward over the corpus callosum, which it supplies, to reach its major territory: the frontal pole, the upper portion of the anterolateral frontal lobe, and the medial surface of the cerebral hemisphere including the paracentral lobule.

Occlusion of the proximal segment of the ACA is rare. Isolated occlusion of the medial lenticulostriate arteries is likely to result from primary lipo-hyalinosis, or mi-croatheroma (Fisher, 1969, 1979), rather than from embolism. The expected clinical syndrome is characterized by arm and face weakness, usually accompanied by dysarthria (Critchley, 1930; Rascol et al., 1982). Embolism is likely to produce variable size infarctions affecting the corpus callosum and the cortical areas supplied by the ACA (Figure 26-8). The inclusion of the genu and body of the corpus callosum in such infarction produces striking behavioral abnormalities, as a result of an interruption of connections between the two hemispheres: ideomotor dyspraxia affecting the left ("non-dominant" or "minor") limbs is evidenced by the inability to perform skillful movements on verbal command, writing is difficult with the left hand, and complex tactile stimuli applied to those limbs cannot be named aloud or matched with printed names (Geschwind and Kaplan, 1962; Geschwind, 1965, 1975). The clinical manifestations that result from embolic occlusion of hemispheric branches of the ACA are quite variable and involve combinations of contralateral hemiparesis and sensory loss predominating in the leg; abulia; amnestic syndromes; urinary incontinence; and abnormal reflexes (grasping, sucking) (Critchley, 1930). In bilateral infarction along the ACA distribution from either multiple bilateral emboli or occlusion of a single "azygous" artery supplying both

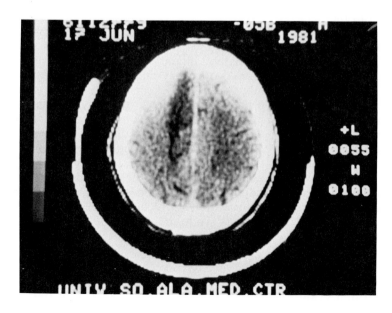

Figure 26-8. CT scan of infarction in the distribution of the left anterior cerebral artery.

hemispheres (Berman et al., 1980), profound abulia results, with the development of a state of "akinetic mutism."

POSTERIOR CEREBRAL ARTERY

This artery is second in frequency of occlusion by emboli, accounting for approximately 10% of the cases (Mohr et al., 1978a). The posterior cerebral artery (PCA) usually arises from the basilar artery, but is a branch of the internal carotid in 10% of cases. It supplies the midbrain and thalamus via two groups of small, deep penetrating branches that arise from the trunk, the thalamoperforator and thalamogeniculate arteries (Hayman et al., 1981). The PCA cortical surface territory includes the inferomedial portions of the temporal and occipital lobes, including the calcarine cortex.

From an anatomical–angiographic point of view, Goto et al. (1979) have divided the PCA into four segments: interpeduncular, crural, ambient, and cortical. In 38 cases, they found that occlusion occurred most commonly in the crural segment, and the site and extent of infarction was determined by the pattern of collateral circulation: when collateral flow was prominent, infarcts were confined to the thalamus, when collateral flow was poor, the infarcts involved both the thalamus and the cortical surface. In five of thirty-eight cases there was a massive infarction in both the deep and superficial PCA territories, the remaining 33 cases showed variable degrees of partial collateralization.

In a rare, non-collateralized occlusion of the PCA trunk, infarction of both the deep and superficial territories occurs (Figure 26-9), producing a syndrome that mimics MCA occlusion. Should the process be limited to the thalamoperforate branches alone, the resulting small deep infarct affects only the thalamus, and produces the classic "thalamic syndrome" of Dejerine and Roussy (1906): contralateral loss of superficial and deep sensation, mild hemiparesis, slight ataxia and choreathetoid movements, homonymous hemianopia, and agonizing, burning spontaneous pain ("thalamic pain syndrome").

More often, the cortical territory of the PCA is infarcted. When infarction is restricted to the calcarine cortex, a contralateral homonymous hemianopia, unaccompanied by other deficits, occurs. Commonly, collateral flow from the ACA across the cuneus spares the upper bank of the calcarine cortex; in such cases the infarct may be confined to the lower bank and presents only as a contralateral upper quadrantic homonymous defect, a sign that requires careful clinical examination, since the patient may not be aware of the deficit. Larger infarcts involving the lingual and fusiform gyri produce more complex neurobehavioral syndromes. Prominent among them are an agitated delirium accompanied by an exaggeration of responses to external stimuli, along with auditory or visual hallucinations and memory loss (Horenstein et al., 1967). The memory loss can acquire dramatic severity, with a total inability to form new memories and variable degrees of retrograde amnesia (Mohr et al., 1971). This state has usually been associated with bilateral medial temporal lobe lesions (Milner, 1966), but occasional cases of unilateral dominant hemisphere lesion have been documented (Mohr et al., 1971; Caplan and Hedley-White, 1974; Benson et al., 1974). In addition, lesions involving the dominant hemisphere can produce defects in the discrimination and naming of colors (Geschwind and Fusillo, 1966; Mohr et al., 1971), as well as frank amnestic aphasia in cases of large infarcts (Wyllie, 1894; Victor et al., 1961).

Bilateral infarction in the PCA distribution is commonly due to embolism (Symmonds and Mackenzie, 1957) and can produce dramatic instances of cortical blindness, in which unawareness of the defect may be present, followed by prominent confabulation (Anton's syndrome). Occasionally, the behavioral abnormalities do not include cortical blindness, but rather a combination of visual and visuomotor defects included as elements of Balint's syndrome (Balint, 1909).

Lacunes

Lacunar infarcts represent about 10% of strokes, and one out of every seven cerebral

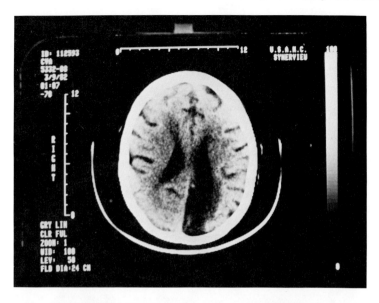

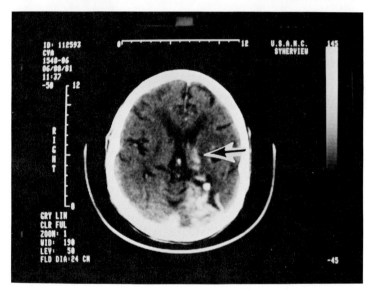

Figure 26-9. (A) CT scan with infarction in the cortical territory of the left posterior cerebral artery. (B) CT scan after intravenous contrast infusion showing enhancing infarct in both the cortical (occipital) and thalamic (arrow) distribution of the left posterior cerebral artery.

infarcts corresponds to this type (Kunitz et al., in press). Approximately two-thirds of patients with lacunes are hypertensive, and in 32% there is an association with diabetes (Mohr et al., 1982). This stroke type shares with atherothrombosis its rarity in the young adult age group, since 90% of the cases occur in patients older than 50 (Kunitz et al., in press).

The pathogenesis of lacunes is occlusion of the perforating cerebral arteries by either "lipohyalinosis" (Fisher, 1969), a form of segmental arterial degeneration related to chronic hypertension, or "microatheroma" (Fisher, 1979) involving the small perforating arteries. When perforators originating from the stems of the anterior, middle, and posterior cerebral arteries and the basilar artery are occluded, a small, 2- to 15-mm-diameter infarct ("lacune") results (Figure 26-10). The corresponding clinical syndromes are well-recognized clinicopathological entities, as observed by C.M. Fisher (1965a, b,

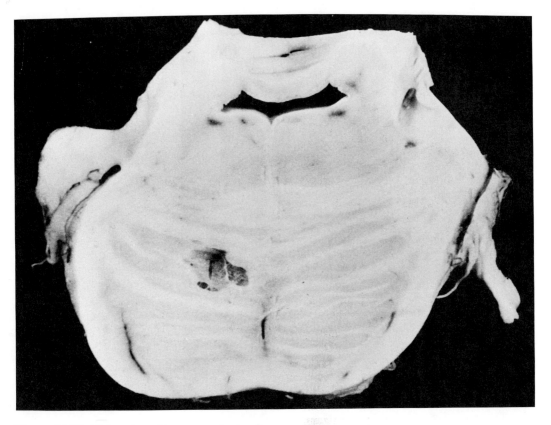

Figure 26-10. Old cavitated lacune at the level of the paramedian basis pontis.

1967, 1978a, b) and co-workers (Fisher and Curry, 1965; Fisher and Cole, 1965; Mohr et al., 1977).

Clinically, the different lacunar syndromes have a number of features in common. Transient ischemic attacks precede them in about 20% of the cases, less often than in large artery atherosclerosis (50%), but more often than in cerebral embolism (5%) (Mohr et al., 1978a; Kunitz et al., in press). In about one-third of the cases, the deficit progresses over several hours after onset, not uncommonly continuing for 24 hours or more after admission to the hospital. The sudden onset commonly associated with stroke in general occurs in only 50 to 60% of the cases (Mohr et al., 1978a; Kunitz et al., in press). The remainder correspond to those with onset during sleep, without further progression. The clinical course is usually one of improvement after a few days from stabilization of the neurological deficit, and the speed of recovery is related to the completeness of the initial deficit; that is, those patients with initially partial syndromes show the fastest and most complete recoveries. Because of the small size of the infarcts and their tendency toward recovery of function, mortality is the lowest (5%) of all stroke types (Mohr et al., 1982).

The clinical presentation in lacunar infarction varies according to the perforating artery involved. In occlusion of a middle cerebral perforator ("lenticulostriate") artery, the lacune is confined to the basal ganglia or the genu or posterior limb of the internal capsule. This infarct causes the most common lacunar syndrome, *pure motor hemiparesis* (PMH), which accounted for 68% of the lacunar strokes in the NINCDS Stroke Data Bank (Kunitz et al., in press). Pure motor hemiparesis, as the result of an infarct in the posterior limb of the internal capsule, leads to hemiparesis or hemiplegia involving the arm, leg, face, and trunk, accompanied by mild dysarthria without sensory deficit, visual field defect, aphasia, or alteration of consciousness (Fisher and Curry, 1965). A syndrome with identical characteristics can result from a lacune at the level of the basis pontis, whereas PMH secondary to medullary pyramidal infarction spares the face (Ropper et al., 1979). The distribution of the motor deficit in PMH is subject to considerable variation: some cases conform to the expected comparable degree of weakness of the arm, leg, and face, whereas others show a surprising predominance for the arm and/or face, and even the leg, with relative sparing of other segments (Rascol et al., 1982; Donnan et al., 1982; Mohr et al., 1982). These variations probably reflect differences in the size and location of the lacunes along the genu and posterior limb of the internal capsule.

Other lacunar syndromes in the lenticulo-striate territory are less common and not áso well characterized as PMH. These include the *dysarthria–clumsy hand syndrome* (Fisher, 1967), in which severe dysarthria, facial palsy, and tongue paresis are associated with clumsiness and mild weakness of the hand, due to a lacune involving the genu and anterior limb of the internal capsule (Spertrell and Ransom, 1979); *hemichorea–hemiballismus* (Kase et al., 1981b), from putaminal and caudate lacunes, with sparing of the internal capsule; mutism, or anarthria, from bilateral, non-simultaneous, capsular lacunes (Fisher, 1979). In the latter, a pseudobulbar syndrome may develop, with anarthria or severe dysarthria accompanied by dysphagia, bilateral spasticity, bilateral Babinski sign, paroxysms of inappropriate crying or laughter, and short-stepped gait. This vascular syndrome, the "lacunar state," must be differentiated from other causes of gait disturbance in the elderly.

Occlusion of a perforating branch originating from the posterior cerebral artery results in a *pure sensory stroke* (Fisher, 1965b, 1978a), a form of lacunar stroke that represented only 9% of the cases in the NINCDS Stroke Data Bank (Kunitz et al., in press). Characterized by a hemisensory syndrome involving the face, limbs, and trunk, it is at times remarkably well defined along the midline of the body. This contrasts with a perfect preservation of motor strength, visual fields, speech function, and level of consciousness. Lesions are found in the ventral posterior thalamic nuclei. In very rare instances, this striking sensory syndrome is accompanied by a mild and transient hemiparesis, and autopsy has documented a slight involvement of the posterior limb of the internal capsule adjacent to the expected lacune on the ventral posterior nucleus of the thalamus (Mohr et al., 1977).

Occlusion of perforating pontine branches of the basilar artery can be associated with several lacunar syndromes. These infarcts are most commonly confined to the basis pontis, in which the descending corticospinal tracts and the exiting cerebellopontine fibers represent most of its volume, along with the pontine nuclei. Involvement of tegmental structures by pontine lacunes occurs rarely (Fisher, 1977). Lacunar syndromes due to basis pontis lesions include PMH and dysarthria–clumsy hand syndrome, both clinically indistinguishable from capsular infarct syndromes. A third syndrome, *homolateral ataxia and crural paresis* ("ataxic hemiparesis") (Fisher and Cole 1965; Fisher, 1978b), has been correlated with basal pontine lacunar infarcts. It presents with a particular combination of hemiparesis that affects the leg more than the arm or face, in association with marked cerebellar ataxia of the weak limbs, out of proportion with the degree of paresis. This is particularly obvious at the level of the upper limb, which is usually slightly weak. Pathologically, lacunes have been documented at paramedian and lateral locations in the basis pontis contralaterally to the affected limbs.

The diagnosis of lacunar infarction is usually made on purely clinical grounds. A normal electroencephalogram supports a clinical diagnosis of lacunes (Caplan and Young, 1972), since the same motor or sensory syndrome due to cortical surface infarction would be associated with focal

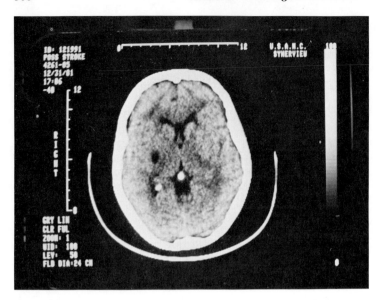

Figure 26-11. CT scan with low-density lacunar infarction in the right basal ganglia, adjacent to the posterior limb of the internal capsule.

slowing. CT scan provides the positive diagnosis of lacunar infarction (Fig. 26-11). Despite variation in size and location of these infarcts, 50 to 70% of them can now be detected if CT scans are performed within 10 days of onset (Weisberg, 1979, 1982; Pullicino et al., 1980; Rascol et al., 1982; Donnan et al., 1982; Kunitz et al., in press). Those likely to be missed are smaller than 2 mm or located at the level of the pons, where artifact usually precludes visualization of small, nonhemorrhagic lesions. Angiography is of little use in the evaluation of lacunar strokes, except when an unusually large lacune is detected by CT scan. The latter may indicate that the vessel is occluded proximally, at its origin from the main cerebral artery stem, and atherosclerosis may be the causal factor.

Intracerebral Hemorrhage

Intracerebral hemorrhage (ICH) accounts for 10 to 12% of strokes (Mohr et al., 1978a; Kunitz et al., in press). Arterial hypertension is the leading risk factor (Fisher, 1961, 1971), and it plays a role for most ICH, being present in 72 to 81% of the cases (Kunitz et al., in press). Hypertensive ICH occurs in all age groups, but the majority of the cases (78%) occur in the fifth through the seventh decade (Ku-

nitz et al., in press), which represents a shift of at least one decade down in the distribution curve of ICH as compared with the occlusive strokes. A racial distribution, with predominance in blacks, has been observed (Gross et al., in press), and has been related to a higher frequency of uncontrolled hypertension.

Intracerebral hemorrhage occurs predominantly in the deep portions of the cerebral hemispheres, the putamen accounting for 35 to 50% of the cases (Hier et al., 1977; Mohr et al., 1978a; Kase et al., 1982; Kunitz et al., in press) (Table 26-3). The second site of preference varies in different series, between the subcortical

Table 26-3. Intracerebral hemorrhage distribution by site over a three and a half year period, at the University of South Alabama.*

Site	Number of Cases	Total Cases (%)
Putaminal	31	33
Lobar	22	23
Thalamic	19	20
Cerebellar	7	8
Pontine	6	7
Miscellaneous	8	9
Total	93	100

*From Kase et al., 1982.

white matter and the cerebellum (Mohr et al., 1978a; Kase et al., 1982). The thalamus and pons follow, with frequencies of 15 and 5%, respectively (Mohr et al., 1978a; Kase et al., 1982). Different forms of ICH have some clinical features in common: ICH occurs characteristically in activity, and onset during sleep is virtually unknown; the clinical course is one of gradual and smooth progression in two-thirds of the cases, the deficit being maximal from the onset in the remainder (Mohr et al., 1978a; Kunitz et al., in press); a regressive course in the acute phase is not encountered; some degree of decreased alertness is present on admission in 60% of the cases. Coma on admission has been correlated with ventricular extension of the hemorrhage, large size of the hematoma, and a poor prognosis (Hier et al., 1977). Headache and vomiting occur in 36 and 44% of the cases, respectively, which stresses the point that absence of headache or vomiting does not rule out ICH (Mohr et al., 1978a). Seizures at the onset of ICH are uncommon, occurring in 7 to 14% of the cases (Aring, 1964; Mohr et al., 1978a).

The different anatomical varieties of ICH account for several distinctive clinical syndromes. In the *putaminal* form, involvement of the internal capsule by the expanding hematoma produces a dense flaccid hemiplegia with a hemisensory syndrome and homonymous hemianopia, along with either a global aphasia in dominant hemisphere hematomas or hemi-inattention in non-dominant ones. A supratentorial type of gaze palsy to the contralateral side is the rule, the eyes being conjugately deviated toward the side of the lesion in the resting state. Pupillary size and reactivity to light are usually normal, unless uncal herniation occurs, in which case signs of an ipsilateral third nerve palsy will be present. These abnormalities in oculomotor function are uniformly associated with large hematomas and poor prognoses. Seemingly, total unilateral motor deficit and coma both correlate with large hematoma size and poor functional and vital prognosis (Hier et al., 1977). On the other hand, tiny hematomas can present with pure motor hemiparesis

and evolve in a surprisingly benign fashion (Tapia et al., 1983).

Thalamic hemorrhage is characterized clinically by hemiparesis or hemiplegia in 100% of the cases, virtually all of them with an associated severe hemisensory syndrome (Walshe et al., 1977; Barraquer-Bordas et al., 1981). The severity and distribution of motor and sensory symptoms are similar to those of putaminal hemorrhage; thus they do not help in the differential diagnosis. A homonymous hemianopia is an uncommon finding and tends to be transient. The landmark in the clinical presentation of thalamic hemorrhage is a characteristic combination of upward gaze palsy with miotic unreactive pupils (Walshe et al., 1977). The upward gaze palsy results in an ocular position at rest of conjugate downward deviation.

Some CT aspects of thalamic hemorrhage are of interest: the high frequency of ventricular extension (reflecting the location of the hematoma immediately adjacent to the third ventricle), and the resulting high frequency (about 25%) of hydrocephalus (Barraquer-Bordas et al., 1981) (Fig. 26-12). Treatment of the latter may allow a successful therapeutic intervention in thalamic hemorrhage (Waga et al., 1979). In addition, CT information on the size of the hematoma has prognostic significance; hematomas larger than 3.3 cm were uniformly fatal, whereas all cases with hematomas smaller than 2.7 cm survived in the series of Walshe et al. (1977).

Lobar ICH (also called "slit" hemorrhage) occurs in the subcortical white matter of the cerebral lobes, usually extending longitudinally in a plane parallel to the overlying cortex. They can be located in all cerebral lobes, but have a predilection for the parietal lobe and the adjacent temporal and occipital lobe (Furlan et al., 1979; Kase et al., 1982).

The etiological factors in lobar ICH may differ from those of other forms of ICH, in particular with regard to a less prominent role of arterial hypertension, with significant numbers due to arterial-venous malformations (AVM) (8 to 9%), tumors (7 to 9%), and blood dyscrasias or anticoagulation (5 to 20%), leaving a large group (around 20%) in whom the mechanism for

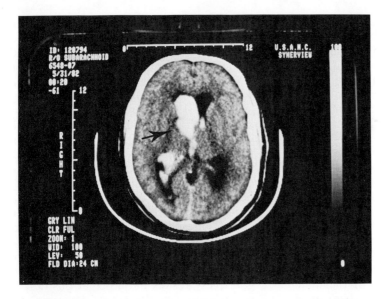

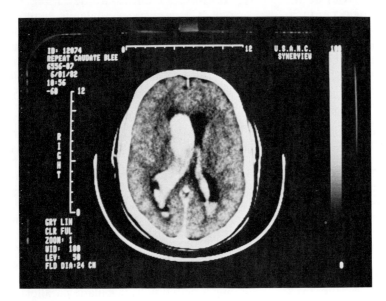

Figure 26-12. (A) CT scan of right anterior thalamic hemorrhage (arrow), with ventricular extension. (B) Massive ventricular hemorrhage with hydrocephalus of lateral ventricles.

the ICH remains unknown (Ropper and Davis, 1980; Kase et al., 1982).

The neurological deficits in lobar ICH depend on the location and size of the hematoma: a sudden hemiparesis, which is more severe in the arm, with ability to walk intact, in frontal hematomas; combined sensory and motor deficits and visual field defects, in parietal hematomas; fluent paraphasic speech with poor comprehension and relatively spared repetition, in left temporal lobe hematomas; homonymous hemianopia, occasionally accompanied by

mild sensory changes, in occipital lobe hematomas (Ropper and Davis, 1980). The prognosis in lobar hematomas is usually less grave than in other forms of ICH (Ropper and Davis, 1980; Kase et al., 1982). The outcome in lobar ICH correlates with the volume of the hematoma by CT. Although small hematomas are regularly associated with good prognosis, the large ones carry a 60% mortality rate. Selected patients with a large hematoma may benefit from surgical clot evacuation, in particular when clinical deterioration continues after admission (Kase et al., 1982).

Cerebellar hemorrhage represents between 5 and 15% of ICH cases (Fisher et al., 1965b; Ott et al., 1974; Kase et al., 1982). The prognosis is good after prompt surgical intervention. The characteristic manifestation at onset is a sudden inability to stand and walk, due to severe disequilibrium, which is commonly associated with headache, vomiting, and dizziness. The physical findings are those of unilateral cerebellar deficit along with variable signs of ipsilateral tegmental pontine involvement (Fisher et al., 1965b; Ott et al., 1974; Brennan and Bergland, 1977), including peripheral facial palsy, ipsilateral horizontal gaze palsy, depressed corneal reflex, and miosis. Along with these focal manifestations, patients with cerebellar hemorrhage may present with variable degrees of decreased alertness.

The clinical course in cerebellar hemorrhage is notoriously unpredictable (Fisher et al., 1965b; Ott et al., 1974): patients who are alert or drowsy on admission can deteriorate suddenly to coma or death without warning, whereas others in a similar clinical status have an uneventful course with complete recovery of function (Fig. 26-13). Although most cases deteriorate early in the course, occasional cases have shown fatal decompensations at a later stage (Brillman, 1979). A prediction of the type of course cannot be made based on clinical parameters, but CT scan provides some useful early predictors of clinical course (Little et al., 1978): hematomas of 3 cm or more in diameter, obstructive hydrocephalus, and ventricular extension, all correlate with a tendency toward deterioration, and thus require surgical intervention. Those lacking these features tend to have a benign course and outcome, and surgical evacuation is not generally required (Heiman and Satya-Murti, 1978).

The least common and most dramatic form of ICH *pontine hemorrhage* results from the rupture of intraparenchymal mid-pontine branches that originate in the basilar artery. This leads initially to hematoma formation around the junction of tegmentum and basis pontis, from where the mass grows into its final oval or round shape, with destruction of most of the pontine parenchyma. This results in the classic combination of signs of involvement of cranial nerve nuclei, long tracts, auto-

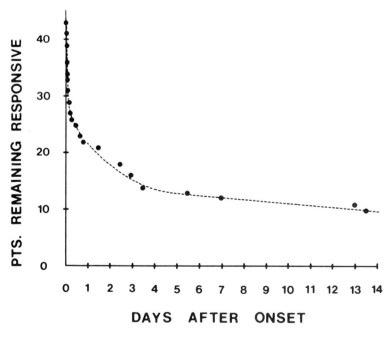

Figure 26-13; Progression to coma as a function of time from onset of cerebellar hemorrhage. Within two days of onset, one-half of the patients have lapsed into coma. (From Ott et al., 1974.)

nomic centers, and structures responsible for maintenance of consciousness (Oku-dera et al., 1978). In addition to this more familiar variety of bilateral massive pon-tine hemorrhage, examples of unilateral or incomplete bleeds occasionally occur. These less common, incomplete forms occur as either unilateral tegmental–basi-lar hematomas or purely tegmental ones (Kase et al., 1980; Caplan and Godwin, 1982). They present acutely with a variety of sensory and motor symptoms, such as facial–appendicular numbness or paresis, in addition to headache, dizziness, and vomiting. Neurological findings are ocu-lomotor abnormalities in various com-binations, such as the "one-and-a-half syndrome," horizontal gaze palsy with isolated contralateral sixth nerve palsy, partial unilateral involvement of vertical eye movements, and ocular bobbing. In addition, trigeminal and facial nuclei are affected bilaterally or, more frequently, unilaterally, along with signs of involve-ment of the pyramidal and cerebellar tracts (Kase et al., 1980; Caplan and Godwin, 1982). Coma, pinpoint pupils, decerebrate rigidity, and hyperthermia are not prominent features of these in-complete forms of pontine ICH.

Although the vital prognosis of pontine hemorrhage as a group remains poor, the growing recognition of these partial forms is now delineating a clinical syndrome of non-lethal pontine hemorrhage (Payne et al., 1978; Kase et al., 1980; Caplan and Godwin, 1982).

Subarachnoid Hemorrhage

Most often the result of a ruptured congeni-tal berry aneurysm, subarachnoid hem-orrhage (SAH) is almost equally distrib-uted in the four decades between ages 30 and 70 (Kunitz et al., in press), and as many as 12% of the cases of SAH collected in the NINCDS Stroke Data Bank project (Ku-nitz et al., in press) occurred in patients younger than 30. On the other hand, cases in elderly patients (70 and older) accounted for less than 6%. Clearly, SAH is a com-mon cause of stroke in the young, being relatively rare in elderly populations.

The most common sites for aneurysm

Table 26-4. Distribution of cerebral aneurysms by artery.

Artery	Symon (1976) (%)	Locksley (1966) (%)
Anterior communicating	39.1	28.0
Distal anterior cerebral	1.6	2.6
Middle cerebral	18.3	20.0
Posterior communicating	32.5	25.0
Terminal carotid	5.0	9.0
Posterior circulation	3.3	3.5

are in the circle of Willis, in the internal carotid, anterior communicating, and middle cerebral artery (Table 26-4). In general, aneurysms less than 3 mm in diameter have a very low risk of rupture, the risk increasing significantly when they reach diameters of 10 mm or more (Wiebers et al., 1981). These lesions are rarely symptomatic prior to their rupture, unless one is so large as to produce erosion of adjacent bone or mass effect. Rupture of the aneurysm characteristically causes the sudden onset of a brutal headache, frequently accompanied by vomiting, and followed by loss of consciousness. As the blood diffuses through the subarachnoid space, the patient will awaken to complain of headache and a stiff neck, and show focal symptoms and signs if an intracere-bral hematoma accompanies the rupture. Such hematomas are uncommon, since the rupture site of the aneurysm, although always in the subarachnoid space, is only occasionally so oriented as to direct blood into the adjacent brain. The most valuable diagnostic test is CT scanning, which fre-quently documents not only the presence of blood in the basal cisterns and convex-ity, but even the aneurysm itself (Ghosh-hajra et al., 1979) and the intracerebral hematoma that may accompany aneurysm rupture (Fig. 26-14).

In addition to the presence of an asso-ciated intracerebral hematoma, SAH can be followed by a number of complications (Crowell and Zervas, 1979). These include (1) aneurysmal re-rupture; (2) obstruction of CSF flow in the subarachnoid space, resulting in communicating hydrocephalus; and (3) vasospasm, which may be suffi-

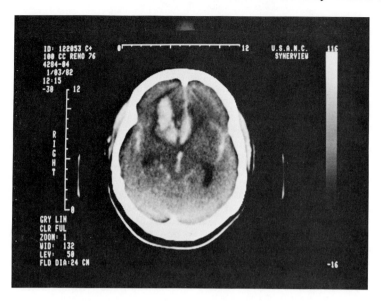

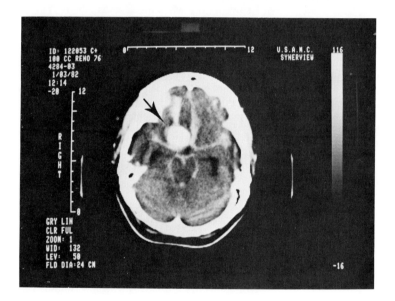

Figure 26-14. (A) CT scan with diffuse subarachnoid hemorrhage and left frontal intraparenchymal hematoma. (B) After contrast infusion, a large enhancing aneurysm is seen at the level of the right internal carotid artery bifurcation (arrow).

ciently severe to produce ischemic brain infarction (its severity is closely correlated with the thickness of the blood layer around a given artery) (Fisher et al., 1980). Symptoms due to vasospasm ordinarily are delayed between three and fourteen days following aneurysm rupture (Fisher et al., 1980). When clinical symptoms of focal deficit appear, vasospasm is always evident angiographically (Fisher et al., 1980) and is expected to have reduced the regional cerebral blood flow in the symptomatic artery to critically insufficient levels.

References

Ackerman, R.H. (1979). A perspective on noninvasive diagnosis of carotid disease. Neurology 29, 615–622.

Ackerman, R.H. and Taveras, J. (1975). Supratrochlear and supraorbital artery flow patterns in carotid disease: Bedside detection and arteriographical correlation. Stroke 6, 228 (Abstr.).

Archer, C.R. and Horenstein, S. (1977). Basilar artery occlusion. Clinical and radiological correlation. Stroke 8, 383–390.

Aring, C.D. (1964). Differential diagnosis of

cerebrovascular stroke. Arch. Int. Med. 113, 195–199.

Balint, R. (1909). Seelenlähmung des "Schauens," optische Ataxie, räumliche Störung der Aufmerksamkeit. Monatsschr. Psychiat. Neurol. 25, 51–81.

Barraquer-Bordas, L., Illa, I., Escartin, A., Ruscalleda, J., and Marti-Villalta, J.L. (1981). Thalamic hemorrhage. A study of 23 patients with diagnosis by computed tomography. Stroke 12, 524–527.

Benson, D.F., Marsden, C.D., and Meadows, J.C. (1974). The amnestic syndrome of posterior cerebral artery occlusion. Acta Neurol. Scand. 50, 133–145.

Berman, S.A., Hayman, L.A., and Hinck, V.C. (1980). Correlation of CT cerebral vascular territories with function: I. Anterior cerebral artery. Amer. J. Neuroradiol. 1, 259–263.

Biemond, A. (1951). Thrombosis of the basilar artery and the vascularization of the brain stem. Brain 74, 300–317.

Bogen, J.E. and Bogen, G.M. (1976). Wernicke's region—where is it? Ann. N.Y. Acad. Sci. 290, 834–843.

Brennan, R.W. and Bergland, R.M. (1977). Acute cerebellar hemorrhage: Analysis of clinical findings and outcome in 12 cases. Neurology 27, 527–532.

Brice, J.G., Dowsett D.J., and Lowe R.D. (1964). Hemodynamic effects of carotid artery stenosis. Br. Med. J. 2, 1363–1366.

Brillman, J. (1979). Acute hydrocephalus and death one month after nonsurgical treatment for acute cerebellar hemorrhage. J. Neurosurg. 50, 374–376.

Brown, J.W. (1972). Aphasia, Apraxia, and Agnosia. C. C. Thomas, Springfield, Ill.

Caplan, L.R. (1973). The frontal-artery sign—a bedside indicator of internal carotid occlusive disease. New Eng. J. Med. 288, 1008–1009.

Caplan, L.R. (1979). Occlusion of the vertebral or basilar artery. Follow up analysis of some patients with benign outcome. Stroke 10, 277–282.

Caplan, L.R. (1980). "Top of the basilar" syndrome. Neurology 30, 72–79.

Caplan, L.R. and Godwin, J.A. (1982). Lateral tegmental brainstem hemorrhages. Neurology 32, 252–260.

Caplan, L.R. and Hedley-White, T. (1974). Cuing and memory dysfunction in alexia without agraphia—a case report. Brain 97, 251-262.

Caplan, L.R. and Rosenbaum, A.E. (1975). Role of cerebral angiography in vertebro-basilar occlusive disease. J. Neurol. Neurosurg. Psychiat. 38, 601–612.

Caplan, L.R. and Sergay, S. (1976). Positional cerebral ischemia. J. Neurol. Neurosurg. Psychiat. 39, 385–391.

Caplan, L.R. and Young, R.R. (1972). EEG findings in certain lacunar stroke syndromes. Neurology 22, 403 (Abstr.).

Castaigne, P., Lhermitte, F., Gautier, J.C., Escourolle, R., and Derouesne, C. (1970). Internal carotid artery occlusion: A study of 61 instances in 50 patients with post-mortem data. Brain 93, 231–258.

Castaigne, P., Lhermitte, F., Gautier, J.C., Escourolle, R., Derouesne, C., Agopian, P., and Popa, C. (1973). Arterial occlusions in the vertebro-basilar system. A study of 44 patients with post-mortem data. Brain 96, 133–154.

Critchley, M. (1930). The anterior cerebral artery and its syndromes. Brain 53, 120–165.

Crowell, R. M. and Zervas, N.T. (1979). Management of intracranial aneurysm. Med. Clin. N. Amer. 63, 695–713.

Currier, R.D. (1969). Syndromes of the medulla oblongata. In Handbook of Clinical Neurology, Vol. 2, Ch. 10, P.J. Vinken and G.W. Bruyn, Eds. North-Holland Publ. Co., Amsterdam, pp. 217–237.

Damasio, H. and Damasio, A.R. (1980). The anatomic basis of conduction aphasia. Brain 103, 337–350.

Damasio, H., Damasio, A.R., Hamsher, K., and Varney, N. (1979). CT scan correlates of aphasia and allied disorders. Neurology 29, 572 (Abstr.).

Dejerine, J. (1914). Semiologie des affections du système nerveux. Masson et Cie. ed., Paris.

Dejerine, J. and Roussy, G. (1906). Le syndrome thalamique. Rev. Neurol. (Paris) 12, 521–532.

Donnan, G.A., Tress, B.M., and Bladin, P.F. (1982). A prospective study of lacunar infarction using computerized tomography. Neurology 32, 49–56.

Duncan, G.W., Gruber, J.O., Dewey, C.F., Myers, G.S., and Lees, R.S. (1975a). Evaluation of carotid stenosis by phonoangiography. New Eng. J. Med. 293, 1124–1128.

Duncan, G.W., Parker, S.W., and Fisher, C.M. (1975b). Acute cerebellar infarction in the PICA territory. Arch. Neurol. 32, 364–368.

Duncan, G.W., Pessin, M.S., Mohr, J.P., and Adams, R.D. (1976). Transient cerebral ischemic attacks. Adv. Int. Med. 21, 1–20.

Escourolle, R., Hauw, J.J., Der Agopian, P.,

and Trelles, L. (1976). Les infarctus bulbaires. Etude des lésions vasculaires dans 23 observations. J. Neurol. Sci. 28, 103–113.

Fisher, C.M. (1951). Occlusion of the internal carotid artery. Arch. Neurol. Psychiat. 69, 346–377.

Fisher, C.M. (1957). Cerebral thromboangiitis obliterans. Medicine (Baltimore) 36, 169–209.

Fisher, C.M. (1961). The pathology and pathogenesis of intracerebral hemorrhage. In "Pathogenesis and Treatment of Cerebrovascular Disease", Ch. 12, W.S. Fields Ed. Charles C. Thomas, Springfield, Ill, pp. 295–317.

Fisher, C.M. (1965a). Lacunes: Small deep cerebral infarcts. Neurology 15, 774–784.

Fisher, C.M. (1965b). Pure sensory stroke involving face, arm, and leg. Neurology 15, 76–80.

Fisher, C.M. (1967). A lacunar stroke. The dysarthria-clumsy hand syndrome. Neurology 17, 614–617.

Fisher, C.M. (1969). The arterial lesions underlying lacunes. Acta Neuropathol. (Berlin) 12, 1–15.

Fisher, C.M. (1970). Facial pulses in internal carotid artery occlusion. Neurology 20, 476–478.

Fisher, C.M. (1971). Pathological observations in hypertensive cerebral hemorrhage. J. Neuropathol. Exptl. Neurol. 30, 536–550.

Fisher, C.M. (1975). Clinical syndromes of cerebral thrombosis, hypertensive hemorrhage, and ruptured saccular aneurysm. Clin. Neurosurg. 22, 117–147.

Fisher, C.M. (1977). Bilateral occlusion of basilar artery branches. J. Neurol. Neurosurg. Psychiat. 40, 1182–1189.

Fisher, C.M. (1978a). Thalamic pure sensory stroke: A pathologic study. Neurology 28, 1141–1144.

Fisher, C.M. (1978b). Ataxic hemiparesis. Arch. Neurol. 35, 126–128.

Fisher, C.M. (1979). Capsular infarcts. Arch. Neurol. 36, 65–73.

Fisher, C.M. and Adams, R.D. (1951). Observations on brain embolism with special reference to the mechanism of hemorrhagic infarction. J. Neuropathol. Exptl. Neurol. 10, 92–94.

Fisher, C.M. and Caplan, L.R. (1971). Basilar artery branch occlusion: A cause of pontine infarction. Neurol. 21, 900–905.

Fisher, C.M. and Cole, M. (1965). Homolateral ataxia and crural paresis. A vascular syndrome. J. Neurol. Neurosurg. Psychiat. 28, 48–55.

Fisher, C.M. and Curry, H.B. (1965). Pure motor hemiplegia of vascular origin. Arch. Neurol. 13, 30–44.

Fisher, C.M., Gore, I., Okabe, N., and White, P.D. (1965). Atherosclerosis of the carotid and vertebral arteries—extracranial and intracranial. J. Neuropathol. Exptl. Neurol. 24, 455–476.

Fisher, C.M., Karnes, W.E., and Kubik, C.S. (1961). Lateral medullary infarction—the pattern of vascular occlusion. J. Neuropathol. Exptl. Neurol. 20, 323–379.

Fisher, C.M., Kistler, J.P., and Davis, J.M. (1980). Relation of cerebral vasospasm to subarachnoid hemorrhage visualized by computed tomographic scanning. Neurosurgery 6, 1–9.

Fisher, C.M., Ojemann, R.G., and Roberson, G.H. (1978). Spontaneous dissection of cervico-cerebral arteries. Can. J. Neurol. Sci. 5, 9–19.

Fisher, C.M., Picard, E.H., Polak, A., Dalal, P., and Ojemann, R.G. (1965b). Acute hypertensive cerebellar hemorrhage: Diagnosis and surgical treatment. J. Nerv. Ment. Dis. 140, 38–57.

Furlan, A.J., Whisnant, J.P., and Elveback, L.R. (1979). The decreasing incidence of primary intracerebral hemorrhage: A population study. Ann. Neurol. 5, 367–373.

Gacs, G., Merei, F.T., and Bodosi, M. (1982). Balloon catheter as a model of cerebral emboli in humans. Stroke 13, 39–42.

Gautier, J.C., Rosa, A., and Lhermitte, F. (1975). Auscultation carotidienne. Corrélations chez 200 patients avec 332 angiographies. Rev. Neurol. (Paris) 131, 175–184.

Geer, J.G., McGill, H.C., Robertson, W.B., and Strong, J.P. (1968). Histologic characteristics of coronary artery fatty streaks. Lab. Invest. 18, 565–570.

Geschwind, N. (1965). Disconnexion syndromes in animals and man. Brain 88, 585–644.

Geschwind, N. (1975). The apraxias: Neural mechanisms of disorders of learned movements. Amer. Sci. 63, 188–195.

Geschwind, N. and Fusillo, M. (1966). Color naming defects in association with alexia. Arch. Neurol. 15, 137–146.

Geschwind, N. and Kaplan, E. (1962). A human cerebral deconnection syndrome. Neurology 12, 675–685.

Ghatak, N.R. (1975). Pathology of cerebral embolization caused by nonthrombotic agents. Human pathol. 6, 599–610.

Ghoshhajra, K., Scotti, L., Marasco, J., and Baghai-Naiini, P. (1979). CT detection of intracranial aneurysms in subarachnoid hemorrhage. Amer. J. Roentgenol. 132, 613–616.

Gore, I. and Collins, D.P. (1960). Spontaneous atheromatous embolization. Review of the literature and report of 16 additional cases. Amer. J. Clin. Pathol. 33, 416–426.

Goto, K., Tagawa, K., Uemura, K., Ishii, K., and Takahashi, S. (1979). Posterior cerebral artery occlusion: Clinical, computed tomographic, and angiographic correlation. Radiology 132, 357–368.

Gross, C.R., Kase, C.S., Mohr, J.P., Cunningham, S.C., and Baker, W.E. (1984). Stroke in south Alabama: Incidence and diagnostic features. Stroke (in press).

Hansen, B.S. and Marquardsen, J. (1977). Incidence of stroke in Frederiksberg, Denmark. Stroke 8, 663–665.

Hauw, J.J., Der Agopian, P., Trelles, J.L., and Escourolle, R. (1976) Les infarctus bulbaires. Etude systematique de la topographie lésionnelle dans 49 cas. J. Neurol. Sci. 28, 83–102.

Hayman, L.A., Berman, S.A., and Hinck, V.C. (1981). Correlation of CT cerebral vascular territories with function: II. Posterior cerebral artery. Amer. J. Neuroradiol. 2, 219–225.

Heilman, K.M. and Valenstein, E. (1979). Clinical Neuropsychology. Oxford University Press, New York.

Heiman, T.D. and Satya-Murti, S. (1978) Benign cerebellar hemorrhages. Ann. Neurol. 3, 366–368.

Herman, B., Schulte, B.P.M., van Luijk, J.H., Leyten, A.C.M., and Frenken, C.W.G.M. (1980). Epidemiology of stroke in Tilburg, The Netherlands. The population-based stroke incidence register: 1. Introduction and preliminary results. Stroke 11, 162–165.

Heros, R.C. (1979). Cerebellar infarction resulting from traumatic occlusion of the vertebral artery. J. Neurosurg. 51, 111–113.

Heros, R.C. (1982). Cerebellar hemorrhage and infarction. Stroke 13, 106–109.

Hier, D.B., Davis, K.R., Richardson, E.P., and Mohr, J.P. (1977). Hypertensive putaminal hemorrhage. Ann. Neurol. 1, 152–159.

Hinton, R.C., Mohr, J.P., Ackerman, R.H., Adair, L.B., and Fisher, C.M. (1979). Symptomatic middle cerebral artery stenosis. Ann. Neurol. 5, 152–157.

Horenstein, S., Chamberlain, W., and Conomy, J. (1967). Infarction of the fusiform and calcarine regions: Agitated delirium and hemianopia. Trans. Amer. Neurol. Assoc. 92, 85–89.

Javid, H., Ostermiller, W.E., and Hengesh, J.W. (1970). Natural history of carotid bifurcation atheroma. Surgery 67, 80–86.

Jones, H.R., Millikan, C.H., and Sandok, B.A. (1980). Temporal profile (clinical course) of acute vertebrobasilar system cerebral infarction. Stroke 11, 173–177.

Jones, H.R., Siekert, R.G., and Geraci, J.E. (1969). Neurologic manifestations of bacterial endocarditis. Ann. Int. Med. 71, 21–28.

Kase, C.S., Maulsby, G.O., and Mohr, J.P. (1980). Partial pontine hematomas. Neurology 30, 652–655.

Kase, C.S., Maulsby, G.O., DeJuan, E., and Mohr, J.P. (1981b). Hemichorea-hemiballism and lacunar infarction in the basal ganglia. Neurology 31, 452–455.

Kase, C.S., Varakis, J.N., Stafford, J.R., and Mohr, J.P. (1983). Medial medullary infarction from fibrocartilaginous embolism to the anterior spinal artery. Stroke 14, 413–418.

Kase, C.S., White, R.L., Vinson, T.L., and Eichelberger, R.P. (1981a). Shotgun pellet embolus to the middle cerebral artery. Neurology 31, 458–461.

Kase, C.S., Williams, J.P., Wyatt, D.A., and Mohr, J.P. (1982). Lobar intracerebral hematomas: Clinical and CT analysis of 22 cases. Neurology 32, 1146–1150.

Kistler, J.P., Lees, R.S., Friedman, J., Pessin, M.S., Mohr, J.P., Roberson, G.H., and Ojemann, R.G. (1978). The bruit of carotid stenosis versus radiated basal heart murmurs. Differentiation by phonoangiography. Circulation 57, 975–981.

Kreindler, A. and Fradis, A. (1968). Performances in aphasia. Gauthier-Villars, Paris.

Kubik, C.S. and Adams, R.D. (1946). Occlusion of the basilar artery: A clinical and pathological study. Brain 69, 73–121.

Kunitz, S.C., Gross, C.R., Heyman, A., Kase, C.S., Mohr, J.P., Price, T.R., and Wolf, P.A. (1984). The Pilot Stroke Data Bank: Definition, design, and data. Stroke (in press).

Kurtzke J.F. (1969). Epidemiology of Cerebrovascular Disease. Springer-Verlag, Berlin.

Lees, R.S. and Kistler, J.P. (1978). Carotid Phonoangiography. In "Noninvasive Diagnostic Techniques in Vascular Disease," E. Bernstein, Ed. C.V. Mosby, St. Louis, pp. 187–194.

Lehrich, J.R., Winkler, G.F., and Ojemann, R.G. (1970). Cerebellar infarction with brainstem compression.. Diagnosis and surgical treatment. Arch. Neurol. 22, 490–498.

Leicester, J., Sidman, M., Stoddard, L.T., and Mohr, J.P. (1971). The nature of aphasic responses. Neuropsychologia 9, 141–155.

Lhermitte, F., Gautier, J.C., Derouesne, C., and Guiraud, B. (1968). Ischemic accidents in the middle cerebral artery territory. Arch. Neurol. 19, 248–256.

Liepmann, H. (1915). Diseases of the Brain. In C.W. Burr Ed. Curschmann's Textbook on Nervous Diseases, Vol. 1, Blakiston, Philadelphia, pp. 467–480.

Little, J.R., Tubman, D.E., and Ethier, R. (1978). Cerebellar hemorrhage in adults. Diagnosis by computerized tomography. J. Neurosurg. 48, 575–579.

Locksley, H.B. (1966). Report on the cooperative study of intracranial aneurysms and subarachnoid hemorrhage. Section V, Part 1: Natural history of subarachnoid hemorrhage, intracranial aneurysms and arteriovenous malformations. J. Neurosurg. 25, 219–239.

Luria, A. R. (1966). Higher Cortical Functions in Man. Basic Books, New York.

Matsumoto, N., Whisnant, J.P., Kurland, L.T., and Okazaki, H. (1973). Natural history of stroke in Rochester, Minnesota, 1955 through 1969: An extension of a previous study, 1945 through 1954. Stroke 4, 20–29.

Mazzochi, F. and Vignolo, L.A. (1979). Localisation of lesions in aphasia: Clinical-CT scan correlations in stroke patients. Cortex 15, 627–653.

Milner, B. (1966). Amnesia following operations on the temporal lobes. In "Amnesia", C.M.W. Whitty and O.L. Zangwill, Eds. Butterworth, London, pp. 109–133.

Mizutani, T., Lewis, R.A., and Gonatas, N.K. (1980). Medial medullary syndrome in a drug abuser. Arch. Neurol. 37, 425–428.

Mohr, J.P. (1969). Distal field infarction. Neurology 19, 279 (Abstr.).

Mohr, J.P. (1973). Rapid amelioration of motor aphasia. Arch. Neurol. 28, 77–82.

Mohr, J.P. (1979). Neurological complications of cardiac valvular disease and cardiac surgery including systemic hypotension. In "Handbook of Clinical Neurology", Vol. 38, P.J. Vinken and G.W. Bruyn, Eds. North-Holland Publ. Co., Amsterdam, pp. 143–171.

Mohr, J.P. (1980). The vascular basis of Wernicke aphasia. Trans. Amer. Neurol. Assoc. 133–137.

Mohr, J.P. (1982). Lacunes. Stroke 13, 3–11.

Mohr, J.P., Caplan, L.R., Melski, J.W., Goldstein, R.J., Duncan, G.W., Kistler, J.P., Pessin, M.S., and Bleich, H.L. (1978a).

The Harvard cooperative stroke registry: A prospective registry. Neurology 28, 754–762.

Mohr, J.P. and Kase, C.S. (1983). Cerebrovascular Disorders. In The Clinical Neurosciences, R.N. Rosenberg, Ed., Churchill Livingstone, New York.

Mohr, J.P., Kase, C.S, Meckler, R.J., and Fisher, C.M. (1977). Sensorimotor stroke due to thalamocapsular ischemia. Arch. Neurol. 34, 739–741.

Mohr, J.P., Kase, C.S., Wolf, P.A., Price, T.A., Heyman, A., Dambrosia, J.H., and Kunitz, S. (1982). Lacunes in the NINCDS Pilot Stroke Data Bank. Ann. Neurol. 12, 84 (Abstr.).

Mohr, J.P., Leicester, J., Stoddard, L.T., and Sidman, M. (1971). Right hemianopia with memory and color deficits in circumscribed left posterior cerebral artery territory infarction. Neurology 21, 1104–1113.

Mohr, J.P., Pessin, M.S., Finkelstein, S., Funkenstein, H.H., Duncan, G.W., and Daris, K.R. (1978b). Broca aphasia: Pathologic and clinical aspects. Neurology 28, 311–324.

Momose, K.J. and Lehrich, J.R. (1973). Acute cerebellar infarction presenting as a posterior fossa mass. Radiology 109, 343–352.

Moncada, S. and Vane, J.R. (1978). Unstable metabolites of arachidonic acid and their role in haemostasis and thrombosis. Br. Med. Bull. 34, 129–135.

Moscow, N.P. and Newton, T.H. (1973). Angiographic implications in diagnosis and prognosis of basilar artery occlusion. Amer. J. Roentgenol. 119, 597–604.

Naeser, M.A. and Hayward, R.W. (1978). Lesion localization in aphasia with cranial computed tomography and Boston Diagnostic Aphasia Exam. Neurology 28, 545–551.

National Heart and Lung Institute Task Force on Arteriosclerosis (1971). National Institute of Health, Bethesda, Maryland, Department of Health, Education and Welfare Publ. No. (NIH) 72–219.

Okudera, T., Uemura, K., Nakajima, K., Fukasawa, H., Ito, Z., and Kutsuzawa, T. (1978). Primary pontine hemorrhage: Correlations of pathologic features with postmortem microangiographic and vertebral angiographic studies. Mt. Sinai J. Med. 45, 305–321.

Ott, K.H., Kase, C.S., Ojemann, R.G., and Mohr, J.P. (1974). Cerebellar hemorrhage: Diagnosis and treatment. Arch. Neurol. 31, 160–167.

Patrick, B.K., Ramirez-Lassepas, M., and

Snyder, B.D. (1980). Temporal profile of vertebrobasilar territory infarction. Prognostic implications. Stroke 11, 643–648.

Payne, H.A., Maravilla, K.R., Levinstone, A., Heuter J., and Tindall, R.S.A. (1978). Recovery from primary pontine hemorrhage. Ann. Neurol. 4, 557–558.

Peltier, L.F., Collins, J.A., Evarts, C.M., and Sevitt, S. (1974). Fat embolism. Arch. Surg. 109, 12–16.

Pessin, M.S., Duncan, G.W., Mohr, J.P., and Poskanzer, D.C. (1977). Clinical and angiographic features of carotid transient ischemic attacks. New Eng. J. Med. 296, 358–362.

Pessin, M.S., Duncan, G.W., Davis, K.R., Hinton, R.C., Roberson, G.H., and Mohr, J.P. (1980). Angiographic appearance of carotid occlusion in acute stroke. Stroke 11, 485–487.

Pessin, M.S., Hinton, R.C., Davis, K.R., Duncan, G.W., Roberson, G.H., Ackerman, R.H., and Mohr, J.P. (1979). Mechanisms of acute carotid stroke. Ann. Neurol. 6, 245–252.

Pullicino, P., Nelson, R.F., Kendall, B.E., and Marshall, J. (1980). Small deep infarcts diagnosed on computed tomography. Neurology 30, 1090–1096.

Rascol, A., Clanet, M., Manelfe, C., Guiraud, B., and Bonafe, A. (1982). Pure motor hemiplegia: CT study of 30 cases. Stroke 13, 11–17.

Roch-LeCours, H. and Lhermitte, F. (1976). The pure form of the phonetic disintegration syndrome (pure anarthria). Brain Lang. 3, 88–113.

Ropper, A.H. and Davis, K.R. (1980). Lobar cerebral hemorrhages: Acute clinical syndromes in 26 cases. Ann. Neurol. 8, 141–147.

Ropper, A.H., Fisher, C.M., and Kleinman, G.M. (1979). Pyramidal infarction in the medulla: A case of pure motor hemiplegia sparing the face. Neurology 29, 91–95.

Scotti, G., Spinnler, H., Sterzi, R., and Vallar, G. (1980). Cerebellar softening. Ann. Neurol. 8, 133–140.

Sherman, D.G., Hart, R.G., and Easton, J.D. (1981). Abrupt change in head position and cerebral infarction. Stroke 12, 2–6.

Spertrell, R.B. and Ransom, B.R. (1979). Dysarthria-clumsy hand syndrome produced by capsular infarct. Neurology 6, 264–268.

Sundt, T.M., Whisnant, J.P., Piepgras, D.G., Campbell, J.K., and Holman, C.B. (1978). Intracranial bypass grafts for vertebralbasilar ischemia. Mayo Clin. Proc. 53, 12–18.

Symmonds, C. and Mackenzie, I. (1957). Bilateral loss of vision from cerebral infarction. Brain 80, 415–454.

Symon, L. (1976). Subarachnoid haemorrhage from intracranial aneurysm and angioma. In "Cerebral Arterial Disease", Ch. 12, R.W.R. Russell, Ed. Churchill Livingstone, New York, p. 231–261.

Sypert, G.W. and Alvord, E.C. (1975). Cerebellar infarction. A clinicopathologic study. Arch. Neurol. 32, 357–363.

Tapia, J.F., Kase, C.S., Sawyer, R.H., and Mohr, J.P. (1983). Hypertensive putaminal hemorrhage presenting as pure motor hemiparesis, Stroke 14, 505–506.

Ueda, K., Omae, T., Hirota, Y., Takeshita, M., Katsuki, S., Tanaka, K., and Enjoji, M. (1981). Decreasing trend in incidence and mortality from stroke in Hisayama residents, Japan. Stroke 12, 154–160.

Victor, M., Angevine, J.B., and Mancall, E.L. (1961). Memory loss with lesions of the hippocampal formation. Arch. Neurol. 5, 244-263.

Waddington, M.M. and Ring, B.A. (1968). Syndromes of occlusions of middle cerebral artery branches. Angiographic and clinical correlation. Brain 91, 685–696.

Waga, S., Okada, M., and Yamamoto, Y. (1979). Reversibility of Parinaud syndrome in thalamic hemorrhage. Neurology 29, 407–409.

Walshe, T.M., Davis, K.R., and Fisher, C.M. (1977). Thalamic hemorrhage: A computed tomographic-clinical correlation. Neurology 27, 217–222.

Weisberg, L.A. (1979). Computed tomography and pure motor hemiparesis. Neurology 29, 490–495.

Weisberg, L.A. (1982). Lacunar infarcts. Clinical and computed tomographic correlations. Arch. Neurol. 39, 37–40.

Wiebers, D.O., Whisnant, J.P., and O'Fallon, W.M. (1981). The natural history of unruptured intracranial aneurysms. New Eng. J. Med. 304, 696–698.

Wolf, P.A., Dawber, T.R., Thomas, H.E., Colton, T., and Kannel, W.B. (1977). Epidemiology of Stroke. In Advances in Neurology, Vol. 16, R.A. Thompson and J.R. Green, Eds. Raven Press, New York.

Wyllie, J. (1894). The Disorders of Speech. Oliver & Boyd, Edinburgh.

27. Cerebrovascular Diseases in the Elderly: Rehabilitation

JOHN E. SARNO

In view of the fact that most stroke patients are in the older age range, one may conclude that much of what has been written on the subject of stroke rehabilitation pertains to the geriatric patient. In one large series of 578 patients, 76.5% were between the ages of 60 and 99 (Moskowitz et al., 1972). Yet to my knowledge, there has been no study concerned exclusively with the rehabilitation of the elderly stroke patient. Studies specifically addressed to the ability to predict which patients are appropriate for rehabilitation services have failed to produce clear-cut guidelines and have not identified age as a negative prognostic factor (Lehmann et al., 1975; Gersten, 1975; Anderson et al., 1974). It has been stated (Anderson and Kottke, 1978) that any patient who can comprehend and follow two- or three-step verbal or nonverbal directions and can remember what has transpired from one day to the next should be given a trial of rehabilitation, and in a brief time will demonstrate whether or not he/she is an apt candidate. This attitude seems logical, since chronological age does not define the patient's physiological and psychological condition nor the severity and location of the lesion, factors that would appear to be important in the outcome of rehabilitation.

Since the elderly patient is not disqualified from attempts at rehabilitation because of age per se, it behooves the practitioner to study each one according to the details of his case. This is appropriate in the interest of both science and humanitarianism. When age is reflected in deteriorated physiology or psychology, the unsuitability for rehabilitation efforts is apparent.

Another question of a general nature has to do with what might be coldly termed the "cost effectiveness" of rehabilitation services. This has wide ramifications involving such factors as availability of medical services, competition for those services, money to pay for them, and cultural and social practices. Studies have indicated that adequate numbers of patients live long enough to warrant rehabilitation measures so that they can be sufficiently independent to live outside of an institution, thereby reducing the cost of their care to society (Anderson et al., 1977). It has been further pointed out that the high cost of rehabilitation services is amply repaid by the lower costs of maintaining such an individual later (Kottke, 1974). Whether or not these conclusions can be substantiated, there is little question that rehabilitation services are humanitarian. One does not question the high cost of cardiac surgery, for example, because it has become an imperative when indicated, and it would be considered barbaric to deprive someone of such a procedure. With some change in attitude, the same might be said of the stroke patient. Assisting someone to a greater measure of independence, interest, and dignity in the remaining years of life should rank as highly as any other medical objective. What can justifiably be questioned and still requires a great deal of study is how to provide these services in the most parsimonious and effective way. Although there have been claims that stroke patients can be adequately rehabilitated at a reasonable cost (Feigenson, 1981; Lehmann et al., 1975), clinical experience suggests that the problem is more complex than it appears, since most of these studies are concerned with physical accomplishments, important to be sure, but by no means the complete story. An example of the point is the report of Andrews and Stewart (1979) that stroke patients were more independent in a treatment setting than they were at home, preferring to depend on family members to assist them than to put their newly learned skills to use. On the other hand, Anderson et al. (1977) have demonstrated that patients who are properly trained and followed with adequate psychosocial support do maintain their gains; the value of this study is enhanced by the fact that the criteria for success included certain "quality of life" measures as well as physical measures.

Thus, experience to date does not disqualify the elderly stroke patient from receiving rehabilitation services. Although the aged are not usually at a life-stage where employment, which is the ultimate rehabilitation goal, is an issue, they deserve to be assisted to as independent, satisfying, and dignified a life as can be provided by modern medicine. Because of wide variation in physiological and social factors, it should be assumed that all elderly patients, except the demented or psychotic, are entitled at the least to a trial of rehabilitation.

The material that follows has been organized according to a temporal format rather than the more usual system-by-system treatment. This approach was chosen because it seems more likely to highlight the most important elements of the rehabilitation process. Recovery will be discussed within a framework of three phases: an early phase beginning at the point at which the patient has stabilized medically and may be out of bed for varying periods during the day, extending to the time when the basic skills of transferring, walking, and self-care have been acquired. The end-point of this phase is not always clear cut and raises questions about the capacity of the patient for further improvement and the ability of the health care system to provide further services. These kinds of questions should be addressed and clarified if possible. This phase usually occupies the first six months, post-onset.

The second or intermediate stage extends roughly from the sixth to the twelfth month. It is the period during which the patient is first exposed to life in the home and the community. Some form of treatment or psychosocial attention may be provided, but more often than not, it is unavailable.

The third phase encompasses that indeterminate period that comprises the remainder of the patient's life.

Phase One

One of the primary concerns of the early phase of rehabilitation is the prevention of contractures or deformities resulting from malposition of limb segments. These include shortening of the Achilles tendon on the hemiparetic side; knee and hip flexion contractures; finger, wrist, or elbow flexion contractures; and stretching of the glenohumeral joint capsule, with subluxation of the humeral head. All these deformities except the last can be avoided by appropriate nursing and physical therapeutic attention. They are more likely to occur in the patient who spends a great deal of time in bed or immobile.

It is common practice to attempt to prevent subluxation of the humeral head through the use of slings, some of which are elaborate devices. The literature is contradictory on the efficacy of slings; it is the author's impression that subluxation cannot be prevented. If there is sufficient tone in the muscles that hold the humeral head in the glenoid fossa, the deformity will not occur; if not, stretching will occur despite the best sling. It may be of value to encourage contraction of the shoulder musculature many times during the day, although reminders to exercise are usually required. However, it has not appeared that subluxation of the shoulder adversely affects function. It is usually present in association with severe paresis of the limb, in which case its occurrence is academic. A sling may be useful for other reasons: to prevent edema in the dependent hand or to give the patient better balance in early walking attempts. Some patients reject slings for either physical or psychological reasons and in our experience there is no sufficiently compelling indication for their use to force the issue.

Moskowitz and Porter (1963) have described peripheral neuropathies in the paretic upper limb. Though these are relatively uncommon, one should be aware of the possibility so that measures can be taken to avoid unnecessary complications.

The so-called shoulder–hand syndrome has been mentioned as a serious complication in the hemiparetic upper limb (Moskowitz et al., 1958). It is difficult to be sure of the existence of a reflex sympathetic dystrophy in patients who may have pain for other reasons. The diagnosis should perhaps be reserved for those with unequivocal spotty demineralization of the carpal bones. We have seen a number of stroke patients with the tension myositis syndrome (TMS) (J. Sarno, 1981), who have had shoulder, arm, and hand pain. The syndrome is most likely an autonomically mediated ischemic phenomenon and is induced by anxiety; it occurs in patients of all ages (J. Sarno, 1981), although there are no statistics on its incidence in stroke patients. The great anxiety of many patients makes its occurrence logical and the ability to diminish the symptomatology with appropriate treatment further supports the diagnosis. Although it is mediated autonomically, sympatholytic drugs have not been helpful. Counseling and physical therapy have been found to be effective, the latter consisting of heat modalities and massage and vigorous exercise, when possible, to reduce local ische-

mia. Since TMS is a species of sympathetic dystrophic process, it is not far removed pathologically from the traditional diagnosis of reflex sympathetic dystrophy, and the physical treatment is similar.

Prevention of foot-drop and some of the flexion deformities noted above often require the use of splints, particularly for periods when the limb is at rest. These may be required for many months in the upper limb, particularly, when spasticity is severe. They are rarely necessary for the ankle, once active rehabilitation has begun. Orthotic devices for the ankle to facilitate walking will be discussed later.

The Motor System

Let us turn now to a consideration of the motor deficit associated with stroke and what can be done to modify it. The various clinical syndromes have been described elsewhere in this volume, but two prime questions remain to be answered: What is the character of the motor deficit produced by the stroke? and What, if anything, can be done to ameliorate it?

The paper by Twitchell in 1951, describing the restoration of motor function following hemiplegia, remains the most authoritative guide to what can be expected in the natural evolution of a stroke. A great deal has been learned about the functon of the motor system since that paper was published, but to my knowledge, no report has improved on Twitchell's description. More recently, Kottke (1975) reviewed contemporary concepts of sensorimotor function, particularly in dissolution, and advanced his views on how disordered motor function could be improved through "neurophysiological therapy."

Drawing on these papers, let us look at the stroke patient during the earliest phase of rehabilitation, for it is during this period that the motor picture will stabilize and the job of physical restoration will be defined. Following a brief period of flaccidity in the involved limbs, the patterns of motor activity follow an orderly sequence in which spasticity, reflex movements, and willed voluntary movement coexist in varying degrees, depending upon the magnitude of recovery (Twitchell, 1951). Twitchell points out that even when the patient recovers rapidly and completely, close observation reveals a regular sequence of events that characterize recovery. He plotted the appearance of finger jerks, spasticity, proprioceptive facilitation, the traction response, flexor and extensor synergies, voluntary willed movement, tactile facilitation, and the grasp reflex and described a variety of recovery courses. Further, the appearance and persistence of these various phenomena can be roughly correlated with recovery of voluntary movement.

In most cases, flaccidity lasted for 48 hours; spasticity was noted to appear between two to twenty days, and the first voluntary movements from six to thirty-three days after onset.

The early appearance and mildness of spasticity and resistance to passive stretch presages better eventual voluntary control, as do the early appearance of proprioceptive facilitation and the traction response, the latter two being the most dependable prognosticators. It was noted that recovery events in the upper limb were associated with prehension and that the flexor synergy was, therefore, pre-eminent there. In the leg, extensor patterns were dominant, undoubtedly related to the reflex mechanism of walking.

A concept of clinical importance reiterated by Twitchell (originally advanced by Walshe and further clarified by Sherrington) asserts that spasticity is not a phenomenon apart from willed movement, and therefore capable of being modified independently, but rather that it represents diffuse hyperactivity resulting from the loss of cerebral control and must be harnessed if possible.

One fact of great clinical significance rarely mentioned in the literature is that severity of spasticity increases with anxiety. This appears to be true of all abnormal involuntary movements associated with alterations of brain function (for example, tremor, chorea, athetosis, ataxia); more broadly applied, the severity of all kinds of neural deficits intensifies and the quality of performance deteriorates with anxiety. Since this is to some extent true also of the non-brain–damaged, it is understandable; however, the phenomenon may make the difference between functioning and not functioning in certain circumstances, or it may significantly modify function. It is thus very important clinically.

The richness of detail in Twitchell's study is no doubt of greater interest to the neurophysiologist than the clinician. From a practical point of view, lower limb function is generally better preserved than is arm function; in both cases, weakness is more marked distally than proximally. Because of reflex phenomena, patients can often walk despite little or no voluntary power during the early months after onset.

Traditional methods of physical and occupational therapy have emphasized restoration or maintenance of a normal range of motion, improvement of function through strengthening paretic limbs, using the non-hemiplegic limbs in a compensatory fashion, and practice in the performance of such basic activities as walking, dressing, and grooming. However, as knowledge of the motor system has increased, treatment approaches have emerged in which rationales focus on various aspects of this new knowledge. Implicit in these methods is the idea that motor deficits can be circumvented or overcome through prolonged treatment, in the course of which more normal patterns become established. Fundamental to therapies based upon this concept are certain assumptions:

1. Impaired motor function can be augmented by facilatory or inhibitory reflexes.
2. These reflexes exert their effect by utilizing "unused" intact pathways in the central nervous system (for example, the extrapyramidal), producing motor activity that approximates that which existed prior to brain damage.
3. To see results, these reflex patterns must be joined to volitional efforts and repeated many times over (a million repetitions is an oft-used figure).
4. In time, the process comes under greater volitional control and reflexes need no longer be used to initiate motor activity.
5. Undesirable involuntary movements, such as ataxia, spasticity, and dystonia, can be modified through the elicitation

of certain spinal reflexes, to inhibit the unrestricted excitation occasioned by brain damage.

A variety of workers have developed treatment systems based upon different aspects of this general concept. These include Fay (1954), Kabat (1965), Bobath (1979), and Kottke (1975). Although the neurophysiological concepts for these therapeutic techniques are probably sound, based as they are upon the laboratory work of reputable neurophysiologists, the therapeutic hypotheses derived from them require validation. To my knowledge, there are no controlled studies that demonstrate the effectiveness of any one of these systems. This is unfortunate, since there is good anecdotal evidence that some of them are effective. For the most part, these therapies have been carried out primarily by their originators, but in recent years they have been more generally used. Practical problems are formidable, the chief among these being the length of time and expense required. There is little doubt that those patients fortunate enough to be the recipients of such treatment profit both physically and psychologically, but whether physical improvement can be attributed to the use of these techniques per se remains to be demonstrated. For a more detailed discussion of both conventional and facilitation therapeutic techniques, the reader may wish to consult Kottke (1975), Swenson (1978), and Harris (1978).

What seems quite clear is that the stroke patient in the early phase of rehabilitation requires a physical program with certain specific goals: to maintain full range of motion; to enhance volitional motor activity, generally; to improve walking ability; to improve functional dexterity of the involved upper limb, if possible; and to work on producing independence in all of the so-called activities of daily living, including the ability to transfer, groom, bathe, dress, and eat. The latter are still primarily the result of teaching the patient compensatory or adaptational techniques, rather than restoring function in the involved limbs. These training programs are carried out by physical and occupational therapists whose skills and devotion are important factors in the degree of success achieved by the patient.

Brief mention should be made of the importance of orthotic devices to assist walking. What is required is a light, comfortable device that will resist a deforming posture of the foot–ankle complex while the patient is walking. Experience suggests that plastic devices probably serve best with this population of patients (J. Sarno, 1973; J. Sarno and Lehneis, 1971), for they are light, cosmetically acceptable, and mechanically sound. There are three basic devices: the posterior leaf spring (PLS) orthosis designed to prevent the foot-drop occasioned by weakness of the dorsiflexors of the foot; the spiral orthosis for patients with more global weakness of the foot–ankle musculature; the solid ankle orthosis for those patients in whom the deforming effect of severe spasticity requires the elimination of all ankle movement so that there is adequate stability during the stance phase of gait on the involved side. Not infrequently, patients who would otherwise qualify for a PLS or spiral orthosis have a marked tendency to equinovarus posturing throughout the gait cycle and require a modification to counteract this tendency; hence, there are hemi-PLS and hemi-spiral orthoses so designed to more effectively maintain the foot in a neutral, and therefore more stable position. It is rarely desirable to employ an orthotic device to prevent knee buckling during the stance phase on the paretic side, since this usually impedes more than it helps attempts at walking. Often the patient will develop the capacity to bear weight on the involved leg over time. This may occur despite the total absence of voluntary power through the influence of spinal and supraspinal reflexes that tend to produce reflex extension in the involved limb. In fact, this extensor posture tends to persist throughout the gait cycle, interfering with the movement of the leg forward during the swing phase of gait.

Because advances in the rehabilitation of the stroke patient have been slow and fragmented, there is considerable variation in the type and effectiveness of physical restoration programs in rehabilitation settings. To a large extent, physical restoration may represent the totality of rehabilitation efforts in patients without speech disorders; speech therapy for the latter is now commonly employed. For example, in a report on outcome studies and guidelines for alternative levels of care for stroke patients (Feigenson, 1981), the outcome measures used to predict success in rehabilitation were ADL (activities of daily living) status, ambulation ability, and length of hospital stay. One cannot criticize this, for physical restoration is basic. There are, however, other factors that strongly affect the quality of the elderly stroke patient's life, to which we shall address ourselves.

Emotional Sequelae

Let us now consider a subject of major importance in the recovery and rehabilitation process: the effect of a stroke on personality and emotional behavior. The literature on the subject, combined with clinical experience, suggests that emotional reactions play a dominant role throughout the recovery process, since they will largely determine the degree of effort put forth by the patient as well as his/her adaptation to persistent deficits and continuing physical and social restrictions.

Immediately after onset, patients may be confused or apathetic, but as awareness increases, these give way to a variety of reactions. Anxiety, in some patients to the point of terror (Hodgins, 1964), is common and may express itself as inattentiveness, insomnia, psychosomatic phenomena, phobias, obsessional states, or neurasthenia. Catastrophic reactions, first described by Goldstein (1942), are particularly liable to occur in patients with left hemisphere pathology, many of whom are aphasic; they are characterized by uncontrollable emotional outbursts, some of which may be violent (Gainotti, 1972).

One of the most pervasive and destructive emotional responses is depression. Horenstein (1970) suggested that it represented a grief reaction, characteristic of any catastrophic illness, and related in severity to the quality and quantity of the neural deficit, level of awareness, premorbid capacity for adaptation, intellectual level, and feelings of self-worth. These, in turn, are further modified by the patient's personal and social situation, the loss of accustomed roles in the family and the community, and the quality of family relationships. Ullman (1962) found that the persistence of disability (including aphasia) usually led to feelings of depression, hopelessness, and futility. He, too, described depression in stroke as reactive, but distinct from that seen in the usual psychiatric population, in that real problems made it difficult to distinguish between appropriate feelings of despair and depression attributed to premorbid personality.

Denial of illness based upon psychological, rather than perceptual phenomena has been described by a number of workers (Horenstein, 1970; Baretz and Stephenson, 1976; Gainotti, 1972; Ullman, 1962; Weinstein and Kahn, 1955). Though it is of practical importance in that it may retard progress in the treatment program, Baretz and Stephenson (1976) see it as a necessary stage for many patients who would otherwise be overwhelmed by depression. It is essential that those treating the patient recognize this and deal with it constructively, rather than allow the therapeutic relationship to deteriorate as a result of the patient's resistance or hostility (Baretz and Stephenson, 1976; Horenstein, 1970).

A psychoanalytically oriented analysis of a group of aphasic patients revealed a tendency to regressive behavior with manifestations of dependency, denial, projection, and exaggeration of deficits (Friedman, 1961). Most of these patients tended to avoid personal contact because of marked loss of self-esteem.

A study of emotional behavior correlated with locus of lesion found that those with left hemishere damage manifested catastrophic or anxiety-depression symptoms more commonly than those with nondominant hemisphere pathology; the latter had indifference reactions more frequently (Gainotti, 1972). There were further differences resulting from the absence, presence, and type of aphasia. These observations suggest that the right hemisphere may play a role in the elaboration of emotional responses, whereas the left side appears to monitor emotionality.

Latent psychosis precipitated by a stroke and psychiatric hospitalization due to deep depression secondary to aphasia have been described (Ullman, 1962).

An almost universal complaint among stroke patients is that of fatigue. It is common during the early months, but it may persist, sometimes for years. A metabolic explanation has never been demonstrated, suggesting that it may be a response to anxiety and/or depression.

Experience suggests that the management of the emotional reactions to stroke is best incorporated in the patient's daily therapeutic regimen (Horenstein, 1970). That is, the attending physician and the therapists working with the patient must be sensitive to his/her feelings and try to modify them by reassurance, information, and, perhaps best of all, commiseration, for the devastated patient responds better to this than expressions of hopefulness and "be of good cheer." Personal accounts of the stroke experience (Wint, 1967) document the depth of feelings of depression, hopelessness, and loneliness, and patients derive comfort from knowing that those around them are aware of those feelings.

Aphasia

The literature on recovery and rehabilitation in aphasia since World War II is based on the study of post-stroke patients primarily; the majority of these are in the older age group. Whether or not chronological age has an effect on recovery has never been resolved, some investigators stating that it has an effect (Sands et al., 1969) and others that it is a weak factor (Basso et al., 1979; Culton, 1969; Kertesz and McCabe, 1977). Only one study has addressed the question directly, with the conclusion that chronological age has no effect on recovery (M.T. Sarno, 1980).

The subject is difficult to study because of methodological problems, lack of consensus on what constitutes recovery, and the like. A comprehensive review of the subject of recovery and rehabilitation may be found in M.T. Sarno (1981). Also included in the same review (M.T. Sarno,

1981) is a detailed discussion of the principles and practices of speech therapy for aphasia. It is a complicated subject, since there are a multitude of therapeutic techniques, although two mainstreams can be identified: (1) pedagogical methods, which are generally based upon the concept that aphasia represents a "loss" of language, and (2) stimulation techniques, which are based on the concept that impaired access to language is the physiopathology responsible for aphasia.

M.T. Sarno (1981) has suggested that therapy for aphasia should be viewed as a comprehensive, dynamic rehabilitation process in which the aphasia therapist (usually a speech pathologist) must develop an individual program for each patient; the program is designed to facilitate and stimulate language use, to be responsive to the psychological stages through which the patient evolves, and to avoid intensifying frustration, low self-esteem, depression, and other negative reactions. Repetition and reinforcement, the use of cues to enhance responses, and the abandonment of techniques viewed as meaningless by the patient are all essential ingredients in the design of a language rehabilitation program.

Speech therapy should be started early on a one-to-one basis and should include group therapy as soon as possible. The decision to terminate is often difficult and should depend more on emotional and social factors than on linguistic achievements. Viewed in this light, speech therapy may go on for long periods, well beyond the time span identified as the first phase of rehabilitation. The early months are very important, however, for establishing a basis for hope and continuing effort by the patient.

Sensory, Visual, Perceptual, and Cognitive Disorders

There is an impressive list of other disorders associated with stroke (as well as other forms of brain damage); these have engaged the attention of clinicians and academicians for many years. They are all of practical importance to those individuals who attempt to resume vocational roles, particularly roles that are intellectually demanding; some may be problematic to the person who does manual work. Only a few are of importance to most elderly stroke patients, whose primary requirements are self-care and the ability to interact socially. Though these disorders have been the subject of much research and conjecture, there is very little in the literature detailing their practical impact on patients and the possibilities of remediation. Reference to contemporary textbooks of human neuropsychology (Hécaen and Albert, 1978; Heilman and Valenstein, 1979) indicates that there are a multitude of disorders associated with brain damage that are of academic interest. Some of these are recognized as clinically important, according to present standards of practice; it may be that greater understanding of these phenomena will lead to better recognition and remediation by clinicians.

It is of interest to reflect on the fact that, in this, as in most fields of medicine, basic research has been done primarily by academicians and is, therefore, not generally responsive to clinical needs. The result is that the focus of most studies has been on description, physiology, localization, and theories of function. All of these represent the foundation for rational management and therapy, but require a collaboration between research worker and clinician, which does not generally happen at this time.

Sensory Function

Sensory deficits following stroke may involve all modalities, although only position sense appears to be a practical problem. Appreciation of touch, pain, and temperature are rarely totally lost, and patients, therefore, are not usually greatly hindered by these deficits. On the other hand, the loss of proprioceptive function in either the upper or lower limb is sometimes a great problem. An occasional patient with fairly well-preserved motor power in the leg may encounter much difficulty walking due to the imposition of a severe proprioceptive loss and some with poor power may not walk at all. Upper limb function

may be similarly affected, with a marked reduction in the functional capacity of the limb, despite adequate motor power.

The most common problem involving the special senses is visual impairment. A visual field defect is usually homonymous and often represents a practical problem, particularly in the elderly, less alert patient. Bumping into objects in the involved peripheral field, leaving food on one side of the plate, missing one side of the written page, and the like are common occurrences. Training to learn to scan the involved field is sometimes helpful. These patients should never drive an automobile.

Diplopia, nystagmus, opthalmoplegias, and unilateral blindness due to occlusion of the ophthalmic artery are less common.

The visual manifestations of unilateral spatial agnosia (neglect) are tantamount to a homonymous field defect, since the patient acts as though he does not perceive objects or occurrences in the involved peripheral field, as described above. Indeed, hemianopia and neglect often coexist. Neglect almost always involves the left half of space and is generally thought to be due to a lesion involving the right parietotemporal–occipital junction (Hécaen and Albert, 1978). Diller and Weinberg (1977) have described a program designed to ameliorate this condition. Tactile and auditory neglect have been described, but have not been found to be of clinical importance in the elderly stroke patient.

Perception

Disorders of perception, which probably represent a failure of high level integration of sensory stimuli, are common and sometimes of practical importance to the stroke patient. They tend to improve with time, but may persist. Two of these, constructional apraxia and dressing apraxia, are associated with right hemisphere lesions, although the former is seen also with left-brain damage. It is thought that constructional problems following left hemisphere lesions may be due to a motor executory defect as opposed to a deficit in visuospatial perception in right-brain lesions (Hécaen and Albert, 1978).

Of the two disorders, dressing apraxia is

of greater clinical significance, since it contributes to the patient's dependency. The results of treatment are variable; we are unaware of studies dealing with the subject. The presence of constructional apraxia is significant only to the patient who has vocational or avocational aspirations that depend upon an accute perception of two- or three-dimensional relationships. We recall a draftsman with right-brain damage due to stroke who encountered great conceptual difficulties when he attempted to render architectural drawings. Contrary to the experimental observation (Hécaen and Assal, 1970) that right-brain damaged patients with this disorder do not improve with practice, this patient was able to function eventually after a prolonged, intensive effort. In this same category are non-aphasic reading problems, in which patients skip letters, words, or lines, and a group of visual-perceptual difficulties, such as an inability to read graphs or charts, enter columns of figures, or perform hand activities that require accurate eye–hand coordination. These are likely to be of greater importance to younger stroke patients with vocational aspirations, but they apply also to the elderly stroke patient in the performance of a variety of daily activities.

Praxis

Limb dyspraxias may substantially contribute to impaired upper limb function. First described by Liepmann (1908), contemporary thinking places the lesion for the disorder in the dominant premotor area, but there must also be an intact corpus callosum to transmit stimuli to the premotor area of the opposite hemisphere (usually the right) (Geschwind, 1975). This pathological location explains the frequent association of limb dyspraxia with aphasia, but there is thought to be no physiological relationship between the two. The manifest problem is that the individual has difficulty executing learned movements.

Varying combinations of motor, proprioceptive, dyspraxic, and visual–perceptual deficits can represent a formidable deterrent to effective upper limb function.

In well-established rehabilitation programs, it is routine to mount a treatment program addressed to this problem. These programs are generally based upon in-depth evaluations, which employ standardized tests for motor status, tactile sensation, kinesthetic awareness and position sense, stereognosis, double simultaneous stimulation, visual fields, spatial relationships, eye–hand coordination, kinesthetic motor skills, ideational and ideomotor praxis, and constructional praxis. The treatment programs are usually developed by an occupational therapist, who generally has a strong sense of contributing to the patient's emotional and physical well-being. Needless to say, practical function is the primary goal.

Cognition

The most devastating of post-stroke cognitive disorders, aphasia, has been discussed. Its great importance is reflected in the extensive literature on the subject since the late nineteenth century. But what of other intellectual functions? By comparison, the literature is sparse.

A recent review (Hamsher, 1981) of the relationship between intelligence and aphasia is relevant, since it discusses contemporary concepts of the nature of intelligence within the context of brain damage. Hamsher concludes from the evidence that right hemisphere damage produces deficits in nonverbal intelligence and left brain damage impairs verbal intelligence, except that patients with receptive language disorders (usually associated with left hemisphere lesions) appear to have problems in both verbal and nonverbal spheres.

Practically, the clinician should be guided by the results of such standardized tests as the Wechsler Adult Intelligence Scale (WAIS), Raven's Progressive Matrices, and Bender Gestalt. Experience suggests, however, that one must accept the results of these tests with caution, since some patients may have significant problems despite good scores. We recall a physician with right-brain damage from a stroke with a full-scale score of 138 on the WAIS, who was unable to practice medicine because of poor judgment. Many high level executives are unable to function adequately after stroke, although they appear to be normal and act normally. In general, the more intellectually demanding the profession, the less likely it is that the patient will be able to perform at premorbid levels.

Personal accounts of aphasic patients invariably describe memory deficits (Wint, 1967; Moss, 1976; Dahlberg, 1977). Gardner and Winner (1981) have discussed the effects of brain damage on musical, literary, and graphic art abilities. It is of interest that damage to either hemisphere may result in a disturbance in each of these artistic forms; the nature of the disturbance differs in quality, however, depending on which hemisphere is damaged.

Rehabilitation of cognitive deficits remains virtually unexplored. In the elderly stroke patient, who is not likely to resume professional work, there seems little reason to attempt remediation except in aphasia. For those who have continuing vocational aspirations, the physician must use his knowledge of the nature of cognitive impairment, derived from both tests and experience, to guide the patient in his decisions. Often a trial experience on the job is the only way to determine whether or not the patient can perform adequately. Actual remediation in the form of helping the patient function better on specific tasks remains an experimental process.

This discussion of the first phase of stroke rehabilitation is concluded with a word of caution. One must not follow temporal imperatives too closely. Many patients are simply not ready for rehabilitative efforts during the first six months; they are more appropriately treated later, as their emotional, motor, or cognitive status improves. Not infrequently, such patients are placed in programs prematurely, use up their financial resources, and have nothing left at a later time when they might derive greater benefit from treatment. It requires fortitude to resist the requests of family and other referral sources for treatment, but it may be clearly in the patient's interest to do so. They must be convinced that nothing will be lost if treatment is postponed to a later, more appropriate time.

Phase Two

Thus far we have concerned ourselves with the first phase of rehabilitation, extending to about six months post-onset, and it would appear that most of the important factors have been discussed, leaving little else to consider. As has been pointed out, this early period often represents the full extent of rehabilitation efforts, with therapeutic and economic realities permitting no further services. The economic reasons are obvious and no doubt pre-eminent. However, there are few studies in the literature that address this subject and/or recommend continuing therapy for the stroke patient, aside from those mentioned above relating to continuing motor training (for example, Kottke, 1975; Bobath, 1979) and speech therapy for aphasics.

There is very likely a deeply held, but unexpressed bias that the elderly stroke patient, having run his race, does not require further attention. One cannot dictate cultural mores and, financial consideration aside, they dictate society's attitude toward such individuals as the elderly stroke patient.

Assuming the ideal, there is a great deal to be done with the stroke patient during the second and third rehabilitation phases. Here is a typical scenario: the patient, a man aged 71, returns home about 5 months after onset of a left hemisphere stroke. He is fortunate enough to have a healthy spouse; he lives on the second floor of a two-family house; income consists of social security for both husband and wife plus modest savings. The patient walks with the help of a plastic orthosis and regular cane. He is moderately aphasic, able to communicate with his wife at a simple level, but unable to compose a letter; reading skill is adequate for simple material only. The right arm is essentially without function. Before the stroke, this man enjoyed walking, working with his hands around his apartment and on a small plot of ground, reading, and playing with his grandchildren when they visited. He often helped his wife with shopping and sometimes with meal preparation. Walking is safe and adequate but laborious, certainly not conducive to the resumption of his old schedule of a brisk walk each day. He returns home disappointed that he has not recovered fully, devastated by his inability to converse freely, feeling enormously unworthy over the loss of his ability to be the man about the house, the fixer, the gardener, and the helper. Though he is fairly competetent at self-care, he still needs his wife's assistance in bathing and a few dressing skills like tying shoe laces and doing up certain buttons, adding to his feelings of low self-esteem. All these feed a pervasive depression, with a resultant lack of energy, which further reduces his ability and desire to do things. His wife, who always depended upon him, both physically and emotionally, feels overwhelmed with the new burdens placed upon her and becomes depressed and anxious about what will become of them.

Who can help in ameliorating this situation? Some of the problems are medical, but the more difficult ones are social and psychological. In an ideal setting, the kind envisioned in a comprehensive rehabilitation program, it is possible to make inroads on some of these problems. Since the literature does not address itself to this situation, specifically, one must deal with it anecdotally.

Taking physical matters first, experience suggests that walking ability may be enhanced through the application of such techniques as espoused by Bobath (1979) or Kottke (1975), over a protracted period of time. Teaching better gait patterns and reducing the effect of spastic components is both physically and psychologically uplifting for the patient and may bring him to the point where he is willing to try resuming his old walking habits, starting modestly and gradually increasing his range. Clinically, an additional three to six months of physical therapy to accomplish this end is reasonable and appropriate. Whether it is economically feasible is another question. To avoid repetition, this question of economic practicality will apply to all considerations of continuing therapy.

Improvement in walking ability has also been reported through selective blocking of peripheral nerves in the leg with phenol, most notably the tibial (Petrillo et al.,

1980). This diminishes spastic manifestations. Selective nerve blocks in the arms have been similarly employed to decrease the deforming effects of spasticity, with the end in view of easing dressing and hygiene tasks and making the limb more comfortable and more cosmetically acceptable.

Another therapeutic technique for improving motor performance of both the lower and upper limbs is variously identified as EMG feedback, EMG training, sensory feedback, or biofeedback training. It is based upon the principle that EMG visual and acoustic signals can be used to enhance normal motor function by stimulating volitional movement and/or suppressing undesirable involuntary activity, which in the case of most stroke patients, is spasticity. The neural mechanism underlying the process is still unclear. The method has been used to improve motor function at the ankle, specifically, diminishing foot-drop, to reduce spasticity and enhance hand function, and to reduce subluxation of the humerus from the glenohumeral joint (Basmajian, 1981; Brudny et al., 1979). In view of the variable success in the traditional treatment of these problems, this technique is widely employed. The second six months post-onset is a good time to try EMG feedback training, since the period of spontaneous neural restitution has passed.

There is rarely enough time during the initial phase of rehabilitation to fully develop upper limb function through training. A comprehensive rehabilitation program should be designed to continue treatment beyond six months and to meet specific needs. These include neuromuscular re-education, training in coordination and dexterity, activities of daily living, home-making, public transportation usage, and the development of avocational interests.

Returning to the subject of speech therapy for aphasia, a recent study has suggested that one is likely to see greater improvement in global aphasic patients during the second six as opposed to the first six months, post-onset (M. T. Sarno and Levita, 1979). Non-fluent aphasics continued to improve at the same rate during the second period, and the fluent aphasics tended to plateau. Though many patients remain severely impaired, it would appear that continuing speech therapy has both linguistic and psychological value.

Emotional reactions, such as depression, low self-esteem, and feelings of loss, discouragement, and apathy, tend to intensify during the second six months post-onset, as described in the example above. This is sometimes associated with improvement in cognitive function. It is the time, therefore, when psychological counseling for both patient and family may become critical. It is also the time when an effort must be made to increase the patient's social and community activities. Fatigue, shame, and practical impediments (for example, transportation) may discourage such efforts; involvement of the psychosocial staff is often needed to motivate and facilitate it. Hospital or community-based clubs (for example, stroke clubs) often provide a good setting for this kind of activity. The patient who returns to a community where religious or civic groups are active in the interest of the disabled is fortunate, but such communities are rare.

In summary, the second six months post-stroke may be a period of significant improvement in specific skills if the patient continues to receive professional help. It is almost always a time of deepening emotional trouble and increasing isolation, requiring, therefore, the continuation of specific therapies as well as psychological and social assistance.

Phase Three

This post-stroke period encompasses the remainder of the patient's life. A number of studies have documented the fact that a significant population of patients will survive a stroke and, therefore, continue to be a medical and social responsibility (Anderson et al., 1977; Gresham et al., 1979), often for many years. As pointed out earlier, patients who receive adequate training and are properly followed in their homes after discharge achieve and maintain satisfactory levels of physical function (Anderson et al., 1977). For a long time, physical competence was considered the only measure of successful rehabilitation.

More recently it has been suggested that social and psychological factors may be the prime indicators of success, since they determine the all-important quality of life of the surviving patient. Exemplifying this is a report based upon stroke survivors in the well-known Framingham cohort (Labi et al., 1980). The study revealed that many patients, despite physical competence, did not resume a normal social life; women and patients with more education, statistically, had greater problems in this regard. Another surprising finding was that patients who lived alone had better social reintegration than patients who lived with their families. Feelings of stigma, depression, low self-esteem, low levels of energy, the tendency of old friends to avoid such patients, and many other factors no doubt contribute to this situation (Isaacs et al., 1976; Brocklehurst et al., 1981; Labi et al., 1980).

Hyman (1972) found that a variety of social–psychological phenomena adversely influenced rehabilitation outcome, including self-esteem, feelings of stigma, certain attitudes toward illness, and dependency.

Clinical experience supports the implication of these studies: social and psychological factors are probably the major determinants of rehabilitation success. This leads, in turn, to the conclusion that there must be greater involvement of social and psychiatric workers in the care of these patients, particularly in the later phases.

What of the question of continuing physical treatment in this third phase? There would be no question of ongoing physical restoration therapy if it could be demonstrated conclusively that further return of function might be expected. A number of physiologists and clinicians have addressed themselves to this question, and there are certain indications that the brain has the capacity for improving function beyond the immediate postictal period, although many of the pertinent studies have been conducted in laboratory animals and may not be applicable to man. There is no gain-saying that some experienced clinicians have observed improvement in function extending over years, lending credence to the suggestion that there are neuroplastic processes at work. The subject has been reviewed and it is suggested that collateral sprouting (reactive synaptogenesis) and unmasking may be two such processes (Bach-y-Rita, 1981). The former refers to "sprouting from intact cells to a denervated region after some or all of its normal input has been destroyed" (Laurence and Stein, 1978). Unmasking is hypothesized as the activation of previously unused neural pathways under the stimulus of damage to the normal systems, or compensatory hyperactivity in those portions of the system that are not damaged. It is implied in both that effort is imperative, that increased function requires repetitive stimulation of the system, an idea reinforced by clinical experience. Meaningless "exercises" appear to have no capacity to improve function. Regarding age, Bach-y-Rita (1981) suggests that morphological plasticity appears not to be lost in the aged brain, citing Buell and Coleman (1976). However, there may be factors at work in elderly patients, such as fatigue, other medical conditions, and depression, which limit their ability to put forth the required effort. Clinically, this appears to be a potent factor. Although the will to live may be strong, the ability to struggle is often absent. One often observes a circular process in which anxiety and depression over lost abilities lead to an intensification of pathological features (for example, spasticity), as well as psychosomatic manifestations (for example, pain), with a further reduction in functional ability that suggests a progressive neural lesion. Paradoxically, this may be a greater problem late in the course of the illness, perhaps because the initial optimism for full recovery has been lost. Once more, one is impressed with the ability of psychological factors to dominate physical ones.

Conclusion

It is clear from the foregoing that rehabilitation of the brain-damaged is a complicated, time-consuming, expensive process, in which there is a great need for further research and planning. Because it extends beyond the usual domain of medicine there is some question as to who should assume responsibility for the process. In view of the basically medical nature of stroke, and the many disorders it produces, it seems appropriate that medicine should lead in the rehabilitation effort. The philosophically most desirable role of medicine is that it should be responsible for the well-being of the total individual, a challenge that is formidable in the care of the stroke patient.

References

Anderson, E., Anderson, T.P., and Kottke, F.J. (1977). Stroke rehabilitation: Maintenance of achieved gains. Arch. Phys. Med. Rehab. 58, 345–352.

Anderson, T.P., Bourestom, N., Greenberg, F.R., and Hildyard, V.G. (1974). Predictive factors in stroke rehabilitation, Arch. Phys. Med. Rehab. 55, 545–553.

Anderson, T.P. and Kottke, F.J. (1978). Stroke rehabilitation: A reconsideration of some common attitudes. Arch. Phys. Med. Rehab. 59, 175–181.

Andrews, K. and Stewart, J. (1979). Stroke recovery: He can but does he? Rheum. Rehab. 18, 43–48.

Bach-y-Rita, P. (1981). Central nervous system lesions: Sprouting and unmasking in rehabilitation. Arch. Phys. Med. Rehab. 62, 413–417.

Baretz, R.M. and Stephenson, G.R. (1976). Unrealistic patient. N.Y.S. J. Med. 76, 54–57.

Basmajian, J.V. (1981). Biofeedback in rehabilitation: A review of principles and practices. Arch. Phys. Med. Rehab. 62, 469–475.

Basso, A., Capitani, E., and Vignolo, L. (1979). Influence of rehabilitation on language skills in aphasic patients. Arch. Neurol. 36, 190–196.

Bobath, B. (1979). The application of physiologic principles to stroke rehabilitation. The Practitioner 223, 793–794.

Brocklehurst, J.C., Morris, P., Andrews, K., Richards, B., and Laycock, P. (1981). Social effects of stroke. Soc. Sci. Med. 15A, 35–39.

Brudny, J., Korein, J., Grynbaum, B.B., Belandres, P.V., and Gianutsos, J.G. (1979). Helping hemiparetics to help themselves. JAMA 241, 814–818.

Buell, S.J. and Coleman, D.P. (1976). Dendritic growth in aged human brain and failure of growth in senile dementia. Science 206, 854–856.

Culton, G. (1969). Spontaneous recovery from aphasia. J. Sp. Hear. Res. 12, 825–832.

Dahlberg, C.C. (1977). Stroke. Psychology Today 2, 121–128.

Diller, L. and Weinberg, J. (1977). Hemiinattention in rehabilitation: The evolution of a rational remedial program. In Advances in Neurology, E.A. Weinstein and R.P. Friedlan, Eds. Raven Press, New York.

Fay, T. (1954). The use of pathological and unlocking reflexes in the rehabilitation of spastics. Amer. J. Phys. Med. 33, 347–352.

Feigenson, J. (1981). Stroke rehabilitation outcome studies and guidelines for alternative levels of care. Stroke 12, 372–375.

Friedman, M.H. (1961). On the nature of regression in aphasia. Arch. Gen. Psychiat. 5, 60–64.

Gainotti, G. (1972). Emotional behavior and hemispheric side of lesion. Cortex 8, 41–55.

Gardner, H. and Winner, E. (1981). Artistry in aphasia. In Acquired Aphasia, M.T. Sarno, Ed. Academic Press, New York.

Gersten, J.W. (1975). Rehabilitation potential. In Stroke and its Rehabilitation, S. Licht, Ed. Waverly Press, Baltimore.

Geschwind, N. (1975). The apraxias: Neurological mechanisms of disorders of learned movement. Amer. Sci. 63, 188–195.

Goldstein, K. (1942). After Effects of Brain Injuries in War. Grune & Stratton, New York.

Gresham, G.E., Phillips, T.F., Wolf, P.A., McNamara, P.M., Kannel, W.B., and Dawber, T.R. (1979). Epidemiologic profile of long-term stroke disability. Arch. Phys. Med. Rehab. 60, 487–491.

Hamsher, K. (1981). Intelligence and aphasia. In Acquired Aphasia, M.T. Sarno, Ed. Academic Press, New York.

Harris, F.A. (1978). Facilitation techniques in therapeutic exercise. In Therapeutic Exercise, J.V. Basmajian, Ed. Waverly Press, Baltimore.

Hécaen, H. and Albert, M.L. (1978). Human Neuropsychology. J. Wiley, New York.

Hécaen, H. and Assal, G. (1970). A comparison of construction deficits following right and left hemispheric lesions. Neuropsychologia 8, 289–304.

Heilman, K.M. and Valenstein, E. (1979). Clinical Neuropsychology. Oxford University Press, New York.

Hodgins, E. (1964). Episode. Atheneum, New York.

Horenstein, S. (1970). Effects of cerebrovascular disease on personality and emotionality. In Behavioral Change in Cerebrovascular Disease, A.L. Benton, Ed. Harper & Row, New York.

Hyman, M.D. (1972). Social psychological determinants of patients' performance in stroke rehabilitation. Arch. Phys. Med. Rehab. 53, 217–226.

Isaacs, B., Neville, Y., and Rushford, I. (1976). The stricken: The social consequences of stroke. Age Ageing 5, 188–192.

Kabat, H. (1965). Proprioceptive facilitation in therapeutic exercise. In Therapeutic Exercise, S. Licht, Ed. E. Licht, New Haven, Conn.

Kertesz, A. and McCabe, P. (1977). Recovery patterns and prognosis in aphasia. Brain 100, 1–18.

Kottke, F.J. (1974). Historia obscura hemiplegiae. Arch. Phys. Med. Rehab. 55, 4–13.

Kottke, F.J. (1975). Neurophysiologic therapy for stroke. In Stroke and its Rehabilitation, S. Licht, Ed. Waverly Press, Baltimore.

Labi, M.L.C., Phillips, T.F., and Gresham, G.E. (1980). Psychosocial disability in physically restored long-term stroke survivors. Arch. Phys. Med. Rehab. 61, 561–565.

Laurence, S. and Stein, D.G. (1978). Recovery after brain damage and concept of localization of function. In Recovery from Brain Damage, S. Finger, Ed. Plenum Press, New York.

Lehmann, J.F., DeLateur, B.J., Fowler, R.S. Jr., Warren, C.G., Arnhold, R., Schertzer, G., Hurka, R., Whitmore, J.J., Masock, A.J., and Chambers, K.H. (1975). Stroke rehabilitation: Outcome and prediction. Arch. Phys. Med. Rehab. 56, 383–389.

Liepmann, H. (1908). Drei Aufsätze aus dem Apraxiegebiet. Karger, Berlin.

Moskowitz, E., Bishop, H.F., Pe, H., and Shibutani, K. (1958). Posthemiplegic reflex sympathetic dystrophy. J.A.M.A. 167, 836–838.

Moskowitz, E., Lightbody, F.E.H., and Freitag, N.S. (1972). Long-term follow-up of the post-stroke patient. Arch. Phys. Med. Rehab. 53, 167–172.

Moskowitz, E. and Porter, J.I. (1963). Peripheral nerve lesions in the upper extremity in hemiplegic patients. New Eng. J. Med. 269: 776–778.

Moss, S. (1976). Notes from an aphasic psychologist, or different strokes for different folks. In Recovery in Aphasics, Y. Lebrun and R. Hooks, Eds. Swetz and Zeitlinger, B.V., Amsterdam.

Petrillo, C. Chu, D.S., and Davis, S.W. (1980). Phenol block of the tibial nerve in the hemiplegic patient. Orthopedics 3(9), 871–874.

Sands, E., Sarno, M.T., and Shankweiler, D. (1969). Long-term assessment of language function in aphasia due to stroke. Arch. Phys. Med. Rehab. 50, 203–207.

Sarno, J.E. (1973). Below knee orthoses: A system for prescription. Arch. Phys. Med. Rehab. 54, 458–552.

Sarno, J.E. (1981). Etiology of neck and back pain: An autonomic myoneuralgia? J. Nerv. Ment. Dis. 169, 55–59.

Sarno, J.E. and Lehneis, H.R. (1971). Prescription considerations for below knee orthoses. Arch. Phys. Med. Rehab. 52, 503–510.

Sarno, M.T. (1980). Language rehabilitation outcome in the elderly aphasic patient. In Language and Communication in the El-derly, L.K. Obler and M.L. Albert, Eds. Heath, Lexington, Mass.

Sarno, M.T. (1981). Recovery and rehabilitation. In Acquired Aphasia, M.T. Sarno, Ed. Academic Press, New York.

Sarno, M.T. and Levita, E. (1979). Recovery in treated aphasia in the first year post-stroke. Stroke 10, 663–670.

Swenson, J.R. (1978). Therapeutic exercise in hemiplegia. In Therapeutic Exercise, J.V. Basmagian, Ed. Waverly Press, Baltimore.

Twitchell, T.E. (1951). The restoration of motor function following hemiplegia in man. Brain 74, 443–480.

Ullman, M. (1962). Behavioral Change in Patients Following Strokes. C.C. Thomas, Springfield, Ill.

Weinstein, E. and Kahn, R. (1955). Denial of Illness. C.C. Thomas, Springfield, Ill.

Wint, G. (1967). The Third Killer. Abelard-Schuman, New York.

Index

Page numbers in *italics* indicate illustrations.
Page numbers followed by *t* indicate tables.